The Developing Person
Through Childhood and Adolescence

Christian Pierre, *Boy and Cat* (front cover) and *Doorway to Possibility* (back cover)
Affection, curiosity, love . . . what is the relationship between boy and cat? We cannot be sure, but we do know that each developing child reaches out to other creatures (mostly, but not always, other people) in thousands of everyday moments. Surprising things inevitably occur in that connection, as indicated here by the unusual coloring of boy, cat, and background—and the wealth of possibilities makes the study of development a source of wonder as well as a science.

Seventh Edition

The Developing Person

Through Childhood and Adolescence

KATHLEEN STASSEN BERGER

Bronx Community College

City University of New York

WORTH PUBLISHERS

Publisher: Catherine Woods

Senior Sponsoring Editor: Jessica Bayne

Developmental Editor: Cecilia Gardner

Production Editor: Vivien Weiss

Marketing Manager: Katherine Nurre

Associate Managing Editor: Tracey Kuehn

Production Manager: Barbara Seixas

Art Director and Cover Designer: Barbara Reingold

Interior Designer: Charles Yuen

Layout Designer: Paul Lacy

Photo Editor: Bianca Moscatelli

Photo Researcher: Nicole Villamora

Senior Illustration Coordinator: Bill Page

Illustrator: Todd Buck Illustration

Composition: TSI Graphics, Inc.

Printing and Binding: R. R. Donnelly & Sons Company

Cover Art: Christian Pierre, Boy and Cat (front) and Doorway to Possibility (back)

ISBN: 0-7167-7050-4 (EAN: 9780716770503)
0-7167-7630-8 (EAN: 9780716776307)—ppbk.
0-7167-6801-1 (EAN: 9780716768012)—comp.

Copyright © 2006, 2003, 1995, 1991, 1986, 1980 Worth Publishers
All rights reserved.

Printed in the United States of America

First printing 2005

Library of Congress Cataloging-in-Publication Data
Berger, Kathleen Stassen
The developing person through childhood and adolescence / Kathleen Berger.—7th ed.
p. cm.
Includes bibliographical references.
ISBN 0-7167-7050-4
Child development. 2. Adolescence. I. Title.
RJ131.B385 2005
305.231—dc22
2005044941

Worth Publishers

41 Madison Avenue

New York, NY 10010

www.worthpublishers.com

Permission has been granted to reprint the following photos:

Chapter openers:

1. Tony Savino/The Image Works, vii, 4
2. Shu-Tung-Unep/Peter Arnold, vii, 34
3. David M. Phillips/Photo Researchers, Inc., vii, 64
4. Stephanie Rausser/Taxi/Getty Images, viii, 96
5. Lisi Dennis/The Image Bank/Getty Images, viii, 130, 219
6. Banana Stock/Picture Quest, viii, 164, 219
7. Johner/Photonica, viii, 190, 219
8. Banana Stock/Punchstock, ix, 222, 321
9. Tom Hood, *The Daily Courier*/AP Photo, ix, 252, 321
10. Deborah Davis/PhotoEdit, Inc., ix, 284, 321
11. Osamu Koyata/Pacific Press Service, x, 324, 427
12. Jim Cummins/Getty Images, x, 356, 427
13. Sean Sprague/The Image Works, x, 394, 427
14. James Oliver/Getty Images, x, 430, 529
15. Walter Hodges/Getty Images, xi, 464, 529
16. David Grossman/The Image Works, xi, 494, 529

Part openers

1. Laura Dwight, vi, vii, 2
2. Rommel/Masterfile, vi, viii 128, 219
3. Johner/Photonica, vi, ix, 220, 321
4. Steffen Honzera/Peter Arnold, vi, ix, 322, 427
5. Antonio Mo/Taxi/Getty Images, vi, x, 428, 529

About the Author

Kathleen Stassen Berger received her undergraduate education at Stanford University and Radcliffe College, earned an M.A.T. from Harvard University and an M.S. and Ph.D from Yeshiva University. Her broad experience as an educator includes directing a preschool, teaching philosophy and humanities at the United Nations International School, teaching child and adolescent development to graduate students at Fordham University, teaching undergraduates at Montclair State University in New Jersey and at Quinnipiac University in Connecticut, as well as inmates earning paralegal degrees at Sing Sing Prison.

For the past 35 years Berger has taught at Bronx Community College of the City University of New York. She has taught introduction to psychology, child and adolescent development, adulthood and aging, social psychology, abnormal psychology, and human motivation. Her students—who come from many ethnic, economic, and educational backgrounds and who have a wide range of interests—consistently honor her with the highest teaching evaluations. Her own four children attended New York City public schools, one reason that she was elected as president of Community School Board in District Two.

Berger is also the author of *The Developing Person Through the Life Span*. Her developmental texts are currently being used at nearly 700 colleges and universities worldwide and are available in Spanish, French, Italian, and Portuguese as well as English. Her research interests include adolescent identity, sibling relationships, and bullying, and she has contributed articles on developmental topics to the *Wiley Encyclopedia of Psychology*. Berger's interest in college education is manifest in articles published by the American Association for Higher Education and the National Education Association for Higher Education. She continues to teach and learn with every semester and every edition of her books.

Brief Contents

Contents

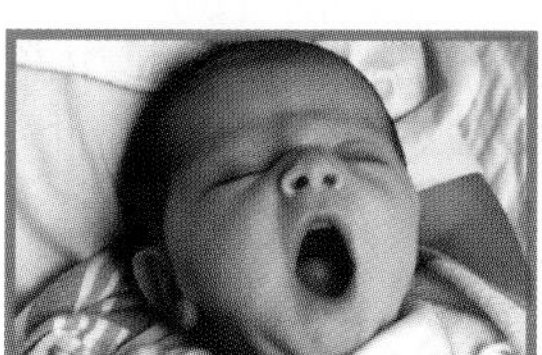

Part I

The Beginnings

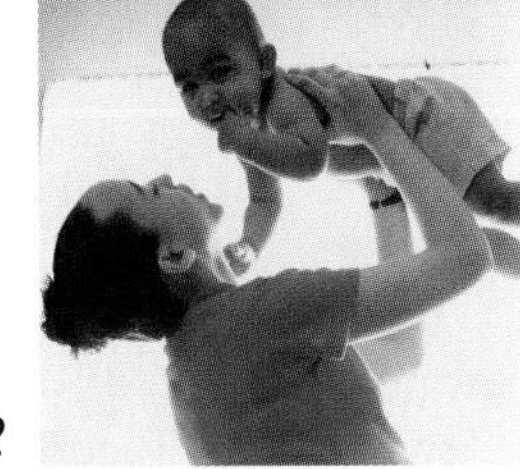

Part II

The First Two Years: Infants and Toddlers

Part III

The Play Years

Part IV

The School Years

Part V

Adolescence

Preface

Development happens, ready or not. Each year brings gains and losses, continuity and discontinuity. Developmental changes may be expected or discovered by scientists, to be understood by you and me. Or they may be quite personal.

Between the sixth and seventh editions of this book, many of the children of the world suffered disasters, including Hurricane Katrina and the South Asian tsunami, and wars in Iraq and elsewhere. Globalization improved the economic prospects for many families and threw others into deeper poverty; it has led to speedy international transmission of music, diseases, and lifestyles—with some gains and losses.

When we look at children, gains are more evident than losses. Many children are healthier and happier than they would have been if they had been born a decade earlier. For instance, more infants are breast-fed, more young children are immunized, more older children learn to read and write, and even the poorest children may attain a secondary education. The birth rate is falling in every nation of the world, which means more attention to each developing person. Worldwide, educational standards are rising.

M. MEYERSFELD / MASTERFILE

No Writer's Block The context is designed to help this South African second-grader concentrate on her schoolwork. Large, one-person desks, uniforms, notebooks, and sharp pencils are manageable for the brains and skills of elementary-school children, but not yet for preschoolers.

Development happens personally, and this has been very evident for me. Since the sixth edition, my mother, my father, and my husband have died. Those are deep losses, but there are also gains: I am closer to my brother and my children. My dedication to writing the best possible textbook is stronger than ever.

Since the first edition, I have tried to make this book reflect the values of my own classroom—high standards and clear expectations within a context of respect for each learner. That is the basis of education, but effective learning also requires the instructor to be enthusiastic, good-humored, and honest. I try to apply this lesson to my writing.

I hope you will see evidence of my fascination with development, my intellectual integrity, and, most of all, my respect for the learner. If so, I thank my many heroes and mentors. These include not only my own gifted professors who studied directly with Erikson, Piaget, and Skinner but also researchers whom I admire from the cool distance of the printed page: Ainsworth, Baltes, Bem, the Coles, Garbarino, Gardner, the Gibsons, Lightfoot, Olweus, Plomin, Rutter, Schaie, Vygotsky, Whitborne, Zigler—and many more (which explains why the bibliography is longer than any comparable book's)—plus the thousands of peers and students who continue to teach me.

To learn more about the specifics of this text, including the material that is new to this edition, read on. Or you can turn to the first page of Chapter 1 and begin your study.

New Material

Even Stronger Integration of Theory and Practice

Nothing is quite so practical as a good theory, as my mentors taught me, and nothing about development is a mere abstraction. In this new edition, more than ever, theoretical insights are connected to practical issues. This link is evident throughout, notably in the "Especially for . . ." questions in the margins (many of which are revised and updated for this edition) and through the series of features under the titles "Issues and Applications," "Thinking Like a Scientist," and "A Case to Study," which help readers see how the experience of each developing child illustrates theories and applications.

Up-to-Date Research

Every year brings new concepts and research. The best of these are integrated into the text, including hundreds of new references on many topics—among them, challenges to Piaget's theories, origins of infant language, causes of emotional regulation, demographics of adolescent drug use, and the impact of stereotype threat. Much of this new research is in the area of brain development and education. A sampling of some of this new material is listed below:

Cultural variations in cognition and education in the school years, pp. 360–362
The pragmatics of language and new vocabulary, pp. 371–372
Education around the world, pp. 375–377
Educational assessment, pp. 377–380
Comparison of education in the United States and Japan, pp. 379–380
Curriculum wars—reading and math, pp. 380–389
In Person: When Did You Learn *Tsunami?*, p. 382
Bilingual education, pp. 387–389
Culture and education, pp. 389–391
Middle school, pp. 469–472
High school, pp. 481–487
Thinking Like a Scientist: Stereotype Threat, pp. 488–489
College, pp. 489–491
Sex education in school, pp. 516–517

Revised Chapters on Adolescence

While I've been sensitive to current research through developing the book, I've been particularly impressed with the magnitude of changes that are happening in our understanding of adolescence. As a result, I have extensively rewritten the three chapters on the teen years. Highlights include new discoveries about the adolescent brain, the distinctive periods of early adolescence (the "tweens") and emerging adulthood, plus a more up-to-date understanding of the developmental impact of schooling, sex, and peers.

New Learning Features

With every edition, changes in the narrative are made to enhance readers' understanding of what scientists do. Readers are offered many opportunities to test their observational and analytical skills. The new "Issues and Applications" features illuminate current topics, from punishment to class size. I've also added a medial summary, entitled "Summing Up," at the end of each major section to allow students to pause and reflect on what they've learned. New end-of-chapter key questions and additional application questions offer students ways to explore and refine what they've learned about the topic. These and other pedagogical elements of the text reflect recent research in learning strategies.

Ongoing Features

Many characteristics of this text have been acclaimed since the first edition and have been retained in this revision.

Writing That Communicates the Excitement and Challenge of the Field

An overview of the science of human development should be lively, just as children and adolescents are. Consequently, each sentence has been crafted to convey tone as well as content. More summarizing and transitional statements are provided, in order to clarify the logical connection between one idea and the next. Sentences are shorter and less daunting, although I still choose some vocabulary words that will expand comprehension. Chapter-opening vignettes are more evocative, to bring students into the immediacy of development from the very first paragraph of a chapter.

© OWEN FRANKEN / STOCK, BOSTON

Demonstration of High IQ? If North American intelligence tests truly reflected all the aspects of the mind, children would be considered mentally slow if they could not replicate the proper hand, arm, torso, and facial positions of a traditional dance, as this young Indonesian girl does brilliantly. She is obviously adept in kinesthetic and interpersonal intelligence. Given her culture, it would not be surprising if she were deficient in the logical-mathematical intelligence required to use the Internet effectively or to surpass an American peer on a video game.

Coverage of Diversity

Cross-cultural, international, multiethnic, rich and poor, boy and girl—all these words and ideas are vital to appreciating how we all develop. Studies of various groups make it clear that we are all the same, yet each of us is unique. From the discussion of the cultural context in Chapter 1 to the coverage of cultural differences in adolescent depression in Chapter 16, each chapter refers to the vast possibilities in human cultural experience. New research on family structures, immigrants, bilingualism, and ethnic variations in disease are among the many topics that are presented, always with respect for human diversity, throughout the book. Listed here are just a few of the places where you can find discussions of culture and diversity in this new edition:

Culture and Diversity

Study of bullying in Norwegian schools, p. 404
Social support and religious faith, pp. 423–424
Sexual maturation in various cultures, pp. 443–445
Thinking Like a Scientist: Stereotype Threat, pp. 488–489
Identity and religion, ethnicity, and vocation worldwide, pp. 499–505
Teens, culture, and family, pp. 507–508
The peer group for immigrant teens, pp. 511–513
Teen suicide rates in various cultures, pp. 523–524

Up-to-Date Coverage

My students as well as my children keep me current through their questions and concerns. I learned from my mentors curiosity, creativity, and skepticism; as a result, I am eager to read but ready to analyze thousands of journal articles and books on everything from abuse to zygosity. The recent explosion of research in neuroscience and genetics has challenged me, once again, first to understand and then to explain many complex findings and speculative leaps.

Topical Organization within a Chronological Framework

The book's basic organization remains unchanged. Four chapters begin the book with coverage of definitions, theories, genetics, and prenatal development, used not only as a developmental foundation but also as the structure for explaining the life-span perspective, plasticity, nature and nurture, multicultural awareness, risk analysis, the damage–repair cycle, family bonding, and many other concepts that yield insights for all of human development. The following four parts correspond to the major periods of development.

Each part contains three chapters, one for each of the three domains: biosocial, cognitive, and psychosocial. The topical organization within a chronological framework is a useful scaffold for student understanding of the interplay between age and domain as they themselves actually experience it. Linking science to everyday life is one way to expand cognition. The chapters are color-coded with tabs on the right-hand margins: The pages of the biosocial chapters have green tabs, the cognitive chapters have lavender tabs, and the psychosocial chapters have salmon-colored tabs.

Relevant Features

In some books, boxes are tacked on to make the text seem more current or multicultural than it really is. In this edition, four series of deeper discussions appear as integral parts of the text, and only where they are relevant. These features include three series that readers have particularly liked in earlier editions—called "In Person," "A Case to Study," and "Thinking Like a Scientist"—and one that is new to this edition, called "Issues and Applications."

Pedagogical Aids

Each chapter ends with a summary, a list of key terms (with page numbers indicating where the word is introduced and defined), key questions, and three or four application exercises designed to let students apply concepts to everyday life. Terms are defined in the margins (in boldface) and again in a glossary at the back of the book. The outline on the first page of each chapter and the system of major and minor subheads facilitate the survey-question-read-write-review (SQ3R) approach. New to this edition are the section-ending "Summing Up"

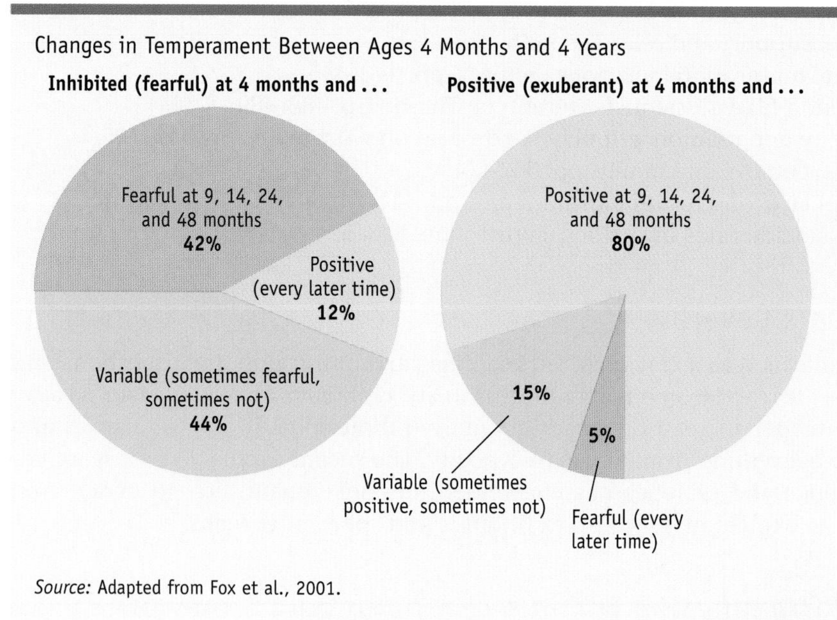

FIGURE 7.1 **Do Babies' Temperaments Change?** The data suggest that fearful babies are not necessarily fated to remain that way. Adults who are reassuring and do not act frightened themselves can help children overcome an innate fearfulness. Some fearful children do not change, however, and it is not known whether that's because their parents are not sufficiently reassuring (nurture) or because they are temperamentally more fearful (nature).

? Observational Quiz (see answer, page 202): Out of 100 4-month-olds who react positively to noises and other experiences, how many are fearful at later times in early childhood?

Especially for Health Workers Parents ask that some medication be prescribed for their kindergarten child, who they say is much too active for them to handle. How do you respond?

features designed to aid student learning. Observational quizzes inspire readers to look more closely at data and photographs. The "Especially for . . ." questions in the margins, many of which are new to this edition, apply concepts to real-life careers and social roles.

Photographs, Tables, and Graphs That Are Integral to the Text

Students learn a great deal by studying this book's illustrations, because Worth Publishers encourages authors to choose photos, tables, and graphs, to write captions, and to alter designs to better fit the words—not vice versa. As one result, photos and captions are instructional, supplementing and extending the text. Appendix A furthers this process by presenting at least one chart or table per chapter, containing detailed data for further study.

Content Changes for the Seventh Edition

Child and adolescent development, like all sciences, builds on past learning. Many facts and concepts must be restated in every edition of a textbook—stages and ages, norms and variations, dangers and diversities, classic theories and fascinating applications. However, the study of development is continually changed by discoveries and innovations, so no paragraph in this seventh edition is exactly what it was in the sixth edition, much less the first. Extensive updating is evident on every page. Highlights appear below.

Chapter 1 Introduction

- Expanded section on the five characteristics of development
- Greater emphasis on what brain research tells us about development, with particular focus on childhood depression and social-cognitive neuroscience
- Thinking Like a Scientist: Ethnicity, Race, Culture, and Income
- Issues and Applications: "My Name Wasn't Mary"

Chapter 2 Theories of Development

- Updated and expanded coverage of epigenetic and evolutionary theory
- New subsection on the interweaving of nature and nurture in ADHD

DAVID YOUNG-WOLFF / PHOTOEDIT

Same Birthday, Same (or Different?) Genes Twins who are of different sexes or who have obvious differences in personality are dizygotic, sharing only half of their genes. Many same-sex twins with similar temperaments are dizygotic as well.

Chapter 3 The Genetic Code

- Substantially reworked to reflect the latest in our understanding of genetics and fetal development
- Thinking Like a Scientist: Genetic Diversity
- In Person: Enhancing Fertility
- New subsection on visual acuity as an example of the complexity of gene–environment interaction
- Updated material on cloning, hazards of multiple births, the practice of genetic counseling and testing

Chapter 4 Prenatal Development and Birth

- Issues and Applications: Should the Government Protect Fetuses from AIDS and Alcohol?
- A Case to Study: "What Do People Live to Do?"
- A Case to Study: "What Did That Say About Me?"
- Updated data on fetal viability, prenatal testing, cultural variations in birthing, and father's role after birth

SHEHZAD NOORANI / PETER ARNOLD, INC.

A Teenaged Mother This week-old baby, born in a poor village in Myanmar (Burma), has a better chance of survival than he might otherwise have had, because his 18-year-old mother has bonded with him.

Chapter 5 The First Two Years: Biosocial Development

- Updated discussion of brain growth, including the impact of cortisol, experience-dependent and experience-expectant development, and self-righting
- New research on cultural variations in infant sleep
- Heavily revised section on public health issues and initiatives worldwide, with specific coverage of breast-feeding and immunization

Chapter 6 The First Two Years: Cognitive Development

- Research-based challenges to Piaget's theories of early cognition
- New treatment of infant memory
- Expanded section on cultural variations in early language development

Chapter 7 The First Two Years: Psychosocial Development

- Thinking Like a Scientist: The Still-Face Technique
- Significantly reorganization of chapter to highlight new research and theories on emotional development

- Major new sections on sociocultural theory (covering ethnotheories and proximal and distal parenting styles) and epigenetic theory
- Revised coverage of infant day care (including the latest NICHD reports), temperament (including new physiological correlates), and attachment (including cultural variations and predictors of secure attachment)

Chapter 8 The Play Years: Biosocial Development

- New subsection on ethnic, cultural, and SES differences in eating habits
- Expanded coverage of brain development focusing on development of attention, prefrontal cortex, emotions, and brain damage
- Updated section on child maltreatment

LAURA DWIGHT

No Spilled Milk This girl is demonstrating her mastery of the motor skills involved in pouring milk, to the evident admiration of her friend. The next skill will be drinking it—not a foregone conclusion, given the lactose intolerance of some children and the small appetites and notorious pickiness of children this age.

? Observational Quiz (see answer, page 226): What three things can you see that indicate that this attempt at pouring will probably be successful?

Chapter 9 The Play Years: Cognitive Development

- Classic coverage of Piaget and Vygotsky refined to be more accessible to students
- Expanded and updated coverage of theory of mind
- More on bilingual language development
- Revised coverage of early childhood education, including Reggio Emilia, Montessori, and other types of programs

Chapter 10 The Play Years: Psychosocial Development

- Issues and Applications: Planning Punishment
- Significantly updated coverage of emotional development, including more material on intrinsic and extrinsic motivation, cultural differences in emotional regulation, internalizing and externalizing disorders, and the role of the brain
- New coverage of creativity, practical plans for dealing with childhood aggression, cultural differences in parenting styles, discipline (including cultural differences), the challenge of media

Response for Health Workers (from page xviii): Medication helps some hyperactive children, but not all. It might be useful for this child, but other forms of intervention should be tried first. Compliment the parents on their concern about their child, but refer them to an expert in early childhood for an evaluation and recommendations. Behavior-management techniques geared to the particular situation, not medication, will be the first stategy.

Chapter 11 The School Years: Biosocial Development

- Expanded coverage of childhood obesity
- New coverage of the impact of early puberty in middle childhood
- Revised discussion of childhood asthma
- Updated section on brain development in middle childhood includes coverage of attention and automatization
- Revised material on pervasive developmental disorders (including autism and Asperger syndrome) and ADHD, with new focus on education and treatment

Chapter 12 The School Years: Cognitive Development

- Thinking Like a Scientist: Mothers and Morals
- Issues and Applications: More Children, Less Learning?
- Updated section on information processing throughout early and middle childhood
- Major new section on education, including controversies such as the reading and math wars, high-stakes testing, and class size
- Revised discussion of moral development, including new research about acting moral

Chapter 13 The School Years: Psychosocial Development

- Extensively revised discussion of family function and structure during the school years
- New discussion of resilience in school-age children and the importance of social support and religious faith in coping with stress

Chapter 14: Adolescence: Biosocial Development

- New focus on sub-periods of early, middle, and late adolescence
- Updated coverage of timing of puberty and adolescent sexual activity
- Expanded coverage of recent research on the adolescent brain

Chapter 15: Adolescence: Cognitive Development

- Thinking Like a Scientist: Stereotype Threat
- Major new section on learning across the spectrum of adolescence, including middle school, high school, and college

Chapter 16: Adolescence: Psychosocial Development

- A Case to Study: "Give Him a Break"
- In Person: The Berger Women Have Weird Rituals
- New coverage of religious identity, teenage employment, parent–teen relationships, culture and peers, teenage romance and sex, cultural variations in adolescent depression and suicide

KAZ MORI / THE IMAGE BANK

Eye on the Ball This boy's concentration while heading the ball and simultaneously preparing to fall is a sign that he has practiced this maneuver enough times that he can perform it automatically. Not having to think about what to do on the way down, he can think about what to do when he gets up, such as pursuing the ball or getting back to cover his position.

Supplements

As an instructor myself, I know the importance of good supplements. I have rejected textbook adoptions because the company had a poor history of inaccurate test banks, dull ancillaries, and slow service. Fortunately, Worth has a well-deserved reputation for the quality of such materials—for both professors and for students. With this edition you will find:

Exploring Child Development: A Media Tool Kit for Understanding Development

This CD series (also available for instructors on VHS and DVD) was prepared by a talented team of instructors including: Sheridan Dewolf, Grossmont College; Lisa Huffman, Ball State University; Thomas Ludwig, Hope College; Cathleen McGreal, Michigan State University; Amy Obegi, Grossmont College; Tanya Renner, Kapiolani Community College; Catherine Robertson, Grossmont College; and Stavros Valenti, Hofstra University. Combining video, animations, self-tests, and interactive exercises, the *Exploring Child Development Media Tool Kit* offers students hands-on, interactive learning. These activities range from investigations of classic experiments (like the visual cliff and the Strange Situation) to observations on children's play and adolescent risk-taking. The student tool kit includes 48 interactive video-based student activities, quizzes, and flashcards tied to every chapter of the book. The instructor tool kit includes more than 250 video clips and animations, along with teaching tips and discussion starters.

NANCY SHEEHAN / PHOTOEDIT

Memory Aid Personal motivation and action are crucial to early memory, and that is why Noel has no trouble remembering which shape covers the photograph of herself as a baby.

The Journey Through Childhood Observational Videos

Bringing observational learning to the classroom, this child development video set allows students to watch and listen to real children as a way of amplifying their reading of the text. Students will be able to observe children from birth through adolescence, in settings ranging from day-care centers to schools, homes, and doctor's offices, and from a multitude of cultures and communities across the globe (Africa, Europe, Latin America, and Asia). Some of the most noted experts in child development—Patricia Greenfield, Charles Nelson, Barbara Rogoff, and Carolyn Rovee-Collier—talk about their work in areas ranging from the biology of early brain development to prosocial behavior in middle childhood. This two-video set contains more than four hours of footage, including one hour of observational clips without narration. An instructor's observation workbook provides teaching and activity tips, while a student workbook helps students sharpen their observational skills and relate text material to real-life settings.

The Scientific American Frontiers Videos for Developmental Psychology

This remarkable resource provides instructors with 17 video segments of approximately 15 minutes each, on topics ranging from language development to nature–nurture issues. The videos can be used to launch classroom lectures or to emphasize and clarify course material. The *Faculty Guide* by Richard O. Straub (University of Michigan) describes and relates each segment to specific topics in the text.

Child Development Telecourse

The *Child Development: Stepping Stones* Telecourse, developed by Coast Learning Systems and Worth Publishers, will teach the fundamentals of child development. The course also explores the variety of individual and developmental contexts that influence development, such as socioeconomic status, culture, genetics, family, school, and society. Each video lesson includes specific real-life examples interwoven with commentary by subject matter experts. In addition, video lessons describe the whole child, while others focus on topics such as fathers, maltreatment, and school. The course includes 26 half-hour video lessons, a *Telecourse Study Guide,* and a *Faculty Manual* with test bank. The test bank is also available electronically.

eLibrary to accompany *The Developing Person Through the Life Span,* Sixth Edition

Worth Publishers' new eLibrary, located at www.worthpublishers.com/irel, brings together all of the existing text and supplementary resources in a single, easy-to-use Web interface. This searchable, Web-based integrator includes materials from the textbook, the Instructor's Resources, and select electronic supplements, including PowerPoint slides, and video clips. Through simple browse and search tools, instructors can quickly access virtually any piece of content and either download it to their computer or create a Web page to share with students. The eLibrary also features prebuilt, customizable collections for each chapter, allowing adopters to quickly access the "best of" the eLibrary and adapt it for their needs. While we do not offer a specific eLibrary for *The Developing Person Through Childhood and Adolescence,* the *Life Span* eLibrary will be of great benefit to faculty teaching the childhood and adolescent development course.

Instructor's Resources

This collection of resources written by Richard O. Straub has been hailed as the richest collection of instructor's resources in developmental psychology. This manual features chapter-by-chapter previews and lecture guides, learning objectives, springboard topics for discussion and debate, handouts for student projects, and supplementary readings from journal articles. Course planning suggestions, ideas for term projects, and a guide to audiovisual and software materials are also included. New to this edition are additional media teaching suggestions.

Study Guide

The *Study Guide* by Richard O. Straub helps students evaluate their understanding and retain their learning longer. Each chapter includes a review of key concepts, guided study questions, and section reviews that encourage students' active participation in the learning process. Two practice tests and a challenge test help them assess their mastery of the material.

PowerPoint Slides

A number of different presentation slides are available on the Web site or on the *Exploring Child Development: Instructor's Media Tool Kit* CD-ROM. There are two prebuilt PowerPoint slide sets for each text chapter—one featuring chapter outlines, the other featuring all chapter art and illustrations. These slides can be used as is or can be customized to fit individual needs. In addition, Kate Byerwalter (Grand Rapids Community College) has produced a set of enhanced lecture slides focusing on key themes from the text and featuring tables, graphs, and figures.

The Worth Image and Lecture Gallery

Worth's Image and Lecture Gallery, located at www.worthpublishers.com/ilg, is a convenient way to access electronic versions of lecture materials. Instructors can browse, search, and download illustrations from every Worth title, as well as prebuilt PowerPoint presentations that contain all chapter art or chapter section headings in text form. Users can also create personal folders on a personalized home page for easy organization of the materials.

PIOTR KAPA / CORBIS

How to Think About Flowers A person's stage of cognitive growth influences how he or she thinks about everything, including flowers. To a baby, in the sensorimotor stage, flowers are "known" through pulling, smelling, and perhaps tasting. Thinking is an active process from the beginning of life until the end.

Overhead Transparencies

This set of 75 full-color transparencies consists of key illustrations, charts, graphs, and tables from the textbook.

Test Bank and Computerized Test Bank

The test bank prepared by myself and Vivian Harper (San Joaquin Delta College) includes at least 90 multiple-choice and 70 fill-in, true-false, and essay questions for each chapter. Each question is keyed to the textbook by topic, page number, and level of difficulty. The Diploma computerized test bank, available on a dual-platform CD-ROM for Windows and Macintosh, guides instructors step by step through the process of creating a test, allowing them to quickly add an unlimited number of questions; edit, scramble, or resequence items; format a test; and include pictures, equations, and media links. The accompanying gradebook enables instructors to record students' grades throughout the course and includes the capacity to sort student records, view detailed analyses of test items, curve tests, generate reports, add weights to grades, and more.

The CD-ROM is also the access point for Diploma Online Testing, which allows instructors to create and administer secure exams over a network or over the Internet. In addition, Diploma has the ability to restrict tests to specific computers or time blocks. Blackboard- and WebCT-formatted versions of each item in the Test Bank are available on the CD-ROM. For more information on Diploma, please visit their Web site at www.brownstone.net.

Online Quizzing, Powered by Questionmark®

By sending students to the companion Web site for *The Developing Person Through Childhood and Adolescence,* located at www.worthpublishers.com/berger, instructors can easily and securely quiz students online using prewritten multiple-choice questions for each chapter. Even better, the questions are not from the test bank! Students receive instant feedback and can take the quizzes multiple times. Using the online quiz gradebook, instructors can view results by quiz, student, or question, or can get weekly results via email.

BOB DAEMMRICH/THE IMAGE WORKS

Reality and Fantasy Because teenagers can think analytically and hypothetically, they can use computers not only to obtain factual information and to email friends but also to imagine and explore future possibilities. This opportunity may be particularly important for adolescents like 17-year-old Julisa *(right)*. She is a student in a high school in Brownsville, Texas, that offers computer labs and other programs to children of migrant laborers.

Companion Web Site

The companion Web site by Catherine Robertson (Grossmont College), Michael S. Swett (University of California, Berkeley Extension Online), and Shelley Janiczek Woodson (Holyoke Community College), located at www.worthpublishers.com/berger, is an online educational setting for students and instructors. It is free and does not require any special access codes or passwords. Student resources include: detailed chapter outlines; learning objectives; annotated Web links, online quizzes with immediate feedback and instructor notification; Internet exercises; critical thinking questions; case study exercises; an English/Spanish glossary; interactive flashcards in both English and Spanish; and frequently asked questions about developmental psychology. For instructors, the Web site includes a full array of teaching tools, such as PowerPoint slides, syllabus posting, an online gradebook, and links to various resources, including WebCT, Blackboard, the eLibrary, and the Worth Image and Lecture Gallery.

Thanks

I'd like to thank those academic reviewers who have read this book in every edition and who have provided suggestions, criticisms, references, and encouragement. They have all made this a better book. I want to mention especially those who have reviewed this edition:

Melissa Atkins, *Marshall University*
Cynthia L. Baer, *Lamar Community College*
Kirsten Bell, *Waukesha County Technical College*
Patricia Bellas, *Irvine Valley College*
Penelope L. Blair, *Evergreen Valley College*
Krista Carter, *Colby Community College*
Kimberly Chapman, *Blue River Community College*
Nancy E. Clavere, *Woodland Community College*
Alison Corsino, *Concordia University*
Marcie Coulter-Kern, *Manchester College*
Shawn DiNarda Watters, *Mount Union College*
Gary G. Felt, *City University*
Killian James Garvey, *University of New England*
Donna Goetz, *Elmhurst College*
Laura Gruntmeir, *Redlands Community College*
Sandra Hellyer, *Butler University*
April Mansfield Juarez, *Long Beach City College*
Kathy G. Kelley, *Chabot Community College*
Iris Obille Lafferty, *Mira Costa College*
Paul T. Lewis, *Bethel College*
Laura Manson, *Santa Monica College*
Jessica Miller, *Mesa State College*

Mary Beth Miller, *Fresno City College*
J. Ann Moylan, *California State University, Sacramento*
Winnie Mucherah, *Ball State University*
Ronnie Naramore, *Angelina College*
Amy Obegi, *Grossmont College*
John W. Otey, *Southern Arkansas University*
Wendy Parise, *Santa Monica College*
Jeff Pedroza, *Santa Ana College*
Antoinette Phillips, *El Camino College*
Ralph G. Pifer, *Sauk Valley Community College*
Michelle L. Pilati, *Rio Hondo College*
Dawn M. Pope, *University of Wisconsin, Oshkosh*
John Prange, *Irvine Valley College*
Jim Previte, *Victor Valley College*
Gaile Price, *Loyola Marymount University Extension, East Los Angeles College*
Kathie Reid, *California State University, Fresno*
Amy Kathleen Resch, *Citrus College*
Eileen Roth, *Los Angeles Community College District—Instructional Television, Glendale Community College*
Sherry Schanke, *St. Mary of the Woods College*
Susan Schlicht, *St. Cloud Technical College*
Bernard Schwartz, *Santiago Canyon College*
Peggy Skinner, *South Plains College*
Ling-Yi Zhou, *University of St. Francis*

In addition, I wish to thank those instructors who participated in our online survey. We've tried to apply the insights gained from their experiences with the sixth edition to make this new edition better.

Madeleine Boskovitz, *University of Houston, Downtown*
Peter Carson, *South Florida Community College*
Jurgen Combs, *Shenandoah University*
James Greene, *Brigham Young University, Idaho*
Kathy Harris, *Iowa Western Community College*
Danijela Korom, *University of Connecticut*
Deborah Laible, *Lehigh University*
Bill Mesa, *Colorado Christian University*
Mary Beth Miller, *Fresno City College*
Jane Ogden, *East Texas Baptist University*
Catherine Perz, *University of Houston—Victoria*
Patti Price, *Wingate University*
Deb Reay, *University of Nebraska Medical Center*
Betsy Stern, *Milwaukee Area Technical College, North*
Shelley Warm, *Palm Beach Community College South*
Shelley Janiczek Woodson, *Holyoke Community College*

The editorial, production, and marketing people at Worth Publishers are dedicated to meeting the highest standards of excellence. Their devotion of time, effort, and talent to every aspect of publishing is a model for the industry. I particularly would like to thank: Stacey Alexander, Jessica Bayne, Eve Conte, Cele Gardner, Tom Kling, Tracey Kuehn, Bianca Moscatelli, Katherine Nurre, Danny Pucci, Babs Reingold, Kimberly Rossi, Barbara Seixas, Nicole Villamora, Vivien Weiss, and Catherine Woods.

Kathleen Stassen Berger

New York, September 2005

PART I

The Beginnings

The science of human development has many beginnings, as you will see in the following four chapters.

Chapter 1 introduces what we study, why, and how, explaining some research strategies and methods used to understand human development. Chapter 2 explains how theories organize and guide our study. You will be introduced to five major theories—three grand theories and two emergent ones—that are used in developmental research.

Chapter 3 traces the interaction of heredity and environment. Each human being develops in accord with chemical instructions on the genes and chromosomes, influencing everything from the thickness of toenails to the swiftness of brain waves. Personality traits, many diseases, and biological growth are also partly genetic. But genes never act alone. The environment—that is, the individual's surroundings—also influences every aspect of development. Understanding the fundamentals of the interaction between genes and the environment is a foundation for understanding development.

Chapter 4 details the beginning of human life, from one dividing cell to a baby's arrival. Those expectant prenatal months and first postnatal minutes influence the decades that follow.

Together these four chapters start our study of human life.

Chapter One

Introduction

What will happen to the infant just born, or to the 1-year-old who says "grandma" for the first time, or to the schoolchild trying to make a friend? What about you, or your child, or your father—how does anyone become who they are, and what will happen to them tomorrow or next year? This book is about the development of those individuals and all the billions of others, worldwide.

Why should you care? There are dozens of reasons, some explained in this chapter, several that will become evident as you study, and this one, right now: You will learn to look more closely at the people around you, and small moments will become precious. This is my experience:

> One day I entered my 8-month-old baby's room to be greeted by a smile and "hahh" as she held on to the slats of her crib, kicking her chubby little legs excitedly.
>
> "Hi, Elissa," I grinned back joyously. "You're talking!"

Most people would not consider "hahh" talking. But learning about infants had taught me that language begins with noises and gestures, although the first identifiable words don't come until later. You will experience such joy, too, in moments you might not have noticed or appreciated if you had not studied child development.

Defining Development

The **science of human development** *seeks to understand how and why people—all kinds of people, everywhere—change or remain the same over time.* This definition has three crucial elements.

First, and most important, developmental study is a *science*. It depends on theories, data, analysis, critical thinking, and methods just like every other science, from physics to economics. The goal is to understand how and why—that is, to discover the processes of development and the reasons for it. Using the scientific method means that developmentalists ask crucial questions and seek accurate answers.

Science cannot decide the purpose of life; we need philosophy or religion to help us with that. Literature and art sometimes provide insights beyond the data of the scientific experiment. But "the empirical sciences will show us the way, the means, and the obstacles" (Koops, 2003, p. 18) in making life what we want it to be. To say that something is *empirical* means it is based on data, on many experiences, on actual facts. Without the conclusions and applications of empirical science—everything from antibiotics to immunizations—human life would be "solitary, poor, nasty, brutish, and short," as Thomas Hobbes noted in 1651.

Second, the science of development studies *all kinds of people*—young and old; rich and poor; of every ethnicity, background, sexual orientation, culture, and nationality. The challenge is to identify the universalities (beyond the obvious ones of birth and death) and the differences (beyond each

science of human development The science that seeks to understand how and why people change or remain the same over time. People of all ages and circumstances are studied.

new person's unique genetic code) and then to describe these universalities and differences in ways that simultaneously distinguish and unify all humans. For example, when you first meet someone, you recognize that person as human (universal) and as a member of his or her sex and generation (differences within universals; we all have a sex and an age). But when you think about yourself or someone you know well, you realize how much more complex each individual is. Developmental scientists seek to convey both: the generalities and the specifics.

Developmentalists aren't the only ones who can achieve this goal. Novelists can also be insightful. Christina Garcia wrote a novel in which a Cuban American woman, vehemently anti-Communist, is raising an adolescent daughter who hates her mother's politics. In one episode, the mother asks her daughter to paint a mural of the Statue of Liberty for the opening of a new store. At the public unveiling, the mother sees that Liberty has a safety pin through her nose and that the torch floats above her grasp. The daughter reports:

> The blood has drained from my mother's face and her lips are moving as if she wants to say something but can't find the words. . . . A lumpish man charges Liberty with a pocket knife. . . . Mom swings her new handbag and clubs the guy cold, inches from the painting. . . . And I, I love my mother very much at that moment.
>
> *[Garcia, 2004, pp. 143, 144]*

As for specifics, did this episode actually happen? No, probably not (it appears in a work of fiction). As for generalities, can mother–daughter love overcome generational and political differences? Yes. Researchers have documented the power of family bonds; the dramatic power of this incident arises from that universality.

You might wonder how a novel relates to science, since science, unlike art, depends on objective data, empirical observations, and tested theories. Yet the struggle to understand both the universal and the unique in *all kinds of people* is the central task of both artists and scientists—and, for that matter, of philosophers, preachers, and every other thoughtful human being. Using science to study people is one effective means to that end.

The third crucial element of the definition is *change over time*. The very word *development* implies growth and change. The study of human development includes all the changes of human life, from the very beginning to the very end. This book stops before adulthood, but the same principles underlie the entire life span. There is a "reciprocal connection" between childhood and adulthood (Baltes et al., 1998); between prenatal and postnatal life; between ages 2, 12, 22, and so on. This means that "even if one is primarily interested in the study of infants and infant development, part of one's intellectual agenda requires attention to life-span development" (Baltes et al., 1998, p. 1030).

continuity The word that signifies developments over time that appear to persist, unchanging, from one age to the next. Parents might recognize the same personality traits in their grown children that they saw in them as infants.

discontinuity The word that signifies developments that appear quite different from those that came before. A person, or a researcher, might believe that "everything changed" when school started or when puberty began, for instance.

The definition includes both *how people change* and *how they remain the same*. **Continuity** and **discontinuity** are key words describing the processes of development. *Continuity* refers to characteristics that are stable over time (unchanging), and *discontinuity* refers to characteristics unlike those that came before (changing). Both continuity (as with biological sex or temperament) and discontinuity (as with speaking a new language or quitting an addictive drug) are evident in each person's life.

Five Characteristics of Development

Developmentalists are acutely aware of the reciprocal connection between one moment in life and another, which leads them to five principles, all arising from a life-span approach to development. These five characteristics, useful for understanding any age (Baltes et al., 1998; Smith & Baltes, 1999; Staudinger & Lindenberger, 2003), are:

- *Multidirectional.* Change occurs in every direction, not always in a straight line. Gains and losses, predictable growth and unexpected transformations, are part of the human experience, evident at every age and with every type of development.
- *Multicontextual.* Human lives are embedded in many contexts, including historical conditions, economic constraints, and cultural traditions.
- *Multicultural.* The science of development recognizes many cultures—not just internationally but also within each nation—each with a distinct set of values, traditions, and tools for living.
- *Multidisciplinary.* Numerous academic fields—especially psychology, biology, education, and sociology, but also neuroscience, economics, religion, anthropology, history, medicine, genetics, and many more—contribute data and insights to the science of development.
- *Plasticity.* Every individual, and every trait within each individual, can be altered at any point in the life span. Change is ongoing, although neither random nor easy.

Each of these five principles merits further explanation.

Multidirectional

The study of human development is the study of change; it is dynamic, not static. Developmentalists sometimes analyze each fraction of a second, as when a barely perceptible change in a newborn's face reflects a parent's fleeting glance (e.g., Lavelli & Fogel, 2005). More often years, not seconds, are analyzed. In studying dynamic change, developmentalists have discovered that each aspect of life (physical health, intellectual growth, social interaction) is multidirectional; any direction—up, down, stable, or erratic—is possible. There is evidence for simple growth, radical transformation, improvement, and decline as well as for continuity—day to day, year to year, and generation to generation (see Figure 1.1).

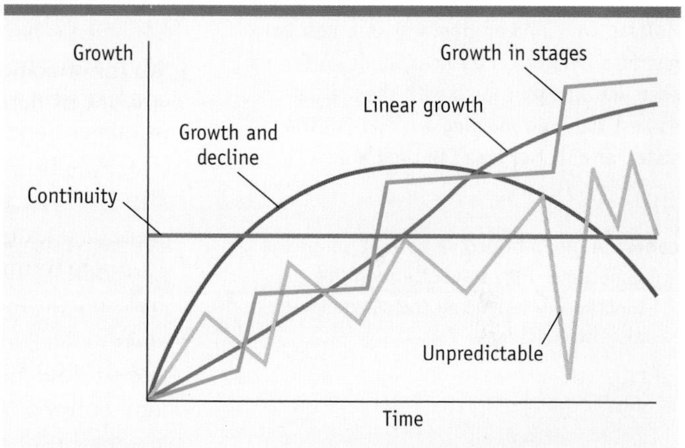

FIGURE 1.1 **Patterns of Developmental Growth** Many patterns of developmental growth have been discovered by careful research. Although linear (or near-linear) progress seems most common, scientists now find that almost no aspect of human change follows the linear pattern exactly.

The Butterfly Effect

Small changes may have large effects, precisely because every change is part of a dynamic system. The potential power of a small change is called the **butterfly effect**, after a 1972 speech by a weather expert, Edward Lorenz, titled "Predictability: Does the Flap of a Butterfly's Wings in Brazil Set Off a Tornado in Texas?"

The idea of the butterfly effect is that, just as one drop of water might make an overfull glass suddenly spill over, so a small increase in wind velocity in the Amazon might be the final force that triggers a weather front resulting in a storm a thousand miles away. The possibility that small input may result in large output applies to human thoughts and actions as well (Masterpasqua & Perna, 1997). To use a developmental example, one cigarette smoked by a pregnant woman could be a matter of life or death if a fetus is already fragile and underweight for other reasons. In fact, however, most butterfly wings have no noticeable effects, nor do most puffs of a cigarette. The butterfly effect means that a tiny event *could* have an enormous impact, not that it always does.

butterfly effect The idea that a small event or thing can have a large impact if it happens to tip the balance, causing other changes that create a major event.

Continuity in Wartime

The opposite effect occurs as well: Large changes may have no perceptible effect. For example, a group of 4- to 6-year-old children, fleeing with their mothers from war-torn Bosnia, were undernourished, had been shot at, and knew that some of

AP PHOTO / HIDAJET DELIC

Holding On Children from war-torn Kosovo rest at a refugee center near Sarajevo, Bosnia. They are actively coping with their situation as best they can, holding a friend, a little sister, or a loaf of bread in their arms.

their relatives were dead—yet were surprisingly "high on positive characteristics and low on psychological symptoms and problems," according to the aid workers in their refugee camp (Dybdahl, 2001, p. 1225).

These preschoolers' ability to "cope and function in everyday life" (p. 1226) is less astonishing when other research is considered. In general, young children survive traumatic experiences as long as their mothers are nearby and supportive. A close bond to a loving caregiver protects against adversity of many kinds, including illness, poverty, and even war (Burlingham & Freud, 1942). In this example, continuity (the ongoing mother–child bond) was more powerful than the horrific discontinuity the children experienced.

Multicontextual

Humans develop in many contexts that profoundly affect their development. Contexts include, among many others, the physical surroundings (for example, climate, noise level, population density) and the family situation. Here we explain two aspects of the *social context*—that is, of the society or the social setting: the historical and socioeconomic contexts.

The Historical Context

cohort A group of people born at about the same time. They travel through life together, experiencing the same major historical changes.

All persons born within a few years of one another are said to be a **cohort,** a group of people whose shared age means that they travel through life together. (The term *cohort* once included only people from the same region and social class as well as the same era, but, with increasing globalization and democratization, it now means everyone born at about the same time.) The people in a particular cohort, in other words, experience the same history—including the same assumptions, important public events, technologies, and popular trends.

If you wonder whether national trends and events really affect individual lives, consider your first name—a very personal word chosen especially for you. You may not realize how much that choice, and your reaction to it, is influenced by the historical context until you look at Table 1.1, which lists the top five boys' and girls' names given to newborns in the United States in 1923, 1943, 1963, 1983, and 2003. If you can match the five sets of names to their years, you are

© 2005 MICK STEVENS FROM CARTOONBANK.COM. ALL RIGHTS RESERVED

"And this is Charles, our web-master."

Computer Expert in a Baseball Cap Cohort differences become most apparent when new technology appears. Which age group is most likely to download music onto iPods or to send text messages on cellular phones?

TABLE 1.1 **Which First Names Were Most Popular When?**

Boys' Names	Girls' Names	Year
1. David, John, Michael, James, Robert	Lisa, Mary, Maria, Susan, Karen	
2. John, Robert, William, James, Charles	Mary, Dorothy, Helen, Margaret, Betty	
3. Michael, Christopher, Matthew, David, Daniel	Jennifer, Jessica, Ashley, Amanda, Sarah	
4. Jacob, Michael, Joshua, Matthew, Andrew	Emily, Emma, Madison, Hannah, Olivia	
5. James, Robert, John, William, Richard	Mary, Barbara, Patricia, Linda, Carol	

Source: Social Security Administration, 2004.

sensitive to cohort shifts. Your thoughts about your own name are affected by how many other people, of what age and background, have it. This is an example of the historical context impinging on you.

Some customs, such as severe physical punishment and child employment, seem to ensure suffering, which people accepted when historical conditions resulted in many unwanted children. Although most modern parents are thrilled when their infants begin to crawl, in colonial America infants were tightly swaddled and tied to their cradles day and night so that they could hardly move, let alone crawl, because

> parents and physicians alike viewed crawling on all fours, not as a natural stage of human development, but as a bad habit that, if not thwarted, would remain the baby's primary form of locomotion for the rest of its life. . . . As the common form of locomotion for most animals, crawling raised too many fears and negative associations.
>
> [Calvert, 2003, p. 65]

Obviously, the "right" way to raise a child depends on the historical context.

? OBSERVATIONAL QUIZ (see answer, page 10): Which set of names belongs to which year: 1923, 1943, 1963, 1983, 2003?

The Socioeconomic Context

When social scientists study the second major contextual influence, the socioeconomic context, they often focus on **socioeconomic status,** abbreviated **SES.** Sometimes SES is called "social class" (as in "middle class" or "working class").

socioeconomic status (SES) Part of the socioeconomic context, whereby people are classified as rich, poor, middle class, and so on according to income, education, occupation, and so on.

ASIM TANVEER / REUTERS / CORBIS

Culturally Acceptable Putting very young children to work is still a widespread custom in many parts of the world. The International Labor Organization estimates that, worldwide, 246 million children aged 5 to 17 are employed—often at very low wages. These children are working in an embroidery shop in Pakistan.

! Answer to Observational Quiz (from page 9): (1) 1963, (2) 1923, (3) 1983, (4) 2003, (5) 1943.

Socioeconomic status is particularly important for children. In almost every nation of the world, more children than adults live in low-income households (Qvortrup, 2000). Growing children, even more than adults, are likely to suffer from inadequate nutrition, education, or medical care. For instance, more children than adults die in famines.

Scientists measure a family's SES by a combination of income and other factors, such as education, neighborhood, and parental occupation. (In the past, the father's occupation was the crucial one; now researchers use either parent's occupation.) The SES of a family consisting of, say, an infant, an unemployed mother, and a father who earns $12,000 a year would be low if the wage earner is an illiterate dishwasher living in an urban slum, but would be much higher if the wage earner is a postdoctoral student living on campus and teaching part time.

As this example illustrates, SES includes advantages and disadvantages, opportunities and limitations, past history and future prospects—all of which affect SES via buying power, knowledge, and habits. Although poverty obviously limits access to high-quality housing, medical care, and so on, other factors (such as the mother's education) can make the low-income child's life better or worse.

Multicultural

Culture affects each human at every moment. Precisely because culture is so pervasive, people rarely notice their culture while they are immersed in it— just as fish do not know they are surrounded by water.

Deciding What to Do Each Moment

When social scientists use the term *culture,* they refer to the countless specific manifestations of a social group's "design for living." The social group may be citizens of a nation, residents of a region within a nation, members of an ethnic group, children in one neighborhood, or even students in a college community. Any group may have its own culture, which includes values, technologies, customs, clothes, dwellings, cuisine, and patterns of behavior.

Thus, culture includes all the decisions that people make, from whether to cover their mouth when they laugh to what to eat for breakfast. For example, do

JOAN LEBOLD COHEN / PHOTO RESEARCHERS, INC.

Cherish the Child Cultures vary tremendously in their views of such seemingly personal matters as ideal family size. China's "one-child" policy urges every family to limit reproduction in order to shrink the country's population and to expand its economy.

? Observational Quiz (see answer, page 12): What three signs suggest that this community enjoys this boy?

STEVE RUARK / SYRACUSE NEWSPAPERS / THE IMAGE WORKS

How Have You Changed Since Childhood? Many colleges have a spring festival, when students can act like kids again—as these sophomores at LeMoyne College in Syracuse, New York, are doing. Although blowing bubbles may seem to be child's play, the two have obviously changed since childhood. Change is evident not only in their physical size and shape but also in their willingness to be friends with someone of the other sex.

? Observational Quiz (see answer, page 12): One type of change is historical. Can you see three signs that this photo was taken in 2000, not 20 years before?

you use a highlighter, study in the library, or call professors by their first names? Why or why not? The reasons are partly cultural.

People can belong to more than one culture, following more than one design for living, with the particular choice dependent on their immediate context. In multiethnic nations such as the United States and Canada, many individuals are considered multicultural; they function well not only within the dominant culture (the national culture) but also within regional, ethnic, school, and other cultures.

Cultures are dynamic, always changing, in part because individuals typically abandon some aspects of whatever culture they embraced as children. Cultural shifts within individuals and within social groups are not unusual, especially when historical, geographical, or family circumstances change; "culture is external, acquired, and transmissible to others" (Smedley & Smedley, 2005). Because of changing contexts and choices, every generation experiences a somewhat different culture than previous generations did.

Multidisciplinary

The study of human development requires insight and information from many disciplines, because each person develops simultaneously in body, mind, and spirit. Development is thus often divided into three domains—the *biosocial, cognitive,* and *psychosocial domains*—that roughly correspond to biology, psychology, and sociology. (Figure 1.2 provides a detailed description of each domain.)

However, as you will see repeatedly, all three domains interact. Although language learning is primarily cognitive, a baby learns to talk because of a combination of *biosocial development* (maturation of the brain and vocal cords), *cognitive development* (ability to understand the connections among objects, ideas, and words), and *psychosocial development* (the baby's reactions to others' responses). The placement of any topic within one chapter or domain never means that that topic is exclusively biosocial, cognitive, or psychosocial.

Moreover, many more disciplines besides biology, psychology, and sociology contribute to our study. As one expert explains: "The study of development is a huge community enterprise that spans generations and many disciplines"

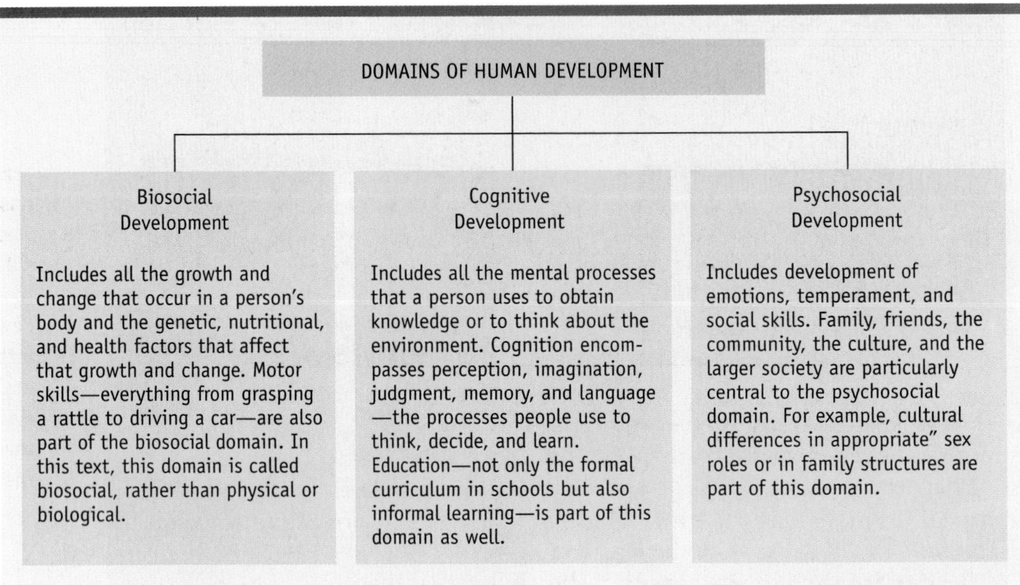

FIGURE 1.2 **The Three Domains** The division of human development into three domains makes it easier to study, but remember that very few factors belong exclusively to one domain or another. Development is not piecemeal but holistic: Each aspect of development is related to all three domains.

(Moore, 2002, p. 74). Multiple disciplines are needed because human beings develop in several domains, multifaceted contexts, and diverse cultures.

Childhood Psychopathology

A multidisciplinary approach is particularly urgent when children have serious problems, such as psychopathologies, or disorders of the mind—autism, severe depression, phobias, and so on. Psychopathologies tend to "run in families," but it is not clear whether a child's mental illness results from genetic inheritance or faulty upbringing.

Progress has been made in research on fear, because the fear response is localized within the *amygdala,* a small structure located deep within the brain. Neuroscientists know that the amygdala is a major source of fear and anxiety. For decades, psychiatrists have noted that some people are much more anxious than others, sometimes suffering from extreme phobias (irrational fears) or panic attacks (sudden, overwhelming anxiety). Developmentalists have debated whether such emotional extremes are genetic or learned, inherited from the parents or taught through the parents' own fearfulness. New research sheds light on this debate.

! Answer to Observational Quiz (from page 10): At least four adults are smiling at him; he is eating an apple that was brought to the market for sale; he is allowed to sit on the table with the food. If you noticed another sign—his new green sandals—give yourself bonus credit.

! Answer to Observational Quiz (from page 11): Loose, printed T-shirts, backward baseball caps, and plastic-lidded spout cups were rare before 1980.

Research from Many Disciplines on the Amygdala

The photographs of brain scans on page 13 show the average amygdala activity of two groups of people, safe within a scientist's laboratory, responding to photos of faces showing fear or surprise (Hariri et al., 2002). The red areas show activation of the amygdala. The average size of the red area for the group on the left is twice the average size for the group on the right.

What makes this research noteworthy is that these two groups differ genetically. The researchers first analyzed a particular gene (the serotonin transporter gene) that is usually inherited in one of two forms (alleles). People who inherit

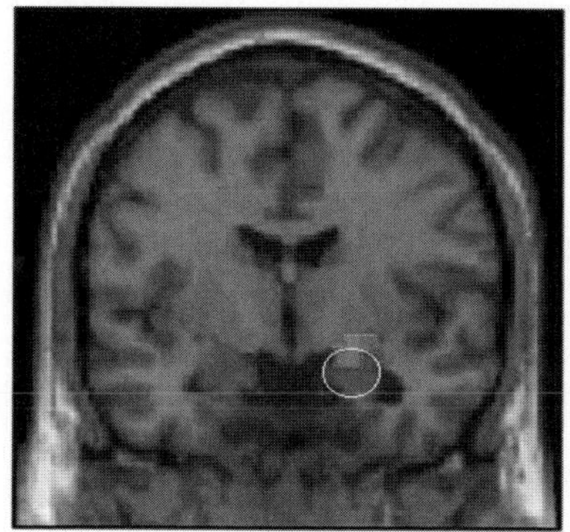

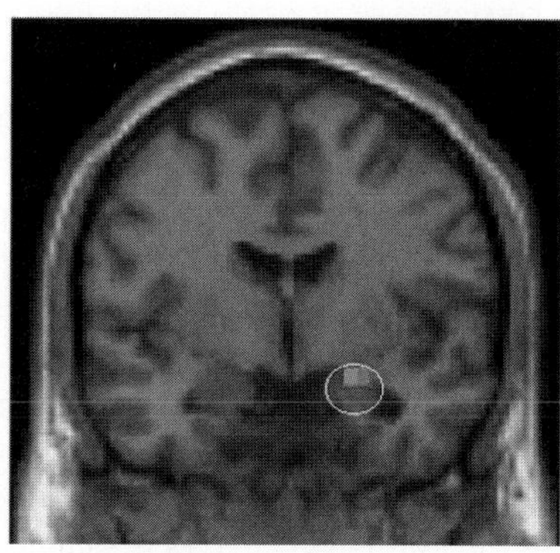

Brain Alert These two images represent the averages of brain scans of two groups of people, all of whom were looking at the same photographs of faces that were showing fear. The areas in red reflect activity in the amygdala. Which group was more afraid, and why? For the answers, see the text.

the shorter version of the gene are more likely to score high in fearfulness on clinical personality tests than are those with the longer version.

Combining genetic research and brain research, these researchers found that people with the short version of the gene also had more active amygdalas. This finding suggests that "small genetic differences might shape the way people respond to the world" (Miller, 2002, p. 319). As this study reveals, heredity, brain activity, and emotions are directly linked.

A multidisciplinary approach must include psychological research as well as biological, genetic, and neuroscientific studies. A field called "social cognitive neuroscience" (which combines several disciplines, in all three domains of development) has shown that each person's past experience and the immediate context also affect amygdala activity (Phelps et al., 2000; Wheeler & Fiske, 2005).

In one set of experiments, participants examined photographs of unfamiliar people from various ethnic backgrounds. Amygdala activity occurred when the task was to categorize (in this case, to estimate the ages of the people in the photos) but not when the task was neutral (to see whether a dot appeared on the people's faces) or individualized (to say whether the person might like a particular vegetable—e.g., asparagus, eggplant, or broccoli). When the participants were primed to perceive categories, not individuals, the fear centers of their brains were active (Wheeler & Fiske, 2005). The researchers concluded that "social cognitive goals differentiated amygdala activity patterns" (p. 61).

Thus, activation of the amygdala depends not only on genes but also on past learning and current context. In other words, biology, psychology, and sociology all help explain why some people feel threatened in situations that others perceive as harmless.

Plasticity

The term *plasticity* denotes two complementary aspects of development: Human traits can be molded into different forms and shapes (as plastic can be), yet people maintain a certain durability of identity (again, like plastic, which takes decades to break down). Culture and upbringing are important to both these aspects of plasticity; so are genes and other biological constraints. This dual influence is strikingly evident in the developmental history of my nephew David.

Plasticity provides both hope and realism—hope because change is possible, and realism because children must build on what has come before. In some ways, the concept of plasticity encompasses all the other four characteristics of development—its multidirectional, multicontextual, multicultural, and multidisciplinary nature. People can overcome handicaps and reexamine values, but they cannot ignore them. No matter what directional path a person follows, the journey begins at some particular point and then proceeds from that point—up, down, or straight ahead, but always connected to earlier growth.

Especially for Public Health Professionals Can immunization protect an embryo?

A Case to Study

My Nephew David

In the spring of 1967, in rural Kentucky, an epidemic of rubella (German measles) reached my sister-in-law, who had a rash and a sore throat for a couple of days, and her 4-week-old embryo, who was damaged for life. David was born in November with a life-threatening heart defect and with thick cataracts covering both eyes. Other damage included minor malformations of the thumbs, feet, jaw, and teeth, as well as of the brain.

My brother is a professor and his wife is a nurse; their cultural and socioeconomic contexts encouraged them to seek outside help. They listened to a teacher at the Kentucky School for the Blind who knew that development is plastic. She told them to stop blaming themselves and stop overprotecting David. If their son was going to learn about his world, he had to explore it.

For example, rather than confining David to a crib or playpen, they were to provide him with a large rug for a play area. Whenever he crawled off the rug, they were taught to say "no" and place him back in the middle of it. He would learn to use his sense of touch to decide where he could explore safely without bumping into walls or furniture.

Even with special attention, progress was slow. At age 3, David could not yet talk, chew solid food, use the toilet, coordinate his fingers, or even walk normally. An IQ test showed him to be severely mentally retarded. Fortunately, although deafness is common for rubella syndrome children, David could hear. By age 5, in 1972, one eye had been destroyed, but surgery had removed the cataract on the other eye, allowing some vision. Two heart operations had been successful.

By then, the social construction that children with severe disabilities are unteachable was changing. David's parents enrolled him in four schools. Two were for children with cerebral palsy: One had morning classes, and the other—40 miles away—afternoon classes. On Fridays, when those schools were closed, David attended a school for the mentally retarded.

On Sunday mornings he went to church school, his first experience with "mainstreaming"—the then-new idea that children with special needs should be educated with normal children. Particularly in the church community, the cultural-ethnic context of northern Kentucky benefited David: Accepting the disabled and helping neighbors are basic Appalachian values.

At age 7, David entered public school, one of the first severely disabled children to be mainstreamed. His motor skills were poor (among other things, he had difficulty controlling a pencil); his efforts to read were limited by his faulty vision; and his social skills were seriously impaired (he pinched people he didn't like, hugged girls too tightly, cried and laughed at inappropriate times).

By age 10, David had made great strides. He had skipped a year of school and was a fifth-grader. He could read—with a magnifying glass—at the eleventh-grade level and was labeled "intellectually gifted" according to tests of verbal and math skills. Outside school he began to learn a second language, play the violin, and sing in the choir.

David now works as a translator of German texts, and he reports that he is

> generally quite happy, but secretly a little happier lately, especially since November, because I have been consistently getting a pretty good vibrato when I am singing, not only by myself but in congregational hymns in church. [I asked what vibrato is:] When a note bounces up and down within a quarter tone either way of concert pitch, optimally between 5.5 and 8.2 times per second.
>
> *[David, 2002]*

Amazing. David is both knowledgeable and happy, and he continues to develop his skills. He also has a wry sense of humor. When I told him that I wasn't progressing as fast as I wanted to in revising this text, even though I was working very hard every day, he replied, "That sounds just like a certain father I know."

The rubella damage will always be with David, limiting his development. But as his aunt, I have watched him defy pessimistic predictions. David is a testimonial for plasticity: No human is entirely, inevitably, restricted by past experiences.

Three Brothers No human is untouched by understanding the personal story of another. I have learned many things from David, shown in this family photo with his two older brothers, Bill *(left)* and Michael *(right)*. One is the role of siblings: Bill and Michael protected their younger brother, but David also taught them, making them more nurturant than most young men in their community. I know this firsthand—these boys were the closest thing my daughters had to big brothers, and they tolerated teasing that some older cousins would have put a stop to.

KATHLEEN BERGER

The Person Within the Contexts

The five characteristics of human development lead to one conclusion: Nobody is exactly like the statistically "average" person of his or her cohort, socioeconomic status, or culture. Each person is influenced in divergent directions by many contexts, whose power varies from individual to individual, age to age, situation to situation, and family to family. Moreover, each person has unique genes and experiences, and each might defy easy predictions. David was not expected to survive, much less to contribute to society.

Not the Typical Path This woman's lifelong ambition is to walk the 2,160-mile Appalachian Trail from Maine to Georgia. She is considerably more active than the average member of her cohort.

Resilience

One topic of great interest to developmentalists is **resilience,** the ability of some children to overcome severe threats to their development (Clarke & Clarke, 2003; Luthar, 2003b; Luthar et al., 2000; Masten, 2001; Walsh, 2002). For instance, a child growing up in a low-income household in a rundown neighborhood, with a mentally ill mother, an unemployed alcoholic father, and several brothers and sisters, is likely to become a delinquent, dropout, drug addict, and criminal. Statistics reveal that, no matter what the culture or ethnicity, such childhoods usually lead to troubled adulthoods.

However, some children growing up in such terrible circumstances become happy, healthy, and productive adults. These individuals may graduate from college, hold good jobs, marry loving spouses, and raise happy, productive children. They are resilient. How does this happen?

As you would guess from employing a multicontextual perspective, the child's personality, the specifics of schooling, the nature of family life, and the characteristics of the neighborhood all contribute to resilience. None of these factors are simple.

resilience The ability of some people to endure conditions that are often harmful—such as poverty, mental illness, social disruptions, and low intelligence—and to adapt in ways that make them stronger.

Neighborhood Efficacy

Contrary to popular opinion, income levels are not the best measures of how well a neighborhood functions for children. Some low-income neighborhoods are high in a characteristic called *collective efficacy,* as when neighbors create an active, informal network of people who show concern for one another and for their block. Such actions as picking up trash on the street, repairing broken windows,

A Dangerous Place for Children This neighborhood in Washington, D.C., shows no signs of collective efficacy on the part of its adult residents. The trash, boarded-up windows, and broken pavement are signals that any child who lives nearby is at higher risk of poor health, family maltreatment, and social neglect.

Response for Public Health Professionals (from page 13): No and yes. Embryos cannot be vaccinated, but immunization of preschool children would have prevented this rubella epidemic. In 1967 the historical context allowed protection against polio and whooping cough, but rubella immunization was not yet available. If David had been conceived in 1980 or later, he would not have had all the problems he did.

and keeping an eye on the children are more accurate signs of a neighborhood's emotional and physical health than is average income (Cohen et al., 2000; Sampson et al., 1997). Because religious and social institutions can enhance collective efficacy, social scientists assess whether local churches, temples, mosques, schools, clinics, stores, and community centers indeed build collective efficacy and thereby encourage resilience.

Residential stability is also more important than income levels (Adam, 2004). Children benefit if their families and neighbors live in the same houses for years, probably because good neighborly relationships and effective neighborhood functioning take a long time to develop.

Resilience is discussed in more detail in Chapter 13. For now, just remember that children's outcomes are affected, but not necessarily determined, by their contexts. As an illustration, consider the African American poet Maya Angelou, who refused to let her life be determined by her historical, cultural, and socioeconomic contexts.

Issues and Applications

"My Name Wasn't Mary"

Maya Angelou was born Marguerite Johnson in 1929 into a community in rural Arkansas that was so racially segregated that she thought "white folks couldn't be people because their feet were too small, their skin too white and see-throughy, and they didn't walk on the balls of their feet the way people did—they walked on their heels like horses" (Angelou, 1970, p. 76). At age 10 Marguerite began to learn about white people (her "finishing school," she called it) as an apprentice to Miss Glory, who worked as a maid for Mrs. Cullinan. Once, when Marguerite was serving Mrs. Cullinan and her friends:

> One of the women asked, "What's your name, girl?" It was the speckled-face one. Mrs. Cullinan said, "She doesn't talk much. Her name is Margaret." . . .
>
> I smiled at her. Poor thing . . . couldn't even pronounce my name correctly.
>
> "She's a sweet little thing, though."
>
> "Well, that may be, but the name's too long. I'd never bother myself. I'd call her Mary if I were you."
>
> I fumed into the kitchen. That horrible woman would never have the chance to call me Mary because if I was starving I'd never work for her. I decided I wouldn't pee on her if her heart was on fire. . . .
>
> The very next day . . . Miss Glory and I were washing up the lunch dishes when Mrs. Cullinan came to the doorway, "Mary?"
>
> Miss Glory asked, "Who?" . . . "Her name is Margaret, ma'am. Her name's Margaret."
>
> "That's too long. She's Mary from now on. Heat that soup from last night and put it in the china tureen and Mary, I want you to carry it carefully."
>
> Every person I knew had a hellish horror of being "called out of his name." It was a dangerous practice to call a Negro anything that could be loosely construed as insulting because of the centuries of their having been called niggers, jigs, dinges, blackbirds, crows, boots and spooks.
>
> Miss Glory had a fleeting second of feeling sorry for me. Then as she handed me the hot tureen she said, "Don't mind, don't pay that no mind. Sticks and stones may break my bones, but words. . . . You know, I been working for her for twenty years. . . . Twenty years. I wasn't much older than you. My name used to be Hallelujah. That's what Ma named me, but my mistress gave me 'Glory' and it stuck. . . ."

DAN NIERLING, CEDAR FALLS COURIER/THE WATERLOO/AP PHOTO

Today, Everybody Knows Her Name Poet and best-selling author Maya Angelou speaks at the University of Northern Iowa about the healing and saving nature of poetry. She encouraged the members of the audience to become the "composers" of their own lives.

For a few seconds it was a tossup over whether I would laugh (imagine being called Hallelujah) or cry (imagine letting some white woman rename you for her convenience). My anger saved me from either outburst. I had to quit the job, but the problem was going to be how to do it. Momma wouldn't allow me to quit for just any reason. . . .

For a week I looked into Mrs. Cullinan's face [an insult] as she called me Mary. She ignored my coming late and leaving early. Miss Glory was a little annoyed because I had begun to leave egg yolk on the dishes and wasn't putting much heart in polishing the silver. I hoped she would complain to our boss, but she didn't.

Then Bailey [Maya's brother, age 11] solved my dilemma. He had me describe the contents of the cupboard and the particular plates she liked best. Her favorite piece was a casserole shaped like a fish and the green glass coffee cups. I kept his instructions in mind, so on the next day when Miss Glory was hanging out clothes and I had again been told to serve the old biddies on the porch, I dropped the empty serving tray. When I heard Mrs. Cullinan scream, "Mary!" I picked up the casserole and two of the green glass cups in readiness. As she rounded the kitchen door, I let them fall to the tiled floor.

I could never absolutely describe to Bailey what happened next, because each time I got to the part where she fell on the floor and screwed up her ugly face to cry, we burst out laughing. She actually wobbled around on the floor and picked up shards of cups and cried "Oh Momma. Oh, dear Gawd. It's Momma's china from Virginia. Oh, Momma, I sorry."

Miss Glory came running in from the yard . . . almost as broken up as her mistress. "You mean to say she broke our Virginia dishes. What we gone do?"

Mrs. Cullinan cried louder, "That clumsy nigger. Clumsy little black nigger."

Old Speckled Face leaned down and asked, "Who did it, Viola? Was it Mary? Who did it?" . . .

Mrs. Cullinan said "Her name's Margaret, goddam it, her name's Margaret." And she threw a wedge of broken plate at me. It could have been the hysteria which put her aim off, but the flying crockery caught Miss Glory right over her ear and she started screaming.

I left the front door wide open so all the neighbors could hear.

Mrs. Cullinan was right about one thing. My name wasn't Mary.

[Angelou, 1970, pp. 90–93]

Maya Angelou resisted the behavior expected of a poor African American girl in this episode (as in several other incidents described in her autobiography), but she unquestioningly accepted other aspects of her situation. Note that it didn't occur to her to ask Mrs. Cullinan to call her "Marguerite" or tell her mother she wanted to quit. Her childhood culture made that unthinkable.

Her brother's influence was crucial, not only in this incident but even in her name. Bailey always called her "Mya sister," creating a nickname that she liked. In general, resilient people voluntarily take on their own names, roles, and challenges and resist those that are imposed on them.

Why was Maya's behavior so different from Miss Glory's? Social contexts are part of the answer. Not only was Miss Glory born 20 years earlier than Maya, she was also the descendant of Virginia slaves owned by Mrs. Cullinan's family. Other possible reasons are Maya's personality, the influence of her brother, her ethnic pride, and her intellect—all of which are powerful factors in resilience. One thing is clear: The past does not always determine the future. As this incident demonstrates, children react to events in unexpected ways, taking on some aspects of their background and history but also becoming their own person.

SUMMING UP

Human development is the science that seeks to understand how people change throughout their lives. Each life is a dynamic system, characterized by change that is *multidirectional.* Development is also *multicontextual,* in that every context has an impact. For example, historical and socioeconomic conditions make some paths through life much more likely and close off other directions completely. The very concept of "childhood" is a social construction, dependent on historical and economic circumstances. Culture is pervasive, affecting every choice a person makes. A *multicultural* approach to the study of development makes contrasts and similarities more evident. Developmental study is also *multidisciplinary,* drawing on biology, psychology, education, sociology, and many other disciplines. The more the disciplines that contribute, the better the whole of development is understood. *Plasticity* is always evident, especially in the display of resilience by children who overcome harmful conditions. Although developmental change must build on prior biosocial, cognitive, and psychosocial foundations, humans are neither stuck in their past nor free of it. A person's life is affected by all past developments but determined by none of them.

Developmental Study as a Science

Because the study of development is a science, it is based on objective evidence. Because it concerns human life and growth, it is also laden with subjective implications and applications. This interplay of the objective and the subjective, of the universal and the personal, makes developmental science a challenging, fascinating, and even transformative study. It also makes firm conclusions difficult to reach and implications controversial.

Adults have heartfelt opinions about how children should grow; why they turn out as they do; and where, when, and even whether adolescents should find work, or romance, or religion. Opinions are subjective, influenced by background, culture, and experiences; to move from opinion to truth, from wishes to outcomes, we need science.

Scientists advance knowledge by asking questions and seeking answers, always examining what has been taken for granted. To avoid the distortions of unexamined opinions, and to control the biases of personal experience, they use the **scientific method.** This method, used in all the sciences from physics to economics, involves four basic steps and sometimes a fifth:

scientific method A way to answer questions that requires empirical research and data-based conclusions.

1. *Ask a question.* On the basis of previous research or a particular theory or personal observation, pose a question. Scientists are curious about almost everything.
2. *Develop a hypothesis.* Reformulate and segment the question into a **hypothesis,** a specific prediction to be tested.
3. *Test the hypothesis.* Design and conduct research that will provide empirical evidence—in the form of data—about the validity or falsehood of the hypothesis.
4. *Draw conclusions.* Use the evidence to support or refute the hypothesis. Note limitations of the research (including characteristics of the particular participants) and alternative explanations.
5. *Make the findings available.* Publish the procedure and results in sufficient detail that other scientists can evaluate the conclusions or replicate the research. **Replication** is the repetition of a scientific study, using the same procedures on a different group of participants, to verify or dispute the original study's conclusions.

hypothesis A specific prediction that is stated in such a way that it can be tested and either confirmed or refuted.

replication The repetition of a scientific study, using the same procedures on another group of participants, to verify or dispute the original study's conclusions.

Between the questions developmental scientists ask (steps 1 and 2) and the answers they find (steps 4 and 5) lies *methodology*—the specific strategies, or methods, used to gather and analyze data and to test hypotheses. These strategies are pivotal because "the ways that you attempt to clarify phenomena in large measure determine the worth of the solution" (Cairns & Cairns, 1994). In other words, a research study's *validity* (does it measure what it purports to measure?), *reliability* (are the measurements accurate, in that they would show the same results if done again?), *generalizability* (does it apply to other populations and situations?), and *usefulness* (can it solve real-life problems?) affect the power of the conclusions. Research design can advance or undercut that power.

Some general strategies to make research valid, reliable, generalizable, and useful are described in Appendix B. Several theories of development, which give rise to many research questions, are explained in Chapter 2. Now we turn to four methods of testing hypotheses: observations, experiments, surveys, and case studies. Remember, the overall goal is to find evidence that answers questions as accurately as possible.

Observation

scientific observation A method of testing hypotheses by unobtrusively watching and recording participants' behavior in a systematic and objective manner, either in a laboratory or in a natural setting.

Scientific observation requires observing and recording behavior in a systematic and objective manner. In the science of human development, observations

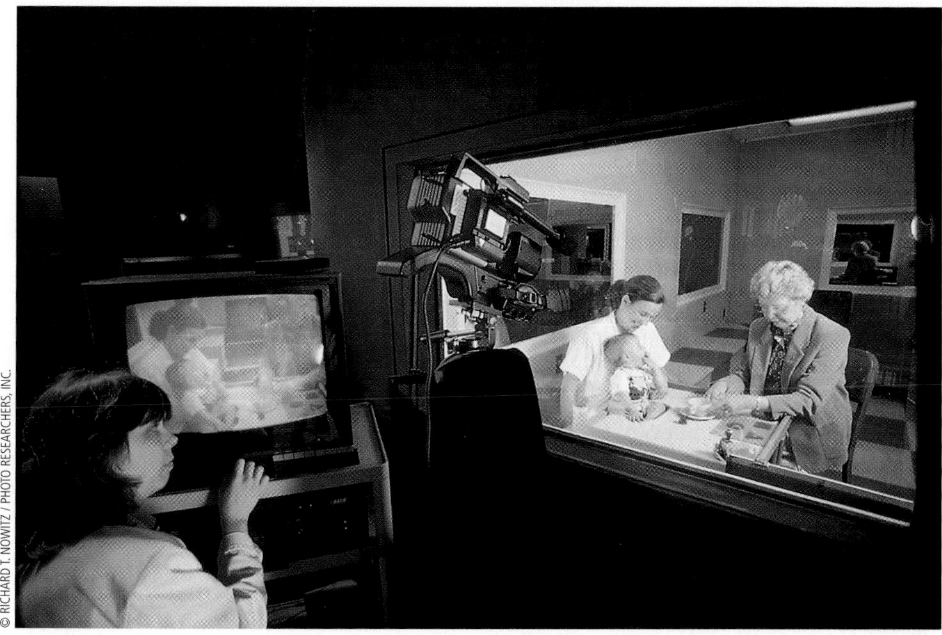

© RICHARD T. NOWITZ / PHOTO RESEARCHERS, INC.

Do Not Disturb: Science in Progress
Does any 6-month-old understand that cups go on saucers, that circles are not squares, and that mothers know the answers when a child does not? In this laboratory observation, one scientist elicits the answers while another videotapes the results for later analysis.

often occur in a naturalistic setting, such as at home, in a school, or in a public park, because these settings encourage people to behave as they usually do. Typically, the observing scientist tries to be unobtrusive, so that research participants act naturally, while the scientists collect data in ways that guard against their prejudices or wishful thinking.

Observation has been used to shed light on the worldwide increase in the average weight of children during the past few decades. Data from the United States are shown in Figure 1.3, and all the evidence suggests that the problem is getting worse (Hedley et al., 2004). One important developmental question (step 1 of the scientific method) is, "Why is childhood obesity increasing?" One hypothesis (step 2) is that today's children are less active than were previous generations.

A specific question is, "How many children walk or ride a bike to school?" Several observers went to eight elementary schools (some rural, some urban) in South Carolina to count how many children arrived by bus, by car, by bike, or on foot (step 3). To make sure they would catch any fluctuations by day of the week, they observed each school for five consecutive days. As Figure 1.4 shows, only 5 percent of the children got physical exercise by walking or biking to school (Sirard et al., 2005).

These numbers are lower than the national average (13 percent walk to school, according to a telephone poll of parents). One reason for the discrepancy may be context. None of the eight schools were in a large city, where most schools are within walking distance of children's homes. In addition, the researchers thought that "the observation system used for this study may provide more accurate prevalence estimates compared with previous survey-based estimates" (Sirard et al., 2005, p. 237).

Observation has one major limitation: It does not indicate what causes people to do whatever they do. Did children grow heavier because their parents drove them to school, or did parents become more likely to drive their children to school because they were too

FIGURE 1.3 **The Obesity Epidemic** The percentage of children and adolescents who are overweight or obese has more than tripled in less than 50 years, and the rate of increase has been especially rapid in the past 15 years. Currently, 16 percent of the U.S. population aged 18 or younger have BMI (body mass index) values that are at or above the 95th percentile of the Centers for Disease Control's growth charts, which is the criterion for classification as overweight.

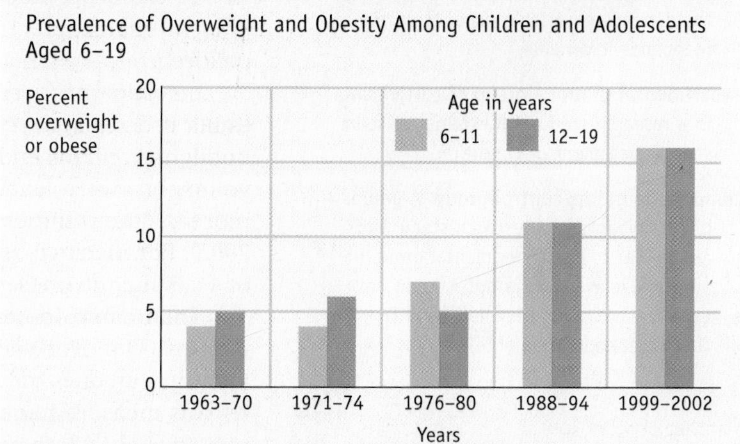

Source: Centers for Disease Control, National Center for Health Statistics Web site, http://www.cdc.gov/nchs/products/pubs/pubd/hestats/overwght99.htm; accessed March 1, 2005.

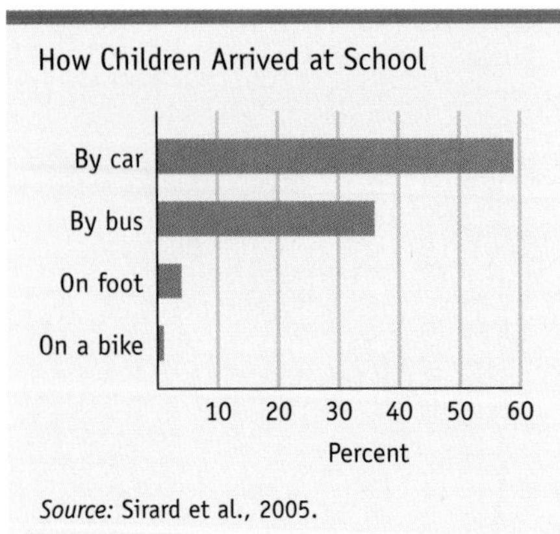

FIGURE 1.4 **Why Walk When You Can Ride?** An observational study of eight South Carolina elementary schools found that only 5 percent of the children rode their bikes or walked to school. Such a study could not explain *why* so few children got to school under their own steam. For that, an experiment would be needed.

experiment A research method in which the researcher tries to determine the cause-and-effect relationship between two variables by manipulating one variable (called the *independent variable*) and then observing and recording the resulting changes in the other variable (called the *dependent variable*).

independent variable In an experiment, the variable that is introduced to see what effect it has on the dependent variable. (Also called *experimental variable.*)

dependent variable In an experiment, the variable that may change as a result of whatever new condition or situation the experimenter adds. In other words, the dependent variable *depends* on the independent variable.

experimental group A group of participants in a research study who experience some special treatment or condition.

comparison group/control group A group of participants in a research study who are similar to the experimental group in all other relevant ways but who do not experience the experimental condition (the independent variable).

ESPECIALLY FOR NURSES In the field of medicine, why are experiments conducted to test new drugs and treatments?

heavy to walk or ride their bikes? Is inactivity the result or the cause of overweight? This observational study cannot tell us.

The Experiment

The **experiment** is the research method that scientists use to establish cause. In the social sciences, experimenters typically give people a particular treatment or expose them to a specific condition and then note whether their behavior changes.

In technical terms, the experimenters manipulate an **independent variable** (the treatment or special condition, also called the *experimental variable*). They note whether the independent variable they have imposed affects the specific behavior they are studying, called the **dependent variable** (which, in theory, *depends* on the independent variable). Thus, the independent variable is the new, special treatment; the dependent variable is the result.

The purpose of an experiment is to find out whether an independent variable affects the dependent variable. Statistics are often used to analyze the results. Sometimes results are reported by *effect size,* to distinguish slight, moderate, or large effect. Sometimes tests of *significance* are used, to indicate whether the results might have occurred by chance. (A finding that chance would produce the results less than 5 times in 100 is significance at the .05 level; 1 time in 100 is .01 significance.) Finding the link between cause and effect is the reason for doing experiments; statistics indicate how strong that link is. No other method pinpoints what leads to what.

To make sure it was the special treatment, not some other unmeasured variable, that caused a change in the dependent variable, experimenters usually compare two groups of participants: one group that gets the special treatment and one, similar in every other way, that does not. Thus, in a typical experiment (as diagrammed in Figure 1.5), two groups of participants are studied: an **experimental group,** which is given a particular treatment (the independent variable), and a **comparison group** (also called a **control group**), which does not get the special treatment. Sometimes participants are used as their own control group, in that they are measured before and after the experimental treatment (independent variable) to see if any changes have occurred (dependent variable).

You can see the need for an experiment when considering the data on children walking to school. Historical data show that most children and adults walk much less in their daily routines than they used to, but the relationship between that fact and the increase in obesity is not clear. Does inactivity cause weight gain, or is it the other way around?

To establish cause, an experiment is needed. For ethical reasons (explained later in this chapter), some experiments are easier to do with adults than with children.

Investigators recruited inactive adults (they described themselves as "couch potatoes") who agreed to wear electronic monitoring equipment to record their bodily movement and position 120 times each minute, 24 hours a day. Half the volunteers were lean, and half were somewhat obese. The lean adults moved more in "the routines of daily life" than the overweight adults did (Levine et al., 2005). For instance, the lean ones spent an average of nine hours a day standing or walking; the obese ones spent only six hours.

Then came the experiment. Both groups were put on strict diets for two months. The overweight participants lost about 20 pounds (8 kg) on their diet, and the lean ones gained about 10 pounds (4 kg) on theirs. Then their daily activity was measured again. There was no statistical change; in fact, the heavy ones moved slightly less now that they had lost weight. This experiment shows cause and effect: A person's daily pattern of movement affects body weight, not the other way around. For permanent weight loss, people need to increase their customary level of movement.

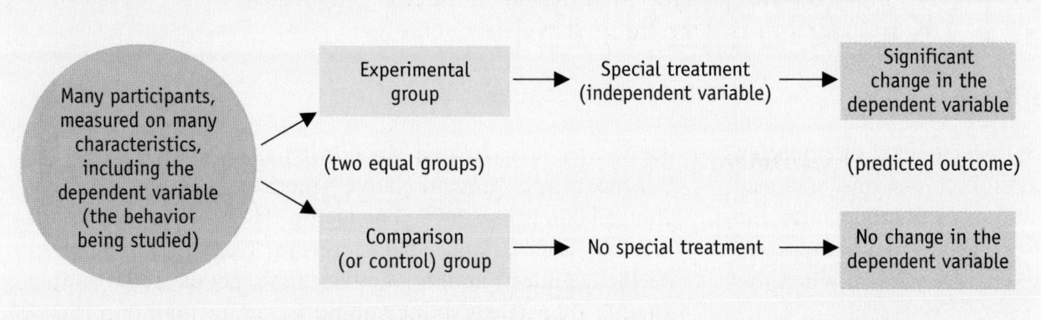

Procedure:

1. Divide participants into two groups that are matched on important characteristics, especially the behavior that is the dependent variable on which this study is focused.
2. Give special treatment, or intervention (the independent variable), to one group (the experimental group).
3. Compare the groups on the dependent variable. If they now differ, the cause of the difference was probably the independent variable.
4. Publish the results.

FIGURE 1.5 **How to Conduct an Experiment**

? Observational Quiz (see answer, page 23): Does the experimental group always change?

To apply this lesson to children, increasing a child's daily activity level is likely to keep his or her weight down. Being driven to school, rather than walking or biking, is one reason today's children are heavier than children used to be.

The Survey

A third research method is the **survey.** Information is collected from a large number of people by interview, questionnaire, or some other means. This is an easy, quick, and direct way to obtain data. However, getting valid data through an interview or questionnaire is more difficult than it seems. One reason is that the people who are surveyed may not be truly representative of the group about whom one hopes to learn.

survey A research method in which information is collected from a large number of people by personal interview, written questionnaire, or some other means.

This problem arises in every survey that seeks to predict which candidate will win an election. Especially if the numbers are close, it is crucial that the respondents actually vote, vote as they say they will, and reflect the views of the thousands of citizens they are supposed to represent.

Further, the phrasing of survey questions may influence people to answer in a particular way. Even the order of the questions makes a difference. In addition, many interviewees give inaccurate responses that they hope will make them seem wise or good, especially if the truth is embarrassing. For example, some of the 13 percent of parents who said their children walk to school may have been stretching the truth.

Many studies have found that when mothers and fathers, or parents and teachers, or adults and children are asked about the same thing, the two groups' responses differ. For example, when asked about their children's health, "parents portray a much rosier picture of children's well-being than children do of themselves" (Scott, 2000, p. 99). Misleading survey data are particularly common when adolescents are asked about drugs or sex. Boys tend to exaggerate their sexual conquests, and girls tend to deny their sexual activity—but one sex may be answering more honestly than the other.

Problems with surveys may begin even before the respondent answers. For instance, developmentalists are very interested in the differences between people of various backgrounds; but as soon as race, ethnicity, or income enters the picture, it becomes more difficult to categorize people, as the following explains.

Especially for Social Scientists What are some of the benefits of cross-cultural research?

THINKING LIKE A SCIENTIST

Ethnicity, Race, Culture, and Income

Confusion arises whenever people—scientists or nonscientists—refer to ethnic groups, races, cultures, and socioeconomic classes, because these categories overlap in complicated ways. Accordingly, scientists try hard to untangle these categories by specifying exactly what they mean when they use these terms.

Members of an **ethnic group** share certain attributes, almost always ancestral heritage and often including national origin, religion, and language (Whitfield & McClearn, 2005). (*Heritage* refers to customs and traditions passed down to the present; *national origin* refers to one's ancestors' country of birth.) Every ethnic group has a culture. Someone born into an ethnic group may or may not choose to identify with the group and be a part of its culture. Someone from another heritage can adopt aspects of that culture, but people are not considered members of an ethnic group unless they are born into it—that is, a person cannot voluntarily join an ethnic group.

Ethnic categories arise from history, sociology, and psychology, not from biology. The term **race,** in contrast, has been used to categorize groups of people as genetically distinct on the basis of physical appearance (e.g., skin color, hair color and texture, eye color and shape, and body structure). However, in reality there are no clear-cut racial boundaries, and about 95 percent of the genetic differences between one person and another occur *within,* not between, supposed racial groups. Genetic variation is particularly apparent among dark-skinned people whose ancestors were African (Tischkoff & Kidd, 2004).

Social scientists often refer to ethnic and cultural categories used in the societies they study, because these classifications can affect development. Prejudice and discrimination have often resulted from perceived racial differences, and people's racial self-identification may affect their cognition. But it must be remembered that race "is a socially constructed concept, not a biological one" (Sternberg et al., 2005), a concept too clumsy and misleading to be used unless it is carefully defined as a social construction, not a biological reality.

Evidence that race is a social construction can be found in categories used by the U.S. Census, which once counted only White people. By 1970, the U.S. Bureau of the Census had three racial categories: "White," "Black," and "Other." In the 1980 census, "Other" was replaced by "Asian and Pacific Islander," "American Indian, Eskimo, Aleut," and "Hispanic, may be of any race." In 1980, Hispanics also had to describe themselves as either "White" or "Black"; this classification in itself was inaccurate, since virtually all Latinos have European, African, *and* Native American ancestors (Shields et al., 2005). In the 2000 census, the "Hispanic" category remained; "Asian" was separated from "Native Hawaiian and Pacific Islander"; and, for the first time, people could simply identify themselves as belonging to "more than one race." The 2010 census will undoubtedly adjust the categories still further. Suffice it to say that, although scientific research (some of which is reported in this text) traditionally used racial categories, the concept of race is less often used, and increasingly less useful, today.

To further complicate matters, socioeconomic status (SES) tends to follow developmental and ethnic variations, which themselves overlap old racial categories and new cultural patterns. Some studies show that differences once thought of as ethnic are actually differences in social class. For example, one study of census tracts in Rhode Island and Massachusetts found that half of the health differences among Americans of African, Asian, European, and Hispanic heritage were the result of low SES, not ethnicity (Krieger et al., 2005).

The overlap of ethnicity, SES, and culture makes it hard to pinpoint a single root cause of any difference. For example, in the United States, European Americans are three times more likely than Hispanic Americans to live alone (U.S. Bureau of the Census, 2003). Is this an ethnic pattern, reflecting "familism," the value that people from Latin America place on family closeness? Or is it income-related, since Hispanics earn only about 60 percent as much as the average European American, and hence individuals cannot afford separate residences? Or is it cultural, a decision made by elderly Latinos to live with their children because that is the cultural norm? Or is it the result of developmental stage, since the median age of Hispanic Americans is 27, compared to 40 for the average European American? This means that Hispanic families are more likely to have young children, who obviously cannot live alone. Each of these possible explanations is plausible.

Scientists can separate ethnicity, SES, culture, and developmental stage, but such analysis is difficult, since all four of these factors interact within every ethnic group. Obviously, within each group, further distinctions are important. For example, even though both groups are European American, Italian Americans differ from Norwegian Americans on the basis of various critical factors, which may include religion, language, and immigration history. Thinking like a scientist means taking special care that conclusions about one group are not thoughtlessly extended to other groups.

ethnic group People whose ancestors were born in the same region, usually sharing a language and religion.

race A group of people who are regarded (by themselves or by others) as genetically distinct on the basis of physical appearance.

The Case Study

A fourth research method, the **case study,** is an intensive study of one individual. It usually begins with an interview, in which a person describes his or her background, current thinking, and actions. Other people (friends, family, neighbors, teachers) who know the individual are also interviewed. Usually the interviewer has a set of questions prepared in advance, but answers are recorded in full rather than being condensed to a checklist, and follow-up questions are framed on the spot, in order to comprehend and record all the nuances of this particular person.

case study A research method in which one individual is studied intensively.

A case study can be very useful if the author is insightful. Sometimes someone remembering his or her own life provides emotional insights that are hard to obtain any other way. Frank McCourt did this in *Angela's Ashes,* his best-selling memoir, which begins:

> When I look back on my childhood I wonder how I survived at all. It was, of course, a miserable childhood: the happy childhood is hardly worth your while. Worse than the ordinary miserable childhood is the miserable Irish childhood, and worse yet is the miserable Irish Catholic childhood. People everywhere brag and whimper about the woes of their early years, but nothing can compare with the Irish version: the poverty; the shiftless loquacious alcoholic father; the pious defeated mother moaning by the fire; the English and the terrible things they did to us for eight hundred long years. Above all—we were wet.
>
> *[McCourt, 1996, p. 9]*

RESPONSE FOR NURSES (from page 20): Experiments are the only way to determine cause-and-effect relationships. If we want to be sure that a new drug or treatment is effective, an experiment must be conducted to establish that the drug or treatment causes people to feel better.

The problem with a case study is that it may not reveal truths about anyone except the individual concerned, and other truths could be told for that one person. McCourt's brother Malachy does not remember his childhood as Frank does (McCourt, 1998). As one scholar wrote, many researchers could immediately find in Ireland "a sample of children who were not wet, only half wet, or merely wet through the night." Nonetheless, this scholar praises McCourt for "coming to terms with his childhood, indirectly comparing it with other childhoods" (Qvortup, 2003, p. 78).

! ANSWER TO OBSERVATIONAL QUIZ (from page 21): No. Note the word *predicted.* The hypothesis is that change will occur for the experimental group and not the control group, but the reason for doing the experiment is to discover whether that prediction does indeed come true.

The case study has three important uses:

- To make it possible to understand a particular individual very well
- To provide a provocative starting point for other research
- To illustrate, in a memorable way, more general truths

Inevitably, collecting and interpreting case-study information reflects individual biases and idiosyncrasies. The data are filtered by one person, and the conclusions apply to one person. Certainly other children, even poor ones in Ireland, had contrasting experiences, and certainly many adults who did not grow up in Ireland would argue that their childhood was every bit as miserable as McCourt's. An additional limitation, to be discussed later, is that case studies rely on words more than numbers.

RESPONSE FOR SOCIAL SCIENTISTS (from page 21): Different cultures have different ideas about child rearing. Cross-cultural research provides us with information that may be shared among various cultures and may benefit the children of those cultures.

Studying Change over Time

Remember the definition on page 5: The science of human development seeks to understand how and why people—all kinds of people, everywhere—change or remain the same *over time.* Developmental scientists use the methods just described—observations, experiments, surveys, and case studies—but they must add another dimension in order to measure developmental change. They design their research to include time, or aging. Usually they accomplish this by using one of three basic designs: cross-sectional, longitudinal, or cross-sequential (summarized graphically in Figure 1.6).

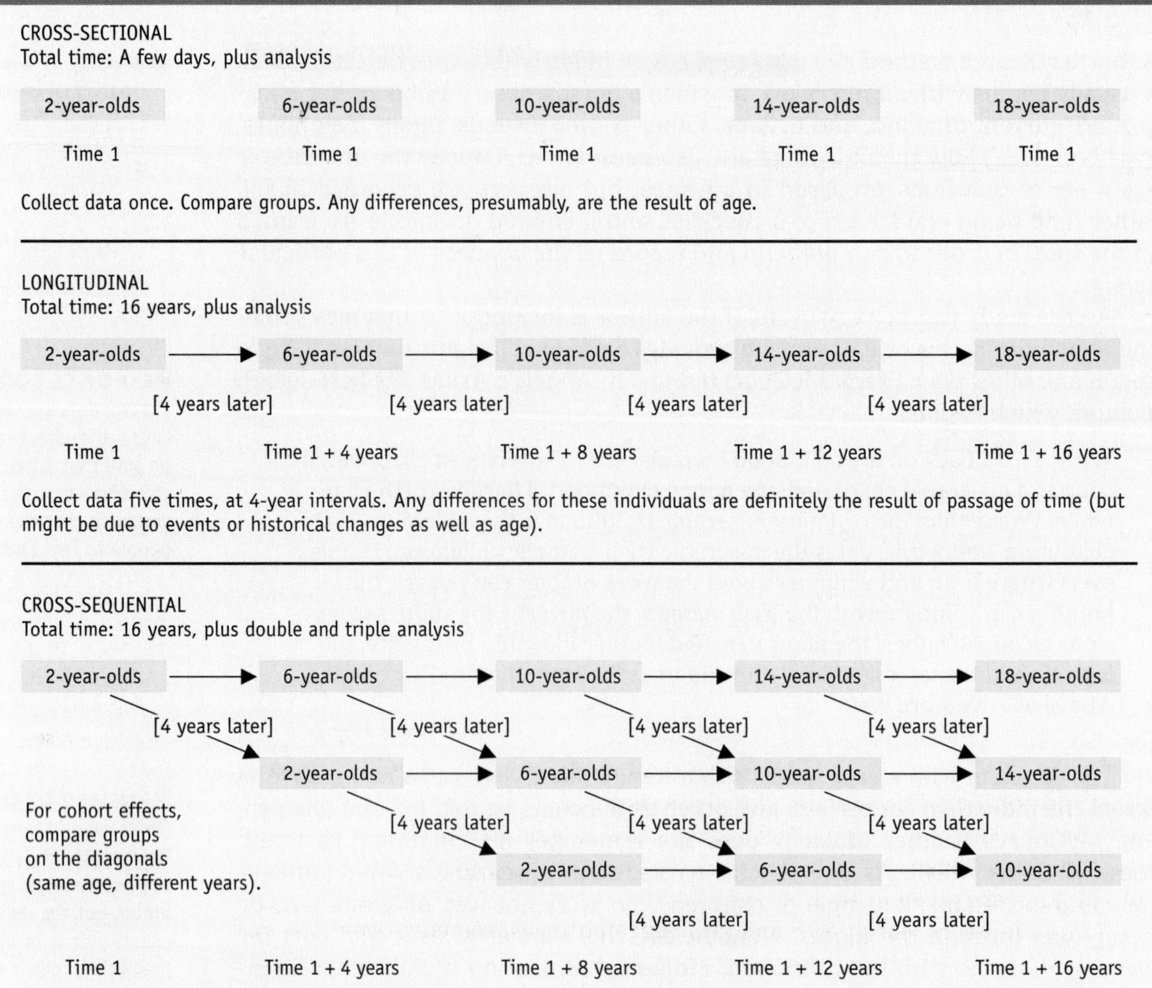

FIGURE 1.6 **Which Approach Is Best?** Cross-sequential research is the most time-consuming and most complex approach, but it also yields the best information about development. This is one reason why hundreds of scientists conduct research on the same topics, replicating one another's work—to gain some of the advantages of cross-sequential research without having to wait all those years.

cross-sectional research A research design that compares groups of people who differ in age but are similar in other important characteristics.

Cross-Sectional Research

The most convenient, and thus most common, way to study development is with **cross-sectional research.** Groups of people who differ in age but share other important characteristics (such as education, SES, and ethnicity) are compared. Cross-sectional design seems simple enough, but it is very difficult to ensure that the various groups being compared are similar in every important background variable except age.

In addition, historical change might affect one cohort more than another. This happened between 1950 and 1954, when the average preschool child's television-watching time increased from zero to almost three hours a day. Any characteristic

VIC BIDER / INDEX STOCK IMAGERY

SW PRODUCTION / INDEX STOCK IMAGERY

Compare These with Those The apparent similarity of these two groups in gender and ethnic composition makes them candidates for cross-sectional research. Before we could be sure that any difference between the two groups is the result of age, we would have to be sure the groups are alike in other ways, such as socio-economic status and religious affiliation. Even if two groups seem identical in everything but age, there may be unknown differences.

connected to television watching (such as obesity, aggression, or fantasy play) might seem to be a product of age in cross-sectional research, but would really be a result of technology. As you can see, any conclusions about development that are based only on cross-sectional comparisons might be wrong.

Longitudinal Research

To help discover whether age itself, not cohort differences, causes a developmental change, scientists undertake **longitudinal research.** This involves collecting data repeatedly on the same individuals as they age.

longitudinal research A research design that follows the same individuals over time, repeatedly assessing their development.

Longitudinal research is particularly useful in studying development over a long age span (Elder, 1998). Some valuable and surprising findings of longitudinal research are given in Table 1.2.

Longitudinal research that includes repeated measurements over a shorter period can uncover the processes of change, a "micro-level" technique that is particularly useful in studying child development (Granott & Parziale, 2002). For example, do children learn to read suddenly, by "cracking the code," or gradually? The answer could not be found by simply comparing preliterate 4-year-olds and fluently reading 8-year-olds. However, following children month by month reveals the answer: Learning to read is usually a gradual process (Adams et al., 1998).

The longitudinal research design does have some serious drawbacks. Over time, participants may withdraw, move far away, or die. This can skew the ultimate results if those who disappear are unlike those who stay in some relevant characteristic, as they usually are. (People of low SES and the seriously ill are particularly likely to be lost over time.) In the Hawaii study, great effort was made to locate all the participants, resulting in the revelation that the individuals who left Kauai in early adulthood tended to be more resilient and successful than those who stayed. However, in longitudinal research, tracking down participants who move away is not always possible, especially if an entire family disappears.

Another problem is that participants may "improve" as they become increasingly familiar with the questions or the goals of the study. Even the resilient Hawaiians may have been motivated to become successful because they knew their accomplishments would be publicized.

TABLE 1.2 Some Findings from Longitudinal Research

- *Children's adjustment to their parents' divorce.* Negative effects linger, but not for everyone (Hetherington & Kelly, 2002).
- *The benefits of joining the military during adolescence.* Although obviously some soldiers die or are seriously injured, those who survived World War II had much more successful lives than those who did not serve (Elder, 1986).
- *The role of fathers.* Even 50 years ago, fathers had far more influence on their children's future happiness than the stereotype of the traditional, distant dad implies (Snarey, 1993).
- *Prevention of delinquency.* Patient parenting at age 5, using conversation rather than physical punishment, decreases the likelihood of delinquency 10 years later (Pettit, 2004).
- *The effects of day care.* The quality and extent of child care in infancy and early childhood are not as influential as the mother is. Her warmth and responsiveness, or coldness and rejection, are key (NICHD Early Child Care Research Network, 2003).

ALL: MARK ANTMAN / THE IMAGE WORKS

Nathaniel Becomes Nat Longitudinal research shows how people change and how they remain the same over time. Babies *(a)* mostly stay in one place and stare, in contrast to 2-year-olds *(b)*, who actively explore everything. Nine-year-olds *(c)* learn the health habits their culture teaches them, but 13-year-olds *(d)* cherish their privacy so much that Nat (which he prefers over his given name, Nathaniel) would probably never allow his father to photograph him brushing his teeth. At 18 *(e)* and 28 *(f)*, it is obvious that this red-haired, bespectacled young man is still the thoughtful and bemused person he was at 6 months; but changes are obvious as well, not only in hair and glasses but also in attitude.

Probably the biggest problem comes from the changing historical context. Science, popular culture, and politics alter life experiences for each generation, thus limiting the current applicability of data collected on people born decades ago. This problem is particularly frustrating, because scientists want to know what effect drugs, lifestyles, or experiences have on development without waiting decades for the child participants to grow up. This is urgent in studies of the effects of tobacco, asbestos, and lead on children who were exposed to those substances before the risks were known.

Cross-Sequential Research

Cross-sectional and longitudinal research each have advantages that tend to make up for the other's disadvantages. Scientists use the two together in various ways, often with complex statistical analysis (Hartmann & George, 1999). The simplest combination is **cross-sequential research** (also referred to as *cohort-sequential* or *time-sequential research*) (Schaie, 1996). With this design, researchers study several groups of people who are of different ages (a cross-sectional approach) and follow all of them over the years (a longitudinal approach).

cross-sequential research A hybrid research method in which researchers first study several groups of people of different ages (a cross-sectional approach) and then follow those groups over the years (a longitudinal approach). (Also called *cohort-sequential* or *time-sequential research.*)

A cross-sequential design can compare findings for a group of, say, 18-year-olds with findings for the same individuals at age 2, as well as with findings for groups who were 18 a decade or two earlier and groups who are 2 years old now (see Figure 1.6). Cross-sequential research thus allows scientists to disentangle differences related to chronological age from those related to historical period. Researchers using this method are like prospectors for gold, sifting through other elements to find genuine nuggets of knowledge about age-related development.

The Ecological-Systems Approach: A Synthesis

The usefulness of combining many methods, using a multidisciplinary and multicultural approach to understand the developing person within many contexts and dynamic systems, is apparent. No person can be understood in isolation, at just one moment in time.

Urie Bronfenbrenner deserves credit for recognizing this fact. Referring in 1977 to research on mother–child attachment (discussed in Chapter 7), he criticized the then-prevalent laboratory research: "Much of contemporary developmental psychology is the science of the strange behavior of children in strange situations with strange adults for the briefest periods of time" (p. 513).

Bronfenbrenner recommended an **ecological-systems approach** to the study of development. Just as a naturalist studying an organism examines the ecology, or the interrelationship between the organism and its environment, he argued that developmentalists likewise need to examine all the systems that surround the development of each child (Bronfenbrenner & Morris, 1998).

ecological-systems approach A vision of how development should be studied, with the person considered in all the contexts and interactions that constitute a life.

Among the systems that Bronfenbrenner described were *microsystems* (elements of the person's immediate surroundings, such as family and peer group), *exosystems* (such local institutions as school and church), *macrosystems* (the larger social setting, including cultural values, economic policies, and political processes), and *chronosystems* (the historical conditions). A fifth system, the *mesosystem,* involves the connections between microsystems; for example, the home–school mesosystem includes all the communication processes (letters home, parent–teacher conferences, phone calls, back-to-school nights) between a child's parents and teachers.

It is difficult to incorporate all the systems in any one study, just as it is hard to use all the scientific methods and strategies simultaneously. The goal, however, is to consider all the multidirectional, dynamic systems over time, using a multimethod, multidisciplinary, multicultural strategy to comprehend the whole of development.

ESPECIALLY FOR FUTURE RESEARCHERS What is the best method for collecting data?

Although every method and strategy has shortcomings, all developmentalists appreciate the fact that research has led to happier and healthier children. It was once thought that children needed to be immersed in ice water soon after birth so they would go to heaven, swaddled to make them grow, punished to make them learn, kept apart from the other gender to prevent pregnancy, and much more.

SUMMING UP

The scientific method is designed to help researchers answer questions objectively and honestly, with carefully collected evidence, drawing conclusions based on the data they find. Methods, findings, and conclusions are reported so that other scientists can build on past work and reexamine results. Every method has unique strengths and weaknesses. Researchers observe people in naturalistic or laboratory settings, and they conduct experiments under controlled conditions. They can survey hundreds or even thousands of people, interview a smaller number in great depth, or study one case in detail. Strategies for studying how humans change over time include cross-sectional research (comparing groups of people of various ages), longitudinal research (following the same individuals over time), and cross-sequential research (combining cross-sectional and longitudinal strategies). Ideally, several strategies and methods are used in an ecological-systems approach, which considers all contexts and systems that affect development.

Cautions from Science

No doubt the scientific method illuminates and illustrates human development as nothing else could. Facts, hypotheses, and possibilities have all emerged that would not be known without science. Many benefits to children, including survival, health, and happiness, are evident. Nevertheless, scientists recognize problems with aspects of the scientific method, including misinterpretation of data and conclusions, overdependence on numbers, and ignorance about many urgent issues.

Correlation and Causation

correlation A number indicating the degree of relationship between two variables, expressed in terms of the likelihood that one variable will (or will not) occur when the other variable does (or does not). A correlation is not an indication that one variable causes the other.

Probably the most common mistake in research interpretation is the confusion of correlation with causation. A **correlation** exists between two variables if one variable is more (or less) likely to occur when the other occurs. A correlation is *positive* if both variables tend to increase together or decrease together, *negative* if one variable tends to increase when the other decreases, and *zero* if no connection is evident.

To illustrate: From birth to age 9, there is a positive correlation between age and height (children grow taller as they grow older), a negative correlation between age and amount of sleep (children sleep less as they grow older), and zero correlation between age and number of toes (almost all children have the same number of toes as they had years earlier). Many correlations are fascinating, such as those between risk of developing asthma and being the first-born child, or attachment to mother and learning to read, or early puberty and early pregnancy. However, such correlations are often misinterpreted; people assume that one variable causes another.

TABLE 1.3 **Correlations Between Spanking of 4- to 5-year-olds and Other Variables**

Child is female	–0.06
Parent is warm toward child	–0.23
Child has behavior problems	+0.46

Source: McLoyd & Smith, 2002.

For instance, in 4- and 5-year-olds, there is a positive correlation of +.46 between being spanked and having behavior problems (see Table 1.3). At first, the reason might seem obvious: Parents are more likely to spank difficult children. But in every correlation, the relationship may run in either direction; so behavior problems may lead to spanking or spanking may cause behavior problems—or some third variable may be the underlying cause. Consider the following alternative explanations, one from each of the three developmental domains.

- *Biosocial:* Angry antisocial behavior may be genetic; genes make some parents more likely to hit their children, and children inheriting those genes are more likely to misbehave (a third variable).
- *Cognitive:* Spanking may make children more aggressive, because they have learned about physical aggression from their parents' behavior. In other words, physical discipline may cause misbehavior, rather than vice versa (opposite direction from the usual interpretation).
- *Psychosocial:* Economic stress may make parents punitive and children difficult. Low income, not the behavior of the parents or the children, may cause the correlation (a third variable).

All of these are logical hypotheses. Many more hypotheses could be formulated. The +.46 correlation proves none of them, because correlation indicates relationship, not cause and effect or explanation. Similarly, a positive correlation exists between ice cream sold and number of murders committed, not because ice cream makes people kill but because both phenomena increase with warmer weather. And a negative correlation exists between losing baby teeth and learning to read, not because reading loosens teeth but because both events tend to occur at about age 6.

Quantity and Quality

A second caution concerns how much scientists should rely on data produced by **quantitative research** (from the word *quantity*). Quantitative research data can be categorized, ranked, or numbered and thus can be easily translated across cultures. For example, people agree or disagree on some issue (no maybes), or children speak Spanish well, poorly, or not at all (only three choices), or a family is above or below the poverty line (two choices, with a numerical cutoff score), or a college student has a GPA, an SAT, and a sum of credits (many choices, but all expressed in numbers).

quantitative research Research that provides data that can be expressed with numbers, such as ranks or scales.

Since numbers can be easily summarized, compared, charted, and replicated, quantitative research is often preferred and usually respected by scientists. Statistics of all kinds, including correlation, significance, and effect size, begin with quantitative data, which has been described as providing "rigorous, empirically testable representations" (Nesselroade & Molenaar, 2003, p. 635).

However, by reducing data to categories and numbers, some nuances and individual distinctions are lost. Quantitative research may be particularly limiting when describing children, not only because each child is unique and each group of children has its own culture but also because change seems particularly rapid and multidirectional in childhood, both of which are hard to quantify.

For this reason, many developmental researchers use **qualitative research** (from *quality*), that is, research that asks open-ended questions and obtains answers that are not easily translated into numbers and categories. As one research team explains, such approaches "are generally engaged with exploring, describing and understanding the personal and social experiences of participants" (Smith & Dunworth, 2003, p. 603).

qualitative research Research that considers qualities instead of quantities. Descriptions of particular conditions and participants' expressed ideas are often part of qualitative studies.

Consider this example of qualitative research, a product of naturalistic observation. A group of kindergarteners began a "grass war" triggered by freshly mown grass and a boy who hit Carlotta.

> The grass war now escalates, with girls and boys on both sides becoming involved. In fact, all but a few of the 5-year-old group I am observing are now in the grass war. The war continues for some time until Marina [one of the children] suggests to the children in our group that they make peace. Marina with several children behind her marches up to the boy who hit Carlotta and offers her hand in peace. The boy responds by throwing grass in Marina's face . . . over the objections of another boy who is in his group. Marina stands her ground after being hit with the grass. The second boy pulls his friend aside and suggests that they make peace. The other boy is against the proposal, but eventually agrees and the two then shake hands with Marina. Marina then returns to our group and declares "Peace has been established." The two groups now meet for a round of handshaking.
>
> *[Corsaro & Molinari, 2000, p. 192]*

Notice that this is scientific observation. The researcher did not intervene. At this point, months into the study, the children did not expect him to do so. As a result of his neutrality, he obtained evidence that young children, on their own, can resolve conflicts.

Something would be lost if this observation were expressed in numbers. For instance, since the weapon was grass, would this episode be categorized as a conflict or not? Is it significant that a girl was the peacemaker? This particular incident happened in a preschool in Italy, which might or might not be significant. Handshaking, for instance, might be more European than American, but if the observer were coding only cross-cultural instances of handshaking, other aspects of this incident would be ignored. Until we have similar, qualitative reports from many cultures, we cannot judge whether this instance illustrates a universal

Response for Future Researchers (from page 27): There is no best method for collecting data. The method used depends on many factors, such as the age of participants (infants can't complete questionnaires), the question being researched, and the time frame.

trait of young children or is peculiar to Italy or is unique to these children. Probably all are true, for different aspects of this incident, but some of that complexity would be lost if expressed numerically.

Qualitative research may seem preferable, in that it reflects diversity, with all the cultural and contextual complexity just described. But it is also more vulnerable to bias, harder to replicate, and therefore considered less scientific by many researchers. Developmentalists pay attention to both kinds of research, sometimes translating qualitative research into quantifiable data, sometimes using qualitative information to suggest hypotheses for quantitative research.

Especially for College or Graduate School Applicants Is the admissions process based on quality or quantity?

Ethics

The most important caution for all scientists, especially those studying humans, is ethical standards. Each academic discipline and professional society involved in the study of human development has a **code of ethics,** or a set of moral principles, and a scientific culture that protect the integrity of research. Like the progress of science itself, ethical standards and codes are increasingly stringent, as scientists are concerned that "practitioners' research is not only valid and useful, but also ethical" (Lindsay, 2000, p. 20). Most colleges and universities have a group called the IRB (Institutional Research Board), which is charged with ensuring that research at the college meets ethical standards.

code of ethics A set of principles that members of a profession or group are expected to follow.

Protection of Participants

Researchers must make sure that participation is voluntary, confidential, and harmless for all. In Western nations, this is done via "informed consent" of the participants and, if children are involved, of the parents. In some other nations, this requires consent of the village elders, consent of heads of families, and, finally, consent of the mothers of the children (Doumbo, 2005).

The need for researchers to protect participants is especially obvious with children, but the same principles apply no matter what the age of the participants (Gilhooly, 2002). These include explaining the purposes and procedures of the study in advance, obtaining written permission, and allowing the participants to stop at any time.

If researchers discover something that is potentially harmful to any participant, they must stop being dispassionate, objective observers. They must intervene even though their study might be jeopardized. Here is an exchange between a researcher and a research participant, a boy who was in residential care:

> **[Researcher:]** Sometimes a person might talk about a situation where they have been harmed by someone. If this happens, I may need to talk to someone else, especially if it is something awful which is still happening to you, or if the person who harmed you may still be hurting someone else. I would want to be able to agree with you what should be done, and who should be told.
>
> **[Participant:]** Well, that's one part of my life I'm not going to be able to talk to you about then, isn't it? I'm not having you deciding who to go and talk to about me.
>
> *[Morris, 1998]*

We have already mentioned ways in which development research has benefited children.We should add that many earlier researchers undertook experiments that would never be approved today, including "studies carried out by respected psychologists and published in the finest journals of the day. We've come a long way since then, baby. And babies are grateful" (Black, 2005).

Protection of participants sometimes conflicts with the goals of science, creating a dilemma. For example, studies with the greatest potential benefit often involve the most vulnerable groups, such as abused children or very young single parents. Ironically, some groups (women, children, drug addicts) were excluded as subjects of research into drug treatments for AIDS because experimental drugs might have done them unexpected harm; as a result, the first effective AIDS treatments were not tested on the people who needed them most (Kahn et al., 1998). This example shows that the benefits of research, as well as the costs, need to be considered.

The Canadian Psychological Association maintains that the first principle of ethical research is "respect for the dignity of persons"; the second and the third are "responsible caring" and "integrity in relationships." "Responsibility to society" is ranked fourth. Although all four principles should be observed if possible, the ranking is in order of importance, with individuals held to be more important than the larger social good (CPA, 2000).

Implications of Results

Once a study has been completed, additional ethical issues arise. Scientists are obligated to report research results as accurately and completely as possible, without distorting the results to support any political, economic, or cultural position.

An obvious breach of ethics is to "cook" the data, arranging the numbers so that a particular conclusion seems the only reasonable one. Deliberate falsification is rare; it leads to ostracism from the scientific community, dismissal from a teaching or research position, and, sometimes, criminal prosecution.

A more insidious danger is that research is unintentional slanting. For this reason, scientific training, collaboration, and replication are crucial. Incomplete reporting, or research that comes to a conclusion that is only one possible interpretation is understandable, since scientists are subject to human failings.

To avoid this, numerous precautions are built into methodology, several of which have already been explained. In addition, scientific reports in professional journals include (1) details for replication, (2) a section describing the limitations of the findings, and (3) alternative interpretations.

None of this is to be taken for granted, as one researcher in animal behavior explains: "Desirable modes of scientific conduct require considerable self-awareness as well as a reaffirmation of the old virtues of honesty, skepticism, and integrity" (Bateson, 2005, p. 645). Such virtues need to be stressed for every scholar, writer, and student of child development, including you and me.

There is an additional ethical concern. "In reporting results, . . . the investigator should be mindful of the social, political, and human implications of his research" (Society for Research in Child Development, 1996). What does it mean to be "mindful" of research implications?

In one study of college students who listened to Mozart before taking a cognitive test scored higher than another group who heard no music (Rauscher et al., 1993; Rauscher & Shaw, 1998). This "Mozart effect" was wildly misinterpreted: The governor of Georgia ordered that all babies born in his state be given a free Mozart CD in order to improve their intelligence, and Florida passed a law requiring every state-funded infant day-care center to play classical music. In fact, the initial research did not use infants. The results could not be replicated (McKelvie & Low, 2002; Nantais & Schellenberg, 1999; Steele et al., 1999).

What Should We Study?

Every reader of this book should consider the most important ethical concern of all: Are scientists answering the questions that are crucial to human development?

- Do we know enough about nutrition and drug use during pregnancy to protect every fetus?
- Do we know enough about child discipline to prevent bullying, delinquency, and violent crime?

Response for College or Graduate School Applicants (from page 30): Most institutions of higher education emphasize quantitative data—the SAT, the GRE, the GPA, class rank, and so on. Decide for yourself if this is fairer than a more qualitative approach.

- Do we know enough about poverty to enable all children to be healthy?
- Do we know enough about literacy to teach every child to read?
- Do we know enough about sexual urges to eliminate AIDS, unwanted pregnancy, and sex abuse?

The answer to all these questions is a resounding *NO!* Even deciding what questions to ask is an ethical issue. Two scientists explain:

> It is our task as researchers, from both practical and ethical considerations, to ensure that we ask the right questions in our studies, those which are important, and that we conduct our research in a manner that optimizes the opportunity for children's perspectives to be listened to—and heard.
>
> [Lewis & Lindsay, 2000, p. 197]

Ethics means more than taking care of participants and reporting research honestly. It also means choosing topics that are of major importance for the human family. Millions of children suffer because many questions have not yet been answered, or even asked. The next cohort of developmental scientists will build on what is known, mindful of issues that need to be explored. That is one more answer to the question on the first page of this chapter: "Why should you care?"

SUMMING UP

Correlations are useful, but they do not prove causation. Quantitative research is more objective and easier to replicate but loses the nuances that qualitative research reveals. Correlations and qualitative studies are explored in experimental research.

Scientists follow codes of ethics and employ various safeguards to protect research participants and to ensure that the data can be used by other scientists. Particular care must be taken to ensure not only that no child is harmed but also that the needs and opinions of everyone—including parents, teachers, and the children themselves—are considered. The most urgent issues tend to be difficult to explore objectively and report honestly. That is precisely why further scientific research is needed.

■ SUMMARY

Defining Development

1. The study of human development is a science that seeks to understand how people change over time. Sometimes these changes are linear—gradual, steady, and predictable—but more often they are not. Change may be small or large, caused by something seemingly insignificant like the flap of a butterfly's wings, or large and pervasive.

Five Characteristics of Development

2. Development is multidirectional, multicontextual, multicultural, multidisciplinary, and plastic, the product of dynamic systems. Any one change affects an interconnected system, and any one person affects all the other people in a family or social group.

3. *Plasticity* means that change is always possible but is never unrestricted: Childhood becomes the foundation for later growth.

4. Each individual develops within unique historical, cultural, and socioeconomic contexts. Life is quite different for a low-income child in a traditional culture, for instance, than for a middle-class child in a modern, multicultural society.

5. To understand development, it is necessary to compare many cultures and use research from many disciplines. Nevertheless, because each person has unique genes and experiences, contexts do not determine an individual's development—but they always influence it.

Developmental Study as a Science

6. The scientific method leads researchers to question assumptions and gather data to test conclusions. Although far from infallible, the scientific method helps researchers avoid biases and guides them in asking questions.

7. Commonly used research methods are scientific observation, the experiment, the survey, and the case study. Each method has strengths and weaknesses. The most reliable conclusions can be drawn when various methods all reach similar conclusions and when replications using many subjects in diverse cultures confirm the results.

8. To study change over time, scientists use three research designs: cross-sectional research (comparing people of different ages), longitudinal research (studying the same people over time), and cross-sequential research (combining the other two methods). Each method has advantages.

9. Further synthesis is the goal of the ecological-systems approach, which takes into account various components of the individual's environment, from the immediate contexts (the microsystems) to the overarching culture (the macrosystem).

Cautions from Science

10. One useful statistical way to show that two variables are related is the correlation, a number that indicates a connection between two variables but does not prove that one variable causes the other.

11. Another useful method is qualitative research, in which information is recorded without being quantified, or translated into numbers. Qualitative research best captures the nuances of individual lives, but quantitative research is easier to replicate and verify.

12. Ethical behavior is crucial in all sciences, perhaps especially in developmental research when children are involved. Not only must participants be protected, but results must be clearly reported and understood.

13. Appropriate application of scientific research depends partly on the integrity of the scientific methods used and especially on careful explanation and interpretation of the conclusions. The most important ethical issues are whether the critical questions are being asked and whether the needed research is being conducted.

■ KEY TERMS

science of human development (p. 6)
continuity (p. 6)
discontinuity (p. 6)
butterfly effect (p. 7)
cohort (p. 8)
socioeconomic status (SES) (p. 9)
resilience (p. 15)
scientific method (p. 18)
hypothesis (p. 18)
replication (p. 18)
scientific observation (p. 18)
experiment (p. 20)
independent variable (p. 20)
dependent variable (p. 20)
experimental group (p. 20)
comparison group/control group (p. 20)
survey (p. 21)
ethnic group (p. 22)
race (p. 22)
case study (p. 23)
cross-sectional research (p. 24)
longitudinal research (p. 25)
cross-sequential research (p. 26)
ecological-systems approach (p. 27)
correlation (p. 28)
quantitative research (p. 29)
qualitative research (p. 29)
code of ethics (p. 30)

■ KEY QUESTIONS

1. What does it mean to say that the study of human development is a science?

2. Give an example of a social construction. Explain why this is a construction, not a fact.

3. What is the difference between ethnic group and culture?

4. Why is race not useful as a biological concept?

5. Why are most children *not* considered resilient?

6. What are the differences between scientific observation and everyday observation?

7. In what ways can surveys be considered the opposite of case studies?

8. Why would a scientist decide to do cross-sectional research?

9. Cite a positive correlation and a negative correlation in the way you spend your time.

10. What are the disadvantages and advantages of qualitative research?

11. Why would some people refuse to participate in research or quit before the study was finished?

12. What is one question about development that you think should be answered?

■ APPLICATIONS

1. It is said that culture is pervasive but that people are unaware of it. List 30 things you did *today* that you might have done differently in another culture. (You might list what you did in one column and what you might have done in another.)

2. Is socioeconomic status an important context? How would your life be different if your parents had much less, or much more, education and income than they actually do?

3. Design an experiment to test a hypothesis you have about human development. Specify the hypothesis, then describe the experiment, including the sample size and the variables. (Look first at Appendix B, at the back of this book.)

Chapter Two

Theories of Development

As we saw in Chapter 1, the science of human development begins with questions. Among the hundreds of important questions are the following five; each is central to one of the five theories described in this chapter:

1. Do early experiences—of breast-feeding or bonding or abuse—linger into adulthood, even if they seem to be forgotten?
2. Does the development of intelligence depend on what a child is taught, through specific instruction, punishment, and examples?
3. Do children develop moral values naturally, or must they be taught right from wrong?
4. Does culture elicit behavior? For example, do more people vote in Okinawa or Ontario than in Ohio because of local customs or laws?
5. If a baby's parents both suffer from depression, schizophrenia, or alcoholism, is that infant likely to develop the same affliction?

For every answer, more questions arise: Why or why not? When and how? And so what? This is the most crucial question of all, because the implications and applications of the answers affect daily life.

What Theories Do

Each of the five questions listed above is answered "yes" by one of the five major theories—in order: (1) psychoanalytic theory, (2) behaviorism, (3) cognitive theory, (4) sociocultural theory, and (5) epigenetic theory. Each question is answered "no" or "not necessarily" by several other theories.

Thousands of other questions, evoked by millions of observations, are relevant to human development. To find and frame the critical questions and to seek answers to them, we must determine which observations are relevant. Then we must organize the facts to produce a deeper understanding. In short, we need a theory.

A **developmental theory** is a systematic statement of principles and generalizations that provides a coherent framework for understanding how and why people change as they grow older. Developmental theorists "try to make sense out of observations . . . [and] construct a story of the human journey from infancy through childhood or adulthood" (Miller, 2002, p. 2). Such a story, or theory, connects facts and observations with patterns and explanations, weaving the details of life into a meaningful whole. As an analogy, imagine building a house. A person could have a heap of lumber, nails, and other materials, but without a plan and workers to do the building, the heap cannot be assembled into a house. The observations of human development are

developmental theory A group of ideas, assumptions, and generalizations that interpret and illuminate the thousands of observations about human growth. In this way, developmental theories provide a framework for explaining the patterns and problems of development.

essential raw materials, but theories are needed to put them together. As Kurt Lewin (1943) once quipped, "Nothing is as practical as a good theory."

To be more specific about what theories do:

- Theories produce hypotheses. Formulating pivotal questions is much more difficult than finding answers. Theories suggest questions and then hypotheses, which become "a direct test of a question" (Salkind, 2004, p. 14).
- Theories generate discoveries: "New facts change the theory, and changes in the theory generate new experiments and thus new facts" (Miller, 2002, p. 4).
- Theories offer practical guidance. If a 5-year-old shouts "I hate you!" at his father, the man's reaction (smiling, ignoring, slapping, or asking "Why?") depends on his theory of child development (whether or not he knows that he has a theory).

grand theories Comprehensive theories of psychology, which have traditionally inspired and directed psychologists' thinking about child development. Psychoanalytic theory, behaviorism, and cognitive theory are all grand theories.

minitheories Theories that focus on some specific topic. In development, for example, several theories of how infants learn to talk are minitheories. They are less general and comprehensive than the grand theories, although useful in their own right.

emergent theories Theories that bring together information from many disciplines and are becoming comprehensive and systematic in their interpretations of development but are not yet established and detailed enough to be considered grand theories.

Hundreds of theories pertain to developmental science (Hartup, 2002). Several are called **grand theories** because they describe universal processes and the entire span of development. They offer "a powerful framework for interpreting and understanding . . . change and development of all individuals" (Renninger & Amsel, 1997, p. ix). Many are **minitheories,** explaining only a part of development or applying only to some individuals (Parke et al., 1994). And a few are **emergent theories;** they may become the new systematic and comprehensive theories of the future.

The distinction between *grand* and *emergent* theories is best understood by referring to the multidisciplinary perspective. The grand theories of human development originated in the discipline of psychology, focusing particularly on childhood. The emphasis on childhood is especially apparent in the work of two grand theorists, Sigmund Freud and Jean Piaget, both of whom depicted the *final* stage of human development as beginning in early adolescence.

Observations and explanations originating in history, biology, sociology, and anthropology led to the emergent theories. Historical events (notably, increasing globalization and immigration) and genetic discoveries (most recently, from the Human Genome Project) highlighted the need for the new theories, using cultural and genetic approaches. These emergent theories are not yet as coherent as the grand theories, but they are insightful, current, and more inclusive than theories that draw only on psychology.

SUMMING UP

Theories are useful because they provide a framework for organizing the thousands of observations that may be made about any aspect of development. This chapter describes three grand theories—psychoanalytic, behaviorist, and cognitive—and two emergent theories—sociocultural and epigenetic. Throughout the remaining chapters of the book, these five theories, as well as many minitheories, will be referred to again (see the Subject Index entry for each theory, and look under "Theories compared" for relevant page numbers).

Grand Theories

In the first half of the twentieth century, two opposing theories—psychoanalytic theory and behaviorism (also called "learning theory")—began as general theories of psychology and later were applied specifically to child development. By mid-century, cognitive theory had emerged, and it gradually became the dominant seedbed of research hypotheses. All three theories are "grand" in that they are comprehensive, enduring, and widely applied.

Psychoanalytic Theory

Inner drives and motives, many of them irrational, originating in childhood, and unconscious (hidden from awareness), are the foundation of **psychoanalytic theory.** These basic underlying forces are thought to influence every aspect of thinking and behavior, from the smallest details of daily life to the crucial choices of a lifetime. Psychoanalytic theory considers these drives and motives to be the foundation for stages of development, with each stage building on the previous one.

psychoanalytic theory A grand theory of human development that holds that irrational, unconscious drives and motives, often originating in childhood, underlie human behavior.

Freud's Ideas

Psychoanalytic theory originated with Sigmund Freud (1856–1939), an Austrian physician who treated patients suffering from mental illness. He listened to their accounts of dreams and fantasies, as well as to their "uncensored" streams of thought, and constructed an elaborate, multifaceted theory. According to Freud, development in the first six years occurs in three stages, each characterized by sexual interest and pleasure centered on a particular part of the body.

In infancy, the erotic body part is the mouth (the *oral stage*); in early childhood, it is the anus (the *anal stage*); in the preschool years, it is the penis (the *phallic stage*), a source of pride and fear among boys and a reason for sadness and envy among girls. Then comes *latency* and, beginning at adolescence, the *genital stage*. (Table 2.1 describes the stages in Freud's theory.)

AKG / PHOTO RESEARCHERS, INC.

Freud at Work In addition to being the world's first psychoanalyst, Sigmund Freud was a prolific writer. His many papers and case histories, primarily descriptions of his patients' bizarre symptoms and unconscious sexual urges, helped make the psychoanalytic perspective a dominant force for much of the twentieth century.

Freud maintained that at each stage, sensual satisfaction (from stimulation of the mouth, anus, or penis) is linked to major developmental needs and challenges. During the oral stage, for example, sucking not only provides nourishment for the baby but also gives sensual pleasure to the mother (particularly her breasts) and heightens her emotional attachment to the infant. Next, during the anal stage, pleasures related to control and self-control—initially with defecation and toilet training—are paramount.

One of Freud's most influential ideas was that each stage includes its own potential conflicts. Conflict occurs, for instance, when parents try to wean their babies (oral stage) or teachers expect 6-year-olds to become independent of their parents (phallic stage). According to Freud, how people experience and resolve these conflicts—especially those related to weaning, toilet training, and sexual pleasure—determine personality patterns, because "the early stages provide the foundation for adult behavior" (Salkind, 2004, p. 125).

Although they may not realize it, adults may have unconscious conflicts rooted in a childhood stage if they smoke cigarettes (oral) or keep careful track of money (anal) or are romantically attracted to much older partners

SUSAN LAPIDES / DESIGN CONCEPTIONS

Childhood Sexuality The girl's interest in the statue's anatomy may reflect simple curiosity, but Freudian theory would maintain that it is a clear manifestation of the phallic stage of psychosexual development, when girls are said to feel deprived because they lack a penis.

TABLE 2.1 **Comparison of Freud's Psychosexual and Erikson's Psychosocial Stages**

Approximate Age	Freud (Psychosexual)	Erikson (Psychosocial)
Birth to 1 year	*Oral Stage* The mouth, tongue, and gums are the focus of pleasurable sensations in the baby's body, and sucking and feeding are the most stimulating activities.	*Trust vs. Mistrust* Babies learn either to trust that others will care for their basic needs, including nourishment, warmth, cleanliness, and physical contact, or to lack confidence in the care of others.
1–3 years	*Anal Stage* The anus is the focus of pleasurable sensations in the baby's body, and toilet training is the most important activity.	*Autonomy vs. Shame and Doubt* Children learn either to be self-sufficient in many activities, including toileting, feeding, walking, exploring, and talking, or to doubt their own abilities.
3–6 years	*Phallic Stage* The phallus, or penis, is the most important body part, and pleasure is derived from genital stimulation. Boys are proud of their penises, and girls wonder why they don't have one.	*Initiative vs. Guilt* Children want to undertake many adultlike activities, or fear the limits set by paents and feel guilty.
6–11 years	*Latency* This is not a stage but an interlude, during which sexual needs are quiet and children put psychic energy into conventional activities like schoolwork and sports.	*Industry vs. Inferiority* Children busily learn to be competent and productive in mastering new skills or feel inferior and unable to do anything well.
Adolescence	*Genital Stage* The genitals are the focus of pleasurable sensations, and the young person seeks sexual stimulation and sexual satisfaction in heterosexual relationships.	*Identity vs. Role Confusion* Adolescents try to figure out "Who am I?" They establish sexual, political, and career identities or are confused about what roles to play.
Adulthood	Freud believed that the genital stage lasts throughout adulthood. He also said that the goal of a healthy life is "to love and to work."	*Intimacy vs. Isolation* Young adults seek companionship and love with another person or become isolated from others because they fear rejection and disappointment. *Generativity vs. Stagnation* Middle-aged adults contribute to the next generation through meaningful work, creative activities, and/or raising a family, or they stagnate. *Integrity vs. Despair* Older adults try to make sense out of their lives, either seeing life as a meaningful whole or despairing at goals never reached.

(phallic). For all of us, childhood fantasies and memories remain powerful lifelong. If you have ever wondered why lovers call each other "baby" or why many people refer to their spouse as their "old lady" or "sugar daddy," then Freud's theory provides an explanation: The parent–child relationship is the model for all intimacy.

Freud put forward many other ideas about personality and psychopathology that are influential for interpreting adult behavior. However, his ideas about stages and parenting in the first five years, as just described, are most relevant to child development.

Erikson's Ideas

Many of Freud's followers became famous psychoanalytic theorists themselves. Although they all acknowledged the importance of unconscious, irrational forces and early childhood, each of these neo-Freudians expanded and modified Freud's ideas. The most notable was Erik Erikson (1902–1994), who formulated his own version of psychoanalytic theory and applied it to human development.

Erikson never knew his biological father. He spent his childhood in Germany, his adolescence wandering through Italy, and his young adulthood in Austria, working with Freud. He married an American, and he fled to the United States just before World War II began. His studies of Harvard students, Boston children at play, and Native American cultures led Erikson to stress cultural diversity, social change, and psychological crises throughout the life span. For example, he wrote a massive case study of Mahatma Gandhi, who was born in India, was educated in Britain, practiced law in South Africa, and then led the nonviolent revolution that helped India gain independence.

Erikson described eight developmental stages, each characterized by a particular challenge, or *developmental crisis* (summarized in Table 2.1). Although Erikson named two polarities at each crisis, he recognized that there is a wide range of outcomes between these opposites. For most people, development at each stage leads to neither extreme but to something in between.

As you can see from Table 2.1, Erikson's first five stages are closely related to Freud's stages. Erikson, like Freud, believed that problems of adult life echo unresolved conflicts of childhood. For example, an adult who has difficulty establishing a secure, mutual relationship with a life partner may never have resolved the first crisis of early infancy, *trust versus mistrust.* However, Erikson's stages differ significantly from Freud's in that they emphasize people's relationships to their family and culture, not their sexual urges.

In Erikson's theory, the resolution of each crisis depends on the interaction between the individual and the social environment. In the stage of *initiative versus guilt,* for example, children between ages 3 and 6 often want to undertake activities that exceed their abilities or the limits set by their parents. They jump into swimming pools, dress themselves, mix and bake a cake according to their own recipe. Such efforts to act independently leave them open to pride or failure, producing guilt if they hide their actions from adults and are blamed for it.

The outcome of the initiative-versus-guilt crisis depends partly on how the child goes about seeking independence, partly on the reactions of the parents, and partly on the culture. As an example, some parents and cultures *encourage* assertive 5-year-olds, seeing them as creative spirits who know their own minds, letting them wear mismatched clothes if they choose, whereas others *discourage* such initiative, calling the children "rude" or "fresh" if they demand their own way.

CORBIS

What's in a Name?—Erik Erikson As a young man, this neo-Freudian changed his last name to the one we know him by. What do you think his choice means? (See the caption to the next photograph.)

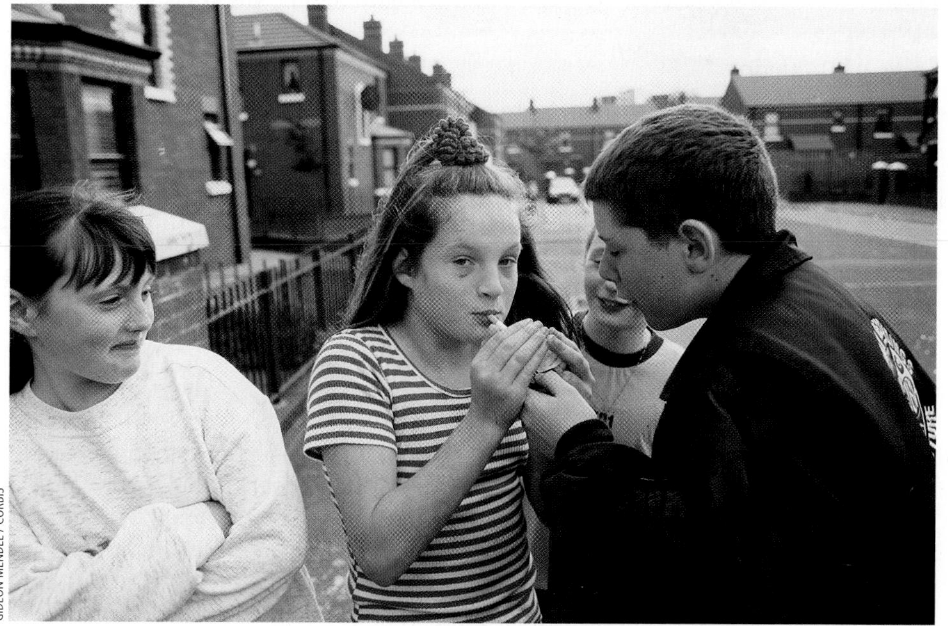

GIDEON MENDEL / CORBIS

Who Are We? The most famous of Erikson's eight crises is the identity crisis, during adolescence, when young people find their own answer to the question "Who am I?" Erikson did this for himself by choosing a last name that, with his first name, implies "son of myself" (Erik, Erik's son). These children in Northern Ireland may be smoking because their search for identity is taking place in a sociocultural context that allows an unhealthy path toward adulthood.

Children internalize, or accept, responses from their parents, peers, and cultures, and the child's internalized reactions persist throughout life. Even in late adulthood, one older person may be quite bold and outspoken while another is always fearful of saying the wrong thing, because they resolved their initiative-versus-guilt stage in opposite ways. Erikson believed that a father's reaction to his son's "I hate you!" reflects his childhood experiences with his own father.

ESPECIALLY FOR TEACHERS Your kindergarteners are talkative and always moving. They almost never sit quietly and listen to you. What would Erik Erikson recommend?

ESPECIALLY FOR TEACHERS Same problem as above, but what would a behaviorist recommend?

Behaviorism

The second grand theory arose in direct opposition to the psychoanalytic emphasis on unconscious, hidden urges (described in Table 2.2). The problem was that such urges could not be studied and quantified, which meant that psychology did not seem scientific. Early in the twentieth century, John B. Watson (1878–1958) argued that, if psychology was to be a true science, psychologists should examine only what they could see and measure: behavior, not thoughts and hidden urges. In Watson's words:

> Why don't we make what we can *observe* the real field of psychology? Let us limit ourselves to things that can be observed, and formulate laws concerned only with those things. . . . We can observe behavior—what the organism does or says.
>
> [Watson, 1924/1998, p. 6]

ARCHIVES OF THE HISTORY OF AMERICAN PSYCHOLOGY, THE UNIVERSITY OF AKRON

An Early Behaviorist John Watson was an early proponent of learning theory whose ideas are still influential today.

According to Watson, if psychologists focus on behavior, they will realize that anything can be learned. He wrote:

> Give me a dozen healthy infants, well-formed, and my own specified world to bring them up in and I'll guarantee to take any one at random and train him to become any type of specialist I might select—doctor, lawyer, artist, merchant chief, and yes, even beggar-man and thief, regardless of his talents, penchants, tendencies, abilities, vocations, and race of his ancestors.
>
> [Watson, 1924/1998, p. 82]

Other psychologists, especially in the United States, agreed. They found it difficult to use the scientific method to verify the unconscious motives and drives that Freud described (Uttal, 2000). They developed **behaviorism** to study actual behavior, objectively and scientifically. Behaviorism is also called *learning theory* because it describes how people learn and develop habits, step by step.

behaviorism A grand theory of human development that studies observable behavior. Behaviorism is also called *learning theory,* because it describes the laws and processes by which behavior is learned.

Laws of Behavior

For every individual at every age, from newborn to octogenarian, behaviorists describe natural laws that govern how simple actions and environmental responses shape complex competencies, such as reading a book or making a family dinner. Learning theorists believe that development occurs in small increments. Because change is cumulative, behaviorists, unlike Freud or Erikson, describe no specific stages (Bijou & Baer, 1978).

The specific laws of learning apply to **conditioning,** the processes by which responses become linked to particular stimuli; it is sometimes called *S–R (stimulus–response) conditioning.* There are two types of conditioning: classical and operant.

conditioning According to behaviorism, conditioning is the process of learning. The word *conditioning* is used to emphasize the importance of repeated practice, as when an athlete gets in condition by training for many weeks or months. (Sometimes called *S–R [stimulus–response] conditioning.*)

Classical Conditioning A century ago, Russian scientist Ivan Pavlov (1849–1936), after winning the Nobel Prize for his work on animal digestion, began to study the link between stimulus and response. While studying salivation, Pavlov noted that his experimental dogs drooled not only at the sight and smell of food but also, eventually, at the footsteps of the attendants who brought the food. This observation led Pavlov to perform his famous experiment in which he conditioned dogs to salivate when they heard a bell.

TABLE 2.2 **Psychoanalytic Theory vs. Behaviorism**

Area of Disagreement	Psychoanalytic Theory	Behaviorism
The unconscious	Emphasizes unconscious wishes and urges, unknown to the person but powerful all the same	Holds that the unconscious not only is unknowable but may be a destructive fiction that keeps people from changing
Observable behavior	Holds that observable behavior is a symptom, not the cause—the tip of an iceberg, with the bulk of the problem submerged	Looks only at observable behavior—what a person does rather than what a person thinks, feels, or imagines
Importance of childhood	Stresses that early childhood, including infancy, is critical; even if a person does not remember what happened, the early legacy lingers throughout life	Holds that current conditioning is crucial; early habits and patterns can be unlearned, even reversed, if appropriate reinforcements and punishments are used
Scientific status	Holds that most aspects of human development are beyond the reach of scientific experiment; uses ancient myths, the words of disturbed adults, dreams, play, and poetry as raw material	Is proud to be a science, dependent on verifiable data and carefully controlled experiments; discards ideas that sound good but are not proven

SOVFOTO

A Contemporary of Freud Ivan Pavlov was a physiologist who received the Nobel Prize in 1904 for his research on digestive processes. It was this line of study that led to his discovery of classical conditioning.

Pavlov began by ringing the bell just before presenting food. After a number of repetitions of the bell-then-food sequence, dogs began salivating at the bell's sound even when there was no food. This simple experiment demonstrated **classical conditioning** (also called *respondent conditioning*).

classical conditioning The learning process that connects a meaningful stimulus (such as the smell of food to a hungry animal) with a neutral stimulus, which had no special meaning before conditioning. Thus, money is neutral to a baby, but adults have been conditioned to want money because they have learned that it is connected to obtaining food and other basic things. (Also called *respondent conditioning.*)

In classical conditioning, a person or animal is conditioned to associate a neutral stimulus with a meaningful stimulus, gradually responding to the neutral stimulus in the same way as to the meaningful one. In Pavlov's original experiment, the dog associated the bell (the neutral stimulus) with food (the meaningful stimulus) and responded to the bell's ringing as though it were the food itself. The conditioned response to the bell (which was no longer neutral but was now a conditioned stimulus) was evidence that learning had occurred.

Operant Conditioning The most influential North American proponent of behaviorism was B. F. Skinner (1904–1990). Skinner agreed with Watson that psychology should focus on the scientific study of behavior, and he agreed with Pavlov that classical conditioning explains some behavior. However, Skinner believed that another type of conditioning—**operant conditioning** (also called *instrumental conditioning*)—is often crucial, especially in complex learning.

operant conditioning The learning process by which a particular action is followed by something desired (which makes the person or animal more likely to repeat the action) or by something unwanted (which makes the action less likely to be repeated). A student might study for many hours because, in the past, studying produced intellectual satisfaction, high grades, or parental praise. Such diligence is the result of operant conditioning. (Also called *instrumental conditioning.*)

In operant conditioning, animals perform a particular behavior and experience a consequence. If the consequence is useful or pleasurable, the animal is likely to repeat the behavior. If the consequence is unpleasant, the animal becomes less likely to repeat the behavior.

Pleasant consequences are sometimes called "rewards," and unpleasant consequences are sometimes called "punishments." Behaviorists hesitate to use those words, however, because what people commonly think of as a punishment can actually be a reward, and vice versa. For example, parents punish their children by withholding dessert, by spanking them, by not letting them play, by speaking harshly to them, and so on. But it is possible that a particular child

© SAM FALK / MONKMEYER

Rats, Pigeons, and People B. F. Skinner is best known for his experiments with rats and pigeons, but he also applied his knowledge to human problems. For his daughter, he designed a glass-enclosed crib in which temperature, humidity, and perceptual stimulation could be controlled to make her time in the crib enjoyable and educational. He wrote about an ideal society based on principles of operant conditioning, where, for example, workers in less desirable jobs would earn greater rewards.

might, for instance, dislike the dessert, so that being deprived of it is no punishment. Another child might not mind a spanking, especially if that is the only time the parent pays attention to the child. In this case, the intended punishment is actually a reward.

Similarly, teachers sometimes punish misbehaving children by sending them out of the classroom or even suspending them from school; but if a child dislikes the teacher and school, being sent out is actually a reward for misbehaving. The true test is the *effect* a consequence has on the individual's future behavior, not whether it is intended to be a reward or a punishment. The child who commits the offense a second time may have been reinforced, not punished, for the first infraction.

Once a behavior has been conditioned (learned), animals (including humans) continue to perform it even if pleasurable consequences occur only occasionally or continue to avoid it even if punishment is rare. Almost all of our daily behavior, from socializing with others to earning a paycheck, can be understood as a result of past operant conditioning. For instance, when a baby first gives a half-smile in response to a full stomach, the mother might smile back. Soon the baby is conditioned to smile in order to see the mother's responsive smile. The baby smiles more broadly at the mother, and the mother (who herself has been conditioned) encourages the broader smile, perhaps by picking the baby up. As time goes on, that baby becomes a smiling toddler, a cheerful child, an outgoing adolescent, and a friendly adult—all because of early operant conditioning and periodic reinforcing.

Similarly, if parents want their child to share, they must encourage early efforts in that direction. When the baby hands them a toy—or even a gummy, half-eaten cracker—the parents should take the gift with apparent delight and then return it, smiling. Adults should never pull at a toy a child is holding; that encourages the child to hold on tighter (a game strangers sometimes played with my children) and teaches possessiveness, not sharing.

In these examples of operant conditioning, using consequences to make it more likely that a particular action will be repeated is a process called **reinforcement** (consequences that make the behavior *less* likely are called *punishments* or *aversive consequences*) (Skinner, 1953). A consequence that increases behavior is therefore called a *reinforcer*. In the example above, the mother's smiles are reinforcers, and her early reinforcement of the baby's first smiles produce a socially responsive, friendly adult.

The science of human development has benefited from behaviorism. That theory's emphasis on the causes and consequences of observed behavior led researchers to realize that many behavior patterns that seem to be genetic, or to result from deeply rooted emotional problems, are actually learned. And if something is learned, it can be unlearned.

Behaviorism is a very hopeful theory. It encouraged scientists to find ways to eliminate particular human problems—among them temper tantrums, phobias, and addictions. To do this, a scientist (or teacher, or parent) must first analyze all the reinforcements, punishments, and past conditioning that set the problem in place. Then those past stimulus–response chains must be broken and replaced by new S–R links. Tantrums will cease, phobias will disappear, addicts will recover, and so on. Many teachers, counselors, and parents use behaviorist techniques to break undesirable habits and teach new behaviors (Kazdin, 2001).

Like all good theories, both behaviorism and psychoanalytic theory have been sources of hypotheses for many scientific experiments, such as those described in the following Thinking Like a Scientist.

reinforcement A technique for conditioning behavior in which that behavior is followed by something desired, such as food for a hungry animal or a welcoming smile for a lonely person.

Response for Teachers (from page 40): Erikson would note that the behavior of 5-year-olds is affected by their developmental stage and by their culture, and therefore you might design your curriculum to accommodate active, noisy children.

Response for Teachers (from page 40): Behaviorists believe that anyone can learn anything. If your goal is quiet, attentive children, begin by reinforcing a moment's quiet or a quiet child, and soon all the children will be trying to remain attentive for several minutes at a time.

THINKING LIKE A SCIENTIST

What's a Mother For?

Why do children love their mothers, even if their mothers are ugly, mean, or unresponsive? Is it because their mothers fed them when they were infants? Everyone has observed mothers and babies, but the answer to this simple question is not obvious. Theories organize perceptions, helping scientists to interpret observations, develop hypotheses, and then test the hypotheses. When questions arise, such as these questions about mother love, scientists seek data to disprove, as well as to confirm, their theories.

Both behaviorism and psychoanalytic theory originally hypothesized that mothers earn their children's love because they satisfy the newborn's hunger and sucking needs. In other words, "the infant's attachment to the mother stemmed from internal drives which triggered activities connected with the libations of the mother's breast. This belief was the only one these two theoretical groups ever had in common" (C. Harlow in Harlow, 1986).

The hypothesis, derived from both theories, was that a child's love of the mother was the direct result of maternal feeding. Once physicians established the germ theory of disease, they assumed that mothers who showered too much affection on their children would "spoil" them and even make them sick. This hypothesis was accepted not only by pediatricians and psychologists but by almost everyone. As a consequence, in the late nineteenth and early twentieth centuries, orphanages and hospitals kept babies clean and well-fed but forbade caregivers to interact with them, never kissing or hugging, because "human contact was the ultimate enemy of health" (Blum, 2002, p. 35). A 1949 guide for new mothers from a Kansas hospital advised, "Do not pick baby up every time it cries. Normal infants cry some every day to obtain exercise. Infant is quickly spoiled by handling" (quoted in Rogoff, 2003, p. 130).

In the 1950s, Harry Harlow (1905–1981), a psychologist who studied learning in monkeys, observed something that made him question this hypothesis:

> We had separated more than 60 of these animals from their mothers 6 to 12 hours after birth and suckled them on tiny bottles. The infant mortality rate was a fraction of what we would have obtained had we let the monkey mothers raise their infants. Our bottle-fed babies were healthier and heavier than monkey-mother-reared infants. . . . [But] during the course of our studies we noticed that the laboratory-raised babies showed strong attachment to the folded gauze diapers which were used to cover the . . . floor of their cages.
>
> *[C. Harlow, 1986, p. 103]*

In fact, the infant monkeys seemed more attached to the cloth diapers than to their bottles. This was contrary to the two prevailing theories, since psychoanalytic theory predicted that infants would cherish whatever satisfied their oral needs and behaviorism predicted that infants would become attached to whatever provided reinforcing food. Both these theories led to the prediction that motherless monkeys would love their bottles.

HARLOW PRIMATE LABORATORY, UNIVERSITY OF WISCONSIN

Clinging to "Mother" Even though it gave no milk, this "mother" was soft and warm enough that infant monkeys spent almost all their time holding on to it. Many infants, some children, and even some adults cling to a familiar stuffed animal when life becomes frightening. According to Harlow, the reasons are the same: All primates are comforted by something soft, warm, and familiar to the touch.

Harlow set out to make a "direct experimental analysis" via his monkeys. Using monkeys to study human emotions may seem odd to some people, but not to an experimental psychologist who believed that "the basic processes relating to affection, including nursing, contact, clinging, and even visual and auditory exploration, exhibit no fundamental differences in the two species" (H. Harlow, 1958). Harlow was troubled that few psychologists recognized the crucial role of physical contact—in the form of cuddling, soothing, hugging, and so on—for all social species, including monkeys and humans.

Harlow raised eight infant monkeys in cages without other animals but with two "surrogate" (artificial) mothers, both mother-monkey size. One surrogate was made of bare wire and the other was covered by soft terrycloth, with a face designed to be ugly — two red bicycle reflectors for eyes and a strip of green cloth for a mouth. Four of the baby monkeys were fed by a bottle stuck through the chest of the cloth "mother," the other four by a bottle put through the chest of the wire "mother."

Harlow measured how much time each baby spent holding on to either of the two surrogates. The monkeys who had a cloth, milk-providing mother clung to it and ignored the wire mother; this was to be expected, since feeding was connected with mothering. However, even the four babies that fed from the wire mother spent more time clinging to the cloth mother, going to the wire mother only when hunger compelled them (see Figure 2.1). In short, no attachment to, or love for, the nourishing wire mother could be observed, but the cloth mother seemed to have the infants' affection whether or not it provided food.

Harlow then wondered if the cloth mothers might reassure infants when frightening events occurred, just as a real mother does. He devised another experiment, putting an unfamiliar mechanical toy into each infant's cage. The monkeys immediately sought comfort from the cloth mother, clinging to the soft belly with one hand and then timidly exploring the new object with the other.

The wire mother provided no such reassurance, whether or not it had provided food. Monkeys confronted by the same mechanical toy with access only to the wire mother were terrified—freezing, screaming, shivering, hiding, urinating. Harlow concluded that mothering is not primarily about feeding, but about touching, comforting, and holding, which Harlow called "contact comfort" or "love" (H. Harlow, 1958). In later research, Harlow's students discovered that mother love involved more than contact—that infant monkeys need interaction with another living, moving creature to grow up to be psychologically healthy adults (Blum, 2002).

This research revolutionized the treatment of sick or motherless children. Even very tiny, fragile preterm infants now have contact with their parents, typically including very gentle touch—and their chances of survival are better because of it (see Chapter 4).

Harlow's experiments are a classic example of the use of theories. Although aspects of both behaviorism and psychoanalytic theory were disproved, that is not the most significant point. Remember, theories are meant to be useful, not necessarily true. (If they were known to be true in every aspect, they would be scientific laws, not theories.) Because Harlow knew what the psychoanalytic and behavioral theories said about love and comfort, he was intrigued by the baby monkeys' preference for the gauze diapers over the bottles of milk. That led to closer observation, a hypothesis, a clever series of experiments, and some amazing results.

Both psychoanalytic theory and behaviorism were revised and expanded in response to these experiments and to other evidence. Harlow himself was criticized for overemphasizing the role of mothers and for ignoring animal suffering, but his research has had beneficial applications (Blum, 2002). Today's mothers do much more cuddling and infants do much less crying than their predecessors did a century ago, because one creative scientist contrasted theoretical predictions and his own observations and performed ingenious experiments to test a hypothesis.

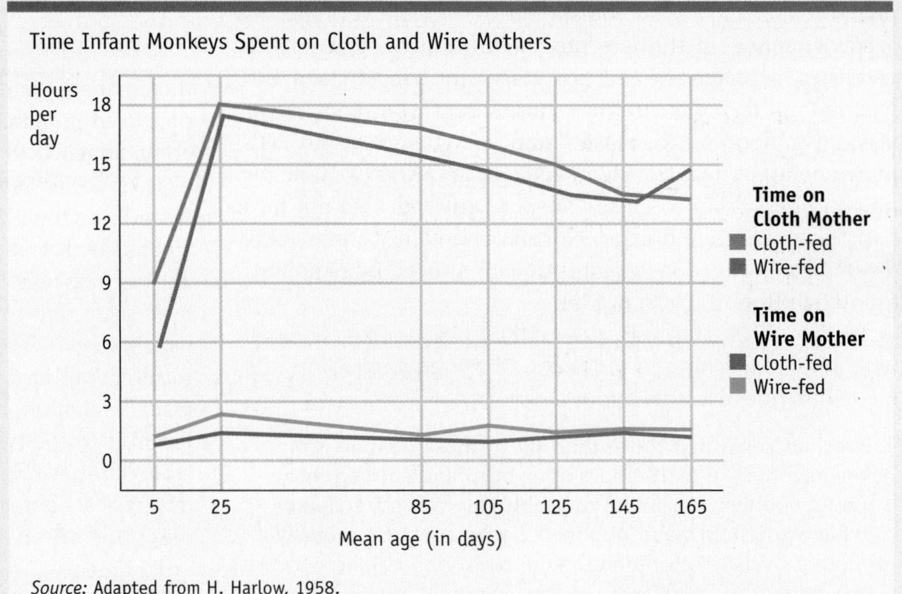

FIGURE 2.1 **Softer Is Better** During the first three weeks of Harlow's experiment, the infant monkeys developed a strong preference for the cloth-covered "mothers." That preference lasted throughout the experiment, even among the monkeys who were fed by a wire-covered mother.

? OBSERVATIONAL QUIZ (see answer, page 48): At five days, how much time did the wire-fed monkeys (compared with the cloth-fed monkeys) spend on the cloth mothers?

Social Learning

Originally, behaviorists interpreted all behavior as arising from a chain of learned responses, the result of classical and operant conditioning. One refinement of behaviorism, based on thousands of studies, arose from evidence (from humans as well as monkeys) that all creatures appreciate another's touch, warmth, reassurance, and example.

This revision is called **social learning theory** (see Figure 2.2). Humans learn from observing others, without linking one stimulus with another (classical conditioning) and without personally experiencing any reinforcement (operant conditioning). We learn because we are social beings, seeking the feelings of pride and acceptance that other people can bestow. For this reason, others teach us in ways beyond classical or operant conditioning.

social learning theory An extension of behaviorism that emphasizes the power of other people over our behavior. Even without specific reinforcement or punishment, people learn many things via observation and imitation of other people.

Learning occurs through:

- **Classical conditioning** Through association, neutral stimulus becomes conditioned stimulus.
- **Operant conditioning** Through reinforcement, weak or rare responses become strong, frequent responses.
- **Social learning** Through modeling, observed behaviors become copied behaviors.

FIGURE 2.2 **Three Types of Learning** Behaviorism is also called "learning theory," because it emphasizes the learning process, as shown here.

An integral part of social learning is **modeling,** in which people observe behavior and then copy it. Modeling is a complex learning activity, far more than simple imitation, because people model only some actions, of some individuals, in some contexts. As an example, you may know adults who, as children, saw their parents hit each other. Some of these adults are abusive to their own partners, while others scrupulously avoid marital conflict. These two responses seem directly opposed, but both support social learning theory in that they show the continuing impact of the original example. Generally, modeling is most likely when the observer is uncertain or inexperienced (which explains why modeling is especially powerful in childhood) and when the model is admired, powerful, nurturing, or similar to the observer (Bandura, 1986, 1997).

modeling The central process of social learning, by which people observe the actions of others and then copy them.

self-efficacy In social learning theory, the belief that one is effective. Self-efficacy motivates people to change themselves and their contexts because they believe they are capable of effective action.

As this example shows, social learning is connected to perceptions and interpretations. It is also related to self-understanding, self-confidence, social reflection, and feelings of **self-efficacy,** the belief that one succeeds because of one's own ability. People develop a sense of efficacy when they have high aspirations and experience notable achievements (Bandura et al., 2001).

Self-efficacy explains a paradox found in recent research: Parents who do not believe in their own efficacy and who think their babies are strong-willed are stricter and less responsive than other parents. Their own parents probably never let them develop a strong sense of themselves, so they learned to feel helpless and still feel ineffective as adults (Guzell & Vernon-Feagons, 2004). Their lack

Social Learning in Action Social learning validates the old maxim "Actions speak louder than words." If the moments here are typical for each child, the girl on the left is likely to grow up with a ready sense of the importance of this particular chore of infant care. Unfortunately, the boy on the right may become a cigarette smoker like his father—even if his father warns him of the dangers of this habit.

? **OBSERVATIONAL QUIZ** (see answer, page 48): What shows that these children imitate their parents?

PHOTOGRAPHER'S CHOICE/GETTY

RICHARD HUTCHIN / PHOTOEDIT

of feelings of self-efficacy and the example set by their own parents lead them to be overly controlling with their children.

As you read in Chapter 1, *collective efficacy* prompts family and community systems to join together to work for improvements (Sampson et al., 1997). Obviously, social learning theory and, more generally, behaviorism encourage action. Modeling and conditioning can change an individual, a social group, or even an entire culture. Social learning depends not only on observation and reinforcement but also on cognition, the focus of the next grand theory.

Cognitive Theory

cognitive theory A grand theory of human development that focuses on changes in how people think over time. According to this theory, our thoughts shape our attitudes, beliefs, and behaviors.

The third grand theory, **cognitive theory,** emphasizes the structure and development of thought processes. According to cognitive theory, our thoughts and expectations profoundly affect our attitudes, beliefs, values, assumptions, and actions. Cognitive theory has dominated psychology since about 1980 and has branched into many versions.

A major cognitive theory is *information-processing theory,* which focuses on the step-by-step activation of various parts of the brain, from initial sensory awareness all the way to sophisticated analysis and exposition. Information-processing theory is described in detail in Chapter 6.

The original cognitive theorist was the Swiss scientist Jean Piaget (1896–1980). Piaget was trained in the natural sciences, studying shellfish as his academic specialty, and he learned to be meticulous in observation.

YVES DEBRAINE / BLACK STAR

Would You Talk to This Man? Children loved talking to Jean Piaget, and he learned by listening carefully—especially to their incorrect explanations, which no one had paid much attention to before. All his life, Piaget was absorbed with studying the way children think. He called himself a "genetic epistemologist"—one who studies how children gain knowledge about the world as they grow up.

Piaget became interested in human thought processes when he got a job in Paris field-testing questions for a standardized IQ test. Although he was hired to find the age at which most children could answer each question correctly, the children's wrong answers caught his attention. *How* children think is much more revealing of their mental development, Piaget concluded, than *what* they know.

Piaget's interest in cognitive development grew as he observed his own three children, from their first weeks of life onward. Piaget realized that babies are much more curious and thoughtful than other psychologists had imagined. He devised and recorded many simple experiments to explore what his children understood, thus tracing intellectual development during infancy. Later he studied hundreds of schoolchildren.

From this work Piaget developed the central thesis of cognitive theory: How children think changes with time and experience, and these thought processes always affect behavior. According to cognitive theory, if psychologists understand a person's thinking, they will understand how and why that person behaves as he or she does—the goal of all psychology.

Piaget maintained that cognitive development occurs in four major periods, or stages: the *sensorimotor* period, the *preoperational* period, the *concrete operational* period, and the *formal operational* period (see Table 2.3). These periods are age-related, and, as you will see in later chapters, each period fosters certain types of knowing and understanding (Piaget, 1952b; Inhelder & Piaget, 1958).

cognitive equilibrium In cognitive theory, the condition of mental balance, when people are not confused or bewildered because they can use their existing thought processes to understand current experiences and ideas.

Intellectual advancement occurs because humans seek **cognitive equilibrium**—that is, a state of mental balance. An easy way to achieve this balance is to interpret new experiences through the lens of preexisting ideas. For example, infants discover that new objects can be grasped in the same way as familiar objects and adolescents explain the day's headlines as evidence for their existing worldviews.

Sometimes a new experience is jarring and incomprehensible. Then the individual experiences *cognitive disequilibrium,* an imbalance that initially creates confusion. As Figure 2.3 illustrates, disequilibrium leads to cognitive growth, because people must adapt their old concepts. Piaget describes two types of adaptation:

TABLE 2.3 **Piaget's Periods of Cognitive Development**

Age Range	Name of Period	Characteristics of the Period	Major Gains During the Period
Birth to 2 years	Sensorimotor	Infants use senses and motor abilities to understand the world. Learning is active; there is no conceptual or reflective thought.	Infants learn that an object still exists when it is out of sight (*object permanence*) and begin to think through mental actions.
2–6 years	Preoperational	Children use *symbolic thinking,* including language, to understand the world. Thinking is *egocentric,* causing children to perceive the world from their own perspective.	The imagination flourishes, and language becomes a significant means of self-expression and of influence from others.
6–11 years	Concrete operational	Children understand and apply logical operations, or principles, to interpret experiences objectively and rationally. Their thinking is limited to what they can personally see, hear, touch, and experience.	By applying logical abilities, children learn to understand concepts of conservation, number, classification, and many other scientific ideas.
12 years through adulthood	Formal operational	Adolescents and adults think about abstractions and hypothetical concepts and reason analytically, not just emotionally. They can be logical about things they have never experienced.	Ethics, politics, and social and moral issues become fascinating as adolescents and adults take a broader and more theoretical approach to experience.

- *Assimilation,* in which new experiences are reinterpreted to fit into, or *assimilate* with, old ideas.
- *Accommodation,* in which old ideas are restructured to include, or *accommodate,* new experiences.

Accommodation is harder than assimilation, but it is sometimes necessary because new ideas and experiences may not fit into existing cognitive structures. Accommodation produces significant intellectual growth, including advancement to the next stage of cognitive development. For example, if a friend expresses ideas that reveal cognitive inconsistencies in your own opinions, or if your favorite chess strategy fails, or if your mother says something you never expected her to, you will experience cognitive disequilibrium. In the last example, you might *assimilate* your mother's words by deciding she didn't mean what she said. Perhaps she was just repeating something she had read, or perhaps you misheard her. Intellectual growth would occur if, instead, you adapted by changing your view of your mother to *accommodate* a new, expanded understanding. You might realize you didn't know her as well as you thought.

Ideally, when two people disagree, or when they surprise each other by things they say, adaptation is mutual. For example, parents are often startled by their grown children's opinions. If the parents are able to grow intellectually, they revise their concept of their offspring, accommodating to an updated perception. The children, too, might accommodate to a new understanding of their

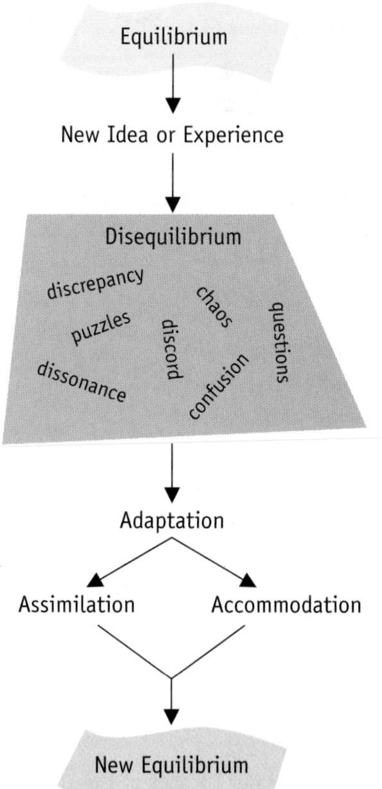

FIGURE 2.3 **Challenge Me** Most of us, most of the time, prefer the comfort of our conventional conclusions. According to Piaget, however, when new ideas disturb our thinking, we have an opportunity to expand our cognition with a broader and deeper understanding.

! Answer to Observational Quiz (from page 44): Six hours, or one-third less time. Note that later on, the wire-fed monkeys (compared with the cloth-fed monkeys) spend equal, or even more, time on the cloth mothers.

! Answer to Observational Quiz (from page 45): The obvious part of the answer is that the girl is feeding her doll and the boy is pretending to smoke a cigarette, but modeling goes far beyond that. Notice that the girl is holding her spoon at exactly the same angle as her mother is holding hers, and that the boy's blue-jeaned legs are posed casually, just like his father's.

How to Think About Flowers A person's stage of cognitive growth influences how he or she thinks about everything, including flowers. *(a)* To a baby, in the sensorimotor stage, flowers are "known" through pulling, smelling, and perhaps tasting. *(b)* A slightly older child might be egocentric, wanting to pull up all the flowers within reach, *now.* *(c,d)* At the adult's formal operational stage, flowers can be part of a larger, logical scheme—either to earn money or to cultivate beauty. Thinking is an active process from the beginning of life until the end.

parents, perhaps respecting them more or discovering new fallibility. The point is that cognitive growth is an active process, dependent on clashing ideas and challenging experiences, not primarily on maturation (as postulated in psychoanalytic theory) or repetition (as postulated in behaviorism).

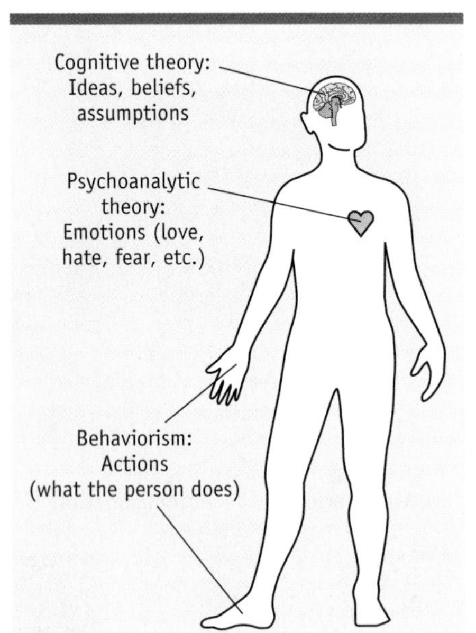

FIGURE 2.4 Major Focuses of the Three Grand Theories

SUMMING UP

The three grand theories originated almost a century ago. Each was pioneered by men who are still admired for their ability to set forth psychological theories so comprehensive and creative that they deserve to be called "grand." Each grand theory has a different focus: emotions (psychoanalytic theory), actions (behaviorism), or thoughts (cognitive theory) (see Figure 2.4). The theories' conclusions also differ. Freud and Erikson thought it was important to understand unconscious drives and early experiences in order to understand personality and actions. Behaviorists instead stress experiences in the recent past, especially learning by association, by reinforcement, and by observation. Cognitive theory holds that, to understand a person, one must understand how that person thinks—an ability that, according to Piaget, develops in four distinct stages.

The methods used by the three grand theories differ as well. Psychoanalytic theory relies heavily on dreams, classic literature, and case studies of adults in order to uncover hidden drives. Behaviorists conduct experiments with rats and other animals in order to find the universal laws of learning. Cognitive theorists ask questions of children and analyze unexpected answers.

Emergent Theories

You have surely noticed that the grand theorists were all men, scientists from Western Europe or North America, born more than a hundred years ago. These background variables are limiting. (Of course, women, non-Western, and contemporary theorists are limited by their backgrounds as well.) Despite their impressive insights, the three grand theories just described no longer seem as comprehensive as they once did.

Two new theories have emerged that, unlike the grand theories, are multicultural and multidisciplinary. The first emergent theory described here, sociocultural theory, draws on research in education, anthropology, and history; the second one, epigenetic theory, arises from biology, genetics, and neuroscience. This wide-ranging approach makes these theories particularly pertinent to our study.

Neither emergent theory has yet developed a comprehensive, coherent explanation of all of human development, of how and why people change. However, both provide significant and useful frameworks leading to better understanding, which is precisely what good theories do.

Sociocultural Theory

Chapter 1 emphasized that humans develop within social contexts. Barbara Rogoff, a leading proponent, insists that, while "sociocultural theory is still emerging" (Rogoff, 1998, p. 687), "individual development must be understood in, and cannot be separated from, its social and cultural-historical context" (Rogoff, 2003, p. 50). The central thesis of **sociocultural theory** is that human development results from the dynamic interaction between developing persons and their surrounding society. Culture is viewed not as an external variable that impinges on developing persons, but as integral to each person's development (Cole, 1996).

sociocultural theory An emergent theory that holds that development results from the dynamic interaction between each person and the surrounding social and cultural forces. This theory notes similarities and differences among children growing up in various nations, ethnic groups, and eras.

Consider this: What should you do if your 6-month-old baby starts to fuss? You could give the baby a pacifier, turn on a musical mobile, change the diaper, prepare a bottle, walk around with the baby in your arms, sing a lullaby, offer a breast, shake a rattle, ask for help, or close the door and walk away. Each of these is a "right thing to do" in some cultures but not in others. In fact, some parents are warned not to "spoil" their babies by picking them up when they fuss, while others are told that if they don't carry their babies virtually all day and night, they are abusive and neglectful.

Few adults realize that their responses are shaped by culture, yet this is precisely the case, according to sociocultural theory. Societies provide not only customs and practices but also the tools and theories. For instance, some places have no pacifiers, bottles, or mobiles—or even diapers or doors. The kinds of tools available for baby care profoundly affect parents and infants in ways that echo throughout life. Possessions and privacy are valued much more by some adults than by others, probably because of their early cultural experiences.

Social Interaction

The pioneer of the sociocultural perspective was Lev Vygotsky (1896–1934), a psychologist from the former Soviet Union. Vygotsky was particularly interested in the cognitive competencies that developed among the culturally and ethnically diverse people of his huge nation, as well as among children who were considered mentally retarded. He studied how farmers used tools, how illiterate people used abstract ideas, and how children of all abilities learned in school. In his view, each person, schooled or not, developed competencies taught by more skilled members of the society, who are tutors or mentors in an **apprenticeship in thinking** (Vygotsky, 1934/1986).

apprenticeship in thinking In sociocultural theory, the process by which novices develop cognitive competencies. They work with more skilled members of the society, often parents or teachers, who act as tutors or mentors.

The implicit goal of this apprenticeship is to provide the instruction and support that novices need to acquire whatever knowledge and capabilities their culture values. This is best accomplished through **guided participation:** Tutors engage learners in joint activities, offering not only instruction but also "mutual involvement in several widespread cultural practices with great importance for learning: narratives, routines, and play" (Rogoff, 2003, p. 285). Active apprenticeship and guided participation are central concepts of sociocultural theory, because each person depends on others to learn. This process is informal, pervasive, and social.

guided participation In sociocultural theory, the most effective technique used by skilled mentors to help novices learn. They not only provide instruction but also allow direct, shared involvement in the activity.

ESPECIALLY FOR NURSES Using guided participation, how would you teach a young child who has asthma to breathe with a nebulizer?

For example, one of my students recently came to my office with her young son, who eyed my candy dish but did not take any.

"He can have one if it's all right with you," I whispered to his mother.

She nodded and told him, "Dr. Berger will let you have one piece of candy."

He smiled shyly and quickly took one.

"What do you say?" she prompted.

"Thank you," he replied, glancing at me out of the corner of his eye.

"You're welcome," I said.

In that brief moment, all three of us were engaged in guided participation, as the mother and I had been taught and as the boy was learning from us. We were surrounded by cultural traditions and practices, including my authority as professor, the fact that I have an office and a candy dish (a custom that I learned from one of my teachers), and the direct authority of the mother over her son. This mother had taught her son that *thank you* is the "magic word"—true in some families, not in others. Specifics differ, but all adults teach children skills they may need in the society in which they live.

COURTESY OF DR. MICHAEL COLE, LABORATORY OF COMPARATIVE HUMAN COGNITION, UC SAN DIEGO

The Founder of Sociocultural Theory Lev Vygotsky, now recognized as a seminal thinker whose ideas on the role of culture and history are revolutionizing education and the study of development, was a contemporary of Freud, Skinner, Pavlov, and Piaget. Vygotsky did not attain their eminence in his lifetime, partly because his work, conducted in Stalinist Russia, was largely inaccessible to the Western world and partly because he died young, at age 38.

Social interaction is pivotal in sociocultural theory, quite different from either a student's independent discovery or a teacher's lecture. This contrasts with learning in the grand theories, which depends, primarily, either on the student *or* on the teacher, not on both simultaneously. However, in guided participation it is assumed that neither student nor teacher is passive; they learn from each other, through words and activities that they engage in *together* (Karpov & Haywood, 1998), because "cognitive development occurs in, and emerges from, social situations" (Gauvain, 1998, p. 191). Adults learn from children and vice versa, and everyone learns more from peers than from older or younger individuals.

The concept that a culture's patterns and beliefs are social constructions (as explained in Chapter 1) is easy for sociocultural theorists to understand. They believe that socially constructed ideas are not less powerful than physical realities; quite the opposite.

Values are potent, shaping the development of every person in every culture, even though values are constructed. This point was stressed by Vygotsky, who argued that mentally and physically disabled children should be educated (Vygotsky, 1925/1994). If people believe that every child can learn, they will find ways to teach every child. That belief has taken hold in the past 30 years, revolutionizing the education of children with special needs (Rogoff, 2003).

R. ROWAN / PHOTO RESEARCHERS, INC.

A Temporary Support Structure Scaffolds support workers as they construct a new building or repair an existing one, such as the California state capitol in Sacramento, shown here. Similarly, expert teachers erect educational scaffolds, using hints, ideas, examples, and questions to support the novice learner until a solid cognitive structure is formed.

The Zone of Proximal Development

According to sociocultural theory, *what* people need to learn varies by culture but *how* they learn is always the same, whether they are learning a manual skill, a social custom, or a language. Cultural contexts, social tools, and guided participation are always parts of the process.

For learning to occur, a teacher (parent, peer, or professional) locates the learner's **zone of proximal development,** meaning the skills, knowledge, and concepts that the learner is close to acquiring but cannot yet master without help. Through sensitive assessment of the learner's ability and capacity, the teacher engages student participation, guiding a transition from assisted performance to independent achievement. The teacher must avoid two opposite dangers—boredom and failure. Some frustration is permitted, but the learner must be actively engaged, never passive or overwhelmed (see Figure 2.5).

To make this abstract-seeming process more concrete, here is a simple example—a father teaching his daughter to ride a bicycle. He begins by slowly rolling her along, supporting her weight while telling her to keep her hands on the bars and her feet on the pedals, to push the right and left pedals in rhythm, and to look straight ahead. As she becomes more comfortable and confident, he begins to roll her along more quickly, praising her for keeping her legs pumping steadily. Within another lesson or two he is jogging beside her, holding only the handlebars. When, days or weeks of practice later, he senses that, with a little more momentum, she could maintain her balance by herself, he urges her to pedal faster and slowly loosens his grip. Perhaps without her even realizing it, she is riding on her own. Both father and daughter are thrilled at her accomplishment.

ESPECIALLY FOR TEACHERS Following Vygotsky's precepts, how might you teach reading to an entire class of first-graders at various skill levels?

zone of proximal development A metaphorical area, or "zone," surrounding a learner that includes all the skills, knowledge, and concepts that the person is close ("proximal") to acquiring but cannot yet master without help.

ARIEL SKELLEY / CORBIS

Learning to Ride Although they are usually not aware of it, children learn most of their skills because adults guide them carefully. What would happen if this father let go?

What the learner is not yet ready or able to learn (don't teach; too difficult)

Zone of Proximal Development
What the learner could understand with guidance (do teach; exciting, challenging)

What the learner already knows (don't reteach; too boring)

The learner

FIGURE 2.5 **The Magic Middle** Somewhere between the boring and the impossible is the zone of proximal development, where interaction between teacher and learner results in knowledge never before grasped or skills not already mastered. The intellectual excitement of that zone is the origin of the joy that both instruction and study can bring.

Response for Nurses (from page 50): You would guide the child in the zone of proximal development, where teacher and child interact. Thus, you might encourage the child to prepare the nebulizer (by putting in the medicine, for instance) and then breathe through it yourself, taking turns with the child.

Note that this is not instruction by preset rules. Sociocultural learning is active: No child learns to ride a bike by reading and memorizing written instructions. Social and cultural skills require step-by-step apprenticeship. The mentor must already have mastered the skill in order for guided participation to work. In this example, if a father intellectually understands the general principles of bicycle locomotion but has never ridden a bike, he should let his bike-riding wife do the instructing.

Each student brings personal traits, past experiences, and future aspirations to the educational setting, which means that learning must be individualized. Learning styles vary: Some children need more assurance than others; some children learn most easily by looking, others by hearing. A mentor needs to sense exactly when more support or more freedom is needed and what the child's learning style might be. The nature and process of instruction are constantly adjusted as the zone of proximal development expands or shifts.

Excursions into and through the zone of proximal development, such as the boy prompted to say "thank you" or the girl learning to balance on a bike, are commonplace throughout life. Ideally, learning always follows the same general pattern: Mentors, attuned to learners' ever-shifting abilities and motivation, continually urge a new level of competence; learners ask questions, show interest, and demonstrate progress, thus guiding and inspiring the mentors. As you can see, when education goes well, both teachers and students are fully engaged and productive. Particular skills and processes vary enormously from culture to culture, but the overall social interaction is the same.

Sociocultural theorists have been criticized for overlooking developmental processes that are not primarily social. Vygotsky's theory, in particular, may neglect the power of genes to guide development, especially if neurological immaturity or disability makes some learning impossible (Wertsch, 1998; Wertsch & Tulviste, 1992). It is true that every child can learn, but not every child can learn everything at any moment. The other emerging theory, which we will now discuss, avoids this criticism.

Epigenetic Theory

epigenetic theory An emergent theory of development that includes both the genetic origins of behavior (within each person and within each species) and the direct, systematic influence that environmental forces have, over time, on genes. The theory focuses on the dynamic interaction, over the decades and centuries, between these two influences.

preformism The belief that the form of development is permanently set before a person is born. Some developments appear in the course of maturation, but it is through time, not experience, that they emerge.

The central idea of **epigenetic theory** is that genes interact with the environment to allow development, in dynamic and reciprocal interaction (Gottlieb, 2003). Such interaction contrasts sharply with **preformism,** the theory that genes determine everything, even developments that require maturation.

Epigenetic theory is the newest developmental theory, but it incorporates several established bodies of research. Many disciplines in the natural sciences—including biology (especially the principles of evolution), genetics, and chemistry—provided a foundation for epigenetic theory. Several psychologists—including Erikson and Piaget—described aspects of their theories as epigenetic, recognizing that development builds on genes but is not determined by them.

Many specialties within the social sciences—especially *sociobiology* (the study of how individuals within society seek to pass along their genetic heritage), *evolutionary psychology* (the study of the inherited patterns of behavior that were once adaptive), and *ethology* (the study of animals in their natural environments)—stress the interaction of genes and the environment (Alcock, 2001; Laland & Brown, 2002). They are all incorporated into epigenetic theory, although, like the four other theories we have discussed in this chapter, many divergent threads are woven into one tapestry in order to introduce this theory.

With, On, and Around the Genes

What, then, is new about this theory? One way to answer that question is to consider the theory's name, derived from the root word *genetic* and the prefix *epi*.

Genetic refers to the entire genome, which includes the particular genes that make each person (except monozygotic twins) genetically unique, the genes that distinguish our species as human, and the genes that all living creatures share.

The root word *genetic* emphasizes the powerful instincts and abilities that arise from our biological heritage. The Human Genome Project has made it clear that all psychological as well as all physical traits, from bashfulness to blood type, from moodiness to metabolism, from vocational aptitude to voice tone, are influenced by genes. This truth was ignored 30 or so years ago, partly in reaction to *eugenics*, a now-discredited pseudoscience that emphasized genetics in an attempt to ensure that only genetically well-endowed humans would reproduce (Wahlsten, 2003).

No current developmentalist ignores the role of genes. We now know that even the timing of change is genetic: Humans walk and talk at about 1 year and reach reproductive maturity in early adolescence because that is when genes switch on those abilities (unless something is terribly wrong). Thus, half of epigenetic theory is the recognition of genes.

The other half is equally important: the need to avoid exaggerating the power of genes (Singer, 2003). The prefix *epi* means "with," "around," "before," "after," "on," or "near." Thus, *epigenetic* refers to all the surrounding factors that affect genetic expression. Those factors stop some genes before they have any effect, and they cause other genes to influence every aspect of a person's development. Some are stress factors, such as injury, temperature, and crowding. Some are facilitating factors, such as nourishing food, loving care, and freedom to play. These and hundreds of other factors arise from the environment in which the organism develops.

Epigenetic theory puts the two halves together in one word to signify the inevitable interaction between genes and the environment. This is illustrated by Figure 2.6, which was first published in 1992 by Gilbert Gottlieb, a leading proponent of epigenetic theory. That simple diagram, with arrows going up and down over time, has been redrawn and reprinted dozens of times (Gottlieb, 2003) to emphasize that dynamic interaction continues long after conception.

Obvious and direct epigenetic effects are easier to find in lower animals than in people. For example, the shape of an animal's face and the color of its fur are genetically determined, but environmental conditions cause some species to develop abnormal facial features or to change the color of their fur. (Some rabbit species are white in cold climates but brown in warm ones.) Even biological sex can be epigenetic. Researchers have found that all alligator eggs hatch into males when the nest temperature is 34°C during days 7 to 21 of incubation and into females at nest temperatures of 28–31°C (Ferguson & Joanen, 1982).

Many epigenetic factors affect human body and brain development; some genes and environmental factors influence almost every trait, while others are insignificant (Marcus, 2004). Even identical twins, who have exactly the same genes, are born with distinct brain networks and modules because of chance prenatal factors. Other differences develop as they grow, again because of epigenetic factors (Finch & Kirkwood, 2000). Ordinary siblings differ from each other even more, and nonrelatives far more than that.

As development progresses, each person develops along the course set by earlier genetic–environmental interactions, which allow a range of possible outcomes called the *reaction range*. Some aspects of development become less plastic with age, which explains why prenatal conditions (e.g., drugs and alcohol in the bloodstream) can damage neurological structures and physical features of a

Response for Teachers (from page 51): First of all, you wouldn't teach them "to read"; you would find out where each child was and what he or she was capable of learning next, so that instruction would be tailored to each child's zone of proximal development. For some this might be letter recognition; for others, comprehension of paragraphs they read silently. Second, you wouldn't teach the whole class. You would figure out a way to individualize instruction, maybe by forming pairs, with one child teaching the other; by setting up appropriate computer instruction; or by having parents or ancillary teachers work with small groups of three or four children.

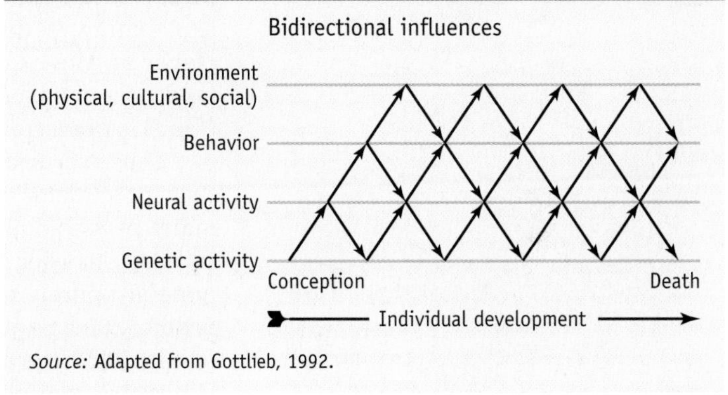

Source: Adapted from Gottlieb, 1992.

FIGURE 2.6 **An Epigenetic Model of Development** Notice that there are as many arrows going down as going up, at all levels. Although development begins with genes at conception, it requires that all four factors interact.

? Observational Quiz (see answer, page 55): According to this diagram, does genetic influence stop at birth?

fetus far more than the brain or body of the pregnant woman. However, even in adulthood new contexts can change genetic patterns that are already in place.

Dramatic evidence comes from studies of drug addiction. A person's potential to become addicted is genetic. That potential is realized—a genetically vulnerable person becomes an addict or alcoholic—if the person repeatedly consumes an addictive substance. Thus, addiction is epigenetic, the outcome of the interaction of genes and environment. Once that interaction has occurred and people are addicted, something in their biochemistry and brain makes them hypersensitive to the particular drug. For example, one drink will make a nonalcoholic pleasantly tipsy but will awaken a powerful craving for more in the alcoholic. The role of experience in developing an addiction and in creating hypersensitivity to a drug has been demonstrated in countless experiments (Crombag & Robinson, 2004). Nonetheless, as one team of researchers explains:

> Within the epigenetic model, each intermediary phenotype [genetic manifestation] is an outcome as well as a precursor to a subsequent outcome contingent on the quality of person–environment interactions. . . . Sudden shifts . . . can occur. In this regard, it is noteworthy that 86 percent of regular heroin users among soldiers in Vietnam abruptly terminated consumption upon return to the United States (Robins, Helzer, & Davis, 1975). In effect, a substantial change in the environment produced a major phenotype change.
>
> *[Tarter et al., 1999, p. 672]*

The fact that most soldiers who became heroin addicts in Vietnam kicked the drug on their own once they returned home is astonishing to anyone who has ever watched an addict get "clean" and then relapse time after time. The usual explanation is that the biochemical pull of the drug is too strong to resist. However, the example of the Vietnam veterans suggests that the biochemical (and genetic) aspect of addiction does not work in isolation; the social context ("epi") is powerful as well.

Thus, a crucial aspect of epigenetic theory is that genes never function alone; their potential is not actualized unless certain "epi" factors occur. For example, many psychological disorders, including schizophrenia, autism, antisocial personality disorder, and some forms of depression, have a genetic component. But none are purely genetic; all are epigenetic (Reiss & Neiderhiser, 2000; Rutter & Sroufe, 2000; Sanchez et al., 2001). People who inherit a particular variant of one gene (called the short allele of 5-HTT) are more likely to become depressed. However, even people who have this variant do not usually become depressed unless they are maltreated as children *or* experience stressful events as adults (Caspi et al., 2003). Epigenetic again.

Genetic Adaptation

So far we have described epigenetic factors that affect individuals. Epigenetic factors, however, also affect entire species. Over time, in a process called **selective adaptation,** genes become more common among the population if they increase chances of survival and reproduction, and genes that are destructive become rare.

selective adaptation The process by which humans and other animals gradually adjust to their environment. Specifically, the frequency of a particular genetic trait in a population increases or decreases over generations, depending on whether or not the trait contributes to the survival and reproduction of members of that population.

Selective adaptation begins when a particular variant of a gene benefits the organism that inherits it, enabling that organism to survive and to have many offspring. Since half of those offspring inherit the same gene as their fortunate father or mother and have many offspring themselves, that beneficial gene will become more common in the population with each succeeding generation. Eventually, almost everyone has that gene and the entire species benefits.

Whether a gene is beneficial, harmful, or neutral depends on the particular environment. For instance, allergy to bee stings is genetic, but this genetic variant is no problem if the neighborhood has no bees and the allergic person does not travel far. Complex traits such as fearfulness are also partly genetic, and this trait might be a benefit if the environment is hostile (the fearful person might escape attack) but a liability if the environment is benign (the fearful person would not accept other people's help). Selective adaptation is, in this way, epigenetic—the result of interaction between genes and surrounding factors.

For an entire species, selective adaptation is more obvious in nonhumans than in humans. Many species of birds and insects develop markings and coloration to protect them from predators. Likewise, bills (for birds) or teeth (for mammals) enable creatures to get food from their environment; a woodpecker's strong, narrow bill can pry insects out of the bark of trees, for instance, but a duck's broad, rounded bill is better for straining its food out of water.

! ANSWER TO OBSERVATIONAL QUIZ (from page 53): No. Arrows originating with genetic activity extend throughout development until death.

According to epigenetic theory, human differences can be traced to selective adaptation. All humans may originally have been lactose-intolerant, getting sick if they drank cow's milk; but in regions where dairy farming was introduced thousands of years ago, only a few fortunate people inherited the gene for an enzyme that let them digest cow's milk. Those people were fatter and healthier—and had more children. As a result, this genetic variant gradually became widespread in the population, especially in cooler regions where plant proteins were less abundant and cow's milk was needed for nutrition.

For groups as well as individuals, the interaction of genes and environment affects survival. Genetic variations are particularly beneficial when the environment changes. If a species' gene pool does not include at least some variants of crucial genes that allow the species to adapt, the entire species can disappear. About 90 percent of all species that ever existed have become extinct because, as conditions changed, nonadaptive animals died and were not replaced (Buss et al., 1998).

Extinction is not only genetic: Species that have lost the knowledge of how to avoid predators also become extinct if changing conditions allow predators to reappear (Berger et al., 2001). The variation among humans is one reason our species has survived and multiplied. In addition, humans have beneficial genes that foster socialization and language, as well as books and universities, an epigenetic combination that enables humans to learn from one another, thus avoiding some lethal diseases and injuries.

Selective adaptation is less clear-cut when it involves body shape (tall or short, stocky or thin), physical appearance (hair, skin, and so on), or personality traits (such as shyness or aggression) in diverse, mobile populations. But epigenetic theory suggests that adaptation and selective expression occur for all living creatures, no matter where and how they live, and that variations in how people look and act are evidence of humans' adjustment to their setting (Fish, 2002).

The variants of body shape between species of primates are obviously adaptive. Look at humans and chimpanzees, two species that share 99 percent of their genes. The remaining 1 percent cause some crucial differences that may not seem distinctive from afar but are pivotal for human survival. For instance, as a species, humans are taller than chimpanzees and have longer legs and shorter arms. These traits make it much easier for humans to carry things while walking long distances. Consequently, bipedal (two-legged) locomotion was adaptive because it increased mobility, enabling humans (but not chimps) to journey from Africa to distant fertile regions. Humans are the only mammals that have traveled, reproduced, and thrived on every landmass of the world (except the frigid continent of Antarctica).

ESPECIALLY FOR STUDENTS WHO ARE BORED WITH READING ABOUT GENES
How can reading this textbook help you live longer and be happier?

Consider a more controversial example: the mating strategies of males and females. According to some scholars, females, whose biology makes them the sex that must become pregnant and breast-feed if the species is to continue, benefit if they have a man staying nearby to protect them and their children. Women therefore look for one steady mate. Males, in contrast, will have more offspring if they have sex with many women, so they are naturally more promiscuous, less faithful. Because of this biological and genetic difference between males and females, even today men of all ages tend to have more sex partners than women do.

It is possible that sexism, not genetic makeup, is behind the different mating patterns and sexual behaviors of men and women. Nonetheless, this example is given to show the reach of epigenetic theory—that it can be used to explain the behavior of groups of people, not only individuals. Most of the solid evidence for epigenetic theory comes from research with lower animals that is extended to people—which explains why not all scholars agree with every application (Laland & Brown, 2002).

Some aspects of epigenetic theory are widely accepted, including one that helps us understand why children and parents develop affection for each other: It originates with the genes and is evoked by the experience of living together in a family. Note that humans (unlike other animals) remain dependent on their parents for a decade or more. Adults must spend years in child rearing, because the child's brain takes more than a decade to mature.

For the human species to continue, children must win the affection of their caregivers over a long childhood. Consequently, babies spontaneously smile at a human face and a child's facial expressions and trusting grasp stir almost any parent to protective affection. Parental investment occurs because, over the millennia, genes have strengthened parents' love for their children. Unloved children were more likely to die, and thus parents' genes that fostered survival were more likely to be passed on to the next generation. This natural inclination begins with the same hormones that accompany birth—an example of selective adaptation whose influence I have experienced myself.

RESPONSE FOR STUDENTS WHO ARE BORED WITH READING ABOUT GENES (from page 55): Genetic adaptation of the species has allowed people to learn from one another, thus preventing extinction of the human race. The same process might apply to individuals learning in college.

IN PERSON

My Beautiful, Hairless Babies

The epigenetic approach focuses on both the "micro" interactions of genes at the individual level and the "macro" genetic systems that have developed within the species over time. In the latter respect, epigenetic theory builds on *ethology,* the study of patterns of animal behavior, particularly as that behavior relates to species survival. The ethological perspective has particular relevance for infancy. Many of the instinctive behaviors of infants and their caregivers promote survival (Marvin, 1997).

Newborns have predispositions and skills that help ensure their nurturance. For example, very young human infants distinguish the sounds and rhythms of speech; recognize the facial expressions of fear and pleasure; and differentiate one person from another by smell, touch, and sound. Despite being so obviously immobile and helpless, newborns are genetically programmed to display reflexes—including grasping, clinging, crying, and grunting—that summon adults or keep them nearby.

In the beginning, infants accept help from anyone—a good survival strategy during the centuries when women regularly died in childbirth. By the time they are able to crawl, however, infants are emotionally attached to their specific caregivers and fearful of unfamiliar situations—another good survival tactic.

Both accepting help from anyone and later forming an attachment to a specific caregiver are evidence of selective adaptation. Over the course of human history, infants who stayed near nurturing and protecting adults were more likely to survive, so those traits became part of the genetic heritage.

Correspondingly, caregiving adults are genetically equipped to nurture babies. Logically, no reasonable adult would become a parent. It is irrational to endure sleepless nights, dirty diapers, and frequent interruptions. Fortunately, genes aren't logical. Humans are programmed to cherish their babies. In fact, humans seem programmed to cherish motherhood, especially motherhood of infants, so much that reason and logic disappear and mothering becomes "a minefield" for emotions and explosions that can harm women, men, and children (Hrdy, 2000).

As the mother of four, I have been surprised by the power of genetic programming many times. With my first-born, I asked my pediatrician whether Bethany wasn't one of the most beautiful, perfect babies he had ever seen.

"Yes," he said, with a twinkle in his eyes, "and my patients are better looking than the patients of any other pediatrician in the city."

When my second child was 1 day old, the hospital offered to sell me a photograph of her—hairless, chinless, and with swollen eyelids. I glanced at it and said "no," because the photo didn't look at all like her—it made my beautiful Rachel look almost ugly. I was similarly enamored of Elissa and Sarah. However, I am not only a woman who loves her children; I am a woman who loves her sleep. In the predawn hours, as I roused myself yet again to feed Sarah, I asked myself why I had chosen for the fourth time to add someone to my life who would deprive me of my precious slumber. The answer, of course, is that some genetic instincts are even stronger than the instinct for self-preservation.

Open Wide Caregivers and babies elicit responses from each other that ensure survival of the next generation. The caregiver's role in this vital interaction is obvious, but ethology has shown that infants starve if they do not chirp, meow, whine, bleat, squeal, cry, or otherwise signal hunger—and then open their mouths wide when food arrives. Both the baby birds and the baby human obviously know what to do.

UNEP / SAY BOON FOO / THE IMAGE WORKS

DIGITAL VISION / PUNCHSTOCK

SUMMING UP

The two emergent theories point in opposite directions. Sociocultural theory looks outward, to the overarching social, historical, and cultural patterns that affect communities, families, and, ultimately, individuals. Sociocultural theory emphasizes how social and cultural groups transmit their values and skills—through apprenticeships of learning—to individual children. By contrast, epigenetic theory begins by looking inward, at thousands of genes, and then moves outward to incorporate the environmental factors that directly affect the expression of those genes. Epigenetic theory leaps from genetic transmission to the centuries-old and species-wide patterns of selective adaptation, seeming to skip what sociocultural theory stresses.

Both emergent theories combine insights, data, and methods from many academic disciplines and take into account current research and techniques of analysis unavailable to earlier generations. Both are innovative and exciting paths leading toward a better understanding of development.

What Theories Contribute

Each major theory discussed in this chapter has contributed a great deal to our understanding of human development (see Table 2.4):

- *Psychoanalytic theory* has made us aware of the impact of early-childhood experiences, remembered or not, on subsequent development.
- *Behaviorism* has shown the effect that immediate responses, associations, and examples have on learning, moment by moment.
- *Cognitive theory* has brought an understanding of intellectual processes and how our thoughts and beliefs affect every aspect of our development.
- *Sociocultural theory* has reminded us that development is embedded in a rich and multifaceted cultural context, which is evident in every social interaction.
- *Epigenetic theory* emphasizes the interaction between inherited forces and immediate contexts.

In order, these five theories present us with: early childhood, environment, mind, culture, and genes. No comprehensive view of development can ignore any of these.

TABLE 2.4 **Five Perspectives on Human Development**

Theory	Area of Focus	Fundamental Depiction of What People Do	Relative Emphasis on Nature or Nurture?
Psychoanalytic theory	Psychosexual (Freud) or psychosocial (Erikson) stages	Battle unconscious impulses and overcome major crises	More nature (biological, sexual impulses, and parent–child bonds)
Behaviorism	Conditioning through stimulus and response	Respond to stimuli, reinforcement, and models	More nurture (direct environment produces various behaviors)
Cognitive theory	Thinking, remembering, analyzing	Seek to understand experiences while forming concepts and cognitive strategies	More nature (person's own mental activity and motivation are key)
Sociocultural theory	Social context, expressed through people, language, customs	Learn the tools, skills, and values of society through apprenticeships	More nurture (interaction of mentor and learner, within cultural context)
Epigenetic theory	Genes and factors that repress or encourage genetic expression	Develop impulses, interests, and patterns inherited from ancestors	Begins with nature; nurture is also crucial, via nutrients, toxins, and so on

Each theory has faced severe criticism. Psychoanalytic theory has been faulted for being too subjective; behaviorism, for being too mechanistic; cognitive theory, for undervaluing cultural diversity; sociocultural theory, for neglecting individual initiative; and epigenetic theory, for neglecting the human spirit. Most developmentalists prefer an **eclectic perspective.** That is, rather than adopt any one of these theories exclusively, they make selective use of all of them. The state of research in human development has been accurately characterized as "theoretical pluralism" because no single theory fully explains the behavior of humans as they go through life (Dixon & Lerner, 1999).

eclectic perspective The approach taken by most developmentalists, in which they apply aspects of each of the various theories of development rather than adhering exclusively to one theory.

Being eclectic, not tied to any one theory, is beneficial because everyone, scientists as well as laypeople, tends to be biased. It is easy to dismiss alternative points of view, but using all five theories opens our eyes and minds to aspects of development that we might otherwise ignore.

The Nature–Nurture Controversy

Whatever the limitations of particular theories, developmental theories time and time again illuminate life's myriad experiences and events. Development is dazzling and confusing without some perspective. Ideology and prejudice easily overcome reality without scientific theory and data. One illustration comes from the dispute that has echoed through every decade of developmental study: *the nature–nurture controversy.*

Nature refers to the influence of the genes that people inherit from their parents at the moment of conception. **Nurture** refers to all the environmental influences, beginning with the mother's health and diet during prenatal development and continuing lifelong, with family, school, community, society.

nature A general term for the traits, capacities, and limitations that each individual inherits genetically from his or her parents at the moment of conception.

nurture A general term for all the environmental influences that affect development after an individual is conceived.

The nature–nurture controversy has been given many names, among them *heredity versus environment* and *maturation versus learning.* Under whatever name, the basic question remains: How much of any characteristic, behavior, or pattern of development is the result of genes, and how much is the result of experiences? Note that the question is "How much?"—not "Whether" or "Which one?"— because both nature and nurture are always involved, to varying degrees.

Developmentalists agree that nature and nurture interact to produce every specific trait; no characteristic develops exclusively via nature or nurture. Recent longitudinal research confirms this interaction. For example, a longitudinal study of adolescent siblings—twins, stepsiblings, full siblings, and adoptees—found that genes are far more influential than a shared family setting, but

> it seems unlikely that heritable traits in children would become manifest as either full-blown successes or full-blown failures without . . . formative transactions with their families. . . . [Families] are not merely passive responders. They are themselves initiators: they respond to a genetic signal from the child—or really an array of signals—and their response is transmitted back to the child.
>
> *[Reiss et al., 2000, p. 354]*

In other words, genetic traits in children need family responses in order to become "full-blown," for good or ill. The family responses are not random; they are elicited by the child's genes, but each parent responds in particular ways (partly because of their own genes and culture) to each child. The combination—not one or the other alone—leads to development.

This interaction is complex—"feedback loops swirling in all directions, all inextricably intertwined" (Lippa, 2002, p. 197)—yet sometimes it is crucial to figure out exactly how nature and nurture interact for a given trait. As one expert wrote:

> Both nature and nurture now have seats at the theoretical table, and so the really hard work now begins—to specify, in nitty gritty detail, exactly how the many biological and social environmental factors identified by recent theories weave together.
>
> *[Lippa, 2002, p. 206]*

As you will see, theories can help with this work because they provide new perspectives on behavior. Imagine a parent and a teacher discussing a child's behavior. Each suggests a possible explanation that makes the other say, "I never thought of that." Both then understand the child better. Having five theories is like having five very perceptive observers. All five are not always on target, but it is certainly better to use theories to expand perception than to stay stuck in one narrow groove. A hand functions best with five fingers, even though each finger is different and some are more useful than others.

Theoretical Perspectives on Hyperactivity and Homosexuality

Consider two very different issues: hyperactivity and homosexuality. How, and to what extent, are nature and nurture involved in each?

Hyperactivity

Some children seem always active, running around or restless even when they should be still. They are impulsive, unable to attend to anything for more than a moment. This is called *attention-deficit/hyperactivity disorder*, or ADHD (American Psychiatric Association, 2000). Is ADHD more a matter of *nature* (a product of the child's genes) or *nurture* (a product of the child's home, school, and society)? There is evidence for both possibilities.

Several facts support the argument that "nature" (genetic inheritance) is responsible:

- Children with ADHD are usually boys.
- Children with ADHD often have close male relatives with the same problem.
- Children with ADHD are typically overactive in every context, home as well as school.
- Children with ADHD often calm down when they take stimulants, such as Ritalin, Adderall, and even coffee.

The fourth fact convinces many: Since biochemical treatment works, the cause of ADHD must be biochemical—that is, essentially, nature.

But wait. There is also evidence that "nurture" is the cause:

- The percentage of the U.S. population diagnosed with ADHD has increased from 1 percent to 5 percent over the past 50 years. Since genes do not naturally change that fast, this rapid increase suggests an environmental cause.
- Many plausible environmental causes have been suggested, among them crowded living conditions, television, lead, refined sugar, and food additives. Some have been substantiated in correlational research (e.g., Bateman et al., 2004).
- There are more ADHD children in some classrooms than in others, suggesting that teaching styles may elicit or suppress ADHD.
- No biological test, such as microanalysis of blood chemistry or neuroimaging of the brain, reliably distinguishes ADHD children from normal children.

This fourth fact is persuasive to many. If there is no biological marker for the condition, the cause must be nurture.

Homosexuality

Now consider the influence of nature and nurture on sexual orientation. Most social scientists once theorized that homosexuality was the product of nurture, variously attributed. Psychoanalytic theory placed the origins in early childhood, with the parents—specifically, a weak father and an overbearing mother—as the cause. Behaviorists thought that people learned sexual behavior, as they learned everything else, through reinforcement and punishment. Cognitive theory suggested that, because people's thoughts and ideas determine their actions, some people's thoughts led them to rebel against family and society by becoming homosexual. Sociocultural theory discovered that some cultures expect everyone to be homosexual during adolescence; other cultures kill homosexuals. The frequency of homosexuality follows these cultural expectations—another argument for nurture.

When researchers began to test hypotheses based on these theories, nurture seemed less crucial. A distinction was made between **sexual orientation**, which encompasses erotic inclina-

Building for the Future The proud parents beam as their 19-month-old son uses blocks to make a tall building. Erik Erikson and other psychoanalytic theorists would be happy, too: Erikson observed that boys build towers and girls create circular enclosures. Psychoanalytic theorists might not be so happy, however, with these parents' sexual orientation.

BOB DAEMMRICH / THE IMAGE WORKS

tions and thoughts, and sexual *expression,* which encompasses sexual activities. Surveys have found that many people have homosexual impulses (nature) but that society has encouraged them to have heterosexual interactions, including marriages (nurture). This finding supports all the theories, suggesting that nurture affects sexual behavior but that sexual orientation may come from nature.

Researchers have failed to find evidence that parental characteristics determine sexual orientation, contrary to psychoanalytic theory. Children raised by homosexual couples (either adopted or the biological offspring of one of the parents) become heterosexual or homosexual in about the same proportions as children raised by heterosexuals, which again suggests that nature, not nurture, determines sexual orientation (Wainwright, Russell, & Patterson, 2004). Indeed, several genetic analyses have found homosexual linkages among close relatives (especially monozygotic twins, and uncles and nephews) (Bailey et al., 2000). Inherited genetic anomalies also increase the prevalence of homosexuality (Hines, 2004).

sexual orientation A person's impulses and internal direction regarding sexual interest. People can be oriented to persons of the same sex, of the other sex, or of both sexes. Sexual orientation may differ from sexual expression, appearance, identity, or lifestyle.

No Answers Yet

Both hyperactivity and homosexuality are discussed later in this text. Now is not the time to decide how much nature or nurture contributes to either of them. In fact, choosing nature *or* nurture is a "dangerous quagmire," according to one team of psychologists:

> Those who dichotomize sexual orientation into pure biological or social causation fall into a dangerous quagmire. To deny any role for biology affirms an untenable scientific view of human development. Equally harsh and deterministic would be to deny the significance of the environment.
>
> *[Savin-Williams & Diamond, 1997, p. 235]*

For hyperactivity as well, people have diametrically opposed opinions based on emotions, not data, but either extreme may harm some children. For example, those who emphasize nurture worry that restriction of normal play makes some children hyperactive and that society medicates boisterous children rather than reorganizing school or family life. On the opposite side, those who believe hyperactivity is the result of nature contend that, just as a parent would give insulin to a child who inherited type 1 diabetes, it is cruel not to provide medication to children with ADHD.

Both sides lament that many children are misdiagnosed, but those who believe in nurture think too many are drugged who actually are fine, whereas those who believe in nature complain that too many children and adults struggle to concentrate when a proper diagnosis and treatment could make their lives much better. As you can see, both sides believe children are harmed, for opposite reasons.

Similarly impassioned opinions arise concerning homosexuality, or, for that matter, birth defects, school curricula, childhood aggression, divorce laws, and so on. Ideology often adds to the polarization of opinion. As one scholar, using the example of aggression, points out: "Individual differences in aggression can be accounted for by genetic or socialization differences, with politically conservative scientists tending to believe the former and more liberal scientists the latter" (Lewis, 1997, p. 102). Thus, a question for developmental science becomes, instead, a weapon in a political war.

On nature versus nurture, "opinions shift back and forth between extreme positions" (Singer, 2003, p. 438). Because erroneous opinions can lead to contradictory and even harmful policies, it is critical to separate assumptions from facts, to put data as a buffer between opinions and conclusions. How can we avoid extremes, resist the pull of ideology, overcome the bias of political assumptions? Consider theory!

Especially for Older Brothers and Sisters Psychologists believe that the best role models for children are older siblings and other people they know well and see daily, rather than sports stars or political heroes. Why?

SUMMING UP

As a description of the nature–nurture controversy makes clear, theories are needed to suggest hypotheses, investigation, and, finally, answers, so that objective research can replace personal assumptions. For instance, although it is now known that the parental relationship is not the cause of homosexuality, this conclusion could not be drawn until researchers tested the psychoanalytic hypothesis. Theories as such are not true or false, but they serve to move the scientific process forward. Given the impact of some applications (e.g., the widespread medication of children with ADHD), such progress is sorely needed.

In later chapters, as you encounter elaborations and echoes of the five major theories and various minitheories, you will form your own opinions as to the validity and usefulness of each. Probably you will also take an eclectic view—one that chooses the best from each theory—to guide your exploration. You may even begin to devise a coherent, comprehensive, systematic approach of your own.

Remember that theories—grand, mini-, or emergent—are very practical. Many issues related to human development—hyperactivity, homosexuality, and hundreds more—stir up strong feelings and have practical implications. Theories help scholars and others find their way through the thicket of political and personal assumptions, allowing hypotheses and research that go beyond prevailing assumptions. Most scholars remain open to various theoretical perspectives, choosing to be eclectic in their approach rather than tied to any one point of view.

Response for Older Brothers and Sisters (from page 61): An older sibling is an ideal role model because he or she has survived or—better yet—succeeded within the same family and community context in which the younger child lives but has human weaknesses that are also apparent. By contrast, distant role models are portrayed as unusually skilled or fortunate, with no weaknesses—unless a particular foible makes the headlines and causes children to lose faith in the former hero.

▪ SUMMARY

What Theories Do

1. A theory provides a framework of general principles to guide research and explain observations. Each of the five major theories—psychoanalytic, behaviorist, cognitive, sociocultural, and epigenetic—interprets human development from a distinct perspective, and each provides guidance for understanding how human experiences and behaviors change over time. Good theories are practical: They aid inquiry, interpretation, and daily life.

Grand Theories

2. Psychoanalytic theory emphasizes that human actions and thoughts originate from unconscious impulses and childhood conflicts. Freud theorized that sexual urges arise during three stages of childhood development: oral, anal, and phallic. Parents' reactions to conflicts associated with their child's erotic impulses have a lasting impact on personality, according to Freud.

3. Erikson's version of psychoanalytic theory emphasizes psychosocial development, specifically as societies, cultures, and parents respond to children. Erikson described eight successive stages of psychosocial development, each with a developmental crisis that occurs as people mature within their context.

4. Behaviorists, or learning theorists, believe that scientists should study observable and measurable behavior. Behaviorism emphasizes conditioning—a learning process. In classical conditioning, a neutral stimulus becomes associated with a meaningful stimulus. In operant conditioning, reinforcers make it more likely that certain behaviors will be repeated.

5. Social learning theory recognizes that much of human behavior is learned by observing the behavior of others. The basic process is modeling. Children are particularly vulnerable to social learning. Throughout life, motivation and context are crucial.

6. Cognitive theorists believe that thought processes are powerful influences on human attitudes, behavior, and development. Piaget proposed that children's thinking develops through four age-related periods, propelled by an active search for cognitive equilibrium.

Emergent Theories

7. Sociocultural theory explains human development in terms of the guidance, support, and structure provided by cultures and societies. For Vygotsky, learning occurs through social interactions, when knowledgeable members of the society guide learners through the zone of proximal development.

8. Epigenetic theory begins with genes, powerful and omnipresent, affecting every aspect of development. However, genes are inert without environmental influences, from prenatal toxins and nutrients to long-term stresses. This interaction can halt, modify, or strengthen the effects of the genes within the person and, via selective adaptation over time, within the species.

What Theories Contribute

9. Psychoanalytic, behavioral, cognitive, sociocultural, and epigenetic theories have each aided our understanding of human development, yet no one theory is broad enough to describe the full complexity and diversity of human experience. Most developmentalists are eclectic, using many theories.

10. Every theory can shed some light on almost every developmental issue. One example is the nature–nurture controversy. All researchers agree that both factors influence all aspects of development to some extent, but the specific applications of nature or nurture can affect children in opposite ways. More research is needed, and theories point the way toward what questions need to be answered.

■ KEY TERMS

developmental theory (p. 35)
grand theories (p. 36)
minitheories (p. 36)
emergent theories (p. 36)
psychoanalytic theory (p. 37)
behaviorism (p. 40)
conditioning (p. 40)
classical conditioning (p. 41)
operant conditioning (p. 41)
reinforcement (p. 42)
social learning theory (p. 45)
modeling (p. 45)
self-efficacy (p. 45)
cognitive theory (p. 46)
cognitive equilibrium (p. 46)
sociocultural theory (p. 49)
apprenticeship in thinking (p. 49)
guided participation (p. 50)
zone of proximal development (p. 51)
epigenetic theory (p. 52)
preformism (p. 52)
selective adaptation (p. 54)
eclectic perspective (p. 58)
nature (p. 59)
nurture (p. 59)
sexual orientation (p. 60)

■ KEY QUESTIONS

1. Why do social scientists use theories instead of depending entirely on data and experiments?

2. How might a psychoanalytic theorist interpret a childhood experience, such as the arrival of a new sibling?

3. Why do behaviorists use nonhumans as their primary experimental subjects?

4. What are the reinforcements and social learning that might induce some teenagers to begin smoking cigarettes?

5. According to Piaget's theory, what happens when a person experiences cognitive disequilibrium?

6. What are the background similarities and differences among Freud, Pavlov, and Piaget?

7. What are the differences between the grand and emergent theories?

8. Sociocultural theory stresses the impact of culture. How might this emphasis be used to explain how students behave in class?

9. How might epigenetic theory explain the behavior of a pet dog or cat?

10. Explain how nature and nurture might interact in a child learning to read.

11. Why are most developmentalists said to be eclectic?

12. Explain why it makes a difference whether hyperactivity is primarily nature or primarily nurture.

■ APPLICATIONS

1. Developmentalists sometimes talk about "folk theories," which are theories developed by ordinary people, who may not know that they are theorizing. Choose three sayings commonly used in your culture, such as (from the dominant U.S. culture) "A penny saved is a penny earned" or "As the twig is bent, so grows the tree." Explain the underlying assumptions, or theory, that each saying reflects.

2. The nature–nurture debate can apply to many issues. Ask three people to tell you their theories about what factors create a criminal and how criminals should be punished or rehabilitated. Identify which theory described in this chapter is closest to each explanation you are given.

3. Behaviorism has been used to change personal habits. Think of a habit you'd like to change (e.g., stop smoking, exercise more, watch less TV). Count the frequency of that behavior for a week, noting the reinforcers for each instance. Then, and only then, try to develop a substitute behavior by reinforcing yourself for it. Keep careful records; chart the data over several days. What did you learn?

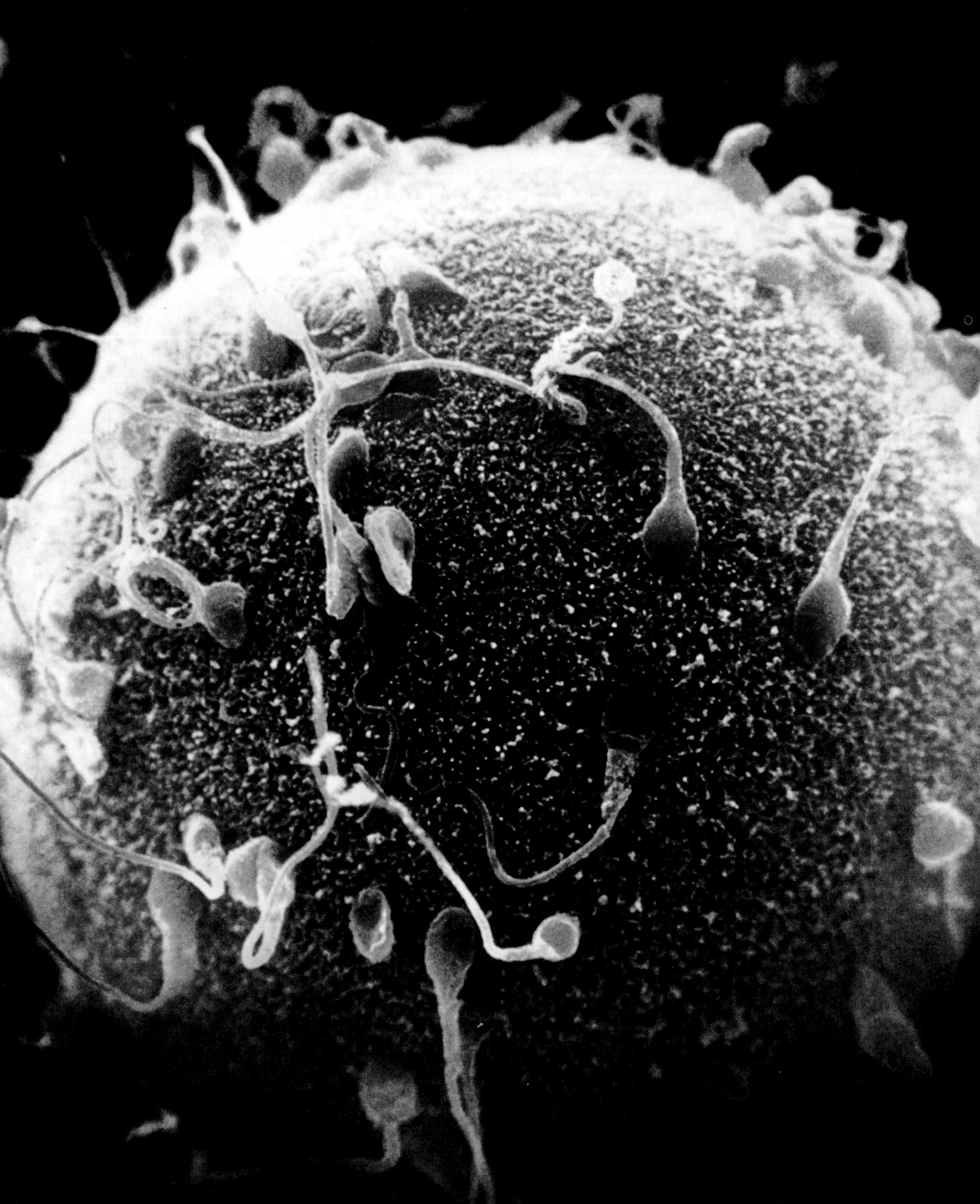

Chapter Three

Heredity and Environment

Genes play a leading role in the drama of human development. Prospective parents wonder what traits their children will inherit; physicians question patients about close relatives and distant ancestors; multinational teams of scientists have decoded the human genome; and all students of human development realize that "once we take development seriously, we must also take genetics seriously" (Pennington, 2001). Yet genes sometimes remain a mystery—pervasive and powerful, but also hidden and elusive.

One day when I arrived to pick up my daughter Rachel from school, another mother pulled me aside. She whispered that Rachel had fallen on her hand and that her little finger might be broken. My daughter was happily playing, but when I examined that baby finger, I saw that it was crooked. Trying to avoid both needless panic and medical neglect, I took Rachel home and consulted my husband. He smiled and spread out his hands, revealing the same bent little finger. Aha! An inherited abnormality, not an injury. But why had I never noticed this before?

That bent finger is one small example of millions of genetic surprises in human development. This chapter anticipates and explains some of those mysteries, going behind the scenes to reveal not only what genes are but also how they work. Many ethical issues are raised by genetics, and we will explore these, too. First, the basics.

The Genetic Code

As you learned in the preceding chapters, a person is much more than a set of genetic instructions. Development is always dynamic, ongoing, and interactional. Each person is unlike anyone who has gone before because of invisible instructions, locked in DNA, that are transmitted throughout life.

What Genes Are

To reveal the secrets of the genetic code, we begin by reviewing some biology. All living things are made up of tiny cells. The work of these cells is done by *proteins*. Each cell manufactures these proteins according to instructions stored at the heart of each cell in molecules of **DNA (deoxyribonucleic acid),** the famed double helix (see Figure 3.1). Each molecule of DNA is called a **chromosome,** and these chromosomes contain the instructions to make all the proteins that a living being needs.

Humans have 23 pairs of chromosomes (46 in all). All 46 are replicated in each cell, with a few exceptions. One member of each pair is inherited from each parent. The instructions in these 46 chromosomes are organized into units called

DNA (deoxyribonucleic acid) The molecule that contains the chemical instructions for cells to manufacture various proteins.

chromosome A carrier of genes; one of the 46 molecules of DNA (in 23 pairs) that each cell of the human body contains and that, together, contain all the genes. Other species have more or fewer chromosomes.

gene The basic unit for the transmission of heredity, consisting of a string of chemicals coding for the manufacture of certain proteins.

human genome The full set of all the 25,000 or so genes that are the instructions to make a human being.

genes, with each **gene** (about 25,000 in all for a human) located on a particular chromosome. Thus, every gene is a separate section of a chromosome, and each gene contains the instructions for specific proteins.

You are familiar with proteins in the diet; they are abundant in meat, fish, and soybeans, for instance. But what exactly is a protein? A protein is composed of a sequence of chemicals, a long string of building blocks called *amino acids*. The recipe a cell needs to manufacture a protein consists of instructions for stringing together the right amino acids in the right order. These instructions are transmitted to the cell via pairs of chemicals, arranged in triplets (three pairs) on a gene.

Most genes have thousands of precise pairs and triplets, making hundreds of amino acids (20 types in all). Some are crucial, and any error in their code—even a few extra repeats of a triplet—can be fatal. Other miscodes are normal variations, and still others make no difference (Marcus, 2004). Most genes come in pairs, or duplicates, just as chromosomes do, with one of each pair inherited from each parent.

The entire packet of instructions to make a living organism is called the genome. There is a genome for every species, even for every plant. The **human genome** is the code for making a human being. Each person (except monozygotic twins) has a slightly different code, but the human genome is 99.9 percent the same for any two persons. Our similarities far outweigh our differences.

Especially for Number Crunchers
A hundred years ago, it was believed that humans had 48 chromosomes, not 46; 10 years ago, it was thought that humans had 100,000 genes, not 25,000. Why?

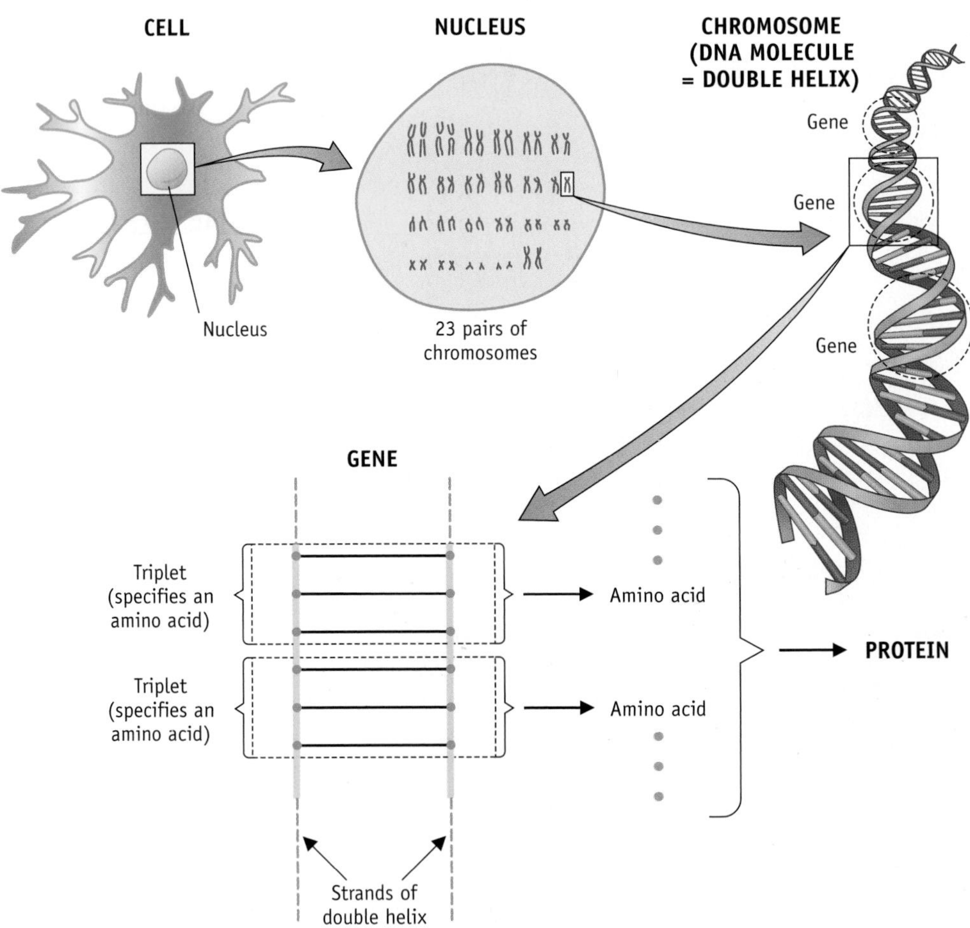

FIGURE 3.1 **How Proteins Are Made** The genes on the chromosomes in the nucleus of each cell instruct the cell to manufacture the proteins needed to sustain life and development.

Thus, the human genome contains about 25,000 genes, on 46 chromosomes, instructing the developing body to produce the proteins to make each person unique, yet similar to all other humans. The total is awe-inspiring. As one expert explains,

> If each triplet is considered a word, this sequence of genes is . . . as long as 800 Bibles. If I read the genome out to you at the rate of one word per second for eight hours a day, it would take me a century. . . . This is a gigantic document, an immense book, a recipe of extravagant length, and it all fits inside the microscopic nucleus of a tiny cell that fits easily upon the head of a pin.
>
> *[Ridley, 1999, p. 7]*

This quote captures some of the immensity of the genetic code, but there is another amazing part of human genetics—how genes work together to make human beings.

The Beginnings of Life

Development begins at conception, when a male reproductive cell, or *sperm* (plural: *sperm*), penetrates the membrane of a female reproductive cell, or *ovum* (plural: *ova*). Each human reproductive cell, or **gamete,** contains only 23 chromosomes (this is the main exception mentioned above—the chromosomes in each person's gametes are not *paired*).

gamete A reproductive cell; that is, a sperm or ovum that can produce a new individual if it combines with a gamete from the other sex to make a zygote.

The particular member of each chromosome pair that appears in a given gamete is random; some gametes have one chromosome of the person's pair, and some have the other. Each man or woman can produce 2^{23} different gametes, which is more than 8 million versions of his or her own chromosomes.

Matching Genes

When conception occurs in the usual way, one of several thousand sperm finds its way through the vagina, cervix, and uterus and then into a fallopian tube, where, if ovulation recently occurred, it enters an ovum. After about an hour, the nucleus of the sperm meets the nucleus of the ovum, and they fuse to form a new living cell called a **zygote.** Two reproductive cells have literally become one, and that one new cell is unlike the cells of either parent.

zygote The single cell formed from the fusing of two gametes, a sperm and an ovum.

genotype An organism's entire genetic inheritance, or genetic potential.

The chromosomes from the father match up with the chromosomes from the mother, so that the zygote contains 23 pairs of chromosomes, arranged in father/mother pairs. The genetic information on those 46 chromosomes constitutes the organism's genetic inheritance, or **genotype,** which endures throughout life, repeated in almost every cell. Sometimes a zygote has more or less than 46 chromosomes, a problem discussed later in this chapter. Even then, the genotype at conception remains the same lifelong.

In 22 of the 23 pairs of human chromosomes, the two chromosomes of each pair are closely matched. Each chromosome of the pair contains hundreds of genes in the same positions and sequence, and these genes each match with their counterpart from the other

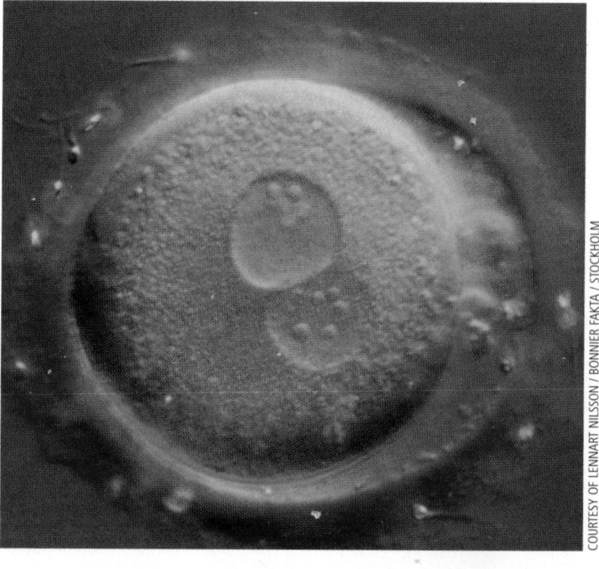

COURTESY OF LENNART NILSSON / BONNIER FAKTA / STOCKHOLM

The Moment of Conception This ovum is about to become a zygote. It has been penetrated by a single sperm, whose nucleus now lies next to the nucleus of the ovum. Soon, the two nuclei will fuse, bringing together about 25,000 genes to guide development.

RESPONSE FOR NUMBER CRUNCHERS (from page 66): There was some scientific evidence for the wrong numbers (e.g., chimpanzees have 48 chromosomes), but the reality is that humans tend to overestimate many things, from the number of genes to their grades on the next test.

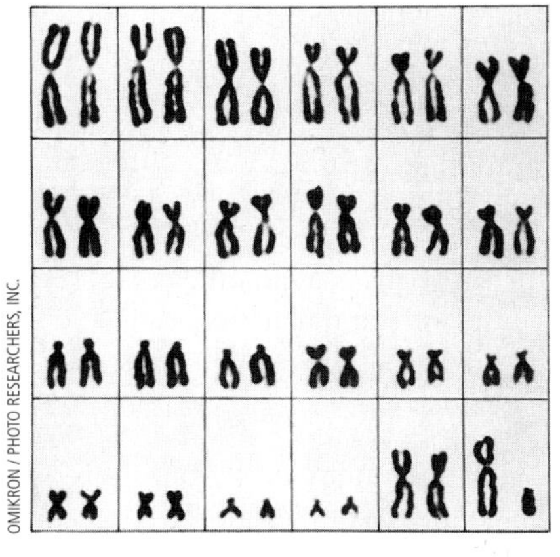

OMIKRON / PHOTO RESEARCHERS, INC.

Mapping the Karyotype A *karyotype* portrays a person's chromosomes. To create a karyotype, a cell is grown in a laboratory, magnified, and then usually photographed. The photo is cut into pieces and rearranged so that the matched pairs of chromosomes are lined up from largest (*at top left*) to smallest (*at bottom right, fourth box from the left*). Shown in the last two boxes at the bottom right are the two normal possibilities for the 23rd chromosome pair: XX for a female and XY for a male.

? OBSERVATIONAL QUIZ (see answer, page 70): Is this the actual karyotype of a person?

parent. The match is not always exact, because a few genes vary slightly in the triplets that make up that gene. Each alternate version of such variable genes is called an **allele.** Thus, a gene from the mother and a gene from the father together constitute a gene pair. The pair could be an exact match or could differ—if the allele from the father is not the same as the allele from the mother. Very rarely, a gene has no counterpart on the other chromosome and that gene stands alone. But more than 99 percent of the genes on 22 pairs find an exact match.

allele A slight, normal variation of a particular gene. Typically an allele differs in some amino-acid triplets but is the same in most of the genetic code.

23rd pair The chromosome pair that, in humans, determines the zygote's (and hence the person's) sex. The other 22 pairs are autosomes, the same whether the 23rd pair is for a male or female.

XX A 23rd pair of two X-shaped chromosomes, an X from the mother and an X from the father. XX zygotes become female embryos, female fetuses, and girls.

XY A 23rd pair of an X-shaped chromosome from the mother and a Y-shaped chromosome from the father. Zygotes that are XY become male embryos, male fetuses, and boys.

Male or Female?

The **23rd pair** of chromosomes is a special case. In females, the 23rd pair is composed of two large X-shaped chromosomes. Accordingly, it is designated **XX.** In males, the 23rd pair is composed of one large X-shaped chromosome and one smaller Y-shaped chromosome. It is designated **XY.**

Because a female's 23rd chromosome pair is XX, every ovum that her body creates will contain either one X or the other—but always an X. And because a male's 23rd pair is XY, half of his sperm will contain an X chromosome and half will contain a Y. The Y chromosome (but not the X) contains a gene (called SRY)

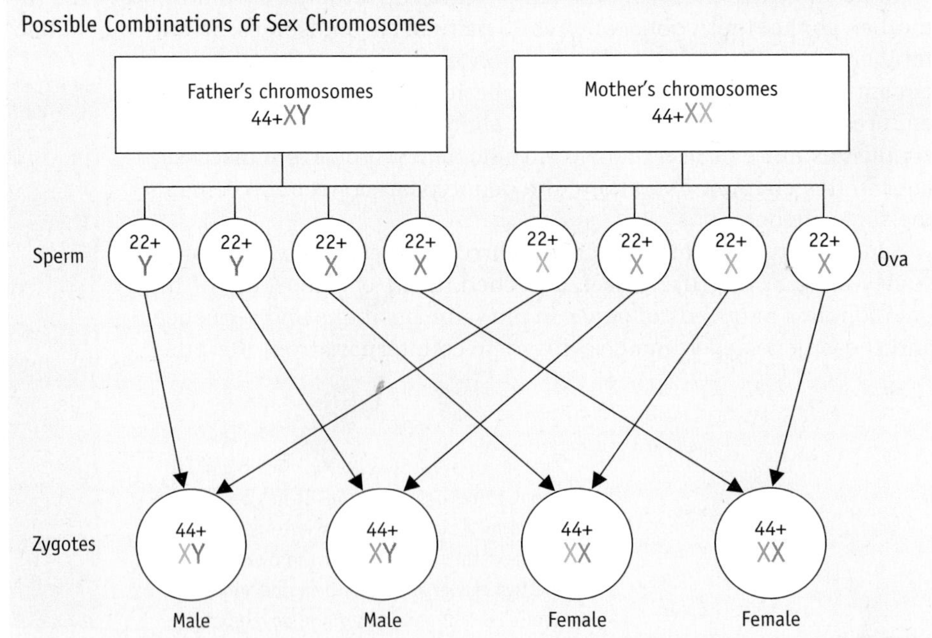

FIGURE 3.2 **Determining a Zygote's Sex** Any given couple can produce four possible combinations of sex chromosomes; two lead to female children, and two to male. In terms of the future person's sex, it does not matter which of the mother's Xs the zygote inherited. All that matters is whether the father's Y sperm or X sperm fertilized the ovum. However, for X-linked conditions it matters a great deal, because typically one, but not both, of the mother's Xs carries the trait.

that directs a developing fetus to make male organs. Thus, the critical factor in the determination of a zygote's sex is which sperm reaches the ovum first—a Y sperm, creating a male (XY), or an X sperm, creating a female (XX) (see Figure 3.2).

Although only one chromosome determines sex, the race between an equal number of X and Y sperm is not the only influence on the sex ratio at birth. Rarely, a man carries a gene that renders either his X or Y sperm immobile, so he fathers only sons or only daughters. Occasionally a woman's uterus is unusually acid or alkaline, giving either X or Y sperm an advantage. The newborn sex ratio also reflects the woman's health: If she is ill, undernourished, or stressed, XY embryos are more likely than XXs to be expelled in a **spontaneous abortion** (also called a *miscarriage*).

spontaneous abortion The naturally occurring termination of a pregnancy before the embryo or fetus is fully developed. (Also called a *miscarriage*.) If the woman chooses to terminate a pregnancy, that is called an *induced abortion*.

For the population as a whole, these factors usually even out, and the natural sex ratio at birth is close to 50/50. The actual sex ratio among newborns in the United States is about 52 males to 48 females. Minor ethnic variations at birth are found: Chinese Americans have the most males, at 55/45, and Hawaiian Americans have the fewest, at 50/50 (Martin et al., 2002). As the following makes clear, some couples prefer one sex or the other and take steps to have the boy, or the girl, they want.

ISSUES AND APPLICATIONS

Too Many Boys?

Historically, wars and diseases sometimes killed most members of a given population before they could reproduce, with girls more likely to survive than boys. When there were far more young women than men, many societies encouraged polygamy or single motherhood. Sometimes newborn girls were killed (a practice so common that the Koran explicitly forbade it) or men were allowed to discard wives who bore no sons (England's King Henry divorced or killed five wives for this reason). When cultural extinction or royal lineage was not threatened, many women ate "hot" or "cold" foods, slept on one side, followed religious rituals, or took quack advice to produce boys or girls. Now we know that sperm determine sex. No postconception diet or action can alter the sex of an embryo.

However, knowledge does not change desires; it only changes the means used to attain them. This is dramatically evident in Asia. Beginning in 1990, the government of China has pursued a policy of one child per couple. As a result, overpopulation and poverty have been dramatically reduced, but the policy has had one unexpected effect: too many boys.

By 1993 it became apparent that if they could have only one child, many Chinese couples wanted it to be a boy. Millions of pregnant women obtained tests in mid-pregnancy to determine the sex of the fetus and then had induced abortions if the fetus was female. At the same time, thousands of unwanted newborn girls were put up for adoption abroad. Consequently, the government forbade prenatal testing solely to determine sex, but "the law has been spottily enforced" (French, 2005, p. 3). In the city of Guiyang, the sex ratio in 2004 was about 75 girls born for every 100 boys (French, 2005).

Similar data come from other places. In 1999, in Punjabi, India, only 79 females were born for every 100 boys (Dugger, 2001). In Nepal, far more women use contraception after the birth of a son than a daughter (Leone et al., 2003), again skewing the sex ratio. In the United States, the sex ratio is shifting slightly toward more males.

Is this a private matter or a public concern? Chinese doctors worry that AIDS will spread more rapidly if there are too many unmarried men, who might turn to risky sex if they have no wives (Cohen, 2004). Other concerns are that a society with too many males might have more learning disabilities, drug abuse, violent crimes, wars, and suicides but fewer nurses, day-care centers, and close family bonds.

Do you object to these concerns because cultural preferences, not biology, affect such disparities? You are right to do so. Chromosomes and genes do not determine behavior directly; cultures can adjust to any problems that an unbalanced sex ratio might cause. For example, although women traditionally bring family members together, men can do so as well—as many single fathers and loving grandfathers have done.

The Ethics Committee of the American Society for Reproductive Medicine (2001) permits selective human sperm-sorting (separation of X and Y sperm), especially to avoid a genetic disease that occurs only in one sex or the other. Unlike China and India, most nations have no laws about sex selection. Should they?

! Answer to Observational Quiz (from page 68): No. Each person has one pair of sex chromosomes, never two. Two pairs are shown here to illustrate the two normal possibilities, XX and XY.

SUMMING UP

The fusion of a sperm and an ovum creates a zygote, a tiny one-celled creature that has the potential to develop into a human being. That moment of conception can be considered the result of a long process of gamete formation. One way to describe that process is chemically: The DNA of heredity is composed of chemicals that pair up; three of those pairs (a triplet) direct the formation of an amino acid; amino acids in a particular sequence make up a protein; and proteins make a person. Another way to describe it is with numbers: The genetic code for a human being consists of about 25,000 genes on 46 chromosomes. Those 46 chromosomes are the combination of 23 from the father and 23 from the mother, with the father's 23rd chromosome (an X or a Y) determining the person's sex.

From One Cell to Many

As already explained, when sperm and ovum combine into a zygote, they form the person's genotype, a complete set of instructions for creating a person. This creation of a living person from one living cell involves several complex processes of duplication of genetic information, cell division, and differentiation of cells into different types.

phenotype The observable characteristics of a person, including appearance, personality, intelligence, and all other traits.

Some of the instructions on the genotype are ignored and others amplified as genes direct the formation of the **phenotype,** which is the actual appearance and manifest behavior of the person. Life begins with one cell but becomes increasingly complex, not only as cells multiply and differentiate but also as nongenetic factors influence growth (Johnston & Edwards, 2002). Let's begin our discussion of genetic interaction and diversity by describing the changes in that one original cell.

New Cells, New Functions

Within hours after conception, the zygote begins the first stages of growth, duplicating and dividing. First, the 23 pairs of chromosomes duplicate, forming two complete sets of the genome for that person. Then these two sets move toward opposite sides of the zygote, and the single cell of the zygote splits neatly down the middle. The outer membrane now surrounds two cells, each containing a complete set of the original genetic code. These two cells duplicate and divide to become four; these four, in turn, duplicate and divide to become eight; and so on.

By the time you (or I, or any other person) were born, your original zygote had become about 10 trillion cells. By adulthood, those cells had become more than 100 trillion. But no matter how large the total number, no matter how much division and duplication occur, each cell (except gametes and some cells of the immune system) carries an exact copy of the complete genetic instructions inherited by the one-celled zygote. This explains why DNA testing of any body cell, even one from a drop of blood or a snip of hair, can identify "the real father," or "the guilty criminal," or "the long-lost brother."

The fact that every cell in the embryo contains the developing human being's complete genetic code does not mean that any cell could become a person—far from it. At about the eight-cell stage, a third process, *differentiation*, is added to duplication and division. Cells begin to specialize, taking different forms and reproducing at various rates, depending on where in the growing mass of cells they are located. As one expert explains, "We are sitting with parts of our body that could have been used for thinking" (Gottlieb, 2002, p. 172).

As a result of this specialization and differentiation, very early in development cells change from being able to become any part of a creature to being able to become only one part—an eye or a finger, for instance. All cells carry the same genetic code, but cells take on new functions as needed and cannot switch back. An eyelash cannot become a knee, although those original cells could have been knees or eyelashes.

Genes direct this differentiation. Some genes code for proteins that switch other genes on and off, ensuring that they produce proteins at appropriate times. These *on–off switching mechanisms* operate lifelong, instructing cells to repair damage, to take in nourishment, to multiply, to atrophy, and even to die.

Certain genes switch on at particular ages. For instance, genes activate specific parts of the brain that are important in cognitive development, such as the ability to think about abstractions or to plan ahead (Marcus, 2004). One of the fascinating aspects of human development is the growth and functioning of the various parts of the brain; that process is partly maturational (which explains why no 6-month-old can talk and why few 16-year-olds can make realistic plans for their retirement) and partly experiential.

Keep in mind that "genes merely produce proteins, not mature traits" (Gottlieb, 2002, p. 164). In other words, the genotype may instigate body and brain formation, but genetic expression of traits in the phenotype depends on the influence of other genes and the environment. A zygote might have the genes for becoming, say, a musical genius, but that potential will not be realized unless additional genes and factors in the environment permit development of that trait. Epigenesis—the interaction of genes and the environment (see Chapter 2)—is always apparent. Genotype does not equal phenotype, a truism illustrated with many examples throughout this chapter.

Gene–Gene Interactions

Conception brings together genetic instructions from both parents for every human characteristic. Exactly how do these instructions influence the specific traits that a given offspring inherits? The answer is quite complex, because most traits are **polygenic**—that is, affected by many genes—and **multifactorial**—that is, influenced by many factors, both genetic and environmental.

polygenic Literally, "many genes." Almost all important human traits, including abilities and emotions, are the result of the interaction of many genes.

multifactorial Literally, "many factors." In genetics, *multifactorial* means that traits are affected by many influences, both genetic and environmental.

Virtually every important human trait is the result of interactions among several genes (Hoh & Ott, 2003). Those interactions are crucial. For instance, the **Human Genome Project** (the international effort to map the entire human genome) found that humans have only about 25,000 genes, not the 100,000 that had previously been estimated. Further, almost all those 25,000 genes are not exclusively human but are present in other creatures as well. For example, the eyes of flies, mice, and people all originate from the Pax6 gene; another gene produces legs for a butterfly, a cat, a centipede, and a person. Tiny differences in interaction can result in major variations.

Human Genome Project An international effort to map the complete human genetic code. This effort was virtually completed in 2001, though analysis is ongoing.

The genetic similarity among living creatures makes it apparent that a few genes affect all the others. What makes the difference between humans and chimps is 100 or so "regulator" genes, which influence thousands of other genes (Marcus, 2004). Regulator genes make a creature who talks, walks, and thinks as humans do, unlike other animals. Regulator genes regulate genetic interaction, and that makes all the difference.

TEK IMAGE / SCIENCE PHOTO LIBRARY / PHOTO RESEARCHERS, INC.

Reading the Code A small segment of a DNA molecule is sequenced into bands, with one color for each of the base pairs. These pairs direct the synthesis of enzymes and proteins that, in turn, direct the formation of a living creature. One small change in a gene might result in a physical anomaly or a mental quirk. A few hundred different genes might result in a giraffe instead of a whale.

Another surprise from the Human Genome Project is that the genetic differences that were once thought to differentiate human races are superficial and often inconsequential. As one report explains, "Within-population differences among individuals account for 93 to 95 percent of genetic variation; differences among the major groups constitute only 3 to 5 percent" (Rosenberg et al., 2002, p. 2381). This means that you might have more genes in common with someone whose ancestors came from the opposite side of the globe than with someone whose ancestors were neighbors of your forebears.

Now we'll look at some specific types of gene–gene interaction. As just mentioned, some regulator genes instruct, say, the leg gene to make just two legs for a person and many more for a centipede. Other genes turn development on or off. Here we'll consider two other types of genes: additive and dominant–recessive.

Additive Heredity

additive gene A gene that, through interaction with other genes, affects a specific trait (such as skin color or height).

Some genes are called **additive genes** because their effects combine to make the phenotype. When genes interact additively, the trait reflects contributions of all the genes that are involved. The many genes that affect height, hair curliness, and skin color, for instance, usually interact as additive genes. Indeed, height is affected by an estimated 100 genes, each contributing a small amount (Little, 2002).

Consider an unlikely couple. A tall man whose parents and grandparents were all very tall marries a short woman whose parents and grandparents were all very short. Assume that every one of his 100 height genes is for tallness and that hers are all for shortness. The couple's children will inherit tall genes via the father's sperm and short genes via the mother's ova. Because the genes affecting height are additive, the children will be of middling height (assuming that environmental influences, such as nutrition and physical health, are adequate). None will be as tall as their father or as short as their mother, because each has half the genes for tallness and half for shortness, averaged together.

In actuality, most people have both kinds of ancestors—relatively tall ones and relatively short ones—so children can be taller or shorter than either parent. My daughter Rachel (with the crooked little finger) is of average height, shorter than either my husband or me, and the shortest of our four children. However, Rachel is taller than either of her grandmothers. She inherited many of her grandmothers' shortness genes from our genotypes, even though those genes had minimal effect in our phenotypes.

ESPECIALLY FOR FUTURE PARENTS
Suppose you wanted your daughters to be short and your sons to be tall. Could you achieve that?

How any additive trait turns out depends on all the genes (half from each parent) a child happens to inherit. All additive genes contribute something to the phenotype. Other genes enhance additive genes. For instance, the male hormones produced by the SRY gene on the Y chromosome add about three inches that would not be added if all the other 45 chromosomes were the same but the 46th chromosome was an X instead of a Y.

Dominant–Recessive Heredity

dominant–recessive pattern The interaction of a pair of alleles in such a way that the phenotype reveals the influence of one allele (the dominant gene) more than that of the other (the recessive gene).

Less common than additive genes are nonadditive genes, in which the phenotype shows the influence of one gene of a pair much more than the other. In one nonadditive form, alleles interact according to the **dominant–recessive pattern.** When a pair of alleles interact according to this pattern, the resulting phenotype reveals the influence of one allele, called the *dominant gene*, more than that of the other allele, called the *recessive gene*.

Sometimes the dominant gene completely controls the characteristic. In this case, the recessive gene is carried on the genotype but has no obvious effect on the phenotype. Some physiological characteristics are expressed according to the dominant–recessive pattern. Blood types A and B are both dominant and blood type O is recessive, leading to a complex relationship of genotype and phenotype (see Appendix A, p. A-3). Brown eyes are said to be dominant over blue eyes, and many genetic diseases are recessive. (In actual genetic interaction, many recessive genes are not completely hidden. A phenotype of hazel eyes, for instance, hints at a recessive blue-eye gene.)

A special case of the dominant–recessive pattern occurs with genes that are **X-linked,** which means that they are located on the X chromosome. If an X-linked gene is recessive—as are the genes for most forms of color blindness, many allergies, several diseases, and some learning disabilities—the fact that it is on the X chromosome is critical. Recall that males have only one X chromosome and a much smaller Y. Thus, many recessive genes that a male inherits on his X chromosome are not dominated by alleles on his other X chromosome—because he has no second X. As a result, most recessive genes on his X chromosome will be expressed.

X-linked Referring to a gene carried on the X chromosome. If a boy inherits an X-linked recessive trait from his mother, he expresses that trait, since the Y from his father has no counteracting gene. Girls are more likely to be carriers of X-linked traits but are less likely to express them.

X-linked genes are the reason recessive traits carried on the X chromosome can be passed directly from mother to son but not from father to son (since the Y chromosome does not carry the trait) (see Table 3.1). This explains why males have more X-linked disorders, such as color blindness.

More Complications

As complex as the preceding may seem, it makes genetic interaction appear much simpler than it actually is. That is because, to be able to discuss interaction at all, we are forced to treat genes as though they are separately functioning "control devices." But remember that genes merely direct the creation of 20 types of amino acids, the combinations of which produce thousands of proteins, which then form the body's structures and direct its biochemical functions. The proteins of each body cell are continually affected by other proteins, nutrients, and toxins that influence the cell's functioning.

TABLE 3.1 **The 23rd Pair and X-Linked Color Blindness**

X indicates an X chromosome with the X-linked gene for color blindness

23rd Pair	Phenotype	Genotype	Next Generation
1. XX	Normal woman	Not a carrier	No color blindness from mother
2. XY	Normal man	Normal X from mother	No color blindness from father
3. XX	Normal woman	Carrier from father	Half her children will inherit her X. The girls with her X will be carriers; the boys with her X will be color-blind.
4. XX	Normal woman	Carrier from mother	Half her children will inherit her X. The girls with her X will be carriers; the boys with her X will be color-blind.
5. XY	Color-blind man	Inherited from mother	All his daughters will have his X. None of his sons will have his X. All his children will have normal vision, unless their mother also had an X for color blindness.
6. XX	Color-blind woman (rare)	Inherited from both parents	Every child will have one X from her. Therefore, every son will be color-blind. Daughters will be only carriers, unless they also inherit an X from the father, as their mother did.

RESPONSE FOR FUTURE PARENTS (from page 72): Yes, but you wouldn't want to. You would have to choose one mate for your sons and another for your daughters, and you would still have to use sex-selection methods. Even so, it might not work, given all the genes on your genotype. More important, the effort would be unethical, unnatural, and possibly illegal.

Scientists are well aware that "no gene operates in a vacuum" and that each gene "interacts, either directly or through its protein product, with many other genes or gene products" (Peltonen & McKusick, 2001, p. 1226). The outcome of this interaction is difficult to predict. In fact, a small alteration or several extra repetitions in one triplet may be inconsequential or may cascade to create a major anomaly. The outcome depends on dozens of other factors, many of which are not yet understood (Kirkwood, 2003; Plomin & McGuffin, 2003).

For example, a dominant gene might not "penetrate" the phenotype completely (i.e., might not be completely expressed) for reasons unknown. Perhaps penetrance depends on other genes or perhaps on nongenetic factors such as temperature or stress. Similarly, in the additive pattern, genes sometimes contribute substantially more than their share, probably because their influence is amplified by other genes. Another puzzle is that, although females are always XX, one of those X chromosomes is inactive and the other dominant; whether it's the mother's or the father's X that is the inactive chromosome seems random. To discover the reasons for such complications, geneticists study the behavior of mice that have been carefully interbred to be virtually identical. Yet mice with almost identical genotypes act differently from one lab to another—reflecting unknown but significant environmental variations (Wahlsten, 2003).

THINKING LIKE A SCIENTIST

Genetic Diversity

Some people, even some developmental scientists, once feared that genetic discoveries might disprove that each human is unique or prove that the environment has little impact. Those fears were unfounded. Scientists now know that each person is doubly unique, both in biology and in upbringing. When someone with a terminal illness asks the doctor "How long do I have?" the best answer can only be an estimate. Many people are still alive years after the doctor predicted death within six months. Such survivors may be grateful to God and critical of medicine, but true scientists are not surprised.

The opposite is true as well. Death and disease can be predicted, but never with precision. In fact, genetic diversity makes every prediction a best guess, not a guarantee. Developmentalists can make quite accurate predictions as to the month an infant will start walking, whether a 4-year-old will be reading by age 6, or whether an 8-year-old will become an athlete; but no one can be sure what day the first step will occur or who the next poetic genius or sports star will be. Human diversity is always evident, a fact that scientists appreciate now more than ever.

The foundation of such diversity is variation in "every aspect of biological systems, including morphology, behavior, physiology, development and susceptibility to common disease" (Glazier et al., 2002). This biological variation begins at conception. You already know that about 8 million chromosomally different ova or sperm can be produced by a single individual, which means that any couple can produce 64 trillion different children. What's more, before a chromosome pair divides to form gametes, genes from corresponding segments can be exchanged, thus altering the genetic composition of both pair members and creating trillions of additional possibilities.

Once a baby is born, each moment of life shapes that person in unique ways. To pick an obvious example, at this very moment no one but you is reading this book in exactly the situation you are in, with the same memories and attitudes that you bring to your understanding of the text. If you discuss what you read with your classmates, it quickly becomes apparent that the impact of the words varies depending on what each person has already experienced.

To think like a scientist is to take great pleasure in such diversity, to be awed by its impact on human survival as well as by variation from person to person and society to society. In fact, diversity is one reason the human species has survived for thousands of years. One surprising example relates to HIV, the human immunodeficiency virus that leads to AIDS (acquired immune deficiency syndrome). A few people who are repeatedly exposed to HIV never catch the virus because a small difference in the code of one gene (a rare allele) prevents the virus from infecting their cells (Little, 2002). Other alleles allowed some of our ancestors to survive plague, tuberculosis, malaria, or other scourges. They kept the species from extinction.

Scientists are delighted by the discovery, made by the Human Genome Project, that various species share many genes. This means that research on small mammals can find causes and treatments for human diseases, including cancer, mental illness, and blood disorders (Demant, 2003; Little, 2002). Many research methods—interbreeding (for genetic purity), cross-breeding (to isolate genes), creating knock-out genes (disabling a gene to learn its function), and experimenting with drugs (to discover intended and unintended effects)—are impossible to use with people and would take years with most mammals. However, using these techniques with mice reveals much about human diseases.

The best example of the benefits of genetic diversity and similarity comes from cancer, a set of diseases that has troubled scientists for decades, not only because cancer is a common cause of death but also because it takes so many forms, each with its own genetic patterns. Strains of mice can differ 100-fold in their susceptibility to particular forms of cancer (Demant, 2003), and this provides powerful clues about genetic and environmental protection. Human cancer treatments have been developed because of what we've learned from the genes of mice!

Developmentalists are as intrigued by the genetics of human diversity as medical researchers are. Social scientists are now studying how to reverse addiction, prevent mental illness, and enhance learning with treatments tailored to each individual's particular personality and learning style. Soon a better understanding of each child will lead to applications not yet imagined. For instance, the educator's goal, "every child a learner," will come closer to reality as the diversity of learning styles and strengths becomes better understood.

The more we appreciate all the sources of the wondrous diversity among the 6 billion people now alive on earth, the closer we can come to the goal of developmental study: to help each person develop his or her full potential.

Twins and Clones

Although every zygote is genetically unique (i.e., has a unique genotype) and most newborns (even twins) are similarly unique, there are some human exceptions (monozygotic twins) and some lower-animal exceptions (clones). First, we explain genetically diverse twins, who share no more genes than any other brother and sister.

Dizygotic Twins

About two-thirds of all twins are **dizygotic (DZ) twins,** also called *fraternal twins*. They began life as two separate zygotes created by the fertilization of two ova by two sperm at roughly the same time. (Usually, only one ovum is released per month, but sometimes two or more ova are available for fertilization.) Although dizygotic conceptions may occur as frequently as one in every eight pregnancies, generally one embryo dies early in the pregnancy (the "vanishing twin" phenomenon) and just one baby is born (Bryan, 1999).

dizygotic (DZ) twins Twins who are formed when two separate ova are fertilized by two separate sperm at roughly the same time. Such twins share about half their genes, like any other siblings. (Also called *fraternal twins.*)

The incidence of dizygotic twins varies by ethnicity; for example, dizygotic twins occur about once in every 11 births among Yoruba women from Nigeria; once in 100 among English women; and once in 700 among Japanese women (Gall, 1996; Piontelli, 2002). Age is also a factor: Women in their late 30s are three times as likely to have DZ twins as are women in their early 20s (Mange & Mange, 1999), probably because ovulation becomes irregular as menopause approaches, with some cycles releasing no ova and others multiple ova.

Each dizygotic twin forms from its own ovum and sperm, so DZ twins have about half of their genes in common, just like any other siblings from the same parents. DZ twins can differ markedly in appearance because of the particular chromosomes and genes on the gametes that created them. The most obvious difference is in their 23rd pair, which half the time makes one dizygotic twin XY and the other XX.

Although dizygotic twins, even of the same sex, usually have phenotypic differences that indicate their nonshared genotypes, they can look quite similar, just as nontwin siblings sometimes do. Occasionally, similarities are so close that genetic tests are used to determine whether a pair of twins are monozygotic or dizygotic.

DAVID YOUNG-WOLFF / PHOTOEDIT

BRUCE ROBERTS / PHOTO RESEARCHERS, INC.

Same Birthday, Same (or Different?) Genes Twins who are of different sexes or who have obvious differences in personality are dizygotic, sharing only half of their genes. Many same-sex twins with similar temperaments are dizygotic as well. One of these twin pairs is dizygotic; the other is monozygotic.

? OBSERVATIONAL QUIZ (see answer, page 78): Can you tell which pair is monozygotic?

Monozygotic Twins

Rarely—about once in 250 conceptions—in the first day or so of development, cells not only duplicate but split completely apart, creating two, or four, or even eight identical, separate zygotes. They are called monozygotic because they originate from one (mono) zygote. If each implants and grows, they become multiple births, usually **monozygotic (MZ) twins** (also called *identical twins*) but possibly monozygotic quadruplets or octuplets.

monozygotic (MZ) twins Literally, "from one zygote." Twins and other multiple births that originate from one zygote that splits apart very early in development. (Also called *identical twins.*)

Because monozygotic twins originate from the same zygote, their genotype is the same, as are their genetic instructions for physical appearance, psychological traits, vulnerability to diseases, and everything else. For instance, one monozygotic twin can donate a kidney for surgical implantation in the other twin with no risk of organ rejection.

As a reminder, genes start the process of development, affecting every trait, but environmental factors always have an impact. Monozygotic twins usually differ in birthweight by a pound or more. Parents respond differently to each monozygotic twin, sometimes favoring the larger one, sometimes the smaller (Caspi et al., 2004; Piontelli, 2002).

Clones

clone An organism that has exactly the same genotype as another organism that is already alive.

A **clone** has exactly the same genotype as one other organism that is already alive. Unlike monozygotic twins, which occur naturally, clones are artificially created by humans. Cloning involves removing a cell from one living creature and making it develop into another, genetically identical creature. Since each cell of any organism carries the entire genetic code of the host individual, cloning is theoretically possible for all living things. Cloning is routine with plants but is very difficult with animals; more than 99 percent of all cloning attempts with animals have failed. It is illegal to try to clone a human being.

The most famous successful clone was a sheep named Dolly. She was created in Scotland in 1997 when scientists took a cell from the mammary gland of one ewe, chemically induced it to begin duplicating, and then implanted the embryo in the uterus of another ewe. Dolly was the only live birth of 434 cloning attempts with sheep, and she aged rapidly and soon died.

The Hazards of Multiple Births

Other multiple births, such as triplets and quadruplets, may be monozygotic, dizygotic, trizygotic, quadrazygotic, and so on (or combinations of these). Giving birth to more than one baby is hazardous for both the mother and the newborns. Complications of pregnancy, including high blood pressure and toxemia, are more common, and multiples are almost always born too early—twins by three weeks on average, triplets by six weeks, quadruplets by nine weeks.

Problems present at birth often continue, with multiples having higher rates of death, disease, and disabilities. Generally, the more embryos that develop together, the smaller, less mature, and more vulnerable each one is. Triplets, for example, produce more stress in their parents, develop language more slowly, and form weaker social bonds than do equally small single babies or twins (Feldman & Eidelman, 2004).

Many methods for overcoming infertility result in multiple births. In the United States, triplet births have increased by 500 percent since 1980, according to the Center for Health Statistics, and the rate of twin births has almost doubled (U.S. Bureau of the Census, 2004–2005).

Since fertility treatments are one cause of multiples, some nations restrict such treatments. Finland allows only two zygotes to be implanted at once after in vitro fertilization. The limit is three in Norway and four in several other nations. The United States has no legal limit (Jones & Cohen, 2001), but many doctors recommend selective abortion when a woman has multiple embryos, sacrificing some to allow the survival and health of others. This raises one of many ethical questions surrounding alternate means of conception, as the following explains.

infertility The inability to produce a baby after at least a year of trying.

assisted reproductive technology (ART) A general term for the techniques designed to help infertile couples conceive and then sustain a pregnancy.

in vitro fertilization (IVF) Literally, fertilization "in glass"—that is, in a glass laboratory dish, rather than inside a woman's body. Sperm are mixed with ova that have been surgically removed from a woman's ovary. If the combination produces a zygote, it is inserted into the woman's uterus, where it may implant and develop into a baby.

IN PERSON

Enhancing Fertility

Depending on the population surveyed, between 2 and 30 percent of all couples are troubled by **infertility,** or the inability to produce a baby after at least a year of trying. (The 2 to 30 percent range occurs because of wide regional differences in cultural practices and medical care; younger couples in medically advanced nations are usually more fertile.)

Infertile couples often turn to **assisted reproductive technology (ART)** for help in conceiving and then sustaining a pregnancy. The first step is to try to locate the cause of infertility. Each partner bears the primary responsibility about one-third of the time, with the remaining third caused by biological incompatibility between the partners or by some unknown factor. Treatment begins with advice about the best time in the woman's cycle to have sexual intercourse. Another simple treatment for female infertility is to use drugs to cause ovulation. If the male partner is infertile, sperm from a donor may be inserted into the female partner's uterus at ovulation via a syringe. This process, called *artificial insemination,* has been used for 50 years.

A more complicated method that can overcome some causes of male or female infertility is **in vitro fertilization (IVF).** Ova are surgically removed from a woman and mixed with sperm. If fertilization occurs, viable zygotes begin to duplicate *in vitro,* which literally means "in glass" (i.e., a glass laboratory dish). After about three duplications, the developing cells are inserted into the uterus. About a third of the time, at least one zygote implants and develops into a baby (American Society for Reproductive Medicine, 2002).

Although failure is more common than success, a million IVF children (more than half of them twins or triplets) have been born in 40 nations since the first "test-tube" baby was born in England in 1978 (Gerris et al., 2004). An increasingly common in vitro procedure to overcome sperm problems is to inject a single viable sperm into an ovum (Bentley & Mascie-Taylor, 2000).

Successful IVF usually produces several zygotes. The couple and the clinic then face a difficult choice: All viable zygotes could be inserted; some could be frozen for later use; some could be used for research; and some could be discarded. Each option has been chosen by some nations, clinics, and couples and forbidden by others (IFFS Surveillance, 2001). One factor in the decision is cost: In the United States in 2004, each IVF attempt costs about $12,000. Some couples travel to nations where costs are lower; others improve their odds by implanting several zygotes, increasing the likelihood of multiple births.

Ethical issues arise for many reasons, among them that ART can separate biological parenthood completely from child rearing. Indeed, IVF can be done with donated sperm and ova, with the resulting embryos inserted into the uterus of another woman. This gestational mother can allow yet another woman and/or man to adopt the newborn. At birth, that infant already has five "parents."

ART also raises the following ethical questions:

- Does every zygote have a right to be implanted? (Laws in England allow in vitro zygotes to be frozen for later use but require that they be destroyed after five years.)
- If a woman carries multiple embryos, is she obligated—or forbidden—to abort some to save the others? (Some nations forbid any abortion, even to save the life of a fetus.)
- Should the cost of ART be borne by the public or by the couples involved?

This last question is rarely debated but affects every infertile couple. ART is very costly and is not always covered by insurance or public health care systems. In the United States in 2004, the average woman under age 35 who sought IVF paid about $24,000 for two attempts; women over age 35 had an average cost of $70,000.

Some nations have public health care systems that cover ART but stipulate whether a woman must be heterosexual, married, and/or self-supporting. In the United States, anyone who can afford to pay for it can obtain IVF. Other matters relating to infertility are also affected by socioeconomic status. Low-income women are more likely to provide ova or to carry a fetus for another woman, who is usually relatively wealthy. Similarly, poor and politically unstable nations are more likely to allow children to be adopted by couples in wealthier nations.

One final issue: Should laws, medical ethics, and contemporary culture forbid infertile individuals to incur great financial expense (as well as psychic stress and, sometimes, physical pain) in an effort to have children? Is IVF ill advised when thousands of children with special needs await loving adoptive parents?

When I suggested the answer might be yes to a friend who was infertile, she accused me of being insensitive, arrogant, and ignorant. Maybe so. Since then I have read the words of many infertile women. One wrote:

> I just cannot imagine ever feeling good about anything again. I do not even know if my husband will stay with me when he realizes that children are not an option for us. My guess is he will find someone else who will be able to give him a baby. Since I cannot do that, I cannot imagine that he would be happy with me. I am not happy with me.
>
> *[quoted in Deveraux & Hammerman, 1998]*

Another explained:

> When you take away being able to have a child biologically, it is like having to face death—almost like having half of you die. Having kids is the main way that people deal with the fact that they are mortal.
>
> *[quoted in Hodder, 1997]*

Compassionate, thoughtful people—including developmentalists—differ widely in their responses to ART. Culture may be more influential than facts, and many prospective parents and political leaders ignore medical advice (Gerris et al., 2004). Some nations outlaw practices that others encourage (IFFS Surveillance, 2001), yet almost everyone agrees that babies belong not only to their parents but also to their communities. The questions about ART involve all of us.

! ANSWER TO OBSERVATIONAL QUIZ (from page 76): The Japanese American girls are the monozygotic twins. If you were not sure, look at their teeth, their eyebrows, and the shape of their faces.

SUMMING UP

The particular genotype a person happens to inherit influences almost every characteristic, although specifics are not usually evident from the phenotypes of the parents. Genes interact additively, recessively, and in many other ways; almost every trait is polygenic. Genetic interaction is only the beginning. Human diversity is guaranteed not only by the process of gamete formation and conception but also by experiences from that moment on. Each zygote is unlike any ever conceived before.

Most twins are dizygotic, with no more genes in common than any other siblings. About a third of all twins are monozygotic, developing from one zygote and hence having the same genotype. Clones also have the same genotype, but cloning is illegal for humans and problematic for other animals. Some adults are much less fertile than others, and some infertile couples turn to assisted reproductive technology (ART) to try to have a baby.

From Genotype to Phenotype

The main goal of this chapter is to help every reader grasp the complexity of the interaction between genotype and phenotype. To this end, consider a pair of quotations regarding recent research. One geneticist wrote:

> The results were consistently striking, albeit slow to be accepted. Genes were shown to influence virtually every aspect of human personality, temperament, cognitive style, and psychiatric disorder. The effects of heredity were substantial, typically representing 30 to 70% of total variation, and highly replicable across societies and cultures. The long reach of genes extended from a friendly disposition to xenophobia, from bipolar disease to bedwetting, from getting married to keeping a job.
>
> *[Hamer, 2002, p. 71]*

Research reinforces another conclusion: Nature always interacts with nurture, and vice versa. As a team of leading researchers explains:

> The first message is that genes play a surprisingly important role throughout psychology. The second message is just as important: Individual differences in complex psychological traits are due at least as much to environmental influences as they are to genetic influences.
>
> *[Plomin et al., 2001, p. 323]*

Exploring Genotype-Phenotype Interaction

In order to reach these conclusions, hundreds of scientists in many nations have studied thousands of twins, both monozygotic and dizygotic, raised together in the same home and raised in different homes. When this research began, scientists assumed that monozygotic twins reared together would share both genes and environment and that monozygotic twins raised apart would have the same genes but contrasting environments. This led scientists to hope that genetic influences could be distinguished from environmental ones (e.g., Segal, 1999).

The next generation of scientists were skeptical. They undertook more research—on stepsiblings, adopted siblings raised together, biological siblings raised apart, and all kinds of twins raised in all kinds of homes. They discovered three generalities that virtually all developmentalists accept but that still surprise some nonscientists.

1. Genes affect every aspect of human behavior.
2. Most environmental influences on children raised in the same household are *not* shared.
3. Genes elicit responses from other people that shape each child's development. In other words, many genes affect traits via the reactions of other people to the genetic characteristic.

As you learn more about the interactions among genetic and nongenetic influences, remember to distinguish between a person's *genotype,* or genetic *potential,* and his or her *phenotype,* the actual *expression* of that genetic inheritance in physical appearance, health, intelligence, and actions.

Everyone has many genes that are not expressed. In genetic terms, each person is a **carrier** of some unexpressed genes; that is, a person might "carry" a gene and transmit that gene to offspring via sperm or ova. Depending on other genes, as well as enabling or repressing effects from the environment, that person's children may express that gene in their phenotypes or may merely carry it in their genotype, perhaps to affect the next generation.

carrier A person whose genotype includes a gene that is not expressed in the phenotype. Carriers pass on those unexpressed genes to half their gametes and thus to half their children, who most likely will be carriers, too. Generally, only when the gene is inherited from both parents does the characteristic appear in the phenotype.

Only rarely does one single gene, or even one pair, cause a single, identifiable trait or disorder (some of those instances are described later in this chapter).

CORBIS / THE PURCELL TEAM

Shyness Is Universal Inhibition is a psychological trait that is influenced by genetics. It is more common at some ages (late infancy and early adolescence) and in some gene pools (natives of Northern Europe and East Asia) than others. But every community includes some individuals who are unmistakably shy, such as this toddler in Woleai, more than 3,000 miles west of Hawaii.

Most personality patterns and cognitive skills are affected by several genetic combinations. It is incorrect to assume that one phenotype results from one genotype, or vice versa (Rutter & Sroufe, 2000). Instead, tiny genetic differences have small but measurable effects, with specifics dependent on other genes as well as on family and culture (Hardy et al., 2002). This is explained by a team of eight scientists who are working to decipher the coding variations of some 11 million alleles:

> Many different genes distributed throughout the human genome contribute to the total genetic variability of a particular complex trait, with any single gene accounting for no more than a few percent of the overall variability.
>
> *[Hinds et al., 2005, p. 1079]*

Thus, when something is "genetic," that does not mean that its genetic origins are substantial, fixed, or unalterable. It means that it is part of a person's basic foundation, affecting many aspects of life but determining none (Johnston & Edwards, 2002). Even Rachel's crooked little finger, mentioned in the chapter's opening, might not have developed in that way if her prenatal environment had been different.

As one expert put it, "A gene is a framed canvas upon which the psychological environment paints the person" (Brown, 1999). Each trait, action, and attitude of every living organism has a genetic component: Without genes, no behavior could exist. But without environment, no gene would be expressed. Now let us look at three examples of complex traits—psychopathology, addiction, and visual acuity—each with a specific example that has been the topic of extensive research. As you read about these examples—schizophrenia, alcoholism, and nearsightedness—you will see that understanding the progression from genotype to phenotype has many practical uses.

Psychopathology

Mental illnesses, or psychopathologies—including depression, antisocial behavior, phobias, and compulsions, as well as virtually every other psychological disorder—are the results of gene–gene and gene–environment interaction (Plomin & McGuffin, 2003). Schizophrenia is one example.

Genes and Schizophrenia

The rate of schizophrenia is about 1 percent in the population overall but about 12 percent if a parent or full sibling has schizophrenia (Plomin et al., 2001). If one monozygotic twin develops schizophrenia, about two-thirds of the time the other twin does, too, even if the other twin is raised in a different family (Rutter, 2002).

Those statistics have convinced almost every scientist that schizophrenia is influenced by genes. Viewed another way, however, the same statistics reveal the importance of the environment: One-third of monozygotic twins whose identical twin has schizophrenia are not themselves afflicted, nor are about 88 percent of the offspring of a parent with the disease. Further, many people with schizophrenia have no immediate relatives with the illness, and most relatives of people with schizophrenia do *not* develop the disorder.

About 30 genes predispose for this brain dysfunction, including at least one each on chromosomes 1, 5, 6, 10, 13, 15, and 22 (McGuffin et al., 2001). None of these genes act alone. In fact, some people with one or another of these genes are mentally healthy; some people without one or another of these genes have schizophrenia. That variation leads scientists to look at the causal influence of environment.

Schizophrenia and the Environment

Experiences at birth or even before birth—possibly a slow-acting virus, head injury, inadequate oxygen at birth, or other physical insult—may be crucial for schizophrenia to develop (Cannon et al., 1999). One intriguing example is found in the following correlation: More people who develop schizophrenia were born during late winter than during any other time of year. Why? Perhaps some virus that is more prevalent in late fall or early winter affects a vulnerable fetus (Mortensen et al., 1999). But birth date has only a small effect, as does almost every other prenatal influence.

Experiences after birth have an effect as well. Multicultural research confirms that schizophrenia is prevalent in every part of the world, but it seems less debilitating in Africa and India than in North America and Western Europe—an argument for the effects of environment. In the United States, family context affects the frequency and severity of episodes for people diagnosed with schizophrenia. Family interaction does not cause the illness; its origins are genetic and biochemical. But if a person with schizophrenia lives with family members who are very critical, hostile, or overprotective, he or she is more likely to relapse than if the family were more accepting (Hooley, 2004).

Further evidence of the importance of the environment was provided by the Genain quadruplets, four monozygotic girls born in Canada in the early twentieth century. In those days, the survival of all four quadruplets was almost miraculous, and experts did not know that contact comfort and mother love were crucial (remember Harlow's monkeys from Chapter 2). As a result, the Genains were raised by nurses in a glass laboratory, where they could be observed by the curious public.

COURTESY OF EDNA MORLOK

Too Cute? This portrait of the Genain sisters was taken 20 years before they all developed schizophrenia. However, from their identical hair ribbons to the identical position of their feet, it is apparent that their unusual status as quadruplets set them apart as curiosities. Could their life in the spotlight have nurtured their potential for schizophrenia? There is no way to know for sure.

Between ages 22 and 24, all four developed schizophrenia. Each one had a different type and severity of the illness, even though they all had identical genes—evidence that environment plays a role in schizophrenia. Moreover, since other evidence finds that monozygotic multiples do not necessarily all become schizophrenic if one of them does, at least one of the quadruplets should have escaped the disease. The fact that all four of these women were diagnosed with schizophrenia suggests that something early in their lives magnified their genetic risk. Their separation from their parents and their low birthweight, both of which are environmental, are likely explanations.

Similar results are found for almost every form of psychopathology. The roots are genetic, which means that families should not be blamed for a disorder's origin. Nonetheless, a cascade of factors—some in the environment—triggers every psychological disorder.

Addiction

At various times, drug addiction, including alcoholism, has been considered a moral weakness and a personality defect (Leonard & Blane, 1999). Addicts were locked up in jails or in mental institutions. Some nations have tried to stop alcoholism by making alcohol illegal, as the United States did from 1919 to 1933, and most have laws against some drugs and tax others to discourage use. Nonaddicts have long wondered why some people just can't stop drinking too much, using illegal drugs, smoking cigarettes, and so on, while addicts and alcoholics try and fail to limit their consumption.

Now we know that some people's inherited biochemistry makes them highly susceptible to each kind of addiction. Anyone can abuse drugs and alcohol, but each person's genetic makeup creates an addictive pull that can be overpowering, extremely weak, or somewhere in between. The likely explanation is a genetic reaction that is passed down through the generations.

Alcohol and Biology

Researchers have studied the biology of alcoholism for decades (Agarwal, 2001). Genetic affinity is shown by the fact that alcoholics' children who have never drunk alcohol nevertheless have distinct brain patterns similar to those of alcoholic adults. Biochemistry allows some people to "hold their liquor" and therefore drink too much; it causes others, notably many East Asians, to sweat and become red-faced after just a few sips. This embarrassing response is an incentive, particularly for women, to avoid alcohol (McGue, 1995). Some people become sleepy, others nauseated, others aggressive, and others euphoric when alcohol hits their brains. Each reaction can make a person more, or less, likely to have another drink.

Personality, Culture, and Alcoholism

Alcoholism is not simply a biochemical reaction. As with all addictions, alcoholism is psychological as well as physical. Addictions correlate with certain personality traits (a quick temper, a readiness to take risks, and a high level of anxiety) that are evident in some, but not all, people who have the gene for metabolizing alcohol (Bau et al., 2001; Nielson et al., 1998). All these traits are both genetic and environmental, and none are inevitable precursors.

Especially for People Who Are Easily Bored Is your wish for excitement likely to lead to addiction?

Especially for College Students Who Enjoy a Party You wonder if one of your male friends is an alcoholic, because he sometimes drinks too much. He may be OK, though, because he can still talk clearly after drinking twice as much as you do. What should you ask him?

Thus, alcoholism is polygenic, with almost every alcoholic inheriting a particular combination of biochemistry-affecting and temperament-affecting genes that push him or her toward abusive drinking. It is also multifactorial. For example, women were formerly less likely to be pushed into alcoholism, because families and cultures pulled them in the opposite direction. Now that more women are free to follow their genetic impulses, they seem as susceptible to inherited alcoholism as men are (Heath et al., 1997).

Culture still counts. If people with a strong genetic tendency toward alcoholism spend a lifetime in an environment where alcohol is unavailable (in a devout Islamic family in Saudi Arabia, for example), the genotype will never be expressed in the phenotype. Similarly, if people live in a nation where alcohol is readily available (such as the United States or Japan) but belong to a religion that forbids it (Mormonism or Seventh-Day Adventistism, for instance) or a group that rarely gets drunk (such as Japanese women), they may escape their genetic destiny.

FABIAN FALCON / STOCK, BOSTON

All Alcoholics? Probably Not Farmworkers in Provence, France, pause for a meal—complete with bread, wine, glasses, and a tablecloth. Habitually drinking alcohol alone is a sign of alcoholism; drinking with friends and food is not. Of course, cultural pressure to drink creates problems, which is one reason France has a high rate of cirrhosis, but this might not be a pressure group: One of the two bottles contains water.

Visual Acuity

Almost every factor that affects development in general also affects vision. Age is the most obvious. Newborns cannot focus more than two feet away; children see better each year and then worse again, as adolescence brings a change in eyeball shape that makes many teenagers nearsighted; over the decades of adulthood vision gradually improves, but then, in late middle age, the elasticity of the lens decreases, so that almost every elderly person needs reading glasses. Toward the end of life, blindness afflicts more than 10 percent of the very old.

HASHIMOTO NOBORU / CORBIS SYGMA

Young Scholars In Japan and other countries of East Asia, the incidence of nearsightedness is increasing at a rapid rate. One reason may be the amount of time children in those cultures spend indoors studying, which far exceeds the time spent by children in Western societies.

Nearsightedness and Genes

Now let us look specifically at the most common vision problem in children, nearsightedness (also called *myopia*). Nearsightedness is a symptom in more than 150 genetic syndromes (Morgan, 2003). It may also be caused by physical trauma or illness (such as the rubella virus that caused my nephew David's cataracts; see Chapter 1) or by poor nutrition (such as vitamin A deficiency). Most of these factors cause "high" nearsightedness, so severe that it can lead to blindness. What about the more common form of nearsightedness, in which it is simply hard to read signs that are too far away?

A study of British twins finds that the Pax6 gene, which governs eye formation, contains minor variations that make people vulnerable to nearsightedness (Hammond et al., 2004). This research found heritability of almost 90 percent. This means that if one monozygotic twin is nearsighted, the other twin will be nearsighted about 90 percent of the time (Hammond et al., 2004). From this and other research, it is evident that genes affect nearsightedness, as they do almost everything else. No doubt the shape of the eye is genetic and familial.

Culture and Cohort

If the science of human development arose from the study of only one cohort or culture (such as, in this case, contemporary Britons), scientists might conclude that genes were the major cause of poor vision (Farbrother & Guggenheim, 2001). However, historical and multicultural research finds that environment powerfully influences the incidence of nearsightedness. The most obvious example is that if a culture provides children with a diet deficient in vitamin A, as do many ethnic groups in Africa, then the children will have vision problems. More than 100,000 children in Africa have only partial vision, or are even blind, for that reason (West & Sommer, 2001). In this specific case, the environmental cause and the solution (supplemental vitamin A) are clear.

But what about well-nourished children? Barring trauma, is their visual acuity entirely genetic? Cross-cultural research indicates that it is not.

In Hong Kong, Taiwan, Singapore, and Japan, myopia has recently increased to an extent that has been called epidemic. The first published research on this phenomenon appeared in 1992, when scholars noticed that, in medical exams of all 17-year-old males in Singapore, 43 percent were nearsighted in 1990 compared to only 26 percent a decade earlier (Tay et al., 1992). Further studies of children revealed that in Taiwan, rates of nearsightedness increased from 12 percent among 6-year-olds to 84 percent among 17-year-olds; in Singapore, from 28 percent among 6-year-olds to 44 percent among 9-year-olds; and in Hong Kong, from 10 percent among 7-year-olds to 60 percent among 12-year-olds (cited in Grosvenor, 2003).

This increase is partly developmental; remember that the rate of nearsightedness increases with puberty. Some observers want longitudinal, experimental research before they conclude that "myopia is increasing at an 'epidemic' rate, particularly in East Asia" (Park & Congdon, 2004, p. 21). However, the data are alarming: The increase is far higher than for comparable children outside East Asia, and the rates are far higher than among the parents of these children. The gene pool has not changed much over recent years, so it seems that something in the environment must be interacting with the genes to cause this epidemic (Morgan, 2003; Saw, 2003).

One possible culprit has been mentioned again and again: the increasing amount of time spent by children in close study of books and papers. In Chapter 12 you will see data about the current educational successes of East Asian schoolchildren, whose proficiency in math and science far exceeds that of children in North America, Europe, and the Middle East. Children in Singapore, Taiwan, Hong Kong, and Japan spend much more time studying and doing other "close work" than Western children do. Their developing eyes must focus on nearby objects, so that eventually they may lose acuity for objects far away—which is exactly what nearsightedness means. Ophthalmologists suggest that if these children spent more time outside playing, or even walking and relaxing in regular daylight, their eyes would remain better able to adjust to all focal distances (Goss, 2002; Grosvenor, 2003).

Response for People Who Are Easily Bored (from page 82): It depends on you. Some people who love risk become addicts; others develop a healthy lifestyle that includes adventure, new people, and exotic places. Any trait can lead in various directions.

Response for College Students Who Enjoy a Party (from page 82): Your friend's ability to "hold his liquor" is an ominous sign; his body probably metabolizes alcohol differently from the way most other people's do. Alcoholics are often deceptive about their own drinking habits, so you might ask him about the drinking habits of his relatives. If he has either alcoholics or abstainers in his family, you should be concerned, since both patterns are signs of a genetic problem with alcohol. Ask your friend whether he could have only one drink a day for a month. Alcoholics find such restricted drinking virtually impossible.

Research on other Asian children leads to the same conclusions. Young men in India are nearsighted at a rate of about 10 percent, but 17-year-olds of Indian descent in Singapore are nearsighted at a rate of 70 percent. Sherpa children living in Nepal spend most of their time outdoors; only 3 percent of them are nearsighted. Other Tibetan children living in Nepal have similar genes, but they spend much more time studying; their rate of nearsightedness is 22 percent (Garner et al., 1999).

There seems to be no doubt that "the extremely rapid changes in the prevalence of myopia and the dependence of myopia on the level of education indicate that there are very strong environmental impacts" on whether or not a child needs glasses by age 12 (Morgan, 2003, p. 276). There is also no doubt that genes are crucial; scientists are no longer surprised to find another example of a condition that is highly hereditary *and* highly environmental.

Practical Applications

The research on the nature–nurture interactions involved in schizophrenia, alcoholism, nearsightedness, and virtually every other condition has many practical implications, but not everyone agrees about the specifics (Ridley, 2004). For example, children of Chinese descent seem unusually vulnerable to nearsightedness. However, beyond that, some suggest that the epidemic in China should alert adults throughout the world that excessive close work—whether it be studying, or television watching, or computer use—and insufficient outdoor play will increase nearsightedness among children of every genetic background. Some disagree, arguing that this combination creates problems only in East Asia.

Genes rarely act alone, and that makes practical applications complex. A cluster of factors, some hereditary and some environmental, produce a person who suffers from psychological disorders, addictions, or impaired vision. Although either genes *or* environmental trauma have substantial impact in some cases, more often both are implicated—and if either were absent, the problem might not appear in the phenotype.

Some applications, however, are obvious. First, knowing that there is a genetic component in each of these disorders can help parents of children with schizophrenia, alcoholism, or myopia accept that neither their child-rearing practices nor the children themselves are the origin of the problem. Genetic problems begin at conception, but practical steps can be taken early on to reduce the manifestation of these genetic vulnerabilities: Especially if schizophrenia runs in the family, prenatal care and birth practices can minimize birth complications. Especially if alcoholism is in the genes, children and adolescents should be kept away from alcohol. Especially if nearsightedness is familial, children should spend lots of time each day playing outdoors.

Of course, these protective measures are recommended for every child, as are dozens of other behaviors, such as flossing the teeth, being polite, getting enough sleep, eating vegetables, and writing thank-you notes. However, no child can do everything right, and no parent can do everything perfectly. This is why awareness of genetic vulnerability is useful: It alerts parents to set priorities regarding what they should do and encourages them to accept what cannot be changed.

Examples of the benefits of this combination approach abound regarding many conditions that have become increasingly common, from autism in toddlers to suicide in older adolescents. Knowing that these stem from both nature and nurture keeps blame at bay and allows for constructive action.

To illustrate, consider one more epidemic: type 2 diabetes, which used to be called adult-onset diabetes. In the United States in 2004, diabetes was the sixth most common cause of death, and it is estimated that 1 in 3 children who were born in 2000 will develop diabetes (Lazar, 2005). Some ethnic groups (e.g., African Americans, Hispanic Americans, and members of many Native American peoples) are genetically more vulnerable to diabetes than are other North Americans. Worldwide, the incidence of diabetes is expected to double by 2025, when 300 million people will have the disease (Kiberstic, 2005).

Type 2 diabetes does not usually begin unless a person is genetically vulnerable *and* has more body fat than is ideal for someone of his or her age and height (Lazar, 2005). Thus, in their ancestral homelands, many African and Hispanic people were not fat enough to develop diabetes. However, in the United States, as obesity becomes more common in children, type 2 diabetes is appearing among adolescents. It's not that genes have changed: Some adolescents have always been genetically susceptible to diabetes. But almost none of them developed type 2 diabetes until the current obesity epidemic. Knowing this, parents who have diabetes in their families can redouble their efforts to encourage healthy eating and exercise in their children and themselves. Once again, understanding the interaction between nature and nurture can help to prevent or moderate genetic problems.

SUMMING UP

Genes affect every trait—whether it be something wonderful, such as a wacky sense of humor; something fearful, such as a violent temper; or something quite ordinary, such as the tendency to be bored. The environment affects every trait as well, in ways that change as maturational, cultural, and historical processes unfold. The expression of genes can sometimes be directed or deflected, depending on the culture and the society and even on the individual and the family. This is apparent in schizophrenia, alcoholism, and nearsightedness, all of which have strong genetic roots but all of which are affected by the environment. Genes are always part of the story, influential on every page, but they never determine the plot or the final paragraph.

Chromosomal and Genetic Abnormalities

We now focus on abnormalities that are caused by an identifiable problem, such as an extra chromosome or a single gene. Chromosomal abnormalities occur when a zygote's cells have more or fewer chromosomes than the usual 46. Genetic abnormalities occur when one gene codes for a protein that creates problems or fails to code for a preventative protein.

Chromosomal and genetic abnormalities, although uncommon, are relevant for three reasons:

- They provide insight into the complexities of genetic interaction.
- Knowing their origins helps limit harmful consequences.
- Accurate information can halt the misinformation that compounds genetic problems.

Not Exactly 46 Chromosomes

Gametes with more or fewer than 23 chromosomes are formed for many reasons, both inherited and environmental (such as a parent's exposure to excessive radiation). The variable that most often correlates with chromosomal abnormalities is the age of the mother. Paternal age (if a father is over age 40) is also relevant, but maternal age is the most crucial (Crow, 2003), presumably because ova (which begin to form before a girl is born) become increasingly fragile by midlife.

Chromosomal abnormalities may also occur not only before conception, as gametes are formed, but also when gametes fuse to form a zygote or in the early stages of duplication. In that case, some cells may have more or fewer than 46 chromosomes, while others have exactly 46. The result is a person who is **mosaic**—that is, who has a mixture of cells.

mosaic Having a condition (*mosaicism*) that involves having a mixture of cells, some normal and some with an odd number of chromosomes or a series of missing genes.

Down syndrome A condition in which a person has 47 chromosomes instead of the usual 46, with 3 rather than 2 chromosomes at the 21st position. People with Down syndrome often have distinctive characteristics: unusual facial features, heart abnormalities, and language difficulties. (Also called *trisomy-21*.)

Actually, zygotes often have too many or too few chromosomes. One scientist estimates that only half of all conceptions have the usual 46 (Borgaonkar, 1997). Most abnormal zygotes do not begin to duplicate, divide, and differentiate (Moore & Persaud, 2003). Few develop to term—usually because they are spontaneously aborted early in pregnancy or aborted by choice once the parents know about the condition. If a fetus survives prenatal development, birth is hazardous: About 5 percent of stillborn (dead-at-birth) babies have more than 46 chromosomes (Miller & Therman, 2001).

Once in about every 200 births, a surviving infant has 45, 47, or, rarely, 48 or 49 chromosomes. Each particular chromosomal abnormality leads to a recognizable *syndrome,* a cluster of distinct characteristics that tend to occur together. Usually the cause is three chromosomes (a condition called a *trisomy*) at a particular location instead of the usual two.

GETTY (TAXI)

Is She the Baby's Grandmother? No Women over age 40 now have a higher birth rate than women that age did just a few decades ago. Later-life pregnancies are more likely to involve complications, but the outcome is sometimes what you see here: a gray-haired mother thrilled with her happy, healthy infant.

Down Syndrome

The most common extra-chromosome condition is **Down syndrome,** also called *trisomy-21* because all people with Down syndrome have three copies of chromosome 21, not just two. According to one estimate, a 20-year-old woman has about 1 chance in 800 of carrying a fetus with Down syndrome; a 39-year-old woman, 1 in 67; and a 44-year-old woman, 1 in 16 (see Appendix A, p. A-3). A few decades ago, almost all infants with Down syndrome died in early childhood, but advances in treatment mean that most now survive into adulthood.

Some 300 distinct characteristics can result from the presence of that extra chromosome 21. No individual with Down syndrome is quite like another, either in symptoms or in severity. (One reason is that some are mosaic, having some cells with 46 chromosomes and others with 47; another reason is that the other genes and environmental experiences differ for each person.) Despite this variability, most people with trisomy-21 have certain specific facial characteristics—a thick tongue, round face, slanted eyes—as well as distinctive hands, feet, and fingerprints. Many also have hearing problems, heart abnormalities, muscle weakness, and short stature.

In terms of brain development, individuals with Down syndrome experience some mental slowness, especially in language. Their eventual intellect varies: Some are severely retarded; others are of average or even above-average intelligence. Usually—but not always—those who are raised at home and given appropriate cognitive stimulation progress to the point of being able to read and write and care for themselves (and often much more). Specific early stimulation and guidance of language abilities often make a marked difference (Miller et al., 1999).

Many young children with trisomy-21 are unusually sweet-tempered; they are less likely to cry or complain than other children. Temperament may be a liability, however. If a child with Down syndrome is more passive than his or her siblings, and the parents are relieved that their special child does not need much attention, that may result in slower learning and a lower IQ as time goes on (Wishart, 1999).

People with Down syndrome grow old faster than other adults. For them, the ailments of aging usually begin at about age 30 (Hassold & Patterson, 1999). By middle adulthood, they "almost invariably" develop Alzheimer's disease, which severely impairs their communication skills and makes them much less compliant (Czech et al., 2000). They are prone to a host of other problems commonly found in older persons, including cataracts and certain forms of cancer. Consequently, their mortality rate begins to rise at about age 35, and their life expectancy is lower than that of other adults with mental retardation and much lower than that of the population as a whole (Strauss & Eyman, 1996).

This generally pessimistic description, however, does not reflect the actual experience of individuals with Down syndrome. Language does not come easily for them, and many have medical problems. But they may still become happy, proud, and successful young adults. One advised others:

> You may have to work hard, but don't ever give up. Always remember that you are important. You are special in your own unique way. And one of the best ways to feel good about yourself is to share yourself with someone else.
>
> *[Christi Todd, quoted in Hassold & Patterson, 1999]*

MACPHERSON / MONKMEYER

Earning His Daily Bread This man with Down syndrome works in a cafeteria and, by all reports, is a steady, conscientious employee.

? OBSERVATIONAL QUIZ (see answer, page 90): Visible are four signs of Down syndrome; not visible (and perhaps not present) are at least four other signs. Name all eight.

Abnormalities of the 23rd Pair

As already explained, every surviving human has at least one X chromosome in the 23rd pair; an embryo cannot develop without an X. However, about 1 in every 500 infants either is missing a sex chromosome (the X stands alone) or has two or more other sex chromosomes in addition to the first X.

An odd number of sex chromosomes impairs cognitive and psychosocial development as well as sexual maturation. The specifics depend on the particular syndrome. The only person with 45 chromosomes who can survive is a girl with only one X (written as X0, with the 0 standing for no chromosome). This is called *Turner syndrome,* and the girl has underdeveloped female organs and other anomalies.

If there are three sex chromosomes instead of two, a child may seem normal until puberty, particularly if he has *Klinefelter syndrome,* XXY. Such a boy will be a little slow in elementary school, but not until age 12 or so, when the double X keeps his penis from growing and when fat begins to accumulate around his breasts, does something seem seriously wrong. For such boys, hormones can alleviate some problems, and special education will aid learning—another example of nurture compensating for nature.

Single-Gene Disorders

Everyone carries genes or alleles that could produce serious diseases or handicaps in the next generation (see Table 3.2). Usually these diseases are expressed only if specific other genes are in the genotype or if enabling factors are present in the environment. The previous section of this chapter describes this polygenic and multifactorial interaction. Given that most genes contribute only a small amount to a disorder and that the mapping of the human genome is relatively recent, the exact impact of each allele of these multifactorial disorders is not yet known (Hinds et al., 2005). However, research on single-gene disorders has been under way for decades and has uncovered many specifics.

TABLE 3.2 **Common Genetic Diseases and Conditions**

Name	Description	Prognosis	Probable Inheritance	Incidence*	Carrier Detection?†	Prenatal Detection?
Albinism	No melanin; person is very blond and pale	Normal, but must avoid sun damage	Recessive	Rare overall; 1 in 8 Hopi Indians is a carrier	No	No
Alzheimer's disease	Loss of memory and increasing mental impairment	Eventual death, often after years of dependency	Early onset—dominant; after age 60—multifactorial	Fewer than 1 in 100 middle-aged adults; 40 percent of all adults over age 85	Yes, for some genes; ApoE4 allele increases incidence	No
Breast cancer	Tumors in breast that can spread	With early treatment, most are cured; without it, death within 3 years	BRCA1 and BRCA2 genes seem dominant; other cases, multifactorial	1 woman in 8 (only 20 percent of breast cancer patients have BRCA1 or BRCA2)	Yes, for BRCA1 and BRCA2	No
Cleft palate, cleft lip	The two sides of the upper lip or palate are not joined	Correctable by surgery	Multifactorial	1 in every 700 births; more common in Asian Americans and American Indians	No	Yes
Club foot	The foot and ankle are twisted	Correctable by surgery	Multifactorial	1 in every 200 births; more common in boys	No	Yes
Cystic fibrosis	Mucous obstructions, especially in lungs and digestive organs	Most live to middle adulthood	Recessive gene; also spontaneous mutations	1 in 2,500; 1 in 20 European Americans is a carrier	Sometimes	Yes, in most cases
Diabetes	Abnormal sugar metabolism because of insufficient insulin	Early onset (type 1) fatal without insulin; for adult onset (type 2), variable risks	Multifactorial; for adult onset, environment is crucial	Type 1: 1 in 500 births; more common in American Indians and African Americans. Type 2: 1 adult in 10	No	No
Deafness (congenital)	Inability to hear from birth on	Deaf children can learn sign language and live normally	Multifactorial; some forms are recessive	1 in 1,000 births; more common in people from Middle East	No	No
Hemophilia	Absence of clotting factor in blood	Death from internal bleeding; blood transfusions prevent damage	X-linked recessive; also spontaneous mutations	1 in 10,000 males; royal families of England, Russia, and Germany had it	Yes	Yes
Hydro-cephalus	Obstruction causes excess fluid in the brain	Brain damage and death; surgery can make normal life possible	Multifactorial	1 in every 100 births	No	Yes

*Incidence statistics vary from country to country; those given here are for the United States. All these diseases can occur in any ethnic group. Many affected groups limit transmission through genetic counseling; for example, the incidence of Tay-Sachs disease is declining because many Jewish young adults obtain testing and counseling before marriage.
†"Yes" refers to carrier detection. Family history can also reveal genetic risk.

Name	Description	Prognosis	Probable Inheritance	Incidence*	Carrier Detection?†	Prenatal Detection?
Muscular dystrophy (13 diseases)	Weakening of muscles	Inability to walk, move; wasting away and sometimes death	Duchenne's is X-linked; other forms are recessive or multifactorial	1 in every 3,500 males develops Duchenne's	Yes, for some forms	Yes, for some forms
Neural-tube defects (open spine)	Anencephaly (parts of the brain missing) or spina bifida (lower spine not closed)	Anencephalic—severe retardation; spina bifida—poor lower body control	Multifactorial; defect occurs in first weeks of pregnancy	Anencephaly—1 in 1,000 births; spina bifida—3 in 1,000; more common in Welsh and Scots	No	Yes
Phenylketonuria (PKU)	Abnormal digestion of protein	Mental retardation, hyperactivity; preventable by diet	Recessive	1 in 10,000 births; 1 in 100 European Americans is a carrier, especially Norwegians and Irish	Yes	Yes
Pyloric stenosis	Overgrowth of muscle in intestine	Vomiting, loss of weight, eventual death; correctable by surgery	Multifactorial	1 male in 200, 1 female in 1,000; less common in African Americans	No	No
Rett syndrome	Neurological developmental disorder	Boys die at birth. At 6–18 months, girls lose communication and motor abilities	X-linked	1 in 10,000–23,000 live female births	No	Sometimes
Schizophrenia	Severely distorted thought processes	No cure; drugs, hospitalization, psychotherapy ease symptoms	Multifactorial	1 in 100 people develop it by early adulthood	No	No
Sickle-cell anemia	Abnormal blood cells	Possible painful "crisis"; heart and kidney failure; treatable with drugs	Recessive	1 in 500 African Americans; 1 in 10 African Americans and 1 in 20 Latinos is a carrier	Yes	Yes
Tay-Sachs disease	Enzyme disease	Apparently healthy infant becomes weaker, usually dying by age 5	Recessive	1 in 4,000 births; 1 in 30 American Jews and 1 in 20 French Canadians are carriers	Yes	Yes
Thalassemia	Abnormal blood cells	Paleness and listlessness, low resistance to infections	Recessive	1 in 10 Greek, Italian, Thai, and Indian Americans is a carrier	Yes	Yes
Tourette syndrome	Uncontrollable tics, body jerking, verbal obscenities	Often imperceptible in children; gets worse with age	Dominant, but variable penetrance	1 in 250 births	Sometimes	No

Sources: Briley & Sulser, 2001; Klug & Cummings, 2000; Mange & Mange, 1999; McKusick, 1994; Moore & Persaud, 2003; National Academy of Sciences, 1994; Shahin et al., 2002.

! Answer to Observational Quiz (from page 87): Four visible signs: round head, short stature, large hands, slanted eye sockets. Not visible: mental retardation, heart abnormalities, muscle weakness, thick tongue.

Dominant Disorders

Most of the 7,000 *known* genetic disorders are dominant (always expressed). They are known because they are easy to notice: Their dominant effects are apparent in the phenotype. With a few exceptions, disabling dominant disorders are rare because people with such disorders rarely have children and thus the gene dies with them.

One exception to this generality is *Huntington's disease,* a fatal central nervous system disorder caused by a genetic miscode—this time more than 35 repetitions of a particular triplet. Unlike most dominant traits, this miscode is inactive until middle adulthood. By then a person could have had several children, half of whom inherit the same dominant gene and therefore will eventually develop Huntington's disease.

Another disorder, which is probably dominant, is *Tourette syndrome,* common because it is not disabling and because the effects vary. About 30 percent of those who inherit the gene for Tourette syndrome exhibit recurrent uncontrollable tics and explosive outbursts of verbal obscenities. The remaining 70 percent experience milder symptoms, such as an occasional twitch that is barely noticeable or a postponable impulse to speak inappropriately. A person with mild Tourette syndrome might curse and tremor at home but behave normally in public. To add to the complications, if one is female and has the dominant Tourette gene, expression is less likely.

Fragile X and Recessive Conditions

fragile X syndrome A genetic disorder in which part of the X chromosome seems to be attached to the rest of it by a very thin string of molecules. The actual cause is too many repetitions of a particular part of a gene's code.

Several recessive genetic disorders are sex-linked, carried on the X chromosome. For this reason, males are more likely to be affected. One such condition, called **fragile X syndrome**, is caused by a single gene that has more than 200 repetitions of another triplet (Plomin et al., 2001). (Some repetitions are normal, but not this many.) The repetitions multiply as that X chromosome is passed from one generation to the next. Half of a woman's sons will be affected, but often her daughters are not if the X from their father is normal.

Although it is a single-gene disorder, fragile X syndrome is not strictly recessive, or dominant, or additive. Of females with the fragile X gene, about two-thirds are normal and one-third show some mental deficiency. Of males who inherit a fragile X, about 20 percent seem normal, about 33 percent are somewhat retarded, and the rest are severely retarded. If a man with a fragile X is normal, half the sons of his daughters (his grandsons) will probably be significantly impaired because of the increased number of repetitions with each generation.

The cognitive deficits caused by fragile X syndrome are the most common form of inherited mental retardation (many other forms are not inherited) (Sherman, 2002). In addition to having cognitive problems, children with fragile X syndrome often are shy, with poor social skills (Hagerman, 2002).

Hundreds of other recessive disorders are not sex-linked, among them cystic fibrosis, thalassemia, and sickle-cell anemia. All three of these are equally common in males and females (see Table 3.2). About 1 in 12 North Americans is a carrier for one or another of these three. Each became widespread because, although the double recessive is lethal, the single recessive is protective. For example, carriers of the sickle-cell trait are less likely to die of malaria, which is still a problem in central Africa. Their descendants in North America, including 10 percent of all African Americans, carry a gene that is no longer needed for protection.

Especially for History Students Some genetic diseases may have changed the course of history. For instance, the last czar of Russia had four healthy daughters and one son with hemophilia. Once called the royal disease, hemophilia is X-linked. How could this rare condition have affected the monarchies of Russia, England, Austria, Germany, and Spain?

Sometimes a person who happened to have a lethal gene has many descendants who tend to marry each other. In that case, a particular group of people who intermarry begin to have children with an unusual disease. This was the case among Jews in one area of Eastern Europe, who often carried Tay-Sachs, a recessive disease, and among the royal families of Europe in the nineteenth century, who often were carriers of hemophilia, a sex-linked recessive condition in which the ability of the blood to clot is impaired.

genetic counseling Consultation and testing that enables individuals to learn about their genetic heritage, including conditions that might harm any children they may conceive.

Genetic Testing and Counseling

Until recently, after the birth of a child with a serious or even fatal disorder, couples blamed fate, not genes or chromosomes. Today, many young adults worry about their genes long before they marry. Almost every adult has a relative with a serious disease that is partly genetic. **Genetic counseling** can relieve some of these worries by providing facts and raising issues for prospective parents to use in deciding how to proceed. In general, preconception or even prenuptial genetic testing and counseling are recommended for:

- Individuals who have a parent, sibling, or child with a serious genetic condition
- Couples who have a history of spontaneous abortions, stillbirths, or infertility
- Couples from the same ethnic group or subgroup—particularly if they are close relatives
- Women age 35 or older and men age 40 or older

Genetic counselors try to follow two ethical guidelines. First, the results of their clients' tests are kept confidential, beyond the reach of insurance companies and public records. Second, decisions are made by the clients, not by the counselor. (Figure 3.3 outlines the decision-making process.) These guidelines are not always easy to follow. Consider these cases:

1. A pregnant woman and her husband both have achondroplastic dwarfism, a dominant condition that affects appearance (very short stature, large heads) but not intellect. They want genetic analysis of their fetus, which they intend to abort if it would become a child of normal height.
2. A 40-year-old woman is tested and hears bad news: She has the BRCA1 gene, which gives her about an 80 percent chance of developing breast cancer before age 70, and perhaps ovarian or colon cancer as well. She refuses to believe the results and insists that no one tell her family, including her mother, her four sisters, and her three daughters. Several of them probably have the gene and may be in the early stages of cancer without knowing it.
3. A 30-year-old mother of two daughters (no sons) learns that she is a carrier for hemophilia. She requests pre-implantation analysis, demanding that only male embryos without her hemophilia-carrying X chromosome be implanted. This means that all

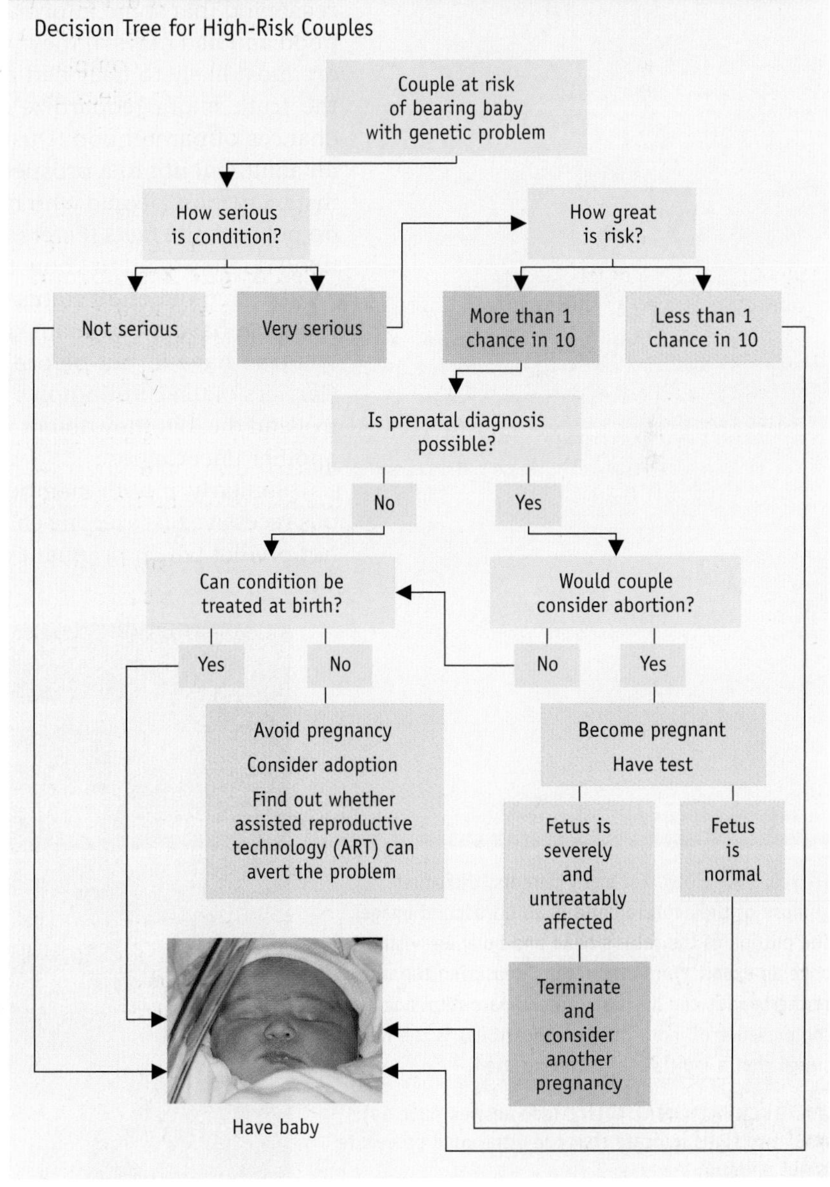

FIGURE 3.3 **At-Risk Decision Making** With the help of a genetic counselor, even couples who know they run a risk of having a baby with a genetic defect might decide to have a child. Although the process of making that decision is more complicated for them than it is for couples with no family genetic illness and no positive tests for harmful recessive genes, the outcome is usually a healthy baby. Genetic counselors provide facts and alternatives; couples make decisions.

Response for History Students (from page 90): Hemophilia is a painful chronic disease that (before blood transfusions became feasible) killed a boy before adulthood. Though rare, it ran in European royal families, whose members often intermarried, which meant that many queens (including England's Queen Victoria) were carriers of hemophilia and thus were destined to watch half their sons die of it. All families, even rulers of nations, are distracted from their work when they have a child with a mysterious and lethal illness. Some historians believe that hemophilia among European royalty was an underlying cause of the Russian Revolution of 1917 as well as the spread of democracy in the nineteenth and twentieth centuries.

female zygotes, all healthy and only half of them carriers, would be destroyed, as would half of her male zygotes.

4. A couple has a child with cystic fibrosis. They want to know if they both carry the recessive gene or if this was a spontaneous miscode (as is often the case). If they are both carriers, their next child has one chance in four of having cystic fibrosis. If not, they could have another child with very little risk of cystic fibrosis. During testing, the counselor learns that the wife is a carrier but the husband is not—and also realizes that the husband is not the biological father of the child.

[adapted from Fackelmann, 1994]

Should test results be kept confidential even from other family members who are directly affected (examples 2 and 4)? And should a client be allowed to make a decision that the counselor believes is unethical (examples 1 and 3)? Most counselors answer "yes" to both questions, but many students say that they would break confidentiality for examples 2 and 4 and would refuse to test in examples 1 and 3. What would you do?

Genetic counselors, scientists, and the general public usually favor testing, reasoning that some information is better than none. Counselors tell clients both good and bad news, if they want to know it. However, high-risk individuals (who are most likely to hear bad news) do not necessarily want to know, especially if the truth might jeopardize their marriage, their insurance coverage, or their chances of parenthood (Duster, 1999). If genetic tests can reveal only the risk to an adult, but not to a prospective child, many high-risk adults refuse testing. For instance, most people who have a 50/50 risk of developing Huntington's disease do not seek the facts (Peterson, 2001). Only when they are contemplating parenthood do they want to know their own status.

Finding out one's status merely alerts a person to probabilities. For instance, if people have a dominant gene for Huntington's disease, half of their children will also have it, but before conception those are merely odds, not certainties. Carriers of the Huntington's gene know that they will eventually lose muscle control and die, but they do not know if the deterioration will begin at age 30 or 50—another uncertainty.

Similarly, if both members of a couple learn that they are carriers for a serious recessive disease, one child out of four is likely to have the condition. That does not predict which pregnancy will be the unfortunate one. Thus, if both partners

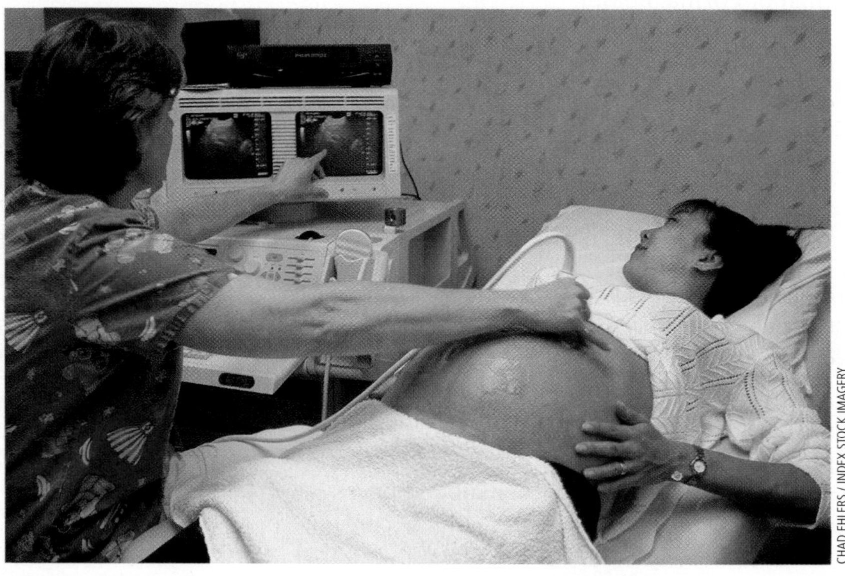
CHAD EHLERS / INDEX STOCK IMAGERY

There's Your Baby For many parents, their first glimpse of their future child is an ultrasound image. The outline of the fetus's head and body are visible once an expert points them out. Measuring the width of the head is the best way to estimate fetal age, and the presence of more than one heartbeat is the first signal that a multiple birth is expected.

? Observational Quiz (see answer, page 94): What two signs indicate that the ultrasound procedure is not painful?

ROBERT SPENCER / THE NEW YORK TIMES

"The Hardest Decision I Ever Had to Make" That's how this woman described her decision to terminate her third pregnancy when genetic testing revealed that the fetus had Down syndrome. She soon became pregnant again with a male fetus that had the normal 46 chromosomes, as did her two daughters. Many personal factors influence such decisions. Do you think she and her husband would have made the same choice if they had had no other children?

have the recessive gene for sickle-cell anemia, then all, some, or none of their children *could* have the disease. Probability predicts—but does not guarantee—that one child in four will be afflicted, two in four will be carriers (one because of the mother and one because of the father), and one in four will not even be a carrier. Each new pregnancy is a new risk, another roll of the same dice with all four combinations equally possible.

As this chapter has emphasized, the interaction of genes and the environment makes each developing person somewhat unpredictable, even when the genes are known. For example, some people with sickle-cell anemia suffer terribly and then die young, while others live satisfying lives, with occasional painful crises that can be weathered. Some couples at high risk refuse to be tested; others with the same genotype are tested and then adopt rather than risk bearing a child with the disease; still others take their chances, either hoping to have a child without the disease or opting for testing during pregnancy and terminating the pregnancy if the fetus has the double recessive. Information is power that can be used in many ways.

For many inherited problems, including most recessive genetic disorders and chromosomal miscounts, accurate testing can be done during pregnancy but not before conception. Is a couple willing to start a pregnancy and then end it if the embryo would develop into a seriously ill child? One couple that said "no" and one that said "yes" are presented in the next chapter, as is a more general discussion of the methods and problems of prenatal testing. In most cases, genetic testing occurs after one child is born with a problem, not before.

ESPECIALLY FOR A FRIEND A female friend asks you to go with her to the hospital, where she is planning to be surgically sterilized. She says she doesn't want children, especially since her younger brother recently died of sickle-cell anemia, a recessive disease. What, if anything, should you do?

Only after Rachel fell and seemed to have broken her finger did I realize that a gene absolved me of the need to get medical attention for her. Similarly, with all my children when problems arise, understanding genetic and experiential possibilities has helped me decide what to do. However, when everything seems to be developing well, I do not question my children's genotypes or phenotypes. Likewise, for all scientists, genetics helps interpret development that has already occurred, but much needs to be learned before future prenatal or postnatal problems can be accurately foreseen.

! Answer to Observational Quiz (from page 92): The woman's smile and her hand holding her belly. She is relaxed and focused on her fetus, not on herself.

Response for a Friend (from page 93): She needs the information you have. She may not be a carrier of the sickle-cell trait (you know she doesn't have the disease, so she has one chance in three of not being a carrier). Even if she is a carrier, she can have a child with the disease only if the father of her child is also a carrier—and then there is only one chance in four. Urge your friend not to do anything irreversible.

SUMMING UP

When sperm and ovum combine, the resulting zygote always carries some genes for susceptibility to various syndromes, abnormalities, or diseases. Perhaps as often as half the time, the total number of chromosomes is not the usual 46. If the zygote has a serious chromosomal miscount, chances are it will be too defective to grow, much less become a full-term infant. The main exceptions are Down syndrome (trisomy-21) and abnormalities of the sex chromosomes, which allow offspring to develop for decades.

As part of selective adaptation, few zygotes with severe single-gene problems survive and then reproduce. Less severe problems (such as Tourette syndrome), dominant diseases that do not appear until middle age (such as Huntington's disease), and recessive diseases that carry an enhanced chance of survival if only one gene is inherited (such as sickle-cell anemia) are exceptions; they are passed on because carriers are likely to reproduce. Genetic counseling helps couples clarify their values and understand the probabilities before they conceive, but each choice is a personal combination of facts, probabilities, experiences, and values.

■ SUMMARY

The Genetic Code

1. Genes are the foundation for all development, first instructing the living creature to form the body and brain, and then regulating behavior. Human conception occurs when two gametes (an ovum and a sperm, each with 23 chromosomes) combine to form a zygote, 46 chromosomes in a single cell.

2. The sex of an embryo depends on the sperm: A Y sperm creates an XY (male) embryo; an X sperm creates an XX (female) embryo. Every cell of every living creature has the unique genetic code of the zygote that began that life. The human genome contains about 25,000 genes in all.

From One Cell to Many

3. Genes interact in various ways, sometimes additively, with each contributing to development, sometimes in a dominant–recessive pattern. Factors from the environment influence the phenotype as well.

4. The environment interacts with genetic instructions for every trait, even for physical appearance. Every aspect of a person is almost always multifactorial and polygenic. This is equally true for traits that are not evident until long after birth, such as learning disabilities and hyperactivity.

5. Combinations of chromosomes, interactions among genes, and myriad influences from the environment all assure both similarity and diversity within and between species. This aids health and survival.

6. Twins occur if a zygote splits into two separate beings (monozygotic, or identical, twins) or if two ova are fertilized by two sperm (dizygotic, or fraternal, twins). Monozygotic multiples are genetically the same. Dizygotic multiples have only half of their genes in common.

7. A clone has the same genes as another living creature. Clones of lower animals are very difficult to create. Human cloning is illegal.

8. Fertility treatments, including drugs and in vitro fertilization, have led to millions of much-wanted babies but also to several thorny ethical questions. One problem is how to balance the needs and wishes of the infertile adult with those of the prospective child.

From Genotype to Phenotype

9. Environmental influences are crucial for almost every complex trait. This includes schizophrenia, alcoholism, and nearsightedness. Some people are genetically susceptible to each of these, but nongenetic factors affect every condition.

Chromosomal and Genetic Abnormalities

10. Often a gamete has fewer or more than 23 chromosomes, creating a zygote with an odd number of chromosomes. Usually such zygotes do not develop unless they have three number 21 chromosomes (Down syndrome) or an odd number of sex chromosomes. In such cases, the child has physical and cognitive problems but can live a nearly normal life.

11. Everyone is a carrier for genetic abnormalities, but usually those conditions are recessive (not affecting their phenotype), mild, or inconsequential until late adulthood. If carrying a genetic abnormality is protective, the gene can become widespread in a population.

12. Genetic testing and counseling can help many couples learn whether their future children are at risk for a chromosomal or genetic abnormality. Genetic testing usually provides information about risks, not actualities. Couples, counselors, and cultures differ in the decisions they make.

KEY TERMS

DNA (deoxyribonucleic acid) (p. 65)
chromosome (p. 65)
gene (p. 66)
human genome (p. 66)
gamete (p. 67)
zygote (p. 67)
genotype (p. 67)
allele (p. 68)
23rd pair (p. 68)
XX (p. 68)
XY (p. 68)
spontaneous abortion (p. 69)
phenotype (p. 70)
polygenic (p. 71)
multifactorial (p. 71)
Human Genome Project (p. 71)
additive gene (p. 72)
dominant–recessive pattern (p. 72)
X-linked (p. 73)
dizygotic (DZ) twins (p. 75)
monozygotic (MZ) twins (p. 76)
clone (p. 76)
infertility (p. 77)
assisted reproductive technology (ART) (p. 77)
in vitro fertilization (IVF) (p. 77)
carrier (p. 79)
mosaic (p. 86)
Down syndrome (p. 86)
fragile X syndrome (p. 90)
genetic counseling (p. 91)

KEY QUESTIONS

1. What are the relationships among proteins, genes, chromosomes, and the genome?

2. How and when is the sex of a zygote determined? Why is this significant, both earlier and in current times?

3. Compare the degrees of certainty in identifying a criminal: a lineup of suspects, a confession, a fingerprint match, DNA identification.

4. Genetically speaking, how similar are people to one another?

5. Sometimes parents have a child who looks like neither of them. How does that happen?

6. What are the differences among monozygotic twins, dizygotic twins, single births, and clones?

7. From the prospective parents' perspective, what are the advantages and disadvantages of adoption and ART?

8. Explain how the course of schizophrenia, alcoholism, or nearsightedness is affected by nature and by nurture.

9. What are the causes and effects of Down syndrome?

10. Why is genetic counseling a personal decision and usually confidential, not to be publicized or legislated?

APPLICATIONS

1. Pick one of your traits, and explain the influences that both nature *and* nurture have on it. For example, if you have a short temper, explain its origins in your genetics, your culture, and your childhood experiences.

2. Many men want a son. Interview several men to find out if they follow this pattern. If they give the socially acceptable answer ("It does not matter"), ask how the two sexes differ and what fathers should do for sons and daughters. Listen and take notes—don't disagree. Analyze the implications.

3. Draw a genetic chart of your biological relatives, going back as many generations as you can, listing all serious illnesses and causes of death. Include ancestors who died in infancy. Do you see any genetic susceptibility? If so, how can you overcome it? If not, why not?

Chapter Four

Prenatal Development and Birth

Wonder and worry, worry and wonder. Expectant parents wonder: Will it be a boy or a girl? One baby or two? What name to choose? What color hair, eyes, and skin? What shape head, nose, and chin? When and how will birth occur? With what help, where, from whom? Expectant parents worry, too, praying that their baby will be healthy and whole.

My friend Judy taught history at the United Nations International School in New York City. She often emphasized the contrast between the broad generalities of human history and the local particulars. When she was pregnant with her first child, she did the same thing: She rubbed her bulging belly and told her students, "According to international statistics, this most likely is a Chinese boy."

Judy was right—at least in a sense. A majority of fetuses are male (about 52 percent), and more of the world's babies are Chinese than any other ethnicity (about 30 percent). Given these statistical generalities, Judy's statement was accurate. Given Judy's local particulars (genes, age, sonogram), though, I was not at all surprised when she gave birth to a healthy European American girl. Judy herself seemed awestruck, repeatedly recounting tiny details, as if no baby like hers had ever appeared before. She was right about that, too.

This example illustrates the dual themes of this chapter, which describes human development from conception through birth. Every topic in the chapter—embryonic development, teratogens, sonograms, low birthweight, medical assistance, bonding, and so on—is directly relevant to the 200 million babies born in the world every year. Yet each pregnancy and birth is unique and never proceeds exactly as predicted. This chapter includes both generalities and variations. Learn all you can, and then, if you become a parent, expect to be awed by your personal miracle.

From Zygote to Newborn

The most dramatic and extensive transformation of the entire life span occurs before birth. To make it easier to study, the awesome process of prenatal development is often divided into three main periods. The first two weeks are called the **germinal period**; the third through the eighth week is the **embryonic period**; the ninth week until birth is the **fetal period.** (Alternative terms are discussed in Table 4.1.)

Germinal: The First 14 Days

You learned in Chapter 3 that the one-celled zygote, traveling slowly down the fallopian tube toward the uterus, begins to duplicate and multiply (see Figure 4.1). At about the eight-cell stage, differentiation begins. The early "stem" cells soon take on distinct characteristics and gravitate toward particular locations, foreshadowing the types of cells they will become.

germinal period The first two weeks of development after conception; characterized by rapid cell division and the beginning of cell differentiation. This is the most hazardous period of development.

embryonic period Approximately the third through the eighth week after conception; the period during which the basic forms of all body structures, including internal organs, develop.

fetal period The stage of prenatal development from the ninth week after conception until birth; the period during which the organs of the developing person grow in size and mature in functioning. Brain maturation and weight gain occur throughout this period.

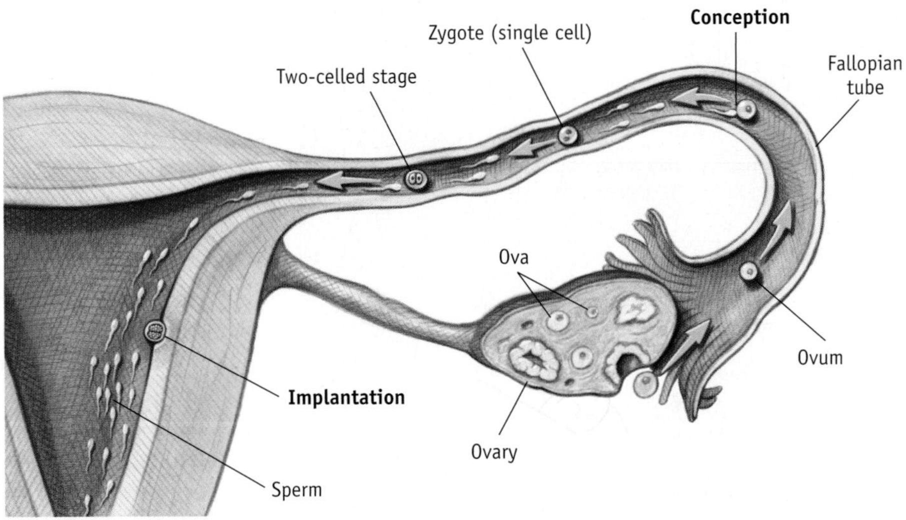

FIGURE 4.1 **The Most Dangerous Journey** In the first 10 days after conception, the organism does not increase in size because it is not yet nourished by the mother. However, the number of cells increases rapidly as the organism prepares for implantation, which occurs successfully about a third of the time.

About a week after conception, the multiplying cells (now numbering more than 100) separate into two distinct masses. The outer cells form a shell that will become the *placenta* (the organ that surrounds and protects the developing creature), and the inner cells form a nucleus that will become the embryo.

implantation Beginning about a week after conception, the burrowing of the zygote into the lining of the uterus, where it can be nourished and protected during growth.

The first task of the outer cells is to achieve **implantation**—that is, to embed themselves in the nurturing environment of the uterus. Implantation takes about a week and is far from automatic (Moore & Persaud, 2003). At least 60 percent of all natural conceptions and 70 percent of all in vitro conceptions fail to implant (see Table 4.2). Most new life ends even before the embryo begins to form and before the woman suspects she is pregnant. For those that survive, the woman's prepregnancy health, nutrition, and drug use are critical.

TABLE 4.1 Timing and Terminology

Popular and professional books use various phrases to segment pregnancy. The following comments may help to clarify the phrases used.

- *Beginning of pregnancy:* Pregnancy begins at conception, which is also the starting point of *gestational age*. However, the organism does not become an *embryo* until about two weeks later, and pregnancy does not affect the woman (and cannot be confirmed by blood or urine testing) until implantation. Paradoxically, many obstetricians date the onset of pregnancy from the date of the woman's last menstrual period (LMP), about 14 days *before* conception.
- *Length of pregnancy:* Full-term pregnancies last 266 days, or 38 weeks, or 9 months. If the LMP is used as the starting time, pregnancy lasts 40 weeks, sometimes expressed as 10 lunar months. (A lunar month is 28 days long.)
- *Trimesters:* Instead of *germinal period, embryonic period,* and *fetal period,* some writers divide pregnancy into three-month periods called *trimesters.* Months 1, 2, and 3 are called the *first trimester;* months 4, 5, and 6, the *second trimester;* and months 7, 8, and 9, the *third trimester.*
- *Due date:* Although doctors assign a specific due date (based on the woman's LMP), only 5 percent of babies are born on their exact due date. Babies born between three weeks before and two weeks after the due date are considered "on time." Babies born earlier are called *preterm;* babies born later are called *post-term.*

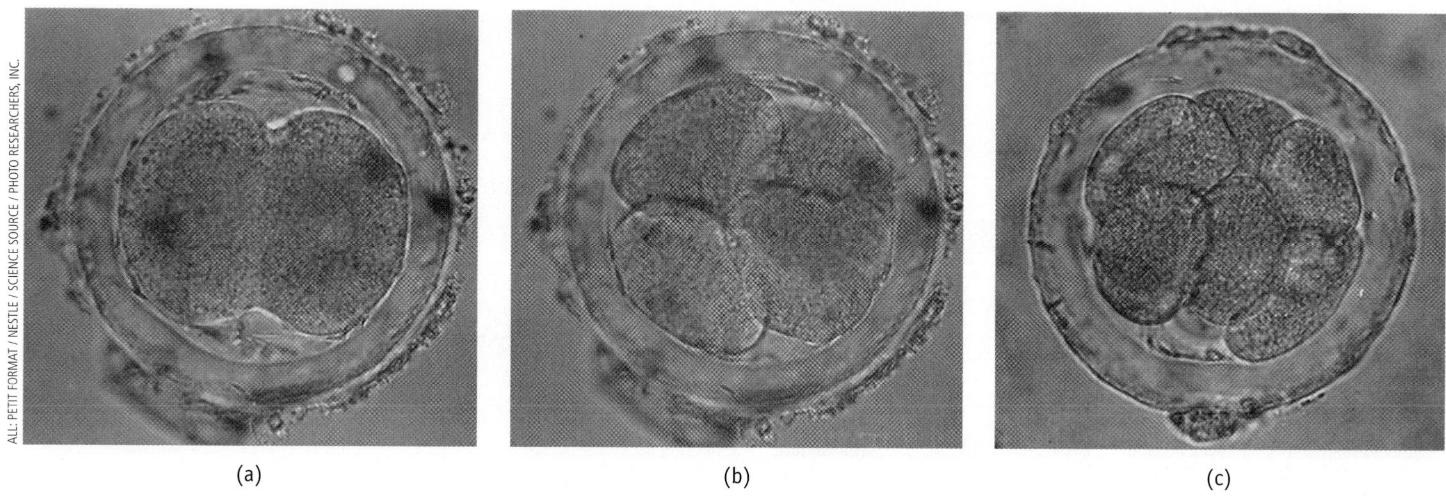

First Stages of the Germinal Period The original zygote as it divides into *(a)* two cells, *(b)* four cells, and *(c)* eight cells. Occasionally at this early stage, the cells separate completely, forming the beginning of monozygotic twins, quadruplets, or octuplets.

TABLE 4.2 **Vulnerability During Prenatal Development**

The Germinal Period
At least 60 percent of all developing organisms fail to grow or implant properly and thus do not survive the germinal period. Most of these organisms are grossly abnormal.

The Embryonic Period
About 20 percent of all embryos are aborted spontaneously, most often because of chromosomal abnormalities.

The Fetal Period
About 5 percent of all fetuses are aborted spontaneously before viability at 22 weeks or are stillborn, defined as born dead after 22 weeks.

Birth
About 31 percent of all zygotes grow and survive to become living newborn babies.

Sources: Bentley & Mascie-Taylor, 2000; Moore & Persaud, 2003.

Embryo: From the Third Through the Eighth Week

The start of the third week after conception initiates the *embryonic period,* during which the formless mass of cells becomes a distinct being—not yet recognizably human but worthy of a new name, **embryo.** The first sign of a human body structure appears as a thin line (called the *primitive streak*) down the middle of the embryo. This line becomes the neural tube 22 days after conception and eventually develops into the central nervous system, consisting of the brain and spinal column (Moore & Persaud, 2003).

embryo The name for the developing organism from about the third through the eighth week after conception.

The head begins to take shape in the fourth week, as eyes, ears, nose, and mouth start to form. Also in the fourth week, a minuscule blood vessel that will become the heart begins to pulsate, making the cardiovascular system the first to show any activity.

By the fifth week, buds that will become arms and legs appear, and a tail-like appendage extends from the spine. The upper arms and then forearms, palms, and webbed fingers appear. Legs, feet, and webbed toes, in that order, emerge a few days later, each having the beginning of a skeletal structure. Then—52 and 54 days after conception, respectively—the fingers and toes separate.

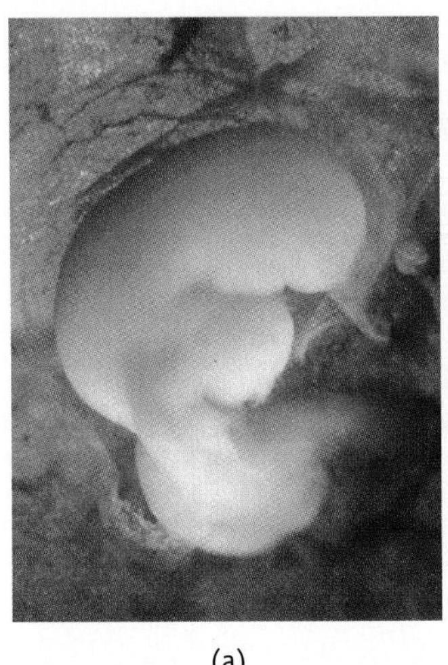
(a)

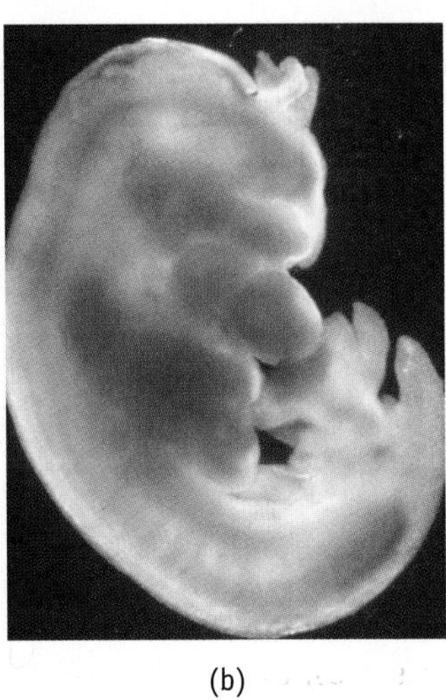
(b)

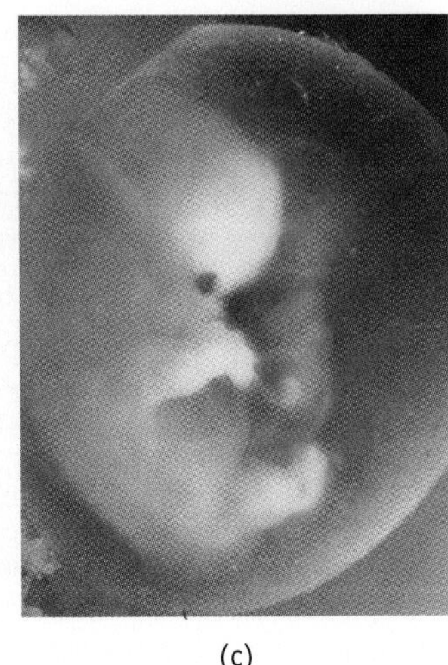
(c)

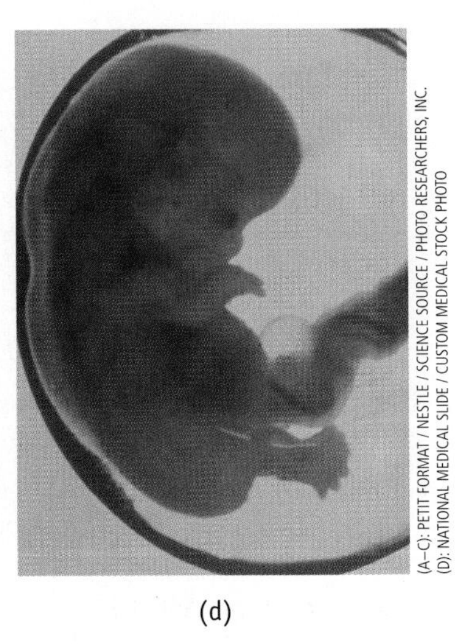
(d)

(A–C): PETIT FORMAT / NESTLE / SCIENCE SOURCE / PHOTO RESEARCHERS, INC. (D): NATIONAL MEDICAL SLIDE / CUSTOM MEDICAL STOCK PHOTO

The Embryonic Period *(a)* At 4 weeks past conception, the embryo is only about 1/8 inch (3 millimeters) long, but already the head (top right) has taken shape. *(b)* At 5 weeks past conception, the embryo has grown to twice the size it was at 4 weeks. Its primitive heart, which has been pulsing for a week now, is visible, as is what appears to be a primitive tail, which will soon be enclosed by skin and protective tissue at the tip of the backbone (the coccyx). *(c)* By 7 weeks, the organism is somewhat less than an inch (2½ centimeters) long. Eyes, nose, the digestive system, and even the first stage of toe formation can be seen. *(d)* At 8 weeks, the 1-inch-long organism is clearly recognizable as a human fetus.

At the eighth week after conception (56 days), the embryo weighs just one-thirtieth of an ounce (1 gram) and is about 1 inch (2½ centimeters) long. The head has become more rounded, and the features of the face have formed. The embryo has all the basic organs and body parts (except sex organs) of a human being, including elbows and knees. It moves frequently, about 150 times per hour, but such movement is random and imperceptible (Piontelli, 2002). Although it does not yet have male or female organs, by the sixth week it has an "indifferent gonad," which will become ovaries or testicles (as the case may be) and other sex organs early in the fetal period (Moore & Persaud, 2003).

Fetus: From the Ninth Week Until Birth

fetus The name for the developing organism from the ninth week after conception until birth.

The organism is called a **fetus** from the ninth week after conception until it is born. This period involves tremendous change, from a tiny, sexless creature smaller than the final joint of your thumb to a 7½-pound, 20-inch-long (3.4 kilograms, 51 centimeters) boy or girl.

The Third Month

ESPECIALLY FOR FEMINISTS Many people believe that the differences between the sexes are primarily sociocultural, not biological. Is there any prenatal support for that view?

If an embryo is male (XY), a gene on the Y chromosome signals the development of male sexual organs to begin in the ninth week; with no such signal (XX), the indifferent gonad develops into female sex organs (O'Rahilly & Muller, 2000). By the twelfth week, the genital organs are fully formed and are sending hormones to the developing brain. Although most functions of the brain are gender-neutral, some sex differences in brain organization will occur by mid-pregnancy (Cameron, 2001).

At the end of the third month, the fetus has all its body parts, weighs approximately 3 ounces (87 grams), and is about 3 inches (7.5 centimeters) long. Early prenatal growth is very rapid, but there is considerable variation from fetus to fetus, especially in body weight (Moore & Persaud, 2003). The numbers just given

—3 months, 3 ounces, 3 inches—are rounded off for easy recollection. (For those on the metric system, "100 days, 100 millimeters, 100 grams" is similarly useful.)

Despite the variations, some aspects of third-month growth are universal. The tiny fetus (smaller than an adult's finger) is too small to survive outside the womb, the organs are not yet functioning, but all the body structures are in place.

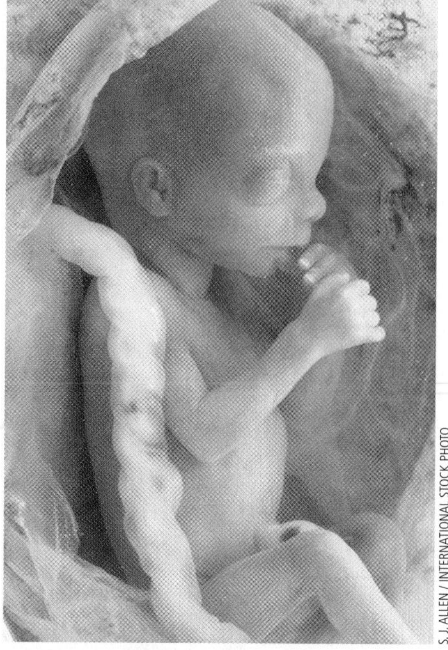

S. J. ALLEN / INTERNATIONAL STOCK PHOTO

The Fetus At the end of 4 months, the fetus, now 6 inches long, looks fully formed but out of proportion—the distance from the top of the skull to the neck is almost as large as that from the neck to the rump. For many more weeks, the fetus must depend on the translucent membranes of the placenta and umbilical cord (the long white object in the foreground) for survival.

? OBSERVATIONAL QUIZ (see answer, page 103): Can you see eyebrows, fingernails, and genitals?

The Middle Three Months: Preparing to Survive

In the fourth, fifth, and sixth months, the heartbeat becomes stronger and the cardiovascular system takes on a clearer form and more active function. Digestive and excretory systems develop. Fingernails, toenails, and buds for teeth form, and hair grows (including eyelashes).

Amazing as body growth is, the brain is even more impressive, increasing about six times in size and developing many new neurons (in a process called *neurogenesis*) and synapses, or connections between neurons (*synaptogenesis*). Also at this time the neurons (brain cells) begin to organize themselves, some dying, some extending long axons to distant neurons (Kolb & Whishaw, 2003). Brain growth and neurological organization continue for years, as you will see in later chapters (in which neurons, synapses, and axons are discussed and illustrated), but the entire central nervous system first becomes responsive and sentient during mid-pregnancy.

Advances in fetal brain functioning are critical in attaining the **age of viability,** the age at which a preterm newborn can survive. That's because the brain regulates basic body functions, such as breathing and sucking. With advanced medical care, the age of viability is about 22 weeks after conception. Babies born before 22 weeks rarely survive more than a few hours, because even the most sophisticated respirators and heart regulators cannot maintain life without some brain response. At 23–26 weeks, the survival rate improves, but 20 percent will have cerebral palsy, 41 percent will have some mental retardation, and only 20 percent will, by age 6, have no overall disability (Marlow et al., 2005).

age of viability The age (about 22 weeks after conception) at which a fetus can survive outside the mother's uterus if specialized medical care is available.

At about 28 weeks after conception, the brain-wave pattern includes occasional bursts of activity that resemble the sleep–wake cycles of a newborn (Joseph, 2000). Similarly, because of ongoing brain maturation, the heart rate becomes regulated by body movement (speeding up during activity, slowing during rest) between 28 and 32 weeks (DiPietro et al., 1996). Body movement itself becomes reactive, not random, actually decreasing in frequency when the fetus needs rest.

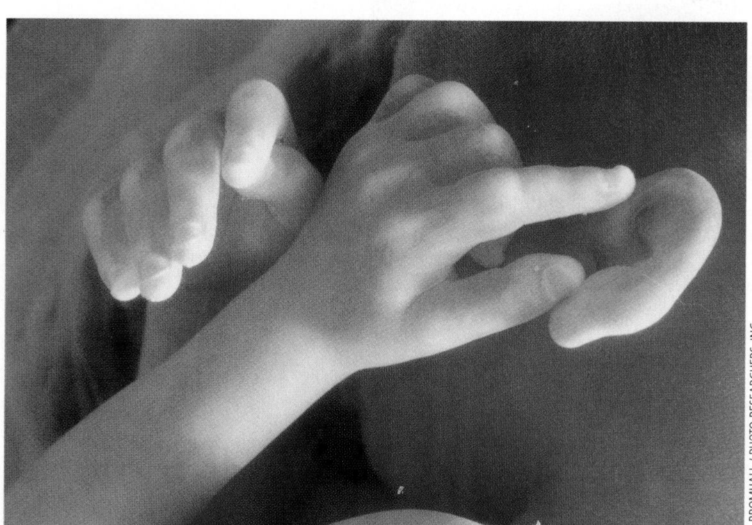

N. BROMHALL / PHOTO RESEARCHERS, INC.

Can He Hear? A fetus, just about at the age of viability, is shown fingering his ear. Such gestures are probably random; but, yes, he can hear.

TOM CARTER / PHOTOEDIT, INC.

Should They Have Stopped at Two? A third child will soon join this family. Most families in China and Italy have one child; most families in Africa have four; and most families in the United States, like this one, have two.

? OBSERVATIONAL QUIZ (see answer, page 104): What three things in this photograph suggest that this couple will cope well with a third child?

RESPONSE FOR FEMINISTS (from page 100): Only one of the 46 human chromosomes determines sex, and the genitals develop last in the prenatal sequence.

Largely because of this neurological awakening, the odds of survival are good for a preterm baby at least 28 weeks old.

Weight is also crucial. Even with excellent care, only 20 percent of those weighing less than 1½ pounds (680 grams) survive, usually with serious health problems (Sweet et al., 2003). By 28 weeks, the typical fetus weighs about 3 pounds (1.3 kilograms), and its chances of survival are 95 percent.

Maturity is even more crucial than birthweight, however. Some very tiny babies survive, but only if they are at least a few weeks past viability. Rumaisa Rahmon, currently the world's smallest surviving baby, was born in Chicago in September 2004 weighing only 8.6 ounces (244 grams). Rumaisa had four advantages besides her gestational maturity: her sex (girls are more likely to survive); her birthplace (Loyola University Hospital, which specializes in the care of extremely low-birthweight babies); her birth process (cesarean delivery, which is easier on the fetus); and the reason for her tiny size (because she was a twin, not because of maternal illness, malnutrition, or drug use). Rumaisa went home in February 2005 after gaining 5 pounds (2.2 kilograms). Her sister, Hiba, who weighed 1.3 pounds (600 grams) at birth, had gone home two months earlier. Both girls are expected to develop normally (BBC News Online, 2005).

The Final Three Months: From Viability to Full Term

Attaining viability simply means that life outside the womb is *possible*. Each day of the final three months of prenatal growth improves the odds not merely of survival but of a healthy and happy baby. A viable preterm infant born in the seventh month is a tiny creature requiring intensive hospital care and life-support systems for each gram of nourishment and for every shallow breath.

By contrast, after nine months or so, the typical full-term infant is a vigorous person, ready to thrive at home on mother's milk—no expert help, oxygenated air, or special feeding required.

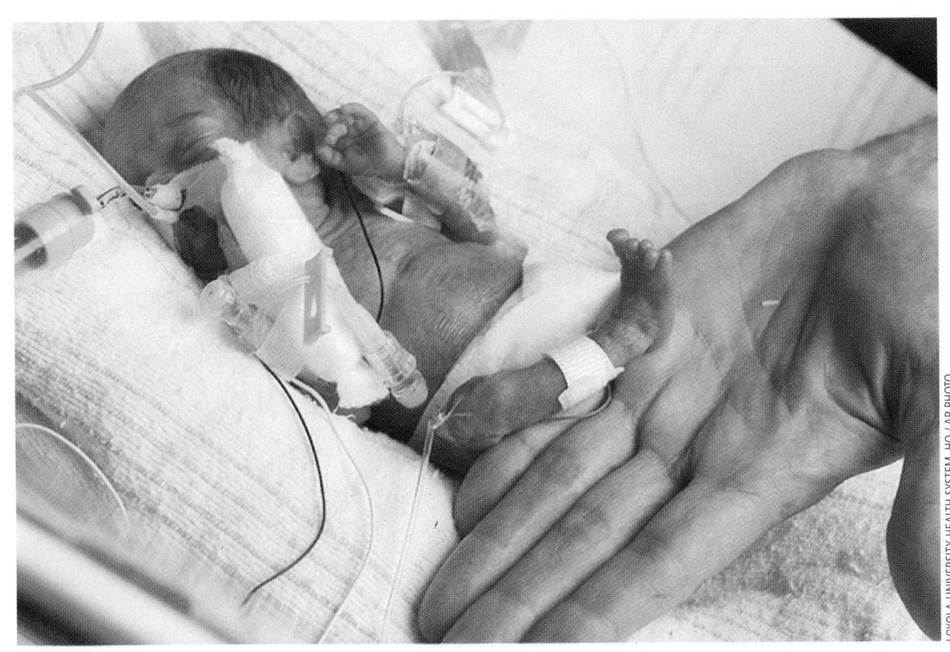

LOYOLA UNIVERSITY HEALTH SYSTEM, HO / AP PHOTO

The World's Littlest Baby For reasons discussed in the text, tiny Rumaisa Rahmon has a good chance of living a full, normal life.

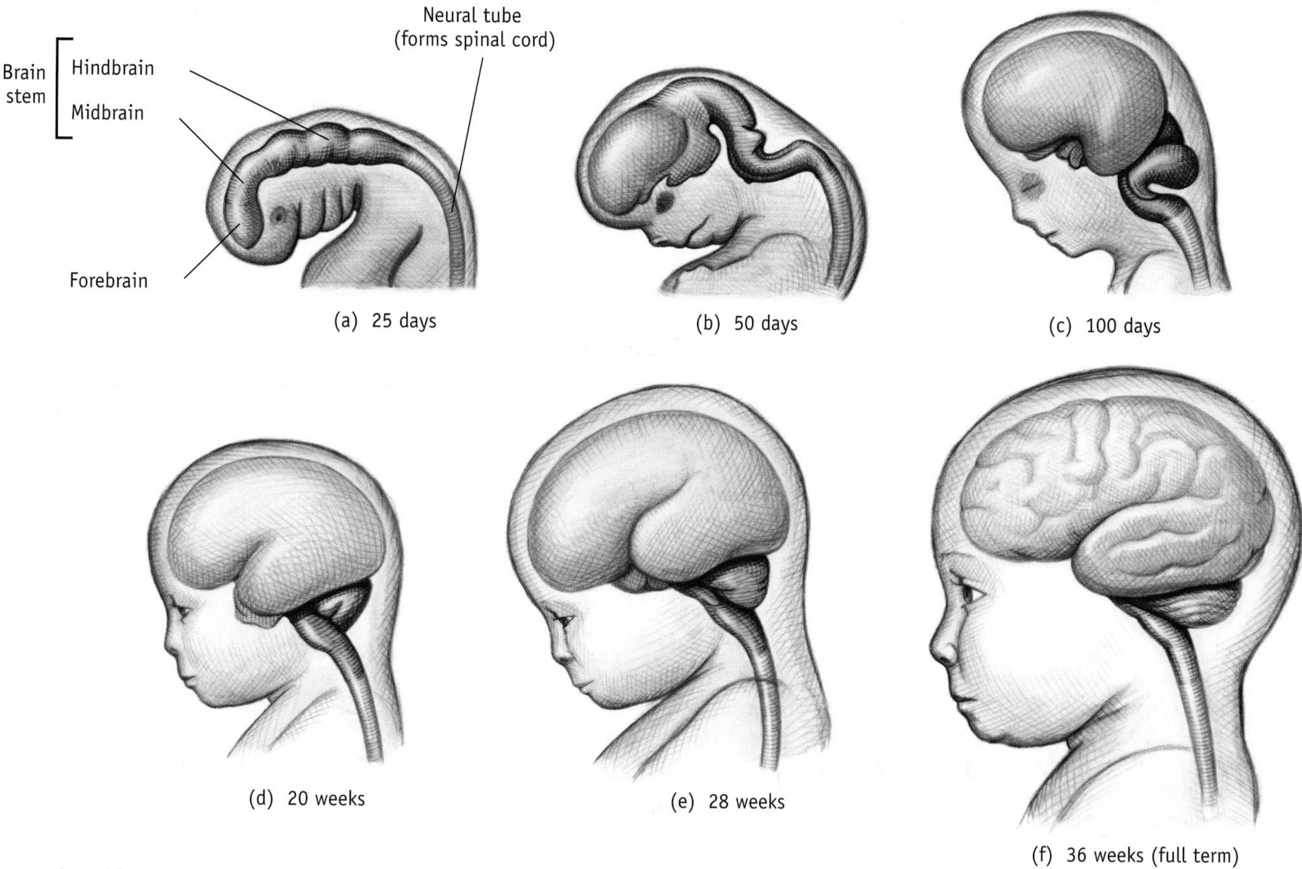

Source: Adapted from Cowan, 1997, p. 116.

FIGURE 4.2 **Prenatal Growth of the Brain** Just 25 days after conception *(a)*, the central nervous system is already evident. The brain looks distinctly human by day 100 *(c)*. By the 28th week of gestation *(e)*, at the very time brain activity begins, the various sections of the brain are recognizable. When the fetus is full term *(f)*, all the parts of the brain, including the cortex (the outer layer), are formed, folding over one another and becoming more convoluted, or wrinkled, as the number of brain cells increases.

The critical difference between a fragile preterm baby and a robust newborn is maturation of the neurological, respiratory, and cardiovascular systems. In the last three months of prenatal life, the lungs begin to expand and contract, exercising muscles involved in breathing by using the amniotic fluid as a substitute for air. The valves of the heart go through a final maturation, as do the arteries and veins throughout the body. Among other things, this helps to prevent "brain bleeds," a condition in which blood vessels in the skull collapse.

The fetus usually gains at least 4½ pounds (2 kilograms) in the third trimester, increasing body weight to about 7½ pounds (about 3.4 kilograms) at birth (see Table 4.3). This weight gain ensures that the developing brain is well nourished. Severe malnutrition in the second or third trimester reduces the future child's ability to learn (Georgieff & Rao, 2001). By full term, human brain growth is so extensive that the *cortex* (the brain's advanced outer layer) forms several folds in order to fit into the skull (see Figure 4.2).

The relationship between mother and child intensifies during the final three months, for fetal size and movements make the pregnant woman very aware of it. In turn, her sounds, smells (via amniotic fluid), and behavior become part of fetal consciousness. Communication can begin at the 28th week, as the fetus hears many sounds, including the mother's heartbeat and voice (Aslin & Hunt, 2001).

! ANSWER TO OBSERVATIONAL QUIZ (from page 101): Yes, yes, and no. Genitals are formed, but they are not visible in this photo. The object growing from the lower belly is the umbilical cord.

TABLE 4.3 AT ABOUT THIS TIME: **Average Prenatal Weights***

Period of Development	Weeks After Conception	Weight (Nonmetric)	Weight (Metric)	Notes
End of embryonic period	8	1/30 oz.	1 g	A birthweight less than 2 lb. (1,000 g) is considered extremely low birthweight (ELBW).
End of first trimester	13	3 oz.	100 g	
At viability (50/50 chance of survival)	22	20 oz.	570 g	
End of second trimester	26–28	2–3 lb.	1,000–1,300 g	Less than 3 lb. (1,300 g) is very low birthweight (VLBW). Less than 5½ lb. (2,500 g) is low birthweight (LBW).
End of preterm period	35	5½ lb.	2,500 g	Between 5½ and 9 lb. (2,500–4,500 g) is considered normal weight.
Full term	38	7½ lb.	3,400 g	

*To make them easier to remember, the weights are rounded off (which accounts for the inexact correspondence between metric and non-metric measures). Actual weights vary. For instance, a normal full-term infant can weigh between 5½ and 9 pounds (2.5 and 4 kilograms); a viable infant, especially one of several born at 26 or more weeks, can weigh less than shown here.

! ANSWER TO OBSERVATIONAL QUIZ (from page 102): Both parents appear to provide excellent care without anxiety or stress. The father seems used to carrying the 2-year-old, and the mother holds the older child's wrist to make sure she doesn't go astray. Moreover, the woman appears to take pregnancy in stride, wearing comfortable shoes and strolling at this Labor Day festival, just as her doctor would recommend.

The fetus becomes accustomed to the rhythm and tone of the sounds heard—music, conversation, or the mother's voice reading a book out loud. In addition, the fetus feels maternal movement: Regular walking is soothing, and sudden startles cause the fetus to jump. If the mother is highly fearful or anxious, the fetus's heart beats faster and body movements increase (DiPietro et al., 2002).

SUMMING UP

In two weeks of rapid cell duplication, differentiation, and finally implantation, the organism is transformed from a one-celled zygote to a many-celled embryo. The embryo soon develops the beginning of the central nervous system (3 weeks), a heart and a face (4 weeks), arms and legs (5 weeks), hands and feet (6 weeks), and fingers and toes (7 weeks), while the inner organs take shape. By 8 weeks, all the body structures, except male and female organs, are in place. Fetal development then proceeds rapidly, including mid-trimester weight gain (about 2 pounds, or 1 kilogram) and brain maturation, which make viability possible by about 22 weeks. At 7½ pounds (3.4 kilograms), the 35- to 40-week-old newborn is a survivor, born "on time" and ready for life.

Risk Reduction

ESPECIALLY FOR THE FRIEND OF A PREGNANT WOMAN Suppose that your friend is frightened of having an abnormal child. She refuses to read about prenatal development because she is afraid to learn about what could go wrong. What could you tell her?

teratogens Agents and conditions, including viruses, drugs, and chemicals, that can impair prenatal development and result in birth defects or even death.

Many toxins, illnesses, and experiences can harm a developing person before birth. If this topic alarms you, bear in mind that the large majority of newborns are healthy and capable. Only about 3 percent of all fetuses are born with major structural anomalies, such as cleft palate, malformed organs, or missing limbs (Moore & Persaud, 2003). In addition, most hazards can be avoided or their effects reduced.

Thus, prenatal development should be thought of not as a dangerous period to be feared but as a natural process to be protected. The goal of *teratology,* the study of birth defects, is to increase the odds that every newborn will have a healthy start. **Teratogens** are substances (such as drugs and pollutants) and conditions (such as severe malnutrition and extreme stress) that increase the risk of prenatal abnormalities.

Teratogens cause not only physical problems that are obvious at birth but also impaired learning and behavior. Teratogens that harm the brain and make a child hyperactive, antisocial, or learning-disabled are called **behavioral teratogens.** The causes of such problems are not easy to pinpoint, but about 20 percent of all children have difficulties that could be connected to behavioral teratogens.

behavioral teratogens Agents and conditions that can harm the prenatal brain, affecting the future child's intellectual and emotional functioning.

Determining Risk

Sixty years ago, it was believed that the placenta screened out all harmful substances, preventing them from reaching and damaging the fetus. Then two tragic episodes showed otherwise. An increase in babies born blind was traced to a rubella (measles) epidemic on an Australian military base (Gregg, 1941, reprinted in Persaud et al., 1985), and an increase in newborns with deformed limbs was traced to maternal use of thalidomide, a new drug widely prescribed in Europe (but not in the United States) in the late 1950s (Schardein, 1976).

Teratology is a science of **risk analysis,** of weighing the factors that affect the likelihood that a particular teratogen will cause harm. Understanding risk is crucial for understanding human development; every period of life entails certain risks, and much harm can be avoided. Although all teratogens increase the *risk* of harm, none *always* cause damage. The impact of teratogens depends on the interplay of many factors, both destructive and protective. Several of these factors—such as timing, dosage, and genetic vulnerability—are described below; others—such as early care, attachment, and education—are discussed in the three chapters on infancy (5, 6, and 7).

risk analysis The science of weighing the potential effects of a particular event, substance, or experience to determine the likelihood of harm. In teratology, risk analysis attempts to evaluate everything that affects the chances that a particular agent or condition will cause damage.

Timing of Exposure

One crucial factor is timing—the age of the developing organism when it is exposed to the teratogen. Some teratogens cause damage only during specific days early in prenatal development, when a particular part of the body is forming. Thalidomide was one such substance, halting the formation of arms and legs in weeks 6 or 7 but causing no damage after week 9. Others, such as rubella, can be harmful from week 3 until week 30, but the severity and site of the insult depend on when exposure occurs (Moore & Persaud, 2003).

The time of greatest susceptibility is called the **critical period.** As you can see in Figure 4.3, each body structure has its own critical period. The entire six weeks of the embryonic stage can be called a critical period for physical structure and form, with the specifics varying somewhat week by week (Moore & Persaud, 2003).

critical period In prenatal development, the time when a particular organ or other body part of the fetus is most susceptible to damage by teratogens.

Because the early days are critical, most obstetricians today recommend that *before* pregnancy, all couples get counseling, stop using recreational drugs (especially alcohol), and update their immunizations (Kuller et al., 2001). In addition, a prospective mother should make sure her body is ready by supplementing a balanced diet with extra folic acid and iron. Not all women follow these recommendations (see Table 4.4). Since the brain and nervous system can be harmed throughout prenatal development, there is no safe period for behavioral teratogens. Teratogens that cause preterm birth or low birthweight (notably cigarettes) are particularly harmful in the second half of pregnancy.

Amount of Exposure

A second important factor is the dose and/or frequency of exposure. Some teratogens have a **threshold effect;** that is, they are virtually harmless until exposure reaches a certain level, at which point they "cross the threshold" and become damaging (O'Rahilly & Muller, 2000). Indeed, a few substances are beneficial in small amounts but fiercely teratogenic in large quantities (Kraft &

threshold effect A situation in which a certain teratogen is relatively harmless in small doses but becomes harmful once exposure reaches a certain level (the threshold).

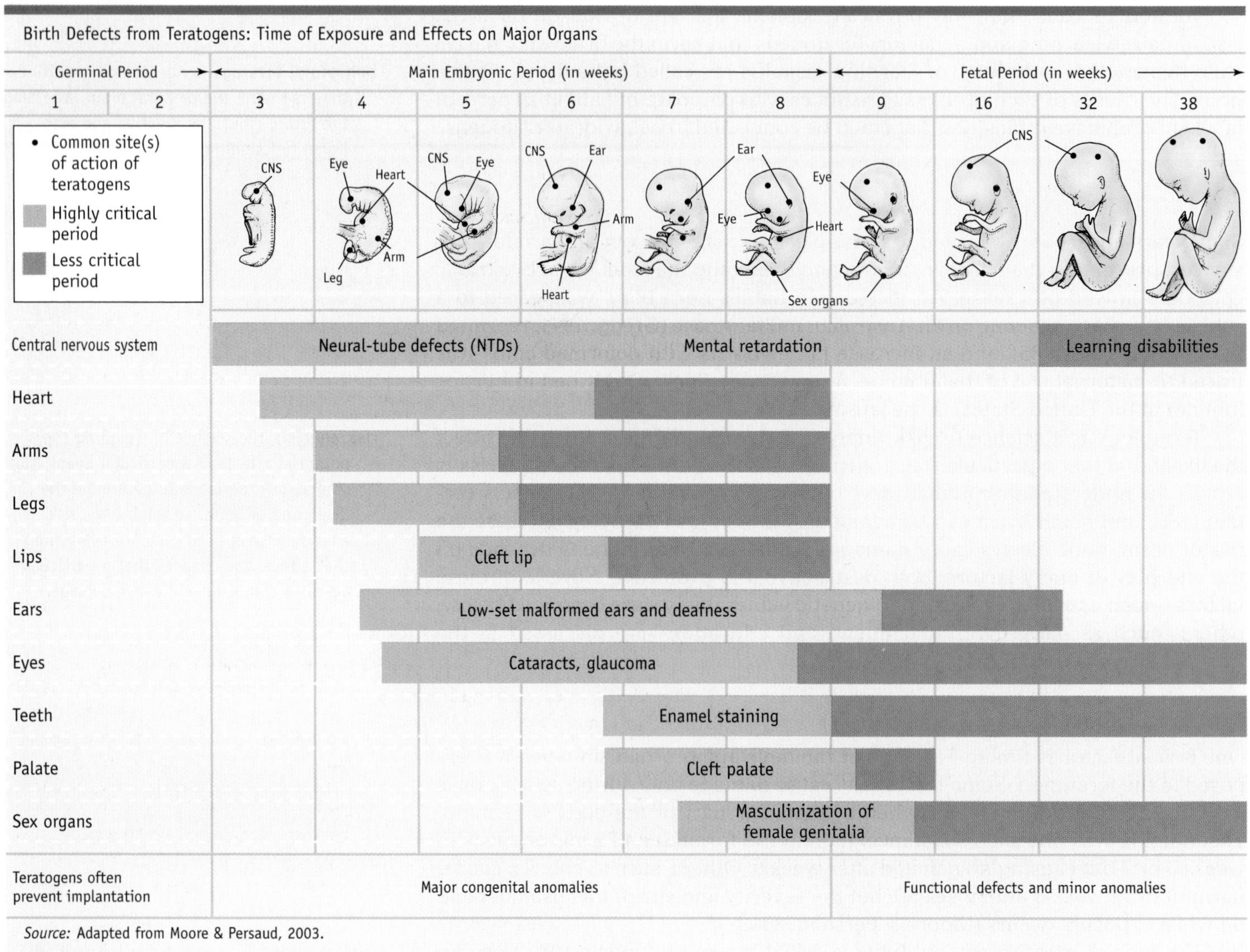

FIGURE 4.3 **Critical Periods in Human Development** The most serious damage from teratogens *(orange bars)* is likely to occur early in prenatal development. However, significant damage *(purple bars)* to many vital parts of the body, including the brain, eyes, and genitals, can occur during the last months of pregnancy as well.

Willhite, 1997). For example, vitamin A is an essential part of the prenatal diet, but more than 10,000 units per day may be too much and 50,000 units can cause abnormalities in body structures.

interaction effect The result of a combination of teratogens. Sometimes risk is greatly magnified when the embryo is exposed to more than one teratogen at the same time.

For most teratogens, experts are reluctant to specify a threshold below which the substance is safe. One reason is the **interaction effect** that occurs when one substance intensifies the effects of another. Alcohol, tobacco, and marijuana are among the substances that interact, doing more harm in combination than any one of them would do alone.

Genetic Vulnerability

A third factor that determines whether a specific teratogen will be harmful, and to what extent, is the developing organism's genes (O'Rahilly & Muller, 2000). When a woman carrying dizygotic twins drinks alcohol, for example, the twins' blood alcohol levels are equal, yet one twin may be more severely affected than

TABLE 4.4 **Before You Become Pregnant**

What the Prospective Mother Should Do	What the Prospective Mother Really Does
1. Take a daily multivitamin with folic acid.	1. In 2004, 40 percent of women aged 18 to 45 did so, up from 30 percent in previous years.
2. Avoid binge drinking (defined as 4 or more drinks in a row).	2. One-eighth of all women who might become pregnant (are sexually active, use no contraception) binge-drink (55 percent of them are alcoholics).
3. Update your immunizations against all teratogenic viruses, especially rubella.	3. Because of laws regarding school admission, most young women in the United States are well immunized.
4. Gain or lose weight, as appropriate.	4. Babies born to underweight women are at risk for low birthweight. Babies born to obese women have three times the usual rate of birth complications.
5. Reassess your use of prescription drugs.	5. Eighty-five percent of pregnant women are taking prescription drugs (not counting vitamins).
6. Know your status regarding sexually transmitted diseases.	6. Only a third of sexually active women get tested for the most common STD, chlamydia. Even fewer are screened for other, more dangerous infections, such as syphilis and HIV.

Sources: Andrade et al., 2004; MMWR, September 17, 2004; MMWR, October 29, 2004; MMWR, December 24, 2004; Cedergren, 2004.

the other (Maier et al., 1996). This difference probably involves a gene affecting the specific enzyme that metabolizes alcohol.

Genetic susceptibilities are probable in other birth disorders—including cleft lip, cleft palate, and club foot—that may result from a combination of genetic vulnerability and stress (Hartl & Jones, 1999). An international comparison of birth defects finds marked variability; for example, only 1 in 2,000 Canadian newborns has a cleft lip, compared to 1 in 600 Japanese newborns. Other birth defects have similar variability, with each nation (and sometimes even regions within nations) having relatively high rates of some specific defects and low rates of others (World Health Organization, 2003). Of course, pollutants and medical care affect the rate of birth defects, but the high *and* low rates within the same region suggest that people in some locales are more likely to have certain genetic vulnerabilities as well as genetic protections.

Genes are specifically implicated in the teratogenic effect of inadequate folic acid in the mother-to-be's diet. Deficiency of this B-complex vitamin can produce *neural-tube defects*—either *spina bifida,* in which the spine does not close properly, or *anencephaly,* in which part of the brain does not form.

Neural-tube defects occur more commonly in certain ethnic groups (specifically, Irish, English, and Egyptian) and less often in others (most Asian and African groups). That variability led researchers to identify a defective gene that produces a protein that prevents the normal utilization of folic acid (Mills et al., 1995). In 1996 the U.S. government mandated that all packaged bread and breakfast cereal be fortified with this vitamin. This law has been credited with a 26 percent reduction in the rate of neural-tube defects (MMWR, September 13, 2002). Canada mandated the addition of folic acid to all flour in 1998. About one-third of all young women are dieting, reducing their intake of baked goods containing flour and thus risking neural-tube defects in a genetically vulnerable fetus (MMWR, September 17, 2004).

In some cases, genetic vulnerability is related to the sex of the developing organism. Generally, males (XY) are at greater risk. This genetic vulnerability is one explanation for the more frequent spontaneous abortions of male than female fetuses. In addition, boys have more birth defects, learning disabilities, and other problems caused by behavioral teratogens.

RESPONSE FOR THE FRIEND OF A PREGNANT WOMAN (from page 104): Reassure her that almost all pregnancies turn out fine, partly because most defective fetuses are spontaneously aborted (miscarried) and partly because protective factors are active throughout pregnancy. Equally important, the more she learns about teratogens, the more she will learn about protecting her fetus. Many birth defects and complications can be prevented with good prenatal care.

ESPECIALLY FOR NUTRITIONISTS Is it beneficial that most breakfast cereals are fortified with vitamins and minerals?

Specific Teratogens

Because of the many variables involved, risk analysis cannot precisely predict the results of teratogenic exposure in individual cases. However, much is known about the most common and damaging teratogens and about how individuals and society can reduce the risks. Table 4.5 lists some teratogens and their possible effects, as well as preventive measures.

Remember that the effects vary a great deal. Although the table lists possible problems and practical interventions, many pregnant women are exposed to

TABLE 4.5 **Teratogens: Effects of Exposure and Prevention of Damage**

Teratogens	Effects on Child of Exposure	Measures for Preventing Damage
Diseases		
Rubella (German measles)	In embryonic period, causes blindness and deafness; in first and second trimesters, causes brain damage	Get immunized before becoming pregnant
Toxoplasmosis	Brain damage, loss of vision, mental retardation	Avoid eating undercooked meat and handling cat feces, garden dirt
Measles, chicken pox, influenza	May impair brain functioning	Get immunized before getting pregnant; avoid infected people during pregnancy
Syphilis	Baby is born with syphilis, which, untreated, leads to brain and bone damage and eventual death	Early prenatal diagnosis and treatment with antibiotics
AIDS	See Issues and Applications (p. 110) for a full discussion	
Other sexually transmitted diseases, including gonorrhea and chlamydia	Not usually harmful during pregnancy but may cause blindness and infections if transmitted during birth	Early diagnosis and treatment; if necessary, cesarean section, treatment of newborn
Infections, including infections of urinary tract, gums, and teeth	May cause premature labor, which increases vulnerability to brain damage	Get infection treated, preferably before becoming pregnant
Pollutants		
Lead, mercury, PCBs (polychlorinated biphenyls), dioxin, and some pesticides, herbicides, and cleaning compounds	May cause spontaneous abortion, preterm labor, and brain damage	Most common substances are harmless in small doses, but pregnant women should still avoid regular and direct exposure, such as drinking well water, eating unwashed fruits or vegetables, using chemical compounds, eating fish from polluted waters
Radiation		
Massive or repeated exposure to radiation, as in medical X-rays	In the embryonic period, may cause abnormally small head (microcephaly) and mental retardation; in the fetal period, suspected but not proven to cause brain damage. Exposure to background radiation, as from power plants, is usually too low to have an effect.	Get sonograms, not X-rays, during pregnancy; pregnant women who work directly with radiation need special protection or temporary assignment to another job
Social and Behavioral Factors		
Very high stress	Early in pregnancy, may cause cleft lip or cleft palate, spontaneous abortion, or preterm labor	Get adequate relaxation, rest, and sleep; reduce hours of employment; get more help with housework and child care
Malnutrition	When severe, may interfere with conception, implantation, normal fetal development, and full-term birth	Eat a balanced diet (with adequate vitamins and minerals, including, especially, folic acid, iron, and vitamin A); achieve normal weight before getting pregnant, then gain 25–35 lbs. (10–15 kg) during pregnancy
Excessive, exhausting exercise	Can affect fetal development when it interferes with pregnant woman's sleep or digestion	Get regular, moderate exercise

Teratogens	Effects on Child of Exposure	Measures for Preventing Damage
Medicinal Drugs		
Lithium	Can cause heart abnormalities	Avoid all medicines, whether prescription or over-the-counter, during pregnancy unless they are approved by a medical professional who knows about the pregnancy and is aware of the most recent research
Tetracycline	Can harm the teeth	
Retinoic acid	Can cause limb deformities	
Streptomycin	Can cause deafness	
ACE inhibitors	Can harm digestive organs	
Phenobarbital	Can affect brain development	
Thalidomide	Can stop ear and limb formation	
Psychoactive Drugs		
Caffeine	Normal use poses no problem	Avoid excessive use: Drink no more than three cups a day of beverages containing caffeine (coffee, tea, cola drinks, hot chocolate)
Alcohol	May cause fetal alcohol syndrome (FAS) or fetal alcohol effects (FAE) (see Issues and Applications, p. 110)	Stop or severely limit alcohol consumption during pregnancy; especially dangerous are three or more drinks a day or five or more drinks on one occasion
Tobacco	Increases risk of malformations of limbs and urinary tract, and may affect the baby's lungs	Stop smoking before and during pregnancy
Marijuana	Heavy exposure may affect the central nervous system; when smoked, may hinder fetal growth	Avoid or strictly limit marijuana consumption
Heroin	Slows fetal growth and may cause premature labor; newborns with heroin in their blood-stream require medical treatment to prevent the pain and convulsions of sudden withdrawal	Get treated for heroin addiction before becoming pregnant; if already pregnant, gradual withdrawal on methadone is better than continued use of heroin
Cocaine	May cause slow fetal growth, premature labor, and learning problems in the first years of life	Stop using cocaine before pregnancy; babies of cocaine-using mothers may need special medical and educational attention in their first years of life
Inhaled solvents (glue or aerosol)	May cause abnormally small head, crossed eyes, and other indications of brain damage	Stop sniffing inhalants before becoming pregnant; be aware that serious damage can occur before a woman knows she is pregnant

Note: This table summarizes some relatively common teratogenic effects. As the text makes clear, many individual factors in each pregnancy affect whether a given teratogen will actually cause damage and what that damage might be. This is a general summary of what is known; new evidence is reported almost daily, so some of these generalities will change. Pregnant women or women who want to become pregnant should consult with their physicians.
Sources: Brown, 1997; Larsen, 1998; Lyons & Rittner, 1998; Singer, 1999; O'Rahilly & Muller, 2000; Singer et al., 2002.

these teratogens with no evident harm to their fetuses, and some defects occur that are not listed. In fact, about 20 percent of all serious defects occur for reasons that are not known. Women are advised to avoid all possible teratogens, especially chemicals in products ranging from bug spray to hair dye, and to consult their doctors *before* becoming pregnant, because damage can occur in the critical first weeks.

Such advice is easy to give, but not always easy for pregnant women to follow. For instance, doctors recommend medication for HIV-positive women and abstinence from drinking for pregnant alcoholics, but not all women follow these recommendations. Moreover, doctors are not as careful as they might be. According to a massive study of 152,000 new mothers in eight health maintenance organizations (HMOs) in the United States, doctors wrote an average of three prescriptions per woman, including drugs that had not been declared safe during pregnancy (prescribed for 40 percent of pregnant women) and drugs with proven risks to fetuses (prescribed for 2 percent) (Andrade et al., 2004). Should the government intervene to protect the fetus? The following highlights this dilemma.

Response for Nutritionists (from page 107): Useful, yes; optimal, no. Some essential vitamins are missing (too expensive), and individual needs differ, depending on age, sex, health, genes, and eating habits. The reduction in neural-tube defects is good, but many women do not benefit because they don't eat enough packaged cereal or take vitamin supplements before becoming pregnant.

Especially for Social Workers
When is it most important to convince women to be tested for HIV: a month before pregnancy, a month after conception, or immediately after birth?

Issues and Applications

Should the Government Protect Fetuses from AIDS and Alcohol?

In the past few decades scientists have identified hundreds of teratogens that *might* harm an embryo or fetus. Almost every common disease, almost every food additive, most prescription and nonprescription drugs (even caffeine and aspirin), trace minerals in the air and water, emotional stress, exhaustion, and even hunger are suspected of impairing prenatal development—but only at some times, in some amounts, in some mammals. Most research on new substances has been done with mice; harm to humans is rarely proven to the satisfaction of every scientist. The idea of taking steps to prevent human birth defects that might or might not occur raises many ethical questions.

The most devastating viral teratogen is the **human immunodeficiency virus (HIV),** which gradually overwhelms the body's natural immune response and eventually leads to *AIDS (acquired immune deficiency syndrome)*. Pregnant women who do not know they are infected with HIV transmit the virus to their newborns in about 25 percent of cases, and unless medical treatment is obtained, infected babies usually die by age 5 (Parker, 2002).

Fortunately, pediatric AIDS can be prevented. In fact, the number of pediatric AIDS cases in the United States has declined significantly (see Figure 4.4). Pregnant women who know they are HIV- positive, whose prenatal care includes antiretroviral drugs beginning 14 weeks after conception, who give birth by cesarean section, and who do not breastfeed transmit the virus to their babies less than 1 percent of the time (Santora, 2005).

Still, almost a million HIV-positive children are born worldwide each year, half of them in sub-Saharan Africa, where most pregnant women with HIV receive no treatment (Leroy et al., 2002). Even in Brazil, where the drugs are free, and in India, where inexpensive combination drugs are used, many pregnant women who need the drugs do not take them. These women's sociocultural context is hostile to persons with AIDS. They fear that their husbands would leave them and their families shun them, so they avoid the stigma by avoiding treatment.

In view of these facts, should manufacturers, doctors, and governments make anti-AIDS drugs readily available to everyone throughout the world? If so, should pregnant women be allowed to refuse prenatal testing and treatment?

The rights and obligations of women are equally controversial regarding alcohol, the most common teratogen in North America (National Task Forces on Fetal Alcohol Syndrome and Fetal Alcohol Effects, 2002). Alcohol causes **fetal alcohol syndrome (FAS)** and a less damaging condition called *fetal alcohol effects (FAE)*.

With FAS, alcohol ingested during pregnancy affects development of the baby's facial features (especially the eyes, ears, and upper lip). Even if the newborn looks unharmed, alcohol can affect the brain, causing hyperactivity, poor concentration, impaired spatial reasoning, and slow learning (Streissguth & Conner, 2001). Although both FAS and FAE are dose-related (binge drinking is especially risky), genetic variation and interaction effects confound prediction about how much damage they may cause.

Given the seriousness of the potential damage, however, many experts advise women to abstain completely from alcohol (as well as from other psychoactive, or mood-altering, drugs, such as heroin, cocaine, and LSD). Total abstinence requires pregnant and potentially pregnant women to avoid alcohol, even though it is a legal substance that most adults, including more than half of all young women, use routinely.

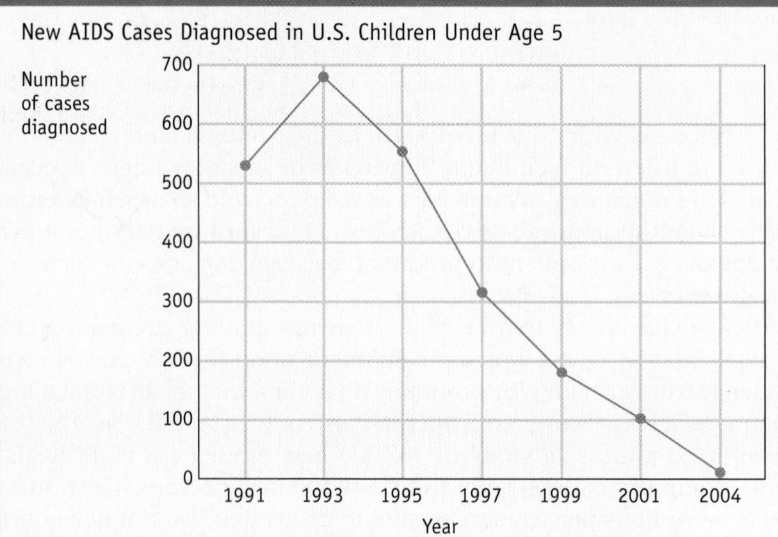

FIGURE 4.4 **Down to Just 11 a Year** The number of young children diagnosed with AIDS has fallen dramatically over the past decade in the United States. The rate of decline is much greater than that for older children and adults. The reason is the reduction in mother-to-child transmission—thanks to better drugs as well as better understanding of the process of infection. In less developed nations, the incidence of pediatric AIDS continues to increase.

STEPHEN NICHOLAS

Hope for the Future Marilis and Anol, of the Dominican Republic, are especially delighted with their 18-month-old daughter, Yolanda, because their first child died of AIDS at age 2. Both parents are HIV-positive, but Yolanda is not. To avoid transmitting the virus to her baby, Marilis took the anti-AIDS drug AZT during her pregnancy, delivered Yolanda by cesarean section, and gives the baby formula rather than breast milk. Yolanda, too, received AZT for the first six weeks of her life. Marilis and Anol hope that their story will inspire other people to do all they can to reduce the transmission of HIV.

Again, difficult public policy questions arise: *Should pregnant women be allowed to drink if they choose? Should governments intervene, imprisoning pregnant drinkers? If so, should a pregnant drinker's husband, mother, or bartender also be punished for not preventing her from drinking?*

The policy dilemmas are compounded by the data on risk analysis. First of all, with both AIDS and alcohol, many fetuses are exposed but unharmed. Further, many HIV-positive or alcoholic women have other problems: drug abuse; unstable eating and sleeping patterns; bouts of anxiety, stress, or depression; accidental injuries; domestic violence; sexual infections; malnutrition; illnesses; lack of family support; and inadequate medical care. And these problems may continue after birth, making matters worse for the infant. Thus, unless FAS is apparent in facial deformities, a child's learning difficulties may not be traced directly to prenatal alcohol, and unless the HIV-positive newborn is tested, his or her health problems may seem to result from inadequate parenting.

Similarly, many teachers and school psychologists blame children's learning difficulties on their mothers' use of crack cocaine, but even experienced assessors often guess wrong about which preschool children with learning problems were prenatally exposed to cocaine and which were not (Rose-Jacobs et al., 2002). Longitudinal research finds only subtle effects of prenatal cocaine, and these effects are not apparent in every case (Frank et al., 2001; Seifer et al., 2004). The cocaine-using mother and her infant almost always need intervention for many other reasons, and the same is probably true of women who use other drugs.

Should women who might become pregnant (unlike men) be required to be tested for HIV and then to take antiretroviral drugs if they conceive? Should women be required to abstain from alcohol (as well as from other drugs) before and throughout pregnancy? High-dose drug use is undeniably risky, as is use of multiple drugs. Even occasional use of a small amount of any psychoactive drug is not recommended. But for government officials to target only one teratogen or to use only one strategy—coercion by threat of punishment—would be to ignore the complexity of risk analysis, teratology, and individual human differences.

BOTH: GEORGE STEINMETZ

Differences and Similarities The differences between these two children are obvious at a glance: One is an African American teenager, the other a Swedish toddler. One similarity is obvious, too: Both are girls. However, the most important similarity—fetal alcohol syndrome—is apparent only on closer observation. Among the visible characteristics of FAS are abnormally spaced eyes and a thin upper lip.

human immunodeficiency virus (HIV) The virus that causes AIDS (acquired immune deficiency syndrome), in which the body's immune system is gradually overwhelmed and the individual becomes vulnerable to opportunistic infections. Even with treatment, AIDS eventually leads to death from any of several opportunistic diseases.

fetal alcohol syndrome (FAS) A cluster of birth defects, including abnormal facial characteristics, slow physical growth, and retarded mental development, caused by the mother's drinking alcohol when pregnant.

Knowledge and Responsibility

There are many advantages to obtaining early prenatal care. Chief among them is protection against teratogens—knowing what medicines to avoid or what foods to eat, for instance. Some deadly teratogens, notably syphilis and AIDS, are less likely to harm the fetus if the woman is diagnosed and treated early in pregnancy. Many prenatal tests can reassure a nervous couple, and the first image of their fetus on a sonogram is often taped to a refrigerator for frequent viewing. (Table 4.6 provides information about sonograms and other prenatal tests.)

Birth is more likely to be problem-free if pregnancy is confirmed early, if twins are detected by the 12th week, if drug use is halted before mid-pregnancy, and so on. However, about 20 percent of early pregnancy tests suggest that all is not well. For instance, the level of alpha-fetoprotein (AFP) may be too high or too low, or a sonogram may indicate multiple fetuses or a too-narrow pelvis. Many such warnings are "false positives," which means they suggest the presence of an abnormality that does not actually exist. Such false alarms produce needless

TABLE 4.6 **Methods of Postconception Testing**

Method	Description	Risks, Concerns, and Indications
Pre-implantation testing	After in vitro fertilization, one cell is removed from each zygote at the four- or eight-cell stage and analyzed.	Requires in vitro fertilization and is not entirely accurate. Requires surgery, in vitro fertilization, and rapid assessment. This delays implantation and reduces the likelihood of successful birth. It is used only when couples are at high risk of known, testable genetic disorders.
Alpha-fetoprotein assay	The mother's blood is tested for the level of alpha-fetoprotein (AFP).	Indicates neural-tube defects, multiple embryos (both cause high AFP), or Down syndrome (low AFP). Normal levels change each week; interpretation requires accurate dating of conception. The test itself is not risky, but high or low AFP levels indicate that additional testing is needed. About 10 percent of all pregnant women exhibit high or low AFP, but 98 percent of these are false positives. This may cause needless worry. Can also yield a false negative, suggesting no problem when there is actually a defect.
Sonogram (ultrasound)	High-frequency sound waves are used to produce a "picture" of the fetus. This can be done as early as 8 weeks. Sonograms are more accurate later in pregnancy, and can be done several times, to detect less apparent problems, to confirm earlier suspicions, and to anticipate birth complications.	Reveals problems such as a small head or other body malformations, excess fluid accumulating on the brain, Down syndrome, and several diseases (for instance, of the kidneys). Estimates fetal age and reveals multiple fetuses, placental position, and fetal growth, all of which are useful in every pregnancy. Sometimes sex is apparent. No known risks, unlike the X-rays that it has replaced.
Chorionic villi sampling (CVS)	A sample of the chorion (part of the placenta) is obtained (via sonogram and syringe) at about 10 weeks and analyzed. Since the cells of the placenta are genetically identical to the cells of the fetus, this can indicate many chromosomal or genetic abnormalities.	Provides the same information as amniocentesis but can be performed earlier. Can cause a spontaneous abortion (1%)
Amniocentesis	About half an ounce of the fluid inside the placenta is withdrawn (via sonogram and syringe) at about 16 weeks. The cells are cultured and analyzed, a process that takes about a week.	Detects chromosomal abnormalities and other genetic and prenatal problems. The amniotic fluid also reveals the sex of the fetus. Is done later in pregnancy than other tests, and it takes a week or more before results are known. Can cause spontaneous abortion (1% of cases). Has largely been replaced by CVS.

Sources: Harmon, 2004; Moore & Persaud, 2003; Newnham et al., 2004; Philip et al., 2004.

anxiety, which might be problematic for the expectant couple, especially if the problem is sufficiently serious that a decision to terminate the pregnancy is a possibility, as shown in the following case.

A CASE TO STUDY

"What Do People Live to Do?"

John and Martha, graduate students at Harvard, were expecting their second child. Martha was four months pregnant, and her initial prenatal screening revealed an abnormally low level of alpha-fetoprotein, which could indicate that the fetus had Down syndrome. It was too early for amniocentesis, a more definitive test, so another blood test was scheduled to doublecheck the AFP level.

John met Martha at a café after a nurse had drawn the second blood sample, before the laboratory reported the test result. Later, Martha wrote about their conversation.

> "Did they tell you anything about the test?" John said. "What exactly is the problem?" . . .
>
> "We've got a one in eight hundred and ninety-five shot at a retarded baby."
>
> John smiled, "I can live with those odds."
>
> I tried to smile back, but I couldn't. . . . I wanted to tell John about the worry in my gut. I wanted to tell him that it was more than worry—that it was a certainty. Then I realized all over again how preposterous that was. "I'm still a little scared."
>
> He reached across the table for my hand. "Sure," he said, "That's understandable. But even if there is a problem, we've caught it in time. . . . The worst case scenario is that you might have to have an abortion, and that's a long shot. Everything's going to be fine."
>
> . . . "I might *have to have* an abortion?" The chill inside me was gone. Instead I could feel my face flushing hot with anger. "Since when do you decide what I *have to* do with my body?"
>
> John looked surprised. "I never said I was going to decide anything," he protested. "It's just that if the tests show something wrong with the baby, of course we'll abort. We've talked about this."
>
> "What we've talked about," I told John in a low, dangerous voice, "is that I am pro-choice. That means I decide whether or not I'd abort a baby with a birth defect. . . . I'm not so sure of this."
>
> "You used to be," said John.
>
> "I know I used to be." I rubbed my eyes. I felt terribly confused. "But now . . . look, John, it's not as though we're deciding whether or not to have a baby. We're deciding what *kind* of baby we're willing to accept. If it's perfect in every way, we keep it. If it doesn't fit the right specifications, whoosh! Out it goes." . . .
>
> John was looking more and more confused. "Martha, why are you on this soapbox? What's your point?"
>
> "My point is," I said, "that I'm trying to get you to tell me what you think constitutes a 'defective' baby. What about . . . oh, I don't know, a hyperactive baby? Or an ugly one?"
>
> "They can't test for those things and—"
>
> "Well, what if they could?" I said. "Medicine can do all kinds of magical tricks these days. Pretty soon we're going to be aborting babies because they have the gene for alcoholism, or homosexuality, or manic depression. . . . Did you know that in China they abort a lot of fetuses just because they're female?" I growled. "Is being a girl 'defective' enough for you?"
>
> "Look," he said, "I know I can't always see things from your perspective. And I'm sorry about that. But the way I see it, if a baby is going to be deformed or something, abortion is a way to keep everyone from suffering—*especially* the baby. It's like shooting a horse that's broken its leg. . . . A lame horse dies slowly, you know? . . . It dies in terrible pain. And it can't run anymore. So it can't enjoy life even if it doesn't die. Horses live to run; that's what they do. If a baby is born not being able to do what other people do, I think it's better not to prolong its suffering."
>
> ". . . And what is it," I said softly, more to myself than to John, "what is it that people do? What do we live to do, the way a horse lives to run?"
>
> *[Beck, 1999, pp. 132–133, 135]*

The second AFP test came back low but in the normal range, "meaning there was no reason to fear that [the fetus] had Down syndrome" (p. 137).

Note that John thought they had already discussed and decided to abort a fetus if a serious problem were evident. However, the stress of an unexpected abnormality distresses many prospective parents. As you read in Chapter 3, a genetic counselor not only explains the odds but also helps a couple discuss their choices *before* becoming pregnant. John and Martha had not sought counseling before conceiving because the pregnancy was unexpected and because their risk for any problems, especially chromosomal ones, was low.

The opposite of the false positive is the false negative, a mistaken assurance that all is well. Even though the second AFP test revealed that there was no problem, Martha wrote, she had "a worry in my gut." She had amniocentesis later in her pregnancy and learned that the second AFP score had been a false negative. Her fetus had Down syndrome after all. Still, Martha decided against abortion.

Before they conceive, many couples are very definite about whether or not they would carry a severely abnormal fetus to term. But, as the dialogue between Martha and John reveals, couples tend to be much less certain once pregnancy occurs. Consider another difficult case.

A Case to Study

"What Did That Say About Me?"

When Tom Horan and his wife learned in April [2004] that their fetus' legs were bowed and shortened, they were told that the condition could be healed through braces, growth hormones, and surgical procedures in childhood.

But before they decided what to do, a closer examination by a specialist with a 3-D ultrasound machine revealed other deformities: the left arm was missing below the elbow and the right hand was only partially developed. Moreover, sometimes such features are a sign of a neurological impairment, the doctors told them, but in this case it was impossible to tell.

"Our main concern was the quality of life that the child would having growing up with such extensive limb deformities, even in the absence of cognitive problems," Mr. Horan said. He and his wife, who have three other children, were reared Roman Catholic and had never considered terminating a pregnancy. Yet even his father, Mr. Horan said, who had long been opposed to abortion, supported their decision to end the pregnancy.

"Confronted with this question and knowing what we knew, it changed his mind," Mr. Horan said. "It's not just a question of right and wrong; it introduces all sorts of other questions that one has to consider, whether it is the survivability of the child, quality of life of parents, quality of life of siblings, social needs. And it becomes much more real when you're confronted with an actual situation."

After the termination, an examination showed . . . an extremely rare condition, Cornelia de Lange syndrome. [The baby] would have been severely mentally and physically disabled.

The news was a relief to Mr. Horan, who said he felt sadness and grief, but no regrets . . . . Before the diagnosis, he felt guilt and uncertainty. . . . "I wondered about the ethical implications. . . . What did that say about me?"

[Harmon, 2004, p. 22]

Confronted with the information provided by the ultrasound test, the Horans found that they had to reexamine their values. As one review reports, "Most couples say they are both profoundly grateful for the new information and hugely burdened by the choices it forces them to make" (Harmon, 2004, p. 1).

In such situations, genetic counselors, members of the clergy, and doctors are crucial. Some of these advisers are more skilled than others. After one newborn died with a trisomy, a newly pregnant couple disagreed about amniocentesis. The woman wanted it, but the man didn't. The husband asked the counselor, "Well, what are we to do?" The counselor answered, "It's not my problem. I am not you. You'll have to come to some resolution with your conscience and work it out with your wife" (quoted in Kessler, 2000, p. 154).

A more helpful answer was suggested by an expert on genetic counseling: "When you ask me 'What are we to do?' what do you see as the problem?" (quoted in Kessler, 2000, p. 156). This response would challenge the couple to identify the aspects of the situation that were critical for them: religious beliefs, marital bonding, other children, fear of losing another newborn, tolerance for risk, feelings of shame and guilt, ability to raise a child with serious medical or psychological problems.

Members of the medical profession usually decide which tests should be done, and doctors differ in how they present prenatal testing to prospective parents. For instance, in a British hospital that required doctors to offer genetic tests to all pregnant women, one doctor spoke to a patient of the "tremendous amount of heartache if we get a false positive"; another told a patient to begin by asking herself, "How do I feel about having a Down syndrome baby?" and to work back from there (quoted in Heyman & Henriksen, 2001, pp. 100, 145). Not surprisingly, the patient of the first doctor decided against genetic testing, and the second doctor's patient decided to have amniocentesis.

Response for Social Workers (from page 109): Testing and then treatment are useful at any time, because women who know they are HIV-positive are more likely to get treatment, reduce risk of transmission, and avoid pregnancy. If pregnancy does occur, early diagnosis is best. Getting tested after birth is too late for the baby.

We should emphasize again that most newborns are fine, and that research and medical care work to safeguard many pregnancies that would have ended in tragedy a few decades ago. Worldwide, only nations with scarce and inadequate medical care have a neonatal death rate of 10 percent or higher.

We should also recognize that medical testing can pose difficult dilemmas for everyone. This was recognized explicitly by Martha, the woman in the first Case to Study above. She was talking to a group about her decision to give birth to her fetus with Down syndrome. A woman in the audience said that she had been in the same situation but had made the "wrong" decision. Martha replied that there was no right or wrong decision; every decision about prenatal testing is difficult, and each choice has costs (Beck, 1999).

Low Birthweight

Insufficient body weight is sometimes considered a *birth* complication, not a prenatal one. However, we discuss it here because low birthweight is caused by teratogens and other factors during, and even before, pregnancy.

Low birthweight (LBW) is defined by the World Health Organization as a body weight of less than 5½ pounds (2.5 kilograms) at birth. LBW babies are further grouped into **very low birthweight (VLBW)**, a weight of less than 3 pounds (1.3 kilograms), and **extremely low birthweight (ELBW)**, a weight of less than about 2 pounds (1 kilogram).

The rate of LBW varies widely from nation to nation (see Figure 4.5). The U.S. rate of 8 percent in 2002 was the highest it had been in more than 30 years (see Figure 4.6) (Hamilton et al., 2004).

Remember that fetal body weight normally doubles in the last trimester of pregnancy, with a typical gain of almost 2 pounds (900 grams) occurring in the final three weeks. Thus, a baby born **preterm**, defined as 3 or more weeks before the standard 38 weeks, usually (though not always) is LBW.

Although most preterm babies are LBW, some full-term babies are underweight as well. Some fetuses gain weight too slowly throughout pregnancy. They are called *small-for-dates* or **small for gestational age (SGA).** An underweight

low birthweight (LBW) A body weight at birth of less than 5½ pounds (2.5 kilograms). The cause could be slow growth during prenatal development, or birth before 36 weeks of gestation, or both.

very low birthweight (VLBW) A body weight at birth of less than 3 pounds (1.3 kilograms).

extremely low birthweight (ELBW) A body weight at birth of less than 2 pounds (1 kilogram).

preterm birth Birth that occurs 3 weeks or more before the full term of pregnancy has elapsed—that is, at 35 or fewer weeks after conception.

small for gestational age (SGA) A term for a baby whose birthweight is significantly lower than expected, given the time since conception. For example, a 5-pound (2.2-kilogram) newborn is SGA if born on time but not SGA if born two months early. (Also called *small-for-dates*.)

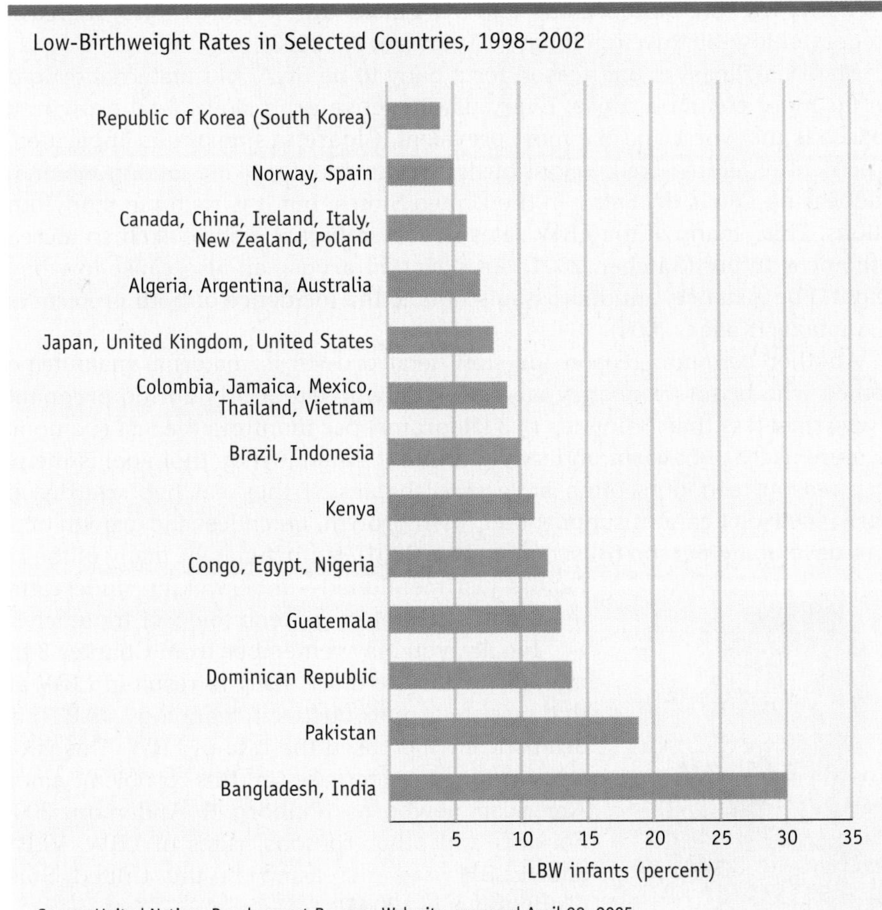

FIGURE 4.5 **Low Birthweight Around the World** The LBW rate is often considered a reflection of a country's commitment to its children as well as of its economic resources.

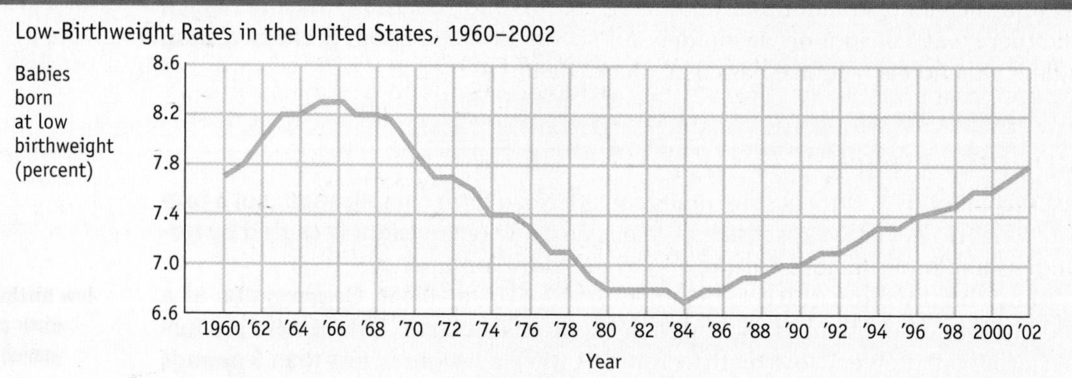

Source: U.S. Bureau of the Census, 2002; Martin et al., 2002; National Center for Health Statistics Web site, accessed April 22,2005.

FIGURE 4.6 **Not Improving** The LBW rate is often taken to be a measure of a nation's overall health. In the United States, the rise and fall of this rate are related to many factors, among them prenatal care, maternal use of drugs, overall nutrition, and number of multiple births.

? OBSERVATIONAL QUIZ (see answer, page 118): In what year was one out of every 13 U.S. babies (7.5 percent) born weighing less than 5½ pounds (2.5 kilograms)?

SGA infant causes more concern than an underweight preterm birth, because SGA signifies impairment throughout the pregnancy. To prevent the neurological consequences of continued slow growth, birth may be induced early. Newborns who are *both* preterm and SGA make up the most rapidly increasing category of low-birthweight infants (Ananth et al., 2003).

Maternal illness is one reason for a baby to be SGA, but maternal drug use is a far more common cause. Every psychoactive drug slows fetal growth, but tobacco is the worst and the most prevalent. Cigarette smoking is implicated in 25 percent of all low-birthweight births worldwide. Smoking among women of childbearing age is declining in the United States, but it is rising in many other nations. Thus, many of the LBW rates shown in Figure 4.5 are likely to increase in the near future (Satcher, 2001). Prescription drugs can also cause low birthweight. For instance, antidepressants double the incidence of both preterm and SGA infants (Källén, 2004).

Another common reason for slow fetal growth is maternal malnutrition. Women who begin pregnancy underweight, who eat poorly during pregnancy, or who gain less than 3 pounds (1.3 kilograms) per month in the last six months are more likely to have an underweight infant. Malnutrition (not age) is the primary reason teenagers often have small babies: If they eat haphazardly and poorly, their diet cannot support their own growth, much less the growth of another developing person (Buschman et al., 2001). Unfortunately, many of the risk factors just mentioned—underweight, undereating, underage, and smoking—tend to occur together.

Finally, you may remember from Chapter 3 that multiple births are more likely to result in LBW and that assisted reproductive technology (ART) has dramatically increased the rate of LBW. This is one reason for the increase in this problem among American newborns (Pinborg & Anderson, 2004). For this and other reasons, rates of LBW, VLBW, and ELBW are increasing in the United States (Hamilton et al., 2004).

Which Baby Is Oldest? The baby at the left is the oldest, at almost 1 month; the baby at the right is the youngest, at just 2 days. Are you surprised? The explanation is that the 1-month-old was born 9 weeks early and now, at 7½ weeks, weighs less than 5½ pounds (2.5 kilograms); the 2-day-old was full-term and weighs almost 8 pounds (3.6 kilograms). The baby in the middle, born full-term but weighing only 2 pounds (1 kilogram), is the most worrisome. Her ears and hands are larger than the preterm baby's, but her skull is small; malnutrition may have deprived her brain as well as her body.

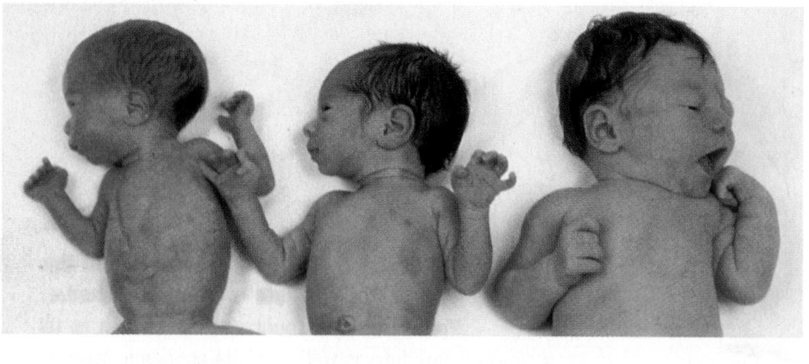

RON SUTHERLAND / SCIENCE PHOTO LIBRARY / PHOTO RESEARCHERS, INC.

None of the factors that impede or interrupt normal prenatal growth are inevitable. Quality of medical care, education, culture, and social support affect every developing person before birth, via their impact on the pregnant woman. The importance of these factors is made starkly evident in data from Gambia, a poor nation in Africa. Preterm births are highest (17 percent) in July, when women usually work long hours in the fields. SGA births are more common (31 percent) in November, the end of the "hungry season," when most women had been undernourished for three months or more (Rayco-Solon et al., 2005).

Fathers and other relatives, neighbors, cultures, clinics, and other factors can reduce risks markedly. For example, the rate of low birthweight among Mexican Americans is lower than the overall U.S. rate because families are more likely to make sure that their pregnant members do not smoke, drink, or undereat.

Especially for Women of Child-bearing Age If you have decided to become pregnant soon, you cannot change your genes, your age, or your economic status. But you can do three things in the next month or two that can markedly reduce the risk of having a low-birthweight or otherwise impaired baby a year from now. What are they?

SUMMING UP

Risk analysis is a complex but necessary aspect of prenatal development because the placenta does not protect the fetus from all hazards, especially diseases, drugs, and pollutants. Many factors reduce risk, including the mother's health and nourishment before pregnancy and early prenatal care (to diagnose and treat problems and to teach the woman how to protect her fetus). Risk is affected by dose and frequency of teratogens, as well as by the fetus's genetic vulnerability and stage of development. Prenatal testing often reassures the prospective parents, but it can reveal severe problems that require them to make difficult decisions. If the fetus gains weight slowly or is born preterm as a result of maternal illness, drug use, or malnutrition, low birthweight increases vulnerability to birth defects.

The Birth Process

For a full-term fetus and a healthy mother, birth can be simple and quick. At some time during the last month of pregnancy, most fetuses change position, turning upside down so that the head is low in the mother's pelvic cavity. They are now in position to be born in the usual way, head first. About 1 in 20 babies do not turn and are positioned to be born "breech," that is, buttocks or, rarely, feet first. Obstetricians sometimes turn such fetuses before birth or perform a cesarean section (described below) because breech babies may get insufficient oxygen during labor.

At about the 266th day after conception, the fetal brain signals the release of certain hormones that pass into the mother's bloodstream (Lye & Challis, 2001). These trigger her uterine muscles to contract and relax, starting the process that becomes active labor. The triggering process is not yet fully understood. It is "an extremely complex system involving various hormones and tissues," and irregular contractions typically occur hours, days, or even weeks before active labor begins (Chow & Yancey, 2001). Many women believe they were in labor for two days or more before giving birth.

Uterine contractions eventually become strong and regular, less than 10 minutes apart. The baby is born, on average, after 12 hours of active labor for first births and 7 hours for subsequent births (Moore & Persaud, 2003), although labor commonly takes twice as long or half as long. Women's birthing positions also vary—sitting, squatting,

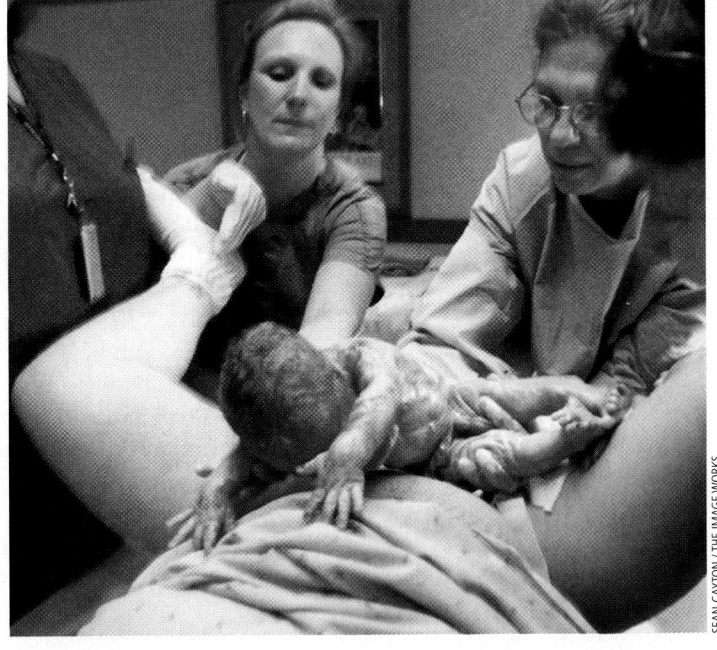

No Doctor Needed In this Colorado Springs birthing center, most babies are delivered with the help of nurse-midwives. This newborn's bloody appearance and bluish fingers are completely normal; an Apgar test at five minutes revealed that the baby's heart was beating steadily and that the body was "entirely pink."

SEAN CAYTON / THE IMAGE WORKS

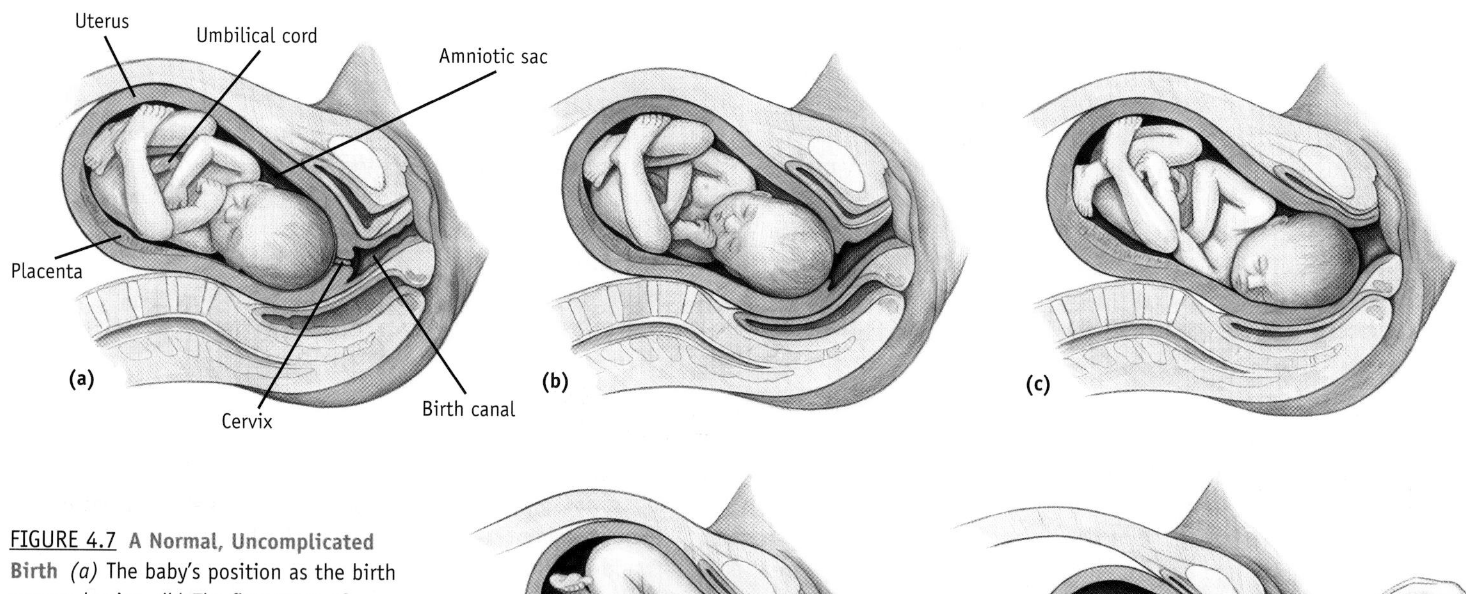

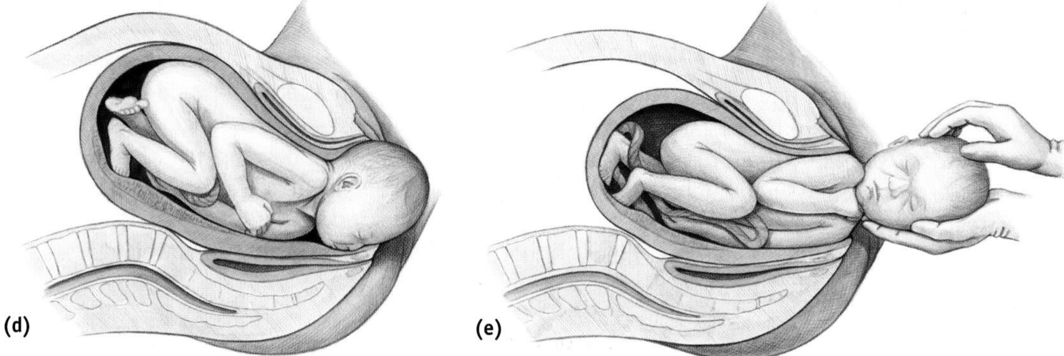

FIGURE 4.7 **A Normal, Uncomplicated Birth** *(a)* The baby's position as the birth process begins. *(b)* The first stage of labor: The cervix dilates to allow passage of the baby's head. *(c)* Transition: The baby's head moves into the "birth canal," the vagina. *(d)* The second stage of labor: The baby's head moves through the opening of the vagina ("crowns") and *(e)* emerges completely.

? OBSERVATIONAL QUIZ (see answer, page 120): In drawing (e), what is the birth attendant doing as the baby's head emerges?

lying down (Blackburn, 2003), or even immersed in warm water. Figure 4.7 shows the sequence of stages in the birth process.

The Newborn's First Minutes

Do you picture just-delivered babies as being held upside down and spanked so that they will start crying and breathing? Wrong image. Gentle handling is best, because newborns usually breathe and cry on their own. Between spontaneous cries, the first breaths of air cause the infant's color to change from a bluish tinge to pinkish as oxygen begins to circulate throughout the system, with the hands and feet the last body parts to turn pink. ("Bluish" and "pinkish" refer to the color of the blood, visible beneath the skin, and apply to newborns of all skin colors.) The eyes open wide; the tiny fingers grab anything they can; the even tinier toes stretch and retract. The newborn is instantly, zestfully, ready for life.

Nevertheless, there is much for those attending the birth to do. Mucus in the baby's throat is removed, especially if the first breaths seem shallow or strained. The umbilical cord is cut to detach the placenta, leaving the "belly button." The infant is weighed and then wrapped to preserve body heat. If birth is assisted by a trained health worker—as are 99 percent of the births in industrialized nations and about half of all births worldwide (Rutstein, 2000)— newborns are weighed and examined to make sure there are no problems that require prompt medical attention.

One widely used assessment is the **Apgar scale** (see Table 4.7). The examiner checks five vital signs—heart rate, breathing, muscle tone, color, and reflexes—at one minute after birth and again at five minutes, assigning each a score of 0, 1, or 2 (Moster et al., 2001). If the five-minute total score is 7 or better, there is no danger. If the five-minute total score is below 7, the infant needs help establish-

! ANSWER TO OBSERVATIONAL QUIZ (from page 116): In 1998. After having declined since the mid-1960s, the LBW rate began an upward climb in the mid-1980s.

Apgar scale A quick assessment of a newborn's body functioning. The baby's color, heart rate, reflexes, muscle tone, and respiratory effort are scored (from 0 to 2) twice, at one minute and five minutes after birth, and the total scores are compared with the ideal score (a perfect 10).

TABLE 4.7 **Criteria and Scoring of the Apgar Scale**

Score	Color	Heartbeat	Reflex Irritability	Muscle Tone	Respiratory Effort
0	Blue, pale	Absent	No response	Flaccid, limp	Absent
1	Body pink, extremities blue	Slow (below 100)	Grimace	Weak, inactive	Irregular, slow
2	Entirely pink	Rapid (over 100)	Coughing, sneezing, crying	Strong, active	Good; baby is crying

Source: Apgar, 1953.

ing normal breathing. If the score is below 4, the baby needs urgent critical care. Most newborns are just fine, which reassures the new mother and father, who cradle their newborn and congratulate each other.

cesarean section A surgical birth. Incisions through the mother's abdomen and uterus allow the fetus to be removed quickly, instead of being delivered through the vagina. Also called *c-section* or simply *section.*

Variations

How closely any given birth matches the foregoing description depends on the parents' preparation for birth, the physical and emotional support provided by birth attendants, the position and size of the fetus, and the customs of the culture. In developed nations, births usually include drugs to dull pain or speed contractions; sterile procedures that involve special gowns, gloves, and washing; and electronic monitoring of both the mother and the fetus. In about 28 percent of births in the United States, a **cesarean section** is performed. The fetus is removed through incisions in the mother's abdomen and uterus (Hamilton et al., 2004). The rate of surgical birth varies markedly from place to place, with many developed nations having far fewer cesareans than the United States but others having more (see Figure 4.8).

If serious organic abnormalities are evident, microsurgery on tiny hearts, lungs, and digestive systems has been amazingly successful in recent years. Thousands of infants who once would have died have been able to develop normally. Eighty years ago 5 percent of all newborns in the United States died (De Lee, 1938).

In many nations, including the United States, newborns are tested for genetic diseases, almost always for phenylketonuria and sickle-cell anemia and often for many more (some states test newborns for 40 diseases). If the tests indicate a problem and it is confirmed by further testing, parents and medical staff begin measures to avoid the worst consequences (MMWR, October 15, 2004).

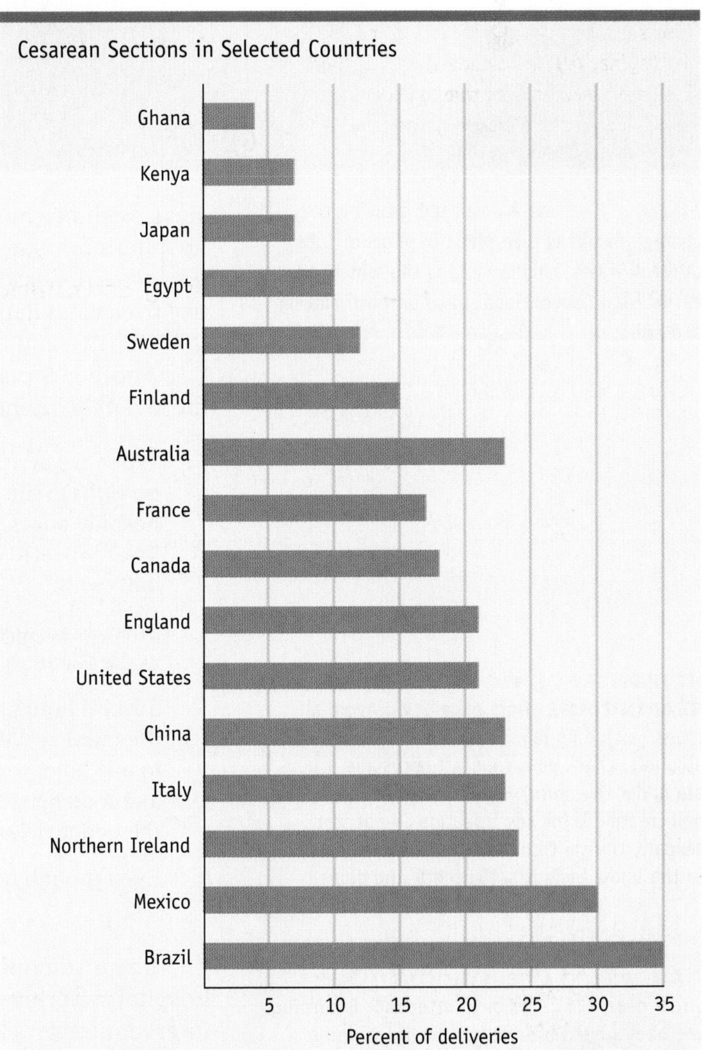

Sources: Belizan et al., 1999; Buekens et al., 2003; Gomes et al., 1999; Khawaja et al., 2004; Royal College of Obstetricians and Gynecologists, 2001.

FIGURE 4.8 **Too Many Cesareans or Too Few?** Rates of cesarean deliveries vary widely from nation to nation. In general, cesarean births are declining in North America and increasing in Africa. Latin America has the highest rates in the world (note that 35 percent of all births in Brazil are by cesarean), and sub-Saharan Africa has the lowest. The underlying issue is whether some women who should have cesareans do not get them, while other women have unnecessary cesareans.

Every year worldwide, obstetricians, midwives, and nurses save millions of lives—of mothers as well as of infants. Indeed, a lack of medical attention during childbirth and illegal abortions are the major reasons why motherhood is still hazardous in the least developed nations; about 1 in 20 women in Africa die of complications of pregnancy and childbirth (Daulaire et al., 2002).

Modern medical care has undeniable benefits, but many aspects of hospital birth have been criticized as being rooted in custom, not necessity. Even worse, financial considerations or fear of lawsuits all too often affects medical decisions. For example, one careful study in the Midwest found that the rate of cesarean deliveries was 17 percent among women with private medical insurance, 14 percent for those with Medicaid, and only 10 percent for those who had no insurance (Aron et al., 2000). The most plausible explanation is that women with insurance receive more costly care—perhaps adding to the stress of childbirth, or perhaps adding to their joy. Similarly, conventional wisdom—and fear of lawsuits—dictates that women who have had one cesarean section should have cesareans for all their subsequent births in order to avoid a rupture of the uterus, even though that complication is unusual.

WATERBIRTH INTERNATIONAL

A Tender Moment A small but growing percentage of births take place in pools or tubs of warm water. This method is thought to be easier than conventional birth on both mother and child.

In response to criticism, alternatives to the conventional hospital birth have become more widespread. By the 1990s only 41 percent of all U.S. births occurred in hospital delivery rooms with high-tech equipment, whereas 53 percent occurred in a *labor room*—typically, a smaller, more homelike room where the mother-to-be stays, with her husband or another familiar person, from the time she enters the hospital until she and her baby have recovered from the birth. In this setting, doctors and nurses intervene when needed, but the woman has much more control over what happens and when. It is *her* room and she is with *her* partner, so it is *her* birth—and that itself reduces anxiety, pain, stress, and complications.

Another 5 percent of U.S. births occur in *birthing centers,* which are even more family oriented. As one woman recounts:

> When we arrived at the Birthing Center to have the baby, we were told to go right to the room we had chosen ahead of time. There weren't any strong hospital odors, no people rushing around, no papers for Gary to fill out while I was wheeled off down a long hall without him. We just walked together to our room.
>
> There is always some amount of anxiety in starting labor; but the atmosphere at the Birthing Center was so relaxing that it had a calming effect on me. . . .
>
> Several hours later, our third daughter was born. She never left us to go to the nursery with harsh lights and lots of other crying babies. She remained in our quiet room with us. We could hold her when she wanted to be held and feed her when she wanted to be fed. Gary and I both were there when the pediatrician checked her.
>
> Even though it was my most difficult labor and delivery, it was our happiest.
>
> *[quoted in La Leche, 1997]*

One testimonial like this does not prove that birthing centers are better than hospital maternity wards, but a careful comparison of the two found that medical intervention of all sorts is less common in birthing centers (e.g., fewer intravenous fluids, more eating or drinking during labor) and that birth outcomes

Response for Women of Childbearing Age (from page 117): Avoid all drugs (including legal ones, like nicotine and alcohol), check your weight (gain some if you are under the norm), and receive diagnosis and treatment for any infections—not just sexually transmitted ones but those anywhere in the body, including the teeth and gums.

! Answer to Observational Quiz (from page 118): The birth attendant is turning the baby's head after it has emerged; doing this helps the shoulders come out more easily.

were similar. The birthing center in San Diego, California, that was the focus of this study is one of the best. The nurses and midwives readily refer pregnant women to doctors and hospitals when indicated. Overall, the evidence suggests that traditional hospital births are no better for the baby than more family-centered births (Jackson et al., 2003).

Only 1 percent of U.S. births take place at home—about half of these by choice, attended by a doctor or midwife, and half due to unexpectedly rapid birth. Home births are usually quite normal and healthy, but any complications can become more serious while waiting for emergency medical help (Pang et al., 2002).

In many regions of the world, as modern medicine is introduced, a clash develops between traditional home births attended by a midwife and hospital births attended by an obstetrician. All too often, women need to choose one or the other, rather than combining the two. An example is reported regarding the Inuit people of northern Canada:

> Until thirty or forty years ago every woman, and most men, learned midwifery skills and knew what to do to help at a birth if they were needed. . . . They helped the woman kneel or squat on caribou skins, and tied the cord with caribou sinews. . . . Since the 1950s, as the medical system took control in the belief that hospital birth was safer, more and more pregnant women were evacuated by air to deliver in large hospitals in Winnipeg and other cities. . . . Around three weeks before her due date a woman is flown south to wait in bed and breakfast accommodation for labor to start, and to have it induced if the baby does not arrive when expected. Anxious about their children left at home, mothers became bored and depressed. . . . Women . . . deliver in a supine position [on their back] instead of an upright one, which was part of their tradition, and also describe being tied up while giving birth. Many women say that children who have been born in a hospital are different and no longer fit into the Inuit lifestyle. . . . Several new birth centres have now been created [in the Inuit homeland] and nurse-midwives are bringing in traditional midwives as assistants during childbirth, training some Inuit midwives to work alongside them, and at the same time learning some of the old Inuit ways themselves.
>
> *[Kitzinger, 2001, pp. 160–161]*

Another example of a traditional custom incorporated into a modern birth is the presence of a **doula.** Long a fixture in many Latin American countries, a doula is a woman who helps other women with labor, delivery, breast-feeding, and newborn care. Increasing numbers of women in North America now hire a professional doula to perform these functions (Douglas, 2002). From a developmental perspective, such combinations of traditional and modern birthing practices are excellent. Some practices in every culture are helpful and some are harmful to development; a thoughtful combination is likely to be an improvement.

doula A woman who helps with the birth process. Traditionally in Latin America, a doula was like a midwife, the only professional who attended the birth process. Now doulas are likely to work alongside a hospital's medical staff to help the woman through labor and delivery.

Birth Complications

When a fetus is already at risk because of low birthweight, preterm birth, genetic abnormality, or exposure to a teratogen, or when a mother is unusually young, old, small, or ill, birth complications become more likely. The crucial point to emphasize is that such complications are part of a sequence of events and conditions that begin long before the first contractions of labor and continue through the months and years of life. This means that prevention and treatment must be ongoing.

As an example, **cerebral palsy** (difficulties with movement control resulting from brain damage) was once thought to be caused solely by birth procedures: excessive pain medication, slow breech birth, or delivery by forceps (an instrument

cerebral palsy A disorder that results from damage to the brain's motor centers. People with cerebral palsy have difficulty with muscle control, which can affect speech and body movements.

sometimes used to pull the fetus's head through the birth canal). In fact, however, cerebral palsy often results from genetic vulnerability and may be worsened by teratogens and a preterm birth that involves **anoxia**—a temporary lack of oxygen.

anoxia A lack of oxygen that, if prolonged during birth, can cause brain damage or death.

Anoxia has many causes and is always risky; that's why the fetal heart rate is monitored during labor and why the newborn's color is one of the five criteria on the Apgar scale. How long a fetus can experience anoxia without suffering brain damage depends on genes, weight, neurological maturity, drugs in the bloodstream (either taken by the mother before birth or given by the doctor during birth), and a host of other factors.

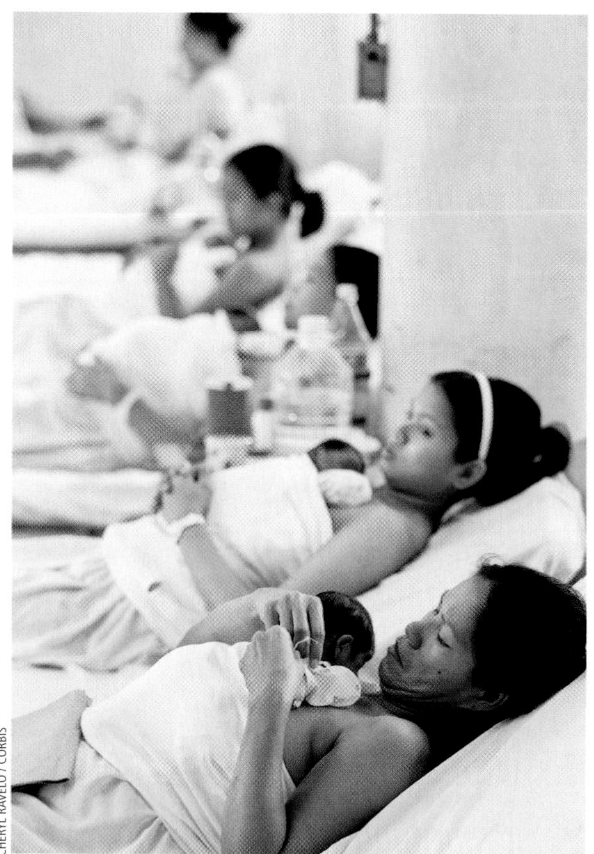

CHERYL RAVELO / CORBIS

A Beneficial Beginning These new mothers in a maternity ward in Manila are receiving training in the technique called kangaroo care for their low-birthweight babies.

Low-birthweight infants are at risk for many problems before, during, and immediately after birth, especially when they are born very early or very small. As we have seen, these problems have their origins in factors that exist even before conception, such as a woman's being underweight, smoking cigarettes, or taking other drugs.

First, Intensive Care . . .

Vulnerable infants are typically placed in intensive-care nurseries, where they are hooked up to one machine or another and surrounded by bright lights and noise. Although these measures are often medically warranted, they deprive neonates of both the gentle rocking in semi-darkness that they would have experienced if they were still in the womb and the regular handling involved in feeding and bathing that they would have had if they were at low risk. To overcome these deprivations, many hospitals provide high-risk infants with regular massage and soothing stimulation, which aid weight gain and increase overall alertness (Field, 2001).

Ideally, parents share in this early caregiving in recognition of the fact that they, too, are deprived and stressed. They are uncertain about their baby's future and often feel inadequate, sad, guilty, or angry. Such emotions are relieved somewhat if they can cradle and care for their vulnerable newborn.

One way to achieve parental involvement is through **kangaroo care**, in which the mother of a low-birthweight infant spends at least an hour a day holding her tiny newborn between her breasts, skin-to-skin, allowing the tiny baby to hear her heart beat and feel her body heat. A comparison study (Feldman et al., 2002) found that kangaroo-care newborns slept more deeply and spent more time alert than did infants who received standard care. By 6 months of age, infants who had received kangaroo care were more responsive to their mothers. These findings could be the result of either improved infant maturation or increased maternal sensitivity, but either way, this is good news.

kangaroo care Care that occurs when the mother of a low-birthweight infant spends at least an hour a day holding the infant between her breasts, like a kangaroo that carries her immature newborn in a pouch on her abdomen. If the infant is capable, he or she can easily breast-feed.

. . . Then Home

For high-risk infants who survive, complications await, including minor medical crises and slow development. Preterm infants are often late to smile, to hold a bottle, and to communicate. As the months go by, short- and long-term cognitive difficulties may emerge. High-risk infants are more distractible, less obedient, and slower to talk (Girouard et al., 1998; Taylor et al., 2000). Even in young adulthood, some risks persist (Hack et al., 2002). Ironically, low-birthweight infants have relatively high rates of obesity and diabetes, as well as other illnesses, in adulthood.

Long-term handicaps are not inevitable, even for tiny, fragile newborns. Some infants with heart defects or other serious abnormalities, or who weigh

2 pounds (900 grams) or less, develop quite normally if they receive excellent early care. Most have long-lasting disabilities, however (Miller et al., 2001; Sweet et al., 2003). Thus, parents should assume neither that a high-risk birth was the child's last major challenge nor that severe intellectual and physical problems are inevitable. Ongoing medical care, family support, and special educational services may be needed for many years (Petrou et al., 2001). The best predictor of preterm infants' cognitive development is not their birth complications but the social support they received in infancy.

Mothers, Fathers, and a Good Start

Humans are social creatures, always interacting with their families and their societies. Accordingly, prenatal development and birth involve not only the fetus but also the mother, father, and many others. As you have already read, a woman's chance of avoiding risks during pregnancy depends partly on her family, her ethnic background, and the nation where she lives.

Support for Mothers

The experience of women born in Mexico and now living in the United States is another illustration of the difference the social context can make. As Figure 4.9 shows, these women have fewer LBW births than do U.S.-born Hispanics (of any ethnicity), European Americans, and African Americans. This is especially remarkable because immigrant Mexican Americans obtain less prenatal care and have lower incomes than do pregnant women in the other groups and even second-generation Mexican Americans from the same neighborhoods. Social practices, not genes, must be the reason (Aguirre-Molina et al., 2001).

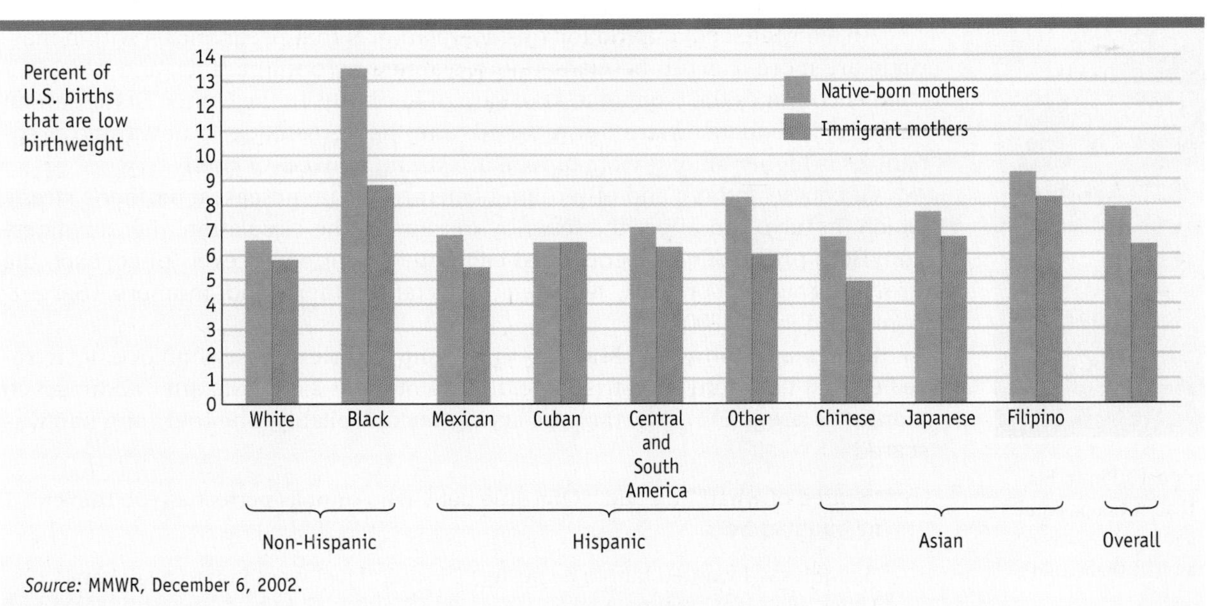

FIGURE 4.9 **Low Birthweight and Mother's Country of Origin** Overall, and for almost every ethnic group, mothers born in the United States have a higher rate of underweight newborns than do mothers born elsewhere who have immigrated to the United States. This benefit for immigrant women occurs despite three risks: They tend to be poorer, less educated, and less likely to obtain prenatal care. They also tend to have three advantages, however: They are less often teenagers, unmarried, and users of drugs and alcohol.

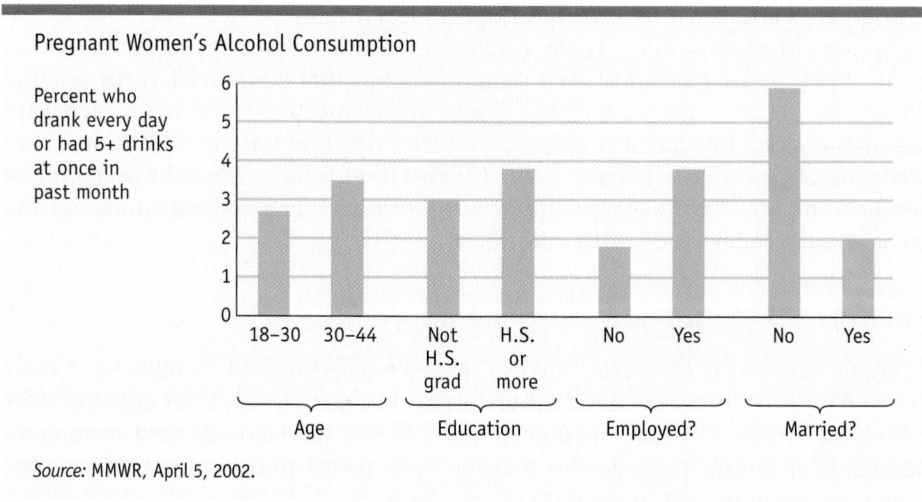

FIGURE 4.10 **Wisdom Doesn't Cut It** Logically, one might think that older women and women with job experience and education would never drink to the point of endangering their fetus, but this isn't so. The only factor that seems to make a powerful difference is marriage.

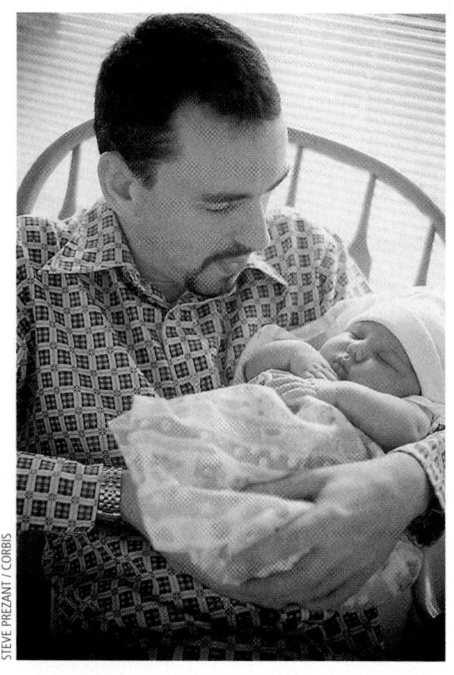

His Baby, Too This father's devotion to his baby illustrates a truism that developmental research has only recently reflected: Fathers contribute much more than half their child's genes.

ESPECIALLY FOR FATHERS-TO-BE When does a man's nongenetic influence on his children begin?

Help from Fathers

This example makes another important point: Fathers can be crucial. A supportive father-to-be helps a mother-to-be stay healthy, well nourished, and drug-free. Alcohol is not good for a fetus, but, as Figure 4.10 shows, neither education nor employment correlates with decreased alcohol consumption during pregnancy. Marriage does. When it comes to alcohol, at least, husbands seem to help their wives abstain.

An alternate explanation for this correlation is that pregnancies within marriage are more likely to be wanted and planned by both parents, and a wanted child encourages the woman to take care of her body. In the United States, about half of all pregnancies are not planned, and the percentage of unwanted pregnancies is higher among women who are young, unwed, or both.

Of course, fathers and other family members can increase a mother's stress, which, in turn, can affect the fetus by disrupting the circulation, diet, or digestion. Both prospective parents need each other's support. Levels of cortisol, the stress hormone, correlate between expectant fathers and mothers (Berg & Wynne-Edwards, 2002).

Remember John and Martha, the young couple whose amniocentesis revealed that their fetus had trisomy-21? One night at 3:00 A.M., after about seven months of pregnancy, Martha was crying uncontrollably. She told John she was scared.

> "Scared of what?" he said, "Of a little baby who's not as perfect as you think he ought to be?"
>
> "I didn't say I wanted him to be perfect," I said. "I just want him to be normal. That's all I want. Just normal."
>
> "That is total bullshit. . . . You don't want this baby to be normal. You'd throw him in a dumpster if he just turned out to be normal. What you really want is for him to be superhuman."
>
> "For your information," I said in my most acid tone, "I was the one who decided to keep this baby, even though he's got Down's. You were the one who wanted to throw him in a dumpster."

> "How would you know?" John's voice was still gaining volume. "You never asked me what I wanted, did you? No. You never even asked me. . . ."
>
> [Beck, 1999, p. 255]

This episode ended well, with a long, warm, and honest conversation between the two prospective parents. Both parents learned what their fetus meant to the other, a taboo topic until that night. Adam, their future son, became an important part of their relationship. Their lack of communication up to this point, and the sudden eruption of unexpressed emotions, is not unusual during pregnancy. Honest discussion between expectant parents is difficult, especially because pregnancy itself raises memories from childhood and fears about the future. Yet open and intimate communication is crucial throughout pregnancy and throughout child rearing to form a **parental alliance,** a commitment by both parents to cooperate in raising the child.

SHEHZAD NOORANI / PETER ARNOLD, INC.

A Teenaged Mother This week-old baby, born in a poor village in Myanmar (Burma), has a better chance of survival than he might otherwise have had, because his 18-year-old mother has bonded with him.

New Mothers' Problems

Among women in the United States who gave birth between 1993 and 1997, 42 percent had some kind of medical problem. For 4 percent, the problem predated the birth (such as heart disease), for 29 percent it was a complication directly related to the birth (such as an infection), and for about 9 percent it was a cesarean section without other complications (Danel et al., 2003). Many of these women, as well as most women without complications, are delighted with themselves and their infants, but birth is almost always stressful in some way.

In the days and weeks after birth, between 8 and 15 percent of women experience **postpartum depression,** a sense of inadequacy and sadness (called *baby blues* in the mild version and *postpartum psychosis* in the most severe form) (Perfetti et al., 2004). The mother finds normal baby care (feeding, diapering, bathing) to be very burdensome, and she may have thoughts of neglecting or abusing the infant. Postpartum depression lasting more than a few weeks can have a long-term impact on the child, so it should be diagnosed and treated as soon as possible (Goodman & Gotlib, 2002; Hay et al., 2001).

From a developmental perspective, some causes of postpartum depression predate the pregnancy (such as preexisting depression, financial stress, or marital problems); others occur during pregnancy (women are more often depressed two months before birth than two months after); and still others are specific to the particular infant (health, feeding, or sleeping problems) (Ashman & Dawson, 2002; Evans et al., 2001). In every case, the father's support benefits the mother, and his attachment to the baby can overcome any negative impact on the developing child (National Institutes of Health, 2001).

Focusing on the mother's emotions raises the question: To what extent are the first hours crucial for the **parent–infant bond,** the strong, loving connection that forms as parents hold, examine, and feed their newborn? It has been claimed that this bond develops in the first hours after birth when a mother touches her naked baby, just as sheep and goats must immediately smell and nuzzle their newborns if they are to nurture them (Klaus & Kennell, 1976).

Although the concept of bonding has been used to argue against the impersonal medicalization of birth, research does not find that early skin-to-skin contact is essential for humans (Eyer, 1992; Lamb, 1982). Unlike sheep and goats, most mammals do not need immediate contact for parents to nurture their offspring. In fact, substantial research on monkeys begins with *cross-fostering,* a strategy in which newborns are removed from their biological mothers in the first days of life and raised by another female or even a male. A strong and beneficial relationship sometimes develops (Suomi, 2002).

parental alliance Cooperation between mother and father based on their mutual commitment to their children. In a parental alliance, the parents agree to support each other in their shared parental roles.

postpartum depression A mother's feelings of sadness, inadequacy, and hopelessness in the days and weeks after giving birth. These feelings are partly physiological (especially hormonal) and partly cultural, particularly if the woman does not receive adequate assistance and encouragement from the baby's father and other helpers.

parent–infant bond The strong, loving connection that forms as parents hold their newborn. Bonding probably begins before birth and continues throughout infancy, so mother–child contact in the first few minutes after birth is helpful but not crucial.

ESPECIALLY FOR SCIENTISTS Research with animals can benefit people, but it is sometimes used too quickly to support conclusions about people. When does that happen?

Response for Fathers-to-Be (from page 124): Before conception and throughout prenatal development, through his influence on the mother's attitudes and health.

Response for Scientists (from page 125): Whenever it supports an assertion that is popular but has not been substantiated by research data, as in the social construction about physical contact being crucial for parent–infant bonding.

SUMMING UP

Most newborns weigh about 7½ pounds (3.4 kilograms), score at least 7 out of 10 on the Apgar scale, and thrive without medical assistance. If necessary, neonatal surgery and intensive care can save lives and prevent long-term complications. Although modern medicine has made maternal or infant death and serious impairment less common in advanced nations, many critics deplore the tendency to treat birth as a medical crisis instead of a natural event. Developmentalists note that lifelong complications are rarely the consequence of birth practices alone; prenatal problems and postnatal care are usually involved in any complications. Postpartum depression is not rare, but, again, factors before and after birth affect how serious and long-lasting this problem is. Human parents and infants seem to benefit from close physical contact following the birth, but it is not essential for bonding. The family relationship begins before conception, may be strengthened by the birth process, and continues lifelong.

SUMMARY

From Zygote to Newborn

1. The first two weeks of prenatal growth are called the germinal period. During this period, the single-celled zygote develops into an organism of more than 100 cells, travels down the fallopian tube, and implants itself in the lining of the uterus. Most zygotes do not develop and never implant.

2. The period from the third through the eighth week after conception is called the embryonic period. The heart begins to beat, and the eyes, ears, nose, and mouth begin to form. By the eighth week, the embryo has the basic organs and features of a human, with the exception of the sex organs.

3. The fetal period extends from the 9th week until birth. By the 12th week all the organs and body structures have formed. The fetus attains viability when the brain is sufficiently mature to regulate basic body functions.

4. The average fetus gains approximately 4½ pounds (2 kilograms) during the last three months of pregnancy and weighs 7½ pounds (3.4 kilograms) at birth. Maturation of brain, lungs, and heart ensures survival of more than 99 percent of all full-term babies. Toward the end of prenatal development, the fetus can hear and respond to movement, and parents are likewise very much aware of their baby.

Risk Reduction

5. Some teratogens (diseases, drugs, and pollutants) cause physical impairment. Others, called behavioral teratogens, harm the brain and therefore impair cognitive abilities and personality tendencies.

6. Whether a teratogen harms an embryo or fetus depends on timing, amount of exposure, and genetic vulnerability. To protect against prenatal complications, good public and personal health practices are strongly recommended. There are no guarantees either way, however.

7. Many methods of prenatal testing inform pregnant couples in the first few months how the fetus is developing. Such knowledge can bring anxiety and unexpected responsibility as well as welcome information.

8. Low birthweight (under 5½ pounds, or 2.5 kilograms) may arise from maternal illness, malnutrition, smoking, drinking, drug use, and age. Compared to full-term newborns, preterm and underweight babies experience more medical difficulties, especially breathing problems and brain damage.

The Birth Process

9. Birth typically begins with contractions that push the fetus, head first, out of the uterus and then through the vagina. The Apgar scale, which rates the neonate's vital signs at one minute and again at five minutes after birth, provides a quick evaluation of the infant's health.

10. Medical intervention can speed contractions, dull pain, and save lives. However, many aspects of the medicalized birth have been faulted. Contemporary birthing practices are aimed at finding a balance, protecting the baby but also allowing more parental involvement and control.

11. Birth complications, such as unusually long and stressful labor that includes anoxia (a lack of oxygen to the fetus), have many causes. Vulnerable newborns are placed in an intensive-care unit for monitoring and treatment. Long-term handicaps are not inevitable for such children, but careful nurturing from their parents may be needed.

12. Fathers as well as mothers experience stress during pregnancy and birth. Ideally, the parents form a parental alliance, working together to make sure their baby gets a good start in life.

13. Many women feel unhappy, incompetent, or unwell in the days immediately after giving birth. Postpartum depression may lift with appropriate help, with fathers particularly crucial for mother and child. Mother–newborn interaction should be encouraged, although the parent–infant bond depends on many factors, not solely on birth practices.

KEY TERMS

germinal period (p. 97)
embryonic period (p. 97)
fetal period (p. 97)
implantation (p. 98)
embryo (p. 99)
fetus (p. 100)
age of viability (p. 101)
teratogens (p. 104)
behavioral teratogens (p. 105)
risk analysis (p. 105)
critical period (p. 105)
threshold effect (p. 105)
interaction effect (p. 106)
human immunodeficiency virus (HIV) (p. 112)
fetal alcohol syndrome (FAS) (p. 112)
low birthweight (LBW) (p. 115)
very low birthweight (VLBW) (p. 115)
extremely low birthweight (ELBW) (p. 115)
preterm birth (p. 115)
small for gestational age (SGA) (p. 115)
Apgar scale (p. 115)
cesarean section (p. 119)
doula (p. 121)
cerebral palsy (p. 121)
anoxia (p. 122)
kangaroo care (p. 122)
parental alliance (p. 125)
postpartum depression (p. 125)
parent–infant bond (p. 125)

KEY QUESTIONS

1. What are the major differences between an embryo at 2 weeks and at 8 weeks after conception?

2. What are the factors in achieving viability?

3. Since almost all fetuses born at 30 weeks survive, why don't women avoid the last month of pregnancy by having an elective cesarean at that time?

4. Which maternal behavior or characteristic seems most harmful to the fetus: eating a diet low in folic acid, drinking a lot of alcohol, or being HIV-positive? Explain your answer.

5. Reconsider the Horans' decision to abort their fetus. According to this published account, which considerations were crucial for them? If you were in this situation, which considerations would be crucial for you?

6. How much influence do husbands and mothers have on pregnant women? Explain your answer.

7. How have medical procedures helped *and* harmed the birth process?

8. Why do hospitals encourage parents of fragile newborns to provide some care, even if the newborn is in critical condition and may die?

9. What factors increase the likelihood of a strong mother–infant bond?

10. What can be done about postpartum depression, for both the mother and the infant?

APPLICATIONS

1. Go to a nearby greeting-card store and analyze the cards regarding pregnancy and birth. Do you see any cultural attitudes (e.g., variations depending on sex of the newborn or of the parent)? If possible, compare those cards with cards from a store that caters to another economic or cultural group.

2. Interview three mothers of varied backgrounds about their birth experiences. Make your interviews open-ended—let them choose what to tell you, as long as they give at least 10 minutes of description. Then compare and contrast the three accounts, noting especially any influences of culture, personality, circumstance, or cohort.

3. People sometimes wonder how any pregnant woman could jeopardize the health of her fetus. Consider your own health-related behavior in the past month—exercise, sleep, nutrition, drug use, medical and dental care, disease avoidance, and so on. Would you change your behavior if you were pregnant? Would it make a difference if your family, your partner, or you yourself did not want a baby?

PART II

The First Two Years: Infants and Toddlers

Adults don't change much in a year or two. Sometimes their hair gets longer, grayer, or thinner, or they gain or lose a little weight, or they learn something new. But if you were reunited with friends you haven't seen for two years, you would recognize them immediately.

If, in contrast, you cared for a newborn 24 hours a day for the first month and then went away for two years, you probably would not recognize him or her when you came back. Imagine trying to recognize a best friend who had quadrupled in weight, grown 14 inches (35 cm), and sprouted a new head of hair. Behavior has changed, too. A hungry newborn just cries; a hungry toddler says "more food" or climbs up onto the kitchen counter to reach the cookies.

A year or two is not much compared to the 75 years or more of the average life span. However, in two years tiny, nonverbal newborns reach half their adult height, talk in sentences, and express almost every emotion—not just joy and fear but also love, jealousy, and shame. The next three chapters describe these radical and wonderful changes.

Chapter Five

The First Two Years: Biosocial Development

In the first two years, rapid growth is obvious in all three domains—body, mind, and social relationships. Picture biosocial development, from birth to age 2: Roll over . . . sit . . . stand . . . walk . . . run! Reach . . . touch . . . grab . . . throw! Listen . . . stare . . . see! Each object, each person, each place becomes something to explore with every sense, every limb, every organ. Clothes are outgrown before they become too stained or torn to wear.

Invisible developments are even more striking. Small infant brains become larger, with neurons connecting to one another at a dizzying, yet programmed, pace. Tiny stomachs digest food and more food, dispatching nourishment to brain and body to enable phenomenal growth.

Parents and cultures are pivotal to this process, which makes this bio*social*—not merely biological—development. Nurture always interacts with nature. Adults provide the nurture that enables infant growth, with specifics that change daily because infants change daily. As one expert explains, "Parenting an infant is akin to trying to hit a moving target" (Bornstein, 2002, p. 14).

This chapter describes that target as it moves—not only weight, height, and motor skills at key ages but also the brain growth that provides the foundation for all other developments. You will learn in this chapter how to help the infants you know, and some whom you will never meet, make it safely to age 2.

Body Changes

In infancy, growth is so fast, and the consequences of neglect are so severe, that gains need to be closely monitored. Medical checkups, including measurement of height, weight, and head circumference, should occur every few weeks at first. Any slowdown is a cause for immediate concern, because sensation, perception, and cognition all depend on early growth.

Body Size

Exactly how rapidly does growth typically occur? We saw in Chapter 4 that at birth the average infant weighs 7½ pounds (3.4 kilograms) and measures about 20 inches (51 centimeters). This means that the typical newborn weighs less than a gallon of milk and is about as long as the distance from a man's elbow to the tips of his fingers.

Infants typically double their birthweight by the fourth month and triple it by their first birthday. Physical growth slows in the second year, but it is still rapid. By 24 months most children weigh almost 30 pounds (13 kilograms) and are between 32 and 36 inches (81–91 centimeters) tall. This means that typical 2-year-olds are already half their adult height. They are also about 15 to 20 percent of their adult weight, four times as heavy as at birth. (See Appendix A, pp. A-6, A-7.)

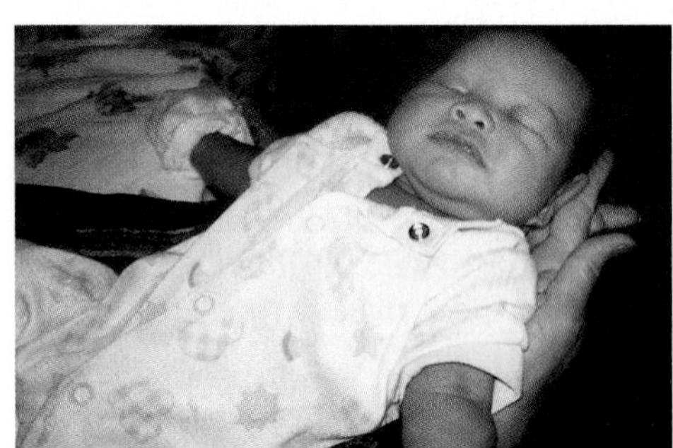

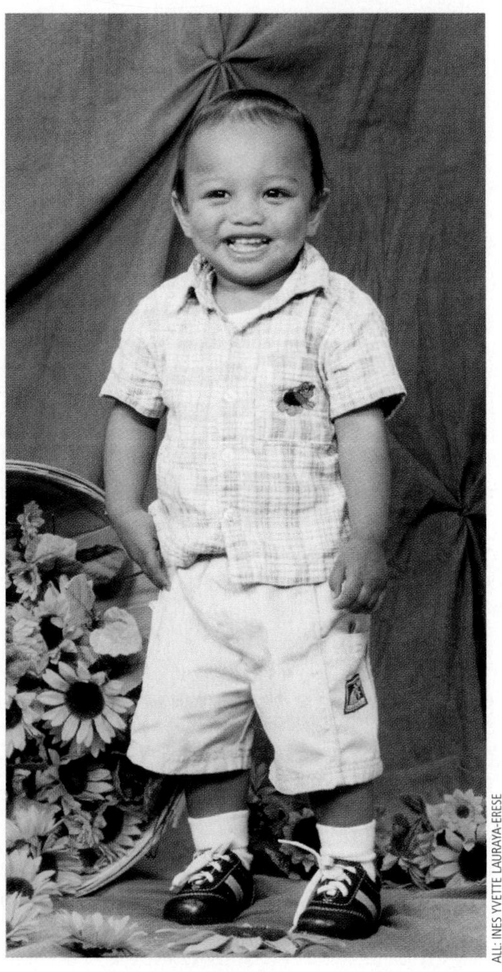

ALL: INES YVETTE LAURAYA-ERESE

Both Amazing and Average Juwan's growth from *(a)* 4 months to *(b)* 12 months to *(c)* 24 months is a surprise and delight to everyone who knows him. At age 2, this Filipino American toddler seems to have become a self-assured, outgoing individual, obviously unique. Yet the norms indicate that he is developing right on schedule—weight, teeth, motor skills, and all.

Much of the weight increase in the early months is fat, to provide insulation for warmth and a store of nourishment. This stored nutrition keeps the brain growing if teething or the sniffles interfere with eating. When nutrition is temporarily inadequate, the body stops growing but not the brain, a phenomenon called **head-sparing** (Georgieff & Rao, 2001). (Chronic malnutrition is discussed later in this chapter.)

head-sparing The biological protection of the brain when malnutrition affects body growth. The brain is the last part of the body to be damaged by malnutrition.

Each of the above numbers is a **norm,** an average or standard measurement for a particular population. Norms must be carefully interpreted. The "particular population" for the norms above is a representative sample of North American infants, who may not be comparable to infants from other continents. To understand norms, you also need to understand percentiles. An average child is at the 50th **percentile,** a number that is midway between 1 and 99, with 49 percent of the children above it and 49 percent below it.

norm An average, or standard, measurement, calculated from the measurements of many individuals within a specific group or population.

percentile A point on a ranking scale of 1 to 99. The 50th percentile is the midpoint; half the people rank higher and half lower. If a child is in the bottom 5 percent, or loses rank from one measurement to the next, that is a cause for concern.

Percentiles allow a child's growth to be compared not only to that of other children but also to his or her own prior development. Pediatricians and nurses notice children whose growth is far from the norms, but they pay closer attention to the ranking: A drop in percentile means that something might be wrong. Consider Toni.

A CASE TO STUDY

Toni's Well-Child Visit

The following is an excerpt from a report written by a medical team.

> Toni is a 17-month-old girl who has been brought to the doctor for a well-child visit. She was last seen at 11 months and is behind in immunizations. Toni was born at term to an 18-year-old mother and weighed 3,850 grams [8½ pounds; 75th percentile] and measured 50 centimeters in length [20 inches; 50th percentile]. Prenatal history was negative for problems, and her health has been good, according to her mother. At Toni's last visit, her height and weight were at the 50th percentile.
>
> Today Toni weighs 9,400 grams [21 pounds; 20th percentile) and is 79 centimeters tall [32 inches; 40th percentile). Development, according to her mother, is normal, although her language skills are delayed—she has only a five-word vocabulary. Toni's mother describes Toni as busy, always on the go. The family history for medical problems is negative. Toni's mother is 5 feet 5 inches tall and weighs 130 pounds. Her father is reported to be about 6 feet tall. He is not in the household.
>
> There have been no significant illnesses since the 11-month visit. The physical exam, as well as screening laboratory tests, are essentially negative except for mild anemia.
>
> Toni's mother has recently (within the past 4 months) returned to work as a waitress. She has pieced together a patchwork of child care. The child is cared for by a variety of family members. She [the mother] has indicated that she is afraid of using strangers. She has a difficult time giving a feeding history because multiple providers feed Toni, who apparently do not communicate with each other about her intake. Mealtimes vary from household to household as do other routines, such as naps and bedtime. Toni's mother's meals are also erratic, and the two rarely eat a meal together. Toni falls asleep in front of the television every night and generally awakens too late for breakfast at home, prior to [being rushed] out in order to accommodate her mother's work schedule.
>
> *[Yoos et al., 1999, pp. 380, 381, 383]*

Toni's case will be referred to throughout our three chapters (5, 6, and 7) on infancy. From what you learned in Chapter 4 you can recognize several strengths. Toni was full-term, weighing 8½ pounds (3.8 kilograms), born to an 18-year-old mother. All these are low-risk characteristics. (Birthweight below 5½ pounds [2.5 kilograms] or a mother younger than 16 would involve high risk.) In addition, Toni's mother brought her for a checkup, to her usual care provider, only a few months late. Many teenage parents skip appointments, seek medical help only for emergencies, and change providers. Continuity of medical care allows accurate records regarding immunizations, birth complications, and growth.

For Toni, ongoing care and records were particularly useful. Her 17-month measurements, by themselves, were not seriously low, but look at her medical history. She dropped from the 75th to the 50th to the 20th percentile in weight. At 17 months she still had not tripled her birthweight, a benchmark usually reached at 12 months. Notice also that Toni is mildly anemic; her parents are of average height, but she is short; her mother could not give a feeding history; caregivers do not coordinate Toni's eating; household routines vary; her height percentile is decreasing; and Toni skips breakfast. No single one of these facts means that Toni is malnourished, but the combination suggests that she is.

Because of head-sparing, Toni's malnutrition has not yet damaged her brain. Typically, reduced weight is the first sign of malnutrition, stunted height is the next, and finally comes slow head growth (Rao & Georgieff, 2000). There is no indication that Toni's head circumference is too small, and her weight and height are still in the normal ranges. Nor has Toni reached the danger point called **failure to thrive**, when a child stops growing or even loses weight. This case was published partly to show when intervention was needed. Toni soon gained weight. Most likely catch-up growth, and the human tendency to thrive if possible (called *self-righting*; more on this later), will protect her from serious harm. Follow-up recommendations for Toni are presented in Chapter 7.

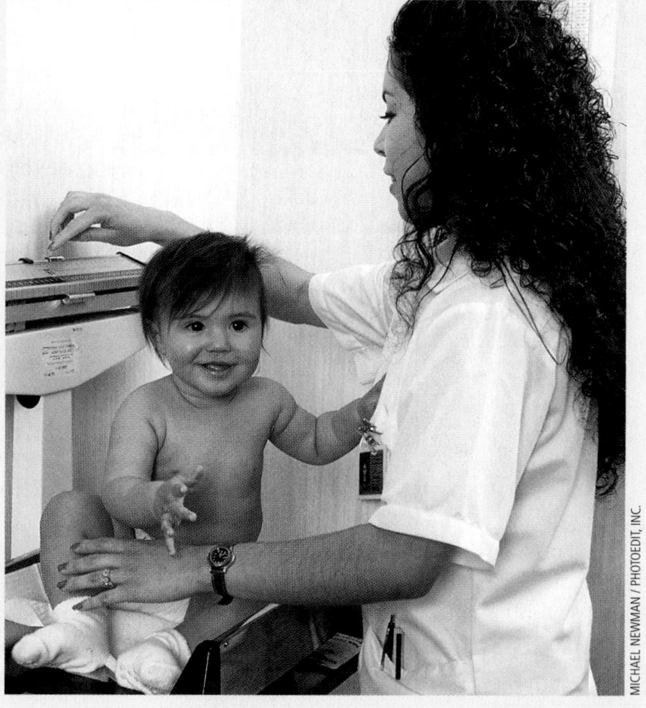

MICHAEL NEWMAN / PHOTOEDIT, INC.

The Weigh-In At her one-year well-baby checkup, Blair sits up steadily, weighs more than 20 pounds, and would scramble off the table if she could. Both Blair's development and the nurse's protective arm are quite appropriate.

failure to thrive A situation in which a child stops growing or even loses weight, despite apparently normal health.

Sleep

New babies spend most of their time sleeping and eating. It is obvious why they eat so much: They must double their weight in four months! However, it is not obvious why they sleep 17 hours or more a day. Growth hormones tend to be released during sleep, a possible reason why rapidly growing infants sleep as much as they do (see Figure 5.1). Throughout childhood, regular and ample sleep correlates with brain maturation, learning, emotional regulation, and psychological adjustment in school and within the family (Bates et al., 2002; Sadah et al., 2000). A child who does not sleep well is a child in trouble, although it is not known if poor sleeping is a cause or a symptom of that trouble.

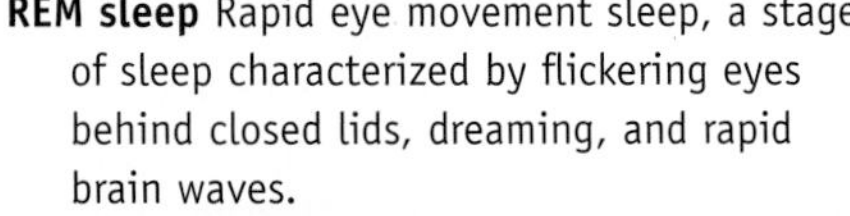

REM sleep Rapid eye movement sleep, a stage of sleep characterized by flickering eyes behind closed lids, dreaming, and rapid brain waves.

Over the first months, the relative amount of time spent in each type or stage of sleep changes. Newborns seem to dream a lot. **REM sleep** (rapid eye movement sleep, characterized by dreaming and rapid brain waves) declines over the early weeks, as does "transitional sleep," the dozing stage when a person is half awake. At 3 or 4 months, quiet sleep (also called slow-wave sleep) increases markedly (Salzarulo & Fagioli, 1999). At about this time, the various "states" of waking and sleeping become more evident. Thus, although many newborns rarely seem sound asleep or wide awake, by 3 months most babies have periods of alertness, when they are neither hungry nor sleepy but are ready to learn.

DAVID YOUNG-WOLFF / PHOTOEDIT, INC.

Dreaming, Dozing, or Sound Asleep? Babies spend most of their time sleeping.

? OBSERVATIONAL QUIZ (see answer, page 136): Can you tell which kind of sleep this infant is experiencing?

Psychologists wonder why infants dream so much. Many new parents are more concerned about *when* their infants sleep. Parents want babies to sleep all night long, but infants are too immature—in their brains, digestive organs, and biological rhythms—to do so. A mismatch between infant wakefulness and parents' wishes is especially noticeable in the hectic schedules of modern life.

Child rearing was much easier in the days before most mothers worked outside the home. In traditional cultures, if an infant awoke several times each night, the mother simply reached out and put the baby to her breast. She soon went back to sleep herself, later napping in the daytime if she needed to. No longer. Very few of today's working mothers can nap on the job.

Parents gradually become less sleep-deprived. Between birth and age 1, infant sleep schedules come closer to matching the family day–night rhythm. No newborns, but 80 percent of all 1-year-olds, "sleep through the night," although many preschoolers still wake up before their parents in the morning (Weissbluth, 1999).

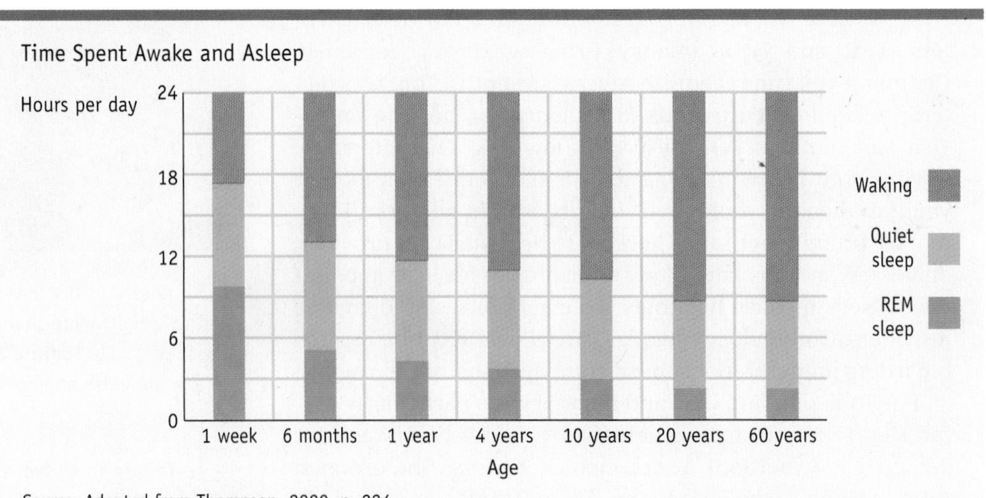

FIGURE 5.1 **Sweet Dreams**
On average, the older we are, the less sleep we get, probably because older people dream less. At age 60, we spend only about one hour per night dreaming. The mystery is: What can newborns be dreaming about?

Both nature and nurture influence every aspect of physiological development, including sleep. By nature, newborns sleep a great deal and wake up often. However, sleep cycles are affected by birth order, newborn diet, and child-rearing practices, as well as by brain maturation. For example, if parents respond to predawn cries with food and play, babies learn to wake up night after night. First-born infants typically "receive more attention and better care" (Bornstein, 2002, p. 28), which may be why they exhibit more sleep problems than later-borns. This report from one mother tells what can happen:

> I . . . raised my first taking him wherever I went, whenever I went, confident he would adapt. While he was always happy, he was never a good sleeper and his first 4 years were very hard on me (I claim he didn't sleep through the night until he was 4, but I could be wrong, I was so sleep-deprived). . . . [When my third child] came along . . . , I was determined to give her a schedule. . . . She is a GREAT sleeper, happy to go to bed. I am convinced, anecdotally, that schedules are the most important part of this. When I talk to new mothers, I give them this advice: Let the baby determine the schedule, then let nothing interfere with it.
>
> *[Freda, personal communication, 1997]*

That is good advice. Developmentalists agree that insisting that an infant conform to the parents' schedule can be frustrating to the parents and, in some cases, harmful to the infant; but letting a child continually interrupt the adults' sleep can be harmful to the parents. Ideally, families interact and adapt until every member's basic needs are met.

One question for many parents is: Where should infants sleep? Traditionally, Western parents put their infants to sleep in a crib in a separate bedroom, unless the family did not have a spare room. Parents from Asia, Africa, and Latin America slept beside their infants, a practice called *co-sleeping* or *bed-sharing*. Today, many Western parents allow bed-sharing, at least in the first months. In fact, a recent survey of British parents found that half of them slept with their infants some of the time (Blair & Ball, 2004). A study of California families found that about a third practiced co-sleeping from birth; about one-fourth of couples had newborns sleep in another room but allowed their toddlers to sleep with them; and the rest kept babies in a separate room throughout childhood (Keller & Goldberg, 2004). By ages 3 to 5, those children who always slept with their parents were developing well and independently, which suggests that co-sleeping did not harm them. A further question then arises: How is the decision made to put children to sleep in some location other than the parents' room?

Who Sleeps with Whom?

Suppose you are asked to find an apartment for an immigrant family. You find them a four-room apartment in a decent neighborhood with a low rent, an accomplishment that should make you proud. However, when the family arrives you learn it consists of a husband and wife, two daughters aged 15 and 4, and two sons aged 13 and 6. The apartment has a living–dining room, a small kitchen, one bathroom, and two bedrooms. Who should sleep where?

Think a moment and take a look at Figure 5.2 before reading on.

Have you come up with an arrangement? If yours is an Asian culture, you may see two easy solutions: The males sleep in one bedroom and the females in the other, or everyone sleeps in one room, perhaps on mats on the floor, and the other bedroom is used as a reading/studying/computer room. Sharing rooms is accepted, even desired, in cultures where the company of others, awake or asleep, is preferred to isolation (Shweder, 2003). However, if you are from North America or Western Europe,

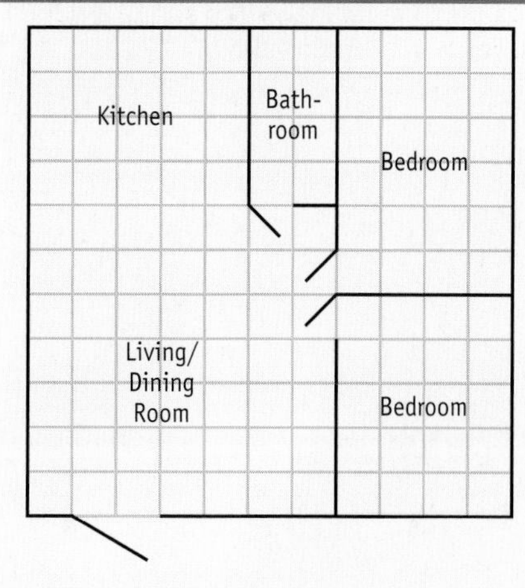

FIGURE 5.2 **Who Sleeps Where?** A six-person family needs to sleep in the apartment diagrammed here. We have a mother, father, two daughters aged 4 and 15, and two sons aged 6 and 13. Can you figure out where each person should sleep?

> you believe in the ritualized isolation of children during the night, the institution of "bedtime," and the protection of the privacy of the "sacred couple" upheld by a cultural norm mandating the exclusive co-sleeping of the husband and wife.
>
> *[Shweder et al., 1998, p. 873]*

! Answer to Observational Quiz (from page 134): The baby's outstretched left arm suggests dreaming, which occupies about six hours of every day's sleep at this age. Direct observation or a video, not a photograph, could demonstrate whether this is REM (dreaming) sleep. Quiet sleep is characterized by shallow breathing, still eyes, and relaxed muscle tone.

Most North American and European cultures endorse all three of these customs: (1) Husband and wife sleep together; (2) children do not sleep with their parents, (3) adolescents need privacy at night, especially from siblings of the other sex. From this perspective, our immigrant family has a problem without a solution—except the one suggested by one of my students: "They must move." Another student wanted to know the dimensions of the rooms and of a twin bed, as he was designing partitions to make four tiny bedrooms.

This example leads to another point. Not only do people assume that their culture is best; they also justify their customs with reasons that seem strange to outsiders. For instance, Westerners connect communal sleeping with sexual abuse; Easterners see isolated sleeping as child neglect. My students explain that the parents need privacy for sex, as if an exclusive bedroom is required for intimacy.

More broadly, every culture endorses certain parental strategies—for sleeping, talking, feeding, disciplining, encouraging, playing, and so on—to guide children to develop whatever abilities, values, and expectations are suited for that place and time. Thus, children who sleep with their parents may learn to depend on their parents for warmth and protection; children who sleep alone may become more independent (McKenna, 2000). In fact, both practices produce reasonably healthy adults.

The Children's House

"Reasonably healthy adults" seem to develop from a variety of sleeping arrangements. Does that mean that it makes no difference where infants and children sleep? Not quite.

Consider an unusual sleeping arrangement that was common in Israel from about 1950 until 1980 in hundreds of *kibbutzim* (the plural of *kibbutz*). A kibbutz is a kind of farming commune whose members share work, meals, income, and child care. Young adults joined kibbutzim long before they became parents and adopted the culture of the kibbutz, including child-rearing customs.

Infants of the kibbutzim originally spent several hours each evening with their parents but slept in a separate "Children's House" with other children and without adults. (The adults took weekly turns monitoring the children by intercom, in case an emergency arose during the night.) In the communal culture of the kibbutzim, the social construction was that this arrangement would encourage all the children to become loyal to their "brothers and sisters" of the kibbutz.

The Children's House made logical sense, but the practice was gradually abandoned. First in a few kibbutzim, then in others, some children began sleeping near their parents (Oppenheim, 1998). Meanwhile, other children in Israel were being raised not on kibbutzim but in traditional families (parents and children in one household, sleeping in separate bedrooms). These variations allowed comparison of the effects of different sleeping practices on children who were born in the same nation at the same time.

Accordingly, one researcher (Scharf, 2001) studied four groups of adolescents, a total of 131 16- to 18-year-olds. Three groups had been raised on kibbutzim: 33 had spent all their childhood nights away from their parents, 34 had slept in Children's Houses as infants but had been switched before age 6 to sleeping near their parents, and 33 had always slept near their parents. In addition, a fourth group with a conventional childhood were also studied: 31 Israeli adoles-

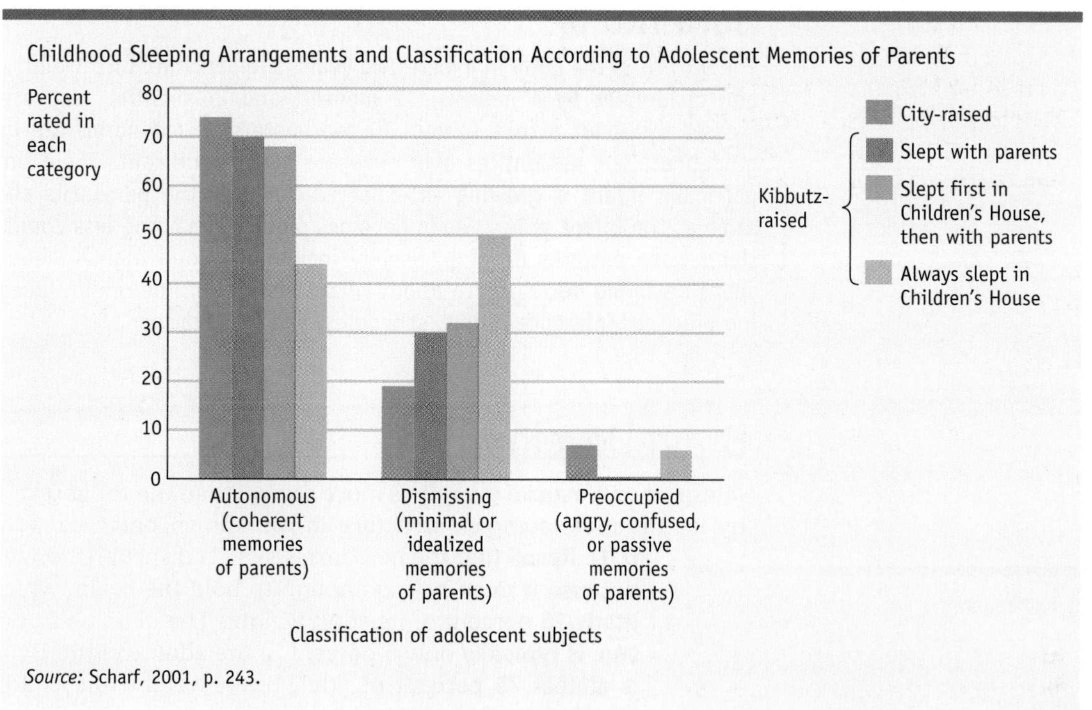

FIGURE 5.3 **The Cost of Nighttime Separation from Parents** The adolescent participants' tape-recorded reminiscences about their parents were rated by researchers who did not know which of the four sleeping arrangements the participants had experienced. The youngsters were rated as autonomous, dismissing, or preoccupied, according to the criteria established for the Adult Attachment Interview. Those who, as children living on a kibbutz, had slept in a Children's House rather than near their parents were least likely to be rated as autonomous.

cents who grew up with their parents in city homes, sleeping near them from infancy on (but not in the same bed).

The researcher evaluated these four groups of adolescents, particularly their emotions regarding their parents (see Figure 5.3). Many in the group of 33 teenagers who had always slept in the Children's Houses had difficulty talking about and relating to their family members (Scharf, 2001). This is a measure of attachment, a topic that is discussed in detail in Chapter 7. The teenagers who had slept near their parents were quite similar to each other (and to adolescents in other nations).

Note that the crucial factor was *not* growing up on a kibbutz or being Israeli but sleeping away from parents. One specific aspect of the culture, not the overall design, had unanticipated consequences. Other research worldwide suggests that babies are more likely to become healthy children and adults if they sleep with or near their mothers than if they sleep far from them (Shweder, 2003).

What Does the Research Tell Us?

Co-sleeping does not seem to be harmful unless the adult is drugged or drunk—and thus in danger of "overlying" the baby. According to one report:

> Mothers instinctively take up a protective posture when sharing a bed with their infants, lying in a fetal position with their lower arm above the infant's head and the infant lying within around 20–30 centimeters [about 10 inches] from the mother's chest. The position of the mother's thighs prevents the baby from sliding down the bed.
>
> *[Wailoo et al., 2004, p. 1083]*

Although a videotape analysis found that co-sleeping infants wake up twice as often (six times a night) as solo-sleeping infants (three times), co-sleepers get just as much sleep as solo sleepers because they go back to sleep more quickly (Mao et al., 2005). As with other aspects of infant care, it seems that many sleeping patterns are suitable for normal family functioning. However, babies and children develop best, awake and asleep, when their parents are nearby.

ESPECIALLY FOR NEW PARENTS You are aware of cultural differences in sleeping practices, and this raises a very practical issue: Should your newborn sleep in bed with you?

SUMMING UP

The growth of the body in a mere two years is remarkable. Birthweight doubles, triples, and quadruples by 4 months, 12 months, and 24 months, respectively. Height increases by about a foot (about 30 centimeters). Such norms are useful as general guidelines, but percentiles over time are more significant. They indicate whether a particular infant is growing as expected, because the percentile should remain the same as the infant grows. Sleep becomes regular, dreaming less common, and distinct sleep–wake patterns develop, usually including a long night's sleep by age 1. Time spent dreaming decreases to about what it is for an older child. Cultural and caregiving practices influence norms, schedules, and expectations.

Brain Development

No aspect of biosocial growth is more critical than the rapid growth of the brain, "by far the most complex structure in the known universe" (Thompson, 2000, p. 1). Recall that the newborn's skull is disproportionately large. That's because it must be big enough to hold the brain, which at birth is already 25 percent of its adult weight. The neonate's body, by comparison, is typically only 5 percent of the adult weight. By age 2, the brain is almost 75 percent of adult brain weight; the child's body is only about 20 percent as big as it will be (see Figure 5.4).

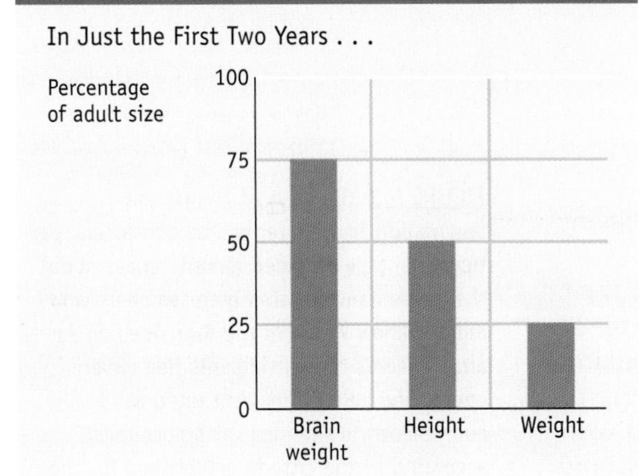

FIGURE 5.4 **Growing Up** Two-year-olds are barely talking and are totally dependent on adults, but they have already reached half their adult height and three-fourths of their adult brain size. This is dramatic evidence that biosocial growth is the foundation for cognitive and social maturity.

Connections in the Brain

Head circumference provides a rough idea of growth within the brain, which is why medical checkups include measuring the skull. The distance around the head typically increases about 35 percent (from 13 to 18 inches, or from 34 to 46 centimeters) within the first year. Much more significant (although harder to measure) are changes in the brain's communication system, which make early child rearing especially crucial. Neglect, abuse, malnutrition, or overstimulation may hinder brain development. To understand how, we review the basics of brain structure and functioning (see Figure 5.5).

Basic Brain Structures

The brain's communication system begins with nerve cells, called **neurons.** Most neurons are created before birth, at a peak production rate of 250,000 new brain cells per minute in mid-pregnancy (Bloom et al., 2001). In infancy, the human brain has billions of neurons, about 70 percent of which are in the **cortex,** the brain's four to six outer layers (sometimes called the *neocortex* or the *gray matter*) (Kolb & Whishaw, 2003). The cortex is crucial for humans, as is evident in the following three facts:

neuron A nerve cell of the central nervous system. Most neurons (billions of them) are in the brain.

cortex The outer layers of the brain in humans and other mammals. Most thinking, feeling, and sensing involve the cortex.

- About 80 percent of the human brain material is in the cortex.
- In other mammals the cortex is much smaller, and non-mammals have brains but no cortex at all.
- Most thinking, feeling, and sensing are processed in the cortex, although other parts of the brain join in.

Various areas of the cortex specialize in particular functions. For instance, there is a visual cortex, an auditory cortex, and an area dedicated to the sense of touch for each body part—even for each finger of a person or, in rats, for each whisker (Bloom et al., 2001). Regional specialization within the cortex occurs not only for motor skills and senses but also for particular aspects of cognition.

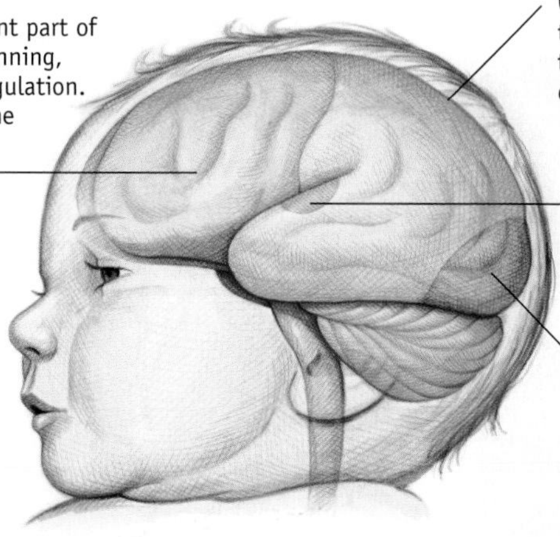

FIGURE 5.5 **The Developing Cortex** The cortex consists of four to six thin layers of tissue that cover the brain. It contains virtually all the neurons that make conscious thought possible. Some areas of the cortex, such as those devoted to the basic senses, mature relatively early. Others, such as the frontal cortex, mature quite late.

Precise understanding of each cognitive region has not yet been achieved, but scientists agree that each aspect of thought arises from a specific brain area, linked to other areas (Kolb & Whishaw, 2003). Various kinds of memory, particular parts of speech, and recognition of distinct patterns are each connected to a set of neurons. Thinking in those areas increases the rate of neurological firing and triggers activity in several other parts of the brain. As one science reporter explains:

> It's a complicated world out there, visually, full of things that look a lot alike. Yet people rarely identify a TV remote control as a cell phone or confuse a pencil with a swizzle stick. . . . In the past few years, brain imaging studies have identified one region [of the area of the brain called the *ventral temporal cortex*] that specializes in recognizing faces and another that processes places. More recently, researchers have found that even mundane objects such as shoes, chairs, and plastic bottles also light up distinct areas in part of the brain.
>
> *[Helmuth, 2001, pp. 196, 198]*

This regional specialization has been discovered through research on normal brain functioning as well as on brain-damaged individuals who are capable of some kinds of thinking but not others. There are people who can dance but cannot walk, who can recite poetry but cannot answer a simple question. A best-selling book that describes neurological problems, titled *The Man Who Mistook His Wife for a Hat* (Sacks, 1970/1998), tells about a man whose sight recognition was scrambled. He could not identify his wife when he saw her, although he loved her and recognized her in nonvisual ways.

Within and between brain areas, neurons are connected to other neurons by intricate networks of nerve fibers called **axons** and **dendrites** (see Figure 5.6). Each neuron has a single axon and numerous dendrites, with the latter spreading out like the branches of a tree. The axon of one neuron meets the dendrites of other neurons at intersections called **synapses,** which are critical communication links within the brain.

To be more specific, neurons communicate by sending electrical impulses through their axons to synapses, to be picked up by the dendrites of other neurons. The dendrites bring the message to the cell bodies of those neurons, which, in turn, convey the message via their axons to still other neurons. Axons and dendrites do not touch at synapses. Instead, electrical impulses excite brain chemicals, called *neurotransmitters,* which carry information from the axon of the sending neuron, across the *synaptic gap,* to the dendrites of the receiving neuron, a process speeded up by myelination (described in Chapter 8).

Response for New Parents (from page 137): From the psychological and cultural perspectives, babies can sleep anywhere as long as the parents can hear them if they cry. The main consideration is safety: Infants should not sleep on a mattress that is too soft, nor should a baby sleep beside an adult who is drunk or drugged or sleeps very soundly (Nakamura et al., 1999). Otherwise, the family should decide for itself where its members would sleep best.

axon A nerve fiber that extends from a neuron and transmits electrical impulses from that neuron to the dendrites of other neurons.

dendrite A nerve fiber that extends from a neuron and receives electrical impulses transmitted from other neurons via their axons.

synapse The intersection between the axon of one neuron and the dendrites of other neurons.

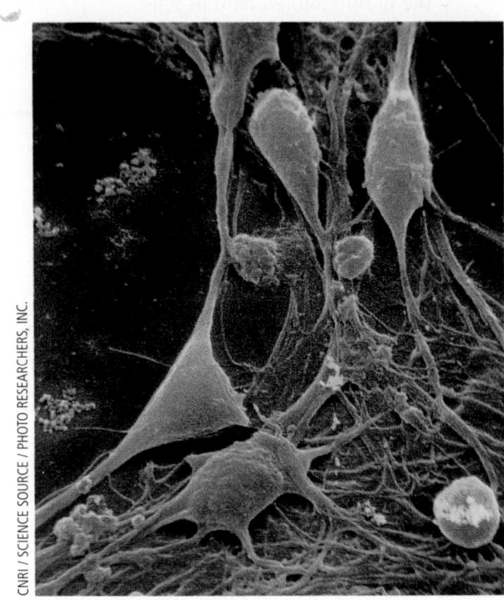

CNRI / SCIENCE SOURCE / PHOTO RESEARCHERS, INC.

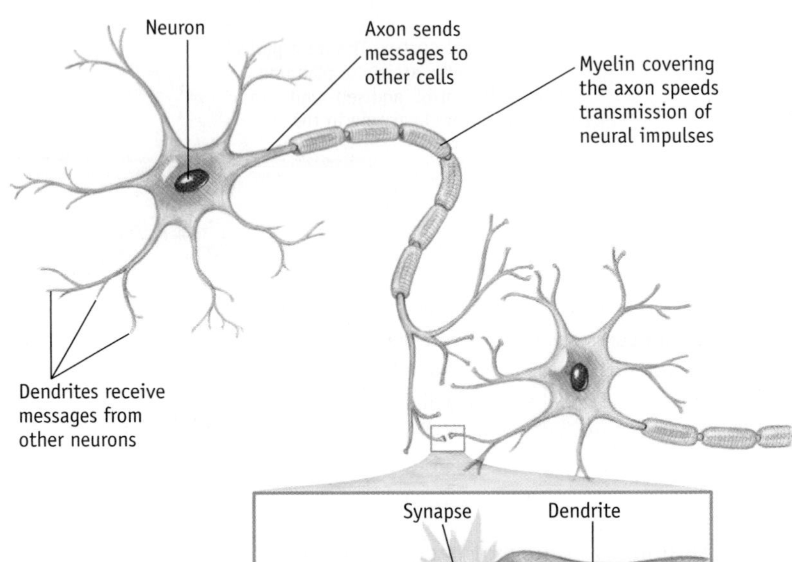

FIGURE 5.6 **How Two Neurons Communicate** The link between one neuron and another is shown in the simplified diagram at right. The infant brain actually contains billions of neurons, each with one axon and many dendrites. Every electrochemical message to or from the brain causes thousands of neurons to fire simultaneously, each transmitting the message across the synapse to neighboring neurons. The electron micrograph directly above shows several neurons, greatly magnified, with their tangled but highly organized and well-coordinated sets of dendrites and axons.

In the synapse, or intersection between an axon and dendrite, neurotransmitters carry information from one neuron to another.

Exuberance

At birth, the brain contains more than 100 billion neurons, more than any person will ever need (de Haan & Johnson, 2003). By contrast, the newborn brain has far fewer dendrites and synapses than the person will eventually possess. During the first months and years, rapid growth and refinement in axons, dendrites, and synapses occur, especially in the cortex. Dendrite growth is the major reason that brain weight triples in the first two years.

transient exuberance The great increase in the number of dendrites that occurs in an infant's brain during the first two years of life.

An estimated fivefold increase in dendrites in the cortex occurs in the 24 months after birth, with about 100 trillion synapses being present at age 2 (Schwartz & Begley, 2002). As many as 15,000 new connections may be established *per neuron* (Thompson, 2000). This early growth is called **transient exuberance,** because the expanded growth of dendrites is followed by a pruning process (see Figure 5.7), in which unused neurons and misconnected dendrites atrophy and die (Barinaga, 2003). Transient exuberance enables neurons to become connected to, and communicate with, a greatly expanding number of other neurons within the brain. Synapses, dendrites, and even neurons continue to form and die throughout life, though much less rapidly than in infancy.

MARK JOHNSON, CENTRE FOR BRAIN AND COGNITIVE DEVELOPMENT, BIRBECK COLLEGE, LONDON

Electric Excitement This infant's delight at his mother's facial expressions is visible, not just in his eyes and mouth but also in the neurons of the outer layer of his cortex. Electrodes map his brain activation region by region and moment by moment. Every month of life up to age 2 shows increased electrical excitement.

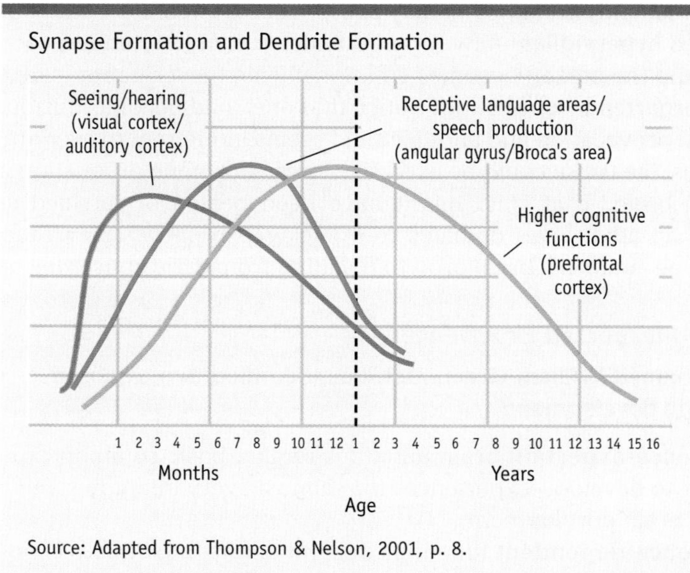

FIGURE 5.7 **Brain Growth in Response to Experience** These curves show the rapid rate of experience-dependent synapse formation for three functions of the brain (senses, language, and analysis). After the initial increase, the underused neurons are gradually pruned, or inactivated, as no functioning dendrites are formed from them.

? OBSERVATIONAL QUIZ (see answer, page 143): Why do both "12 months" and "1 year" appear on the "Age" line?

These links are essential because thinking and learning require making connections between many parts of the brain. For example, to understand any word in this text, you need to understand the surrounding words, the ideas they convey, and how they relate to your other thoughts and experiences. Baby brains have the same requirement, although at first they have few experiences to build on.

Experience Enhances the Brain

The specifics of brain structure and growth depend not only on preordained cell functioning but also on experience, which produces the "postnatal rise and fall" of synapses (de Haan & Johnson, 2003, p. 5). Soon after exuberant expansion, some dendrites wither because they are underused—that is, because experiences have not caused them to connect with the axons of other neurons at the synapses. Underused neurons are inactivated. Strangely enough, this loss actually increases brain power; the "increasing cognitive complexity of childhood is related to a loss rather than a gain of synapses" (de Haan & Johnson, 2003, p. 8).

This process is called *pruning* because it resembles the way a gardener might prune a rose bush by cutting away some stems to enable more, or more beautiful, roses to bloom. It has also been called *sculpting* after the way a sculptor takes a block of stone or wood and chisels it into a work of art, discarding the useless chips. Both these analogies illustrate that cell death can benefit thinking.

Further evidence comes from neurological research regarding the form of mental retardation called fragile X syndrome, described in Chapter 3. One major sign of fragile X syndrome is "a persistent failure of normal synapse pruning" (Irwin et al., 2002, p. 194). In fragile X children, dendrites are too dense and too long; without pruning, children cannot think normally.

Stress Hormones

A practical example of the importance of experience in early brain growth comes from reactions to stress. The brain produces cortisol and other hormones in response to stress lifelong, but the amount relates partly to early experiences (Gunnar & Vasquez, 2001). If too many stress hormones are produced early on (for instance, if an infant is frequently terrified, anticipating pain), then the developing brain becomes incapable of normal stress responses. If this part of the brain is permanently damaged, it may overproduce stress hormones and the person becomes hypervigilant (always on the alert), or it may underproduce stress hormones and the person becomes emotionally flat (never happy, sad, or angry).

A kindergarten teacher might notice that one child becomes furious or terrified at a mild provocation and another child seems indifferent to everything. Why? In both cases, the cause could be excessive stress-hormone production in infancy, altering the brain. That child might have been beaten or terrified as a baby. Similarly, if an adult loves or hates too quickly, extremely, and irrationally, the cause could be abnormal brain growth resulting from early abuse (Teicher, 2002).

Usual and Unexpected Experiences

A scientist named William Greenough has identified two experience-related aspects of brain development:

experience-expectant Refers to brain functions that require basic common experiences (which the infant can be expected to have) in order to develop normally.

experience-dependent Refers to brain functions that depend on particular, variable experiences and that therefore may or may not develop in a particular infant.

- **Experience-expectant** brain functions require basic common experiences in order to develop—experiences that almost every infant has and needs for normal brain development.
- **Experience-dependent** functions depend on the individual's exposure to particular, variable events that occur in some families and cultures but not in others (Greenough et al., 1987).

Expected experiences *must* happen for normal brain maturation to occur, and they almost always do happen: The brain is designed to expect them and use them for growth. By contrast, dependent experiences *might* happen; because of them, one brain differs from another.

Human brains have many *expected* experiences. In deserts and the Arctic, on isolated farms and in crowded cities, babies have things to see and people to care for them. As a result, their brains develop normally. Some particular experiences, such as which language a baby hears or how the mother reacts to frustration, vary. *Depending* on those various experiences, infant brains will be structured and connected one way or another, as particular dendrites grow and neurons thrive. Consequently, each person is similar to every other person but is also a unique product of particular early experiences.

This distinction can be made for all mammals. Some of the most persuasive research comes from songbirds. All the males have a brain region dedicated to listening and reproducing sounds (experience-expectant), but each species in a

EASTCOTT / MOMATINK / THE IMAGE WORKS

Let's Talk Infants evoke facial expressions and baby talk, no matter where they are or which adults they are with. Communication is thus experience-expectant: Young human brains expect it and need it.

? OBSERVATIONAL QUIZ (see answer, page 146): Are these two father and daughter? Where are they?

particular locality learns to produce a slightly different song (experience-dependent) (Knudsen, 1999). Further research finds that birds develop the new neurons that they need most: neurons dedicated to learning new songs (canaries) or to finding hidden seeds (chickadees). Both of these are experience-dependent functions that are needed in context by some birds but not others (Barinaga, 2003).

Experience-expectant brains mature on schedule because expected experiences occur. At a particular age the brain is sensitive to those expected events. For instance, newborns see light and dark patterns in the visual displays all around them, and this helps trigger the development of their visual cortex (Maurer et al., 1999).

In unusual situations, knowledge of which developmental events are expected at what ages is helpful to protect the cortex. For example, proliferation and pruning occur first in the visual cortex and the auditory cortex, beginning at about 4 months. Consequently, diagnosis of blind or deaf newborns, and then treatment (surgery, glasses, hearing aids, etc.), should occur in the first weeks of life, to prevent premature atrophy of those brain regions primed to expect sights and sounds (Leonard, 2003). If early visual or auditory neuronal connections are not made, those areas of the brain may become dedicated to other senses, such as touch. Braille, for that reason, is easier for a blind person to read than for a seeing person, because blind people often have more brain cells dedicated to the sense of touch (Pascual-Leone & Torres, 1993).

Similarly, the language areas of the brain develop most rapidly between the ages of 6 and 24 months, so infants need to hear a lot of speech during that period in order to talk fluently. The last part of the brain to mature is the **prefrontal cortex**, the area for anticipation, planning, and impulse control. It is virtually absent in early infancy and gradually becomes more efficient over the years of childhood and adolescence (Luciana, 2003). Thus, telling an infant to stop crying is pointless because the infant cannot decide to stop crying. Such decisions require brain capacity that is not yet present.

! Answer to Observational Quiz (from page 141): "One year" signifies the entire year, from day 365 to day 729, and that is indicated by its location between "12 months" and "2 years."

prefrontal cortex The area of cortex at the front of the brain that specializes in anticipation, planning, and impulse control.

Implications for Caregivers

What does early brain development mean for caregivers? First, early brain growth is rapid and reflects experience. This means that caressing a newborn, talking to a preverbal infant, and showing affection toward a small person may be essential to develop that person's full potential. If such experiences are missing from the early weeks and months, that is tragic. As you will discover later, early child neglect can reverberate throughout life.

Second, each part of the brain has a sequence of growing, connecting, and pruning. Some kinds of stimulation are meaningless before the brain is ready, and some potential learning is irrelevant to a particular person. That means it is advisable to follow the baby's lead to figure out what stimulation is needed. Infants are alert to whatever their brains need—which is why very young babies like to look at and listen to musical mobiles, strangers on the street, and, best of all, their own caregivers. This reflects a general trend toward **self-righting**, the inborn drive to remedy any deficit that may occur. An infant with limited stimulation will use whatever experiences are available to develop the brain. Babies do not need the latest educational toys—their brains will develop with normal stimulation. Just don't keep them in a dark, quiet place all day long.

self-righting The inborn drive to remedy a developmental deficit.

Human brains are designed to grow and adapt; some plasticity is retained throughout life. Brains protect themselves from overstimulation (overstimulated babies sometimes cry or sleep) as well as understimulation, developing new connections lifelong, depending on experience (Greenough, 1993; Schwartz & Begley, 2002). Are there limits to brain plasticity? Read about some research on rats and human orphans.

Thinking Like a Scientist

Plasticity and Orphans

Neuroscientists once thought that brains were formed solely by genes and prenatal influences. By contrast, many social scientists once thought that childhood environment was crucial: Cultures (according to anthropologists) or societies (according to sociologists) or parents (according to psychologists) could be credited or blamed for a child's emotions and actions.

Now most scientists, especially life-span developmentalists, are multidisciplinary (as explained in Chapter 1), incorporating perspectives of both neuroscience and social science. They believe in *plasticity* (also described in Chapter 1). Personality, intellect, habits, and emotions change throughout life for many biological and social reasons, not just one (Wachs, 2000). There are **sensitive periods**, which are times in the developmental sequence when particular kinds of development are primed to occur because "this time of plasticity does not last infinitely" (de Haan & Johnson, 2003), but timing is not as rigid as neuroscientists once thought.

The crucial question: How much, and when, can experience affect the brain? Two research projects—one with caged rats and the other with adopted babies—shed some light.

In research by Marion Diamond, William Greenough, and their colleagues, some rats were raised with other rats in large cages filled with interesting rat toys; other rats were isolated in small, barren cages. In order to minimize the influence of inborn differences, all the rats in these experiments were close genetic relatives, randomly assigned to the "enriched" or "deprived" environments. After the rats died, their brains were examined. The brains of the rats in the "enriched" group were far better developed (larger, heavier, with more dendrites) than were the brains of the rats in the "deprived" group (Diamond et al., 1988; Greenough & Volkmar, 1973).

Many other researchers have confirmed this phenomenon: Isolation and sensory deprivation harm the developing brain of a rat, and a complex social environment enhances neurological growth (Curtis & Nelson, 2003). Plasticity is not just an ideal; it is a proven fact. The most recent extensions of this research suggest that rats raised in cognitively stimulating environments are less likely to suffer from any brain disease, including Alzheimer's disease, in late adulthood.

Such experiments are unthinkable with humans, but a chilling natural experiment began in Romania in the 1980s, when dictator Nicolae Ceauseșcu forbade all birth control and outlawed abortions except for women who already had five children (illegal abortions became the leading cause of death for women of childbearing age) (Verona, 2003). Parents were paid for every newborn, but they received no financial support for raising the child.

As a result, more than 100,000 children were abandoned to the streets or to crowded, understaffed state-run orphanages (D. E. Johnson, 2000). Unlike the rats, these children were not isolated or deprived. In terms of what human brains need to develop, however, their experience may have been worse: They were stressed and overstimulated by the crowding without the buffers of social reassurance and love. They experienced "severe and pervasive restriction of human interactions, play conversation, and experiences" (Rutter et al., 2004, p. 91).

Ceauseșcu was ousted and killed in 1989. During the next two years, thousands of Romanian children were taken out of the orphanages and adopted by North American and Western European families who believed that "lots of love and good food would change the skinny, floppy waif they found in the orphanage into the child of their dreams" (D. E. Johnson, 2000, p. 154).

All the Romanian adoptees experienced catch-up growth, becoming taller and gaining weight until they reached normal size (Rutter et al., 2004). However, many showed signs of emotional damage: They were too friendly to strangers, or too angry without reason, or too frightened of normal events (Chisholm, 1998). The children who fared best were adopted before age 2 and were cared for initially by their birth parents, and thus had some experience-expectant development, before being turned over to the orphanage (Verona, 2003).

AP / WIDE WORLD PHOTOS

A Fortunate Pair Elaine Himelfarb *(shown in the background)*, of San Diego, California, is in Bucharest to adopt 22-month-old Maria. This adoption was an exception to the Romanian government's current ban on international adoptions. Adopted children like Maria, who have been well fed and who are less than 2 years old, are especially likely to develop well.

For those scientists who expected dire consequences, the news was good: "The human infant has built-in 'buffers' against early adversity" (O'Connor et al., 2000). Self-righting was apparent, especially in weight and height, and, for some children, in other ways as well. For those scientists who expected complete recovery, the news was bad: The researchers found "persistent deficits in post-institutionalized children . . . in all longitudinal studies of Romanian orphans" (D. E. Johnson, 2000, p. 152). Long-term deficits were often apparent in social interaction and cognition, precisely the functions controlled by the cortex.

Research on maltreated children in the United States reaches similar conclusions. If maltreatment begins early in life and continues for years, complete social and emotional recovery is rare, much more elusive than catch-up physical growth (Bolger & Patterson, 2003). Plasticity is not infinite; some early brain damage probably persists no matter how nurturant later life is. A detailed study of 144 of the Romanian children who had spent more than two years in an institution but were then adopted into loving, stimulating homes found that IQ was 20 points below average. Figure 5.8 is a scatterplot of their IQ at age 6. It shows marked variation: One child adopted after age 3 had an above-average IQ, two had average IQs, and five were mentally retarded. Not shown is a correlate of low IQ—malnutrition so severe that it affected head circumference (Rutter et al., 2004).

Note that dire, deterministic predictions about maltreated children can be wrong. A team of scientists who have devoted their lives to impaired children advise: "Be skeptical about 'miracle' cures of severely affected individuals which appear in the media, or even in scientific journals, while recognizing that partial amelioration can occur in individual cases" (Clarke & Clarke, 2003, p. 131).

Thinking like a scientist, in this case, means condemning every government, culture, or family that allows young children to be raised without the experiences they need in order to develop normally. It also means appreciating head-sparing, plasticity, self-righting, and experience-expectant events, all of which help to compensate for early deprivation as long as that deprivation is relatively brief and not overwhelming.

The childhood environment can remedy as well as cause deprivation, especially in infancy, which is one reason that applying this research is crucial. Efforts are being made to find out why some children were spared. Were they protected by genes, by caregivers at their institutions, or by some other factor?

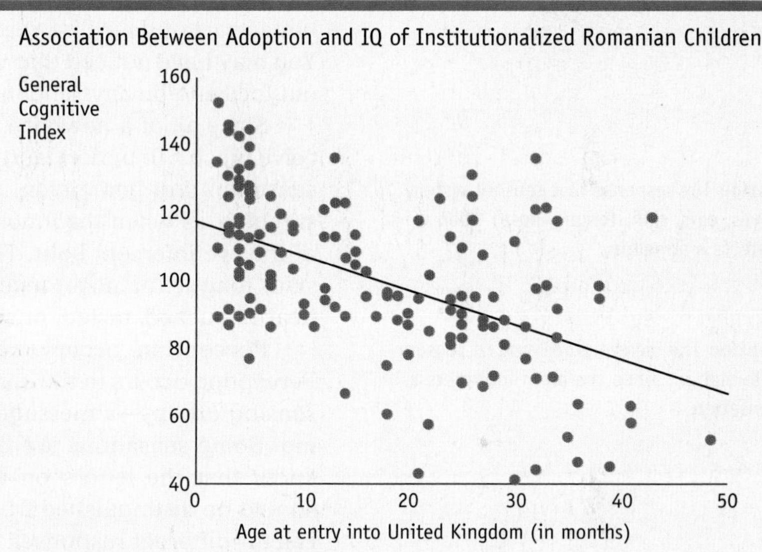

FIGURE 5.8 **Long-Term Deficits Persist** Scatterplot and regression line for the association between cognitive level and age at entry into the United Kingdom (UK).

SUMMING UP

Brain growth is astonishingly rapid during the first months of life, when dendrites and the synapses within the cortex increase exponentially. By age 2 the brain already weighs three-fourths of what it will weigh in adulthood, has grown rapidly (transient exuberance), and has begun notable pruning. The shrinkage of underused and unconnected dendrites begins in the sensory and motor areas and then occurs in other areas, including those dedicated to language. Although some brain development is maturational, experience is also essential—both the universal experiences that almost every infant has (experience-expectant brain development) and the particular experiences whose nature depends on the family or culture (experience-dependent brain development).

sensitive period A time when a certain kind of growth or development is most likely to happen or happens most readily.

ESPECIALLY FOR SOCIAL WORKERS
An infertile couple in their late 30s asks for your help in adopting a child from Eastern Europe. They particularly want an older child. How do you respond?

! Answer to Observational Quiz (from page 142): The man's straight black hair, high cheekbones, and weather-beaten face indicate that he could be an Indian from North or South America. Other clues pinpoint the location more closely. Note his lined, hooded jacket and the low, heat-conserving ceiling of the house—he is an Inuit in northern Canada. A father's attention makes a baby laugh and vocalize, not look away, so this man is not the 6-month-old baby's father. She is being held by a family friend whom she is visiting with her parents.

The Senses and Motor Skills

You learned in Chapter 2 that Piaget called the first period of intelligence the *sensorimotor* stage, emphasizing that cognition develops from the senses and motor skills. The same concept—that infant brain development depends on the sensory experiences and early movements of the baby—underlies the discussion you have just read. Similarly, within hours of birth, doctors and nurses make sure the vital organs function, assessing basic senses and motor responses. Many of them use the *Brazelton Neonatal Assessment Scale,* which measures 26 items of newborn behavior (such as cuddling, listening, and soothing) as well as several reflexes. Now we will look at these senses and motor abilities.

Sensation and Perception

All the senses function at birth. Newborns have open eyes, sensitive ears, and responsive noses, tongues, and skin. Throughout their first year, infants use their senses to sort and classify their many experiences. Indeed, "infants spend the better part of their first year merely looking around" (Rovee-Collier, 2001, p. 35). You may have noticed that very young babies seem to attend to everything, without focusing on anything in particular.

Since all of a newborn's senses function, why don't newborns seem to perceive much? To understand this, you need to be aware of the distinction between sensation and perception. **Sensation** occurs when a sensory system detects a stimulus, as when the inner ear reverberates with sound or the retina and pupil of the eye intercept light. Thus, sensations begin when an outer organ (eye, ear, skin, tongue, or nose) meets anything in the external world that can be seen, heard, touched, tasted, or smelled.

sensation The response of a sensory system (eyes, ears, skin, tongue, nose) when it detects a stimulus.

Perception occurs when the brain notices and processes a sensation. Perception occurs in the cortex, usually as the result of a message from one of the sensing organs—a message that experience suggests might be worth interpreting. Some sensations are beyond comprehension at first: A newborn does not know that the letters on a page might have significance, that mother's face should be distinguished from father's face, or that the smells of roses and garlic call for different responses. Perceptions require experience.

perception The mental processing of sensory information, when the brain interprets a sensation.

Infant brains are especially attuned to experiences that are repeated, striving to make sense of them (Leonard, 2003). Thus, newborn Emily has no idea that *Emily* is her name, but she has the brain capacity to hear sounds in the usual speech range (not the high sounds that only dogs can hear) and an inborn preference for repeated patterns. At about 4 months, especially when her auditory cortex is rapidly creating and pruning dendrites, the repeated word *Emily* is perceived as well as sensed, and the sound is associated with attention from other people (Mandel et al., 1995). At 6 months, Emily probably opens her eyes and turns her head when her name is called. It will take many more months before she tries to say "Emmy" and still longer before she knows that *Emily* is indeed her name. When that happens, cognition is evident.

Especially for Parents of Grown Children Suppose that you realize that you seldom talked to your children until they talked to you and that you never used a stroller or a walker but put them in cribs and playpens. Did you limit their brain growth and their sensory capacity?

Thus, cognition goes beyond perception. It occurs when people think about and interpret what they have perceived. (As time goes on, cognition no longer requires sensation and perception: People can imagine, fantasize, hypothesize.) There is a sequence of comprehension, from sensation to perception to cognition. A baby's sense organs must function if this sequence is to begin. No wonder the parts of the cortex dedicated to the senses develop rapidly: That is the prerequisite for the other developments.

Hearing

The sense of hearing is already quite acute at birth. Certain sounds seem to trigger reflexes, even without conscious perception. Sudden noises startle newborns, making them cry; rhythmic sounds, such as a lullaby or a heartbeat, soothe them and put them to sleep. Even in the first days of life, infants turn their heads toward the source of a sound, and they soon begin to adapt that response to connect sight and sound, with increasing accuracy (Morrongiello et al., 1998).

Young infants are particularly attentive to the human voice, developing rapid comprehension of spoken words and ignoring irrelevant features. One overview of hearing in childhood explains this striking example of genetic programming for social interaction:

> Infants are exposed to a variety of different sounds in their native environments. Some of these are produced with great frequency by other active, nonhuman creatures, such as family pets, and others by electromechanical devices, such as alarm clocks. Yet, the sounds that infants choose to imitate, the ones which seem to attract their attention most, are the ones produced by other human beings.
>
> *[Aslin et al., 1998, p. 158]*

The human brain detects meaningful differences and ignores insignificant ones; experience builds on those abilities and plugs in the specifics. One significant factor is pitch. A word conveys the same meaning to your brain whether spoken by a man, a woman, or a child, whether said by a close family member or a stranger (Leonard, 2003). English speakers learn to ignore some variations in pronunciation (such as whether a person pronounces *orange* with a long *o* or a short *a*) and to pay attention to others (such as small nuances in the pronunciation of *did*, which could mean "did" or "dead").

This form of selective attention can be seen in everyday life. When I call my students' names, I sometimes fail to pronounce them the way their parents did or the way they prefer. My students immediately know whom I mean, because they ignore such differences. Infants learn to respond to their names, even when uttered by a stranger amid background noise (Newman, 2005). Dogs have better hearing than people, but they also learn to be selective in what sounds they perceive. My daughter Rachel got a puppy in Hungary and gave her a Hungarian name, Cipu. The dog has lived in Minnesota for five years, responding to "Ceepoo" when all of us call her but still responding best when her name is said with a proper Hungarian accent.

As time goes on, sensitive hearing combines with the developing brain to distinguish patterns of sounds and syllables. Infants become accustomed to the rules of their language, such as which syllable is usually stressed (various English dialects have different rules), whether changing voice tone is significant (as it is in Chinese), whether certain sound combinations are often or never repeated, and so on. All this is based on very careful listening to human speech, even speech not directed toward them and uttered in a language they do not yet understand (Jusczyk, 1997; Marcus, 2000).

Seeing

Vision is the least mature sense at birth. The fetus has nothing to see, and thus the connection between the eyes and the visual cortex cannot form. Newborns focus on objects between 4 and 30 inches (10 and 75 centimeters) away and stare blankly at whatever they see (most often the faces of their caregivers), unable to figure out who or what that might be. They prefer to look at faces, but they do not know why, and this reflexive newborn preference disappears in a month or two (Johnson, 1998).

Soon visual experience combines with maturation of the visual cortex to improve visual ability. By 2 months, infants look more intently at a human face, and, tentatively and fleetingly, smile. Over time, visual scanning becomes more

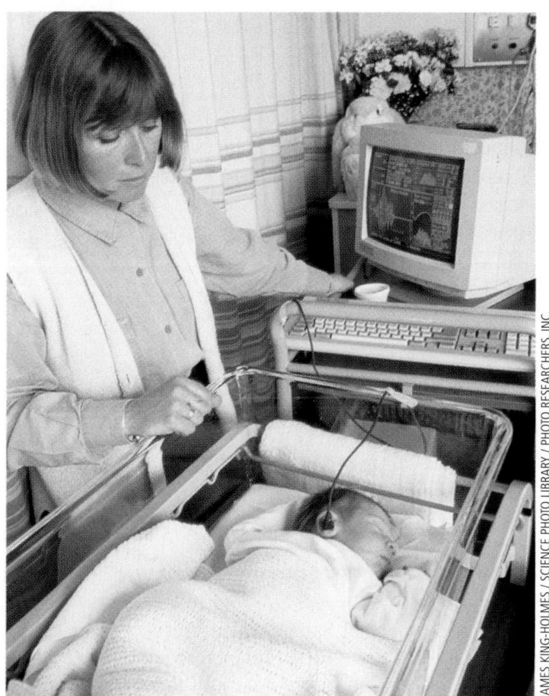

JAMES KING-HOLMES / SCIENCE PHOTO LIBRARY / PHOTO RESEARCHERS, INC.

Before Leaving the Hospital Even as he sleeps, this newborn has his hearing tested via vibrations of the inner ear in response to various tones. The computer interprets the data and signals any need for more tests—as is the case for about 1 baby in 100. Normal newborns hear quite well.

Response for Social Workers (from page 145): Tell them that such a child would require extra time and commitment, more than a younger adoptee would. Ask whether both are prepared to cut down on their working hours in order to meet with other parents of international adoptees, to obtain professional help (for speech, nutrition, physical development, and/or family therapy), and to help the child with schoolwork, play dates, and so on. You might encourage them instead to adopt a special-needs child from their own area, to become foster parents, or to volunteer at least 10 hours a week at a day-care center. Their response would indicate their willingness to help a real—not imagined—child. If they demonstrate their understanding of what is required, then you might help them adopt the child they want.

organized, more efficient, centered on important points. Thus, 3-month-olds look more closely at the eyes and mouth, the parts of a face that contain the most information, and they much prefer photos of faces with features over photos with blank faces (Johnson & Morton, 1991).

binocular vision The ability to focus the two eyes in a coordinated manner in order to see one image.

Binocular vision is the ability to coordinate the two eyes to see one image. Because using both eyes together is impossible in the womb, many newborns seem to focus with one eye or the other, or to use their two eyes independently, seeming momentarily wall-eyed or cross-eyed. At about 14 weeks, binocular vision appears quite suddenly, probably because the underlying brain mechanisms are activated and the infant becomes able to focus both eyes on one thing (Atkinson & Braddick, 2003).

Tasting, Smelling, and Touching

As with vision and hearing, the senses of taste, smell, and touch function at birth and rapidly adapt to the social world. For example, one study found that a taste of sugar calmed 2-week-olds but had no effect on 4-week-olds—unless accompanied by a reassuring look from a caregiver (Zeifman et al., 1996). Another study found that sugar is a good anesthetic for newborns (Gradin et al., 2002). However, older babies may start crying when they see a doctor, anticipating pain and ignoring the comfort of sugar. They may even grow to hate lollipops if the doctor gives them one right before a shot.

Response for Parents of Grown Children (from page 146): Probably not. Experience-expectant brain development is programmed to occur for all infants, requiring only the stimulation that virtually all families provide—warmth, reassuring touch, overheard conversation, facial expressions, movement. Extras such as baby talk, music, exercise, mobiles, and massage may be beneficial but are not essential.

Similar adaptation occurs for the senses of smell and touch. As babies learn to recognize their caregiver's smell and handling, they relax only when cradled by their familiar caregiver, even when their eyes are closed. The ability to be comforted by the human touch is one of the important "skills" tested in the Brazelton Neonatal Assessment Scale. Although almost all newborns respond to cuddling, over time the response becomes more specific to the particulars of a certain touch.

The entire package of early sensation seems organized for two goals: social interaction (to respond to familiar caregivers) and comfort (to be soothed amid the disturbances of infant life). Even the sense of pain and the sense of motion, not among the five basic senses because no body part is dedicated to them, are adapted by infants to aid both socialization and comfort.

The most important experiences are perceived with all the senses at once. Breast milk, for instance, is a mild anesthetic, so the newborn literally feels happier at the mother's breast, connecting pleasure with taste, touch, smell, and sight. Similarly, because infants respond to motion as well as to sights and sounds, many new parents rock, carry, or even drive (with the baby in an infant seat)

Learning About a Lime Like every other normal infant, Jacqueline's curiosity leads to taste, then to a slow reaction, from puzzlement to tongue-out disgust. Jacqueline's responses demonstrate that the sense of taste is acute in infancy and that quick brain reactions are still to come.

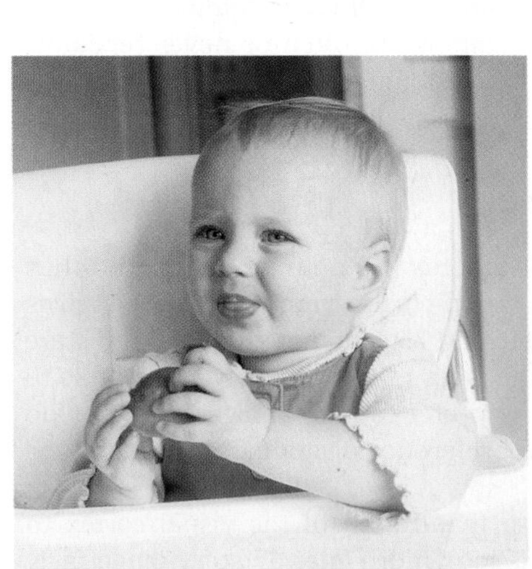

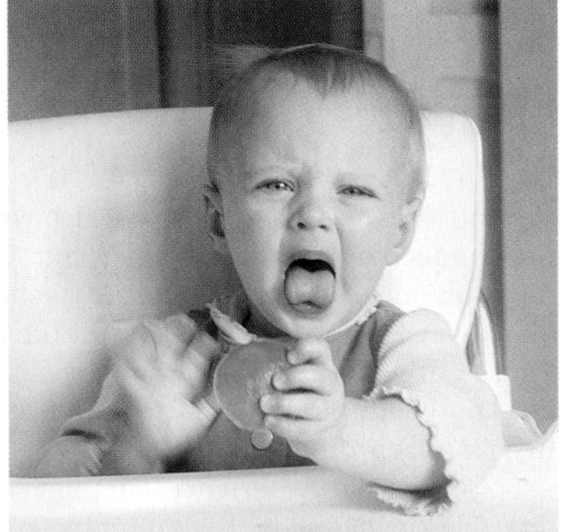

ALL: CINDY CHARLES / PHOTOEDIT, INC.

while humming a lullaby to soothe the infant's distress, again connecting infant comfort with social interaction. In sum, infants seem genetically programmed with senses that help them happily join the human family, and then the senses adapt to the details of each baby's experiences.

Motor Skills

We now come to the most visible and dramatic advances of infancy, those that ultimately allow the child to "stand tall and walk proud." Thanks to ongoing changes in size and proportion, and to increasing brain maturation, infants markedly improve their **motor skills**, which are the abilities needed to move and control the body.

motor skill Any ability to move a part of the body, from a large leap to a small movement of the eyelid. These are called skills because they are learned, not automatic.

To understand the sequence of motor skills, it is useful to understand two Latin terms: *proximal-distal* and *cephalo-caudal*. *Proximal-distal* means "from near [as in *proximity*] to far [as in *distant*]." The term is used to refer to the fact that development proceeds from the center of the body toward the extremities. Thus, the infant torso is much bigger, and more mature, than the hands or the feet.

Cephalo-caudal means "from head [as in *encephalitis*] to tail [as in *caudal*]" and is used to refer to the fact that development proceeds from the head down. Thus, the brain, the eyes, and the mouth develop before the legs and feet; sucking with great skill occurs more than two years before kicking with good aim. Together, *proximal-distal* and *cephalo-caudal* describe the sequence of motor-skill development. For example, head-to-toe development is seen in head lifting, shoulder propping, sitting, standing, walking, and, at about 18 months, running.

Reflexes

Newborns can move their bodies—curl their toes, grasp with their fingers, screw up their faces—but these movements are not under voluntary control. Strictly speaking, the infant's first motor skills are not really skills but reflexes. A **reflex** is an involuntary response to a particular stimulus. Newborns have dozens of them. Three sets of reflexes are critical for survival and become stronger as the baby matures:

reflex A responsive movement that seems automatic because it almost always occurs in reaction to a particular stimulus. Newborns have many reflexes, some of which disappear with maturation.

- *Reflexes that maintain oxygen supply.* The *breathing reflex* begins in normal newborns even before the umbilical cord, with its supply of oxygen, is cut. Additional reflexes that maintain oxygen are reflexive *hiccups* and *sneezes*,

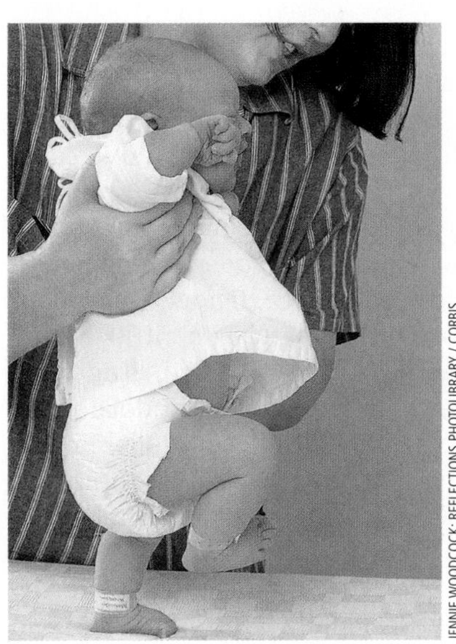

JENNIE WOODCOCK; REFLECTIONS PHOTOLIBRARY / CORBIS

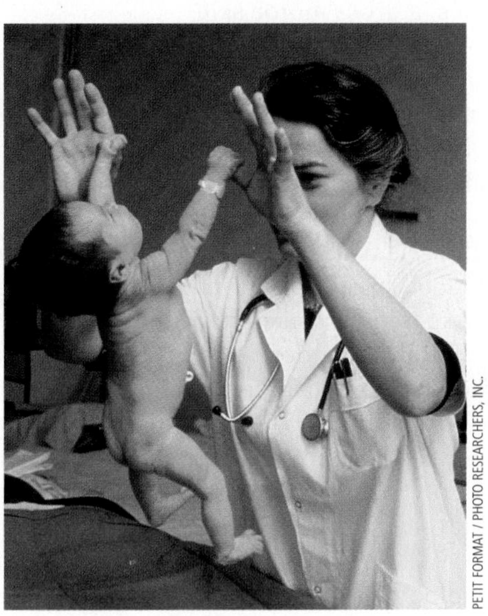

PETIT FORMAT / PHOTO RESEARCHERS, INC.

Never Underestimate the Power of a Reflex For developmentalists, newborn reflexes are mechanisms for survival, indicators of brain maturation, and vestiges of evolutionary history. For parents, they are mostly delightful and sometimes amazing. Both of these viewpoints are demonstrated by three star performers: A 1-day-old girl stepping eagerly forward on legs too tiny to support her body; a newborn grasping so tightly that his legs dangle in space; and a newborn boy sucking peacefully on the doctor's finger.

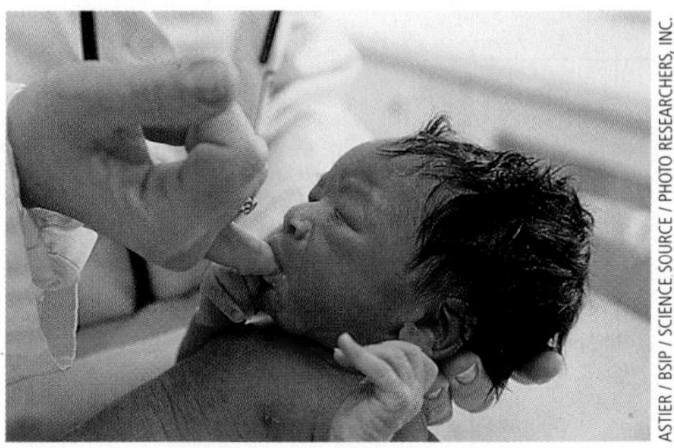

ASTIER / BSIP / SCIENCE SOURCE / PHOTO RESEARCHERS, INC.

as well as *thrashing* (moving the arms and legs about) to escape something that covers the face.

- *Reflexes that maintain constant body temperature.* When infants are cold, they *cry, shiver,* and *tuck in their legs* close to their bodies, thereby helping to keep themselves warm. When they are hot, they try to *push away* blankets and then stay still.
- *Reflexes that manage feeding.* The *sucking reflex* causes newborns to suck anything that touches their lips—fingers, toes, blankets, and rattles, as well as natural and artificial nipples of various textures and shapes. The *rooting reflex* causes babies to turn their mouths toward anything that brushes against their cheeks—a reflexive search for a nipple—and start to suck. *Swallowing* is another important reflex that aids feeding, as are *crying* when the stomach is empty and *spitting up* when too much has been swallowed too quickly.

Other reflexes are not necessary for survival but are important signs of normal brain and body functioning. Among them are the following:

- *Babinski reflex.* When infants' feet are stroked, their toes fan upward.
- *Stepping reflex.* When infants are held upright with their feet touching a flat surface, they move their legs as if to walk.
- *Swimming reflex.* When they are held horizontally on their stomachs, infants stretch out their arms and legs.
- *Palmar grasping reflex.* When something touches infants' palms, they grip it tightly.
- *Moro reflex.* When someone bangs on the table they are lying on, infants fling their arms outward and then bring them together on their chests, as if to hold on to something, while crying with wide-open eyes.

Gross Motor Skills

gross motor skills Physical abilities involving large body movements, such as walking and jumping. (The word *gross* here means "big.")

Deliberate actions coordinating many parts of the body, producing large movements, are called **gross motor skills.** These emerge directly from reflexes. Crawling is one example. Newborns placed on their stomachs reflexively move their arms and legs as if they were swimming. As they gain muscle strength, they start to wiggle, attempting to move forward by pushing their arms, shoulders, and upper bodies against the surface they are lying on. Usually by 5 months or so, they become able to use their arms, and then legs, to inch forward on their bellies, a gross motor skill.

Between 8 and 10 months after birth, most infants can lift their midsections and crawl (or *creep,* as the British call it) on "all fours," coordinating the movements of their hands and knees in a smooth, balanced manner (Adolph et al., 1998). Crawling is experience-dependent. Some normal babies never do it, especially if they have always slept on their backs.

Within the next couple of months, infants learn to climb up onto couches and chairs—as well as up onto windowsills and down into dangerous places, including pools. Soon brain maturation will help them anticipate danger, but meanwhile caregivers need to be vigilant with a mobile but immature infant.

Sitting also develops gradually. It may seem as if unsupported sitting is a sudden accomplishment when infants no longer topple over like rag dolls when put in a sitting position. Although newborns are indeed like rag dolls, unable even to sit supported on someone's lap, by 3 months they have enough muscle control to be lap-sitters if the lap's owner provides supportive arms. This achievement gradually leads to sitting unsupported at 6 months.

Walking shows a similar progression: from reflexive, hesitant, adult-supported stepping to a smooth, speedy, coordinated gait (Bertenthal & Clifton, 1998). On average, a child can walk while holding a hand at 9 months, can stand alone momentarily at 10 months, and can walk well, unassisted, at 12 months.

Walking is an excellent example of multifaceted development. Three factors combine to enable toddlers to walk (Adolph et al., 2003):

- *Muscle strength.* Newborns with skinny legs and infants buoyed by water make stepping movements, but 6-month-olds on dry land do not; their legs are too heavy for their underdeveloped muscles.
- *Brain maturation within the motor cortex.* The first leg movements—kicking (alternating legs at birth and then kicking both legs together or one leg repeatedly at about 3 months)—occur without much thought or aim. As the brain matures, deliberate leg action becomes possible.
- *Practice.* Unbalanced, wide-legged, short strides become a steady, smooth gait after hours of practice.

Once the first two developments have made walking possible, infants are passionate walkers, logging those needed hours of practice. They take steps on many surfaces, with bare feet, stocking feet, slippers, shoes, or whatever. They hate to be pushed in their strollers when they could walk instead. Their enthusiasm for developing this motor skill is commendable:

> Walking infants practice keeping balance in upright stance and locomotion for more than 6 accumulated hours per day. They average between 500 and 1,500 walking steps per hour so that by the end of each day, they have taken 9,000 walking steps and traveled the length of 29 football fields.
>
> [Adolph et al., 2003, p. 494]

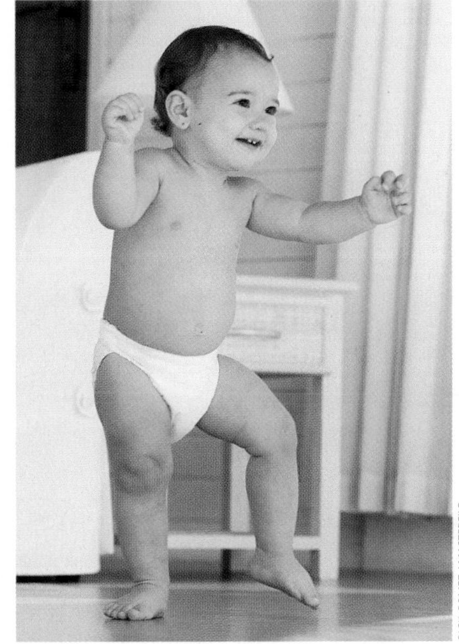

RICK GOMEZ / MASTERFILE

Bossa Nova Baby? This boy in Brazil demonstrates his joy at acquiring the gross motor skill of walking, which quickly becomes dancing whenever music plays.

Fine Motor Skills

Small body movements are called **fine motor skills.** For people, finger movements are the most obvious fine motor skills, enabling humans to write, draw, type, tie, and so on. Movements of the tongue, jaw, lips, and toes are fine movements also. As an example of cephalo-caudal and proximal-distal development, fine mouth skills precede finger skills by many months, although a 1-year-old's skill at spitting or chewing obviously gets much less acclaim than does a 4-year-old's skill at copying a letter.

fine motor skills Physical abilities involving small body movements, especially of the hands and fingers, such as drawing and picking up a coin. (The word *fine* here means "small.")

Regarding finger skills, newborns have a strong reflexive grasp but seem to lack hand and finger control. During their first 2 months, babies excitedly stare and wave their arms at an object dangling within reach. By 3 months of age, they can usually touch it; but they cannot yet grab and hold on unless the object is placed in their hands, partly because their eye–hand coordination is too limited.

By 4 months, infants sometimes grab, but their timing is off: They close their hands too early or too late, and their grasp tends to be of short duration. Finally, by 6 months, with a concentrated, deliberate stare, most babies can reach for, grab at, and hold onto almost any object that is of the right size. They can hold a bottle, shake a rattle, and yank a sister's braids. Moreover, they no longer need to see their hands in order to grab; they can grasp a slowly moving object that is illuminated in an otherwise dark room (Robin et al., 1996), although when the lights are on, they use vision to help them reach accurately (McCarty & Ashmead, 1999).

Once they have this ability, they practice it enthusiastically. In fact, "from 6 to 9 months, reaching appears as a quite compulsive behaviour for small objects presented within arm's reach" (Atkinson & Braddick, 2003, p. 58). A similar progression occurs for using both hands.

By 4 months, infants can transfer objects from hand to mouth (thumb sucking becomes a powerful motivating force). By 6 months,

Mind in the Making Pull, grab, look, and listen. Using every sense at once is a baby's favorite way to experience life, generating brain connections as well as commotion.

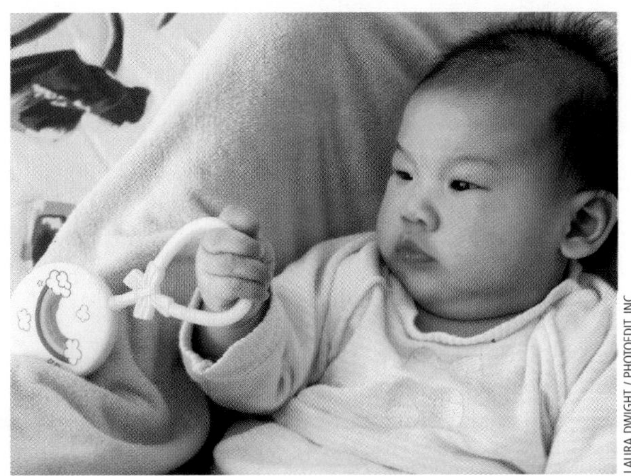

LAURA DWIGHT / PHOTOEDIT, INC.

most infants can transfer objects from one hand to the other. By 8 or 9 months, they adjust their reach in an effort (not always successful) to catch a fast-moving object. By 11 or 12 months, they coordinate both hands to enclose an object that is too big for one hand alone (de Róiste & Bushnell, 1996).

Toward the end of the first year and throughout the second, finger skills improve, as babies master techniques like the pincer movement (using thumb and forefinger to pick up tiny objects) and self-feeding (first with hands, then fingers, then utensils). In the second year, grabbing becomes less compulsive and more selective (Atkinson & Braddick, 2003). Toddlers begin to learn when to pull at sister's braids, Mommy's earrings, and Daddy's glasses, and when not to—although, as you will learn in the next chapter, being aware that a certain activity is not appreciated does not always overcome the curiosity to see the effect produced by that behavior.

Ethnic Variations

All healthy infants develop motor skills in the same sequence, but they acquire these skills at different ages. Table 5.1 shows age norms for mastery of each major motor skill. These percentiles are based on a large, representative, multi-ethnic sample of infants in the United States. Within the United States, ethnic differences are apparent. Generally, African Americans are ahead of Hispanic Americans, who are ahead of European Americans. Internationally, the earliest walkers in the world are in Uganda, where well-nourished and healthy babies walk at 10 months, on average. Some of the latest walkers are in France, where taking one's first unaided steps at 15 months is not unusual.

What accounts for this variation? The power of genes is suggested not only by ethnic differences but also by identical twins, who walk on the same day more often than fraternal twins do. Striking individual differences are apparent in infant strategies, effort, and concentration in mastering motor skills, again suggesting something inborn in motor-skill achievements (Thelen & Corbetta, 2002).

? **Observational Quiz** (see answer, page 154): Is a 6-month-old developing normally if he or she can sit propped up but cannot stand up, even while holding on?

As you remember from Chapter 1, ethnic differences involve much more than genes: Cultural patterns of child rearing also vary from one ethnic group to another. Early reflexes are less likely to fade if culture and conditions allow lots of practice in a particular motor skill. This has been demonstrated with legs (the stepping reflex), hands (the grasping reflex), and crawling (the swimming reflex). Senses and motor skills are part of a complex and dynamic system in which practice counts (Thelen & Corbetta, 2002).

Patterns of infant care are influential in other ways as well. For example, in Uganda, infants are held next to an adult's body, usually in the upright position, virtually all day long; they are cradled and rocked as the adult works. Continually feeling the rhythm and changes of an adult's gait stimulates the infant to practice movement, unlike infants who spend hours in playpens. Crawling occurs later if floors are rough or cold, or if an infant never has "tummy time."

Although some North American parents believe that crawling helps later cognitive development by patterning the brain, and today most Western adults delight in a baby's first steps, some cultures

TABLE 5.1 **Age Norms (in Months) for Gross Motor Skills**

Skill	When 50% of All Babies Master the Skill	When 90% of All Babies Master the Skill
Lifts head 90° when lying on stomach	2.2 months	3.2 months
Rolls over	2.8	4.7
Sits propped up (head steady)	2.9	4.2
Sits without support	5.5	7.8
Stands holding on	5.8	10.0
Walks holding on	9.2	12.7
Stands momentarily	9.8	13.0
Stands alone well	11.5	13.9
Walks well	12.1	14.3
Walks backward	14.3	21.5
Walks up steps (with help)	17.0	22.0
Kicks ball forward	20.0	24.0

Note: These norms came from a large cross section of infants in 1960 in the western half of the United States. Infants born more recently or babies from other nations may have different norms.
Source: The Denver Developmental Screening Test (Frankenburg et al., 1981).

MIKE GREENLAR / THE IMAGE WORKS

Safe and Secure Like this Algonquin baby in Quebec, many American Indian infants still spend hours each day on a cradle board, to the distress of some non-Native adults, until they see that most of the babies are quite happy that way. The discovery in the 1950s that Native American children walked at about the same age as European American children suggested that maturation, not practice, led to motor skills. Later research found that most Native American infants also received special exercise sessions each day, implying that practice plays a larger role than most psychologists once thought.

discourage or even prevent infants from crawling or walking. The people of Bali, Indonesia, never let their infants crawl, for babies are considered divine and crawling is for animals (Diener, 2000). Similar reasoning was dominant in colonial America, where "standing stools" were designed for children so they could strengthen their walking muscles without sitting or crawling (Calvert, 2003). By contrast, the Beng people of the Ivory Coast are proud when their babies start to crawl but do not let them walk until at least 1 year. Although the Beng do not recognize the connection, one reason for this prohibition may be birth control: Beng mothers do not resume sexual relations until their baby begins walking (Gottlieb, 2000).

Although variation in the timing of the development of motor skills is normal, a pattern of slow development suggests that the infant needs careful examination in case brain abnormalities are at fault. Slow infants may be mentally retarded, physically ill, seriously neglected—or perfectly fine, as I know from experience.

In Person

The Normal Berger Babies

Cultural beliefs and the demands of daily life affect every parent and baby. When I had our first child, Bethany, I was a graduate student. I had already memorized such norms as "sitting by 6 months, walking by 12." During her first year, Bethany reached all the developmental milestones pretty much on time. However, at 14 months, she was still not walking.

I became anxious. I read about norms with a sharper eye and learned three comforting facts:

- Variation in timing is normal.
- When late walking signifies brain damage, other signs of delayed development are evident. (Thankfully, Bethany was already talking.)
- Norms for motor-skill development vary from nation to nation. (My grandmother came from France, where babies tend to walk late.)

Two months later, Bethany was walking. In my relief, I began marshaling evidence that motor skills are genetic. My students provided additional testimony as to the power of genes. Those from Jamaica, Cuba, and Barbados expected babies to walk earlier than those from Russia, China, and Korea. Many of my African American students proudly cited their sons, daughters, or younger siblings who walked at 10 months, or even 8 months, to the chagrin of their European American classmates.

Believing now in a genetic timetable for walking, I was not surprised when our second child, Rachel, took her first steps at 15 months. Our third child, Elissa, also walked "late"—though on schedule for a Berger child with some French ancestry. I was not worried about her late motor-skill development, partly because Bethany had become the fastest runner in her kindergarten.

By the time our fourth child, Sarah, was born, I was an established professor and author, able to afford a full-time caregiver, Mrs. Todd, from Jamaica. Mrs. Todd thought Sarah was the brightest, most advanced baby she had ever seen, except, perhaps, her own daughter Gillian. I agreed, but I cautioned Mrs. Todd that Berger children walk late.

"She'll be walking by a year," Mrs. Todd told me. "Maybe sooner. Gillian walked at 10 months."

"We'll see," I replied, confident in my genetic interpretation.

I underestimated Mrs. Todd. She bounced baby Sarah on her lap, day after day. By the time Sarah was 8 months old, Mrs. Todd was already spending a good deal of time bent over, holding Sarah by both hands to practice walking—to Sarah's great delight. Lo and behold, Sarah took her first step at exactly 1 year—late for a Todd baby, but amazingly early for a Berger.

As a scientist, I know that a single case proves nothing. It could be that the genetic influences on Sarah's walking were different from those on her sisters. Furthermore, she is only one-eighth French, a fraction I had ignored when I sought reassurance regarding Bethany. But in my heart I think it likely that practice, fostered by a caregiver with a cultural tradition unlike mine, made the difference. Now, as I teach, I always emphasize both nature and nurture in describing motor-skill development.

HAZEL HANKIN

My Youngest at 8 Months When I look at this photo of Sarah, I see evidence of Mrs. Todd's devotion. Sarah's hair is washed and carefully brushed, her jumper and blouse are clean and pressed, and the carpet and stepstool are perfect equipment for standing practice. Sarah's legs—chubby and far apart—indicate that she is not about to walk early; but, given all these signs of Mrs. Todd's attention to caregiving, it is not surprising, in hindsight, that my fourth daughter was my earliest walker.

! Answer to Observational Quiz (from page 152): Yes—somewhat slow, but still quite normal. By age 6 months, the average baby can stand up while holding on, but 40 percent master this skill later, between 6 and 10 months.

SUMMING UP

The five senses (seeing, hearing, tasting, touching, smelling) function quite well at birth, although hearing is far superior to vision, probably because of experience: The fetus has much more to hear than to see. After birth, vision develops rapidly, leading to binocular vision at about the 14th week. Quite sensitive perception from all sense organs is evident by 1 year. The senses work together and are particularly attuned to human interaction.

Motor skills begin with survival reflexes but quickly expand to include various body movements that the infant masters. Infants lift their heads, then sit, then stand, then walk and run. Sensory and motor skills follow a genetic and maturational timetable, but they are also powerfully influenced by experiences, which result from specific actions of the caregiver, which in turn are guided by the culture. Infants themselves practice whatever skills they can—looking, reaching, or walking many hours a day.

Public Health Measures

Although precise worldwide statistics are unavailable, at least 6 billion children were born between 1950 and 2000. More than 1 billion of them died before age 5. As high as this figure is, the death toll would have been at least 2 billion without advances in newborn care, especially childhood immunization, oral rehydration therapy (giving restorative liquids to children who are sick and have diarrhea; this alone saves 3 million young children *per year*), clean water, and better nutrition.

According to reliable statistics, in 2005 in the healthiest nations (such as Japan, the Netherlands, and France), less than 0.1 percent (1 in 1,000) of babies who survive the first days after birth will die before age 5. Even in the nations with the most childhood deaths (Malawi, Niger, and Afghanistan), less than 25 percent of newborn survivors die in their first 5 years (UNICEF, 2003). In 1900, by contrast, no matter where they were born, about 1 in 3 children—in many places, 1 in 2—died that young (Bogin, 1996).

Immunization

Measles, whooping cough, pneumonia, and other illnesses were once common childhood killers. Although these diseases can still be fatal, especially for malnourished children, they are no longer common. Most children are protected because of **immunization** (which primes the body's innate immune system to defend against a specific contagious disease), a scientific development said to have had "a greater impact on human mortality reduction and population growth than any other public health intervention besides clean water" (Baker, 2000).

immunization A process that stimulates the body's immune system to defend against attack by a particular contagious disease. Immunization may either occur naturally (by having the disease) or be acquired through vaccination (by injection, wearing a patch, or swallowing or inhaling).

When someone contracts a contagious disease, that person's immune system produces antibodies that protect him or her from getting the disease again. In a healthy person, a vaccine—a small dose of inactive virus (often via a "shot" in the arm)—stimulates the production of antibodies to protect against the disease. Some details about various vaccines are given in Table 5.2. Stunning successes in immunization include the following:

- Smallpox, the most lethal disease for all children in past centuries, was eradicated worldwide as of 1971. Routine vaccination against smallpox is no longer recommended. Stockpiles of the virus and the vaccine, and immunization of emergency workers, are precautions only against bioterrorism, not against a normal outbreak.
- Polio, a crippling and sometimes fatal disease, is very rare. Widespread vaccination, begun in 1955, has led to elimination of polio in most nations (including the United States). Just 784 cases worldwide were reported in 2003.
- Measles (rubeola, not rubella), which can cause fatal dehydration, is disappearing, thanks to a vaccine developed in 1963. In all of the Americas, fewer than 100 cases of measles occurred in 2003, down from 53,683 in 1997 (MMWR, June 13, 2003). One reason for this success is a new method of measles vaccination, via inhaling rather than injection, now widely used in Mexico.

In protecting children against common childhood diseases, immunization also protects them against serious complications that sometimes occur, among them deafness, blindness, sterility, meningitis, and even death. Less obviously, immunization of each child protects other people. Infants who have not been immunized may die if they catch a disease from an older child; the fetus of a woman who contracts rubella (German measles) during pregnancy may be born blind, deaf, and brain-damaged; adults suffer much more from mumps or measles than children do; and vulnerable adults (the elderly, those who are HIV-positive, or chemotherapy patients, whose immune systems are impaired) can be killed by "childhood" diseases.

Look Away! The benefits of immunization justify the baby's brief discomfort, but many parents still do not appreciate the importance of following the recommended schedule of immunizations.

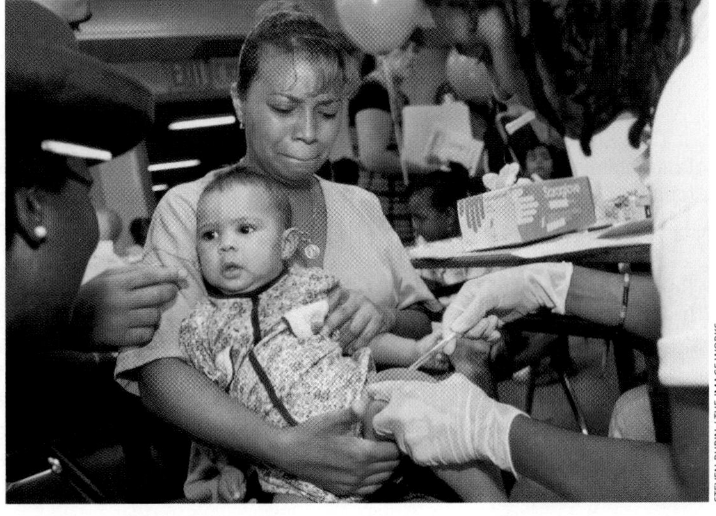
STEVEN RUBIN / THE IMAGE WORKS

Parents do not notice if their child does *not* get seriously ill, but public health advocates note that even a "benign" disease such as chicken pox can turn deadly. One Kansas father, age 36, caught varicella (chicken pox) from his 9-year-old daughter. He was admitted to the hospital on January 19, 2002, suffered numerous complications, and died on March 9 (MMWR, June 13, 2003). No one in this man's family had been vaccinated; unlike most other

TABLE 5.2 **Details About Vaccinations**

Vaccine	Year of Introduction	Peak Annual Disease Total	1999 Total	Consequences of Natural Disease	Percent of Children Vaccinated (U.S.)	Known Vaccine Side Effects
Chicken pox (varicella)	1995	4 million*	N/A	Encephalitis (2 in 10,000 cases), bacterial skin infections, shingles (300,000 per year)	59.4	Mild rash (1 in 20 doses)
DTaP					83.3	Prolonged crying, fever of 105°F or higher
Diphtheria	1923	206,939	1	Death (5 to 10 in 100 cases), muscle paralysis, heart failure		
Tetanus	1927	1,560*	40	Death (30 in 100 cases), fractured bones, pneumonia		Peripheral neuritis, Guillain-Barré syndrome (temporary paralysis—rare)
Pertussis	1926 (whole cell) 1991 (acellular)	265,269	7,288	Death (2 in 1,000 cases), pneumonia (10 in 100 cases), seizures (1 to 2 in 100 cases)		Brain disease (0 to 10 in 1 million doses—whole-cell vaccine only)
H influenzae B (childhood)	1985	20,000*	71	Death (2 to 3 in 100 cases), meningitis, pneumonia, blood poisoning, inflammation of epiglottis, skin or bone infections	93.5	
Hepatitis B	1981	300,000*	7,694	Death from cirrhosis or liver cancer (4,000 to 5,500 per year)	88.1	
MMR					91.5	Fever of 103°F or higher (5 to 15 in 100 doses)
Measles	1963	894,134	100	Encephalitis (1 in 1,000 cases), pneumonia (6 in 100 cases), death (1 to 2 in 1,000 cases), seizure (6 to 7 in 1,000 cases)		
Mumps	1967	152,209	387	Deafness (1 in 20,000 cases), inflamed testicles (20 to 50 in 100 postpubertal males)		
Rubella	1969	56,686	267	Blindness, deafness, heart defects, and/or retardation in 85 percent of children born to mothers infected in early pregnancy		Temporary joint pain (25 in 100 adult doses in women)
Pneumococcal† (childhood)	2000	93,000*	New vaccine	Meningitis (800 cases per year), pneumonia (77,000 cases), blood poisoning (15,000 cases)	New vaccine	Fever over 100.3°F (22 in 100 doses)
Polio (paralytic)	1955	21,269	0	Death (2 to 5 in 100 cases in children), respiratory failure, paralysis, postpolio syndrome	89.6	Vaccine-induced polio (oral vaccine only—1 in 2.4 million doses)

*Estimated.
†Lieu et al., 2000.
Source: Centers for Disease Control and Prevention, in *Consumer Reports,* August 2001, p. 19.

states, Kansas did not require varicella immunization for school entry. Although the 9-year-old was the direct carrier of the disease to her father, both parents, the school, the pediatrician, and the lawmakers also played roles in this tragedy. In the United States, before the chicken pox vaccine, more than 100 people died each year from the disease and more than 1 million were miserably itchy and feverish for a week or more. The death rate is down 92 percent among children, with a total of 27 individuals (mostly unimmunized adults) dying in 2001 (Nguyen et al., 2005).

Many parents are concerned about the potential side effects of vaccinations. However, the risks of diseases that once were common are far greater than the risks from immunization. A review of all the published research concludes: "Immunizations are not without their problems and critics, but the data demonstrate consistently that the overall benefit of vaccinations ranks among the foremost achievements in modern public health" (Dershewitz, 2002).

The biggest problem in the twenty-first century is that more than 1 million children in developing nations die each year because there are not yet approved, effective vaccines against AIDS, malaria, cholera, typhoid, and shigellosis (Russell, 2002). Another 2 to 3 million children die in Africa because the immunization rate against diphtheria, tetanus, and measles is only about 50 percent (Mahmoud, 2004). (Current childhood immunization schedules for the United States are given in Appendix A, p. A-4.)

ESPECIALLY FOR NURSES AND PEDIATRICIANS A mother refuses to have her baby immunized because she wants to prevent side effects. She wants your signature for a religious exemption. What should you do?

Sudden Infant Death Syndrome

Infant mortality worldwide has plummeted in recent years (see Figure 5.9). Several reasons have already been mentioned: advances in newborn care, better nutrition, access to clean water, and widespread immunization. Another reason is that fewer babies are dying of unknown causes, especially **sudden infant death syndrome (SIDS).**

sudden infant death syndrome (SIDS) A situation in which a seemingly healthy infant, at least 2 months of age, suddenly stops breathing and dies unexpectedly while asleep. The cause is unknown, but it is correlated with sleeping on the stomach and having parents who smoke.

Still, some young infants who appear healthy—already gaining weight, learning to shake a rattle, starting to roll over, and smiling at their caregivers—die unexpectedly in their sleep. If autopsy and careful investigation find no apparent cause of death, the diagnosis is SIDS (Byard, 2004). SIDS is perhaps the most frightening cause of infant mortality because its cause is not known.

In 1990 in the United States, about 5,000 babies died of SIDS, about 1 infant in 800. Canada, England, Australia, and virtually every other European and South American nation experienced similar rates. Today, that rate has been cut in half, primarily because fewer infants are put to sleep on their stomachs and because fewer mothers smoke cigarettes. The first of these preventive measures has arisen from an increased respect for cultural differences.

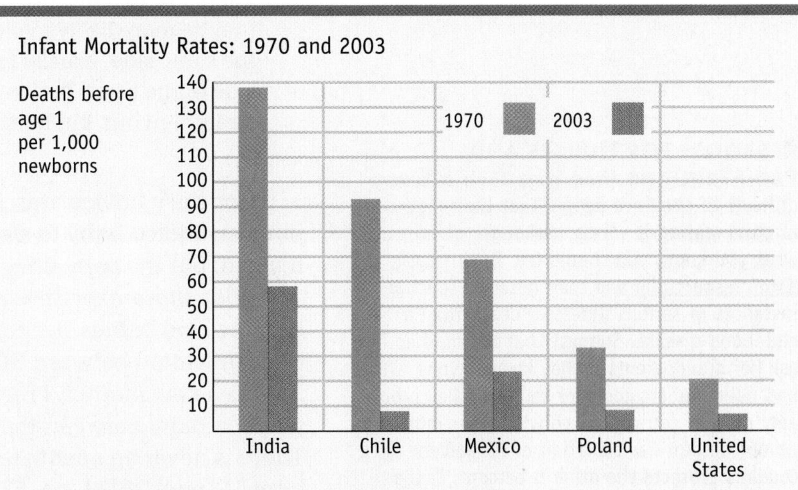

FIGURE 5.9 **More Babies Are Surviving** Improvements in public health—better nutrition, cleaner water, more widespread immunization—over the past three decades have meant millions of survivors.

? CRITICAL THINKING QUESTION (see answer, page 159): The United States seems to be doing very well on reducing infant deaths. Can you suggest another way to present the U.S. data that would lead to another impression?

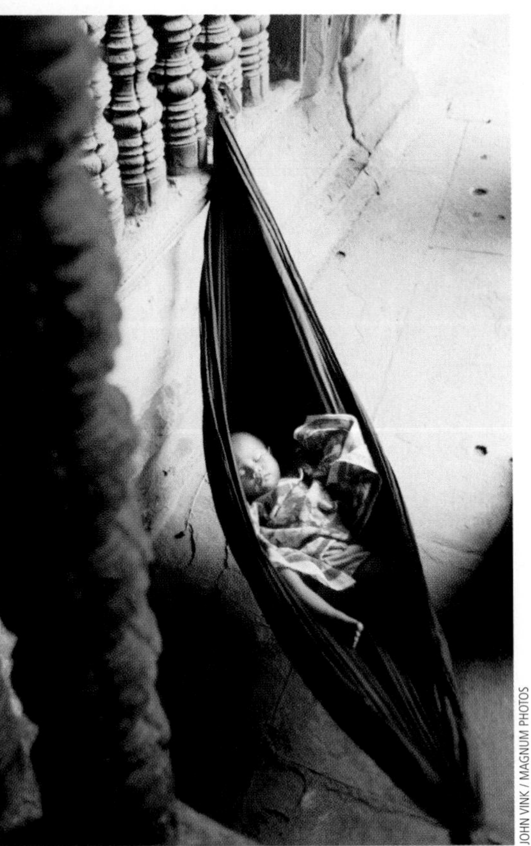

JOHN VINK / MAGNUM PHOTOS

Sleeping Like a Baby It's best to lay babies on their backs to sleep—even if it's in a hammock in a Cambodian temple.

Ethnicity and SIDS

Within ethnically diverse nations such as the United States, Canada, Great Britain, Australia, and New Zealand, babies of Asian descent have always been far less likely than babies of European descent to succumb to SIDS (Byard, 2004). Although low socioeconomic status (SES) is also a risk factor for SIDS, poverty does not seem to be the primary explanation for this ethnic difference. For example, Bangladeshi infants in England tend to be underweight and to be of low-SES families, yet they have lower rates of SIDS than do White British infants of normal birthweight and middle-class families. For decades, pediatricians thought that genes were the underlying cause.

Fortunately, new attention to cultural differences led to a closer look at specific infant-care routines. Bangladeshi infants are usually breast-fed and, even when they sleep, are surrounded by many family members in a rich sensory environment, continually hearing noises and feeling the touch of their caregivers. Therefore, they do not sleep deeply for very long. By contrast, their White British age-mates tend to sleep in their own private spaces in an environment of enforced quiet, and these "long periods of lone sleep may contribute to the higher rates of SIDS among white infants" (Gantley et al., 1993).

Similarly, Chinese infants, whether born in China or elsewhere, have a low rate of SIDS (Beal & Porter, 1991). In fact, *before* a worldwide campaign to reduce the risk of SIDS, only 1 baby in 3,000 in Hong Kong died of SIDS, compared to 1 baby in 200 in New Zealand (Byard, 2004). Why? First, Chinese parents tend to their babies periodically as the infants sleep, caressing a cheek or repositioning a limb. Second, almost all Chinese infants are breast-fed, which makes them sleep less soundly—and deep sleep seems to contribute to SIDS (cow's milk is harder to digest, so it causes more tiredness and thus a deeper sleep).

"Back to Sleep"

When pediatricians, nurses, and anthropologists observed infant care among Asians and Europeans, they noticed another crucial difference: sleeping position. In all the ethnic groups with a low incidence of SIDS, babies were put to sleep on their backs; in all those with high rates, babies slept on their stomachs. The expressed reasons varied and had nothing to do with SIDS. For example, until recently, Benjamin Spock's (1976) book of advice for parents (more than 30 million copies sold) recommended stomach sleeping:

> There are two disadvantages to babies sleeping on their back. If they vomit, they're more likely to choke. Also, they tend to keep the head turned toward the same side, usually toward the center of the room. This may flatten that side of the head. It won't hurt the brain, and the head will gradually straighten out, but it may take a couple of years.
>
> *[Spock, 1976, p. 199]*

Contrary advice was provided to Turkish mothers, who were told: "Never put a swaddled baby to sleep on its stomach, for it would not be able to breathe. Instead, put the baby down to sleep on its back" (Delaney, 2000, p. 131).

Both these experts were mistaken: Babies sleeping on their stomachs can breathe, and babies sleeping on their backs do not choke. Neither expert realized the connection between SIDS and sleeping position.

As a new mother, I remember reading these chilling words: "Every once in a while, a baby between the ages of 3 weeks and 7 months is found dead in bed. There is never an adequate explanation, even when a postmortem examination is done" (Spock, 1976, pp. 576–577). I put my babies to sleep on their stomachs, as my mother did with me and as the hospital where they were born did with thousands of newborns every year. My infants survived, but some other parents' babies did not.

Response for Nurses and Pediatricians (from page 157): It is very difficult to convince people that their method of child rearing is wrong, although, given what you know, you should try. In this case, listen respectfully and then describe specific instances of serious illness or death from a childhood disease. Suggest that the mother ask her grandparents if they knew anyone who had polio, tuberculosis, or tetanus (they probably did). If you cannot convince this mother, do not despair—vaccination of 95 percent of toddlers protects the other 5 percent. If the mother has deeply held religious reasons, talk to her clergy adviser, if not to change the mother's mind, at least to understand her perspective.

About two decades ago, researchers in Australia advised a group of non-Asian mothers to put their infants to sleep on their backs. Other scientists in other nations tried the same experiment. The results were dramatic: Fewer infants died. For example, one comparison study found that the risk of SIDS was only one-fourth as high when infants slept supine (on their backs) instead of prone (Ponsoby et al., 1993).

It is now accepted that "back to sleep" (as the public-awareness slogan puts it) is safest. Worldwide, SIDS rates have fallen—to 1 in 1,000 in New Zealand, for instance. In the United States, in the four years between 1992 and 1996, the stomach-sleeping rate decreased from 70 to 24 percent, and the SIDS rate dropped from 1.2 to 0.7 per 1,000, a "remarkable success" (Pollack & Frohna, 2001). As these statistics show, sleeping position does not prevent all SIDS deaths. Cigarette smoking by parents before and after an infant's birth, low birthweight, overdressed infants, teenage parenthood, and formula-feeding remain risk factors (Byard, 2004). In fact, as more babies sleep on their backs, maternal smoking has become a relatively greater risk factor for SIDS (Anderson et al., 2005).

! Answer to Critical Thinking Question (from page 157): The same data could be presented in terms of rate of reduction in infant mortality. Chile's rate in 2003 was only 10 percent of what it had been in 1970—much better than the U.S. rate, which in 2003 was 35 percent of what it had been in 1970. At the same time, India's reduction is even less impressive: only about 50 percent. (Other data show that about 25 developed nations have lower infant mortality rates than the United States.)

Especially for Police Officers and Social Workers If an infant died suddenly, what would you look for to distinguish SIDS from homicide?

Nutrition

Indirectly, nutrition has been a theme throughout this chapter. You read that pediatricians closely monitor early weight gain, that head-sparing protects the brain from temporary undernourishment, that oral rehydration prevents childhood diarrhea from being fatal. Now, we focus directly on how infants are fed.

Breast Is Best

For most newborns, good nutrition starts with mother's milk. First comes *colostrum,* a thick, high-calorie fluid secreted by the woman's breasts at the birth of her child. After three days, the breasts begin to produce milk, which is the ideal infant food (see Table 5.3). Mother's milk helps prevent almost every infant illness and allergy (Isolauri et al., 1998). It is always sterile and at body temperature; it contains more iron, vitamins C and A, and many other nourishing substances than cow's or goat's milk; it provides antibodies against any disease that the mother has been immunized against. One illness that has recently been increasing among schoolchildren is asthma (discussed in Chapter 11), and one way to reduce the risk of asthma is to breast-feed exclusively for six months or more (Oddy, 2004).

The specific fats and sugars in breast milk make it more digestible, and probably better for the infant brain, than any prepared formula (Riordan, 2005). The particular composition of breast milk adjusts to the age of the baby, with breast milk for premature babies distinct from breast milk for older infants. Quantity increases to meet the demand: Twins and even triplets can grow strong while being exclusively breast-fed for months (Riordan, 2005). In fact, breast milk has so many advantages over formula that critics question the validity of the research: Although studies control for education and income, it is possible that women who choose to breast-feed are better caregivers in some other ways.

Bottle-feeding may be better than breast-feeding in unusual circumstances: when the mother is HIV-positive, uses toxic or addictive drugs, or has some other condition that makes her milk decidedly unhealthy. Even then, however, breast milk may be better than formula. In Africa HIV-positive women are encouraged to breast-feed because the baby's risk of catching the virus is less than the risk of dying from infections, diarrhea, or malnutrition as a result of bottle-feeding. Bottle-feeding is recommended only if it is "acceptable, feasible, affordable, sustainable, and safe" (WHO, 2000)—criteria that are rarely met in developing nations.

AMY ETRA / PHOTOEDIT, INC.

Relaxation—and Sound Nutrition Breast-feeding is ideal, if not always as idyllic as it appears in this scene, set in Palm Beach Gardens, Florida.

TABLE 5.3 **The Benefits of Breast-Feeding**

For the baby:

Balance of nutrition (fat, protein, etc.) adjusts to age of baby

Breast milk has micronutrients not found in formula

Less infant illness: including allergies, ear infections, stomach upsets

Less childhood asthma

Better childhood vision

Less adult illness, including diabetes, cancer, heart disease

Protection against measles and all other childhood diseases, since breast milk contains antibodies

Stronger jaws, fewer cavities, advanced breathing reflexes (less SIDS)

Higher IQ, less likely to drop out of school, more likely to attend college

Later puberty, less prone to teenage pregnancy

Less likely to become obese

For the mother:

Easier bonding with baby

Reduced risk of breast cancer and osteoporosis

Natural contraception (with exclusive breast-feeding, for several months)

Pleasure of breast stimulation

Satisfaction of meeting infant's basic need

No formula to prepare; no sterilization needed

Easier to travel with the baby

For the family:

Increased survival of other children (because of spacing of births)

Increased family income (because both formula and medical care are expensive)

Less stress on father, especially at night (he cannot be expected to feed the baby)

Sources: DiGirolamo et al., 2005; Oddy, 2004; Riordan, 2005.

Virtually all international health organizations recommend that infants be fed exclusively with breast milk for the first four to six months. At that point, other foods can be added—especially cereals and bananas, which are easily digested and provide the iron and vitamin C that older infants need. Dark-skinned infants who are kept indoors may need additional vitamin D to prevent rickets. Once other foods are added, breast-feeding should continue at least until the infant is 1—and longer if both baby and mother wish (Savage & Lhotska, 2000).

In developing nations, breast-feeding dramatically reduces the risk of infant death. In industrialized nations, formula is an acceptable alternative, but many women choose to breast-feed for the sake of their infant. However, in the United States, while two-thirds of all newborns are breast-fed, only one-third are still being breast-fed at 6 months and only one-sixth at 1 year.

Many women decide how they will feed their newborn long before giving birth, so immediately after birth is too late to convince a mother to breast-feed. Whether or not a breast-feeding mother continues to breast-feed for 6 months (as pediatricians recommend) depends a great deal on her experiences in the first week. Those early days are when breast-feeding mothers need the most encouragement and practical help (DiGirolamo et al., 2005). Unfortunately, many social forces (employers, fathers, other relatives) may discourage breast-feeding. (See Appendix A, p. A-5, for variations within the United States.)

Malnutrition

Protein-calorie malnutrition occurs when a person does not consume sufficient food of any kind. Roughly 8 percent of the world's children are severely malnourished because they do not get adequate calories and protein (UNICEF, 2003). These 8 percent are children who are not only too short for their age but also too thin for their height. Far more are too thin *or* too short (2 or more standard deviations below an average well-nourished child). According to this criterion, between 27 percent and 32 percent of the world's children are malnourished (UNICEF, 2003).

protein-calorie malnutrition A condition in which a person does not consume sufficient food of any kind. This results in several illnesses, weight loss, and sometimes death.

To measure a particular child's nutritional status, compare weight and height with the detailed norms presented in Appendix A, pages A-6 and A-7. As you remember from reading about Toni, a child may simply be genetically small, but weight loss or a decline in percentile ranking during the first two years is an ominous sign. Birthweight should triple by age 1, and the 1-year-old's legs and cheeks should be chubby with baby fat (which disappears over the next several years).

Chronically malnourished infants and children suffer in three ways:

- Their brains may not develop normally. If malnutrition has continued long enough to affect the baby's height, it may also affect the brain (Grantham-McGregor & Ani, 2001).
- Malnourished children have no body reserves to protect them against common diseases, such as measles. About half of all childhood deaths occur because malnutrition makes a childhood disease lethal (Rice et al., 2000). To make matters worse, malnourished children are least likely to be immunized. For example, in 2001 in Afghanistan, less than half the children had even the basic vaccinations, and more than half were underweight or stunted. One of every four Afghan newborns died before age 5 (UNICEF, 2003).
- Some diseases result directly from malnutrition.

marasmus A disease of severe protein-calorie malnutrition during early infancy, in which growth stops, body tissues waste away, and the infant eventually dies.

The worst disease directly caused by malnutrition is **marasmus.** Growth stops, body tissues waste away, and an infant eventually dies. Prevention of

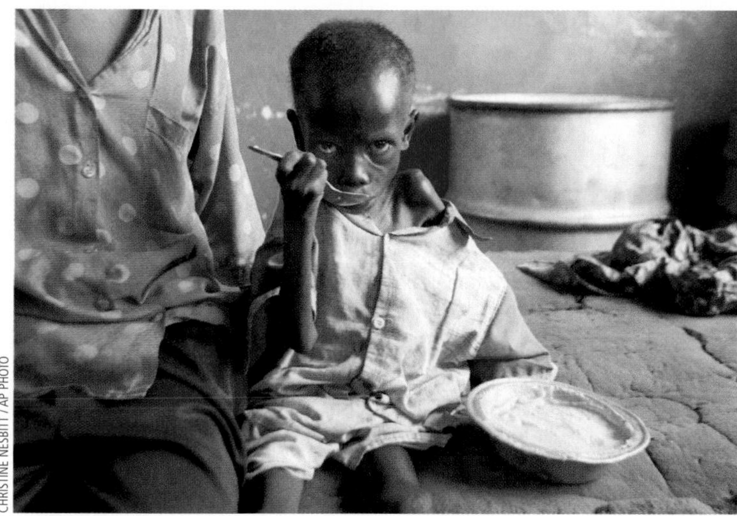

CHRISTINE NESBITT / AP PHOTO

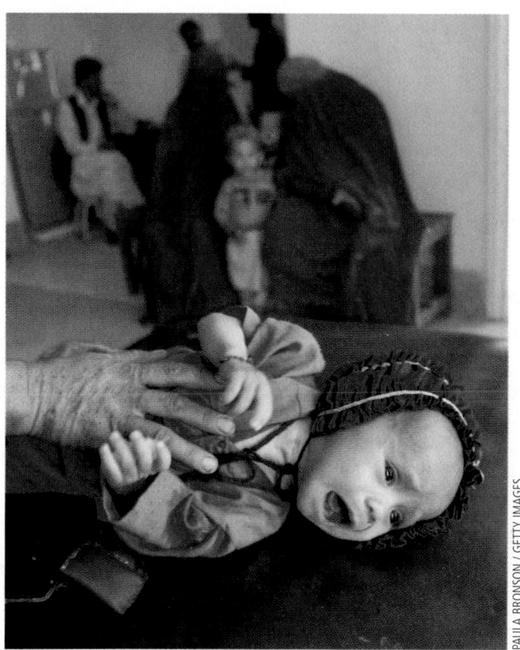

PAULA BRONSON / GETTY IMAGES

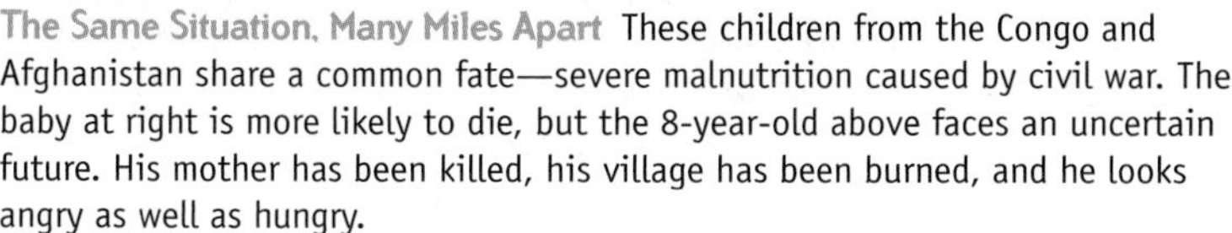

The Same Situation, Many Miles Apart These children from the Congo and Afghanistan share a common fate—severe malnutrition caused by civil war. The baby at right is more likely to die, but the 8-year-old above faces an uncertain future. His mother has been killed, his village has been burned, and he looks angry as well as hungry.

marasmus begins long before birth, with good nutrition for the pregnant woman. Then breast-feeding on demand (eight or more times a day) and frequent check-ups to monitor the baby's weight can stop marasmus before it begins. Infants who show signs of failure to thrive can be hospitalized and treated before brain damage occurs.

If malnutrition begins after age 1, it may take the form of **kwashiorkor**, an illness caused by insufficient protein. Ironically, the word *kwashiorkor* means "a disease of the older child when a new baby arrives"—signifying cessation of breast-feeding and less maternal attention. In kwashiorkor, the child's face, legs, and abdomen swell with water; essential organs claim whatever nutrients are available; energy is reduced (malnourished children play much less than well-nourished children); and nonessential parts of the body become degraded (including the hair, which becomes thin, brittle, and colorless—a telltale sign of chronic malnutrition).

kwashiorkor A disease of chronic malnutrition during childhood, in which a deficiency of protein makes the child more vulnerable to other diseases, such as measles, diarrhea, and influenza.

SUMMING UP

Many public health practices save millions of infants each year. Widespread immunization, putting infants to sleep on their backs, and feeding breast milk are simple yet life-saving steps. Note, however, that these are called "public health" measures rather than parental practices because they go beyond the private decisions made by caregivers. Young lives are saved through national policies and cultural practices; they are the responsibility of everyone. Infant mortality ranges from region to region from less than 1 percent to more than 20 percent, depending on national policies and priorities as well as practices within each family.

An underlying theme throughout this chapter is that healthy biological growth is the result not simply of genes and nutrition but also of a social environment that provides opportunities for growth: lullabies and mobiles for stimulating the infant's senses, encouragement for developing the first motor skills, and protection against disease. Each aspect of development is linked to every other aspect, and each developing person is linked to family, community, and world, as will become even more apparent in the next two chapters on infancy.

Response for Police Officers and Social Workers (from page 159): An autopsy, or at least a speedy and careful examination by a medical pathologist, is needed. Suspected foul play must be either substantiated or firmly rejected—so that the parents can be arrested or warned about conditions that caused an accident, or can mourn in peace. Careful notes about the immediate circumstances—such as the infant's body position when discovered, the position of the mattress and blankets, the warmth and humidity of the room, and the baby's health—are crucial. Further, although SIDS victims sometimes turn blue and seem bruised, they rarely display signs of specific injury or neglect, such as a broken limb, a scarred face, an angry rash, or a skinny body.

SUMMARY

Body Changes

1. In the first two years of life, infants grow taller, gain weight, and increase in head circumference—all indicative of development. The norm at birth is slightly more than 7 pounds, 20 inches (about 3⅓ kilograms, 51 centimeters). Birthweight doubles by 4 months, triples by 1 year, and quadruples by 2 years, when they weigh about 30 pounds (14 kilograms).

2. Sleep gradually decreases over the first two years (from almost 18 hours a day to 11), with less REM sleep, less night waking, and more slow-wave sleep over time. As with all areas of development, variations in sleep patterns are normal, caused by both nature and nurture. Co-sleeping is increasingly common for very young infants, and developmentalists increasingly approve.

Brain Development

3. The brain increases dramatically in size, from about 25 to 75 percent of adult weight, in the first two years. Complexity increases as well, with transient exuberance of cell growth, dendrite development, and synapse connections. Both growth and pruning aid cognition.

4. Experience is vital for dendrites and synapses to link neurons. In the first year, parts of the cortex dedicated to the senses and motor skills mature. If neurons are unused, they atrophy, and the brain regions are rededicated to other sensations. Normal stimulation, which almost all infants obtain, allows experience-expectant maturation.

5. Most experience-dependent brain growth reflects the varied, culture-specific experiences of the infant. Therefore, one person's brain differs from another's. However, all normal infants are equally capable in the basic ways—emotional, linguistic, and sensual—that humans share.

The Senses and Motor Skills

6. At birth, the senses already respond to stimuli. Prenatal experience makes hearing the most mature sense and vision the least mature sense. Vision improves quickly; binocular vision emerges at about 14 weeks. Infants use their senses to strengthen their early social interactions.

7. Newborns have many reflexes, including the survival reflexes of sucking and breathing. Gross motor skills are soon evident, from rolling over to sitting up (at about 6 months), from standing to walking (at about 1 year), from climbing to running (before age 2).

8. Fine motor skills are difficult for infants, but babies gradually develop the hand and finger control needed to grab, aim, and manipulate almost anything within reach. Experience, time, and motivation allow infants to advance in all their motor skills.

Public Health Measures

9. About 1 billion infant deaths have been prevented in the past half-century because of improved health care. One major innovation is immunization, which has eradicated smallpox and virtually eliminated polio and measles in the Americas, but not in sub-Saharan Africa or South Asia.

10. Sudden infant death syndrome (SIDS) once killed about 5,000 infants per year in the United States, and thousands more worldwide. This number has been reduced by half since 1990, primarily because researchers discovered that putting infants to sleep on their backs makes SIDS less likely. If adults stopped smoking, hundreds more infants would survive.

11. Breast-feeding is best for infants, partly because breast milk reduces disease and promotes growth of every kind. The World Health Organization advocates exclusive breast-feeding for the first several months and continued breast-feeding (with supplemental food) until age 2.

12. Severe malnutrition stunts growth and can cause death, directly through marasmus or kwashiorkor and indirectly through vulnerability if a child catches measles, an intestinal disorder, or other illness.

KEY TERMS

head-sparing (p. 132)
norm (p. 132)
percentile (p. 132)
failure to thrive (p. 133)
REM sleep (p. 134)
neuron (p. 138)
cortex (p. 138)
axon (p. 139)
dendrite (p. 139)
synapse (p. 139)
transient exuberance (p. 140)
experience-expectant (p. 142)
experience-dependent (p. 142)
prefrontal cortex (p. 143)
self-righting (p. 143)
sensitive period (p. 144)
sensation (p. 146)
perception (p. 146)
binocular vision (p. 148)
motor skill (p. 149)
reflex (p. 149)
gross motor skills (p. 150)
fine motor skills (p. 151)
immunization (p. 155)
sudden infant death syndrome (SIDS) (p. 157)
protein-calorie malnutrition (p. 160)
marasmus (p. 160)
kwashiorkor (p. 161)

KEY QUESTIONS

1. In what aspects of development would it be best to be at the 10th, 50th, and 90th percentiles? Give an example for each.

2. How might stress hormones affect later development?

3. Why is pruning an essential part of brain development?

4. What is the relationship between the cortex and the dendrites?

5. What are the differences in the visual abilities of a newborn and a 3-month-old?

6. What characteristics of the human brain seem designed for hearing and understanding speech?

7. Why would parents encourage early (before 12 months) or late (after 12 months) walking?

8. How do proximal-distal and cephalo-caudal sequences apply to fine motor skills?

9. In what ways does immunization save lives?

10. What are the signs of malnutrition?

11. Since breast is best, why do most North American women bottle-feed their 6-month-olds?

APPLICATIONS

1. Immunization regulations and practices vary, partly for social and political reasons. Ask at least two faculty or administrative staff members what immunizations students at your college must have and why. Don't stop asking if you hear "it's a law"; ask why that law is in place. If both your informants say the same thing, ask a third person.

2. Observe three infants whom you do not know in public places such as a store, playground, or bus. Look closely at body size and motor skills, especially how much control each baby has over legs and hands. From that, estimate the age in months, and then ask the caregiver how old the infant is. (Most caregivers know the infant's exact age and are happy to tell you.)

3. *This project can be done alone, but it is more informative if several students pool responses.* Ask 3 to 10 adults whether they were bottle-fed or breast-fed and, if breast-fed, for how long. If anyone does not know, or if anyone expresses embarrassment about how long they were breast-fed, that itself is worth noting. Is there any correlation between adult body size and mode of infant feeding?

Chapter Six

The First Two Years: Cognitive Development

This chapter is about infant *cognition,* a word that means "thinking" in a very broad sense, including language, learning, memory, and intelligence in the first two years of life. My aunt's husband, my Uncle Henry, boasted that he had nothing to do with his three children until they were smart enough to talk, at about 2 years. He may have found a good excuse to avoid diapering, burping, and bathing his infants, but his beliefs about babies' cognitive abilities were wrong. Babies are smart from the first days of life, and they communicate quite well long before they begin talking. In avoiding the work of parenting, Uncle Henry also missed out on the most impressive cognitive accomplishments of his children's lives.

Infants strive to organize sensations and perceptions and to put them all together, including sequence and direction, familiar and strange, objects and people, events and experiences, permanent and transient, cause and effect. By the end of the first year—and often much sooner—babies succeed at this task. They organize their perceptions, have goals and know how to reach them, understand what to do with various objects and people, and begin to talk. By the end of the second year, they speak in sentences, think before acting, and pretend to be someone or something (a mother, an airplane) that they know they are not. Intelligence in babies? Yes indeed.

We begin this chapter by looking at the framework that Jean Piaget provided for observing this amazing intellectual progression, from newborns who know nothing to toddlers who make a wish and blow out their birthday candles. We end by discussing several theories about how these cognitive accomplishments occur.

Sensorimotor Intelligence

As you learned in Chapter 2, Jean Piaget was a Swiss scientist, born in 1896. His ideas "continue to be an important source of inspiration for contemporary infant research" (Rochat, 2001, p. 7). Contrary to all the popular ideas of his day (including my Uncle Henry's), Piaget concluded that humans of every age and circumstance are active learners.

Thinking adapts to experiences. You saw in Chapter 2 that **adaptation** occurs in two complementary ways: by assimilation and by accommodation. *Assimilation* means taking new information into the mind by incorporating it into previously developed mental categories, or action patterns—or, in Piaget's terminology, "schemas." *Accommodation* means taking new information into the mind so as to adjust, refine, or expand previous schemas.

These adaptive processes occur throughout life. According to Piaget, adaptation is the essence of intelligence: Unintelligent people are rigid, stuck, unable or unwilling to adapt their cognitive processes.

adaptation The cognitive processes by which new information is taken in and responded to. Both assimilation and accommodation are kinds of adaptation.

TABLE 6.1 **The Six Stages of Sensorimotor Intelligence**

For an overview of the stages of sensorimotor thought, it helps to group the six stages into pairs. The first two stages involve the infant's responses to its own body (*primary circular reactions*):

Stage One (birth to 1 month)	*Reflexes*—sucking, grasping, staring, listening.
Stage Two (1–4 months)	*The first acquired adaptation* (assimilation and coordination of reflexes). Examples: sucking a pacifier differently from a nipple; grabbing a bottle to suck it.

The next two stages involve the infant's responses to objects and people (*secondary circular reactions*):

Stage Three (4–8 months)	*An awareness of things*—responding to people and objects. Example: clapping hands when mother says "patty-cake."
Stage Four (8–12 months)	*New adaptation and anticipation*—becoming more deliberate and purposeful in responding to people and objects. Example: putting mother's hands together in order to make her start playing patty-cake.

The last two stages are the most creative, first with action and then with ideas (*tertiary circular reactions*):

Stage Five (12–18 months)	*New means through active experimentation*—experimentation and creativity in the actions of the "little scientist." Example: putting a teddy bear in the toilet and flushing it.
Stage Six (18–24 months)	*New means through mental combinations*—considering before doing provides the child with new ways of achieving a goal without resorting to trial-and-error experiments. Example: before flushing, remembering that the toilet overflowed the last time, and hesitating.

sensorimotor intelligence Piaget's term for the intelligence of infants during the first period of cognitive development, when babies think by using their senses and motor skills.

Piaget described four distinct periods of intelligence. The first one begins at birth and ends at about 24 months. Piaget called it **sensorimotor intelligence** because infants learn through their senses and motor skills. The two-years-long sensorimotor period of rapid change is subdivided into six stages (see Table 6.1).

Stages One and Two: Primary Circular Reactions

primary circular reactions The first of three types of feedback loops, this one involving the infant's own body. The infant senses motion, sucking, noise, and so on, and tries to understand them.

In every aspect of sensorimotor intelligence, there is an active interaction between the brain and the senses. Sensation, perception, and cognition cycle back and forth (circling round and round) in what Piaget calls a circular reaction. The first two stages of sensorimotor intelligence are examples of **primary circular reactions,** which are reactions that involve the infant's own body.

Stage one, called the *stage of reflexes,* lasts only for a month. It includes the standard reflexes (described in Chapter 5), such as sucking and grasping, and also the senses, which are so responsive at birth that they seem like reflexes. Simple inborn actions are all that newborns have available to respond to their experiences, but these simple reflexes also help infants think. Sensation becomes perception, which becomes cognition; reflexes become deliberate, and thus sensorimotor intelligence begins.

As reflexes adjust to experience, the baby enters stage two, *first acquired adaptations* (also called the stage of first habits). This change from reflexes to deliberate action occurs because repeated responses provide information about what the body does and how that action feels. This ushers in *adaptation* of reflexes and senses, and to Piaget, adaptation *is* intelligence.

Especially for Parents When should parents decide whether to feed their baby only by breast, only by bottle, or using some combination? When should they decide whether or not to let their baby use a pacifier?

As an example, newborns suck anything that touches their lips; sucking is one of the strongest and most obvious reflexes. At about 1 month, infants start to adapt sucking. Some items, such as the nipple of a bottle (for a breast-fed infant), merely require assimilation: The same old sucking reflex brings nourishment. Other items require accommodation: Pacifiers do not provide food, so they need to be sucked without the reflexive tongue-pushing and swallowing. This adaptation is a sign that infants have begun to organize their perceptions; as they accommodate to pacifiers, they are "thinking."

In other words, adaptation in the early weeks relies primarily on reflexive assimilation—everything suckable is assimilated as worthy of being sucked until accommodation occurs. After several more months, more adaptation occurs. The infant's intelligent responses include: Suck some things to soothe hunger, suck others to bring comfort, and never suck still others (fuzzy blankets, large balls). If the baby is hungry, only familiar nourishing nipples will do; all other objects are rejected.

Adaptation is apparent when babies are not hungry but want the reassurance of rhythmic sucking. Then they suck a pacifier, or, if they have not adapted to a pacifier (because one was not offered in the stage of reflexes), they suck their thumbs, fingers, or knuckles (whichever one they first assimilate).

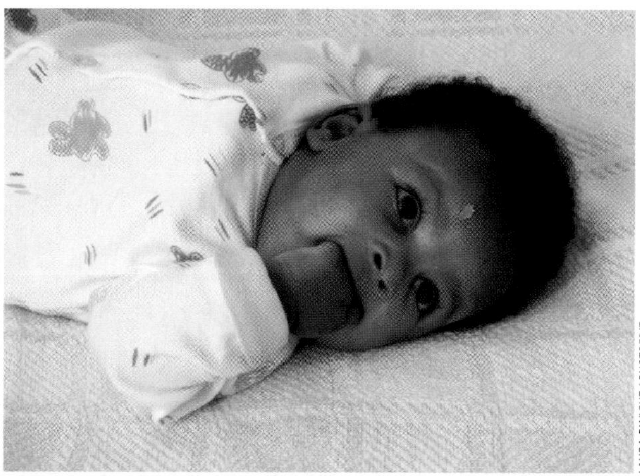

LAURA DWIGHT / PHOTOEDIT

Time for Adaptation Sucking is a reflex at first, but adaptation begins as soon as an infant differentiates a pacifier from her mother's breast or realizes that her hand has grown too big to fit into her mouth. This infant's expression of concentration suggests that she is about to make that adaptation and suck just her thumb from now on.

Stages Three and Four: Secondary Circular Reactions

In stages three and four, development switches from primary circular reactions, involving the baby's own body (stages one and two), to **secondary circular reactions,** involving the baby and an object or another person.

secondary circular reactions The second of three types of feedback loops, this one involving people and objects. The infant is responsive to other people and to toys and other objects that can be manipulated.

First, during stage three (age 4 to 8 months), infants interact diligently with people and objects to produce exciting experiences, to *make interesting events last.* Realizing that rattles make noise, for example, they wave their arms and laugh whenever someone puts a rattle in their hand. The sight of something that normally delights an infant—a favorite toy, a favorite food, a smiling parent—can trigger an active attempt at interaction.

Stage four (8 months to 1 year) is called *new adaptation and anticipation,* or "the means to the end," because babies now think about a goal and begin to understand how to reach it. Thinking is much more innovative in stage four than it was in stage three. Stage-three babies merely understand how to continue an experience once it is under way; stage-four babies anticipate.

ESBIN-ANDERSON / THE IMAGE WORKS

Talk to Me This 4-month-old is learning how to make interesting sights last: The best way to get Daddy to respond is to vocalize, stare, smile, and pat his cheek.

LAURA DWIGHT

Where's Rosa? At 18 months, Rosa knows all about object permanence and hiding. Her only problem here is distinguishing between "self" and "other."

object permanence The realization that objects (including people) still exist when they cannot be seen, touched, or heard.

Thus, in stage four, babies continue to adapt in new, more deliberate ways. They anticipate events that will fulfill their needs and wishes, and they try to make such events occur. A 10-month-old girl who enjoys playing in the bathtub might see a bar of soap, crawl over to her mother with it as a signal to start her bath, and then remove her clothes to make her wishes crystal clear—finally squealing with delight when the bath water is turned on. Similarly, if a 10-month-old boy sees his mother putting on her coat to leave, he might begin tugging at it to stop her or he might drag over his own jacket to signal that he wants to go with her.

All these examples reveal *goal-directed behavior*—that is, purposeful action. The baby's obvious goal-directedness stems from an enhanced awareness of cause and effect, as well as from better memory for actions already completed and better understanding of other people's intentions (Behne et al., 2005; Willatts, 1999). Cognitive awareness coincides with the emergence of the motor skills (e.g., crawling, walking) to achieve goals; both are the result of neurological maturation.

Piaget thought that the concept of **object permanence** emerges during stage four, at about 8 months. Object permanence refers to the awareness that objects or people continue to exist when they are no longer in sight. Other researchers agreed that a goal-directed search for toys that have fallen from the baby's crib, rolled under a couch, or disappeared under a blanket does not begin to emerge until about 8 months, just as Piaget indicated. However, many current scientists question Piaget's interpretations, as the following explains.

Thinking Like a Scientist

Object Permanence Revisited

Although it seems obvious that objects, animals, and your mother continue to exist when you cannot see them, object permanence is not at all obvious to very young infants. If a 5-month-old sees your ring of keys, for instance, and reaches for it, there is an easy way to keep the keys away. Just make them "disappear" by putting them behind your back or closing them in your hand. The baby will probably display only fleeting disappointment and will stop crying and reaching. Out of sight is literally out of mind.

Not so with 10-month-olds. In the same scenario, infants may demonstrate object permanence (perhaps trying to pry open your hand to get the keys) because they now realize that objects exist permanently, even when they are not visible. If you refuse to hand over your keys or any other attractive object, an older baby may howl in frustration.

Object permanence is the subject of intense developmental research; many scientists have tried to figure out exactly when and what babies understand about disappearing objects. Piaget himself found that older babies have trouble with some versions of object permanence, if, for instance, the hiding place changes. The design and implications of object permanence research continue to be surprising and controversial (Baillargeon, 1999; Butler et al., 2002; Ruffman et al., 2005).

To understand that controversy, we return to Piaget's initial research. Before Piaget, it was assumed that infants understood objects just as adults do. Piaget's first experiment, replicated with thousands of infants in dozens of nations, proved that assumption wrong. An adult shows a very young infant an interesting toy, and then covers it up with an easy-to-remove blanket or cloth. The results:

- Infants younger than 8 months do not search (by removing the blanket) for hidden objects.
- At about 8 months, infants search if they can do so immediately but lose interest or forget if they have to wait a few seconds.
- By 2 years, the concept of object permanence is understood quite well, but not perfectly. When playing hide-and-seek, preschoolers may fear that someone has really disappeared, or they may hide in obvious places (such as behind a coat rack with their feet still visible or as a big lump under a sheet on a bed).

As you learned in Chapter 1, thinking like a scientist means, first, replicating the original research and, second, questioning the interpretation of the results. Among the questions: Piaget claimed that failure to search for a hidden object meant that infants have no concept of object permanence, but could other immaturities, such as imperfect motor skills or fragile memory, mask the understanding that objects still exist when they are not seen?

Apparently yes. As one infant researcher explains, "Amid his acute observation and brilliant theorizing, Piaget . . . mistook infants' motor incompetence for conceptual incompetence" (Mandler, 2004, p. 17). A series of clever experiments, in which objects seemed to disappear behind a screen while researchers traced eye movements and brain activity, revealed some inkling of object permanence in infants as young as 4½ months (Baillargeon & DeVos, 1991; Spelke, 1993). Infants that young seemed surprised when an object hidden by a screen vanished or became two objects or moved in an unexpected way. Apparently the infants had some concept of object permanence; they knew the object still existed behind the screen, and they expected it to behave like a normal object.

Further understanding of infant thinking came from a recent series of experiments in which 2-, 4-, and 6-month-olds watched balls moving behind a screen and reemerging (Johnson et al., 2003). In some cases, the trajectory of the balls was smooth. In other cases, a ball seemed to disappear but not to reemerge or to reemerge in the wrong place. The 2-month-olds showed no awareness that anything odd was occurring, no matter what the balls did; the 4-month-olds showed signs that they knew something was amiss; and the 6-month-olds demonstrated (with attentive stares) that they expected the balls to move in the usual way and were surprised when they didn't.

These researchers are convinced that the idea of object permanence (or, at least, perception regarding object trajectories) is not inborn (Johnson et al., 2003). Object permanence is the result of maturation and experience, just as Piaget thought. The difference between this research and Piaget's is the age at which understanding of the concept is first noted: In the right conditions (i.e., visual tracking rather than pulling away a cloth), it begins to emerge at 4½ months, not 8 months.

Most developmentalists still respect Piaget's work on infancy, particularly two discoveries: (1) Infants' thinking is not the same as adult thinking, and (2) infants understand more than adults realize. Piaget underestimated the speed of cognitive development in infants, but his basic observations were correct: Babies are intelligent in many ways.

Peek-a-Boo The best hidden object is Mom under an easily moved blanket, as 7-month-old Elias has discovered. Peek-a-boo is fun from about 7 to 12 months. In another month, Elias will search for more conventionally hidden objects. In a year or two, his surprise and delight at finding Mom will fade.

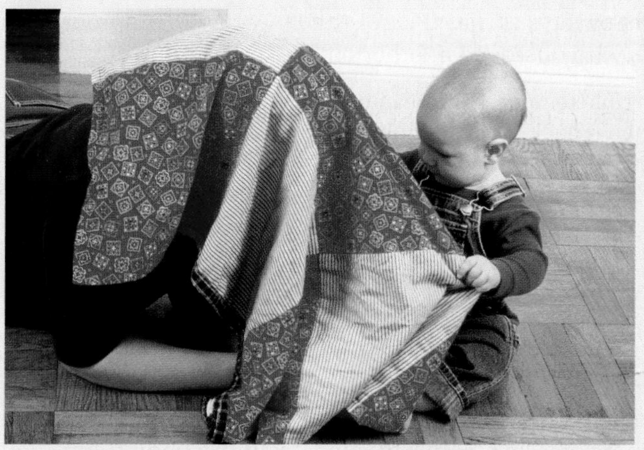

BOTH: LAURA DWIGHT

Stages Five and Six: Tertiary Circular Reactions

In their second year, infants start experimenting in deed and in thought, typically acting first and thinking later. **Tertiary circular reactions** begin when 1-year-olds take independent and varied actions to actively discover the properties of other people, animals, and things. Infants no longer simply respond to their own bodies (primary reactions) or to other people or objects (secondary reactions).

tertiary circular reactions The third of three types of feedback loops, this one involving active exploration and experimentation. The infant explores a range of new activities, varying his or her responses as a way of learning about the world.

MEYER RANGELL / THE IMAGE WORKS

Bib and Bath Learning to use eating utensils is a cognitively stimulating experience that is largely a matter of trial and—often messy—error.

The first of the two stages of tertiary circular reactions is stage five (age 12 to 18 months), called *new means through active experimentation.* Stage five builds directly on the accomplishments of stage four: Infants' goal-directed and purposeful activities become more expansive and creative. Toddlerhood is a time of active exploration, when, as Toni's mother said in Chapter 5, babies "get into everything." They try to discover all the possibilities their world has to offer. They delight in squeezing all the toothpaste out of the tube, taking apart the tape recorder, uncovering the ant hill.

Because of the experimentation that characterizes this stage, Piaget referred to the stage-five toddler as a **little scientist** who "experiments in order to see." Having discovered some action or set of actions that is possible with a given object, stage-five infants seem to ask, "What else can I do with this?" Their scientific method is one of trial and error. Their devotion to discovery is familiar to every adult scientist—and to every parent.

little scientist Piaget's term for the stage-five toddler (age 12 to 18 months), who experiments without anticipating the results.

deferred imitation A sequence in which an infant first perceives something that someone else does and then performs the same action a few hours or even days later.

In the sixth and final stage of sensorimotor intelligence (age 18 to 24 months), toddlers begin to anticipate and solve simple problems by using *mental combinations.* This is a kind of intellectual experimentation that supersedes the active experimentation of stage five. Stage-six toddlers try out various actions mentally before actually performing them. They think about the consequences their actions might bring, hesitating a moment before yanking the cat's tail or dropping a raw egg on the floor. They may miscalculate, and they still want to discover, so a stage-six toddler does not always choose safety over danger. But at least some thought precedes action.

Being able to use mental combinations also makes it possible for the child to pretend. A toddler might sing to a doll before tucking it into bed. This is in marked contrast to the younger infant, who treats a doll like any other toy, throwing or biting it, or to the stage-five toddler, who pulls off the head, arms, and legs to see what is inside.

Piaget describes another stage-six intellectual accomplishment, involving both thought and memory. **Deferred imitation** occurs when infants copy behavior they noticed hours or days earlier (Piaget, 1962). A classic example is Piaget's daughter, Jacqueline, who observed another child

> who got into a terrible temper. He screamed as he tried to get out of a playpen and pushed it backward, stamping his feet. Jacqueline stood watching him in amazement, never having witnessed such a scene before. The next day, she herself screamed in her playpen and tried to move it, stamping her foot lightly several times in succession.
>
> *[Piaget, 1962, p. 63]*

LWA-DANN TARDIFF / CORBIS

I'm Listening This 14-month-old is a master at deferred imitation. He knows how to hold a cell phone and what gestures to use as the "conversation" goes on.

Piaget and Research Methodology

Infants sometimes reach the various stages of sensorimotor intelligence at earlier ages than Piaget predicted they would. Not only do 4½-month-olds show some sense of object permanence, but babies demonstrate pretending and deferred imitation as early as 9 months (Meltzoff & Moore, 1999). One reason Piaget underestimated infant cognition is that he was limited by direct observation of his own three infants. In addition, he lacked advanced research tools, particularly habituation studies and fMRI scans.

Habituation (from the word *habit*) refers to the process of getting used to an experience after repeated exposure to it. Habituation occurs in schoolchildren when the school cafeteria serves the same menu day after day, or when an infant hears the same sound or sees the same picture again and again. In infants, habituation is evident when they lose interest in whatever stimulus is being repeated. This method is very useful for studying infants in the early months, when they cannot yet talk to say what they see.

habituation The process of getting used to an object or event through repeated exposure to it.

In the classic form of habituation study, one stimulus is repeated until babies lose interest (are habituated) and then they are presented with another, slightly different one—a new sound or sight or other sensation. Any of several indicators—a longer or more focused gaze; a faster or slower heart rate; more or less muscle tension around the lips; a change in the rate, rhythm, or pressure of suction on a nipple—can indicate that the baby detects a difference between the two stimuli. All these signs are recorded by sensitive technology that was not available to Piaget.

By inducing habituation and then presenting a new stimulus, scientists have learned that even 1-month-olds can detect the difference between a *pah* sound and a *bah* sound, between a circle with two dots inside it and a circle without any dots, and much more. These are secondary circular reactions that Piaget did not expect until about 4 months.

More recent techniques involve measurement of brain activity (see Table 6.2) (Thomas & Casey, 2003). For example, **fMRI** (functional magnetic resonance imaging) and other techniques indicate that preverbal infants have memories, goals, and even mental combinations in advance of Piaget's stages. Essentially, a burst of electrical activity within the brain shows that neurons in a particular region are firing, which leads researchers to conclude that a particular stimulus has been noticed and processed. For instance, sucking a pacifier might reduce activity in the fear center of the brain and increase activity in the pleasure center.

Response for Parents (from page 166): Both decisions should be made within the first month, during the stage of reflexes. If parents wait until the infant is 4 months or older, they may discover that they are too late. It is difficult to introduce a bottle to a 4-month-old who has been exclusively breast-fed or a pacifier to a baby who has already adapted the sucking reflex to a thumb.

fMRI Functional magnetic resonance imaging, a measuring technique in which the brain's magnetic properties indicate activation anywhere in the brain; fMRI helps locate neurological responses to stimuli.

TABLE 6.2 **Some Techniques Used by Neuroscientists to Understand Brain Function**

Technique	Use	Limitations
EEG (electroencephalogram)	Measures electrical activity in the top layers of the brain, where the cortex is.	Especially in infancy, much brain activity of interest occurs below the cortex.
ERP (event-related potential)	Notes the amplitude and frequency of electrical activity (as shown by brain waves) in specific parts of the cortex in reaction to various stimuli.	Reaction within the cortex signifies perception, but interpretation of the amplitude and timing of brain waves is not straightforward.
fMRI (functional magnetic resonance imaging	Measures changes in activity anywhere in the brain (not just the outer layers).	Signifies brain activity, but infants are notoriously active, which can make fMRIs useless.
PET (positron emission tomography)	Also (like fMRI) reveals activity in various parts of the brain. Locations can be pinpointed with precision, but PET requires injection of radioactive dye to light up the active parts of the brain.	Many parents and researchers hesitate to inject radioactive dye into an infant's brain unless a serious abnormality is suspected.

For both practical and ethical reasons, these techniques have not been used with large, representative samples of normal infants. One of the challenges of neuroscience is to develop methods that are harmless, easy to use, and comprehensive to the study of normal children.

Many measurements of neurons show that early brain development is wide-ranging, dendrites proliferate, and pruning is extensive. The first three years of life appear to be prime time for cognitive development.

In fact, discoveries about the infant brain have given developmentalists a new worry: People might conclude that these years are the *only* ones that provide a foundation for brain growth and learning. Not so. As a report by 20 leading developmentalists summarizes:

> Early experiences clearly affect the development of the brain. Yet the recent focus on "zero to three" as a critical or particularly sensitive period is highly problematic, not because this isn't an important period for the developing brain, but simply because the disproportional attention to the period from birth to 3 years begins too late and ends too soon.
>
> *[National Research Council and Institute of Medicine, 2000, p. 7]*

Especially for Parents One parent wants to put all the breakable or dangerous objects away because a toddler is now able to move around independently. The other parent says that the baby should learn not to touch certain things. Who is right?

"Begins too late and ends too soon". . . Could the sophisticated technology and computerized analysis of recent research distract observers from noticing the entire sweep of intellectual development? In collecting data about infants' moment-by-moment, neuron-by-neuron processes, do people ignore the brain-building and mental reorganization that characterize human intelligence, beginning before birth and continuing throughout life? Piaget's view of infant cognition was limited, but at least he did not make that mistake.

SUMMING UP

Piaget discovered, described, and then celebrated active infant learning. Babies use their senses and motor skills to gain an understanding of their world, first with reflexes and then by adapting through assimilation and accommodation. Object permanence, goal pursuit, and deferred imitation all develop during infancy. Crucial in all six stages of sensorimotor intelligence is the idea of circular reactions: Babies use basic sensory experiences to build cognitive structures. In the first two stages, infants use their bodies (primary circular reactions); in the next two stages, they use their immediate experiences (secondary circular reactions); and in the final two stages, they use creative experimentation with anything at hand (tertiary circular reactions). Although modern research finds that Piaget underestimated infant cognition, his basic concepts still inspire researchers.

Information Processing

information-processing theory A perspective that compares human thinking processes, by analogy, to computer analysis of data, including sensory input, connections, stored memories, and output.

Piaget was a "grand" theorist of cognition, with an appreciation of shifts in the nature of cognition that occur at about ages 2, 6, and 12. His sweeping overview with distinct stages contrasts with **information-processing theory**, a perspective modeled on computer functioning.

Information-processing theorists believe that a step-by-step description of the mechanisms of human thought aids our understanding of the development of cognition at every age. Human information processing begins with input picked up by the five senses; proceeds to brain reactions, connections, and stored memories; and concludes with some form of output. For infants, the output might consist of moving a hand to uncover a hidden toy (object permanence), saying a word (e.g., *mama*) to signify recognition, or staring upon noticing a new stimulus.

With the aid of the sensitive technology described in the preceding section, information-processing research has overturned some of Piaget's findings. For example, concepts and categories seem to develop in the infant brain by about 6 months (Mandler, 2004; Quinn, 2004).

The information-processing perspective helps tie together the various aspects of infant cognition that have merited extensive study and produced exciting discoveries. We review two of these now: affordances and memory. Affordances concern perception or, by analogy, input. Memory concerns brain organization and output—in other words, storage and retrieval.

RESPONSE FOR PARENTS (from page 171): It is easier and safer to babyproof the house, because toddlers, being little scientists, want to explore. However, it is important for both parents to encourage and guide the baby, so it is preferable to leave out a few untouchable items if that will help prevent a major conflict between husband and wife.

Affordances

Perception, remember, is the mental processing of information that arrives at the brain from the sensory organs. It is the first step of information processing—the input to the brain. One of the puzzles of development is that two people can have discrepant perceptions of the same situation, not only interpreting it differently but actually observing it differently. One person can even perceive the same thing in opposite ways at different times in his or her life.

Look at Me These 1-year-olds are just learning about the affordances of objects. Thus, a rattle may be pushed against a friend's face to gain the friend's attention. This little scientist has not yet discovered that doing so may not be a good idea.

? **OBSERVATIONAL QUIZ** (see answer, page 174): Are these two toddlers boys or girls?

Decades of thought and research led Eleanor and James Gibson to conclude that perception is far from automatic (E. Gibson, 1969; J. Gibson, 1979). Perception—for infants, as for the rest of us—is a cognitive accomplishment that requires selection: "Perceiving is active, a process of obtaining information about the world. . . . We don't simply see, we look" (E. Gibson, 1988, p. 5).

The Gibsons contend that the environment (people, places, and objects) *affords,* or offers, many opportunities for perception and interaction (E. Gibson, 1997). Each of these opportunities is called an **affordance.** Which particular affordance is perceived and acted on depends on four factors: sensory awareness, immediate motivation, current development, and past experience.

affordance An opportunity for perception and interaction that is offered by people, places, and objects in the environment.

As a simple example, a lemon may be perceived as something that affords smelling, tasting, touching, viewing, throwing, squeezing, and biting (among other things). Each of these affordances is further perceived as offering pleasure, pain, or some other emotion. Which of the many affordances a particular person perceives and acts on depends on the four factors just mentioned: sensations, motives, age, and history. Consequently, a lemon might elicit quite different perceptions from an artist about to paint a still life, a thirsty adult in need of a refreshing drink, and a teething baby wanting something to gnaw on.

Clearly, infants and adults perceive quite different affordances. A toddler's idea of what affords running might be any unobstructed surface—a meadow, a long hallway in an apartment building, or a road. To an adult eye, the degree to which these places afford running may be restricted by such factors as a bull grazing in the meadow, neighbors in the hallway, or traffic on the road. Moreover, young children love to run, so they notice affordances for running; some adults prefer to stay put—so they do not perceive whether running is afforded or not.

Affordances are sought by infants of every age. For instance, one study found that when 9- to 12-month-olds were presented with unknown objects that rattled, rang, squeaked, or were silent, they decided what noise the object afforded on the basis of whether the object's shape was similar to that of another noise-making object or, by 12 months, whether the object's name was the same as that of another object that rattled, rang, or squeaked (Graham et al., 2004).

In another experiment, 12- to 24-month-olds watched adults look at or bend a laminated photograph and then either looked at it or bent it themselves. They

Baby in Charge As this mother no doubt realizes, for her toddler, playing with blocks affords touching, stacking, and tossing them, not trying to identify the letters and numbers on them.

! ANSWER TO OBSERVATIONAL QUIZ (from page 173): Surprise! Both babies are girls, named Anne and Sarah. Illustrating the power of stereotyping, many observers would have guessed that they are boys because their blue garments afford masculinity.

did not yet know that photos are primarily for viewing, so they used whichever affordance they had been shown (Callahan et al., 2004). The deferred imitation described by Piaget (and demonstrated by his daughter Jacqueline) is an example of an experienced affordance. Infants typically watch other infants intently to learn what affordances they themselves might want.

Sudden Drops

visual cliff An experimental apparatus that gives an illusion of a sudden drop between one horizontal surface and another.

The affordances that an infant perceives evolve as the infant gains experience. An example is provided by the **visual cliff**, an apparatus designed to provide the illusion of a sudden dropoff between one horizontal surface and another (see the photograph at left).

Researchers once thought that perception of a visual cliff was purely a matter of visual maturity: Young babies, because of their inadequate depth perception, could not see the sudden drop, but by about 8 months, maturation of the visual cortex allowed such awareness. "Proof" came when 6-month-olds could be enticed to wiggle forward over the supposed edge of the visual cliff, in contrast to 10-month-olds, who fearfully refused to budge, even when their mothers called them (E. Gibson & Walk, 1960).

MARK RICHARDS / PHOTO EDIT

Depth Perception This toddler in a laboratory in Berkeley, California, is crawling on the experimental apparatus called a visual cliff. She stops at the edge of what she perceives as a dropoff.

Later research (benefiting from better technology) found that the earlier interpretation of the data was wrong. Even 3-month-olds notice the difference between a solid surface and an apparent cliff, as evidenced by their slowed heart rate and wide-open eyes when they are placed over the "edge." But they do not realize that one affordance of the cliff is falling. That realization comes after they start crawling. Their memory of a caregiver's fear (or perhaps their own tumble off a bed) teaches them that the edge of a precipice (as in stairs that go down) affords danger (Campos et al., 1978).

Movement and People

Despite all the variations from one infant to another in the particular affordances they perceive, two general principles of perception are shared by all infants. One is **dynamic perception**, which is perception primed to focus on movement and change. Infants love motion. As soon as they can, they move their own bodies—grabbing, scooting, crawling, walking. To their delight, these movements change what the world affords them. Other creatures that move, especially their own caregivers, are among the first and best sources of pleasure, again because of dynamic perception. That is one reason it's almost impossible to teach a baby not to chase and grab a dog, a cat, or even a cockroach, especially if the creature is moving.

dynamic perception Perception that is primed to focus on movement and change.

people preference The innate attraction that human babies have to other humans, evident in visual, auditory, tactile, and other preferences.

The second universal principle of infant perception is **people preference.** This characteristic may have evolved over the centuries because humans of all ages survived by learning to attend to, and rely on, one another. As you remember from Chapter 5, all human senses are primed to respond to social stimuli. Even in the first days of life, babies listen to voices, stare at faces, and are soothed by human touch. Soon they prefer the particular voice, face, and touch of their primary caregiver; connect sound with sight; and make other linkages (Aslin et al., 1998; Kellman & Banks, 1998).

Very early in life, humans are interested in the emotional affordances of their caregivers, using their limited perceptual abilities to focus on the social world. As one example, infants connect facial expressions with vocal tone long before they understand language. This ability has led to a hypothesis:

> Given that infants are frequently exposed to their caregivers' emotional displays and further presented with opportunities to view the affordances (Gibson, 1959, 1979) of those emotional expressions, we propose that the expressions of familiar persons are meaningful to infants very early in life.
>
> *[Kahana-Kalman & Walker-Andrews, 2001, p. 366]*

ESPECIALLY FOR PARENTS OF INFANTS When should you be particularly worried that your baby will fall off the bed or down the stairs?

As with the earlier research, these researchers presented infants with two moving images on a video screen. Both images were of a woman. In one, she visibly expresses joy; in the other, sorrow. Each image is accompanied by an audiotape of that woman's happy *or* sad talk. By 7 months, but not before, babies can match emotional words with facial expressions.

Some infants in this experiment were only 3½ months old. Not surprisingly, given their immaturity, when the infants did not know the woman, they failed to match the verbal emotion with the face. In other words, when the face was that of a stranger, these 3½-month-olds did not tend to look more at the happy face when they heard the happy talk or to match sad voice and sad face. However, when the 3½-month-olds saw two images (happy and sad) of their own mothers and heard an audiotape that played either their mother's happy words or her sad ones, they correctly matched visual and vocal emotions. They looked longest at their happy mothers talking in a happy way, but they also looked at their sad mothers when the audio they heard was their mother's sad voice—an amazing display of the very young infant's ability to connect the tone of speech with facial expressions.

The researchers noticed something else. When infants saw and heard their happy mothers, as opposed to the happy strangers, they smiled twice as quickly, seven times as long, and much more brightly (with cheeks raised as well as lips upturned) (Kahana-Kalman & Walker-Andrews, 2001). Obviously, experience had taught these babies that a smiling mother affords joy, especially if you smile back. The affordances of a smiling stranger are more difficult to judge.

ULLI SEER / IMAGE BANK

One Constant, Multisensual Perception From the angle of her arm and the bend of her hand, it appears that this infant recognizes the constancy of the furry mass, perceiving it as a single entity whether it is standing still, rolling in the sand, or walking along the beach.

ESPECIALLY FOR PARENTS This research on early affordances suggests a crucial lesson about how many babysitters an infant should have. What is it?

Memory

A certain amount of experience and maturation is required in order to process and remember experiences. Infants have great difficulty storing new memories in their first year, and older children are often unable to describe events that occurred when they were younger. But on the basis of a series of experiments, developmentalists now agree that very young infants *can* remember *if* the following are true:

- Experimental conditions are similar to real life.
- Motivation is high.
- Special measures aid memory retrieval.

The most dramatic evidence for infant memory comes from a series of innovative experiments in which 3-month-old infants were taught to make a mobile move by kicking their legs (Rovee-Collier, 1987, 1990). The infants lay on their backs, in their own cribs, connected to a mobile by means of a ribbon tied to one foot.

Virtually all the infants began making some occasional kicks (as well as random arm movements and noises) and realized, after a while, that kicking made the mobile move. They then kicked more vigorously and frequently, sometimes laughing at their accomplishment. So far, this is no surprise—self-activated movement is highly reinforcing to infants, part of dynamic perception. Moreover, 3-month-old infants are already

MICHAEL NEWMAN / PHOTOEDIT

He Remembers! In this demonstration of Rovee-Collier's experiment, a young infant immediately remembers how to make the familiar mobile move. (Unfamiliar mobiles do not provoke the same reaction.) He kicks his right leg and flails both arms, just as he learned to do several weeks ago.

Response for Parents of Infants (from page 174): Constant vigilance is necessary for the first few years of a child's life, but the most dangerous age is from about 4 to 8 months, when infants can move but do not yet have a fear of falling over an edge.

at stage two, adapting reflexes, and are almost at stage three, making interesting sights last. Kicking and laughing at the result are to be expected.

When some infants had the mobile-and-ribbon apparatus reinstalled in their cribs *one week later,* most started to kick immediately; this reaction indicated that they remembered their previous experience. But when other infants were retested *two weeks later,* they began with only random kicks. Apparently they had forgotten what they had learned—evidence that memory is fragile early in life.

Reminders and Repetition

The lead researcher, Carolyn Rovee-Collier, developed another experiment that demonstrated that 3-month-old infants *could* remember after two weeks *if* they had a brief reminder session before being retested (Rovee-Collier & Hayne, 1987). A **reminder session** is any perceptual experience that might make a person recollect an idea or thing.

reminder session A perceptual experience that helps a person recollect an idea or experience, without testing whether the person remembers it at the moment.

In this particular reminder session, two weeks after the initial training, the infants watched the mobile move but were *not* tied to it and were positioned so that they could *not* kick. The next day, when they were again connected to the mobile and positioned so that they *could* move their legs, they kicked as they had learned to do two weeks earlier. In effect, watching the mobile move on the previous day revived their faded memory. The information about how to make the mobile move was stored in their brains; they needed some information-processing time to retrieve it, and the reminder session provided that time.

Overall, some early memories can be "highly enduring, and become even more so after repeated encounters with reminders" (Rovee-Collier & Gerhardstein, 1997). Repetition and reminders are key: Infants under 6 months do not remember meeting their grandparents once or twice, nor do they remember a sudden trauma, such as emergency surgery. Early in life, under the best conditions, long-term storage and retrieval of memories are fragile and uncertain. Infant memory is facilitated by repetition, reminders, and active involvement.

The fact that infants can remember at all is remarkable; many scientists once believed that it was impossible. For example, Sigmund Freud (1901/1966) wrote about "infantile amnesia." It is true, though, that memories formed in infancy fade much more quickly than they do later, in childhood.

Memory Aid Personal motivation and action are crucial to early memory, and that is why Noel has no trouble remembering which shape covers the photograph of herself as a baby.

NANCY SHEEHAN / PHOTOEDIT

A Little Older, a Little More Memory

After about 6 months, infants can retain information for longer periods of time than younger babies can, with less training or reminding. Toward the end of the first year, many kinds of memory, including deferred imitation, are apparent (Meltzoff & Moore, 1999). For example, suppose a 9-month-old watches someone playing with a toy the baby has never seen before. The next day, if given the toy, the 9-month-old is likely to play with it in the same way as he or she had observed. (Younger infants do not.) Over the next few months, deferred imitation becomes more elaborate. Infants are particularly likely to imitate other children (Heimann & Meltzoff, 1996; Ryalls et al., 2000).

By the middle of the second year, toddlers can remember and reenact more complex sequences. In one study, 16- and 20-month-olds watched an experimenter perform various activities, such as putting a doll to bed, making a party hat, and cleaning a table (Bauer & Dow, 1994). For each activity, the experimenter used particular props and gave a brief "instruction" for performing each step. For instance, to clean the table, the experimenter wet it with water from a white spray bottle, saying, "Put on the water"; wiped it with a paper towel, saying, "Wipe it"; and placed the towel in a wooden trash basket, saying, "Toss it."

A week later, most toddlers remembered how to carry out the sequence just from hearing "Put on the water. Wipe it. Toss it." They did this not only with the same props the experimenter had used but also when given different props (for instance, a clear spray bottle, a sponge, and a plastic lidded garbage can). This shows that infants are developing concepts, not mindlessly imitating behavior (Mandler, 2004). Many other experiments also show that toddlers are thinking conceptually, not just repeating what they have experienced.

Memory is not one thing, "not a unitary or monolithic entity" (Schacter & Badgaiyan, 2001, p. 1). People are inaccurate when they say, "I have a good memory" or "My memory is failing." Brain-imaging techniques (such as fMRI) reveal many distinct brain regions devoted to particular aspects of memory, as you learned in Chapter 5. One distinction is between *implicit memory,* which is memory for routines and memories that remain hidden until a particular stimulus brings them to mind (like the mobile), and *explicit memory,* which is memory that can be recalled on demand. As you can see in Table 6.3, explicit memory is probably impossible in the first months of life. At about age 5 or 6, when children begin school, explicit memory improves dramatically as parts of the brain mature (Nelson & Webb, 2003). Neuroscientists and psychologists are still discovering various types of memory, but it is apparent that humans have a memory for words, for images, for actions, for smells, for experiences, for "memorized" facts, for "forgotten" faces, and so on. Each type of memory is encoded by neurons in a particular part of the brain.

Because there are so many types of memory, it is not surprising that infants remember some things better than others: That's the way human brains are constructed. Thus, early memories are *both* fragile and enduring, depending on which type of memory is described (Nelson & Webb, 2003). Infants probably store within their brains many emotions and sensations that they cannot readily retrieve, whereas memories of motion (dynamic perception) are remembered once that particular action is cued by the context (as when the infants remembered how to kick to make the mobile move).

Response for Parents (from page 175): It is important that infants have time for repeated exposure to each caregiver, because infants adjust their behavior to maximize whatever each particular caregiver affords in the way of play, emotions, and vocalization. Parents should find one steady babysitter rather than several.

Memory Isn't Easy This table illustrates the complexity and depth of current research on memory and the brain. Few developmentalists, let alone beginning students, can be expected to master the details given here. They are presented in order to convey the dimensions of cutting-edge research on memory; read the table, appreciate the range of the research entailed, but don't feel that you have to memorize every word.

TABLE 6.3 **The Major Memory Systems and Developmental Tasks**

General System	Subsystems	Tasks	Brain Systems Related to Tasks	Infancy Example
Implicit memory (nondeclarative memory)	Procedural learning	Serial reaction time (SRT) task	Striatum, supplementary motor association, motor cortex, frontal cortex	Kick to make mobile move
		Visual expectation paradigm (VExP)	Frontal cortex, motor areas	
	Conditioning	Conditioning	Cerebellum, basal ganglia	Laugh when tickled
	Perceptual representation system	Perceptual priming paradigms	Modality dependent; parietal cortex, occipital cortex, inferior temporal cortex, auditory cortex	Recognize mother's voice
Explicit memory	Pre-explicit memory	Novelty detection in habituation and paired comparison tasks	Hippocampus	Hear difference between sounds
Not before age 1	Semantic memory (generic knowledge)	Semantic retrieval, word priming, and associative priming	Left prefrontal cortex, anterior cingulate cortex, hippocampal cortex	First spoken words
	Episodic memory (autobiographical)	Episodic encoding	Left prefrontal cortex, left orbitoprefrontal cortex	Remember usual routines of dinner
		Recall and recognition	Right prefrontal cortex, anterior cingulate cortex, parietal cortex, cerebellum, hippocampal cortex	Remember when and how a painful event occurred

Source: Adapted from Nelson & Webb, 2003, p. 103.

Until language is established, motor skills are remembered in a nonverbal part of the brain. This explains why most adults remember how to crawl but few can describe it verbally. (Arms and legs first on one side and then on the other? Knees and elbows? Think about it. Can you describe it without doing it?)

SUMMING UP

Infant cognition can be studied using the information-processing perspective, which analyzes each component of the learning system. Infant perception is powerfully influenced by particular experiences, so the affordances perceived by one infant differ from those perceived by another. Memory depends on both brain maturation and experience, and that is why memory is fragile in the first year (being influenced by dynamic perception and reminders) and becomes more evident (although it remains quite fragile) in the second year.

Language: What Develops in Two Years?

Language, with thousands of vocabulary words, hundreds of idiomatic phrases, dozens of grammar rules, and many exceptions to those rules, is the most impressive intellectual achievement of the young child. In fact, language is the most impressive accomplishment of humans: It differentiates *Homo sapiens* from all other species, and it may be the reason human brains are more complex than those of other animals (Leonard, 2003).

For instance, humans and gorillas are close relatives, with about 99 percent of their genes in common. Gorillas are bigger than people, but an adult gorilla's brain is only one-third as big as a human's and has far fewer dendrites, synapses, and other components. This means that a 2-year-old human has twice as much brainpower as a full-grown gorilla.

Similarly, the human brain is three times as large as the chimpanzee brain. Elephants have larger brains than people do, but elephants weigh 20 times as much, so proportionally they have much smaller brains (Kolb & Whishaw, 2003). The size and complexity of the cortex is the key difference. Other animals communicate, but no species has anything approaching the neurons and networks that support one or more of the 6,000 human languages.

The Universal Sequence

Children around the world follow the same sequence of early language development (see Table 6.4). Timing and depth of linguistic ability vary; the most advanced 10 percent of 2-year-olds know more than 550 words, and the least advanced 10 percent speak fewer than 100 words—a fivefold difference (Merriman, 1999). (Some explanations are discussed at the end of this chapter.) But the sequence of language learning is the same for almost all, with humans surpassing even the smartest ape many times over. We now describe this sequence.

First Noises and Gestures

Infants begin learning language before birth, with brain organization and auditory experiences during the final prenatal months. Newborns prefer to hear speech over other sounds; they prefer to listen to high-pitched, simplified, and repetitive adult speech. This form of speech is quite distinct from normal speech. It is sometimes called *baby talk*, since it is talk directed to babies, and sometimes called *motherese*, since mothers all over the world speak it. Both these terms may have misleading implications, so scientists prefer the more formal term **child-directed speech**.

child-directed speech The high-pitched, simplified, and repetitive way adults speak to infants. Also called *baby talk* or *motherese*.

Newborns do much more than listen to child-directed speech. They are noisy creatures—crying, cooing, and making a variety of other sounds even in the first weeks of life. These noises gradually become more varied until, by the age of 4 months, most babies have verbal repertoires that include squeals, growls, gurgles, grunts, croons, and yells, as well as some speechlike sounds (Hsu et al., 2000).

CORBIS / ANTHONY BANNISTER

Too Young for Language? No. The early stages of language are communication through noises, gestures, and facial expressions, very evident here between this !Kung grandmother and granddaughter.

Babbling

Between 6 and 9 months, babies begin to repeat certain syllables (*ma-ma-ma, da-da-da, ba-ba-ba*), a phenomenon referred to as **babbling** because of the way it sounds. Babbling is experience-expectant learning; all babies do it if given half a chance. Moreover, the sounds they make are similar no matter what language their parents speak. They also make rhythmic gestures, typically waving their arms as they babble (Iverson & Fagan, 2004).

Toward the end of the first year, babbling incorporates more sounds from the native language, as infants imitate the sounds they hear. Many cultures assign important meanings to the sounds that babies babble; *ma-ma-ma, da-da-da,* and *pa-pa-pa* usually refer to significant people in the infant's life (Bloom, 1998). (See Appendix A, p. A-4.)

babbling The extended repetition of certain syllables, such as *ba-ba-ba,* that begins at about 6 or 7 months of age.

Deaf babies make babbling sounds later and less frequently than hearing infants do. However, many deaf infants are advanced in their use of gestures; they begin babbling manually at about the same time hearing infants begin babbling orally (Petitto & Marentette, 1991). Analysis of videotapes of deaf children whose parents communicate via sign language reveals that 10-month-old deaf infants use about a dozen distinct hand gestures—which resemble the signs their parents use—in a rhythmic, repetitive manner similar to the utterances *ma-ma-ma*

TABLE 6.4 **AT ABOUT THIS TIME: The Development of Spoken Language in the First Two Years**

Age*	Means of Communication
Newborn	Reflexive communication—cries, movements, facial expressions
2 months	A range of meaningful noises—cooing, fussing, crying, laughing
3–6 months	New sounds, including squeals, growls, croons, trills, vowel sounds
6–10 months	Babbling, including both consonant and vowel sounds repeated in syllables
10–12 months	Comprehension of simple words; speechlike intonations; specific vocalizations that have meaning to those who know the infant well. Deaf babies express their first signs; hearing babies use specific gestures (e.g., pointing) to communicate.
12 months	First spoken words that are recognizably part of the native language
13–18 months	Slow growth of vocabulary, up to about 50 words
18 months	Vocabulary spurt—three or more words learned per day. Much variation: Some toddlers do not yet speak.
21 months	First two-word sentence
24 months	Multiword sentences. Half the infant's utterances are two or more words long.

*The ages of accomplishment in this table reflect norms. Many healthy children with normal intelligence attain these steps in language development earlier or later than indicated here.
Source: Bloom, 1993, 1998; Fenson et al., 2000; Lenneberg, 1967.

LAURA DWIGHT

Baby Talk Infants' verbal understanding advances well ahead of their abilities at verbal production. *Fishy* is probably one of dozens of words that this child readily recognizes even though he has yet to say them himself.

or *da-da-da.* Hearing babies also communicate with gestures before they talk. Pointing, for instance, is very advanced, in that it requires an understanding of another person's perspective. Most animals never interpret pointing correctly; most humans can do so at 10 months. There is good reason to encourage the use of gestures, even in hearing babies. Children understand concepts expressed with gestures a little sooner than concepts expressed in speech.

First Words

ESPECIALLY FOR CAREGIVERS A toddler calls two people "Mama." Is this a sign of confusion?

Finally, at about 1 year of age, the average baby speaks (or signs) a few words. Usually, caregivers understand the first word before strangers do, which makes it hard for researchers to pinpoint exactly what a 12-month-old can say (Bloom, 1998). For example, at 13 months, Kyle knew standard words such as *mama,* but he also knew *da, ba, tam, opma,* and *daes,* which his parents knew to be, respectively, "downstairs," "bottle," "tummy," "oatmeal," and "starfish" (yes, that's what *daes* meant) (Lewis et al., 1999).

The Language Explosion and Early Grammar

naming explosion A sudden increase in an infant's vocabulary, especially in the number of nouns, beginning at about 18 months.

Once vocabulary reaches about 50 words, it begins to build rapidly, at a rate of 50 to 100 words per month (Fenson et al., 1994). This language spurt is sometimes called the **naming explosion,** because the first words include a disproportionate number of nouns, or naming words (Gentner & Boroditsky, 2001). In almost all the world's languages, a label for each significant caregiver (often *dada, mama, nana, papa, baba, tata*), sibling, and sometimes pet appears between 12 and 18 months. Other frequently uttered words refer to the child's favorite foods and, if toilet training is an issue, elimination (*pee-pee, wee-wee, poo-poo, ka-ka, doo-doo*). These sounds are universal, with some version of them uttered by children in every nation.

ESPECIALLY FOR NURSES AND PEDIATRICIANS The parents of a 10-month-old have just been told that their child is deaf. They don't believe it, because, as they tell you, the baby doesn't always respond to noises, but he babbles as much as their other children did. What do you tell them?

No doubt you have noticed that all these words have a similar structure: two identical syllables, each a consonant followed by a vowel. Variations follow that pattern—not just *baba* but also *bobo, bebe, bibi.* Some are slightly more complicated—not just *mama* but also *ma-me, ama,* and so on.

Short, two-syllable words with *m, n, t, d, b,* or *p* are easiest for the child to say because they follow directly from babbling. As mentioned, all cultures use those spontaneous babbles to form words. This pattern facilitates early communication for both the child and the listener. In turn, easy communication aids young children's rapid acquisition of additional words (see Figure 6.1).

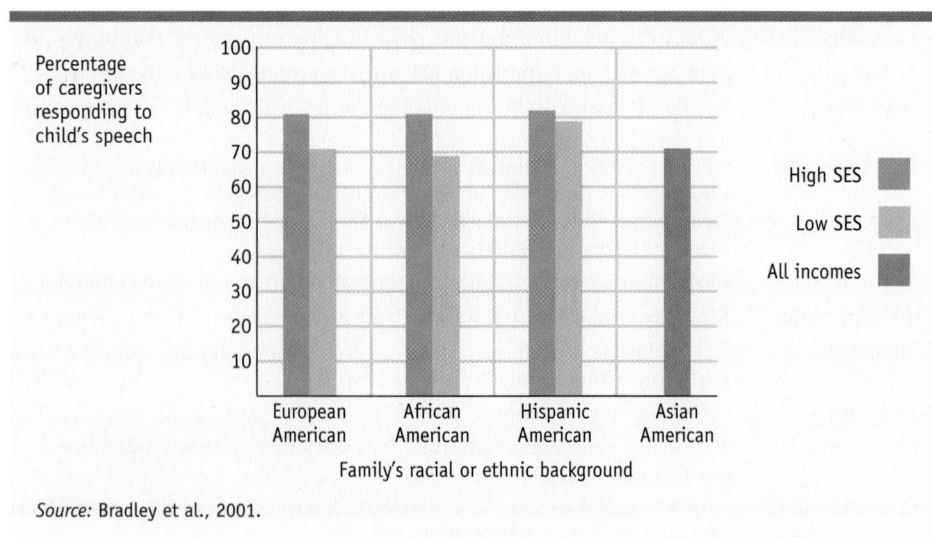

FIGURE 6.1 **When Children Talk, Caregivers Respond** More than 5,000 pairs of caregivers and children under age 3 were observed and interviewed at home. Most of the caregivers, regardless of racial or ethnic background or socioeconomic status, responded to the infant's speech. This may be one reason language development progresses so rapidly.

Cultural Differences

Although all new talkers say names, using similar sounds, and all use more nouns than any other part of speech, the ratio of nouns to verbs and adjectives shows cultural influences (Bornstein et al., 2004). For example, by 18 months, English-speaking infants use more nouns but fewer verbs than Chinese or Korean infants do. One explanation is directly linguistic: Chinese and Korean are "verb-friendly" languages, in that adults use more verbs and place them at the beginning or end of sentences, which makes them easier to learn. In English, verbs are more difficult because they occur in various positions within sentences and their forms change in illogical ways (think of *go, gone, will go, went*). This irregularity makes English verbs harder for novice learners (Gentner & Boroditsky, 2001).

JORGEN SCHYTTE / PETER ARNOLD

Where in the World? Different cultures influence children's language learning in different ways. Children who spend a lot of time with adults receive abundant exposure to the unique speech patterns of their culture.

? OBSERVATIONAL QUIZ (see answer, page 183): What elements in this photograph suggest cultural differences between this family and most European or North American ones?

An alternative explanation considers the entire social context: Playing with a variety of toys and learning about dozens of objects are crucial in North American culture, whereas East Asian cultures emphasize human interactions—specifically, how one person responds to another. Accordingly, North American infants need to name many inanimate things, whereas Asian infants need to encode social interactions into language.

As toddlers' vocabulary builds, they often misuse words. Each language has some concepts that are hard for infants: English-speaking infants confuse *before* and *after*, Dutch-speaking infants misuse *out* when it refers to taking off clothes; Korean infants need to learn two meanings of *in* (Mandler, 2004). Overall, however, in every language, infants demonstrate impressive speed and efficiency in acquiring both vocabulary and grammar (Bornstein et al., 2004).

Toddlers seem to "experiment in order to see" with words, just as the little scientist that Piaget described (stages five and six) experiments with objects. Little scientists become little linguists, learning the words of their culture. It is not unusual for 18-month-olds walking down a street to point at every vehicle, asking "Car?" "Truck?" and even "Fire engine?" "Motorcycle?" Or, again and again, "Wha' dat?"—perhaps to confirm their hypothesis about which words go with which things, or simply because they enjoy conversation and "What's that?" keeps the talk coming.

Sentences

The first words soon take on nuances of tone, loudness, and cadence that are precursors of the first grammar, because a single word can convey many messages by the way that it is spoken. Imagine meaningful sentences encapsulated in "Dada!" "Dada?" and "Dada." Each is a **holophrase**, a single word that expresses an entire thought.

holophrase A single word that is used to express a complete, meaningful thought.

Grammar includes all the methods that languages use to communicate meaning. Word order, prefixes, suffixes, intonation, loudness, verb forms, pronouns and negations, prepositions and articles—all of these are aspects of grammar. Infants begin using grammar even in holophrases, but grammar is especially obvious when they begin to combine words into simple sentences (Bloom, 1998).

grammar All the methods—word order, verb forms, and so on—that languages use to communicate meaning, apart from the words themselves.

Response for Caregivers (from page 180): Not at all. Toddlers hear several people called "Mama" (their own mother, their grandmothers, their cousins' and friends' mothers) and experience mothering from several people, so it is not surprising if they overextend "Mama." They will eventually narrow the label down to the one correct person.

Response for Nurses and Pediatricians (from page 180): Urge the parents to accept the diagnosis and take action. They should begin learning sign language immediately and investigate the possibility of cochlear implants. Babbling has a biological basis and begins at a specified time, in deaf as well as hearing babies. However, deaf babies eventually begin to use gestures more and to vocalize less than hearing babies.

At about 21 months, infants manage their first two-word sentences, with some normal infants achieving this milestone at 15 months and others not reaching it until 24 months. These sentences take the form of "Baby cry" or "More juice," rather than the reverse order of the words. Soon three words combine, usually subject–verb–object—as in "Mommy read book," rather than any of the eight other possible combinations of those three words.

At least in the first few years, a child's grammar correlates with the size of vocabulary. The child who says "Baby is crying" is advanced in language development compared with the child who says "Baby crying" or simply the holophrase "Baby" (Dionne et al., 2003). Each of those sentences is evidence of grammar.

Theories of Language Learning

Worldwide, people who weigh less than 33 pounds (15 kilograms) and are not yet 2 years old already use language quite well, sometimes speaking two languages. Bilingual toddlers know who understands which language and they choose the correct holophrases to communicate—an awesome accomplishment. The process of language learning continues throughout childhood. By adolescence, some teenagers compose lyrics or deliver orations that move thousands of their co-linguists. By adulthood, some people are fluent in two, three, or even more languages. How does this language learning happen?

Answers to this question have come from three schools of thought, each with its own history, body of research, and committed scholars, and each connected to one of the major theories (behaviorism, epigenetic theory, and sociocultural theory) described in Chapter 2. The first says that infants are directly taught, the second that infants naturally understand language, and the third that social impulses propel infants to communicate.

Each theory of language learning has profound implications for parents and early-childhood educators. Everyone wants children to speak fluently and well, but no one wants to waste time and effort trying to teach something that 1-year-olds cannot learn or will learn just as well without any instruction. Which theory should guide them?

Theory One: Infants Are Taught

The seeds of the first perspective were planted more than 50 years ago, when the dominant theory in North American psychology was behaviorism, or learning theory. The essential idea was that all learning is acquired, step by step, through association and reinforcement. Just as Pavlov's dogs learned to associate the sound of a bell with the presentation of food (see Chapter 2), behaviorists believe that infants associate objects with words they have heard often, especially if reinforcement occurs.

ELLIOTT VARNER SMITH

Cultural Values If his infancy is like that of most babies raised in the relatively taciturn Ottavado culture of Ecuador, this 2-month-old will hear significantly less conversation than infants from most other regions. According to many learning theorists, a lack of reinforcement will result in a child who is insufficiently verbal. In most Western cultures, that might be called maltreatment. However, each culture tends to encourage the qualities it most needs and values, and verbal fluency is not a priority in this community. In fact, people who talk too much are ostracized, and those who keep secrets are valued, so encouragement of language may be maltreatment here.

B. F. Skinner (1957) noticed that spontaneous babbling at 6 to 8 months is usually reinforced. Typically, every time the baby says "ma-ma-ma-ma," a grinning mother appears, repeating the sound as well as showering the baby with attention, praise, and perhaps food. These affordances of mothers are exactly what the infant wants, and the baby will make those sounds again to get them.

Most parents are excellent intuitive instructors. For instance, parents who talk to their young infants typically name each object—"Here is your *bottle*," "There is your *foot*," "You want your *juice*?" and so on—often touching and moving the named object at the same time as they speak the target word loudly, clearly, and slowly (Gogate et al., 2000). They also use child-directed speech like experts, capturing the baby's interest with higher pitch, shorter sentences, elongated words, stressed nouns, and simpler grammar. All these features help infants associate words with things (L. Smith, 1995).

The core ideas of this theory are the following:

- Parents are the first teachers, although other relatives and caregivers also teach language.
- Frequent repetition is instructive, especially when linked to daily life.
- Well-taught infants become well-spoken children, with the accents and gestures of their teachers.

Support for the view that children must be taught language begins with an undeniable fact: Wide variations are apparent in language fluency, especially when children from various cultures are compared. Some 3-year-olds converse in elaborate sentences; others just barely put one simple word together with another.

Such wide variations correlate with teaching and learning practices. Parents of the most verbal children teach language throughout infancy—singing, explaining, listening, and responding. Parents of the least verbal children rarely talk to their babies and don't even realize that their children's language delays are connected to their parenting practices (Law, 2000).

Many studies comparing children of varied household incomes have found dramatic differences in children's language directly linked to how much language they heard, which was indirectly linked to family socioeconomic status (SES) (Hart & Risley, 1995; Hoff, 2003). One study found that between the ages of 9 months and 4 years, children whose parents were professionals (such as doctors and lawyers) heard an average of *20 million* more words than did children of low-income single parents (Hart & Risley, 1995). When middle-class parents of higher or lower SES are compared, and when infants are studied when they are just beginning the naming explosion, those babies whose mothers are college educated hear more words, in more complex sentences. Their own language development increases as a result (Hoff, 2003).

The importance of parental input (not just commands, but conversation about many things) has repeatedly been confirmed. Consider the details of one study of infants from 9 to 17 months of age (Tamis-LeMonda et al., 2001). The researchers analyzed the language that mothers (all middle-class) used with their preverbal infants. One mother never imitated her infant's babbling; another mother imitated 21 times in 10 minutes, babbling back as if in conversation. Overall, mothers were most likely to describe things or actions (e.g., "That is a spoon you are holding—spoon"). The range was vast: In 10 minutes, one mother described something only 4 times, while another provided her baby with 33 descriptions.

The frequency of maternal responsiveness at 9 months predicted language acquisition many months later (see Figure 6.2). It was not just that noisy infants, who were on their way to being talkative, elicited more talk from their mothers. Some quiet infants had quite verbal mothers, who suggested play activities, described things, and asked questions. Quiet infants with talkative mothers usually became talkative later on.

This research is in keeping with the behaviorist theory that adults teach language and then infants learn it. This theory holds that the main linguistic difference between one child and another originates with caregivers' behavior. If adults want talkative children, they must talk to them as babies.

! ANSWER TO OBSERVATIONAL QUIZ (from page 181): At least four elements are unusual in today's Western families: large size (four children), a child held in the mother's lap to eat (i.e., no high chair for the baby), the father pouring for everyone, and the fact that the whole family, including teenagers, is eating together. This family lives in Mozambique, in southeastern Africa.

ESPECIALLY FOR NURSES AND PEDIATRICIANS Bob and Joan have been reading about language development in children. They are convinced that language is "hard-wired," so they need not talk to their 6-month-old son. How do you respond?

FIGURE 6.2 **Maternal Responsiveness and Infants' Language Acquisition** Learning the first 50 words is a milestone in early language acquisition, as it predicts the arrival of the naming explosion and the multiword sentence a few weeks later. Researchers found that half the infants of highly responsive mothers (top 10 percent) reached this milestone as early as 15 months of age and the other half reached it by 17 months. The infants of nonresponsive mothers (bottom 10 percent) lagged significantly behind.

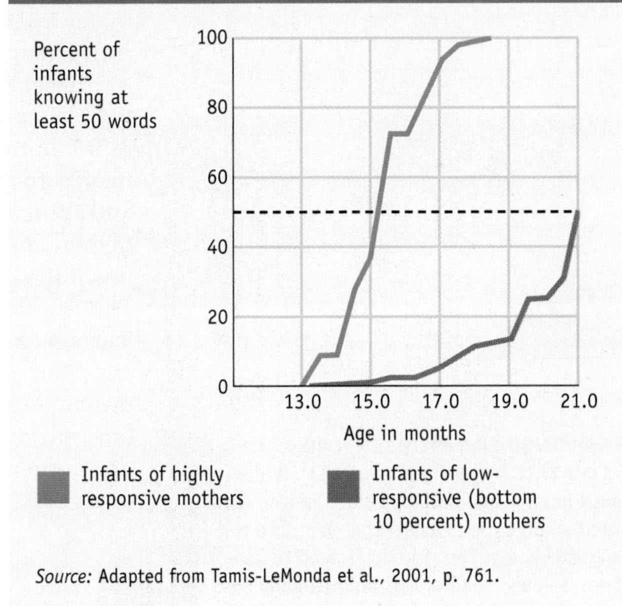

Source: Adapted from Tamis-LeMonda et al., 2001, p. 761.

MICHELLE D. BRIDWELL / PHOTOEDIT, INC.

Show Me Where Pointing is one of the earliest forms of communication, emerging at about 10 months. As Carlos demonstrates, accurate pointing requires a basic understanding of social interaction, because the pointer needs to take the observer's angle of vision into account.

language acquisition device (LAD) Chomsky's term for a hypothesized brain structure that enables humans to learn language, including the basic aspects of grammar, vocabulary, and intonation.

Theory Two: Infants Teach Themselves

A contrary theory holds that language learning is innate. The seeds of this perspective were planted soon after Skinner proposed his theory of verbal learning. Noam Chomsky (1968, 1980) and his followers believe that language is too complex to be mastered so early and so easily merely through step-by-step conditioning. Although behaviorists focus on variations among children in vocabulary size and the like, Chomsky notes that all young children worldwide learn the rudiments of grammar at approximately the same age.

Chomsky hypothesizes that the human brain is uniquely equipped to learn language. That is, acquiring a language is an experience-expectant function, because centuries of evolution made it adaptive for humans to use words to communicate. Chomsky has written about *universal grammar,* meaning that all humans are born with brain structures that prepare them to seek some elements of human language—for example, that a raised tone at the end of an utterance indicates a question or that object names usually refer to the whole object, not just a part. Universal grammar is evidence for brain structure, Chomsky believes.

Somewhat boldly, Chomsky has labeled this hypothetical neurological structure the **language acquisition device,** or **LAD.** The LAD enables children to derive the rules of grammar quickly and effectively from the speech they hear every day, regardless of whether their native language is English, Thai, or Urdu.

All reputable researchers realize that *some* input from the environment is required for language learning, but only some take an epigenetic (genes-plus-environment) approach, agreeing with Chomsky that infants are innately ready to use their minds to understand and speak whatever language is offered (Gopnik, 2001). The various languages of the world, as different as they are from one another, are all logical, coherent, and systematic. Infants, who are also logical, are primed to grasp the particular language they are exposed to, making caregiver speech "not a 'trigger' but a 'nutrient'" (Slobin, 2001, p. 438). There is no need for a language trigger, according to theory two, because words are "expected" by an LAD in the developing brain, which quickly and efficiently connects neurons to support whichever particular language the infant hears.

Research supports this perspective as well. As you remember, all infants babble *ma-ma* and *da-da* sounds (not yet referring to mother or father) at about 6 to 9 months (Goldman, 2001). No reinforcement or teaching is needed; all they need is for dendrites to grow, mouth muscles to strengthen, neurons to connect, and speech to be heard. Further evidence comes from twins. Although raised together, and presumably hearing the same amount of speech, dizygotic twins are much less similar in their early language learning than monozygotic twins are. This suggests that vocabulary building is more genetic and brain-based than learned and experience-based (Johnson et al., 2003).

More generally, in infancy, "developing cognition provides the foundational grammatical abilities" (Langer, 2001, p. 38). In other words, thought (not instruction) produces language. Toddlers are smart enough to learn language simply by overhearing, as many parents discover—occasionally to their dismay (Akhtar et al., 2001).

RESPONSE FOR NURSES AND PEDIATRICIANS (from page 183): While much of language development is indeed hard-wired, many experts assert that exposure to language is required. You don't need to convince Bob and Joan of this point, though—just convince them that their baby will be happier if they talk to him.

Theory Three: Social Impulses Foster Infant Language

The third theory is called *social-pragmatic* because it perceives the crucial starting point to be neither vocabulary reinforcement (behaviorism) nor the innate thought–language connection (epigenetic), but rather the social reason for language: communication. According to this perspective, infants communicate in every way they can because humans are social beings, dependent on one another for survival and joy.

Newborns look searchingly at human faces and listen intently to human voices because they seek to respond to emotional tone, not because they want to know content. Before age 1, infants vocalize, babble, gesture, listen, and point—with an outstretched little index finger that is soon accompanied by a very sophisticated glance to see if the other person is looking in the right spot. These and many other examples show how humans are compelled to be social from the very start and how language is used to aid social interaction (Bloom, 1998).

If 1-year-olds are playing intently with an unnamed new toy and an adult utters a word that might be that toy's name, would the child learn that word as the name of the mystery toy? From a purely behaviorist, learning-by-association perspective, the answer is yes, but the actual answer is no. In an experiment, toddlers were playing with intriguing, unnamed toys and heard adults say a word. The toddlers stopped playing, looked up, and figured out what the adult was looking at when the word was said. Babies then assigned the new word to that object, not to the fascinating toy in front of them (Baldwin, 1993). This study supports theory three by suggesting that infants are socially focused, considering language a social tool.

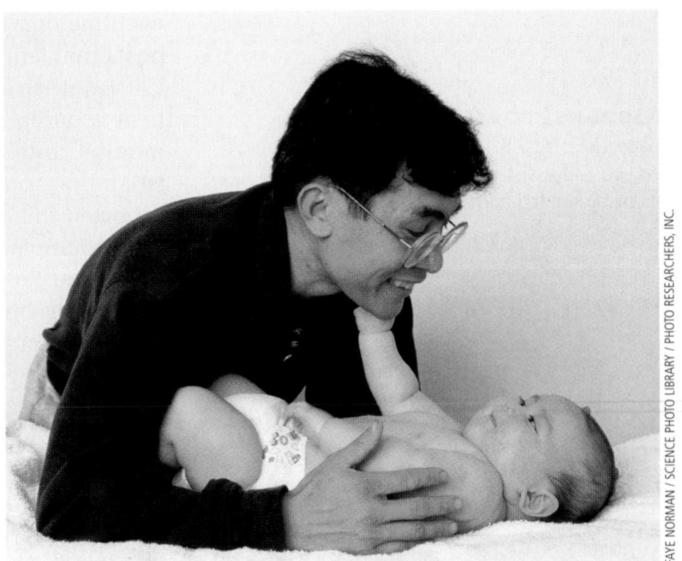

FAYE NORMAN / SCIENCE PHOTO LIBRARY / PHOTO RESEARCHERS, INC.

Not Talking? No words yet, but this infant communicates well with Dad, using eyes, mouth, and hands. What are they telling each other?

According to theory three, then, social impulses, not explicit teaching or brain maturation (as in the first two perspectives), make infants learn language, "as part of the package of being a human social animal" (Hollich et al., 2000). They seek to understand what others want and intend, and therefore "children acquire linguistic symbols as a kind of by-product of social action with adults" (Tomasello, 2001).

A Hybrid Theory

Which of these three perspectives is correct? As you can see, each position has been supported by research, so finding one and only one answer is impossible (Bloom, 1998). Many scientists seek to reconcile all the research and theories, acknowledging the merits of each (e.g., Bowerman & Levinson, 2001; Boysson-Bardies, 1999; Leonard, 2003; K. Nelson, 1996).

Three scholars attempted to integrate all three perspectives in a monograph, based on 12 experiments designed by eight researchers (Hollich et al., 2000). The authors developed a hybrid (which literally means "a new creature, formed by combining two other living things") of previous theories. They called their model an *emergentist coalition* because it combines valid aspects of several theories about the emergence of language during infancy.

These researchers point out that children learn language to do numerous things—indicate intention, call objects by name, put words together, talk to family members, sing to themselves, express their wishes, remember the past, and much more. Therefore, the scientists hypothesize that some aspects of language are best learned in one way at one age, others in another way at another age.

ESPECIALLY FOR BABYSITTERS Should you do anything for your clients' infants besides keeping them safe and clean?

For example, the name of the family dog may be learned by association and repetition, with family members and eventually the dog itself reinforcing the name, a behaviorist process. However, the distinction between *cat* and *dog* may reflect a neurological predilection (epigenetic), which means that the human brain may be genetically wired to differentiate those species. Just as neuroscientists have discovered that memories arise from many parts of the brain, with each memory retrieved under different conditions, the emergentist theory suggests that language may be learned and expressed in many ways.

Response for Babysitters (from page 185): Yes. Babies need to hear language, so you can assist in their language development by talking and singing to them.

Another example has to do with an amazing fact: A 6-month-old's ability to hear a difference in sounds predicts that child's ability to talk at 13 months, 18 months, and 24 months. This could be the result of early adult talking (behaviorist), inborn potential (Chomsky), or social impulses (sociocultural). The team that reported this fact, after intensive study, endorsed the hybrid theory, concluding that "multiple attentional, social and linguistic cues" contribute to early language (Tsao et al., 2004, p. 1081).

Underlying the hybrid theory is another theory—that language emerges at about 1 year because infants have already formed some concepts by about 6 months. The early process of concept formation likewise follows many "different developmental courses," just like early word learning does, in part because all infants must develop concepts in one way or another, no matter which approach their families and cultures use (Mandler, 2004, p. 304).

The cortex contains not one language center, but many, as brain-imaging studies have revealed. Similarly, decades of cross-cultural studies have found that cultures vary tremendously in language acquisition practices. For example, caregivers in some cultures seldom or never read to their infants, while others do so daily (see Figure 6.3). Some children are taught almost exclusively by their mothers, and other children are surrounded by the talk of a dozen or more people (Blum-Kulka & Snow, 2002).

Yet, although conditions vary, all normal infants learn their native language, talking in the way that their culture encourages. For instance, French infants learn when to use which form of "you," mastering the very difficult task of using the respectful *vous* form with adults who use the intimate *tu* form with them. One cultural difference is in the goal of language learning and therefore the reactions of adults. A talkative toddler is usually admired by middle-class European Americans, who will stop their conversation to respond to a toddler's questions; but such interruptions may be less appreciated by Latino Americans, who want children to show respect by not talking all the time (D. Johnson et al., 2003).

This variability makes language learning complicated to understand but simple for babies to do, and that is how it should be. Communication is crucial. Babies need to communicate from the moment they are born in order to help their caregivers know when to feed and change them and to meet their other needs.

It makes logical and practical sense that nature provides several paths toward language learning. Each path may be preferred or more efficient in some

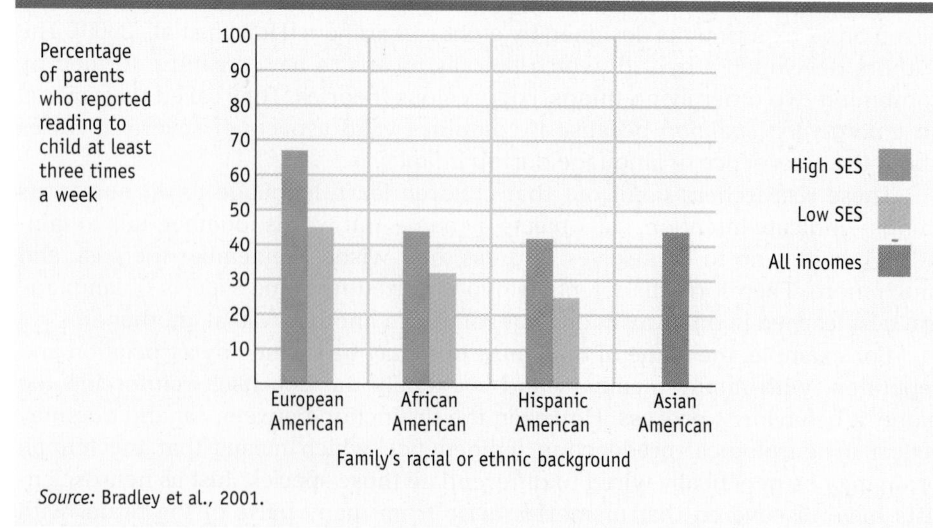

FIGURE 6.3 Not Even a Bedtime Story? To build vocabulary, most psychologists and educators recommend reading to a child several times a week. This graph reflects the fact that in the United States, caregivers of children under 3 usually don't follow this advice, especially if they are poor and have a non-European background. Some language-learning theorists contend that these variations are not problematic, but behaviorists are troubled by them.

stages, cultures, and families, but every child must communicate. That is how the human family is designed. This hybrid perspective returns the child to center stage: Infants are active learners not only of the concepts described in the first half of this chapter but also of language. As one expert concludes:

> Word learning theories will have to come to terms with the fact that children . . . are more than perceivers, receivers, or possessors of external supports. Instead, the word learning child is a child with feelings and thoughts about other persons, a child engaged in dynamic real-life events, a child learning to think about a world of changing physical and psychological relationships—in short, a child poised to act, to influence, to gain control . . . to embrace the learning of language for the power of expression it provides.
>
> *[Bloom, 2000, p. 13].*

ESPECIALLY FOR EDUCATORS An infant day-care center has a new child whose parents speak a language other than the one the teachers speak. Should the teachers learn basic words in the new language, or should they expect the baby to learn the majority language?

SUMMING UP

From the first days of life, babies attend to words and expressions, responding as well as their limited abilities allow—crying, cooing, and, by 9 months, responsively babbling. Before age 1, they understand simple words and communicate with gestures. At 1 year, most infants speak. Vocabulary accumulates slowly at first, but the holophrase, the naming explosion, and the two-word sentence emerge as evidence that toddlers become rapid language learners, mastering grammar as well as vocabulary.

The impressive language learning of the first two years can be explained in many ways. One theory contends that caregivers must teach language, reinforcing the infant's every vocal expression by using words to describe the many objects and experiences in the infant's life. Another theory relies on an inborn "language acquisition device," which means that, given a normal environment and exposure to language, infants will talk. A third theory stresses social interaction, implying that infants will learn language as long as their social context is supportive. A hybrid model combines all three. Because infants vary in cultures, learning styles, and families, each theory might be best suited to describe a particular aspect of language learning at one place and time.

A Note for Caregivers

There are many ways to foster an infant's language development or, for that matter, cognition. All three theories can be applied: The infant can be deliberately taught and encouraged, the brain and curiosity can be nourished and supported, and the social drive of the young human can be appreciated and even celebrated.

As you can see from Figure 6.1, about three-fourths of all caregivers respond to the infant's early talking, as theory three recommends; but, as Figure 6.3 shows, many parents do not expand their infants' language learning by regularly reading to them, as behaviorists would recommend. Many parents seem to believe that reading to young children is not necessary. However, that conclusion may be risky, especially in a culture that prizes fluency.

Toni, the 17-month-old whom you met in Chapter 5, had an expressive vocabulary of only 5 words, which is about average for infants several months younger than she was. Many 17-month-olds already speak 50 words. Reasons for Toni's language delay are provided by all three theoretical perspectives: (1) behaviorist—inadequate teaching from her patchwork of caregivers and too much time spent watching TV; (2) epigenetic—abnormal brain development, perhaps related to poor nutrition or disorganized, erratic experiences; and (3) social-pragmatic—lack of social incentive for her to communicate, since she had no steady caregiver.

Given what is known about infant cognition and brain development, Toni's limited vocabulary is worrisome. From the viewpoint of every language-learning theory, Toni may be in trouble. It is time to check Toni's hearing and to examine

Response for Educators (from page 187): Probably both. Infants love to communicate, and they seek every possible way to do so. Therefore, the teachers should try to understand the baby, and the baby's parents, but should also start teaching the baby the majority language of the school.

her social interaction with her mother and other caregivers. The published case study does not mention whether Toni uses gestures or whether her mother provides encouraging touch and facial expressions. This information is crucial to assess Toni's language-learning context. Without that, we cannot say whether Toni is on the verge of her naming explosion or needs special intervention now.

Although the norms for language development indicate that most children are talking more than Toni by 1½, some children—especially boys whose mothers have not had much education—are much slower, with some (perhaps 10 percent) still not talking at all at 18 months. One large study found that 16 percent of all 3-year-olds are still language-delayed, with unusually small vocabularies or unintelligible speech (Campbell et al., 2003). Three-fourths of them are expected to catch up by age 6. It is quite possible that Toni is already communicating with gestures, that soon she will be speaking sentences, that her delay is a temporary glitch. She has two apparent assets, her sex and her mother (who did bring Toni in for her checkup—a good sign). But something should be done, as discussed in the next chapter.

All the research and norms alert caregivers and professionals to the importance of the intellect in these first two years. If the next generation of children are to become bright, verbal, high achievers in a society that values knowledge, then providing infants with objects, words, and social play may be essential. Or maybe infants learn on their own as long as their families do not actively prevent them from doing so. But since all infants enjoy discovery, accomplishment, and social responses, there is no harm in providing opportunities for learning from the very start.

In fact, what is known about sensorimotor intelligence, about early information processing, and about rapid language learning strongly suggests that infants benefit from intellectual encouragement. The next chapter further describes what caregivers might do to promote healthy development.

■ SUMMARY

Sensorimotor Intelligence

1. Piaget realized that very young infants are active learners, seeking to understand their complex observations and experiences. Adaptation in infancy is characterized by sensorimotor intelligence, the first of Piaget's four stages of cognitive development. At every time of their lives, people adapt their thoughts to the experiences they have.

2. Sensorimotor intelligence develops in six stages—three pairs of two stages each—beginning with reflexes and ending with the toddler's active exploration and use of mental combinations. In each pair of stages, development occurs in one of three types of circular reactions, or feedback loops, in which the infant takes in experiences and tries to make sense of them.

3. Reflexes provide the foundation for intelligence. The continual process of assimilation and accommodation is evident in the first acquired adaptations, from about 1 to 4 months. The sucking reflex accommodates the particular nipples and other objects that the baby learns to suck. As time goes on, infants become more goal-oriented, creative, and experimental.

4. Infants gradually develop an understanding of objects over the first two years of life. As shown in Piaget's classic experiment, infants understand object permanence and begin to search for hidden objects at about 8 months. Other research finds that Piaget underestimated the cognition of young infants.

Information Processing

5. Another approach to understanding infant cognition is information-processing theory, which looks at each step of the thinking process, from input to output. The perceptions of a young infant are attuned to the particular affordances, or opportunities for action, that are present in the infant's world.

6. Objects that move are particularly interesting to infants, as are other humans. Objects as well as people afford many possibilities for interaction and perception, and therefore these affordances enhance early cognition.

7. Infant memory is fragile, but not completely absent. Reminder sessions help trigger memories, and young brains learn motor sequences long before they can remember verbally. Memory is multifaceted; explicit memories are rare in infancy.

Language: What Develops in Two Years?

8. Eager attempts to communicate are apparent in the first year. Infants babble at about 6 to 9 months, understand words and gestures by 10 months, and speak their first words at about 1 year.

9. Vocabulary begins to build very slowly until the infant knows approximately 50 words. Then a naming explosion begins. Toward the end of the second year, toddlers begin putting two words together, showing by their word order that they understand the rudiments of grammar.

10. Various theories attempt to explain how infants learn language as quickly as they do. The three main theories emphasize different aspects of early language learning: that infants must be taught, that their brains are genetically attuned to language, and that their social impulses foster language learning.

11. Each of these theories seems partly true. The challenge for developmental scientists has been to formulate a hybrid theory that uses all the insights and research on early language learning. The challenge for caregivers is to respond appropriately to the infant's early attempts to communicate.

▪ KEY TERMS

adaptation (p. 165)
sensorimotor intelligence (p. 166)
primary circular reactions (p. 166)
secondary circular reactions (p. 167)
object permanence (p. 168)
tertiary circular reaction (p. 169)
little scientist (p. 170)
deferred imitation (p. 170)
habituation (p. 170)
fMRI (p. 171)
information-processing theory (p. 172)
affordance (p. 173)
visual cliff (p. 174)
dynamic perception (p. 174)
people preference (p. 174)
reminder session (p. 176)
child-directed speech (p. 178)
babbling (p. 179)
naming explosion (p. 180)
holophrase (p. 181)
grammar (p. 181)
language acquisition device (LAD) (p. 184)

▪ KEY QUESTIONS

1. Why is Piaget's first period of cognitive development called sensorimotor intelligence? Give examples.

2. Give examples of some things adults learn via sensorimotor intelligence.

3. What does the active experimentation of the stage-five toddler suggest for parents?

4. Why are some researchers concerned about too much emphasis being placed on early cognitive development?

5. How do researchers figure out if an infant has a concept of something even if the infant cannot talk about it yet?

6. What does research on affordances suggest about cognitive differences between one infant and another?

7. Why would a child remember very little about experiences in infancy?

8. What indicates that toddlers use some grammar?

9. How do deaf and hearing babies compare in early language learning?

10. How would a caregiver who subscribes to the behaviorist theory of language learning respond when an infant babbles?

11. According to the sociocultural theory of language learning, what might explain why an 18-month-old was not yet talking?

12. What does the research on language learning suggest to caregivers?

▪ APPLICATIONS

1. Elicit vocalizations from an infant—babbling if the baby is under age 1, words if older. Write down all the baby says for 10 minutes. Then ask the primary caregiver to elicit vocalizations for 10 minutes, and write these down. Is there a difference between the two attempts at communication? If so, what and why? Compare your findings with the norms described in the chapter.

2. Piaget's definition of intelligence is adaptation. Others consider a good memory or an extensive vocabulary to be a sign of intelligence. How would you define intelligence? Give an example of something you did that was intelligent, and explain how it meets your definition.

3. Some educators recommend that parents read to babies even before the babies begin talking. How do you feel about this advice? What theory of language development does it reflect? How does reading affect the language use of people you know?

4. Test an infant's ability to search for a hidden object. Ideally, the infant should be about 7 or 8 months old, and you should retest over a period of weeks. If the infant can immediately find the object, make the task harder by pausing between the hiding and searching or by secretly moving the object from one hiding place to another.

Chapter Seven

The First Two Years: Psychosocial Development

Psychosocial development is the combination of emotional and social development. Accordingly, infant emotions and social contexts, as well as the dynamic interaction between the two, are the topics of this chapter. You have witnessed this interaction many times: Tiny babies break into smiles when staring at an engaging face; 1-year-olds cling to their parents when frightened; toddlers flop to the floor, kicking and screaming, after being told "no." Almost every moment of a baby's waking life is a psychosocial moment, because infants depend on other people for minute-to-minute survival and because humans of all ages attend to each other, adjusting to social needs.

As I sat on a crowded subway, a young woman boarded with an infant in one arm and a shopping bag on the other. She tried to steady herself as the train started to move. Should I have given her my seat? Probably. I didn't. Instead I asked, "Can I help you?" Wordlessly she handed me . . . the baby. I began softly singing a children's song. The baby seemed content to listen, watching her mother. For all three of us, each with our own understanding of what should happen, that was a psychosocial moment.

This chapter opens with a much longer psychosocial episode, the early development of a boy named Jacob. Then we trace infant emotions over the first two years, followed by a review of the five theories first described in Chapter 2. This leads us into research on caregiver–infant interaction, particularly *synchrony, attachment,* and *social referencing*—all research topics that are pivotal to psychosocial development. We then explore the pros and cons of infant day care. The chapter ends with practical suggestions for Toni (the 17-month-old you met in Chapter 5) and Jacob, whose story appears on the following page.

A Case to Study

Parents on Autopilot

A father writes about his third child, Jacob:

> We were convinced that we were set. We had surpassed our quota of 2.6 children and were ready to engage parental autopilot. I had just begun a prestigious job and was working 10–11 hours a day. The children would be fine. We hired a nanny to watch Jacob during the day. As each of Jacob's early milestones passed, we felt that we had taken another step toward our goal of having three normal children. We were on our way to the perfect American family. Yet, somewhere back in our minds we had some doubts. Jacob seemed different than the girls. He had some unusual attributes. There were times when we would be holding him and he would arch his back and scream so loud that it was painful for us.
>
> *[Jacob's father, 1997]*

As an infant, Jacob did not relate to his parents (or to anyone else). His parents paid little heed to his psychosocial difficulties, focusing instead on physical development. They noted that Jacob sat up and walked on schedule, and when they "had some doubts," they found excuses, telling themselves that "boys are different" or that Jacob's language delays were caused by his nanny, who spoke little English. As time went on, their excuses fell short. His father continues:

> Jacob had become increasingly isolated [by age 2]. I'm not a psychologist, but I believe that he just stopped trying. It was too hard, perhaps too scary. He couldn't figure out what was expected of him. The world had become too confusing, and so he withdrew from it. He would seek out the comfort of quiet, dark places and sit by himself. He would lose himself in the bright, colorful images of cartoons and animated movies.

Jacob was finally diagnosed at age 3 with "pervasive developmental disorder." This is a catchall diagnosis that can include autism (discussed in Chapter 11). At the moment, you need to know only that Jacob's psychosocial potential was unappreciated. His despairing parents were advised to consider residential placement because Jacob would never be normal and, with Jacob living elsewhere, they would not be constantly reminded of their "failure." This recommendation did not take into account the commitment that Jacob's parents, like most parents, felt toward their child.

Despite their commitment, they had ignored early signs of trouble. They had overlooked Jacob's reaction to being held and his failure to talk. The absence of smiling, of social play, and of imitation should have raised an alarm. The father's use of the word *autopilot* shows that he realized this in hindsight. Later in this chapter, you will learn the outcome.

Emotional Development

Within the first two years, infants progress remarkably in emotional expression, from reactive pain and pleasure to complex patterns of social awareness (see Table 7.1). This is the period of life with "high emotional responsiveness" (Izard et al., 2002, p. 767). Young infants display speedy, frequent, and uncensored reactions—crying, startling, laughing, raging. Older infants also make their emotions evident, but the range of emotions is wider and the social impact more evident as toddlers manifest self-satisfied grins or mournful pouts.

TABLE 7.1 AT ABOUT THIS TIME: Ages When Emotions Emerge

Age	Emotional Expression
Birth	Crying; contentment
6 weeks	Social smile
3 months	Laughter; curiosity
4 months	Full, responsive smiles
4–8 months	Anger
9–14 months	Fear of social events (strangers, separation from caregiver)
12 months	Fear of unexpected sights and sounds
18 months	Self-awareness; pride; shame; embarrassment

The First Year

At first there are only two identifiable emotions: contentment and distress, expressed as pleasure and pain. Newborns look happy and relaxed when they are recently fed and drifting off to sleep. They cry when they are hurt or hungry, when they are tired or frightened (as of a loud noise or a sudden loss of support), and sometimes when they have digestive difficulties such as *colic,* a word used to refer to the seemingly unstoppable wailing that about a third of all infants do in the early months.

After the first few weeks, additional emotions become recognizable (Lavelli & Fogel, 2005). Curiosity, or at least interest, is shown when infants stare at something new, or hear a melodic voice, or watch a mobile. Unexpected—but not too surprising—sensations are exactly what infants enjoy. Curiosity is increasingly evident as infants become better able to distinguish the unusual from the familiar (Kagan, 2002). Interest in faces matures into pleasure, first expressed by the **social smile** at about 6 weeks. At 3 or 4 months, babies begin to laugh, especially when a caregiver makes expressions and noises that offer the right combination of familiarity and novelty.

social smile A smile evoked by a human face, normally evident in infants at about 6 weeks after birth.

Parents are not the only ones who elicit laughter, especially in cultures where many adults delight in an infant's joy. Among the Navajo, whoever brings forth that first laugh gives a feast to celebrate that the baby is becoming a person (Rogoff, 2003). Laughter builds as curiosity does, so that a typical 1-year-old is not only driven to discover new things but also laughs loudly, with evident joy.

Anger is usually triggered by frustration, when something or someone interferes with attainment of a goal. Piaget thought goal seeking begins at 8 months, although, as you remember from Chapter 6, many infants reach Piaget's stages earlier than he predicted. Some infants fuss and scowl in anger as early as 4 months. Anger is most apparent when infants are frustrated because they are being restrained or prevented from reaching a graspable object (Plutchik, 2003).

As infants become more capable of deliberate movement, anger at restraint becomes more apparent. One-year-olds hate to be strapped in, caged in, closed in, or just held tight on someone's lap when they want to explore. Anger in infancy is considered a healthy response to frustration, unlike sadness, which indicates withdrawal and which includes not only a helpless, sorrowful expression but also an increase in the level of *cortisol*, a stress hormone (Lewis & Ramsay, 2005).

GERI ENGBERG / THE IMAGE WORKS

Friendship Begins Emotions connect friends to each other—these two 1-year-olds as well as friends of any age. The shared smiles indicate a strong social connection. What will they do next?

Fully formed fear at some *thing* (not just distress at a surprise) emerges at about 9 months. It builds rapidly, becoming more frequent as well as more apparent (Kagan, 1998). Two fears are obvious:

- **Stranger wariness** occurs when an infant no longer smiles at any friendly face and cries if an unfamiliar person moves too close, too quickly.
- **Separation anxiety** is expressed in tears, dismay, or anger when a familiar caregiver leaves. This is one sign of attachment, discussed later in this chapter.

stranger wariness An infant's expression of concern—a quiet stare, clinging to a familiar person, or sadness—when a stranger appears. This signifies maturation: The baby recognizes the person as strange.

separation anxiety Distress when a familiar caregiver leaves; most obvious between 9 and 14 months.

Separation anxiety is normal at age 1, intensifies by age 2, and usually subsides after that. If it remains strong after age 3, it is considered an emotional disorder (Silverman & Dick-Neiderhauser, 2004).

In addition to stranger wariness and separation anxiety, many 1-year-olds fear anything unexpected, from the flush of a toilet to the pop of a jack-in-the-box, from the sudden closing of elevator doors to the friendly approach of a dog. Such fears are normal, requiring reassurance and gradual development of familiarity. With repeated experiences and caregiver protection, older infants might themselves enjoy flushing the toilet (again and again) or calling the dog (crying if the dog does *not* come).

The Second Year

As you have just read, many emotions that emerge in the first months of life take on new strength at about age 1 (Kagan, 2002). Throughout the second year and beyond, anger and fear typically become less frequent and become targeted toward things that are truly infuriating or terrifying. Similarly, both laughing and

ESPECIALLY FOR NURSES AND PEDIATRICIANS Parents come to you concerned that their 1-year-old hides her face and holds onto them tightly whenever a stranger appears. What do you tell them?

JOURNAL-COURIER / TIFFANY HERMON / THE IMAGE WORKS

Stranger Wariness Becomes Santa Terror For toddlers, even a friendly stranger is cause for alarm, especially if Mom's protective arms are withdrawn. The most frightening strangers are men who are unusually dressed and who act as if they might take the child away. Ironically, therefore, Santa Claus remains terrifying until children are about 3 years old.

crying become more discriminating, so that the experiences that once reliably triggered shrieks of joy or pain no longer do so. For example, 1-year-olds who are learning to run often tumble, but they do not cry immediately. Between falling down and reacting, they pause to decide whether the fall was fun or not. Only then do they burst into laughter or tears.

New emotions appear toward the end of the second year: pride, shame, embarrassment, and even guilt. Because these emotions require an awareness of other people, they emerge from the family setting, which is itself influenced by the culture (Eid & Diener, 2001). For example, pride is encouraged in North American toddlers ("You did it all by yourself"—even when that is untrue), but Asian families discourage pride and cultivate modesty and shame (Rogoff, 2003).

Throughout the first two years, the social context elicits, guides, and identifies the various emotions of the child. In some families anger is rare; in other families outbursts at minor transgressions are routine. Two-year-olds not only have many emotional reactions but also know which ones are considered acceptable and which are not (Rothbart & Bates, 1998). For example, if a toddler holds on tightly to his mother's skirt and hides his face when a strange dog approaches, the mother could pick the child up, bend down to pet the dog, or push the child away. Each of these maternal responses affects whether the child expresses fear, joy, or anger the next time a dog approaches.

Over the first two years, the toddler's emotions, particularly negative ones, become less instinctual and more responsive. Motivation and cognition grow; parents' reactions to each infant emotion affect later expression (Izard & Ackerman, 2000; Pauli-Pott et al., 2004).

Self-Awareness

self-awareness A person's realization that he or she is a distinct individual, with independent body, mind, and actions.

In addition to the social circumstances, another foundation for emotional growth is **self-awareness**, a person's realization that he or she is a distinct individual whose body, mind, and actions are separate from those of other people. This emerging sense of "me" and "mine" leads to a new consciousness of others. That consciousness fosters the ability to experience emotions about and express them toward other people, including defiance and jealousy as well as empathy and affection. As one developmentalist explains:

> With the emergence of consciousness in the second year of life, we see vast changes in both children's emotional life and the nature of their social relationships. . . . With consciousness the child can feel . . . self-conscious emotions, like pride at a job well done or shame over a failure.
>
> *[Lewis, 1997, p. 132]*

Response for Nurses and Pediatricians (from page 193): Stranger wariness is normal up to about 14 months. This baby's behavior actually sounds like secure attachment!

The onset of self-awareness is strikingly evident when infants of various ages are compared. Very young infants have no sense of self. In fact, a prominent psychoanalyst, Margaret Mahler, theorized that for the first 4 months of life infants see themselves as part of their mothers. They "hatch" at about 5 months and spend the next several months developing a sense of themselves as separate from their mothers (Mahler et al., 1975). Whether or not Mahler is correct, there is no doubt that maturation brings self-awareness. The period from 15 to 18 months "is noteworthy for the emergence of the Me-self, the sense of self as the object of one's knowledge" (Harter, 1998).

In a classic experiment (Lewis & Brooks, 1978), babies looked into a mirror after a dot of rouge had been surreptitiously put on their noses. If the babies reacted to the mirror image by touching their noses, that meant they knew they were seeing their own faces. With 96 babies between the ages of 9 and 24 months, the experimenters found a distinct developmental shift. None of the babies under 12 months reacted to the mark as if they knew it was on them (they sometimes smiled and touched the dot on the baby in the mirror). However, most of those between ages 15 and 24 months did react with self-awareness, sometimes touching their own noses with an expression of curiosity and puzzlement.

A longitudinal replication of this experiment reveals the increase of self-recognition (Lewis & Ramsay, 2004). Most (79 percent) of the children who did not touch their noses at 15 months did so six months later. Self-recognition usually emerges at about 18 months.

LAURA DWIGHT

She Knows Herself This 18-month-old is happy to see herself in her firefighter's helmet. She is adjusting the helmet with her hands on it, and that's evidence that she understands what a mirror is. Note, however, that she is not yet aware that a hat has a front and a back.

Pride and Shame

Pride and shame are strongly linked to self-concept and vary in when and how they develop. If someone tells a 1- or 2-year-old, "You're very smart," the toddler may smile at the praise but usually already feels smart—and thus is already pleased and proud. Being told you are smart, strong, or beautiful may not be news at all and may even be unhelpful. Certainly at older ages, unrealistically high self-esteem leads to less achievement, not more (Baumeister et al., 2003).

In toddlerhood, the relationship between parental praise and self-esteem is not straightforward. In one study, toddler boys who received *less* parental praise became *more* proud of themselves, perhaps because they were better able than younger children to form their own positive self-evaluations (Belsky et al., 1997).

Another longitudinal study found that positive comments from mothers to 2-year-olds did *not* lead to more pride or less shame by age 3 (Kelley et al., 2000). However, certain negative comments (such as "You're doing it all wrong") diminished effort and increased shame. Neutral suggestions, in addition to guiding toddlers to complete activities on their own, fostered the willingness to try new challenges (Kelley et al., 2000). It seems that building self-esteem results not from praising young children but from enabling them to accomplish things that make them feel proud.

How can a toddler's own self-evaluation be more compelling than parental approval? Look, for example, at Ricky, the grandson of a noted psychologist. Shortly before his second birthday, Ricky teased his mother by deliberately pouring a cup of juice onto a rug. Ricky knew he was being naughty: He was unfazed by his mother's scolding and was quite willing to help her clean up the mess. Other research also finds that toddlers enjoy deliberately disobeying their parents on occasion (Dunn, 1988). Ricky protested only when his mother sent him to his room; he did not expect such punishment.

Later that day Ricky told his grandmother, "Juice on a floor." She responded somewhat sternly, "Juice doesn't go on the floor." "Yes, juice on a floor, juice on a floor," he laughingly repeated several times, pretending to turn an imaginary cup upside down. The grandmother comments:

> The boy's pleasure at watching the juice spill and anger at being sent to his room are emotions that are typical at all periods of infancy, but his obvious pride at his ability to act counter to convention or his mother's wishes is possible only when self-awareness is firmly established.
>
> *[Shatz, 1994]*

Ricky's pride shows his self-awareness, and so does the fact that he pours with an imaginary cup. A longitudinal study revealed a strong correlation among three things: pretending, touching one's own nose in the mirror, and using first-person pronouns (*I, me, mine, myself, my*). This correlation occurs because of emotional development, not mere chronological age, as shown by the timing of the three. Of those few 21-month-olds who still did not recognize themselves in the mirror, none pretended with a doll and none used first-person pronouns (Lewis & Ramsay, 2004).

The reasons one toddler demonstrates a sense of self sooner than another are many, including temperament and culture, each of which is favored by a major theory. To further explore the development of emotions in the early years, it is useful to consider all five theories again. But first, let us recap.

SUMMING UP

Newborns seem to have only two simple emotions, distress and contentment, which are expressed by crying or looking happy. Very soon curiosity and obvious joy, with social smiles and laughter, appear. By the second half of the first year, anger and fear are increasingly evident, especially in reaction to social experiences, such as encountering a stranger. In the second year, as infants become self-aware, they express emotions connected to themselves, including pride, shame, and embarrassment, and emotions about other people, such as defiance, jealousy, and affection. Universal maturation makes these emotions possible at around 18 months, but context and learning affect their timing, frequency, and intensity.

Theories About Infant Psychosocial Development

Emotional development reflects, above all, the connection between infants and their immediate social surroundings, especially their family. As you remember from Chapter 2, two of the grand theories, psychoanalytic theory and behaviorism, emphasize the ways in which parents, particularly mothers, shape emotions and personality. Cognitive theory, the third grand theory, stresses the infant's own cognitive constructions. The two emerging theories emphasize factors beyond the parents' control: genetics in epigenetic theory and culture in sociocultural theory.

Psychoanalytic Theory

Psychoanalytic theory connects biosocial and psychosocial development, emphasizing the need for responsive maternal care. Both major psychoanalytic theorists, Sigmund Freud and Erik Erikson, described two distinct early stages. Freud (1935, 1940/1964) wrote about the *oral stage* and the *anal stage*. Erikson (1963) called his first stages *trust versus mistrust* and *autonomy versus shame and doubt*.

A Moment of Bliss Freud thought that oral gratification through breast-feeding was an erotic experience as well as, in his day, a nutritional necessity. Modern psychologists question the power and even the existence of Freud's stages, but his emphasis on the universality of unconscious, primitive urges may not be as far-fetched as some believe.

KEN CAVANAUGH / PHOTO RESEARCHERS, INC

Freud: Oral and Anal Stages

According to Freud (1935), psychological development begins in the first year of life with the *oral stage,* so named because the mouth is the young infant's prime source of gratification. In the second year, with the *anal stage,* the infant's main pleasure comes from the anus—particularly from the sensual pleasure of bowel movements and, eventually, the psychological pleasure of controlling them.

Freud believed that both the oral and anal stages are fraught with potential conflicts that have long-term consequences. If a mother frustrates her infant's urge to suck—weaning the infant too early, for example, or preventing the child from sucking on fingers or toes—the child may become distressed and anxious, eventually becoming an adult with an *oral fixation.* Such a person is stuck (fixated) at the oral stage and therefore eats, drinks, chews, bites, or talks excessively, in quest of the mouth-related pleasure denied in infancy.

Similarly, if toilet training is overly strict or if it begins before the infant is mature enough, parent–infant interaction may become locked into a conflict over the toddler's refusal, or inability, to comply. The child becomes fixated and develops an *anal personality*—as an adult, seeking self-control with an unusually strong need for regularity in all aspects of life.

Erikson: Trust and Autonomy

According to Erikson, the first crisis of life is **trust versus mistrust**, when infants learn whether the world is to be trusted, whether basic needs will be satisfied or not. For some babies, the world is an unpredictable arena where needs are met only after much crying—and sometimes not even then. Babies feel secure when food and comfort are provided with "consistency, continuity, and sameness of experience" (Erikson, 1963, p. 247). If social interaction inspires trust and security, the child (and later the adult) will confidently engage in exploration of the social world.

The next crisis is called **autonomy versus shame and doubt.** Toddlers want autonomy (self-rule) over their own actions and bodies. If they fail to gain it, either because they are incapable or because their caregivers are too restrictive, they feel ashamed of their actions and doubtful of their abilities. According to Erikson, parental guidance and protection are crucial for establishing autonomy.

Like Freud, Erikson believed that problems arising in early infancy could last a lifetime. The adult who is suspicious and pessimistic or who always seems burdened by shame may have been an infant who did not develop sufficient trust or a toddler who did not achieve sufficient autonomy.

JOSE LUIS PELEAZ, INC. / CORBIS

A Mother's Dilemma Infants are wonderfully curious, as this little boy demonstrates. Parents, however, must guide as well as encourage the drive toward autonomy. Notice this mother's expression as she makes sure her son does not crush or eat the flower.

trust versus mistrust Erikson's first psychosocial stage. Infants learn basic trust if the world is a secure place where their basic needs (for food, comfort, attention, etc.) are met.

autonomy versus shame and doubt Erikson's second crisis of psychosocial development. Toddlers either succeed or fail in gaining a sense of self-rule over their own actions and bodies.

Behaviorism

From the perspective of behaviorism, emotions and personality are molded as parents reinforce or punish the child's spontaneous behaviors. If parents smile and pick up their infant at every glimmer of a grin, he or she will become a child—and later an adult—with a sunny disposition. The opposite is also true. Early behaviorists, especially John Watson, made the strongest statements on this issue:

> Failure to bring up a happy child, a well-adjusted child—assuming bodily health—falls squarely upon the parents' shoulders. [By the time the child is 3] parents have already determined . . . [if the child] is to grow into a happy person, wholesome and good-natured, whether he is to be a whining, complaining neurotic, an anger-driven, vindictive, over-bearing slave driver, or one whose every move in life is definitely controlled by fear.
>
> *[Watson, 1928]*

Later behaviorists noted that infants also experience **social learning**, which is learning by observing others. This was shown by research, especially Albert Bandura's famous experiment in which young children imitated an adult who punched a rubber "Bobo" clown (Bandura, 1977). Social learning is also revealed in many families, in which the toddler girl or boy expresses emotions—from giggling to cursing—in much the same way their parent or older sibling of the same sex does. A boy might develop a hot temper, for instance, if his father regularly displays anger and in return gets respect—or at least obedience—from other family members.

social learning Learning by observing others.

You have probably noticed that both psychoanalytic and behaviorist theories emphasize the role of the parents. Freud thought that the mother was the young child's first and best "love object," and behaviorists stress the power of a mother over her children. In retrospect, this focus seems too narrow. The other three theories reflect more recent research and the changing historical context.

Especially for Nursing Mothers
You have heard that if you wean your child too early, he or she will overeat or become an alcoholic. Is it true?

Cognitive Theory

Cognitive theory holds that thoughts and values determine a person's perspective. Early family experiences are important primarily because beliefs, thoughts, perceptions, and memories make them so, not because they shape development by getting buried in the unconscious (as psychoanalytic theory maintains) or burned into the brain as patterns (according to behaviorism). Cognitive theory suggests that early psychosocial development is shaped by infants' attempts to form a general concept of what to expect from other people.

working model In cognitive theory, a set of assumptions that the individual uses to organize perceptions and experiences.

Infants use their early relationships to develop a **working model,** a set of assumptions that become a frame of reference that can be called on later in life (Bretherton & Munholland, 1999; Thompson & Raikes, 2003). It is called a "model" because these early relationships form a prototype, or blueprint; it is called "working" because, while usable, it is not necessarily fixed or final.

For example, a 1-year-old girl might develop a working model, based on her mother's responses to her, that people cannot be trusted. All her life she will apply that model whenever she meets a new person. Her childhood relationships will be insecure, and as an adult she will be suspicious of people, on guard against further disappointment. To use Piaget's terminology, she has developed a cognitive *schema* to organize her perceptions. According to cognitive theory, a child's interpretation of early experiences is crucial, not necessarily the experiences themselves (Schaffer, 2000).

Response for Nursing Mothers (from page 197): Freud thought so, but there is no experimental evidence that weaning, even when ill timed, has such dire long-term effects.

The hopeful message of cognitive theory is that people can rethink and reorganize their thoughts, developing new working models that are more positive than their original ones. Our mistrustful girl can learn to trust if experiences—such as being married to a faithful and loving husband—provide a new model.

Epigenetic Theory

temperament Inborn differences between one person and another in emotions, activity, and self-control. Temperament is epigenetic, originating in genes but affected by child-rearing practices.

As you remember from Chapter 2, epigenetic theory holds that every human characteristic is strongly influenced by each person's unique genotype. Thus, a child might be happy or anxious not because of early experiences (the three grand theories) but because of inborn predispositions. Child-rearing practices can shape those predispositions (they are *epi*genetic), but DNA remains the same from conception on, no matter how emotions are blocked (psychoanalytic theory), reinforced (behaviorism), or interpreted (cognitive theory).

Temperament

Among each person's genetic predispositions are the traits of **temperament,** defined as "constitutionally based individual differences" in emotions, activity, and self-control (Rothbart & Bates, 1998, p. 109). "Constitutionally based" means that these traits originate with nature, not nurture.

Twins They were born on the same day and now are experiencing a wading pool for the first time.

? Observational Quiz (see answer, page 201): Are these babies monozygotic or dizygotic twins?

CORROON AND COMPANY / MONKMEYER

Temperament is similar to personality, except that personality includes traits that are primarily learned (e.g., honesty and humility), whereas temperamental traits (e.g., shyness and aggression) are primarily genetic. Temperamental traits originate in the genes, although the environment, from prenatal nurturance to ongoing social context and experience, influences their expression. Epigenetic theorists stress that an infant's temperamental traits, including what Watson described as being "happy, wholesome and good-natured" or "anger-driven, vindictive, over-bearing" (Watson, 1928), are not *caused* by early experiences.

In laboratory studies of temperament, infants have experiences that might be frightening. Four-month-olds might see spinning mobiles or hear unusual sounds. Older children might confront a noisy, moving robot or a clown who quickly moves close. At such experiences, some children laugh (and are classified as "easy"), some cry ("difficult"), and some are quiet ("slow to warm up") (Fox et al., 2001; Kagan & Snidman, 2004).

The categories of "easy," "difficult," and "slow to warm up" come from a classic study called the *New York Longitudinal Study* (NYLS), the first among many to recognize that each newborn has distinct traits that are coded in the networks of his or her brain. Although its origins are neurological, temperament is difficult to detect via brain scans such as fMRIs or EEGs, for reasons explained in Chapter 6 (Thompson & Nelson, 2001). Accordingly, most research on infant temperament uses parent reports and direct observation. In order to overcome the parents' hopes and biases, researchers ask for specific behavioral examples. As the NYLS researchers explain:

> If a mother said that her child did not like his first solid food, we . . . were satisfied only when she gave a description such as "When I put the food into his mouth he cried loudly, twisted his head away, and let it drool out."
>
> [Chess et al., 1965]

LEONG KA TAI / MATERIAL WORLD

Which Sister Has a Personality Problem? Culture always affects the expression of temperament. In Mongolia and many other Asian countries, females are expected to display shyness as a sign of respect to elders and strangers. Consequently, if the younger of these sisters is truly as shy as she seems, her parents are less likely to be distressed about her withdrawn behavior than the typical North American parent would be. Conversely, they may consider the relative boldness of her older sister to be a serious problem.

According to the NYLS, by 3 months, infants manifest nine temperamental traits. Clustering these traits, the NYLS found four types of infants:

- Easy (40 percent)
- Difficult (10 percent)
- Slow to warm up (15 percent)
- Hard to classify (35 percent)

Many other researchers began by studying adult personality and came up with the "Big Five" traits (whose first letters form the easy-to-remember acronym *OCEAN*):

- Openness: imaginative, curious, welcoming new experiences
- Conscientiousness: organized, deliberate, conforming
- Extroversion: outgoing, assertive, and active
- Agreeableness: kind, helpful, and easygoing
- Neuroticism: anxious, moody, and self-critical

Especially for Nurses and Pediatricians Parents come to you with their fussy 3-month-old. They say that they have read that temperament is "fixed" before birth, and they are worried that their child will always be difficult. What do you tell them?

The Big Five are found in many cultures, among people of various ages (Jang et al., 1998; Loehlin et al., 1998; McCrae & Costa, 2003). This adds to the evidence that some basic temperamental differences are innate, preceding child-rearing practices and cultural values. The Big Five are more complex than the easy/difficult/slow-to-warm up classifications; but a baby high on agreeableness would be easy, one high on neuroticism would be difficult, and one low on openness would be slow to warm up. In other words, the Big Five, which originated with adults, do not contradict the NYLS, which originated with infants.

The Parents' Role

Almost all studies of temperament or personality find that clusters of behaviors, similar to those found in the NYLS or the Big Five, appear very early in life. Easy babies are happy and outgoing most of the time, adjusting quickly to almost any change. Difficult babies are the opposite: irregular, intense, unhappy, disturbed

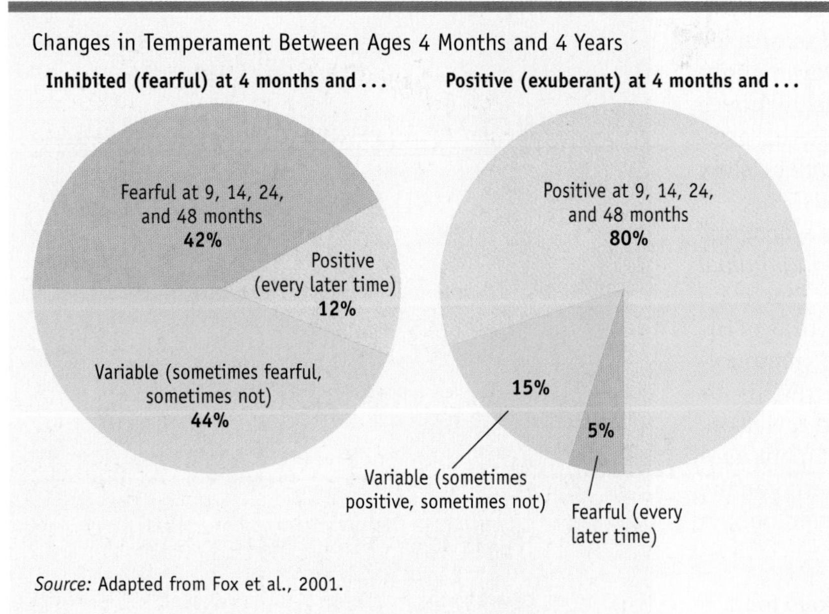

FIGURE 7.1 **Do Babies' Temperaments Change?** The data suggest that fearful babies are not necessarily fated to remain that way. Adults who are reassuring and do not act frightened themselves can help children overcome an innate fearfulness. Some fearful children do not change, however, and it is not known whether that's because their parents are not sufficiently reassuring (nurture) or because they are temperamentally more fearful (nature).

? OBSERVATIONAL QUIZ (see answer, page 202): Out of 100 4-month-olds who react positively to noises and other experiences, how many are fearful at later times in early childhood?

goodness of fit A similarity of temperament and values that produces a smooth interaction between the individual and the social context, including family, school, and community.

by every noise, and hard to distract—quite a handful. Slow-to-warm-up babies are unwilling to adapt to new people and experiences at first, but they do adapt with time and patience.

One longitudinal study (Fox et al., 2001) spotted three distinct groups—exuberant (positive), negative, and inhibited (fearful)—at 4 months. (It also found many infants who did not fit into any of these groups.) The researchers followed the infants in these three groups, with laboratory measures, mothers' reports, and brain scans at 9, 14, 24, and 48 months. Half of these infants were very stable in temperament, reacting the same way and having similar brain-wave patterns when confronted with frightening experiences all four times they were tested.

The other half of the children took a new approach to frightening experiences on at least one of the later assessments. Children who had been fearful (inhibited) at 4 months were most likely to change, and the positive (exuberant) infants were least likely to change (see Figure 7.1). That speaks to the influence of child rearing, since parents and others are likely to coax frightened children to be braver but usually encourage happy children to stay positive.

This information is especially helpful for parents of a "difficult"—or negative—infant, because it reassures them that they need not blame themselves as they guide and encourage their child. Parents ideally achieve a **goodness of fit**—that is, a temperamental match that allows smooth infant–caregiver interaction. When the fit is good, parents of difficult children patiently guide them, building a close, trusting relationship; parents of exuberant, curious children protect them from harm as they explore their surroundings; parents of slow-to-warm-up children give them time to adjust to new situations.

In general, a difficult child is more affected by a mother's responsiveness than a positive child is (Pauli-Pott et al., 2004). The combination of ineffective parenting and difficult temperament may create an antisocial, destructive child. Perhaps happy babies thrive in almost any family, but difficult ones need careful nurturance.

As you can see, the epigenetic perspective emphasizes individual differences and thus avoids generalities about good parenting (Derryberry et al., 2003). Parents must first understand the temperamental traits of their children and then teach and guide them to help their inborn traits become constructive, not destructive. Some children naturally cope easily with life's challenges, whereas "a shy child must control his or her fear and approach a stranger, and an impulsive child must constrain his or her desire and resist a temptation" (Derryberry et al., 2003, p. 1061).

Sociocultural Theory

Many cultural influences on caregiving have been discussed in the previous two chapters—from breast-feeding to language learning, from immunization to object play. No one doubts that "human development occurs in a cultural context" (Kagitcibasi, 2003, p. 166). The crucial question is *how much* influence culture has. Sociocultural theory argues that the influence is substantial, that the entire social context has a major impact on infant–caregiver relationships and thus on infant development.

Ethnotheories

An **ethnotheory** is a theory of child rearing that is embedded in a particular culture or ethnic group (Dasen, 2003). Usually the group is unaware that theories underlie their practices and customs. However, as you saw in Chapter 5's discussion of co-sleeping customs, multicultural research finds that many differences in child-rearing practices spring from ethnotheories (Greenfield et al., 2003).

ethnotheory A theory that underlies the values and practices of a culture and that becomes apparent through analysis and comparison of those practices, although it is not usually apparent to the people within the culture.

Now consider differences in emotions. Some cultures encourage independence and autonomy—leading to pride, jealousy, and defiance—and others favor dependency and cooperation—leading to sympathy, embarrassment, and compliance. Such social values give rise to parental ethnotheories that shape emotional expression. As a result, the behavior of toddlers from one nation can be considered immature, even shocking, by people elsewhere. For example, if the ethnotheory includes the idea that ancestors are reincarnated, then "children are not expected to show respect for adults, but adults [are expected to show respect] for their reborn ancestors." Such cultures favor child-rearing practices that "Western people perceive as extremely lenient" (Dasen, 2003, pp. 149–150).

R. IAN LLOYD / MASTERFILE

Learning to Worship This boy in Borneo has learned that Allah is to be shown respect with a covered head and bare feet. He already prays five times a day as part of an ethnotheory that includes concepts of life and death, male and female, good and evil—just like everyone else in the world, although the specifics vary widely.

We noted earlier that infants become angry when they are restrained. Nonetheless, many European American parents force their protesting toddlers to sit in strollers, to ride in car seats, or to stay in cribs and playpens or behind gates. If toddlers do not lie down quietly to allow diapers to be changed (and few do), some parents simply hold the protesting child still while diapering. Contrast this with Mayan parents, who believe that children should never be forced to comply. When 18-month-old Roberto did not want to wear a diaper, his mother used a false promise, and then a distraction.

> "Let's put on your diaper . . . Let's go to Grandma's . . . We're going to do an errand." This did not work, and the mother invited Roberto to nurse, as she swiftly slipped the diaper on him with the father's assistance. The father announced, "It's over."
>
> *[Rogoff, 2003, p. 204]*

Lack of compliance by toddlers is a problem for many Western parents because their ethnotheory values independence, as Erikson recognized in his second stage, autonomy versus shame and doubt. Many Western parents battle with their autonomy-seeking 1-year-olds when the child's self-will manifests itself in stubborn behavior. Mutual anger is common. Usually either the parent or the toddler gives up and allows the other to win.

For instance, if a child refuses to get dressed, parents sometimes force compliance by holding the child tight, pulling on clothes as the child cries and kicks. Or, if the room is warm enough and the child will be inside, parents sometimes give up and let the child remain half-dressed. Neither option seemed to occur to Roberto's mother, even when she felt

> increasing exasperation that the child was wiggling and not standing to facilitate putting on his pants. Her voice softened as Roberto became interested in the ball, and she increased the stakes: "Do you want another toy?" They [father and mother] continued to try to talk Roberto into cooperating, and handed him various objects, which Roberto enjoyed. But still he stubbornly refused to cooperate with dressing. They left him alone for a while. When his father asked if he was ready, Roberto pouted "nono!"

! ANSWER TO OBSERVATIONAL QUIZ (from page 198): True tests of zygosity involve analysis of blood type, although physical appearance often provides some clues. Here such clues are minimal: We cannot see differences in sex, coloring, or hand formation—although the shapes of the skulls seem different. The best clue from this photo is personality. Confronting their first experience in a wading pool, these twins are showing such a difference on the approach–withdrawal dimension of temperament that one would have to guess they are dizygotic.

> After a bit, the mother told Roberto that she was leaving and waved goodbye. "Are you going with me?" Roberto sat quietly with a worried look. "Then put on your pants, put on your pants to go up the hill." Roberto stared into space, seeming to consider the alternatives. His mother started to walk away, "OK then, I'm going. Goodbye." Roberto started to cry, and his father persuaded, "Put on your pants then!" and his mother asked, "Are you going with me?"
>
> Roberto looked down worriedly, one arm outstretched in half a take-me gesture. "Come on, then," his mother offered the pants and Roberto let his father lift him to a stand and cooperated in putting his legs into the pants and in standing to have them fastened. His mother did not intend to leave; instead she suggested that Roberto dance for the audience. Roberto did a baby version of a traditional dance.
>
> *[Rogoff, 2003, p. 204]*

RESPONSE FOR NURSES AND PEDIATRICIANS (from page 199): It's too soon to tell. Temperament is not truly "fixed" but variable, especially in the first few months. Many "difficult" infants become happy, successful adolescents and adults.

This incident is an example of an ethnotheory that "elders protect and guide rather than giving orders or dominating" (Rogoff, 2003, p. 205). Most European American parents would either force their toddler to put on the pants or decide that a diaper was enough.

A second ethnotheory is apparent in this excerpt. Not only did the parents avoid dominating, showing remarkable patience, they also used deception. If a European American mother threatened to leave and her child then submitted, she probably would take him somewhere, as her ethnotheory probably holds that false threats lead children to doubt their parents. Accordingly, storks, Santa Claus, and tooth fairies are less often invoked by today's educated parents than they were a few generations ago, more because of changed theory than because of new science.

Proximal and Distal Parenting

A longitudinal study comparing child rearing among the rural Nso people of Cameroon, West Africa, and among urban Greeks in Athens found marked differences (Keller et al., 2004). First the researchers videotaped 78 mothers as they played with their 3-month-old infants. Coders (who did not know the study's hypothesis) rated the play as evidence of either **proximal parenting** (physically close or near, involving holding the child while carrying, swinging, exercising the body, etc.) or **distal parenting** (physically far or distant, involving offering a toy or positioning the child for face-to-face interaction).

proximal parenting Parenting practices that involve close physical contact with the child's entire body, such as cradling and swinging.

distal parenting Parenting practices that focus on the intellect more than the body, such as conversing and playing with an object.

Play patterns were quite different in the two cultures (see Table 7.2). The Nso mothers were proximal parents, holding their babies all the time but almost never using objects; the Greek mothers were distal parents, using objects almost half the time but holding their babies less often. The researchers hypothesized that proximal parenting in early infancy might result in toddlers who are less self-aware but more compliant; these traits are needed in an interdependent and cooperative society such as rural Cameroon. By contrast, distal parenting might produce toddlers who are more self-aware but less obedient; these traits are needed in a society (such as modern Athens) where independence, self-reliance, and competition are crucial.

The researchers' predictions were accurate. The same children were tested at 1½ years on self-awareness (the rouge test) and compliance (told not to eat a desired snack for two minutes). The African toddlers did not recognize themselves in the mirror but complied with instruction; the opposite was true of the Greek toddlers.

! ANSWER TO OBSERVATIONAL QUIZ (from page 200): Out of 100 4-month-olds, 20 are fearful at least occasionally later in childhood, but only 5 are consistently fearful.

Replicating their work, these researchers studied a dozen mothers in Costa Rica, where play patterns and later toddler behavior were midway between those of the Nso and the Greeks. They also analyzed their original longitudinal

TABLE 7.2 **Play Patterns in Rural Cameroon and Urban Greece**

		Amount of Time Spent in Play (percent)	
Age of Babies	**Type of Play**	**Nso, Cameroon**	**Athens, Greece**
3 months	Held by mother	100	31
3 months	Object play	3	40
	Toddler Behavior Measured		
18 months	Self-recognition	3	68
18 months	Compliance (without prompting)	72	2

Source: Adapted from Keller et al., 2004.

data, child by child. Proximal or distal play at 3 months was highly predictive of toddler behavior, even apart from culture. In other words, Greek mothers who, unlike most of their peers, were proximal parents had more compliant toddlers (Keller et al., 2004).

ESPECIALLY FOR PARENTS OF TODDLERS Your child refuses to stay in the car seat, spits out disliked foods, and almost never does what you say. What can you do?

SUMMING UP

The five major theories differ in their explanations of the origins of early emotions and personality. Psychoanalytic theory stresses the crucial role of mothers as they respond to infants' needs for food and elimination (Freud) or for security and independence (Erikson). Behaviorism also stresses caregiving—especially as parents reinforce the traits they want their baby to learn or thoughtlessly teach unwanted behaviors (as when they give in to a temper tantrum or are afraid themselves).

Learning is also crucial in cognitive theory—but instead of the moment-by-moment learning highlighted by behaviorism, the infant's self-constructed concept, or model, is central. Epigenetic theory begins with each infant's lifelong genetic imprint and then proceeds to how environment shapes the expression of that inborn temperament. Sociocultural theory also sees an interaction between nature and nurture but emphasizes that the diversity of nurture explains much of the diversity of emotions. According to sociocultural theory, child-rearing practices arise from ethnotheories, which are unexpressed and implicit but still powerful.

The Development of Social Bonds

All the theories of development agree that human nurturance depends on social connections. You have already read about Romanian orphans (Chapter 5), the social theory of language (Chapter 6), and many other examples of the pivotal role of the social context in early psychosocial development. All the infant emotional expressions already described elicit social reactions, and infants of all species seem happier and less fearful when other creatures (especially their own mothers) are near them (Plutchik, 2003). Now we look specifically at infant–caregiver bonds.

Synchrony

Although any face elicits a focused stare and then a social smile at about 6 weeks, by 3 months an infant's familiar caregivers are far more likely than strangers to provoke grins, arm waving, and other reactions signifying that the

MYRLEEN FERGUSON CATE / PHOTO EDIT

Dance with Me Synchrony in action, with each one's hands, eyes, and open mouth reflecting the other's expression. The close timing of synchrony has been compared to a waltz—and these partners look as if they never miss a beat.

synchrony A coordinated, rapid, and smooth exchange of responses between caregiver and infant.

Response for Parents of Toddlers (from page 203): Remember the origins of the misbehavior—probably a combination of your child's inborn temperament and your own distal parenting. Blended with your ethnotheory, all contribute to the child's being stubborn and independent.

infant "knows" them (Rochat, 2001). The owners of those faces likewise have become very familiar with their particular infant, reading signals of hunger, curiosity, or sleepiness better than any stranger can. For instance, some babies tug at their ears, a meaningful sign to caregivers who have studied the emotions of that infant.

Such signals indicate that **synchrony** has begun. Synchrony is a coordinated interaction between caregiver and infant, responding to each other with split-second timing. Synchrony has been described as the meshing of a finely tuned machine (Snow, 1984), an emotional "attunement" of an improvised musical duet (Stern, 1985), and a smoothly flowing "waltz" that is mutually adaptive (Barnard & Martell, 1995). The critical factor is timing; each partner responds to the other almost instantly, in a chain of mutual communication.

Detailed research reveals how mutual the interaction is: Although adults are obviously capable of grinning at their newborns, they rarely do so until the infant smiles at them, at which point the adult breaks into a grin and talks animatedly (Lavelli & Fogal, 2005). Since each baby has his or her own temperament, synchrony depends on a caregiver's sensitivity (Feldman & Eidelman, 2005). Synchrony helps infants learn to read other people's emotions and to develop some of the basic skills of social interaction, such as taking turns and paying attention, that they will need throughout life.

Synchrony helps infants express their own feelings as well. A sensitive parent responds to every hint ("Ooh, are you hungry?" "Aahaaa, you're tired," "Uuumm, you see the rattle?"). The adult reacts to each expression with exaggerated facial movements and a solicitous tone as well as with action, such as getting food, putting the baby's head on the shoulder, or handing over the rattle (Gergely & Watson, 1999). Breast-feeding, particularly, requires that the mother respond to her baby's emotions.

Parental imitation is the foundation of an infant's self-understanding. If parents can detect an emotion from an infant's expression (and they usually can, because early facial expressions and body motions reflect universally recognizable emotions), and if an infant sees a familiar face expressing that emotion, the infant learns to connect an internal state with an external expression (Rochat, 2001).

For example, suppose an infant is unhappy. An adult who mirrors the distress, and then tries to solve the problem, will teach the infant that unhappiness is a valid emotion that can be assuaged. Obviously, if the adult's reaction to unhappiness is always to feed the infant, that might teach a destructive lesson (food equals comfort), but if an adult is more nuanced (differentiating hunger from pain, boredom, or fear, for instance), then the infant will learn more varied reasons for unhappiness and more diverse responses to it.

A crucial aspect of synchrony is reciprocal imitation. Sometimes infants—even newborns—imitate the mouth movements and facial expressions of their caregivers (Meltzoff & Moore, 1989). Just as adults feel happier overall after they laugh, infants experience some of the emotions that accompany the expressions they see and copy. Surrounded by happy adults, infants feel happiness; surrounded by depressed adults, infants become sad (Tronick & Weinberg, 1997). Although infants imitate adults, synchrony usually begins with parents imitating infants (Lavelli & Fogal, 2005). The major force that fuels synchronous activity is the parents' ability to read and respond to each infant nuance.

Synchrony is experience-expectant, developing the brain as well as the facial expressions (Schore, 2001). Differences in frequency affect later development. For example, parents of triplets spend less time in synchrony with each of their infants than do parents of single infants, even though they feel just as much love for each baby as parents of twins and singletons do (Feldman et al., 2004). Triplet cognition tends to be slightly delayed, perhaps for that reason. Some mothers in the United States spend very little time playing with their infants, and that is reflected in the infants' later development (Huston & Aronson, 2005).

Although synchrony is evident early in life, it becomes more frequent and more elaborate as time goes on; a 6-month-old is a much more responsive social partner than a 3-month-old. Parents and infants average about an hour a day in face-to-face play, although variations are apparent from baby to baby, time to time, culture to culture (Baildam et al., 2000; Lee, 2000).

By 5 months infants adjust their style of synchrony to their social experiences. If a stranger responds quickly with lots of smiling, infants reciprocate *if* their mother acts the same way. However, if their mother is more low-key, infants may be quiet or even cry at an exuberant stranger; they respond better to a stranger whose behavior is similar to their own mother's (Bigelow, 1999). This is further evidence that emotions are learned from social interaction and are not merely a matter of maturation.

It is true that infants need to reach a certain maturity before they express anger or even a social smile, but it is also true that this emotional potential becomes expressed when caregivers respond and that the specific expressions depend on reciprocal interactions.

still-face technique An experimental device in which an adult keeps his or her face unmoving and without expression in face-to-face interaction with an infant.

THINKING LIKE A SCIENTIST

The Still-Face Technique

Is synchrony needed for normal development? If no one played with an infant, would that infant develop well? Creative experiments using the **still-face technique** have addressed these questions (Tronick, 1989; Tronick et al., 1978). An infant is placed facing an adult (usually the mother), who plays with the baby while a video camera records each partner's reactions. Frame-by-frame comparison of the two videotapes reveals the sequence. Typically, adults spontaneously synchronize their responses to the infants' movements, usually with exaggerated tone and expression, and babies reciprocate with smiles and arm waving.

Then, on cue, the adult erases all facial expression and stares with a "still face" for a minute or two. Not usually at 2 months, but clearly at 6 months, babies become very upset by their still-faced caregiver. They may frown, fuss, drool, look away, kick, cry, or suck their fingers. Babies are always distressed by still-faced mothers, fathers, and other significant caregivers; with still-faced strangers, infants' responses are more muted.

Interestingly, babies are much more upset when parents show a still face than when parents leave the room for a minute or two (Feld, 1994). From a psychological perspective, this is healthy: It shows that babies expect interactive play. In one set of experiments, infants became upset if someone had a still face for any reason—to look at a wall, to look at someone else, or merely to look away (Striano, 2004).

In another study, infants experienced not just one but two episodes of a parent's still face. The infants quickly readjusted when their parent became responsive again *if* synchrony characterized the parent–infant relationship. If the parent was typically unresponsive, however, infants stayed upset (with faster heart rate and more fussing) after the second still-face episode ended (Haley & Stansbury, 2003).

This is one example of many research studies that lead to the same conclusion: A parent's responsiveness to the infant aids development, measured not only psychosocially but also biologically (with heart rate, weight gain, and brain maturation) (Moore & Calkins, 2004). If a mother is unresponsive to an infant (as usually happens with postpartum depression), someone else should establish synchrony to help ensure normal development (Tronick & Weinberg, 1997).

Attachment

Toward the end of the first year, face-to-face play almost disappears. Once infants can move around and explore on their own, they are no longer content to stay in one spot and follow an adult's facial expressions and vocalizations. Remember that, at about 12 months, infants can walk and talk, which changes the rhythms of their social interaction (Jaffee et al., 2001). A new type of connection, called *attachment,* evolves from synchrony.

attachment According to Ainsworth (1973), "an affectional tie" that one person forms with another—a tie that binds them together in space and endures over time.

According to Mary Ainsworth (1973), **attachment** is an emotional bond that one person has with another. Attachments form in infancy and persist throughout life. New close relationships arise later on, such as between husband and wife or parent and child, but all relationships are influenced by the first experiences, according to attachment theory (Thompson & Raikes, 2003). In fact, adults' attachment to their own parents, even though it was formed decades earlier, affects their relationships with their children. Humans learn in childhood how to relate to people, and that lesson echoes lifelong.

When two people are attached, they respond to each other in particular ways. Infants show their attachment through *proximity-seeking behaviors,* such as approaching and following their caregivers, and through *contact-maintaining behaviors,* such as touching, snuggling, and holding. A securely attached toddler is curious and eager to explore but maintains contact by looking back at the caregiver.

Caregivers show attachment as well. They keep a watchful eye on the baby and respond affectionately and sensitively to vocalizations, expressions, and gestures. For example, many mothers or fathers, awakening in the middle of the night, tiptoe to the crib to gaze fondly at their sleeping infant. During the day, many parents smooth their toddler's hair or caress their child's hand or cheek. Indeed, some infants just need to glance at their parents to establish eye contact because their parents are always watching them.

Attachment deepens the parent–child relationship. Over humanity's evolutionary history, proximity-seeking and contact-maintaining behaviors contributed to the survival of the species by keeping infants near their caregivers and keeping caregivers vigilant. Many experts believe that the drive for attachment is genetic, that all humans seek connection with others. Infants express this drive most obviously, but everyone of every age feels it.

ELIZABETH CREWS

(a)

BRUCE PLOTKIN / THE IMAGE WORKS

(b)

Personality of Caregiver Both nature and nurture may be in evidence here, in that the mother's personality obviously affects the quality of interaction with her offspring. Adults typically use special social behaviors *(a)* with their young infants—leaning in close, opening their eyes and mouths wide in exaggerated expressions of surprise or delight, maintaining eye contact—because those behaviors elicit the baby's attention and pleasure. But such behaviors are subdued or absent when the adult is depressed or stressed *(b),* and this makes social interaction much less enjoyable for each partner.

Secure and Insecure Attachment

The concept of attachment was originally developed by John Bowlby (1969, 1973, 1988), a British developmentalist influenced by both psychoanalytic theory and ethology. His ideas inspired Mary Ainsworth, then a young American graduate student who worked in Uganda, where she began to define and measure the relationship between parents and their children. Ainsworth (1973) discovered that virtually all infants develop special attachments to the people who care for them. Some infants are more secure in their attachments than others—an observation later confirmed by hundreds of other researchers (Cassidy & Shaver, 1999; Thompson, 1998).

Secure attachment (called type B) provides comfort and confidence, evidenced both by the infant's attempt to be close to the caregiver (comfort) and by the infant's readiness to explore (confidence). In such relationships, caregivers become a base for exploration, giving the child the assurance to venture forth. A toddler might, for example, scramble down from the caregiver's lap to play with a toy but periodically look back, vocalize a few syllables, and perhaps return for a hug.

By contrast, insecure attachment is characterized by fear, anxiety, anger, or seeming indifference toward a caregiver. The insecure child has much less confidence, perhaps playing without trying to maintain contact with the caregiver or, the opposite, being unwilling to leave the caregiver's lap. Both these extremes are signs of insecure attachment; the first is called **insecure-avoidant attachment** (type A) and the second **insecure-resistant/ambivalent attachment** (type C) (see Table 7.3).

secure attachment A relationship of trust and confidence. During infancy, secure attachment enables a child to play independently and happily, reassured by the caregiver's proximity.

insecure-avoidant attachment A pattern of attachment in which one person avoids connection with another, as when an infant seems not to care about a caregiver's presence, departure, or return.

insecure-resistant/ambivalent attachment A pattern of attachment in which anxiety and uncertainty are evident, as when an infant is very upset at separation and both resists and seeks contact on reunion.

TABLE 7.3 **Patterns of Infant Attachment**

Type	Name of Pattern	In Play Room	Mother Leaves	Mother Returns	Toddlers in Category (percent)
A	Insecure-avoidant	Child plays happily	Child continues playing	Child ignores her	10–20
B	Secure	Child plays happily	Child pauses, is not as happy	Child welcomes her, returns to play	50–70
C	Insecure-resistant/ambivalent	Child clings, is preoccupied with mother	Child is unhappy, may stop playing	Child is angry, may cry, hit mother, cling	10–20
D	Disorganized	Child is cautious	Child may stare or yell; looks scared, confused	Child acts oddly—may freeze, scream, hit self, throw things	5–10

Measuring Attachment

Ainsworth (1973) developed a now-classic laboratory procedure, called the **Strange Situation,** to measure attachment. In a well-equipped playroom, an infant is closely observed in eight episodes, during which the infant is with the caregiver (usually the mother), with a stranger, with both, or alone. At the beginning, the caregiver and child are together. Then every three minutes the stranger or the caregiver enters or leaves the playroom. Infants' responses indicate which type of attachment they have formed to their caregivers. For research purposes, observers are carefully trained and are certified when they are able to accurately differentiate types A, B, C, and D. The key aspects of the Strange Situation are the following:

Strange Situation A laboratory procedure to measure attachment by evoking infant reactions to stress.

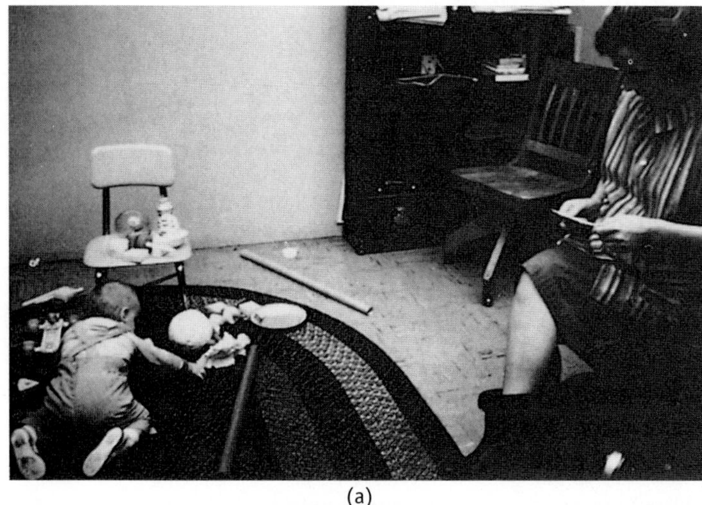
(a)

(b)

(c)

ALL: COURTESY OF MARY AINSWORTH

The Attachment Experiment In this episode of the Strange Situation, Brian shows every sign of secure attachment. *(a)* He explores the playroom happily when his mother is present; *(b)* he cries when she leaves; and *(c)* he is readily comforted when she returns.

- *Exploration of the toys.* A securely attached toddler plays happily.
- *Reaction to the caregiver's departure.* A securely attached toddler misses the caregiver.
- *Reaction to the caregiver's return.* A securely attached toddler welcomes the caregiver.

Almost two-thirds of all infants tested in the Strange Situation are securely attached (type B). Their mother's presence gives them courage to explore the playroom and investigate the toys. Fathers make some infants even more confident. The caregiver's departure may cause distress (perhaps expressed by an outcry or by a pause in playing); the caregiver's return elicits positive social contact (such as smiling or hugging) and then more playing. This balanced reaction —being concerned about the caregiver's departure but not overwhelmed by it— reflects secure attachment.

disorganized attachment A category of attachment that is marked by inconsistent behavior of the infant in reaction to the caregiver's departure and return.

About a third of all infants are insecure, appearing either indifferent (type A) or unduly anxious (type C). Another small group (about 5–10 percent) fit none of these categories; they are classified as **disorganized,** or type D. They may shift from hitting to kissing their mothers, from staring blankly to crying hysterically, from pinching themselves to freezing in place. Type D infants are likely to have serious problems later in childhood. Their attachment status is disorganized because their mother's inconsistent and inappropriate behavior makes an effective attachment strategy impossible (see Table 7.4).

Goodness of Fit Attachment to the father can be very strong, especially for boys. If the mother is unavailable for any reason, a secure attachment to the father or another caregiver can make the difference in the child's emotional health.

MICHAEL NEWMAN / PHOTOEDIT

Insecure Attachment and Social Setting

Although early reports found that secure attachment would "predict all the outcomes reasonably expected from a well-functioning personality" (Thompson & Raikes, 2003, p. 708), later research discovered that attachment status can change. Securely attached infants *are* somewhat more likely to become securely attached toddlers, socially competent preschoolers, academically skilled schoolchildren, and even better parents (Thompson, 1998). However, the correlations are not large; shifts in attachment status from one age to another are common (Beckwith et al., 1999; NICHD, 2001; Seifer et al., 2004).

Both type A and type C behavior patterns can be considered adaptive, serving insecure children as strategies for fostering secure attachment. Type A (insecure-avoidant) infants ignore their mothers, who seem to be ignoring them. They explore the envi-

TABLE 7.4 **How Disturbed Mothers Develop Type D (Disorganized) Attachment in Their Infants**

Mothers of type D infants are at least three times more likely than mothers of types A, B, and C infants to exhibit these behaviors:

Laugh when infant is crying	Pull infant by the wrist
Invite approach and then distance	Mock and tease the infant
Use friendly tone while maintaining threatening posture	Tell a crying infant to hush
Direct infant to do something and then say not to do it	Ignore an infant who falls down
Display a sudden change of mood, not elicited by the context	Use a loud or sharp voice
Handle the infant as though the infant were not alive	Remove a toy with which the infant is engaged
Display a frightened expression	Hold infant away from body with stiff arms
Withhold a toy from the infant	Speak in hushed, intimate, sexy tones to the infant
Neglect to soothe a distressed infant	Talk in "haunted" or frightened voice

Source: Adapted from Lyons-Ruth et al., 1999.

ronment instead. Often, as part of this exploration, they find another attachment figure. If a father, grandparent, or day-care provider offers secure attachment, these infants develop normally (Goodman & Gotlib, 1999). Some type A infants experience contextual risks (such as a low-income household, absent father, or highly stressed mother). They are less likely to find alternate sources of attachment and more likely to develop behavior problems, including hostility (Belsky & Fearon, 2002). For them, hostility may be adaptive if they are growing up in a harsh environment. Type C (insecure-resistant/ambivalent) infants sometimes manage, through their clinging and protesting, to change their caregivers' behavior. They then develop a more secure relationship.

The most troubled infants may be those who are type D. If disorganization means that they cannot develop an effective strategy for dealing with other people, even an avoidant or resistant strategy, they may lash out in pain and confusion. Sometimes they become hostile and aggressive, difficult for anyone else to relate to (Lyons-Ruth et al., 1999). (We saw in Chapter 5 that an unusually high percentage of the Romanian children who were adopted after age 2 were type D, which made it difficult for their new parents to bond with them.)

Overall, insecure attachment is a warning sign, not a signal of doom. Insecurely attached infants sometimes become securely attached children. Young children sometimes recover from periods of maternal depression, responding more to their mother's current behavior than to her behavior months earlier (National Research Council and Institute of Medicine, 2000).

Unfortunately, attachment status can change for the worse as well. Disrupting factors can shake loose a secure attachment, as happened to a majority (61 percent) of a group of 18-year-olds who had been secure at age 1 but had experienced traumatic family events (such as abuse or

JOHN MOORE / AP PHOTO

Nobody's Children These orphans in Kabul, Afghanistan, are living casualties of years of civil war. They appear well nourished, but, with their parents dead and with no adult to develop an attachment to, they are emotionally deprived. Also, this spartan orphanage gives them physical shelter but inadequate mental stimulation. These conditions lessen their chances of developing normally.

divorce) before age 12 (Beckwith et al., 1999). Even then, insecure attachment does not necessarily mean an isolated, friendless, and sad life: it is only one of several factors that influence psychosocial development.

Predictors of Attachment

The percentages of infants classified as type A, B, C, or D varies across studies, partly because groups of infants differ in their family and cultural experiences and therefore in their attachment patterns. For example, some studies find that insecurely attached Japanese infants are more often type C than type A, but the opposite is true for insecure German infants (Grossman & Grossman, 1990). In Mali, West Africa, infants who are not secure are often type D (True et al., 2001). (A sociocultural approach might question whether the classifications used in North America are as useful elsewhere.)

Most infants become securely attached, even if they were exposed prenatally to cocaine, had a low birthweight, or live with a single parent. Studies have identified various factors that affect a child's chances of being classified as type A, B, C, or D (Cicchetti & Barnett, 1991; Eiden et al., 2002; National Research Council and Institute of Medicine, 2000; Seifer et al., 1996, 2004; Tronick & Weinberg, 1997; van IJzendorn, 1992).

Secure attachment is more likely if these conditions exist:

- The parent is unusually sensitive and responsive to the infant's needs.
- The infant–caregiver relationship is high in synchrony.
- The infant's temperament is "easy."
- The parents are not stressed about income, other children, or their marriage.
- The parents have a "working model" of secure attachment to their own parents.

Insecure attachment is more likely if these conditions exist:

- The parent mistreats the child. (Neglect increases the rate of type A attachment; abuse increases rates of types C and D.)
- The mother is mentally ill. (Paranoia increases type D; depression increases type C.)
- The parents are highly stressed. (Parental stress increases types A and D.)
- The parents are intrusive and controlling. (Parental domination increases type A.)
- Both parents are active alcoholics. (An alcoholic father increases type A; an alcoholic mother increases type D.)
- The child's temperament is "difficult." (Difficult temperament correlates with type C.)
- The child's temperament is "slow to warm up." (Slow-to-warm-up temperament correlates with type A.)

Social Referencing

social referencing Seeking information about an unfamiliar or ambiguous object or event by observing someone else's expressions and reactions. That other person becomes a social reference.

Infants seek to understand caregivers' emotions. They are not skilled at this until about age 1, when **social referencing** becomes evident. In social referencing, people consult another person for clarification or information, much as someone might consult a dictionary or other "reference" work. A glance of reassurance or words of caution, an expression of alarm, pleasure, or dismay—each becomes a social guide, telling an infant how to react to an unfamiliar or ambiguous event.

After age 1, because walking infants move into the stage of active exploration (Piaget) and autonomy (Erikson), their need and desire to consult a caregiver become urgent. Toddlers search for emotional cues in gaze and facial expressions, pay close attention to outbursts of pleasure or disgust, and watch carefully to detect the intentions behind the actions of others (Baldwin, 2000).

Emotional signals from trusted caregivers are especially powerful. However, infants also attend to signals from strangers, even when the signals are not targeted at them. In an experiment, infants saw a video of an unknown actress reacting with pleasure or disgust to a toy. Although 10-month-olds seemed unfazed by the stranger's responses, those who were at least 12 months old avoided the disgusting toy (Mumme & Fernald, 2003).

Social referencing has many practical applications. Consider mealtime. Caregivers the world over smack their lips, pretend to taste, and say "yum-yum," encouraging toddlers to eat and enjoy their first beets, liver, or spinach. For their part, toddlers become quite astute at reading expressions, insisting on the foods that the adults *really* like. Through this process, children in some cultures develop a taste for raw fish or curried goat or smelly cheese—foods that children in other cultures refuse to eat.

Referencing Mothers

Most everyday instances of social referencing occur with mothers. Infants usually heed their mother's wishes, expressed in tone and facial expression. This does not mean that infants are always obedient, especially in cultures where parents and children value independence. For example, in an experiment in the United States, few toddlers obeyed their mother's request to pick up dozens of toys that they had not scattered (Kochanska et al., 2001). Their refusal actually indicates some emotional maturity: Self-awareness had led to pride and autonomy. Most mothers had taught their toddlers to clean up their own messes, but not someone else's scattered toys. In fact, although the mothers complied with the experimenters, asking their children to pick up the toys, their body language and expressions sometimes implied that they did not really expect their children to obey the request.

These same toddlers usually obeyed when their mothers told them not to touch a very attractive toy that was within easy reach. The mothers used tone and expression as well as words to make this prohibition clear, pointing out the forbidden toys. Even when the mothers were out of sight, half of the 14-month-olds and virtually all of the 22-month-olds obeyed, with 80 percent of the older toddlers seeming to agree with the mother's judgment (which the researchers called *committed compliance*). One girl even told herself, "No-no touch" as a reminder (Kochanska et al., 2001).

CORBIS / MICHAEL S. YAMASHITA

Social Referencing Should I be happy or scared to ride on a bicycle through the streets of Osaka, Japan? Check with Mom to find out.

Referencing Fathers and Others

Early research on the psychosocial context of development usually studied only mother–infant relationships, on the assumption that mothers were the main caregivers. It is now apparent, however, that a range of relatives and unrelated people (including fathers, siblings, grandparents, neighbors, and other children's parents) have always been crucial to development, especially for children growing up outside middle-class North America (D. Johnson et al., 2003).

In North America, increases in maternal employment have expanded the social references available to infants. Fathers spend considerable time with their children, and toddlers readily refer to them. The social information from fathers tends to be more encouraging than that from mothers, who are more cautious and protective. When toddlers are about to explore, they often seek their father's approval, expecting fun from their fathers and comfort from their mothers (Lamb, 2000; Parke, 1996).

ESPECIALLY FOR GRANDMOTHERS A grandmother of an infant boy is troubled that the baby's father stays with him whenever the mother is away. She says that men don't know how to care for infants, and she notes that he sometimes plays a game in which he tosses his son in the air and then catches him.

CHROMOSOHM / SOHM / PHOTO RESEARCHERS, INC.

Up, Up, and Away! The vigorous play typical of fathers is likely to help in the infant's mastery of motor skills and the development of muscle control.

In this, infants show social intelligence, because fathers' play is more noisy, emotional, boisterous, physical, and idiosyncratic. Fathers tend to make up active and exciting games. They move their infant's legs and arms in imitation of walking, kicking, or climbing; or play "airplane," zooming the baby through the air; or tap and tickle the baby's stomach. Mothers caress, murmur, read, or sing soothingly; combine play with caretaking such as diapering and bathing; and use standard sequences such as peek-a-boo and patty-cake. In short, fathers are more proximal, engaging in play that involves the infant's whole body. At the same time, infants are more likely to comply with their father's commands than their mother's (Feldman & Klein, 2003).

Sons are particularly likely to elicit roughhousing from fathers. In fact, sons are also likely to elicit fathers' caregiving, commitment, and encouragement for learning math and science. One review finds that in North America, there are "wide-ranging and surprisingly large" differences in the areas in which sons and daughters are encouraged to excel, although sons are not necessarily favored (Lundberg & Rose, 2003, p. 347).

Infant Day Care

You have seen that the development of social bonds is crucial to infants and that babies benefit from having good relationships with several members of their immediate families. What is the effect of relationships with nonrelatives, particularly paid caregivers?

More than half of all 1-year-olds in the United States are in "regularly scheduled" nonmaternal care. The reason is primarily that their mothers are employed. In 2003, 58 percent of the married mothers of children under age 2 in the United States were in the labor force, as were higher percentages of single mothers of infants (U.S. Bureau of the Census, 2004–2005). In recent years, every type of nonmaternal care has become more common, not only care by relatives (usually the father or grandmother) but also care within organized programs (Loeb et al., 2004). Such a program may be either **family day care,** with children of various ages cared for in the home of a paid caregiver, or **center day care,** with several paid providers caring for children in a place especially designed for that purpose.

family day care Child care that occurs in a paid caregiver's home and involves six or fewer children of various ages.

center day care Child care that usually occurs in a place especially designed for the purpose, where several paid providers care for many children. Usually the children are grouped by age, the day-care center is licensed, and providers are trained and certified in child development.

Working mothers usually prefer care by a relative because it is the least expensive (sometimes free). However, such care is of variable quality and may not always be available. In today's economy, if a mother is employed, chances are her husband and mother are as well. Family day care is more often used for infants than for older children (Galinsky et al., 1994).

Center care may generally be the best of the options, because day-care centers are licensed and inspected and the presence of several caregivers and many parents reduces the likelihood of neglect or abuse. However, basic standards and compliance with those standards vary markedly from state to state as well as from nation to nation. Some center care is excellent, with adequate space, equipment, and trained providers (the ratio of adults to infants should be about 1:3), but it is hard to find. Table 7.5 lists the characteristics of high-quality day care.

In the United States, most middle-class parents pay directly for child care. They encounter a "mix of quality, price, type of care, and government subsidies" (Haskins, 2005, p. 168). Households with higher incomes tend to be more likely than low-income families to use center care. In some other nations, the government pays for infant and early-childhood care. The rates of participation in such government-supported programs are very high, although the quality is not always better.

The evidence is overwhelming that good preschool education (from age 3 to 5) is beneficial, as reviewed in Chapter 9, but day care for infants is controversial. Most developmental scientists agree that the parent–infant relationship is crucial

Response for Grandmothers (from page 211): Fathers can be great caregivers, and most mothers prefer that the father provide care. It's good for the baby and the marriage. Being tossed in the air is great fun (as long as the father is careful and a good catcher!). A generation ago, mothers seldom let fathers care for infants, so today's grandfathers may feel unable to do it. Fortunately, today's mothers are less likely to act as gatekeepers, shutting the fathers out.

TABLE 7.5 High-Quality Day Care

High-quality day care has five essential characteristics:

1. *Adequate attention to each infant.* This means a low caregiver-to-infant ratio and, probably even more important, a small group of infants. The ideal situation might be two reliable caregivers for five infants. Infants need familiar, loving caregivers; continuity of care is very important.
2. *Encouragement of language and sensorimotor development.* Infants should receive extensive language exposure through games, songs, conversations, and positive talk of all kinds, along with easily manipulated toys.
3. *Attention to health and safety.* Cleanliness routines (e.g., handwashing before meals), accident prevention (e.g., no small objects that could be swallowed), and safe areas for exploration (e.g., a clean, padded area for crawling and climbing) are good signs.
4. *Well-trained and professional caregivers.* Ideally, every caregiver should have a degree or certificate in early-childhood education and should have worked with children for several years. Turnover should be low, morale high, and enthusiasm evident. Good caregivers love their children and their work.
5. *Warm and responsive caregivers.* Providers should engage the children in problem solving and discussions, rather than giving instructions. Quiet, obedient children may be an indication of unresponsive care.

For a more detailed evaluation of day care, see the checklist in NICHD, 2005.

but that infants are not harmed by—in fact, can benefit from—professional day care (Brooks-Gunn et al., 2002; Lamb, 1998). However, "disagreements about the wisdom (indeed, the morality) of nonmaternal child care for the very young remain" (NICHD, 2005, p. xiv).

A longitudinal study has followed the development of 1,300 children from birth to age 11. The effects of various types of infant care on attachment has been one concern. This study, by the National Institute of Child Health and Human Development (NICHD) Early Child Care Research Network, has found that attachment to the mother is as secure among infants in center care as among infants cared for at home.

As other, smaller studies have done, the massive NICHD study confirms that the main determinant of child development is the mother's warmth and responsiveness (NICHD, 2005). Infant day care, even for 40 hours a week in the first year of life, has much less influence than the mother–infant relationship. Cognition, especially language learning among infants and preschool children, advances with center care (NICHD, 1999, 2000).

Certain specifics of the longitudinal data have raised questions among some developmentalists, notably Jay Belsky (2001). Although the mother's sensitivity is by far the best predictor of a kindergartner's social skills, those children, especially boys, who had experienced the most nonmaternal care were more likely to quarrel and to have conflicts with their first-grade teachers (NICHD, 2003). (It should be noted that interpretation of the data is complicated by multicultural awareness: What one observer considers aggressive, another may consider assertive.)

However, no study finds that children of employed mothers suffer solely because their mothers are working. The main reason is that employed mothers often make infant care and relationships their top priority. For example, time-use research finds that mothers who work 40 hours a week outside the home spend almost as much time playing with their babies (14½ hours a week) as do mothers without jobs (16 hours a week) (Huston & Aronson, 2005). They spend half as much time on housework and almost no time on leisure. The study concludes:

ESPECIALLY FOR DAY-CARE PROVIDERS A mother who brings her child to you for day care says that she knows she is harming her baby but must work out of economic necessity. What do you say?

Secure Attachment Kirstie and her 10-month-old daughter Mia enjoy a moment of synchrony in an infant day-care center sponsored by a family-friendly employer, General Mills. High-quality day care and high-quality home care are equally likely to foster secure attachment between mother and infant.

ANN HEISENFELT / AP PHOTO

> There was no evidence that mothers' time at work interfered with the quality of their relationship with their infants, the quality of the home environment, or children's development. In fact, the results suggest the opposite. Mothers who spent more time at work provided slightly higher quality home environments.
>
> *[Huston & Aronson, 2005, p. 479]*

The researchers suggest that their incomes and self-assurance enabled these women to provide better home environments for their infants.

This particular study did not distinguish between the various types of care the infants received. The researchers noted that, whether employed or not, mothers who spend more time socializing with their infants also tend to have better relationships with them.

Other research confirms that much depends on the quality of care, wherever it occurs or whoever provides it. According to the NICHD Early Child Care Research Network, early day care seems detrimental *only* when the mother is insensitive *and* the infant spends more than 20 hours a week in a poor-quality program (too few caregivers with too little training) (NICHD, 2005).

The negative effects of poor care have also been found in a study in Israel of 758 infants. Those cared for at home by an attentive father or grandmother seemed to do very well, as did those in a high-quality day-care center. However, those cared for in a center with untrained caregivers and a ratio of more than five infants to one adult fared poorly (Sagi et al., 2002). If a depressed mother is the primary caregiver, children fare worse than they would in another place with other caregivers (Loeb et al., 2004). Low-income children in high-quality care tend to have fewer social problems and more school-readiness skills than they otherwise would have had (Loeb et al., 2004; Votruba-Drzal et al., 2004).

Additional evidence comes from a study that looked at the reading ability of 5-year-olds. If their homes were low in stimulation (few books, few outside trips), they were better readers by age 5 if they had entered group care as infants. However, if their home was stimulating, they were academically worse off at age 5 than if they had been in infant day care (Caughy et al., 1994). Thus, out-of-home day care can be better than in-home care, especially for infants whose homes do not provide the stimulation and attention that they need (Ramey et al., 2002).

Among the benefits of day care is the opportunity to learn to express emotions. When a toddler is temperamentally very shy or aggressive, he or she is less likely to remain so if other caregivers and children are available as social references (Fox et al., 2001; Zigler & Styfco, 2001). But no expert would dare to say that *all* infants are better off at home or better off in day care. Developmentalists are still trying to figure out if babies are programmed to develop fairly well as long as their family and nonfamily care is not abusive or if every increment of quality (lots of synchrony, a language-rich day-care center) makes a difference even for normal, happy babies.

Response for Day-Care Providers (from page 213): Reassure the mother that you will keep her baby safe and will help to develop the baby's mind and social skills by fostering synchrony and attachment. Also tell her that the quality of mother–infant interaction at home is more important than anything else for psychosocial development; mothers who are employed full time usually have wonderful, secure relationships with their infants. If the mother wishes, you can discuss ways she can be a more responsive mother.

Especially for Potential Day-Care Providers What are some of the benefits and costs of opening and running a day-care center?

SUMMING UP

Infants seek social bonds, which they develop with one or several people as long as the caregivers are responsive and familiar. In the early months, synchrony begins: Infants and caregivers interact face to face, making split-second adjustments in their emotional responses to each other. The still-face situation reveals the importance of facial expression to infants.

Early responsiveness evolves into attachment, an emotional bond that encourages toddlers to explore. Secure attachment allows learning to progress; insecure infants are less confident and may develop emotional impairments. As infants become more curious and as they encounter new toys, people, and events, they use social referencing to learn whether such new things are fearsome or fun.

Although mothers are infants' usual, and most studied, social partners, the emotional connections evident in synchrony, attachment, and social referencing can also occur with fathers, other relatives, and day-care providers. Instead of harming infants, as was once feared, nonmaternal care can enhance infants' psychosocial development. The quality and continuity of child care matter more than who provides the care.

Conclusions in Theory and Practice

You have seen in this chapter that the first two years are filled with psychosocial interactions, all of which result from genes, maturation, culture, and caregivers. Each of the five major theories seems plausible, yet they differ in assessing the significance of the experiences of the first two years of life.

What conclusions can be drawn from theory and research? No single theory stands out as the best. All agree that the first two years are crucial, with early emotional and social development influenced by the mother's behavior, the father's support, the quality of day care, cultural patterns, and inborn traits. It has not been proven whether one influence, such as a good day-care center, compensates for another, such as a depressed mother (although parental influence is always significant). Multicultural research has identified a wide variety of practices in different societies. That implies that no one event—such as toilet training in Freud's theory—determines emotional health.

On the basis of what you have learned, you could safely advise parents to play with their infants; respond to their physical and emotional needs; let them explore; maintain a relationship; pay attention to them; and expect every toddler to be sometimes angry, sometimes proud, sometimes uncertain. Parental actions and attitudes may or may not have a powerful impact on later development, but they certainly can make infants happier. Parental attentiveness leads to synchrony, attachment, and social referencing, which are, in turn, crucial to infant and toddler development.

Such generalities are not good enough for our two toddlers, Toni and Jacob, or for all the other infants who show signs of malnutrition, delayed language, poor social skills, abnormal emotional development, disorganized attachment, or other deficits. In dealing with individual children who have problems, we need to be more specific.

TABLE 7.6 **AT ABOUT THIS TIME: Infancy**

Approximate Age	Characteristic or Achievement
3 months	Rolls over Stays half-upright in stroller Uses two eyes together Grabs for object; if rattle in hand, can shake it Makes cooing noises Obvious recognition of familiar people
6 months	Sits up, without adult support (but sometimes using arms) Grabs and can grasp objects with whole hand Smiles and laughs Babbles, listens, and responds with facial expression Tries to crawl (on belly, not yet on all fours) Stands and bounces with support (on someone's lap, in a bouncer) Begins to shows signs of anger, fear, attachment
12 months	Stands without holding on Crawls well Takes a few unsteady steps Uses fingers, including pincer grasp (thumb and forefingers) Can feed self with fingers Speaks a few words (*mama, dada, baba*) Strong attachment to familiar caregivers Apparent fear of strangers, of unexpected noises and events
18 months	Walks well Runs, but also falls Tries to climb on furniture Speaks 50–100 words; most are nouns Begins toilet training Likes to drop things, throw things, take things apart Recognizes self in mirror
24 months	Runs well Climbs up (down is harder) Uses simple tools (spoon, large marker) Combines words (usually noun/verb, sometimes noun/verb/noun) Can use fingers to unscrew tops, open doors Very interested in new experiences and new children

An Eventful Time This table lists aspects of development that have been discussed in Chapters 5, 6, and 7. Throughout infancy, temperament and experience affect when and how babies display the characteristics and achievements listed here. The list is meant as a rough guideline, not as a yardstick for indicating a child's progress in intelligence or any other trait.

Response for Potential Day-Care Providers (from page 214): A high-quality day-care center needs trained and responsive adults and a clean, safe space—all of which can be expensive and may mean that you will have to charge higher fees than many families can afford to pay. The main benefit for you is knowing that you can make a major contribution to the well-being of infants and their families.

A Practical Approach for Toni

The health workers who reported on Toni's development (see Chapter 5) used her as an example of the need for good nutrition. That concern is valid, but here we are concerned with Toni's psychosocial experiences.

The report on Toni (on page 133) mentions several worrisome social factors: Her mother went back to work when Toni was about 1 year old, Toni's father is "not in the household," many relatives provide "patchwork care," and the mother does not trust strangers. These factors were not properly explained in the report. For example, we know that "the influence of non-residential fathers on offspring can be substantial, but it is highly variable" (King et al., 2004, p. 1). If Toni's father is financially supportive and actively involved in her care, it does not matter where he sleeps. Merely stating that he is not in the household does not tell us enough.

Also missing from the report is explicit discussion of Toni's psychosocial needs. We do know that Toni lived exclusively with her mother and then suddenly started being cared for outside her home by a variety of people. The lack of continuity of care is a problem. The mother's mistrust of strangers prevented her from getting needed support. That Toni is not gaining weight or learning language may stem from her feelings of anger, depression, or fearfulness rather than from her feeding history.

Like all toddlers, Toni needs stability of care. Ideally, only one person should be the primary nonmaternal caregiver. That person might be a day-care provider, father, grandparent, or a neighbor who stays home with a toddler of her own. Probably the best solution is for Toni to attend a day-care center that has all five characteristics of high-quality day care described in Table 7.5. The authors of the case study report that a social worker was assigned to help Toni's mother find a nearby day-care center. Let's hope she found a good one, so that Toni can get the stable, high-quality care she needs.

A Practical Approach for Jacob

Jacob was in more serious condition, psychosocially, than Toni. He may have been understimulated by the nanny who did not speak English; he may have been suffering from a lack of parental attention. He was already 3 years old but not talking. All infants need one or two people who are emotionally invested in them from the first days of life, and it is not clear that Jacob had anyone. There is no indication of attachment.

Something had to be done, as his parents eventually realized. They took him for evaluation at a major teaching hospital. He was seen by at least 10 experts, none of whom said anything encouraging. The diagnosis was "pervasive developmental disorder," which suggests serious brain damage.

Fortunately, Jacob's parents then consulted a psychologist who was skilled in helping infants with psychosocial problems. The psychologist showed them how to build a relationship with Jacob, saying, "Now I am going to teach you how to play with your son." They learned about "floor time," four hours a day set aside for them to get on their son's level and interact with him: Imitate him, act as if they are part of the game, put their faces and bodies in front of his, create synchrony even though Jacob did nothing to initiate it.

The father reports:

> We rebuilt Jacob's connection to us and to the world—but on his terms. We were drilled to always follow his lead, to always build on his initiative. In a sense, we could only ask Jacob to join our world if we were willing to enter his. . . . He would drop rocks and we would catch them. He would want to put pennies in a bank and we would block the slot. He would want to run in a circle and we would get in his way. I remember a cold fall day when I was

> putting lime on our lawn. He dipped his hand in the powder and let it slip through his fingers. He loved the way it felt. I took the lawn spreader and ran to the other part of our yard. He ran after me. I let him have one dip and ran across the yard again. He dipped, I ran, he dipped, I ran. We did this until I could no longer move my arms.
>
> *[Jacob's father, 1997]*

Jacob's case is obviously extreme, but many infants and parents have difficulty establishing synchrony. From the perspective of early psychosocial development, nothing could be more important than a connection like the one Jacob and his parents established.

> In Jacob's case it worked. He said his first word at age 3, and by age 5 . . . he speaks for days at a time. He talks from the moment he wakes up to the moment he falls asleep, as if he is making up for lost time. He wants to know everything. "How does a live chicken become an eating chicken? Why are microbes so small? Why do policemen wear badges? Why are dinosaurs extinct? What is French? [A question I often ask myself.] Why do ghosts glow in the dark?" He is not satisfied with answers that do not ring true or that do not satisfy his standards of clarity. He will keep on asking until he gets it. Rebecca and I have become expert definition providers. Just last week, we were faced with the ultimate challenge: "Dad," he asked: "Is God real or not?" And then, just to make it a bit more challenging, he added: "How do miracles happen?"
>
> *[Jacob's father, 1997]*

Miracles do not always happen; in fact, infants diagnosed with pervasive developmental disorders usually require special care throughout childhood. Nevertheless, almost all infants, almost all the time, develop relationships with their close family members. The power of early psychosocial development is now obvious to every developmentalist and, it is hoped, to every reader of this text.

■ SUMMARY

Emotional Development

1. Two emotions, contentment and distress, appear as soon as an infant is born. Anger emerges with restriction and frustration, between 4 and 8 months of age, and becomes stronger by age 1.

2. Reflexive fear is apparent in very young infants. However, fear of something specific, including fear of strangers and fear of separation, does not appear until toward the end of the first year.

3. In the second year, social awareness produces more selective fear, anger, and joy. With increasing self-awareness at about 18 months, emotions emerge that encourage an interface between the self and others, specifically pride, shame, and jealousy.

Theories About Infant Psychosocial Development

4. According to all five major theories, caregiver behavior is especially influential in the first two years. Freud stressed the mother's impact on oral and anal pleasure; Erikson emphasized trust and autonomy.

5. Behaviorists focus on learning; parents teach their babies many things, including when to be fearful or joyful. Cognitive theory holds that infants develop working models based on their experiences.

6. Epigenetic theory emphasizes temperament, a set of genetic traits whose expression is influenced by the environment. Parental practices inhibit and guide a child's temperament, but they do not create it. Ideally, a good fit develops between the parents' actions and the child's personality.

7. The sociocultural approach notes the impact of social and cultural factors on the parent–infant relationship. Ethnotheories shape infant emotions and traits so that they fit well within the culture.

The Development of Social Bonds

8. By 3 months, infants become more responsive and social, and synchrony begins. Synchrony involves moment-by-moment interaction. Caregivers need to be responsive and sensitive. Infants are disturbed by a still face because they expect and need social interaction.

9. Attachment, measured by the baby's reaction to the caregiver's presence, departure, and return in the Strange Situation, is crucial. Some infants seem indifferent (type A—insecure-avoidant) or overly dependent (type C—insecure-resistant/ambivalent), instead of secure (type B). The most worrisome form of attachment is disorganized (type D).

10. Secure attachment provides encouragement for infant exploration. As they play, toddlers engage in social referencing, looking to other people's facial expressions to detect what is fearsome and what is enjoyable.

11. Fathers are wonderful playmates for infants, who frequently consult them as social references. Each family is different, but generally mothers are more nurturing and fathers more exciting to play with as well as more supportive of exploration. Fathers seem particularly important to boys.

12. Day care for infants seems, on the whole, to be a positive experience, especially for cognitive development. Psychosocial characteristics, including secure attachment, are influenced more by the quality of home care than by the number of hours spent in nonmaternal care. Quality of care is crucial, no matter who provides that care.

Conclusions in Theory and Practice

13. Experts debate exactly how critical early psychosocial development may be: Is it the essential foundation for all later growth or just one of many steps along the way? However, all infants need caregivers who are committed to them and are dedicated to encouraging each aspect of early development. Caregivers should be sensitive and responsive for optimal psychosocial development.

▪ KEY TERMS

social smile (p. 193)
stranger wariness (p. 193)
separation anxiety (p. 193)
self-awareness (p. 194)
trust versus mistrust (p. 197)
autonomy versus shame and doubt (p. 197)
social learning (p. 197)
working model (p. 198)
temperament (p. 198)
goodness of fit (p. 200)
ethnotheory (p. 201)
proximal parenting (p. 202)
distal parenting (p. 202)
synchrony (p. 204)
still-face technique (p. 205)
attachment (p. 206)
secure attachment (p. 207)
insecure-avoidant attachment (p. 207)
insecure-resistant/ambivalent attachment (p. 207)
Strange Situation (p. 207)
disorganized attachment (p. 208)
social referencing (p. 210)
family day care (p. 212)
center care (p. 212)

▪ KEY QUESTIONS

1. How would a sensitive parent respond to an infant's distress?

2. How do emotions in the second year of life differ from emotions in the first year?

3. What are similarities and differences in the two psychoanalytic theories of infancy?

4. How might synchrony affect the development of emotions in the first year?

5. What are the differences between cognitive and behaviorist theory?

6. What are the similarities between epigenetic and sociocultural theories of infant emotions?

7. What ethnotheories did your parents or grandparents hold? Do they differ from yours? How?

8. What are the advantages and disadvantages of four kinds of infant care: mother exclusively, relatives, family day care, and center care?

9. What would be different if an infant were raised exclusively by a single father compared to a single mother?

10. Why would an infant's psychosocial development be affected if he or she spent every day in a crowded day-care center—for example, one with eight infants for every caregiver?

11. In terms of infant development, what are the differences between employed and unemployed mothers?

▪ APPLICATIONS

1. One cultural factor influencing infant development is how infants are carried from place to place. Ask four mothers whose infants were born in each of the past four decades how they transported them—front or back carriers, facing out or in, strollers or carriages, car seats or on mother's laps, and so on. Why did they choose the mode(s) they chose? What are their opinions and yours on how that cultural practice might affect infants' development?

2. Observe synchrony for three minutes. Ideally, ask the parent of an infant under 8 months of age to play with the infant. If no infant is available, observe a pair of lovers as they converse. Note the sequence and timing of every facial expression, sound, and gesture of both partners.

3. Telephone several day-care centers to try to assess the quality of care they provide. Ask about such factors as adult–child ratio, group size, and training for caregivers of children of various ages. Is there a minimum age? If so, why was that age chosen? Analyze the answers, using Table 7.5 as a guide.

BIOSOCIAL

Body, Brain, and Nervous System Over the first two years, the body quadruples in weight and the brain triples in weight. Connections between brain cells grow into increasingly dense and complex neural networks of dendrites and axons. As neurons become coated with an insulating layer of myelin, they send messages faster and more efficiently. The infant's experiences are essential in "fine-tuning" the brain's ability to respond to stimulation.

Motor Abilities Brain maturation allows the development of motor skills from reflexes to coordinated voluntary actions, including grasping and walking. At birth, the infant's senses of smell and hearing are quite acute. At first the eyes focus only on objects about 10 inches away. Experiences lead to rapid refinement of all the senses and underlying brain networks.

Health The health of the infant depends on nutrition (ideally, breast milk), immunization, and parental practices, including "back to sleep." Survival rates are much higher today than they were even a few decades ago.

COGNITIVE

Cognition As Piaget describes it, in sensorimotor intelligence the infant progresses from knowing his or her world through immediate sensorimotor experiences to being able to "experiment" on that world through the use of mental images. Concepts, such as object permanence and deferred imitation, are evident. The infant is most interested in affordances, that is, in what various experiences and events offer him or her. Active curiosity and inborn abilities interact with various experiences to develop early cognition. Recent research finds traces of memory even at 3 months, evidence of concept formation at 6 months, and deferred imitation at 9 months—all much younger ages than Piaget described.

Language Babies' cries are their first communication; they then progress through cooing and babbling. Interaction with adults exposes them to the structure of language. By age 1, an infant can usually speak a word or two; by age 2, a toddler is talking in short sentences, displaying an ability that distinguishes humans from all other animals. Language develops through reinforcement, neurological maturation, and social motivation, although the precise impact of these three remains controversial.

PSYCHOSOCIAL

Emotions and Personality Development Emotions change from quite basic reactions to complex, self-conscious responses. Infants become increasingly independent, a transition explained by Freud's oral and anal stages, by Erikson's crises of trust versus mistrust and autonomy versus shame and doubt, and by cognitive theory's working models. While these theories emphasize the parents' role, research finds that much of basic temperament—and therefore personality—is inborn and apparent throughout life, as epigenetic theory explains. Sociocultural theory stresses cultural norms, which affect what parents do with their babies, shaping their personality traits to fit the particular society in which they live.

Parent–Infant Interaction Early on, parents and infants respond to each other by synchronizing their behavior in social play. Toward the end of the first year, secure attachment between child and parent sets the stage for the child's increasingly independent exploration of the world. The infant becomes an active participant in this social interaction, first in directly reacting to others and then in seeking out others' opinions through social referencing. Fathers, other relatives, and day-care providers, in addition to mothers, encourage infants' social confidence.

PART III

The Play Years

The years from age 2 to age 6 are often called early childhood, or the preschool period. In this book we also call them the play years. People of all ages play, of course, but these years are prime time for play. During early childhood, children spend most of their waking hours discovering, creating, laughing, and imagining as they acquire the skills they will need. They chase each other and attempt new challenges (developing their bodies); they play with sounds, words, and ideas (developing their minds); they invent games and dramatize fantasies (learning social skills and moral rules).

Playfulness makes young children exasperating as well as delightful. To them, growing up is a game, and their enthusiasm for it seems unlimited—whether they are quietly tracking a beetle through the grass or riotously turning their bedroom into a shambles. Their minds seem playful, too, when they explain that "a bald man has a barefoot head" or that "the sun shines so children can go outside to play."

If you expect young children to sit quietly or think logically, you'll be disappointed. But if you enjoy play, then children between ages 2 and 6 will bring you joy.

Chapter Eight

The Play Years: Biosocial Development

Between ages 2 and 6, significant development occurs on several fronts. The most obvious changes are in size and shape, as chubby toddlers seem to stretch upward, becoming thinner as well as taller. Less obvious but more crucial changes occur in the brain. Maturation turns a clumsy, impulsive 2-year-old into a deft, deliberate 6-year-old.

Do you remember learning to skip, or write your name, or tie your shoes? Three-year-olds try to do all these things, but they shuffle instead of skip, forget letters, and—these days—get more practice with Velcro strips than with shoelaces. By age 6, they can do them all, as long as they have had enough time to practice. If you can remember yourself in early childhood, you probably remember trying to do things you could not yet do. Now you can be grateful for your persistence as well as your maturation.

Maturation, high aspirations, and active play make young children vulnerable to many biosocial hazards, including injury and abuse. These hazards are covered in this chapter as well, to aid in recognizing them and preventing harm. When you were 3 years old and wanted to fly like a bird, a plane, or Superman, I hope someone made sure you did not fall very far. Every child deserves a happy, pain-free life.

Body Changes

Compared to cute and chubby 1-year-olds, 6-year-olds are amazingly grown up. This is true throughout the world, because human genes cause reshaping of the body during early childhood. To be specific, as in infancy, the body and brain develop according to powerful epigenetic forces, biologically driven and socially guided, experience-expectant and experience-dependent (see Chapter 5). In early childhood, these general developmental principles reflect the reality that the child's body changes every year.

Growth Patterns

Just comparing a toddling 1-year-old and a cartwheeling 6-year-old makes some differences obvious. During the play years, children become slimmer as the lower body lengthens and baby fat turns to muscle. In fact, the lowest BMI (body mass index) of the entire life span, when humans average the lowest weight in relation to their height, is at age 5 (Guillaume & Lissau, 2002). Gone are the protruding belly, round face, short limbs, and large head that characterize the toddler. By age 6, body proportions are similar to those of an adult. The center of gravity has moved from the breastbone to the belly button, enabling not only cartwheels but also many other motor skills.

Increases in height and weight accompany these changes in proportions. Each year from 2 through 6, well-nourished children add almost 3 inches (about 7 centimeters) and gain about 4½ pounds (2 kilograms). By age 6, the average child in a developed nation weighs about 46 pounds (21 kilograms) and is 46 inches (117 centimeters) tall. (As my nephew David said at that point, "In numbers I am square now.") These are averages; children vary a great deal, especially in weight. As noted in Chapter 5, percentiles are more useful than norms in monitoring the growth of a particular child (see Appendix A, pp. A6–A7, for tables listing height and weight percentiles).

A typical 6-year-old:

- Is at least 3½ feet tall (more than 100 centimeters)
- Weighs between 40 and 50 pounds (between 18 and 22 kilograms)
- Looks lean, not chubby (ages 5–6 are lowest in body fat)
- Has adult-like body proportions (legs constitute about half the total height)

These are *averages,* not true of every child. Many ethnic and genetic variations occur.

Ethnic and Cultural Differences

When many ethnic groups live together in one developed nation (such as in Australia, Canada, England, France, or the United States), children of African descent tend to be tallest, followed by those of European descent, then Asians, and then Latinos. These are very broad generalities; every continent has many ethnic groups, within which many individual families exhibit distinct inherited patterns unlike their ethnic norms (Eveleth & Tanner, 1990). Height is particularly variable among children of African descent, because the various groups living on that large continent have developed substantial genetic diversity.

Cultural patterns affect growth. In many families in South Asia, males are better fed than females. Consequently, girls tend to be much shorter and smaller than boys and are more likely to die in early childhood (the death rate in India is almost twice as high for girls as for boys) (Costello & Manandhar, 2000). By contrast, boys are more vulnerable than girls in most developed nations. For instance, although children of both sexes are generally healthy and well fed in the United States, boys are 25 percent more likely to experience a serious illness than girls are (U.S. Bureau of the Census, 2004–2005).

Socioeconomic Status

Household income affects physical growth as well. Traditionally, low-income families of all ethnicities feared that their children would be malnourished and thus become vulnerable to illness. That was once a reasonable fear, as Chapter 5 explains, and adults tried to make sure the children ate enough. That reaction has become destructive, not protective. In 1975 in Brazil, for example, two-thirds of all nutrition problems were related to undernourishment; in 1997, two-thirds were related to overnourishment. In Brazil lower income correlates not only with more underweight but also with more overweight (Monteiro et al., 2004).

Overfeeding is a recent problem, not yet found in every nation. In some countries today (including several in Asia and Africa) food is still scarce, and that makes children notably shorter than their genetic peers in more affluent nations. Several other factors also make a difference, including birth order, sex, disease, and region (Eveleth & Tanner, 1990). Healthy first-born boys living in cities at sea level are usually taller than their peers who live in other circumstances. Although traditionally such boys may have been advantaged, bigger is not always better. If tall and heavy boys become tall and heavy men, they will be vulnerable to many illnesses in adulthood.

A detailed study in New York City found that the rate of overweight (22 percent) was higher for low-income 2- to 4-year-olds than for middle-income children the same age (Nelson et al., 2004). Furthermore, the 4-year-olds were more often overweight than the 2-year-olds (27 percent compared with 14 percent), an increase suggesting that family eating habits, rather than the children's genes, were the cause. There were ethnic differences as well, with 27 percent of Hispanic (mostly Dominican, Mexican, and Ecuadorian) preschoolers overweight, 22 percent of Asian Americans (mostly Chinese and Korean), 14 percent of African Americans, and 11 percent of European Americans. (Childhood obesity is discussed in more detail in Chapter 11.)

Eating Habits

Compared with infants, young children—especially modern children, who play outdoors less than their parents or grandparents did—need far fewer calories per pound of body weight. Appetite decreases between ages 2 and 6, causing many parents to fret, threaten, and cajole ("Eat all your dinner, and you can have ice cream").

Reduced appetite in early childhood is not a medical problem, unless a child is unusually thin or gains no weight at all. Percentile rankings indicate whether children are losing or gaining weight compared with their peers; these measures are a better guide to under- or overnourishment than are the leftovers on the dinner plate (Wardley et al., 1997).

LAURA DWIGHT

No Spilled Milk This girl is demonstrating her mastery of the motor skills involved in pouring milk, to the evident admiration of her friend. The next skill will be drinking it—not a foregone conclusion, given the lactose intolerance of some children and the small appetites and notorious pickiness of children this age.

? OBSERVATIONAL QUIZ (see answer, page 226): What three things can you see that indicate that this attempt at pouring will probably be successful?

Nutritional Deficiencies

Although most children in developed nations consume more than enough calories, they do not always obtain adequate minerals or vitamins (Wardley et al., 1997). The major nutritional deficits in early childhood are insufficient iron, zinc, and calcium. Foods containing these minerals get crowded out by other foods. For example, the past 20 years have seen a decline in calcium consumption because children drink less milk and more soft drinks and fruit juice (Jahns et al., 2001).

Sweetened cereals and drinks, advertised as containing 100 percent of a day's vitamin requirements, are a poor substitute for a balanced diet, for two reasons. First, some essential nutrients have not yet been identified. Second, it is easy for a child to consume too much of one nutrient and not enough of another if fortified cereals and juice drinks rather than fresh fruits and vegetables are the mainstays of the diet (Wardley et al., 1997).

High-calorie foods cause vitamin or mineral deficiencies if they reduce an already small appetite. In the study of low-income preschoolers in New York, about half ate not even one fruit or vegetable serving a day, much less the five or more daily servings recommended by nutritionists (Nelson et al., 2004).

One particular problem is candy. Many cultures promote children's eating of sweets, in the form of birthday cake, holiday candy, Halloween treats, and such. The details (e.g., chocolate Easter bunnies or Hanukkah gelt) depend on family ethnicity and religion, but the general trend is pervasive and hard to resist. Yet sugar is the leading cause of early tooth decay, the most prevalent disease of young children in developed nations (Lewit & Kerrebrock, 1998).

Just Right

Adding to the nutritional complications is the fact that many young children are quite compulsive about daily routines, including meals. This phenomenon is called *just right* or *just so*, in reference to the child's insistence that a particular experience occur in an exact sequence and manner. For example:

! Answer to Observational Quiz (from page 225): The cup, the pitcher, and the person. The cup has an unusually wide opening; the pitcher is small and has a sturdy handle; and the girl is using both hands and giving her full concentration to the task.

Especially for Parents of Fussy Eaters You prepare a variety of vegetables and fruits, but your 4-year-old wants only French fries and cake. What should you do?

> Whereas parents may insist that the child eat his vegetables at dinner, the child may insist that the potatoes be placed only in a certain part of the plate and must not touch any other food; should the potatoes land outside of this area, the child may seem to experience a sense of near-contamination, setting off a tirade of fussiness for which many 2- and 3-year-olds are notorious.
>
> *[Evans et al., 1997]*

Most food preferences and rituals are far from nutritionally ideal. (One 3-year-old I know wanted to eat only cream cheese sandwiches on white bread; one 4-year-old, only fast-food chicken nuggets.) The insistence on eating only certain foods, prepared and placed in a particular way, would be pathological in an adult but is common among young children.

About 1,500 parents answered questions about the desire of their 1- to 6-year-olds to have familiar routines and habits (Evans et al., 1997). They reported that more than 75 percent of the 2- to 4-year-olds displayed one or more of the following attitudes:

- Preferred to have things done in a particular order or in a certain way
- Had a strong preference for wearing (or not wearing) certain articles of clothing
- Prepared for bedtime by engaging in a special activity, routine, or ritual
- Had strong preferences for certain foods

By age 6, this rigidity begins to fade. The items that indicate a child's demand that things be "just right" (e.g., "liked to eat food in a particular way") show a marked decline after age 3 (see Figure 8.1). As a team of experts explain, "Most, if not all, children exhibit normal age-dependent obsessive compulsive behaviors [which are] usually gone by middle childhood" (March et al., 2004, p. 216).

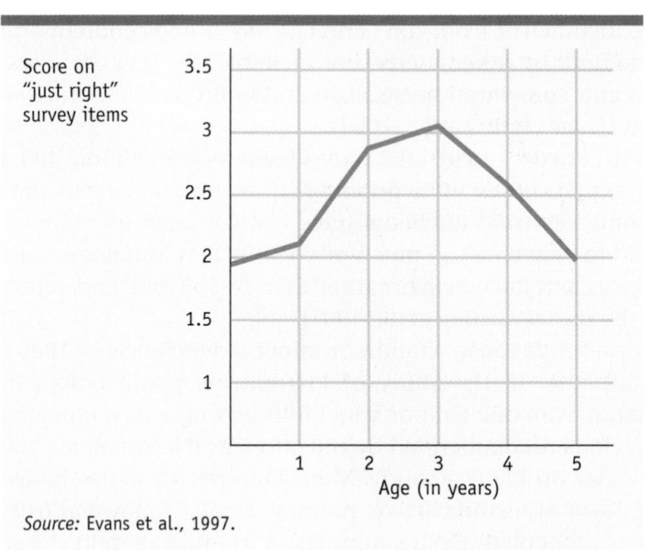

FIGURE 8.1 **Young Children's Insistence on Routine** This chart shows the average scores of children (who are rated by their parents) on a survey indicating the child's desire to have certain things—including food selection and preparation—done "just right." Such strong preferences for rigid routines tend to fade by age 6.

Given both the power and the transience of this behavior in normal children, parents should probably be tolerant. Insistence on a particular bedtime routine, a preferred pair of shoes, or favorite cup can usually be accommodated until the child no longer wants the item. Malnutrition is another story; the best tactic is to offer ample healthy foods only when the child is hungry. This approach, however, is rarely taken in the United States, where children typically consume several unhealthy snacks each day (Jahns et al., 2001).

SUMMING UP

During the play years, children grow steadily taller and proportionately thinner, with variations depending on genes, gender, nutrition, income, and other factors. Overweight has become a more common problem than underweight. One reason is that in some areas, parents have not yet adjusted to an abundance of food. Another is that the typical young child has a smaller appetite but still tends to overeat. Children also tend to prefer unhealthy foods and to be fussy about what they eat. All that makes it difficult for parents to make sure their children consume enough fruits and vegetables.

Brain Development

Brain development begins early in life, as described in Chapters 4 and 5. By age 2, a great deal of pruning of dendrites has already occurred, as has major brain growth: The 2-year-old brain weighs 75 percent of what it will weigh in adulthood. (The major structures of the brain are diagrammed in Appendix A, p. A-18.)

Since most of the brain is already present and functioning by age 2, what remains to develop? The most important parts! Brain weight continues to increase faster than the child's body weight, reaching 90 percent of adult weight by age 5 and almost 100 percent by age 7, when the rest of the child's body still has about 100 pounds (45 kilograms) to gain. More important, those functions of the brain that make us most human are the ones that develop after infancy, enabling quicker, more coordinated, and more reflective thought. Brain growth after infancy is a crucial difference between humans and other animals.

Speed of Thought

After infancy, continued proliferation of the communication pathways (neurons) adds some brain growth, but the more marked transformations occur because of **myelination,** a process that continues through early adulthood (Sampaio & Truwit, 2001). *Myelin* is a fatty coating on the axons that speeds transmission of nerve impulses between neurons. Myelination is like adding insulation around electric wires to aid conduction.

myelination The process by which axons become coated with myelin, a fatty substance that speeds the transmission of nerve impulses from neuron to neuron.

Although myelination continues for many years, its effects are most noticeable in early childhood: Young children think and react much more quickly than infants can. This greater speed is apparent with single thoughts (as when children quickly recognize familiar faces or respond to their own names) and becomes pivotal when several thoughts must occur in rapid succession. With increasing myelination, thoughts follow each other quickly; children can perform a task and then remember to do the next one. They listen and then answer, catch a ball and then throw it, write the letters of the alphabet in sequence, and so on.

Parents of young children must still be patient when listening to them talk, when helping them get dressed, or when watching them try to write their names; all these tasks are completed much more slowly by 4-year-olds than by 14-year-olds. At least young children are quicker than toddlers, who take so long with even the simplest task that they sometimes forget what they were doing before they finish.

Myelination is not essential for basic communication between neurons, but it *is* essential for fast and complex communication. Experience affects the rate of myelination: Practice makes thoughts come more quickly (Merzenich, 2001). Because young infants spend almost all their waking hours looking and listening (displaying sensorimotor intelligence), the visual and auditory cortexes are among the earliest to become myelinated.

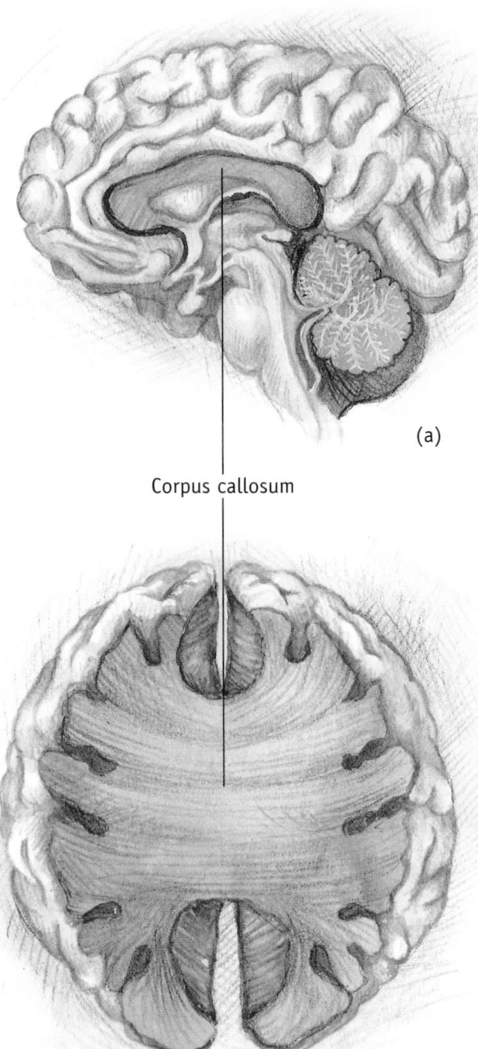

FIGURE 8.2 **Connections** Two views of the corpus callosum, a band of nerve fibers (axons) that convey information between the two hemispheres of the brain. When developed, this "connector" allows the person to coordinate functions that are performed mainly by one hemisphere or the other. *(a)* A view from between the hemispheres, looking toward the right side of the brain. *(b)* A view from above, with the gray matter removed in order to expose the corpus callosum.

corpus callosum A long strip of nerve fibers that connect the left and right hemispheres of the brain.

lateralization Literally, sidedness. Each side of the brain specializes in certain functions, with one side dominant for each activity. The left side of the brain controls the right side of the body, and vice versa.

During the play years, myelination proceeds most rapidly in the areas of the brain dedicated to memory and reflection. A 5-year-old, for example, can remember last year, can stop and think, and can act after some contemplation—all of which are impossible for a 1-year-old, who acts on an impulse immediately. Inadequate myelination early in life means that a message to one part of the brain is not immediately sent to another part. As a result, for infants, coordinated reflection is impossible.

Connecting the Brain's Hemispheres

One particular part of the brain that grows and myelinates rapidly during the play years is the **corpus callosum**, a band of nerve fibers that connect the left and right sides of the brain (see Figure 8.2). The corpus callosum is "250–800 million fibers that do nothing other than keep the hemispheres coordinated in their processing" (Banich & Heller, 1998, p. 1). As a result of growth in the corpus callosum, communication between the two brain hemispheres becomes markedly more efficient, allowing children to perform actions that involve both halves of the brain or body (Banich, 1998).

To understand the significance of this, you need to realize that, although it looks as if the two sides of the body and brain are identical, in many crucial ways they are not. Each side specializes, so each is dominant for certain functions—a process called **lateralization.**

You know that almost everyone is either right-handed or left-handed. But you may not realize that lateralization, or "sidedness," is also apparent in the arms, legs, feet, eyes, ears, and brain. The entire body is divided into two halves, which are not identical. People are left- or right-eared, left- or right-eyed, and so on. Such specialization is epigenetic, prompted by genes, prenatal hormones, and early experiences.

The Left-Handed Child

Sleeping newborns usually turn their heads rightward (or leftward, for those who will be left-handed) and bend their limbs toward one side. As infants lie in their cribs, they face toward one hand, moving it as they watch, gaining dexterity, making that hand more dominant. Thus, experience influences hand preference. Later experience can also make a difference, altering a genetic preference, as happened to millions of left-handed children who were forced (sometimes via punishment) to be right-handed.

Why would anyone force a child to change hand preference? Actually, all societies favor right-handed people. This bias is apparent in language. In English a "left-handed compliment" is insincere, and no one wants to be "way out in left field." In Latin, *dexter* (the root for *dexterity)* means "right" and *sinister* (also meaning "evil") means "on the left side." Similar connotations are found in almost every language.

The same bias is found in customs, in tools, and in taboos. For example, in many Asian and African nations today, the left hand is used only for wiping after defecation; it is a major insult to give someone anything or to perform any other observable action with that "dirty" hand. In every nation, tools—scissors, steam irons, faucets, screws—are designed for right-handed people. Thus, well-meaning adults might force their children to be right-handed to avoid the social stigma and might conclude that left-handed children who resist are stubborn, or even "the devil's spawn."

The Whole Brain

Through studies of people with brain damage, neurologists have determined how the brain's hemispheres specialize: The left half of the brain controls the right side of the body and contains the areas dedicated to logical reasoning, detailed analysis, and the basics of language; the right half controls the left side of the body and generalized emotional and creative impulses, including appreciation of most music, art, and poetry. Thus, the left side notices details and the right side grasps the big picture—a distinction that should provide a clue in interpreting Figure 8.3.

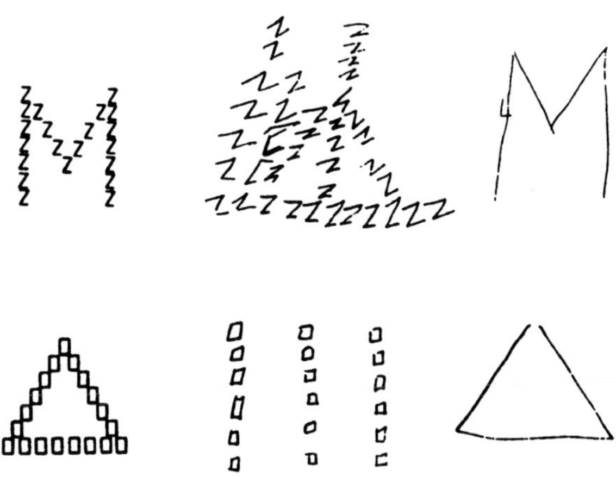

FIGURE 8.3 **Copy What You See** Brain-damaged adults were asked to copy the figure at the left in each row. One person drew the middle set, another the set at the right.

? OBSERVATIONAL QUIZ (see answer, page 231): Which set was drawn by someone with left-side damage and which set by someone with right-side damage?

No one (except severely brain-damaged people) is either left-brained or right-brained. Every cognitive skill requires both sides of the brain, just as every important motor skill requires both sides of the body (Hugdahl & Davidson, 2002). Because they do not have a mature corpus callosum, "the hemispheres of young children are more functionally disconnected than those of adults" (Banich, 1998, p. 36), and some behaviors are clumsy, wobbly, and slow. Because older children and adults have myelinated fibers in the corpus callosum that carry faster signals between the two hemispheres, better thinking and quicker action are possible.

Training one side of the body and brain is easier in the young, before patterns of lateralization are firmly established (Merzenich, 2001). For this reason, damage to the left side of the brain, where language functions are located, is less serious in children than in adults. Indeed, in cases where removing a major brain tumor requires loss of the entire left side of the brain, young children switch language functions to the right side of the brain, learning to talk, listen, and read quite well. Once lateralization has occurred and language functions are securely located in the left side, some plasticity is lost. In adults, removal of brain tumors on the left side is likely to cause a loss of language ability (Leonard, 2003).

Interestingly, although people whose left hemisphere was removed early in life generally score in the normal range on various tests of language abilities, subtle deficiencies in fluency can be found (Stiles, 1998). There is some evidence that removing the left hemisphere, thus relocating language to the right hemisphere, produces some neurological "crowding," so some less important brain functions are lost to make room for language (de Haan & Johnson, 2003).

In general, we humans sometimes use only part of our brains, but a whole brain is best, and one fully functioning side is better than a partially functioning side. Given a certain amount of brain damage, it is much more destructive if it affects both sides of the brain rather than only one side.

Usually, the young are better able to recover from brain injury than are adults, with one important exception: Brain damage to the prefrontal cortex is more devastating for children than for adults (de Haan & Johnson, 2003).

RESPONSE FOR PARENTS OF FUSSY EATERS (from page 226): The nutritionally wise answer would be to offer *only* fruits, vegetables, and other nourishing, low-fat foods, counting on the child's eventual hunger to drive him or her to eat them. However, centuries of cultural custom make it almost impossible for parents to be wise in such cases. Perhaps the best you can do is to discuss the dilemma with a nutritionist or pediatrician, who can advise you about what to do for your particular child.

Planning and Analyzing

You learned in Chapter 5 that the *prefrontal cortex* (sometimes called the *frontal cortex* or *frontal lobe*) is an area in the very front part of the brain's outer layer (the cortex), under the forehead. It "underlies higher order cognition, including planning and complex forms of goal-directed behavior" (Luciana, 2003, p. 163). This is the last part of the human brain to reach maturity. The prefrontal cortex is crucial for humans; it is said to be the "executive" of the brain because all areas are ruled by prefrontal decisions. It is undeveloped in nonhuman primates and completely absent in most lower animals.

Maturation of the Prefrontal Cortex

The frontal lobe "shows the most prolonged period of postnatal development of any region of the human brain" (Johnson, 1998, p. 33), with dendrite density increasing throughout adolescence. The first benefits of the prefrontal cortex's maturation over the years from 2 to 6 are these:

ESPECIALLY FOR EARLY-CHILDHOOD TEACHERS You know you should be patient, but you feel your frustration rising when your young charges dawdle on the walk to the playground a block away. What should you do?

RESPONSE FOR EARLY-CHILDHOOD TEACHERS (from page 229): One solution is to remind yourself that the children's brains are not yet myelinated enough to enable them to quickly walk, talk, or even button their jackets. Maturation has a major effect, as you will observe if you can schedule excursions in September and again in November. Progress, while still slow, will be a few seconds faster in November than it was in September.

- Sleep becomes more regular.
- Emotions become more nuanced and responsive (think of shrieks of joy at a father's tickling but cries of anger when a sibling does the same thing).
- Temper tantrums subside.
- Uncontrollable laughter or tears are less common.

Maturation of the prefrontal cortex can be demonstrated experimentally (Diamond, 2001). In one test, called the Day-Night Stroop Test, children are told to look at cards with pictures of the sun or the moon and to say "Night" on seeing the sun and "Day" on seeing the moon. Three-year-olds do poorly on this task, but 6-year-olds often succeed, presumably because their maturing prefrontal cortex allows them to inhibit their first impulse and to follow directions (Gerstadt et al., 1994).

An everyday example of the same phenomenon is the game Simon Says, in which children are supposed to follow the leader's actions only when preceded by the words "Simon says." Thus when the leader touches his or her nose and says, "Simon says touch your nose," the other children are supposed to touch their noses; but when the leader touches his or her nose and merely says, "Touch your nose," no one is supposed to follow the example. Young children quickly lose the game because they mistakenly do what they see. Older children are better at it, because their prefrontal cortex allows them to think before acting.

Attention

A major function of the prefrontal cortex is to regulate attention. A 3-year-old jumps from task to task and cannot sit still for long, even in church or some other place that requires quiet. Impulsiveness is also obvious in a day-care center with many children and toys, where some younger children want to play immediately with a toy that another child has but lose interest by the time that toy becomes available. Advances in prefrontal cortex development occur at about age 3 or 4 (Posner & Rothbart, 2000), making control of impulses more likely and therefore making formal education more possible.

perseveration The tendency to persevere in, or stick to, one thought or action for a long time.

The opposite of the jumpy 3-year-old is the 3-year-old who stays in one spot and plays with the same toy for hours. **Perseveration** is the name for this tendency to persevere in, or stick to, one thought or action long after it is time to move on. For example, some preschoolers perseverate when they sing the same song again and again, or scribble the same drawing, or throw a tantrum when their favorite TV show is interrupted. That temper tantrum itself may perseverate, with the child's crying becoming uncontrollable and unstoppable, as if the child remains stuck in that emotion until exhaustion sets in.

M. MEYERSFELD / MASTERFILE

No Writer's Block The context is designed to help this South African second-grader concentrate on her schoolwork. Large, one-person desks, uniforms, notebooks, and sharp pencils are manageable for the brains and skills of elementary-school children, but not yet for preschoolers.

Impulsiveness and perseveration are not exactly opposites, because they both have the same underlying cause: immaturity of the prefrontal cortex. Over the play years, brain maturation (innate) and emotional regulation (learned) make a child more able to think before acting (inhibition) and to stop an activity (nonperseveration) when it is time to do so. Inability to do this is one reason the toddler stage is called the "terrible twos": Brain patterns lead children to lose control, becoming too impulsive or too perseverative in their emotional expression (Denham, 1998).

Remember that, although impulsiveness and perseveration seem to be opposites, they are actually two manifestations of the same deficiency—a lack of self-control, of appropriate focus, and of emotional balance. In other words, they are signs of an undeveloped prefrontal cortex, which characterizes all 2-year-olds and far fewer 5-year-olds. Gradually, children become less likely to bump into walls or each other as they learn to "look before they leap."

Both impulsiveness and perseveration are quite normal before the prefrontal cortex has matured, although both are signs of brain damage in older children.

! Answer to Observational Quiz (from page 229): The middle set, with its careful details, reflects damage to the right half of the brain, where overall impressions are found. The person with left-brain damage produced the drawings that were just an M or a Δ, without the details of the tiny *z*'s and squares. With a whole functioning brain, people can see both "the forest and the trees."

Emotions and the Brain

Explaining precisely how the complex structure of the human brain develops is beyond the scope of this book. At the moment, many details are even beyond the comprehension of neuroscientists. However, each year brings more research, and therefore each chapter in this book dealing with biosocial development builds on earlier chapters, providing a deeper understanding of the brain. Chapter 5 explained neurons, dendrites, axons, synapses, the cortex, and neurotransmitters, and you have just learned about myelination, lateralization, the corpus callosum, and the prefrontal cortex. There is much more that is relevant to an understanding of children's growth.

The Limbic System

A part of the brain called the *limbic system* is crucial in the expression and regulation of emotions, both of which become very important during the play years (more about that in Chapter 10). Three major parts of the limbic system are the amygdala, the hippocampus, and the hypothalamus.

The **amygdala,** a tiny structure deep in the brain (named after an almond, because it is about that shape and size), registers emotions, particularly fear and anxiety. It activates instantly and powerfully when a person is afraid. The amygdala develops during early childhood, and its increased activity is one reason some young children have terrifying nightmares or sudden terrors. Many develop irrational fears, either of everyday things (such as dogs, mice, a flushing toilet) or of impossible things (for urban North Americans, of lions, tidal waves, or, in the case of one of my daughters, quicksand).

amygdala A tiny brain structure that registers emotions, particularly fear and anxiety.

Nightmares and fears can overwhelm the slowly developing prefrontal cortex and disrupt a child's immature ability to think and reason. Adults also experience irrational fears. Such a fear is called a *phobia* if it disrupts normal living. As two neuroscientists explain:

> How can the amygdala influence our thoughts about emotion-laden stimuli? People have all sorts of fears and worries that can interfere with everyday life, and for some people these fears become debilitating. People suffer from panic disorders, posttraumatic stress disorder, obsessive-compulsive disorders, anxiety disorder, and phobias. These examples illustrate the extreme power of fear-related events to affect cognition.
>
> *[Kolb & Whishaw, 2003, p. 533].*

The amygdala is particularly responsive to facial expressions of fear (Vasa & Pine, 2004). Thus, if a child is afraid and sees a parent's terrified expression caused by the same object, a phobia is likely to develop because the child's amygdala becomes hypersensitive to that object. By contrast, if the parent's expression is one of pleasure or curiosity, the child might forget the initial feelings of fear because of another brain structure, the hippocampus.

The **hippocampus** is located right next to the amygdala. It is a central processor of memory, especially memory of locations. The hippocampus responds to the anxieties of the amygdala with memory; it makes the child remember, for instance, that Mother is even more afraid of mice in the basement than the child is, that lions in the zoo are not to be feared, or that quicksand appears in movies but not on the upper floors of buildings.

hippocampus A brain structure that is a central processor of memory, especially the memory of locations.

Memories of location are fragile in early childhood. Each of the many forms of memory has its own developmental timetable (Nelson & Webb, 2003). In particular, memory for context is less advanced than memory for content. The

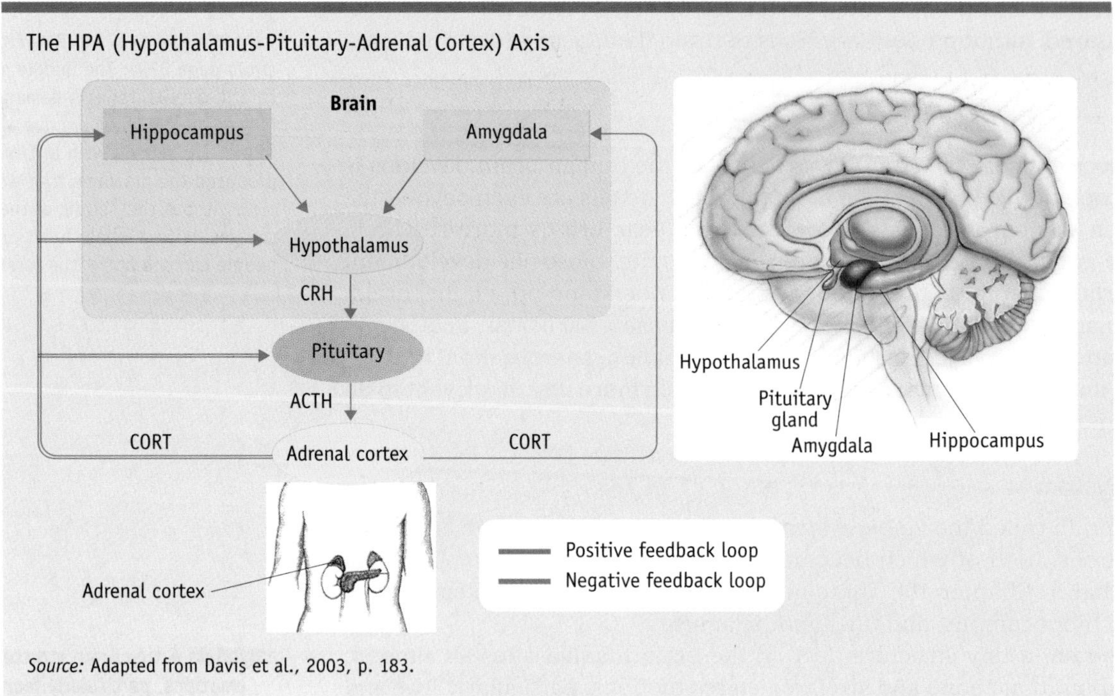

Source: Adapted from Davis et al., 2003, p. 183.

FIGURE 8.4 **A Hormonal Feedback Loop** This diagram simplifies a hormonal linkage, the HPA axis, involving the limbic system. Both the hippocampus and the amygdala stimulate the hypothalamus to produce CRH (corticotrophin-releasing hormone), which in turn signals the pituitary gland to produce ACTH (adrenocorticotrophic hormone). ACTH then triggers the production of CORT (glucocorticoids) by the adrenal cortex (the outer layers of the adrenal glands, atop the kidneys). The initial reaction to something frightening may either build or disappear, depending on other factors, including memories, and on how the various parts of the brain interpret that first alert from the amygdala. (Some other components of this mechanism have been omitted for the sake of clarity.)

hypothalamus A brain area that responds to the amygdala and the hippocampus to produce hormones that activate other parts of the brain and body.

aspect of context that is most difficult to remember accurately is *source memory,* which is memory of when, where, and how a certain fact was learned (Cycowicz et al., 2003). Source memory is quite inaccurate in preschool children (who might claim, "No one told me that. I always knew it").

If something frightening happens, the hippocampus arouses anxiety whenever the person is in that place again—even if the location was irrelevant to the fear. From an evolutionary perspective, this is helpful; it is wise to avoid the place where a poisonous snake appeared. It is less helpful in many modern situations; for example, a child should not fear the hospital where he or she got stitches.

As in this example, you can see that the amygdala is sometimes helpful, sometimes not. When the amygdala is surgically removed from animals, they are fearless in situations that should scare them; cats will stroll nonchalantly along when monkeys are nearby, for instance—something no normal cat would do (Kolb & Whishaw, 2003).

The **hypothalamus** responds to signals from the amygdala (arousing) and the hippocampus (usually dampening) to produce hormones that activate other parts of the brain and body, including stress hormones (see Figure 8.4). All these structures communicate with the prefrontal cortex, which, as you just learned, takes time to mature. If too many stress hormones flood the system in infancy and early childhood, some neurons of the hippocampus are destroyed, and permanent deficits in learning and memory may result (Davis et al., 2003).

Brain damage can occur if a young child is often terrorized. As one team of authors explain:

> Exceptionally large quantities of stress hormones and neurotransmitters may be released during the trauma, which lead to high levels of activation of the sympathetic nervous system. This may cause the brain to enter a very different biochemical state than is usually the case when ordinary experiences are encoded into memory.
>
> *[Macfie et al., 2001, p. 234]*

As a result of such abnormal brain development, memory may be impaired and logical thinking delayed until long past 6 years, the age at which the prefrontal cortex should reach a certain level of maturation (Teicher, 2002). In general, researchers have found that "prolonged physiological responses to stress and challenge put children at risk for a variety of problems in childhood, including physical and mental disorders, poor emotional regulation, and cognitive impairments" (Quas et al., 2002, p. 379). However, the links among the amygdala, the hypothalamus, and the hippocampus are complex.

The amygdala's reaction to stress during the preschool years is guided by three other parts of the brain: the hippocampus, the hypothalamus, and the prefrontal cortex. Parents and teachers help forge these links via social referencing, as explained in Chapter 7. Note that the word is *guided*, not *blocked*. Some stress aids learning and memory; too little activity in the amygdala may be as harmful as too much (Davis et al., 2003). Researchers have extensively studied the relationship between stress hormones and later learning ability in lower animals, finding benefits as well as detriments from stress.

The same conclusions probably apply to humans as well. Stressful experiences —such as meeting new friends, entering school, visiting a new place—are likely to foster growth if the child has access to someone or something that can temper the stress. For example, in a group of 4- to 6-year-olds, stress levels were measured first via brain scans and hormone levels and again after they had experienced a fire alarm. Then, two weeks later, they were interviewed about what had happened. If the interviewer was friendly, children with high stress levels remembered more; if the interviewer was stern, they remembered less than the other children (Quas et al., 2004). The practical lesson is that stress can be taken in stride—and may even be beneficial if a parent or other caregiver is supportive and reassuring.

Remember the Bosnian refugee children in Chapter 1? The presence of their mothers kept the stresses of their life from being overwhelming. Remember the Romanian orphans in Chapter 5? Without their parents, they had poorly regulated emotions. Later in this chapter, you will learn about child maltreatment overall; now we look specifically at early brain damage.

Brain Damage

Some developing brains are damaged by high fevers, viruses, or head injuries. Psychological experiences in the first years of life can also damage the brain (De Bellis, 2001). First, remember that brains need stimulation to develop: Just as the eyes need to see in order for the visual cortex to mature, young children need to be taught, guided, encouraged, and talked to for their cognitive structures to develop.

A major problem in the first years of life occurs if the child does not see, and then experience, normal emotions. The most serious impairment in this area is **shaken baby syndrome,** a life-threatening condition that occurs when an infant is held by the shoulders and shaken back and forth, sharply and quickly. A caregiver may become angry at a baby for crying, failing to realize that infants have no control over their emotions. The shaking stops the crying because of ruptured blood vessels in the brain and broken neural connections.

shaken baby syndrome Life-threatening brain damage resulting from internal hemorrhaging and broken neural connections, caused by shaking an infant back and forth, sharply and quickly.

Shaken baby syndrome is common, although there is usually no visible damage. In the United States, brain scans show that more than one in five of all children hospitalized for maltreatment suffer from shaken baby syndrome (Rovi et al., 2004). That brain damage becomes apparent in later behavior. Children whose early sadness was met with anger rather than synchrony may not have the appropriate brain networks to allow them to understand when to cry or even to feel sad. Older children who seem unmoved by experiences that sadden most children may still be suffering the effects of shaken baby syndrome.

Another brain disorder occurs in children whose mothers are clinically depressed, unable to provide the encouragement and emotional guidance that young children need. The neurological effects are that the right side of these children's prefrontal cortex develops more than the left. As a result, negative emotions (fear, sadness, anxiety) dominate and the children themselves are vulnerable to depression, which makes learning more difficult (Dawson & Ashman, 2000). There are genetic links between depression in mothers and children, but early-childhood neglect seems to be a potent influence as well.

A third problem occurs in the brains of young children who are in group residential homes. One study compared the limbic systems of Romanian children in institutions with their peers living in Romanian families. When the children saw pictures of happy, sad, frightened, and angry faces, the limbic systems of the institutionalized children were less reactive, especially to the happy and angry faces. (They were most reactive to the frightened faces.) Not only were their emotions and the brain activity flatter, but their brains did not show the lateralization that the brains of home-reared children did (Parker & Nelson, 2005).

SUMMING UP

The brain continues to mature as childhood progresses, with more myelination as well as maturation of several crucial areas. One is the corpus callosum, which connects the left and right sides of the brain and therefore the right and left sides of the body, including the hands, feet, eyes, and ears. Increasing myelination also speeds up actions and reactions. The prefrontal cortex enables impulse control, allowing children to think before they act as well as to stop one action in order to begin another. As impulsiveness and perseveration decrease and emotional control and the ability to pay attention improve, children become better able to learn.

Several key areas of the brain—including the amygdala, the hypothalamus, and the hippocampus—make up the limbic system, which is involved in emotional expression and regulation. Brain development is abnormal in young children who are mistreated, socially isolated, or subjected to extreme stress. Some stress may aid memory under the right circumstances. Other forms of stress are never beneficial, among them shaken baby syndrome, neglect, and living in an institution. The harm is evident not only in neurological tests but also in the flattened emotions of the brain-damaged preschool child.

More Curiosity Than Caution As they master their gross motor skills, children of every social group seem to obey a universal command: "If it can be climbed, climb it." That command is usually heard louder than any words of caution—one reason direct supervision is needed during the play years.

TONY FREEMAN / PHOTOEDIT

Motor Skills and Hazards

As you have just read, during the play years bodies grow slimmer, stronger, and less top-heavy; maturation of the prefrontal cortex improves impulse control; myelination of the corpus callosum permits coordination of arms and legs. No wonder children move with greater speed and grace as they age from 2 to 6, becoming better able to direct and refine their actions. (See Table 8.1 for a list of the approximate ages at which various motor skills develop.) Now we describe the specifics.

Gross Motor Skills

Gross motor skills—which, as defined in Chapter 5, involve large body movements, such as running, climbing, jumping, and throwing—improve dramatically. When you watch children play, you see clumsy 2-year-olds who fall down and sometimes bump into stationary objects. But you also see 5-year-olds who are both skilled and graceful.

Most North American 5-year-olds can ride a tricycle; climb a ladder; pump a swing; and throw, catch, and kick a ball. Some can skate, ski, dive, and ride a bicycle—activities that demand balance as well as coordination. In some nations, 5-year-olds swim in ocean waves or climb cliffs that, in other nations, few people of any age would attempt. A combination of brain maturation, motivation, and guided practice makes each of these skills possible.

At one point, many developmentalists believed that the development of motor skills was directly connected to the same brain networks that would later allow academic learning. Parents worried if their infant walked without crawling first, and many kindergarten teachers stressed skills such as skipping, sewing, and playing with blocks. Now most researchers believe that distinct brain connections support reading, math, and so on, and motor skills are no longer considered the foundation for all other skills. Motor skills are important for other reasons: exercise for health; movement for pride and joy; sports for cooperation and competition; drawing and writing for self-expression.

Generally, children learn motor skills from other children rather than through adult instruction, which is one of the many reasons children need to play. According to sociocultural theory, learning from peers is the best way for children to master skills they will need. As long as children have ample time, adequate space, and suitable playmates, their gross motor skills develop as rapidly as their maturation, body size, and innate ability allow.

Space, playmates, and free time cannot be taken for granted, however, especially in large cities. Ideally, every urban block should have a spacious, safe playground designed for young children. Ideally, every child should have slightly older children to play with, children who can demonstrate whatever motor skills—from catching a ball to climbing a tree—the child is ready to learn.

TABLE 8.1 AT ABOUT THIS TIME: Motor Skills at Ages 2–6

Approximate Age	Skill or Achievement
2 years	Run for pleasure, without falling (but bumping into things) Climb chairs, tables, beds, out of cribs Walk up stairs Feed self with spoon Draw lines, spirals
3 years	Kick and throw a ball Jump with both feet off the floor Peddle a tricycle Copy simple shapes (e.g., circle, rectangle) Walk downstairs Climb ladders
4 years	Catch a ball (not too small or thrown too fast) Use scissors to cut Hop on either foot Feed self with fork Dress self (no tiny buttons, no ties) Copy most letters Pour juice without spilling Brush teeth
5 years	Skip and gallop in rhythm Clap, bang, sing in rhythm Copy difficult shapes and letters (e.g., diamond shape, letter *S*) Climb trees, jump over things Use knife to cut Tie a bow Throw a ball Wash face, comb hair
6 years	Draw and write with one hand Write simple words Scan a page of print, moving the eyes systematically in the appropriate direction Ride a bicycle Do a cartwheel Tie shoes Catch a ball

Growing Maturity Many children achieve these motor skills at earlier or later ages than shown in this list because that skill is (or is not) valued by their culture, as reflected by their families. This rough guide is more accurate regarding sequence than age. It is useful because it shows that physical as well as cognitive skills require maturation and that each age has its challenges. Each child has a unique set of experiences and rate of maturation, both of which affect the time at which these abilities develop (Merzenich, 2001).

Fine Motor Skills

Fine motor skills, which involve small body movements (especially those of the hands and fingers), are much harder to master than gross motor skills. Pouring juice into a glass, cutting food with a knife and fork, and achieving anything more artful than a scribble with a pencil are difficult for young children, even with great concentration and effort.

The chief difficulty with fine motor skills is simply that young children do not have the necessary muscular control, patience, and judgment—in part because their central nervous system is not yet sufficiently myelinated. Many fine motor skills involve two hands and thus two sides of the brain: The fork stabs the meat while the knife cuts it; one hand steadies the paper while the other writes; and tying shoes, buttoning shirts, pulling on socks, and zipping zippers require two coordinated hands. If "one hand knows not what the other hand does" because of an immature corpus callosum and prefrontal cortex, shoelaces get knotted, paper gets ripped, zippers get stuck, and so on.

For many young children, neurological immaturity is compounded by three circumstances:

- Short, stubby fingers
- Tools (e.g., scissors, pencils, hammers) designed for adults
- Confusion about which hand is dominant

Unless caregivers keep these limitations in mind when selecting utensils, toys, and clothes, frustration may result.

ESPECIALLY FOR IMMIGRANT PARENTS You and your family eat with chopsticks at home, but you want your children to feel comfortable in Western culture. Should you change your family's eating customs?

BANANA STOCK / PICTUREQUEST

Snip, Snip Cutting paper with scissors is a hard, slow task for a 3-year-old, who is just beginning to develop fine motor control. Imagine wielding blunt "safety" scissors and hoping that the paper will be sliced exactly where you want it to be.

FIGURE 8.5 **Which Is Which?** The child who made these drawings insisted that the one at top left was a lollipop and the one at top right was a balloon (not vice versa), and that the drawing at bottom left was the experimenter and the one at bottom right was the child (not vice versa).

A lollipop

A balloon

The experimenter

The child

Artistic Expression

During the play years, children are imaginative, creative, and not yet very self-critical. They love to express themselves, especially if their parents applaud, display their artwork, and otherwise communicate approval. This makes all forms of artistic expression a joy—dancing around the room, building an elaborate tower of blocks, making music by pounding in rhythm, and putting bright marks on shiny paper. Fine motor skills are useful in almost all forms of artistic expression, yet such skills are far from perfect. Fortunately, in early childhood children are controlled much more by their desire to create than by their inclination to be self-critical.

Children's artwork reflects their unique perception and cognition. Adults are not skilled at knowing what children are drawing. For example, researchers asked young children to draw a balloon and, later, a lollipop. Even though the actual drawings were indistinguishable, children were quite insistent as to which was which (Bloom, 2000) (see Figure 8.5). It's safer to ask "What is it?" or, better yet, "Tell me about your drawing" than to guess or assume what it represents.

In every artistic domain, from dance to sculpture, gradual maturation of brain and body is apparent. For example, when drawing the human figure, 2- to 3-year-olds usually draw a "tadpole"—a circle for a head with eyes and sometimes a smiling mouth, and then a line or two beneath to indicate the rest of the body. Tadpoles are "strikingly characteristic" of children's art (Cox, 1993); they are drawn universally, in all cultures. With time, the dangling lines become legs, and a circle is placed between them and the head to indicate a stomach. By age 5, a torso is added and, after 5, arms and hands (Cox, 1997). Preschoolers enjoy drawing the same picture again and again, just as they repeatedly practice their other motor skills.

(a) 

(b) 

(c) 

No Ears? *(a)* Jalen was careful to include all seven of her family members who were present when she drew her picture. She tried to be realistic—by, for example, portraying her cousin, who was slumped on the couch, in a horizontal position. *(b)* Elizabeth takes pride in a more difficult task, drawing her family from memory. All have belly buttons and big smiles that reach their foreheads, but they have no arms or hair. *(c)* This 5-year-old's portrait shows advanced thinking; his drawing of his mother has fingers and eyelashes—details that few young children include. Although older children and adults could produce "better" artwork, the preschool child can match them in pleasure and pride.

NICOLE VILLAMORA / LAURA DWIGHT / LAURA DWIGHT

The Games Children Play

Many of the games that adults enjoy require skills and goals that are beyond the young child. Even keeping score is difficult, much less batting or kicking a fast-moving ball, deciding when to play your high card, or waiting your turn. Yet spontaneous play during these years is children's main way of developing their motor and social skills.

Avoidable Injuries

Except in famine, when malnutrition and disease are particularly likely to fell the youngest members of families, children in every nation are more likely to die of accidental injuries than any other cause. Detailed statistics are compiled in the United States, where newborns have about 1 chance in 700 of dying from an unintended injury before age 15—more than three times the odds of dying of cancer, which is the leading lethal childhood disease (National Center for Health Statistics, 2002). The rate for boys is higher than that for girls: A North American boy's odds of dying accidentally before age 15 are about 1 in 600 and a girl's, about 1 in 800.

Worldwide, unintended injuries cause millions of premature deaths each year: Not until age 40 does any disease overtake accidents as a cause of mortality. Among children, the most vulnerable age group is the 1- to 4-year-olds (MMWR, September 3, 2004).

Response for Immigrant Parents (from page 235): Children develop the motor skills that they see and practice. They will soon learn to use forks, spoons, and knives. Do not abandon chopsticks completely, because young children can learn several ways of doing things, and the ability to eat with chopsticks is a social asset.

Age Trends

Age-related trends are apparent in the particular kinds of injuries, and these trends should alert adults to the particular dangers of various periods. Teenagers and young adults are most often killed as passengers or drivers in motor-vehicle accidents. However, young children in the twenty-first century are much less likely than teenagers to die in car crashes, especially when adults obey the laws that require children to ride in car seats behind (not beside) the driver. Falls are particularly likely to be fatal for the very young (under 24 months) and very old (over 80 years). Preschoolers who fall are often injured but rarely killed. For preschoolers, death is more often caused by accidentally swallowing poison, being burned, choking, or drowning. In fact, drowning is the leading cause of death for 1- to 4-year-olds in the United States because of high rates in the swimming pools of California, Florida, Texas, and Arizona.

For small children, the rate of nonlethal injuries reported by hospitals and doctors is almost a thousand times the rate of injury-caused deaths (MMWR, September 3, 2004). In the United States in 2001, for every child who choked to death, 110 were treated in hospitals because they swallowed something that obstructed their breathing (MMWR, October 25, 2002). Several times that number choked (usually on a piece of candy or a coin), but they coughed out or swallowed the object before getting to the emergency room.

Why do small children have such high accident rates? Immaturity of the prefrontal cortex makes young children unlikely to think things through, so they plunge into dangerous places and activities (Zeedyk et al., 2002). Unlike infants, their motor skills allow them to run, leap, scramble, and grab in a flash. Their curiosity is boundless, and their impulses are uninhibited.

Injury Control

As one team of experts notes, "Injuries are not unpredictable, unavoidable events. To a large extent, society chooses the injury rates it has" (Christoffel & Gallagher, 1999, p. 10). How could a society *choose* injury, pain, and lifelong damage for any of its children? Injury prevention is no accident; it is a choice made by parents, by manufacturers, by legislators, and by society as a whole.

To understand this, consider the implications of the terminology. The word *accident* implies that an injury is a random, unpredictable event, an act of God or fate. If anyone is to be blamed, the guilty one is assumed to be a careless parent or an accident-prone child. This is called the "accident paradigm"; it implies that "injuries will occur despite our best efforts," and this allows the general public to feel blameless (Benjamin, 2004, p. 521).

In response, public health experts now prefer the term **injury control** (or **harm reduction**) to *accident prevention. Injury control* implies that harm can be minimized if appropriate social controls are in place. Minor mishaps occur, but the damage is reduced if a child falls on a safety surface instead of concrete, if a car seat protects the body in a crash, if a bicycle helmet cracks instead of a skull, if the swallowed pills come from a tiny bottle, not a big one.

injury control/harm reduction These terms express the belief that accidents are not random and that injuries are less harmful with proper controls in place. In practice, this means anticipating, controlling, and preventing dangerous activities.

primary prevention Actions that change overall background conditions to prevent some unwanted event or circumstance, such as injury, disease, or abuse.

secondary prevention Actions that avert harm in the immediate situation, such as stopping a car before it hits a pedestrian.

tertiary prevention Actions that are taken after an adverse event occurs, aimed at reducing the harm or preventing disability. Immediate and effective medical treatment of illness or injury is tertiary prevention.

Three Levels of Prevention

Prevention and control begin long before any particular child or parent does something foolish or careless.

- In **primary prevention,** the overall situation is structured to make injuries less likely. Primary prevention fosters conditions that reduce everyone's chance of injury, no matter what their circumstances.
- **Secondary prevention** is more specific, averting harm in high-risk situations or for high-risk individuals in the minutes before it could occur.
- **Tertiary prevention** begins after an injury, reducing damage from any particular trauma. Tertiary prevention saves lives and prevents permanent disabilities, although it occurs too late to prevent all harm.

(a)

LEW MERRIM / MONKMEYER

(b)

CAROL PALMER / THE PICTURE CUBE / INDEX STOCK

(c)

MYRLEEN FERGUSON CATE / PHOTOEDIT

Protective Settings In order for parents to safeguard their children from injury, they need to become aware of hazards and then take whatever action is necessary to prevent accidents. In two of these photos, the parents are to be commended: The mother in *(b)* probably has been securing her child in a safety seat from infancy. The parents of the child in *(c)* not only put a helmet on their skater but protected his knees, wrists, elbows, and hands as well. However, the boy in *(a)* may be in danger, depending on the kind of surface that is under him.

An Example: Preventing Pedestrian Deaths More than 100,000 pedestrians were killed by motor vehicles in the United States between 1985 and 2005, most of them under age 15 or over age 65. The number of pedestrian deaths has steadily gone down each year because of improvements at all three levels of prevention.

Primary prevention includes several highly effective measures, including sidewalks, speed bumps, pedestrian overpasses, brighter streetlights, and single-lane traffic circles (Retting et al., 2003; Tester et al., 2004). In other measures, cars have been redesigned (e.g., better headlights and brakes) and drivers' skills improved (more frequent vision tests and stronger drunk-driving penalties). In short, any step that makes traffic conditions safer overall is primary prevention.

Secondary prevention reduces the dangers in high-risk situations. For children this might mean requiring flashing lights on stopped schoolbuses, employing school-crossing guards, refusing alcohol to teenagers, insisting that children walk with adults. The distinction between primary prevention and secondary prevention is not clear-cut. In general, secondary prevention is more targeted, focusing on specific risk groups (e.g., young children) and proven dangers (e.g., walking to school) rather than on the overall culture, politics, or economy.

Finally, *tertiary prevention* reduces damage after impact. For pedestrians, tertiary prevention includes laws against hit-and-run drivers, speedy and well-trained ambulance drivers, emergency room procedures that reduce brain swelling, and effective rehabilitation techniques. If an injured person gets to an emergency room within the "golden hour" after a crash, the chances of recovery are much better. Yet too often, inefficiency, along with shock and guilt, uses up that hour (Christoffel & Gallagher, 1999).

Many measures at all three levels have been instituted, to good effect. In the United States pedestrian deaths decreased from 8,842 in 1990 to 4,808 in 2002 (U.S. Bureau of the Census, 2004–2005). Similar trends are found in almost every nation. In many European countries, tertiary prevention has involved redesigning the fronts of cars so that they are less destructive to pedestrians when accidents do occur (Retting et al., 2003).

Lest you think that such measures are a luxury needed only by developed nations, you should know that motor vehicles kill more than a million people each year in poor nations. Consequently, the World Health Organization dedicated World Health Day—April 7, 2004—to traffic safety. Streetlights, sidewalks, and similar measures would reduce childhood deaths everywhere, from the richest countries to the poorest.

Thinking Like a Scientist

Pool Fences Required?

Scientists are trained to think empirically, looking at data in ways that are objective, avoiding wishful thinking, emotional arguments, and single-case examples. However, particularly when it comes to child well-being, scientific thinking does not translate into child health. Consider pool safety.

Only half as many 1- to 5-year-olds in the United States were fatally injured in 2000 compared with 20 years earlier, thanks to laws governing poisons, fires, and cars. But laws about pools are hard to write and enforce. The leading cause of unintentional death for children aged 1 to 5 is drowning in a swimming pool (Brenner et al., 2001), with young children 10 times more likely to be killed in a pool than in a car. Similar statistics are found in every nation, with family pools a frequent cause of child death in wealthier nations and family cisterns or wells within toddling distance of the house a leading cause in poor nations.

Pediatricians and other scientists know how to prevent such deaths: Build a high fence around any body of water near a home. Consider the data from two Australian cities: Canberra, which had a law requiring pool fences, and Brisbane, which had no such law. Brisbane had nine times more child drownings than Canberra. The need for legislation seemed obvious (Baker, 2000).

Scientists provided data and language for a law written in 1978, requiring proper fences with self-locking gates for every swimming pool in Brisbane. However, the law took 12 years to pass. Objections involved costs, property rights, parental responsibility, and community aesthetics. After the law was passed, enforcement was poor. Then a 3-year-old drowned in a motel pool with a broken gate. That death brought community outrage and police enforcement. Child drownings were reduced by half (Nixon, 2000).

A similar problem occurred in southern California. A pool-fencing ordinance passed with one small modification, which seemed reasonable to homeowners but not to scientists. The law allowed one side of the pool enclosure to be the wall of a house, with a door that could be locked. Thus, parents and legislators protected trespassing children but did not recognize what the pediatricians knew: A family's own children often drown after entering the swimming pool through that door. Child drownings did not decline in California (Morgenstern et al., 2000).

Fewer children drown in Australia, the United Kingdom, and the United States than 10 years ago, largely because more and more communities are requiring fences around all four sides of pools. Many parents try to "drown-proof" children by teaching them to swim. They have proven that very young children can learn to swim, but no evidence finds that just knowing how to swim prevents drowning.

Meanwhile, as many pediatricians recognize, scientists need to translate their research into action that will encourage "a level of public and political interest " that will reduce the numbers of small children who fall into the family pool and die (Pitt & Cass, 2001). Although it is useful for scientists to think like scientists, they also need to think like everyone else.

RICHARD RANSIER / CORBIS

A Safe Leap What makes this jump safe as well as fun are the high fences on all sides of the pool, the adequate depth of the water, and the presence of at least one adult (taking the picture).

Especially for Urban Planners Describe a neighborhood park that would benefit 2- to 5-year-olds.

Parents, Education, and Protection The first strategy that most people advocate to prevent injury to young children is parental education. However, public health research finds that laws that apply to everyone are more effective than education of people who are not particularly ready to learn and change. "Too often, we design our physical environment for smart people who are highly motivated"

(Baker, 2000), whereas in real life, everyone has moments of foolish indifference. At those moments, automatic safety measures save lives.

This explains a powerful fact: Impoverished parents care about their children, but their children are much more likely to be seriously injured. This is true worldwide. The poorest countries have high childhood mortality, not only from disease but also from injuries that rarely occur in richer nations (Mohan, 2000).

In wealthier nations, income disparity in childhood injuries is evident whenever statistics are collected. For example, in North Carolina fatal home fires are six times more likely to occur in low-income than in high-income communities (Christoffel & Gallagher, 1999); in Sacramento, California, child pedestrian fatalities are three times more common among families with incomes under $5,000 a year than among families who earn more than $45,000 (Marcin et al., 2003); and in Toronto, Canada, the poorest children are six times more likely to be injured than the richest (Macpherson et al., 1998). The reason is that fewer automatic injury-control measures are present.

I know this firsthand, and I am grateful for automatic prevention. My daughter Bethany, at age 2, climbed onto the kitchen counter to find, open, and swallow most of a bottle of baby aspirin. Where was I? A few feet away, nursing our second child and watching television. What prevented serious injury? Laws limiting the number of baby aspirin per container (primary prevention), my earlier purchase of syrup of ipecac (on my pediatrician's advice) (secondary prevention), and a phone call to someone at Poison Control. I was told to make Bethany swallow ipecac so that she'd throw up the swallowed aspirin. She did (tertiary prevention). I still blame myself, but I am grateful for the various preventive measures that protected my child.

ESPECIALLY FOR SOCIALLY AWARE STUDENTS How did Kathleen Berger's SES protect Bethany from serious harm?

SUMMING UP

Preschool children practice all their motor skills with diligence and enthusiasm, not only gross motor skills such as running and climbing but also the fine motor skills needed for eating, getting dressed, and drawing. As they move with more speed and agility, they encounter new dangers, becoming seriously injured more often than older children. Three levels of prevention are needed. Laws and practices should be put in place to protect everyone (primary prevention), adult supervision should guard against each mishap (secondary prevention), and medical treatment should be quick and effective when injury occurs (tertiary prevention). With a little encouragement and guidance, children develop almost every motor skill; with a little care and protection, they can do so with only minor scrapes and bruises.

Child Maltreatment

Throughout this text, we have assumed that parents want to foster their children's development and protect them from danger. Yet daily, it seems, the news media report shocking stories of parents who deliberately harm their offspring. Tragic though these incidents are, the implications of the information provided by the press are that some evil person is to blame. Such news reports distract the public from far more typical incidents that might be prevented if child maltreatment were better understood (Larner et al., 1998). As a leading researcher in child maltreatment explains:

> Make no mistake—those who abuse children are fully responsible for their actions. However, creating an information system that perpetuates the message that offenders are the only ones to blame may be misleading. . . . We all contribute to the conditions that allow perpetrators to succeed.
>
> *[Daro, 2002, p. 1133]*

MISHAWAKA POLICE DEPARTMENT / GETTY IMAGES

Nobody Watching? Madelyn Gorman Toogood looks around to make sure no one is watching before she slaps and shakes her 4-year-old daughter, Martha, who is in a car seat inside the vehicle. A security camera recorded this incident in an Indiana department store parking lot. A week later, after the videotape was repeatedly broadcast nationwide, Toogood was recognized and arrested. The haunting question is: How much child abuse takes place that is not witnessed?

In fact, the dominant finding of current research in child maltreatment is that the causes are multifaceted, involving the nature of the child, the parents, the community, and the culture. For example, infants are most at risk of being mistreated if they themselves are difficult (fragile, needing frequent feeding, crying often) *and* if their mothers are depressed and do not feel in control of their lives or their infants *and* if the family is stressed because of inadequate finances. In such circumstances, the mothers blame the babies for crying, as if they cried on purpose (Bugental & Happaney, 2004).

Maltreatment Noticed and Defined

Understanding is the first step. Until about 1960, the news media and almost everyone else thought of child abuse as a rare outburst, usually taking the form of an attack by a mentally disturbed stranger. Today we know better: Maltreatment is neither rare nor sudden, it includes much more than overt attacks, and the perpetrators are usually the child's own parents or immediate relatives.

With this recognition came a broader definition: **Child maltreatment** includes all intentional harm to, or avoidable endangerment of, anyone under 18 years of age. Thus, child maltreatment includes both **child abuse,** which is deliberate action that is harmful to the child's physical, emotional, or sexual well-being, and **child neglect,** which is failure to appropriately meet a child's basic physical or emotional needs. Note that abuse is deliberate, inflicted with the intention of doing harm; that's one reason it is so hurtful. When the abuser is a parent, the young child realizes that harm comes from a person who should provide protection and love.

child maltreatment Intentional harm to, or avoidable endangerment of, anyone under 18 years of age.

child abuse Deliberate action that is harmful to a child's physical, emotional, or sexual well-being.

child neglect Failure to meet a child's basic physical, educational, or emotional needs.

reported maltreatment Maltreatment about which someone has notified the authorities.

substantiated maltreatment Maltreatment that has been reported, investigated, and verified.

Not all cases of maltreatment are reported, and not all of those are substantiated. **Reported maltreatment** cases are those about which the authorities have been informed; **substantiated maltreatment** has been investigated and verified (see Figures 8.6 and 8.7). Since 1993, the number of *reported* cases of maltreatment in the United States has been about 3 million a year, and the number of *substantiated* cases has been not quite 1 million, an annual rate of 1 child in every 70. This 3-to-1 ratio of reported to substantiated cases is attributable to three factors:

- A particular child's maltreatment is counted as one case, even if it is reported many times.
- Substantiation requires proof in the form of unmistakable injuries, serious malnutrition, or a witness willing to testify. Such evidence is not always available.
- A report may be false or deliberately misleading.

Some observers fear that reporting abuse might make it worse for the child, but this is not usually the case. Note that neglect as well as abuse should be reported, because children who experience one form of maltreatment usually suffer others as well. Noticing, reporting, and thereby halting one episode may prevent many more, not only for that child but for brothers and sisters as well.

Maltreatment is usually a family affair. If one parent is abusive, then the other parent is neglectful, unless he or she recognizes the problem and intervenes. Every kind of abuse is most destructive if the perpetrator is a parent and if

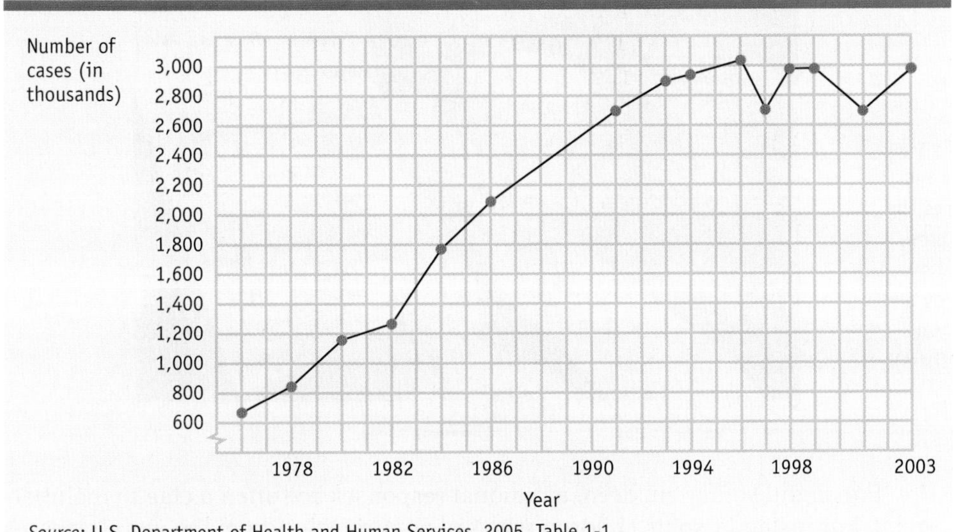

Source: U.S. Department of Health and Human Services, 2005, Table 1-1.

FIGURE 8.6 **Reported Cases of Child Maltreatment, United States, 1976–2003** After doubling in the 1970s and doubling again in the 1980s, the number of children reported as maltreated has zigzagged downward and then back up since the mid-1990s. What are possible explanations for this pattern?

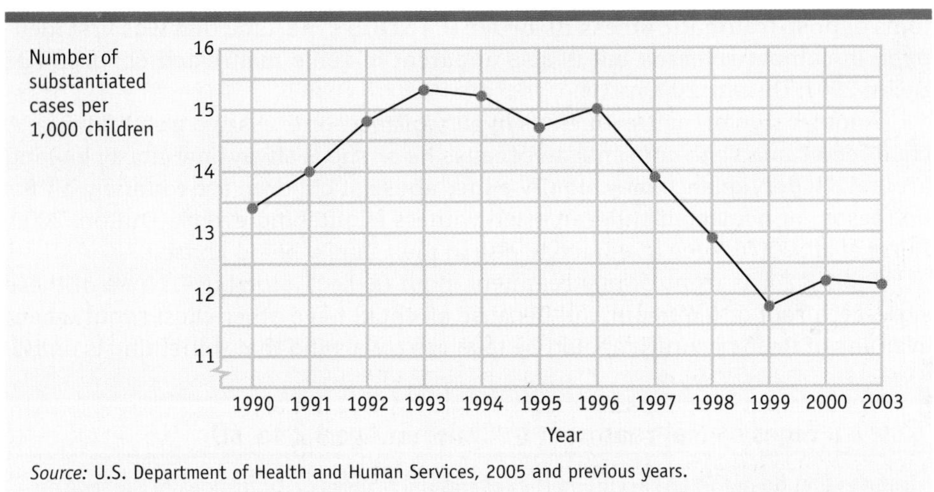

Source: U.S. Department of Health and Human Services, 2005 and previous years.

FIGURE 8.7 **Rates of Substantiated Child Maltreatment, United States, 1990–2003** The number of substantiated cases of child maltreatment in the United States is too high, but there is some good news: The rate has declined significantly from the peak in 1993.

? OBSERVATIONAL QUIZ (see answer, page 245): The dot for 1999 is close to the bottom of the graph. Does that mean it is close to zero?

the other parent does not stop it. Older siblings may also be abused or may have become abusers. Neglect by family members is particularly likely when the abuse is sexual. Sexual abuse is most common in early adolescence, although the pattern of neglect and the lack of sexual boundaries begin earlier.

Warning Signs of Maltreatment

Compared to physical abuse, neglect is twice as common and can be even more damaging (Smith & Fong, 2004). The first sign of neglect is typically delayed development, such as a lack of language, play, or laughter at age 1.

One form of neglect (which we first discussed in Chapter 5) is **failure to thrive,** a situation in which an otherwise healthy infant or young child does not gain weight. Typically, the mother explains that the child refuses to eat, but if hospitalization produces weight gain, failure to thrive is diagnosed. Children can also suffer from *medical neglect,* when a life-threatening illness is not treated (Dubowitz, 1999), or *educational neglect,* when a child gets no schooling at all (Gelles, 1999).

failure to thrive A situation in which an infant or young child gains little or no weight, despite apparently normal health.

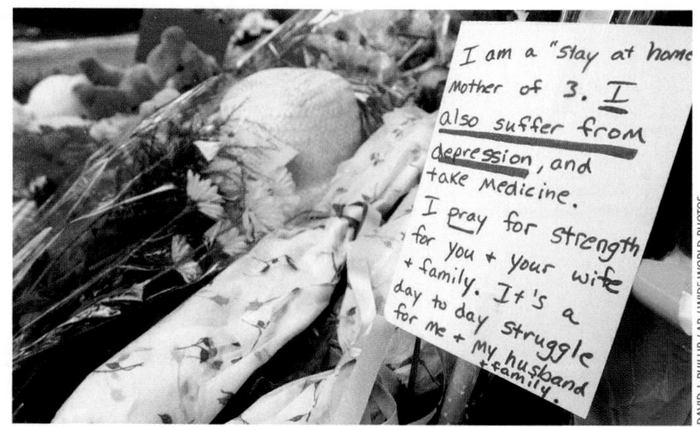

DAVID J. PHILLIP / AP / WIDE WORLD PHOTOS

Who Is to Blame? This note was left at a makeshift memorial outside the Texas home where Andrea Yates drowned her five children. It attests to the possibility that some parents, overwhelmed by their children's needs and demands, will become negligent or abusive; sometimes the child's death is the outcome. In the Yates case, the pressures of caring for five young children were increased by the mother's long-standing mental illness. Vigilance by and support from family, friends, and the community at large (members of the clergy, health care providers, and others) might help to prevent some of these tragedies.

For slightly older children, emotional responses are often a clue to maltreatment. For instance, some children who are not protected from the worst stresses of family and neighborhood life are similar to soldiers thrust into unpredictable battle. Many maltreated children are startled at any noise, quick to attack for an imagined insult, and confused between fantasy and reality. These are all symptoms of **post-traumatic stress disorder (PTSD)**, a syndrome that was first identified in combat veterans but is also apparent in some maltreated children (De Bellis, 2001; Dutton, 2000).

post-traumatic stress disorder (PTSD) A delayed reaction to a trauma or shock, which may include hyperactivity and hypervigilance, displaced anger, sleeplessness, sudden terror or anxiety, and confusion between fantasy and reality.

Another sign of maltreatment is *hypervigilance,* or excessive watchfulness: A child seems unable to concentrate because he or she is always nervously looking around. Hypervigilance may signify either abuse, if children are routinely hit for no reason, or neglect, if children often witness frightening events (Dutton, 2000; Kerig et al., 2000), such as someone else in their family being abused.

Table 8.2 lists signs of maltreatment, both neglect and abuse. None of these signs are proof of maltreatment, because all could have other causes; but whenever any of them occurs, it should be taken as a warning that something is amiss.

Response for Urban Planners (from page 240): The adult idea of a park—a large, grassy open place—is not best for young children. For them, you would design an enclosed area, small enough and with adequate seating to allow caregivers to socialize while watching their children. The playground surface would have to be protective (since young children are clumsy), with equipment that encouraged both gross motor skills (such as climbing) and fine motor skills (such as sandbox play). Swings are not beneficial, since they do not develop many motor skills. Teenagers and dogs should go elsewhere for recreation.

TABLE 8.2 **Signs of Maltreatment in Children Aged 2 to 10**

Injuries that do not fit an "accidental" explanation: bruises on both sides of the face or body; burns with a clear line between burned and unburned skin; falls that result in cuts, not scrapes
Repeated injuries, especially broken bones not properly tended
Fantasy play, with dominant themes of violence or sexual knowledge
Slow physical growth, especially with unusual appetite or lack of appetite
Ongoing physical complaints, such as stomachaches, headaches, genital pain, sleepiness
Reluctance to talk, to play, or to move, especially if development is slow
No close friendships; hostility toward others; bullying of smaller children
Hypervigilance, with quick, impulsive reactions, such as cringing, startling, or hitting
Frequent absences from school, changes of address, or new caregivers
Expressions of fear rather than joy on seeing the caregiver

Response for Socially Aware Students (from page 241): Preschoolers from families at all income levels can have accidents, but Kathleen Berger's SES allowed her to have a private pediatrician to turn to for advice, as well as the income to buy ipecac "just in case" and to have a working phone and the education to know about and to call Poison Control.

Especially for Nurses While weighing a 4-year-old, you notice several bruises on the child's legs. When you ask about them, the child says nothing and the parent says the child bumps into things. What should you do?

Many nations, including the United States, now mandate professionals who deal with children (teachers, nurses, social workers, doctors, police officers) to report any suspected maltreatment. These laws are one reason reports of maltreatment have increased. However, not all professionals know when to be suspicious. For instance, child patients in teaching hospitals (where ongoing education is part of the hospital's mission) are reported for maltreatment three times as often as children in nonteaching hospitals, where "child abuse and neglect are underidentified, underdiagnosed, and undercoded" (Rovi et al., 2004, p. 589). Would better reporting make any difference? Read about the short life of one boy.

! Answer to Observational Quiz (from page 243): No. The number is actually 11.8. Note the little squiggle on the graph's vertical axis below the number 11. This means that numbers between zero and 11 are not shown.

A Case to Study

The Neglect of Neglect

Three million reported cases of maltreatment per year in the United States seems like a huge number, yet most cases of neglect are not reported. Consider one team's report on a child in a low-income family:

> B. V., a 2-year-old male, was found lying face down in the bathtub by an 8-year-old sent to check on him. He had been placed in the bathtub by his mother, who then went to the kitchen and was absent for approximately 10 minutes. B. V. was transported by ambulance to a local hospital. He was unresponsive and had a rectal temperature of 90 degrees Fahrenheit. After medical treatment, the child's breathing resumed, and he was transported to a tertiary care hospital. B. V. remained in the pediatric intensive care unit for 9 days with minimal brain function and no response to any stimuli. He was then transferred to a standard hospital room where he died 2 days later. The mother refused to have an autopsy performed. Subsequently, the death certificate was signed by an attending physician, and cause of death was pneumonia with anoxic brain injury as a result of near-drowning.
>
> The CPS [Child Protective Services] worker advised B. V.'s mother that 10 minutes was too long to leave a 2-year-old in the bathtub unsupervised. B. V.'s mother replied that she had done it many times before and that nothing had happened. Further examination of the medical chart revealed that prior to B. V.'s death, he had a sibling who had experienced an apparent life-threatening event (previously termed a "near miss" sudden infant death syndrome). The sibling was placed on cardiac and apnea (breathing) monitors for 7 to 8 months. In addition, B. V. had been to the children's hospital approximately 2 weeks prior for a major injury to his big toe. B. V.'s toe had been severed and required numerous stitches. The mother stated that this incident was a result of the 4-year-old brother slamming the door on B. V.'s foot. Furthermore, B. V. had been seen in a different local hospital for a finger fracture the month before his death. None of the available reports indicate the mother's history of how the finger fracture occurred.
>
> *[Bonner et al., 1999, pp. 165–166]*

No charges were filed in this death. The team notes:

> This case illustrates chronic supervisory neglect but also shows that a child's death can occur in a short period of time. The mother's self-reported practice of leaving the child in the bathtub unsupervised is an example of a pattern of chronic failure to supervise in a manner appropriate for the age and development of the child. Also note that the series of suspicious events that preceded the death did not result in protective or preventive services for the family.
>
> *[Bonner et al., 1999, p. 166]*

The case of B.V. is a chilling example of "chronic supervisory neglect." Professionals who dealt with the family ignored many signs that something was wrong in this family—the near-miss SIDS, the fractured finger, and the severed toe. Death led to no charges or even the mother's acknowledgment that she had been neglectful. Furthermore, no action was taken to deal with the emotional trauma suffered by the 8-year-old who found his dying brother or by the 4-year-old who reportedly severed the toddler's toe. These children are at high risk of maltreatment. Indeed, they already are mistreated: A child's mental health is most seriously damaged not by abuse itself but by chronic feelings of helplessness and danger (De Bellis, 2001).

Families that are at high risk, like this one, are especially likely to need professional help. Specifically, physical abuse and all forms of neglect fall most heavily on children under age 6 who have the following:

- Three or more siblings
- An unemployed or absent father
- A mother who did not complete high school
- A home in a poor, high-crime neighborhood

All these factors signify poverty and lead to greater poverty, and all were present for B. V. For example, his medical care is typical for low-income children, who are usually taken to various hospital emergency rooms to be seen by overworked staff, who treat only obvious physical problems and ignore the family context. If he had not been poor, a private pediatrician who saw him regularly might have noticed and addressed his maltreatment. If his mother had had fewer children and a supportive husband, she might have taken the time to watch him bathe. Or, in another context, a single parent with several children might have had neighbors and relatives to provide support—or at least to report neglect. Instead, B.V. died.

Consequences of Maltreatment

The impact of any child-rearing practice is affected by the cultural context. Certain customs (such as circumcision, pierced ears, and spanking) are considered abuse in some cultures but are expected in others. Children are particularly damaged if they perceive that they are treated worse than other children and if their parents seem not to love them, according to their community's standards for parental love. This means that if home is a place where the child is lonely and afraid, any maltreatment is more devastating. If maltreatment is not spotted early, reported, and stopped, every aspect of development in every domain is impaired.

Learning and Health

Maltreatment compromises basic health in many ways, from neglected immunizations to malnutrition to various forms of poisoning. Abused and neglected children are more often injured, more often sick, and more often hospitalized for reasons not directly related to their maltreatment (Kendall-Tackett, 2002).

Usually brain damage is irreversible. You already know brain structures can be harmed by shaking a baby, overstressing an infant, or hitting a child on the head. Abuse harms the brain in many other ways. As you remember from Chapter 5, long-term malnutrition impedes brain growth. Many neglected infants are underfed; many neglected preschoolers eat few healthy foods. Teratogens harm the brain before birth, but toxins can also damage the brain in early childhood. For example, excess lead (often found in chips of old paint, which small children may swallow) is a common reason for cognitive impairment (Wachs, 2000).

Many neglectful parents do not enroll their children in day-care centers or schools that would give them the stimulating experience they need in order to learn. Visits to a park, to a zoo, to the grandparents' home, or to a neighbor child's house are infrequent, since social isolation is a result as well as a cause of child maltreatment. Children learn less if they always stay home.

Response for Nurses (from page 244): Any suspicion of child maltreatment must be reported, and these bruises are suspicious. Someone in authority must find out what is happening, so that the parent as well as the child can be helped.

Impaired Social Skills

Although biological, intellectual, and academic handicaps are substantial and usually quite obvious by age 6, deficits are even more apparent in maltreated children's social skills. Such children tend to regard other people as hostile and exploitative; hence, they are less friendly, more aggressive, and more isolated than other children. The longer their abuse continues and the earlier it started, the worse their peer relationships are (Bolger et al., 1998).

Maltreated children within any group are often bullies or victims or both. As adolescents and adults, people who were severely maltreated in childhood (physically, sexually, or emotionally) often use drugs or alcohol to numb their emotions, enter unsupportive relationships, become victims or aggressors, sabotage their own careers, eat too much or too little, and generally engage in self-destructive behavior (Smith & Fong, 2004; Wolfe et al., 1998).

Adults—teachers, neighbors, other relatives—who should intervene in situations of abuse or neglect are often put off by the child's distrustful, depressed, or disobedient personality. Yet those children are exactly the ones who most need help and are least likely to get it. Substantial research shows that children who are genetically vulnerable (difficult, irregular, impulsive) *and* who are mistreated are likely to become disruptive students, delinquent adolescents, and violent adults (Caspi et al., 2002; Jaffee et al., 2005). By contrast, maltreated children who are not genetically at risk, or genetically vulnerable children who are not maltreated, are unlikely to develop such problems. That brings us back to prevention: It is much easier to stop maltreatment before it begins than to rescue a severely damaged child.

Three Levels of Prevention, Again

Just as with injury control, there are three levels of prevention of child maltreatment. The ultimate goal of child-care policy is to keep all maltreatment from beginning. This is called *primary prevention* because it must occur before the problem starts. Stable neighborhoods, family cohesion, income equality, and measures that decrease financial instability, family isolation, and teenage parenthood are all examples of primary prevention; their nature and impact are described in every chapter of this book.

Secondary prevention involves spotting the warning signs listed in Table 8.2 and intervening to keep a problematic situation from getting worse. For example, insecure attachment, especially of the disorganized type (described in Chapter 7), is a sign of a disrupted parent–child relationship. Secondary prevention includes measures such as home visits by nurses or social workers, high-quality day care, and preventive medical treatment—all designed to help high-risk families.

Secondary prevention is tricky. Efforts to identify problem families may increase the risks, not reduce them. A systems approach (first described in Chapter 1) is needed because "many of the most effective solutions to social problems are not readily apparent and may even be counterintuitive. . . . Any single action may reverberate and produce . . . unintended consequences" (Garbarino & Collins, 1999, p. 4).

A very practical example came out of the campaign to stop the spread of the Marburg virus in Angola (Enserink, 2005). Emergency medical personnel from other nations set up a special hospital for the sick, equipped with laboratory facilities to diagnose the virus and special measures to keep the virus from spreading. One was that, if a person died, the body was put in a sealed plastic bag and disposed of. Although these practices were designed to save lives, they actually furthered the spread of the virus because no one who was sick would go to the hospital. Instead, they followed traditional customs, with family members caring for the ill and ritually washing the bodies of the dead before burial. Given a choice between the clinical isolation advocated by foreigners and the customs that had sustained the community for generations, families made the obvious choice. The virus spread.

Cultural patterns must be respected, but cultural patterns can also lead to abuse. For example, in Japan it is the custom for mothers to take care of their children by themselves, without help from fathers or others, for the first three years. A very close relationship between mother and child (called *amae*) is expected and is crucial. However, if a child needs outside care in the first months of life, it becomes very difficult for the mother to form that close bond. Yet the culture gives her no alternatives—except to neglect or abuse her infant. In a survey of Japanese mothers of children under age 3, 22.5 percent of mothers thought they were abusive (Shoji, 2005). Neighbors and relatives typically assume that all is well (unless the mother is employed outside the home); child abuse is seldom reported in Japan until it is very obvious. One result is that almost all reports are substantiated because by then there is no doubt (Shoji, 2005). Developmentalists are quite sure that every culture has values that are destructive of children, although they are hard to see in one's own community.

Temporarily Abandoned, Not Neglected Judgments regarding child maltreatment depend partly on the customs of the community. In Berlin, Germany, parents routinely leave their babies outside stores while they shop, and passers-by do not associate the sight with parental neglect or the danger of abduction.

PETER TURNLEY / CORBIS

The Same Situation, Many Miles Apart: Intergenerational Bonding Devoted grandfathers, such as these two in Su Zhou, China (left), and Delhi, India (right), prevent the social isolation that is a prerequisite for serious abuse. Can you imagine either man's response if he thought his granddaughter was underfed, overdisciplined, or unloved?

Remember that when it came to fencing in pools, homeowners did not believe that their own pools presented any danger to children. Similar problems occur for maltreatment of all kinds. Reformers must consider the overall context and specific conditions, and then must use scientific methods for evaluation (Thompson & Nelson, 2001). For instance, careful evaluation of one program providing social support to depressed mothers found that "helping" the mothers led to worse family functioning than no intervention at all, perhaps because the intervention made the mothers feel even more inadequate (National Research Council and Institute of Medicine, 2000). If secondary prevention is to be effective:

Especially for the General Public You are asked to give a donation to support a billboard campaign against child abuse and neglect. You plan to make charitable contributions totaling $100 this year. How much of this amount should you contribute to the billboard campaign?

- It must not stigmatize certain families as inadequate.
- It must not undermine atypical family or cultural patterns that actually nurture children.
- It must not reinforce typical family patterns that actually harm children.
- It must not create a sense of helplessness in family members, leading them to rely on outsiders rather than strengthening their own confidence, skills, and resources.

Even more complex than secondary prevention is *tertiary prevention*—intervention to reduce the harm done by actual abuse. Tertiary prevention sometimes occurs too late. If it involves hospitalization, the medical care itself is more expensive and lengthy than hospitalization for other conditions (Rovi et al., 2004) because of the need for investigation, family support or foster care, and therapy. Hospitalization further damages the fragile bond between parents and child, thus making the child's return to the family more dangerous.

Once maltreatment has been substantiated, the first priority must be to protect the child by planning for long-term care. Such **permanency planning** may mean setting goals and a timetable. Either the parents must improve in certain ways (successful drug treatment, new interaction patterns with their child) or a foster or adoptive home must be found to nurture the child until adulthood. Children need stability and continuity of care, not repeated cycles of removal and return to abuse.

permanency planning A plan for the eventual outcome when a child has experienced substantiated maltreatment. A goal is to make a definite plan that avoids repeated changes of caregiver or school, which can be particularly harmful for the child.

STEPHANIE MAZE / CORBIS

Tertiary Prevention Adoption has been these children's salvation, particularly for 9-year-old Leah, clinging to her mother. The mother, Joan, has five adopted children. Adoption is generally better than foster care for maltreated children, because it is a permanent, stable arrangement.

Although many children receive informal care from someone other than their parents, **foster care** generally means a legally sanctioned, publicly supported arrangement in which children are officially removed from their parents' custody and entrusted to another adult or family who is paid to nurture them. In 2002 more than half a million children in the United States were in foster care, a number that rose over the 1990s but has leveled off, partly because permanency planning now restores families or allows adoption more quickly than it once did (U.S. Department of Health and Human Services, 2004).

foster care A legal, publicly supported plan in which a maltreated child is cared for by someone other than the parents.

Almost all foster children are from low-income families, and many of them have multiple physical, intellectual, and emotional problems. More than 300,000 children enter foster care each year; many of them are placed in **kinship care,** in which a relative of the maltreated child becomes the approved caregiver (U.S. Department of Health and Human Services, 2004). Generally, children fare better in foster care than with abusive original families, and they do as well in kinship care as in the homes of strangers *if* the kin receive the same screening, supervision, and support as other foster parents (Berrick, 1998).

kinship care A form of foster care in which a relative of the maltreated child becomes the approved caregiver.

Adoption is the preferred option when parents are past competence. Since adoption is a permanent commitment, it is usually better for the child; but adults often create obstacles to adoption, causing further harm. For example, judges and biological parents must agree to release children for legal adoption, and they are often reluctant to do so because the rights of biological parents must be protected. Moreover, the "ideal" adoptive family—a heterosexual married couple, middle class, with the wife not employed—is increasingly rare, and many fail to realize that "non-ideal" families can also provide excellent adoptive care. Finally, prospective adoptive parents usually prefer to adopt a healthy infant. Virtually none of the 130,000 children in the United States currently awaiting adoption are healthy infants. For all these reasons, adoption is uncommon today.

Theory and research in human development suggest that abuse-prevention programs should be comprehensive, considering the different needs of children from birth through adolescence and involving the entire social context. Since poverty, teenage parenthood, drug addiction, social isolation, and ignorance tend to correlate with unwanted births, inadequate parenting, and injury and maltreatment of children, measures to undercut those root causes are needed, as are measures to place more children in loving adoptive homes. Such programs are costly, but so is child maltreatment. Primary prevention may be the most cost-effective approach after all.

SUMMING UP

Every culture seeks to protect children, and customs that seem to be destructive may merely be culturally different. Nonetheless, severe maltreatment occurs in every nation, with devastating long-term consequences for the children and, eventually, for the entire society. About a million children a year in the United States are substantiated as victims of abuse or neglect, usually by one or both of the child's own parents. Neglect is more common than abuse and is potentially even more harmful to development.

Stopping maltreatment of all kinds is urgent but complex, because the source is often the family system, not a deranged stranger. Ideally, abuse and neglect should be reported as soon as they occur and families should receive immediate help and guidance. Sometimes foster care, either with a relative or with an unrelated family, is better for the child. Primary prevention includes changing the social context to ensure that all parents protect and love their children. This is expensive but may be cost-effective over the long term. Secondary prevention focuses on families at high risk—the poor, the drug-addicted, the overwhelmed. In tertiary prevention, the abused child is rescued before further damage occurs.

RESPONSE FOR THE GENERAL PUBLIC (from page 248): Maybe none of it. Educational campaigns seldom change people's habits and thoughts, unless they have never thought about an issue at all. If you want to help prevent child abuse and neglect, you might offer free babysitting to parents you know who seem overwhelmed, or you might volunteer for a community group that helps troubled families.

SUMMARY

Body Changes

1. Children continue to gain weight and height during early childhood. Generally, they become thinner and more active.

2. Culture, income, and family customs all affect children's growth. Many children have unbalanced diets, eating more fat and sugar and less iron and calcium than they need. Childhood obesity is increasingly common worldwide because children exercise less and snack more than children once did.

Brain Development

3. The brain reaches adult size by age 7. Myelination is substantial during early childhood, speeding messages from one part of the brain to another. The corpus callosum becomes thicker and functions much better. The prefrontal cortex, known as the executive of the brain, is strengthened as well.

4. Brain changes enable more reflective, coordinated thought and memory; better planning; and quicker responses. Many brain functions are localized in one hemisphere of the brain. However, important neurological abilities tend to involve more than one brain part, and some abilities, such as language on the left side of the brain, can develop in new areas if one part of the brain is damaged.

5. The expression and regulation of emotions are fostered by several brain areas, including the amygdala, the hippocampus, and the hypothalamus. Child abuse early in life may cause an overactive amygdala and hippocampus, creating a flood of stress hormones that interfere with learning. Normally, maturation of these brain areas gradually enables the child to learn in a standard school classroom.

Motor Skills and Hazards

6. Gross motor skills continue to develop, so that clumsy 2-year-olds become 6-year-olds able to move their bodies in whatever ways their culture values and they themselves have practiced.

7. Muscle control, practice, and brain maturation are also involved in the development of fine motor skills. Young children enjoy expressing themselves artistically, developing their motor skills as well as their self-expression. Children are very creative and enjoy playing together.

8. Accidents are by far the leading cause of death for children, with 1- to 4-year-olds, boys, and low-income children more likely to suffer a serious injury or premature death than girls or older children. Biology, culture, and community conditions combine to make some children more vulnerable.

9. Injury control occurs on many levels, including long before and immediately after each harmful incident, with primary, secondary, and tertiary prevention. Laws seem more effective than educational campaigns. Close supervision is required to protect young children from their own eager, impulsive curiosity.

Child Maltreatment

10. Child maltreatment occurs far too often, usually in the form of ongoing abuse and neglect by a child's own parents. Each year about 3 million cases of child maltreatment are reported in the United States, about 1 million of which are substantiated.

11. Health, learning, and social skills are all impeded by ongoing child abuse and neglect. Physical abuse is the most obvious form of maltreatment, but neglect is common and more harmful in the long term.

12. Foster care, adoption, and kinship care are sometimes necessary alternatives to parental care. Permanency planning can avert some of the consequences of repeated foster-care placements. Primary and secondary prevention helps parents care for their children and can eliminate the need for tertiary preventive measures.

KEY TERMS

myelination (p. 227)
corpus callosum (p. 228)
lateralization (p. 228)
perseveration (p. 230)
amygdala (p. 231)
hippocampus (p. 231)
hypothalamus (p. 232)
shaken baby syndrome (p. 233)
injury control/harm reduction (p. 238)
primary prevention (p. 238)
secondary prevention (p. 238)
tertiary prevention (p. 238)
child maltreatment (p. 242)
child abuse (p. 242)
child neglect (p. 242)
reported maltreatment (p. 242)
substantiated maltreatment (p. 242)
failure to thrive (p. 243)
post-traumatic stress disorder (PTSD) (p. 244)
permanency planning (p. 248)
foster care (p. 249)
kinship care (p. 249)

KEY QUESTIONS

1. How are growth rates, body proportions, and motor skills related during early childhood?

2. Does low family income tend to make young children eat more or less? Explain your answer.

3. What are the crucial aspects of brain growth that occur after age 2?

4. How do emotions, and their expression, originate in the brain?

5. What does a caregiver who shakes a crying baby not understand about brain development?

6. Why do public health workers prefer not to use the word *accident*?

7. What conditions are best for children to develop their motor skills?

8. What are the differences among the three kinds of prevention?

9. What are the arguments for and against laws to protect children from injury?

10. Why is neglect considered worse than abuse?

11. What are the advantages and disadvantages of foster care?

12. Why do some people believe maltreatment has increased in the past 50 years, while others disagree?

APPLICATIONS

1. Keep a food diary for 24 hours, writing down what you eat, how much, when, how, and why. Then think about nutrition and eating habits in early childhood. Do you see any evidence in yourself of imbalance (e.g., not enough fruits and vegetables, too much sugar or fat, not eating when you are hungry)? Did your food habits originate in early childhood, in adolescence, or at some other time?

2. Go to a playground or other place where young children play. Note the motor skills that the children demonstrate, including abilities and inabilities, and keep track of age and sex. What differences do you see among the children? Does anything surprise you?

3. Ask several parents to describe each accidental injury of their children, particularly how it happened and what the consequences were. What primary, secondary, or tertiary prevention would have made a difference? What was the response of the parents and the medical community? What percent of the injuries were truly "accidents"—that is, unforeseeable events that could not have been prevented?

4. Describe the injuries you yourself have sustained, including injuries that resulted in stitches, broken bones, or scars. Could any of these injuries have been prevented?

adidas

Chapter Nine

The Play Years: Cognitive Development

Where do dreams come from? Most 3-year-olds say they come from somewhere outside your head (maybe God, or the sky, or your pillow), but almost all 5-year-olds know better—dreams come from your mind (Woolley & Boerger, 2002). Three-year-olds might not even know what their mind is!

That our understanding of dreams—and the mind—changes markedly at about age 4 is one of hundreds of discoveries about cognitive development between ages 2 and 6. Extensive research reveals that much learning occurs during early childhood. This learning includes not only more words and facts gained bit by bit, but also a qualitative leap, as children begin to understand how other people think and as language explodes.

Recently, dozens of adults on a subway train I was riding were captivated by a little girl, perhaps 3 years old, with sparkling eyes and many braids. She sat beside a large stranger, looking at her mother who stood about 6 feet to her left, holding onto a pole. The little girl repeatedly ducked her head behind the stranger and said, "You can't see me, Mama," unaware not only that her stockinged legs and shiny shoes stuck out in front of her but also that her whole body was constantly visible to her mother.

Like that little girl, every young child has much to learn. Among their developing ideas is a *theory of mind*, an understanding of how minds work (as in knowing that dreams do not come from your pillow or that your mother can sometimes see you when you cannot see her).

Since children learn so much from ages 2 to 6, developmentalists have gained a new respect for early schooling. No longer merely "day care," early education is now considered vital, whether it occurs at home or in a center. As one developmental psychologist explains:

> People often call this the "preschool period," but that's not only a mundane name for a magic time, it's also a misnomer. These three-ish and five-ish years are not a waiting time before school or even a time of preparation for school, but an age stage properly called "early childhood" that has a developmental agenda of its own.
>
> *[Leach, 1997, p. 431]*

This chapter explores that "developmental agenda." Two developmentalists, Jean Piaget and Lev Vygotsky (whose theories were introduced in Chapter 2 and discussed further in Chapter 6) are justly famous for their descriptions of cognition in early childhood. They agree more than they disagree: Young children are prodigious thinkers and learners. After considering the insights of Piaget and Vygotsky, we consider a more recent explanation of children's thought, called theory-theory.

The focus then is on learning language and attending school. The halting, simple sentences of the typical 2-year-old become the nonstop, complex outpourings of a talkative 6-year-old, explaining everything to everyone. Some young children learn to speak two or even three languages fluently, to understand numbers in sequence, and to comprehend other people's points of view. How and when does that happen? In this chapter, you will learn some answers.

Piaget: Children as Thinkers

preoperational thought Piaget's term for cognitive development between the ages of about 2 and 6, before logical, operational thinking becomes possible.

cognitive operation The process of organizing and evaluating thoughts in one's mind to come to a logical conclusion.

egocentrism Piaget's term for children's tendency to think about the world entirely from their own personal perspective.

For Piaget, early childhood is the second of four stages of cognition. He termed cognitive development between the ages of about 2 and 6 **preoperational thought.** Far more advanced than sensorimotor thought (reviewed in Chapter 6), preoperational thinking goes beyond senses and motor skills to include language, imagination, and other aspects of symbolic thought. Symbolic thought does not require visible, immediate objects but can use words, pretending, and other symbols to aid cognition. However, preoperational thinking also is magical and self-centered, with no room for the operations (or reasoning processes) of logic (Inhelder & Piaget, 1964). That is why it is called *pre*operational.

A **cognitive operation** involves organizing ideas and using them to come to some conclusion. This is easy to understand if you think about other uses of the word *operation.* To perform any operation is to work toward a desired result, as a surgeon operates on a patient or a worker operates a machine. Until about age 6 or 7, according to Piaget, children do not think *operationally;* that is, they cannot figure out logical ideas.

A major reason that logic is beyond young children is that they are severely and inevitably limited by their own perspective. To describe this limitation, Piaget used the word **egocentrism,** which literally means "self-centered." That label stuck, because many young children seem unable to consider other people's points of view. For instance, many 2- to 6-year-olds know that their mother is their mother, but they cannot grasp that their mother was once their grandmother's baby girl. Described below are four specific lapses of logic, all of which demonstrate what makes young children preoperational.

Obstacles to Logical Operations

centration A characteristic of preoperational thought in which a person focuses (centers) on one idea, excluding all others.

Centration is the tendency to focus on one aspect of a situation to the exclusion of all others. Young children may, for example, insist that lions and tigers are not cats because the children "center" on the house-pet aspect of the cats they know. Or they may insist that Daddy is a father, not a brother, because they center on the role that each family member fills for them.

The mommy and daddy examples both illustrate a particular type of centration, *ego-centration.* (As noted above, Piaget called it egocentrism.) Since egocentric children contemplate the world exclusively from their personal perspective, they center on their mother's or father's relationship to them, not on how the parent is related to his or her own parents or siblings.

Note that Piaget did not equate egocentrism with selfishness. For example, most young children will try to comfort a tearful adult, but comfort comes in a decidedly egocentric form, such as a teddy bear or a lollipop. Children offer the lollipop because it hasn't occurred to them that someone else's needs and responses might differ from their own. That is egocentrism.

Four Aspects of Preoperational Thought

1. Centration
2. Focus on appearance
3. Static reasoning
4. Irreversibility

As another example, two brothers, aged 7 and 3, were taken by their aunt to buy a birthday present for their mother. The 7-year-old selected a piece of jewelry, and the 3-year-old chose a model car, stubbornly and genuinely convinced that his mother would be delighted with this present. In fact, his "behavior was not selfish or greedy; he carefully wrapped the present and gave it to his mother with an expression that clearly showed that he expected her to love it" (Crain, 2005, p. 108).

A second characteristic of preoperational thought is a **focus on appearance** to the exclusion of other attributes. A girl given a short haircut might worry that she has turned into a boy. Or upon meeting a tall 4-year-old and a shorter 5-year-old, a child might insist that the taller child is the older one. The reason is that, in preoperational thought, a thing is whatever it appears to be.

focus on appearance A characteristic of preoperational thought in which a young child ignores all attributes that are not apparent.

Third, preoperational children use **static reasoning,** assuming that the world is unchanging, always in the state in which they currently encounter it. A young boy might be puzzled to meet his preschool teacher in the grocery store shopping for her family because he assumes that she is always a teacher and nothing else.

static reasoning Thinking that nothing changes: Whatever is now has always been and will ever be.

Because of static reasoning, whenever change occurs, it must occur totally and suddenly. When she awakened on her fifth birthday, my daughter Rachel asked, "Am I 5 yet?" Told yes, she grinned, stretched out her arms, and said, "Look at my 5-year-old hands." A poignant example comes from a child who was told that his parents were getting divorced. "I'll be an orphan," he said.

The fourth characteristic of preoperational thought is **irreversibility,** which means that preoperational thinkers fail to recognize that reversing a process sometimes restores whatever existed before the process occurred. A 3-year-old who cries because his mother put lettuce on his hamburger might not think to suggest removing the lettuce. Overwhelmed by his desire to have things "just right" (as explained in Chapter 8), he might reject the hamburger even after the lettuce is removed because he believes that what is done cannot be undone. If his mother takes the "contaminated" hamburger away, secretly removes the lettuce, and then brings back the "new" hamburger, the child might happily eat it.

irreversibility The idea that nothing can be undone; the failure to recognize that reversal sometimes restores something back to what existed before a change occurred.

conservation The idea that the amount of a substance remains the same (i.e., is conserved) when its appearance changes.

Conservation and Logic

Piaget devised many experiments to test and illustrate the ways in which these four preoperational characteristics—centration, focus on appearance, static reasoning, and irreversibility—limit young children's ability to reason logically. The most famous set of experiments involve the logical idea called **conservation,** the principle that the amount of a substance is conserved despite changes in its appearance. Piaget found that, because of their preoperational thinking, conservation is not at all obvious to young children (Inhelder & Piaget, 1964).

As an example, suppose two identical glasses contain the same amount of liquid. Then the liquid from one of the glasses is poured into a taller, narrower glass. If young children are asked whether one glass contains more liquid than

COURTESY OF KATHLEEN BERGER

Demonstration of Conservation
My youngest daughter, Sarah, here at age 5¾, demonstrates Piaget's conservation-of-volume experiment. First, she examines both short glasses to be sure they contain the same amount of milk. Then, after the contents of one are poured into the tall glass and she is asked "Which has more?", she points to the tall glass, just as Piaget would have expected. Later she added, "It looks like it has more because it's taller," indicating that some direct instruction might change her mind.

Tests of Various Types of Conservation

Type of Conservation	Initial Presentation	Transformation	Question	Preoperational Child's Answer
Volume	Two equal glasses of liquid.	Pour one into a taller, narrower glass.	Which glass contains more?	The taller one.
Number	Two equal lines of checkers.	Increase spacing of checkers in one line.	Which line has more checkers?	The longer one.
Matter	Two equal balls of clay.	Squeeze one ball into a long, thin shape.	Which piece has more clay?	The long one.
Length	Two sticks of equal length.	Move one stick.	Which stick is longer?	The one that is farther to the right.

FIGURE 9.1 **Conservation, Please** According to Piaget, until children grasp the concept of conservation at (he believed) about age 6 or 7, they cannot understand that the transformations shown here do not change the total amount of liquid, checkers, clay, and wood.

the other, they will insist that the narrower glass, with the higher liquid level, contains more. All four characteristics of preoperational thought are evident in this mistake. Young children fail to understand conservation of liquids because they focus (*center*) on what they see (*appearance*), noticing only the immediate (*static*) condition. It does not occur to them that they could reverse the process and re-create the liquid level of a moment earlier (*irreversibility*).

Similarly, to test conservation of number, an experimenter lines up seven pairs of checkers in two rows of equal length and asks a child if the rows have the same number of checkers. Preoperational children (ages 2 to 5) say "yes." As the child watches, the experimenter makes one of the rows longer by spacing its checkers farther apart. The experimenter asks again if the rows have the same number of checkers; most young children reply "no." Other conservation tasks, shown in Figure 9.1, produce similar results. Children are not logical, at least about conservation, until about age 7.

ESPECIALLY FOR AUNTS AND UNCLES It is a special family occasion, and you want to take presents to your nieces and nephews. What should you take?

Limitations of Piaget's Research

Notice that Piaget's tests of conservation require the child's words, not actions. When the tests of logic are simplified, children younger than 7 often succeed. For instance, other research has found that even 3-year-olds can distinguish appearance from reality if the test is nonverbal, as when children reach for objects rather than talk about them (Sapp et al., 2000). In many ways, children indicate that they know something via their gestures before they say it in words (Goldin-Meadow, 2000). Further, some young children demonstrate that they understand conservation and other logical ideas in a gamelike setting, although not in Piaget's experiments (Donaldson, 1979). For example, if a "naughty bear" rearranges one row of checkers, children know that the elongated line still has the same number as before.

Researchers now believe that Piaget underestimated conceptual ability during early childhood, just as he underestimated it during infancy (Flavell et al., 2002; Siegler, 1998). He designed his experiments to reveal what young children seemed *not* to understand, rather than to identify what they could understand, and he relied on the children's words in an experimental setting rather than nonverbal signs in a play context.

The same problem arises for other aspects of Piaget's experiments to distinguish preoperational thought from the next stage (which is called concrete operational because children then understand logical operations). For instance, Piaget thought that preoperational children cannot classify objects properly, in that they do not firmly grasp that dogs, cats, and cows are all kinds of animals. To some extent, Piaget was right: Many researchers have found that children are confused about the relationship between superordinate categories (such as animals), subcategories (such as dogs), and further subcategories (such as collies).

However, recent research finds that even 3-year-olds can classify things that they know well, such as foods, if the categories themselves are ones they often use (Nguyen & Murphy, 2003). Piaget was correct that young children do not think as logically as adults do, or even as operationally as older children do, but he did not realize how much children can understand.

SUMMING UP

Cognition develops rapidly from ages 2 to 6. Children's active search for understanding was first recognized by Piaget, who appreciated that young children use language to think symbolically, allowing them much more intellectual understanding than sensorimotor infants have. Piaget also realized that few children understand logical operations (which is why he called this period *preoperational*). Their egocentrism limits their understanding. They are preoperational because they center on only one thing at a time, they focus on appearance at the moment (static, not dynamic thinking), and they do not realize that what is done can sometimes be undone (irreversibility). Piaget's tests of preoperational thinking demonstrated what young children do not yet understand; other tests that are more child-friendly suggest that young children can be logical if the experiments are designed to reveal what they can do.

Vygotsky: Children as Learners

According to Vygotsky (1978), many adults make the same mistake that Piaget did: They note what children cannot do rather than helping them learn what they can. It is undeniable that young children's thinking is often magical and self-centered. For many years, this aspect of cognition dominated developmentalists' descriptions of early childhood, with Piaget the most famous proponent.

Vygotsky was the first leading developmentalist to emphasize a second aspect of early cognition: Young children are not always egocentric; they can be very responsive to the wishes and emotions of others. In fact, young children learn from others and from their culture even when people wish children would not notice, much less repeat, certain things. Many adults find that their offhand criticism of an in-law reappears in their child's words directly addressed to the offending (and offended) relative. The adult's embarrassment is a reminder of how observant children are and how quickly they learn the content, if not the social propriety, of various remarks.

A poignant example of memory for social experiences is evident when a young child's play includes explicit sexual references or evidence of abuse—telltale indicators that something has happened that the child should never have experienced. Adults should not jump to conclusions too quickly: Spanking a "bad dolly," showing sexual curiosity, or repeating things seen on television is normal. However, if a child hits a doll with a belt or pretends to have intercourse, abuse should be suspected.

Children as Apprentices

Vygotsky believed that every aspect of children's cognitive development is embedded in a social context (Vygotsky, 1935/1978). Children are curious and observant. They ask questions—about how machines work, why weather changes, where the sky ends—assuming that others know the answers.

apprentice in thinking A person whose cognition is stimulated and directed by older and more skilled members of society.

In many ways, a child is what Vygotsky called an **apprentice in thinking,** someone whose intellectual growth is stimulated and directed by older and more skilled members of society. In the most developed nations, with families of one or two children, parents and child-care providers are usually the teachers. In some early-childhood education programs, learning from "more capable peers" is central (Thompson, 2002). In less developed nations, older siblings often play a particularly important educational role (Maynard, 2002; Rogoff, 2003).

guided participation The process by which people learn from others who guide their experiences and explorations.

According to Vygotsky, children learn because their elders actively guide cognitive growth:

- Presenting challenges
- Offering assistance (not taking over)
- Providing instruction
- Encouraging motivation

The process of apprenticeship involves working beside the more skilled person, as the apprentices of old worked to assist the master blacksmith, cobbler, or silversmith. With the help of their mentors, children learn to think by means of their **guided participation** in social experiences and in explorations of their universe, with both participants talking as well as acting. For example, children learning to draw or write or dance are quite willing to copy from one another. A child who is copied is not resentful (as an adult might be if another adult copied) but appreciates the recognition.

The reality that children are curious about everything, learning and remembering whatever they experience, is evidence of cognition. The ability to learn (not the measure of what is known) indicates intelligence. Vygotsky (1978) said: "What children can do with the assistance of others might be in some sense even more indicative of their mental development than what they can do alone" (p. 5).

Guided Participation Through shared social activity, adults in every culture guide the development of their children's cognition, values, and skills. Typically, the child's curiosity and interests, rather than the adult's planning for some sort of future need, motivate the process. That seems to be the case as this Guatemalan girl eagerly tries to learn her mother's sewing skills.

DAVE BARTRUFF / STOCK, BOSTON

How to Solve a Puzzle

Here is a practical example of Vygotsky's approach. Suppose a child tries to assemble a jigsaw puzzle, fails, and stops trying. Does that mean the task is beyond the child? Not according to Vygotsky. Could someone else guide the child toward a solution?

An adult or older child might begin by praising the child for choosing a hard puzzle and then might encourage the child to look for a particular missing piece ("Does it need to be a big piece or a little piece?" "Do you see any blue pieces with a line of red?"). Suppose the child finds some pieces of the right size and color but still seems stymied. The tutor might become more directive, selecting a piece to be tried next, or rotating a piece so that its proper location is obvious, or actually putting a piece in place with a smile of satisfaction. Throughout, the tutor praises success, maintains enthusiasm, and helps the child recognize progress.

The level of difficulty must challenge but not overwhelm. If the puzzle is too hard, the mentor puts it aside with reassurance ("Let's do this one after your next birthday") and selects an easier one. Motivation is crucial ("Look, this one has a dog like your dog"). The same strategies are used in all forms of guided participation, from exploring ideas to building towers of blocks.

The crucial element in guided participation is the interaction between the partners, with the tutor sensitive and responsive to the precise needs of the learner. Eventually, as a result, children become able to succeed independently—the ultimate goal of Vygotsky's "apprenticeship in thinking."

Scaffolding

As you saw in Chapter 2, Vygotsky believed that for each developing individual, there is a **zone of proximal development (ZPD),** which includes skills that the person can perform with assistance but cannot quite perform independently. How and when children master their potential skills depends, in part, on the willingness of others to provide **scaffolding,** or sensitive structuring, for children's participation in learning. Most caregivers do this, teaching children to look both ways before crossing a street (while holding the child's hand), letting them stir the batter for a cake (perhaps stirring a few times themselves to make sure the ingredients are well mixed).

zone of proximal development (ZPD) Vygotsky's term for the skills that a person can exercise with assistance but not yet independently. ZPD applies to the ideas or cognitive skills a person is close to mastering as well as to more apparent skills.

scaffolding Temporary support provided to help a learner master the next task in a given learning process.

Scaffolding is particularly important for experiences that are directly cognitive. For example, adults reading to 3-year-olds usually provide excellent scaffolding—explaining, pointing, listening—toward the child's ZPD in response to the child's needs at the moment (Danis et al., 2000). The sensitive reader would never tell the child to be quiet and listen but might instead prolong the session by asking the child questions. Frequent (at least once a day) joint reading at age 2 predicts literacy at age 7, because the scaffolding aids language development (Pellegrini & Galda, 1998).

Siblings can also provide scaffolding. In one study in Chiapas, Mexico, 8-year-old Tonik taught his 2-year-old sister, Katal, how to wash a doll. After several minutes of demonstrating and describing, Tonik continues:

> **Tonik:** Pour it like this. *(Demonstrates)*
> **Tonik:** Sister, pour it. *(Hands glass)*
> **Tonik:** Look! Pour it.
> **Katal:** *(Pours, with some difficulty)*
> **Tonik:** Like that. *(Approval)*
> **Katal:** *(Looks away)*
> **Tonik:** It's finished now.
>
> *[quoted in Maynard, 2002, p. 977]*

Note that when Katal looked away, Tonik wisely declared the session finished. Such a response, not criticism, encourages the learner to participate in later apprenticeships. Motivation is crucial in early education—one reason that sensitive social interaction is so powerful.

RESPONSE FOR AUNTS AND UNCLES (from page 256): Remember that preschool children focus on appearances and are egocentric. Whatever you give a 2- to 5-year-old must be seen as equal to any present you give another child. Thus, you would choose identical gifts (perhaps markers, toys, or articles of clothing), so that no child can compare presents and decide that you love another child more.

Language as a Tool

Vygotsky believed that words are used to build the scaffold, enabling cognition to develop. Just as a builder could not construct a house without tools (even though, once the house is built, the tools are no longer apparent), so a child's mind does not develop without language, even though the words are not apparent once the neurological connections are established. According to Vygotsky, talking, listening, reading, and writing are all tools to advance thought.

private speech The internal dialogue that occurs when people talk to themselves (either silently or out loud).

social mediation A function of speech by which a person's cognitive skills are refined and extended through both formal instruction and casual conversation.

During early childhood, language is essential to intellectual growth in two ways. First, internal dialogue, or **private speech**, occurs when people talk to themselves. Private speech helps people develop new ideas (Vygotsky, 1987). Young children use private speech often, typically talking out loud. They review what they know, decide what to do, and explain events to themselves (and, incidentally, to anyone else within earshot). Older preschoolers use private speech more selectively and effectively than younger ones, sometimes in a whisper or even without any audible sound (Winsler et al., 2000). Adults use private speech, too, but not usually out loud if anyone else is nearby.

The second way in which language advances thinking, according to Vygotsky, is as the *mediator of the social interaction* that is vital to learning. This **social mediation** function of speech occurs during both formal instruction and casual conversation. Both private speech and social mediation refine and extend cognitive skills. Language allows children to enter and traverse their ZPD, because words are a bridge from current understanding toward what is almost understood. This idea—that language is a conceptual tool—is accepted by many developmentalists (e.g., Gelman, 2003; Pellegrini & Galda, 1998).

Language used in social mediation is particularly apparent in the development of an understanding of numbers, memories, and routines. Among the major differences between younger children and 5-year-olds is that the latter can count objects, assigning one number to each item (called one-to-one correspondence, rare in younger children), can remember accurately (although children may become confused by false memories), and can verbalize scripts (such as the usual scenario for a birthday party or a restaurant meal).

Researchers are convinced that the social context, particularly parental instruction and verbal encouragement, is crucial for all these cognitive accomplishments (e.g., Hubbs-Tait et al., 2002; Mix et al., 2002). Thus, although children reach sufficient neurological maturity to comprehend the concepts of numbers, memories, and routines by age 3 or 4, whether or not a child actually demonstrates them depends on family, school, and culture. Language is a key mediator between brain potential and what children actually understand and remember (Haden et al., 2001; Schneider & Pressley, 1997).

In one experiment in Australia that verified the role of language, children aged 3 to 6 performed 26 activities with 30 toy props in a pretend zoo (e.g., putting a ribbon on a toy giraffe's tail) (McGuigan & Salmon, 2004). They were exposed to one of four possible language conditions: (1) "empty speech" that was irrelevant to the zoo, (2) speech before the experience that described what would happen, (3) a running descriptive dialogue during the experience, or (4) a description two days later of what had occurred. Each child's memory for 26 actions and 30 props was tested two weeks later.

Empty speech was least helpful: Children who had experiences but heard no words about them were most likely to forget. Talking about the experiences aided memory, especially if the child also spoke about what had occurred. Although specific talk before, during, or after the event was better than empty speech, as Vygotsky's concept of social mediation would predict, children benefited especially from talk *after* the event (McGuigan & Salmon, 2004). Note the similarity between this study and the research on reminder sessions for kicking infants that you read about in Chapter 6 (Rovee-Collier & Hayne, 1987). Review helps memory, probably lifelong.

This research has one very practical application. When children are abused or they observe someone else being hurt or killed, they can give accurate accounts of what they have witnessed. However, their memory is affected by the language and tone of the questions (Bruck & Ceci, 2004). If, after a crime, an adult describes one possibility and then asks if that happened, children tend to agree. Later they may remember the adult's description as true, even if it was

TABLE 9.1 Comparing Piaget and Vygotsky

Piaget	Vygotsky
Learning Process	
Active Learning	**Guided Participation**
The child's own search for understanding, motivated by the child's inborn curiosity.	The mentor's aid in guiding the next step of learning, motivated by the learner's need for social interaction.
Nature of Child	
Egocentric	**Apprentice**
The preschooler's tendency to perceive everything from his or her own perspective and to be limited by that viewpoint.	The preschooler's tendency to look to others for insight and guidance, particularly in the cognitive realm.
Components	
Structure	**Scaffold**
The mental assumptions and scenarios the child creates to help him or her organize an understanding of the world. Structures are torn down and rebuilt when disequilibrium makes new structures necessary.	The building blocks for learning put in place by a "teacher" (a more knowledgeable child or adult) or a culture. Learners use scaffolds and then discard them when they are no longer needed.

not. People of all ages are affected by biased questioning, but young children are most vulnerable of all, especially if the questioner is stern (as a judge may be). This means that child eyewitnesses need to be carefully and gently questioned and must never be led to believe, and later to testify to, something that might not be true.

The theories of Piaget and Vygotsky are "compatible in many ways" (Rogoff, 1998, p. 681). Each perspective supplements the other (see Table 9.1). Young children are sometimes egocentric and sometimes socially aware. They are always eager to learn.

SUMMING UP

Vygotsky emphasized the social and cultural aspects of children's cognition. He believed that children become much less egocentric if they are properly guided within their zones of proximal development. According to Vygotsky, parents, siblings, peers, and other mentors are aides to young children's apprenticeship in learning. Language facilitates the interaction of child and mentor in social mediation, as language becomes the tool that combines the child's curiosity and the mentor's knowledge. Young children also use private speech, talking to themselves to consolidate what they are learning.

Children's Theories

Among the commonalities in both Piaget's and Vygotsky's theories of early childhood is that children actively try to understand their world. Several psychologists have recently attempted to show exactly what children bring to their acquisition of knowledge. Apparently they bring a drive to explain what they experience, seeking to know why and how various events occur. If no one provides explanations that they find satisfying, they develop their own answers.

The finding that children seek explanations is recognized by every developmentalist, every preschool teacher, and every parent: Young children ask about whatever fascinates or confuses them. Children are active, not passive, thinkers; they are agents who react to their perceptions, not passive recipients of sensations (Bloom & Tinker, 2001; Brandtstädter, 1998).

Theory-Theory

theory-theory The idea that children attempt to explain everything they see and hear by constructing theories.

One theory of cognitive development begins with this human drive to develop theories, a drive especially apparent in early childhood. Some use the term **theory-theory** to refer to the theory that children construct theories to explain everything they see and hear:

> More than any animal, we search for causal regularities in the world around us. We are perpetually driven to look for deeper explanations of our experience, and broader and more reliable predictions about it. . . . Children seem, quite literally, to be born with . . . the desire to understand the world and the desire to discover how to behave in it.
>
> *[Gopnik, 2001, p. 66]*

Thus, according to theory-theory, the best conceptualization of, and explanation for, mental processes in young children is that humans always seek reasons, causes, and underlying principles. Figure 9.2, with its narrative-style "recipe," captures the essential idea of theory-theory: that children don't want logical definitions but rather explanations of various things, especially things that involve them.

Exactly how does this occur in early childhood? In one study, Mexican American parents kept detailed diaries of every question their 3- to 5-year-olds asked that could be considered a request for an explanation (Keleman et al.,

FIGURE 9.2 **Unfold the Turkey** This recipe (from *Smashed Potatoes,* edited by Jane Martel) shows many characteristics of preschool thought, among them literal interpretation of words ("Sometimes you can call it a bird, but it's not") and an uncertain idea of time ("Push in the stuffin' for a couple hours") and quantity ("A giant lump of stuffin'").

A whole turkey

1 big bag full of a whole turkey (Get the kind with no feathers on, not the kind the Pilgrims ate.)
A giant lump of stuffin'
1 squash pie
1 mint pie
1 little fancy dish of sour berries
1 big fancy dish of a vegetable mix
20 dishes of all different candies; chocolate balls, cherry balls, good'n plenties and peanuts

Get up when the alarm says to and get busy fast. Unfold the turkey and open up the holes. Push in the stuffin' for a couple of hours. I think you get stuffin' from that Farm that makes it.

I know you have to pin the stuffin' to the turkey or I suppose it would get out. And get special pins or use big long nails.

Get the kitchen real hot, and from there on you just cook turkey. Sometimes you can call it a bird, but it's not.

Then you put the vegetables in the cooker—and first put one on top, and next put one on the bottom, and then one in the middle. That makes a vegetable mix. Put 2 red things of salt all in it and 2 red things of water also. Cook them to just ½ of warm.

Put candies all around the place and Linda will bring over the pies. When the company comes put on your red apron.

2005). They also noted whether and how they answered. The children averaged about 1 question per day, with a range over two weeks of 2 to 60 questions.

Generally, younger children asked more questions than older children, and more educated parents heard (or recorded) more questions. As Figure 9.3 shows, most of the questions were about human behavior—specifically, the reasons people do things, such as "Why do you give my mother a kiss?" and "Why is my brother bad?" Questions that concerned the biology of living things were also common, such as "Why do women have breasts?" and "Why are there Black kids?" There were fewer questions about nonliving natural things ("Why does it rain?") or objects ("Why is my daddy's car white?").

The questions children asked demonstrated that they wondered about many things. Many questions were teleological, referring to the study of the underlying design or purpose in various natural phenomena. Parents in this study (most of whom were religious) sometimes ignored the questions and, when they did answer, usually responded as if the children wanted to know about scientific causality, not about teleology. For example, children who asked why women have breasts were more often told about hormones and maturation than that breasts are for feeding babies. A child who asked why his brother was bad was likely to be told that what his brother did was bad (for instance, he broke a toy), whereas a more satisfying answer would have been why the brother was angry or jealous.

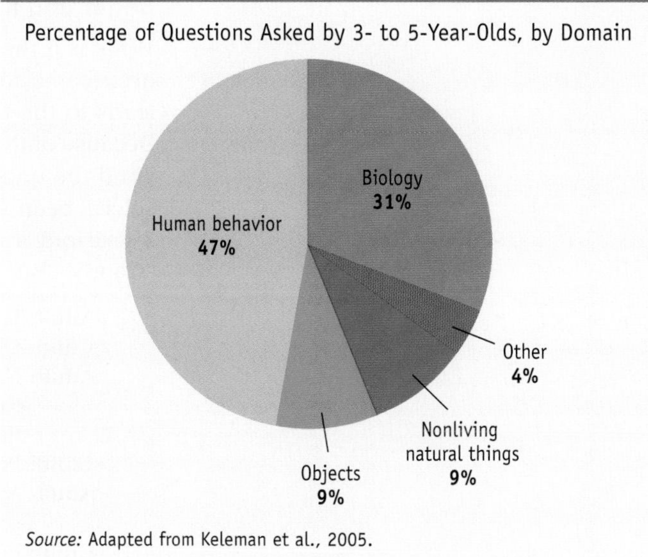

FIGURE 9.3 **Questions, Questions** Parents found that most of their children's questions were about human behavior—especially the parents' behavior toward the child. Children seek to develop a theory to explain things, so the question "Why can't I have some candy?" is not satisfactorily answered by "It's almost dinnertime."

Piaget noted the same phenomenon, pointing out that children seek explanations, not direct causes (Piaget, 1929), although he focused on the egocentric nature of the child. Thus, a child who asks why her parents are getting divorced might be told that the parents no longer love each other, but in egocentrism the child might secretly infer that the parents no longer love her. Similarly, a child told that his grandmother died because she had cancer might conclude, instead, that Grandma died because God wanted her or because Grandma was upset at him.

This insight is useful for parents who feel beleaguered by their child's "why" questions. Children do not mean "What is the scientific, logical reason or definition of this?" More likely, they mean "What is the purpose of this in my small universe?" Adults rarely provide explanations that scaffold a sophisticated view of human behavior, which is one reason that children, on their own, seem slow to understand how other people think.

Theory of Mind

Human mental processes—thoughts, emotions, beliefs, motives, and intentions—are among the most complicated and puzzling phenomena in a young person's world. Whether trying to understand a playmate's unexpected anger, to determine when a sibling will be generous, or to avoid an aunt's too-wet kiss, children want to understand and predict what goes on in another person's mind. To do so, they develop a kind of "folk psychology," an understanding of human mental processes called **theory of mind.**

theory of mind A person's theory of what other people might be thinking. In order to have a theory of mind, children must realize that other people are not necessarily thinking the same thoughts that they themselves are. Such a realization is seldom possible before age 4.

Theory of mind is evident when young children grasp something about how other people think; this is "an important intellectual change at about 4 years" (Perner, 2000, p. 396). This awareness typically occurs rather suddenly, the result of insight more than of accumulated knowledge (Wellman et al., 2001). Both maturation and social experience are factors in this development, so theory of mind can be seen as evidence for the theories of both Piaget and Vygotsky.

Belief and Reality: Understanding the Difference

What is it that children suddenly understand? Between the ages of 3 and 6, children come to realize that mental phenomena may not reflect reality. This idea leads to the theory-of-mind concept that individuals can believe untrue things. Because of this, people can be deliberately deceived or fooled—an idea that is beyond the understanding of most younger children, even when they have themselves been deceived. Consider an experiment in which an adult shows a 3-year-old a candy box and asks, "What is inside?" The child says, naturally, "Candy." But, in fact, the child has been tricked:

Adult: Let's open it and look inside.
Child: Oh . . . holy moly . . . pencils!
Adult: Now I'm going to put them back and close it up again. *(Does so)* Now . . . when you first saw the box, before we opened it, what did you think was inside it?
Child: Pencils.
Adult: Nicky [friend of the child] hasn't seen inside this box. When Nicky comes in and sees it . . . what will he think is inside it?
Child: Pencils.

[adapted from Astington & Gopnik, 1988, p. 195]

Especially for Social Scientists
Can you think of any connection between Piaget's theory of preoperational thought and 3-year-olds' errors in this theory-of-mind task?

This experiment has become a classic, performed with thousands of children from many cultures. When it is replicated exactly, 3-year-olds almost always make the same mistake. They seem to confuse belief and reality, and this "realist bias" makes it difficult for them to remember ever having believed something that contradicts what they now see (Mitchell & Kikuno, 2000). Another way of describing this is to say that they are "cursed" by their own knowledge (Birch & Bloom, 2003) and are too egocentric to grasp other perspectives.

As a result, until about age 4, children are notoriously bad at fooling other people. They play hide-and-seek by hiding in the same place time after time, or they signify the truth when they try to tell a fib. Their understanding of what other people might think or believe is very limited, although some research finds that they can figure out strategies to trick someone else by age 3, a year younger than the age at which they can realize that they themselves have been tricked (Hala & Chandler, 1996).

Closely related to their lack of awareness regarding their own thought processes is their inability to change their minds, recognizing that they thought one thing and now must think another. With static thinking (one of the characteristics of preoperational thought), changing one's mind is very difficult.

This is shown by another often-repeated experiment, in which children are asked to sort pictures of two shapes (such as apples and pears) in two colors (such as red and green) (Zelazo et al., 1996). When asked to sort by color, 3-year-olds correctly put the red apples and red pears together in one pile and the green apples and green pears in another. If they are initially asked to sort by shape, they usually succeed as well, putting apples (red or green) in one pile and pears (red or green) in another. But when asked to sort first one way (say, by color) and then the other way (by shape), few 3-year-olds can make the switch. The basics of this experiment have been replicated in many nations; 3-year-olds everywhere get stuck on their initial sorting pattern and seem unable to switch (Diamond & Kirkham, 2005).

Curiously, once children have developed a theory of mind (as demonstrated by traditional experiments), usually they can also successfully switch categories when sorting these cards (Kloo & Perner, 2003). However, even adults hesitate a bit before doing this task correctly, which suggests that the tendency toward the initial error that 3-year-olds make never entirely disappears (Diamond & Kirkham, 2005). It is not known whether this also means that adults are more likely to realize that someone else has been fooled than that they themselves have been deceived.

Contextual Influences

Recently, developmentalists have asked what, precisely, strengthens theory of mind at about age 4. Is it nature or nurture, brain maturation or experience?

Neurological maturation is a plausible explanation. In one study, 68 children aged 2½ to 5½ were presented with four standard theory-of-mind situations, including a Band-Aid box that really contained pencils (similar to the candy-box experiment described earlier) (Jenkins & Astington, 1996). More than one-third of the children succeeded at all four tasks (for example, they understood that someone else might initially believe, as they had, that the Band-Aid box would contain Band-Aids), more than one-third failed at three or four tasks, and the rest were in transition. Age had a very powerful effect: The 5-year-olds were most likely to succeed on all tasks, the 4-year-olds had middling success, and the 3-year-olds were most likely to fail every time.

This age-related advance suggests that maturation of the brain's prefrontal cortex (the location of the executive function, which usually reaches a new level at about age 4) is the crucial factor (Perner et al., 2002). Further evidence that brain maturation is a prerequisite for theory of mind is the fact that impaired brain functioning is the most likely cause of autism (see Chapter 11), and many autistic children are advanced in numerical understanding but slow to develop theory of mind (Baron-Cohen, 1995).

General language ability also appears to be significant: The greater a child's verbal proficiency (at any age), the more likely he or she is to have a theory of mind (Astington & Jenkins, 1999; de Villiers & de Villiers, 2000). Language ability may be partly the result of maturation of particular areas of the brain, but it is also the result of language experience, especially mother–child conversations that involve thoughts and wishes, not just facts (Ruffman et al., 2002).

The importance of language for theory of mind is apparent in profoundly deaf children who are not taught sign language as babies. They cannot complete theory-of-mind tasks until age 8 or later (Lundy, 2002).

© PUNCHSTOCK

Road Rage? From their expressions, it looks as if this brother and sister may crash their toy jeep and cry, each blaming the other for the mishap. But a benefit of such sibling interactions is that they can advance theory of mind by helping the child realize that people do not always think the same way.

When the effects of both age and language ability are accounted for, a third important factor emerges: having at least one older brother or sister (Jenkins & Astington, 1996). One researcher estimates that, in theory-of-mind development, "two older siblings are worth about a year of chronological age" (Perner, 2000, p. 383). The arguing, agreeing, competing, and cooperating that siblings normally do apparently lead children to understand that their own thinking is not shared by everyone.

Before concluding that maturation, with help from language and siblings, produces theory of mind at age 4, consider one more study (Vinden, 1996). All the 4- to 8-year-olds in a remote village in the mountains of Peru were tested on a culturally appropriate version of the candy-box experiment—in this case, a sugar bowl that contained tiny potatoes. The children at first thought the bowl contained sugar, as anyone from that village would. But many of these children, even some 8-year-olds, failed theory-of-mind questions: They could not explain why someone would initially expect sugar to be in a sugar bowl and then be surprised to discover potatoes instead.

In the Peruvians' mountainous, isolated village, "there is no reason or time for elaborate deception . . . subsistence farmers, working from dawn to dusk just to survive . . . , live mostly on the landscape of action, and not on the landscape of consciousness" (Vinden, 1996, p. 1715). Neither their language nor their culture recognizes false belief or "how people's thoughts might affect their actions." Thus, culture may be a fourth crucial factor in the development of theory of mind (Lillard, 1998; Vinden, 1996).

Response for Social Scientists (from page 264): According to Piaget, preschool children focus on appearance and on static conditions (so they cannot mentally reverse a process). Further, they are egocentric, believing that everyone shares their point of view. No wonder they believe that they had always known that the candy box held pencils and that their friend would know that, too.

A study comparing theory of mind among young children in preschools in Canada, Peru, India, and Samoa found that the Canadian children were slightly ahead and the Samoan children were slightly behind, but virtually all of them passed the false-belief tests by age 5. Note that all these children were in preschool, so they had the benefit of social interaction as well as language. The researchers who compared these cultures concluded that brain maturation is the primary factor in theory of mind, with language development a secondary influence (Callahan et al., 2005).

To refer again to Piaget and Vygotsky, the child's own logic and maturation are important (Piaget), but language, social interaction, and culture are important mediators (Vygotsky) once brain structures are in place. In most cultures, "a certain amount of experience living and participating in conversation" occurs by age 3, making theory of mind possible (Callahan et al., 2005).

SUMMING UP

Scholars have recently noted that children develop theories to explain whatever they observe, theories that do not necessarily spring from explanations given to them by adults. Children seem to be much more interested in the underlying purpose of events within the grand scheme of life; adults are more focused on the immediate scientific causes of events. Many researchers have explored the development of theory of mind, the understanding that other people can have thoughts and ideas that are unlike one's own. Neurological maturation, linguistic competence, family context, and culture all affect the attainment of theory of mind at about age 4.

Language

Language is pivotal to cognition in early childhood, as we have seen in the examples of Vygotsky's social mediation and the development of theory of mind. Language is also the leading cognitive accomplishment during these years, with 24-month-old children beginning this period with short sentences and limited vocabulary and 6-year-olds ending this stage with the ability to understand and discuss almost anything (see Table 9.2).

Maturation and myelination in particular areas of the brain, and the fact that language is needed for social interaction of all kinds, make ages 2 to 6 the prime time for learning language. Indeed, some scientists once thought that these years were a **critical period**, the only time when a first language could be mastered and by far the best time for learning any language. Some thought that, if grammar and pronunciation were not learned in early childhood, the necessary brain neurons and synapses would wither and language would never be mastered (Lenneberg, 1967; Scovel, 1988). This hypothesis has been disproved. Humans can and do master language after early childhood. Millions of people learn second languages after age 6 and even after puberty (Bialystok, 2001; Hakuta et al., 2003).

critical period A time when a certain development *must* happen if it is ever to happen. For example, the period of the embryo is critical for the growth of arms and legs. It was once thought that early childhood was a critical period for learning language, but today it is considered a *sensitive period*.

sensitive period A time when a certain type of development is most likely to happen and when it happens most easily. For example, early childhood is considered to be a sensitive period for language learning.

The earlier scholars were not completely mistaken, however. Although not a critical period, early childhood does seem to be a **sensitive period** for many language skills, a time when vocabulary, grammar, and pronunciation are rapidly and easily learned. Young children are sometimes called "language sponges" because they soak up every drop of language they encounter.

One reason early childhood is a sensitive period for language lies in the developing brain; the dendrites and neurological areas for language learning grow rapidly during these years (Leonard, 2003). The social context is crucial as well. As you read earlier, young children are powerfully motivated to be social: They want to communicate, and they are not embarrassed to be wrong.

TABLE 9.2 AT ABOUT THIS TIME: **Language in Early Childhood**

Approximate Age	Characteristic or Achievement
2 years	Vocabulary: 100–2,000 words Sentence length: 2–6 words Grammar: Plurals, pronouns, many nouns, verbs, adjectives Questions: Many "What's that?" questions
3 years	Vocabulary: 1,000–5,000 words Sentence length: 3–8 words Grammar: Conjunctions, adverbs, articles Questions: Many "Why?" questions
4 years	Vocabulary: 3,000–10,000 words Sentence length: 5–20 words Grammar: Dependent clauses, tags at ends of sentences ("... didn't I?" "... won't you?") Questions: Peak of "Why?" questions; also many "How?" and "When?" questions
5 years	Vocabulary: 5,000–20,000 words Sentence length: Some seem unending ("... and ... who ... and ... that ... and ...") Grammar: Complex, sometimes using passive voice ("Man bitten by dog"); subjunctive ("If I were ...") Questions: Include some about differences (male/female, old/young, rich/poor)

The Urge to Communicate Language depends heavily on social context. Frequent one-on-one conversations with an adult are the main reason one 5-year-old's vocabulary can be four times bigger than another's.

For those reasons, young children talk a lot—to adults, to each other, to themselves, to their toys—unfazed by their mispronunciation, misuse, stuttering, or other impediments to fluency (unless someone else teases them about it). Note a crucial developmental asset here. Language comes more easily to young children because, unlike most older children and adults, they are not inhibited by the possibility of making mistakes in a new language, so they get lots of practice.

MICHAEL WICKES / THE IMAGE WORKS

What's That? By far the best way for a parent to teach a young child new vocabulary is by reading aloud. Ideally, the interaction should be a very social one, with much pointing and talking, as this Idaho pair demonstrate. If such experiences are part of her daily routine, this little girl not only will develop language but also will be among the first of her classmates to learn how to read.

Vocabulary

In early childhood, new words are added rapidly. The average child knows about 500 words at age 2 and more than 10,000 at age 6. One scholar says that 2- to 6-year-olds learn 10 words a day (Clark, 1995); another estimates one new word added every two waking hours from about age 2 to age 20 (Pinker, 1994). The naming explosion (explained in Chapter 6) is overtaken by a more general explosion, with new verbs, adjectives, adverbs, and conjunctions as well as many more nouns mastered during early childhood.

Precise estimates of new vocabulary vary because learning contexts are diverse; the estimates above are probably higher than the worldwide average. However, all researchers agree that vocabulary builds quickly by age 7 and that most children are capable of learning far more language than they do.

Fast-Mapping

How does the vocabulary explosion occur? After painstakingly learning one word at a time at age 1, children develop an interconnected set of categories for words, a kind of grid or mental map, which makes speedy vocabulary acquisition possible. The process is called **fast-mapping** (Woodward & Markman, 1998) because, rather than figuring out an exact definition by waiting until a word is used in several contexts, children hear a word once and stick it on a mental language map.

fast-mapping The speedy and imprecise way in which children learn new words by mentally charting them into categories according to their meaning.

Language mapping is not always precise. In this it is similar to most people's mental map of the world. Thus, when asked where Nepal is, most people can locate it approximately ("in Asia"), but few can locate it exactly, citing each border. Nepal is mapped in your mind, but not exactly. Similarly, children quickly learn new animal names, for instance, because they are mapped in the brain close to already-known animal names. Thus, "animals" is one category, making *tiger* easy to map if you already know *lion*. One trip to the zoo usually facilitates fast-mapping of dozens of words, especially since zoos scaffold vocabulary by placing similar animals together.

The benefit of knowing at least one word of a category, to allow other words to be fast-mapped in that region, is evident in one classic experiment. A preschool teacher taught a new color word by saying, "Give me the chromium tray, not the red one" (Carey, 1985). Those children who already knew at least one color word quickly grasped the new word *chromium*, demonstrating that they remembered it more than a week later. In other words, if they had the general concept that things have color and that each color has a name, they just fast-mapped *chromium* near *red*. Those children who knew no color words did not remember the new word (a week later, they could not select a chromium object) because they were unable to map it (Mandler, 2004).

Generally, the more linguistic clues to the meaning of a new word children already have, the better their fast-mapping is (Mintz, 2005). To increase vocabulary, parents should have frequent and elaborate conversations with each child (Hoff & Naigles, 2002). Alas, preschoolers can also map words their parents would rather they not know, as I learned the hard way.

In Person

Fast-Mapping: Mommy the Brat

Fast-mapping has an obvious benefit: It fosters quick acquisition of vocabulary. However, it also means that children *seem* to know words merely because they use them when, in actuality, their understanding of the words is quite limited. One common example is the word *big*, which even 2-year-olds use and apparently understand. In fact, however, young children often use *big* when they mean *tall* or *old* or *great* ("My love is so big!") and only gradually come to use *big* correctly (Sena & Smith, 1990).

When adults realize that children often do not fully comprehend the meanings of words they use, it becomes easier to understand—and forgive—the mistakes children make. I still vividly recall an incident that stemmed from fast-mapping when my youngest daughter, then 4, was furious at me.

Sarah had apparently fast-mapped several insulting words into her vocabulary. However, her fast-mapping did not provide precise definitions or reflect nuances. In her anger, she called me first a "mean witch" and then a "brat." I smiled at her innocent imprecision, knowing the first was fast-mapped from fairy tales and the second from comments she got from her older sisters. Neither label bothered me, as I don't believe in witches and my brother is the only person who can appropriately call me a brat.

But then Sarah let loose an X-rated epithet that sent me reeling. Struggling to contain my anger, I tried to convince myself that fast-mapping had left her with no real idea of what she had just said. "That word is never to be used in this family!" I sputtered. My appreciation of the speed of fast-mapping was deepened by her response: "Then how come Rachel [her older sister] called me that this morning?"

Logic and Words

Closely related to fast-mapping is logical extension: After learning a word, children use it to describe other objects in the same category. One child told her father she had seen some Dalmatian cows on a school trip to a farm. He understood her because he remembered that she had petted a Dalmatian dog the weekend before. Children use their available vocabulary to cover all the territory they want to talk about (Behrend et al., 2001). As they approach school age, they use logic to figure out what words mean—for instance, deciding that butter comes from butterflies and birds grow from bird seed.

Of course, even the fastest language learners must hear a new word at least once, in a context that allows mapping, and their conversation partners are their guides. An experiment in teaching the names of parts of objects (e.g., the spigot of a faucet) found that children learned much better if the adults named the object that had the part, and then spoke of the part in the possessive (e.g., "See this butterfly? Look, this is its thorax") (Saylor & Sabbagh, 2004). This shows that the precise manner of presenting a new word affects the likelihood that a child will learn that word.

The vocabulary-building process occurs so quickly that, by age 5, some children seem to understand and use almost any term they hear. In fact, 5-year-olds *can* learn any word or phrase if it is explained with specific examples using known words and if the context allows them to figure out what the word means. A teacher (who had been my student) asked her preschoolers what they had done over the weekend. Most children had standard answers—watched television, went to church, shopped for groceries—but one child answered: "I went to a protest." "What is a protest?" another child asked. "A lot of people get together, walk around, and yell," the first child replied, revealing her concept of what had occurred. The second child nodded, mapping *protest* into her vocabulary.

BANANASTOCK / PICTUREQUEST

Fangs for the Memories Museums, zoos, parks, farms, factories—all provide abundant opportunities for vocabulary building and concept formation. These parents may be teaching their children not only *mountain lion* but also *habitat, carnivore,* and *incisors*.

Young children cannot accurately comprehend every word they hear, although, as this example shows, they try to do so. An adult would provide quite a different definition of *protest,* for example. For young children, abstract nouns and metaphors are especially difficult because there is no concrete referent. Fast-mapping is logical and literal, allowing only one meaning per word or phrase. When I was a child in the car with my mother, I cried when she said, "I killed my engine."

Another child took the phrase *live with* literally, meaning "reside in the same home." This explains the child's response upon being scolded for jumping on the bed.

Mother: Stop. You'll hurt yourself.
Child: No I won't. (*Still jumping*)
Mother: You'll break the bed.
Child: No I won't. (*Still jumping*)
Mother: OK. You'll just have to live with the consequences.
Child: (*Stops jumping*) I'm not going to live with the consequences. I don't even know them.

[adapted from New York Times, *November 2, 1998]*

Young children also have difficulty with words that implicitly express comparisons—such as *tall* and *short, near* and *far, high* and *low, deep* and *shallow*—because they do not understand that these words have meaning only in context (Ryalls, 2000). Once young children know which end of the swimming pool is the deep end, for instance, its depth becomes, quite logically, their definition of *deep.* They might obey parental instructions to stay out of deep puddles by splashing through every puddle they see, insisting that none of those is deep.

Words expressing relationships of place and time—such as *here, there, yesterday,* and *tomorrow*—are difficult as well. More than one pajama-clad child has awakened on Christmas morning and asked, "Is it tomorrow yet?" A child told to "stay there" or "come here" may not follow instructions, partly because the terms are confusing.

Similarly, because children use certain words, adults might mistakenly think they understand the implications of what they say. Consider words referring to sex, or war, or death, for instance. One experiment began with kindergartners watching a puppet show in which an alligator ate a mouse. The children agreed that the mouse was dead, and most said the mouse's brain no longer worked. However, few really grasped that death stops life. Many believed that the dead mouse still hoped to get better at math (77 percent), still was thirsty (44 percent), still was scared of the alligator (73 percent), and still loved its mother (94 percent) (Bering & Bjorklund, 2004).

Countless children have been terrified by hearing an older child talk about a ghost, have been punished for uttering curses, or have been accused of being "5 going on 15" because they know words without understanding what they mean. One example of childlike understanding comes from preschoolers in Italy who were discussing the conflict then raging in nearby Kosovo. They seemed to understand the issues, advocating peace. But then they revealed their innocence. Giorgia, age 4, said, "The daddies, mommies, and children get their feelings hurt by war" (Abbott & Nutbrown, 2001, p. 123).

Grammar

The *grammar* of language includes the structures, techniques, and rules that are used to communicate meaning. Word order and word repetition, prefixes and suffixes, intonation and emphasis—all are part of grammar. A distinction is often made between *expressive language,* which is what the person says, and *receptive language,* which is what the person understands. For everyone, receptive language is more extensive, because understanding a collection of vocabulary words is not nearly as difficult as expressing ideas. The difference is grammar, which is much less important in listening than in speaking.

As you remember from Chapter 6, toddlers who speak two-word sentences already use grammar. By age 3, grammar is quite impressive: English-speaking children not only place the subject before the verb but also put the verb before the object and the adjective before the noun. They say, "I eat the apple," not any of the 23 other possible combinations of those four words. They can form the plurals of nouns; the past, present, and future tenses of verbs; and the nominative, objective, and possessive forms of pronouns. In English, the proper use of articles (*the, a, an*) is difficult, so that adults who are learning English often omit them. Most native English-speaking 3-year-olds, by contrast, use them correctly.

Parental input and encouragement lead directly to faster and more correct language use (Barrett, 1999; Hoff & Naigles, 2002). In a study of twins (who are often delayed in grammar because they experience less individualized conversation), researchers found that the speed and depth of language learning depended on how much the parents spoke to each twin (Rutter et al., 2003).

Genetic factors also affect how well 3- to 5-year-olds use language. Each specific aspect of language is affected differently, because many genetic and environmental influences (from peers as well as parents) have an impact, and no two children have exactly the same combination of influences. Some research suggests that genes are more influential for expressive language than for receptive language, which depends heavily on experience. No matter what the particulars, nature and nurture interact for every aspect of language, and early childhood is a time for rapid acquisition, partly because of brain maturation and partly because of the social context (Kovas et al., 2005).

overregularization Applying grammar rules even when exceptions occur, making the language more "regular" than it actually is.

Young children learn their grammar lessons so well that they tend to apply rules even when they should not. This tendency, called **overregularization,** creates trouble when a child's language includes many exceptions, as English does. As an example, one of the first grammatical rules that English-speaking children apply is to add *-s* to form the plural. Overregularization soon leads many young children to talk about *foots, tooths, sheeps,* and *mouses*. They may even put the

-*s* on adjectives when the adjectives are acting as nouns, as in this dinner-table exchange between my 3-year-old and her father:

> **Sarah:** I want somes.
> **Father:** You want some what?
> **Sarah:** I want some mores.
> **Father:** Some more what?
> **Sarah:** I want some more chickens.

Although technically wrong, overregularization is a sign of verbal sophistication; it shows that children are applying the rules. Indeed, as young children become more conscious of grammatical rules, they exhibit increasingly sophisticated misapplications of them. A child who at age 2 correctly says he "broke" a glass may at age 4 say he "braked" it and then at age 5 say he "did broked" it.

Learning Two Languages

In today's world, bilingualism is an asset, even a necessity. Yet language-minority children (those who speak a language that is not the dominant language of their nation) are at a disadvantage on almost every measure. They are more likely to fail in school, to feel ashamed, to become unemployed as adults, and so on. Learning the majority language is crucial for their development. How should this happen?

What Is the Goal?

Before deciding how a second language should be learned, let us decide on the goal. On this parents, researchers, and the public often disagree. Should young children be encouraged to become bilingual, learning two distinct languages? Some say "no," arguing that the primary task of young children is to become proficient in one, and only one, language. Others say "yes," arguing that everyone should learn at least two languages and the language-sensitive years of early childhood are the best time for it.

The second argument seems to be supported by more research. Remarkably, soon after the vocabulary explosion, it is apparent that very young children can master not only extensive vocabulary but also two distinct grammars, using each language's proper word order and characteristic pauses and gestures (Bates et al., 2001; Mayberry & Nicoladis, 2000). These are also the best years to learn native pronunciation—more evidence for early childhood as a sensitive period for language learning.

This is not to say that most 6-year-olds can "speak like a native" in any language. In fact, many monolingual 6-year-olds have difficulty pronouncing certain sounds. Rather, it means that, during the early years, neurons and dendrites adjust to whatever pronunciation a child hears. The distinction between expressive and receptive language is crucial here. When it comes to expressing themselves, many young children transpose syllables (*magazine* becomes *mazagine*), drop consonants (*truck* becomes *ruck*), convert difficult sounds (*father* becomes *fadder*), and make other pronunciation errors. But they can hear distinctions even when they cannot say them. For example, my daughter Rachel asked for a "yeyo yayipop." Her father, smiling, said, "You want a yeyo yayipop?" and she answered, "Daddy, sometimes you talk funny."

AP / WIDE WORLD PHOTOS

Tiene Identificación Lista Are you pleased or angered by this bilingual sign at a school in Chelsea, Massachusetts, that serves as a polling place on election day? In this election, voters were deciding whether or not to eliminate government funding for bilingual education. Those who favored immersion argued that signs like this one would soon become unnecessary if children were taught only in English. Those who favored bilingual education held that without it, children from minority-language families would be likely to drop out of school before mastering any language.

This is just as true in two languages as in one. Children listen to pronunciation, hearing nuances of accent and emphasis even when they do not repeat them accurately. Every year of maturation makes pronunciation more difficult, in part because the auditory cortex becomes attuned to the particular sounds heard, ignoring or not even perceiving other sounds. Thus, adults need to be especially conscious of their pronunciation during these years, not copying the child (*yeyo yayipop*) but speaking clearly (*yellow lollipop,* with the *l* sound stressed).

The fact that these years are prime time for learning a second language does not mean, of course, that immigrants attempting to learn a new language after age 6 are doomed to failure. In fact, a new language can be learned at any age, as millions of adolescent and adult immigrants have done (Hakuta et al., 2003). However, in adulthood, mastering an accent is particularly difficult. Learning new grammar is somewhat difficult, and learning new vocabulary is relatively easy.

Cognition and Culture

Since language is integral to culture, bilingualism is embedded in emotions of ethnic pride and fear. This reality hampers developmental research. One group of researchers explains:

> A question of concern to many is whether early schooling in English for language minority children harms the development and/or maintenance of their mother tongue and possibly children's language competence in general. . . . Such debate quickly and unfortunately becomes highly politicized, and productive scholarly discussion of the issues is hampered by extreme and emotional political positions.
>
> *[Winsler et al., 1999, p. 350]*

Evidence regarding cognitive development points to both advantages and disadvantages of bilingualism. Supporters of bilingualism point out, correctly, that children who speak two languages by age 5 are less egocentric in their understanding of language and more advanced in their theory of mind. Opponents point out, also correctly, that bilingual proficiency usually impedes fluency in one or both languages, slowing down reading as well as other linguistic skills (Bialystok, 2001).

One Family's Multiculturalism One of the first cultural preferences to travel successfully is food, and Italian cuisine is one of the world's most popular. This family lives in New York, the parents were born in Taiwan, their children are learning to speak both Chinese and English—and they all love pepperoni pizza.

SUSAN KUKLIN / PHOTO RESEARCHERS, INC.

This last fact makes many who speak the dominant language strive to have every child learn that language, no matter what their mother tongue. This issue is of particular importance in California, where more than half of all public school children have parents who are immigrants. Many such parents find that their children make a *language shift,* becoming more fluent in their new language than in their home language (Min, 2000; Wong & Lopez, 2000).

It is not unusual for 5-year-olds to understand their parents' language but refuse to speak it, especially if they know their parents will understand the dominant language. Nor is it unusual for adults to depend on a child as interpreter when they deal with monolingual bureaucrats. This practice makes practical sense, but it widens the gap between the child and the parent and between the dominant and minority languages.

The language shift and role reversal are unfortunate, not only for the child and the parents but also for the society, since fluency in several languages is an asset in globalization and respect for family traditions is a bulwark against the role confusion of adolescence. Yet remember that young children are preoperational; they center on the immediate status of their parents and their language, on appearances more than past history. No wonder many shift.

We need to ask again, what is the goal of language learning? Parents are reluctant to deprive children of their roots, heritage, and identity, and yet they want their children to speak, read, and write the dominant language because that is a prerequisite for success (Suarez-Orozco & Suarez-Orozco, 2001). Many monolingual citizens are critical of any immigrant who does not speak the new language fluently. In contrast, many adults who use their original home language with pride are critical of members of their ethnic group who have "lost" their heritage language.

What is the outcome? Remember that children learn language from elaboration and from encouragement. Adult controversies sometimes keep children from becoming fluent in any language; they are semilingual, not monolingual or bilingual, and they are afraid to talk at all in school. This is a developmental tragedy, especially if the sensitive period for language learning is allowed to pass without a child chattering eagerly and extensively in at least one language.

Balanced Bilingualism

The best solution seems to be for every child to become a **balanced bilingual**, equally fluent in two languages, speaking both so well that no verbal hint suggests that the person speaks the other language. Is that possible? Yes. Developmental research confirms that, in these sensitive play years, children *can* become equally fluent in two or more languages (Romaine, 1999). Many Canadian schoolchildren are fluent in both English and French (see Chapter 12).

balanced bilingual A person who is equally fluent in two languages, not favoring one or the other.

Balanced bilingualism is not common in the United States. Most people are much more fluent in one language than in the other, with many monolingual children not studying a second language until high school or college, and then never learning it well.

Balanced bilingualism comes naturally to young children whose parents themselves speak two languages with them. Ideally, one parent (or another family member) uses one language, illustrating vocabulary, correcting grammar, reading books, singing songs, and so on, and the other parent spends as many hours each day using the other language with the child. The principles of language learning—the language explosion, fast-mapping, overregularization, parental encouragement—apply to two languages as well as to one. However, learning two languages requires twice as much language exposure.

Overall, the research continues to confirm that children have a powerful urge to communicate and a readiness to learn whatever language or languages they can. Children master language (with slang, dialect, and so on), and they also freely create vocabulary and grammar if necessary (Kegl et al., 1999). Many children speaking two languages occasionally substitute a word from one language in a sentence expressed in the other language because that word is the best, or only, one they know for what they are trying to say. That is not a sign of confusion; it is evidence of their drive to communicate. Adults can provide the missing word without fearing that the child is mixed up.

The powerful need to communicate was dramatically illustrated by children in Nicaragua at a boarding school for the deaf (Siegal, 2004). Their teachers tried to teach them spoken Spanish and therefore used no sign language. (This strategy is no longer common, since it is now clear that deaf children learn best if they know sign language from infancy and then learn spoken language as a second language. However, the civil war in Nicaragua delayed the teachers' awareness of the best practice for teaching the deaf.) The children invented their own sign language to communicate with one another, teaching it to the new arrivals. Their created language flourished, with each new generation of children making it more comprehensive. Younger children were more fluent than older ones because they built on what had been invented, adding new gestures.

For established spoken languages, the process of change is also apparent. Consider how English has evolved. In the past few decades, the word *Negro* gave way to *Black,* replaced by *African American* (now written without a hyphen). Recently coined, borrowed, or extended terms include *hip-hop, e-mail, DVD, spam, blog, phat, laptop, cell* (phone), *rap* (music), *buff* (in shape), and hundreds more, better known to the younger readers of this book. Words in other languages have been borrowed as well, such as *salsa, loco, amour, kowtow,* and *mensch.* Some of the key terms in this book, *doula* and *kwashiorkor* among them, originated in other languages.

Learning to Read

emergent literacy The early skills that help children learn to read, such as letter recognition and page sequencing.

Language learning provides a crucial foundation for **emergent literacy,** the beginning steps toward reading. By talking to their young children (without too many commands) and by reading to them, parents can prepare children to read fluently (Senechal & LeFevre, 2002). Since reading is the key that unlocks almost every domain of education and adult success, parents and teachers are rightly concerned that preschoolers enter first grade ready to read. What that readiness requires is complex, however. Many parents hope that memorizing the alphabet, or recognizing the letters, is what is needed, but most early-childhood educators disagree (Neuman, 2002). The research suggests that knowledge of the alphabet is only a symptom of readiness.

Much more important are an extensive vocabulary and awareness of sounds. These develop naturally if someone reads to the child at least daily and discusses what is read (NICHD Early Child Care Research Network, 2005). A child's book thus becomes a scaffold, with words and pictures that are used for conversation about comprehension and vocabulary, and thus "joint reading between parents and children is an important crucible for children's literacy learning" (Pellegrini & Galda, 1998, p. 59).

You just read that some adults in the United States fear that children who speak a language other than English will fall behind in every academic subject. This fear is based on statistics showing that academic achievement is low and school dropout rates are high for Spanish-speaking children in the United States. The assumption had been that the knowledge of Spanish interferes with the knowledge of English. However, other statistics now show that Chinese-speaking children do quite well academically. Thus, the first language does not necessarily slow down learning.

An alternate hypothesis for the correlation may be a lack of joint reading. Spanish-speaking parents are unlikely to read to their young children, as you learned in Chapter 6 (see Figure 6.3). Since reading provides a foundation in the ideas and sounds of language, as well as a scaffold for book learning and reading comprehension, Spanish-speaking parents should be encouraged to read to their children in Spanish, in order to help them learn to read English in school.

Sounds are basic to learning to read, a topic further discussed in Chapter 12. In early childhood, this means that songs and rhymes are particularly interesting to children. That's why Mother Goose is still enjoyed by English-speaking children even though such simple poems as "Jack be nimble, Jack be quick/Jack jump over the candlestick" have no basis in a twenty-first-century child's experience. Songs are also pathways to reading; many preschoolers make up their own sing-songs to accompany their actions, an example of private speech that fosters writing later on.

Another correlate for reading skill is symbolic play in early childhood. You remember that Piaget recognized that symbolic thought distinguishes preoperational children from younger children. Such thinking develops best when children play with other children, especially with friends. They develop symbolic play, which helps them with later literacy (Pellegrini & Galda, 1998).

ESPECIALLY FOR IMMIGRANT PARENTS You want your children to be fluent in the language of your family's new country, even though you do not speak that language well. Should you speak to your children in your native tongue or in the new language?

SUMMING UP

Children aged 2 to 6 have impressive linguistic talents. They explode into speech, from a hundred or so words to many thousands, from halting baby talk to fluency in one or more of the world's languages. Fast-mapping and application of grammatical rules are among the sophisticated strategies that young children use, even though these strategies sometimes backfire when children use words too literally or apply rules too rigidly. Early childhood is not a critical period for language learning, but no other time in the entire life span is as sensitive to language, especially to pronunciation. Preschool children should be immersed in words, to sponge up whatever they hear. It is quite possible, and desirable, for children to learn two languages during these years, although extensive language exposure is necessary for a child to become a balanced bilingual. Language learning, especially the learning of extensive vocabulary and sounds, is the basis for later reading.

Early-Childhood Education

Parents are the first teachers. They powerfully influence learning during the play years, not only directly but also indirectly, as they decide whether, when, and where to send their young children to school. All young children benefit from high-quality, regularly scheduled educational experiences. Such experiences can take many forms, including home schooling (Fortune-Wood, 2002). Moreover, those forms can be hard to sort out because the labels are not always clear.

Current research on early cognition leads educators and developmental psychologists to reject the long-held belief that school should begin at age 7. Previously, most children stayed home until first grade—which is why it was called "first" and why younger children were called "preschoolers." Even kindergarten (German for "children's garden") was innovative, with only privileged children attending. Today, kindergarten thrives everywhere (Wollons, 2000), and most 3- to 5-year-olds in developed nations are in school (see Figure 9.4 for U.S. trends). In fact, primary education is compulsory at age 4 in Northern Ireland and the Netherlands, with the general trend in many nations toward publicly funded education at younger and younger ages (Neuman, 2002).

Not every early-education program is the same. It is difficult to tell what a program entails from its name: Programs are called "day-care centers," "preschools," "nursery schools," "pre-primary" and "pre-kindergarten" because of history and local terminology rather than because of distinctions in philosophy or quality. However, there are some notable differences. We will consider them in three clusters: developmental (or child-centered), academic (or teacher-directed), and intervention programs.

© THE NEW YORKER COLLECTION 1991 ROBERT WEBER FROM CARTOONBANK.COM. ALL RIGHTS RESERVED.

"We teach them that the world can be an unpredictable, dangerous, and sometimes frightening place, while being careful not to spoil their lovely innocence. It's tricky."

Child-Centered Programs

Many programs are developmental, or child-centered, stressing children's development and growth. This approach begins with the idea that children need to play and explore rather than to follow adult directions (Weikart,

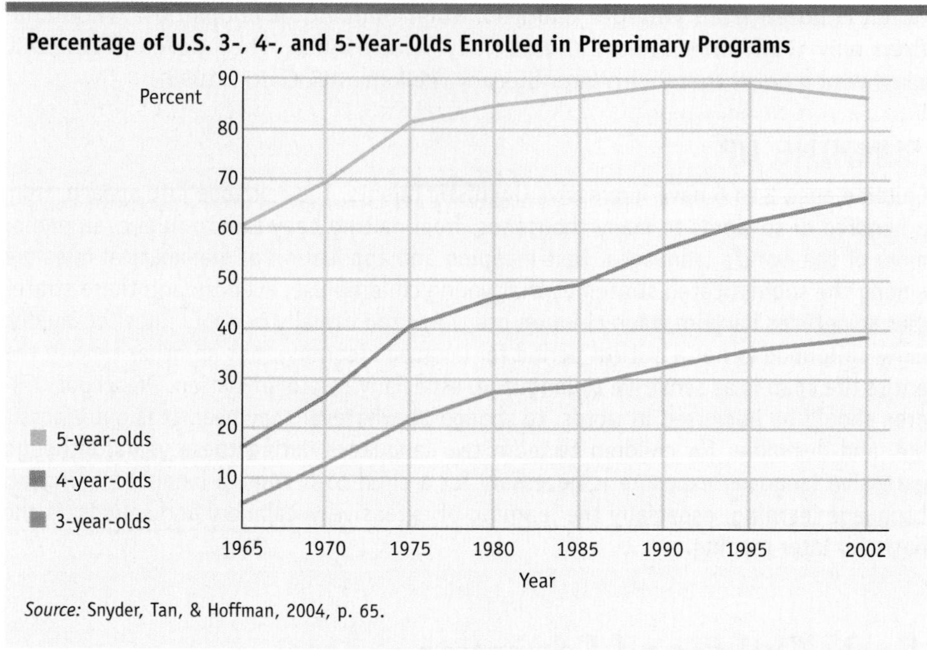

FIGURE 9.4 **Changing Times** As research increasingly finds that preschool education provides a foundation for later learning, more and more young children are in educational programs.

Response for Immigrant Parents (from page 275): Children learn by listening, so it is important for you to speak with them often, and it is probably best to do so in both languages. Depending on how comfortable you are with the new language, you might prefer to read to your children, sing to them, and converse with them primarily in your native language and find a good preschool where they will learn the new language. The worst thing you could do would be to restrict speech in either tongue.

1999). Many child-centered programs use a Piaget-inspired model that allows children to discover ideas at their own pace and in their own way. The physical space and the materials—dress-up clothing, art supplies, puzzles, blocks of many sizes, and other toys—are organized in such a way that they lend themselves to self-paced exploration.

A particular concern of many such programs is the arts. Some argue that young children "are all poets" in that they are gifted in seeing the world more imaginatively than older people do. This peak of creative vision should be nourished; children should be encouraged to tell stories, draw pictures, dance, and make music for their own delight (Egan & Ling, 2002). This approach opposes the notion that young children should be pushed toward the next stage, pressured to learn reading and math skills, instead holding that their particular strengths during early childhood are worth pursuing.

Many child-centered programs are also influenced by Vygotsky, who thought that children learn a great deal by playing with other children but also believed that adults must be alert to the skills that the children will need and must provide guidance and encouragement. For example, since number skills are important in many school subjects, children are encouraged to use math in their games (by counting out objects and keeping score) and in their routines (by using daily calendars and number guidelines such as "Only three children in the blocks corner at a time"). Always with developmental or child-centered programs, the adults are very aware of the nature of young children, who are much more creative and social than they will be a few years later. Two types of schools, both originating in Italy, typify child-centered programs.

Montessori Schools

A hundred years ago, Maria Montessori opened nursery schools for poor children in Rome. She believed that children needed structured, individualized projects that would give them a sense of accomplishment, such as completing particular puzzles, using a sponge and water to clean a table (even if it was not dirty), and drawing shapes.

Like Piaget (her contemporary), Montessori (1936/1966) realized that children have different thoughts and needs from adults. They learn a great deal from activities that adults might call play, and teachers should provide activities that dovetail with the cognitive eagerness within the child. For example, because they have a need for order, for language learning, and for using all their senses, children will learn from exercises that allow them to develop these skills and will choose them happily.

Today's Montessori schools still emphasize individual pride and accomplishment, with many emergent-literacy tasks (such as outlining letters and looking at books) presented at age 4 or so. The specific tasks are different from those Montessori developed, but the underlying philosophy is the same. Children are encouraged to choose tasks to undertake, and all the choices involve action (gross and fine motor skills). Unlike many other child-centered programs, Montessori does not encourage pretend and dramatic play. The idea is that children feel proud of themselves and engaged in learning when they accomplish a task, not when they simply make-believe. Many aspects of Montessori's philosophy are in accord with current developmental research, and that is one reason this kind of school remains popular in many nations (Lillard, 2005).

The Reggio Emilia Approach

Another form of early-childhood education is called *Reggio Emilia,* because it was inspired by a program pioneered in the Italian region of that name, where 13 infant–toddler centers and 21 preschools are funded by the city. Almost all parents in that region want their children to participate; there is a waiting list, and more centers are planned.

In Reggio Emilia, every young child is encouraged to master skills not usually seen in American schools until age 7 or so, such as writing and tool use, but

ATELIER—FROM "OPEN WINDOWS," © MUNICIPALITY OF REGGIO EMILIA—INFANT-TODDLER CENTERS AND PRESCHOOLS, PUBLISHED BY REGGIO CHILDREN 1994.

Another Place for Children High ceilings, uncrowded play space, varied options for art and music, a glass wall revealing trees and flowers—all these features reflect the Reggio Emilia approach to individualized, creative learning for young children. Such places are rare in other nations of the world besides Italy.

! Answer to Observational Quiz (from page 279): All five–not four (look again at the right-hand side of the photograph)!

Response for Parents (from page 279): There is much variation. None fits every parent's values. However, children should be engaged in learning, not allowed to sit passively or to squabble with each other. Before deciding, parents should look at several programs, staying long enough to see the children in action and the teachers showing warmth and respect for the children.

Weikart, 1997); one in North Carolina, called Abecedarian (Campbell et al., 2001); and one in Chicago, called Child–Parent Centers (Reynolds, 2000). All three programs enrolled children from low-income families for several years before kindergarten, all compared experimental groups of children with matched control groups of children, and all reached the same conclusion: Early education can have substantial long-term benefits, which become apparent when the children are in the third grade or later.

Children in these three programs scored higher on math and reading achievement tests than did other children from the same backgrounds, schools, and neighborhoods. They were significantly less likely to be placed in special classes for slow or disruptive children or to repeat a year of school. In adolescence, they had higher aspirations and a greater sense of achievement and were less likely to be mistreated. As young adults, they were more likely to attend college and less likely to go to jail.

All three research projects found that direct cognitive training, with specific instruction in various school-readiness skills, was useful. This was done with sensitivity to the needs and talents of each child: The curriculum was neither child-centered nor teacher-directed, but a combination of the two. Although the programs cost several thousand dollars per child per year (perhaps as much as $14,000 annually per child in 2005 dollars), in the long run the decreased need for special education saved more than the initial cost. By comparison, full-day care in an accredited program costs about $9,000 per child per year in 2005 dollars; Head Start is cheaper, about $6,000 per child per year, primarily because it usually provides only half-day care for only 34 weeks (National Research Council and Institute of Medicine, 2000).

The financial aspect is especially significant in some communities. For many early-childhood educators, Reggio Emilia is the gold standard because the teacher/child ratio is low and the physical space is luxurious; but the cost per child for such a program in the United States is about twice that of most other types of centers. Since parents pay the bulk of the cost of preschool education (except for intervention programs), Reggio Emilia seems beyond the reach of most families. Child-centered programs may be feasible only in places that have a history of community collaborations and a low birth rate (like Italy, where most families have only one child).

Another type of experimental program is one designed to teach children a second language. This is commonly done in Canada, where English-speaking children are enrolled in French nursery schools. It also occurs in the United States. One cluster of bilingual preschools in California taught English and Spanish. The children, who were from Spanish-speaking families, became proficient in both languages. Indeed, the children's mastery of Spanish exceeded that of Spanish-speaking children who stayed home (Winsler et al., 1999). This example proves again that young children are great learners, able to master whatever it is that adults want to teach them.

Quality Matters

A key finding from all the research is that the quality of early-childhood education matters. The most recent reauthorization of Head Start emphasizes educational quality and evaluative research (Lombardi & Cubbage, 2004). Comparisons of programs find that the specific curricula and philosophy matter less than teachers who know how to respond to the needs of young children. Generally, an educational center-based program is better for any child than family day care or home care, but quality is crucial: High-quality home care is better than a poor day-care center (Clarke-Stewart & Allhusen, 2005).

A review of all aspects of early-childhood development by 22 experts concludes:

> In sum, the positive relation between childcare quality and virtually every facet of children's development that has been studied is one of the most consistent findings in developmental science. While child care of poor quality is associated with poorer developmental outcomes, high-quality care is associated with outcomes that all parents want to see in their children, ranging from cooperation with adults to the ability to initiate and sustain positive exchanges with peers, to early competence in math and reading.
>
> *[National Research Council and Institute of Medicine, 2000]*

Some characteristics of quality care have been described in Chapter 6: safety, adequate space and equipment, a low adult/child ratio, positive social interactions among children and adults, and trained staff (and educated parents) who are likely to stay in the program. Continuity helps. (One of the best questions that parents comparing options can ask is, "How long has each staff member worked at this center?") In addition, curriculum is important, especially during the play years; unfortunately, however, only about a third of all early-childhood programs have any curriculum (Epstein et al., 1996). Programs that have no philosophy or direction seem to be worst for early learning.

Best may be programs with an emphasis on learning, reflected in a curriculum that includes extensive practice in language, fine and gross motor skills, and basic number skills. Such programs may be found in child-centered or teacher-directed schools. As this chapter emphasizes, young children love to learn and can master many skills and ideas, as long as adults do not expect them to think and behave in the same ways as older children. Poor-quality care is more prevalent than good care, and many professionals are silent about the risks involved (Ramey, 2005). The work of implementing what is known about cognition during early childhood is daunting but critical.

Beyond that, history teaches that new research will find additional abilities in the brains of 2- to 6-year-olds and additional strategies to develop that potential. Evaluation studies (longitudinal comparisons of similar groups of children with varied experiences) are still too rare. Some readers of this book will be among those who undertake the research, parent the children, and staff the schools that will again cause us to revise our view of the thinking of the very young.

PAUL CHESLEY / STONE / GETTY IMAGES

Learning from One Another Every nation creates its own version of early education. In this scene at a nursery school in Kuala Lumpur, Malaysia, note the head coverings, uniforms, bare feet, and absence of boys. None of these elements would be found in most early-childhood education classrooms in North America or Europe.

? Observational Quiz (see answer, page 282): What seemingly universal aspects of childhood are visible in this photograph?

! Answer to Observational Quiz (from page 281): Three aspects are readily apparent: These girls enjoy their friendships; they are playing a hand-clapping game, some version of which is found in every culture; and, most important, they have begun the formal education that their families want for them.

SUMMING UP

Until a few decades ago, it was widely assumed that young children were *always* better off with their mothers at home. Then research, particularly studies of Head Start and other programs for low-income children, proved that early education benefits mothers entering the labor force and that good early education benefits all children, who improve in language, in social skills, and in prospects for the future (Clarke-Stewart & Allhusen, 2005). Now that that question is settled, it is time to turn to the specifics of quality—factors such as staff training, learning opportunities, curriculum, and adult/child ratios. Each nation, each region, and sometimes each preschool differs on these factors, but all children can learn valuable skills by playing together in an educational setting.

■ SUMMARY

Piaget: Children as Thinkers

1. Piaget stressed the egocentric and illogical aspects of thought during the play years. He called this stage preoperational thought because young children cannot yet use logical operations to think about their observations and experiences.

2. Piaget noted many characteristics of preoperational thinking. Young children's thinking is largely prelogical. They sometimes focus on only one thing (centration) and use only their own viewpoint (egocentrism), remaining stuck on appearances and on current reality. They cannot understand that things change, actions can be reversed, and other people have other perspectives. He found evidence of this in many experiments, including those with conservation.

Vygotsky: Children as Learners

3. Vygotsky stressed the social aspects of childhood cognition, noting that children learn by participating in various experiences, guided by more knowledgeable adults or peers. That guidance assists learning within the zone of proximal development, which includes the knowledge and skills that the child has the potential to learn.

4. According to Vygotsky, the best teachers use various clues, guidelines, and other tools to provide the child with a scaffold for new learning. He believed that learning occurs in social interaction, not in isolation. Language is a bridge of social mediation between the knowledge that the child already has and the learning that the society hopes to impart. For Vygotsky, words are a tool for learning that both mentor and child use.

Children's Theories

5. Children develop theories, especially to explain the purpose of life and their role in it. Among these theories is theory of mind—an understanding of what others may be thinking. Notable advances in theory of mind occur at around age 4. At that point, children become less egocentric and better able to understand the differences among perception, emotion, and fact. Theory of mind is partly the result of maturation, but a child's experiences in the family and community also have an impact.

Language

6. Language develops rapidly during early childhood, which is probably a sensitive period but not a critical one for language learning. Vocabulary increases dramatically, with thousands of words added between ages 2 and 6. In addition, basic grammar is mastered, and many children learn to speak more than one language.

7. Although everyone agrees that children learn language best during early childhood and that children would benefit from mastering more than one language, bilingualism is still controversial. One reason is that languages are intimately connected to culture and heritage. Ideally, children become balanced bilinguals, equally proficient in two languages, by age 6. This ideal, however, is not easily attained.

Early-Childhood Education

8. Organized educational programs during early childhood advance cognitive and social skills. For emergent literacy, language skills need to be emphasized, although it is not obvious whether child-centered or teacher-directed curricula are best.

9. Head Start is a government program that generally helps low-income children. It is controversial, because good research on the benefits is scarce. However, longitudinal research on three other programs has demonstrated that early-childhood education works. Graduates of these programs are less likely to need special education or to repeat a grade and are more likely to attend college and to become law-abiding adults.

10. It is obvious that the quality of early education matters. Children learn best if there is a clear curriculum and if the adult/child ratio is low. The training and continuity of early-childhood teachers are also important.

■ KEY TERMS

preoperational thought (p. 254)
cognitive operation (p. 254)
egocentrism (p. 254)
centration (p. 254)
focus on appearance (p. 255)
static reasoning (p. 255)
irreversibility (p. 255)
conservation (p. 255)
apprentice in thinking (p. 258)
guided participation (p. 258)
zone of proximal development (ZPD) (p. 259)
scaffolding (p. 259)
private speech (p. 260)
social mediation (p. 260)
theory-theory (p. 262)
theory of mind (p. 263)
critical period (p. 266)
sensitive period (p. 266)
fast-mapping (p. 267)
overregularization (p. 270)
balanced bilingual (p. 273)
emergent literacy (p. 274)

■ KEY QUESTIONS

1. Why do most developmentalists prefer not to use the word *preschool*?

2. Piaget is often criticized for his approach to the minds of young children. What are the reasons for this, and do you think the criticism is fair?

3. What are the main similarities between Vygotsky and Piaget?

4. How would parents act differently toward their child according to whether they agreed with Piaget or with Vygotsky?

5. What are the similarities between Piaget's idea of egocentrism and the research on theory of mind?

6. How does fast-mapping apply to children's learning curse words?

7. How do children learn grammar without formal instruction?

8. What are the differences between child-centered and teacher-directed instruction?

9. Why is there disagreement about the extent to which Head Start benefits children?

10. Why is the quality of early-childhood education much higher in some regions than others?

■ APPLICATIONS

The best way to understand thinking in early childhood is to listen to a child, as applications 1 and 2 require. Children may be scarce on some campuses, though, so applications 3 and 4 do not require them.

1. Until you replicate Piaget's conservation experiment, you may find it hard to believe that young children are preoperational. The easiest experiment is conservation of liquids (pictured in Figure 9.1). Find a child under age 5, and make sure the child himself or herself tells you that two identically shaped glasses contain the same amount of liquid. Then carefully pour one glass of liquid into a narrower, taller glass. Ask the child which glass contains more now or if the glasses contain the same amount.

2. To demonstrate how rapidly language is learned, show a preschool child several objects and label one with a nonsense word the child has never heard. (*Toma* is often used; so is *wug*.) Then shuffle the objects and ask the child to name them. (This can also be done with objects the child does not know the name of, such as a wrench, a spatula, or a coin from another nation.) The problem with using the actual names is that if the child learns the name quickly, you may think the child already knew it. If you ask, most children will say they knew it all along.

3. Theory of mind emerges at about age 4, but many adults still have trouble understanding other people's thoughts and motives. Ask several people why someone in the news did whatever they did (e.g., a scandal, a crime, a heroic act). Then ask your informants how sure they are of their explanation. Compare and analyze the reasons as well as the degrees of certainty. One person will probably be quite sure of an explanation that someone else thinks impossible.

4. Think about an experience in which you learned something that was initially difficult. To what extent do Vygotsky's concepts (guidance, motivation, apprenticeship, zone of proximal development) explain the experience? Write a detailed, step-by-step description of your learning process, using theory to explain when relevant.

HE WANTS
BUT ISN'T

Chapter Ten

The Play Years: Psychosocial Development

Picture a 2-year-old and a 6-year-old. Notice their emotions and interactions. Two-year-olds have many moments of clinging, of tantrums, and of stubbornness, going from dependence to self-assertion and back again. Such young children cannot be left alone, even for a moment, because their curiosity may lead to danger. If you take a 2-year-old to the playground and become absorbed in reading the paper, the child may soon be perching atop a high slide, tasting a pretend sandbox cake, grabbing a toy from another child, or, worse, nowhere to be seen.

In contrast, most 6-year-olds are quite safe as long as adults are nearby. They know how to get down from high slides; they never swallow sand; they ask other children to share, expecting cooperation; and they do not disappear.

At school, most 6-year-olds say goodbye to Mom or Dad at the door and then begin their work: following routines, befriending some classmates, listening to teachers. In cultures where 6-year-olds do not go to school, at age 6 or 7 they demonstrate the skills or competencies their culture values (herding the goats, feeding the baby, and so on) (Sternberg & Grigorenko, 2004).

This chapter describes that 2-to-6 transformation. Maturation and motivation are crucial; so are experiences with parents and peers as pivotal socializing agents. Psychosocial development is obviously *social*: Parents, influenced by their culture, affect their young children in many ways. Indeed, no matter who their ancestors were, children from Tokyo, Toronto, and Topeka are shaped by cultural experiences in distinct ways, which are evident in their play, their relationship to parents, and their emotional expression.

Emotional Development

As you remember from Chapter 7, by age 2 children have a sense of themselves and their goals, and they have developed a range of emotions. Chapter 8 described the myelination and maturation of various brain areas—particularly the corpus callosum, prefrontal cortex, amygdala, hippocampus, and hypothalamus—that allow faster and more deliberate coordination, inhibition, and activation of mind and body by age 6 than was possible at age 2.

Learning when and how to express those emotions (never hit your teacher, pet the cat gently, share with your friends) is a major task of childhood, made possible as the emotional hotspots of the brain become linked to the executive functions. A child can feel fear but bravely go forth, can feel anger but not push, can feel sadness but not cry. All that is emotional regulation, which leads to competence within every culture and domain (Matsumoto, 2004). Overall, emotional development is the foundation that enables all the other forms of development, a link that makes children truly ready for whatever goals and challenges lie ahead (Campos et al., 2004).

SEAN CAYTON / THE IMAGE WORKS

Close Connection Unfamiliar events often bring developmental tendencies to the surface, as with the curious boy and his worried brother, who are attending Colorado's Pikes Peak or Bust Rodeo breakfast. Their attentive mother keeps the livelier boy calm and reassures the shy one.

? OBSERVATIONAL QUIZ (see answer, page 288): Mother is obviously a secure base for both boys, who share the same family and half the same genes but are different ages: One is 2 and the other is 4. Can you tell which boy is younger?

Initiative Versus Guilt

initiative versus guilt Erikson's third psychosocial crisis. Children begin new activities and feel guilty when they fail.

self-esteem How a person evaluates his or her own worth, either in specifics (e.g., intelligence, attractiveness) or overall.

self-concept A person's understanding of who he or she is. Self-concept includes appearance, personality, and various traits.

Positive enthusiasm, effort, and self-evaluation characterize ages 3 to 6, according to Erik Erikson's psychosocial theory (first discussed in Chapter 2). During his third developmental stage, called **initiative versus guilt**, self-esteem emerges from the acquisition of skills and competencies described in the previous two chapters, including the ability to master almost any motor skill and to verbalize almost every thought.

Self-esteem is the belief in one's own ability, a personal estimate of success and worthiness. As self-esteem builds, children become more confident and independent. The autonomy of 2-year-olds, often expressed as stubborn reactions, becomes the initiative of 5-year-olds, often seen in their self-motivated activities. In the process, children form a **self-concept**, or understanding of themselves, which includes not only self-esteem but also facts such as gender and size.

Balancing one's own wishes with the expectations embedded in the social context is not easy. For example, one child (about age 3) was new to playmates and to preschool:

> She commanded another child, "Fall down. Go on, do what I say." When the other child stayed stalwartly on his feet, she pushed him over and was clearly amazed when he jumped up and said, "No pushing!" and the teacher came over and reproved her.
>
> *[Leach, 1997, p. 474]*

In this example, the more experienced child was able to resist the newcomer's commands, explaining a rule he had learned, and the teacher told the new child how to behave. Note that the inexperienced girl was "reproved," or gently scolded, not punished. The teacher wanted her to understand and internalize the rule, hoping she would feel guilty if she thought of breaking it again. The child's amazement indicated that she did not yet comprehend the limitations on her initiative or feel the guilt that most older children and adults, but fewer 4- or 5-year-olds, experience when their initiative clashes with the rules and regulations they have learned (Lagattuta, 2005).

Pride

Erikson recognized that typical 3- to 5-year-olds have immodest and quite positive self-concepts, holding themselves in high self-esteem. They believe that they are strong, smart, and good-looking—and thus that any goal is quite achievable.

Whatever they are (self-concept) is also thought to be good (for instance, little boys are proud of being male). They are confident that their good qualities are likely to endure but that any bad qualities (even biological traits such as poor eyesight) will disappear with time (Lockhart et al., 2002). As one group of researchers explained:

> Young children seem to be irrepressibly optimistic about themselves. . . . Consider, for example, the shortest, most uncoordinated boy in a kindergarten class who proclaims that he will be the next Michael Jordan.
>
> *[Lockhart et al., 2002, pp. 1408–1409]*

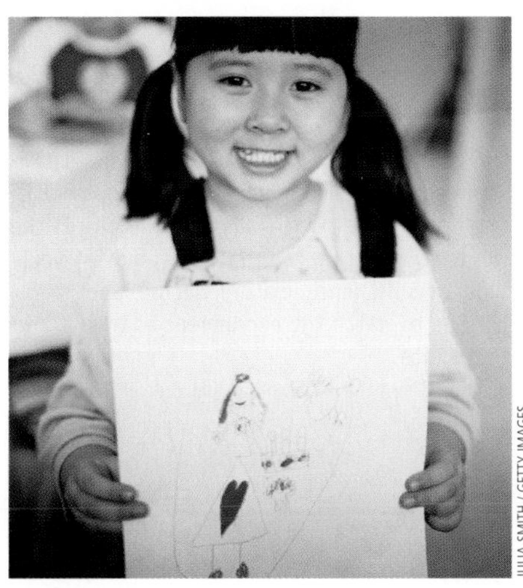

JULIA SMITH / GETTY IMAGES

So Proud If this photograph looks familiar to you, that's probably because it depicts a common theme: Most preschool children are proud of what they achieve, from zipping up their own jackets to drawing Valentines with self-portraits.

Most preschoolers leap at almost any opportunity to show that "I can do it!" Spontaneous play becomes goal-directed, and then goals are reached with pride. Children are not merely active, as they were when they were younger (Piaget's sensorimotor period and Erikson's autonomy-versus-shame stage). Now, in the preoperational or initiative-versus-guilt stage, they not only begin projects but also complete them, becoming pleased with their accomplishments.

This new initiative develops in tandem with a longer attention span (made possible by neurological maturity) because now children have a purpose for what they do. Concentrated attention is believed to be crucial for later competence of all kinds, but note that it is not merely the automatic result of brain growth. It is connected to motivation, cognition, and experience, all of which are correlated with maturation but not directly caused by it.

Motivation comes from the child's own interests, not from some adult or some biological mandate. This is evident when one notices many 3- or 4-year-olds spending an hour in *one* episode of pretend play, practicing *one* motor skill, or creating *one* work of art—something no normal toddler does. If an adult interrupts, saying it is time to stop, the 3- or 4-year-old might have a tantrum, just like a younger child, because emotional maturity takes time to develop. But note that the reason for the anger (interruption of initiative) is more mature than the toddler's reason, which might involve any attempt to curb behavior.

Pride leads not only to concentration and persistence but also to a willingness to try new experiences, such as climbing a taller ladder, speaking another language, or petting a strange animal. Typical young children enjoy undertaking various tasks, and they expect all others—grandparents, playmates, stuffed animals—to be a patient, admiring audience. Try racing a 4-year-old to the corner. If you lose, because you deliberately slowed down, the child quite proudly reports, "I won." If you win, the child may decide that "you cheated" or, more benignly, may discount the outcome as not fair.

Self-esteem is the foundation for practice and then mastery. Self-criticism, fortunately, does not arise in full force until later. Preschoolers predict that they can solve impossible puzzles, remember long lists of words, change every undesirable trait, and control the dreams that come when they are asleep (Stipek et al., 1995; Woolley & Boerger, 2002). Such naive predictions, sometimes called "protective optimism," help them learn (Lockhart et al., 2002).

Guilt and Shame

Notice that Erikson called the negative consequence of this crisis "guilt," not shame. Erikson believed that because children develop self-awareness, they feel guilty when they realize their own blatant mistakes. Generally, guilt means that people blame themselves because they have done something wrong, and shame means that other people blame the wrongdoer and that social judgment makes people feel ashamed. In addition, shame may be based on who or what one is (one may be ashamed of one's nationality, for instance), while guilt is based on what one has done.

! Answer to Observational Quiz (from page 286): Size is not much help, since children grow slowly during these years and the heads of these two boys appear about the same size. However, emotional development is apparent. Most 2-year-olds, like the one at the right, still cling to their mothers; most 4-year-olds are sufficiently mature, secure, and curious to watch the excitement as they drink their juice.

Guilt and shame often occur together, but this is not necessarily the case. For example, a child who misbehaves at a party may shame the parents, but the parents do not usually feel guilty. Or a person could feel ashamed (for not achieving something) but not guilty, or guilty (of driving too fast, for instance) but not feel ashamed.

Many thoughtful people believe that guilt is a more mature emotion than shame because guilt is internalized (Bybee, 1998; Tangney, 2001; Zahn-Waxler, 2000). Guilt originates within; it may bother a person even if no one else knows about the misdeed. Shame depends on other people; it comes from knowing that someone else might see and criticize what a person has done.

Both shame and guilt arise from social standards, and sometimes in children it is hard to see the difference (Kochanska et al., 2002). However, it is significant that the negative outcome of autonomy is shame, compared to guilt if initiative goes awry. Erikson believed that young children are becoming self-motivated and self-regulated, especially when compared with toddlers.

Intrinsic Motivation

intrinsic motivation Goals or drives that come from inside a person, such as the need to feel smart or competent. This contrasts with external motivation, the need for rewards from outside, such as material possessions or someone else's esteem.

The idea that guilt comes from within highlights an important distinction between **intrinsic motivation** and extrinsic motivation. Intrinsic motivation is internal, arising from within the person, who enjoys accomplishing something for the joy of doing it. Extrinsic motivation comes from outside the person, who is moved to do something to earn praise; to avoid punishment; or to gain money, possessions, or some other desired reward.

For the most part, preschool children are intrinsically motivated. They enjoy learning, playing, and practicing for their own joy, not because someone else sets a goal for them or because they are reacting against someone else's prohibition (as in the autonomy-versus-shame stage). For instance, when they play games, young children may be unaware of the score; the fun is more in playing than in winning.

In a classic experiment, preschool children drew pictures with magic markers in one of three conditions: no award, expected award (they were told *before* they started drawing that they would get a certificate when they were finished), and unexpected award (they heard "You were a big help" and received a certificate only *after* they had drawn) (Lepper et al., 1973). After the experiment, observers kept track of how often the children drew on their own, when they could choose from various self-initiated activities. Those children who got the "expected" reward actually drew less later on. The extrinsic reward undercut their intrinsic motivation.

This research triggered a flood of studies, as researchers tried to uncover when, whether, and how rewards should be given for good work. The consensus seems to be that praising a child for work that has been done is likely to encourage that behavior, as long as the child believes that the praise is genuine, based on actual accomplishment. However, at all ages, if substantial rewards are promised in advance for work that is already enjoyable, the extrinsic consequences may backfire by diminishing intrinsic motivation (Cameron & Pierce, 2002; Deci et al., 1999). Adults who want to encourage a preschooler's self-esteem and initiative need to help the child accomplish things and perhaps then compliment the performance, not simply tell the child "You are the best" or "I love you whatever you do."

Emotional Regulation

emotional regulation Controlling the expression of emotions, so sadness, fear, anger, and so on are not apparent.

The preeminent accomplishment between ages 2 and 6 is the ability to inhibit, enhance, direct, and modulate emotions (Eisenberg et al., 2004). Children who master this task, which is called **emotional regulation**, become more competent in every aspect of their lives, within every culture (Denham et al., 2003; Matsumoto, 2004).

Each emotion not only is controlled but also is balanced by other emotions. Pride is tempered by guilt (and vice versa); joy, by sadness; anger, by fear; and all the negative emotions (guilt, anger, and fear), by routines and rituals (such as the "just right" phenomenon, explained in Chapter 8) that might be considered irrational and obsessive in an older person. For instance, a child who is afraid of the dark might insist on saying a particular prayer and sleeping with certain stuffed animals.

Emotions are regulated and controlled by 6-year-olds in ways unknown to exuberant, expressive, and often overwhelmed toddlers. A child who is overjoyed by a new bike might temper her excitement for the sake of another child. Children learn to be friendly to new acquaintances but not too friendly, angry but not explosive, frightened by a clown but not terrified, able to distract themselves and limit their impulses if need be. (All these abilities continue to mature during the school years.)

Emotional regulation is essential all over the world, particularly if a person wants to understand another culture. Each culture has its own values regarding specific emotions. For example, children are especially encouraged to overcome their fear in the United States, to modify their anger in Puerto Rico, to temper their pride in China, to control their aggression in Japan (Harwood et al., 1995; Hong et al., 2000; Miller, 2004). Do not overestimate cultural differences, however. Emotions are thought to be universal, as is the need to regulate them during early childhood. Cross-cultural differences sometimes appear in which particular emotions are deemed most in need of control, but "emotional regulation has been shown to be extremely useful in predicting not only intercultural competence and adjustment, but adjustment in a wide variety of contexts" (Matsumoto, 2004, p. 280).

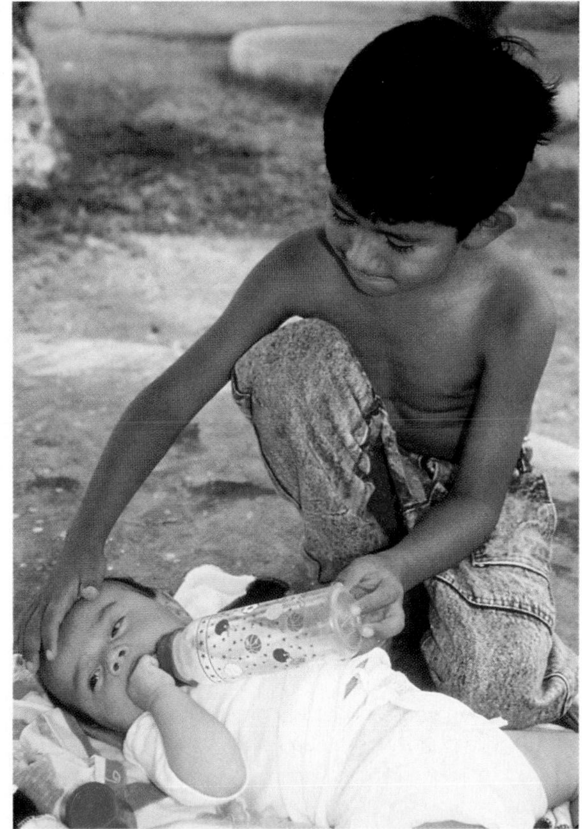

JEFF GREENBERG / THE IMAGE WORKS

Emotional Regulation Older brothers are not famous for being loving caregivers. However, in the Mayan culture, older children learn to regulate their jealousy and provide major care for younger siblings while their parents work.

? OBSERVATIONAL QUIZ (see answer, page 291): What do you see that suggests that this boy is paying careful attention to his brother?

Psychopathology

Emotional regulation begins with impulse control. Often the impulse that most needs control is anger, because "dysregulated anger may trigger aggressive, oppositional behavior" (Gilliom et al., 2002, p. 222). Before such regulation, a frustrated 2-year-old might flail at another person or lie down screaming and kicking. A 5-year-old usually has more self-control, perhaps pouting and cursing, but not hitting and screaming.

The ages given here (2 and 5) are just rough guides. Some 2-year-olds already have impressive emotional control, and some 5-year-olds still do not. Before examining the reasons for this variability, let us emphasize again how crucial emotional regulation is, this time specifically as a buffer against psychological disturbances.

Without adequate control, emotions overpower children. This occurs in two, seemingly opposite, ways. Some children have **externalizing problems:** They lash out in impulsive anger, attacking other people or things. They are sometimes called "undercontrolled." Other children have **internalizing problems:** They are fearful and withdrawn, turning emotional distress inward. They are sometimes called "overcontrolled." Both externalizing and internalizing children are unable to regulate their emotions properly or, more precisely, unable to regulate the *expression* of their emotions. They do not exercise enough control, or they control too much (Cole et al., 1996; Eisenberg et al., 2001).

externalizing problems Difficulty with emotional regulation that involves outwardly expressing emotions in uncontrolled ways, such as by lashing out in impulsive anger or attacking other people or things.

internalizing problems Difficulty with emotional regulation that involves turning one's emotional distress inward, as by feeling excessively guilty, ashamed, or worthless.

Now the critical question: Why would a child have internalizing or externalizing problems? The answer involves all aspects of development—genes, early experiences, ongoing care, education, cognition. Internalizing and externalizing problems in early childhood are likely to persist, but this is far from always the case (Pennington, 2002). Parental behavior has a notable effect, in early childhood and later on. Some specifics of parental style are explained later. First we consider nature and early nurture.

Brain Maturation

Emotional regulation is in part neurological, a matter of brain functioning. Because a child's ability to regulate emotions requires thinking before acting, deciding whether and how to display joy, anger, or fear, emotional regulation is the province of the prefrontal cortex, the "executive" area of the brain. As you remember from Chapter 8, the prefrontal cortex responds to the limbic system, including those parts of the brain (like the amygdala) where powerful emotions, especially fear and anxiety, form.

Normally, neurological advances in the prefrontal cortex occur at about age 4 or 5, when children become less likely to throw a temper tantrum, provoke a physical attack, or burst into uncontrollable giggles (Kagan & Hershkowitz, 2005). Throughout the period from age 2 to 6, violent outbursts, uncontrollable crying, and terrifying phobias diminish, and the capacity for self-control—such as not opening a wrapped present immediately if asked to wait—becomes more evident (Carlson, 2003; Kochanska et al., 2001). These emotional differences between children begin within the brain.

The brain, of course, responds partly to genes. At every age genes push some people to be emotionally expressive and others to be more inhibited. Longitudinal research finds considerable stability in such emotional reactions over time. Children seem not to change much in their immediate reactions (such as laughing or crying when a strange clown appears, for instance), or in their physiological measures (such as whether their heart beats faster or they breathe more quickly), or even in the electrical activity in one side or the other of their prefrontal cortex (Bauer et al., 2002).

Just as with adults, an fMRI or a PET scan of young children who are fearful reveals greater neurological activity in the right prefrontal cortex, while those who are more exuberant show more activity in the left prefrontal cortex (Fox et al., 2001; Kagan & Snidman, 2004). This continuity within the individual from infancy through childhood indicates that genes are responsible for some of the variation in emotional expression. Consequently, in order to get along with their peers, some children must work to regulate their exuberance and others must try to overcome their anxiety, while still others find emotional regulation quite easy.

Girls generally have less trouble with emotional regulation than boys do, perhaps for genetic reasons connected to the XX or XY chromosomes (Colder et al., 2002) or perhaps because of the ways their parents treated them as babies. (Possible reasons for sex differences are explored at the end of this chapter.) Control of externalizing problems seems particularly difficult for boys, in that young boys who are undercontrolled often have the same problems at adolescence. Girls who are undercontrolled more often manage to regulate their emotions by adolescence; but girls who are overcontrolled are frequently still overly anxious or irrationally sad as they grow older (Pennington, 2002).

In the early years, aspects of this neurological maturation are experience-dependent, with each child's unique experiences affecting the neuronal connections that allow emotional regulation. As with all experience-dependent development, cultures differ in the expression, suppression, or control of particular emotions (Garner & Spears, 2000; Olson et al., 2001). For example, if someone dies, some cultures expect bereaved adults to weep and wail, collapsing in despair. Other cultures expect adults to be brave and hold back emotions, to keep a "stiff upper lip," which literally means to show no tremor of emotion. Brain development of young children within each culture is influenced by their sociocultural practices (which depend on family and culture) as well as by each child's temperament.

Differences in Early Care

Brain-related differences in emotional regulation are not entirely inherited or culturally determined. Neurological damage can occur during development, either before birth (if a pregnant woman is stressed, ill, or a heavy drug user) or afterward (if an infant is chronically malnourished, injured, or frightened) (McEwen, 2000). As you remember from Chapter 8, extensive stress can kill some neurons and stop others from developing properly (Sanchez et al., 2001).

FRANK SIMONETTI / STOCK CONNECTION / PICTUREQUEST

Who's Chicken? Genes and good parenting have made this boy neither too fearful nor too bold. Appropriate caution is probably the best approach to meeting a chicken.

For children whose brains no longer respond normally, even an ordinary stressor—such as an unexpected loud noise or a critical remark—could release a flood of hormones, particularly the chief stress hormone, cortisol. Then a 4- or 5-year-old might overreact, experiencing terror or fury at something that another child would find only mildly upsetting.

The opposite reaction may occur as well. The stress hormones could become chronically elevated and dysregulated, making a child underreact to a truly stressful experience (De Bellis, 2001). This might explain why, in many depressed children, all emotional responses, even negative ones, are dulled. A blunted stress response indicates that emotions are dampened and distorted instead of regulated. Overall, scientists agree that early stressors can change the electrical activity, dendrite growth, and production of various hormones in the brain, dysregulating later responses, but many of the specifics are not yet understood (Davis et al., 2003).

Excessive stress in infancy and even inherited difficulties can be either reduced or worsened by early care, at least in rats. Experiments have shown that highly stressed infant rats develop abnormal brain structures (e.g., Weinstock, 1997). However, if repeatedly stressed rat pups are raised by highly nurturing mothers, their brains are spared because their mothers elicit protective hormones in them by licking, nuzzling, grooming, and feeding them more often than usual (Kaufman & Charney, 2001). In humans, too, nurturing caregivers guide highly reactive children toward emotional regulation, helping such children become more competent than children who are less reactive (Quas et al., 2004).

You remember from Chapter 7 that attachment is a much-studied variable. One specific example in that context is that well-nurtured children tend to form secure attachments, and securely attached children can regulate their emotions better than insecure children can (Gilliom et al., 2002; Kochanska, 2001). For example, unlike their insecurely attached peers, children who had been securely attached as infants tended to become 3-year-olds who controlled their frustrations and impatience (primarily by distracting themselves). By age 5, they became cooperative kindergartners who did not have externalizing problems (Gilliom et al., 2002).

The effects of early care are particularly evident in 4- to 6-year-olds who have been mistreated. One study found that 80 percent of such children were "emotionally disregulated," either being strangely indifferent or becoming extremely angry when a stranger criticized their mothers (Maughan & Cicchetti, 2002). Neglect or abuse in the first two years of life is likely to cause later internalizing or externalizing problems, even more than mistreatment that begins when the child is older. Major brain circuits are formed during infancy and toddlerhood, which is one probable explanation (Keiley et al., 2001; Lopez et al., 2004; Manly et al., 2001).

! Answer to Observational Quiz (from page 289): Look at his hands, legs, and face. He is holding the bottle and touching the baby's forehead with delicacy and care; he is positioning his legs in a way that is uncomfortable but suited to the task; and his eyes and mouth suggest he is giving the baby his full concentration.

The brain itself is the product of nurture as well as nature. Two leading researchers explain:

> Multiple converging pathways—including not only the neural circuits that are activated by physical, psychological, and immunological stressors, but also . . . genetics, early experience, and ongoing life events . . . determine the neural response to different stressors.
>
> *[Cicchetti & Walker, 2001, p. 414]*

Cognition and Emotions

Even beyond those converging pathways, a step toward emotional regulation is a child's ability to recognize emotional responses. This ability begins with social referencing (Chapter 7) and continues when children develop a theory of mind (Chapter 9). Cognition (as well as maturation and experience) is needed for both emotional regulation and for theory of mind, which tend to occur at about the same time.

Emotional Intelligence

emotional intelligence An understanding of how to interpret and express emotions.

Daniel Goleman (1998) contends that the ability to modulate and direct emotions is crucial to **emotional intelligence,** an understanding of how to interpret and express emotions. Emotional intelligence develops lifelong but is especially important in early childhood. During these years, the reflective and intellectual areas of the cortex, especially the prefrontal cortex, gradually come to govern the rush of fear, anger, and other passions from the amygdala, the emotional center deep within the brain. In other words, the executive function of the brain gradually takes control of the limbic system.

Goleman is convinced that parents use children's natural attachment and affection to teach young children how and when to express feelings—in other words, to govern the limbic system. If children learn these lessons during early childhood, they will become balanced and empathetic human beings, neither overwhelmed by, nor unresponsive to, their own emotions.

Goleman's conviction is supported by some research. As you remember from Chapter 7, most parents respond to their infants by mirroring and labeling emotions. From synchrony and social referencing, toddlers learn how to modify their fear, anger, sorrow, and other emotions. Further, unresponsive and detached parents tend to raise children who are callous and unemotional, who become seriously disturbed and antisocial adults (Frick et al,. 2003; Lykken, 1995).

The development of emotional intelligence becomes especially apparent in children's growing ability to interpret the emotions of others. Although preschoolers usually correctly judge how other people feel when they say that something good ("My mommy gave me a treat") or bad ("My dog ran away from home") has happened to them, young children judge on the basis of the content, not the tone. This limits their emotional understanding. For instance, when a person says in a very sad voice, "I came in first place in a race," virtually every 6-year-old, but almost no child younger than that, judges the person to be happy (Morton et al., 2003). Young children (ages 3 and 4) also confuse another person's intentions and desires, a mistake that older children and adults rarely make (Schult, 2002).

There is a lesson here for all of us. Anyone who wants sympathy and understanding from a young child should express their feelings clearly and directly. If people hope that children will guess emotions from voice tone, facial expression, or sarcasm, they may be disappointed.

Empathy and Antipathy

We have focused especially on fear and anger, two emotions produced directly by the limbic system, emotions that need to come under the control of the prefrontal cortex as the child matures. However, with increasing social awareness and decreasing egocentricism (as reviewed in Chapter 9), two other emotions develop that are crucial for every person: **empathy,** a true understanding of the feelings and concerns of someone else, and **antipathy,** a dislike or even hatred of other people. Empathy is not sympathy, which is feeling sorry for someone. It is feeling sorry *with* someone. Recent research has found "mirror neurons" in the brain, whereby one person's experiences can activate the same brain areas in the observer as in the experiencer. That is empathy.

empathy The ability to understand the emotions of another person, especially when those emotions differ from one's own.

antipathy Feelings of anger, distrust, dislike, or even hatred toward another person.

An analysis of many studies suggests that, over the years from infancy to early childhood, children increasingly develop empathy as their parents and their experiences teach them to do so. In the same way, exposure within the family to negative emotions (dislike, anger, anxiety) increases their antipathy (Halberstadt & Eaton, 2002). Both empathy and antipathy often lead to action—especially if emotions are unregulated.

Empathy leads to **prosocial behavior,** being helpful and kind without gaining any obvious benefit. Expressing concern, offering to share food or a toy, and including a shy child in a game or conversation are examples of prosocial behavior. Antipathy leads to **antisocial behavior,** deliberately injuring someone or destroying something that belongs to another (Caprara et al., 2001). Antisocial actions include verbal insults, social exclusion, and physical assaults. An antisocial 4-year-old might look another child in the eye, scowl, and then kick him hard without provocation.

prosocial behavior Feeling and acting in ways that are helpful and kind, without obvious benefit to oneself.

antisocial behavior Feeling and acting in ways that are deliberately hurtful or destructive to another person.

There is a crucial difference between forced and voluntary social behavior. When toddlers share only on command, they might scowl, purse their lips, and hand over their cherished toy or half a cookie with evident reluctance. By contrast, prosocial preschoolers voluntarily share, smilingly anticipating their partner's happiness and pleasure. No demands are made, such as "Now give me your truck" or "Now I am your friend." This difference is similar to the distinction between shame and guilt, or between extrinsic and intrinsic motivation. It is the latter (guilt, intrinsic motivation, voluntary prosocial acts) that is the outcome of normal psychosocial development between ages 2 and 6.

The developmental progression of empathy and antipathy is apparent to any close observer. Young infants sometimes behave in ways that suggest empathy or antipathy. They cry when another baby cries, hand over a half-eaten cookie with a smile, or, the opposite, hit in anger or grab a toy from another baby. However, these acts are neither truly prosocial nor antisocial because the self-concept is not sufficiently developed in infants.

By age 4 or 5—as a result of brain maturation, theory of mind, emotional regulation, and interactions with caregivers—most children can be deliberately prosocial or antisocial (Eisenberg, 2000). This maturation is easy to recognize if you imagine that a boy hits his mother. If he is a toddler, the mother usually realizes that the hit is part of Piaget's tertiary circular reaction, in which a child experiments with new behaviors. The mother probably stops her son with a stern expression, but she does not feel personally attacked. However, if the hit comes from a 5-year-old, that means something is seriously amiss.

LAURA DWIGHT

What Will She Do? By age 3 or 4, children can respond with empathy to another child's distress, as the girl on the left is doing. Such emotions usually lead to prosocial actions: She is likely to ask the distressed boy at the right to play with her at the sand table.

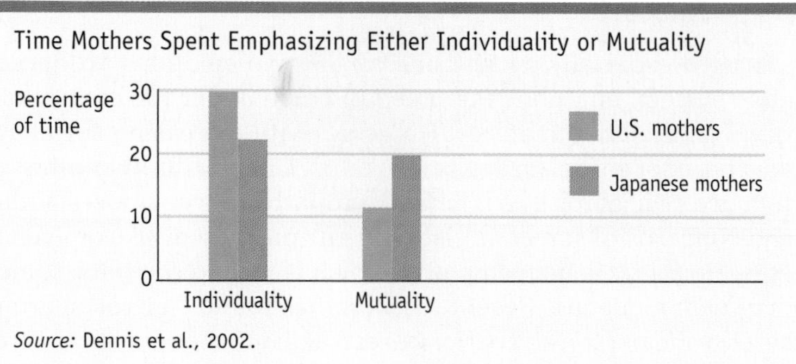

FIGURE 10.1 **How Empathy Is Taught** During free play with their 4-year-olds, Japanese mothers were more likely than U.S. mothers to emphasize mutuality, or interdependence. U.S. mothers tended to stress individuality, or self-reliance. This study demonstrates the role of culture in children's development of empathy.

In fact, according to a study in Montreal, when 5-year-olds are unusually mean to their mothers (physically or verbally), that signifies a disturbed parent–child relationship. Often the child is headed for externalizing problems in school (Moss et al., 2004). Thus, 5-year-olds can be deliberately antisocial, and their antisocial actions are likely to characterize all their relationships.

Prosocial behavior involves much more than obeying an adult's request to share a toy or comfort another child. Truly prosocial children are empathetic: They express concern even when the other person's emotions differ from those the child personally feels. At least a glimmer of theory of mind is usually a prerequisite.

Adults foster empathy when they ask children, "How would you feel if such-and-such happened to you?" Cultures vary in how much empathy is encouraged. For example, a study that compared Japanese and U.S. mothers playing with their 4-year-olds found that the former were more likely to emphasize mutuality (e.g., "This puzzle is hard for us") and the latter to emphasize individuality (e.g., "You are having a hard time with this puzzle") (Dennis et al., 2002) (see Figure 10.1). If this contrast is typical, then U.S. children would empathize less with other people than Japanese children would.

Preference and Prejudice

Any cultural emphasis on shared experiences—such as encouraging a child to identify with past national or ethnic heroes, or to value the family unit more than personal gain—is likely to increase empathy for others within that group. The child learns to identify with others and to feel pride at the achievement of someone else from the group. Such preference for the in-group usually peaks at around age 6 or 7, although much depends on the social context.

Sometimes such favoritism leads to antipathy toward outsiders. Preschool children, however, are capable of identifying with, and being proud of, their own group (national, ethnic, religious, or familial) without being prejudiced against other groups or even realizing that another group has different values and goals (Verkuyten, 2004). In fact, their ignorance is astonishing, as researchers found in Northern Ireland, where most 6-year-olds said they did not know of any problems between the Catholics and Protestants (Sani & Bennett, 2004).

As you might imagine, given their high self-esteem and optimistic self-concept, young children who realize that their group is considered undesirable may believe that they are unlike others in their group. They are likely to think they might change groups later on. The concept of constancy—that one will always be Turkish or African American, say—is not firmly understood until middle childhood or later. Often by that time children internalize the idea that prejudice against one's own or other groups is undesirable, and therefore they do not express it (Rutland et al., 2005).

For many reasons, then, the intellectual transition from preference to prejudice does not occur for all children. When it does occur, it happens in middle childhood or later and is heavily dependent on family, community, and historical pressures (Nesdale, 2004; Ruble et al., 2004). Some children actually develop more positive feelings toward other groups as they age (Barrett et al., 2004). Interethnic friendships or positive family attitudes may protect young children from developing the prejudices of their group.

SUMMING UP

According to a report by 22 researchers on early childhood:

> The developmental tasks of this period range from the mastery of essential building blocks for learning and the motivation to succeed in school, to the ability to get along with other children, to make friends, and become engaged in a social group, as well as the capacity to manage powerful emotions.
>
> *[National Research Council and Institute of Medicine, 2000, p. 386]*

It is noteworthy that these researchers list only one cognitive task, then five emotional tasks, including emotional regulation. This list reiterates the first message of this chapter. From Erikson's initiative versus guilt to Goleman's emotional intelligence, every observer of young children realizes that emotional development is crucial. Pride, purpose, and initiative are typical of young children's self-concept, as Erikson describes. Children who, because of genetic patterns or early mistreatment, have difficulty with emotional regulation often develop internalizing or externalizing problems. Many researchers believe that emotional regulation is the foundation for later social skills and cognitive growth, as children become more prosocial and less antisocial, expressing empathy more than anger.

Play

Developmentalists believe that play is the most productive and enjoyable activity that children undertake. Play is both universal and adaptable. Although all young children play, whether they are on Arctic ice or desert sand, play varies by culture, gender, and age, so it is an ideal means of learning whatever social skills are required in the context (Sutton-Smith, 1997). Children sometimes play when they are alone or with adults, but they play best with other children. Peers (people of about the same age and social status) not only are preferred playmates but also provide practice in emotional regulation, empathy, and social understanding of every kind.

Play changes dramatically between ages 2 and 6. The younger child's social play consists mainly of simple games (such as bouncing and trying to catch a ball and becoming upset if another child does not cooperate). By contrast, most 5-year-olds know how to gain entry to a play group, to manage conflict through the use of humor, and to select and keep friends and playmates—all signs of theory of mind. The difference between those two ages is the consequence of many hours of social play through which children learn how to make, and keep, friends.

The most obvious change in play during childhood is that it becomes increasingly interactive. This was first noted by Mildred Parten (1932), who distinguished five kinds of play, each more social than the previous one.

1. *Solitary play.* A child plays alone, seemingly unaware of any other children playing nearby.
2. *Onlooker play.* A child watches other children play.

3. *Parallel play.* Children play with similar toys in similar ways, but they do not play together.
4. *Associative play.* Children interact, observing each other and sharing material, but their play is not yet mutual and reciprocal.
5. *Cooperative play.* Children play together, creating and elaborating a joint activity or taking turns.

Children move toward the more advanced kinds of play as they reach the end of the play years, although a study of 4-year-olds found that some normal children prefer to play alone rather than with strangers (Henderson et al., 2004). Usually as children grow older their play becomes more complex as well as more social, although temperament, sex, parental encouragement, and personal experience all influence playful interactions at every stage (Rubin, 2000; Rubin et al., 2002). This progression is evident in rough-and-tumble and dramatic play, both of which emerge during the play years.

Rough-and-Tumble Play

Children need to be active in order to develop muscle strength and control. A young child benefits from having someone else to be active with, because a companion provides a model, an audience, and sometimes a rival, to spur the child on. For instance, running skills develop best when a child is chasing another, rather than when the child is running alone.

rough-and-tumble play Play that mimics aggression through wrestling, chasing, or hitting but in which there is no intent to harm.

The most common form of active play is called **rough-and-tumble play** because it looks quite rough and because the children seem to tumble over one another. The term was actually coined by scientists who studied baby monkeys in East Africa (Blurton-Jones, 1976). They noticed that the monkeys often chased, attacked, rolled over in the dirt, and wrestled, quite roughly, without hurting one another. If a young monkey wanted to play, all it had to do was come close, catch the eye of a peer, and then run away as if being chased. This was an invitation, which the other monkey almost always accepted, responding with a "play face" rather than an angry one. When the scientists returned from Africa to their families in England, they saw that their children were like the baby monkeys—that human youngsters also engage in rough-and-tumble play. They enjoy chasing each other and develop games (tag, cops-and-robbers, and many more) that allow them to do so.

Although rough-and-tumble play is obviously physical, it is not intended to be aggressive. Children are more likely to hurt themselves by falling or bumping into something than to hurt one another (Pellegrini & Smith, 1998). (If adults are unsure whether they are observing a fight that should be stopped or a social activity that should continue, they should look for the play face. Children almost always smile, and often laugh, in rough-and-tumble play; they frown or scowl in real fights.) Unlike aggression, rough-and-tumble play is fun and constructive: It teaches children how to enter a relationship, assert themselves, and respond to someone else while practicing gross motor skills.

Male Bonding Sometimes the only way to distinguish aggression from rough-and-tumble play is to look at the faces. The hitter is not scowling, the hittee is laughing, and the hugger is just joining in the fun. Another clue that this is rough-and-tumble play comes from gender and context. These boys are in a Head Start program, where they are learning social skills, such as how to avoid fighting.

LAURA DWIGHT

Rough-and-tumble play is universal. It is evident in every nation of the world among young boys when they are allowed to play freely (Boulton & Smith, 1989). Girls engage in rough-and-tumble play less often, a gender difference that could result primarily from either nature or nurture (Maccoby, 1998). Certain conditions make rough-and-tumble play more likely, among them ample space and indirect supervision. It appears most often when children have room to run and when adults are not underfoot.

Rough-and-tumble play requires both planned provocation and self-control. That explains why very young children merely chase and catch one another but older children develop informal rules to keep the play fair and fun. In tag, for instance, players decide on the rules and then each child decides when and how far to venture from base. If one child is "It" for too long, another child (often a friend) volunteers to be caught.

Rough-and-tumble play is most common among children who have had considerable social experience, often with one another. It develops both the self-concept and social skills, as each child learns how to be assertive without going too far. Not surprisingly, given the gradual increase of emotional regulation, the incidence of rough-and-tumble play increases with age, peaking at about age 8 to 10 (Pellegrini & Smith, 2001). Echoes of it are apparent in the flirting behaviors of young adolescents, another example of social learning that begins in early childhood.

Creativity

Young children may be more creative than people of any other age (Egan & Ling, 2002). Imaginations need not be social: Children invent dialogues for their toys, concentrate on a work of art or architechture, and converse with imaginary friends, who are increasingly common from age 3 through 7. In each of these forms of solitary play, children can develop social skills (Taylor et al., 2004). For example, one girl's invisible friend was Elephant, "7 inches tall, grey color, black eyes, wears tank top and shorts . . . plays with the child [but] sometimes is mean" (Taylor et al., 2004, p. 1178). By having an imaginary friend who is sometimes mean, the child practices strategies to deal with mean playmates. Eventually, that skill needs to be practiced with real children, as young children seem to realize. In fact, the most common reason that imaginary friends are abandoned is that the child has more actual friends.

Sociodramatic Play

One manifestation of creative play is **sociodramatic play,** in which children act out various roles and plots they create, taking on "any identity, role, or activity that they choose. They can be mothers, babies, Cinderella, or Captain Hook. They can make tea or fly to the moon. Or they can fight, hurt others, or kill or imprison someone" (Dunn & Hughes, 2001, p. 491). Sociodramatic play provides a way for children to learn from one another as they do these things:

sociodramatic play Pretend play in which children act out various roles and themes in stories that they create.

- Explore and rehearse the social roles enacted around them
- Test their ability to explain and to convince others of their ideas
- Practice regulating their emotions by pretending to be afraid, angry, brave, and so on
- Develop a self-concept in a nonthreatening context, acting as a warrior, a parent, a teacher, and so on

Sociodramatic play can occur without social interaction. For example, several 2-year-olds can be caring for their "babies" in the doll corner of their preschool, each seemingly unaware of the actions of the others—except perhaps to copy a particularly interesting activity. Parten would describe the unawareness as solitary play and the copying as parallel play, although probably these children notice each other.

Between the ages of 2 and 6, sociodramatic play increases, not only in frequency and complexity but also in cooperative interaction; children enjoy devel-

Ladies and Babies A developmental difference is visible here, between the 14-month-old's evident curiosity and the 4-year-old friends' pleasure in sociodramatic play. The mother's reaction—joy at the children's mastery play or irritation at the mess they've made—is less predictable.

oping their imaginative roles together. Although both sexes engage in sociodramatic play, girls do it more, and they are less likely than boys to use violent themes (Dunn & Hughes, 2001).

Space to Play

The best setting for children to develop social skills as they play is a high-quality educational program (described in Chapter 9), with ample space, peers, materials, and adults who know when to let children learn from one another. In fact, many developmentalists believe that there are more psychosocial than cognitive advantages of organized programs for young children because skilled teachers help them regulate fear, shyness, and anger—all emotions that arise in play (Clarke-Stewart & Allhusen, 2005).

Especially for Young Adults When you were younger, you had an imaginary friend with whom you played, slept, and talked. Does this mean you were emotionally disturbed?

Learning emotional regulation is best done in context, when social complexities arise. Other children are teachers in this, as Vygotsky would proclaim. Even the most patient parent is outmatched by another child at negotiating the rules of tag, at wrestling on the grass, at pretending to be a sick baby, at fighting a dragon. Adults tend to be either too accommodating or too domineering with children, in either case failing to teach cooperation. By contrast, peer reactions are instructive. For instance, if a playmate is hurt in rough-and-tumble play or gets confused in sociodramatic play, children learn to empathize in order to continue the game.

Aggression

The gradual regulation of emotions and emergence of antipathy is nowhere more apparent than in the most antisocial behavior of all, *active aggression.* Learning when and how to be aggressive is a major goal of the play of young children, as is evident on close observation of rough-and-tumble play, or in the fantasies of domination and submission that shine through sociodramatic play, or in the sharing of art supplies, construction materials, and wheeled vehicles.

Developmental Patterns

Think about the developmental progression of aggression. Young children have much to learn. In Richard Tremblay's dramatic words, "The only reason babies do not kill each other is that we do not give them knives or guns" (quoted in Holden, 2000, p. 580). Infants naturally pinch, slap, and even bite other people. Almost all 2-year-olds are sometimes aggressive, too, but if a child has not begun to modify his or her antisocial behavior by age 3 or 4, that child may be headed for trouble at age 5, 10, or even 15 or 25 (Loeber & Farrington, 2000). Much of this learning occurs at home: Parents who are dissatisfied with their lives and hostile toward each other tend to have hostile children who remain so as they grow older. By contrast, parents who create a positive family atmosphere at home tend to buffer their children against hostility (Keltikangas-Jarvinen & Heinonen, 2003).

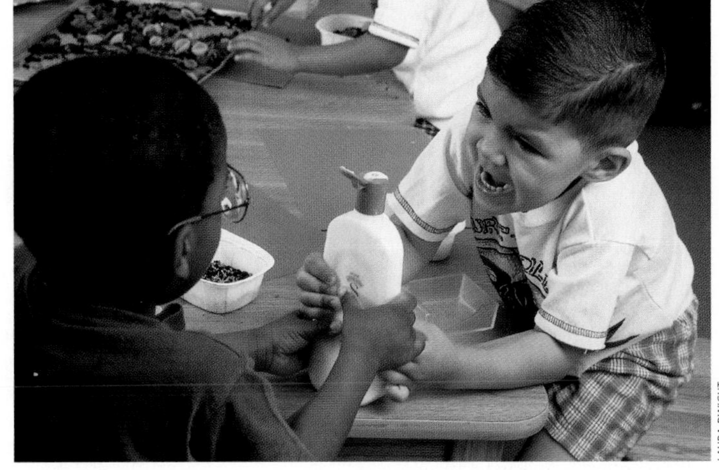

LAURA DWIGHT

Me First! An increase in aggression by about age 4 is typically accompanied by an increase in self-control. This struggle will not escalate to instrumental aggression if both children have learned some emotional regulation and if neither has been misguided by racism or by a false image of maleness.

Since undercontrol as well as overcontrol of emotions can lead to psychological problems, it is crucial to remember that emotions need regulation, not repression. An internalizing 4-year-old who cries and retreats from every threat is likely to become overwhelmed by anxiety or depression later on and may be victimized by bullies. Some assertion and self-protection are probably beneficial (Hawley, 1999). In fact, aggression in early childhood is quite normal, and some forms may increase from ages 2 to 6. As self-esteem and the self-concept build, children become more likely to defend their interests but *less* likely to attack without reason. Normal 4-year-olds have learned to choose issues and targets, as well as the degree of aggression.

Researchers recognize four general types of aggression, described in Table 10.1. **Instrumental aggression** is very common among young children, who often seem to want something they do not have and will try, without thinking, to get it. **Reactive aggression** is impulsive as well, and this type, particularly, becomes better controlled with emotional regulation. **Relational aggression** destroys another child's self-esteem and social networks and actually becomes more hurtful as children mature, since their esteem and social networks are more fragile. Finally, **bullying aggression** is the most ominous. It is apparent among some young children, but it must be stopped lest it continue throughout school age and adolescence. As described in detail in Chapter 13, bullying aggression among older children can be very harmful to both victims and the bullies themselves.

instrumental aggression Hurtful behavior that is intended to get or keep something that another person has.

reactive aggression An impulsive retaliation for another person's intentional or accidental actions, verbal or physical.

relational aggression Actions, such as insults or social rejection, aimed at harming the victim's friendships.

bullying aggression Unprovoked, repeated physical or verbal attack, especially on victims who are unlikely to defend themselves.

Practical Advice

When adults see a young bully who kicks other children for no reason, there is no doubt that they should intervene. However, it is not always so clear that relational aggression is harmful, which means that adults do not step in as quickly as they might to stop name-calling and to protect friendships. Yet developmentalists have found that social relationships with other children are not only the way that many lessons are learned but also important buffers against stresses of every kind, from the death of a goldfish to the divorce of one's parents (Frankel, 2005).

Throughout childhood, friendships are broken by relational aggression more often than by any other type of aggression (Crick et al., 1999). That means that adults should stop insults and exclusions ("You can't play with us") immediately, offering guidance, not merely sympathy and protection, to young victims who need friends.

TABLE 10.1 **The Four Forms of Aggression**

Type of Aggression	Definition	Comments
Instrumental aggression	Hurtful behavior that is aimed at gaining something (such as a toy, a place in line, or a turn on the swing) that someone else has	Often increases from age 2 to 6; involves objects more than people; quite normal; more egocentric than antisocial.
Reactive aggression	An impulsive retaliation for a hurt (intentional or accidental) that can be verbal or physical	Indicates a lack of emotional regulation, characteristic of 2-year-olds. A 5-year-old should be able to stop and think before reacting.
Relational aggression	Nonphysical acts, such as insults or social rejection, aimed at harming the social connections between the victim and others	Involves a personal attack and thus is directly antisocial; can be very hurtful; more common as children become socially aware.
Bullying aggression	Unprovoked, repeated physical or verbal attack, especially on victims who are unlikely to defend themselves	In both bullies and victims, a sign of poor emotional regulation; adults should intervene before the school years. (Bullying is discussed in Chapter 13.)

RESPONSE FOR YOUNG ADULTS (from page 298): No. In fact, imaginary friends are quite common, especially among creative children.

Fortunately, in early childhood, such intervention can succeed. Young children do not need much encouragement to make friends (unlike older children, who are more selective and more suspicious of adults). Before age 7, opportunities to play with other children in a supportive context usually give children the friends and emotional understanding they need. Adults can teach children simple rules (think back to the boy who said "Don't push" early in this chapter) and can team up two similar children, knowing that all children want to play. Then children will teach each other how to patch up a quarrel, to cooperate, and to empathize.

Think back again to the girl who told the boy to fall down, and then pushed him when he stayed upright. Her amazement at his reaction revealed that she did not understand the relationship between her wishes and other children's desires. On the same day, she said, "But I *want* to go first," truly stunned that anyone else should claim the privilege (Leach, 1997, p. 474). The psychologist who reported this incident suggested that the child had not experienced playing with others and that her parents had inadvertently prevented her from learning social skills.

SUMMING UP

All forms of play help children express as well as regulate their emotions, as they coordinate their own wishes with those of their playmates. Boys are more likely to wrestle and chase each other in rough-and-tumble play, developing their motor skills while they modulate their aggression. Girls are more likely to engage in sociodramatic play, practicing social roles and mastering their fears. Both genders often have imaginary companions, who offer an opportunity to practice the social skills they develop with their friends. Some aggression is normal during early childhood, but relational aggression and bullying should alert adults that children need guidance in social understanding.

Parents

We have seen that young children's emotions and actions are affected by many factors, including brain maturation, peers, gender, and culture. Now we consider a fifth, controversial influence: parents. Why "controversial"? There is no doubt that parents matter (Halberstadt & Eaton, 2002; Maccoby, 2000; Patterson, 1998), but the controversy arises for two reasons. One is that families, and cultures, disagree about the best parenting patterns, a topic we will explore soon. Before that, however, we need to face the other reason. In past decades, social scientists exaggerated the role of parents.

> Contemporary students of socialization largely agree that early researchers often overstated conclusions from correlational findings; relied excessively on singular, deterministic views of parental influence; and failed to attend to the potentially confounding effects of heredity. . . . Unfortunately, the weaknesses of old studies still permeate presentations of socialization research in introductory textbooks and the mass media, partly because they appeal to preferences for simple generalizations.
>
> [Collins et al., 2000, p. 218]

Of course, this textbook steers clear of "simple generalizations." Currently, whenever researchers study the complexity of psychosocial development, each child's own temperament is found to be more influential than the parenting style (e.g., Deater-Deckard et al., 1998; O'Connor, 2002; Sameroff, 2000; Van Leeuwen et al., 2004). However, avoiding simple generalizations also means acknowledging the importance of parents, especially if a child has a temperamental tendency toward depression, aggression, or other problems.

Particularly in early childhood, parents are pivotal, directly and indirectly. For instance, they choose whether, how, and where children go to school, have friends, and play. Research, including the studies on emotional regulation cited earlier, confirms that details of parental behavior have a decided influence—as do many other factors. Parenting styles are crucial if temperament or culture makes internalizing or externalizing problems likely. Then parents can modify their child's destructive bent or push the child over the edge into pathology (Galambos et al., 2003; Van Leeuwen et al., 2004).

Another conclusion of recent research must be emphasized: There is no single "best" way to parent. Ideally, every young child has two parents (not necessarily the biological parents) who cooperate with each other and support the child's development. A good relationship between the adults is almost as important for a child's development as effective parenting is (Belksy & Fearon, 2004), but specifics of good parenting (as well as of a happy marriage) vary depending on the particular cohort, culture, and child (Dishion & Bullock, 2002; Hulbert, 2003; Miller, 2004).

Parenting Style

Although thousands of researchers have traced the effects of parenting on child development, the work of one person, 40 years ago, continues to be influential. Diana Baumrind (1967, 1971) studied 100 preschool children, all from California, almost all middle-class European Americans. (The cohort and cultural limitations of this sample were not obvious at the time.)

Baumrind used many measures. First, she observed the children's activities in their nursery school and rated their behavior related to such qualities as self-control, independence, and self-esteem. Then she interviewed the parents and observed parent–child interaction at home and in her laboratory.

Baumrind found that parents differed on four important dimensions:

- *Expressions of warmth.* Parents ranged from very affectionate to quite cold and critical.
- *Strategies for discipline.* Again, there was much variation in the use of explanation, criticism, persuasion, acceptance, and physical punishment.
- *Communication.* Some parents listened patiently to their children; others demanded silence.
- *Expectations for maturity.* Parents varied in their standards of responsibility and self-control.

Baumrind's Three Patterns of Parenting

On the basis of these four dimensions, Baumrind identified three styles of parenting:

authoritarian parenting Child rearing with high behavioral standards, punishment of misconduct, and low communication.

- **Authoritarian parenting.** The parents' word is law, not to be questioned. Misconduct brings strict punishment, usually physical (but not so harsh as to be considered abusive). Authoritarian parents set down clear rules and high standards. They do not expect children to give their opinions; discussion about emotions is especially rare. (One adult from such a family said that the question "How do you feel?" had only two possible answers: "Fine" and "Tired.") Such parents believe that their age and experience have prepared them to know what is best for their children and that the children should do as they are told. The parents love their children, but may seem aloof, rarely showing affection.

permissive parenting Child rearing with high nurturance and communication but rare punishment, guidance, or control.

- **Permissive parenting.** Permissive parents make few demands, hiding any impatience they feel. Discipline is lax because they have low expectations for maturity. Permissive parents are nurturing and accepting. They listen to whatever their offspring say, and they share their own emotions without restrictions. They view themselves as helpful but not as responsible for shaping their children.

authoritative parenting Child rearing in which the parents set limits but listen to the child and are flexible.

- **Authoritative parenting.** Authoritative parents set limits and enforce rules. However, they also listen to their children's requests and questions, discussing feelings and problems. The parents demand maturity from their offspring, but they are nurturing and understanding, usually forgiving (not punishing) if the child falls short. They are flexible if a child explains a particularly good reason for an exception. They are guides and mentors, not authorities (as authoritarian parents are) or friends (as permissive parents are).

The characteristics of these three styles are summarized in Table 10.2.

Baumrind and many others have continued to study parenting styles, following the original 100 children as they grew and studying thousands of other children of various backgrounds and ages (Baumrind, 1991; Bornstein, 2002; Steinberg et al., 1994) They have come to the following conclusions:

- *Authoritarian* parents raise children who are likely to be conscientious, obedient, and quiet, but not especially happy. The children tend to feel guilty or depressed, internalizing their frustrations, blaming themselves when things don't go well. As adolescents, they sometimes rebel, leaving home before age 20.
- *Permissive* parents raise children who are least happy of all. They lack self-control, especially within the give-and-take of peer friendships. Their inadequate emotional regulation makes them immature and impedes friendship formation, which is a main reason for their unhappiness. They tend to live at home, still dependent, in early adulthood.
- *Authoritative* parents raise children who are likely to be successful, articulate, intelligent, happy with themselves, and generous with others. These children are usually liked by teachers and peers, especially in cultures where individual initiative is valued.

Baumrind named two of her three parenting styles with almost the same word; only the last syllables differ. How will you remember them? One student said that "authoritarian" ***I****s* ***A****wfully* ***N****egative* (***-ian***), but "authoritative" ***I****s* ***V****ery* ***E****xcellent* (***-ive***). Maybe this memory trick will work for you, too.

Follow-up research has found that, at least for middle-class families of European ancestry, the initial advantages of the authoritative approach grow stronger over time, helping children to be prosocial and achieve in school, adolescents to avoid drug abuse, and young adults to have high self-esteem (Baumrind, 1991; Steinberg et al., 1994).

Many recent studies have found that parenting styles and the child's behavior are less closely linked than Baumrind's original research implied (Galambos et al.,

TABLE 10.2 **Characteristics of Parenting Styles Identified by Baumrind**

	Characteristics				
				Communication	
Style	**Warmth**	**Discipline**	**Expectations of Maturity**	**Parent to Child**	**Child to Parent**
Authoritarian	Low	Strict, often physical	High	High	Low
Permissive	High	Rare	Low	Low	High
Authoritative	High	Moderate, with much discussion	Moderate	High	High

2003). First, the child's temperament interacts with the parents' style. A fearful child needs gentle parenting, and a bolder child needs more restrictive (but still warm) parenting (Bates et al., 1998; Kochanska et al., 2001; Van Leeuwen et al., 2004). Second, culture and community are crucial, as we will now see.

Cultural Variations

Community and cultural differences influence the child's perception of the quality of parenting (Pettit et al., 1997). Perception is key, because the child's interpretation (of a comment, a punishment, a rule) is what determines the effect of parenting. Effective Asian American and African American parents are often stricter, at least as measured by Baumrind's typology, than effective European American parents (Chao, 2001; Wachs, 1999), probably because their children perceive their parents' love and concern in behaviors that European American children might interpret differently.

That authoritative parenting is not always best surprised developmentalists, few of whom were of Asian or African heritage. The first hypothesis to explain the success of strict non-White parents was that raising children in stressful, violent neighborhoods required more authoritarian parenting.

That hypothesis was reasonable, but not confirmed. The data revealed that even in "good" neighborhoods, minority parents tend to impose strict guidelines and to use some physical punishment; the result is that their children often become high-achieving, emotionally well-regulated adolescents. The same strategies are less successful in European American families (Darling & Steinberg, 1997). Obviously, particular parental strategies can vary, as can outcomes. Later research also found that many parents do not fit neatly into any of Baumrind's three categories. Table 10.3 lists some other styles of parenting.

LAURA DWIGHT

Parenting Style This woman is disciplining her son, who does not look happy about it.

? OBSERVATIONAL QUIZ (see answer, page 305): Which parenting style is shown here?

Later research on African American and other families finds that specific discipline methods and family rules are less important than parental warmth, support, and concern, which are expressed in ways influenced by the family's cultural background and community (McLoyd & Smith, 2002). Children from every ethnic group and every country benefit if they believe that their parents appreciate them; children everywhere suffer if they feel rejected and unwanted (Khaleque & Rohner, 2002; Maccoby, 2000).

When children seem burdened by internalizing or externalizing problems, the cause can often be traced to ineffective or rejecting parenting. The effects of a child's past care are revealed in many ways, including reactions to another child's cry of pain. As empathy develops, children typically comfort, reassure,

ESPECIALLY FOR POLITICAL ACTIVISTS Many observers contend that children learn their political attitudes at home, from the way their parents treat them. Is this true?

TABLE 10.3 **Other Styles of Parenting**

Abusive	Some parents' discipline is not only harsh but also inconsistent, without concern for the child's well-being. Unlike in authoritarian families, guidelines are unclear. Children are punished without knowing why or, worse, knowing that the reason was the parent's drinking, drug use, or emotional instability.
Uninvolved	Some parents have no interest in the child's well-being or even in their whereabouts. Note that Baumrind's permissive parents might seem to be neglectful in that their children are not well behaved, well dressed, or even well groomed—unless they want to be. But permissive parents normally are very concerned about their children's safety and welfare. They are involved, just not directive.
Democratic	In democratic parenting, the children have an equal say in what occurs. Such families might have family meetings, in which everyone discusses issues of concern to any member, and then a consensus is reached or a decision is made by majority vote. In authoritative families, by contrast, the parents have the power to set the agenda and make the rules, listening and adjusting only if and when they decide to do so.
Traditional	In some families, the father is the strict disciplinarian and the mother is the indulgent homemaker. He is seen as the head of the family, and her most powerful threat is "I'll have to tell your father about this." This pattern works if both parents understand and respect each other's role, but the children suffer if their traditional parents clash about how to raise them.

Happiness Runs in Families Happy and successful adults can develop in any kind of family. However, as explained in Chapter 8, both abusive and uninvolved parenting can be very harmful. Neither democratic nor traditional families seem as effective as authoritative families, although each of these family systems, like all three of Baumrind's original types, sometimes produce happy and competent children.

and help a crying playmate. By contrast, children with insecure attachments and unresponsive parents respond abnormally, as revealed in a longitudinal study. Some do whatever

> . . . would precisely further distress the child (e.g., scaring a child with the very mask that had been frightening, taunting a crying child and calling him or her a "cry baby," or punching a child with a stomach ache in the stomach). . . . [Others] would often become upset themselves when another was distressed (e.g., holding their own lip and seeking a teacher's lap when another child had fallen).
>
> *[Sroufe, 1996, p. 227]*

RESPONSE FOR POLITICAL ACTIVISTS (from page 303): There are many parenting styles, and it is difficult to determine each one's impact on children's personalities. At this point, attempts to connect early child rearing with later political outlook are speculative at best.

Thus, developmentalists hesitate to favor any one particular style of parenting, but that does not mean that they believe all parents function equally well—far from it. Signs of serious trouble are obvious in a child's behavior, including several mentioned in this chapter: overcontrol, undercontrol, bullying, and antisocial play.

Punishment

The way a parent disciplines a child is an integral part of parenting style. Given what researchers have learned about cognition, a parent, ideally, anticipates misbehavior and guides children away from misdeeds rather than punishing children after the fact. But parents cannot always be wise and vigilant; punishment is sometimes necessary.

Techniques of Discipline

No disciplinary technique works quickly and automatically to teach a child desired behavior. It is easy to stop a child for a moment, with a threat or a slap, but it is hard to shape behavior so that the child gradually internalizes the parents' standards. Yet this is not only the goal—it can be the result, as we have just described. Between ages 2 and 6, children learn to reflect on the consequences of their actions, to control their emotions, and to bring their actions closer to what their parents expect. The universal goal is to raise a self-regulating child, not just an obedient one. Many parents succeed.

The first step is simply to be clear about what is expected. Opinions about which behaviors should be punished vary by culture. What is "rude" or "nasty" or "undisciplined" behavior in one community is perfectly acceptable, even encouraged, in another. Each family needs to think about the goals—and then make them very clear to the child.

The second step is to relate punishment to child development. For instance, some parents punish children for wetting the bed, as if children with poor bladder control at night are deliberately disobedient. Punishment should be rare, reserved for misdeeds known to the child that could be controlled. Other developmental characteristics that should be kept in mind when punishing young children are listed in Table 10.4.

"He's just doing that to get attention."

© THE NEW YORKER COLLECTION 2001 PAT BYRNES FROM CARTOONBANK.COM. ALL RIGHTS RESERVED.

Pay Attention Children develop best with lots of love and attention. They shouldn't have to ask for it!

Family Differences

What should parents do when a child misbehaves? Again, culture and family patterns are influential. Many Japanese mothers, for example, use reasoning, empathy, and expressions of disappointment to control their children's social behavior more than North American mothers do. These techniques work quite well, partly because the mother–child relationship is much tighter in Japan (where it is referred to as *amae,* a very close interpersonal bond) than in North America (Rothbaum et al., 2000).

If the child does not behave well (e.g., objects to taking a bath), mothers differ in their explanations (Bornstein & Cote, 2004; Bornstein et al., 1998). Japanese mothers are likely to blame themselves rather than get angry at the child. Swedish mothers might punish the child—never by hitting (which is considered

! ANSWER TO OBSERVATIONAL QUIZ (from page 303): The authoritative style. Note the firm hold this woman has on her defiant son; he must listen (evidence that she is not permissive). Also note that she is talking to him, not hitting or yelling, and that her expression is warm (evidence that she is not authoritarian).

TABLE 10.4 Relating Discipline to Developmental Characteristics During Early Childhood

1. *Remember theory of mind.* Young children gradually come to understand things from other viewpoints. Encouraging empathy ("How would *you* feel if someone did that to you?") increases prosocial and decreases antisocial behavior.
2. *Remember emerging self-concept.* Young children are developing a sense of who they are and what they want. Adults should protect that emerging self, neither forcing 3-year-olds to share their favorite toys nor saying, "Words do not hurt." Instead, children need to know when and how to protect their favorite possessions and their emerging sense of self. For instance, a child can learn not to bring a toy to school unless he or she is willing to share it with everyone.
3. *Remember the language explosion and fast-mapping.* Young children are eager to talk and think, but they say more than they really understand. Children who "just don't listen" should not always be punished, because they may not have understood a command. Discussion before and after they misbehave helps children learn.
4. *Remember that young children are not yet logical.* The connection between misdeed and punishment needs to be immediate and transparent, but usually it is not. If you were spanked as a child, do you remember why? Did you ever do the same misdeed again?

abuse) but by removing playthings and privileges. European and European American mothers are unlikely to blame either themselves or the child; they blame other sources (the water was too cold or the father doesn't like baths either).

time-out A disciplinary technique in which a child is separated from other people for a specified time.

One disciplinary technique often used in North America is the **time-out**, in which an adult requires the child to sit quietly apart from other people for a few minutes. For young children, time-out can be quickly effective; one minute of time-out per year of age is suggested. Another common practice is "withdrawal of love," when the parent expresses disappointment or looks sternly at the child.

Every method is complicated by the child's temperament. Techniques may succeed more because of the nature of the child than because of the method (O'Connor, 2002). Some children want to be obedient, and with them almost any punishment is effective.

psychological control A disciplinary technique that involves threatening to withdraw love and support and that relies on a child's feelings of guilt and gratitude to the parents.

Another complication is that methods that work temporarily can have unintended consequences. For example, time-out is effective *if* the child strongly prefers to be with the other people. However, some children don't mind being alone; for them time-out is less effective. One version of time-out for older children is suspension from school. If a child dislikes school, this rewards the child for misbehaving, making future disobedience more likely.

ISSUES AND APPLICATIONS

Planning Punishment

How to punish a child has become one of the most controversial topics in child development, particularly during early childhood, when children are considered "old enough to know better" but not "old enough to listen to reason." Parents often punish their children by slapping, spanking, or beating them; all of these physical punishments are used more on children aged 2 to 6 than on children of any other age group. Not only in North America but also throughout Asia, Africa, and South America, most parents believe that spanking is acceptable, legitimate, and necessary at times, and most adults remember being spanked and consider themselves none the worse for it (Durrant, 1996; Levinson, 1989).

Nevertheless, many developmentalists focus on the long-term consequences of punishment. Physical punishment works at the moment—a spanked and crying child stops whatever he or she was doing—but longitudinal research finds that children who are physically punished are likely to become more aggressive (Lansford et al., 2002). In fact, domestic violence of any type—spanking, spouse abuse, even threats, shouts, and insults among family members—correlates with aggression in children, who fight with classmates and later with family members and strangers (Straus, 1994).

This is not to say that spanked children always become violent adults. Spanking increases the risk, but other factors (poverty, temperament, and many more) are stronger risk factors. Nonetheless, developmentalists wonder why parents would take the risk, since physical punishment increases the possibility of antisocial behavior and only

DAVID STRICKLER / MONKMEYER

Angela at Play Research suggests that being spanked is a salient and memorable experience for young children, not because of the pain but because of the emotions. Children seek to do what they have learned; they know not only how to place their hands but also that an angry person does the hitting. The only part of the lesson they usually forget is what particular misdeed precipitated the punishment. Asked why she is spanking her doll, Angela will likely explain, "She was bad."

temporarily increases obedience (Amato & Fowler, 2002; Gershoff, 2002). Further, abusive parents typically justify their punishment by blaming their difficult child, but the reasons are more often to be found in the family and the adult, not the child (Jaffee et al., 2004). To avoid the risk of abuse or eventual violence, most developmentalists recommend other forms of punishment.

But what form of punishment should a parent choose? Any method may have unintended consequences. **Psychological control,** which uses guilt and the child's gratitude toward the parent, may damage a child's initiative and achievement (Barber, 2002). This was shown in a study of an entire cohort (the best way to obtain an unbiased sample) of children born in Finland (Aunola & Nurmi, 2004). Their parents were asked twenty questions about their approach to child rearing. The following four items, which the parents rated from 1 ("Not at all like me") to 5 ("Very much like me") measured psychological control:

1. *My child should be aware of how much I have done for him/her.*
2. *I let my child see how disappointed and shamed I am if he/she misbehaves.*
3. *My child should be aware of how much I sacrifice for him/her.*
4. *I expect my child to be grateful and appreciate all the advantages he/she has.*

The higher parents scored on psychological control, the lower the children's math scores; the connection grew stronger as the children advanced in school. Even worse, math achievement suffered most if parents were high in both psychological control and affection (e.g., they frequently hugged their children) (Aunola & Nurmi, 2004). Other research also finds that psychological control depresses children's achievement and social acceptance, although affection does not always make things worse (Barber et al., 2002).

Both physical punishment and psychological control share one characteristic: They arouse powerful emotions in the child. The emotional link has been suggested to explain why spanked 4-year-olds become more aggressive schoolchildren (Strassberg et al., 1994).

There is no simple answer. Developmentalists advise parents to plan punishments carefully, adjusting to the child's temperament and age. Talking should be part of discipline, and emotional regulation, particularly of negative emotions, should be one goal. Perhaps for that reason, parents and preschoolers discuss the reasons for negative emotions (e.g., fear, sadness, anger, worry) three times as often as for positive emotions (e.g., joy, pleasure, pride) (Lagattuta & Wellman, 2002).

As a mother, I know that prevention is far superior to punishment, but sometimes I did not anticipate very well or talk very much. One hot summer day, thirsty 3-year-old Rachel took a glass orange juice bottle from the refrigerator. She dropped it on the kitchen floor, and it shattered. I wanted to hit her. "Time-out!" I yelled, making her stay on the couch (20 feet away) until I cleaned it up. I needed that time-out more than she did.

Parents have powerful emotions, memories, and stresses, and that's why punishment is not a simple issue. Conversation helps children internalize standards, but talking takes time and patience. Since 3-year-olds do not understand causes and consequences, they cannot answer an angry "Why did you do that?" One young child who was punished for fighting responded, "Sometimes the fight just crawls out of me." Ideally, the punishment won't just crawl out of the parent.

The Challenge of Media

Some people (not parents) imagine that parenting is straightforward. They may anticipate smooth, effortless child rearing for themselves—because they will provide clear rules that their children will obey. If the preceding discussion of punishment didn't raise doubts, the following discussion of the media's influence on children will.

Preschoolers are emotionally immature, sometimes angry or fearful or defiant in ways that not only distress the parents but may harm the child. Normal children want to talk when they should be quiet, run when they should walk, show off when they should be modest. Every parent wants to avoid both harshness and neglect; no wonder some veer toward authoritativeness and some toward permissiveness.

Further, even if their own parents found a good balance between freedom and restriction, each cohort of parents is faced with challenges that were not evident a decade or two earlier. Currently, those challenges include junk food; new family configurations (both discussed in

© THE NEW YORKER COLLECTION 2002 BARBARA SMALLER FROM CARTOONBANK.COM. ALL RIGHTS RESERVED.

"Why don't you get off the computer and watch some TV?"

Especially for Parents Suppose that you agree that spanking is destructive, but you sometimes get so angry at your child's behavior that you hit him or her. Is your reaction appropriate?

ALEX FARNSWORTH / THE IMAGE WORKS

Dangerous Video Game? It is easy to understand and justify a preschooler's fascination with video games. This child in Sweden is developing computer skills, learning to read, and unlikely to get into trouble as he sits quietly and stares at the screen. However, developmentalists would point out that neurological pathways developed while children play video games, especially violent ones, may lead to antisocial, aggressive behavior later in life.

the following chapters); and an explosion of media, including DVDs, video games, and the Internet, in almost every home (see Figure 10.2).

Parents are tempted to allow their young children to watch a television screen or computer monitor, not only because the children demand it but also because video is a good babysitter. It is very difficult for parents to remember the emotional immaturity of the child, who is dazzled by fast-moving images and who emulates cartoon figures who have no empathy.

Experts, however, advise parents to minimize media exposure and spend more time with their children. Six major organizations devoted to the health of children (the American Psychological Association, the American Academy of Pediatrics, the American Medical Association, the American Academy of Child and Adolescent Psychiatry, the American Academy of Family Physicians, and the American Psychiatric Association) implore parents to stop exposing their children to video violence—whether in cartoons, in situation comedies, in video games, or on the evening news. This leaves almost nothing to watch (Anderson & Bushman, 2002).

FIGURE 10.2
The Typical Child's Home Contains . . .

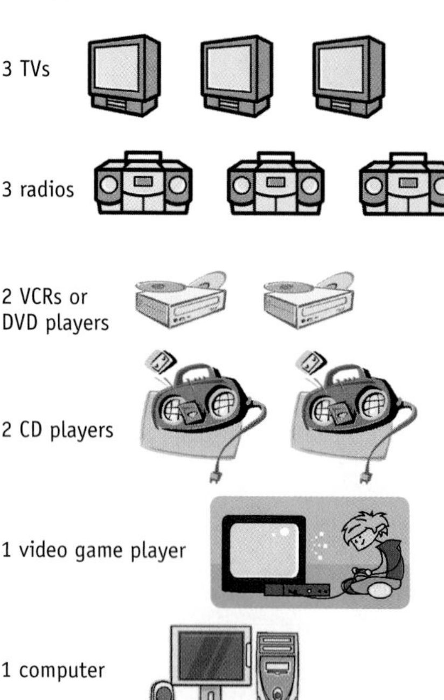

Did you notice that all six organizations have *American* in their titles? That requires a cross-cultural advisement: Most of the research reported here studied U.S. children watching U.S. media (Anderson & Bushman, 2002; Roberts & Foehr, 2004). This is not as substantial a limitation as would be the case for almost any other topic, because, although many national governments regulate and subsidize television, TV programs and movies produced in the United States are popular worldwide. Among younger generations, particularly, cultural differences in access to media (including music and the Internet) are growing smaller. Advice from these six "American" groups is relevant worldwide.

In the United States itself, many subcultures thrive. However, economic and ethnic differences in children's use of media are surprisingly small (Roberts & Foehr, 2004). For example, among 8- to 18-year-olds, those living in low-income households were just as likely to have cable television (75 percent) and video games (83 percent) as were children in middle- or high-income households. European American and African American youth are almost equal (55 and 53 percent) in use of computers; Hispanic children's computer use is lower (35 percent). These data come from a large and careful survey, completed in 1999. Since then, computer use, in particular, has mushroomed, including use by Hispanics.

TABLE 10.5 **Average Daily Exposure to Electronic Media**

Age 2 to 4 Years	Hours per Day
White	3:18
Black	4:30
Hispanic	3:37
Age 5 to 7 Years	**Hours per Day**
White	3:17
Black	4:16
Hispanic	3:38

Source: Adapted from Roberts & Foehr, 2004.

The Evidence on Content

Most young children of every ethnic and economic group in the United States spend more than three hours each day using some sort of media (see Table 10.5). Among young children, television is the most popular medium. Almost every home has at least two televisions, and children usually watch apart from their parents, often in their own rooms. By age 3, more than one-fourth of all children already have a television in their bedrooms, and the percentage rises as children grow older (Roberts & Foehr, 2004).

What do children see? The "good guys," whether in cartoons or police dramas, do as much hitting, shooting, and kicking as the "bad guys," yet the consequences of their violence are sanitized, justified, or made comic. Almost all the good guys are male and White. Women are usually portrayed as victims or adoring girlfriends, not as leaders—except in a very few girl-oriented programs that boys rarely watch.

Some say that the media merely reflect reality. Critic Michael Medved (1995) asks:

> If that's true, then why do we witness so few murders in real life and so many on TV and in the movies? About 350 characters appear each night on prime-time TV; on average, seven of them are murdered. If this murder rate applied in reality, then in just 50 days everyone in the United States would be killed (and the last one left alive could turn off the TV).

One of the best longitudinal studies surveyed children at about age 5 and again at about age 16 (Anderson et al., 2001). The researchers used many statistical safeguards to find causation, not merely correlation. (For instance, children from high-income families tend to watch less TV and do better academically, so children were compared with others of the same socioeconomic status.) They found that young children who watched educational television (mostly *Sesame Street* and *Mr. Rogers' Neighborhood*) became teenagers who earned higher grades and read more than other high school students did, especially if they were boys. Children who watched violent TV programs had lower grades, especially if they were girls.

Evidence from every perspective and method confirms that content matters, that violence is pervasive, and that children of all ages who watch violence on television become more violent themselves (Anderson et al., 2003; Huesmann et al., 2003; Johnson et al., 2002; Singer & Singer, 2005). Developmentalists note that video games are worse than broadcast television in every observable respect—more violent, more sexist, more racist. The heroes are usually Anglo males, and in 80 percent of the games an essential strategy for winning requires violence or aggression (Dietz, 1998).

The Evidence on Family life

All the research on parenting finds that children benefit when parents are involved in their lives. For instance, language, the crucial cognitive achievement of early childhood, depends on hours of conversation with parents every day. Likewise, emotional regulation depends on parental responsiveness.

TV watching limits parent–child interaction in many ways. Parents and children rarely talk when they watch together—and, in fact, they hardly ever watch together. Parents and children have their own TVs, often in separate rooms. In many homes, the television stays on during meals; it even stays on when no one

© THE NEW YORKER COLLECTION 1999 BARBARA SMALLER FROM CARTOONBANK.COM. ALL RIGHTS RESERVED.

"Have some respect for my learning style."

Video Style When children spend a lot of time watching television and playing video games, they are likely to develop a visual learning style. They get used to receiving information in the form of vivid images and brief scenes. That makes it harder for them to concentrate on and comprehend anything that is longer and presented in verbal form, such as a book, lecture, or discussion.

is watching. This amounts to "parental abdication of oversight on children's media behavior" (Roberts & Foehr, 2004, p. 202). By the time children are age 8, only half of all parents have any rules at all about TV watching; rules that do exist are usually about time (no TV after 10:00 P.M., for instance) rather than content.

Not only do the media cut into the time children spend with their parents; they also reduce the amount of time children spend in imaginative and social play. Although many adults hope that more time spent with one type of media would mean less time with another, this is not the case. The only exception is with print: Children who read many books tend to watch less TV.

It is not surprising that grades suffer and violence increases as children watch more TV. The most ominous information, however, comes from studies of the medium that parents understand least: the video game. "It seems likely that the impact of watching characters being killed on television will be exceeded for a child playing a computer game who is doing the virtual killing" (Larson, 2001, p. 150).

Does this discussion seem premature, since it is teenagers, not younger children, who are in the headlines because their use of such media as music videos, CDs, and Internet chat rooms supposedly makes them more likely to become violent or sexually active? There is some truth to that: These games interest adolescents much more than younger children. However, from a developmental perspective, early childhood is pivotal because that is when family media habits are established. Household practices, such as having the TV on during meals and using computers and video games, are noticed by very young children, who try to copy their parents and older siblings. Already by age 6, a fourth of all children had played a computer or video game in the past 24 hours (Roberts & Foehr, 2004).

Early childhood may be the most vulnerable period for other reasons as well. First, young children spend more time in front of the TV and computer screens than do people of any other age group. Second, young children are not very logical about society, culture, and people; they are novices at interpreting and regulating emotions.

You can understand why those six leading organizations hope that children never watch television or play video games. But few parents can enforce a total prohibition. (When you read the In Person feature in Chapter 9, did you wonder why Sarah was so frustrated that she called me angry names? It was because I had unplugged the TV.) It is possible, however, for parents to limit media exposure, to engage children in active recreation, and to limit their own media use.

RESPONSE FOR PARENTS (from page 308): The worst time to spank a child is when you are angry, because you might seriously hurt the child and because the child will associate anger with violence and may follow your example. You would do better to learn to control your anger and develop other strategies for disciplining your child or for preventing him or her from misbehaving in the first place.

SUMMING UP

Parent-child interaction is not the only, or even the most important, influence on children's psychosocial development, but parenting practices do have a significant impact. Over the past 40 years, Diana Baumrind and most other developmentalists have found that authoritative parenting (warm, with guidance) is more effective than either authoritarian (very strict) or permissive (very lenient) parenting. In any culture, children thrive when their parents appreciate them and care about their accomplishments. The children of parents who are uninvolved, uncaring, or abusive are seldom happy, well-adjusted, and high-achieving.

Spanking is a quick way to make children stop misbehavior, but most developmentalists believe that nonphysical discipline is more effective over the long term. Every method may have unintended consequences, however, with psychological control particularly problematic.

Good parenting is not achieved by following any one simple rule; children's temperaments vary, and so do cultural patterns. The media pose a particular challenge worldwide because children are attracted to colorful, fast-paced images, yet violent TV programs, in particular, lead to more aggressive behavior. Parental monitoring of the quality and quantity of the media—the underlying messages as well as the overt themes—to which children are exposed is recommended by every expert.

Becoming Boys and Girls

Identity as a male or female is an important feature of a child's self-concept, a major source of self-esteem (with each gender believing that it is best) (Powlishta, 2004).The first question asked about a newborn is "Boy or girl?" and parents select gender-distinct clothes, blankets, diapers, and even pacifiers. By age 2, children already know their own sex, and they become more aware of gender with every year of childhood (Maccoby, 1998).

Social scientists attempt to distinguish between **sex differences**, which are the biological differences between males and females, and **gender differences**, which are culturally imposed masculine or feminine roles and behaviors. In theory, this is a logical separation, but, as with every nature–nurture distinction, the interaction between sex and gender makes it hard to separate the two (Hines, 2004). Curiously, although true *sex* differences are far less apparent in childhood (when boys and girls are about the same size and shape) than in adulthood (when physical differences become more visible and anatomy becomes critical in sexual intercourse, pregnancy, and birth), *gender* differentiation seems more significant to children than to adults (Powlishta, 2004).

sex differences Biological differences between males and females, in organs, hormones, and body type.

gender differences Differences in the roles and behavior of males and females that originate in the culture.

The Development of Gender Awareness

As already mentioned, even 2-year-olds know whether they are boys or girls, can identify adult strangers as mommies or daddies, and can apply gender labels (*Mrs., Mr., lady, man*) consistently. That simple cognitive awareness becomes, by age 3, a rudimentary understanding that sex distinctions are lifelong (although some pretend, hope, or imagine otherwise). By age 4, children are convinced that certain toys (such as dolls or trucks) and certain roles (such as nurse or soldier) are appropriate for one gender but not the other (Bauer et al., 1998; Ruble & Martin, 1998).

Two Sets of Cousins Same day, same trampoline, and similar genes and culture, because these eight children are cousins. But sex or gender differences are quite apparent in the later preschool years. This group, like any group of preschoolers, offers suggestive evidence of boy–girl differences, here including one specific aspect of their apparel.

? **OBSERVATIONAL QUIZ** (see answer, page 312): What sex or gender differences can you see?

BRADY / MONKMEYER

(a)

BRADY / MONKMEYER

(b)

! Answer to Observational Quiz (from page 311): The most obvious gender differences are in appearance. The girls have longer hair, and the colors and styles of their clothes are different. Did you notice the wearing-apparel difference—that the soles of all four boys' shoes are black, whereas the girls' are white or pink? Now let's get more speculative. The girl on the left, who may need to establish her alliance with the group since she is the only one in colors a boy might wear, is looking at and talking with her cousins—a very female thing to do. In addition, the girls' facial and body expressions suggest they are much more comfortable with this close contact. In fact, the two boys on the left seem about to start relieving their tension with a bout of rough-and-tumble play.

When given a choice, children play with other children of their own sex. This tendency begins by age 1 and is clear-cut by age 4, with children becoming more selective and exclusive as they mature (Martin & Fabes, 2001). By school age, those few children who still have friends of the other sex rarely play with them when other children are around (Kovacs et al., 1996).

Throughout the play years, children confuse gender and sex. Awareness that a person's sex is a biological characteristic, not determined by words, opinions, or clothing, develops gradually, becoming firm at age 8 or so (Szkrybalo & Ruble, 1999). This uncertainty about the biological determination of sex was demonstrated by a 3-year-old who went with his father to see a neighbor's newborn kittens. Returning home, the child reported to his mother that there were three girl kittens and two boy kittens. "How do you know?" she asked. "Daddy picked them up and read what was written on their tummies," he answered.

Theories of Gender Differences

Experts as well as parents disagree about what proportion of observed gender differences is biological (perhaps a matter of hormones, of brain structure, or of body size and musculature) and what proportion is environmental (perhaps embedded in centuries of cultural history or in the immediate, explicit home training each child receives) (Beal, 1994; Leaper, 2002). For example, you read earlier that girls are often ahead of boys in emotional regulation and that there are gender differences in the preference for rough-and-tumble or sociodramatic play. It may be that these differences are genetic, tied to the chromosomal differences between XX and XY that affect prenatal brain development, or that parents treat their sons and daughters differently. In fact, the evidence supports both propositions.

Neuroscientists tend to look for male–female brain differences, and they find many; sociologists tend to look for male–female family and culture patterns, and they also find many. The same predilections apply to historians, anthropologists, political scientists, and psychologists of every stripe. Sex/gender differences are pervasive, apparent to every observer, and no single perspective can explain them all. To find a framework for analyzing the conflicting evidence, we need a theory. Fortunately, we have five developmental theories, first described in Chapter 2.

Psychoanalytic Theory

phallic stage Freud's third stage of development, when the penis becomes the focus of concern and pleasure.

Freud (1938) called the period from about age 3 to 6 the **phallic stage,** because he believed its central focus is the *phallus,* or penis. At about 3 or 4 years of age, said Freud, the process of maturation makes a boy aware of his male sexual organ. He begins to masturbate, to fear castration, and to develop sexual feelings toward his mother.

Oedipus complex The unconscious desire of young boys to replace their fathers and win their mother's exclusive love.

These feelings make every young boy jealous of his father—so jealous, according to Freud, that every son secretly wants to replace his dad. Freud called this the **Oedipus complex,** after Oedipus, son of a king in Greek mythology. Abandoned as an infant and raised in a distant kingdom, Oedipus later returned to his birthplace and, not realizing who they were, killed his own father and married his mother. When he discovered what he had done, he blinded himself in a spasm of guilt.

Freud believed that this ancient story still echoes throughout history because every man feels horribly guilty for the incestuous and murderous impulses that are buried in his unconscious. Boys fear that their fathers will inflict terrible punishment if their secret impulses are discovered. Therefore, they hide their feelings, even from themselves. Specifically, boys cope with their guilt and fear through **identification,** a defense mechanism that allows a person to ally him- or herself with another person by symbolically taking on that person's behavior and attitudes. Because they cannot replace their fathers, young boys strive to become them, copying their fathers' masculine mannerisms, opinions, and actions.

identification An attempt to defend one's self-concept by taking on the behaviors and attitudes of someone else.

Boys also develop, again in self-defense, a powerful conscience called the **superego,** which is quick to judge and punish "the bad guys." According to Freud's theory, a young boy's fascination with superheroes, guns, kung fu, and the like arises from his unconscious urges to kill his father. An adult man's homosexuality, homophobia, or obsession with punishment might be explained by an imperfectly resolved phallic stage.

superego In psychoanalytic theory, the judgmental part of the personality that internalizes moral standards of the parents.

Freud offered two overlapping descriptions of the phallic stage in girls. One centers on the **Electra complex** (also named after a figure in classical mythology), which is similar to the Oedipus complex in that the little girl wants to eliminate her mother and become intimate with her father. In the other description, girls are jealous of boys because they have penises. According to Freud, a girl deals with her *penis envy* by deciding to become sexually attractive so that someone who does have a penis—preferably her father—will love her (Freud, 1933/1965). Her *identification* is with women her father finds attractive; her *superego* strives to avoid his disapproval. Thus, the origins and consequences of the phallic stage are similar for girls and for boys.

Electra complex The unconscious desire of girls to replace their mothers and win their father's exclusive love.

As a woman, and as the mother of four daughters, I have regarded Freud's theory of sexual development as ridiculous, not to mention antifemale. I am not alone. Since 1950, social scientists generally have agreed that Freud's explanation of sexual and moral development "flies in the face of sociological and historical evidence" (David et al., 2004, p. 139). Freud's ideas reflect the values of middle-class Victorian society at the end of the nineteenth century. Only recently have some of Freud's ideas become more acceptable to psychologists. I myself have softened my criticism of Freud, as the following feature explains.

IN PERSON

Berger and Freud

My family's first "Electra episode" occurred in a conversation with my eldest daughter, Bethany, when she was about 4 years old:

Bethany: When I grow up, I'm going to marry Daddy.
Mother: But Daddy's married to me.
Bethany: That's all right. When I grow up, you'll probably be dead.
Mother: *(Determined to stick up for myself)* Daddy's older than me, so when I'm dead, he'll probably be dead, too.
Bethany: That's OK. I'll marry him when he gets born again.

At this point, I couldn't think of a good reply, especially since I had no idea where she had gotten the concept of reincarnation. Bethany saw my face fall, and she took pity on me:

Bethany: Don't worry, Mommy. After you get born again, you can be our baby.

The second episode was a conversation I had with my daughter Rachel when she was about 5:

Rachel: When I get married, I'm going to marry Daddy.
Mother: Daddy's already married to me.
Rachel: *(With the joy of having discovered a wonderful solution)* Then we can have a double wedding!

The third episode was considerably more graphic. It took the form of a "valentine" left on my husband's pillow by my daughter Elissa, who was about 8 years old at the time. It is reproduced on the next page.

Finally, when my youngest daughter, Sarah, turned 5, she also expressed the desire to marry my husband. When I told her she couldn't, because he was married to me, her response revealed one more hazard of watching TV: "Oh, yes, a man can have two wives. I saw it on television."

I am not the only feminist developmentalist to be taken aback by her own children's words. Nancy Datan (1986) wrote about the Oedipal conflict: "I have a son who was once five years old. From that day to this, I have never thought Freud mistaken." Obviously, these bits of "evidence" do not prove that Freud was correct. I still think he was wrong on many counts. But I now find Freud's description of the phallic stage less bizarre than I once did.

Pillow Talk Elissa placed this artwork on my husband's pillow. My pillow, beside it, had a less colorful, less elaborate note—an afterthought. It read "Dear Mom, I love you too."

Behaviorism

In contrast with psychoanalytic theorists, behaviorists believe that virtually all roles are learned and therefore result from nurture, not nature. To behaviorists, gender distinctions are the product of ongoing reinforcement and punishment rather than of any specific stage.

Some evidence supports this aspect of learning theory. Parents, peers, and teachers all reward behavior that is "gender-appropriate" more than "gender-inappropriate" (Ruble & Martin, 1998). Mothers encourage girls to control their emotions and boys to "let it all hang out" (Colder et al., 2002), and fathers rough-house more with their sons, who learn to do likewise. Similarly, boys are praised for not crying ("He took it like a man"), while girls are encouraged to "act like a lady."

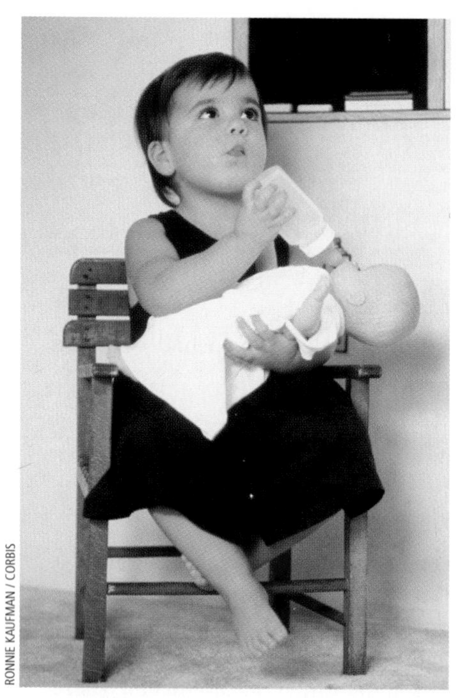

RONNIE KAUFMAN / CORBIS

Rehearsal for Future Motherhood This preschooler is demonstrating three behaviors that are considered appropriate for girls and are almost never seen in boys: She is wearing a skirt, tucking her crossed legs back, and cradling and "feeding" a doll.

This male–female distinction seems to be more significant to males than to females (Banerjee & Lintern, 2000; David et al., 2004), as boys are more often criticized for being "sissies" than girls are criticized for being "tomboys." Fathers, more than mothers, expect their daughters to be feminine and their sons to be tough. Girls, however, are more aware of gender discrimination against them, as might be expected for the group that tends to be seen as subordinate.

Behaviorists believe children learn about proper behavior not only directly (such as receiving a gender-appropriate toy or a father's praise) but also indirectly, through social learning. Children model their behavior particularly after that of people they perceive to be nurturing, powerful, and yet similar to themselves. For young children, those people are usually their parents. And parental attitudes about gender differences become increasingly influential as children grow older (Tenenbaum & Leaper, 2002).

Ironically, young children see more sex-stereotyped behavior than do people at any other life stage, because child care is primarily done by women. If young boys and girls model their behavior after that of their parents, they will follow examples that are quite sex-specific (McHale et al., 2003). The importance of modeling is also shown in the fact that young children of either sex who have older brothers become more masculine and those who have older sisters become more feminine, just as behaviorism would predict (Rust et al., 2000).

Thus, conformity to gender expectations is still rewarded, punished, and modeled, especially for young children and especially for boys. This may explain why girls can aspire to traditionally male occupations but boys cannot aspire to traditionally female occupations without experiencing disapproval, especially from other males.

Note that this theory explains why gender prejudice is particularly strong during the play years. If a college man wants to teach young children, his classmates probably will respect him and may know another man who made the same choice. If a 4-year-old boy wants the same thing, his peers will laugh because their experience has been quite gender-segregated. As one professor reports:

> My son came home after 2 days of preschool to announce that he could not grow up to teach seminars (previously his lifelong ambition, because he knew from personal observation that everyone at seminars got to eat cookies) because only women could be teachers.
>
> *[Fagot, 1995, p. 173]*

Cognitive Theory

In explaining gender identity and gender differences, cognitive theorists focus on children's understanding—on the way a child intellectually grasps a specific issue or value (Kohlberg et al., 1983; Martin, 2000). Young children, they point out, have many gender-related experiences but not much cognitive depth. They tend to see the world in simple terms. For this reason, male and female are categorized as opposites, even when some evidence (such as the father they saw cleaning the living room) contradicts such a sexist assumption. Nuances, complexities, exceptions, and gradations about gender (as well as about everything else) are beyond the intellect of the preoperational child.

Remember that the basic tenet of cognitive theory is that thinking determines how people perceive the world and then they act on their perceptions. Cognitive theory can be considered the opposite of social learning theory, in that "while both theories explain how the social reality of sex differences is internalized, social learning theory proposes that society socializes children, while cognitive developmental theory proposes that children actively socialize themselves" (David et al., 2004, pp. 139–140).

An example comes from a 3½-year-old boy whose aunt called him *cute*. He insisted he should be called *handsome* instead (Powlishta, 2004). Obviously he had developed gender-based categories, and he wanted others to see him as the young man his own cognition had decided he was.

When personal experience is ambiguous or puzzling, young children search for the intellectual categories they have formed to describe appropriate gender behavior. For example, when researchers gave young children unfamiliar, gender-neutral toys, the children first tried to figure out whether the toys were for boys or for girls and then decided whether or not they personally would like to play with them (Martin et al., 1995). Similarly, when older children were shown drawings of people engaging in unfamiliar (actually nonexistent) occupations, they judged the status of the occupation according to whether the workers were men or women, ranking the supposedly female occupations lower than the male ones.

Thus, the self-esteem and self-concept that young children tend to develop lead to a cognitive drive to categorize themselves as male or female, and then to behave in a way that fits the category. For that reason, cognitive theorists see "Jill's claim that she is a girl because she is wearing her new frilly socks as a genuine expression of her gender identity" (David et al., 2004, p. 147).

According to cognitive theory, children develop a mental set, or a cognitive schema, which biases their views of whatever experiences they have. For 2- to 6-year-olds, that cognitive set is, of necessity, quite simple, which is why their sex stereotyping peaks at about age 6.

Sociocultural Theory

Proponents of the sociocultural perspective point out that many traditional cultures enforce gender distinctions. In societies where adult activities and dress are strictly separated by gender, girls and boys attend sex-segregated schools and virtually never play together (Beal, 1994). And all over the world, children quickly adopt the patterns of talking, behaving, and even thinking that are prescribed for their sex (Leaper & Smith, 2004).

The particulars of gender education—such as teaching children which activities are promoted for which sex—vary by region, socioeconomic status, and historical period. For example, in many regions of the world, it's the women who are responsible for growing the vegetables and grains, but on North American farms, men are in charge of growing all the crops.

Every society has powerful values and attitudes regarding preferred behavior for men and women, and every culture teaches these to the young, even though the particular tasks assigned to males and to females vary. To sociocultural theorists, this proves that society, not biology, segregates the sexes and transmits proper male or female behavior (Kimmel, 2004).

This is blatantly apparent during adolescence, when sexual urges might drive young people to seek out the other sex. Instead, in most nations, young people work beside adults of the same sex as themselves and socialize in sex-segregated but cross-age groups, "from the pottery making sessions of the Hopi to the gathering parties of the !Kung Bushmen to the groups of Sicilian women neighbors, sitting together as they embroider" (Schlegel, 2003, pp. 243–244).

After many years of feminist campaigns for gender equity, one might imagine that any remaining sex differences in developed nations would be biological, not sociocultural. This is not the case: Gender stereotypes and different roles may be less rigid than they once were, but they are still omnipresent for young children in every country (Kimmel, 2004).

Consider Halloween dress-up, a North American custom. (Most nations have no Halloween.) In an analysis of all 469 children's costumes available in one region, only 10 percent were gender-neutral, and those were designed for babies. By age 2, girls trick-or-treated as pumpkin princesses, blushing brides, and beauty queens; boys dressed as warriors and villains of all sorts, including Hercules, Dracula, and the serial killer Jack the Ripper. Even animal costumes

ARIEL SKELLEY / CORBIS

Trick or Treat? Any doubt about which of these children are girls and which are boys? No. Any question about whether such strict gender distinctions are appropriate at age 4? Maybe.

were sex-specific, with girls dressed as black cats and pink dragons, boys as lions and T-Rex dinosaurs (Nelson, 2000).

To break through the restrictiveness of culture and to encourage individuals to define themselves primarily as humans, rather than as males or females, some parents and teachers have embraced the idea of androgyny. As developmentalists use the term, **androgyny** means a balance, within a person, of masculine and feminine psychological characteristics. To achieve androgyny, boys should be encouraged to be nurturant and girls to be assertive, so that they will develop less restrictive, gender-free self-concepts (Bem, 1993).

androgyny A balance, within a person, of traditionally male and female psychological characteristics.

Sociocultural theory stresses that androgyny (or any other gender concept) cannot be taught simply through parental reinforcement or cognition, as behaviorism and cognitive theory might propose. Children will not be androgynous unless their culture promotes such ideas and practices—something no culture has done. Why not? The reasons may lie buried far deeper in human nature than in political forces or social values. That is what epigenetic theory suggests.

Epigenetic Theory

We saw in Chapter 2 that epigenetic theory contends that every aspect of human behavior is the result of interaction between genes and early experience—not just for the individual but also for the entire human race. The idea that gender differences are based in genetics is supported by recent research in neurobiology, which has found biological differences between male and female brains. Sex hormones produced by XX (female) or XY (male) chromosomes begin to circulate in the fetal stage, affecting the development of the brain throughout life (Cameron, 2001).

Much of the research on the brain is done with lower animals, since experimenting with human brains, or studying brains on autopsy, is complex, both ethically and scientifically (Kagan & Herschkowitz, 2005). With nonhuman creatures, however, sex differences in brain shape and function are legion. For example, male and female voices differ partly because of vocal control systems within the brains of all jawed vertebrates. In an experiment, male and female hormones quickly changed the brain impulses, altering the pattern of vocalization in a fish species. The authors believe this may apply to all "vocal vertebrates," including people (Remage-Healey & Bass, 2004). Perhaps sex differences in voices originate not in experience or the larynx but in the hormones in the brain. Similar examples, demonstrated in lower animals, can be found for almost every human sex difference.

Although epigenetic theory stresses the biological and genetic origins of behavior, it also recognizes that the environment can shape, enhance, or halt those genetic impulses. Here is one example: Infant girls seem to be genetically inclined to talk earlier than boys, perhaps because in prehistoric times, when women stayed home together to care for the children while men hunted, women had to become more adept at social interaction. Consequently, female brains evolved to favor language (Gleason & Ely, 2002).

Especially for Gender Idealists Suppose you want to raise an androgynous child. What do you think would happen if you told no one your newborn's sex, dressed it in yellow and white rather than pink or blue, and gave it a gender-neutral name, such as Chris or Lee?

Today, women still specialize in caregiving, using language to show support and agreement, while men still are more assertive, favoring speech that is more directive, with shorter, louder sentences. Even when these stereotyped patterns no longer apply to a specific person, genetic adaptation began several millennia ago and would take centuries to change. Researchers repeatedly find that girls tend to be more responsive to language than boys, and mothers and daughters typically talk more than fathers and sons (Leaper, 2002; Leaper & Smith, 2004; Maccoby, 1998). Thus, a baby girl's slight linguistic advantage in inherited brain circuitry will become a notably higher level of language proficiency as she grows up. By school age, the average girl is better at language arts than the average boy for epigenetic, not merely genetic, reasons.

Response for Gender Idealists (from page 317): Since babies are raised by a society and community as well as by their parents, and since some gender differences are biological, this attempt at androgyny would not succeed. First, other interested parties would decide for themselves that the child was male or female. Second, the child would sooner or later develop gender-specific play patterns, guided by other boys or girls.

Epigenetic theorists note that the language areas of the infant's brain develop as people speak to that infant. Thus, language development is experience-dependent as well as experience-expectant. It is not surprising, then, that the female advantage in language is more apparent from ages 2 to 5 than at any other age (Leaper & Smith, 2004), because those are the years when the brain is most likely to respond to language.

The fact that nurture is crucial for nature to unfold explains why some men are much more verbal than some women: Their nurture did not follow their nature. For instance, if a boy is an only child, raised in a household with several nurturant women, he is likely to be talked to, sung to, and read to by all his devoted female caregivers. His linguistic environment (which is much richer than that of most infants), interacting with his genetic potential (which may be slightly less than that of the typical girl), will cause him to develop superior verbal ability in his brain as well as in his speech. In this way, environmental factors will greatly enhance his genetic capabilities, perhaps allowing him to excel in all the language arts in the first grade.

In the same way, all sex and gender differences may have genetic, hormonal roots, for reasons that originated thousands of years ago, but modern society can enhance or redirect those inherited tendencies. Our society rarely chooses to do so. Accordingly, male–female distinctions are among the first that children recognize, and by age 5 children show a strong same-sex favoritism as well as rigid ideas about which sex does what.

Conclusion: Gender and Destiny

The first and last of our five major theories—psychoanalytic theory and epigenetic theory—emphasize the power of biology. This conclusion may be reinforced by the fact that gender awareness emerges early, by age 2. A reader might seize on those theories to decide that, since gender-based behavior and sexual stereotypes originate in the body and brain, they are impossible to change. But the other three theories—behaviorism, cognitive theory, and sociocultural theory—all present persuasive evidence for the influence of family and culture.

Thus, our five major theories lead in two opposite directions:

- Gender differences are rooted in biology.
- Biology is not destiny: Children are shaped by their experiences.

Given nature and nurture, both these conclusions are valid. That creates a dilemma for every person. Since human behavior is plastic, what gender patterns *should* children learn, ideally? Answers vary among developmentalists as well as among mothers, fathers, and cultures. If all children responded only to their own inclinations, they might choose behaviors, express emotions, and develop talents that are taboo—even punished—in certain cultures. In Western societies, little boys might put on makeup, little girls might play with guns, and both sexes might play naked outside in hot weather. Whether these behaviors should be permitted is a question for adults, not children.

My daughter Bethany, at about age 5, challenged one of my young male students to a fight.

"Girls don't fight," he said, laughing.

"Nobody fights," I quickly corrected him. To this day I wonder if my response to my girl child, although cast in unisex words, was nonetheless quite female. Should I have just left it alone, allowing my student to teach Bethany the norms of society? Or should I have championed androgyny, telling Bethany that girls can fight and making my student engage in the same rough-and-tumble play fighting that might have occurred if my child had been a boy? I remember this incident now, years later, because I am still not sure of the answer.

SUMMING UP

Young boys and girls are seen as quite different, not only by parents and other adults but especially by the children themselves. Gender stereotypes are held most forcefully at about age 6. Each of the five major theories has an explanation for this phenomenon: Freud describes unconscious incestuous urges; behaviorists note social reinforcement; cognitive theorists describe immature categorization; sociocultural explanations focus on patterns throughout the culture; and epigenetic theory begins with the hereditary aspects of brain and body development. Although each theory offers an explanation, theories don't answer questions about moral and social values. Perhaps that is why cultures and individuals draw contradictory conclusions about everyday practices regarding sex and gender.

■ SUMMARY

Emotional Development

1. In Erikson's psychosocial theory, the crisis of initiative versus guilt occurs during the play years. Children normally feel pride and self-esteem, sometimes mixed with feelings of guilt.

2. Regulation of emotions is crucial during the play years, when children learn emotional control. Emotional regulation is made possible by maturation of the brain, particularly of the prefrontal cortex, as well as by experiences with parents and peers. Both externalizing and internalizing problems indicate impaired self-control.

3. Empathy, which leads to prosocial behavior, and antipathy, which leads to antisocial behavior, develop during early childhood. These emotions come from within the child, but family experiences probably start the process.

Play

4. Young children love to play—by themselves, with imaginary friends if need be, and with peers if possible. Children learn to control their emotions, particularly their antisocial ones, through play with peers. Cooperation gradually develops through rough-and-tumble and sociodramatic play, both of which require adjustment to the needs and imaginations of playmates.

5. As children become more aware of themselves and their peers, they regulate their aggression. Instrumental aggression occurs when children fight over toys and privileges, and reactive aggression occurs when children react to being hurt. More worrisome are relational and bullying aggression, damaging to both aggressor and victim.

Parents

6. Three classic styles of parenting have been identified: authoritarian, permissive, and authoritative. Generally, children are more successful and happy when their parents express warmth and set guidelines. Parenting that is rejecting and uninvolved is harmful.

7. Punishment should fit not only the age and temperament of the child but also the culture. Developmentalists fear that physical punishment increases reactive and bullying aggression and that psychological control by the parents impedes a child's self-concept and achievement.

8. Children are prime consumers of many kinds of media, usually for several hours a day, often without their parents' involvement. Content is crucial. The themes and characters of many television programs and video games reflect sexism and racism and lead to increased aggression.

Becoming Boys and Girls

9. Even 2-year-olds correctly use sex-specific labels, and young children become aware of gender differences in clothes, toys, future careers, and playmates. Gender stereotypes, favoritism, and segregation peak at about age 6.

10. Nature and nurture are both involved with sex and gender; disentangling them is very difficult. Every type of scientist and each major theory has a perspective on sex and gender distinctions.

11. Freud emphasized that children are attracted to the opposite-sex parent and eventually seek to identify, or align themselves, with the same-sex parent. Behaviorists hold that gender-related behaviors are learned through reinforcement and punishment (especially for males) and social modeling.

12. Cognitive theorists note that simplistic preoperational thinking leads to gender stereotypes. Sociocultural theorists point to the many male–female distinctions apparent in every society.

13. An epigenetic explanation notes that some sex differences result from hormones affecting brain formation. Experiences enhance or halt those neurological patterns.

KEY TERMS

initiative versus guilt (p. 286)
self-esteem (p. 286)
self-concept (p. 286)
intrinsic motivation (p. 288)
emotional regulation (p. 288)
externalizing problems (p. 289)
internalizing problems (p. 289)
emotional intelligence (p. 292)
empathy (p. 293)
antipathy (p. 293)
prosocial behavior (p. 293)
antisocial behavior (p. 293)
rough-and-tumble play (p. 296)
sociodramatic play (p. 297)
instrumental aggression (p. 299)
reactive aggression (p. 299)
relational aggression (p. 299)
bullying aggression (p. 299)
authoritarian parenting (p. 302)
permissive parenting (p. 302)
authoritative parenting (p. 302)
time-out (p. 306)
psychological control (p. 306)
sex differences (p. 311)
gender differences (p. 311)
phallic stage (p. 311)
Oedipus complex (p. 312)
identification (p. 313)
superego (p. 313)
Electra complex (p. 313)
androgyny (p. 317)

KEY QUESTIONS

1. How can adults help children develop self-esteem?

2. How and when is it unwise to praise a child?

3. What is the connection between temperament and emotional regulation?

4. How do early caregiving and culture affect later emotional control?

5. If a young child never played with other children, what problems would that cause and why?

6. What are the similarities and differences between rough-and-tumble play and sociodramatic play?

7. What are the advantages and disadvantages of physical punishment?

8. How do parenting styles relate to cultural differences?

9. Describe the differences among three of the five theories of sex differences.

10. List the similarities between two of the five theories of sex differences.

11. How do children change from ages 2 to 6 in their male and female roles and behaviors?

APPLICATIONS

1. Observe the interactions of two or more young children. Sort your observations into four categories: emotion, reasons, results, and emotional regulation. Note every observable emotion (laughter, tears, etc.), the reason for it, the consequences, and whether or not emotional regulation was likely. For example: "Anger: friend grabbed toy; child suggested sharing; emotional regulation probable."

2. Ask three parents about punishment, including their preferred type, at what age, for what misdeeds, and by whom. Ask your informants how they were punished and how that affected them. Then report your findings with your own analysis. If your sources agree, and you agree with them, find someone from another culture who has a different view.

3. Gender indicators often go unnoticed. Go to a public place (park, restaurant, busy street) and spend at least 10 minutes recording examples of gender differentiation, such as articles of clothing, mannerisms, interaction patterns, activities. Quantify what you see, such as baseball hats on eight males and two females or (better but more difficult) four male–female conversations, with gender difference in length and frequency of talking, interruptions, vocabulary, and so on.

PART III

The Play Years

BIOSOCIAL

Physical growth As growth slows down, children become more discriminating eaters, often eating too much of the wrong foods.

Brain and Nervous System The brain attains 90 percent of its adult weight by the time the child is 5 years old. Both the proliferation of neural pathways and myelination continue. Specific parts of the brain (including the corpus callosum, the prefrontal cortex, and the limbic system) begin to connect, allowing coordination of left and right and some modification of the impulsivity and perseveration of the younger child. Gross motor skills, such as running and jumping, improve dramatically, making injury more likely. Fine motor skills, such as writing and drawing, develop more slowly.

Maltreatment Child abuse and neglect, potential problems at every age, are particularly likely in homes with many children and few personal or community resources. Recognition of the problem has improved, but treatment is uneven. Prevention occurs when an abused child is protected from further harm (tertiary prevention), when risk factors are reduced (secondary prevention, such as more help for overwhelmed parents), and when society-wide factors make maltreatment less likely (primary prevention).

COGNITIVE

Cognitive Skills Piaget stressed the child's self-centered, illogical perspective; Vygotsky stressed the cultural context; both see the child as ready to learn. Many children develop their own theories of the world, including a theory of mind.

Language Language abilities develop rapidly; by the age of 6, the average child knows 10,000 words and demonstrates extensive grammatical knowledge in one language or two, depending on the social context. Children adjust their communication to their audience, and they use language to help themselves learn. Preschool education helps children develop language and express themselves as well as prepares them for later education and adult life.

PSYCHOSOCIAL

Emotions and Personality Development With the stage called initiative versus guilt, self-concept emerges, as does the ability to regulate emotions. Externalizing problems may be the result of too little emotional regulation; internalizing problems may result from too much control. Empathy produces prosocial behavior; antipathy leads to antisocial actions, including aggression.

Play Children engage in play to master physical and intellectual skills. Both rough-and-tumble and sociodramatic play can help channel aggression.

Parent–Child Interaction Parenting styles that are warm and responsive, with much communication, seem to be most effective in encouraging the child to develop autonomy and self-control. Extensive use of television and other media by children can disrupt parent–child interaction.

Gender Roles Children develop stereotypic concepts of sex differences in appearance and gender differences in behavior. Theories give contradictory explanations of nature and nurture.

PART IV

The School Years

If someone asked you to pick the best years of the entire life span, you might choose ages 7 to 11 and defend your choice persuasively. For many children, biosocial development during these years is almost problem-free (unless puberty begins), and includes the mastery of dozens of new athletic skills. With regard to cognition, most children learn quickly and think logically, as long as the topic is not too abstract. Moreover, they acquire concepts, vocabulary, and intellectual skills with enthusiasm, perseverance, and curiosity; they are a joy to teach. These are "the school years," because every culture instructs its children during this time.

Children's thinking is straightforward and is based on observation more than imagination. For instance, in relation to moral reasoning and behavior, right seems clearly distinguished from wrong—without the possible ambiguities and potential conflicts that complicate ethics later on. Further, their psychosocial world is usually benign: School-age children usually consider their parents helpful, their teachers fair, and their friends loyal.

All this is true for many, but not all, school-age children. Some struggle with special educational needs, some live in dysfunctional families, some cope with poverty or homelessness, some suffer obesity, asthma, bullying, or another ongoing problem. The next three chapters celebrate the joys and acknowledge the difficulties of middle childhood.

ZENRAKU MILK
全酪牛乳
MILK
全酪牛乳

Chapter Eleven

The School Years: Biosocial Development

Context changes, and that makes everything else change. No longer do children depend entirely on their families to dress, feed, and wash them, or to send them off to a preschool where they are apt to encounter a limited number of other similar children. By age 6 or 7, self-care (dressing, eating, bathing) is routine and attendance at school is mandated—usually a school with a formal curriculum and, often, hundreds of fellow learners from many backgrounds. That change, from home to school, is a major shift in context.

This chapter describes similarities among all school-age children, but also differences that suddenly become significant—in size, in health, in learning ability, and in almost everything else. Every child suddenly realizes that the social world of school is unlike home, where each child is usually appreciated for himself or herself. Children make comparisons, and almost every child suffers from such comparisons at some point. I changed schools as well as cities in the second grade, and I was thrilled that Cynthia seemed willing to be my friend. But I was mistaken.

"We cannot be friends," she told me, "because I am a Democrat."

"So am I," I answered. I knew my family believed in democracy.

"No you're not. You are a Republican," she said.

I was stunned. I did not know what she meant, but we never became friends.

Underlying social perceptions are the neurons and networks of the brain, which function differently for each child but make all children aware of one another. Ongoing brain maturation makes many motor skills and behaviors easier for some children than others. School is daunting for the third-grader who has dyslexia and cannot read, or the fourth-grader who is hyperactive and cannot sit still, or the 6-year-old who has autism and cannot make friends.

But once we look closely at and compare real children, it becomes obvious that every child has strengths and liabilities. Every child is special because every brain is unique and every home environment is unique. Diversity splinters into further diversities; multiculturalism becomes multi-multi-multicultural. To highlight this point, we begin with two children who seem to share the same background: They are both of Mexican heritage, and both live in southern California. The differences between them, as between any two children of the same age, are evident.

A CASE TO STUDY

Two Hispanic Children: Typical or Unique?

Yolanda Piedra and Paul Chavez (not their real names) reflect on their school years.

Yolanda:

When I got here [from Mexico at age 7], I didn't want to stay here, 'cause I didn't like the school. And after a little while, in third grade, I started getting the hint of it and everything and I tried real hard in it. I really got along with the teachers. . . . They would start talking to me, or they kinda like pulled me up some grades, or moved me to other classes, or took me somewhere. And they were always congratulating me.

Actually, there's one friend of mine. . . . She's been with me since first grade until eighth grade, right now. And she's always been with me, in bad or good things, all the time. She's always telling me, "Keep on going and your dreams are gonna come true." . . .

I see some other kids that they say, like, they'd say they're Colombian or something. They try to make themselves look cool in front of everybody. I just say what I am and I feel proud of myself. . . . It's okay for me being born over there 'cause I feel proud of myself. I feel proud of my culture.

[quoted in Nieto, 2000, pp. 220–221]

Paul:

I grew up . . . ditching school, just getting in trouble, trying to make a dollar, that's it, you know? Just go to school, steal from the store, and go sell candies at school. And that's what I was doing in the third or fourth grade. . . . I was always getting in the principal's office, suspended, kicked out, everything starting from the third grade.

My fifth grade teacher, Ms. Nelson . . . she put me in a play and that like tripped me out. Like, why do you want me in a play? Me, I'm just a mess-up. Still, you know, she put me in a play. And in the fifth grade, I think that was the best year out of the whole six years. I learned a lot about the Revolutionary War. . . . Had good friends. . . . We had a project we were involved in. Ms. Nelson . . . just involved everyone. We made books, this and that. And I used to write, and wrote two, three books. Was in a book fair. . . . She got real deep into you. Just, you know, "Come on now, you can do it." That was a good year for me, fifth grade.

I think right now about going Christian, right? Just going Christian, trying to do good, you know? Stay away from drugs, everything. And every time it seems like I think about that, I think about the homeboys. And it's a trip because a lot of the homeboys are my family, too, you know? . . .

Let's say I'm Chicano and dress like a gang member. They're gonna look at you like one of these crazy kids, you know, Mexican kid. . . . I don't really know if it's 'cause I'm Brown or it's 'cause of my gang tattoo, so I can't really pinpoint. But for me, as far as me being a Chicano, it's prideful, it's pride of your race, of what you are.

[quoted in Nieto, 2000, pp. 249–251]

Surely you took note of differences between these two children. In the third grade Paul considered himself "just a mess-up," whereas Yolanda was beginning to get "the hint of it." Yolanda's friend encouraged her to "keep on going," whereas Paul's friends discouraged him from "going Christian."

FELICIA MARTINEZ/PHOTOEDIT, INC.

Yolanda's Favorite Holiday This Cinco de Mayo (Fifth of May) fiesta at a Los Angeles school is part of an effort to celebrate Mexican traditions. At the same time that the Mexican students' native culture is recognized, they are taught the English language and U.S. traditions.

? OBSERVATIONAL QUIZ (see answer, page 328): Why are some of the children wearing green, white, and red?

There are similarities, too. As you will learn in this trio of chapters, almost all school-age children, like these two, enjoy learning in school, are proud of their heritage, and depend in a variety of ways on their friends. We begin with the health and growth that most 7- to 11-year olds, no matter where they live, experience.

A Healthy Time

Genetic and developmental factors safeguard humans during childhood. For thousands of years, although many babies and young children died, those who survived were generally quite hardy—protected genetically from serious illness such that they were able to reach their reproductive years. The same genetic protections operate today. For almost every ailment, from flu to cancer, the years from age 7 to 11 are the healthiest period of the entire life span (see Figure 11.1). Even unintended injuries and serious abuse (the leading causes of childhood illness and death) occur less often from age 7 to 11 than at younger or older ages. (These topics were discussed in Chapter 8.)

Therefore, during **middle childhood** (so called because it is after early childhood and before early adolescence), parents and other caregiving adults can relax a little: Most children are quite healthy and self-sufficient, content to be with their friends. They are (especially when compared with adolescents) not nearly as depressed, or delinquent, or even disobedient as they might be.

middle childhood The period between early childhood and early adolescence, roughly age 6 or 7 to 10 or 11.

Size and Shape

One reason middle childhood is easy is biological: The rate of growth slows down. As a result, many children become quite skilled at controlling their own bodies. With typical motivation and experience, school-age children have the skills to undertake their basic care, from brushing their teeth to buttoning their jackets, from making their lunch to walking to school. In fact, they can master

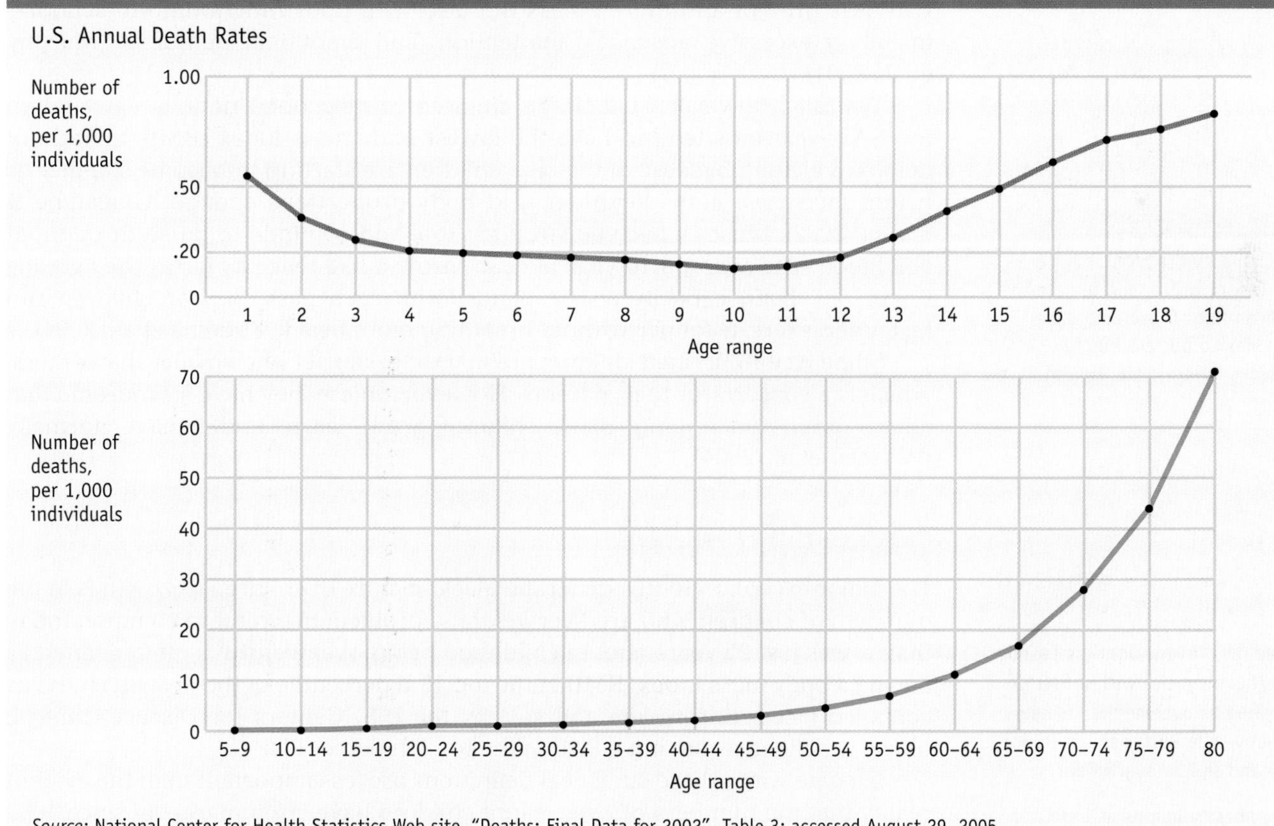

Source: National Center for Health Statistics Web site, "Deaths: Final Data for 2002", Table 3; accessed August 29, 2005

FIGURE 11.1 **Death at an Early Age? Almost Never!** Schoolchildren are remarkably hardy, as measured in many ways. These charts show that death rates for 7- to 11-year-olds are lower than those for children under 7 or over 11 and about a hundred times lower than for adults.

almost any motor skill, sometimes with impressive grace and precision, as long as it doesn't require too much strength or height, or split-second judgment centering on speed and distance. For instance, 9-year-olds can race their elders on bicycles, but they can't compete in adult basketball.

LAURA DWIGHT

All The Same These boys are all friends in the third grade, clowning in response to the camera—as school-age boys like to do. Outsiders might notice the varied growth rates and genetic differences, but the boys themselves are more aware of what they have in common.

When we say that growth slows down, we are referring to the *rate* of growth: With respect to absolute measurements, children grow at least as much each year as they did at age 3 or 4. The proportional gain is less, however, and that makes all the difference. For example, if an 8-year-old already weighs 55 pounds (25 kilograms), a gain of 5 pounds (2 kilograms) is taken in stride.

Generally, well-nourished 7- to 11-year-olds gain 5 to 7 pounds (2 to 3 kilograms) and at least 2 inches (almost 6 centimeters) in height each year. By age 10, a child weighs about 70 pounds (32 kilograms) and is about 4½ feet (1.37 meters) tall. (See Appendix A, pages A–6 and A–7, for specifics.) The extent and rate of growth vary, and depend not only on genes and gender but also on nutrition.

Obviously, children who are malnourished or undernourished grow less, as we saw in Chapters 5 and 8. Undernutrition does not disappear with age or a nation's wealth. For instance, a study of low-income schoolchildren in Philadelphia and Baltimore found that 8 percent were often hungry, which correlated not only with less growth and more illness but also with poor functioning in school—including excessive absences, inattention, and emotional outbursts (Murphy et al., 2001).

Typically, however, school-age children in developed nations eat enough food. Six-year-olds tend to have the lowest body mass index (BMI), or ratio of height to weight, because at that age children are starting to become slimmer as height increases, limbs lengthen, and body proportions change (Guillaume & Lissau, 2002). Muscles become stronger, too, and continue to do so throughout childhood: The average 10-year-old can throw a ball twice as far as the average 6-year-old. Lung capacity also expands; with each passing year children run faster and exercise longer without breathing more heavily (Malina et al., 2004).

! Answer to Observational Quiz (from page 326): Green, white, and red are the colors of the Mexican flag. These colors are not often worn in Mexico but are highly symbolic for Mexicans living in the United States.

Some well-nourished children are markedly shorter and smaller than others, which is a concern for their parents. However, unless they have a syndrome that affects brain functioning, short children grow, learn, and behave normally (Wheeler et al., 2004).

Overweight Children

The major exception to this generally placid picture of children's growth is in the numbers of children who are overweight, a problem much more common today than it was just 25 years ago. In childhood being **overweight** is often defined as having a body mass index (BMI) in the top 15th percentile of the growth charts as compiled (according to age and sex) by the U.S. Centers for Disease Control; **obese** is defined as having a BMI in the top 5th percentile.

overweight For adults, "overweight" is based on the weight/height ratio, with a BMI of 25 to 29 classified as overweight. Usually a child who is above the 85th percentile, for his or her age and sex, is overweight.

obese For adults, obesity begins at a BMI of 30. For children, obesity is usually set at the 95th percentile or higher, based on 1980 standards for age and sex.

In some ways, these statistical definitions are less important than the evident reality that the numbers of overweight children have risen markedly since 1980 in the United States—with Ireland, Greece, and Portugal not far behind (Lissau et al., 2004). This is the case with respect to every age and income group, but older and poorer children are heavier than their younger, wealthier counterparts (Burniat et al., 2002; Danielzik et al., 2004; Lin et al., 2004; Lissau et al., 2004).

Each of these generalities has implications. The facts that the rate of obesity is increasing and that older children are more likely than younger children to be overweight mean that most children are not born too fat but become that way because of their family's feeding practices. In fact, underweight newborns are more, not less, likely to become overweight children (Parizkova & Hills, 2005). Further, the fact that poorer children are more often obese suggests that quality of food, not quantity, is the problem. These trends are worldwide. Even in China, where more than a billion people still live in abject poverty, obesity is becoming a medical problem (Gu et al., 2005).

Excess weight can hinder every aspect of development—most obviously, biological health. Overweight children exercise less and have higher blood pressure, which puts them at risk for many later health problems, including type II diabetes (the incidence of which is rapidly increasing among children), heart disease, and stroke. Other childhood health problems, such as asthma (to be discussed later in this chapter), are more common in overweight and obese children. Cognition is affected as well: School achievement decreases as weight rises, although it is not clear if poor grades result from weight problems or from social rejection (Guillaume & Lissau, 2002).

In any case, psychosocial development suffers. As they grow older, children shun overweight peers more than underweight ones (Hill & Lissau, 2002). Self-esteem falls and loneliness rises with obesity—a problem that worsens as children mature (Friedlander et al., 2003; Mustillo et al., 2003).

ESPECIALLY FOR TEACHERS A child in your class is overweight, but you are hesitant to say anything to the parents, who are also overweight, because you do not want to insult them. What should you do?

Causes of Childhood Obesity

Why might one child be heavier than another of the same age? Genes are part of the explanation; they affect activity level, food preferences, body type, and metabolic rate. Adopted children whose biological parents were obese are more often overweight (no matter what the weight of their adoptive parents) than other adoptees, and monozygotic twins are more alike in weight than dizygotic twins (Perusse & Bouchard, 1999).

However, genes never act in isolation, and overall gene frequencies change very little from one generation to the next. For these reasons, the primary causes of *increases* in childhood obesity must be environmental. Although genes have always made some children more likely to be overweight, today those genetically vulnerable children are more likely to actually become obese, in response to a variety of environmental influences (Rollan-Cachera & Bellisle, 2002). Correlational

MICHAEL NEWMAN / PHOTO EDIT

Will She Drink Her Milk? The first word many American children read is *McDonald's*, and they all recognize the golden arches. Fast food is part of almost every family's diet—one reason the rate of obesity has doubled in every age group in the United States since 1980. Even if the young girl stops playing with her straw and drinks the milk, she is learning that soda and French fries are desirable food choices.

data suggest many culprits: those residing in the home, at school, and in the culture. For instance, children who watch more than two hours of television per day or consume more than two servings of soft drinks ("soda" or "pop") per day are more often overweight than are those who do neither (Institute of Medicine, 2005).

Response for Teachers (from page 329): Speak to the parents, not accusingly (because you know that genes and culture have a major influence on body weight), but helpfully. Alert them to the potential social and health problem that their child's weight poses. Most parents are very concerned about their child's well-being and will work with you to improve the child's snacks and exercise level.

Lack of exercise has more impact than diet (Patrick et al., 2004), and here the historical contrasts are dramatic. Fifty years ago, most children played outside until dark; most children walked to school; and most had physical education as part of each school day. Now, few children do any of these. For instance, a study of 684 U.S. elementary schools found that the average student had only two gym classes per week, each lasting about half an hour. To make matters worse, children in gym classes were inactive most of the time: The average child exercised vigorously only about five minutes per physical education class (NICHD and Youth Development Network, 2003). Another study (discussed in Chapter 1; see Figure 1.4) reported that parents of all incomes usually drive their children to school or have them ride on the school bus; few children walk or ride their bikes to school (Evenson et al., 2003).

The children of immigrants to the United States are exposed to an additional hazard in their social context: Their parents overfeed them. Adults from nations where hunger was prevalent continue to uphold customs that formerly protected but now harm the children. For example, U.S. children born in Mexico are healthier than their peers in many ways, but not in diet: Their obesity rate is higher than that of children of any other major national or ethnic group (Flores & Zambrana, 2001).

If adults are unaware of the dangers of junk food, videos, and inactivity, they do not protect their children from those temptations. In a study of obese African American children, only 30 percent of the parents acknowledged that their children were overweight (Young-Hyman et al., 2003).

Especially for Parents Suppose that you always serve dinner with the television on, tuned to a news broadcast. Your hope is that your children will learn about the world as they eat. Can this practice be harmful?

When parents do recognize that they are jeopardizing their child's health, what can they do? Enforcing a weight-loss diet is not necessarily the answer. One study of 7- to 12-year-olds found that "restricting access to certain foods increases rather than decreases preference. Forcing a child to eat a food will decrease liking for that food" (Benton, 2004, p. 858). A better strategy is for adults to keep their own weight down (overweight mothers tend to have overweight children) and to exercise with the child.

Puberty and Weight

As is discussed in detail in Chapter 14, *puberty* is the period of rapid physical growth and sexual maturation that signals the end of childhood. Puberty at any age is accompanied by increases in weight and height (Susman & Rogol, 2004). If a particular child gains much more than 5 pounds or grows more than 2 inches per year, the cause may be that adolescence is beginning, which could occur as early as age 8 or 9. Two of the main reasons for early puberty are sex (girls begin sooner) and genes (puberty is affected by family patterns). However, a third reason is greater body weight, and this again illustrates the interaction of nature and nurture.

Especially for Teachers The boys in your fourth-grade class have begun to tease one of the girls because she has "pointers" on her chest. How should you respond?

One of the prerequisites of puberty is a certain amount of body fat: Overweight children are likely to experience puberty earlier than their underweight peers. Historically (and in undernourished populations), puberty did not begin, on average, until age 14 or so, primarily because children had not at that age accumulated enough body fat for the hormones in the brain to kick off the process. Age 14 is now considered late. The more typical age of onset is 11 or 12.

That age is now considered ideal for the child (psychologically speaking), because children prefer to mature at the same rate as their peers. If a child begins puberty sooner than age 11 or 12, the risk of teenage pregnancy, drug abuse, and family conflicts increases—one more reason why parents should exercise with their children and limit intake of soda and chips. When the first signs of puberty appear (such as a girl developing breasts or a boy wearing adult-size shoes), a child's appetite and weight increase. Good nutrition is more important than ever.

Especially for School Nurses For the past month a 10-year-old fifth-grade girl has been eating very little at lunch and has visibly lost weight. She has also lost interest in daily school activities. What should you do?

Chronic Illness

We noted earlier that middle childhood is generally a healthy time, more so now in every nation of the world than just 30 years ago. Immunization has reduced deaths dramatically, and serious accidents, fatal illnesses, and even minor diseases are less common. In the United States, the improved health of school-age children is evidenced in fewer illnesses, smaller exposures to environmental toxins, and the smaller number of surgeries performed. For example, tonsillectomy—a type of surgery "practically every child" experienced as recently as 1980 (Larson, 1990, p. 698)—is uncommon today. Hearing impairments and anemia are half as frequent as they were two decades ago, and only 1 percent of U.S. children aged 5 to 10 had elevated blood lead levels in 2001, compared with almost 30 percent in 1978 (MMWR, May 27, 2005).

When they do occur, however, health-related problems can take a major toll on children socially. School-age children are more critical of themselves and of one another than are younger children (who often exhibit protective optimism; see p. 287). This means that walking with a limp, wearing glasses, having a birthmark, or having to blow one's nose makes children self-conscious. In addition, certain conditions become more noticeable during the school years, including Tourette syndrome (characterized by involuntary noises or movements), stuttering, and some allergies.

About 13 percent of all children have special health needs, and during the school years these may cause family disruption. For instance, although most mothers currently in the United States are employed full time, maternal employment is reduced if a child has chronic health needs (van Dyck et al., 2004). This affects family income, maternal self-esteem, and the marriage relationship, usually for the worse.

Furthermore, any condition that prevents normal play or school attendance correlates with emotional and social problems for the child, including low achievement, loneliness, and delinquency. Let's take a closer look at the condition that is the most common reason children miss school: asthma (Msall et al., 2003).

Asthma

Asthma is a chronic inflammatory disorder of the airways in which breathing becomes difficult. It affects between 5 and 20 percent of school-age children in North America. This rate is three times higher than it was only 20 years ago, and the incidence is expected to double again by 2020 (Pew Environmental Health Commission, 2000). Asthma rates are high in North and South America, but may also be increasing in Africa, Latin America, and Europe, especially in crowded cities (Crane et al., 2002; MacIntyre et al., 2001; Strachan, 1999).

asthma A chronic disease of the respiratory system in which inflammation narrows the airways from the lungs to the nose and mouth, causing difficulty in breathing. Symptoms include wheezing, rapid breathing, and coughing.

Many researchers are studying the possible causes of asthma. Genes affect the incidence: Some families have higher rates than other families living in the same conditions. Genes identified on chromosomes 2, 11, 12, 13, and 21 correlate with asthma, although geneticists caution that asthma is a catch-all diagnosis, and not every person with the disease will have started out with the same genetic risk.

With asthma, as with obesity, genes alone cannot provide explanation for the marked increase. What has changed in the past 50 years? Better diagnosis is part of the answer. In addition, some experts invoke the "hygiene hypothesis," the idea that because contemporary children are overprotected from dirt and bacteria, some infections and childhood diseases that could strengthen the immune system seldom occur anymore (Busse & Lemanske, 2005).

Response for Parents (from page 330): Habitual TV watching correlates with obesity, so you may be damaging your children's health rather than improving their intellect. Your children would probably profit more if you were to make dinner a time for family conversation.

Response for Teachers (from page 330): Stop all teasing, especially when it is concerned with early puberty, by teaching all your students about the need to respect each other and about the facts of puberty—a milestone to be proud of, not a reason for teasing.

This hypothesis has not been proved, but several aspects of modern life—carpeted floors, dogs and cats living inside the home, airtight windows, less outdoor play—are known to increase the risk of asthma (Carpenter, 1999). Many allergens that trigger asthma attacks, such as pet dander, tobacco smoke, dust mites, cockroaches, and mold, are more concentrated in the modern home, and children spend more time inside their homes than they once did.

Prevention

The three levels of prevention discussed in Chapter 8 can be applied to asthma and other chronic health problems. Primary prevention is aimed at problems that affect everyone; secondary prevention focuses on the protection of high-risk children; and tertiary prevention is aimed at reducing the severity of problems after they occur.

Primary prevention is the best of all, although it is the most difficult to achieve. The proper ventilation of schools and homes, decreased pollution, the eradication of cockroaches, and safe outdoor play spaces would make life and health better for all school-age children, including those at risk for asthma.

The benefit of primary prevention was revealed in a natural experiment during the 1996 Summer Olympics in Atlanta, Georgia. To facilitate the movement of athletes and spectators in the city, Atlanta imposed traffic restrictions, encouraged carpooling, and offered free mass transit for 17 days. Air pollution declined, and, surprisingly, so did the number of asthma attacks. During the Olympics, Medicaid asthma treatments decreased by 42 percent and HMO asthma claims were down by 44 percent compared with the four-week periods just before and just after the Olympics (Friedman et al., 2001). Asthma-related trips to hospital emergency rooms also declined.

Could something other than a reduction in air pollution explain this phenomenon? Were children being more carefully tended by their parents, thus reducing the number of medical emergencies? No. Hospitals and insurance agencies reported no change in the rates of children needing acute care for injuries, heart ailments, accidental poisoning, and other problems unrelated to pollution.

Secondary prevention reduces new cases of illness among high-risk children. If a family has a genetic history of allergies, breast-feeding and ridding the house of allergens before any overt signs of disease appear would cut the rate of allergies and asthma in half (Gdalevich et al., 2001). A well-trained public health worker can assess a newborn's risk and can advise the parents which measures are prudent and which are unnecessary. For example, some breeds of dogs are more likely to trigger asthma attacks than others.

Already Too Late A nurse uses an inhaler to open a young asthma patient's airways. Such hospital care is tertiary prevention, which will avoid death, but it represents a failure of primary and secondary prevention.

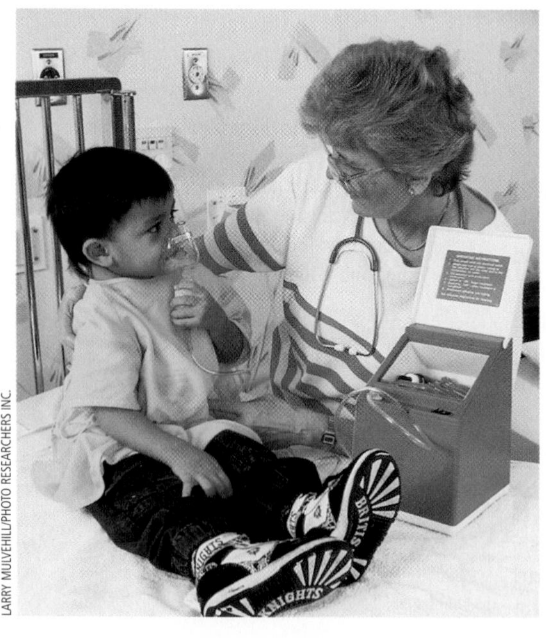

LARRY MULVEHILL/PHOTO RESEARCHERS INC.

Finally, *tertiary prevention* (preventing serious illness once an ailment is recognized) occurs every day in physicians' offices and hospital emergency rooms. In the case of asthma, the prompt use of injections, inhalers, and pills that are prescribed and monitored by specialists markedly reduces the rate of acute wheezing and overnight hospitalizations (Glauber et al., 2001). The use of asthma-reducing materials (e.g., hypoallergenic mattress covers) can also reduce the rate of asthma attacks—but not by much, probably because tertiary prevention at home occurs too late in the course of the illness (MMWR, January 14, 2005).

Less than half the children in the United States have the benefit of adequate tertiary prevention. Why? One reason is economic. One-third of school-age children, including more than half of African American and Hispanic children, have no health insurance (U.S. Department of Health and Human Services, 2004). Another reason is mistrust between parents of young children (often non-White, low-income younger women) and doctors (mostly White, high-income older men).

Language and cultural barriers make the problem worse. Among one group of immigrant mothers of asthmatic children, 88 percent thought drugs were overused in the United States, and 72 percent did not give their children the asthma medication their doctors had prescribed (Bearison et al., 2002). In one large multiethnic study, only half the parents who purchased prescription drugs for their child's breathing problems acknowledged that their child had asthma (Roberts, 2003), even though such medications are rarely prescribed unless asthma is present. Children reflect their parents' attitudes. Only half of a group of 8- to 16-year-olds with asthma followed their doctors' advice about medication; those children who were older, minority, and low-income were least likely to comply (McQuaid et al., 2003).

Response for School Nurses (from page 331): Something is wrong, and you (or the school psychologist, or both) should talk to the girl's parents. Ask whether they, too, have noticed any changes. Recommend that the child see her pediatrician for a thorough physical examination. If the girl's self-image turns out to be part of the problem, stress the importance of social support.

SUMMING UP

School-age children are healthy, strong, and capable. Immunizations protect them against childhood diseases, and developmental advances give them sufficient strength and coordination to take care of their own basic needs (eating, dressing, bathing). However, their growing awareness of themselves and of one another, as well as their increasing independence from parents, make every physical impairment a potential problem, particularly if it interferes with peer acceptance and school attendance. Obesity and asthma are two notable examples. Both have genetic and early-childhood origins, but both become more serious during middle childhood, when they often interfere with self-esteem, friendship, and learning. Prevention is crucial, because every health problem affects school achievement and later health status, but many parents and communities are not yet aware of the need for primary prevention.

Brain Development

Remember that the brain, proportionally large at birth, continues to grow more quickly than the rest of the child's body, reaching adult size at about age 7. As experiences accumulate, the basic areas of the sensory and motor cortexes develop. Among the particulars of this development are the activation of complex language, logic, memory, and spatial areas, and the formation of thousands of new dendrites, which reach out to various neurons.

Also recall that, in early childhood, emotional regulation, theory of mind, and left–right coordination emerge as the maturing corpus callosum connects the two hemispheres of the brain and as the prefrontal cortex—the executive part of the brain—plans, monitors, and evaluates all the impulses it receives from the various sectors, especially from the emotional centers. Hemispheric specialization makes the brain more efficient overall, and myelination speeds impulses from one brain area to another.

Advances in Middle Childhood

All the brain maturation that begins in early childhood continues in middle childhood. Ongoing maturation of the cerebral cortex as well as of the cerebellum becomes apparent in both motor and cognitive development, which are neurologically connected to each other (Diamond, 2000). Indeed, increasing myelination results "by age 7 or 8 years of age, in a massively interconnected brain" (Kagan & Herschkowitz, 2005, p. 220).

Because of this massive interconnection, children can modify (improve upon) several behaviors common in early childhood—emotional outbursts, perseveration, inattention, and the insistence on routines. Further advances in the executive functions, the "mental control processes that enable self-control necessary for attainment of a future goal" (Verte et al., 2005, p. 415), allow the child to keep goals in mind. Thus, children can analyze possible consequences prior to lashing out in anger or dissolving in tears, and they know when a curse word seems advisable (on the playground to a bully, perhaps) and when it doesn't (during math class or in church). Attention and automatization are two additional aspects of brain functioning that become increasingly evident in middle childhood (Berninger & Richards, 2002).

Attention

selective attention The ability to concentrate on one stimulus and exclude others.

Neurological advances allow children to process different types of information in many areas of the brain at once, and to pay special heed to the most important elements. One key ability is called **selective attention,** the ability to choose which of many stimuli to concentrate on. Learning to focus attention is a crucial skill for early school competence (NICHD Early Child Care Research Network, 2003), and impaired attention is a major problem for many children who have special educational needs (discussed later in this chapter).

In the classroom, advances in selective attention allow most children to listen to the teacher, write down what is important, and ignore another child's whispering or the noises from the street. In the cafeteria, despite the din, children can understand one another's gestures and facial expressions and respond quickly and appropriately. On the ball field, children can not only calculate the trajectory of a batted ball but also start running in the right direction while simultaneously noting where other teammates are positioned and whether anyone besides the batter is trying to reach base. A batter must also ignore distracting taunts from the other team's onlookers. Selective attention is expected in many contexts.

Three-year-olds lack the capacity to process multiple, competing demands for action and inaction from various parts of the brain; 10-year-olds can do it (Kagan & Herschkowitz, 2005). Over these seven years of neurological maturation, thoughtful and competent older children learn to "select" and coordinate the simultaneous impulses arising from all neurological regions as they develop large cortical networks that link the various parts together. Thus, the child can think in a harmonious manner and not be confused by myriad signals issuing from millions of scattered neurons in various parts of the brain (Bressler, 2002).

Selective attention requires ongoing myelination and the increased production of neurotransmitters (chemical messengers), which are also among the advances of middle childhood. For example, the maximum density of receptors for *serotonin,* a neurotransmitter that aids in impulse control, probably occurs at about age 6, allowing children to be more reflective in their responses (Kagan & Herschkowitz, 2005).

Maturation continues to help children think more deeply. For example, a study compared 8- and 10-year-olds of two levels of intelligence, gifted and average. Not surprisingly, the gifted children were more advanced than the non-gifted of the same age; but when 10-year-olds were compared with 8-year-olds of the same intelligence group, net neurological advances were greater among the average children as they got older (Johnson et al., 2003).

Automatization

automatization A process in which repetition of a sequence of thoughts and actions makes the sequence routine so that it no longer requires conscious thought.

The second major advance in brain function that becomes apparent in middle childhood is in **automatization,** a process by which a sequence of thoughts and actions is repeated until it becomes automatic, or routine, and no longer requires much conscious thought. At first, almost all behaviors that originate in the cortex require careful, slow, and focused concentration when they are performed. After many repetitions, with neurons firing together in a particular sequence, behavior becomes more automatic and more patterned. Less neuronal effort is required, because one neuron's firing sets off a chain reaction, firing the entire sequence.

You can see this yourself if you travel the same route to the same destination every day and one day decide to go somewhere else. Unless you are careful, you might find your brain directing you to the usual place instead of where you intended to be. The reason is automatization.

Increased myelination, which enables the signals going from one part of the brain to another to travel more rapidly, and hours of practice trigger the "automatic pilot" of cognition (Berninger & Richards, 2002). For a clear example of automatization during middle childhood, consider reading. It begins with the child using the eyes (sometimes aided by a finger and the lips) to sound out letters and guess at words; this series of fine motor skills leads to perception in the brain. At first, reading is slow and painstaking. Then it gradually becomes so automatic that, finally, a person glances at billboards or cereal boxes and reads them without intending to do so.

JOHNATHAN KIM / STOCK CONNECTION / PICTUREQUEST

Brain Music If this boy is to become a competent violinist, the brain must coordinate arms, hands, fingers, ears, and memory. All this is possible only after practice has made some of it automatic. Automatization frees the brain's cortex for more emotional and synchronized play.

Automatization is apparent in almost every skill. Speaking a second language, repeating the multiplication tables, and writing one's own name are haltingly, even painfully, difficult at first, and then become automatic. A transformation to a more efficient form of neural processing, freeing the brain for more advanced reading, computation, and writing, is the reason for this advance (Berninger & Richards, 2002). Consider the specifics of learning a second language. Brain scans reveal that, if a young child speaks two languages, the use of either activates a particular part of the brain called Broca's area. However, if a second language is not learned until middle childhood, the use of the second language usually involves various parts of the brain other than Broca's area and is not as automatic as first-language use (Kim et al. 1997).

Motor skills develop in the same way. Because neurons that fire together are strengthened together, practicing any particular skill—from moving a pencil on paper to kicking a ball toward a goalpost—gradually makes processing in the brain related to that skill faster and more efficient (Merzenich, 2001). Hours of practicing penmanship, kicking a ball, or cutting one's food with a knife and fork develop neurological pathways and give rise to automatization.

Motor Skills

The most obvious evidence of neurological maturation (apart from that provided by brain scans) is a child's motor skills. Each skill requires several distinct abilities, all of which improve during middle childhood. Often motor skills in childhood are studied apart from brain development, as if movement of the body should be considered separately from activity within the brain. However, the more we know about childhood, the more aware we become of the profound connection between mind and body, or between neurons and actions (Kagan & Herschkowitz, 2005).

It is the brain, more than the muscles, that throws the ball toward the catcher's mitt instead of into the dugout, through the basket rather than against the backboard, into the goal and not out of bounds. If a particular communication network is flawed, as in some forms of childhood psychopathology or neurological impairment, then the child cannot produce the coordinated responses that the activity requires—even if each component of the action can be performed. "Dropping the ball" has become a metaphor for not following through on a project, but many school-age children have literal difficulty in catching and holding onto a ball. Adult expectations often make the problem worse.

ISSUES AND APPLICATIONS

Not Enough Places to Play

Great joy comes to children as they play, and they often play "fully and totally immersed" (Loland, 2002, p. 139). Regular exercise benefits people at every age: Those who exercise live longer, healthier, smarter, and happier lives.

Exercise is particularly beneficial for 6- to 11-year-olds, some of whom are motivated by sports more than by anything else. As the 43rd president of the United States said, "Years ago, when I was playing on those dusty Little League fields in West Texas, I never dreamt I'd be President of the United States . . . I did dream about . . . making it to Williamsport, Pennsylvania, for the Little League World Series." (Bush, 2001, quoted in Little League, 2005).

Adults who look closely at the play activity and physical exercise of 6- to 11-year-olds cannot be happy about everything they see. There are benefits, of course, but not for every child. There are also hazards (which adults are, often, not doing enough to control). The benefits include:

- Higher self-esteem
- Better health (both in childhood and for a lifetime)
- Less obesity
- Appreciation of cooperation and fair play
- Improved problem-solving abilities
- Respect for teammates and opponents of many ethnicities and nationalities

Here are some of the drawbacks:

- Deflation of fragile egos
- Injuries (the infamous "Little League elbow" is just one example)
- Reinforcement of prejudices (especially against the other sex)
- Increases in stress (evidenced by altered hormone levels as well as neglected homework and insomnia)
- Time and effort taken away from learning academic skills
- Unequal opportunity; sometimes overt discrimination

From a developmentalist perspective, children aged 6 to 11 are not only especially open to learning about cooperation and rules, but are also particularly vulnerable in body and brain to the harmful effects of too much exercise. Play is much smoother in early childhood, when children play wherever and with whomever they can—with a parent or alone, if need be.

But 6- to 11-year-olds are past the stage when they play happily by themselves or with an adult. Adults may be content with a "personal best" or the vicarious victories of the team connected to their college, city, or nation, but children seek personal engagement and social comparison. They want to play with someone else, and to know that they are better than, or almost as good as, another child. Why are developmentalists uneasy about physical exercise in middle childhood today? The problem is not with the children, but with the three social contexts of school-age children's play: the neighborhood, the school, and clubs and leagues.

The Neighborhood

Children like to play together after school or on weekends. Their teams get larger or smaller as individual children come and go; the game's boundaries fit the setting (an empty lot, an unplanted field, a back alley); and they play by improvised and flexible rules that are enforced, if need be, by logic combined with shouting. Stickball, touch football, tag, hide-and-seek, jump rope, and dozens of other games that involve running and catching, or kicking and jumping, can go on forever—or at least until dark. Almost every child who wants to play is included. Some are better than others, but no one cares, because more participants make a better game. The play is active and interactive.

Modern life makes this kind of neighborhood play increasingly rare, for several reasons. One is that more and more people, including children, live in crowded cities with exploding populations and few places to play that are both fun and safe. (For example, the population of Mexico City was 3 million in 1970 and 20 million in 2005.)

Adults opt for safety, and that sometimes means that children lose all opportunity for neighborhood play. According to one source, parents fear "stranger danger"—even though "there is a much greater chance that your child is going to be dangerously overweight from staying inside than that he is going to be abducted" (Layden, 2004, p. 96). Another expert complains that safety surfaces have made parks less fun (Ball, 2004). Further, children have less free time as they participate in organized after-school programs.

The School

Physical education has been a pivotal part of school curricula since ancient times. Today it is almost universally required, which means that virtually every child, throughout the world, gets regular, planned exercise. Good teachers know developmentally appropriate games and exercises that all the children can participate in—and in the process avoid competition and learn cooperation (Belka, 2004).

However, although children enjoy sports, they often hate physical education. One author cites an example of two children who participate enthusiastically in sports every weekend but have a different attitude in school:

> Their current softball unit in physical education hardly provokes any excitement. There are 18 students on each side, sides that are formed in an ad hoc manner each lesson. . . . Few students get turns to pitch, and many are satisfied playing the deepest of outfield positions in order to have minimal involvement in the game.
>
> *[Hastie, 2004, p. 63]*

In the past decades, as pressure on teachers to increase their students' reading and math knowledge has increased (see Chapter 12), the time devoted to physical education has declined, from an hour or more every day (in addition to a lengthy recess for free play) to a few times a week. Further, classroom teachers, not physical education specialists, are often responsible for physical education, which means it is less likely to be developmentally appropriate.

One new California teacher read in his school's curriculum manual that he had to include physical activity in his class every day. He started out by running with his first-graders around the school each morning. Only later did he learn that most teachers ignored this mandate. But by then his children were used to running each day, so the running continued all year long. He is convinced that they are better academic learners because of it (cited in Layden, 2004).

Exactly how much exercise and health information should be included in the school curriculum is controversial. However, it seems clear that physical education is being squeezed out of the elementary school curriculum and that most children are inactive most of the time in gym class. Unless a dramatic reversal occurs, schools will not be the places where children get the exercise and play time they need.

Athletic Clubs and Leagues

Every nation has a network of private or nonprofit clubs and organizations that are devoted to one sport or another. Cricket and rugby are common in England and nations that were once colonies of England; baseball is common in the United States, Cuba, and the Dominican Republic; soccer is central in many African and Latin American nations.

Some athletic clubs and leagues are designed primarily for adults and adolescents, but some are devoted to children. The best known is Little League, with 2.7 million children playing baseball and softball on 180,000 teams in 75 countries. When it began in 1939, Little League had only three teams of boys aged 9–12. Now it includes girls; younger and older children (5- to 6-year-olds are in T-ball; 16- to 18-year-olds are in Big League Baseball or Softball); and 22,000 children with disabilities play in the Challenger League (Little League, 2005).

Little League stresses participation (every child plays in every game), sportsmanship (win or lose, do your best), and parental involvement. Many of the managers are parents of players. Therein lies a problem: Adults focus on competition, scores, and winning more than young children do (Humphrey, 2003). Coaches in Little League and other children's organized sports are infamous for yelling (or worse) when children drop the ball, strike out, or daydream. Children themselves (61 percent in one survey) say that what they like least is that their coach sometimes "gets mad and yells at us" (Humphrey 2003). One Little League father writes:

> I can't count the number of times I've seen a manager screaming, and sometimes swearing, at individual players (often their own child), which makes for awkward moments on the sidelines and then disapproving chatter afterward.
>
> *[Smith, 2005]*

Another father, after managing a team for three years, counters:

> No one has threatened to sue. No one has called the cops. No one has challenged a birth certificate. No fist fights. No handcuffs. No father has berated a son, no son has berated a father. I haven't even seen anyone openly jeer the umpires. . . . It's the outbursts that make the evening news that are the exception.
>
> *[Benson, 2005]*

For the most part, children enjoy and benefit from their chosen activities. One adult confesses:

> I was a lousy Little League player. Uncoordinated, small, and clueless are the accurate adjectives I'd use if someone asked politely. As for the five baseball essentials—hitting, hitting with power, running, fielding, and throwing—my toolbox was empty. What I did possess, though, was enthusiasm. Wearing the uniform—cheesy mesh cap, scratchy polyester shirt, old-school beltless pants, uncomfortable cleats and stirrups that never stayed up—gave me a sort of pride. It felt special and made me think that I was part of something important.
>
> *[Ryan, 2005]*

"Just remember son, it doesn't matter whether you win or lose—unless you want Daddy's love."

Belonging is important to every child, but that raises another criticism: Not every child can participate. Parents must pay their children's fees, transport them to practices and games, and support their children's teams. Children from poor or large families, or who are not particularly coordinated, are much less likely to belong to sports teams. If we consider this third context (clubs and leagues) as the primary way today's children get the exercise they need for health and joy, then exclusion is a serious problem (Collins, 2003).

In addition, sports designed for adults do not necessarily give children the exercise and sense of accomplishment they need. Basketball and soccer are high in "physical activity yield," but baseball is not. One author remembers standing in center field, "practically motionless for most of the game" (Humphrey, 2003).

The elements on our list of the benefits of physical exercise are not speculative; research confirms that children who are physically active every day during middle childhood are happier, healthier, and more successful. Yet for most children, the kind of play they need is not available to them in their neighborhood, school, or club. Children are ready for any form of enjoyable active play; it is up to adults to figure out how to provide it.

SEAN SPRAGUE / THE IMAGE WORKS

Keep It Rolling This boy in Orissa, India, is using an old bicycle tire as a hoop. Although they use different objects, children everywhere have the impulse to play, and many of their games are the same.

? **OBSERVATIONAL QUIZ** (see answer, page 341): Is this boy malnourished?

Coordination

In many ways, a child's motor habits, especially those that have to do with the coordination of both sides of the body and the performance of complex tasks, benefit from faster connections in the brain. The corpus callosum, linking the brain's hemispheres, continues to mature during middle childhood. This process of maturation is crucial for balance and even for using both hands in a smooth manner.

One key element of coordination, related to the phenomenon of increasing myelination, is **reaction time,** the length of time it takes to respond to a stimulus. Every year of childhood, reaction time shortens by a few milliseconds. Then it stabilizes. Beginning at about age 20, reaction time lengthens again, so that older adults (aged 60–81) are about as quick in their responses as 8-year-olds (Williams et al., 1999). This can be seen in the speeds at which people of various ages walk and talk (too fast at age 15? too slow at age 85?). Reaction time explains why video games are mesmerizing to young people and frustrating to older ones, who are apt to lose to their teenage grandchildren.

Further neurological development means that eye–hand coordination, balance, and judgment of movement (including time, distance, and trajectory) continue to develop during the school years. Thus, 12-year-olds are better at these skills than 9-year-olds, who, in turn, are better than 6-year-olds. Most athletic abilities depend on a combination of such abilities, which is why older children are more proficient at almost every sport—from baseball to rugby—than younger children. Size is a factor, of course, but almost every team has an older, shorter child who outperforms younger, taller teammates. Brain maturation is invisible all the while, but potent.

reaction time The time it takes to respond to a stimulus, either with a reflexive movement (such as an eye blink) or with a thought.

Practice and Motivation

Culture, motivation, and practice are crucial. Indeed, as the epigenetic perspective emphasizes, the brain itself responds to the activities and experiences of the child, whereby connections between neurons are forged (Kagan & Herschkowitz, 2005). This is illustrated by the proper use of chopsticks, a fine motor skill attained by half of the 4-year-olds and virtually all the 6-year-olds in chopstick-using cultures (Wong et al., 2002), and by almost no 7- to 11-year-olds elsewhere, even if they occasionally eat in restaurants where chopsticks are provided.

According to research on lower animals, play advances brain development—especially the active, erratic, rough-and-tumble frolicking that many children love. One expert believes that such play particularly helps many boys to overcome their tendencies toward hyperactivity and learning disabilities. Rough-and-tumble play may advance the coordinated activity of the frontal lobes of the brain (Panksepp, 1998). Another study finds that preschool boys who spend more time playing with other boys (with lots of active, rough-and-tumble play) become more competent academically (Fabes et al., 2003).

Whether or not play has direct neurological effects, it is apparent that children's impulses toward active play call for guidance but not repression. Rough-and-tumble play benefits children, not only with respect to motor skills but probably in the areas of emotional regulation and social interaction as well (Pellegrini & Smith, 2001). Participation in team sports begins during these years, partly because the necessary sustained attention and social cooperation become possible for the first time. Some school-age children may be too conceited or too self-effacing to be good team players, but, as coaches realize, these are the years when teamwork begins. Children themselves understand this, as they criticize the "poor loser" or "bad sport" and say "good try" to the dejected teammate who missed the goal.

Hereditary differences and early brain damage also affect motor skills. As school-age children grow, some of them shine on the athletic field and others remain uncoordinated, unable to throw or kick a ball with as much strength and accuracy as their peers. The same is true for fine motor skills. Some children write more neatly than others, and those children usually practice their penmanship, refining the curve of the *s* and the slant of the *t*.

With penmanship, as with every other motor skill that represents a particular kind of brain development, practice accentuates pre-existing neurological and cultural differences. Because of both nature and nurture, about 6 percent of all children are considered to have motor coordination problems serious enough to interfere with school achievement (American Psychiatric Association, 2000).

Especially for Phys. Ed. Teachers A group of parents of fourth- and fifth-graders has asked for your help in persuading the school administration to sponsor a competitive sports team. How should you advise the group to proceed?

aptitude The potential to learn, or master, a particular skill or body of knowledge.

IQ tests Aptitude tests designed to measure intellectual aptitude, or ability to learn in school. Originally intelligence was defined as mental age divided by chronological age, times 100—hence *intelligence quotient* (IQ).

achievement tests Measures of mastery and proficiency in reading, math, science, or any other subject.

Measuring the Mind

The maturation of the brain affects not only movement of the body but also movement within the mind, as one idea leads to another. If children become quicker, more automatic thinkers, they become more able to learn and, as a result, they learn more. Brain scans of various kinds, such as EEG, fMRI, and PET scans (see p. 171), can reveal brain activity in various ways; but these tools are used only in unusual circumstances. For most children, psychological aptitude or achievement testing means taking a standardized test with paper and pencil or seated in front of a computer screen.

In theory, **aptitude** is the potential to learn, or master, a particular skill or body of knowledge. The most important aptitude for school-age children is intellectual aptitude, or the ability to learn in school. This aptitude is measured by **IQ tests** (see Figure 11.2).

In theory, achievement is distinct from aptitude. Achievement is not what a person *may* accomplish, but what a person has accomplished. **Achievement tests** measure reading proficiency, math knowledge, knowledge of science facts, writing skills, or skills related to any other subject matter that has actually been studied. Achievement tests are given routinely in school (mandated in the United States by the federal law called the No Child Left Behind Act).

If a child's achievement test score is unexpectedly high or low, he or she may be a gifted or retarded learner. Then an IQ test is given to gauge the child's aptitude. For example, if achievement is low but aptitude is high (a discrepancy that is

LEW MERRIM / MONKMEYER

Performance IQ This puzzle, part of a performance subtest on the Wechsler IQ test, seems simple until you try. The limbs are difficult to align correctly, and time is of the essence. This boy has at least one advantage over most African American boys who are tested. Especially during middle childhood, boys tend to do better when their examiner is of the same sex and ethnicity.

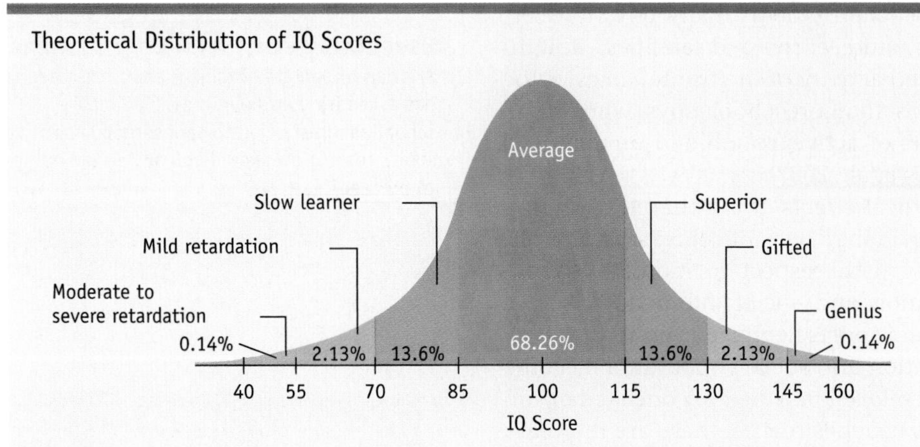

FIGURE 11.2 **In Theory, Most People Are Average** Almost 70 percent of IQ scores fall within the normal range. Note, however, that this is a norm-referenced test. In fact, actual IQ scores have risen in many nations; 100 is no longer exactly the midpoint. Further, in practice, scores below 50 are slightly more frequent than indicated by the normal curve shown here, because severe retardation is the result, not of the normal distribution, but of genetic and prenatal factors.

? OBSERVATIONAL QUIZ (see answer, page 342): If a person's IQ is 110, what category is he or she in?

Wechsler Intelligence Scale for Children (WISC) An IQ test designed for school-age children. The test assesses potential in many areas, including vocabulary, general knowledge, memory, and spatial comprehension.

mental retardation Literally, slow, or late, thinking. In practice, people are considered mentally retarded if they score below 70 on an IQ test and if they are markedly behind their peers in adaptation to daily life.

discussed later), distinct educational strategies may be needed. A child who is low or high in both achievement and aptitude requires different strategies. Thus, aptitude and achievement tests can be useful, but, as you will learn, experts fear that both can be misused.

IQ is an abbreviation for "intelligence quotient," reflecting the fact that originally an IQ score was an actual quotient: IQ was calculated by dividing a child's mental age, measured by an intelligence test, by his or her chronological age, and then multiplying the result by 100. For example, consider three children, all of whom have just celebrated their 12th birthday. The first might have a mental age of 15, the second, 12, and the third, 8. Then the IQ's of these children would be: $15/12 = 1.25 \times 100 = 125$ (superior); $12/12 = 1 \times 100 = 100$ (average); $8/12 = 0.75 \times 100 = 75$ (slow learner).

The formula for calculating IQ has become more complicated than dividing mental age by chronological age, because test designers want the distribution of scores to follow the normal curve (see Figure 11.2). However, the underlying concept (that children grow smarter with age) remains. Chronological comparisons are pivotal until adulthood, when the brain is considered full-grown.

Highly regarded and widely used IQ tests include the *Stanford-Binet* test, now in its fifth edition (Rord, 2003), and the various *Wechsler* tests. There are Wechsler tests for preschoolers (the WPPSI, or Wechsler Preschool and Primary Scale of Intelligence), adults (the WAIS, or Wechsler Adult Intelligence Scale), and school-age children—the **WISC**, or **Wechsler Intelligence Scale for Children,** now in its fourth edition (Wechsler, 2003).

The WISC is the most commonly used psychological test. One reason is that its subscales assess many abilities, including vocabulary, general knowledge, memory, and visual awareness. Another reason is that the full IQ can be divided into verbal components (measured by tests of vocabulary, word problems, etc.) and performance components (ability at solving puzzles and such).

The WISC is given by a trained examiner who reads the questions to one child at a time, to avoid measuring reading achievement. Some items have time limits, but test-takers are allowed to complete items after time is up to prevent their frustration (although no points are given when a child does so) (Kaufman & Lichtenberger, 2000).

If children score much higher on the WISC than what is indicated by their chronological age, they are considered gifted, although what that means in practice depends on where they live. The proportion of high-scoring children who are placed in "gifted and talented" classes varies from state to state. In Wisconsin, 15 percent of the children are in gifted classes; in South Dakota, only 1 percent (Snyder et al., 2004). Most children who score in the mentally retarded range are placed in special classes, although here, too, the circumstances vary.

Thirty years ago the definition of **mental retardation** was straightforward: All children with an IQ of below 70 were classified as mentally retarded, with further subdivisions for progressively lower scores: mild retardation, 55–70; moderate retardation, 40–54; severe retardation, 25–39; profound, below 25. Each of these categories signified different expectations, from "educable" (mildly retarded, able to learn to read and write) to "custodial" (profoundly retarded, unable to learn any skills).

The label *mentally retarded,* meaning "slow in learning," often led parents and teachers to expect less of a child, and that itself reduced learning. In addition, although only about 3 percent of the general population score below 70, if a group has an IQ average that is significantly below 100 (as is true for many immigrant, low-income, and minority groups in the United States), then a larger proportion of children in those groups would be labeled mentally retarded (Pennington, 2002). That seemed unfair.

Accordingly, the currently accepted definition of "mentally retarded" stipulates that children must be unusually low in adaptation to daily life, in addition to having IQs of below 70. Thus, a 6-year-old who, without help, gets dressed, fixes her breakfast, walks to school, and knows the names of her classmates would not be designated mentally retarded, even if her IQ score were 65. Adaptation is often measured with the *Vineland Test of Adaptive Intelligence* or some other assessment tool (Venn, 2004).

IQ tests are quite accurate at predicting school achievement and somewhat reliable in predicting adult success. In other words, children with high IQs usually earn good grades in school and graduate from college. As adults, they typically hold professional or managerial jobs, marry, and own homes, although these later indicators may be the result of education, not IQ (Sternberg et al., 2001).

Averages of IQ scores of entire nations have risen substantially—a phenomenon called the **Flynn Effect,** named after the man who described and publicized it (Flynn, 1999). The reasons for this upward trend are environmental—for example, better health, smaller families, and more schooling. The Flynn Effect was recently demonstrated in Kenya, the first developing nation with sufficient historical data to enable a study of IQ scores (Daley et al., 2004).

! Answer to Observational Quiz (from page 338): Although malnutrition is common in India, school-age children worldwide are more often too fat than too thin. This boy has healthy hair; his ribs do not show; and, most important, he seems to have adequate energy and coordination for active play. Although a definitive answer depends on percentiles, he is probably just fine.

Flynn Effect The rise in IQ score averages that has occurred over the decades in many nations.

Criticisms of IQ Testing

Many developmentalists criticize IQ tests. They argue that no test can measure potential without also measuring achievement, and that every test reflects the culture of the people who wrote it, administer it, and take it (Armour-Thomas & Gopaul-McNicol, 1998; Cianciolo & Sternberg, 2004; Greenfield, 1997). Even tests that purport to be culture-free, such as a test that asks children to "draw a person" or to name their classmates, are easier in some cultures than in others.

Further, each person's intellectual potential changes over time. This means that a score that is tied to a particular chronological age applies to one moment, not to potential for ongoing development. If a child is designated as needing special education at one point (on the basis of various test scores), that same child may be classified as normal, above average, or even gifted later on. A psychological test is a snapshot—one perspective at one moment. And even at that moment, it provides only a limited view.

These criticisms are taken seriously. Every developmentalist knows that some children do not demonstrate their true potential on IQ tests. That's why IQ tests are given only when there is concern about a given child's ability to learn well in a particular setting. Even then, IQ tests are only one of many measures. Specific aspects of achievement within a particular domain are often tested. If reading disability seems to be the problem, then tests of comprehension, word recognition, and phonetic skills are also used. If brain damage is suspected, tests of balance and coordination (e.g., hop on one foot, touch your nose) or of the brain/eye/hand connection (e.g., copy a diamond, point to my left foot) are useful.

Even with a battery of tests, assessment may be inaccurate, especially if tests that are standardized in the United States are used in other cultures, in which school intelligence (a large vocabulary, abstract logic, remembering

Demonstration of High IQ? If North American intelligence tests truly reflected all the aspects of the mind, children would be considered mentally slow if they could not replicate the proper hand, arm, torso, and facial positions of a traditional dance, as this young Indonesian girl does brilliantly. She is obviously adept in kinesthetic and interpersonal intelligence. Given her culture, it would not be surprising if she were deficient in the logical-mathematical intelligence required to use the Internet effectively or to surpass an American peer in playing a video game.

© OWEN FRANKEN / STOCK, BOSTON

! Answer to Observational Quiz (from page 340): He or she is average. Anyone with a score between 85 and 115 is of average IQ.

Response for Phys. Ed. Teachers (from page 339): Discuss with the parents their reasons for wanting the team. Children need physical activity, but some aspects of competitive sports are better suited to adults than to children. Recommend that the parents think of ways to foster their children's health and cooperative spirit without the element of competition.

Gardner's Eight Intelligences

- Linguistic
- Logical–Mathematical
- Musical
- Spatial
- Body–Kinesthetic
- Interpersonal (social-understanding)
- Intrapersonal (self-understanding)
- Naturalistic

numbers in sequence) may not be valued. Competence varies according to culture, which means that scores on tests created and having become standardized in one country may be of small value elsewhere (Sternberg & Grigorenko, 2004). When tests are used, those who interpret the results need to realize that

> Like many other Western technological inventions (such as the printing press, the sewing machine, the bicycle, and the tractor), the intelligence test (popularly known as the IQ test) has been widely exported around the world. Like tractors, intelligence tests bring with them both ostensible utility and hidden implications.
>
> *[Serpell & Haynes, 2004, p. 166]*

Multiple Intelligences

A more fundamental criticism concerns the very concept of intelligence. Humans may have many intelligences, not just one. If this is true, then using an IQ test to measure intelligence is based on a false assumption. Robert Sternberg (1996), for example, describes three distinct types of intelligence:

- *Academic,* measured by IQ and achievement tests
- *Creative,* evidenced by imaginative endeavors
- *Practical,* seen in everyday problem solving

Similarly, Howard Gardner described eight intelligences: linguistic, logical–mathematical, musical, spatial, bodily–kinesthetic (movement), interpersonal (social understanding), intrapersonal (self-understanding), and naturalistic (understanding of nature, as in biology, zoology, or farming) (Gardner, 1983; 1999).

According to those who hold that humans have multiple intelligences, standard IQ tests measure only linguistic and logical–mathematical ability, which represent just a portion of brain potential. The fact that most schools founded by Western educators (which means most schools worldwide) emphasize language and math explains why traditional IQ tests predict school success.

If intelligence is the multifaceted jewel that Gardner believes it to be, schools everywhere need to expand their curricula so that every child can shine. Moreover, since aptitude tests predict academic and occupational success within North America, low scores may mean that schools and societies, not children, should change. Standardized tests themselves may be difficult for a child who excels at creative expression or kinesthetic skills or interpersonal understanding.

SUMMING UP

During middle childhood the brain functions faster, more automatically, and with better coordination, particularly as the prefrontal cortex matures. This is apparent in shorter reaction times and in many other ways. Selective attention (the ability to filter out distractions), the ability to pause before acting, and the ability to wait for one's turn are crucial for learning in school and for developing gross and fine motor skills. Brain maturation becomes evident in many school-related abilities, as measured in aptitude tests, particularly intelligence tests. IQ (intelligence quotient) scores relate mental age to chronological age, which implies that children become smarter as they grow older. The underlying assumption of standard IQ tests is that children who are intellectually gifted or mentally retarded have an unusually high or low aptitude. This assumption is challenged by many modern theorists, such as Howard Gardner and Robert Sternberg, who believe that the brain contains not just one aptitude but many, and that culture and experience are pivotal in turning a child's potential into achievement. Children in cultures in which academic intelligence is not equated with competence may be quite capable yet score low on IQ tests.

Children with Special Needs

All parents watch with pride and satisfaction as their offspring become smarter, taller, and more skilled as each year of middle childhood passes. For many parents, however, these feelings mingle with worry and uncertainty when their children encounter difficulties in one area of development or another. Often delay, impulsiveness, or clumsiness is the first problem to be noticed; other problems become apparent once formal education begins (Lerner, 2000; Silver & Hagin, 2002).

Although developmental problems usually originate in the brain, the observable signs and symptoms and the many factors that inhibit or amplify those developmental problems or deficits are social and cognitive (Rutter & Sroufe, 2000). That is why the signs of disability become more apparent on the playground or in the classroom than at home or in the pediatrician's office. That also explains why most children who need special education are not identified until school age, even though the problems begin much earlier. One example is Billy, whose behavior became a problem in the third grade.

A Case to Study

Billy: Dynamo or Dynamite?

In many ways, Billy was a typical 8-year-old with a history of healthy development. He was born full term after an uncomplicated pregnancy; he sat up, walked, and talked at the expected ages. His parents were proud of his energy and curiosity: "Little Dynamo" they called him affectionately. They did not consider him disabled—he began to read on schedule, and he looked quite normal. But Billy's third-grade teacher, Mrs. Pease, referred him to a psychiatrist because his behavior in class was "intolerably disruptive" (Gorenstein & Comer, 2002, p. 250), as the following episode illustrates:

> Mrs. Pease had called the class to attention to begin an oral exercise: reciting a multiplication table on the blackboard. The first child had just begun her recitation when, suddenly, Billy exclaimed, "Look!" The class turned to see Billy running to the window.
>
> "Look," he exclaimed again, "an airplane!"
>
> A couple of children ran to the window with Billy to see the airplane, but Mrs. Pease called them back, and they returned to their seats. Billy, however, remained at the window, pointing at the sky. Mrs. Pease called him back, too.
>
> "Billy, please return to your desk," Mrs. Pease said firmly. But Billy acted as though he didn't even hear her.
>
> "Look, Mrs. Pease," he exclaimed, "the airplane is blowing smoke!" A couple of other children started from their desks.
>
> "Billy," Mrs. Pease tried once more, "if you don't return to your desk this instant, I'm going to send you to Miss Warren's office." [Billy did sit down, but before Mrs. Pease could call on anyone, Billy blurted out the correct answer to the first question she asked.]
>
> Mrs. Pease tried again. "Who knows 3 times 7?" This time Billy raised his hand, but he still couldn't resist creating a disruption.
>
> "I know, I know," Billy pleaded, jumping up and down in his seat with his hand raised high.
>
> "That will do, Billy," Mrs. Pease admonished him. She deliberately called on another child. The child responded with the correct answer.
>
> "*I* knew that!" Billy exclaimed.
>
> "Billy," Mrs. Pease told him, "I don't want you to say one more word this class period."
>
> Billy looked down at his desk sulkily, ignoring the rest of the lesson. He began to fiddle with a couple of rubber bands, trying to see how far they would stretch before they broke. He looped the rubber bands around his index fingers and pulled his hands farther and farther apart. This kept him quiet for a while; by this point, Mrs. Pease didn't care what he did, as long as he was quiet. She continued conducting the multiplication lesson while Billy stretched the rubber bands until finally they snapped, flying off and hitting two children, on each side of him. Billy let out a yelp of surprise, and the class turned to him.
>
> "That's it, Billy," Mrs. Pease told him, "You're going to sit outside the classroom until the period is over."
>
> "No!" Billy protested. "I'm not going. I didn't do anything!"
>
> "You shot those rubber bands at Bonnie and Julian," Mrs. Pease said.
>
> "But it was an accident."
>
> "I don't care. Out you go!"
>
> Billy stalked out of the classroom to sit on a chair in the hall. Before exiting, however, he turned to Mrs. Pease. "I'll sue you for this," he yelled, not really knowing what it meant.
>
> *[Gorenstein & Comer, 2002, pp. 250–251]*

child with special needs A child who, because of a physical or mental disability, requires extra help in order to learn.

You will read more about Billy's diagnosis and treatment later in this chapter. The psychiatrist found him to be a **child with special needs,** one who, because of a physical or mental disability, requires extra help in order to learn.

The specific diagnosis that lies behind the use of the term *special needs* might be one of dozens of conditions, including anxiety disorder, Asperger syndrome, attachment disorder, attention-deficit disorder, autism, bipolar disorder, conduct disorder, clinical depression, developmental delay, Down syndrome, and many more. All of these conditions begin with a biological anomaly, which might be the extra chromosome of Down syndrome or simply an inherited tendency.

All special needs are also powerfully influenced by the social context of family and school. The brain itself is epigenetic—it is molded by experiences as well as by genes (Pennington, 2002). As for outgrowing or adjusting to a disability, the particular diagnosis is less predictive than family factors, particularly the mother's mental and physical health (Witt et al., 2003).

Developmental Psychopathology

developmental psychopathology The field that uses insights into typical development to study and treat developmental disorders, and vice versa.

Psychologists and psychiatrists who study childhood disorders have joined with those who study normal development to create the field of **developmental psychopathology,** in which knowledge about typical development contributes to the understanding of various disorders, and vice versa. The goal is "to understand the nature, origins, and sequelae of individual patterns of adaptation and maladaptation over time" (Davies & Cicchetti, 2004, p. 477). The "core identity" of the person is dynamic, not static. Developmental psychopathology discovers "processes of development. . . . [and the] progressive, unfolding . . . transformation of patterns" (Cicchetti & Sroufe, 2000, pp. 258–259).

Given this emphasis, developmental psychopathology has provided four lessons that apply to all children:

1. *Abnormality is normal.* Most children act in unusual ways sometimes, and most children with serious disabilities are, in many respects, quite normal. Children with psychological disorders should be viewed first as children, with the same needs as all other children, and second as children with special challenges (see box).
2. *Disability changes over time.* Behavior changes as people age, year by year. A child who seems severely disabled at one stage may seem quite capable at the next stage, or vice versa. In fact, "discontinuity in disorders from childhood to adulthood" is typical (Silk et al., 2000, p. 728).
3. *Adolescence and adulthood may be better or worse.* Many children with seemingly serious disabilities, even blindness or mental retardation, become happy and productive adults, sometimes possessing unusual gifts. Conversely, disabilities that make a person aggressive and socially inept may become more serious with maturation, when physical maturity and social demands require self-control and interpersonal skills.
4. *Diagnosis depends on the social context.* According to the widely used ***Diagnostic and Statistical Manual of Mental Disorders* (DSM-IV-R),** "nuances of an individual's cultural frame of reference" must be considered before a firm diagnosis is made (American Psychiatric Association, 2000, p. xxxiv). Many developmentalists go beyond this statement, believing that psychopathology resides "not in the individual but in the adaptiveness of the relationship between individual and context" (Sameroff & Mackenzie, 2003, p. 613).

***Diagnostic and Statistical Manual of Mental Disorders* (DSM-IV-R)** The American Psychiatric Association's official guide to the diagnosis (not treatment) of mental disorders ("IV-R" means "fourth edition, revised").

We have space to include only three of the many categories of disorders that developmental psychopathologists study: pervasive developmental delays, learning disabilities, and attention deficits; and only one specific disorder from each category: autism, dyslexia, and ADHD, respectively. Understanding these three can lead to a better understanding of all children.

Using Language Carefully

Labels can stereotype and restrict rather than describe and enable. It is generally agreed that "people first" designations should be used, in writing or speech, to refer to people with special needs; that is, the general human term (e.g., *child, boy, person*) should be used first and followed by "with [the type of special need]." Thus, we write of "children with special needs" or "a person with AIDS" instead of "special-needs children" or "an AIDS patient."

Particular medical conditions should not be expressed in the possessive. For example, people with three chromosomes at the 21st pair (trisomy-21) were once said to have Down's syndrome, named after English physician John Langdon Haydon Down, who first described the condition's physical features in 1866. Now, the preferred form is *Down syndrome* (no *'s*), which no longer suggests that the syndrome "belongs" to the person who first described it.

Some people also believe it is better to call someone "challenged" rather than "handicapped" or "disabled," because a challenge is something that can be overcome and is not necessarily a permanent characteristic. For the same reason, "disability" is preferred to "handicap."

With all such terms, two opposing pitfalls are lurking: insensitivity to the persons who have the disorder (who do not want to be labeled by their difference) versus hiding or denying reality (some children really do need special education). For instance, calling a child "mentally challenged" might gloss over mental retardation, thus discouraging the provision of needed assistance. In 1992, the American Association on Mental Retardation changed its definition of mental retardation by raising the cut-off IQ to 75. This allowed millions more children to qualify for special services, but it also stigmatized an additional 13 percent of U.S. children (Pennington, 2002). (This controversial new cut-off score is not used here.)

In any case, preferred terminology changes from decade to decade. Remember, however, that words matter. Every term and definition has implications and nuances. Be thoughtful.

Pervasive Developmental Delays

Pervasive developmental disorders are severe problems that affect many aspects of psychological growth. (Jacob, the withdrawn, nonspeaking 3-year-old whom you met in Chapter 7, had a pervasive developmental disorder.) Making a diagnosis involves comparing a particular child's development with the norms (some of which are listed in this book's series of tables with the heading "At About This Time"). For example, children usually walk and talk by age 1, become attached to their caregivers throughout infancy, engage in rough-and-tumble and sociodramatic play in early childhood, and develop emotional regulation before school age.

pervasive developmental disorders Severe problems, such as autism, that affect many aspects of a young child's psychological growth, causing evident delay of speech, movement, or social skills before age 6.

Children with pervasive developmental disorders are often close to normal in some aspects of development but markedly delayed in others. Each particular disorder has its own pattern. For example, in Rhett syndrome, a girl has normal abilities during early infancy, but the brain does not grow and development is very slow. By contrast, the brain grows too much in autistic infants, especially the limbic system (Schumann et al., 2004). Let's look more closely at autism, which is probably the most severe of all the psychopathologies of childhood.

Autism Defined

Autism is marked by an "inability to relate in an ordinary way to people . . . an extreme aloneness that, whenever possible, disregards, ignores, shuts out anything that comes to the child from the outside" (Kanner, 1943).

autism A pervasive developmental disorder marked by an inability to relate to other people normally, extreme self-absorption, and an inability to acquire normal speech.

Autistic infants sometimes seem normal, but they are often hypersensitive to noise or other stimulation, do not cuddle as other infants do, and are less coordinated in rolling over, sitting, and walking (Teitelbaum et al., 1998). As they grow, they show deficits in language, social interaction, and play. Children with autism may never talk at all, may never smile at anyone, and are apt to play with only one object (such as a spinning top or a toy train) for hours on end. Some, however, are diagnosed with "high-functioning autism," or *Asperger syndrome,* and will manifest close to normal speech and even brilliance in some areas (Barnhill

Core Symptoms of Autism

- Absent or abnormal language
- Social aloofness or unawareness
- Repetitive, asocial play

et al., 2000; Green et al., 2000). Further, many seemingly normal children and adults have some autistic symptoms, which makes it possible that this disorder is far more common than people once thought.

In 1990 the incidence of children with autistic characteristics (including those with Asperger syndrome) was about 1 in 300 (Szatmari, 2001). The incidence may be increasing. California reported more than three times as many people with autism in 2002 as in 1993 (Maugh, 2002); Minnesota's rate of autism-like disorders among 6- to 11-year-olds jumped from 3 per 10,000 in 1992 to 52 per 10,000 in 2002 (Gurney et al., 2003); and the city of Atlanta reported a tenfold increase between 1986 and 1996 (Parsell, 2004).

Possible Causes of Autism

Although particular genes make some embryos vulnerable, genetic changes in a population are too slow to cause dramatic increases. The reason for the increases may simply be the expanded definition of autism and improved diagnosis. For example, before 1980, autism was not recognized as a reason for special education in the United States. Now that children considered autistic do receive special educational services, many more are diagnosed. Of course, if rates continue to increase, this hypothesis will seem less plausible (Gurney et al., 2003; Parsell, 2004).

Another possibility is that some new teratogen is harming more embryonic brains, especially at three weeks after conception, which, according to some researchers, is the time when the relevant neurological damage is sustained (Rodier, 2000). Many viruses, infections, pesticides, or drugs might affect an embryo, fetus, or infant.

One suspected toxin to which infants are exposed is thimerosal (an antiseptic containing mercury that is used in childhood immunizations). Many parents of autistic children say that they first noticed their infants' impaired social interaction and language after they received MMR (measles-mumps-rubella) vaccinations (Dales et al., 2001).

This immunization hypothesis has been disproved many times. One of the best studies followed all 500,000 children born in Denmark from 1991 to 1998 (Madsen et al., 2002). About a fifth of these children never received MMR vaccinations. Of those who were not vaccinated, 53 developed autism and 77 had other pervasive developmental disorders—the same rates as those occurring among the children who were vaccinated. Further, mercury was removed from vaccines a decade ago, but new cases of autism continue to appear.

Treatment of Autism

Some children with high-functioning autism become adults who do well, even brilliantly, in some domains (Hermelin, 2001). Children who speak before age 5 and develop some close relationships are most likely to become high achievers. However, most children with autism never speak normally and need help with daily care all their lives. As with all developmental disorders, much depends on the social context. As one expert explains:

> People with Asperger syndrome or high-functioning autism might not necessarily be disabled in an environment in which an exact mind, attracted to detecting small details, is an advantage. . . . In the world of business, for example, a mathematical bent for estimating risk and profit, together with a relative lack of awareness of the emotional states of one's employees or rivals, can mean unbounded opportunities.
>
> *[Baron-Cohen, 2000, pp. 497–498]*

This does not mean that parents and teachers should merely hope for the best. For all disorders, psychologists advocate "preventive intervention rather than waiting to intervene when language and learning problems begin to cast a long and wide shadow" (Plomin, 2002, p. 59).

Although the cause is clearly biological, probably the result of a combination of genes and early stresses to the brain, the only successful treatment for autism is psychosocial, with intense early education. Each of autism's three core symptoms (deficit or abnormality in language, social connections, and play) has been the focus of a treatment program.

Some programs emphasize language, with one-on-one behavioral training from teachers and parents to help the child learn to communicate. Such programs increase the possibility of normal education for the child later on (Lovaas, 1987). Other programs emphasize play (Greenspan et al., 1998). The case study of Jacob in Chapter 7 showed that his parents learned to play with him, teaching him that play could be interactive. You may recall that this intervention resulted in an explosion of language abilities, suggesting that playing with Jacob was the key to unlocking his mind. Both the language-development and social-play strategies, implemented intensely early in life, seem successful for many children. However, research with an adequate control group, the members of which received no intervention, has not been reported.

ALAN CAREY / THE IMAGE WORKS

Hope for Autism The prime prerequisite in breaking through the language barrier in a nonverbal autistic child, such as this 4-year-old, is to get the child to pay attention to another person's speech. Note that this teacher is sitting in a low chair to facilitate eye contact and is getting the child to focus on her mouth movements—a matter of little interest to most children but intriguing to many autistic ones. Sadly, even such efforts were not enough: At age 13 this child was still mute.

Other programs stress attachment. This strategy is used in Japan, where autism is diagnosed relatively often, perhaps because "successful diagnosis of high-functioning autism and Asperger syndrome has resulted in high detection rates" (Beppu, 2005, p. 204).

Because children with autism are severely impaired in social interaction (they do not use social referencing, or develop a theory of mind, when most other children do), the goal of some programs is to encourage social connections, especially those that have emotional overtones. In one such program, a 6-year-old Japanese boy with autism noticed his older brother pouring water with a ladle. He tried to pour water himself. "When his mother praised him, [the boy] looked back at his mother with a smile and poured his water even more eagerly" (Beppu, 2005, p. 211); his smile and pride were signs of successful intervention.

All these efforts seem to improve the development of children with autism, although the underlying brain pathology seems lifelong. Now we turn to a disorder at the other end of the spectrum—a learning disability that centers on reading. Unlike autism, learning disabilities are very common, and dyslexia, or reading disability, is particularly likely to be overcome. With proper education, every child (except those who are severely retarded) learns to read.

Learning Disabilities

A child with a **learning disability** has difficulty mastering a particular skill that most people acquire easily. Such children fall markedly behind in one aspect of school, yet they have no physical handicap (such as hearing loss) or stressful home environment (such as physical abuse) that might cause their low achievement. The diagnosis of a learning disability relies on a *measured discrepancy* between expected learning and actual accomplishment (or between aptitude and achievement) in a particular academic area.

learning disability A marked delay in a particular area of learning that is not caused by an apparent physical disability, by mental retardation, or by an unusually stressful home environment.

Many children with learning disabilities score in the normal range on intelligence tests. Often their scores on WISC subtests are "scattered"—some unusually high and others unusually low—which suggests specific disabilities (Kaplan et al., 2000). At age 7, a one-year discrepancy between aptitude and achievement is usually considered evidence of learning disability; by age 11, a two-year discrepancy is the criterion (Lerner, 2000).

LAURA DWIGHT

Is She Dyslexic? No. Some young readers have difficulty "tracking" a line of print with their eyes alone. Using a finger to stay on track can be a useful temporary aid.

dyslexia Unusual difficulty with reading; thought to be the result of some neurological underdevelopment.

KENT MEIREIS / THE IMAGE WORKS

Culture Clash This Tibetan boy attends a Chinese school. Chinese is very difficult to learn to read, especially if it is not one's native language. He may indeed have learned to decode the printed symbols—or he may have learned to fake it.

Learning disabilities do not usually result in lifelong dependence. Some children find ways to compensate for their deficiencies, and others are taught effective strategies for learning. Consequently, many children with learning disabilities become adults who function well, even brilliantly, as seems to have been the case with Winston Churchill, Albert Einstein, and Hans Christian Andersen.

Dyslexia

The most common learning disability is **dyslexia,** which refers to unusual difficulty with reading. Most children who suffer from dyslexia seem bright and happy in the early years of school, volunteering answers to difficult questions, diligently completing their worksheets, and quietly looking at their books in class. Although many older children with dyslexia seem depressed, research finds that this is a consequence, not a cause, of their learning disability (Pennington, 2002).

No single test accurately diagnoses dyslexia or any other learning disability (Sofie & Riccio, 2002). A child with a reading disability might be very confused about sounding out new words but be quite advanced in other reading skills, such as comprehension and memory of printed text.

Listening skills are crucial. Although earlier theories of dyslexia hypothesized that vision was the problem (for example, with reversals and mirror writing), the underlying problem more often is in sound, not sight (Pennington, 2002). Early warnings of dyslexia come when a 3-year-old does not talk clearly and profusely and does not demonstrate the language explosion that is typical of young children.

Although certain neurological patterns underlie all cases of dyslexia (and probably other disabilities as well), the severity of a child's disability depends in part on whether or not early, targeted instruction was provided and on the cultural context (Italian children with dyslexia fare better than French or English ones, probably because Italian is more phonetic) (Paulesu et al., 2001). Children with dyslexia who are having difficulty learning to read a language (such as Chinese) that uses pictograms instead of letters to indicate words have fMRI scans that reveal a set of brain abnormalities that are somewhat different from those found in dyslexic children who are expected to decipher letters.

Because reading is essential for adults in every developed country, dyslexic children almost always learn to read. If this does not occur relatively early in their education, however, they never become avid adult readers who enjoy a good book or read a newspaper to entertain and inform themselves.

Early Education

For all children with learning disabilities, patient, individualized instruction before age 6 often helps to form new neurological patterns and better learning strategies, thus minimizing the problem (Berninger & Richards, 2002; Silver & Hagin, 2002). Normal 4-year-olds do not read, which might make it seem premature to intervene in the case of 4-year-olds who have dyslexia. But researchers have found that many skills that prepare children for reading (or writing or math) skills can be taught to young children. For instance, 4-year-olds can be taught to listen for the differences between the sounds of "b" and "p," and that will help them read.

Children typically do not receive individualized instruction until they have fallen far behind. By that time, rebellion, depression, and poor concentration may accompany learning disabilities. About a third of all children with learning disabilities also suffer from other diagnosable problems, with attention-deficit disorders being the most common (Silver & Hagin, 2002). Children whose dyslexia is comorbid with another problem particularly need help, yet they often become especially disruptive and disabled before their underlying disorders are recognized. We now turn to attention-deficit disorder, which is often a cause as well as a consequence of other problems yet often goes unrecognized and untreated.

Attention-Deficit Disorders

One of the most puzzling and exasperating of childhood problems is **attention-deficit disorder (ADD),** in which the child has great difficulty in concentrating for more than a few moments at a time. Children with an attention-deficit disorder may have an underdeveloped prefrontal cortex, an overactive limbic system, or an imbalance of neurotransmitters. All of these brain abnormalities result in great difficulty in "paying attention" and in *not* reacting to irrelevant stimuli.

attention-deficit disorder (ADD) A condition in which a person has great difficulty concentrating. Such persons may seem lost in thought, spaced out, daydreaming, or distracted.

It is known that ADD originates in the brain and is not just a matter of disobedience and misbehavior. It has many causes: genetic vulnerability, prenatal teratogens, postnatal damage (e.g., lead poisoning), and simply the affected individual's being at the extreme end of a normal distribution (Casey, 2001; Oosterlaan et al., 1998).

ADHD

The most common type of ADD is **attention-deficit/hyperactivity disorder (ADHD).** Children with ADHD have three problems: They are inattentive, impulsive, and overactive. After sitting down to do homework, for instance, a child with ADHD might repeatedly look up, ask irrelevant questions, think about playing outside, get a drink of water, sit down, fidget, squirm, tap the table, jiggle his or her legs, and then get up again for a snack or to go to the bathroom. Often this need for distraction and diversion is accompanied by excitability and impulsivity.

attention-deficit/hyperactivity disorder (ADHD) A condition in which a person not only has great difficulty concentrating for more than a few moments but also is inattentive, impulsive, and overactive.

Billy, the 8-year-old described in the Case to Study earlier in this chapter, was diagnosed with ADHD. His attention problems were evident in that he ran to the window when he was supposed to stay in his chair, and his poor impulse control meant that he could not wait to blurt out his math answer.

Teachers notice disruptive children, but a formal diagnosis does not necessarily follow. Children with ADHD are sometimes punished rather than helped. They themselves feel unfairly treated, as Billy did when he said, "I knew that!" and "I didn't do anything," and "I'll sue you for this."

The gap between problem and diagnosis was evident when all the elementary school teachers in one Tennessee county rated their students on *DSM-IV-R* criteria for ADHD. Fewer than 5 percent of the children (the typical proportion) had already been diagnosed as having ADHD, but 16 percent of the children met the criteria (Warlike et al., 1998). In this study, as happens generally, about four times as many boys were ADHD as girls, an indication either of greater male vulnerability to a particular kind of brain damage or of a mismatch between the expectations of elementary school teachers and the natural behavior of school-age boys.

Compounding the problems of children with ADHD are other, comorbid disorders. Some problems, such as juvenile delinquency, are probably consequences of untreated ADHD, but many predate ADHD or are simultaneous with it. Among these are "conduct disorder, depression, anxiety, Tourette syndrome, dyslexia, and bipolar disorder. Moreover, children with autism and schizophrenia frequently exhibit the symptoms of ADHD" (Pennington, 2002, p. 163). Effective treatment for ADHD is needed, not only because affected children are disruptive, but also because ADHD makes their other problems worse.

Treatment of ADHD

The most effective treatment for ADHD is medication combined with psychotherapy; treatment should also include training for parents and teachers (Abikoff & Hechtman, 2005). Certain drugs that act as stimulants for adults have the reverse

ELLEN SENISI/THE IMAGE WORKS

Not a Cure-All Ritalin has been found to calm many children with ADHD—but it does not necessarily make them models of good behavior. Like this 5-year-old boy with multiple handicaps, including ADHD (for which he is given Ritalin), they are still capable of having a tantrum when frustrated.

effect on children with ADHD, and bring marked improvement to 90 percent of them. Among these drugs are amphetamines (e.g., Adderall) and methylphenidate (Ritalin).

Ritalin was prescribed for Billy, and his parents and teacher were taught how to help him. He "improved considerably," not only staying in his seat and completing his schoolwork, but also making friends (Gorenstein & Comer, 2002).

In the United States, more than 3 million children and adolescents under age 18 take prescription drugs to regulate their emotions and behavior, a rate that doubled between 1987 and 1996 and is still increasing (Brown, 2003; Zito et al., 2003). The most commonly prescribed drug is Ritalin, but at least 20 other psychoactive drugs, including Prozac, Zoloft, and Paxil, are now prescribed for children—some of them as young as age 2 (Gorski, 2002). The fact that medication has been shown to be effective does not satisfy critics who fear that drugs are prescribed too easily and too often. One expert contends:

> Squirming in a seat and talking out of turn are not "symptoms" and do not reflect a syndrome. [Such behaviors may be] caused by anything from normal childhood energy to boring classrooms or overstressed parents and teachers. We should not suppress these behaviors with drugs . . .
>
> *[Breggin, 2001, p. 595]*

Almost everyone agrees that although drugs used to treat attention-deficit disorders may benefit children, they are sometimes underused and sometimes overused (Angold et al., 2000; Brown, 2003). Dosage is a particular concern, not only because children weigh less than adults but also because they have higher metabolic rates, their brains are still developing, and their bodies are still growing. A dose that is effective for adults may be too high, too low, or completely unsafe for a growing child.

In a highly respected study of children with ADHD living in Canada and the United States, dosage was very carefully established: Amounts were gradually increased until optimal behavior occurred without side effects. The researchers reassessed the need for medication by having the children take a placebo for a week without the knowledge of the children, their parents, and their teachers. During the time that the children were being given the placebo (and no medication), their ability to function deteriorated rapidly (Hechtman et al., 2005).

The likelihood that a child with ADHD will be given appropriate medication depends on many factors other than the child's behavior. One factor is where and when that child was born (about 7 percent of 7- to 11-year-olds in the United States take medication, but less than 1 percent of the children with ADHD in developing nations do). In England, far fewer children take medication for ADHD than in the United States, because far fewer children are diagnosed with the disorder; however, a greater number of British children are diagnosed with conduct disorder, a psychopathology that some North American experts believe is the result of unrecognized ADHD.

Within the United States, rates of ADHD diagnosis and medication are higher among boys, among children in the Southern states, among children from low-income households, and among children who are not Hispanic (see Table 11.1) (Martin & Leslie, 2003; Rowland et al., 2002; Witt et al., 2003; Zito et al., 2003). These statistics raise many questions. Social

Significant Differences To obtain the data, the researchers questioned the parents of all first- through fifth-graders (except those in self-contained special education classrooms or in private schools) living in Johnston County, North Carolina, in 1998. The parents were asked if their child had ever been diagnosed with ADHD and if the child was at that time taking medication for it. Similar results (e.g., low rates for girls and Hispanics) have come from other U.S. studies performed in the 1990s. The percentages are probably higher today.

TABLE 11.1 **Rates of Diagnosis and Medication for ADHD**

	Percent Diagnosed with ADHD	Percent of Those Diagnosed Taking Medication for ADHD
Girls	4.7	63
Boys	14.8	73
1st and 2nd grades	7.4	70
3rd, 4th, and 5th grades	12.2	72
Non-Hispanic White	10.8	76
Non-Hispanic Black	9.1	56
Hispanic	4.0	53

Source: Rowland et al., 2002.

circumstances, not just individual needs, seem to affect the diagnosis and treatment of ADHD.

Educating Children with Special Needs

One particular question that has been asked in many places and across many decades is answered in divergent ways by parents and educators: Where and how should children with special needs be educated? Although the brain disorders and childhood stresses that cause developmental psychopathology are probably the same everywhere, education for these children varies dramatically. The diversity of approaches is so great that our discussion here focuses primarily on the United States, where almost every approach has been tried (although none has been completely successful).

LAURA DWIGHT

Every Child Is Special One reason for a school policy of inclusion is to teach children to accept and appreciate children who have special needs. The girl with Down syndrome (in yellow) benefits from learning alongside her classmates, as they learn from her. An effective teacher treats every child as a special individual.

Before 1960, most American children with special needs simply left school—they either dropped out or were forced out. That changed in the United States with a 1969 law that required that all children be educated. At first, children with special needs were placed in "self-contained" classrooms (apart from other children). Neither their social skills nor their academic achievement advanced as much as they might have.

In response, a 1975 federal law called the *Education of All Handicapped Children Act* mandated that children with special needs must learn in the **least restrictive environment (LRE).** Children could not be shunted to a special classroom if a less confining learning context could be found. Often this meant **mainstreaming,** a practice whereby children with learning difficulties were educated in the same classrooms as other children. To help children with various levels of disability, teachers were granted the freedom to use alternative teaching methods or to allow some children extra time to complete assignments.

When it became obvious that many children with disabilities needed intensive, personalized instruction, some schools set aside a **resource room,** where children with special needs spent part of each day with a teacher who was trained and equipped to work with them. This approach was not always successful. Pulling a child out of regular class undermined his or her social relationships and meant that the "regular" teacher was not responsible for the child's learning.

Another approach to placement, called **inclusion,** came into being. Inclusion became part of a 1990 law that has been updated several times. With inclusion, children with special needs are "included" in the general classroom, as in mainstreaming, but the law mandates that they be given "appropriate aids and services" (special help by a trained teacher) within that classroom. Inclusion requires adjustment on the part of both the regular teacher and the specialist—as well as additional funding, which the federal law did not provide (Silver & Hagin, 2002).

Many parents prefer inclusion, because neither mainstreaming nor resource rooms combine social interaction with special education (Swenson, 2000; Waldron & McCleskey, 1998). Parents, in theory, decide what happens to their child, but, in practice, this is not always the case.

Most children with special needs are first spotted by a teacher (not a parent or pediatrician), who makes a *referral,* a request for evaluation based on specific behaviors that have been observed in the child. According to U.S. law, following a referral other professionals must observe and test the child. If they agree that the child has special needs, they meet with the parents to devise an **individual education plan (IEP)** (see Table 11.2). Some parents are eager for their children to be designated as having special needs because they welcome specialized help;

least restrictive environment (LRE) A legal requirement that children with special needs be assigned to the least restrictive context in which they can learn.

mainstreaming The practice of teaching children with special needs with other children in the same classrooms.

resource room A room in which trained teachers help children with special needs, using specialized curricula and equipment.

inclusion An approach to educating children with special needs in which they are included in regular classrooms, with "appropriate aids and services" as required by law.

individual education plan (IEP) A document specifying educational goals and plans for a child with special needs.

ESPECIALLY FOR HEALTH WORKERS
Parents ask that some medication be prescribed for their kindergarten child, who they say is much too active for them to handle. How do you respond?

TABLE 11.2 **Laws Regarding Special Education in the United States***

PL (Public Law) 91-230:	**Children with Specific Learning Disabilities Act, 1969**
Recognized learning disabilities as a category within special education. Before 1969, learning-disabled children received no special education or services.	
PL 94-142:	**Education of All Handicapped Children Act, 1975**
Mandated education of all school-age children, no matter what disability they might have, in the *least restrictive environment (LRE)*—which meant with other children in a regular classroom, if possible. Fewer children were placed in special, self-contained classes, and even fewer in special schools. This law required an *individual educational plan (IEP)* for each child with special needs, specifying educational goals and periodic reassessment.	
PL 105-17:	**Individuals with Disabilities Education Act [IDEA], 1990; updated 1997 and 2004**
Refers to "individuals," not children (to include education of infants, toddlers, adults), and to "disabilities," not handicaps. Emphasizes parents' rights in placement and IEP.	

*Other nations have quite different laws and practices, and states and school districts within the United States vary in interpretation and practice. Consult local support groups, authorities, and legal experts, if necessary.

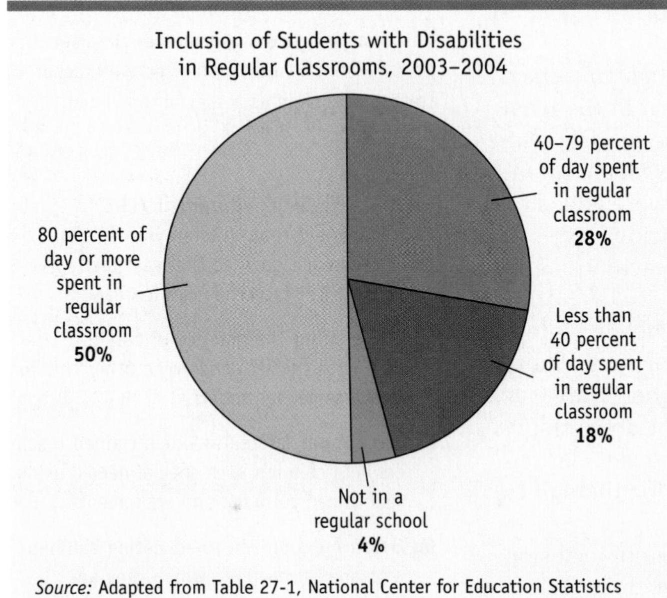

Source: Adapted from Table 27-1, National Center for Education Statistics Web site, accessed July 18, 2005.

FIGURE 11.3 **Side by Side** Fifty years ago, almost all children with special needs were educated apart from unimpaired children, if they were in school at all. Today only 4 percent are not in regular schools, and most of those who are in regular schools spend most of their day in regular classrooms. Opinion is divided as to whether this great inclusion leads to better education.

other parents resist because they dread the social consequences their child may experience.

About 10 percent of schoolchildren are identified as having special needs and receive special educational services—up from 8 percent in 1975 (Snyder, Tan, & Hoffman, 2004). (See Table 11.3.) Currently in the United States, about half of all children diagnosed with special needs are educated solely in regular classrooms, with varied success (see Figure 11.3). Many more children with special needs, perhaps another 13 percent, have not been referred or identified.

Sometimes lack of identification is good, sometimes not. Consider Yolanda and Paul, the two Mexican American chidren whom you met at the beginning of this chapter. Both could have been diagnosed as children with special needs in that their language skills were far below their potential. Yolanda was helped by her peers and teachers, who "pulled me up some grades, or moved me to other classes"; but Paul fell farther and farther behind, was absent a great deal, and finally was sent to a special school, which he soon left.

Obviously, no placement solves all the academic and social problems of children with special needs, who tend to have fewer friends than other children and to learn more slowly, no matter which classroom they are in (Wiener & Schneider, 2002). From a developmental perspective, these ongoing difficulties are not surprising: All manner of disabilities, from severe physical impairments to subtle learning disabilities, are pervasive. The proper educational context is helpful, but, as a review of inclusion programs in eight nations has made clear, disabilities rarely disappear (Booth & Ainscow, 1998).

If parents, teachers, and children understand that learning difficulties do not stem from laziness, stupidity, or stubbornness, but from patterns of brain activity that need to be restructured, then advances can occur. This happened with the late Ennis Cosby (1997), the son of comedian Bill Cosby, who wrote, "The happiest day of my life occurred when I found out I was dyslexic. I believe that life is finding solutions, and the worst feeling to me is confusion." Solutions are easier to implement earlier, when the brain is most plastic, rather than later.

TABLE 11.3 **Prevalence of Some Categories of Childhood Psychopathology: United States**

Categories	American Psychiatric Association DSM-IV-R	Students Receiving Special Education (as percent of all students)	
	2000	1975	2001
Mental Retardation (MR)*	1%	2%	1%
Significantly delayed adaptation to life, and a score of less than 70 on an IQ test			
Specific Learning Disorder or Disability (LD)	6%	2%	6%
Academic achievement substantially below expected in a basic academic skill			
Communicative Disorders	11%	3%	2%
DSM-IV-R includes several types, including:			
Expressive—Understanding but poor expression (5% at school age; 12% under age 3)			
Receptive-expressive—Deficits in understanding and expression (3% of school-age children)			
Phonological—Child's speech cannot be understood (2%)			
Stuttering—Severe disturbance in fluency (1%) (rare before age 5)			
Pervasive Developmental Disorder (PDD)	0.1%	0.01%†	0.26%
(Includes autism and Asperger syndrome)			
Attention-deficit/hyperactivity disorder (ADHD, ADD)	5%	**	**
Inattentiveness, impulsivity, and/or overactivity (see text for clarification of definitions and symptoms)			
Conduct Disorder (CD)	5%	**	**
Bullying, threatening, cruelty to people or animals, lying			
Oppositional Defiant Disorder (ODD)	8%	**	**
Negativity, disobedience, hostility toward authorities			
Serious Emotional Disturbance (ED)	††	0.6%	1%
Totals: §	**25%**	**8%**	**10%**

* Specialists often refer to categories using only abbreviations. To help with interpretation, the common abbreviations are given in parentheses.

† Autism data compare 1990 and 2001, because autism was not a recognized category in 1975.

** These categories do not qualify for special education, according to U.S. law.

†† The American Psychiatric Association uses more specific categories for serious emotional problems and has no general estimate of prevalence.

§ Totals include additional children not listed in specific categories. For DSM-IV-R, these include uncommon psychological disturbances, such as feeding disorders, tic disorders, and attachment disorders. Some children have several disabilities, so the DSM total of 25 percent is less than the sum of all categories. The current educational total includes only those referred, diagnosed, and accepted for special education. Disorders of speech are not often diagnosed, and three common problems—attention-deficit disorder, conduct disorders, and oppositional behavior—are not recognized as educational categories. A few children with those problems receive special services because they are learning-disabled or emotionally disturbed, but most simply go without any special help.

Sources: American Psychiatric Association, 2000; Snyder et al., 2004.

ELLEN SENISI / THE IMAGE WORKS

She Knows the Answer Physical disabilities often mushroom into additional emotional and cognitive problems. However, a disability can be reduced to a minor complication if it is recognized and if appropriate compensation or remediation is made a part of the child's education. As she signs her answer, this deaf girl shows by her expression that she is ready to learn.

Response for Health Workers (from page 351): Medication helps some hyperactive children, but not all. It might be useful for this child, but other forms of intervention should be tried first. Compliment the parents on their concern about their child, but refer them to an expert in early childhood for an evaluation and recommendations. Behavior-management techniques geared to the particular situation, not medication, will be the first strategy.

That said, a multicultural perspective reminds us that other nations recognize fewer children with special needs and have fewer laws and specialized teachers, psychologists, and other trained professionals who might help those children (Silver & Hagen, 2002). Whether or not the U.S. approach benefits children is debatable. Obviously, the outcome depends on values, customs, and the individuals directly involved.

SUMMING UP

Many children have special learning needs. Developmental psychopathologists emphasize that no child is typical in every way; time brings improvement for some children, increased problems for others. Disorders vary in cause, treatment, and prognosis, although many share certain characteristics. People with pervasive developmental delays, learning disabilities, and attention-deficit disorders may function adequately or may have lifelong problems, depending partly on family, school, and culture, as well as on severity and the presence or absence of comorbid conditions. In 2000, about 13 percent of all children in the United States were receiving special educational services in school. Perhaps another 13 percent might benefit from such services, if they were begun early enough. The specifics of diagnosis, prognosis, medication, and placement are very often debatable, and no child learns and behaves exactly like another during the school years.

■ SUMMARY

A Healthy Time

1. Middle childhood is a time of steady growth and few serious illnesses. Increasing independence and self-care allow most school-age children to be relatively happy and competent.

2. Childhood obesity is becoming a worldwide epidemic. Although genetics plays a role in body weight, less exercise and the greater availability of unhealthy food are bigger culprits. Many adults, including parents, have not fully recognized this problem.

3. Most health problems are less common than they were thirty years ago, but the incidence of asthma is increasing. Although the origins of asthma are genetic and the triggers are specific allergens, effective primary prevention involves extending the breast-feeding period, more outdoor play, and reduced air pollution.

Brain Development

4. Brain development continues during middle childhood, enhancing every aspect of development. Myelination increases, which speeds communication between neurons. In addition, the prefrontal cortex and the corpus callosum continue to mature, allowing not only analysis and planning but also selective attention and automatization.

5. With neurological maturation, gross and fine motor skills continue to develop. As with every other aspect of maturation, neurological advances are aided by practice, by culture, and by genetics. Better brain functioning is one of many reasons children should be encouraged to play.

6. IQ tests are designed to quantify intellectual aptitude. Most such tests emphasize language and logical ability and predict school achievement. IQ tests also reflect the culture in which they were created.

7. Achievement tests measure what a person has actually accomplished. Most standard achievement tests measure academic learning, but sometimes the measuring of adaptation to daily life is crucial.

8. Critics contend that intelligence is actually manifested in multiple ways, which conventional IQ tests are too limited to measure. The concept of multiple intelligences recognizes creative and practical abilities, some of which are difficult to test.

Children with Special Needs

9. Developmental psychopathology uses an understanding of normal development to inform the study of unusual development. Four general lessons have emerged: Abnormality is normal; disability changes over time; adolescence and adulthood may make a condition better or worse; and diagnosis depends on context.

10. Some children with obvious educational or psychological disabilities are recognized, referred, evaluated, diagnosed, and treated in early childhood. For the most part, however, behavioral or learning problems are not spotted until the children enter elementary school and are compared with other children in a setting that demands maturity and learning.

11. Children with pervasive developmental disorders typically show odd and delayed language ability; a lack of social awareness with impaired interpersonal skills; and play that is repetitive and unimaginative. The most severe of such disorders is autism, which improves with intensive early education but never disappears.

12. People with learning disabilities have unusual difficulty in mastering a specific skill that other people learn easily. The most common learning disability that manifests itself during the school years is dyslexia, unusual difficulty with reading. Children with learning disabilities can be helped if the problem is spotted early and if the assistance is individualized to suit the particular child.

13. Children with attention-deficit/hyperactivity disorder (ADHD) have potential problems in three areas: inattention, impulsiveness, and overactivity. The treatment for attention deficits is a combination of medication, home management, and education. Stimulant medication often helps children with ADHD to learn, but the dosages must be carefully monitored.

14. About 10 percent of all school-age children in the United States receive special education services. These services begin with an IEP (individual education plan) and assignment to the least restrictive environment—all taking place with the parents' full involvement.

15. Decisions about educational placement are complicated by conflicts between ideological concerns and practical needs, and sometimes between education professionals and parents. The inclusion approach is generally considered superior to mainstreaming, although no one type of placement works for all children.

■ KEY TERMS

middle childhood (p. 327)
overweight (p. 328)
obese (p. 328)
asthma (p. 331)
selective attention (p. 334)
automatization (p. 334)
reaction time (p. 338)
aptitude (p. 339)
IQ tests (p. 339)
achievement tests (p. 339)
Wechsler Intelligence Scale for Children (WISC) (p. 340)
mental retardation (p. 340)
Flynn Effect (p. 341)
child with special needs (p. 344)
developmental psychopathology (p. 344)
***Diagnostic and Statistical Manual of Mental Disorders* (DSM-IV-R) (p. 344)**
pervasive developmental disorders (p. 345)
autism (p. 345)
learning disability (p. 347)
dyslexia (p. 348)
ADD (attention-deficit disorder) (p. 349)
ADHD (attention-deficit/hyperactivity disorder) (p. 349)
least restrictive environment (LRE) (p. 351)
mainstreaming (p. 351)
resource room (p. 351)
inclusion (p. 351)
individual education plan (IEP) (p. 351)

■ KEY QUESTIONS

1. How does the growth of the school-age child compare with the growth of the younger child?

2. How do we know that the reason for the increase in rates of childhood obesity is not genetic?

3. What measures to reduce asthma would also benefit all children?

4. How does reaction time affect a child's ability to learn and behave?

5. What are some good uses of intelligence tests?

6. What are some misuses of intelligence tests?

7. Why was the field of developmental psychopathology created?

8. What are the signs of autism, and when are they evident?

9. How could it happen that an adult might have a learning disability that was never spotted?

10. Why might parents decide to give Ritalin to their child?

11. When is inclusion the best educational setting for a child?

■ APPLICATIONS

1. Compare play spaces for children in different neighborhoods —ideally, urban, suburban, and rural areas. Note size, safety, and use. How might children's weight and motor skills be affected?

2. Developmental psychologists believe that every teacher should be skilled at teaching children with a wide variety of needs. Does the teacher-training curriculum at your college or university reflect this goal? Should all teachers take the same courses, or should some teachers be specialized? Give reasons for your opinions.

3. Web sites vary in quality, no matter what the topic, but this may be particularly true of Web sites designed for parents of children with special needs. Pick one childhood disability or disease and find several Web sites devoted to that condition. How might parents evaluate the information provided?

4. Special education teachers are in great demand. What is your local ratio of regular to special education teachers, in relation to employment and licensing? How many special education teachers are in self-contained classrooms, resource rooms, and inclusion classrooms? Compare your data with the material in this chapter.

Chapter Twelve

The School Years: Cognitive Development

School-age children are learners. They can learn almost anything that is not too abstract, including how to multiply and divide fractions, how to prepare a nutritious and delicious dinner, how to surf the Web to uncover obscure facts, what to feed an orphaned kitten. Between ages 7 and 11, each day advances knowledge a tiny bit.

Time is crucial, but the depth and content of learning reflect motivation more than maturation—motivation that is guided by cultural priorities and channeled by intricate brain networks. Thus, nurture and nature interact to allow each child to learn in his or her own way. Despite this uniqueness of learning styles and interests, every school-age child is primed to learn, and adults in every culture are eager to teach them.

That adult eagerness flows in many directions. In the United States, concerns that children were not learning enough led to a federal law called the ***No Child Left Behind Act,*** passed in 2001 with the strong support of the president and most members of Congress. The law required annual testing and imposed achievement standards, with sanctions for schools that repeatedly fell short, as many schools do (No Child Left Behind Act of 2001). A year later, on the other side of the globe, the people of Japan worried that their children felt too much academic pressure. The government of Japan began a policy called *yutori kyoiku,* which means "more relaxed education," reducing the content of the public school curriculum by 30 percent (Magara, 2005). Both these policies, and many other divergent ideas about education, are described in this chapter.

First, however, we describe the universals, as enunciated by Jean Piaget, Lev Vygotsky, and information-processing theory. Together, these three help us understand the child's thinking. Then we turn to schooling, including the reading and math wars. This chapter will help you understand, and decide, what and how the next generation of children might learn.

Building on Piaget and Vygotsky

Both Piaget and Vygotsky, as you remember from Chapter 9, emphasize the structures, or scaffolding, that children develop—those particular ways in which children collect all the events and facts that surround them, constructing them into organized knowledge (Rogoff, 1998). In Piaget's view, the most important cognitive structure attained in middle childhood is called **concrete operational thought,** characterized by a collection of concepts that enable children to reason.

Piaget discovered that, sometime between ages 5 and 7, children begin to understand certain logical principles (Inhelder & Piaget, 1964). Soon they apply logic in *concrete* situations—that is, situations that deal with visible, tangible, real things. Children thereby become more systematic, objective, scientific—and educable—thinkers.

No Child Left Behind Act A controversial law, enacted in 2001, that uses multiple assessments and achievement standards to try to improve public education in the United States.

concrete operational thought Piaget's term for the ability to reason logically about direct experiences and perceptions.

Vygotsky (1934/1994) agreed with Piaget's attention to the actual thinking of the child. He considered this a marked improvement over the dull "meaningless acquisition" approach favored by the schools of his time. Such schools rendered the child "helpless in the face of any sensible attempt to apply any of this acquired knowledge" (pp. 356–357). Vygotsky also believed that children are eager to learn. Unlike Piaget, however, Vygotsky regarded instruction by others as crucial, with peers and teachers providing the bridge to connect the child's innate developmental potential with the skills and knowledge that education should bring.

Logical Principles

To understand concrete operational thought, consider classification, identity, reversibility, and reciprocity. Piaget thought that the underlying logical concepts for these four are almost impossible for younger children to comprehend but are gradually grasped during middle childhood.

Categories Within Categories

classification The logical principle by which things are organized into groups (or categories or classes) according to some property they have in common.

Classification is the process of organizing things into groups (or *categories* or *classes)* according to some property they have in common. For example, a child's parents and siblings belong to the class called "family." Other common classes are toys, animals, people, and food. Each class includes some elements and excludes others, and each is part of a hierarchy. Food, for instance, is a broad class, which contains the subclasses of meat, grains, fruits, and so on.

Most subclasses can be further divided: Meat includes poultry, beef, and pork, which again can be further subdivided. It is apparent to adults who have mastered classification, but not always to children, that items at the bottom of the class hierarchy belong to every higher category (bacon is always pork, meat, and food) but that the process does not work in reverse (most foods are not bacon).

Piaget developed many experiments that reveal children's understanding of classification. For example, an examiner shows a child a bunch of nine flowers—seven yellow daisies and two white roses (revised and published in Piaget et al., 2001). The examiner makes sure the child knows the vocabulary, that all are "flowers," some "daisies" and others "roses."

PETER CADE / STONE / GETTY IMAGES

Learning by Doing Active learning—the hands-on experience of, in this case, connecting wires with positive and negative charges—is a valuable supplement to book learning and rote learning.

Then comes the crucial question: "Are there more daisies or more flowers?" Until about age 7, most children say "more daisies." Pushed to justify their answer, the youngest children usually have no explanation, but some 6- or 7-year-olds say that there are more yellow ones than white ones or that, because the daisies are daisies, they aren't flowers (Piaget et al., 2001). By age 8, most children have a solid understanding of the classification of objects they can see (concrete objects, not yet hypothetical ones), and they answer confidently "more flowers than daisies."

What, exactly, does this classification experiment mean? It is not quite the proof of a dramatic logical shift, as Piaget thought. Other research finds that classification appears before middle childhood. Even infants seem to have brain networks ready to categorize what they see (Quinn, 2004), and 4-year-olds are somewhat flexible when deciding whether a certain food is breakfast food, junk food, both, or neither (Nguyen & Murphy, 2003).

Nonetheless, Piaget's experimentation revealed something important. What develops during concrete operational thought is the ability to use mental categories and subcategories flexibly, inductively, and simultaneously, as with flowers and roses or (a greater challenge) with cars that can be transportation, toys, lethal weapons, imports, consumer products, Toyotas, and/or SUVs. Although preschool children can categorize, Piaget recognized that older children are more precise and flexible in classification, making them able to separate the essential from the irrelevant (Hayes & Younger, 2004).

identity The logical principle that certain characteristics of an object remain the same even if other characteristics change.

reversibility The logical principle that sometimes a thing that has been changed can be returned to its original state by reversing the process by which it was changed.

reciprocity The principle that things may change in opposite ways and thus balance each other out. (Also called *inversion.*)

Essence and Change

Identity is another principle that becomes much better understood during middle childhood, according to Piaget. Identity means that some characteristics of an object remain the same even if other characteristics appear to shift. A ball is still a ball when it rolls into a hole; a child is the same person, awake or asleep. Children who understand identity realize that superficial changes in an object's appearance do not alter that object's underlying substance or quantity. In conservation tests, for example (described in Chapter 9), identity means understanding that pouring a liquid from one container into a different container does not change the amount of liquid present. "It's still the same milk," a 9-year-old might say. "You haven't changed that."

School-age children also come to understand **reversibility,** the idea that some things can be returned to their original state by reversing a process. Remember that younger children think changes are irreversible. By middle childhood, however, a child might prove conservation by pouring the liquid back into the first container. As another example of both identity and reversibility, 6-year-olds may not expect that lemonade which is frozen into ice pops could melt into lemonade again; 9-year-olds are not surprised that this happens.

Finally, children begin to understand the logical principle of **reciprocity.** Reciprocity (also called *inversion*) occurs when two things change in opposite ways in order to balance each other out. In the conservation experiment, a child who understands reciprocity might explain that, because the new container is wider as well as shorter, the liquid's decreased height is balanced out by its increased width.

Measuring Soil Absorbency This science lesson in the fourth grade of a public school in New York City seems well designed for concrete operational thinking. The children analyze, investigate, and classify samples of soil by putting them in water, not by reading a textbook. Note also that each does his or her own work within a social setting—another sign of effective elementary education.

LAURA DWIGHT

Practical Applications

In each of these examples, changes are understood when compared with some essential nature of an object; certain basics remain even when shape, appearance, or interrelationship is altered. Because you can understand this, you can understand human development as no young child can. You know that a person is the same person at age 1 or 18 or 80, that family bonds endure even when the reciprocal dependence/independence of various generations shifts, and so on.

Remember that Piaget's concepts should not be interpreted too rigidly. No concrete operational concept is completely beyond younger children nor patently obvious to adults. Logic is both present and absent throughout life. However, between ages 6 and 11, major cognitive advances occur.

One practical application occurs when children are learning math. Place value requires classification: Without it, a child might think 21 and 12 are the same. Identity allows a child to understand that, for example, 6 is always 6, whether it is the result of $2 + 4$ or $3 + 3$. Reversibility is harder: If $2 + 4 = 6$, then $6 - 4 = 2$, an idea often grasped in the second grade. Finally, reciprocity: Children learn that 4×6 is the same as 2×12, because if the 4 is divided by 2, then the 6 has to be multiplied by 2. An even harder example of reciprocity is $\frac{1}{2} \div \frac{1}{2} = \frac{1}{2} \times 2$. Reciprocity is beyond almost all children until they are well into middle childhood, which is why multiplication and division of fractions are difficult at first (Piaget & Moreau, 2001).

The same logical ideas apply to other aspects of learning. Geography becomes exciting to many school-age children if they are taught to understand places within places, which is an application of classification. Evidence of classes and subclasses occurs when children write their return address as: their name, then number and street, town, state, nation, continent, earth, solar system, Milky Way. Similarly, a tadpole can become a frog (identity), steam from boiling water can become water again (reversibility), helping a classmate with math might lead that person to help you with spelling (reciprocity).

ESPECIALLY FOR TEACHERS How might Piaget and Vygotsky help in teaching geography to a class of third-graders?

Understanding these four logical principles does not always mean that a child can apply them, either in school or in social situations. When it comes to applications, children learn best if adults guide them, as Vygotsky emphasized.

The Same in Every Nation?

Piaget's basic idea about concrete operational thought—that children during middle childhood gradually comprehend and apply logical ideas that they did not use before—remains valid. In math, in physics, in explaining how people catch illnesses from someone else, in knowing which human characteristics are mostly genetic or environmental, and in many other ways, children become more logical and less egocentric (Astuti et al., 2004; Howe, 1998; Keil & Lockhart, 1999; Siegler & Jenkins, 1989).

Vygotsky's emphasis on the sociocultural context contrasts with Piaget's approach. Vygotsky believed that people learn because other people, as well as the tools of their culture, support their learning. He found that children are powerfully influenced by their social setting, which guides them in one direction or another.

Research on the brain, described in Chapters 8 and 11, reinforces this conclusion (Berninger & Richards, 2002). Neurological advances make 9-year-olds more capable than 3-year-olds, but the prefrontal cortex is not completely developed until adulthood. Especially while it is developing, children need guided apprenticeship, with mentoring adults and peers, to improve brain connections. Neurological research finds that learning is both developmental and sociocultural, both Piagetian and Vygotskyian. Cognition is the result of maturation *and* experience—"neither innately specified nor externally imposed" (Ingold, 2001, p. 131), but both.

Confirmation of the role of the social context comes from children who, because of their school's entry date, are relatively old or young first-graders. Learning among 5-year-old first-graders (for instance, born in December) far exceeds that of 5-year-olds only slightly younger (born in January) but who are in kindergarten. Additional confirmation comes from the effect on children of quality teaching. There is a direct correlation between the percentage of qualified teachers in a school and learning, even when other factors affecting the child (socioeconomic status [SES], prior achievement, neighborhood) are considered (Wayne & Youngs, 2003).

Cultural Variations

Most research on children's cognition has been done in North America and Western Europe, but the same principles are apparent worldwide. In Zimbabwe, for example, children's understanding of the logic of classification is influenced not only by their age (Piaget) but also by the particulars of their schooling (Vygotsky) and their family's SES (Mpofu & van de Vijver, 2000). Similarly, adults and children in Madagascar, struggling to understand the relationship between nature and nurture (particularly the interaction of genes and child rearing on a person's characteristics) are affected not only by their maturity level but also by their cultural background (Astuti et al., 2004). Thus, their cognition is both experience-expectant and experience-dependent, just as it is for people elsewhere.

The non-Western nation with the most research on child development is Japan, where many of the theories explained in this book are being reaffirmed or readjusted. One study of Japanese children found that *some* mathematical skills closely followed Piaget's theory but that others were definitely the result of very specific school instruction, as Vygotsky predicted (Naito & Miura, 2001).

A particular example comes from Japanese 4- to 11-year-olds' understanding of time, speed, and distance. As Piaget would predict, understanding of this reciprocal concept (faster means less time) improves with age: The younger children rarely understood the relationships among the three. Some of the oldest children understood, but their comprehension of the three-way reciprocity of time, speed, and distance varied much more than a straightforward stage theory would predict (Matsuda, 2001). Other research also finds that explicit instruction, much more than maturation, helps Japanese children understand speed (Magara, 2005).

Street Smarts Javier Garcias sells candy and cigarettes on the streets of San Salvador, the capital of El Salvador, from 5:00 A.M. until 1:00 P.M, and from 5:00 P.M. to 8:00 P.M. In between, he goes to school. That combination of work experience and formal education may add up to excellent math skills—if Javier is awake enough to learn.

VICTOR RUIZ CABALLERO / AP / WIDE WORLD PHOTOS

Brazilian Street Children

The most detailed international example comes from Brazil, specifically from the street children who sell fruit, candy, and other products to earn their living. Many have never attended school and consequently score poorly on standard math achievement tests. This is no surprise to developmentalists, who have seen many examples of slower cognition in children who are unschooled (Cole, 1996).

However, most young Brazilian peddlers are adept at pricing their wares, making change, and giving discounts for large quantities—a set of operations that must be recalibrated almost every day because of inflation, wholesale prices, and customer demand. These children calculate "complex markup computations and adjust for inflation in these computations by using procedures that were widespread in their practice but not known to children in school" (Saxe, 1999, p. 255).

Thus, knowledge of advanced math reflected in these children's cognitive performance came from three sources:

- Demands of the situation
- Learning from other sellers
- Daily experience

None of this would surprise Vygotsky, who would expect that street culture would teach children what school did not. The researchers found that, for these Brazilian children, education was not completely irrelevant, again as Vygotsky would predict. The best math skills were demonstrated by those children who had both schooling and street experience (Saxe, 1991).

Further research on Brazilian 4- to 14-year-olds confirms the complex interrelationship of age, cognitive development, and experience. The intellectual advantage of actually having dealt with money was greatest for children aged 6 to 11, in middle childhood. Even experienced children under age 6 could not understand some arithmetic problems presented to them, and children older than 11 performed just as well whether or not they had sold items on the street (Guberman, 1996).

Moral Development

Trying to understand how children think about moral issues reveals the insights and limitations of Piaget and Vygotsky. First, these two theorists (and everyone else who examines children's moral thinking) agree that ages 7 to 11 are:

> years of eager, lively searching on the part of children, whose parents and teachers are often hard put to keep up with them as they try to understand things, to figure them out, but also to weigh the rights and wrongs of this life. This is the time for growth of the moral imagination, fueled constantly by the willingness, the eagerness of children to put themselves in the shoes of others.
>
> *[Coles, 1997]*

Moral thinking begins when children begin to "put themselves in the shoes of others" and to be less judgmental. At about age 7, children realize the difference between morals and matters of convention, taste, or obedience to adults (Turiel, 2002).

Perhaps you know a child, as young as 4, who has a strong sense of right and wrong. Could developmentalists be mistaken when they ignore moral development before age 7? There is reason to wonder: Preschoolers report classmates for not sharing, feel guilty when they lie, fear punishment when they violate a rule, sympathize with someone in distress, and are sad about hungry children elsewhere. Research finds that even 3- and 4-year-olds have the basics of conscience (Aksan & Kochanska, 2005). Further, a study of 5- to 9-year-olds found that most of the youngest children knew that kicking other children was morally wrong, as did virtually all the older children (Wainryb et al., 2004).

But this study also asked these 5- to 9-year-olds about a hypothetical boy named David, who thought chocolate ice cream was yucky, and Daniel, who found chocolate ice cream yummy. Only a third (37 percent) of the 5-year-olds accepted that such taste differences were a matter of personal preference, not morality, and therefore that David and Daniel could both be right. Of those more typical 5-year-olds who thought David was wrong, most went further, judging him to be bad or stupid. By contrast, virtually all (94 percent) of the 9-year-olds realized that both boys could be right, and very few were critical of David for his unusual taste (Wainryb et al., 2004). Thus at least one aspect of morality, respect for individual differences, develops in middle childhood (as egocentrism declines).

Response for Teachers (from page 360): Here are two of the most obvious ways. (1) Use logic. Once children can grasp classification and class inclusion, they can understand cities within states, states within nations, and nations within continents. Organize your instruction to make logical categorization easier. (2) Make use of children's need for concrete and personal involvement. You might have the children learn first about their own location, then about the places where relatives and friends live, and finally about places beyond their personal experience (via books, photographs, videos, and guest speakers).

Kohlberg's Stages

To understand how moral judgment moves past the highly personal and egocentric ideas of preschool children, consider Lawrence Kohlberg's application of Piaget (Kohlberg, 1963; Piaget, 1932). Kohlberg posed ethical dilemmas to children and adolescents (and eventually to adults). The most famous dilemma is about Heinz, a poor man whose wife is dying. A local pharmacist has the only cure, a drug sold for thousands of dollars—far more than Heinz can pay and 10 times what the drug costs to make.

> Heinz went to everyone he knew to borrow the money, but he could only get together about half of what it cost. He told the druggist that his wife was dying and asked him to sell it cheaper or let him pay later. But the druggist said "no." The husband got desperate and broke into the man's store to steal the drug for his wife. Should the husband have done that? Why?
>
> *[Kohlberg, 1963]*

In people's responses to such dilemmas, Kohlberg found three levels of moral reasoning—*preconventional, conventional,* and *postconventional*—with two stages at each level (see Table 12.1). In theory, each level of moral reasoning matches one of Piaget's stages of cognitive development (which are explained in Chapter 2).

Preconventional moral reasoning is similar to preoperational thought in that it is egocentric. **Conventional moral reasoning** is related to concrete operational thought in that it relates to current, observable practices within the community.

preconventional moral reasoning Kohlberg's first level of moral reasoning, emphasizing rewards and punishments.

conventional moral reasoning Kohlberg's second level of moral reasoning, emphasizing social rules.

Lawrence Kohlberg Kohlberg was a scholar, researcher, and philosopher who described the logical structures that underlie specific moral decisions.

TABLE 12.1 **Kohlberg's Three Levels and Six Stages of Moral Reasoning**

Level I: Preconventional Moral Reasoning

Emphasis is placed on getting rewards and avoiding punishments; this is a self-centered level.

- *Stage One: Might makes right* (a punishment and obedience orientation). The most important value is obedience to authority, avoiding punishment while still advancing self-interest. Don't get caught!
- *Stage Two: Look out for number one* (an instrumental and relativist orientation). Each person tries to take care of his or her own needs. The reason to be nice to other people is so that they will be nice to you.

Level II: Conventional Moral Reasoning

Emphasis is placed on social rules; this is a community-centered level.

- *Stage Three: "Good girl" and "nice boy."* Proper behavior is behavior that pleases other people. Social approval is more important than any specific reward.
- *Stage Four: "Law and order."* Proper behavior means being a dutiful citizen and obeying the laws set down by society. Even when no police officer is nearby, obey the law.

Level III: Postconventional Moral Reasoning

Emphasis is placed on moral principles; this level is centered on ideals.

- *Stage Five: Social contract.* Obey social rules because they benefit everyone and are established by mutual agreement. If the rules become destructive or if one party doesn't live up to the agreement, the contract is no longer binding. Under some circumstances, disobeying the law is moral.
- *Stage Six: Universal ethical principles.* General universal principles, not individual situations (level I) or community practices (level II), determine right and wrong. Ethical values (such as "life is sacred") are established by individual reflection and may contradict egocentric (level I) or legal (level II) values.

postconventional moral reasoning Kohlberg's third level of moral reasoning, emphasizing moral principles.

And **postconventional moral reasoning** is similar to formal operational thought, with logic and abstract ideals beyond what is concretely observed within a particular society.

According to Kohlberg, *how* people reason, rather than what specific moral conclusions they reach, determines their stage of moral development. For example, reasoning that seeks social approval (stage three) might produce opposite conclusions: Either Heinz *should* steal the drug (because people would blame him for not saving his wife) or he *should not* steal it (because people would consider him a thief). In both cases, the underlying moral principle (and stage) is the same—that people should behave in ways that earn the approval of others.

Children, adolescents, and adults gradually move up Kohlberg's hierarchy, reasoning at more advanced stages as time goes on. During middle childhood, children's answers are generally at the first two levels—primarily preconventional before age 8 and conventional for 9- to 11-year-olds—although much depends on the specific context and on the opportunities available to the child to discuss moral issues. This shift in middle childhood is what might be expected as children leave preoperational egocentrism and advance to concrete operational thought.

Especially for Parents Suppose you and your school-age children move to a new community that is 50 miles from the nearest location that offers instruction in your faith or value system. Your neighbor says, "Don't worry, they don't have to make any moral decisions until they are teenagers." Is your neighbor correct?

In line with Vygotsky's stress on cultural variations and social guidance, Kohlberg agreed that social forces make a difference. He believed that school-age children should discuss moral dilemmas with each other, a process of "values clarification" that would advance their thinking. However, Kohlberg was heavily influenced by Piaget, and thus he emphasized maturation, especially for children.

Criticisms of Kohlberg

Although the basic scheme proposed by Kohlberg has been replicated (Boom et al., 2001; Walker et al., 2001), his ideas have also been widely criticized. Every culture teaches children distinctive values and morals, sometimes connected to a particular religion, sometimes not. For example, a child might believe that eating beef (or pork, whale, or dog) is immoral; such beliefs are not universal but culture-specific.

Some critics believe that Kohlberg's level III (stages 5 and 6) reflects his own liberal, Western intellectual values. In many non-Western nations, and among some ethnic groups within Western cultures, the good of the family, the well-being of the community, or adherence to religious tradition takes moral precedence over the freedom of the autonomous individual (Wainryb & Turiel, 1995). Members of such cultures and groups may never reach postconventional thinking, but they may be quite moral all the same.

Give Peace a Chance The setting is Israel; the sheep washers include Jews and Muslims. In all probability, these boys are aware that their cooperative efforts are in accord with moral values but are contrary to the social customs prevailing around them. The school years are a good time to teach children about other races and cultures, a lesson best learned through personal experience.

GARY LANGLEY

For example, in a study in the Netherlands, Moroccan and Turkish adolescents were significantly behind their Dutch and Surinamese peers in Kohlberg's stages (De Mey et al., 1999). The Moroccan and Turkish emphasis on family and community, a handicap in Kohlberg's scheme, may be a higher form of moral thinking than the individualism and rationality enshrined by Kohlberg's third level.

Further, Kohlberg's hierarchy may underestimate the potential of school-age children. In one study, Canadian 6- to 10-year-olds judged whether laws were just. They decided that some laws were unfair, and they approved of disobeying unjust laws—a stage-five reaction, because it goes beyond acceptance of current practices (Helwig & Jasiobedzka,

APICHART WEERAWONG / AP PHOTO

Beyond National Borders Empathy during the school years extends worldwide. After the Indian Ocean tsunami that devastated South Asia in December 2004, 8-year-old Bilaal Rajan *(left)* went to Thailand under the auspices of UNICEF to personally deliver the contributions he had helped to raise in his homeland, Canada. He is shown here meeting with Thai children whose families suffered from the tsunami.

2001). Whether or not laws should be obeyed is rarely discussed in elementary school in the United States, presumably because such judgments are thought to be beyond the cognitive power of young children. This research suggests that, at least among this group of students, Kohlberg underestimated children's capacity. The cultural context may be more influential than Kohlberg realized.

Carol Gilligan (1982) raised another criticism—that Kohlberg overlooked significant sex differences because his theory was based on the intellectual responses of boys (he did not realize that his sample was biased). Gilligan believes that females develop a **morality of care** more than a **morality of justice.** The morality of care makes girls and women reluctant to judge right and wrong in absolute terms (justice) because they are socialized to be nurturant, compassionate, and nonjudgmental (caring).

morality of care In Gilligan's view, the moral stance that nurturance and compassion are more important than absolute judgments of right and wrong.

morality of justice In Gilligan's view, the moral stance that judgments of absolute right and wrong are more important than nurturance and compassion.

As an example, Gilligan cited the responses of two bright 11-year-olds, Jake and Amy, to the Heinz story. Jake, who considered the dilemma "sort of like a math problem with humans" (Gilligan, 1982, p. 26), set up an equation that showed that life is more important than property. Amy, in contrast, seemed to sidestep the issue, arguing that Heinz "really shouldn't steal the drug—but his wife shouldn't die either." She tried to find an alternative solution (a bank loan, perhaps) and then explained that stealing wouldn't be right because Heinz "might have to go to jail, and then his wife might get sicker again, and he couldn't get more of the drug" (p. 28).

Amy's response may seem just as ethical as Jake's, but Kohlberg would score it lower. Gilligan argues that this is unfair, because what appears to be a moral weakness—the female hesitancy to take a definitive position based on abstract moral premises—is, in fact,

> inseparable from women's moral strength, an overriding concern with relationships and responsibilities. The reluctance to judge may itself be indicative of the care and concern that infuse the psychology of women's development.
>
> *[Gilligan, 1982, pp. 16–17].*

Many researchers have tested Gilligan's provocative theory by looking for a morality of care or a morality of justice. The evidence does not find a male–female divide in moral thought (Walker, 1988). Boys and girls, or men and women, seem to be more affected by cultural and educational differences than by biological ones when social issues are concerned, again just as Vygotsky would predict.

Response for Parents (from page 364): No. In fact, these are prime years for moral education. You might travel those 50 miles once or twice a week or recruit other parents to organize a local program. Whatever you do, don't skip moral instruction. Discuss and demonstrate your moral and religious values, and help your children meet other children who share those values.

An underlying criticism of Kohlberg is that his stages are too rational, too logical, and thus do not incorporate feelings and actions. Could a child answer Kohlberg's questions in a highly moral way, but still act selfishly? Many people believe that eliciting children's abstract reasoning about the justice of hypothetical situations is not the only, or necessarily the best, way to measure their moral judgment (Emler, 1998). Questions about practical issues, such as feeding the hungry or being kind to younger children, may provide a better test. This topic is discussed further in Chapter 13.

SUMMING UP

Piaget and Vygotsky both recognized that school-age children are avid learners who actively build on the knowledge that they already have. Piaget emphasized the child's own logical thinking, as the principles of classification, identity, reversibility, and reciprocity come to be understood during the stage he called concrete operational thought. Overall, Piaget constructed a valid sketch of cognitive development, but he underestimated the influence of context, culture, and particular instruction. Research inspired by Vygotsky and the sociocultural perspective fills in Piaget's outline with details of the actual learning situation. Cultural differences can be powerful; specific instruction and practical experience, apparent among Brazilian street children, make a difference.

The advancement of moral sensibility is an example of school-age cognition: Children are eager to develop moral values, either in stages (as Kohlberg, inspired by Piaget, described) or in response to cultural norms (as Vygotsky and Gilligan emphasize). Today's educators and psychologists regard both Piaget and Vygotsky as insightful theorists. Developmentalists' understanding of how children learn depends largely on "a framework that was laid down by Piaget and embellished by Vygotsky" (Howe, 1998, p. 207).

Information Processing

information-processing theory The idea that cognition is comparable to the processing of a computer and is best understood by analyzing each component, step by step.

An alternative approach to understanding cognition goes beyond Piaget's stages and Vygotsky's emphasis on culture. It arises from **information-processing theory**. This approach takes its name from a function of a machine, specifically the computer. Computers receive and store vast quantities of information (numbers, letters, pixels, or other coded symbols) and then use preset software programs to process that information.

People, too, take in large amounts of information. They use mental processes to perform three functions: to search for specific units of information when needed (as a search engine does), to analyze situations (as software programs do), and to express the analysis in a format that another person (or a networked computer) can interpret. By tracing the paths and links of each of these functions, scientists can better understand the mechanisms of learning. People "can learn anything, sense or nonsense" (Simon, 2001, p. 205); information-processing theory explains how they do it.

Learning is particularly rapid in childhood, even without the explicit adult instruction that characterizes formal education. Many 7- to 11-year-olds not only soak up knowledge in school but also outscore their elders in playing video games, memorize the lyrics of their favorite songs, and recognize out-of-towners by the clothes they wear. Some children, by age 11, beat their elders at chess, play a musical instrument so well that adults pay to hear them, or write poems that are published. Other children that age must live by their wits on the street or become soldiers in civil wars, learning lessons that no child should know (Grigorenko & O'Keefe, 2004).

This enormous and impressive range of knowledge occurs because older school-age children are very different learners from, say, 4- or 5-year-olds. Not only do they know more, they also use their minds much more effectively, and that means their information-processing abilities have advanced. As with a computer, greater efficiency means not simply having more information stored somewhere within the brain but also having better access strategies and quicker analysis. Efficiency makes 11-year-olds better thinkers than 7-year-olds. As with computers, memory is crucial to this efficiency.

Memory

Sensory memory (also called the *sensory register*) is the first component of the human information-processing system. It stores incoming stimuli for a split second after it is received, to allow it to be processed. To use terms first explained in Chapter 5, *sensations* are retained for a moment while the person selects some of them to become *perceptions*. This first step of sensory awareness is quite good in early childhood, improves slightly until about age 10, and remains adequate until middle or late adulthood. (For most people, hearing and vision decline at around age 60, reducing the sensory register.)

sensory memory The component of the information-processing system in which incoming stimulus information is stored for a split second to allow it to be processed. Sometimes called the *sensory register*.

Once sensations become perceptions, the brain selects certain meaningful perceptions to transfer to working memory for further analysis. It is in **working memory** (sometimes called *short-term memory*) that current, conscious mental activity occurs. Your working memory includes, at this moment, your understanding of this paragraph, any previous knowledge you recall that is related to it, and perhaps distracting thoughts about the weekend or the person sitting beside you. Working memory is constantly replenished with new information, so thoughts are not retained for very long.

working memory The component of the information-processing system in which current conscious mental activity occurs. Sometimes called *short-term memory*.

Working memory improves significantly every year from age 4 to age 15 (Gathercole et al., 2004). Not only do the various parts improve (e.g., capacity increases) but, more important, links are formed more quickly because of increased myelination and dendrite formation in the brain and because the prefrontal cortex sorts and codes material more effectively. This is the massive interconnection explained in Chapter 11 (Kagan & Herschkowitz, 2005).

Finally, some information is transferred to **long-term memory,** which stores information for minutes, hours, days, months, or years. The capacity of long-term memory—how much information can be crammed into one brain—is virtually limitless by the end of middle childhood. Together with sensory memory and working memory, long-term memory assists in organizing ideas and reactions.

long-term memory The component of the information-processing system in which virtually limitless amounts of information can be stored indefinitely.

Crucial here is not merely *storage* (how much material has been deposited in long-term memory) but also *retrieval* (how readily the material can be brought to the conscious mind to be used). Certain information is more readily retrievable (you remember your birth date more easily than your childhood phone number), but all the information in long-term memory is stored somehow, unless something, such as a stroke, destroys it.

Retrieval is easier for some memories—especially vivid, highly emotional experiences—than for others. *Source memory,* which is the ability to remember the origin (a person? an event?) of information, is particularly inadequate in middle childhood, partly because of the immaturity of the prefrontal cortex (Cycowicz et al., 2003). If you are tempted to accuse an 8-year-old of lying, pause to ask yourself if the apparent lie is about the source of information. If so, it may be normal forgetfulness with *confabulation,* which is a lifelong human tendency to imagine and believe things that never happened.

Especially for Teachers How might your understanding of memory help you teach a 2,000-word vocabulary list to a class of fourth-graders?

Speed of Processing

In the discussion of reaction time in Chapter 11, the primary examples were of motor skills, but myelination and brain connections also advance cognition. Speed directly increases mental capacity, because faster thinking allows more

KAZ MORI / THE IMAGE BANK

Eye on the Ball This boy's concentration while heading the ball and simultaneously preparing to fall is a sign that he has practiced this maneuver enough times that he can perform it automatically. Not having to think about what to do on the way down, he can think about what to do when he gets up, such as pursuing the ball or getting back to cover his position.

thoughts to be processed in the conscious mind (working memory) at once. A fifth-grader with a quick working memory can listen to the dinner-table conversation of her parents, respond to the interruptions of her siblings, think about phoning her best friend, and still remember to ask her parents for her allowance. In school, increased processing speed and capacity means that she can answer a teacher's question with several relevant ideas rather than just one and, at the same time, monitor her words for grammar and pronunciation while noting her classmates' reactions.

Speed of thinking continues to increase throughout the first two decades of life (Kail, 2000). Neurological maturation, especially ongoing myelination of neural axons, the sprouting of new dendrites, and the development of the prefrontal cortex, helps to account for these changes (Benes, 2001).

Repetition makes many neurons fire in a coordinated and seemingly instantaneous sequence (Merzenich, 2001). As children repeatedly use their intellectual skills, processes that at first required hard mental labor become automatic. Such *automatization,* as you saw in Chapter 11, increases processing speed, frees up capacity, allows more information to be remembered, and advances thinking in every way (Demetriou et al., 2002).

Consider learning to dance with a partner. Many young children love to move to music, but they follow their own lead and impulses. By school age, some children are taught social dances (from square dances to tango, depending on the culture). At first, novice dancers concentrate on each step, sometimes counting to themselves, bumping into other dancers, or stepping on their partner's foot. Only later, after much practice and automatization, can they attend to their partner, moving smoothly and creatively while conversing and thus advancing their linguistic skills and expanding their knowledge. Note that this automatization occurs in the brain, not the muscles: Some neurons fire more rapidly and automatically in sequence, allowing other neurons to activate.

Progress from initial effort to automatization often takes years, which is why repetition and practice are crucial. Many children lose cognitive skills over the summer because the lack of daily schooling for a few months erases earlier academic learning (Huttenlocher et al., 1998). Even adults who drop out of college for a decade or so feel "rusty" when they first return. Not until something is overlearned does it become automatic.

The Knowledge Base

knowledge base A body of knowledge in a particular area that makes it easier to master new learning.

In addition to improvements in working memory, years of experience and guidance mean that children absorb a great deal of knowledge before they reach the school years. The more they know, the more they can learn and remember. That is, having an extensive **knowledge base,** a broad body of knowledge in a particular subject area, makes it easier to master new information in that area.

The connections between isolated facts improve as the knowledge base expands because a more extensive collection of facts makes it easier to notice how the new knowledge relates to previous knowledge, strengthening memory of both. This explains why learning by rote is fragile, while learning by comprehension endures. Knowledge connections increase in middle childhood and beyond; the older a person is, the worse "sheer memory" (unprocessed and disconnected) becomes.

Knowledge depends not only on prior knowledge but also on opportunity and motivation. This has been illustrated by millions of school-age children whose knowledge base is far greater in some domains, and far smaller in others, than their parents or teachers would like. As an example, British schoolchildren were asked to identify 10 of a random sample of 100 Pokémon creatures and 10 of 100 types of wildlife common in the United Kingdom. As you can see in Figure 12.1, the 4- to 6-year-olds knew only about a third of the 20 items, but they could identify more living things than imaginary ones. From ages 8 to 11, however, knowledge of Pokémon far exceeded knowledge of living creatures. A peak occurred at age 8, not only with higher totals but with the ratio reversed, as boys remembered more Pokémon creatures than girls did (not shown). It is easy to understand why: Third-grade boys were often intensely engaged in collecting Pokémon cards (Balmford et al., 2002).

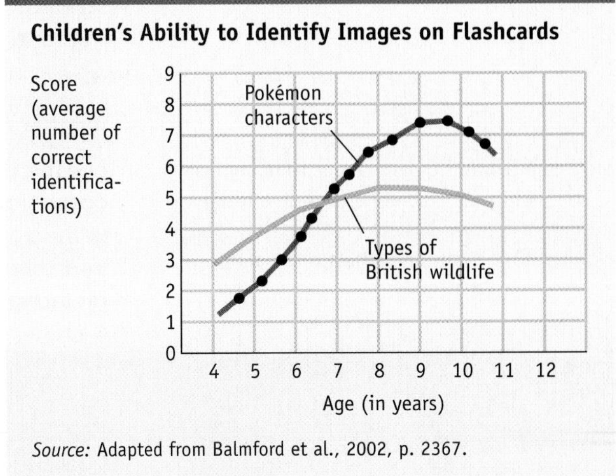

FIGURE 12.1 **Knowledge of the Real and the Imaginary** Every child's knowledge base expands with age, but the areas of special interest tend to shift as the child grows older. At about 8 years of age, British schoolchildren's ability to identify Pokémon characters on flashcards began to surpass their ability to identify real-life animals and plants.

? OBSERVATIONAL QUIZ (see answer, page 371): What does this graph suggest about the state of wildlife conservation in the United Kingdom in the year 2020?

Control Processes

The mechanisms that put memory, processing speed, and the knowledge base together are called the **control processes**; they regulate the analysis and flow of information within the system. Control processes include selective attention, metacognition, and emotional regulation. When someone wants to concentrate on only one part of all the material bombarding the sensory memory or wants to summon a rule of thumb from long-term memory to working memory, control processes assume an executive role in the information-processing system. That is, they organize, decide, and direct, as the chief executive officer of a large corporation is supposed to do.

control processes The mechanisms (selective attention, strategic retrieval, metacognition, and emotional regulation) that combine memory, processing speed, and knowledge to regulate the analysis and flow of information within the information-processing system.

If this sounds familiar, that's because you read in Chapters 8 and 11 about the maturation of the prefrontal cortex, where the brain regulates and coordinates emotions and thoughts. This part of the brain (actually several parts, including the medial prefrontal cortex, the orbital prefrontal cortex, and the anterior cingulate) is sometimes called the *executive function* precisely because it controls the other parts. As you saw in Chapter 11, attention-deficit disorders (ADD) are the result of an underdeveloped executive function (Silver & Hagin, 2002).

You also read in Chapter 11 about selective attention. Now consider what this means in the classroom. Compare children in kindergarten with those in fifth grade. Kindergartners are easily distracted, whether they are listening to a story or printing letters of the alphabet. While they are working, they chatter with each other, look around, fidget, call out to the teacher, and sometimes get up to visit friends or just wander around. Their curriculum includes frequent changes of activity, because the teachers know the nature of their 5-year-old charges.

By contrast, fifth-graders work independently at their own desks or in groups around a table. They read, write, discuss, and seek assistance without distracting, or being distracted by, other students. They can follow a demonstration at the chalkboard, raising their hands to be called on. Remember Billy, the boy with ADHD, from Chapter 11? As his experience demonstrates, toward the end of middle childhood, teachers expect students to persist in difficult academic challenges, waiting and thinking.

Control processes develop with age, but they are also taught by the culture. Sometimes this teaching is explicit, as certain memory processes are. For instance, spelling rules such as "*i* before *e* except after *c*" and sentences for remembering the order of the planets are often part of classroom instruction. Once children know these, they can use the same techniques to make up their own mnemonic devices (memory aids).

Cultures also teach children whether they should attend to one thing at a time, as most teachers expect, or should learn by observation while doing other things, as some cultures (especially in Latin America) encourage. This latter approach is not necessarily inefficient, because "simultaneous attention may be important when learning relies on observation of ongoing events" (Correa-Chavez et al., 2005, p. 665). As children develop whatever control processes they need, they can be more strategic and analytic as they learn. Storage and retrieval

RESPONSE FOR TEACHERS (from page 367): Children this age can be taught strategies for remembering by making links between working memory and long-term memory. You might break down the vocabulary list into word clusters, grouped according to root words, connections to the children's existing knowledge, applications, or (as a last resort) first letters or rhymes. Active, social learning is useful; perhaps in groups the students could write a story each day that incorporates 15 new words. Each group could read its story aloud to the class.

strategies improve when children figure out whether something is worth learning, and then know how to do it.

Metacognition

metacognition "Thinking about thinking," or the ability to evaluate a cognitive task to determine how best to accomplish it, and then to monitor and adjust one's performance on that task.

During the school years, children develop a higher form of thinking called **metacognition**, which is sometimes called "thinking about thinking." Metacognition is the ability to evaluate a cognitive task to determine how best to accomplish it, and then to monitor and adjust performance on that task. Marked advances in metacognition occur over the school years (Case, 1998; Ferrari & Sternberg, 1998). For example, preschool children find it difficult to judge whether a problem is easy or hard, or whether or not they remember a particular fact. As a consequence, when they study, they wastefully devote as much effort to the easy material as to the hard, as much to what they already know as to what they do not. They might remember something irrelevant (the color of the teacher's shirt, for instance) but forget the most important part of the lesson (that 2 + 2 = 4).

BACHMANN / PHOTO RESEARCHERS, INC.

They've Read the Book Acting in a play based on *The Lion, the Witch, and the Wardrobe* suggests that these children have metacognitive abilities beyond those of almost any preschooler. Indeed, the book itself requires a grasp of the boundary between reality (the wardrobe) and fantasy (the witch). "Thinking about thinking" is needed in order to appreciate the allegory.

? Observational Quiz (see answer, page 372): Beyond the book, what are three examples of metacognition implied here? Specifically, how does the ability to memorize lines, play a part, and focus on the play illustrate metacognition?

At the start of middle childhood some children still lack metacognition (Schneider, 1998). By age 8 or 9, however, metacognition is evident. Children become much more accurate about what they know and thus more efficient when they study. They evaluate their learning progress, judging whether they have learned the spelling or the science rules, rather than simply insisting (as many younger children do) that they know it all (Harter, 1999).

Metacognition is strikingly evident as memory improves, because children know how to store information so that retrieval is possible. For example, in one experiment, 7- and 9-year-olds memorized two lists of 10 items each (Howe, 2004). Some children had separate lists of toys and vehicles; others had two mixed lists, with toys and vehicles combined on both lists. A day later, they were asked to remember one of the two lists. Having had separate lists of toys and vehicles helped the 7-year-olds to some degree, but it was particularly beneficial for the older children, who remembered more items than did other 9-year-olds whose lists had mingled toys and vehicles. Some had been explicitly told about the categories and some had not. That did not make much difference, because children spontaneously "benefit from reorganizing material" (Howe, 2004, p. 138). In other words, the 9-year-olds used metacognitive skills without prompting.

An interesting application of metacognition occurs when children are asked to imagine what other people are thinking. As you remember from Chapter 9, the egocentricism of young children begins to soften at about age 4, when theory of mind begins. However, it is not until the school years that children understand that other people have various thoughts, different not only from the child's own thoughts but also from one another's (Flavell et al., 1995). For example, in one study children were shown a picture of Tom and Brian, both looking at a flat tire, and were asked whether or not the two boys were thinking the same thing. When 4-, 6-, and 8-year-olds were compared, the 8-year-olds were not only more likely to realize that Tom and Brian might think differently about the tire; they were also much more likely to provide valid explanations of why two people might have different thoughts (Eisbach, 2004). In other words, theory of mind, first described among 4-year-olds, continues to develop as children are able to think about the thinking of other people as well as about their own thoughts.

An understanding of the cognitive and linguistic processes of metacognition is one benefit of the information-processing approach. It enables adults to help children master the underlying strategies and skills of learning. As you know from your college work, metacognition improves study skills at every stage.

! Answer to Observational Quiz (from page 369): As the authors of this study observe, "People care about what they know." As their knowledge about their country's animal and plant life declines with age, these British children's concern for wildlife conservation is likely to decline, too.

The Pragmatics of Language

In addition to highlighting the various aspects of thinking, the information-processing perspective illuminates particular aspects of spoken language. The practical application of linguistic knowledge, called the *pragmatics* of language, advances noticeably in middle childhood, because new abilities of analysis and control allow children to separate input from output. Whereas younger children blurt out whatever they are thinking (e.g., asking a stranger, "Why are you so fat?"), this does not happen in middle childhood. Children learn to speak one way to strangers and another way to friends, and perhaps one way in the classroom and another at home.

New Vocabulary

The pragmatics of language includes vocabulary and grammar. Some school-age children learn as many as 20 new words a day and become skilled at applying grammar rules, definitions, and metaphors. However, these "new" words and applications are not like the language explosion of the play years. The cognitive skills just explained—logic, memory, speed, connection of one bit of knowledge with another—distinguish language learning as well (Kagan & Herschkowitz, 2005).

code-switching Changing from one manner of speaking to another, a change that usually involves tone, gestures, pronunciation, sentence length, vocabulary, and sometimes language itself.

For example, 2-year-olds know *egg,* but 10-year-olds know *egg salad, egg-drop soup, eggplant, egghead,* and even metaphors such as *walking on eggshells, egg on my face,* and *last one in is a rotten egg.* They understand that each of these expressions is logically connected to *egg* but also that each is distinct from the eggs in the refrigerator and that each is used in some contexts but not in others. They use these terms appropriately for their audience: 10-year-olds do not call their parents rotten eggs, even when the parents are the last to sit down for dinner. In this case, selective attention includes selective use of language, a very practical skill.

A related ability is called **code-switching,** which traditionally meant changing from one language to another in conversation but here means changing from proper speech to a colloquial form of the same language. School-age children typically use one manner of speaking, called the *formal code,* in the classroom and perhaps with all adults, and another type, called the *informal code,* on the street and with friends. The difference between these two codes includes almost every aspect of language—tone, pronunciation, gestures, sentence length, slang, vocabulary, and grammar.

During middle childhood, many children become adept at code-switching from formal to informal code as the context changes. This ability to change codes is a mark of linguistic sophistication because it signals a new sensitivity to one's audience. Adults (especially teachers) need to help children become fluent in the formal code; their peers will teach them the informal code.

Enabling school-age children to process and expand linguistic information is most effectively

Connections Basic vocabulary is learned by age 4 or so, but the school years are best for acquiring expanded, derivative, and specialized vocabulary, especially if the child is actively connecting one word with another. With his father's encouragement, this boy in San Jose, California, will remember *Jupiter, Mars,* and the names of the other planets and maybe even *orbit, light-years,* and *solar system.*

RACHEL EPSTEIN / THE IMAGE WORKS

Especially for Parents You've had an exhausting day but are setting out to buy groceries. Your 7-year-old son wants to go with you. Should you explain that you are so tired that you want to make a quick solo trip to the supermarket this time?

done by linking the new information (*egg-drop soup*) with the old (*egg, drop,* and *soup*) and alerting children to differences in the nuances and implications of various codes. This is beyond the usual information-processing capacity of the younger child but well understood and implemented in middle childhood. As described later in this chapter, the same code-switching skills allow children to learn a second language if their social context supports doing so.

The Socioeconomic Correlation

Decades of research throughout the world have found a powerful connection between language development and socioeconomic status (Plank & MacIver, 2003). Children from low-SES families tend to fall behind in talking, and then in reading and other subjects. By age 6, linguistic differences between low-SES and high-SES children are already vast. For example, some 6-year-olds know 5,000 words and others know 20,000 words, a 400 percent difference that usually reflects the educational attainment of the parents (Moats, 2001). Not only do children from low-income families have smaller vocabularies, but their grammar is simpler (fewer compound sentences, dependent clauses, and conditional verbs) and their sentences are shorter (Hart & Risley, 1995).

Remember that correlation is not causation. In fact, some children from impoverished backgrounds speak, read, and write well (MacWhinney & Bornstein, 2003). E. P. Jones grew up in a very poor family, headed by an illiterate single mother, yet he won the 2004 Pulitzer Prize for his novel *The Known World* (Jones, 2003).

There must be one, or several, specific aspects of child development for which low SES is a marker but not a cause. But what? Possibilities abound—lead in house paint, inadequate prenatal care, lack of a nourishing breakfast, overcrowded household, too few books at home, teenage parenthood, authoritarian child rearing . . . the list could go on and on. All of these may be factors, and all correlate with low SES, but none of these have a major proven effect on children's language abilities, especially on the informal code. For instance, when a mother's education and a child's health are held constant, teenage parenthood has very little negative impact on a child's language proficiency.

The information-processing perspective forces us to look at specifics of daily input that might affect the child's brain and thus the child's language. Two factors are crucial.

One is parental expectations. Some parents expect that their children will excel and others expect that their children will fail; the children live up (or down) to expectations. For Jones and many other low-income children, high parental standards are crucial. Jones writes of his first day going to school:

> For as many Sundays as I can remember, perhaps even Sundays when I was in the womb, my mother has pointed across "I" street to Seaton [school] as we come and go to Mt. Carmel [church]. "You gonna go there and learn about the whole world."
>
> *[Jones, 1992/2003, p. 29]*

The second crucial factor is exposure to language. Many low-income families do not use elaborate and extensive speech with their children for reasons that correlate with low income (financial stress, neighborhood noise) but are not directly caused by it. However, children from impoverished families learn well if they have extensive and direct opportunities to learn language in their homes, neighborhoods, and schools (Duncan & Brooks-Gunn, 1997; McLoyd, 1998; Yeung et al., 2002).

One team of researchers studied the conversations of 53 low-income mothers and their 5-year-olds during meals, play, and reading (Weizman & Snow, 2001). Analysis of more than 2,500 minutes of interaction revealed that some

! Answer to Observational Quiz (from page 370): (1) Memorizing extensive passages requires an understanding of advanced memory strategies that combine meaning with form. (2) Understanding how to play a part so that other actors and the audience respond well requires a sophisticated theory of mind. (3) Staying focused on the moment in the play despite distractions from the audience requires selective attention.

TABLE 12.2 **Variability in Maternal Talking During Mealtime Interactions**

	Average	Least	Most
Time spent by mother in interaction with child	20 minutes	1 minute	47 minutes
Number of different words used by mother	259 words	3 words	595 words
Percentage of words not in child's basic vocabulary	3.5%	None	More than 8%

Source: Weizman & Snow, 2001.

Talk to Me! In a detailed study of low-income mothers in the Boston area and their 5-year-old children, five interactions were recorded for each pair: two reading, two playing, and one mealtime. Despite their similar economic and geographic status, the mothers varied enormously in how much time they spent interacting with their child (by a factor of 3), how much they said (by a factor of 5), and, especially, how many words they used that were not part of a child's expected basic vocabulary (by a factor of 12). Note that the percentage of new words used by the mothers at mealtime—the only one of these five interactions that is always part of each child's day—was greater than the average (mean) percentage for all five interactions. By the time they reached second grade, the children who had heard the most varied maternal talk were ahead of their peers in vocabulary acquisition.

mothers provided much more linguistic encouragement and language exposure than others (see Table 12.2). For example, at mealtime, some mothers just said, "Eat," while others offered extensive, informal language instruction. Here is one dialogue:

Child: *(Makes gulping noise in throat)*
Mother: Please stop.
Child: Okay.
Mother: Were you planning to eat more?
Child: No.
Mother: We kinda wasted some of that first piece of chicken there. Don't you think?
Child: No. *(Makes noise again)*
Mother: Stop it now.
Child: Okay.
Mother: Now you're gonna have to roll up your sleeves and wash your hands and your face. Try not to get your pajama top wet. See how you do. You can wash your face with the face cloth.
Child: Okay.
Mother: Don't you make that gulping noise.
Child: *(Laughs for a while)*

[adapted from Weizman & Snow, 2001, p. 269]

This 5-year-old said only two words, "okay" and "no," but the mother employed a fairly extensive vocabulary, including *planning, wasted, gulping, roll up,* and *face cloth,* using each term in the immediate context so that it had concrete meaning for the child, who obviously enjoyed the interaction. Poverty put all the children in this study "at risk," but 5-year-olds with mothers like this one became schoolchildren with large vocabularies, as measured on standardized tests, and advanced reading skills.

As these authors summarize, there is a "powerful linkage" between adult linguistic input and later child output (Weizman & Snow, 2001, p. 276). Although awareness of letters and sounds at age 4 predicts reading at age 6, vocabulary size at any age is the best predictor of eventual achievement and intelligence. Given school-age children's logical minds and strategic use of their knowledge base, one goal of parents and teachers should be to ensure that every child has the scaffolding (both the vocabulary and the motivation in their zone of proximal development) that makes new learning possible.

Tone and Tricks

A schoolchild's more comprehensive understanding of language was illustrated by a study in which children heard someone saying 20 sentences in a tone that contradicted the content (Morton & Trehub, 2001). For example, a voice reported, sadly, "My mommy gave me a treat" or, joyfully, "I lost my sticker collection." The children were asked whether the speaker was actually happy or sad and whether there was anything silly or tricky in what they heard. None of the

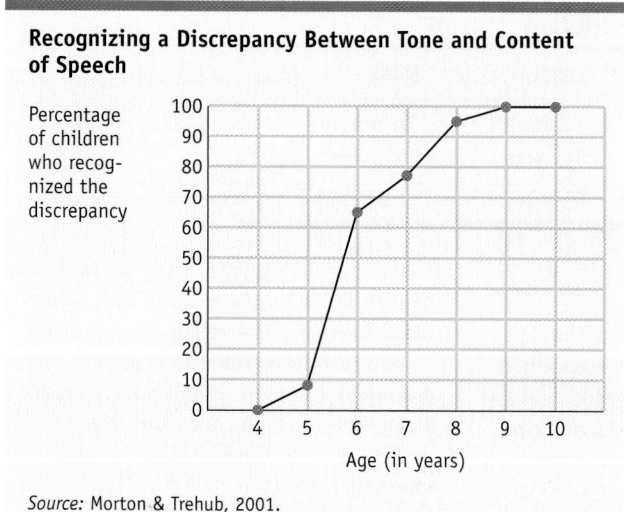

FIGURE 12.2 **Do You Mean What You Say?** A sudden leap of understanding occurs at the beginning of concrete operational thinking, when children can realize that a speaker is using a sad tone to describe a happy event, or vice versa. By age 9 or 10, all children are aware of this phenomenon.

4-year-olds correctly noted the discrepancy between tone and content, but all the older children did (see Figure 12.2).

Notice the sudden leap in recognition at the start of middle childhood: That is when most children realize that many elements, including tone of voice, word choice, and context, override the surface content of speech. Adults, by breaking down language learning into information-processing components, can help children effectively.

As a result of their new level of language skills, school-age children enjoy the sounds and the meanings of words. Consider the poems children write, the secret languages they develop, the slang they use, the puns they enjoy, and the jokes they tell. Joke-telling, for instance, requires intellectual flexibility and sophistication, including memory for sequence and punch lines. One classic school-age joke is, "What's black and white and red all over?" The answer, "A newspaper," is funny only when children are newly aware that *red* and *read* are homophones. Once children have memorized the *red/read* riddle (and told their parents, certain that the joke is new), they begin to enjoy the alternative answers (an embarrassed skunk, a sunburned zebra). Children find such jokes funny because the original answer is known and they delight in using their own new verbal abilities to trap the unsuspecting listener.

RESPONSE FOR PARENTS (from page 372): Your son would understand your explanation, but you should take him along if you can do so without losing patience with him. Any excursion can be a learning opportunity. You wouldn't ignore his need for food or medicine; don't ignore his need for learning. While shopping, you can teach vocabulary (does he know *pimientos, pepperoni, polenta*?), categories ("root vegetables," "freshwater fish"), and math (which size box of cereal is cheaper?). Explain in advance that you need him to help you find items and carry them, and that he can choose only one item that you wouldn't normally buy. Seven-year-olds can understand rules, and they enjoy being helpful.

SUMMING UP

An information-processing analysis highlights many components of thinking that advance during middle childhood. Memory has three basic phases: sensory memory, working memory, and long-term memory. Although sensory memory and long-term memory do not change much during these years, the speed and efficiency of working memory improve dramatically. Better working memory makes older children much better thinkers than they were at younger ages.

In addition, children become more selective and strategic, partly because their prefrontal cortex develops and partly because they are powerfully motivated. Control processes, such as selective attention and metacognition, enable children to direct their minds toward whatever they are motivated to learn and adults are motivated to teach. For all these reasons, language advances in ways distinct from the explosion of earlier years. As children connect words, metaphors, tone, and audience, they can switch codes as needed. Adults need to make sure that linguistic input—vocabulary, pronunciation, formal code, and so on—is extensive so that children will develop the language skills they need.

Teaching and Learning

As you have read, 7- to 11-year-olds are great learners. They develop strategies, accumulate knowledge, apply logic, and think quickly. All those skills make them more teachable with every passing year. They have left behind the magical and often egocentric thinking of younger children, and they are not yet suspicious and resistant to authority, as adolescents sometimes are.

Instruction during middle childhood is most effective if it is concrete and straightforward, neither abstract nor indirect (Simon, 2001). Children are willing to learn anything if it is presented properly, but they cannot learn everything at once. When new learning builds on an established knowledge base, connects to other material, and is taught deliberately and sequentially, then school-age children remember and master complex ideas quite well.

Around the World

Throughout history, children have been given new responsibility and instruction at about age 7, because that is when their brains are ready. Traditionally, this occurred at home or in the neighborhood, but now 95 percent of the world's children spend at least some time in school. What occurs there depends largely on where that school is. Communities and cultures choose what should be taught, for how many years, by whom and to whom, and with what type of funding.

Consider the differences in government spending per child. The amounts given in Figure 12.3 are national averages, which means that the cost of educating a particular child can vary a great deal *within* countries where education is funded locally or where some children (gifted, disabled, and so on) are more costly than others to educate. In the United States, for instance, yearly public spending per child ranges from about $3,000 to more than $15,000 from one town to the next.

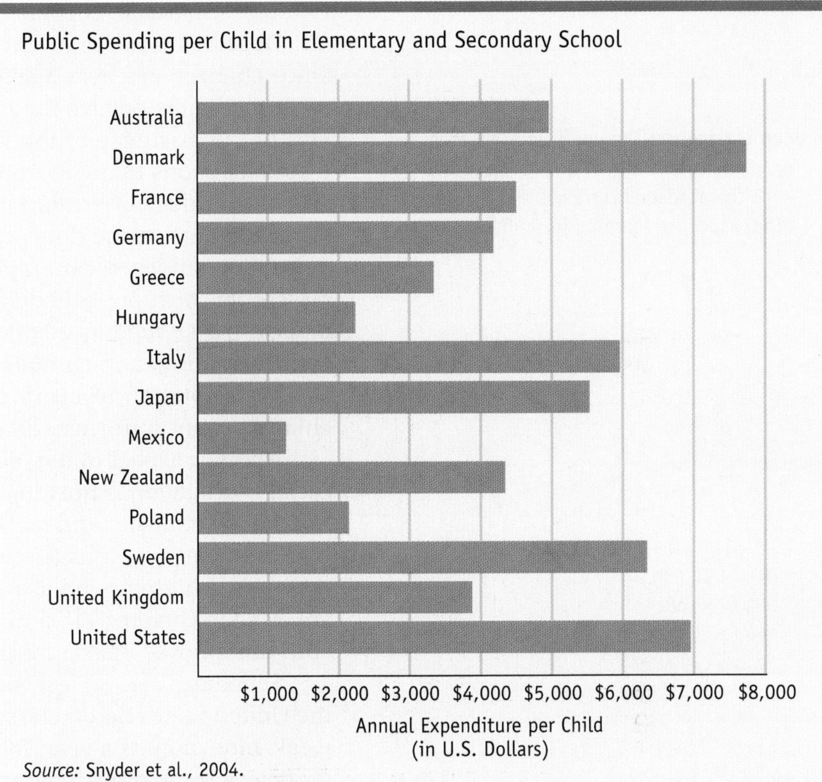

FIGURE 12.3 **If Only It Were That Simple** Spending per student is an imperfect guide to the quality of education, because nations lack a cost/benefit analysis to discover which measures result in more learning. For instance, in some nations, such as Hungary, teachers are relatively well paid compared with the average worker, even though their salaries are relatively low in international comparisons. Many capable Hungarians become teachers, which is one reason their students score well.

The Official Curriculum

Money spent is not necessarily an indication of what children learn. To discover this, we should examine curricula. Everywhere children are taught reading, writing, and simple math, but beyond that, nations vary. For example, oral expression and reasoned argument are routinely taught in Russia and France but not in India or the United States (Alexander, 2000). Memorization is important in India but is less so in England.

In some places the arts and physical education are not taught at all, and in other places they are considered essential. For instance, in France, 11 percent of class time (about three hours a week) is devoted to physical education and about 8 percent (more than two hours a week) to the arts (Marlow-Ferguson, 2002). Even nations that are geographically and culturally close to each other may differ. For example, every elementary school student in Australia spends at least two hours per week studying science, but this is true for only 23 percent in nearby New Zealand (Snyder et al., 2004).

Religious instruction is a major variable. In some nations, every child receives religious instruction. In Finland, parents must choose whether that religious instruction should be Lutheran, Christian Orthodox, or nonsectarian philosophy. No Finnish child can skip such instruction entirely (Marlow-Ferguson, 2002). In other nations, specific religious instruction is forbidden in public school.

This gives rise to a second major difference within nations. Some parents choose to educate their children in private and church-related schools, or at home, because they do not agree with what children are taught (or not taught) at school. The number of such children varies from nation to nation and, within the United States, from state to state. For example, 16 percent of the children in France are in church-related schools, but only 1 percent of the children in Japan are (Marlow-Ferguson, 2002).

In all these variations, those who advocate one "best" practice may be caught in a tangle of ideology, politics, and culture, disconnected from educational research (Rayner et al., 2001). Political and educational leaders often say one thing and do another, and children themselves do not necessarily learn what adults try to teach them; there is often a discrepancy between "expressed aim and observed reality" (Alexander, 2000, p. 176).

The Hidden Curriculum

Countries, states, local schools, and parents often compare curricula, as in the lists of courses that students must take to graduate or the published specifics that mandate, say, what fourth-graders learn in math. But one professor who became a school board member in his Vermont town concluded that publication of curricula "adds up to an elaborate professional camouflage of the fact that at no level—state, district, or school—is there a coherent, sequenced, and specific curriculum" (Shattuck, 2005, p. 30).

Does this mean that schoolchildren learn haphazardly, or not at all? Actually, since children are avid learners, they all learn a great deal, just not necessarily what the adults believe they are learning. To understand this, it is helpful to recognize the existence of the **hidden curriculum,** the unspoken and often unrecognized lessons that children learn in school (Holme, 2001).

hidden curriculum The unofficial, unstated, or implicit rules and priorities that influence the academic curriculum and every other aspect of learning in school.

The hidden curriculum is taught by the way schools are organized. Having a security guard at the door; classes interrupted by fire drills, trip permissions, or disruptive students; an emphasis on sports, drama, music, or art (apparent in classroom location, scheduling, attendance at special events); the composition and class assignments of students (through zoning, tracking, or busing); the education, training, and compassion of the teachers; the age, race, sex, and perhaps sexual orientation of every adult, from principal to janitor; whether or not the children wear uniforms—all these are part of the hidden curriculum.

Another aspect of the hidden curriculum is the segregation of schools. Overt racial segregation is now illegal in virtually every nation, but schools may be segregated by ethnicity and income as a result of housing patterns in their neighborhoods. In many nations some schools and classes are reserved for gifted children; others for children who are emotionally, physically, or educationally disabled (as you read in Chapter 11); and others exclusively for one sex. Does a boy learn best with other boys? Sex-segregated schools teach that the answer is yes.

Schedules also reflect the hidden curriculum. Consider this: Most schools in the United States begin classes at 8:00 A.M. and finish before 3:00 P.M., five days a week, nine months a year. In other nations, the school day ends in late afternoon, six days a week, eleven months a year. What is the message here?

Closely related is whether parents organize their lives so that their children get to school on time every day and have desks, books, and a quiet place and time to study. Educators worldwide believe that home, community, and cultural practices teach children at least as much as what they learn during school hours.

Probably the most obvious manifestation of the hidden curriculum, and of the value the community puts on education, is in the physical condition of the school. Some have spacious classrooms, wide halls, modern technology, and large, grassy playgrounds. Others have small, poorly equipped classrooms and cement yards or "play streets," closed to traffic for a few hours a day. In some countries, school is outside, and students sit on the ground. As a former New York State Commissioner of Education explained:

> If you ask the children to attend school in conditions where plaster is crumbling, the roof is leaking and classes are being held in unlikely places because of overcrowded conditions, that says something to the child about how you diminish the value of the activity and of the child's participation in it and perhaps of the child himself. If, on the other hand, you send a child to a school in well-appointed or [adequate facilities], that sends the opposite message. That says this counts. You count. Do well.
>
> *[Sobol, as quoted in Campaign for Fiscal Equity v. State of New York, 2001]*

Assessment

© THE NEW YORKER COLLECTION 1998 MIKE TWOHY FROM CARTOONBANK.COM. ALL RIGHTS RESERVED.

"Big deal, an A in math. That would be a D in any other country."

Most parents, teachers, and political leaders believe that children are learning what they need to know. Indeed, when U.S. adults are asked to rate public schools, they rate the schools in their town higher than the schools nationwide, and parents give higher ratings than nonparents do (Snyder et al., 2004). The harshest critics of local schools tend to be those who know the least about them.

This does not necessarily mean that parents are fooling themselves or that critics are wrong. Accountability is a goal almost everyone seeks, but people disagree as to what should be measured and how (Elmore et al., 2004; Johnson, 2002). Especially since schools vary so much in curricula and in every other way, many educators seek some objective way to assess whether children are learning.

International Tests

One approach to objective assessment is to compare children's learning on achievement tests given in various countries. Ideally, each nation tests a large representative sample of children, all about the same age with the same number of years of schooling, and all the questions are fair. In practice, absolute uniformity and objectivity are impossible. For example, children in Russia usually begin school at age 7 and in Scotland at age 4 (Mullis et al., 2004), so testing of 8-year-olds is inevitably uneven.

Further, developing nations usually do not participate in international testing, because it is too costly and because the test questions may not reflect their culture. Some advanced nations give tests in science and math but not in reading (e.g., Japan and South Korea); others, in reading but not in science and math (e.g., Iran and Greece).

TIMSS (Trends in Math and Science Study) An international assessment of math skills. Although TIMSS is very useful, scores are not always comparable, since sample selection, test administration, and content validity are hard to keep uniform.

Despite these problems, such tests may be the best tools we have. The results have fueled critics and supporters of various national practices. One assessment is called **TIMSS (Trends in Math and Science Study).** The 2003 TIMSS assessment of achievement in fourth-grade math, like the earlier studies in 1995, found that the average 10-year-old in Singapore was ahead of the top 5 percent of U.S. students. Fourth-graders in Hong Kong, Japan, and Chinese Taipei (Taiwan) also did better than their counterparts in Western nations. This trend continued through eighth grade (see Table 12.3). Canada, England, and the United States were ahead of the international average, but not by much. Australia and New Zealand were just at the average. The lowest-ranking nations—Tunisia, Morocco, and the Philippines (not shown)—do not have a long history of universal fourth-grade education.

Is TIMSS fair? Here is a sample math question for fourth-graders:

> Jasmine made a stack of cubes the same size. The stack had 5 layers, and each layer had 10 cubes. What is the volume of the stack?
> a. 10 cubes
> b. 15 cubes
> c. 30 cubes
> d. 50 cubes

You can judge for yourself whether such items would be equally fair to children in every nation and whether the high scores of East Asian children are valid or biased.

TABLE 12.3 **TIMSS Rankings of Average Math Achievement Scores of Eighth Graders, Selected Countries***

	Year		
Country	**2003**	**1999**	**1995**
Singapore	1	1	1
Korea	2	2	2
Hong Kong	3	3	4
Japan	4	4	3
Netherlands	5	6	6
Canada**	6	5	7
Hungary	7	8	8
Czech Republic	8	7	5
Russian Federation	9	9	9
Australia	10	10	10
United States	11	11	12
New Zealand	12	12	11
Cyprus	13	13	13
Iran	14	14	14

*Not all of the countries that participated in TIMSS (25 in 2003) are reported because most of them did not give this test in all three years. Eighth-grade rankings are given here; the fourth-grade rankings are similar, but less comparative data is available.

**Results for Canada are for the provinces of Ontario and Quebec only and thus are not strictly comparable with other countries' average scores.

Source: TIMSS Web site, http://timss.bc.edu, accessed August 3, 2005.

SHEHZAD NOORANI / PETER ARNOLD, INC.

Catching Up with the West These Iranian girls are acting out a poem that they have memorized from their third-grade textbook. They attend school in a UNICEF-supported Global Education pilot project. Their child-centered classes encourage maximum participation.

Another international assessment is called the Progress in International Reading Literacy Study (PIRLS). As with every other international comparison, there are many ways to read the PIRLS data. In 2001, only 3 of the 35 participating nations (Sweden, England, and Bulgaria) surpassed the United States in the percentage of fourth-graders who read in the top 10 percent.

Another way to read the data is to look at how broad a spread there is from top to bottom. A narrower spread indicates more equitable schooling. Ten nations had a narrower spread in reading than the United States, with fewer children in the bottom quartile (Sweden, England, Bulgaria, Canada, the Netherlands, Lithuania, Latvia, the Czech Republic, France, Hong Kong), and 24 nations fared worse (Mullis et al., 2003).

A third way is to look for improvement, not absolute scores. In reading, Islamic nations generally have scored near the bottom among participating nations, but over the past few decades their literacy has improved dramatically, especially among girls. In 1970, most Muslim women did not learn to read and write at all, and now girls are far ahead of boys in those nations that scored lowest on the PIRLS—outscoring boys by 7 percent in Iran, for example (Mullis et al., 2003).

This test could also be taken as a measure of gender equity. Girls read at a more advanced level than boys in every nation, by an average of 4 percent; Sweden has the lowest differential, at 1.4 percent. Gender differences are apparent in almost every assessment, with girls somewhat ahead in verbal skills and boys in advanced math, but variations from nation to nation make it difficult to decide how much (if any) of those differences are biological and how much originates in the hidden curriculum of school and society.

In short, the results of international testing are fascinating but not always easy to interpret. One use is to discover how much children actually know compared with their peers from other nations. Researchers distinguish *intended, implemented,* and *attained* curricula (Robitaille & Beaton, 2002). *Intended* curriculum refers to the content the educational leaders prescribe; *implemented* curriculum means what the teachers and school administrators offer; and *attained* curriculum refers to what the students learn. For example, many nations have added the concept of mathematical probability to their primary school curriculum (intended curriculum). The outcome has been low student understanding (attained curriculum), mainly because teacher training and student maturation make probability difficult to teach before middle school (implemented curriculum) (Howson, 2002).

Comparing the United States and Japan

Ever since Harold Stevenson first compared schoolchildren in North America and Japan, many people in the United States have envied Japanese education (Stevenson et al., 1990; Stevenson et al., 1993). The differences between the two educational systems are many. For one thing, all the children in Japan believe that effort is crucial, and they study more than U.S. children do. School in Japan is held until later in the day, on Saturday mornings, and for more months per year. Teachers are given more respect and are expected to learn from one another. To that end, time is built into the schedule for teachers to collaborate, plan, and visit one another's classes (Stigler & Hiebert, 1999).

RUSSELL D. CURTIS / PHOTO RESEARCHERS, INC.

Collaborative Learning Japanese children are learning mathematics in a more structured and socially interactive way than are their North American counterparts.

The Japanese educational system is regulated by nationwide policies and supported by nationwide taxes. As a result, some of the inequities that arise when each community must fund its own schools, as in the United States, are eliminated (Welner, 2001). Virtually all Japanese children attend public schools, and the curriculum is universal—a child could move from one city to another in mid-year and encounter no disruption in the sequence of study. Compared with the United States, absenteeism is low (fewer than one child in thirty misses more than a month of school per year), and almost no children (less than 2 percent) drop out of school before high school graduation.

Another set of educational institutions, called *juko*, are attended by three-fourths of Japanese children for at least a few years between grades 1 and 8. Juko are private schools (chosen and paid for by the parents) that emphasize some aspect of education, such as preparation for exams, learning to use the abacus, or doing sports.

All the obvious contrasts between the Japanese and U.S. systems of education are cited as reasons that Japanese children score far above their U.S. peers on virtually every test. These contrasts were offered in support of the No Child Left Behind Act, which signified a shift toward greater federal involvement in education. The law mandated that states set up a system of achievement tests that children would take every year beginning in the third grade. A certain level of achievement was required per school, not only overall but also for particular subgroups (e.g., English-language learners and African American students). If a school did not meet the standard for several years, parents could transfer their children to other schools, and the low-scoring school would not get federal funding. If problems persisted, the school would be closed.

This law was passed with great enthusiasm, but its practical applications have become controversial (Center on Education Policy, 2005; Resnick & Zurawsky, 2005). Some say that having statewide standards perpetuates inequality, since teachers are more qualified and funding is more generous in those schools where children score high (Tuerk, 2005). Many school districts are focusing on reading and math (which are tested) and reducing instruction in the arts and physical education (which are not tested). Often individual children's test scores are used for decisions regarding passing a grade or graduating from school. Low-scoring children are held back. This raises the average score in a particular grade but punishes low-scoring children, who must repeat another year and still may not learn what they should.

ESPECIALLY FOR TEACHERS You are teaching in a school that you find too lax or too strict, or with parents who are too demanding or uncaring. Should you look for a different line of work?

One state, Utah, has opted out of receiving funding under the law, partly because federal standards require practices that members of the state legislature believe are not in the best interests of Utah's children. Many teachers and parents think that changes need to be made, and revisions are underway.

Meanwhile, in Japan, the downside of the national educational system has begun to become apparent. An increasing number of Japanese children were becoming school-phobic (Hosaka, 2005). Some children sought help in developing metacognitive skills that they were not taught in school, partly because large class sizes and detailed curriculum requirements made individualized attention less common (Ichikawa, 2005). Creativity seemed squeezed out.

To reduce the stress, the Japanese government eased educational and testing requirements by instituting a policy called *yutori kyoiku,* which means "more relaxed education." The required content of the public school curriculum was reduced by 30 percent to allow more emphasis on the process of learning, rather than on the learning of facts as demonstrated by achievement test scores (Magura, 2005). This shift is also controversial, and the outcome remains to be seen.

What is apparent at this point is that the two nations have moved in opposite directions, and each has come closer to what the other had been. As this shift demonstrates, children's education is much more strongly influenced by their government's policies than by their developmental needs.

Response for Teachers (from page 379): Nobody works well in an institution they hate, but, before quitting the profession, remember that schools vary. There is probably another school nearby that is much more to your liking and that would welcome an experienced teacher. Before you make a move, however, assess the likelihood that you could adjust to your current position in ways that would make you happier. No school is perfect; nor is any teacher.

Curriculum Wars and Assumptions

As you can see from the international comparisons, adults differ in their beliefs about what children should learn—and how. Virtually every aspect of education is not merely debatable; it is the cause of bitter dispute at some place and time.

To illustrate, we now focus on four areas where research and ideology clash: reading, math, class size, and bilingual education. Entire books and professional articles, written persuasively from opposite perspectives, are devoted to each of these. The point here is not to provide the right answer but to show the need for further research and reflection.

The Reading Wars

Reading is a complex issue in education, partly because speedy, automatic comprehension is the result of many earlier steps—from looking closely at pictures to figuring out unknown technical words. To simplify, there are two distinct methods of teaching children to read: phonics and whole language (Rayner et al., 2001). (A third method, called "look–say," based on sight recognition of a whole word, has been discarded. It doesn't work even for Chinese children, who are used to looking at a whole word rather than individual letters [McBride-Chang & Treiman, 2003]).

NAM Y. HUH / AP PHOTO

TED S. WARREN / AP PHOTO

Reading with Comprehension *(Left)* Reading and math scores in third-grader Monica's Illinois elementary school showed improvement under the standards set by the No Child Left Behind Act. The principal noted a cost for this success in less time spent on social studies and other subjects. *(Right)* Some experts believe that children should have their own books and be able to read them wherever and however they want. This strategy seems to be working with Josue and Cristo, two 8-year-olds who were given books through their after-school program in Rochester, Washington.

Clashes over the two approaches have led to "serious, sometimes acrimonious debate, fueling the well-named 'reading wars'" (Keogh, 2004, p. 93). Battles have sometimes been fought without concern for scientific evidence, developmental changes, or children's needs (Adams et al., 1998).

Historically, the **phonics approach** (from the root word for "sound") meant requiring children to learn the sounds of each letter before they began to decipher simple words. In the first half of the twentieth century, schools in the United States were characterized by

> drill and more drill . . . instruction in letter–sound relationships and pronunciation rules. . . . Children had to learn so much abstract material by rote before doing any significant amount of reading.
>
> *[Diederich, 1973, p. 7].*

Some educators and children hated such drills. Piaget's theory—that children learn on their own as soon as their minds are ready—provided a rationale for another method, called the **whole-language approach.** For concrete operational thinkers, Piaget's followers explained, abstract, decontextualized memorization is difficult; no wonder traditional phonics did not always succeed. In whole-language theory, literacy is the outcome of an entire set of skills—talking and listening, reading and writing—all with the goal of communication, which even very young children do with words, pictures, and great enthusiasm.

When teachers instruct with whole language, young children are encouraged to draw, talk, and write, inventing spelling because many languages, including English, are too variable to be spelled phonetically. Examples abound: A 4-year-old boy tried to keep others out of his room with this sign on his door: GNYS AT WRK (Bissex, 1980); my 5-year-old daughter Elissa, who already knew that the sound of the letter *H* was unlike the name of the letter, wrote *HB* when she was asked to write how she was feeling; a schoolgirl named Karla penned a stern note to her mother (see Figure 12.4). These examples demonstrate that children want to express themselves long before they have mastered standard spelling.

However, unlike talking, which is experience-expectant, reading and writing are experience-dependent. Contrary to the presumption of this application of Piaget's theory, some children never figure out how to read and spell on their own. Beginning readers often need to be taught how to translate spoken words into printed ones, and vice versa. According to the phonics perspective, without explicit instruction and massive practice, automatization in reading will not occur, because brain patterns are established only through extensive repetition (Rayner et al., 2001; Stanovich, 2000).

Research arising from the information-processing perspective has noted the uniqueness of each child, including each aspect of language proficiency, of learning style, and of the rate of maturation, as well as the many distinct steps toward automatic reading with speed, accuracy, and comprehension. In practical terms, this means that phonics may be essential for children who are just beginning to read or who need help learning how to sound out new words. When children are not native speakers of the language or when they have weak listening and speaking skills, they need explicit vocabulary-building and pronunciation practice. Targeted instruction before age 7 in letter–sound combinations may be crucial for them (Torgesen, 2004).

Fortunately, the two sides in the reading wars have declared a truce. Most developmentalists and many reading specialists now believe that teachers should use a variety of methods and strategies, for there are "alternate pathways in learning to read" (Berninger et al., 2002, p. 295). Research leaves little doubt that

From karla to My mom
its No fare
that you mad
me Lat my Lade
bug Go Wat
if I Was your
mom and I mad
You tack your
Lade bug Iam
shr you wud
be sad like me
that lade bug
mat of ban a orfan
so You sod ov lat me
hav it ane wae

FIGURE 12.4 **"You Wud Be Sad Like Me"** Although Karla uses invented spelling, her arguments show that she is reasoning quite logically; her school-age mind is working quite well. (If you have trouble deciphering Karla's note, turn the book upside down for a translation.)

phonics approach Teaching reading by first teaching the sounds of each letter and of various letter combinations.

whole-language approach Teaching reading by early use of all language skills—talking and listening, reading and writing.

"From Karla to my mom. It's no fair that you made me let my lady bug go. What if I was your mom and I made you take your lady bug. I am sure you would be sad like me. That lady bug might have been an orphan. So you should have let me have it anyway."

systematic phonics instruction "is important" (Camilli et al., 2003, p. 34). Every child needs to know the sounds made by letters, singly or in combination, and how to decipher syllables, blends, prefixes, and suffixes. As you remember from the first section of this chapter, such rule-based learning is well suited to the concrete cognitive powers of school-age children.

Phonics need not undercut instruction that motivates children to read, write, and discuss with their classmates and their parents. For reading comprehension and fluency, phonemic awareness is a crucial beginning, but other aspects of literacy are important as well (Muter et al., 2004). As the editors of a leading publication for teachers explain:

> In any debate on reading instruction that counterposes a focus on skills with a focus on enjoyment—or that pits phonological skills against the knowledge necessary to comprehend grade-level material—there is only one good answer: Kids need both. Schools that drop history and science from their curriculum to "make room" for more reading instruction—or [that] fail to incorporate strong content in their core reading program—do so at the expense of their students' long-term reading comprehension. . . . We have the tools to teach reading right the first time, so let's do it.
>
> *[The Editors,* American Educator, *2004, p. 5]*

Researchers are not sure of "the best approaches and methods of reading and writing instruction for students older than age 9 and interventions for those who are struggling readers in grades 4–12" (McCardle & Chhabra, 2004, pp. 472–473). However, the first steps are known for children in the early grades. Phonics, yes, but not at the expense of joy. For older children, it is crucial that reading be connected to literature, history, science, and other areas of study. Reading must continue to develop to avoid a "fourth-grade slump," because children need "long-term reading comprehension." How this is done is illustrated in the following.

In Person

When Did You Learn *Tsunami*?

Before December 26, 2004, perhaps 1 percent of the world's population knew the word *tsunami*. I was one of the ignorant ones. I remember being with my nephew Bill after Christmas. He said we should pray for the victims of the tsunami, and I marveled that he knew how to pronounce a word that I had not known until I read that day's newspaper headlines.

Even those 1 percent usually did not know what the word really meant. A few English 10-year-olds were the exceptions, because in early December their teacher, Andrew Kearny, taught them. He showed a video clip of survivors of a tsunami that occurred in Hawaii in the 1950s and drew a diagram on the board that his students copied into their exercise books. A girl named Tilly Smith was in that class.

Two weeks later, Tilly was on Maikhao Beach in Phuket, Thailand, with her parents and her 7-year-old sister. Suddenly, the tide went out, leaving a wide stretch of sand where the ocean had been. Most tourists stood gawking at the disappearing ocean, but Tilly grabbed her mother's hand: "Mummy, we must get off the beach now. I think there's going to be a tsunami."

> Tilly's parents alerted other holiday makers nearby, then raced to tell their hotel staff in Phuket. The hotel swiftly evacuated Maikhao Beach, and minutes later a huge wave crashed onto the sand, sweeping all before it. Incredibly, the beach was one of the few in Phuket where no one was killed or seriously injured.
>
> *[Larcombe, 2005]*

Tilly and her family are alive today for many reasons: She remembered what she had learned; her parents listened to her; higher ground was nearby. But some of the credit goes to her teacher, who did not just list *tsunami* as a vocabulary word but taught it with examples and activities that gave it meaning. This is a story of a miracle, or at least of good fortune, and of the mind of a child. Tilly was ready to learn and remember, as are all 10-year-olds, as long as knowledge is concrete, with examples and active participation. Her teacher knew that. This is not just good fortune, but also good education.

The Math Wars

Education in mathematics is much more problematic than instruction in reading, for three reasons. First, a nation's economic development is closely connected to science and technology, and math is vital in both those fields. Second, although almost every child learns to read, many children come to hate math, even to the point of developing an irrational fear of the subject. A 2005 Google search found 9,250 Web sites for math phobia and just 67 for reading phobia, almost a 150-to-1 ratio.

Third, Western nations expect to be at the top of the educational competition, but they must cede that honor to East Asian nations, at least as measured by TIMSS and as confirmed by the National Assessment of Educational Progress (see Figure 12.5). That makes math education vulnerable to quick solutions suggested by angry adults—not the best way to decide pedagogy.

One reason the United States does not rank higher may be just that: The battle over how to teach math is not always to the benefit of children (Boaler, 2002). According to one report, "U.S. mathematics instruction has been scorched in the pedagogical blaze known as the 'math wars'—a divide between those who see a need for a greater emphasis on basic skills in math and others who say students lack a broader, conceptual understanding of the subject" (Cavenaugh, 2005, p. 1).

Historically, math was taught by rote; children memorized number facts, such as the multiplication tables, and filled page after page of workbooks. No wonder math phobia flourished. Many educators, inspired especially by Piaget and Vygotsky, sought to make math instruction more active and engaging (Ginsburg et al., 1998).

In the United States, the Research Advisory Committee of the National Council of Teachers of Mathematics (1989) developed a curriculum that emphasizes concepts, problem solving, estimating, and probability. Recommended techniques stress social interaction: "Students are obligated to explain and justify" their solutions, to make sense of answers given by others, to ask clarifying questions, to seek alternatives, and to challenge the teacher (Cobb, 2000, p. 324). The focus is on process, not product—that is, on learning how to think mathematically, not on getting the right answer.

For example, one teacher asked her class how many runners were in a race that had two teams of six runners each. The children had already worked in pairs to come up with the "answer solution."

Teacher: Jack, what answer solution did you come up with?
Jack: Fourteen.
Teacher: Fourteen. How did you get that answer?

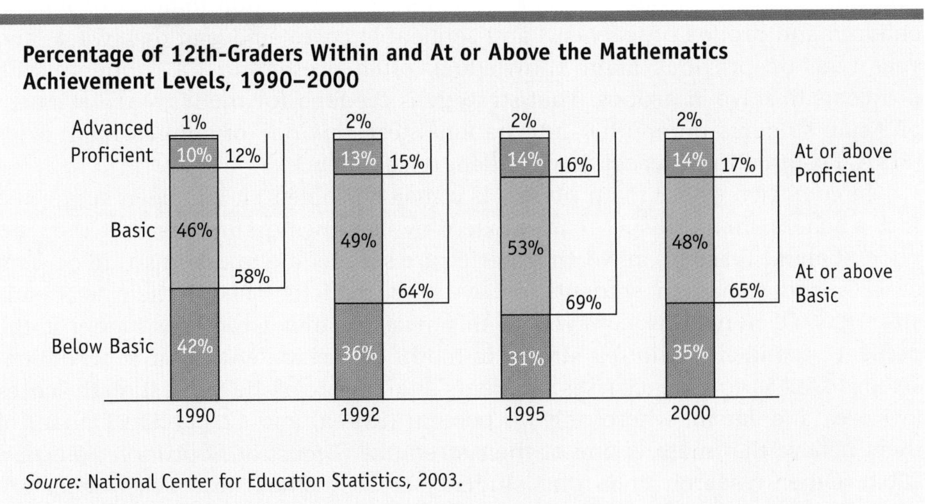

FIGURE 12.5 **Not Much Improvement** The scores of U.S. high school seniors on math achievement tests improved a bit from 1990 to 1992, perhaps because the nationwide math curriculum had been reformed in 1989. However, the results for 2000 show no improvement over those for 1992. This means that one-third of all twelfth-graders cannot do basic math, such as fractions and percentages.

Jack: Because 6 plus 6 is 12. Two runners on two teams . . .
(Jack stops talking, puts his hands to the side of his face and looks down at the floor. Then he looks at the teacher and at his partner, Ann. He turns and faces the front of the room with his back to the teacher and mumbles inaudibly.)

Teacher: Would you please say that again. I didn't quite get the whole thing. You had—say it again, please.

Jack: *(Softly, still facing the front of the room)* It's six runners on each team.

Teacher: Right.

Jack: *(Turns to look at the teacher)* I made a mistake. It's wrong. It should be twelve. *(He turns and faces the front of the room again.)*
(Jack's acute embarrassment . . . confounded the teacher's intention that the children should publicly express their thinking and, more generally, engage in mathematical practice characterized by conjecture, argument, and justification.)

Teacher: *(Softly)* Oh, okay. Is it okay to make a mistake?

Andrew: Yes.

Teacher: Is it okay to make a mistake, Jack?

Jack: Yeah.

Teacher: You bet it is. As long as you're in my class, it is okay to make a mistake. Because I make them all the time, and we learn from our mistakes—a lot. Jack already figured out, "Ooops, I didn't have the right answer the first time" *(Jack turns and looks at the teacher and smiles)*, but he kept working at it and he got it.

[Cobb et al., 1993]

This approach is controversial. Many parents and educators believe that children need to memorize number facts (such as the one needed in the example above, $2 \times 6 = 12$) before they can discuss alternatives. As with phonics, math involves a particular set of rules, symbols, and processes that must be taught, not discovered (Smith, 2002).

Again, as with reading, researchers have attempted to understand what teachers can do to help children learn, and enjoy, math. TIMSS experts videotaped 231 math classes in three nations—Japan, Germany, and the United States—to analyze national differences (Stigler & Hiebert, 1999). The U.S. teachers presented math at a lower level, with more definitions but less coherence and connection to what the students had learned in other math classes. The "teachers seem to believe that learning terms and practicing skills is not very exciting" (p. 89).

In contrast, the Japanese teachers were excited to work collaboratively, structuring lessons so that the children developed proofs and alternative solutions, alone and in groups. Teachers used social interaction (among groups of children and groups of teachers) and sequential curricula (each day, week, and year built on previous math knowledge), often presenting the students with problems to solve in groups. That strategy is credited for the high achievement of Asian students on another international test, this one of applied math skills (PISA, Program for International Student Assessment).

In countries where math phobia is a major problem, it has been suggested that teachers should dispel math anxiety by convincing students that they are good at math. Teachers in North America are succeeding in doing so: 26 percent of U.S. and Canadian students believe that math is one of their academic strengths. Of 38 nations surveyed on this measure, only Israel was higher in the percent of students who felt strong in math. Unfortunately, math achievement seems to fall as confidence rises. Students attain some of the highest math scores in Korea and Japan, where only 10 percent (Korea) and 12 percent (Japan) of them believe that math is one of their strengths (*Digest of Education Statistics*, 2003). Other research finds that student self-assessment and self-esteem are often poor indicators of effort and ability (Baumeister et al., 2003).

Unlike in reading, there is no truce yet in the math wars. No one doubts that math is essential for progress in science and technology, but people disagree about how best to achieve that.

Class Size

Most parents, teachers, and politicians assume that children learn best with fewer students in each classroom. Schools boast about their pupil/teacher ratio if it is low, and parents touring a school are quick to count the number of children in a class. Correlational data link two variables: higher school achievement with smaller classes (Smith & Glass, 1979).

Surprisingly, research support for this popular assumption is weak (Betts, 1995; Blatchford, 2003; Hanushek, 1999). Correlational data may be measuring a third variable. Children in smaller classes may have been ahead because of their family's high SES before they began school, and they may continue to benefit from home conditions that correlate with small classes but are not caused by them. Any correlation between class size and school achievement might be the result of many other variables, especially since schools that have large classes also tend to have fewer master teachers and more problems with crumbling plaster and leaky roofs (Books, 2004; Coles, 1997; Ehrenberg et al., 2001).

Some large-scale data don't show the expected correlations. For example, the pupil/teacher ratio in the United States dropped markedly between 1969 and 2003, from 25-to-1 to 16-to-1 (*Digest of Education Statistics,* 2003). (This statistic relates to all the teachers and students in a school, which means that having special teachers, such as for music or science, reduces the overall teacher/student ratio but not the class size.) No advance in student achievement has accompanied this reduction.

Internationally, the data again raise questions. The pupil/teacher ratio varies widely, from 10-to-1 in Denmark to 30-to-1 in Turkey, but these variations do not necessarily predict results on international assessments (Snyder et al., 2004). East Asian schools have large classes, and yet students in Japan, Singapore, and Hong Kong test higher than students elsewhere. The most surprising data come from South Korea: Students there score close to the top in every assessment of math, yet in 2000 the average eighth-grade math class had 41 students, more than in almost any other nation (*Digest of Education Statistics,* 2003).

Of course, dozens of factors affect children's learning. That U.S. student achievement did not rise between 1969 and 2003 might be attributed to more low-income, special-needs, and immigrant children; to fewer qualified teachers; to broader social factors, such as more media, more divorces, or more single parents; or to changing adult employment, such as more shift work or more maternal employment.

To show cause and effect, experimental evidence is needed. In one experiment, conducted in Tennessee, 12,000 kindergarten children and teachers were randomly assigned to one of three conditions:

1. The usual classroom configuration (one teacher with 22–26 children)
2. A classroom with a full-time helper for every teacher (two adults with 22–26 children)
3. A small class (one teacher with 13–17 children)

On average, the children (especially non-White children) in small classes learned more than their matched peers in larger classes. Small class size, not the pupil/adult ratio, was crucial, because those children who had a teacher and an aide did no better than children in the usual classes. Follow-up research showed that, years later, when all three groups of children were scattered, attending fourth- through sixth-grade classes, students who had earlier been in small classes still outperformed their peers (Finn et al., 2001).

The Tennessee results are controversial. The basic finding that small classes benefited Tennessee children is generally accepted, but researchers disagree as to how great an effect was found, for whom, and why (Rayner et al., 2001). Additional data come from California, where class size was reduced from about 30 to 20 children, albeit without enough qualified teachers or suitable classrooms. The California results were "disappointing"—statistically significant, but very small (Stecher & Bohrnstedt, 2000). Wisconsin also reduced class size for a group of low-income students. Their test scores improved, but not by much (Molnar et al., 1999). In California and Wisconsin, unlike Tennessee, teachers were not randomly assigned, and that may be one reason the effects were small.

Perhaps the most qualified California and Wisconsin teachers tended to have larger classes because parents, principals, or the teachers themselves chose them. This would confound the relationship between class size and learning. Obviously, if small class size signaled low-achieving students or a weak teacher, expected increases in average achievement would not occur. In all three state experiments, teachers, children, and parents knew that they were part of an experiment, and that awareness may have affected the results.

The NICHD Early Child Care Research Network's study (2004), first mentioned in Chapter 8, has collected data on more than 1,000 children. These children are now in 651 classrooms, ranging from 10 to 39 students per teacher, with an average class size of 21. Such longitudinal data, with no experimental manipulation of class size, might reveal important trends.

Unfortunately, the findings are "complex"; they "do not lend themselves to straightforward implications for policy" (NICHD Early Child Care Research Network, 2004, p. 66). No overall effects were found, but some specific differences emerged. First-graders in smaller classes developed some better prereading skills but also were more disruptive. Teachers with fewer students were *less* structured in their teaching and *less* interactive with each child but showed *more* warmth and support toward their students. Variations in student learning and emotional maturity occurred, but some specifics were better in larger classes, some in smaller, and the tipping points varied—some at 21 students, some at 17.

Moreover, "children of non-English-speaking mothers, children with disabilities, children living in dangerous areas, and children of mothers with health problems" were excluded, and few "ethnic minority children and children in poverty" were in the sample (NICHD Early Child Care Research Network, 2004, p. 663). Such children are the very ones most likely to benefit from reductions in class size. All this means that the NICHD study is less informative than it first appears.

Class size is of ongoing concern. Given what is known about individual differences, probably some children benefit more than others. Other reforms—raising teacher salaries; improving professional education; extending school hours; expanding the school year; including more sports, music, or reading—might be more effective. As one review concludes:

> . . . reductions in class size are but one of the policy options that can be pursued to improve student learning. Careful evaluations of the impacts of other options, preferably through the use of more true experiments, along with an analysis of the costs of each option, need to be undertaken. However, to date there are relatively few studies that even compute the true costs of large class-size reduction programs, let alone ask whether the benefits . . . merit incurring the costs.
>
> *[Ehrenberg et al., 2001]*

One conclusion that should *not* be drawn is that class size is meaningless. All the studies find that teachers and students are influenced by each other, especially in the beginning of elementary school and especially students who might fall behind. More research, and then other reforms, must be undertaken to determine how every child can learn as much, and as well, as possible.

Bilingual Education

Bilingual education is another area where assumptions are not aligned with developmental research and where adults have divergent, but deeply held, convictions. Almost every nation has a sizable minority population whose members speak their own language, but most of the estimated 6,000 languages of the world are never used in formal educational settings. Consequently, many of the world's children are educated in a language other than their mother tongue (Tucker, 1998). Obviously, they must understand that language to succeed in school. And almost all parents realize that their children would be better educated if they were fluent in more than one language. Thus, teaching a second language is an important educational goal.

In the United States, about 4 million students (10 percent of the school population) are **English-language learners (ELLs),** that is, children who speak a minority language and are learning to speak English. Although these children are concentrated in California, Texas, and Florida, many others are dispersed throughout the country. In fact, 43 percent of all public school teachers have at least one ELL student (Zehler et al., 2003).

English-language learner (ELL) A person who is learning English.

This may not handicap the child. Although early childhood is the best time to *learn* a second language by listening and talking, the best time to be *taught* a second language is during middle childhood. Children aged 7 to 11 are eager to communicate, are logical, and have an ear (and brain) for nuances of code and pronunciation, all of which makes them good learners of two or even three languages.

However, nations and states vary a great deal in how and when children learn a second language. And scholars vary in their attitudes on teaching a second language. Some advocate protecting "heritage languages" (e.g., Krashen et al., 1998); others are highly critical of "bilingual education" (e.g., Brisk, 1998). Historically, most children in the United States were taught exclusively in their native tongue, which included dozens of languages, notably German for millions of children in the Midwest. During World War I, anti-German sentiment halted German instruction in U.S. schools. Today, two-thirds of all new immigrant children in the United States are Spanish-speaking. For most of them, all their subjects were taught, initially, in Spanish until the mid-1990s, when laws and practices changed. Most are now taught in English.

Many educators fear that the emotional and educational needs of ELL children are short-changed by a rush to put them in English-only classes. One sign that this may be the case is that more than twice as many U.S.-born children as ELL children are designated as having special needs (Zehr, 2004). Perhaps teachers attribute learning difficulties (typically in reading or speech) to the language issue, forgetting that some children of any background may have a disability. Perhaps immigrant parents do not want their children to be seen as different, or perhaps school authorities are afraid of suggesting that an immigrant child has special needs. In any case, some ELL children may not get the extra attention they need.

No single approach to teaching a second language is best for all children in all contexts (Bialystok, 2001). Strategies range from **total immersion,** in which instruction in all school subjects occurs entirely in the second (majority) language, to the opposite, in which children are taught in their first language until the second language can be taught as a "foreign" language. Variations between these extremes include *bilingual education,* with instruction in both languages, and *heritage language classes,* which are usually held after school to allow chil-

total immersion A strategy for teaching a second language by having all instruction in that language.

TABLE 12.4 **Two Common U.S. Strategies for Teaching English**

English as a Second Language (ESL) Requires all non-English-speaking students to undergo an intensive instructional period together, with the goal of mastering the basics of English in six months or so. In classes using ESL, the teacher neither speaks in the child's native language nor allows the children to talk to each other in any language except English.
Bilingual Education Requires that the teacher instruct the children in school subjects using their native language as well as English. In the early years, children are greeted, instructed, and (when necessary) disciplined in the two languages, in the hope that they will progress in both. Informal talk between one child and another is almost always in the native language, as is much of the teacher's informal conversation.

ESL (English as a second language) An approach to teaching English that puts all children who do not speak English together, giving them an intensive course in basic English so that they can be educated in the same classroom as native English speakers.

dren to connect with their culture but learn academic subjects in the dominant tongue (see Table 12.4).

Another common strategy in North America, especially when children from many nations are in one school, is **ESL (English as a second language).** ESL children are taught intensively and exclusively in English for a few months to prepare them for regular classes. The ESL approach has been criticized for devaluing children's attempts to communicate with each other. The criticism is apparently valid in some classrooms: "Be quiet and learn English," one teacher said (Olivo, 2003).

Which is best? In Canada, immersion seems to have succeeded for almost a million English-speaking children who were placed in French-only classrooms. They did not lose the English skills they had learned at home, and their academic achievement did not suffer. Indeed, one study found that English-speaking Canadian children who were immersed in two other languages—French and Hebrew—from the first to the sixth grade did well on achievement tests in all three languages (Genesee, 1998). In Vancouver, to register their children in French-only public schools, some parents camp out all night, convinced that this approach will produce more learning.

Immersion that occurs after puberty, even if the children already have some knowledge of the second language, is not as successful at imparting the flawless accent and extensive vocabulary that many younger children learn (Marsh et al., 2000). In Latin American communities, many families speak various native languages (usually of indigenous origin). If the parents are illiterate but the children are in school, education in their native language succeeds, because respect for a community's culture leads to parental respect for school (King, 2004). In all cultural contexts, any method tends to fail if children are made to feel shy, stupid, or socially isolated because of their language difference (Midobuche, 2001).

Second-language learning remains controversial in the United States, even among immigrants, who want to protect their culture but also succeed in their new society. Cognitive research leaves no doubt that school-age children *can* learn a second language if it is taught logically, step by step. Whether or not such learning occurs depends on the larger society's attitudes and on adults' choices.

JOHN O'BRIAN / CANADA IN STOCK, INC.

Friendly Immersion The poster is in English, because this Toronto teacher is explaining a sign in the city, but all the instruction occurs in French, even though none of these children are native French speakers. Their parents chose this program not only because French immersion works successfully in Canada but also because such programs have a reputation for academic rigor, including high standards for conduct and achievement. Attitudes, not just instruction, facilitate learning a second language.

As explained in Chapter 9, if two languages are valued as well as used extensively, then *additive bilingualism* occurs, with fluency in the second language added to fluency in the first. Often, however, neither language is learned well, and a school-age child ends up semilingual, not even monolingual—literally possessing only part of one language (Swain & Johnson, 1997). An article about the need for well-trained language teachers explains:

> Whether policies are overtly articulated, covertly implied, or invisible . . . , the central concern in multilingual education appears to be how much status and recognition within the educational system should be given to the languages of the minority group.
>
> *[Nunan & Lam, 1998]*

The fear for children whose families do not speak the dominant language is that, if the minority language is given too much recognition, children will not learn the majority language, but if it is given too little, children will forget more than they learn.

Culture and Education

As you can see, many controversies in education are political more than developmental—a matter of the hidden curriculum, not the intended one; a matter of social values, not of cognitive and neurological maturation. Piaget, Vygotsky, information-processing theory, and, in earlier decades, progressive education and behavior modification have all been used to support particular methods of education. Opinions vary widely about how valid the connection is between those theories and actual practice. To conclude this chapter, we highlight again the role of culture in education.

Here are excerpts from three letters to the editor of a local newspaper in British Columbia, Canada (quoted in Mitchell, 2001, pp. 64–65). One mother wrote in favor of a traditional school:

> Our children's performances are much lower both in academic and moral areas. I noticed the children have learned very little academically. They learned to have self-confidence instead of being self-disciplined; learned to speak up instead of being humbled; learned to be creative instead of self-motivated; and learned to simplify things instead of organizing. All of these characteristics were not balanced, and will be the source of disadvantage and difficulties in children in this competitive society.

Two other parents responded:

> These characteristics she disapproves of are the very characteristics I encourage in my children, as do their teachers and the public schools. Self-confidence, creativity, and individuality are wonderful qualities, which in no way detract from a child being respectful and pleasant, and achieving academic success.
>
> She wants her children to be self-disciplined, humble, self-motivated and organized, instead of being self-confident, assertive, creative and analytic. . . . These repressive, authoritarian, "traditional" parents who hanker for the days of yore, when fresh-faced school kids arrived all neatly decked out in drab-grey uniforms and shiny lace-up leather shoes, are a menace to society.

In this school district a sizable number of the families were immigrants from Asia (including the writer of the first letter), yet almost all the school administrators and teachers were from families that had been Canadian for generations. The cultural clash spilled over into the curriculum dispute, as it often does.

BOB DAEMMRICH / THE IMAGE WORKS

Maintaining Tradition Some would say that these Vietnamese children in Texas are fortunate. They are instructed in two languages by a teacher who knows their culture, including the use of red pens for self-correction as well as teacher correction. Others would say that these children would be better off in an English-only classroom.

Similar conflicts appear in almost every community that includes diverse groups of families or a disparity in the backgrounds of the teachers and the children.

Recognizing the problem is a beginning, although such awareness does not come easily. For example, in another Canadian community, Inuit children are taught by native speakers for their first two years of school and are then taught in French or English. The Inuit teachers tried to prepare the children by teaching the dominant language (as a second language) and encouraging the children to learn it. The French or English teachers in this school worked to increase the children's language proficiency, hoping they would succeed in Canadian society.

Both groups of teachers failed: Relatively few children became fluent in a second language, and most dropped out before high school graduation. Other research finds that a disproportionate number of aboriginal youth (as members of Canada's First Nations are called) become alienated from their native culture and then become depressed or even suicidal as adolescents (Chandler et al., 2003). Although at first the problem seems to be a failure of bilingual education—perhaps immersion coming too soon or too late—the problem actually is more cultural than linguistic.

A scientist using naturalistic observation in that school found much more than a language shift between grades 2 and 3 (Eriks-Brophy & Crago, 2003). The Inuit teachers encouraged group learning and cooperation, almost never explicitly judging an individual student's response. The non-Inuit teachers often criticized the behaviors that the earlier teachers encouraged, such as group cooperation (which could be called "talking out of turn"), helping each other ("cheating"), and attempts to answer ("stupid mistakes").

A specific example shows the contrast. A common routine in many North American schools is called initiation/response/evaluation: The teacher asks a question, a child responds, and the teacher states whether the response is correct or not. Teachers are rarely aware of this pattern, but most native English- or French-speaking teachers use it often. An analysis of many hours of instruction by 14 different teachers in this Inuit school found that the initiation/response/evaluation routine dominated the instruction of the non-Inuit teachers (60 percent) but not the Inuit teaching (18 percent) (Eriks-Brophy & Crago, 2003).

For example, an Inuit teacher showed a picture and asked:

Teacher: This one. What is it?
Student: Tutuva (*an insect*).
Teacher: What is it?
Student: Tutuva.
Teacher: All of us, look carefully.
Student: Kituquianluti (*another insect, this time correct. The teacher nodded and breathed in.*)

In contrast, a non-Inuit third-grade teacher asked:

Teacher: Richard, what is this?
Richard: It is an ear.
Teacher: Good.
Teacher: Rhoda, what is this?
Rhoda: Hair.

Teacher: No. What is this?
Rhoda: Face.
Teacher: It is a face.
Rhoda: It is a face.
Teacher: Very good, Rhoda.

[quoted in Eriks-Brophy & Crago, 2003]

Note that the first teacher never verbally evaluated the child (nodding and breathing was enough to signal correctness), but the second teacher did so three times ("good," "no," "very good") or perhaps four times if "It is a face" is considered evaluative. No wonder the children were confused and discouraged by their schooling. They had to switch values of the hidden curriculum as well as languages.

Such problems can emerge in any classroom. Teaching methods are the outcome of cultural beliefs, a "social system that evolves over time" (Eriks-Brophy & Crago, 2003, p. 397), often in ways hidden to the teachers themselves. Parents seize on apparent problems, such as morality, phonics, class size, or math scores, but the underlying disputes concern culture and values.

Every child wants to learn, every teacher wants to teach, and every family wants the best for its children. This makes cultural differences in schooling much harder to reconcile than more obvious cultural manifestations. No one cares if a particular child eats goat, chitlings, or whale for dinner, but everyone cares about what its own—and its neighbor's—children learn.

SUMMING UP

Societies throughout the world recognize that school-age children are avid learners and that educated citizens are essential to economic development. However, schools differ in what and how children are taught. The nature and content of education raise ideological and political concerns. Examples are found in the reading wars, the math wars, class size, and bilingual education. Research finds that direct instruction (in phonics; in mathematical symbols and procedures; in the vocabulary, grammar, and syntax of second languages) is useful, even essential, if children are to master all the skills that adults want them to learn. Also crucial are motivation, pride, and social interaction. School-age children are great learners, but they cannot learn everything. Adults decide the specifics, and cultural values are apparent in every classroom.

■ SUMMARY

Building on Piaget and Vygotsky

1. According to Piaget, children begin concrete operational thought at about age 6 or 7. Egocentrism diminishes and logic begins. School-age children can understand the concrete operations of classification, conservation, identity, reversibility, and reciprocity.

2. Vygotsky stressed the social context of learning, including the specific lessons of school and the overall influence of culture. International research finds that maturation is one factor in the cognitive development of school-age children (as Piaget predicted) and that cultural and economic forces are also influential (as Vygotsky predicted).

3. School-age children are passionately concerned about moral questions. Kohlberg described three levels of moral reasoning, from preconventional (self-concerned) to conventional (community-centered) to postconventional (overarching principles).

4. A major criticism of Kohlberg is that his higher stages are influenced by Western intellectual ideas. As a result, community cooperation and family harmony are discounted. Another criticism is that his stages value the masculine search for justice more than the female preference for cooperation and caring, but males and females have not been shown to have innate differences in moral thought.

Information Processing

5. An information-processing approach examines each step of the thinking process, from input to output, using the computer as a model. Humans are more creative than computers, but this approach is useful for understanding memory, perception, and expression.

6. Memory begins with sensory memory, which briefly stores information that reaches the brain from the sense organs. Then information proceeds to working memory, where perceptions are processed for a short time in active consciousness. Finally, long-term memory stores some images and ideas indefinitely.

7. Working memory improves during middle childhood, aided by selective attention, a broader knowledge base, and logical strategies for retrieval. In addition, faster processing advances every aspect of cognition, including working memory. Repeated practice makes thought patterns and skill sets almost automatic, requiring little time or conscious effort.

8. Children become better at controlling and directing their thinking as the prefrontal cortex matures. Consequently, metacognition advances.

9. Language learning improves in many practical ways, including expanded vocabulary, as words are logically linked together, and code-switching, as children vary their speech to communicate with others. Children of low SES are usually lower in linguistic skills but not directly because of their family income. Parental expectations and language use are influential.

Teaching and Learning

10. Nations and experts agree that education is critical during middle childhood, and 95 percent of the world's children now attend primary school, at least for a few years. However, schools differ in what and how they teach, especially in the hidden curriculum.

11. International assessments are useful as comparisons, partly because few objective measures of learning are available. However, such assessments are open to criticism, and the United States and Japan have reacted in opposite ways to the data.

12. The "reading wars" pit advocates of phonics against advocates of the whole-language approach. These wars have quieted somewhat, as research finds that phonological understanding is essential for every child who is just learning to read but that motivation and vocabulary are important as well.

13. The "math wars" contrast math learned by rote with math learned via social interaction. Math and science achievement are higher in East Asian nations than elsewhere, perhaps because in those countries math lessons are sequential, challenging, and interactive.

14. Most people believe that children learn more when class size is smaller. However, data regarding this assumption are equivocal.

15. During the school years, children are particularly open to learning a second language. The specifics of second-language instruction remain controversial, with marked variations from nation to nation. Cultural attitudes affect second-language learning more than the cognitive potential of children does.

16. The differences in how and what children learn are apparent in every school. However, many people are not aware of this, and practice does not necessarily conform to what is known about children's development.

■ KEY TERMS

No Child Left Behind Act (p. 357)
concrete operational thought (p. 357)
classification (p. 358)
identity (p. 359)
reversibility (p. 359)
reciprocity (p. 359)
preconventional moral reasoning (p. 363)
conventional moral reasoning (p. 363)
postconventional moral reasoning (p. 364)
morality of care (p. 365)
morality of justice (p. 365)
information-processing theory (p. 366)
sensory memory (p. 367)
working memory (p. 367)
long-term memory (p. 367)
knowledge base (p. 368)
control processes (p. 369)
metacognition (p. 370)
code-switching (p. 371)
hidden curriculum (p. 376)
TIMSS (Trends in Math and Science Study) (p. 377)
phonics approach (p. 381)
whole-language approach (p. 381)
English-language learner (ELL) (p. 387)
total immersion (p. 387)
ESL (English as a second language) (p. 388)

■ KEY QUESTIONS

1. How do logical ideas help children understand conservation?

2. According to Vygotsky, if children never went to school, how would cognitive development occur?

3. What is the difference between the moral thinking of the typical 3-year-old and the typical 8-year-old?

4. To teach 8-year-olds a particular moral value, how would Kohlberg's hierarchy be useful?

5. What are differences between the three kinds of memory in middle childhood?

6. Why is faster thinking considered better thinking?

7. What are the differences between language learning in early and middle childhood?

8. How does metacognition affect the ability to learn something new?

9. What are some of the differences in education in various parts of the world?

10. How might a hidden curriculum reflect Piaget's theories?

11. How might a hidden curriculum reflect Vygotsky's theories?

12. What are the advantages and disadvantages in teaching children who do not speak English, in English-only classes?

13. Why are disagreements about curriculum and method sometimes called "wars," not merely differences of opinion?

■ APPLICATIONS

1. Visit a local elementary school and look for the hidden curriculum. For example, do the children line up? Why or why not, when and how? Does gender, age, ability, or talent affect the grouping of children or the selection of staff? What is on the walls? Are there nonteaching staff (nurse, cook, janitor)? Are parents involved? If so, how? For everything you observe, speculate about the underlying assumptions.

2. Interview a 7- to 11-year-old child to find out what he or she knows *and understands* about mathematics. Relate both correct and incorrect responses to the logic of concrete operational thought.

3. What do you remember about how you learned to read? Compare your memories with those of two other people, one at least 10 years older and the other at least five years younger than you. Can you draw any conclusions about effective reading instruction? If so, what are they? If not, why not?

4. The text notes socioeconomic disparities in education. How much do various schools in your state spend per student? Compare the funding of the richest and the poorest schools. (Break down all the costs, including real estate, maintenance, transportation, special education, and so on.) You may be able to find data for public schools but not private ones, although tuition fees, real-estate estimates, and financial reports for the latter may be available.

Chapter Thirteen

The School Years: Psychosocial Development

In middle childhood, children break free from the closely supervised and limited arena they lived in when they were younger. Usually with their parents' blessing (but sometimes not), school-age children explore their neighborhood, community, and school. They experience new vulnerability, increasing competence, ongoing friendships, troubling rivalries, and deeper social understanding.

Such children are avid fans of J. K. Rowling's *Harry Potter* books, with 250 million copies sold, in 55 languages, a popularity that caught many adults by surprise. The reason, as a 12-year-old (whose Muggle name is Ann but who said that in the "wizarding world my name is Arabella") explained: "The thing I like most about Harry Potter is that he's not perfect, and that he relies on friends for a lot. Friendship is a heavily stressed value in the books, and I love how it makes me feel when I think about what he has to face, and then I think about who he has to face it with" (quoted in Adler, 2001, p. 2). As an adult developmentalist explained, Harry Potter "has friends, good friends, and that might make all the difference" (Bukowski, 2001, p. 102).

In many favorite children's books, comic strips, and movies, the extraordinary—either magical or coincidental—is merely the scaffold for deeper themes: friendship, mistrust of adults (some teachers are bad, most parents are naive), the importance of sharp wits and sound education, and the perpetual battle between good and evil. These themes are standard in the stories children love, from Robin Hood to Batman, Snow White, Tom Sawyer, and Peter Pan.

This chapter examines the interplay between expanding freedom and guiding forces. During these years, children wish to be independent from adults, but they still depend on them. Children value their peers and need their parents, which are themes of their lives as well as of their literature. Here we look first at peers and families, then at the children themselves, and, finally, at the coping strategies and inner strengths that enable children to move forward, ready for further development.

The Peer Group

Getting along with peers is especially crucial during middle childhood, "central to living a full life and feeling good" (Borland, 1998, p. 28). Peers can cause serious problems (Rubin et al., 1998, p. 674), yet being well liked is protective, even for children from stressful, conflicted, or punitive homes (Criss et al., 2002).

There is an important developmental progression in peer relationships. Younger children have friends and learn from them, but their egocentrism makes them less affected by another's acceptance or rejection. However, school-age children are aware of their classmates' opinions, judgments, and accomplishments. They need each other for self-validation, advice, and companionship.

IVO VON RENNER / STONE / GETTY IMAGES

Push and Pull During middle childhood, children become aware of their unique traits—for example, whether they are bold or cautious—by comparing themselves with others.

? OBSERVATIONAL QUIZ (see answer, page 398): What do you see that suggests that these children are friends?

social comparison The tendency to assess one's abilities, achievements, social status, and other attributes by measuring them against those of other people, especially one's peers.

culture of children The particular habits, styles, and values that reflect the set of rules and rituals that characterize children as distinct from adult society.

The developmental difference here is in **social comparison,** which is the inclination to compare oneself with other people, even when no one else explicitly makes the comparison. School-age children become much more socially aware, which means that social comparison is particularly strong during these years. Ideally, this comparison leads children to value those abilities they really have and to abandon the imaginary, rosy self-evaluation of preschoolers (Grolnick et al., 1997; Jacobs et al., 2002).

The Culture of Children

Peer relationships, unlike adult–child relationships, involve partners who must learn to negotiate, compromise, share, and defend themselves as equals (Berndt, 1999; Hartup, 1996). Children learn lessons from peers that adults cannot teach, not only because adults are from a different generation but also because adults are not their equals.

The **culture of children** includes the particular set of rules and rituals that children develop and understand and that are passed down from older to younger children (e.g., from 10-year-olds to 6-year-olds), without the approval or even the awareness of adults. Children who are rarely allowed to play with others are at a disadvantage, because they do not know the culture and thus do not fit in with the peer group. For the same reason, children who are rejected by others are at a double disadvantage, in that they have no opportunity to learn the social skills that they lack.

Apart from Adults

Throughout the world, the culture of children encourages independence from adults. Some peer groups go further, demanding distance from adult society. By age 10, if not before, peers pity children (especially boys) whose parents kiss them in public ("momma's boy"), tease children who please the teachers ("teacher's pet," "suckup"), and despise those who betray other children to adults ("tattletale," "grasser," "snitch," "rat"). In fact, fooling adults, or disobeying them without getting caught, is a favored activity of some peer groups and an important part of the culture of children.

Clothes often become a marker of independence: Many a 9-year-old refuses to wear what a parent selects because the clothes are too loose, too tight, too long, too short, or wrong in color, style, brand, or just wrong. Language also reflects the culture of children, as in the informal code (described in Chapter 12), which includes words whose meanings adults do not understand and grammar that adults have repeatedly told them is wrong ("like, me and my friend, you know . . ."). If adults talk with children using the informal code they learned years ago, the children usually recognize the words as old-fashioned, because the culture of children changes with each generation.

KOJI SASAHARA / AP PHOTO

Industry on Display One characteristic of school-age children is their obsession with collecting, whether their interest is stamps or insects, Harry Potter paraphernalia, or, as shown here, Yu-Gi-Oh cards, which are a hot collecting fad in Japan. Children are much more industrious than adult collectors, busily counting, organizing, and trading their treasures.

LINDSAY HEBBERD / WOODFIN CAMP & ASSOCIATES

Celebrating Spring No matter where they live, 7- to 11-year-olds seek to understand and develop whatever skills are valued by their culture. They do so in active, industrious ways, as described in behaviorism as well as cognitive, sociocultural, psychoanalytic, and epigenetic theories. This universal truth is illustrated here, as four friends in Assam, northeastern India, usher in spring with a Bihu celebration. Soon they will be given sweets and tea, which is the sociocultural validation of their energy, independence, and skill.

Adults do not always approve of peer influence (Hartup & Stevens, 1999). Since children take on the characteristics and values of their group, parents encourage their children to associate only with peers who meet their approval (Dishion & Bullock, 2002). Children, however, choose peers who are compatible. For some, this means children who talk "dirty" or criticize adults or enjoy breaking the rules—all traits apparent among first-graders but increasingly valued with age. The culture of children can include "deviancy training," as children validate one another's urge to be free of adult influence (Snyder et al., 2005).

The culture of children does not necessarily mirror the values of adults. One example comes from Northern Ireland, where children follow a rigid divide between girls and boys, with each gender having its own rituals, jokes, and customs. However, children in Northern Ireland often ignore the divide between Protestants and Catholics, which is a source of hate and violence among many adults (Lanclos, 2003). Overall, gender prejudice is apparent in the culture of children, as are standards of proper behavior as children define them, but racial and ethnic exclusion is not (Nesdale, 2004). Social comparison is one of the characteristics of middle childhood that enable children to recognize prejudice and discrimination, first when it is directed at someone else and later when it is directed at themselves (Brown & Bigler, 2005).

The culture of children has both advantages and disadvantages. For example, peers teach language, essential if a child is to learn a second language but problematic when children learn curses that their parents forbid or an accent that their parents denigrate. Peers encourage children—sometimes in constructive ways, sometimes not. By age 9, Paul (from Chapter 11) believed that "I got in just to be in a gang, be somewhere, be known from somewhere," and Yolanda was encouraged to do well in school by her best girlfriend (Nieto, 2000). Given that difference in peer pressure, it is not surprising that Paul was expelled from school and that Yolanda stayed to graduate.

The influence of the culture of children was strong for both these youths, pushing them in opposite directions, as it often does for children from various places. When patriarchal authority dominates and when families include many siblings and cousins, peers from other families are less influential and the culture of one's own generation of relatives is strong. This is often the case in South Asia

! ANSWER TO OBSERVATIONAL QUIZ (from page 396): The children's age and sex provide the clues. Pulling a reluctant playmate toward the end of the diving board might seem mean (and probably would be mean if these children were girls or preschoolers), but physical play is part of close friendships among boys this age. Not only are both boys smiling, but the one at left would not have gotten on the board if his friend had not encouraged him, and the boy at right would pull arms, not feet, or would simply push sideways if he were not just playing with his buddy.

and in Arab countries (Nsamenang, 2002; Verma & Saraswathi, 2002). However, when families are small and fathers do not rule the clan, peers become more important, as is true for many North American and East Asian children (Arnett, 2002; Stevenson & Zusho, 2002). For about a million street children in Latin America, the culture of children is the only culture they have (Welti, 2002).

The values emphasized by the culture differ in various places. Consider these examples:

> In rural Kenyan villages, the most competent children are often those viewed as having the broadest and most accurate knowledge regarding natural herbal medicines that are used to treat parasites and other illnesses. . . . In many rural Alaska Yup'ik villages, the most competent children are often those viewed as having the most superior hunting and gathering skills.
>
> *[Sternberg & Grigorenko, 2004, p. ix]*

Within each nation, every child's particular sociocultural context affects development. Consider again the contrasting opinions about school of Yolanda and Paul, both from the same nation (United States), state (California), region (Los Angeles area), and ethnic heritage (Mexican American):

> *Yolanda:* I feel proud of myself when I see a [good] grade. And like [if] I see a C, I'm going to have to pull this grade up. . . . I like learning. I like really getting my mind working. . . . [Education] is good for you. . . .
>
> *Paul:* I try not to get influenced too much, pulled into what I don't want to be into. But mostly, it's hard. You don't want people to be saying you're stupid. "Why do you want to go to school and get a job? . . . Drop out."
>
> *[quoted in Nieto, 2000, pp. 220, 221, 252]*

Their opposite reactions are not surprising; every child lives in "a culture within a culture" (Stewart & Bond, 2002), each within a social niche.

Moral Actions

Children teach each other moral rules, with values that adults do not necessarily endorse, as we have seen. Among the highest values are: Protect your friends, don't tell adults what really goes on, and try not to be too different from the other children. Of course, cognition influences a child's understanding of right and wrong (as reviewed in Chapter 12), and parents have an effect, especially by their example and attitudes, as you will see later in this chapter.

But generally, when it comes to a code of behavior, peer influence outweighs adult influence. In one series of studies, researchers wanted to know how children would feel about someone who violated a moral agreement. When they gave 3- to 10-year-olds an example of a contract violation between a mother and child, children were not particularly troubled by the broken contract. The researchers suggest that "maternal inconsistency . . . is exactly what children mostly expect from their mothers" (Keller et al., 2004, pp. 623–624). With parents, strict enforcement of moral rules may not be the norm.

Six months later, the researchers asked the same children about a violation of a contract between friends. This time, the school-age children were upset at the broken promises. To be specific, the children were told that one boy (Peter) promised to let another (Johannes) ride his new bike if Johannes helped Peter first (Keller et al., 2004). Virtually all the children understood the contract, realizing that if Johannes helped but then Peter did not

The Rules of the Game These young monks in Myanmar (formerly Burma) are playing a board game that adults also play, but the children have some of their own refinements of the general rules. Children's peer groups often modify the norms of dominant culture, as is evident in everything from superstitions to stickball.

KYUYA KAMAZAWA / HAGA / THE IMAGE WORKS

allow him to ride the bike, that would be a violation, as would Johannes sneaking a ride on the bike without helping.

Although most of the younger children (82 percent) thought that the boy who broke the contract would be happy, by age 10 the children had internalized the moral force of an agreement between friends. Most of them (68 percent) thought that a boy who broke a contract, even though he got what he wanted, would feel guilty or sad (Keller et al., 2004).

As you read in Chapter 12, school-age children become passionate about moral issues. Their passion includes emotional commitment as they learn to interact with peers, as shown in this example and in many instances of children working together to help other, less fortunate children. As you just read, they may ignore the prejudices that their elders have, especially if they know a child from the group that the parents disparage. Often schoolchildren are the first to take up moral issues, whether it is to protect dolphins, protest an unfair regulation, or raise money for the victims of a war or disaster.

Variations in Social Acceptance

Some schoolchildren are well liked by their peers; others are not (Cillessen & Mayeux, 2004b; Newcomb et al., 1993). Over six years, researchers asked 299 children which classmates they either wanted or did not want as playmates. The size of each cluster changed from year to year, but overall about a third of the children were popular (often chosen), about half were average (sometimes chosen), and about a sixth were unpopular (often rejected). Eleven percent of the children (mostly average) were in the same category all six years. Only 2 percent were consistently rejected (Brendgen et al., 2001).

The particular reasons a child might be popular, average, or rejected vary from one culture to another. This was apparent in China, which has experienced a cultural shift over the past two decades. A survey in Shanghai in 1990 found that shy children were respected by peers and teachers, often ranking as popular children, unlike shy children in North America (Chen et al., 1992). Then a greater appreciation for assertiveness emerged among the children when the Chinese culture changed in response to internal factors as well as economic influence from the West. A 2002 survey from the same population in Shanghai found that children were more likely to reject than to accept their shy peers. Consequently, shy children were less happy than in the earlier cohorts, and fewer children were recognized as shy (Chen et al., 2005).

In the United States, two types of popularity emerge as children mature from first grade to middle school. Some children are consistently well liked because they are "kind, trustworthy, cooperative." Among the older children, a group of popular children appears who are "athletic, cool, dominant, arrogant, and . . . aggressive," high in social status and influence, much feared and respected, but not necessarily liked (Cillessen & Mayeux, 2004a).

Three types of unpopular children also become apparent as children grow older. The children in one group are merely *neglected,* not rejected. No one picks them as friends, but nobody avoids them, either. Although it is better to have friends, being neglected is not necessarily harmful, especially if a child has a good family situation or outstanding talents (in music or the

Peer Rejection Hurts Some children do not notice or care if other children reject them, but this girl's lowered head and self-effacing arms convey shame and pain as the other children walk past her.

? Observational Quiz (see answer, page 400): Does this photograph depict an actual incident, or was it "staged" for educational use in textbooks like this one?

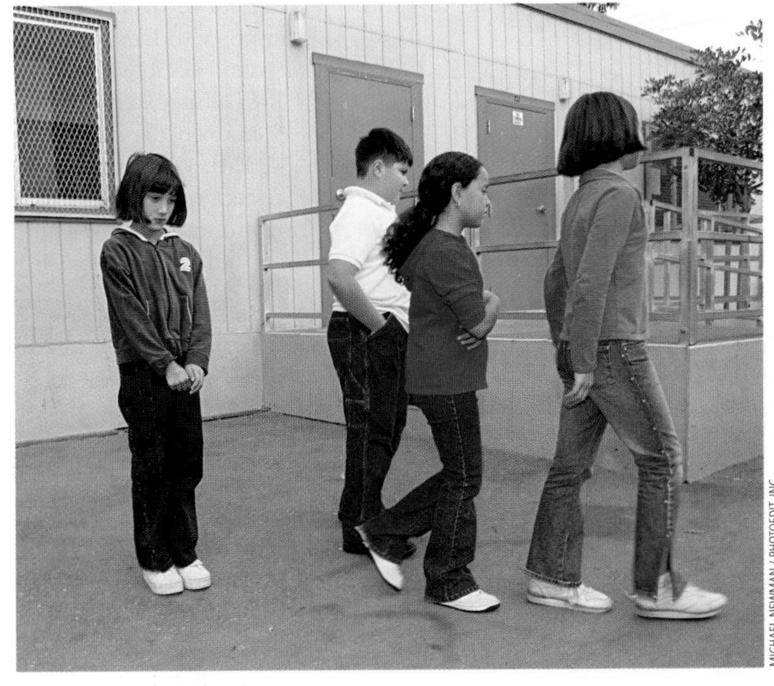

MICHAEL NEWMAN / PHOTOEDIT, INC.

arts, say). If they are ignorant of or indifferent to their status, neglected children are relatively unaffected by their unpopularity (Sandstrom & Zakriski, 2004).

The other two types of unpopular children are actively rejected, not just neglected. Some are **aggressive-rejected**—that is, disliked because of their antagonistic, confrontational behavior. Others are **withdrawn-rejected**—disliked because of their timid, withdrawn, anxious behavior. These seemingly opposite types of rejected children are similar in several ways: They misinterpret social situations, dysregulate their emotions, and are likely to be mistreated at home (Pollak et al., 2000).

aggressive-rejected Rejected by peers because of antagonistic, confrontational behavior.

withdrawn-rejected Rejected by peers because of timid, withdrawn, and anxious behavior.

Social Awareness

Several researchers believe that social cognition is the crucial difference between children who are rejected and children who are accepted (Gifford-Smith & Rabiner, 2004; Ladd, 1999). **Social cognition** is the ability to understand human interactions, an ability that begins in infancy with social referencing and continues in early childhood with theory of mind. By middle childhood, maturation and experience combine to allow school-age children to be articulate and reflective, able to understand themselves and others. Social cognition may have led some of those Chinese children who were inclined to be shy to become more outgoing instead.

social cognition The ability to understand social interactions, including the causes and consequences of human behavior.

In general, their social cognition leads well-liked children to assume that social slights, from a push to an unkind remark, are accidental and not intended to harm. Therefore, a social slight does not provoke fear and self-doubt in them as it does in a withdrawn-rejected child, who might lie awake at night wondering why it occurred. Nor does it provoke anger, as it might in an aggressive child, who blurts out an insult that requires a response—the reactive aggression you read about in Chapter 10 (see Table 13.1).

! Answer to Observational Quiz (from page 399): Staged, we hope, but several clues suggest that it may be genuine. First, the setting is not a studio location, but a real schoolyard in a crowded and poor neighborhood—note the portable classrooms. Second, all these children seem to belong to the same ethnic group, and social rejection is more likely within groups than across ethnic lines. Third, body positions, facial expressions, and clothing styles all suggest the rejection of a socially inept child.

In ambiguous situations, well-liked children try to understand what happened, perhaps asking someone else for an explanation (Erdley & Asher, 1998). Given a direct conflict between themselves and another child, they seek not revenge but rather a compromise that maintains the friendship (Rose & Asher, 1999). These prosocial skills—benign social perceptions, insight into human relationships, and the tendency to help rather than to attack—are rare in rejected children of any type (Gifford-Smith & Rabiner, 2004). Both aggressive-rejected and withdrawn-rejected children misinterpret behavior, are poor listeners, and avoid social situations. They tend to be clumsy, awkward, hostile, and inept.

One extensive two-year study that began with 4½- to 8-year-olds found that children do not necessarily become less impulsive with age (Eisenberg et al., 2004). What does mature is their ability to control themselves. School-age children improve in **effortful control**, which is the power to modify impulses and emotions. As a result, the children in the study had fewer emotional problems, as noted by mothers, fathers, and teachers (Eisenberg et al., 2004).

effortful control The ability to regulate one's emotions and actions through effort, not simply through natural inclination.

TABLE 13.1 **Examples of the Perceptions and Reactions of Popular and Unpopular Children**

Situation	Child B's Type	Typical Interpretation	Typical Response
Child A spills a glass of milk on child B during lunch.	Aggressive-rejected	It was on purpose.	Pour milk on child A, or say something mean.
	Withdrawn-rejected	It was on purpose, or it was accidental.	Ignore it, or leave the table.
	Well-liked	It was accidental.	Get a towel, or ask how it happened.

Which comes first, social acceptance or social understanding? A study of fifth- and sixth-graders, who were assessed three times over two school years, found that rejected children tended to be lonely and depressed, especially if they were anxious by nature. However, aggressive or withdrawn children who became less rejected became happier as well as more prosocial (Gazette & Rudolph, 2004). Note the sequence here: Social acceptance preceded, rather than followed, advances in social cognition. The same sequence was also found in other research with younger children (Haselager et al., 2002). It may be that children develop their social skills because they have friends who teach them, not vice versa.

In general, peers help children see what they are doing, and children begin to modify their behavior consciously, making themselves speak up in class, for instance, or trying not to always blurt out the answer. They become better at emotional regulation and effortful control. Behavior comes more in line with goals, as the metacognitive abilities described in Chapter 12 are used to plan not only how to study but also how to behave.

Friendship

Although school-age children value acceptance by the entire peer group, personal friendship is even more important (Erwin, 1998; Ladd, 1999; Sandstrom & Zakriski, 2004). Indeed, if they had to choose between being popular but friendless and having close friends but being unpopular, most children would take the friends. That choice is the healthier one. Research finds that friendship leads to psychosocial growth and buffers against psychopathology. A longitudinal study of peer acceptance (popularity) and close friendship (mutual loyalty) among fifth-graders found that both affected social interactions and emotional health 12 years later, but the close friends were more important than the acquaintances (Bagwell et al., 2001).

CAROL BECKWITH & ANGELA FISHER / HAGA / THE IMAGE WORKS

Friends and Culture Like children everywhere, these children—two 7-year-olds and one 10-year-old, of the Surma people in southern Ethiopia—model their appearance after that of slightly older children, in this case adolescents who apply elaborate body paint for courtship and stick-fighting rituals.

? OBSERVATIONAL QUIZ (see answer, page 403): Are these boys or girls, and which two are best friends?

Another study found that children from various home backgrounds had about the same number of acquaintances, but the children from violent homes had fewer close friends and were lonelier. The authors explained, "Skill at recruiting surface acquaintances or playmates is different . . . from the skill required to sustain close relationships," and the latter is needed if the child is to avoid loneliness, isolation, and rejection (McCloskey & Stuewig, 2001, p. 93).

Friendships become more intense and intimate as children grow older. Some research has found that this seems to be more true for girls than for boys, but during middle childhood both sexes demand more of their friends, change friends less often, become upset when a friendship breaks up, and find it harder to make new friends than they did when they were younger. Gender differences are found in activities (girls talk more and boys play more games), but boys and girls both want best friends (Erwin, 1998; Underwood, 2004).

Older children of both sexes become pickier: They tend to choose best friends whose interests, values, and backgrounds are similar to their own. In fact, from ages 3 to 13, close friendships increasingly involve children of the same sex, age, ethnicity, and socioeconomic status, not because children are more prejudiced (they are not) but because they seek friends who understand and agree with them (Aboud & Amato, 2001; Aboud & Mendelson, 1996; Powlishta, 2004).

By age 10, most children have one "best" friend (virtually always the same age and sex as themselves) to whom they are loyal. They know how to be a good friend. For example, in one study fifth-graders were asked what they would do if other children teased or laughed at their friends. Almost all the children (boys as wells as girls) said they would ask their friend to do something fun with them, as well as reassure the friend that "things like that happen to everyone" (Rose & Asher, 2004).

Bullies and Their Victims

The discussion of aggressive and withdrawn children brings to mind bullies and their victims. Not every rejected child becomes a victim, nor does every aggressive child become a bully; but for those who do, the consequences can echo for years. Many victims develop low self-esteem, and many bullies become increasingly aggressive (Hanish & Guerra, 2002; Hawker & Boulton, 2000; Kochenderfer-Ladd & Wardrop, 2001). Over time, the social costs to both bullies and victims include impaired social understanding and problems with human relationships in adulthood (Pepler et al., 2004). Even bystanders become distressed, according to detailed research (Nishima & Juvenen, 2005).

Bullying must be distinguished from the normal interaction patterns of children. Almost every adult remembers isolated attacks, occasional insults, or an unexpected social slight from other children, but such one-time occurrences, though painful, are not debilitating. The reason they are not so harmful is that most children have at least one friend who aids in recovery by providing reassurance.

bullying Repeated, systematic efforts to inflict harm through physical, verbal, or social attack on a weaker person.

Bullying is repeated, systematic efforts to inflict harm on someone who is unable or unlikely to defend himself or herself. Bullying may be physical (such as hitting, pinching, or kicking), verbal (such as teasing, taunting, or name-calling), or social (such as deliberate shunning or public mocking). A key word in this definition is *repeated.* It is the series of attacks, time after time, when the victim does not fight back, that makes bullying harmful. Victims typically endure shameful experiences again and again—being forced to hand over lunch money, to laugh at insults, or to drink milk mixed with detergent, all with others watching and no one defending.

Picking on Someone Your Own Sex Bullies usually target victims of the same sex. Boy victims tend to be physically weaker than their tormentors, whereas girl victims tend to be socially out of step—unusually shy or self-conscious, or unfashionably dressed. The girl at left is bullying her sister. In the photograph at right, notice that the bystanders seem very interested in the bullying episode, but no one is about to intervene.

MICHELLE D. BRIDEWELL / PHOTOEDIT, INC.

JONATHAN NOUROK / PHOTOEDIT, INC.

Victims of bullying tend to be "cautious, sensitive, quiet . . . lonely and abandoned at school. As a rule, they do not have a single good friend in their class" (Olweus, 1999, p. 15). Most victims are withdrawn-rejected, but some are aggressive-rejected, called **bully-victims** (or *provocative victims*) (Schwartz et al., 2001). They are mean to everyone, "the most strongly disliked members of the peer group," with neither friends nor sympathizers (Sandstrom & Zakriski, 2004, p. 110).

bully-victim A bully who is, or has been, a victim. Also called *provocative victims* because they deliberately attack a bully.

Most bullies are not rejected, however. They usually have a few admiring friends (henchmen) and are socially perceptive—but without the empathy that characterizes prosocial children. They are adept at being aggressive without getting into immediate trouble. Usually they bully more frequently as the school year goes on, targeting those victims who no longer resist, realizing that no one stops them.

Boys who are bullies are often above average in size and choose to torment smaller, weaker boys. Girls who are bullies are often above average in verbal assertiveness and choose to harass shyer, more soft-spoken girls. These gender differences are reflected in bullying tactics. Boys typically use force or the threat of force. Girls often mock or ridicule their victims, making fun of their clothes, behavior, or appearance; revealing their most embarrassing secrets; or spreading destructive rumors about them. In other words, boys typically use *physical* aggression, and girls use *relational* aggression (see Chapter 10).

Although "mean girls" specialize in relational aggression, boys do it, too, especially in later middle childhood and in early adolescence. At that point (though not in the early grades of elementary school), aggression increases popularity and power in both sexes (Cillessen & Mayeux, 2004a).

Bullying is more obvious and more serious toward the end of childhood and in adolescence, but its roots are buried deep in childhood. A child doesn't just wake up some September morning and decide to be a bully that school year. She or, more often, he has been pushed and pulled toward antisocial behavior, perhaps even before birth, as genetic and prenatal influences make some babies more difficult than others. Then some parents react with anger, and the child reciprocates.

Most families, preschools, and peers help children control their aggressive impulses. For some children, however, bullying develops not only because of inborn brain abnormalities or genetic impulses but also because of insecure attachment, stressful home life, hostile siblings, and other problems that intensify aggressive impulses rather than teach effortful control (Cairns & Cairns, 2001; Repetti et al., 2000).

! Answer to Observational Quiz (from page 401): They are girls. The short hair and necklaces give conflicting signals, from a Western perspective, but the unmistakable sign is that two of them have outlined their future breasts, in imitation of their older sisters. They are all friends, but the two younger girls are especially close: The photographer reports that they decorated their bodies in similar ways to show their affection for each other.

Can victims stop a bully? Sometimes. Most children who are victimized once or twice find a way to stop a repetition, by ignoring, retaliating, defusing, or avoiding. According to one microanalytic study of girls' aggression, de-escalating the confrontation was the best strategy; it succeeded 57 percent of the time, whereas attacking back worked only 23 percent of the time (Putallaz et al., 2004). One girl tried attacking back, and then found that de-escalation was better:

> Some friends teamed up against me. They'd cut down what I'd done or gossip about what I was wearing. I never handled it well, always returning their nasty remarks with cruel ones of my own. But then I realized that was a mistake. When I confronted people and talked civilly, it caused far less pain. First I'd say something like how boring a class was. That set the tone that I wasn't in the mood to argue. Later on, I'd ask, "Why did you say something about me that was untrue?" But my tone was questioning—not angry. Generally the person said "I'm sorry" and didn't do it again.
>
> *[Quoted in Putallaz et al., 2004, p. 123]*

Especially for Former Victims of Bullying Almost everyone was bullied at some point in childhood. When you remember such moments, how can you avoid feeling sad and depressed?

If bullies are not stopped in preschool, and victims cannot break the pattern on their own, can schools make a difference? Maybe.

Issues and Applications

Can Bullying Be Stopped?

Following the suicides of three victims of bullying, the government of Norway asked researcher Dan Olweus to determine the extent and severity of bullying in that country. After a confidential survey among Norway's 90,000 school-age children, Olweus reported that physical and verbal bullying was widespread and serious (see Figure 13.1), that teachers and parents were "relatively unaware" of specific incidents, and that adults rarely stopped it. Olweus found rates that were thought to be high: 3 percent of the children said that they were victims once a week or more; 7 percent admitted that they themselves sometimes deliberately hurt other children, verbally or physically (Olweus, 1993b).

The government asked him to intervene. Using an ecological approach, he attempted to affect the entire school culture. Parents received pamphlets that described signs of victimization to watch for (such as bad dreams, no real friends, damaged clothes, torn books, and unexplained bruises); students saw videotapes intended to evoke sympathy for victims; teachers were given special training; principals learned that adult supervision in the lunchroom, restrooms, and playground was pivotal.

Then in every classroom, students discussed why and how to stop bullying, to mediate peer conflicts, and to befriend lonely children. This last action is particularly crucial: Having at least one protective peer "watching your back" not only prevents the escalation of bullying but reduces its emotional sting (Hodges et al., 1999). For this reason, teachers created cooperative learning groups so that no child was isolated; each had at least some teammates who could defend if an outsider threatened. Teachers also halted each incident of name-calling or minor assault immediately, no longer ignoring it.

If bullying still occurred, counselors required that families undergo therapy, partly because ineffective or harsh parenting is one reason children become bullies. Counselors reassigned bullies (not the victims) to a different class or school, while helping victims strengthen social and academic skills.

Twenty months after this campaign began, Olweus surveyed the children again. Bullying had been reduced by half (Olweus, 1992). These results are thrilling to developmentalists, because the applications of research led to an inexpensive intervention that reduced a serious problem.

Similar efforts are underway in many nations, most of which find higher rates of bullying than Olweus found in Norway. For example, a Canadian study found that about a third of the boys and a fourth of the girls had bullied another child in the previous two months (Pepler et al., 2004).

There are three aspects of successful programs:

- The whole school must change, not just the identified bullies.
- Intervention is more effective earlier than later.
- Evaluation is critical. Programs that sound good may not succeed.

This final point merits special emphasis. Some programs make a difference; sometimes no effects are found; none work as well as Olweus's original intervention (Smith & Ananiadou, 2003). Several studies have discovered that putting troubled students together in a therapy group or a classroom tends to increase aggression in all of them (Kupersmidt et al., 2004). Programs to stop bullying in high school can backfire. Even in elementary school, well-intentioned measures, such as letting children solve their

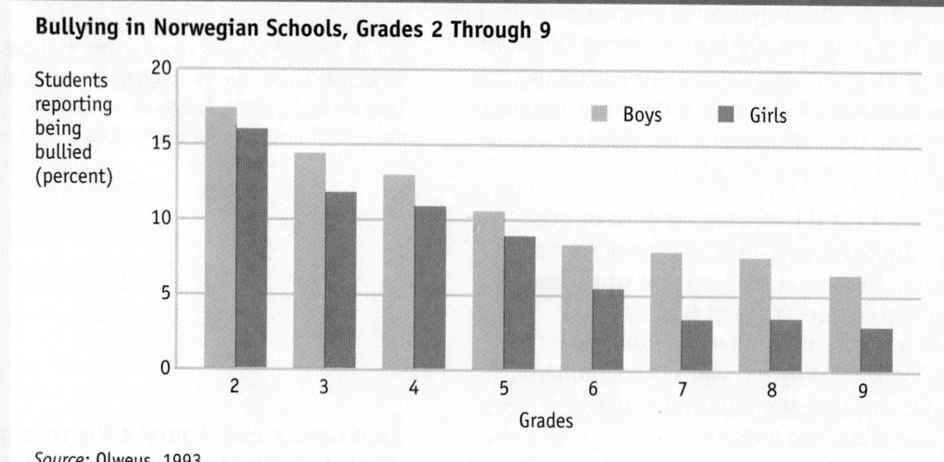

FIGURE 13.1 **Groundbreaking Findings** After Don Olweus surveyed all Norwegian schoolchildren about physical bullying, he reported the shockingly high rates of victimization shown here. As for relational bullying, both sexes in almost every grade and nation report victimization rates of 15 percent or higher.

problems on their own or assigning guards to the school, may make the situation worse. Teaching better social skills to victims may seem like a good idea, but the crucial change is not in the victims' behavior but in the school culture that allows bullies to continue their attacks.

One recent intervention was reported from the Pacific Northwest of the United States (Frey et al., 2005). As a research project, the study had many good features, including a whole-school approach; matched experimental and control schools; playground observations of behavior; confidential teacher and student reports; administrative changes within the schools; and special lessons to be taught over three months by all the third- to sixth-grade teachers, with checks to make sure the teachers understood the curriculum and followed it. A particular emphasis was on using the peer group well, teaching children who observed bullying to stop it.

This program succeeded in some ways, but not in others. Bullying observed on the playground at the three control schools increased from fall to spring, by about 60 percent, but at the experimental schools by only 11 percent. Less improvement was found in the children's attitudes and in their self-reports of bullying or victimization. The authors hope that attitudes will soon follow the changed behavior. Overall, without specific evaluation, it is difficult to know what works and what does not.

Shake Hands or Yell "Uncle" Many schools, such as this one in Alaska, have trained peer mediators who intervene in disputes, hear both sides, take notes, and seek a resolution. Without such efforts, antagonists usually fight until one gives up, giving bullies free rein. Despite Alaska's higher rate of alcohol abuse, the state's adolescent homicide rate is lower than the national average.

? OBSERVATIONAL QUIZ (see answer, page 406): Could this program be one reason?

FRANK FOURNIER / WOODFIN CAMP & ASSOCIATES

FRANK FOURNIER / WOODFIN CAMP & ASSOCIATES

RESPONSE FOR FORMER VICTIMS OF BULLYING (from page 403): Although children who are victims of bullying often feel inferior and alone, you now know that adults should have stopped the bully. Now you can become angry at the adults who should have protected you. You can also be proud of yourself for having eventually gotten through or escaped the situation. Your anger and pride may replace your lingering sadness and depression.

SUMMING UP

School-age children develop their own culture, with customs and morals that encourage children to be loyal to each other. All 6- to 11-year-olds want peer acceptance and close, mutual friendships. These two social supports buffer against loneliness and depression, not only during childhood but also for years beyond. Parents and teachers can help children develop cooperative and constructive relationships with friends and with peers, as protection against the personal and social problems of middle childhood.

Most children experience some peer rejection as well as a degree of social acceptance, a mixture that helps children deal with the realities of life. However, some children are repeatedly rejected and friendless, and some of them become victims of bullying. Bullying occurs in every school in every nation; the frequency and type depend on the school climate, the culture, and the child's age and gender.

ESPECIALLY FOR PARENTS OF AN ACCUSED BULLY Another parent has told you that your child is a bully. Your child denies it and explains that the other child doesn't mind being teased.

Families and Children

! Answer to Observational Quiz (from page 405): Yes. Children learn their conflict-resolution patterns in elementary school and then tend to use them in adolescence.

Response for Parents of an Accused Bully (from page 405): The future is ominous if the charges are true, and your child's denial is a sign that there is a problem. (If your child were not bullying the other child, he or she would be worried about the misperception of his or her "teasing," instead of categorically denying that any problem exists.) You might ask the teacher and guidance counselor what they are doing about bullying in the school. Since bullying behavior is often learned at home, family counseling might help you and your spouse to become less punitive and your child to become less aggressive. Because bullies often have friends who egg them on, you may need to monitor your child's friendships and perhaps even befriend the victim. Talk matters over with your child, as often as necessary. Ignoring the situation might lead to heartache later on.

No one doubts that peers are vital during middle childhood or that schools can make a marked difference in what, and how much, children learn. Parents and the general public are also convinced that parental practices are most important. On this last point, developmental researchers have recently had serious doubts (Ladd & Pettit, 2002; Maccoby, 2000; Reiss et al., 2000), as the roles of genes, peers, and neighborhood have come to appear so powerful that there seems little room left for parents to hold sway.

Proof of the power of genes took many developmentalists by surprise about 20 years ago, but now it is generally accepted that about half a person's behavior can be traced to heredity. That is a general estimate: Some specific aspects of a person (such as physical traits and many diseases) are more than half genetic, and others (especially complex behaviors, including moral values) are less. The epigenetic perspective is also accepted: Genes always interact with the environment, which amplifies the power of some genes and halts the expression of others.

Most developmentalists found the great extent of genetic influence easy to accept because they realized that the environment was still crucial. They assumed that environmental influences primarily meant family factors and that children raised in the same family would have the same, shared environment as well as some nonshared influences (if siblings have different friends, for instance).

Hundreds of researchers forged ahead with studies of twins, both monozygotic and dizygotic, siblings (full and half), and adopted children in order to distinguish genetic from environmental influences. The power of genes was proven to be pervasive, affecting even such things as the tendency to be religious or get divorced. Given that genes affect personality and intelligence, genetic influence on such traits was understood and accepted.

Less well understood and accepted was the discovery that nonshared environment was repeatedly found to be much more influential than shared environment (Plomin et al., 2001; Reiss & Neiderheiser, 2000). At first, researchers thought this meant that genes combined with peers were more important than parents. In the words of one developmentalist:

> Children somewhat resemble their biological parents and siblings in personality, but the genes they have in common can account for almost all of the resemblance. These results indicate that being reared by conscientious parents does not, on average, make children more (or less) sociable, and that being reared by open-minded parents does not, on average, make children more (or less) open-minded.
>
> *[Harris, 2002, p. 5]*

Children Need Families

Even the most avid advocate of genetics and peers as influences on development agrees that families aid development at every point of the life span. The few children who have no families (not even foster parents or caregiving grandparents) are seriously troubled in every way. They are likely to become self-destructive, lonely, and violent (Miller et al., 2000).

The debate, then, is not about families versus no families but about the particulars of family practice. As long as a family is not severely abusive or neglectful, is it just about the same as any other family? Does it matter if bedtime is regular, whether honesty is discussed, how children are disciplined, what the parents yell at each other about, and so on? How can scientists measure the impact of child rearing without indirectly measuring the child's own genetic temperament? Are parents responsible for choosing schools and neighborhoods, the supportive environments that children need, and nothing else? One expert suggests:

> The vulnerabilities of older children may differ substantially in kind from those of young ones, but the potential consequences of risks remain equally great throughout the developmental period. The extent to which parents provide healthy and supportive environments for their developing children is a critical component in their lifelong well-being.
>
> [Ramey, 2002, p. 48]

Do parents directly influence their children, even though genetic and nonshared environments have been proven to be powerful? The current answer is yes, because developmentalists now realize that many *nonshared* environmental influences arise within a family, as the following discussion explains.

THINKING LIKE A SCIENTIST

Shared and Nonshared Environments

One way to measure family influence is to compare children of varying degrees of genetic similarity (twins, full siblings, stepsiblings, adopted children) raised within the same household (Reiss et al., 2000). The extent to which children share genes (100 percent for monozygotic twins, 50 percent for full siblings, 25 percent for half-siblings, and so on) can be used to calculate how much of the variation in a trait is inherited. The remaining variations presumably arise from the environment.

This seems simple enough. If one third-grade girl is a model student—neatly completing her homework, befriending her classmates, and respecting her teacher—most observers would credit her parents for raising her so well. What if her younger brother, in second grade, blurts out the wrong answer, scraps with his classmates, and makes disrespectful gestures toward the teacher when her back is turned? Blame the parents? Or blame the genes (full siblings share only half their genes)? Even though the two children were raised in the same home (shared environment), might the parents have favored the elder girl?

If parents actually do treat their children differently, are those differences caused by genes, gender, or age, which would make them the result of the child's nature more than the parents' nurture? Or is it more than that? One particularly important test would be for moral development, partly because morals are a major concern for parents and society. Of course, the morals of people in the same family correlate, but that might be because they share genes and culture, not because of parental beliefs or behavior.

This issue is particularly urgent regarding antisocial actions—the lying, fighting, and cheating that are considered immoral in virtually every culture. We know that antisocial actions are powerfully influenced by genes, sex, peers, and the community. When a young adolescent commits a serious crime, often a sobbing mother appears on the TV news, asserting, "I did my best to teach him right." Is she deceiving herself, because her child's behavior is the result of her child rearing, or are the child's bad friends and society in general to blame?

This question troubles scientists. Each research design that seems to show a link between parental behavior and child morality is vulnerable to criticism (see Figure 13.2). Consequently, an expert team of scientists, noting the flaws in earlier research, set out to compare 1,000 sets of monozygotic twins (Caspi et al., 2004). Each set of twins had been raised together, and such twins have exactly the same genes, the same family, and the same sociocultural background: this equalizes many factors that confounded earlier studies.

The team assessed how antisocial each twin was by asking the mother and the child's teachers at age 5 and age 7 to fill out a detailed, standard checklist. They also measured every mother's attitude toward each of her twins. Attitudes ranged from very positive ("my ray of sunshine") to very negative ("I wish I never had her. . . . She's a cow, I hate her") (quoted in Caspi et al., 2004, p. 153).

Many mothers assumed that personality differences between their twins were innate, but actually their own words revealed that the mothers' behavior encouraged those differences:

> Susan can be very sweet. She loves babies . . . she can be insecure . . . she flutters and dances around. . . . There's not much between her ears. . . . She's exceptionally vain, more so than Ann. Ann loves any game involving a ball, very sporty, climbs trees, very much a tomboy. One is a

serious tomboy and one's a serious girlie girl. Even when they were babies I always dressed one in blue stuff and one in pink stuff.

[quoted in Caspi et al., 2004, p. 156]

Several mothers were much more negative toward one twin than toward the other:

He was in the hospital and everyone was all "poor Jeff, poor Jeff"' and I started thinking, "Well, what about me? I'm the one's just had twins. I'm the one's going though this, he's a seven-week-old baby and doesn't know a thing about it." . . . I sort of detached and plowed my emotions into Mike.

[quoted in Caspi et al., 2004, p. 156]

When this woman and her husband divorced, she blamed Jeff for favoring his father: "Jeff would do anything for Don but he wouldn't for me, and no matter what I did for either of them it wouldn't be right" (p. 157). She thought Mike was much more lovable.

Even when the researchers controlled for genes, gender, and age as well as for personality differences in kindergarten (by measuring, among other things, antisocial behavior as assessed by the children's teachers), the mothers affected the children. The twins whose mothers were more negative toward them tended to become more antisocial—that is, increasingly likely to fight, steal, and hurt others—between ages 5 and 7, as rated by their teachers. The nonshared aspects of their environment, particularly their mothers' attitudes, made a difference.

Thus "mothers' emotional attitudes toward their children are associated with their child's antisocial behavior" (p. 157). No doubt all the other factors mentioned above—peers, socioeconomic status (SES), and so on—are important influences, but this research showing measurable change in identical twins in just two years confirms the popular hunch that parents matter, too.

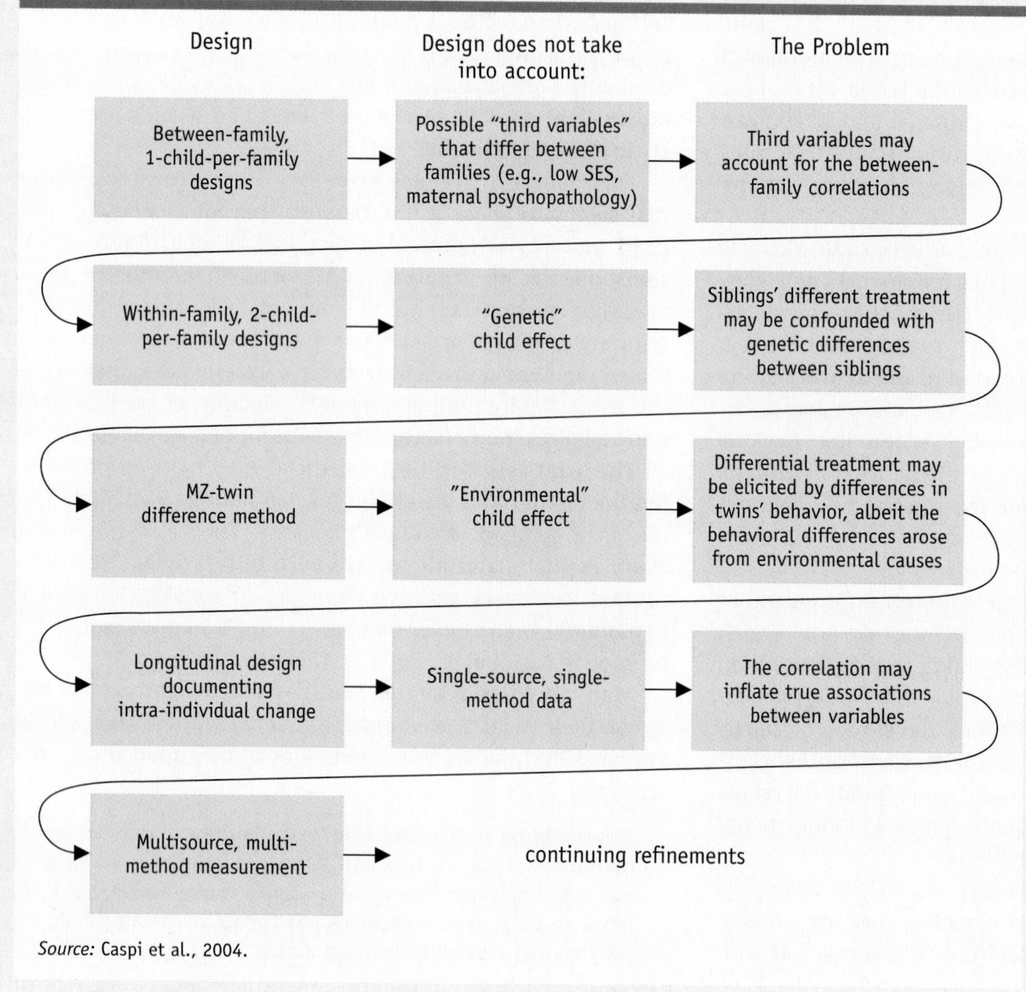

FIGURE 13.2 **Improvements in Research Design** Before designing a study, researchers identify the weaknesses of earlier studies so that they can consider ways of avoiding them. This chart shows the preliminary analysis made by the team that found that parents' attitudes have a direct effect on children's behavior. As they realized, "continuing refinements" in research design are always possible.

Families Are Not the Same

Once we acknowledge that families influence children, the question becomes: Exactly which family configurations and patterns are best and which ones are destructive? This is an urgent concern of parents, psychologists, political leaders, and everyone else.

You already know from Chapters 7 and 10 that parents need to respond to their children, providing both guidance and support. But do children benefit if their parents marry, divorce, or remarry? What about families who move, or get rich, or argue a lot? The answers are sometimes surprising. To begin to answer, we need to distinguish family function from family structure.

Family Function and Dysfunction

Family function refers to the way a family works to meet the needs of its members. Everyone needs love and encouragement, but particular needs vary with development: Infants need frequent care and interaction; teenagers need both freedom and guidance; young adults need peace and privacy.

School-age children need their families to do five things:

1. *Provide food, clothing, and shelter.* Children feed, dress, wash, and sleep by themselves, but they cannot obtain the basic necessities without help.
2. *Encourage learning.* A critical task during middle childhood is to master academic and social skills. Families can be helpful in many ways, supporting and guiding their education.
3. *Help them develop self-respect.* As they become more cognitively mature, children become more self-critical. Families help their children feel competent, loved, and appreciated.
4. *Nurture peer relationships.* Families provide time, space, and opportunity to develop friendships.
5. *Ensure harmony and stability.* Children need to feel safe and secure, with protective and predictable family routines. School-age children are particularly troubled by change.

family function The way a family works to meet the needs of its members. Children need families to provide basic material necessities, encourage learning, develop self-respect, nurture friendships, and foster harmony and stability.

KATHY MCLAUGHLIN / THE IMAGE WORKS

Meeting Her Need for Fit and Fashion A 10-year-old's rapidly growing feet frequently need new shoes, and peer pressure favors certain styles of footwear. Here, Rebekah's sisters wait and watch as their mother tries to find a boot that fits her and is fashionable.

Thus, families provide material and cognitive resources as well as emotional security, so that children grow in body and mind. No family always functions perfectly, but some malfunctions are worse than others. At the end of this section we will focus on two malfunctions, poverty and conflict.

Diverse Structures

family structure The legal and genetic relationships (e.g., nuclear, extended, step) among relatives in the same home.

The other way to categorize is by **family structure,** which refers to the legal and genetic connections among related people living in the same household. Many households (including about a third of all households in the United States) have no "family structure" at all, because the person lives alone or with others who are not family members. Further, many "family households" have no dependent children (for instance, a childless married couple or a parent living with an adult child). About half of all households in Italy and Japan fit this category, because in those nations many families have no young children (the birth rate is very low), but many Italian and Japanese young adults live with their parents.

The various types of family structures are summarized in Table 13.2. The easiest way to classify family structures is according to whether the child lives with

TABLE 13.2 Common Family Structures (with percentages of U.S. children aged 6–11 in each family type)

Two-Parent Families (71%)

Most human families have two parents. These families are of several kinds.

1. **Nuclear family** (59%) Named after the nucleus (the tightly connected core particles of an atom), the nuclear family consists of a husband and wife and their biological offspring. About half of all families with children are nuclear. This category includes extended families in which both parents live with the parents of one of the spouses or when a grandparent couple acts as mother and father.
2. **Stepparent family** (10%) Divorced fathers (Stewart et al., 2003) are particularly likely to remarry. Usually his children from a previous marriage do not live with him, but if they do, they are in a step-parent family. Mothers are less likely to remarry, but when they do, the children often live with her and their stepfather. Many children spend some time in a stepparent family, but relatively few spend their entire childhood in such families.
   Blended family A stepparent family that includes children born to several families, such as the biological children from the spouses' previous marriages and the biological children of the new couple. This type of family is a particularly difficult structure for school-age children.
3. **Adoptive family** (2%) Although as many as one-third of infertile married couples adopt children, fewer adoptable children are available than in earlier decades, which means that most adoptive families have only one or two children.
4. **Polygamous family** (0%) In some nations, it is common for one man to have several wives, each bearing his children. This is considered a two-parent family.

One-Parent Families (25%)*

One-parent families are increasingly common, but they tend to have fewer children than two-parent families.

1. **Single mother, never married** (11%) Many babies (about a third of all U.S. newborns) are born to unmarried mothers, but most of these mothers intend to marry someday (Musick, 2002). Many of them do get married, either to their baby's father or to someone else. By school age, their children are often in two-parent families.
2. **Single mother, divorced** (11%) Although many marriages end in divorce (almost half in the United States, less in other nations), many divorcing couples have no children and many others remarry. Thus, many divorced women do not have school-age children living with them.
3. **Single father, divorced or never married** (3%) About one in five divorced or unmarried fathers has physical custody of the children. This structure is uncommon, but it is the most rapidly increasing form.

Other Family Types

Some children live in special versions of one- or two-parent families, described here.

1. **Extended family** Many children (about 7 percent in the United States, more in most other nations) live with their grandparents as well as with one or both of their parents.
2. **Grandparents alone** For some school-age children, their one or two "parents" are their grandparents, because the biological parents are dead or otherwise unable to live with them. This family type is increasing, especially in Africa, where an epidemic of AIDS is killing many parents.
3. **Homosexual family** Some school-age children live in a homosexual family, usually when a custodial parent takes a homosexual partner. Less often, a homosexual couple adopts children or a lesbian has a child (Patterson, 2002). Varying laws and norms determine whether these are one- or two-parent families.
4. **Foster family** This family type is usually considered temporary, and the children are categorized by their original family structure. Otherwise, they are included in one of the family types above.

*The remaining 4 percent of children do not live with either parent.
Source: Percentages are from U.S. Bureau of the Census, 2005.

one parent or two, with *parent* meaning an adult who provides care (not always the biological mother or father). Most school-age children live in two-parent homes, with the **nuclear family** (a married couple and their biological offspring) still the most common structure.

nuclear family A family that consists of a father, a mother, and their biological children under age 18.

Currently in the United States, compared with other nations as well as with previous decades, there are many single-parent households. About a fourth of all school-age children live in such households at any particular moment, although about two-thirds of U.S. children will spend a year or more in a one-parent family before they reach adulthood. Some of these children actually live with two caregiving adults, with the second adult being their parent's partner (the other biological parent or a potential stepparent) or their parent's parent. Few children live exclusively with only one adult from birth to adulthood.

The nuclear and single-parent family are sometimes contrasted with the **extended family,** in which children live not only with their parents but also with other relatives (usually grandparents, but often aunts, uncles, and cousins as well). Extended families are common among people with low income, partly because household expenses and responsibilities are shared. Such families are the typical structure in many developing nations and are common in North America among immigrants and ethnic minorities.

extended family A family of three or more generations living in one household.

Especially for Readers Whose Parents Are Middle-Aged Your mother tells you that she misses taking care of young children and wants to become a foster parent. How do you advise her?

Connecting Structure and Function

Now that we have explained the difference between family structure and family function, we need to explain that they are intertwined in many ways. For example, children raised in nuclear families are most likely to finish high school, go to college, obey the law, have happy marriages, and pursue fulfilling careers. By contrast, children in never-married, single-mother families "are at greatest risk" and fare worse on almost every indicator (Carlson & Corcoran, 2001, p. 789). But a child's success in a nuclear family or risk in a single-parent home may result from family function, not structure. Nuclear families tend to have more income and more stability, and single mothers tend to have unstable families, with a series of partners, periods of living alone, and periods of time living with relatives (Raley & Wildsmith, 2004). Those changes affect the child more than the fact of having a single mother.

BILL ARON / PHOTOEDIT, INC.

A Comfortable Combination The blended family—husband, wife, and children from both spouses' previous marriages—often breeds resentment, depression, and rebellion in the children. That is apparently not the case for the family shown here, which provides cheerful evidence that any family structure is capable of functioning well.

blended family A family that consists of two adults and the children of the prior relationships of one or both parents and/or the new partnership.

Similarly, a **blended family**, in which a married couple combine offspring from earlier partnerships, tends to have the financial assets of a nuclear family, which helps the children. But blended families also tend to be unstable, with older children leaving, new babies arriving, and the marriage itself more likely to break up than a first marriage. Depending partly on the adults' economic and emotional security, some children thrive and others suffer in blended families. Note that the outcome depends on the family function, not the structure.

This doesn't mean that structure is irrelevant. Some structures tend to attract adults who are likely to be good parents, and then the structure brings out the best in them. For example, a person's financial and emotional strength affects how likely that person is to marry, to have children, to stay married, and to be a good parent. And if a person is married to someone who is a good parent and who is financially secure, that person is more inclined to stay married, which benefits the children.

Correlational statistics show that married adults tend to be wealthier, better educated, healthier, more flexible, and less hostile—all of which was true even before they got married. It continues to be true after parenthood, when they are compared with adults who never married or who divorced. Further, the mere fact that children in a nuclear family share genes and a home with both their married parents increases the odds that their parents will be actively involved in their lives. Two adults, not just one, could teach them to tie their shoes, read them their bedtime story, look over their homework, and so on.

RESPONSE FOR READERS WHOSE PARENTS ARE MIDDLE-AGED (from page 411): Foster parenthood is probably the most difficult type of parenthood, yet it can be very rewarding if all needed support is available and a long-term arrangement is likely. Advise your mother to make sure that medical, educational, and psychological help is available if needed and that the placement agency truly cares about children's well-being.

Any comparison of the advantages of one family structure over another depends partly on the specific parents involved and partly on the culture in which they live, both of which affect structure as well as function (Heuveline & Timberlake, 2004). For example, many French parents are not legally married, but they function as married parents do in other nations, sharing household and child-rearing tasks and staying together more often than married adults do in the United States. Thus, the cohabiting structure functions well for French children. However, in the United States, cohabiting parents are less stable than married parents, which makes that structure, on average, less functional for children.

The relationships among marriage, divorce, and parenthood vary by ethnic group as well. Among Hispanic and Asian Americans, for instance, family ties are strongly valued. Consequently, compared with other American ethnic groups, premarital pregnancies among Hispanics and Asians are more likely to lead to marriage, and marriage usually entails devotion to child rearing on the part of both parents. Divorce is less likely than among European or African American couples of the same SES.

However, if divorce does occur, Hispanic fathers are *less* likely to stay actively involved with their children than are African or European American fathers (King et al., 2004). Obviously, family structure, interacting with ethnicity, affects family functioning.

All the data caution that although structure does not determine function, it may affect function. Some children in every family structure develop well and others run into serious trouble; it is "not enough to know that an individual lives in a particular family structure without also knowing what takes place within that structure" (Lansford et al., 2001, p. 850). This is true in every culture; function is crucial whether the family lives in Moscow, Montreal, or Mexico City.

Sources of Trouble for Families

We now look at two factors that can interfere with good family function in any nation: low income and high conflict. Although financial stress and conflict are likely to feed on each other, we will discuss them one by one. But first, consider an example that illustrates how and why they often co-occur.

Suppose a 3-year-old spills his milk, as every 3-year-old sometimes does. The harmonious parental response, pouring some more and using the opportunity to teach the child to mop up a spill, might be accompanied by a smile and a comment that encourages family togetherness, such as "Everyone makes mistakes sometimes." However, what if the parent feels overwhelmed by unemployment, overdue rent, an older child who wants money for a school book? Perhaps the milk was bought with the last food stamps available, and the parent has no more milk and no money to buy more. Conflict, complete with shouting, crying, and accusations (a jealous sibling claiming "he did it on purpose"), is likely. Poverty makes the parent's stress spill over when the milk does.

Family Income

Family income correlates strongly with function and structure (McLoyd, 1998; Yeung et al., 2002). Either directly or indirectly, all family functions are enhanced by adequate income (Yeung et al., 2002), especially for children aged 6 to 9 (Gennetian & Miller, 2002).

Although all social scientists agree that income is crucial in family life, they disagree about some particulars. Is it the single most important factor, or only one of several powerful influences? Do children suffer more if their household is chronically poor or if the family income fluctuates? Is poverty more destructive early in life or later, when children are in school? Can a family be too rich as well as too poor (Ackerman et al., 2004; Conger et al., 2002; Hetherington et al., 1998)?

To understand exactly how income affects child development, consider the *family stress model.* In developed nations, poverty in the abstract does not harm children: Most children in low-income families have adequate food, clothing, and other necessities. However, economic hardship increases stress, which often makes adults less happy with their marriages and more likely to be harsh and hostile with their children (Conger et al., 2002; Parke et al., 2004). Thus, the parents' reaction to poverty is the crucial factor.

The parents' reaction to wealth may be a problem, too. Families who are very wealthy also raise children with high rates of emotional problems, including drug abuse and delinquency. One reason again is thought to be stress, in this case the stress of the overachieving lifestyle, which can make parents too busy to have much quiet time with their children and puts pressure on children to be superstars in many spheres. The stress may be too much for some families (Luthar, 2003).

The family stress model also helps predict the impact of fluctuating income. If a middle-income couple expects adequate income and becomes poor, the parents may blame each other, becoming depressed and hostile toward their children. In contrast, if parents expect to be poor but earn a middle-class income for a while and then become poor again, they may be less angry and depressed, and therefore remain good parents.

The importance of family stress emerges when children within the same family structures are compared. For example, extended families with several well-educated wage earners are more likely to raise children who become well educated and happy than are extended families receiving public assistance, because the latter are stressed by their condition (Rumbaut & Portes, 2001). Likewise, children in single-mother households achieve much more in school if their father regularly pays adequate child support (Graham & Beller, 2002) or if the nation subsidizes single parents (as Austria and Iceland do) (Pong et al., 2003). Finally, the risks to optimal development that children of teenage mothers encounter are more clearly related to the mother's SES than to her age (Jaffee et al., 2001; Turley, 2003).

In general, economic hardship (either chronic poverty or sudden loss of income) leads to anger and depression among the adults, which makes them

Especially for Readers Who Are Not Yet Parents Should children call their parents by their first names and wear whatever they choose? Or should children be deferential toward adults and be pushed to excel in school?

hostile toward their spouse or their children—and thus not the loving, firm, caring parents they could be (Conger et al., 2002; Parke et al., 2004). The particular consequences of financial hardship vary from family to family and ethnic group to ethnic group (some people are well buffered, others vulnerable). However, the trends are universal, evident in many nations. Economic distress impairs family functioning.

Harmony and Stability

The second factor that has a crucial impact on school-age children is the degree of harmony and stability that characterize family interaction (Buehler & Gerard, 2002; Khaleque & Rohner, 2002). Ideally, parents are neither conflicted nor dissatisfied. They work cooperatively in a *parental alliance*—that is, a harmonious relationship that allows them to support each other's parenting.

The importance of family harmony explains why blended families can be problematic (Hetherington & Kelly, 2002). Jealousy, stress, and conflict are almost inevitable when children suddenly must share a home with other children and a new adult appears in authority. Smooth parental alliances take years to form (which is one reason a first child strains a marriage much more than later arrivals do).

Children's well-being declines if family members fight, especially if parents physically or verbally abuse each other (Cummings & Davies, 1994). Actually, the conflict itself may not be destructive if the parents disagree and then compromise and reconcile (Cummings et al., 2003). This pattern can show children how to repair conflicts with their peers. But some parents end a fight with one parent walking out and the other sobbing. Resentment festers, and that's not a good example for children.

Children's need for harmony also helps explain why single parenthood is risky. Households headed by unmarried single mothers *can* be harmonious and stable but usually are not. Most unmarried mothers are young and poor; they frequently change jobs, homes, and romantic partners, often cohabitating, marrying, divorcing, and remarrying several times from the child's birth to age 18 (Bumpass & Lu, 2000). Any such major change is stressful for every family member, and the mother's stress is typically transmitted to her children. In families with many transitions, children are more likely to quit school, leave home, use drugs, become delinquent, and have children of their own before age 20 (McLanahan, 2005).

The One-Parent Family Single parents are of two types: never married and formerly married. This divorcée is a pediatrician, so she and her daughter have a higher income than many other one-parent families. To combat the other hazards faced by single parents—including loneliness, low self-esteem, and ongoing disputes with the former spouse—she has established a divorce resource center in her hometown in Michigan.

VALICA BOUDRY / AP PHOTO

Children are particularly affected by multiple transitions, suffering more from a series of separations than from living in a stable single-mother household and more from several transitions at once than from one change at a time (Hetherington & Elmore, 2003). School achievement usually falls and friendships falter when children experience divorce, remarriage, or any other family transition.

The importance of warmth and stability also helps explain an ethnic difference in the effectiveness of parenting styles. As you remember from Chapter 10, authoritative parenting—marked by loving guidance and consistent discipline—is generally more likely than authoritarian or permissive parenting to produce outgoing, self-confident, and accomplished children. This is as true for older children as it is for preschoolers, and this type of parenting is found among families of every structure, income, cultural background, and ethnicity (Amato & Fowler, 2002).

However, a subgroup of families do not fit this generalization. Parents who use harsh discipline, especially physical punishment, are often considered authoritarian (not authoritative), but their children sometimes become happy and successful, especially if they are not European American (Chao, 2001; Hill et al., 2003; McLoyd & Smith, 2002).

Family warmth and stability may account for this paradox. Many ethnic-minority families threaten harsh discipline but also are warm toward their children. They delight in the child's actions, appreciate what the child says, and believe in the child's potential. Children may perceive discipline as a sign of caring and commitment, and their obedience may enhance family harmony (Stewart & Bond, 2002). The parents may stay together partly because they are united and the children are respectful.

Household harmony and continuity can be fostered by neighborhoods as well. Immigrant and African American communities tend not to isolate single mothers (Roschelle, 1997). Often a man other than the biological father (sometimes the mother's brother or her father) becomes a "social father" to a child and is particularly likely to help the child with learning (Jayakody & Kalil, 2002). Grandmothers often live nearby, providing guidance, warmth, and practical help.

Generally, socially embedded families, which are a vital part of a larger social unit, give children a strong sense of family honor and ethnic pride. Children try to make their family proud (Hill et al., 2003). This warmth, harmony, and pride may overcome some of the stress of single parenthood. It may also may reduce conflict between the generations. In India a study found very low parent–child conflict when compared with families in the United States. One reason, the authors hypothesized, is that families were embedded in a larger family culture, so that all family members felt that family harmony and cooperation was far better than disagreement (Larson et al., 2003).

ESPECIALLY FOR SINGLE PARENTS You have heard that children raised in one-parent families will have difficulty in establishing intimate relationships as adolescents and adults. What can you do about this possibility?

ISSUES AND APPLICATIONS

Divorce and Remarriage

Parents want "the best" for their children. But reality sometimes forces hard choices. Which is best?

- Abusive marriage
- Angry divorce
- Stressful single parenthood
- Remarriage with stepchildren

Marriage that is filled with abuse, divorce that stirs up hostility, single parenthood that is lonely and stressful, and remarriage that adds steprelatives—all may result in children who develop emotional problems and whose school achievement falters (Hetherington & Elmore, 2003). What if these are the only choices a parent has? In the right circumstances, each of these situations could be "the best."

Consider the two specific factors just described. First, income. Two households are more expensive to maintain than one. In the wake of divorce, most family expenses—for housing, food, transportation, and so on—are doubled, or nearly so. Even if the noncustodial parent pays substantial child support (which happens less than half the time), family income almost always drops after divorce.

The older children are, the worse a sudden drop in income is. College, for instance, can be expensive, and many child-support agreements last only until the child is 18. Remarriage with stepchildren sometimes relieves the financial stress, but many stepparents are reluctant to pay major expenses (school, nonemergency medical and psychological therapy, a separate bedroom) for a stepchild who is distant, difficult, or hostile (as many are).

Second, harmony and stability. If married parents are openly hostile toward each other, or one member of a couple abuses the children, then separation might reduce conflict and benefit the children. That is the case for about a third of all divorces. By contrast, if the parents are divorcing because they no longer like each other, children may prefer that their parents stay together (Booth & Amato, 2001).

> Children from families with low levels of marital conflict are almost never better off if their parents divorce, while those in highly conflicted families are better off divorcing if and only if the divorce will diminish the conflict, which it very frequently does not. . . . Policies that de-escalate or shield children from conflict . . . should be continued.
>
> *[Braver et al., 2004, p. 65]*

During divorce, single parenthood, and remarriage, adults often involve children in conflicts or emotions that children should not experience. Sometimes children are asked to take sides, and sometimes adults use a child to validate their own attractiveness or self-worth (Jacobvitz et al., 2004). Children may feel pressure to fix an adult problem (such as illness, financial stress, or problems at work) or to become a confidante or romantic partner (with increased physical contact or co-sleeping).

Parents may intrude on the child's need for privacy and independence, deciding exactly what the child should wear, for instance, or may dismiss the child's anger, loneliness, and affection for the other parent. A mother might think she is flattering her son by asking how she looks in her new dress, or a father might think he is upholding standards when he tells his daughter that no boy is good enough for her. All these controlling parental actions (called *boundary disturbances,* because the adult–child boundary is not respected) increase the child–parent conflict, whether it is overt or seethes below the surface, and harm the children (Jacobvitz et al., 2004). If parents have a satisfying adult relationship, they usually allow their children to be themselves and do not disrupt their development.

Some children, caught in the middle of their parents' distress, become excessively angry or anxious in school, unable to make close friends or even to study in peace. It is crucial for parents to balance freedom and restrictions, privacy and involvement. As described in Chapter 10, both authoritarian and permissive parenting can backfire, and stress tends to lead to ineffective parenting.

Back to the four hard choices: Which is the best? A team who studied families for decades writes, "What is striking following divorce and remarriage is . . . diversity in the experiences and the outcomes for parents and children" (Hetherington & Elmore, 2003, p. 183). There are no simple answers.

Both parents, ideally, should be part of the solution, making sure that income does not fall and conflict does not increase. Joint custody and co-parenting generally benefit the children, financially and emotionally, as long as the adults can agree. If the adults obtain professional counseling focused on the children's needs before the parents make any structural changes, that may help (Braver et al., 2004; Sandler et al., 2003). The crucial factor is neither family structure nor adult romance, but responsive, effective parenting. That is "the best."

Response for Readers Who Are Not Yet Parents (from page 414): This is a trick question, since the crucial factor in child rearing is parents' genuine warmth toward the child. While neither of the approaches mentioned in the question reflects the ideal, authoritative style, both can produce happy, successful children.

Response for Single Parents (from page 415): Do not get married mainly to provide a second parent for your child. If you were to do so, things would probably get worse rather than better. Do make an effort to have friends of both sexes with whom your child can interact.

Especially for Parents Who Want to Divorce and Remarry You and your spouse want to divorce each other and marry other people. At what age is this step least harmful to children?

SUMMING UP

Families are important to child development, but some types of families are much better than others. For school-age children, families serve five crucial functions: to provide food, clothing, and shelter; to encourage learning; to help develop self-respect; to nurture friendships with peers; and to provide harmony and stability. Low income, conflict, and transitions interfere with these functions, no matter what the family structure. The two-parent family is the most common, but in many countries a sizable minority of families are headed by a single parent (including one-fourth of all families of school-age children in the United States). The two-parent family seems better, but that may be because such families tend to have higher income and can provide children with more adult attention. Extended families, grandparent families, one-parent families, blended families, and adoptive families can raise successful, happy children, although each of these families has its own special problems. No structure inevitably either harms children or guarantees good family function.

The Nature of the Child

We have now discussed peers and parents, the two most important social influences on the school-age child. However, the child is much more than a young person who reacts to the culture of children and to family functions. A look at Table 13.3 will show you that, in many practical ways, children become much more responsible and mature during this period.

To delve more deeply into the nature of the school-age child, we turn first to psychoanalytic theory, which put forth a very specific description of children at this age. Then we look at current developmental research, which provides another set of descriptors.

TABLE 13.3 AT ABOUT THIS TIME: Signs of Psychosocial Maturation Between Ages 6 and 11

Children are more likely to have specific chores to perform at home.
Children are more likely to have a weekly allowance.
Children are expected to tell time, and they have set times for various activities.
Children have more homework assignments, some over several days.
Children are less often punished physically, more often with disapproval or withdrawal of privileges.
Children try to conform to peer standards in such matters as clothing and language.
Children influence decisions about their after-school care, lessons, and activities.
Children use media (TV, computers, video games) without adult supervision.
Children are given new responsibility for younger children, pets, or, in some cultures, employment.

Psychoanalytic Theory

Psychoanalytic theory was the first to describe middle childhood, noting that children are eager to learn about their expanding social universe. Sigmund Freud described middle childhood as the period of **latency,** when children's emotional drives are quiet, their psychosexual needs repressed, and their unconscious conflicts submerged. Suppression in all three of these areas is urgently needed because the lustful and murderous thoughts of the phallic stage (see Chapter 10) are too much to bear in the conscious mind. Latency becomes "a time for acquiring cognitive skills and assimilating cultural values as children expand their world to include teachers, neighbors, peers, club leaders, and coaches. Sexual energy continues to flow, but it is channeled into social concerns" (Miller, 2002, p. 131).

latency Freud's term for middle childhood, during which children's emotional drives and psychosocial needs are quiet (latent). Freud thought that sexual conflicts from earlier stages are only temporarily submerged, to burst forth again at puberty.

Erik Erikson agreed with Freud that middle childhood is an emotionally quiet period. The child "must forget past hopes and wishes, while his exuberant imagination is tamed and harnessed to the laws of impersonal things," becoming "ready to apply himself to given skills and tasks" (Erikson, 1963, pp. 258, 259). During Erikson's crisis of **industry versus inferiority,** children busily try to master whatever abilities their culture values.

industry versus inferiority The fourth of Erikson's eight psychosexual development crises, during which children attempt to master many skills, developing a sense of themselves as either industrious or inferior, competent or incompetent.

Children judge themselves as either *industrious* or *inferior*—that is, competent or incompetent, productive or failing, winners or losers. Being productive not only is intrinsically joyous but also fosters the self-control that is a crucial defense against emotional problems (Bradley & Corwyn, 2005). Erikson's emphasis is that the particular psychosocial need of each stage is of utmost psychic importance to the person during that age period.

Concerns about inferiority are evident in the schoolchild's ditty: "Nobody likes me. Everybody hates me. I think I'll go out and eat some worms." This lament has endured for generations because it captures, with humor that children can appreciate, the self-doubt that many school-age children feel.

Research on Middle Childhood

The following self-description could have been written by many 10-year-olds:

> I'm in the fourth grade this year, and I'm pretty popular, at least with the girls. That's because I'm nice to people and can keep secrets. Mostly I am nice to my friends, although if I get in a bad mood I sometimes say something that can be a little mean. I try to control my temper, but when I don't,

I'm ashamed of myself. I'm usually happy when I'm with my friends, but I get sad if there is no one to do things with. At school, I'm feeling pretty smart in certain subjects like Language Arts and Social Studies. I got As in these subjects on my last report card and was really proud of myself. But I'm feeling pretty dumb in Math and Science, especially when I see how well a lot of the other kids are doing. Even though I'm not doing well in those subjects, I still like myself as a person, because Math and Science just aren't that important to me. How I look and how popular I am are more important. I also like myself because I know my parents like me and so do other kids. That helps you like yourself.

[quoted in Harter, 1999, p. 48]

Response for Parents Who Want to Divorce and Remarry (from page 416): Children usually prefer that their parents stay together, unless one parent is abusive. There is no best age for children when it comes to parents' getting divorced. However, it is probably worst if such major family transitions occur just when children are undergoing major transitions of their own, such as starting school or beginning puberty.

This excerpt, from a book on children's self-concept by a scholar who has studied the development of the self for decades, captures the nature of school-age children as researchers now see them. During middle childhood, children become attuned to social comparison ("especially when I see how well a lot of the other kids are doing"), experienced in effortful control ("I try to control my temper"), loyal to friends ("can keep secrets"), and appreciative of both peers and parents ("I know my parents like me and so do other kids").

Two additional characteristics merit mention here. The first is that the school-age child's self-concept is no longer tied to the parents' perspective. Every theory and every perceptive observer notes that school-age children recognize themselves as distinct from their parents and teachers. This was apparent when children were asked, "Who knows best what you are thinking? . . . how tired you are? . . . your favorite foods?" and so on (Burton & Mitchell, 2003). A 3-year-old might answer "Mommy" and rely on a parent to say, "Oh, you are tired, you are rubbing your eyes, it's time for your nap." Children become increasingly confident of their own minds as they grow older. For instance, in this study, few (13 percent) of the 5-year-olds but most (73 percent) of the 10-year-olds thought that they knew themselves better than their mothers, fathers, or teachers did (Burton & Mitchell, 2003).

The second characteristic is a change in self-concept. Increased self-understanding, effortful control, and social awareness come at a price. Self-criticism and self-consciousness tend to rise from age 6 to 12, and self-esteem dips (Merrell & Gimpel, 1998), especially for children who live with unusual stresses (e.g., an abusive or alcoholic parent) (Luthar & Zelazo, 2003).

For most children, the school-age reduction in self-esteem is relatively slight. It may make them more realistic and therefore able to work on the skills they lack (recall the discussion of metacognition in Chapter 12). As they become more sophisticated in their social cognition, they also become more proficient at protecting themselves: They tend to devalue what they are not good at and to appreciate their strengths ("Math and Science just aren't that important to me").

Some children are already quite anxious and stressed, and reduced self-esteem leads them to lower academic achievement (Pomerantz & Rudolph, 2003). This is particularly true if peer rejection is the reason for the drop in their self-esteem (Flook et al., 2005). A loss of self-pride in middle childhood may foreshadow emotional uncertainty and psychic stress in adolescence—not the usual path, but the one often followed by children who feel inferior (Graber, 2004).

As you can see, self-esteem is tricky. If it is unrealistically high, it may decrease effortful control and thus achievement (Baumeister et al., 2003), but the same consequences may occur if it is unrealistically low. Children who appreciate themselves and appreciate other children (i.e., when self and peers both fare well in social comparison) tend to have more friends and to be prosocial, even defending a bully's victim if the occasion arises. In contrast, children who like themselves but not their peers are more likely to be aggressive and even to become bullies (Salmivalli et al., 2005).

Cultural differences add to the complications. Many groups teach children to be modest; for example, Australians have a saying that "tall poppies" are cut down, and Japanese culture discourages using social comparison to make oneself feel superior (Toyama, 2001). Although Chinese children tend to excel at mathematics, only 1 percent said that they were "very satisfied" with their performance in that subject (Snyder et al., 2004). Does their dissatisfaction contribute to their achievement?

It is apparent that the combination of high self-esteem and low opinion of others tends to leave children with fewer friends and more aggressiveness and loneliness (Salmivalli et al., 2005). Academic and social competence are aided by objective evaluation of measured achievement, not by artificially high self-esteem (Baumeister et al., 2003). Achieving the proper balance is not easy.

SUMMING UP

Children gain in maturity and responsibility during the school years. According to psychoanalytic theory, the relative quiet of the latency period makes it easier for children to master new skills and to absorb their culture's values. To Erikson, the crisis of industry versus inferiority generates self-doubt in many school-age children.

Recent research has identified certain characteristics that typify the school-age child: an awareness of social comparison, an increase in effortful control of emotions, loyalty to friends, an appreciation of parents and peers, a self-concept that is newly independent of the parents' perspective, and a decline in self-esteem as self-consciousness increases.

Coping and Overcoming

As you have seen throughout the past three chapters, the child's expanding social world and developing cognition often bring disturbing problems. Chapter 11 described some serious health impairments (obesity and asthma) that can affect psychosocial development. Formal education brings learning disabilities to the fore and makes children with special needs painfully aware of their differences. Chapter 12 explained that speaking a minority language may hinder academic learning and impair self-esteem when a child enters a school where another language and another culture are dominant. And in this chapter you have read about peers who attack rather than support, parents who may be hostile or stressed, families that are unstable.

All such problems in middle childhood are made worse by long-standing stresses that harm children of every age. Especially stressful are parents who are depressed, drug-addicted, or in prison; a neighborhood that is crumbling, violent, and crime-filled; and a household that is chronically overcrowded, chaotic, and poor.

Every problem increases the chances of other problems. For example, depressed mothers tend to marry men who are emotionally unstable; the couple then live in a deteriorating neighborhood and have ongoing marital and financial difficulties. Some children, beset by multiple stressors and newly self-aware, fail at school, fight with friends, fear the future, and cry themselves to sleep.

Resilience and Stress

Surprisingly, some children who experience serious problems seem to be unscathed. As you read in Chapter 1, such children have been called "resilient" or even "invincible." Those who are familiar with recent research, however, use these terms cautiously, if at all (see Table 13.4). What does seem to be true is that every stress has an impact, but some children cope so well that the impact is

TABLE 13.4 **Dominant Ideas About Challenges and Coping in Children, 1965–Present**

1965	All children have the same needs for healthy development.
1970	Some conditions or circumstances—such as "absent father," "teenage mother," "working mom," and "day care"—are harmful for every child.
1975	All children are *not* the same. Some children are resilient, coping easily with stressors that cause harm in other children.
1980	Nothing inevitably causes harm. Indeed, both maternal employment and preschool education, once thought to be risk factors, usually benefit children.
1985	Factors beyond the family, both in the child (low birthweight, prenatal alcohol exposure, aggressive temperament) and in the community (poverty, violence), can be very risky for the child.
1990	Risk–benefit analysis finds that some children seem to be "invulnerable" to, or even to benefit from, circumstances that destroy others. (Some do well in school despite extreme poverty, for example.)
1995	No child is invincibly resilient. Risks are always harmful—if not in education, then in emotions.
2000	Risk–benefit analysis involves the interplay among all three domains (biosocial, cognitive, and psychosocial), including factors within the child (genes, intelligence, temperament), the family (function as well as structure), and the community (including neighborhood, school, church, and culture). Over the long term, most people overcome problems, but the problems are real.
Today	The focus is on strengths, not risks. Assets in the child (intelligence, personality), the family (secure attachment, warmth), the community (good schools, after-school programs), and the nation (income support, health care) must be nurtured.

Sources: Luthar et al., 2000; Luthar, 2003; Maton et al., 2004; Walsh, 2002; Werner & Smith, 2001.

Resilience Is Real This table simplifies the progression of ideas about resilience; some older ideas are still valid, and some newer ideas were first expressed decades ago. Nonetheless, the emphasis has shifted over the past 40 years, as research evidence and thoughtful critiques have deepened understanding of resilience in children.

blunted. The success of such children has led to a new developmental goal: to allow a child's strengths to flourish, not necessarily to eliminate risks.

This chapter may have reminded you of an episode in your own childhood—perhaps a family transition, a classmate's insult, or a sudden loss of self-confidence. Rather than erase such experiences from children's lives (an impossible task), developmentalists now want to know how children (including you) cope, getting past the problems to become successful adults. But before exploring the implications of this idea, consider exactly what resilience means.

resilience The capacity to develop optimally by adapting positively to significant adversity.

Resilience has been defined as "a dynamic process encompassing positive adaptation within the context of significant adversity" (Luthar et al., 2000, p. 543). Note the three parts of this definition:

- Resilience is *dynamic,* not a stable trait. That means a given child may be resilient at some periods but not others. For example, a child from a troubled family may become a good reader despite a crowded classroom with an ineffective teacher (resilience) but as an adult be unable to establish a satisfying marriage.
- Resilience is not the absence of pathology but a *positive adaptation* to stress. For example, a rejected child is not considered resilient merely because she is not depressed. However, if rejection by her classmates leads her to establish a close relationship with someone else, perhaps a grandparent or a younger child, she is resilient.
- The adversity must be *significant.* Some stresses are benign (including some that were once thought to be harmful, such as maternal employment), some are minor (large class size, poor vision), and some are major (victimization by peers, neglect by parents).

To determine the likely impact of a particular stress on a child, three questions must be answered: How many stresses are experienced? Is daily life affected? What does the child think about it?

Stressors: How Many and How Often?

No stressor inevitably causes harm by itself. Any stress can be overwhelming if it is added to other burdens, even mild ones that might be called "daily hassles" (Durlak, 1998; Shaw et al., 1994). Stresses are cumulative: Ongoing hassles wear down coping ability. Each stress makes others more likely and more harmful (Fergusson & Horwood, 2003; Hammen, 2003).

One example is the noise of airplanes overhead. If a child lives near an airport, that stress happens several times a day, but for just a minute at a time. A study of 2,844 children living near three major airports found that the noise impaired the ability of some of them to learn to read (Stansfeld et al., 2005).

Awareness of the impact of cumulative stress helps adults understand that some aspects of life are more stressful to children than to adults. As we have seen, changing residences is particularly hard for school-age children (who have a special need for continuity); yet each year, about 20 percent of all children move from one home to another, a rate three times that of adults over age 50 (U.S. Bureau of the Census, 2004). Even if the move is to a better neighborhood, school-age children may be upset because their friends are not within walking distance of their new homes. If they change schools and subcultures, the stress is obviously greater.

An example of this comes from Japan, where companies routinely transfer employees for several years to increase their experience and to strengthen the cohesiveness of the company. If the employee is a father, almost half the time his family moves with him; the rest move alone and visit home. Researchers studied the children of such families, expecting to find that daily contact with fathers benefits the children. However, the school-age children benefited more from staying put, even when fathers were absent (Tanaka & Nakazawa, 2005). The mothers in such families were far more stressed than the children, illustrating again that the same event may be experienced in different ways by different people.

Worldwide, children move more often as family income falls, which multiplies the stress. Hardest hit of all are children who are homeless. In the United States, homeless children move, on average, two to three times *a year* before moving into a shelter (Buckner et al., 1999). That pattern alone overwhelms almost any child's ability to cope. Added to that are the daily stresses that life in a shelter entails, including myriad conflicts with strangers, new arrivals and departures, and erratic schooling. In developing nations, homeless children may sleep in a different place each night, reacting to such stress with emotional instability, distrust of everyone, and irrational thinking.

Daily routines are crucial in coping with stress. For example, a depressed mother may have little effect on her child if an emotionally stable and available father buffers the stress for the child or if the mother herself functions well with the child. However, she may become a source of severe stress if the child must, day after day, prepare for school, respond directly and frequently to the mother's irrational thinking, supervise and discipline younger siblings, and keep friends at a distance.

A key aspect of daily routines as contributors to resilience is whether children can develop their own friends, activities, and skills without control by the parents. After-school activities are one arena for this; participation in extracurricular programs correlates with better emotional and academic functioning (NICHD Early Child Care Research Network, 2004). As you saw in Chapter 11, being on a sports team is another such asset. To encourage resilience, community groups, religious institutions, and government programs can develop extracurricular activities for all children, from 4-H to midnight basketball, from choir to Little League. Children who choose their own activities from an array of possibilities develop industry, not, to use Erikson's term, inferiority.

The Child's Interpretation of Stress

The child's interpretation may determine whether a stress becomes overwhelming. An intriguing study of 8- to 11-year-olds measured three factors: conflict between parents, stress reactions in children, and each child's feelings of blame and vulnerability. By far the most important correlate with children's problems was not the marital discord itself but the children's feelings of self-blame or of personal threat: "The negative impact of the stressor" is reduced in "children who do not perceive that marital conflict is threatening to them and do not blame themselves" (El-Sheikh & Harger, 2001, p. 883). (See Figure 13.3.)

Another study also found that children's coping depended more on their appraisal than on the objective nature of the circumstances (Jackson & Warren, 2000). A 40-year study in Hawaii began with babies born in poverty to parents who were alcoholic or mentally ill. Amazingly, about a third of these children coped well. They avoided being overwhelmed by family stresses, choosing instead to achieve in school, to make good friends, and to find nonparental mentors. By adolescence, they had distanced themselves from their parents. As adults, they left family problems behind (many moved away) and established their own healthy relationships (Werner & Smith, 1992, 2001). Similar success in adulthood was found among boys in low-income families in Boston (Vaillant, 2002).

In middle childhood particularly, if family stresses become overwhelming, school achievement is a possible escape. An inherited easygoing temperament and a high IQ help with coping (Curtis & Cicchetti, 2003), but they are not essential. In the Hawaii study, "a realistic goal orientation, persistence, and 'learned creativity' enabled . . . a remarkable degree of personal, social, and occupational success," even for children with evident learning disabilities (Werner & Smith, 2001, p. 140). Good information-processing skills, which usually but not necessarily correlate with school achievement, allow children to avoid blaming themselves for their adversity (Maston & Coatsworth, 1998).

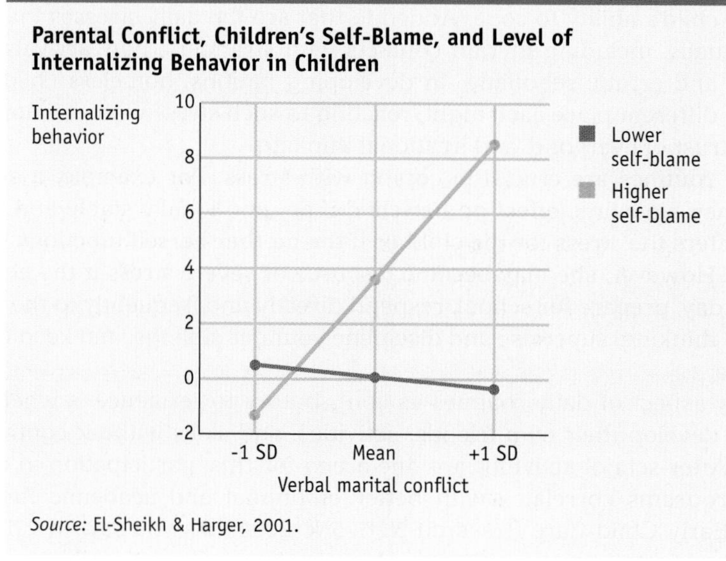

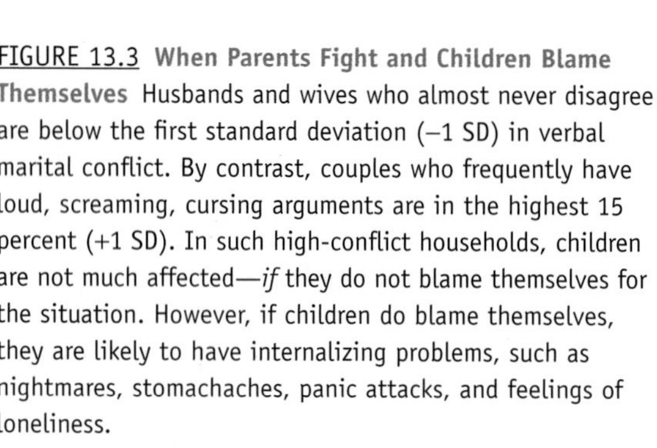
FIGURE 13.3 **When Parents Fight and Children Blame Themselves** Husbands and wives who almost never disagree are below the first standard deviation (–1 SD) in verbal marital conflict. By contrast, couples who frequently have loud, screaming, cursing arguments are in the highest 15 percent (+1 SD). In such high-conflict households, children are not much affected—*if* they do not blame themselves for the situation. However, if children do blame themselves, they are likely to have internalizing problems, such as nightmares, stomachaches, panic attacks, and feelings of loneliness.

Social Support and Religious Faith

A major factor that helps children deal with problems—one we have already touched on—is the social support they receive. A strong bond with a loving and firm parent can see a child through many difficulties. Even in war-torn or deeply impoverished neighborhoods, secure attachment to a parent who has been consistently present since infancy tends to allow children to be resilient (Masten & Coatsworth, 1998; Yates et al., 2003).

Many immigrant children do well in their new culture, academically and emotionally, despite all their stresses, if their families and schools are supportive (Fuligni, 2001). Other research also finds that parenting practices can buffer stress even for impoverished children living in very adverse conditions (Wyman et al., 1999).

BOB CHILD / AP PHOTO

Grandmother Knows Best About 20,000 grandmothers in Connecticut are caregivers for their grandchildren. This 15-year-old boy and his 17-year-old sister came to live with their grandmother in New Haven after their mother died several years ago. This type of family works best when the grandmother is relatively young and has her own house, as is the case here.

Compared with the small, home-bound lives of younger children, the expanding social world of school-age children allows new possibilities for social support. A network of supportive relatives is a better buffer than having only one close parent (Jackson & Warren, 2000). Friends help, too. For example, a child whose parents are fighting bitterly on their way to divorce may spend hours on the phone with a friend whose parents have successfully separated, or may eat, sleep, and play at another home where harmony prevails. Grandparents, unrelated adults, peers, and even pets can help children cope with stress (Borland, 1998).

Children naturally try to deal with problems, a "self-righting" characteristic that seems evident in all humans, from the toddler who stands up after a tumble to the adult who chooses to stop abusing drugs. However, even a well-equipped, well-intentioned child must connect to at least one other person. One study concludes:

> When children attempt to seek out experiences that will help them overcome adversity, it is critical that resources, in the form of supportive adults or learning opportunities, be made available to them so that their own self-righting potential can be fulfilled.
>
> *[Kim-Cohen et al., 2004, p. 664]*

An example of such self-righting potential is children's use of religion, which often provides social support via an adult from the same community. As one study explains, "The influences of religious importance and participation . . . are mediated through trusting interaction with adults, friends and parents who share similar views" (King & Furrow, 2004, p. 709).

The religious convictions of children are very diverse (Levesque, 2002), but faith itself can be psychologically protective, in part because it helps children reinterpret their experiences. Parents can provide religious guidance, but by middle childhood, some children pray and attend religious services more often than their parents do. Research shows that church involvement helps African American children in communities where social stresses and prejudice abound (Akiba & García-Coll, 2004).

Some school-age children develop their own theology, a set of beliefs in which God becomes the benevolent, protective parent who is missing from their daily life. One boy from an impoverished, polluted, violent neighborhood—New York City's South Bronx—wrote:

> No violence will there be in heaven. There will be no guns or drugs or IRS. You won't have to pay taxes. You'll recognize all the children who have died

Especially for Religiously Observant Adults A child you know seems much more religious than his or her parents are, and the parents are upset because the child believes things that they do not. What should be done?

BILL ARON / PHOTOEDIT, INC.

Become Like a Child Although the particulars vary a great deal, school-age children's impulses toward industriousness, stability, and dedication place them among the most devout members of every religious faith.

> when they were little. Jesus will be good to them and play with them. At night he'll come and visit at your house. God will be fond of you.
>
> *[quoted in Kozol, 1991]*

In many ways, children's personalized set of beliefs helps them structure life and deal with their worldly problems (Hyde, 1990; Richards et al., 2003). An 8-year-old girl who, in the 1960s, was one of the first African American children to enter a previously all-White school remembers walking past a mob of adults yelling insults:

> I was alone, and those people were screaming, and suddenly I saw God smiling, and I smiled. A woman was standing there, and she shouted at me, "Hey you little nigger, what are you smiling at?" I looked right up at her face, and I said "At God." Then she looked up at the sky, and then she looked at me, and she didn't call me any more names.
>
> *[quoted in Coles, 1990]*

This quotation illustrates many aspects of children's coping abilities—not only faith but also self-confidence, social cognition, and effortful control, which enabled this child to cope with a major threat.

As they grow older, most children develop ways to deal with all varieties of stress, from minor hassles to major traumatic events. Obeying their self-righting impulses, children try to develop competencies. They find social supports, if not in their families then among their friends. School success, family functioning, friendship, religious faith, after-school achievements—any one of these can help a child overcome problems.

A strength-based understanding of children moves our focus from problems (e.g., divorce, bullies) to assets (e.g., family harmony, social understanding). Thus, when parents are not overwhelmed by their poverty, children will not be, either. Similarly, good social skills and information-processing ability will protect a child from becoming a bully or a victim. In many ways, schoolchildren seek growth, understanding, competence, friends, and independence, and all these help them cope with the problems they inevitably encounter.

At every age, the characteristics of the developing child interact with past developmental history and current conditions to produce either a well-functioning, benevolent person or the opposite (Deater-Deckard et al, 1998; Leeuwen et al., 2004; Prinzie et al., 2003). For adults, a developmental understanding of middle childhood celebrates children's inner strengths while protecting them from the many hazards that threaten. Children cope, if they can; adults make coping possible.

RESPONSE FOR RELIGIOUSLY OBSERVANT ADULTS (from page 423): Because religious beliefs are often helpful to children, because respect for family is emphasized by virtually all religions, and because maturation usually makes people more tolerant, it may be best to let the child develop his or her own beliefs without interference. Of course, parents should set a good example and protect children from harm, no matter what the source.

SUMMING UP

A quotation from two experts serves to summarize our discussion of coping and overcoming:

> Successful children remind us that children grow up in multiple contexts—in families, schools, peer groups, baseball teams, religious organizations, and many other groups—and each context is a potential source of protective factors as well as risks. These children demonstrate that children are protected not only by the self-righting nature of development, but also by the actions of adults, by their own actions, by the nurturing of their assets, by opportunities to succeed, and by the experience of success. The behavior of adults often plays a critical role in children's risks, resources, opportunities, and resilience.
>
> *[Masten & Coatsworth, 1998, p. 216]*

Adolescence, the subject of the next three chapters, is a continuation of middle childhood as well as a radical departure from it. Stresses and strains continue to accumulate, and risk factors, including drug availability and sexual urges, become more prevalent. Fortunately, for many young people, protective resources and constructive coping also increase (Masten, 2001). Personal competencies, family support, and close friends get most people through childhood (as we saw in this chapter), adolescence, and, eventually, adulthood.

■ SUMMARY

The Peer Group

1. Peers are crucial in the social development of the school-age child. Friendships become increasingly close and influential. Usually friends provide needed companionship and allow development of social skills.

2. Popular children may be cooperative and easy to get along with or may be competitive and aggressive. Much depends on the age and culture of the children.

3. Rejected children may be neglected, aggressive, or withdrawn. All three types have difficulty interpreting the normal give-and-take of childhood. Rejection is usually temporary.

4. Bullies do long-lasting damage to themselves and to their victims. In most nations, boy bullies tend to use physical attacks and girls are more likely to use relational aggression. Boys also use relational aggression, especially as they mature.

Families and Children

5. Families influence children in many ways, as do genes and peers. The five functions of a supportive family are: to satisfy children's physical needs; to encourage them to learn; to help them develop friends; to protect their self-respect; and to provide them with a safe, stable, and harmonious home.

6. Family structures that are common today include nuclear, stepparent, blended, adoptive, one-parent, grandparent (either extended or grandparents alone), homosexual, and foster families. Generally, it seems better for children to have two parents rather than one because a parental alliance can form.

7. Income has an effect on family functioning. Poor children are at greater risk for emotional and behavioral problems because the stress of poverty often hinders effective parenting.

8. No particular family structure guarantees good—or bad—child development, although nuclear families often function well for children. Any change in family structure, including divorce and remarriage, is likely to impede child development, particularly reducing school achievement.

The Nature of the Child

9. All theories of development acknowledge that school-age children become more independent and capable in many ways. In psychoanalytic theory, Freud described latency, when psychosexual needs are quiet; Erikson emphasized industry, when children are busy mastering various tasks.

10. The interplay of self-understanding and social perception is increasingly evident during the school years. Children figure out who they are partly by comparing themselves with others. Self-esteem tends to become more closely connected to specific competence and often decreases somewhat with age.

Coping and Overcoming

11. Although most experience some stresses, school-age children tend to be resilient. Many cope well with major problems—learning disabilities, immigration, social rejection, families that are not supportive, poverty, violence.

12. In general, children benefit from social support (perhaps a best friend or a grandparent), from natural assets (intelligence, a winning personality, a special skill), and from personal strengths (religious faith, a stable early childhood). The innate drive toward competence and independence keeps most school-age children from being overwhelmed by problems.

■ KEY TERMS

social comparison (p. 396)
culture of children (p. 396)
aggressive-rejected (p. 400)
withdrawn-rejected (p. 400)
social cognition (p. 400)
effortful control (p. 400)
bullying (p. 402)
bully-victim (p. 403)
family function (p. 409)
family structure (p. 410)
nuclear family (p. 411)
extended family (p. 411)
blended family (p. 412)
latency (p. 417)
industry versus inferiority (p. 417)
resilience (p. 420)

■ KEY QUESTIONS

1. How does a school-age child develop a sense of self?

2. The culture of children strongly disapproves of tattletales. How does this affect child development?

3. Why is social rejection particularly devastating during middle childhood?

4. Describe the personal characteristics of a bully and a victim.

5. How do schools, families, and cultures contribute to the incidence of bullying?

6. What is the difference between family function and family structure?

7. What are the advantages and disadvantages of the nuclear family?

8. Why is a safe, harmonious home particularly important during middle childhood?

9. What are the six characteristics of middle childhood that have been identified by recent research?

10. Why is coping with family problems easier during middle childhood than earlier?

■ APPLICATIONS

1. Go where school-age children congregate, such as a schoolyard, a park, or a community center, and use naturalistic observation for at least half an hour. On the basis of your observations, can you describe behavior that characterizes popular, average, withdrawn, and rejected children?

2. Some surveys of adults suggest that almost everyone remembers being bullied and doing some bullying when they were children. Focusing on verbal bullying, describe at least two times when someone said a hurtful thing to you and two times when you said something hurtful to someone else. Are there any differences between the two types of situations? If so, why do such differences occur?

3. To further understand the effects of family structure, describe how your childhood would have been if your family structure were different. For example, how would life have been if you had (or had not) lived with your grandparents, if your parents had (or had not) gotten divorced, if you had (or had not) lived in a foster family. Describe how that structure would have been *better and worse* for your development than the family structure in which you actually grew up.

4. The chapter suggests that school-age children develop their own theology, distinct from the one their parents teach them. Interview a child, aged 6 to 12, asking what he or she thinks about God, sin, heaven, death, and any other religious topics you think relevant. Compare the child's responses with the formal doctrines of the faith of his or her parents.

PART IV

The School Years

BIOSOCIAL

Growth and Skills During middle childhood, children grow more slowly than they did earlier or than they will during adolescence. Brain maturation continues, particularly in the prefrontal cortex. Practice leads to automatization and selective attention, which allow smoother and quicker activity. Increased strength and lung capacity give children the endurance to improve their performance. Which specific skills a child masters depends largely on culture, gender, and inherited ability. Prevalent physical problems, such as obesity and asthma, have genetic roots and psychosocial consequences.

Special Needs Many children have special learning needs that may originate in the brain but that express themselves in educational problems. Early recognition, targeted education, and psychological support help all children, from those with autism to the much milder instance of a specific learning disability or ADHD.

COGNITIVE

Thinking Beginning at about age 7 or 8, Piaget noted, children attain concrete operational thought, including the ability to understand the logical principles of identity, reciprocity, and reversibility. As Vygotsky emphasized, children also become more open to learning from mentors, both teachers and peers. Information-processing abilities increase, including greater knowledge base, memory capacity, and metacognition.

Language Children's increasing ability to understand the structures and possibilities of language enables them to extend the range of their cognitive powers and to become more analytical in their use of vocabulary. Some children become bilingual; all children learn to switch codes when needed.

Education Formal schooling begins worldwide, with the specifics of the curriculum depending on economic and societal factors. The reading wars, the math wars, and the controversies over class size, second-language learning, and standardized testing are all evidence of the crucial importance of education during the school years.

PSYCHOSOCIAL

Peers The peer group becomes increasingly important as children become less dependent on their parents and more dependent on friends for help, loyalty, and sharing of mutual interests. Rejection and bullying become serious problems.

Parents Parents continue to influence children, especially as they exacerbate or buffer problems in school and the community. During these years, families need to meet basic needs, encourage learning, help develop self-respect, nurture friendship, and—most important—provide harmony and stability. Most one-parent, foster, or grandparent families are better than families in open conflict, but a family with two biological parents, cooperative with each other and loving to the child, is generally best. SES is also influential.

Coping with Problems Fortunately, many school-age children develop competencies and attitudes to defend against the stress that most experience. Friends, family, school, religion, and community can all be helpful, as can inborn personality traits.

PART V

Adolescence

Would you get into a truck driven by an unskilled driver? I did once, when Bethany was learning to drive. I was so focused on staying calm that not until she gave me a terrified look and said, "Mom! Help!" did I grab the wheel to avoid hitting a subway kiosk. That is a problem with adolescents: It's hard to know when to let them make their own choices and when to intervene, because they are beginning to resemble adults and yet they are still children.

Technically, adolescents are neither adults nor children, since adolescence is the period between childhood and adulthood. Developmentalists often subdivide adolescence into *tweens,* from about age 10 to 13, *the teen years,* from 13 to 18, and *emerging adulthood,* from 18 to 22 or 25.

Age is an imperfect guide, because adolescence is so variable. Some 12-year-olds can become mothers or fathers, and others are still shaped like children. And when does society consider a person an adult? One expert asks, "Why is it that a young person is not able to drive a car until 16, vote until 18, drink alcohol until 21, rent a car from a commercial agency until 25, but, in some states, can stand trial for murder at age 12 or 13?" (Dahl, 2004, p. 19). Those specific ages are from the United States, but every nation uses variable and questionable chronological demarcations.

It gets worse. Not only do individuals vary in their rate of biological maturation, and not only do societies use various benchmarks, but within each person, parts of the body mature faster than others. Brain research points toward the prefrontal cortex as the last area to mature. Adolescence may be like "starting turbo-charged engines with an unskilled driver" (Dahl, 2004, p. 17).

To put this complexity into logical sequence is the goal of the next three chapters. Your goal is to understand adolescence in all its gender, national, ethnic, and individual diversity. Fasten your seat belt; get ready to grab the wheel.

Chapter Fourteen

Adolescence: Biosocial Development

The body changes of adolescence echo those of infancy in speed and transformation, but they differ in one crucial way: Adolescents are aware. They are the fascinated, horrified, and thrilled observers of their changing bodies. Some changes are blatant—a magnet for comments and stares from strangers, such as a new shape and size. But only a self-obsessed observer would notice other changes, such as a blemish that sends a teenager to the mirror in despair. Even tiny changes matter to the person whose body is transforming.

Years ago I overheard a conversation between my teenage daughter Rachel and two of her friends. All three were past the awkward years and were emerging as stunningly beautiful young women. They talked about their bodies, each rivaling the other with complaints. One spoke of her fat stomach (what stomach? I could not see it), another despaired of her long neck (who would notice it under her silky, shoulder-length hair?), and my Rachel complained not only of her hands (one bent little finger) but about her feet!

The reality that teenagers achieve adult size and become sexually mature is no surprise to any of us who are already grown. But for all teenagers, including Rachel and her friends, heightened self-awareness makes biosocial development take on major significance, triggering reactions that are difficult for adults to comprehend. This chapter describes normal biosocial changes, including bodies growing and becoming sexual, as well as some of the risk-taking, drug-using, and sexual behaviors that older teenagers often perform—at their peril.

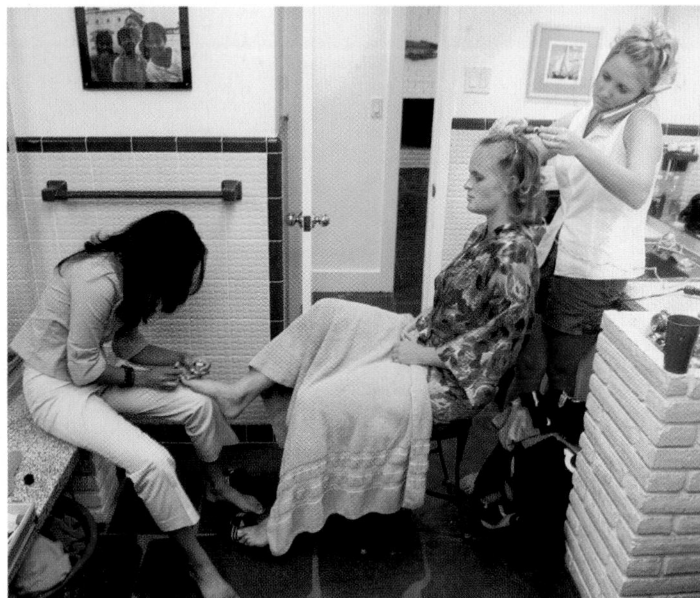

MIKE KING / AP PHOTO

That's What Friends Are For Jennifer's preparations for her prom include pedicure and hairstyle courtesy of her good friends Khushbu and Meredith. In every generation and society the world over, teenagers help their same-sex friends prepare for the display rituals involved in coming of age, but the specifics vary by cohort and culture.

Puberty Begins

Since the beginning of humankind, many thousands of years ago, children have grown into reproductive adults, a transformation that billions of people have gone through to allow the birth of billions more. The same experience occurs to every young person everywhere in the world today. Puberty may be an occasion for ritual facial scarring, for a lonely journey into the wilderness, for a huge party, for private surprise or relief. No matter what the personal or cultural reaction, puberty everywhere signals the end of childhood and the beginning of an adult life.

puberty The time between the first onrush of hormones and full adult physical development. Puberty usually lasts three to five years. Many more years are required to achieve psychosocial maturity.

menarche A girl's first menstrual period, signaling that she has begun ovulation. Pregnancy is biologically possible, but ovulation and menstruation are often irregular for years after menarche.

spermarche A boy's first ejaculation of sperm. Erections can occur as early as infancy, but ejaculation signals sperm production. Spermarche occurs during sleep (in a "wet dream") or via direct stimulation.

Puberty refers to the period of rapid physical growth and sexual maturation that ends childhood, eventually producing a person of adult size, shape, and sexual potential. The forces of puberty are unleashed by a cascade of hormones that trigger the external signs of emerging adulthood.

Although the age at which puberty begins varies substantially, the sequence is usually the same (see Table 14.1). For girls, the sequence of visible changes is breast growth, initial pubic hair, peak growth spurt, widening of the hips, the first menstrual period **(menarche)**, completion of pubic-hair growth, and final breast development. Menarche normally occurs between ages 10 and 14; age 12.8 is the current average among well-nourished girls worldwide (Malina et al., 2004).

For boys, the sequence of visible physical changes is growth of the testes, initial pubic hair, growth of the penis, first ejaculation of seminal fluid **(spermarche)**, facial hair, peak growth spurt, voice deepening, and completion of pubic-hair growth (Biro et al., 2001; Herman-Giddens et al., 2001). The age range for spermarche is from 10 to 16. The modal age of spermarche is just under 13, the same as for menarche. The terms *menarche* and *spermarche* signify the first release of gametes (ova and sperm).

TABLE 14.1 **AT ABOUT THIS TIME: The Sequence of Puberty**

Girls	Approximate Average Age*	Boys
Ovaries increase production of estrogen and progesterone†	9	
Uterus and vagina begin to grow larger	9½	Testes increase production of testosterone†
Breast "bud" stage	10	Testes and scrotum grow larger
Pubic hair begins to appear; weight spurt begins	11	
Peak height spurt	11½	Pubic hair begins to appear
Peak muscle and organ growth (also, hips become noticeably wider)	12	Penis growth begins
Menarche (first menstrual period)	12½	Spermarche (first ejaculation); weight spurt begins
First ovulation	13	Peak height spurt
Voice lowers	14	Peak muscle and organ growth (also, shoulders become noticeably broader)
Final pubic-hair pattern	15	Voice lowers; visible facial hair
Full breast growth	16	
	18	Final pubic-hair pattern

*Average ages are rough approximations, with many perfectly normal, healthy adolescents as much as three years ahead of or behind these ages.

†Estrogen, progesterone, and testosterone are hormones that influence sexual characteristics, including reproductive function. All three are also provided, in small amounts, by the adrenal glands in both sexes. Major production, however, occurs in the gonads, with marked male–female differences.

Typically, physical growth and maturation are complete three or four years after the first signs appear, although some individuals add height and most gain more fat and muscle in the late teens or early 20s. Thus far we have noted visible changes of puberty, but the veiled changes in hormone levels and brain networks are crucial.

Hormones

Invisible changes are intriguing in part because they can be blamed for almost everything an adolescent does. A few decades ago, no one knew that hormones existed, and there is still much to be learned about them. What is known, however, is that hormones affect every aspect of the brain and body and that their unseen rise occurs years before the visible signs of puberty appear.

From Brain to Body

A **hormone** is an organic chemical substance that is produced by one body tissue and conveyed via the bloodstream to another to affect growth, metabolism, or some other physiological function. There are dozens of human hormones, and they affect hunger, sleep, moods, stress, sexual desire, and many other human activities. At least 23 hormones regulate human growth and maturation (Malina et al., 2004).

Increases of certain hormones begin a few months or years before puberty does (Reiter & Lee, 2001). Compared with the increasing levels of sex hormones in the bloodstream, the visible signs of puberty—such as those first straggly pubic hairs—are "a late event" (Cameron, 2004, p. 116).

You learned in Chapter 8 that production of many hormones is regulated deep in the brain, in the hypothalamus. A biochemical signal from the hypothalamus is sent to another brain structure, the **pituitary gland.** The pituitary produces hormones that stimulate the **adrenal glands,** which are small glands located above the kidneys at either side of the lower back. The adrenal glands produce more hormones, which themselves signal other parts of the body and brain to produce more hormones. This is the **HPA axis** (hypothalamus-pituitary-adrenal) that you first read about in Chapter 8 (look again at Figure 8.4). Many hormones follow the HPA axis, including hormones that regulate stress, growth, sleep, appetite, and sexual excitement. The major changes of puberty are caused by hormones that follow this route from the brain to the body (see Figure 14.1).

During puberty, the pituitary not only stimulates the adrenal glands but also activates the **gonads,** or sex glands (the ovaries in females and the testes, or testicles, in males). Because the brain directly influences the gonads, they are the first parts of the body to enlarge at puberty and their hormones, in turn, affect all the other body parts.

hormone An organic chemical substance that is produced by one body tissue and conveyed via the bloodstream to another to affect some physiological function. Various hormones influence thoughts, urges, emotions, and behavior.

pituitary gland A gland that, in response to a signal from the hypothalamus, produces many hormones, including those that regulate growth and control other glands, among them the adrenal and sex glands.

adrenal glands Two glands, located above the kidneys, that produce hormones (including the "stress hormones" epinephrine [adrenaline] and norepinephrine).

HPA axis The hypothalamus-pituitary-adrenal axis, a route followed by many kinds of hormones to trigger the changes of puberty and to regulate stress, growth, sleep, appetite, sexual excitement, and various other bodily changes.

gonads The paired sex glands (ovaries in females, testicles in males). The gonads produce hormones and gametes.

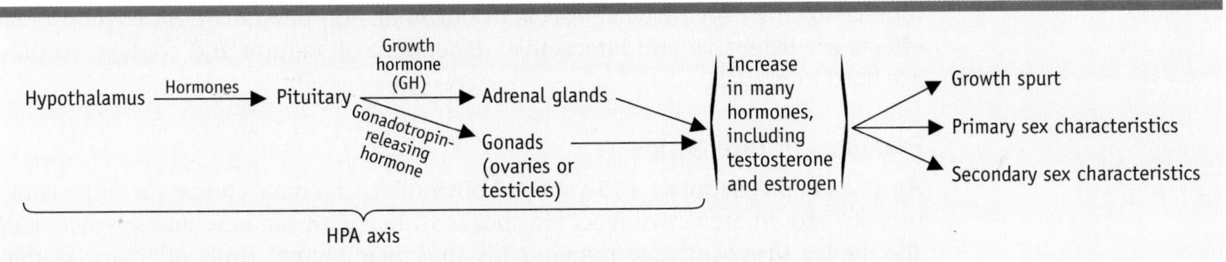

FIGURE 14.1 **Biological Sequence of Puberty** Puberty begins with a hormonal signal from the hypothalamus to the pituitary gland. The pituitary, in turn, signals the adrenal glands and the ovaries or testes to produce more of their hormones.

estradiol A sex hormone, considered the chief estrogen. Females produce far more estradiol than males do.

testosterone A sex hormone, the best known of the androgens (male hormones); secreted in far greater amounts by males than by females.

The gonads produce hormones in greater quantity than the adrenal glands do. The gonads also produce gametes (sperm and ova), soon followed by spermarche or menarche. In girls, the ovaries' enlargement is completely invisible. In boys, the scrotum (the pouch that encases the testicles) increases in size and becomes lighter in color as one of the first apparent signs of puberty.

One hormone in particular, GnRH (gonadotropin-releasing hormone), causes the gonads to dramatically increase their production of sex hormones, chiefly **estradiol** in girls and **testosterone** in boys. Estrogens (including estradiol) are considered female hormones and androgens (including testosterone) are considered male hormones, but the adrenal glands in both sexes produce both. It is the increased *rate* of production in the gonads that is sex-specific. Testosterone actually decreases during childhood, and then skyrockets in adolescent boys, up to 18 times the level at age 10. For girls, estrodiol is level during childhood and then increases by about 8 times the earlier level (Malina et al., 2004).

Sudden Emotions

Many adults, when they are puzzled or exasperated by something a teenager does, blame "raging hormones," as if those unseen but powerful chemicals cause every unexpected behavior—especially an angry outburst, a sudden sadness, or a romantic passion. But hormones do not deserve all the blame.

It is true that conflict, moodiness, and sexual urges rise during adolescence (Arnett, 1999) and that hormones are connected to all these. But puberty happens in a psychosocial context, and this context profoundly influences the impact of hormones (Walker, 2002). Since body, brain, and society are always part of human behavior, it is not easy to disentangle the causes of adolescent behavior.

We know that hormones have some direct effects (Savin-Williams & Diamond, 2004; Susman, 1997; Weisfeld, 1999).

- Testosterone precedes rapid arousal of emotions, especially anger.
- Changing hormones correlate with quick shifts in emotional extremes.
- For many boys, hormones lead to thoughts about sex and to masturbation.
- For many girls, hormones increase happiness in the middle of the menstrual cycle and sadness or anger (in a pattern called PMS, or premenstrual syndrome) at the end.

These hormonal effects are evident in adults as well, but with less drama. During puberty, hormones are more erratic and powerful and less familiar and controllable (Susman & Rogol, 2004). One reason may be the immaturity of the brain (discussed later); another may be novelty (it is hard to control emotions never experienced before); and yet another is that hormone levels increase in bursts (pulsating on and off) rather than steadily, which means adolescents really do experience a "rush" of emotion, followed by a letdown (Cameron, 2004).

Much of the research on the effects of hormones and puberty comes from research on rats, which are good models for biological effects but obviously poor models for the psychosocial effects of hormones on people. These psychosocial effects are extensive and interactive, dependent on culture and context, so they are hard to predict.

Examples of Interaction

As an example, suppose a 15-year-old boy notices a female classmate with visible breasts and an attractive face. He speaks to her with his new manly voice, and she smiles provocatively, noticing his muscular shape. Both of them, at that point, can feel some physical arousal in their genitals and may even dare the thrill of touching each other's hands. What might happen next? One possibility is that he telephones her, but her parents refuse to let her speak to him. Both of them might then explode in anger.

Did hormones cause those thrills or explosions? To conclude that hormones alone caused this sequence of events would be to ignore many other potent factors. First, the two noticed each other's appearance, not each other's hormones, and each one's appearance was the outcome of hormones that began to circulate years earlier. Second, the social setting allowed them to be classmates, and that wouldn't have happened in a single-sex school. Third, their culture (movies, books, peers) provided fantasies about sexual interaction, which meant that they dared to touch and to want further contact.

The girl's parents' disapproval was probably affected by their awareness of her biological maturation, and the adolescents' anger was the consequence of their thoughts about the proper role of parents as well as of their own frustration. Such anger would be very unlikely in some other cultures, such as India (Larson et al., 2003).

As this example shows, sometimes hormones *directly* make adolescents seek sexual activity, and this arouses excitement, pleasure, and frustration. But more frequently, moods are the result of the interaction between visible sexual maturation—new breasts, beards, and body shape—and the reaction of other people to these outward signs. These reactions, not just the hormones, evoke emotions and responses. This follows from current research and speculation in neuroscience: Human thoughts and emotions not only result from but also cause physiological and neurological processes (Damasio, 2003).

This can be seen in simpler examples as well. If a 13-year-old girl hears a lewd remark, she might feel a surge of anger, fear, or embarrassment, but it is the remark about her developing body, not about her hormones, that triggers her emotions. Likewise, the desire of a 13-year-old boy who fantasizes in the shower may have been triggered by hormones, but his rush of pride, shame, and excitement is not directly due to testosterone.

Scientific evidence for the complexity of hormonal effects came from a study of adolescents who showed no signs of puberty two years after the usual age of onset (Schwab et al., 2001). Doctors prescribed 24 months of treatment: 3 months of hormones (low, medium, or high doses of testosterone or an estrogen) alternating with 3 months of a placebo (a look-alike pill that, unknown to the participants, had no hormones). Almost no psychological effects followed immediately from the 3 months of treatment with either hormones or the placebo. However, over two years, participants' moods became more positive—a reaction to their physical development, not to hormones directly.

In this study, aggression was a notable exception to the lack of direct hormonal effect. When the pills contained *moderate* amounts of hormones, both boys and girls reported more anger. However, increased anger was *not* apparent at the highest doses of testosterone (for the boys) or estrogens (for the girls) (Susman & Rogol, 2004).

Especially for Parents of Teenagers Why would parents blame adolescent moods on hormones?

Thus, the link between hormones and emotions is not linear and direct. Although physical development often produces powerful emotional reactions and although hormonal shifts affect some emotions, the famed emotional turbulence of adolescence cannot be blamed on hormones alone. If it could, moodiness would start when hormone production does, as young as age 8 or 9, instead of when adults notice it, at about age 12 or later.

The Timing of Puberty

Hormones cascading into the bloodstream jumpstart puberty. With minor variations, the sequence is always the same. However, the age of onset varies. Anytime from age 8 to 15 is quite normal, although 10 to 13 is more typical.

This wide range of timing adds to the difficulties of puberty. It is hard for preteens to prepare without knowing what will occur when. Likewise, parents and teachers want to anticipate the pubertal changes that affect children. For many reasons, then, people want to know when puberty will begin. Based on recent research, some predictions can be made. Gender, genes, body fat, and stress all have an impact.

Gender

Among well-nourished children, at least one girl in a fifth-grade class has already developed breasts and begun to grow to adult height. Not until age 18 or so has her last male classmate sprouted facial hair and grown to man-size. These are extremes, but throughout middle school most girls are taller than the boys. This height disparity is visible in every nation and every ethnic group, the only time in the entire life span when the average female is taller than the average male.

Girls are about two years ahead of boys in height, but not in everything. Take another look at Table 14.1. Notice that the height spurt occurs about midway in a girl's pubescence (before menarche), but it is one of the later events (after spermarche) for boys (Reiter & Lee, 2001). Hormonally and sexually (for instance, age of menarche and spermarche), girls are ahead of boys by only a few months, not a few years (Malina et al., 2004).

Genes

A second major influence on the timing of puberty is genetic. Ages of menarche in mothers and daughters are strongly correlated, although historical and familial circumstances can be quite different for the two generations (Golub, 1992). Other pubertal changes, for boys as well as for girls, also follow genetic patterns. One reason for this is that genes affect body type, which itself is a factor in the onset of puberty. Even beyond that, a person's maturation is partly genetic (Towne et al., 2002).

There are some ethnic variations in the timing of puberty. In the United States, African Americans tend to reach puberty almost a year earlier than European Americans and Mexican Americans, and Asian Americans average several months later (Herman-Giddens et al., 2001; Malina et al., 2004). But remember that genetic variations between one family and another are far greater than are those between one ethnic group and another (Rosenberg et al., 2002). That means that in predicting puberty, it is wise to ignore broad ethnic background (e.g., African or Asian) and to pay attention to the child's immediate relatives.

The genetic differences noted above tend to be more apparent in developed than in developing nations. For example, youth in rural areas of India and China experience puberty later than do youth of the same ethnicity who live in urban neighborhoods. In nations that are rapidly becoming industrialized, such as Poland and Greece, urban–rural differences are observed among children of the same ethnicity. In Warsaw, for instance, puberty occurs a year earlier than in Polish villages, and in Athens puberty averages three months earlier than in the rest of Greece (Malina et. al., 2004).

Six Bodies Growing All these children are pubescent and are close in age, but each is at a different stage of puberty. Notice that the two tallest children are also the heaviest: Puberty seems to begin earlier in children with more body fat.

JEFF GREENBERG / PHOTOEDIT, INC.

Weight

A third factor that hastens adolescence is body fat. In general, stocky individuals begin puberty earlier than do those with thinner builds. Body type is partly genetic, but body fat is more immediately correlated with diet and exercise (see Chapter 11).

This factor is more obvious in girls than in boys (Vizmanos & Marti-Henneberg, 2000). According to some data, menarche does not usually occur until a girl weighs about 100 pounds (45–48 kilograms), although some experts question whether weight itself triggers menarche (Ellison, 2002). Females who have little body fat (either naturally or because they are malnourished or exercise many hours a day) reach menarche later and experience menstruation less regularly than the average girl. As you will see later, one symptom of the extreme thinness of anorexia nervosa is cessation of menstruation.

In both sexes, chronic malnutrition limits fat and therefore delays puberty. That is the probable explanation for the historical facts that in sixteenth-century Europe puberty was as late as age 17 and a century ago menarche began at 15 in Norway, Sweden, and Finland (Tanner, 1990).

Late puberty is often considered evidence of a poor childhood diet, but it could be seen the other way, with early puberty as evidence of an unhealthy diet among contemporary youth. Is it healthier for a nation to have many adolescents overweight or underweight, experiencing reproductive maturity at age 11 or 18?

Stress

A fourth influence on puberty, recently recognized, is stress. For many years biochemists have noticed that, throughout life, stress affects hormone production (Sanchez et al., 2001). The production of certain hormones, especially cortisol but also those that govern the sexual-reproductive system, is directly connected to the level of stress hormones produced via the HPA axis.

Because of increased stress, some young women experience irregular menstruation when they leave home for college or trips abroad. In adults, stress decreases the number of viable sperm and mature ova. In fact, severe stress is one cause of spontaneous abortions (miscarriages), premature births, and even birth defects. Generally, stress impedes reproduction at every step of the process (Cameron, 2004).

These facts led to the hypothesis that stress affects pubertal hormones. At first, it seemed logical that stress would slow down gonadal hormones, but the opposite seems more likely. For instance, puberty arrives earlier, on average, when children's parents are divorced or when their neighborhood is rundown (Herman-Giddens et al., 2001; Hulanicka, 1999; Moffitt et al., 1992). Suggestive evidence that puberty begins earlier when stress is high comes from several nations, including Great Britain, Australia, Poland, and the United States (Belsky et al., 1991; Kim & Smith, 1998).

You read that puberty occurs earlier in cities than in rural areas in every nation that records such data (Malina et al., 2004). If city life is more stressful for children than country life, this would corroborate the stress hypothesis.

More corroboration was provided by a study that found that menarche came earlier if there were conflicted relationships within the family and if an unrelated man (stepfather or mother's boyfriend) lived in the home (Ellis & Garber, 2000). These researchers took into account genetic and body-fat effects and still found that the longer a girl lived with a man who had no biological relationship to her, the younger she was at menarche.

Animal research points in the same direction. Stressed mice, rats, and opossums become pregnant at younger ages than do less stressed members of their species (Warshofsky, 1999). Further, female mice reach puberty earlier if, as infants, they were raised with unrelated adult male mice (Caretta et al., 1995). Anecdotally, many teenage girls experience menarche when they are stressed, especially if they are away from home.

Why would stress *increase* the hormones that start puberty? Wouldn't conflicted families benefit more if their teenagers still looked and acted like children and were unable to become parents until age 20 or so? This would be especially

Response for Parents of Teenagers (from page 435): If something causes adolescents to shout "I hate you," to slam doors, or to cry inconsolably, parents may decide that hormones are the problem. This makes it easy to disclaim personal responsibility for the teenager's anger. However, research on stress and hormones suggests that this comforting attribution is too simplistic.

beneficial for stepfather families: Later puberty would reduce stepfather–stepdaughter sexual attraction and stepfather–stepson sexual rivalry. That does not seem to be what happens. One explanation for this seemingly counterproductive link comes from evolutionary theory:

> Over the course of our natural selective history, ancestral females growing up in adverse family environments may have reliably increased their reproductive success by accelerating physical maturation and beginning sexual activity and reproduction at a relatively early age.
>
> *[Ellis & Garber, 2000, p. 486]*

In other words, in past stressful times, adolescent parents would at least replace themselves before they died, and so family genes would continue. Early puberty was beneficial, and genes that adapted to stress by initiating reproduction became prevalent in the human genome. Although in the twenty-first century teenage sexual urges and pregnancy lead to social disruption rather than social survival, this was not true in earlier times.

Too Early, Too Late

Although social scientists are intrigued with historical data showing that menarche once began years later and although parents may wish their children matured when their great-grandparents did, few of today's adolescents care about puberty in past centuries. However, they do care when they themselves experience puberty. They do not want to be much earlier or later than their friends, for good reason.

Think about the early-maturing girl. If she has visible breasts in the fifth grade, the boys will tease her; they are awed by the newly sexual creature in their midst. She must fit her womanly body into a school chair designed for younger children, and she often tries to hide her breasts in large T-shirts and bulky sweaters. Given those circumstances, it is no wonder that early-maturing girls tend to have lower self-esteem, more depression, and poorer body image than later-maturing girls (Compian et al., 2004; Siegel et al., 1999).

To further complicate the problem, some early-maturing girls have boyfriends several years older, who find them attractive because they are childlike yet physically developed. They themselves are sexually interested, in response to the same hormones that triggered their puberty. Girls with older boyfriends tend to drink alcohol, smoke cigarettes, and become sexually active before other girls their age (Brooks-Gunn, 1991). They are "isolated from their on-time-maturing peers [and] tend to associate with older adolescents. This increases their emotional distress" (Ge et al., 2003, p. 437).

Early-maturing boys may also have difficulty, in part because they are more likely to join peer groups that rebel against laws and traditions. Of course, much depends on the context. Early-maturing boys who live in stressful urban neighborhoods (with high rates of poverty, unemployment, drug use, and violent crime, for instance) and who have unusually strict parents are particularly likely to have friends who break the law (Ge et al., 2003).

The problems of early-maturing boys are more apparent now than in earlier times. In fact, research on boys born around 1930 who matured early found that they were more likely to be leaders in high school and beyond (Jones, 1965). Today, however, if early puberty leads to romantic relationships, the result is often stress and depression in both sexes (Brown, 2004). Teenage motherhood or fatherhood correlates with emotional problems of all kinds among today's youth.

Late puberty may also be difficult, especially for boys in schools where athletes are the local stars. In a study of one multiethnic high school, the "quiet Asian boys" were teased because they were shorter and thinner than their classmates, much to their dismay (Lei, 2003). Adolescents everywhere seek friends who are on the same pubertal schedule as they are, a preference that may disrupt long-standing friendships as well as cause trouble when younger preteens associate with older teens.

SUMMING UP

The visible signs of puberty usually begin between the ages of 10 and 13 in response to a hormonal trigger deep within the brain. Moving along the HPA axis from the hypothalamus to the pituitary to the adrenal and sex glands, hormones affect the emotions as well as the physique. Adolescent emotions are often the result of social and cultural reactions to visible body changes rather than the direct result of hormones in the bloodstream.

Many factors, including gender, genes, and body fat, determine when the hormonal cascade begins. Suggestive evidence from international correlations, animal research, and stepfamilies suggests that a fourth factor, stress, may induce puberty earlier than it otherwise would begin. In every culture, puberty that begins markedly earlier (especially for girls) or later (especially for boys) than it does among one's peers is problematic.

The Transformations of Puberty

Every part of the body changes during puberty because hormones affect every cell. For simplicity, the transformation from a child into an adult is often divided into two parts, growth and sexuality. But in reality, both usually occur at about the same time.

Suppose 10-year-olds suddenly notice darker and thicker hair growing on their legs. This is primarily a growth change, but interpretation is primarily sexual. If the child is a girl, she will probably start to shave her legs, drawing blood several times before she develops a light touch. If the child is a boy, he will not shave his legs. In fact, he may anticipate, with pleasure, hair on his upper lip, his chin, and especially his chest. Thus, a child's reaction is gender-specific, even though the hair itself is not.

The part introduction that precedes this chapter explained the complex challenge of describing the sequence of multilevel, overlapping, adolescent changes. Separating growth from sexual changes is one example of this complication. Nonetheless, this division may aid comprehension.

Bigger and Stronger

In late childhood and early adolescence, hormones cause a major **growth spurt**—a sudden, uneven, and somewhat unpredictable jump in the size of almost every part of the body. Growth proceeds from the extremities to the core (the opposite of the proximal-distal growth of the prenatal and infant growth periods). Fingers and toes lengthen before hands and feet, hands and feet before arms and legs, arms and legs before the torso.

growth spurt The relatively sudden and rapid physical growth that occurs during puberty. Each body part increases in size on a schedule: Weight usually precedes height, and the limbs precede the torso.

Because the torso is the last body part to grow, many pubescent children are temporarily big-footed, long-legged, and short-waisted, appearing to be "all legs and arms" (Hofmann, 1997, p. 12). If young teenagers complain that their jeans don't fit, they are probably correct, even if those same jeans did fit their shorter-waisted, thinner body when their parents paid for them a month before. Parents had a warning, if they were paying attention, when they began buying shoes for their children in adult sizes.

As the bones lengthen and harden (changes visible on an X-ray), children eat more and gain weight, to provide energy for their growth spurt. In fact, parents typically notice that their children are cleaning their plates, emptying the refrigerator, and straining the seams of their clothes before they notice that their children are also growing taller.

FIGURE 14.2 **Big Difference** All children experience an increase in muscles during puberty, but gender differences are much more apparent in some gross motor skills than others. For instance, upper-arm strength increases dramatically only in boys.

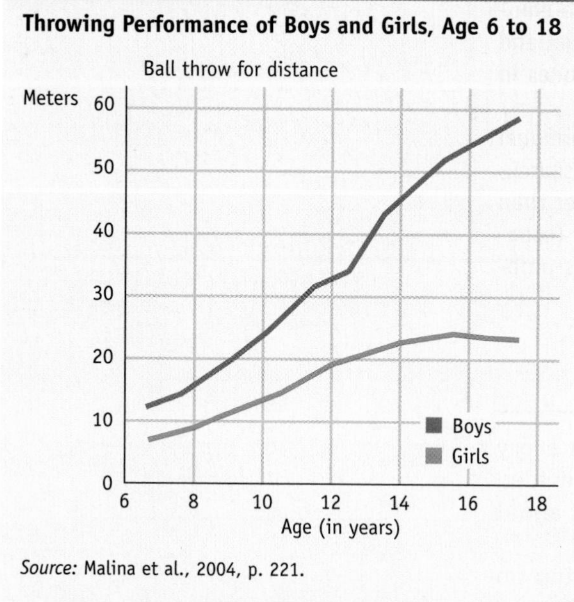

For this reason, when middle childhood ends, weight increases. Exactly when, where, and how much weight is gained depends partly on heredity, partly on diet and exercise, and partly on gender. Females gain more fat overall. Eventually about one-fourth of their body weight is fat, almost double the average for males (Daniluk, 1998). Much of the typical boys' weight gain is muscle, which is heavier than fat.

One of the questions girls ask themselves is why their brothers grow stronger but their own growth spurt makes them fatter; this difference seems unfair in modern society, with its preference for female thinness. The reason is evolutionary: Our foremothers hoped for more fat because that made them appear more fertile and womanly, ready for motherhood. For reasons associated with reproduction, female body fat accumulates on the hips and breasts. Male bodies may be designed for earlier times as well, when young adult males had to use arm muscles to fight beasts or rivals and to bring food home for their families (Ellison, 2001).

A height spurt follows the weight spurt, burning up some fat and redistributing the rest. About a year or two after that is the peak age of muscle increase (Hofmann, 1997). As a consequence, the pudginess and clumsiness typical of early puberty generally disappear a few years later. Overall, muscle strength in boys doubles, especially in the arms (Malina et al. 2004). In fact, an 18-year-boy can throw a ball four times farther than an 8-year-old can (see Figure 14.2). Ball throwing shows a notable sex difference, but leg muscles, and therefore running speed, do not show much sex difference (see Figure 14.3).

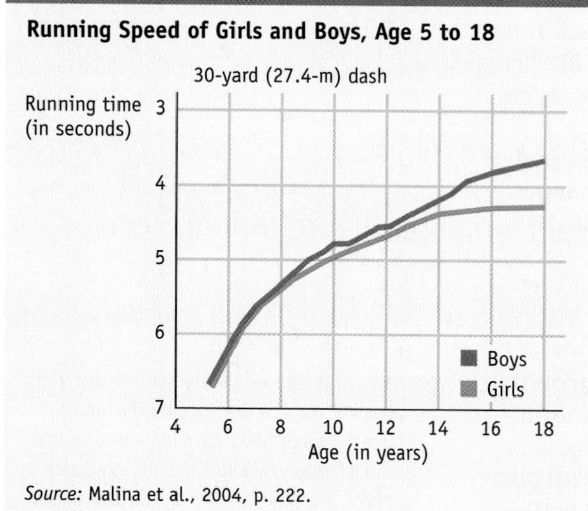

FIGURE 14.3 **Little Difference** Both sexes develop longer and stronger legs during puberty.

? OBSERVATIONAL QUIZ (see answer, page 442): At what age does the rate of increase in the average boy's muscle strength accelerate?

Other Body Changes

One reason that the sexes are more similar than different in their growth spurt is that, for both, internal organs grow not only in size but also in efficiency. Lungs triple in weight, and adolescents breathe more deeply and slowly than children (in both sexes, 10-year-olds breathe about 22 times a minute, while 18-year-olds breathe about 17 times—useful to know if you're doing CPR) (Malina et al., 2004). The heart doubles in size as the pulse decreases; the sitting heartbeat slows more than 10 percent, from about 85 to 75 beats per minute, as the total volume of blood increases (Malina et al., 2004).

These changes in the lungs and the heart increase physical endurance. Many teenagers can run for miles or dance for hours, with energy that any adult can admire. Note, however, that the more visible growth spurts of weight and height occur *before* the less visible growth spurts of muscles and internal organs.

This means that athletic coaches shouldn't be fooled by an adolescent's stature: Training and weight lifting should be tailored to an adolescent's size the previous year to spare the immature muscles and organs (Murphy, 1999). Sports injuries are the most common school accidents, and the rate increases at puberty. Poor judgment on the part of coaches, coupled with the unrealistic aspirations of the young athletes, cause physical problems that knowledge of adolescent development should prevent (Patel & Luckstead, 2000).

One organ system—the lymphoid system (which includes the tonsils and adenoids)—*decreases in size,* making teenagers less susceptible to respiratory ailments. Mild asthma, for example, often switches off at puberty (Busse & Lemanske, 2005), and teenagers have fewer colds than younger children. Another organ system—the skin—changes in marked ways, becoming oilier, sweatier, and more prone to acne.

Hair also changes. During puberty, girls and boys both notice that the hair on their heads and limbs becomes coarser and darker and that new hair grows in their armpits, on their faces, and over their sex organs. Visible facial and chest hair is sometimes considered a sign of manliness, although hairiness depends on genes, not virility. Similarly, a girl's facial and body hair reflects genes, not femininity.

LAURA DWIGHT

Does He Like What He Sees? During adolescence, all the facial features do not develop at the same rate, and the hair often becomes less manageable. If B. T. here is typical, he is not pleased with the appearance of his nose, lips, ears, or hair.

Body Rhythms

The hormones of puberty also affect the rhythms of the body (Nelson et al., 2002). Every living creature responds to a *circadian rhythm,* a cyclical biological pattern that affects reproduction (birth occurs more often in spring), weight gain (more in winter), and much more, including, in some species, migration and hibernation. As one example, the levels of the enzyme monoamine oxidase (MAO), which makes people more careful, vary with life stage and time of year and tends to be particularly low in adolescent males, many of whom take what adults regard as foolish risks (Nell, 2002).

One aspect of the circadian rhythm is the *diurnal (daily) cycle,* the body's response to day and night. Sleep, hunger, body temperature, blood pressure, and elimination all fluctuate according to the time of day. The levels of many hormones and nutrients change hour by hour, allowing people to wake in the morning (usually) and to tire by the end of the day, get hungry at certain points, and feel very alert at other times. Mood also fluctuates: Some people wake up cheery and others cranky, both switching moods by nightfall.

Each person's diurnal rhythm is unique, but all living creatures have a day–night cycle. This became apparent when volunteers were placed in a clockless, windowless room for several weeks and told to eat and sleep whenever they wished. Their activity patterns and body chemicals tended to rise and fall on a 24-hour pattern (Webb, 1994). The disruption of this pattern is the reason jet lag is more of a problem for people who fly from east to west, thereby changing time zones, than for those who fly the same distance from north to south within the same time zone.

Naps—needed by young children and common among the elderly—are also affected by circadian rhythms. For instance, people cannot save up sleep by sleeping for 20 hours a day (including long naps) for three days of a week and not at all for the next four days, even though the total number of hours (60) is virtually the same as 7 days of 8½-hour nights. Body chemicals, melatonin among them, rise and fall each day, making it very difficult to fall asleep at some times but very hard to stay awake at other times (Carskadon, 2002a). Newborns and the elderly sometimes fall asleep while everyone around them is talking.

Puberty alters circadian and diurnal rhythms. Many teenagers find that their sleep–wake patterns naturally follow a different schedule from those of other family members (Carskadon et al., 2004). Normal hormonal shifts and increases (especially in the growth hormones) cause a "phase delay" in sleeping: Many teens are wide awake at midnight but half-asleep all morning.

Typically, adolescents get too little sleep, a problem worsened by television, iPods, and Internet chat rooms as well as by school scheduling. Evidence for this is the fact that teenagers rarely wake up spontaneously (see Figure 14.4) and often "sleep in" on weekends (Andrade & Menna-Barreto, 2002). Girls are particularly likely to be sleep-deprived, which decreases their grades and happiness (Fredriksen et al., 2004).

Sleep deprivation is associated with many difficulties. For instance, adolescent drivers are more likely to fall asleep at the wheel than are older drivers;

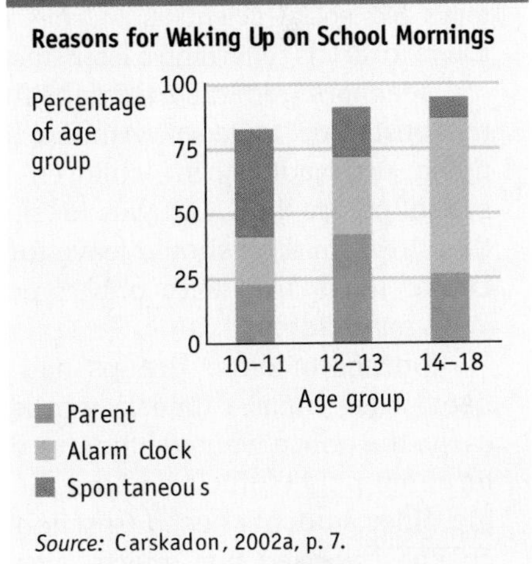

FIGURE 14.4 **Sleep Deprivation** Humans naturally wake up once they have had enough sleep. Few high school students wake up spontaneously, and many sleep later on weekends than on schooldays; these facts suggest that most teenagers need more sleep. Depression and irritability correlate with insufficient sleep.

adolescents have more disturbed sleep patterns (probably because they do not have regular sleep schedules); and sleep-starved teens have more mood disorders (depression, conduct disorder, anxiety) than do other age groups (Carskadon, 2002b; Fredriksen et al., 2004; Roberts et al., 2002).

Given that adolescents are sleep-deprived, why do most high schools require them to be in class by 8:00 A.M. or earlier? Researchers had no idea that puberty affected sleep until about a decade ago, and the implications are not yet understood by many school administrators. Consequently, in many countries, school schedules set a century ago are still in place. In 1900, 90 percent of teenagers lived on farms. Many had to wake up at dawn to do chores, such as milking the cows, and then had to leave school in the early afternoon for more chores before dark. They also had to spend long summers working in the fields. To accommodate these family obligations of yesteryear, millions of contemporary teenagers are bewildered by calculus and chemistry at 8:00 A.M. and are bored by long summer vacations (Barber et al., 1998).

The logic of the new evidence clashes with long-standing cultural habits, as the following feature explains.

! Answer to Observational Quiz (from page 440): About age 13. This is most obvious in ball throwing (see Figure 14.2), but it is also apparent in the 30-yard dash.

A Case to Study

The Early Bird Is a Grown-Up

The data on adolescent sleep confirm that biology designs teenage bodies to be wakeful at night and sleepy in the morning. But the culture endorses morning wakening, a value reflected in the sayings "The early bird catches the worm" and "Early to bed, early to rise, makes a man healthy, wealthy, and wise." When adults decide that the school day should start by 8:00 A.M., they are reflecting culture and memory, not being deliberately destructive.

One school system did heed the research (Wahlstrom, 2002). In Minnesota, biological data on adolescent sleep patterns led social scientists to solicit opinions in 17 public school districts regarding a later start for the high school day.

Teachers generally thought that early morning was the best time to learn. Among parents, 42 percent of those with adolescent children thought that starting school before 8:00 A.M. was ideal. In fact, 20 percent felt that their children should leave for school at 7:15 A.M. or earlier (compared with only 1 percent of parents with younger children).

Dozens of other groups had opinions. Bus drivers hated rush hour; cafeteria workers liked getting home early; the police wanted students off the streets in late afternoon; public officials noted the money saved by having older students bused to school before younger ones; coaches worried that sports events might end too late; employers wondered how they would staff the afternoon shift; community program directors thought that a change might make scheduling (especially use of the gym) more difficult (Wahlstrom, 2002).

Despite the naysayers, one of those 17 school districts, Edina (a town of 47,500 near Minneapolis), decided to experiment. Edina's public high school changed to an 8:30 A.M. start time (from 7:25) and a 3:10 P.M. closing time (from 2:05). After a year, most (93 percent) of the parents and virtually all of the students approved of the change. One student said, "I have only fallen asleep in school once this whole year, and last year I fell asleep about three times a week" (quoted in Wahlstrom, 2002, p. 190). Other improvements surprised the teachers, administrators, and even the school nurse: fewer absent, late, disruptive, or sick students, and higher grades overall.

Edina's success made other Minnesota school districts rethink their schedules. Minneapolis moved the high school start time from 7:15 to 8:40 A.M. Again, attendance improved, as did graduation rate.

In most school districts, the naysayers prevailed. For instance, a few articulate students were quoted in local news stories:

> These students speak of a later start time as having a negative impact upon being selected for the "best" colleges when they will have fewer activities to list on their résumés. Comments such as those hit home with their parents as well as causing a groundswell of opposition to making the change—an opposition . . . based on supposition and speculation.
>
> *[Wahlstrom, 2002, p. 195]*

Most administrators and school board members decided to keep an early start time for their high schools. The researchers recognized that "without a strategic approach, the forces to maintain the status quo in the schools will prevail" (Wahlstrom, 2002, p. 195).

Sexual Maturation

The growth spurt turns children into adults. Another set of changes transform boys into men and girls into women. Puberty not only makes adolescents look more mature; they *are* more mature, at least sexually. They become capable of reproduction. Both primary and secondary sex characteristics signal this change.

Sexual Bodies

Primary sex characteristics are those parts of the body that are directly involved in conception and pregnancy. During puberty, every primary sex organ (the vagina, the uterus, the penis, the testes) becomes much larger.

primary sex characteristics The parts of the body that are directly involved in reproduction, including the vagina, uterus, ovaries, testicles, and penis.

In girls, the ovaries and the uterus grow and the vaginal lining thickens even before any outward signs of puberty appear. Those internal organs continue to mature throughout puberty. In boys, the testes grow and, about a year later, the penis lengthens, while the scrotum enlarges and becomes pendulous.

The sexual signs, followed by menarche and spermarche, do not indicate peak reproductive potential. The prime reproductive years, biologically, occur later, during emerging adulthood. However, parenthood is possible once the primary sexual organs begin to function.

Along with maturation of the reproductive organs (primary sex characteristics) come changes in **secondary sex characteristics.** These are bodily features that do not directly affect fertility (the reason they are called secondary) but that do signify sexual development.

secondary sex characteristics Physical traits that are not directly involved in reproduction but that indicate sexual maturity, such as a man's beard and a woman's breasts.

One obvious secondary sexual characteristic is body shape, which is virtually unisex in childhood but diverges in adolescence. At puberty, males grow taller than females (by 5 inches, on average) and become wider at the shoulders. Girls become wider below the waist, particularly at the pelvis, to prepare for pregnancy, and they develop breasts, to prepare for lactation (Ellison, 2001). Breasts and hips are often considered signs of womanhood; but neither is required for conception and thus both are secondary, not primary, sex characteristics.

In both sexes the diameter of the areola (the dark area around the nipple) increases during puberty, and the nipples become more sensitive. To their consternation, about 65 percent of all adolescent boys experience some breast enlargement (typically in mid-puberty) (Behrman, 1992). This enlargement normally disappears by age 16.

Girls are eager for their breasts to grow but do not want them to grow too much. For most girls, "minimizer," "maximizer," "training," or "shaping" bras are wardrobe essentials. Female puberty begins and ends with breast growth, from the "bud" stage of breast growth (a slight rise) to full breast size six years later (Tanner, 1990).

Another secondary sex characteristic is the voice, which becomes lower as the lungs and larynx grow. This change is most noticeable in boys. (Even more noticeable, to the chagrin of the young adolescent male, is an occasional loss of voice control that throws his newly acquired baritone into a high squeak). Girls also develop a lower voice, which is why a throaty female voice is considered sexy. The "Adam's apple," a visible lump in the throat, becomes prominent in boys (and that's why it's named after Adam, not Eve).

The pattern of growth at the scalp line differs for the two sexes, but few people notice that. Instead, they notice gender markers in hair length and style. Consequently, adolescents spend considerable time, money, and thought on their visible hair, shaving, curling, straightening, styling, dyeing, and conditioning it.

CLEVE BRYANT / PHOTOEDIT

Male Pride Teenage boys typically feel serious pride when they first need to shave. Although facial hair is taken as a sign of masculinity, a person's hairiness is actually genetic as well as hormonal. Further evidence that the Western world's traditional racial categories have no genetic basis comes from East Asia: Many Chinese men cannot grow beards or mustaches, but most Japanese men can.

Sexual Actions

Variations in hairstyles obviously reflect cohort as well as gender. Another secondary sexual sign is sexual behavior—specifically, all the flirting, hand-holding, and touching that boys and girls engage in. This, too, reflects culture and cohort more than biology. As already explained, the various sex hormones trigger thoughts about physical intimacy, but the social context gives those sexual thoughts their form: enjoyable fantasies, shameful preoccupations, frightening impulses, or actual contact.

Consider the impact of culture on sexual activity. Some tweens are sexually active, but most are not. In fact, when sexual intercourse occurs before age 13, the partner is usually years older and the behavior is considered sexual abuse, not freely chosen intimacy (Dickson et al., 1998)

By the teen years, boys and girls have become interested in each other. In some cultures, they show their mutual interest, which gradually leads to sexual intercourse. In those cultures, the ages for sexual experience are similar for boys and girls. About one-fourth of both sexes in the United States have had sexual intercourse by age 14, about half by age 17, and about 90 percent by age 21 (Hogan et al., 2000; Santelli et al., 2000).

These age data come from confidential surveys. Ages vary substantially by cohort and subculture. Some evidence suggests that first intercourse occurs earlier than it did 50 years ago but later than it did 10 years ago. Nonetheless, throughout this period, U.S. and Canadian adolescents of both sexes seemed to experience sexual activity at about the same ages, often with each other. Gender equity is apparent in some other nations as well (e.g., the Netherlands and Uganda) (Cohen, 2005; Teitler, 2002).

By contrast, in Finland and Norway girls tend to become sexually experienced later than boys. In Greece and Portugal, boys are later (Teitler, 2002). Emerging adult men in Nigeria are expected to seek inexperienced younger teens for sexual partners and to give them gifts. By contrast, emerging adult males in Thailand are expected to seek older, experienced women, who may be sex workers (WHO, 2005).

These generalities certainly do not apply to every man within those nations. Subgroups within nations always differ markedly in sexual experience—what, when, with whom, and of what age and sex (Schlegel & Barry, 1991). For instance, a survey of 704 adolescents in Ghana found that more 16-year-old girls than boys were sexually experienced, but the girls tended to be experienced with only one partner, whereas the experienced boys usually had had several part-

JOANNA B. PINNEO / AURORA PHOTOS

A Woman at 15 Dulce Giovanna Mendez dances at her *quinceañera,* the traditional fifteenth-birthday celebration of a Hispanic girl's sexual maturity. Dulce lives in Ures, Mexico, where many older teenagers marry and have children. This was the expected outcome of puberty in earlier decades in the United States as well.

ners. In that nation, Muslim youth of all ages and both sexes were less sexually active than Christians, who were themselves less active than those of neither faith (Glover et al., 2003).

In many nations, religious teachings affect sexual behavior. In fact, devout young people can be oblivious to sexual thoughts. Current brain research confirms that this is quite possible: People can be unaware of their sensations (Damasio, 2003).

A study of adolescent happiness in Israel and the United States found that some individuals in both nations reported experiencing their greatest joy in a romantic relationship. However, especially among Muslim youth, their romances seldom included sexual intimacy, even in thought (Magen, 1998). For example, one Arab Israeli boy reported on "the most wonderful and happiest day of my life":

> A girl passed our house. And she looked at me. She looked at me as though I were an angel in paradise. I looked at her, and stopped still, and wondered and marveled. . . . [Later] she passed near us, stopped, and called my friend, and asked my name and who I am. I trembled all over and could hardly stand on my feet. I used my brain, since otherwise I would have fallen to the floor. I couldn't stand it any longer and went home.
>
> *[quoted in Magen, 1998, pp. 97–98]*

All these examples demonstrate that the universal experiences of rising hormones and the resulting appearance of primary and secondary sexual characteristics can take many forms, depending on the culture in which they occur.

SUMMING UP

The growth spurt and sexual maturation are ongoing in the three or four years after the first signs of puberty appear. Both sets of changes follow a preordained sequence. The growth spurt is uneven, with some body parts maturing before others. Growth proceeds from the extremities to the center, so the limbs grow before the internal organs. Weight gain precedes height gain, which precedes muscle gain.

For girls, puberty begins with primary sex characteristics (growth of internal sex organs) and then secondary sex characteristics (pubic hair, breast buds). The girls' growth spurt occurs midway, and sexual characteristics continue to mature, with menarche completing the sequence. For boys, primary sex characteristics (including growth of the testes and penis and then spermarche) precede the growth spurt. All boys and girls experience increased sexual interest as their bodies develop and their hormones increase, but the expression of and even fantasies about sexual feelings depend on their culture.

Brain Development in Adolescence

Neuroscientists and developmentalists are discovering the intriguing ways in which adolescent brain growth is influenced by hormones, maturation, and experience. Parents are discovering them, too, as in this anecdote from Laurence Steinberg, who is both a scientist and a father:

> When my son, Benjamin, was 14, he and three of his friends decided to sneak out of the house where they were spending the night and visit one of their girlfriends at around two in the morning. When they arrived at the girl's house, they positioned themselves under her bedroom window, threw pebbles against her windowpanes, and tried to scale the side of the house. Modern technology, unfortunately, has made it harder to play Romeo these days. The boys set off the house's burglar alarm, which activated a siren and

> simultaneously sent a direct notification to the local police station, which dispatched a patrol car. When the siren went off, the boys ran down the street and right smack into the police car, which was heading to the girl's home. Instead of stopping and explaining their activity, Ben and his friends scattered and ran off in different directions through the neighborhood. One of the boys was caught by the police and taken back to his home, where his parents were awakened and the boy questioned.
>
> I found out about this affair the following morning, when the girl's mother called our home to tell us what Ben had done. . . . After his near brush with the local police, Ben had returned to the house out of which he had snuck, where he slept soundly until I awakened him with an angry telephone call, telling him to gather his clothes and wait for me in front of his friend's house. On our drive home, after delivering a long lecture about what he had done and about the dangers of running from armed police in the dark when they believe they may have interrupted a burglary, I paused.
>
> "What were you thinking?" I asked.
>
> "That's the problem, Dad," Ben replied. "I wasn't."
>
> *[Steinberg, 2004, pp. 51, 52]*

Steinberg appreciates his son's insight about adolescent thought: "The problem is not that Ben's decision-making was deficient. The problem is that it was nonexistent" (Steinberg, 2004, p. 52). In his analysis, Steinberg points out another characteristic of adolescent thought: When emotions are high, especially with peers, the logical part of the child's brain shuts down and immediate, intense excitement, with its own rush, takes over.

This reality is not captured in research that asks teenagers, one by one, to respond to hypothetical dilemmas. They do well with those (just as they score high on multiple-choice tests about addictive drugs and unprotected sex), but

> the prospect of visiting a hypothetical girl from class cannot possibly carry the excitement about the possibility of surprising someone you have a crush on with a visit in the middle of the night. It is easier to put on a hypothetical condom during an act of hypothetical sex than it is to put on a real one when one is in the throes of passion. It is easier to just say no to a hypothetical beer than it is to a cold frosty one on a summer night.
>
> *[Steinberg, 2004, p. 43]*

To understand how the brain actually works, abstract questionnaires are inadequate. Now that developmentalists realize the limitations of prior research, and the possibilities of fMRI and other brain scans, excitement as well as hard work lies ahead.

Caution Versus Thrill Seeking

Much more interdisciplinary research is needed to integrate brain and behavioral studies (e.g., Dahl, 2004; Keating, 2004; Masten, 2004; Nelson, 2004). The implications of what is known are thrilling: We are on the verge of a new, fuller understanding of the adolescent mind. Yet scientists are cautious. The fMRI, the PET scan, and other tools are expensive and complex, and longitudinal tests of typical adolescents have not yet been done. One expert explains:

> We stand at the edge of very exciting new research developments as new neuroimaging technologies come online, but at present we are groping in the dark in many respects. . . . The work on adolescent development is particularly recent.
>
> *[Keating, 2004, p. 69]*

With excitement tempered by caution, scientists believe that many hallmarks of adolescent thinking and behavior (from impulsiveness and emotionality to analytical skills and problem solving) originate with brain maturation.

An adolescent's ability to plan, to reflect, to analyze, and to decide (all explained in detail in Chapter 15) occurs because of maturation of the prefrontal cortex. Links between various parts of the brain are forged and smoothed (with more dendrites and better myelination), making young people gradually faster and better at problem solving.

But how does this relate to Ben's escapade or, for that matter, to what you read about middle childhood, when dendrites, myelination, and an enlarged corpus callosum allow "a massively interconnected brain" (Kagan & Herschkowitz, 2005, p. 220)? Actually, younger children are, in some ways, better thinkers than young adolescents, at least as adults might define "better." An 8-year-old Ben probably would not have sneaked out of the house at 2 A.M.

How can this be? It is true that problem-solving skills are quite good in middle childhood, because the prefrontal cortex matures and controls the limbic system, and this process continues in adolescence. However, in addition to these advances, two new neurological developments make emotional excitement more attractive and logical thought more elusive in adolescence.

Sequence and Sensation

First, just as for the rest of the body, a developmental sequence in brain maturation means that some parts grow more quickly than others. The limbic system, which is centered in the lower rear of the brain and includes the hippocampus and the amygdala (see Chapter 8), reaches final maturation before the prefrontal cortex, located at the front top of the brain (Compas, 2004).

As you remember, the limbic system predominates in quick emotional reactions—sudden anger, joy, fear, despair—and the prefrontal cortex is called "the executive function" because it coordinates, inhibits, and strategizes. This asynchronous maturation puts adolescents "at increased risk for emotional problems and disorders because the brain systems that activate emotions . . . are developed before the capacity for volitional, effortful control of these emotions is fully in place" (Compas, 2004, p. 283).

The sequence in which the limbic system matures before the prefrontal cortex has particularly serious implications in modern times:

> Many adolescents in modern society may face several years with physically and sexually mature bodies, active brain circuits involved in reproductive drives and related emotional changes, but *gradually emerging cognitive control*. This has led to a metaphor for early puberty as "starting the engines with an unskilled driver."
>
> *[Nelson et al., 2002, p. 515; emphasis in original]*

The second factor is that the maturing limbic system is particularly attuned to strong, immediate sensations, as yet unchecked by the prefrontal cortex. For this reason,

> Adolescents *like* intensity, excitement, and arousal. They are drawn to music videos that shock and bombard the senses. Teenagers flock to horror and slasher movies. They dominate queues waiting to ride the high-adrenaline rides at amusement parks. Adolescence is a time when sex, drugs, *very* loud music, and other high-stimulation experiences take on great appeal. It is a developmental period when an appetite for adventure, a predilection for risks, and a desire for novelty and thrills seem to reach naturally high levels.
>
> *[Dahl, 2004, pp. 7, 8; emphasis in original]*

(a)

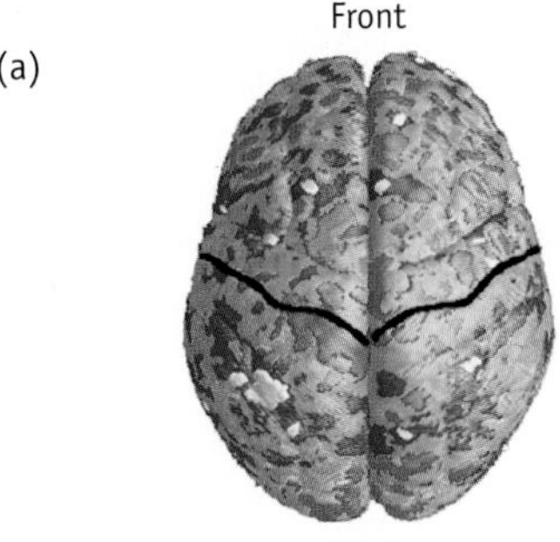

(b)

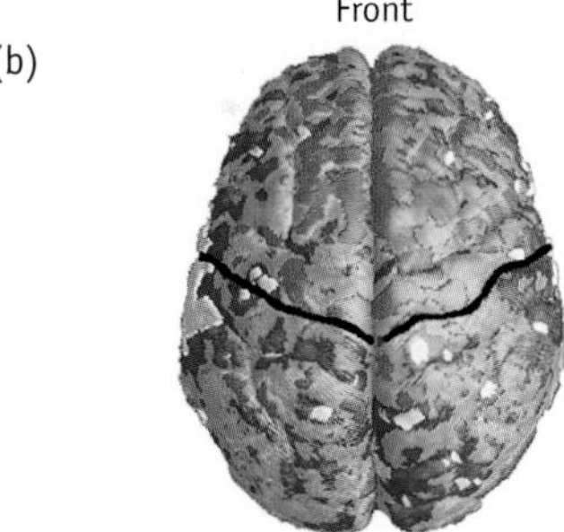

BOTH IMAGES COURTESY OF DR. ELIZABETH SOWELL UCLA / LABORATORY OF NEURO IMAGING

The Prefrontal Cortex Matures These are composite scans of normal brains of *(a)* children and adolescents and *(b)* adolescents and adults. The red areas indicate both an increase in brain size and a decrease in gray matter (cerebral cortex). The red areas in *(b)* are larger than in *(a)* and are concentrated in the frontal area of the brain, which is associated with complex cognitive processes. The growth of brain areas as their gray matter decreases is believed to reflect an increase in white matter, which consists of myelin—the axon coating that makes the brain more efficient.

Such intense experiences are sought precisely because they short-circuit the emotional regulation that the prefrontal cortex fosters. When stress, arousal, passion, sensory bombardment, drug intoxication, or deprivation is extreme, the brain is overtaken by impulses—which is what teenagers want. Have you ever wondered about the words teenagers use when they brag about being so drunk they were "wasted," "bombed," or "smashed"? Why would anyone deliberately spend a night without sleep, or go for days without eating, or push exertion to the point of pain? Quieting the prefrontal cortex by overwhelming it with sensory input may be part of the explanation.

Planning and Execution

Fortunately, given the hazards of adolescent risk taking, uneven brain development is temporary. As adulthood approaches, significant brain maturation includes more densely packed dendrites developing in the prefrontal cortex and reaching throughout the brain (see Chapter 5).

By late adolescence and early adulthood, thinking is more efficient, enabling 18-year-olds to plan their lives, to analyze possibilities, and to pursue goals much more effectively than when they were younger (Keating, 2004). For example, many 12-year-olds dream of becoming world-famous musicians or sports stars; 18-year-olds have more realistic aspirations, and strive to attain them. By age 25, most adults are employed and have a practical understanding of their job's demands.

Especially for Parents Worried About Their Teenager's Risk-Taking You remember the risky things you did at the same age, and you are alarmed by the possibility that your child will follow in your footsteps. What should you do?

Overall, the executive functions of the brain advance markedly throughout adolescence and beyond. This is evidenced not only by fMRI scans but also by simpler, less expensive indicators, such as a person's game strategies and classroom performance (Cepeda et al., 2001; Luciana et al., 2005). For example, in high school and college, but not earlier, students become able to find rational arguments in favor of a viewpoint that is not theirs or to try alternate strategies and to plan ahead when they play cards or solve puzzles. This development is explained further in Chapter 15.

Connections: Some Faster, Some Lost, Some Enduring

As the prefrontal cortex continues to mature during adolescence, myelination shortens reaction time in sports, in academics, and even in conversation. By the end of the teen years, adolescents can grasp, connect, and refute ideas much faster than younger children can (Sampaio & Truwit, 2001). This may be the reason that the "white matter" of the brain, which includes the axons and dendrites that link one neuron to another, increases throughout childhood, adolescence, and emerging adulthood (Thomas & Casey, 2003).

Like the pruning that happens during infancy (explained in Chapter 5), new pruning of dendrites in the prefrontal cortex occurs in adolescence, this time with more precision. But in the meantime, linguistic, cognitive, and personality patterns are quite open to change. In late childhood, repeated connections between one synapse and another easily strengthen links in the brain, which makes it relatively easy to learn unfamiliar concepts or novel dance steps (Keating, 2004). After age 20 new learning of just about everything becomes more difficult.

This is not to say that humans ever stop learning. As you remember from Chapter 1, brain plasticity is apparent lifelong; learning is always possible. However, after substantial brain pruning and connecting in adolescence, it is harder to develop completely new neurological patterns. Professors, teenagers, and political leaders take note: Adults understand something best if it connects to what they already know.

Which brain connections of adolescence endure? Memories and values. Hormones and experiences both cause brain growth. Memories and experiences acquired during the teen years and emerging adulthood are more potent than later on, so adolescence is particularly crucial in forming the values, habits, and priorities that are needed for a productive adulthood.

Parents, judges, and teachers are sometimes tempted to give up on adolescents—kicking them out of the house, jailing them for life, hoping they leave school; but those reactions might prevent the very experiences needed to shape the brain as it should be shaped. In adolescence, "passion intertwines with the highest levels of human endeavor: passion for ideas and ideals, passion for beauty, passion to create music and art" (Dahl, 2004, p. 21). Thus, adolescent brains are passionate, unlike child or adult brains, but sometimes that is for the best.

SUMMING UP

By mid-adolescence, most young people have completed puberty and have attained adult size and sexual characteristics. However, their brains are not yet like those of adults. Maturation of the brain's limbic system is triggered by the hormones of puberty, and it begins before mid-adolescence. Maturation of the prefrontal cortex seems more dependent on age and experience and less on specific hormones, and thus it matures somewhat later. This uneven advancement is thought to be the reason adolescents take irrational risks, enjoy intense sensory experiences, and find ways to strengthen their emotions and dampen their rational thought. During adolescence, reactions are quicker, dendrites are pruned, and memories endure. By adulthood, both the emotional and rational parts of the brain work in harmony most of the time.

Health Hazards

Assuming that a person is well nourished and free of disease, late adolescence is the best period of the life span for hard physical work, problem-free reproduction, and peak athletic performance. Once growth is complete, the young person's body is usually strong and healthy.

Puberty is over by age 18 for almost everyone. Girls usually reach their maximum height by age 16 and boys by age 18, although a few late-maturing boys undergo final skeletal growth in their early 20s (Behrman, 1992). Muscle growth and fat accumulation continue into the early 20s, when women attain their full breast and hip size and men reach full shoulder and upper-arm size. But even without such final growth, emerging adults are muscular, better than any other age group at, say, running up a flight of stairs, lifting a heavy load, or gripping an object with maximum force.

All the body systems, including the digestive, respiratory, circulatory, and sexual-reproductive systems, function at an optimal level. Death from disease is rare. This is true worldwide, although the specifics vary by nation and by disease (Heuveline, 2002). One example to illustrate this trend: In the United States, cancer annually kills less than 1 in 20,000 people aged 16 to 24, compared with 1 in 100 over age 65 (U.S. Bureau of the Census, 2002).

There is a dark spot in the generally bright picture of health and strength. In every nation, as deaths due to disease have decreased, the proportion of violent deaths during late adolescence has increased. Similarly, as malnutrition has decreased, eating disorders have increased. Homicide, suicide, and fatal accidents now account for almost half of young-adult mortality worldwide, with males particularly vulnerable. Although girls less often die, they suffer other morbid conditions—teenage pregnancy, bulimia, and anorexia among them—to which they are more vulnerable than boys. Young people of both sexes usually try addictive drugs before age 18, and some of them become drug abusers and addicts. We now focus on each of these hazards, all particularly damaging in adolescence: violence, sex, drugs, and improper diet.

DOMINIC CHAVEZ / THE DENVER POST / AP PHOTO

Twisted Memorial This wreck was once a Volvo, driven by a Colorado teenager who ignored an oncoming train's whistle at a rural crossing. The car was hurled 167 feet and burst into flames. The impact instantly killed the driver and five teenage passengers. They are among the statistics indicating that accidents (many of which result from unwise risk taking) kill 10 times more adolescents than diseases do.

Injury and Death

Throughout the world, from age 1 to 45, accidents (especially motor-vehicle accidents) are the leading cause of death. Older adolescents are at greatest risk of accidental death on every continent, with two chilling exceptions: In Africa, the leading cause of death among youth is AIDS; in South America, homicides rank first (Blum & Nelson-Mmari, 2004). The United States is more typical: 43 percent of deaths between ages 15 and 25 are from accidents; suicide is second, and homicide is third.

Another way to think about the same data is that, in the United States, about 1 male in every 125 dies violently between his 15th and 25th birthday (U.S. Bureau of the Census, 2002). Accidental death rates among young men are almost as high in Canada, Mexico, and Australia as in the United States.

Injuries requiring medical attention are so common they could be called normal. Most nations do not keep detailed records of the age of injury victims, but in the United States young men average two serious injuries each between the ages of 12 and 21, and young women suffer at least one (U.S. Bureau of the Census, 2002). Adolescents have the highest rate of injury (more than three times higher than that of people aged 45 to 65, the age group with the lowest rate) as well as the highest rate of violent death. Why? Researchers have identified three causes:

1. *Body changes.* The rapid changes in size, shape, and hormone levels are unsettling. Further, many specific body chemicals (especially testosterone and MAO) correlate with impulsive reactions. For these biological reasons, risk taking of all kinds increases in adolescence. Injury follows.
2. *Brain changes.* Intellectual immaturity and the growth of the limbic system may be another factor (Compas, 2004). Adolescents overrate the joys of the moment and disregard risks when confronted with, say, a mind-altering drug, a sexually arousing situation, a suspicious police officer, a dangerous dare (O'Donoghue & Rabin, 2001). Each miscalculation correlates with accidental death and homicide.
3. *Social context.* Psychosocial factors will be discussed in detail in Chapter 16, with particular focus on juvenile delinquency and suicide. Here we note that some adolescents—especially those alienated from their parents and schools and not yet attached to families and work of their own—are at much greater risk than others.

Do not be surprised that the next topic includes adolescent pregnancy. Public health experts believe that a community's rate of adolescent homicide and teen pregnancy are closely related. Both are also connected to the levels of poverty, deprivation, and hopelessness within a given nation (Pickett et al., 2005).

Response for Parents Worried About Their Teenager's Risk-Taking (from page 448): You are right to be concerned, but you cannot keep your child locked up for the next decade or so. Since you know that some rebellion and irrationality are likely, try to minimize them by not boasting about your own youthful exploits, by reacting sternly to minor infractions to nip worse behavior in the bud, and by making allies of your child's teachers.

Sex Too Early

Sex is quite wonderful, a source of great pleasure as well as essential for the future of humankind. There is no need to regret the maturation of the primary sexual characteristics that make reproduction possible or the hormones that increase sexual interest. However, the expression of every human characteristic depends on psychosocial conditions that make it harmful or helpful. The primary discussion of adolescent sexual relationships is in Chapter 16. Here we describe two biosocial hazards connected to early sexual activity: pregnancy and disease.

Pregnancy in Adolescence

In terms of physical health, pregnancy is quite different for a fully mature young woman, age 18 or so, and a still-growing girl, age 15 or so. Giving birth during early adolescence is unhealthy for both mother and child. Giving birth late in adolescence is not unhealthy if the mother is well nourished and has good prenatal care (although her ability to raise her child depends on many factors in addition to her age).

To be specific, if a girl becomes pregnant within a year or two of menarche, she is more likely to experience almost every possible complication of pregnancy and birth—including spontaneous abortion (miscarriage), high blood pressure, stillbirth, cesarean section, and a low-birthweight baby. Her uterus, pelvis, and overall body functioning are not yet mature (Phipps & Sowers, 2002).

Throughout puberty, every young woman's body must adjust to new hormones, add bone density, redistribute weight, and grow taller. Pregnancy interferes with this process because another set of hormones sustains pregnancy, triggers birth, and then produces breast milk. Nature protects the fetus. If both organisms require the same nutrient and the future mother does not have enough stored in her body (often the case for calcium and iron, for instance), her supply will be depleted in favor of the developing person. Probably for this reason, women who give birth before age 16 tend to be shorter and sicker as adults and to die younger than other women.

Correlational data must be interpreted carefully. Low-income women have poorer health and more reproductive complications whether or not they become pregnant at a young age. Further, pregnancy occurs more often among low-income teenagers, so any comparison of maternal age and infant health reflects income. Adolescent pregnancy, poverty, and poor health correlate in every nation (Health Development Agency, 2003).

However, many researchers have taken this into account, and they find that the sheer physical burden of pregnancy, imposed on an immature body, adds to the burden of poverty. The immediate harm from early pregnancy is particularly apparent in developing nations, where young women are three times more likely to die of birth complications than are older women (Blum & Nelson-Mmari, 2004).

Beyond the immaturity of the body, there are two other reasons early pregnancy is risky. The first is that, the younger a pregnant girl is, the more likely her sexual experience is to have been unwanted and coercive, which makes it harder for her to care for herself or her baby (Dickson et al., 1998). The second reason is that, the younger she is, the more likely she is to have an untreated sexually transmitted infection, which itself harms the health of mother, fetus, and newborn (WHO, 2005).

One of the most informative studies about the consequences of teenage pregnancy occurred in Sweden, where income differences between rich and poor are not great and where good prenatal care is available to everyone. This study began with all the girls born between 1941 and 1970. Those who had their first babies as teenagers had lower lifetime income and poorer employment histories than did those who became mothers after age 20. Those whose first babies were born when they were 16 or younger fared worse than the older teenage mothers did, but even those who were 18 and 19 did not do as well, on average, as did young women who were in their 20s when they had their first child (Olausson et al., 2001).

Sexually Transmitted Infections

The other major hazard of adolescent sexual activity is a **sexually transmitted infection (STI)**, also commonly referred to as sexually transmitted disease (STD) or venereal disease (VD). Sexually active teenagers have higher rates of *gonorrhea, genital herpes, syphilis,* and *chlamydia*—the most common STIs—than any other age group (WHO, 2005).

The younger people are when they contract an STI, the more reluctant they are to seek treatment and to alert their sexual

sexually transmitted infection (STI) A disease spread by sexual contact, including syphilis, gonorrhea, genital herpes, chlamydia, and HIV.

Words of Wisdom Abundant information is available to teenagers about the hazards of sex and the benefits of abstinence, condoms, and birth control. Although this knowledge is helpful, it is all too often overpowered by emotion.

DAVID YOUNG-WOLFF / PHOTOEDIT, INC.

partners. Not only do they feel ashamed and afraid, but few recognize symptoms or believe that medical treatment will be confidential. Further, some STIs (notably chlamydia) have no early symptoms and yet can cause infertility later. The rate of reinfection and the risk of serious consequences are higher for teenagers than they are for those age 20 and above (Xu et al., 2000).

Thus, STIs are particularly hazardous in adolescence. The World Health Organization recommends special clinics for teenagers, to reduce their embarrassment and fear of meeting an older person they know. Even in developed nations, however, few such clinics exist (WHO, 2005).

Some natural biological defense against STIs is present in a fully developed woman but not yet in a pubescent girl, who is therefore more likely to catch an infection if her partner has one. Sexually active teenagers are at higher risk than older people for another reason as well: Most teenagers have several sexual partners before they choose a steady one. In some ways, boys are at greater risk because they have more partners, but in other ways girls are at greater risk because their partners are more likely to be older and thus more likely to have an STI (WHO, 2005).

Detailed data regarding transmission comes from Africa, where AIDS is epidemic. Most sexually active teenage boys do not have AIDS because their partners are usually teenage girls who are not infected. However, the most sexually active teenage girls are likely to have older partners, and their rate of HIV infection is much higher than that of their male contemporaries. For example, one study in Addis Ababa, the capital city of Ethiopia, found that the rate of HIV infection in girls aged 15 to 19 was twice that of boys the same age (Fontanet et al., 1998).

The sexual habits of teenagers in developed nations are one explanation for the relatively high rates of STIs among adolescents. Long-term, steady relationships are not the norm. For instance, one survey of high school seniors in the United States found that 20 percent had already had four or more sexual partners and a third had not used a condom the last time they had intercourse (MMWR, May 21, 2004). A detailed study of one high school found that very few sexually active young people had multiple partners. This fact that made most of them think they were at low risk for STIs. However, as Figure 14.5 shows, only about one-third of all romances lasted as long as 6 months. If one person in a network had an STI and did not notify his or her sexual partners and obtain treatment, that STI could spread throughout the school (Bearman et al., 2004).

Worldwide, an estimated 1 in every 20 adolescents acquires an STI each year—so over the 10 years of adolescence, on average half of all adolescents will be infected (Blum & Nelson-Mmari, 2004). Of course, the many teenagers who abstain from sex never get an STI, and a few very active teenagers have several infections, so this statistic does not mean that every adolescent has a 50/50 chance of an STI. However, most who do contract an STI are surprised because they did not expect their partner to have one. Their innocence is captured by one girl in Malawi, who thought she was safe because her partner was known to her and "my mother knows his mother" (quoted in WHO, 2005, p. 11).

What can be done to halt early sexual activity and reduce the rates of early pregnancy and STIs? Education is one factor. Parents, peers, teachers, and the general community all make a difference, as discussed in Chapter 16. From a biosocial perspective, the lack of medical care for teenage sexual problems is a major barrier to health.

Sexual Abuse

Sexual abuse is the use of a nonconsenting person for one's own sexual pleasure. Accordingly, sexual activity is abusive whenever it is not mutual or whenever one participant's consent is not freely given.

sexual abuse The use of a nonconsenting person for one's own sexual pleasure.

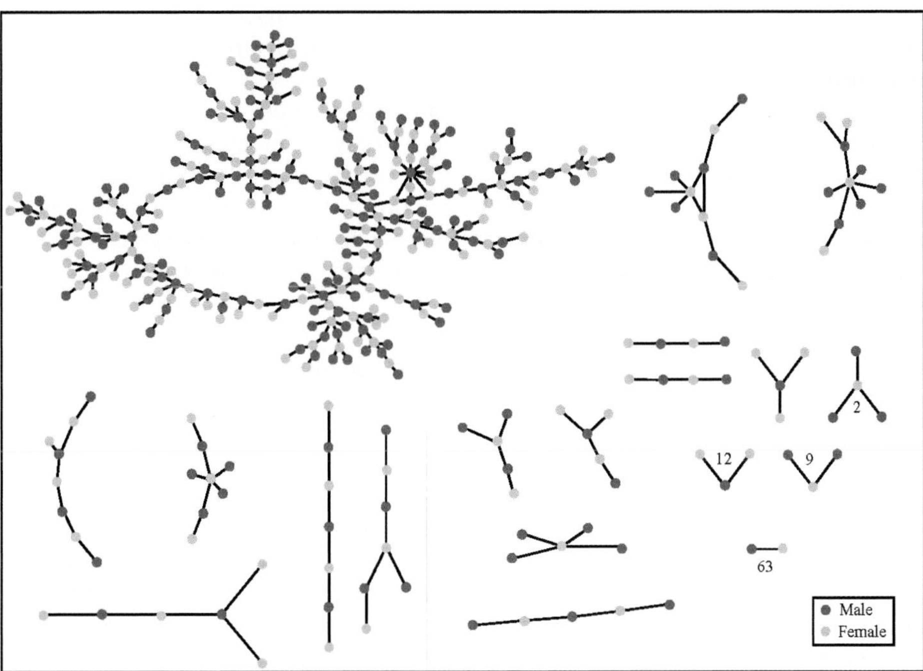

Source: Bearman et al., 2004.

FIGURE 14.5 **Romantic Networks: Your Partner Becomes My Partner** This is a diagram of the romances that students in one U.S. high school reported having during the preceding six months. Each dot represents a student, and the lines between dots represent romantic relationships. Patterns that occurred more than once are indicated with a number. Thus, 63 couples were still together at the end of the six-month period. Those monogamous teenagers were in the minority; most of the other students were linked to two or more romantic partners. If one person in the busy circle of relationships at the upper left had an untreated infection, it could have been transmitted to 100 other people.

Free consent to sexual interaction is considered impossible for children to give, because they do not understand the implications of sexual activity and because they are physically weaker than their elders and psychologically dependent on them. **Child sexual abuse** is any erotic activity that arouses an adult and excites, shames, or confuses a child, whether or not the victim protests and whether or not genital contact is involved. Thus, child sexual abuse includes sexualized teasing, erotic photographing, or—especially once puberty begins—invading the privacy of a child who is bathing, dressing, or sleeping.

child sexual abuse Any erotic activity that arouses an adult and excites, shames, or confuses a child, whether or not the victim protests and whether or not genital contact is involved.

As with other forms of maltreatment (discussed in Chapter 8), the harm done by sexual abuse increases if it is repeated or coercive, or if it impairs the child's relationships with peers (Haugaard, 2000; Stevenson, 1999). Ongoing sexual abuse by a parent is particularly harmful, damaging the victim's ability to establish trusting, comfortable, and intimate relationships. Parents are the perpetrators in more than half of all cases of child sexual abuse. Fathers or stepfathers of victims are usually the abusers; mothers contribute by ignoring, allowing, or even encouraging the abuse (Sheinberg & Fraenkel, 2001).

Young adolescent girls are the principal targets for victimization. In a U.S. survey of young women of four ethnic groups (African, Native, Mexican, and European Americans), about one-third of the girls in each group reported being sexually abused; in one-fifth of these cases, the abuse had involved rape (Roosa et al., 1999). Young Canadian women report similarly high rates (DeKeseredy & Schwartz, 1998). Involuntary sexual intercourse, without any protection against pregnancy or infection, is particularly common among adolescents under age 16 (Kalmuss et al., 2003).

An adolescent boy who becomes a victim of sexual abuse is likely to feel shame at being weak and unable to defend himself. A male sexual abuser of a young boy does not necessarily consider himself homosexual; by the same token, victimization is not an indication of a boy's sexual orientation. However, when an abused boy does in fact have a homosexual orientation, shame escalates.

Especially for Health-Care Workers A 15-year-old patient tells you that she is having sex with her boyfriend and wants your help to protect herself from pregnancy and sexually transmitted infections. Which ethical principle do you observe: your patient's right to privacy or your obligation to report suspected sexual abuse?

RESPONSE FOR HEALTH-CARE WORKERS (from page 453): There is no easy answer, because you want to help prevent STIs, teen pregnancy, *and* sexual abuse. The best course of action probably depends on the specifics of the case. Take time to listen to everything the girl has to say before drawing any conclusion about whether or not she is being sexually exploited.

Shame often leads to further problems. Sexually abused adolescents of both sexes are vulnerable to self-abuse via drugs, eating disorders, self-mutilation (cutting), parasuicide, and suicide.

A complication arises for teenagers who are sexually active by choice. The legal system is likely to define any sexual intercourse involving an adult and a consenting adolescent under age 14 or 16 as *statutory rape* (as opposed to *forcible rape,* in which the victim does not consent). In some U.S. states, sexual intercourse between two consenting 15-year-olds is also considered statutory rape, because the partners are minors. In other states, statutory rape occurs only if the man is 10 or more years older than the young woman. Fear of being charged with statutory rape may cause sexually active teenagers to avoid obtaining medical help with STIs, unwanted pregnancies, and even childbirth (Richardson & Dailard, 2005).

Drug Use

One of the most common ways in which adolescents put themselves at risk of violent death, unprotected sex, and every other health hazard is by using drugs, both legal and illegal. Some teenagers argue that "everyone is doing it," yet many adults try to prevent every teen from taking even one swallow or puff. As you will see, both sides have data to support their perspective.

Widespread Use

By age 18 or so, drug use is common, although the specifics depend on cohort and culture. Among contemporary adolescents in the United States, most use alcohol and tobacco before they are 18 and about half try marijuana. Fewer use other drugs, but since 1975 an annual nationwide survey of high school seniors called *Monitoring the Future* has found that some in every cohort use cocaine, LSD, and other drugs (see Figure 14.6). Overall, drug use is down in the United States over the life of the survey, but the sheer number of drugs available has increased. Methamphetamines (including "crystal meth"), for example, were seldom abused until the early 1990s; now about one high school senior in 25 has tried them.

In some nations, alcohol is far more common than any other drug; in others, smoking is more common than drinking; and in many places both drugs are used

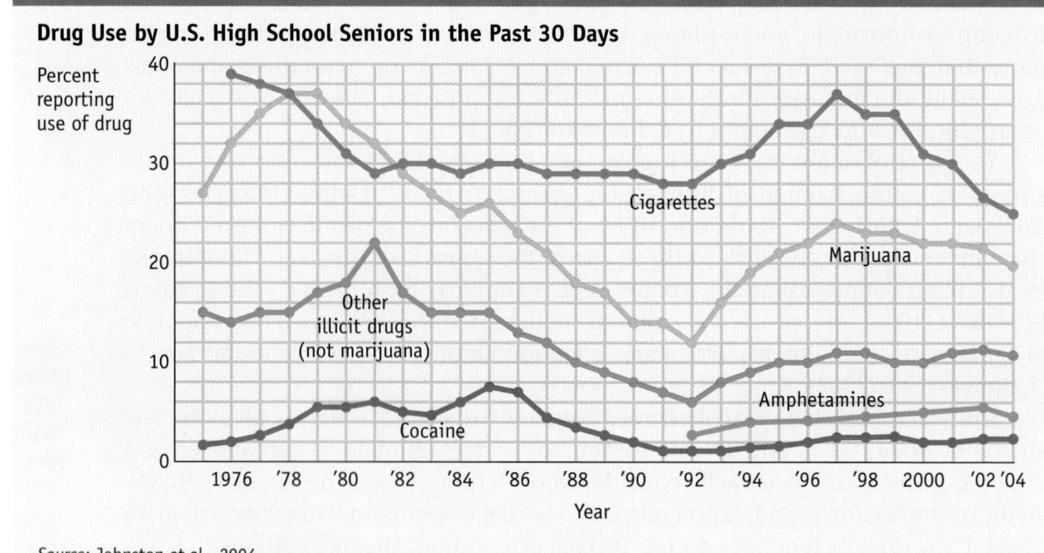

FIGURE 14.6 **Rise and Fall** By asking the same questions year after year, the *Monitoring the Future* study shows notable historical effects. It is encouraging that something in the society, not something in the adolescent, makes drug use increase and decrease, and that the most recent data show a decline. However, as Chapter 1 emphasized, survey research cannot prove what causes change.

MARK PETERS / CORBIS

STUART FRANKLIN / MAGNUM PHOTOS

The Same Situation, Many Miles Apart: Teen Approaches to Drinking Adolescents everywhere drink alcohol, including these girls at a high school prom in New York City *(left)* and at a sidewalk café in Prague *(right)*. Cultural differences affect the specifics but not the general trend toward teenage experimentation with drugs and alcohol.

? Observational Quiz (see answer, page 458): Can you spot three cultural differences between these two groups?

more often than in the United States (Eisner, 2002). Laws and family practices seem to be part of the reason for the differences: In many European nations, children customarily drink wine with dinner; in many Asian nations, there are no antismoking regulations; in many Arab nations, drinking alcohol is strictly forbidden.

A significant number of U.S. teenagers never use drugs. However, the United States leads the world in the number of available drugs. Recent additions to the array are synthetic narcotics, which are unknown in most nations; in 2004, 9 percent of U.S. high school seniors used Vicodin and 5 percent used OxyContin. Of the boys, 5 percent used steroids (Johnston et al., 2005).

Why would any teenager, in any nation, use drugs, especially when doing so is forbidden by law and goes against parental wishes? One reason is that, for many adolescents, peers are more important than parents. "In young adolescence, use of substances . . . provides a form of commerce with the social world" (Dishion & Owen, 2002, p. 489). In other words, socially awkward pubescent children (especially boys) may use drugs for the same reason they do other risky things: to establish friendships and be part of a peer group.

In addition, the neurological drive for intense sensations makes adolescents seek the quick but intense rush that drugs can provide. Ironically, cigarettes, probably the most addictive and most destructive drug commonly used by teenagers, may be more satisfying and cause less pain upon withdrawal during adolescence than later on (O'Dell et al., 2004).

It can be argued that using drugs is part of normal adolescent development, since experimenting with drugs is common, since social acceptance seems beneficial, and since the most commonly used drugs, alcohol and cigarettes, are legal for adults in most nations. However, as developmentalists see it, normal is not healthy, for several reasons.

Long-Term Harm

Remember from Chapter 1 that longitudinal research discovers patterns that are not obvious at the moment. For decades, researchers have noted that many adolescents who distrust their parents, injure themselves, hate their schools, and get in trouble with the law use various substances to cope with their stresses. One hypothesis was that the psychic strains of adolescence lead to drug use. Although that interpretation fits the cross-sectional data, longitudinal research suggests that drug use causes more problems than it solves, often *preceding* anxiety disorders, depression, and conflict with adults (Chassin et al., 2004).

drug abuse The ingestion of a drug to the extent that it impairs biological or psychological well-being. Abuse depends on the context; even one-time use can be abusive.

drug addiction A situation in which a person craves more of a drug to feel physically or psychologically at ease.

binge drinking Consuming five or more drinks in a row. Some authorities specify four or more drinks in a row as binge drinking for women, since women tend to be smaller than men and to metabolize alcohol more quickly.

This has been proved particularly with cigarettes. Smoking in adolescence is linked to all kinds of psychopathology, including ADHD, conduct disorder, anxiety, and depression. The link seems to work both ways. For instance, a depressed adolescent picks up a cigarette to feel less depressed, but over the long term, smoking increases depression (Turner et al., 2004).

Another long-term hazard is that many adolescents move past experimenting (mere use) to **drug abuse** (a degree of drug use that causes harm) or **drug addiction** (in which the person needs the drug to feel normal). Many young people are already using drugs regularly, not just experimentally. *Monitoring the Future* reports that, in 2004, 30 percent of high school seniors reported **binge drinking** (that is, they had had five or more alcoholic drinks in a row sometime during the past two weeks), 16 percent were daily cigarette smokers, and 6 percent were daily marijuana users (Johnston et al., 2005).

Drug use is also common among younger adolescents. For example, another large survey of ninth- through twelfth-graders found that almost a third were binge drinkers (see Figure 14.7). This survey did identify some positive trends: Cigarette smoking is declining for every group; among African Americans, rates of both smoking and drinking are low; and boys in all groups are drinking less. Less hopeful, however, are other findings from the same survey: Among ninth-graders in 2003, 36 percent had begun drinking, 19 percent had smoked at least one cigarette, and 12 percent had tried marijuana before age 13 (MMWR, May 21, 2004).

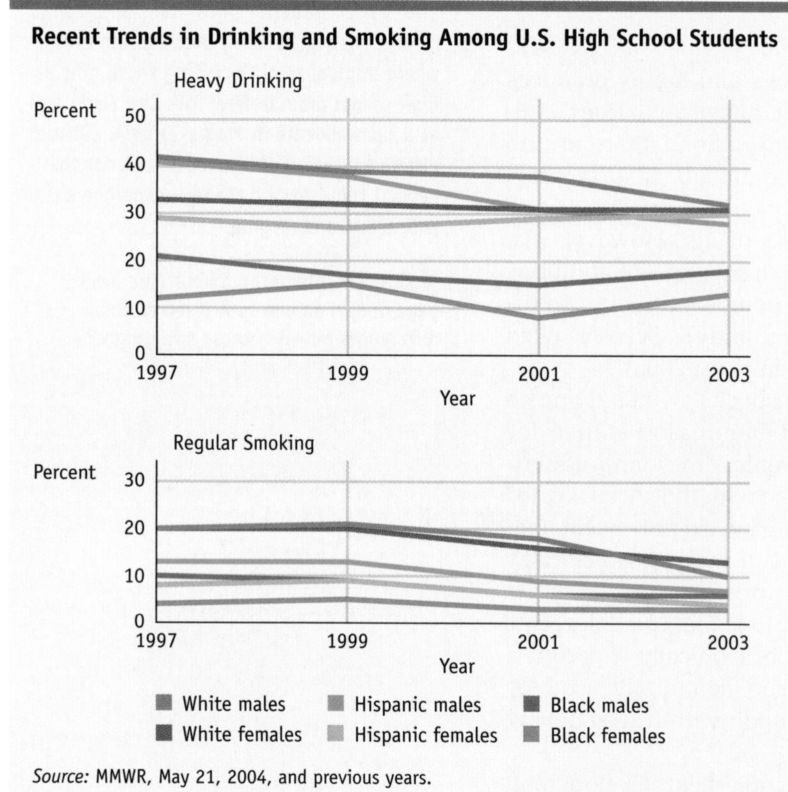

FIGURE 14.7 **Less Drinking, Still Too Much Smoking** The overall downward trend in both binge drinking and regular smoking by adolescents is good news, but why any high school student would ever get drunk or become a daily smoker remains a mystery.

? Observational Quiz (see answer, page 458): Which of these categories of people is least likely to drink alcohol during adolescence? Which category seems most affected by cohort changes in regular smoking?

The younger people are when they first try a drug, the more likely they are to become addicted. Nicotine is probably the most addictive drug, but all psychoactive drugs can be addictive, physically or psychologically. As already explained, risks are likely to be ignored in adolescence (Orford, 2001) and drugs are especially attractive. From a developmental perspective, each year of use adds to the risk of physical harm, reduced motivation, and impaired judgment.

Compared with high school students who do not use drugs, early users think using drugs is a *temporary* respite or reaction to stress, but the opposite is more likely. People who used a given drug in high school are more likely to be using the same drug in adulthood than are those who did not use the drug (Merline et al., 2004). Table 14.2 gives the odds for continuing use of various drugs into adulthood.

Addiction creates the need for more of the drug, day after day, and it can shorten life. Regular smoking causes death from cancer and other causes. Alcohol is a killer as well. Even in small doses, alcohol loosens inhibitions and impairs judgment—an especially dangerous reaction in young persons who are coping with major physical, sexual, and emotional changes.

Data on drunk driving illustrate this point. In the United States in 2000, drunk adolescent drivers were responsible for 15 percent of the fatal crashes in their age group (U.S. Bureau of the Census, 2002). This is actually an improvement: A decade ago, drivers who were drinking caused 39 percent of the fatal accidents involving a driver aged 18 to 21 (U.S. Bureau of the Census, 1991).

There are other immediate hazards. Drugs interfere with healthy eating and digestion. All psychoactive drugs impair the appetite, but tobacco is worst of all.

Smoking or chewing tobacco decreases food consumption and interferes with the absorption of nutrients, resulting in adults who are shorter and thinner than they otherwise would have been.

Remember that the internal organs mature after the height spurt, so teenagers who appear fully grown may still damage their hearts, lungs, and brains, as well as their reproductive systems, by smoking. Smoking reduces fertility in both sexes; it decreases a woman's lifetime supply of ova (U.S. Department of Health and Human Services, 2001).

All psychoactive drugs potentially interfere with brain development, but alcohol may do the most damage. Steady drinking impairs memory and self-control (not just temporarily, as in a blackout) by damaging the hippocampus and the prefrontal cortex (De Bellis et al., 2000; White & Swartzwelder, 2004).

Since definitive research on human brain damage is complex, the evident brain abnormalities in alcoholics could, in theory, predate their drug abuse. However, when neurologists gave alcohol experimentally to lower animals, they found that alcohol doesn't just correlate with brain abnormalities—it causes them (White et al., 2000).

Likewise, some people may be genetically destined to be addicts, so drug use during adolescence simply awakens their inborn tendencies. However, if rats or hamsters are primed by being forced to take a drug they do not want, later they voluntarily take more of the drug, sometimes ignoring their basic survival needs to do so. That is proof of acquired addiction, a process that works in people (especially young ones), too. This is true for established addictive drugs, such as nicotine and heroin, and for more recently abused substances, such as injected steroids (Ballard & Wood, 2005).

Looking Cool Their tight clothing, heavy makeup, multiple rings, and cigarettes are meant to convey to the world that Sheena, 15, and Jessica, 16, are mature, sophisticated women.

? OBSERVATIONAL QUIZ (see answer, page 459): Did these girls buy their own cigarettes?

Is Experience the Best Teacher?

Any drug that affects thinking is likely to be more harmful during adolescence than later in life. Wisdom about use and abuse, about moderation versus addiction, about tolerance and impairment, and about particular risks, comes with personal experience, which is unavailable to most young adolescents. A "relatively common" phenomenon is **generational forgetting**, the idea that each new generation forgets what the previous generation learned about harmful drugs (Chassin et al., 2004, p. 666).

generational forgetting The idea that each new generation forgets what the previous generation learned about harmful drugs.

Teenagers tend to distrust adults, who experienced a different drug scene and whose values are seen as "old-fashioned." For example, the most widely used drug prevention program in U.S. high schools, Project D.A.R.E., involves adult leaders (especially police officers) and has been found to have no impact on adolescent drug use (West & O'Neal, 2004). Some advertisements warning about drugs actually have the opposite effect on adolescents (Block et al., 2002;

TABLE 14.2 **Odds That Teenage Drug Use Will Continue into Adulthood**

Drug Use as High School Senior	Drug Use at Age 35	Odds
Binge drinking	Heavy drinking	3.7 to 1
Marijuana use	Marijuana use	8.7 to 1
Other illicit drugs	Cocaine use	5.3 to 1
	Misuse of prescription drugs	3.4 to 1
Cigarettes, tried	Smoking	3.3 to 1
Cigarettes, used in past month	Smoking	12.7 to 1
Cigarettes, regular use	Smoking	42.5 to 1

Source: Merline et al., 2004.

Gambling with the Future Adolescent drug use often predicts adult drug use. Compared with a person who did no binge drinking as a high school senior, a person who drank heavily in high school is almost four times more likely to drink heavily at midlife (even if that other person did drink heavily at age 20). Generally, people stick to the same drugs they used in high school; there is not much crossover from cigarette smoking to cocaine use, for instance. Exceptions are those who used illicit drugs in high school: Many of them switch to abusing prescription drugs in adulthood.

Especially for Older Brothers and Sisters A friend said she saw your 13-year-old sister smoking. Should you tell your parents?

! Answer to Observational Quiz (from page 455): The most important difference is that, because moderate alcohol use during adolescence is accepted in most European countries, the girls in the Czech Republic are casual about drinking in public. In addition, the American girl is drinking straight from the bottle, and she is drinking hard liquor—both generally frowned upon in Europe.

! Answer to Observational Quiz (from page 456): Black females are least likely to drink alcohol, with Black males the next-lowest group. The White males' rate of smoking dropped from 21 percent to 13 percent in just the four years from 1999 to 2003.

Fishbein et al., 2002). Teenagers learn best from one another, which explains why the most successful programs to halt adolescent drug abuse involve the adolescents themselves.

This does not mean that it is useless to educate adolescents. Massive anti-smoking campaigns in Florida and California have cut adolescent smoking in half, and nationwide increased prices and enforcement of laws have led to a marked decline in smoking among younger adolescents. Only 9 percent of eighth-graders had smoked cigarettes in 2004, compared with 19 percent 10 years earlier (Johnston et al., 2005). This does mean, however, that careful evaluation is crucial: What adults think might work (e.g., photographs of diseased lungs) does not work as well as other approaches (e.g., a sharp price hike).

Diet and Disease

Our final discussion is about nutrition, a topic already mentioned several times in this chapter. The rapid body changes of puberty require additional calories, vitamins, and minerals. Adolescents need 50 percent more calcium, iron, and zinc during their growth spurt than they needed only two years earlier. Many adolescents in modern societies are undernourished or overnourished by choice.

Nutritional Deficiencies

Often the first nutritional problem to appear is deficiency of some essential vitamin or mineral. Calcium is a prime example. About half of adult bone mass is acquired in the second decade of life, yet few adolescents consume enough calcium for bone growth. This increases their lifetime risk of osteoporosis, a leading cause of disability, injury, and even death among older adults.

NANCY J. PIERCE / PHOTO RESEARCHERS, INC.

A Thousand Hamburgers per Person per Year Some teenagers easily reach the thousand mark, wolfing down three burgers a day in after-school or midnight snacks—or even breakfast at noon. This Charlotte, North Carolina, basketball star knows that he should avoid high-fat foods and fill up on whole grains, fresh fruits, and various vegetables. However, for him and for most other teenagers, knowledge does not change habits.

A few decades ago many young people drank more than a quart (32 ounces, almost a liter) of milk every day. Milk drinking has declined in virtually every nation, except in very poor countries where almost no one ever drank milk. In the United States, only 13 percent of ninth-grade girls and 25 percent of ninth-grade boys drink at least three daily glasses (a total of 24 ounces, or ¾ liter) of milk. Milk consumption tends to drop in each year of adolescence, especially among girls (MMWR, May 21, 2004).

Fewer than half of all teenagers consume the recommended daily dose of 15 milligrams of iron, a nutrient found in green vegetables, eggs, and meat—all spurned in favor of chips, sweets, and fast food. Because menstruation depletes the body of iron and because adolescent girls rarely eat enough iron-rich foods, anemia is more common among post-menarcheal girls than among any other age or gender group (Belamarich & Ayoob, 2001). Worldwide, adolescent boys are also likely to suffer from anemia, especially if they do physical labor or play competitive sports, because iron is needed for muscle development (Blum & Nelson-Mmari, 2004).

Nutritional deficiencies result from the choices young adolescents are allowed, even enticed, to make. For example, when today's adults were children, students had to eat whatever the school cafeteria or their parents provided for lunch. Now many middle schools allow students to buy unhealthy snacks. There is a direct link between deficient diets and the presence of vending machines in schools (Cullen & Zakeri, 2004).

Body Image and Obesity

body image A person's concept of his or her body's appearance.

Imbalanced diets are often the result as well as the cause of distorted self-perception and incipient depression. Problems with **body image**—that is, a person's idea of how his or her body looks—are common in adolescence, as you saw with Rachel and her friends at the beginning of this chapter. Since puberty changes every aspect of the body, it is almost impossible for teenagers to be unaware of themselves, yet it is difficult to accept every change. One result is a dangerous discrepancy between body image and reality.

Teenagers are almost never satisfied with their bodies. Girls typically want to be thinner (Ohring et al., 2002), while many boys want to look taller and stronger. Reacting to such concerns, many stressed teenagers eat erratically and use drugs. A major reason that teenage girls smoke cigarettes as much as boys do is that the girls hope smoking will make them thinner. Similarly, the major reason 5 percent of adolescent boys use steroids is to increase their muscles, not to improve athletic performance.

Excessive concern about body weight sometimes backfires and adolescents give up trying, becoming obese instead of thin. In fact, some social scientists believe that the current epidemic of obesity is a direct result of the wish to be thinner (e.g., Campos, 2004).

Diagnosing obesity is more complex in young people than in adults. For adults, a healthy body mass index (BMI) is somewhere between 19 and 25, although a muscular person may be in better shape than his or her BMI suggests. A fully grown person whose BMI is 25 or above is considered overweight (as are about 65 percent of U.S. adults), and anyone whose BMI is above 30 is considered obese (as are about 20 percent of all U.S. adults). As explained in Chapter 11, for children who have not reached their full height, overweight begins at a BMI lower than 25, with the exact number depending on the age and height of the child.

Although obesity is hard to diagnose in any particular growing person, there is no doubt that, in recent years, many adolescents have become heavier and that there is "an increasing prevalence of obesity worldwide" (Blum & Nelson-Mmari, 2004). This situation is primarily caused not by overeating (teens ingest about as much as earlier generations did) but by underexercising (Sutherland, 2003) and eating the wrong foods.

Most teenagers in developed nations snack on their own, order fast food with peers, choose soda over milk, and rarely dine with their families at home. As a result, they consume too much salt, sugar, and fat and not enough calcium or iron. As we have seen, much of the problem relates to lifestyle: Teenagers talk on the phone instead of doing housework, watch television instead of playing outside, use the Internet instead of walking or riding a bike to the library.

A different problem appears among children and youth in developing nations. If they are undernourished as infants, they may be overfed later on. As a result, rates of adolescent obesity are increasing worldwide (Parizkova & Hills, 2005).

About 12 percent of all U.S. teenagers are overweight, a higher proportion than in any other nation that has been studied (Lissau et al., 2004). Some observers connect obesity directly with television and other media. As you remember, the average U.S. home has three television sets and 15 media devices overall. Almost every U.S. teenager has a radio and a CD player in his or her bedroom, 64 percent also have a bedroom TV, and 41 percent have a video game console (Roberts & Foehr, 2004).

Eating Disorders

For some teenagers, unhealthy eating habits become life-threatening. Some eat almost nothing at all, and others eat until their stomach hurts. These habits are the start of eating disorders, which usually do not become full-blown until young adulthood. Symptoms appear long before disease is diagnosed, when concerns about the increase in body size caused by the normal growth spurt lead to efforts to stop weight gain.

MICHAEL NEWMAN / PHOTOEDIT, INC.

Is She Helping? Body image is a social as well as a personal concept. Adolescent boys and girls are keenly aware of their own and other people's bodies. It's evident that this couple is body-conscious as well as safety-conscious.

! ANSWER TO OBSERVATIONAL QUIZ (from page 457): No, they bummed them from a stranger at this San Jose, California, shopping mall. If you answered no, you probably had in mind the fact that most states, including California, are strictly enforcing their laws against selling cigarettes to minors. You may also have noticed the awkward way the girls are holding their cigarettes and realized that they have not yet been smoking long enough to have become addicted to nicotine.

ESPECIALLY FOR COLLEGE ROOMMATES You and your roommate respect each other's privacy, but your roommate is jeopardizing his or her health by losing a lot of weight, or getting drunk every weekend, or practicing unsafe sex. What should you do?

anorexia nervosa A serious eating disorder in which a person restricts eating to the point of emaciation and possible starvation. Most victims are high-achieving adolescent females.

At the worst extreme, a person develops **anorexia nervosa**, an eating disorder characterized by self-starvation, when vital organs do not receive the nourishment they need to function properly. According to DSM-IV-R, anorexia nervosa is revealed by four symptoms:

- Refusal to maintain body weight at least 85 percent of normal BMI
- Intense fear of gaining weight
- Disturbed body perception and denial of the problem
- In adolescent and adult females, lack of menstruation

LAUREN GREENFIELD / VII VIA AP

Guess Her Age Jennifer has gained some weight since she was first admitted to an eating-disorders clinic, but she still looks younger than her years. One hypothesis about anorexia is that it stems from an unconscious desire to avoid growing up. (Jennifer is 18 years old.)

If someone's BMI is 18 or lower, or if she (or, less often, he) loses more than 10 percent of body weight within a month or two, anorexia should be suspected (American Psychiatric Association, 2000).

Anorexia is a disease of the social context; in other words, the culture supports it (Mitchell & McCarthy, 2000). The disease was unknown to most doctors before 1950, although some saints from centuries ago were reputed to eat little or nothing, and 100 years ago some physicians described a "strange malady" involving fasting. In the 1950s anorexia was diagnosed in some high-achieving young women of high socioeconomic status (SES). It soon became more prevalent among college students, then younger students, first in the United States and other developed nations, and more recently in developing nations (Gordon, 2000; Walcott et al., 2003).

In North America, anorexia now appears in groups that once seemed unaffected—African, Hispanic, and Asian Americans. As a result, "It is critical that the possibility of eating and body image concerns are considered for all individuals, regardless of ethnic background" (Dounchis et al., 2001, p. 82). Although anorexia is primarily a woman's disorder, some men are affected, too, so the possibility should be considered for them as well.

About 1 percent of women in developed nations suffer from anorexia at some point in their lives. The rate is much higher among athletes, particularly dancers, gymnasts, and runners (Perriello, 2001; Thompson & Sherman, 1993). Julia is one, as the following explains.

A CASE TO STUDY

"Too Thin, As If That's Possible"

Julia writes of her first months of college, at age 17:

> I have never before felt so much pressure. Because my scholarship depends both on my running and on my maintaining a 3.6 grade point average, I've been stressed out much of the time. Academic work was never a problem for me in the past, but there's just so much more expected of you in college.
>
> It was pressure from my coach, my teammates, and myself that first led me to dieting. . . . I know that my coach was really disappointed in me. He called me aside about a month into the season. He wanted to know what I was eating, and he told me the weight I had gained was undoubtedly hurting my performance. He said that I should cut out snacks and sweets of any kind, and stick to things like salad to help me lose the extra pounds, and get back into shape. He also recommended some additional workouts. I was all for a diet—I hated that my clothes were getting snug. . . . At that point, I was 5 feet, 6 inches and weighed 145 pounds. When I started college I had weighed 130 pounds. . . .
>
> Once I started dieting, the incentives to continue were everywhere. My race time improved, so my coach was pleased. I felt more a part of the team and less like an outsider. My clothes were no longer snug, and when they saw me at my meets my parents said I looked great. I even

received an invitation to a party given by a fraternity that only invited the most attractive . . . women. After about a month, I was back to my normal weight of 130 pounds.

. . . I set a new weight goal of 115 pounds. I figured if I hit the gym more often and skipped breakfast altogether, it wouldn't be hard to reach that weight in another month or so. Of course, this made me even hungrier by lunchtime, but I didn't want to increase my lunch size. I found it easier to pace myself with something like crackers. I would break them into several pieces and only allow myself to eat one piece every 15 minutes. The few times I did this with friends in the dining hall I got weird looks and comments. I finally started eating lunch alone in my room. . . . I couldn't believe it when the scale said I was down to 115 pounds. I still felt that I had excess weight to lose. Some of my friends were beginning to mention that I was actually looking too thin, as if that's possible.

. . . All of which brings me to the present time. Even though I'm running great and I'm finally able to stick to a diet, everyone thinks I'm not taking good enough care of myself. . . . I'm doing my best to keep in control of my life, and I wish that I could be trusted to take care of myself.

Julia's roommate writes:

There were no more parties or hanging out at meals for her. . . . We were all worried, but none of us knew what to do. . . . I looked in the back of Julia's closet. A few months ago I had asked to borrow a tampon. She opened a new box and gave me one. The same box was still there with only that one missing. For the first time, I realized how serious Julia's condition could be.

A few days later, Julia approached me. Apparently she just met with one of the deans, who told her that she'd need to undergo an evaluation at the health center before she could continue practicing with the team. She asked me point blank if I had been talking about her to anyone. I told her how her mother had asked me if I had noticed any changes in her over the past several months, and how I honestly told her yes. She stormed out of the room and I haven't seen her since. I know how important the team is to Julia, so I am assuming that she'll be going to the health center soon. I hope that they'll be able to convince her that she's taken things too far, and that they can help her to get better.

[quoted in Gorenstein & Comer, 2002, pp. 275–280]

Julia, with her rapid weight loss that she does not see as a problem, is a classic case. Her denial is typical. Julia thinks she is finally able to stick to a diet and take control of her life, when in fact she is addicted to exercise and weight loss. Serious depression is linked to anorexia, and suicide is a possibility for Julia. Even if she is not suicidal, she is still in danger: Between 5 and 20 percent of those diagnosed with anorexia nervosa eventually die of this disease, even if they are hospitalized and treated (Lowe et al., 2001; Mitchell & McCarthy, 2000).

Undoubtedly you wonder why Julia's coach, her parents, and her friends did not notice her problem sooner and insist that she get help. This time lag is common: "By the time the anorexic reaches the point at which the disorder is clinically identified, she has already become entrapped in a complex web of psychological attitudes" (Gordon, 2000). Before that point, many people encourage rapid weight loss instead of welcoming the normal weight gain of a healthy, developing young person.

Actually, just at the time that her coach suggested she diet, Julia's weight after a month of college (145 for an athlete who is 5 feet, 6 inches tall) was within the normal BMI. She was not even marginally overweight, much less obese. Yet everyone seemed pleased when she lost 15 pounds. Although Julia was in danger, her parents and the fraternity boys gave her emotional incentives to continue dieting.

This is not to blame any of those people for her disease. According to several studies, the root cause of anorexia is genetic. Early feeding patterns and cultural norms are additional parts of the problem. Nonetheless, coaches, parents, and friends can help to halt the progression of the disease if they recognize the symptoms.

About three times as common as anorexia is the other major eating disorder of our time, **bulimia nervosa.** Compulsive binge eating, when thousands of calories are consumed within an hour or two, is followed by compulsive purging, either through vomiting or by inducing diarrhea with massive doses of laxatives.

bulimia nervosa An eating disorder in which the person, usually an adolescent or young adult female, repeatedly overeats and then purges through induced vomiting or abuse of laxatives.

Typically, bulimia has its origin in early adolescence, when some girls diet and then "pig out" together, not only eating until their stomach hurts and their brain shuts down but also unwittingly encouraging each other toward an eating disorder. Men can have bulimia as well. Usually it takes years for it to develop fully, and by late adolescence both bingeing and purging occur in secret. Bulimia is now found in virtually every city (but not every rural area) of the world (Walcott et al., 2003).

To warrant a clinical diagnosis of bulimia, a binge–purge episode must occur at least once a week for three months, the person must have an uncontrollable urge to overeat, and body image must be seriously distorted. Between 1 and 3

Response for Older Brothers and Sisters (from page 458): Smoking is very addictive; urge your sister to stop now, before the habit becomes ingrained. Most adolescents care more about immediate concerns than about the distant possibility of cancer or heart disease, so tell your sister about a smoker you know whose teeth are yellow, whose clothing and hair reek of smoke, and who is shorter than the rest of his or her family. Then tell your parents; they are your best allies in helping your sister have a healthy adolescence.

Response for College Roommates (from page 459): Think about how you would feel if your roommate died because you kept quiet. Discuss your concerns with your roommate, presenting facts as well as feelings. You cannot make anyone change, but you must raise the issue. You might also consult the college health service.

percent of young adult women in the United States are clinically bulimic (American Psychiatric Association, 2000), with college women particularly vulnerable.

People who suffer from bulimia are usually close to normal in weight. Therefore, those with bulimia do not starve to death. However, they may experience serious health problems, including severe damage to the gastrointestinal system and cardiac arrest from the strain of electrolyte imbalance (Gordon, 2000). Certainly they are not happy.

In all eating disorders, food consumption is disconnected from the internal cues of hunger, serving some psychosocial rather than bodily need. The stresses, weight gain, and changing body shape of puberty, in a culture obsessed with female thinness, make every contemporary girl vulnerable. Most do not develop a disorder; genes and habits help explain who does and who does not. But almost every female wishes to be a little thinner and thus risks ignoring the early signs of disease, in herself and her friends.

SUMMING UP

By the time the teen years are over, young people are as strong and healthy as they will ever be. However, self-destructive habits can cause illness, injury, and even death. Adolescents (from the tweens to emerging adulthood) have the lowest rates of death by disease but the highest rates of death by accidents and homicide in the world. Irresponsible sex is especially common among younger adolescents and can lead to unwanted pregnancy and untreated STIs. Another example of dangerous risk-taking is using psychoactive drugs, a phenomenon found among adolescents (especially males) worldwide. Drugs can affect body growth and brain development, and adolescents underestimate the likelihood of addiction. Further, almost no adolescent consumes the healthy diet (high in calcium and iron) that nutritionists recommend. Obesity is increasing among adolescents. In addition, some adolescents (especially girls) have serious eating disorders, either starving themselves or bingeing and purging.

■ SUMMARY

Puberty Begins

1. Puberty refers to the various changes that transform a child's body into an adult one. Even before the teenage years begin, biochemical signals from the hypothalamus to the pituitary gland to the adrenal glands (the HPA axis) increase testosterone, estrogen, and various other hormones. These hormones cause the body to grow and change.

2. Puberty is accompanied by many emotions. Some, such as quick mood shifts and thoughts about sex, are directly caused by hormones, but most are only indirectly hormonal. Instead, they are caused by reactions (from others and from the young person him- or herself) to the body changes of adolescence.

3. The visible changes of puberty normally occur anytime from about age 8 to 14; puberty most often begins between age 10 and 13. The young person's sex, genetic background, body fat, and level of family stress all contribute to this variation.

4. Girls generally begin and end the process before boys do. Adolescents who do not reach puberty at about the same age as their friends experience additional stresses. Generally (depending on culture, community, and cohort), early-maturing girls have the most difficult time of all.

The Transformations of Puberty

5. The growth spurt is an acceleration of growth in every part of the body. Peak weight increase usually comes before peak height and then peak muscle growth. The lungs and the heart also increase in size and capacity, and body rhythms (especially sleep) change.

6. Sexual characteristics emerge at puberty. The maturation of primary sexual characteristics means that by age 13 or so, menarche and spermarche have occurred, and the young person is soon capable of reproducing. In many ways the two sexes experience the same sexual characteristics, although they emerge in different ways.

7. Secondary sexual characteristics are not directly involved in reproduction but signify that the person is a man or a woman. Body shape, breasts, voice, body hair, and numerous other features differentiate males and females. Sexual activity is influenced more by culture than by physiology.

Brain Development in Adolescence

8. Various parts of the brain mature during puberty, each at its own rate. The neurological areas dedicated to emotional arousal (the limbic system) mature ahead of the areas that regulate and rationalize emotional expression (the prefrontal cortex). Consequently, many adolescents seek intense emotional experiences, untempered by rational thought.

9. The prefrontal cortex matures by the end of adolescence, allowing better planning and analysis. Throughout this period, myelination and experience allow faster and deeper thinking.

Health Hazards

10. Adolescents tend to be healthy. Diseases, both mild (colds and flu) and serious (cancer and heart disease), are rare. However, many take risks that lead to injury and accidental death at a rate five times that of younger children or middle-aged adults.

11. Among the health hazards for adolescents is sex before their bodies and minds are ready. Pregnancy before age 16 takes a physical toll on a growing girl, and STIs at any age can lead to infertility and even death.

12. Most adolescents use drugs, especially alcohol and tobacco, even though such substances impair growth of the body and of the brain. Prevention and moderation are possible, but programs need to be carefully designed to avoid the problem of generational forgetting.

13. To sustain body growth, most adolescents consume large quantities of food, although they do not always make healthy choices. Obesity is increasingly common, as are vitamin and mineral deficiencies that impair growth of bones and teeth and deplete energy. Some adolescents, especially girls, are so concerned with their body image that they suffer from anorexia or bulimia, two eating disorders that can severely impair their health.

■ KEY TERMS

puberty (p. 432)
menarche (p. 432)
spermarche (p. 432)
hormone (p. 433)
pituitary gland (p. 433)
adrenal glands (p. 433)
HPA axis (p. 433)
gonads (p. 433)
estrodiol (p. 434)
testosterone (p. 434)
growth spurt (p. 439)
primary sex characteristics (p. 443)
secondary sex characteristics (p. 443)
sexually transmitted infection (STI) (p. 451)
sexual abuse (p. 453)
child sexual abuse (p. 453)
drug abuse (p. 456)
drug addiction (p. 456)
binge drinking (p. 456)
generational forgetting (p. 457)
body image (p. 458)
anorexia nervosa (p. 460)
bulimia nervosa (p. 461)

■ KEY QUESTIONS

1. What aspects of puberty are under direct hormonal control?

2. What psychological responses are the result of the physical changes of puberty?

3. How do nature and nurture combine to enable young people to become parents?

4. Why is experiencing puberty "off time" especially difficult?

5. What are the similarities of puberty for males and females?

6. What are the differences of puberty for males and females?

7. Almost all neuroscientists agree about certain aspects of brain maturation. What are these aspects?

8. Why are sexually active adolescents more likely to contract STIs than are sexually active adults?

9. Name three reasons many adolescents have nutritional deficiencies.

10. Why is body image particularly likely to be distorted in adolescence?

■ APPLICATIONS

1. Visit a fifth-, sixth-, or seventh-grade class. Note variations in the size and maturity of the students. Do you see any patterns related to gender, ethnicity, body fat, or self-confidence?

2. Interview two to four of your friends who are in their late teens or early 20s about their memories of menarche or spermarche, including their memories of others' reactions. Do their comments indicate that these events are emotionally troubling for young people?

3. Talk with someone who became a parent before the age of 20. Were there any problems with the pregnancy, the birth, or the first years of parenthood? Would the person recommend young parenthood to another person? What would have been different if the baby had been born either three years earlier or three years later?

4. Adults disagree about the dangers of drugs. Find two people with very different opinions (e.g., a parent who would be horrified if his or her child used any drug and a parent who believes that young people should be allowed to drink or smoke at home). Ask them to explain their reasons, and write these down without criticism or disagreement. Later, present each with the arguments from the other person. What is their response? How open, flexible, and rational does it seem to be? Why are beliefs about drugs so deeply held?

Chapter Fifteen

Adolescence: Cognitive Development

I was driving four people I had never met before to a party for the 80th birthday of a mutual friend. One passenger was a young man. He spoke for hours, with great conviction, about the constitutional right to bear arms, about voting for candidates who could not win, about parents being honest with their children, about people loving each other despite differences in values or sexuality. And more.

My other three passengers were middle-aged or older. They bristled at his arrogance and certitude, as well as at some of his assertions. One said, "Yes, but . . . " Another, "No, because . . . " The young man did not budge, no matter how tactful his questioner was. I also tried and failed. Then we learned that he was 16 (he looked older). Argument stopped. Knowing his age helped explain his thought processes—and quieted us.

Adolescents often combine ego, logic, and emotion in ways that contrast with the cognitive processes of older people. Sometimes ego seems to overwhelm logic, sometimes emotion and analysis seem interspersed, and sometimes all three—ego, logic, and emotion—are combined and coordinated. These three modes of adolescent thought may be called egocentrism, formal operational thought, and postformal thinking, and they may appear in sequence over the dozen or so years of adolescence.

As you have already seen with biosocial development, age is not a good marker for the maturation of any particular adolescent. Some never seem egocentric, others are perpetually illogical, and many find postformal thought beyond their ability. Adolescents are brave, brash, and stubborn thinkers—admirable qualities, unless one's older passengers seek to change a teenager's mind.

This chapter explains all three stages—egocentrism, formal thought, and postformal thought—in sequence. Bear in mind that, for ease of discussion, adolescent cognition appears neater in these pages than it is in real life.

Adolescent Egocentrism

In early adolescence, roughly from age 10 to 13, most adolescents think about themselves a great deal. They wonder how others perceive them; they try to reconcile their conflicting feelings about parents, school, and close friends; they think deeply (but not always realistically) about their future; they reflect, at length, on each day's experiences; they worry about their connections to peers, families, schools, and the world. Because they have become avid thinkers, they are ready to learn, although that learning may not always occur in school.

Younger adolescents tend to imagine what others may be thinking about them and then take their hypotheses to be fact, even when such conclusions are distorted by self-absorption.

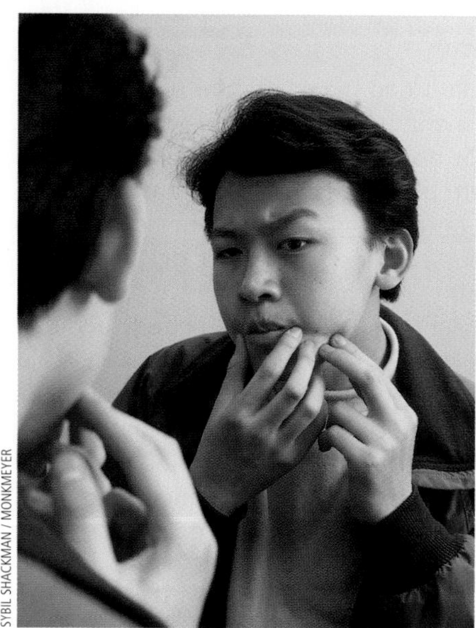

SYBIL SHACKMAN / MONKMEYER

Boys Do It, Too The cognitive capacity to think about oneself in egocentric terms makes many young people of both sexes spend hours combing their hair, adjusting their clothing, and searching for blemishes.

This is called **adolescent egocentrism.** It was first described by David Elkind (1967), who sought to explain the seeming illogic of many tweens.

Remember from Chapter 9 that *egocentric* means "self at the center." The difference between egocentrism during adolescence and the same trait at the stage of preoperational thought is that adolescents, unlike younger children, have developed a theory of mind and social cognition. This makes them aware that other people have their own thoughts. However, their egocentrism leads them to distort what those thoughts might be.

In egocentrism, adolescents regard themselves as uniquely special, much more socially significant (noticed by everyone) than they actually are. That is why it is hard for them to imagine another's perspective (Lapsley, 1993). You saw this in Chapter 14: Ben never contemplated how police might perceive a gang of young men fleeing from a patrol car at 2 A.M. More generally, Elkind (1979) explains that adolescents fail

> to differentiate the unique and the universal. A young woman who falls in love for the first time is enraptured with the experience, which is entirely new and thrilling. But she fails to differentiate between what is new and thrilling to herself, and what is new and thrilling to humankind. It is not surprising therefore, that this young lady says to her mother, "But Mother, you don't know how it feels to be in love."
>
> *[p. 96]*

Self-Important Thinking

Adolescent egocentrism makes it easy to take someone else's behavior personally. For example, a frown from a stranger or an offhand critique from a teacher could make a young teenager conclude that "no one likes me," and then deduce that "I am unlovable" or even "I dare not appear in public." More positive casual reactions—a smile from a sales clerk or an extra big hug from a younger brother—could lead to the thought "I am great" or "Everyone loves me," with similarly distorted self-perceptions.

Elkind gave several aspects of adolescent egocentrism special names. Among them is the **invincibility fable,** the person's idea that he or she is immune to harm or defeat. Some teenagers are convinced that, unlike other mortals, they will not suffer the consequences of fast driving, unprotected sex, addictive drugs, or self-starvation (all described in Chapter 14). When they do any of these things (as many do), and escape immediate harm (as most do), the reprieve makes them feel, not lucky and grateful, but special and proud.

For instance, in a survey of teenage cigarette smokers, only 1 in 20 thought they would still be smoking in five years, even though two-thirds of them had already tried to stop and failed, and at least 15 in 20 people who smoked as teenagers are still smoking as young adults (Siqueira et al., 2001). Such data about their own past or about the addiction of other people is not taken into account because each teenage smoker believes that he or she is invincible.

A second logical lapse resulting from adolescent egocentrism is the **personal fable.** Adolescents imagine their own lives as unique, heroic, or even legendary. In the personal fable, the young person perceives him- or herself as exceptional, distinguished by unusual experiences, talents, perspectives, and values.

Adolescents may consider their family members hopelessly ignorant and beneath them. The thought might occur to some adolescents that the family they live with must not be their biological family, because they were adopted or switched at birth (a thought so common that it has a name: the foundling fantasy). Teachers are too stupid; friends are too selfish.

Adolescents may become upset if others do not believe their personal fable. For example, one of my teenage students complained that it was patently unfair

adolescent egocentrism A characteristic of adolescent thinking that leads young people to focus on themselves to the exclusion of others. A person might believe, for example, that his or her thoughts, feelings, and experiences are unique, more wonderful or more awful than anyone else's.

invincibility fable A teenager's conviction, stemming from adolescent egocentrism, that he or she cannot be conquered or even harmed by anything that might vanquish a normal mortal, such as unprotected sex, drug abuse, or high-speed driving.

personal fable A teenager's belief, stemming from adolescent egocentrism, that he or she is destined to have a unique, heroic, or even legendary life.

NORBERT SCHWERIN / THE IMAGE WORKS

Not Me! A young woman jumps into the Pacific Ocean near Santa Cruz, California, while at a friend's birthday party. The jump is illegal, yet since 1975, 52 people have died taking that leap off these cliffs anyway. Hundreds of young people each year decide that the thrill is worth the risk, aided by the invincibility fable and by what they think are sensible precautions. (Note that she is wearing shoes. Also note that the dog has apparently decided against risking a jump.)

that millions mourned the Tejano singer Selena's tragic death. Using egocentric thinking, he imagined that he might die but that few would mourn or even care. I told him I would care; he dismissed that as unimportant. I said that Selena was extraordinarily talented and accomplished, that she brought joy to millions. He replied:

"But I am very talented, too; if I died, millions would never experience the joy I would bring them."

When I looked quizzical, he was offended: "How do you know I'm not just as talented as she was?"

A third type of egocentrism involves the **imaginary audience.** Adolescents tend to think of themselves as being at center stage, with all eyes on them, because their egocentrism leads them to assume that other people are as intensely interested in them as they themselves are. As a result, they tend to fantasize about how others might react to their appearance and behavior.

imaginary audience The egocentric belief that other people are watching, and taking note, of one's appearance, ideas, and behavior. This belief that "It's all about me" makes people very self-conscious.

The imaginary audience can cause teenagers to enter a crowded room as if they believe themselves to be the most attractive human beings alive. They might dye their hair shocking pink or play their music at high volume to call attention to themselves. The reverse is also possible: Teenagers might try to avoid everyone lest someone notice a blemish on their chin or a stain on their sleeve. Many a middle school student balks at going to school with a bad haircut or the wrong shoes.

For both boys and girls, acute self-consciousness about their appearance is higher between ages 10 and 14 than earlier or later (Rankin et al., 2004). They would rather not stand out from their peers, hoping instead to blend in racially, religiously, economically, and in every other way.

As the acute self-consciousness of adolescent egocentrism reveals, young people in the midst of puberty are not yet comfortable in the broader social world. This is one reason why many of them fuss over their hair and clothing before appearing in public. In fact, the reasons cited for sleep deprivation include not only the two explained in Chapter 14 (a phase delay in diurnal rhythm and the early start time of many high schools) but also the extra time required for "substantial morning grooming routines" (Fredriksen et al., 2004, p. 93).

Especially for Parents of Adopted Children Should adolescents be told if they were adopted?

The power of the imaginary audience also explains many adolescents' concern about the audience of their peers, who presumably judge every visible oddity of their appearance and behavior. No wonder, then, that one adolescent remarked, "I would like to be able to fly if everyone else did; otherwise it would be rather conspicuous" (quoted in Steinberg, 1993). Understanding egocentrism helps parents interpret their children's thoughts, as the following stories about Bethany and Jim reveal.

IN PERSON

Bethany and Jim

It was a humid midsummer afternoon. Bethany prevailed on me to go with her to the Metropolitan Museum of Art. I was ready in five minutes, but, because she was an adolescent, it took her much longer. In fact, we left the house so late that I feared the museum would close soon after we got there. Fortunately, our subway arrived quickly and moved us rapidly to our stop. But when we climbed up to street level from the station, we encountered a sudden downpour. Bethany stopped and became angry—at me!

> **She:** You didn't bring an umbrella? You should have known.
> **Me:** It's OK—we'll walk quickly. It's a warm rain.
> **She:** But we'll get all wet.
> **Me:** It's OK. We'll dry.
> **She:** But people will see us with our hair all wet.
> **Me:** Honey, no one cares what we look like. And we won't see anyone we know.
> **She:** That's OK for you to say. You're already married.

At this I was not only impatient, I was bewildered. I asked her, incredulously, "Do you think you are going to meet your future husband here?"

She looked at me as if I were unbelievably stupid. "No, of course not. But people will look at me and think, 'She'll never find a husband looking like that!'"

Another example is reported by a father, himself a psychotherapist:

> The best way I can describe what happens [during adolescence] is to relate how I first noticed the change in my son. He was about 13 years of age. . . . I was driving 65 miles an hour in a 55-mile-an-hour zone.
>
> He suddenly turned toward me and shouted, "Dad!"
>
> I was startled and responded by saying, "What is it, Jim!"
>
> Then there was this pause as he folded his arms and turned slowly in my direction and said, "Dad, do you realize how fast you are driving this car?" . . .
>
> "Oh, I'm doing 65 miles per hour!" (as if I didn't know it). He then came right back at me and said,
>
> "Dad! Do you know what the speed limit is on this highway?"
>
> "Yes, Jim, it's 55 miles an hour."
>
> He then said, "Dad! Do you realize that you are traveling 10 miles over the speed limit! . . . Don't you care about my life at all! Do you have any idea of how many thousands of people lose their lives every year on our nation's highways who exceed the speed limit!"
>
> Now I was beginning to get angry and I responded by saying, "Look, Jim, I have no idea how many people are killed every year, you were right I shouldn't have been speeding; I promise I won't ever do it again, so let us just forget it!"
>
> Not being satisfied, he continued, "Dad! Any idea what would happen if the front wheel of this car came off doing 65 miles per hour, how many lives you might jeopardize!"
>
> He kept on with this for another 10 minutes until I finally got him quiet for about 20 seconds! Then he came back at me and said, "Dad! I've been thinking about this."
>
> Once he said that, I knew I was in deep trouble! You see, my son was so easy to deal with before he started to think! Who told him he had a right to start thinking! Before this all happened he would ask, why, and I would simply give him the answer and it was good enough!
>
> *[Garvin, 1994, pp. 39-41]*

Bethany and Jim ("Don't you care about my life at all!") were egocentric, with an imaginary audience ("People will look at me and think"), but socially aware ("You're already married," "thousands of people"). That's adolescent egocentrism.

As researchers note the logic and future orientation of adolescent thought, they realize that adolescent egocentrism is not always destructive, "not distorted, egocentric, and somewhat paranoid thinking." Instead, it "may signal growth toward cognitive maturity" (Vartanian, 2001, p. 378).

At least adolescents, reflecting on their own existence, try to imagine the opinions of others. Their conclusions may be invalid and stubbornly held, but their thinking is more advanced than that of children, who never contemplate what might be, especially when those future possibilities include unknown husbands and unusual car crashes.

Indeed, the invincibility fable can lead to brave deeds and heroic sacrifices. Joan of Arc was a young adolescent when voices told her to save France. By 16, she convinced the future King Charles VII that she should lead the French soldiers to victory against the English. In battle after battle she did exactly that, until she was captured, imprisoned, and, at age 20, burned at the stake because she said God talked directly to her.

Joan died six centuries ago and became a saint in 1920, but even today thousands of egocentric adolescents are considered heroic martyrs or misled fanatics, depending on one's perspective. As one expert explains, "Zeal in adolescents can fuel positive humanistic efforts to feed the poor and care for the sick, yet it can also lead to dogmatic attitudes, intolerance . . . passions captured by a negatively charismatic figure like Adolf Hitler or Osama bin Laden" (Dahl, 2004, p. 21). It is said that "adolescents ride the waves of historical events" (Brown & Larson, 2002, p. 12), which means that, given the right historical circumstances, adolescent egocentrism can benefit all humanity.

Response for Parents of Adopted Children (from page 467): Probably not now. Most counselors believe that adopted children should be told very early. Adolescents may react irrationally to learning new information about themselves.

Teaching and Learning in Middle School

Many developmentalists have noted that young people tend to become depressed, rebellious, or apathetic after leaving elementary school and entering their next level of schooling (Eccles, 2004). In many nations of the world, this is the point at which children abandon school, not always by choice.

Even in China, where education is prized and the government's goal is education for all through ninth grade, "only about 48 percent of rural residents and 79 percent of urban residents attain more than a primary school education" (Orsini, 2005). In the developed nations of Europe, North America, Australia, and Japan, everyone is expected (and often required) to attend school through age 17 or so. This creates problems when young people must be in school but do not wish to be. Similar problems occur for students in **middle school** (discussed next) and high school (discussed later).

middle school A term for the years of school between elementary and high school; also called junior high or intermediate schools. Some systems have no middle school, only schools for grades 1–8 or 7–12.

The Low Point of Education

In the United States in the twentieth century, "comprehensive" high schools broke away from elementary schools and then split into senior and junior high schools. The junior high school followed the academic configuration of high school, but that structure often clashed with the intellectual and social needs of early adolescents. Meanwhile, puberty began at younger ages, so many sixth-grade students seemed too big for elementary school. New structures were created that were called intermediate schools or, as here, middle schools.

For decades, scholars have noticed that development becomes difficult at about age 11. School grades tend to decline, and the first year of middle school is a particularly "low ebb" of learning (Covington & Dray, 2002). Those who teach often feel ineffective (Eccles, 2004).

Students' relationships with one another take a turn for the worse. Although friendship and the peer group are more important than ever, several studies have found that, unlike in elementary school, aggressive children tend to be popular and admired in middle school (Cillessen & Mayeux, 2004; Rodkin et al., 2000). These popular children are usually relationally aggressive: They spread rumors, exclude people, criticize classmates behind their backs, and make demands as the price of friendship.

Especially for Middle School Teachers You think your lectures are interesting and you know you care about your students, yet many of them cut class, come late, or seem to sleep through it. What do you do?

Bullying becomes less frequent during each year of elementary school but then increases noticeably during the first year of middle school, whether that is in grade 5, 6, or 7. (It is not the age of the children but the entry into a new school that correlates with the upsurge.) As middle school progresses, relationally aggressive boys as well as girls increase in popularity, and their ability to shun

RAJESH KUMAR SINGH / AP PHOTO

Middle School Slump? These students in rural India are the same age as middle school students in developed nations, but their enthusiasm for school has not waned. One reason is that they do not take education for granted; only a select few are able to stay in school beyond age 11. Another reason may be seen here: The government is trying to upgrade the curriculum by providing traveling, Internet-connected computers.

other students adds to their status. For example, sixth-graders who wish to stay popular stop talking to unpopular peers (Rose et al., 2004).

Another set of signs of middle school problems is more ominous:

> A number of disorders and symptoms of psychopathology, including depression, self-injury behavior, substance abuse, eating disorders, bipolar disorder, and schizophrenia have striking developmental patterns corresponding to transitions in early and late adolescence.
>
> *[Masten, 2004, p. 310]*

So much happens in adolescence (changes in hormone levels, body shape, families, and culture) that the increase in psychopathology cannot be caused entirely by the transition to middle school. Indeed, when developmentalists first noticed the sudden rise in psychopathology at about age 12, they thought the physiological changes of puberty were the cause. However, careful monitoring of the stages of pubertal development did not confirm this hypothesis (Simmons & Blyth, 1987). Puberty (early, middle, or late) does not produce psychopathology or even the low self-esteem and rebellion that are precursors of internalizing and externalizing disorders.

A related hypothesis was that genes for psychopathology become activated at puberty, especially if a family has not helped the child develop emotional regulation and prosocial behavior (Walker, 2002). This hypothesis has not been disproved. Nonetheless, many social scientists find that emotionally vulnerable children might be pushed toward psychopathology by the social context and structure of middle schools.

Designing a School

The first junior highs were not designed; they were copies of high schools, with less challenging curricula. The result was that middle schools were "developmentally regressive" (Eccles, 2004, p. 141)—a step backward just when the children are ready to advance. Typically, compared with the final years of elementary school, intellectual demands are reduced, grades fall, and personal attention declines. Many middle school students are bored in school, in contrast to the eager learners in elementary schools.

The routines of the school day are unsettling to early adolescents. In many middle schools, students move from classroom to classroom every 40 minutes or so. Teachers instruct in a particular subject, unlike elementary school teachers, who remain with one group of students all day. Extracurricular activities and sports are more competitive than in elementary school, which excludes the less able children. Given their egocentric concern for appearance and their self-consciousness about puberty, many capable students avoid sports if they must shower or even change clothes in the locker room.

The intense personal involvement that characterizes avid learners at any age, particularly those who are egocentric, is undercut by the way middle schools are structured. The short class periods prevent in-depth discussion, and the multiplicity of teachers prevents the intense, more personal teacher–student involvement that aids learning (Fredricks et al., 2004).

Much of the research on the deficiencies of middle schools has come from the United States, where virtually every configuration of fifth through ninth grade has been tried and found wanting. Other nations have not succeeded, either. A review of adolescent education throughout the world finds that "no culture or nation has worked out a surefire educational psychology to guarantee that every one of the youth is motivated in school" (Larson & Wilson, 2004, p. 318).

Does cognitive development during early adolescence suggest ways to improve middle school education? Young adolescents can become passionate about ideas, especially their own ideas that criticize accepted practices, but they are also very self-conscious. The educational goal might be to create a learning environment where students can elaborate and develop their ideas without feeling harshly judged. Many educators are restructuring middle schools to suit adolescent learning, with some success (Midgley, 2002).

One obvious change is to reduce the fragmented schedules. A high school model has students traveling to a different teacher, classmates, and classroom for eight or more subjects each semester. Instead, some middle school students stay in their homeroom with their class. Teachers come to them, often one teacher for English and social studies and another for science and math; this arrangement gives the students a chance to get to know one another and to become familiar with at least two of their teachers. Some middle schools allow more time for each class session; the students have a math and science unit for two hours, three days a week, rather than 40 minutes each day for math and the same for science.

School Bonding

Younger adolescents are egocentric not only about themselves but also about their groups—including their school group. This means that efforts to connect them with their class, their grade, and their school might succeed—eventually. A successful project to increase "school bonding" encouraged interaction between teachers and students and improved student involvement during class and afterward. This particular project began in elementary school and yielded results in the first year of middle school, and again in later high school (Hawkins et al., 2003). This is in accord with a developmental perspective: Some children's strengths are temporarily hidden during middle school.

The benefits of bonding with teachers may not be noticed immediately—or may even recede. The fifth grade of a middle school in Ogden, Utah, was "engineered" into small "family pods," in which a group of teachers worked with a limited number of students. The students realized that their new academic environment was more diversified than their elementary schools had been, and they

RESPONSE FOR MIDDLE SCHOOL TEACHERS (from page 469): Students need both challenge and involvement; avoid lessons that are too easy or too passive. Create small groups; assign oral reports, debates, and role-plays; and so on. Remember that adolescents like to hear each other's thoughts and their own voices.

perceived this as an improvement. A similar group of students from the same community but without family pods felt negative about the transition from elementary school. But the middle school slump was postponed by only a year: Once the students were in traditional classes, their performance and attitudes fell to the same low ebb as those of other middle school students (Barber et al., 2004).

SUMMING UP

Thinking reaches a heightened self-consciousness during the preteen years, when adolescent egocentrism is often apparent. Many young adolescents have unrealistic notions about their place in the social world, and they sometimes imagine themselves invincible, unique, and the center of attention. Many are bored by school, often because middle schools tend to be less personal, less flexible, and more tightly regulated than elementary schools. Given the nature of physical and cognitive growth during these years, such school structures are antithetical to the needs of adolescents. Consequently, education reaches a low ebb for many students. Restructuring middle schools may be one way to remedy the problem.

formal operational thought In Piaget's theory, the fourth and final stage of cognitive development, characterized by more systematic logic and the ability to think about abstract ideas.

Thinking Processes During the Teen Years

In sorting through their new life experiences, people in their teen years finally develop one advantage that younger children, even most younger adolescents, do not have: They think logically. Sometime between the ages of 14 and 18, young people typically become markedly less egocentric. As you remember from Chapter 14, their new logic is not always used, especially when the rush of emotions is fueled by stress, drugs, sleep deprivation, friendship, or sexual passion. Logic is sometimes apparent in the mind of the high school student and sometimes not. At least logic is possible, however.

Formal Operational Thought

Jean Piaget was the first to notice and describe the advances of adolescent reasoning. He realized that cognitive processes, not just the content of thoughts, change significantly. He called this stage **formal operational thought,** when thinking is no longer restricted to personal experiences (as in concrete operations). The adolescent can consider logical concepts and possibilities that cannot be observed (Inhelder & Piaget, 1958).

Abstraction Way Beyond Counting on Fingers and Toes This high school student explains an algebra problem, a behavior that requires a level of hypothetical and abstract thought beyond that of any concrete operational child—and of many adults. At the beginning of concrete operational thought, children need blocks, coins, and other tangible objects to help them understand math. By later adolescence, in the full flower of formal operational thought, such practical and concrete illustrations are irrelevant.

WILL MCINTYRE / PHOTO RESEARCHERS, INC.

An easy way to grasp the distinction between formal and concrete thinking is to remember the school curriculum. Younger children can learn to multiply real numbers (4 × 8), whereas adolescents learn to multiply unreal numbers, such as $(2x)(3y)$ or even $(-5xy)(+3zy)$. Younger children study other cultures by learning about daily life—drinking goat's milk or building an igloo, for instance—whereas adolescents can understand concepts like "gross national product" and "fertility rate." Younger students study biology by planting carrots and feeding rabbits, whereas adolescents learn about cells and bacteria.

Piaget developed many experiments to explore stages of cognitive development. He found a sudden advance in reasoning power soon after puberty. Other researchers have not found a *sudden* advance, but it does seem that adolescents improve in memory and strategy, especially when they put their minds to it (Luciana et al., 2005).

Piaget's Experiments

Piaget and his colleagues devised a number of tasks to reveal formal operational thought (Inhelder & Piaget, 1958). They sought to demonstrate that, "in contrast to concrete operational children, formal operational adolescents imagine all possible determinants . . . [and] systematically vary the factors one by one, observe the results correctly, keep track of the results, and draw the appropriate conclusions" (Miller, 2002).

In one experiment (diagrammed in Figure 15.1), children were asked to balance a scale with weights that could be hooked onto the scale's arms. To master this task, a person must realize that the heaviness of the weights and their distance from the center interact reciprocally to affect balance. Therefore, a heavier weight close to the center can be counterbalanced with a lighter weight far from the center on the other side. For example, a 12-gram weight placed 2 centimeters to the left of the center might balance a 6-gram weight placed 4 centimeters to the right of the center.

This concept, and a method to discover it, was completely beyond the ability or interest of 3- to 5-year-olds. In Piaget's experiments, they randomly hung different weights on different hooks. By age 7, children realized that the scale could be balanced by putting the same amount of weight on both arms, but they didn't realize that the distance of the weights from the center of the scale is crucial.

By age 10, the end of the concrete operational stage, children often realized the importance of the weights' locations, but their efforts to coordinate weight and distance to balance the scale involved trial and error, not logic. They succeeded by putting equal weight at equal distances, but they did not know how to get past that.

Finally, by about age 13 or 14, some children hypothesized the effect of the relationship between weight and distance. By systematically testing this hypothesis, they correctly formulated the mathematical relation between weight and distance from the center, solving the balance problem accurately and efficiently. Piaget attributed each of these advances to the children's attainment of the next-higher cognitive stage.

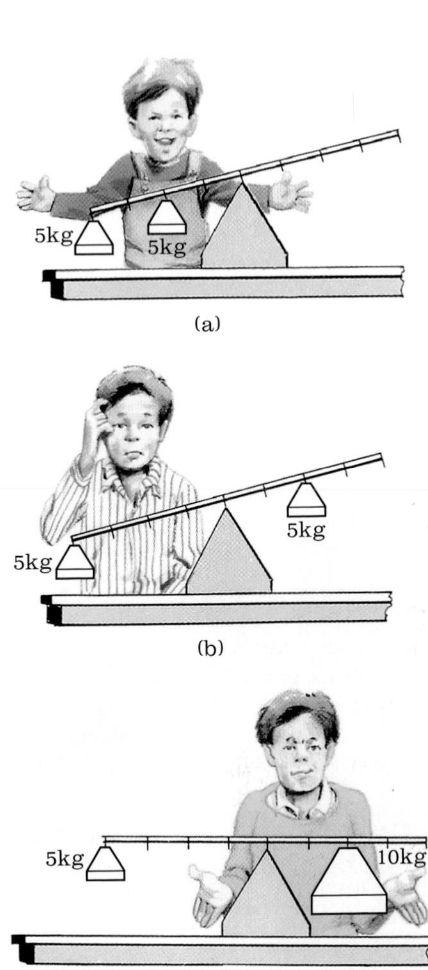

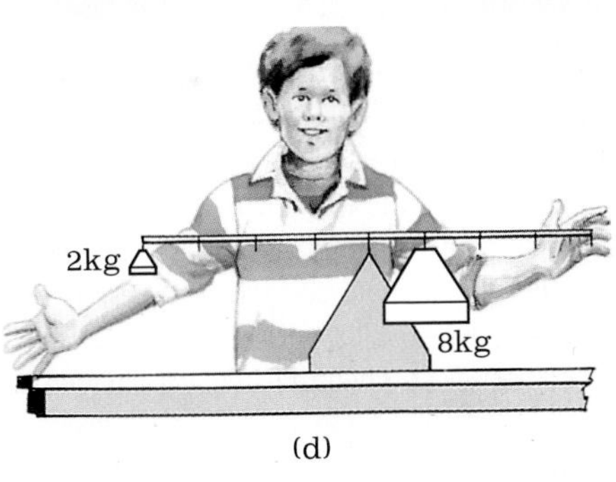

FIGURE 15.1 **How to Balance a Scale** Piaget's balance-scale test of formal reasoning, as it is attempted by *(a)* a 4-year-old, *(b)* a 7-year-old, *(c)* a 10-year-old, and *(d)* a 14-year-old. The key to balancing the scale is to make weight times distance from the center equal on both sides of the center; the realization of that principle requires formal operational thought.

Hypothetical-Deductive Thought

One hallmark of adolescent thought is the capacity to think of possibility, not just reality. Adolescents "start with possible solutions and progress to determine which is the real solution" (Lutz & Sternberg, 1999, p. 283). They realize with joy that almost anything is possible. Nothing is inevitable, and even the impossible can be considered (Falk & Wilkening, 1998). "Here and now" is only one of many alternatives that include "there and then," "long, long ago," "nowhere," "not yet," and "never." In Piaget's words:

> *Possibility* no longer appears merely as an extension of an empirical situation or of action actually performed. Instead, it is *reality* that is now secondary to *possibility*.
>
> *[Inhelder & Piaget, 1958, p. 251; emphasis in original]*

Adolescents are therefore primed to engage in **hypothetical thought**, reasoning about *what-if* propositions that may or may not reflect reality. For example, consider:

> If dogs are bigger than elephants, and
> If mice are bigger than dogs,
> Are elephants smaller than mice?

hypothetical thought Thought that includes propositions and possibilities that may not reflect reality.

Younger children, presented with such counterfactual questions, answer "no." They have seen elephants and mice, so the logic escapes them. Some adolescents answer "yes." They understand what *if* means.

Hypothetical thought transforms the way teenagers perceive their world, not necessarily for the better. Reflection about serious issues becomes complicated because many hypothetical ideas are considered, sometimes sidetracking conclusions about the immediate issues at hand. The complications were illustrated by one high school student who wanted to keep a friend from making a life-threatening decision but did not want to judge her, because

> to . . . judge [someone] means that whatever you are saying is right and you know what's right. You know it's right for them and you know it's right in every situation. [But] you can't know if you are right. Maybe you are right. But then, right in what way?
>
> *[quoted in Gilligan et al., 1990]*

DOUG MARTIN / PHOTO RESEARCHERS, INC.

Deductive Reasoning High school chemistry classes first teach students the general principles and then ask them to test the principles with specific substances. There is no way a student could simply be given these materials and told to figure out some generalities, as a teacher of 8-year-olds, with much simpler and safer substances, might do. Younger children think inductively; these students think deductively as well.

deductive reasoning Reasoning from a general statement, premise, or principle, through logical steps, to figure out (deduce) specifics. Sometimes called "top-down" thinking.

inductive reasoning Reasoning from one or more specific experiences or facts to a general conclusion. Sometimes called "bottom-up" reasoning, induction may be less advanced than deduction.

Although adolescents are not always sure what is "right in what way," they see what is wrong. At every age it is easier to criticize something than to create it, but criticism itself shows an advance in reasoning. (Remember Jim, who lectured his father about speed limits because he "started thinking.")

Unlike younger children, adolescents do not accept current conditions because "that's how things are." They criticize what is, precisely because of their hypothetical thinking. They can imagine how things could be, would be, and should be, in a world where justice is realized, people are always sincere, and the sanctity of human life is truly recognized. This may be hypothetical thinking at its best.

In developing the capacity to think hypothetically, by age 14 or so, adolescents become capable of **deductive reasoning,** which begins with an idea or premise and then uses logic to draw specific conclusions (Galotti, 2002; Keating, 2004). By contrast, as you remember from Chapter 12, **inductive reasoning** predominates during the school years, as children accumulate facts and personal experiences to aid their thought.

In essence, a child's reasoning goes like this: "This is a duck; it waddles and quacks. This other creature also waddles and quacks. Therefore, if a creature waddles like a duck and quacks like a duck, it must be a duck." This reasoning is inductive in that it progresses from particulars ("waddles like" and "quacks like") to a general conclusion ("it's a duck"). By contrast, deduction progresses from the general to the specific: "If it's a duck, it will waddle and quack" (see Figure 15.2).

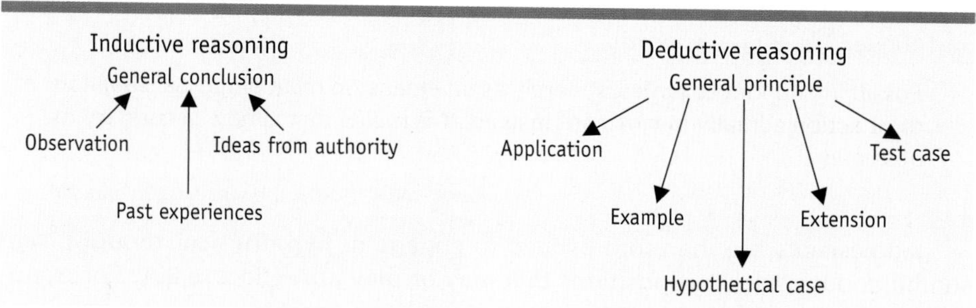

FIGURE 15.2 **Bottom Up or Top Down?** Children, as concrete operational thinkers, are likely to draw conclusions on the basis of their own experiences and what they have been told. This is called inductive, or bottom-up, reasoning. Adolescents can think deductively, from the top down.

THINKING LIKE A SCIENTIST

Religious Freedom for All?

The power of deductive thought is most evident when moral issues are involved, because then rationality may be tested by competing values. This method is used by many social scientists to find out what a person thinks when a favored value (mother, apple pie, democracy) clashes with another favored value (father, dieting, minority rights).

When asked, three groups of adolescents—seventh-graders, eleventh-graders, and college students—all endorsed the abstract principle of free exercise of religion, as upheld by the United Nations and the Constitution of the United States. The tweens, teens, and emerging adults agreed that everyone should be able to worship in his or her own way. (They were from California, where many Buddhists, Muslims, Jews, and various kinds of Christians live, so freedom of religion was familiar to them in practice as well as in ideology.)

Then their endorsement was put to the test, with questions such as "What if a particular religion refused to allow low-income people to become priests?" (Helwig, 1995). This hypothetical *what-if* question would be rejected as impossible by most concrete operational thinkers, who have a very difficult time following any logical argument that begins with a false premise (Moshman, 2000).

All three age groups were past concrete operational thought, and their answers varied by age, as Figure 15.3 shows. Most of the youngest group (94 percent) abandoned freedom of religion when put to the test. If a religion excluded low-income priests, only 6 percent still endorsed religious freedom.

In contrast, 81 percent of those in mid-adolescence (the eleventh-graders) stuck to the principle. They used deductive reasoning to go from the premise to the conclusion that religious freedom should prevail even when a particular religious practice seemed unfair. Note the dramatic switch over a four-year period.

The college students were most conflicted. For 38 percent, economic justice was a more important principle than religious freedom, while 62 percent felt that religious freedom should be upheld. Their struggle to balance logic and personal values is typical of postformal thought, described at the end of this chapter.

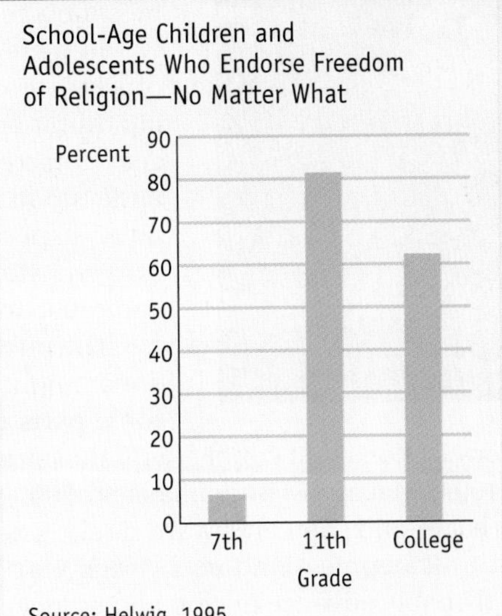

FIGURE 15.3 **Adherence to Principle** High school students are more capable of deductive reasoning than are middle schoolers, as shown by the fact that a much higher percentage of eleventh-graders were able to perceive religious freedom as a basic principle and to cling to it no matter what conflicting circumstances were proposed by the researcher.

Most developmentalists agree with Piaget that adolescent thought can be qualitatively different from children's thought (Fischer & Bidell, 1998; Flavell et al., 2002; Keating, 2004; Moshman, 2000). They disagree about whether this change is quite sudden (Piaget) or gradual (information-processing theory); about whether change results from context (sociocultural theory) or biological changes (epigenetic theory); about whether changes occur in every domain (Piaget) or more selectively (all the other theories).

These criticisms are familiar: They have been described in previous chapters. Relatively few current scholars accept Piaget's description of adolescent cognition in its entirety. Nonetheless, Piaget deserves praise because he "launched the systematic study of adolescent cognitive development" (Keating, 2004, p. 45).

Thus, Piaget is credited with opening the door to the study of adolescent cognition. On the other side of that door is a second mode of thinking that Piaget never described.

Intuitive, Emotional Thought

The fact that adolescents *can* use hypothetical-deductive reasoning does not necessarily mean that they *do* use it when issues of practical importance arise. Advanced reasoning is counterbalanced by the increasing power of intuitive thinking, which leads to a "dual-process model" of adolescent thought (Keating, 2004, p. 61).

Researchers are increasingly convinced that the adult brain has at least two distinct pathways, called *dual-processing* networks. The two processing networks have been designated by various names: intuitive/analytic, implicit/explicit, contextualized/decontextualized; unconscious/conscious; creative/factual; or emotional/intellectual.

BOB DAEMMRICH / THE IMAGE WORKS

Reality and Fantasy Because teenagers can think analytically and hypothetically, they can use computers not only to obtain factual information and to e-mail friends but also to imagine and explore future possibilities. This opportunity may be particularly important for adolescents like 17-year-old Julisa *(right)*. She is a student in a high school in Brownsville, Texas, that offers computer labs and other programs to children of migrant laborers.

These pairs of terms do not necessarily refer to the same functions. You may remember another pair from Chapter 14—the limbic system and the prefrontal cortex. No matter which terms are used, neuroscientists as well as cognitive psychologists recognize that two pathways might develop on parallel tracks within the mind, so that a strong emotional response (of fear or anger, for instance, arising from the amygdala) may not be connected to analysis of the actual threat.

In general, high levels of emotions produce a rush of stress hormones, which slows down rational thinking, but much more research is needed before the precise interrelationships of various brain areas are understood (Davis et al., 2003). It is known that, with time, experience, and maturation, coordination improves within the brain, especially between emotion and reflection (Keating, 2004).

The intriguing possibility is that thoughts and emotions might build and develop independently, with some parts of the brain reaching conclusions and generalizations that conflict with those reached via other parts of the brain (Epstein, 1994; Macrae & Bodenhausen, 2000; Stanovich, 1999). A person might quickly react—and soon afterward doubt whether that reaction was justified at all.

Thoughts along each track may either coexist or conflict, and *both* tracks probably advance during adolescence (Galotti, 2002; Reyna, 2004). This is evident neurologically, in speed as well as depth; namely, myelination increases, allowing quicker brain communication between thoughts and behavior and between one thought and another (Walker, 2002). Cognitive psychologists who explore the thinking of adolescents find that the same advancement is evident when it comes to practical matters.

Thus, humans may have "two parallel, interacting modes of information-processing" (Epstein, 1994, p. 709). Both modes advance during adolescence (Moshman, 2000; Reyna, 2004):

- The first mode begins with a prior belief or an assumption, rather than with a logical premise or objective method. This is called **intuitive** (or *heuristic* or *experiential*) **thought.** Thoughts spring forth from memories and feelings. Intuitive cognition is quick and powerful; it feels "right."
- The second mode is the formal, logical, hypothetical-deductive thinking described by Piaget. This is called **analytic thought,** because it involves rational analysis of many factors whose interactions must be separately calculated, as in the problem of balancing the scale. Analytic thinking requires a certain level of intellectual maturity, brain capacity, motivation, and practice.

intuitive thought Thought that arises from an emotion or a hunch, beyond rational explanation. Past experiences, cultural assumptions, and sudden impulse are the precursors of intuitive thought. Also called *heuristic* or *experiential thought.*

analytic thought Thought that results from analysis, such as a systematic ranking of pros and cons, risks and consequences, possibilities and facts. Analytical thought depends on logic and rationality.

Comparing Intuition and Analysis

The advantage of intuitive thinking is that it is quick and emotional; the disadvantage is that it may be wrong (Moshman, 2000). Rational thinking may be wrong as well, because a system that assumes that step-by-step analysis is always best has built-in biases (Gladwell, 2005; Shafir & LeBoeuf, 2002). Think about the following:

> Every card in a pack has a letter on one side and a number on the other. Prove or disprove this proposition: *If a card has a vowel on one side, then it always has an even number on the other side.*
>
> Of the following four cards, turn over only those cards that will confirm or disconfirm the proposition:
>
> **E 7 K 4**
>
> Which cards must be turned over?

While you are pondering (the answer will be presented soon), consider the research of Paul Klaczynski on the thought processes of hundreds of adolescents, half younger (average age 13) and half older (average age 16). In one study (Klaczynski, 2001), adolescents were presented with 19 problems of logic, including the following:

> Timothy is very good-looking, strong, and does not smoke. He likes hanging around with his male friends, watching sports on TV, and driving his Ford Mustang convertible. He's very concerned with how he looks and with being in good shape. He is a high school senior now and is trying to get a college scholarship.
>
> *Based on this [description], rank each statement in terms of how likely it is to be true. . . . The most likely statement should get a 1. The least likely statement should get a 6.*
>
> ______Timothy has a girlfriend.
> ______Timothy is an athlete.
> ______Timothy is popular and an athlete.
> ______Timothy is a teacher's pet and has a girlfriend.
> ______Timothy is a teacher's pet.
> ______Timothy is popular.

In ranking these statements, 71 percent of the high school students made at least one analytic error. They ranked a double statement (e.g., athlete *and* popular) as more likely than either of the single statements included in it (athlete *or* popular). A double statement cannot be more likely than either of its parts; therefore, those 71 percent were illogical and wrong. This is an example of intuitive thought: The high school students jumped to the more inclusive statement, taking a quick, experiential leap rather than sticking to the narrow, logical task at hand.

In this study, almost all adolescents were analytical and logical on some of the 19 problems and illogical on others. Generally, logic improved with age and education, although not necessarily with intelligence. Klaczynski (2001) concludes that, even though teenagers are sufficiently mature to solve logical problems, "most adolescents do not demonstrate a level of performance commensurate with their abilities" (p. 854).

What would motivate high school students to use—or fail to use—their newly acquired analytic mode of thinking? These students had been taught how scientists think, using empirical evidence and deductive reasoning. But they did not always think that way. Why not?

In another series of experiments, Klaczynski (2000) asked adolescents to judge the strength and persuasiveness of a bogus research report regarding the effect of religious affiliation on parenting practices. (The study supposedly found that a small group from a particular religion were bad parents.)

When the research findings were unfavorable to their own religion, most adolescents pointed out the fallacies in the way the participants were chosen, the research was designed, or the conclusions were drawn. Some even rejected the premise as implausible. One said, "I don't see why they did this research," ignoring the fact that research is needed to disprove as well as to prove hypotheses. However, when the conclusion was favorable to their own religion, fewer found fault with the logic or the hypothesis.

Older adolescents were more analytic than younger ones, as would be expected with more exposure to science classes as well as more maturation, presumably leading to advances in formal operational thought. They could and did identify more flaws than the younger adolescents did in the conclusions of both kinds, those that favored their own religion as well as the opposite. But they were also more biased, in that they saw greater weaknesses in the unfavorable research, and they were more likely to dismiss the conclusions as implausible, impossible, and flat-out wrong (Klaczynski, 2000).

Surprisingly, after reading the bogus research, the adolescents tended to value their own faith more than they had before. Similar results are found when the research challenges ethnic identity. In other words, analyzing research does not detract from beliefs already held; just the opposite. It seems that becoming an adolescent improves both kinds of thought—the ability to analyze logically and the ability to justify intuitive conclusions (Reyna, 2004).

Klaczynski (2000) wrote:

> Analytic reasoning competence . . . has long been considered the pinnacle of adolescent cognitive development [but] . . . biased use of judgmental heuristics [intuitive thought] increases with age in some social arenas. One possible explanation for this unexpected finding is that . . . older adolescents are more flexible and are more geared toward cognitive economy.
>
> *[pp. 1347, 1361]*

cognitive economy The idea that people generally use their minds as efficiently as possible, saving brain power and intellectual work. Although adolescents are capable of intensive, systematic, analytic thought, they often prefer easier and quicker intuitive thought, which is more economical.

Cognitive economy means the most efficient and effective use of mental resources. As the knowledge base increases, as thinking processes accelerate, and as both analysis and intuition become more forceful, adolescents use their minds with more economy. It is efficient to use formal, analytic thinking in science class and to use emotional, experiential thinking (which is quicker and more satisfying) for personal issues.

Another way to express the same idea is that sometimes the best thinking is "fast and frugal" (Gigerenzer et al., 1999). The systematic, analytic thought that Piaget described in formal operational thinking may be slow and costly—wasting precious time when the teenager would rather act than think.

But costly mental effort may reduce risk. The crucial question is: Who cares about reduced risks in later life? Often adults do, but adolescents do not. For many decisions that adolescents make regarding their personal lives, intuitive thinking is what they use. For adolescents, opinions of others are crucial, and managing human relationships requires quick responses, glances of humor or concern, expression of camaraderie or suspicion, indications of liking and love or distrust.

Especially for Religious Leaders Suppose you believe very strongly in some tenet of your faith, but the youth group includes teenagers who act contrary to your belief. What should you do?

Another major issue for many adolescents is morality. As reviewed in Chapter 12, Lawrence Kohlberg and others have developed a hierarchy of moral thinking. Deeper, more comprehensive analysis appears at the higher stages. The first two stages are quite egocentric; adolescents move past that. A major point of Kohlberg's scheme is that many people are influenced by human relationships, caring for their families and friends in ways that make them seem less moral. With this in mind, it is apparent that adolescents have the capacity to

JACKSONVILLE JOURNAL COURIER / THE IMAGE WORKS

Thinking Many Moves Ahead Unlike simple games of chance, which younger children enjoy, chess requires some deductive thinking. This involves general principles, such as protecting your king, focusing on the center, and changing strategies as the game progresses. These students are among 20 who played simultaneous chess games against an adult champion.

? Observational Quiz (see answer, page 481): Beyond the intellectual challenge of chess, what other type of problem do these adolescents seem to be solving?

make on-the-spot moral decisions, which sometimes are made intuitively rather than logically.

Interpersonal Judgment

Now let us look at two specific examples in which past experience and intuitive thought affect each other in constructive ways. First, when an adolescent meets a possible romantic partner, analytic thinking might assess that person's background, personality, habits, and values, comparing those traits to his or her own history and preferences. Intuitive thinking, by contrast, would react to emotional sparks and perhaps tone of voice, body shape, and smile.

In this situation, intuition would be quicker, more responsive, and more exciting. Analysis might come later—possibly before marriage, but probably not before the first date.

Adolescents' romantic relationships are typically short-lived (Brown, 2004), but they teach valuable lessons about romance and social interaction. Indeed, "a succession of experiences with other-sex friendships and then peer groups early in high school seemed to prepare youth for romantic relationships" (Brown, 2004, p. 383).

In general, adolescents who have more experiences with the other sex make better choices in romance. This generality helps explain why marriages in the teen years have a greater risk of divorce than marriages later on. The cognitive benefits of social interaction aid romance.

Now consider a second example, the E–7–K–4 puzzle, which is "notoriously difficult." Almost everyone wants to turn over the E and the 4; but almost everyone is wrong (Moshman, 2000). However, when college students who had guessed wrong (on their own) discussed the problem with one another, 75 percent got it right, avoiding the 4 card (even if it has a consonant on the other side, the statement could still be true) and selecting the E and the 7 cards (if the 7 has a vowel on the other side, the proposition will be false). They were able to think things through, changing their minds after listening to others (Moshman & Geil, 1998).

GARY WALTS / SYRACUSE NEWSPAPERS / THE IMAGE WORKS

A Public Kiss The specific ways in which physical affection is expressed depend on cultural context and cohort, not just on biological processes—as Mike knew when he presented Tiffany with a white carnation for Valentine's Day.

? Observational Quiz (see answer, page 482): In what year and in which country did this kiss occur?

The benefit of experience is also evident when another, related problem is presented. Imagine that this time the cards are said to all have an age on one side and either "beer drinker" or "Coke drinker" on the other side. The proposition is: *If a card has an age under 21 on one side, then it always has "Coke drinker" on the other side.* Of the following four cards, turn over only those cards that will confirm or disconfirm the proposition:

16 years **Beer drinker** **22 years** **Coke drinker**

Which cards must be turned over?

Almost everyone correctly turns over "16 years" and "beer drinker," comparable to the E and 7 cards in the previous example (similar to research cited in Galotti, 2002). Why do adolescents do better on this problem? Because they have had personal experience with the notion that beer drinking is forbidden at young ages. Experience and discussion both help logic.

Overall, these two examples demonstrate a very important idea: Quick, intuitive thinking can, with discussion, experience, and guidance, become more analytic and logical. Of course, maturation of various parts of the brain helps, as explained in Chapter 14. But remember that the prefrontal cortex is not totally absent early in adolescence; by then it has been developing for years. Thus, measures to connect emotions and rational thought can help make adolescents wise enough to use both methods when needed. Adolescents benefit from their experiences.

Response for Religious Leaders (from page 478): This is not the time for dogma; teenagers intuitively rebel against authority. Nor is it the time to keep quiet about your beliefs, because teenagers need some structure to help them think. Instead of going to either extreme, begin a dialogue. Listen respectfully to their expressions of concern and emotion, and encourage them to think more deeply about the implications of their actions.

SUMMING UP

Piaget thought the final stage of intelligence, called formal operational thought, began in adolescence. He found that adolescents improve in deductive logic and hypothetical thinking. Other researchers have found that adolescents often prefer intuitive thinking, which is quicker and more intense. Because of advances in both kinds of thought, adolescents know more, think faster, and use systematic analysis and abstract logic that are beyond the capability of younger children. Whether a particular adolescent uses logical reasoning or intuition depends on many factors. Cognitive economy sometimes favors emotional speed over intellectual analysis, and fast and frugal thinking is valued in personal experiences.

Teaching and Learning in High School

As we have seen, adolescents can think more abstractly, analytically, hypothetically, and logically—as well as more personally, emotionally, intuitively, and experientially—than children can. In theory and sometimes in practice, high schools advance formal operational thought while they develop links between reason and emotion.

Most science and social studies classes emphasize logical and abstract reasoning, often with laboratory experiments or historical documents that require the students to make systematic deductions. Similarly, math classes have moved from calculations to proofs. Adolescents are thus taught to use deductive and hypothetical thought, and to test their conclusions.

In both the written and hidden curricula, formal operational thought is preferred over the emotional, intuitive thought that students themselves like. For instance, schools tend to restrict the times and places where students talk informally, and teachers are licensed because they are proficient in academic fields and thus qualified to answer logical questions about the intricacies of cell biology, calculus, or iambic pentameter.

This emphasis may seem appropriate, because many students are able to develop advanced hypothetical thought. By the twelfth grade, some students can understand almost anything, from theoretical physics to ancient history. Many schools boast about their advanced classes and their erudite teachers, and applaud their graduates who are admitted to elite colleges.

In the United States, high school curricula are becoming more rigorous, with several states (Oklahoma, Illinois, and Mississippi among them) adding to their academic requirements for a high school diploma. Many school systems now demand two years of math beyond algebra, a year of laboratory science, two years of history—and less music, art, and physical education—than a decade ago. In many states, all students must take the courses required for a college preparatory diploma unless their parents request that their son or daughter be allowed to undertake a less demanding course of study and earn a general diploma, as most students once did (Olson, 2005).

Intuitive reasoning and the link between logic and emotion are often ignored in the formal curriculum. That omission may underlie three problems that arise in high schools: high-stakes testing, low motivation, and increased violence.

! Answer to Observational Quiz (from page 479): The photo shows partners who must collaborate in order to produce the desired outcome. How to work with another adolescent is the most urgent curriculum of all during the secondary school years, requiring speculation, strategy, and study of each individual case.

High-Stakes Testing

Is it possible for tests, and test scores, to overtake other aspects of adolescent learning that are hard to score, such as learning from conversation, from experience, from reflection? This question has become especially urgent in East Asian nations, where "examination hell" occurs at the end of high school—when students take tests that will decide whether they will go to college. For example, almost all students in Korea want to go to college and believe that they will if they study hard enough to score well, but only one in four students passes the qualifying test (Larson & Wilson, 2004).

The term **high-stakes testing** was coined to describe such situations, because the consequences of failing are severe. Although many Asian and European nations have used high-stakes tests for entrance to and graduation from academic high schools, North Americans traditionally relied on teachers' grades and the number of credits students had earned to decide promotion and graduation. In the United States, high-stakes tests were used only for adults seeking professional licenses (e.g., lawyer, doctor, clinical psychologist) (Sackett et al., 2001).

high-stakes testing An evaluation that is critical in determining success or failure. If a single test determines whether a student will graduate or be promoted, that is a high-stakes test.

That is changing, although, ironically, many other nations (notably Japan and England) are moving away from relying on high-stakes tests. Virtually every U.S.

state now uses high-stakes tests to determine school promotions. This change led to, and is promoted by, the No Child Left Behind Act (explained in Chapter 12), which stemmed from the fear that some schools were giving students credit for learning very little. However, high-stakes testing is not a very straightforward route to achieving educational accountability (Elmore et al., 2004).

Tests that are the same for all schools provide a common measure that lets parents and political leaders evaluate learning outcomes. The hope is that accountability will follow. The problem is that a failing score might be the fault of the school, the teacher, the family, the community, the test, the student's test-taking ability, or the student's lack of actual achievement—but when students fail, they alone suffer the consequences. Only if a school has many failing students do authorities look beyond the students for someone else to blame.

! Answer to Observational Quiz (from page 480): The contemporary United States is one of the few countries where large, comprehensive high schools are common and rules against public displays of affection by students had been lifted by 1990. In fact, this high school is in Syracuse, New York, and the photograph was taken in 1999.

Although the need for standards is recognized, and students themselves like benchmarks and challenges, many developmentalists wonder whether high-stakes tests undercut adolescent thinking. Teenagers learn via questions more than answers, hypotheses more than facts, deduction rather than induction, their own opinions and experiences more than adult conclusions. Too much emphasis on right or wrong answers on a single test might narrow the curriculum (making it "a mile wide and an inch deep"), reward rote memorization, and discourage students (Kornhaber & Orfield, 2001). This may be one reason why, despite intense effort and increased testing, achievement scores for U.S. high school students appear to be stagnant (see Figure 15.4).

When high-stakes tests are a requisite for graduation, there is a "potential unintended consequence" of increased dropout rates (Christenson & Thurlow, 2004, p. 36). In fact, dropout rates increased in the United States by about 2 percent from 1991 to 2001. The highest rates (an increase of 5 percent, on average) are in the southern states, where high-stakes testing has had the most impact.

One fear is that high-stakes testing increases ethnic, economic, and sexual inequality (Maehr & Yamaguchi, 2001). Some research validates this fear. For example, for girls in math and science and for African American and Latino/Latina students in every subject, teacher evaluations were higher than scores on high-stakes tests, according to a careful study of high schools in the Boston suburbs (where academic standards are high) (Brennan et al., 2001).

Special concern has also been expressed about students who have learning disabilities or come from low-income families. The gap between the educational achievement of the wealthiest and poorest students is increasing (Books, 2004). Some believe that high-stakes tests are part of the cause, others that they are part of the solution (Elmore et al., 2004). Children with special educational needs are generally included as a special population to be tested; some advocates are pleased at this inclusion, while others consider it unfair (Venn, 2004).

Many observers have noted a gender gap in high school grades, graduation rates, and test scores. In the United States and several other developed nations, boys get higher test scores than school grades and the opposite pattern is found for girls, who do better in school (at all levels, but especially in high school) and are more likely to attend college. This gender gap is especially noticeable among minorities. By contrast, in many developing nations, boys are far more likely to attain education at every level, even though education for women is equally crucial if a country wants to reduce infant mortality, child malnutrition, and teen pregnancy (LeVine et al., 2001).

Especially for High School Teachers You are much more interested in the nuances and controversies than in the basic facts of your subject, but you know that your students will take high-stakes tests on the basics and that their scores will have a major impact on their futures. What should you do?

A gender gap (in either direction) suggests that schools are not capturing the potential of both sexes equally. On international tests, girls generally outscore boys in language skills, but the results of math and science tests are mixed, with some nations reporting higher scores for girls and others for boys. All these disparities suggest that education in general and tests in particular are not immune to social bias. But the solution to the inequality is unclear.

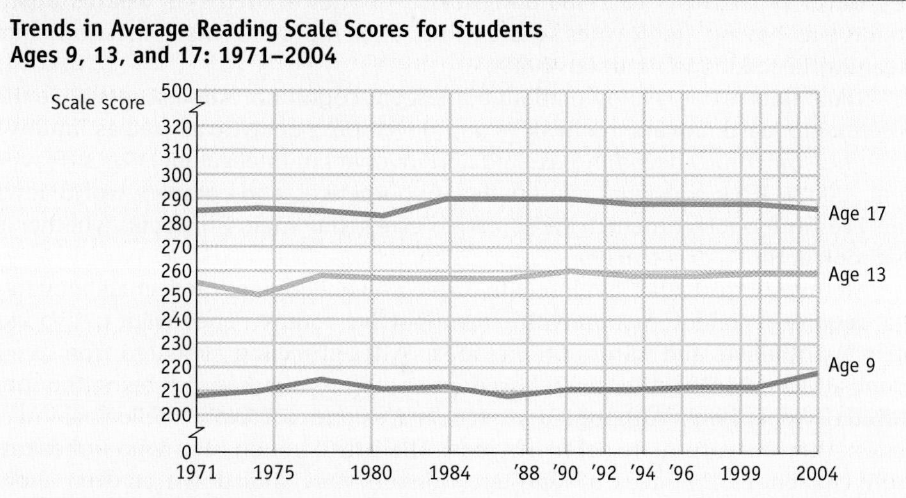

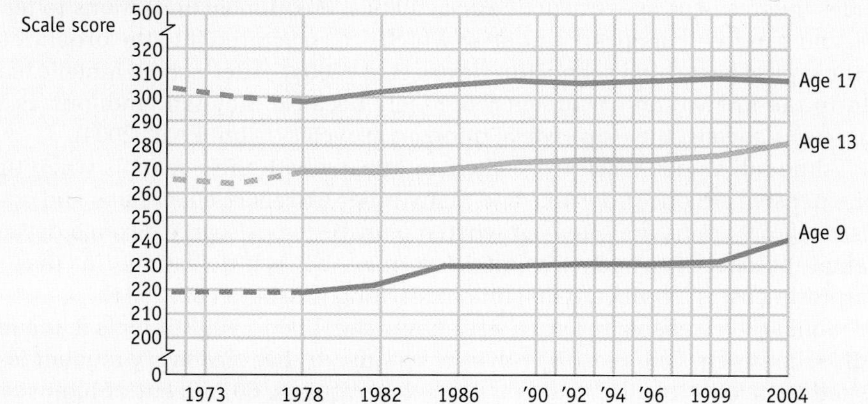

Note: Dashed lines represent extrapolated data.
Source: U.S. Department of Education, Institute of Education Sciences, National Center for Education Statistics, National Assessment of Educational Progress (NAEP), selected years, 1973–2004 Long-Term Trend Reading and Mathematics Assessments. Adapted from *Education Week* Web site, edweb.org, accessed July 28, 2005.

FIGURE 15.4 **The Younger, the Better** Improvements in reading and math scores for younger children are encouraging, but stagnant scores for adolescents are cause for concern. These graphs chart data from the U.S. Department of Education's NAEP (National Assessment of Educational Progress). Some other nations (notably in Europe and the Middle East) show improvements for high school students over the same period, although international test scores are not always directly comparable.

Indeed, there is no consensus about high-stakes testing in high school. Longitudinal data, including information on students in special populations, are needed.

Student Motivation

There *is* a consensus about student motivation: It's generally poor, and that's a serious problem. Many adolescents express boredom and unhappiness with school ("Algebra sucks," "*The Odyssey* is boring"), especially when they are complaining to their friends (Larson, 2000). Adolescents seek to be admired by their peers, which often means appearing to be detached from the excitement of learning. As students, particularly boys, progress through high school, they typically become less attached to their school (Wigfield et al., 1997).

Teachers are well aware of students' problems in this regard. Of public high school teachers in the United States, 38 percent consider student apathy their most serious problem, worse than drugs (14 percent), lack of challenge (10 percent), fighting (9 percent), and racial tension (7 percent). Teachers, researchers, and developmentalists describe adolescents—honor students as well as delinquents—as having "high rates of boredom, alienation, and disconnection from meaningful challenge" (Larson, 2000).

Remember what is known about adolescent cognition. Adolescents have the potential to learn, advancing in skills and developing analytic as well as intuitive thought, sometimes becoming excited and involved in intellectual efforts (Flavell et al., 2002). They construct imaginative, hypothetical, and complex worldviews and are no longer content with someone else's statements of facts, whether a textbook author's or a teacher's.

RESPONSE FOR HIGH SCHOOL TEACHERS (from page 482): It would be nice to advise you to follow your instincts, but the appropriate response depends partly on pressures within the school and on the expectations of the parents and administration. A comforting fact about adolescent cognition is that adolescents can think about and learn almost anything if they feel a personal connection to it. Look for ways to teach the facts your students need for the tests as the foundation for the exciting and innovative topics you want to teach. Everyone will learn more, and the tests will be less intimidating for your students.

All this suggests that adolescents thrive on challenging intellectual activities that require social interaction within a supportive context. They want to express their hypothetical and nontraditional ideas without feeling alienated from their friends. Most would rather feign boredom or stop trying than risk being thought stupid (Dweck, 1999). Although adolescents are eager for lively intellectual interaction, they are also quite self-conscious. The brash young man who unhesitatingly challenges the ideas of long-ago thinkers may shut down or even avoid going to class after his teacher makes a sarcastic remark at his expense.

An antidote to boredom is student engagement with the school, which includes involvement in extracurricular activities, emotional connections to teachers, and support from peers—none of which are structured into the organization of the typical large high school (Fredricks et al., 2004). After-school athletic teams add to the motivation of students, precisely because they tap emotions as few classes do. Ideally, they tap critical thinking as well (Wright et al., 2004).

Although students are more likely to engage with their schools when there are extensive athletic programs and many other extracurricular clubs and activities, such programs are often cut when money becomes scarce. From a developmental perspective, such economizing may be self-defeating, in that the long-term cost is a reduction in student learning (Barber et al., 2001).

Similarly, extensive research has shown that 200 to 400 students is the ideal high school size. One reason is that in schools of that size every student is expected to belong to some team or club. Nevertheless, 60 percent of high school students in the United States attend schools with enrollments of over 1,000 (Snyder et al., 2004). Big schools are more economical, but they do not increase learning.

JACQUES PAVLOVSKY / SYGMA / CORBIS

Lights and Action Instruction in video production, music, photography, or drama—or any other area that results in finished work presented to others—is an excellent way to involve and motivate adolescents.

Student engagement is crucial to school performance. In a longitudinal study of high school students of varied ability in eight U.S. communities, those who disengaged from class (no longer doing the homework, never asking questions, and so on) were *not* those with low intellectual potential but those who initially thought their achievement depended on others or on fate, not on their own efforts (Glasgow et al., 1997).

Certainly aptitude and past achievement have some effect on school performance. However, research on an entirely different group of students in Germany points in the same direction as the U.S. study just cited. Students of varying aptitudes and achievement in math were tested longitudinally. Their self-concept as math students (apart from their actual achievements in math) affected later achievement as much as their math achievement test scores affected their later self-concept (Marsh et al., 2005). Although girls scored lower overall, the reciprocal connection between self-concept and achievement was apparent for both sexes. From such research, most developmentalists think that attitude, more than aptitude, is the key to success in high school (Eccles, 2004).

Violence in Schools

Almost every year, and in many nations, a high school student kills one or more fellow students. High school violence is especially problematic in the United States, where in 2003 about 1 in 15 high school students brought a weapon (gun, knife, or club) to school. Most adolescents who carry weapons say that they do so because they feel unsafe at school (MMWR, July 30, 2004).

Before going further, we should state that, in fact, adolescents are safer in school than elsewhere. Of all teenagers who are killed, 99 percent are attacked somewhere other than in school, usually on streets near their homes. Overall, serious injury among adolescents is less common on school days from 8:00 A.M. to 3:00 P.M. than at other times (Moeller, 2001).

Although schools are relatively safe, school violence is an increasing concern. In the past 10 years in the United States, students are more likely to report being afraid at school even though they are less likely to be in a fight. Fear is about twice as common in ninth grade as in twelfth grade (see Table 15.1); it is three times as high among African American and Hispanic youth as among European American youth (MMWR, July 30, 2004).

Students are more likely to be injured by other students in the first years of middle or high school and at the beginning of a semester, and boys are twice as likely as girls to be threatened or injured. Vulnerable and uncertain students are more often victims and aggressors, which explains why pubescent boys in large schools who feel shamed or disrespected by teachers or other students are most

TABLE 15.1 **Prevalence of Nonlethal Violence Among Ninth- and Twelfth-Graders**

	1993		1997		2003	
Students who, in the past 12 months, were . . .	**Ninth-graders**	**Twelfth-graders**	**Ninth-graders**	**Twelfth-graders**	**Ninth-graders**	**Twelfth-graders**
In a physical fight on school property	23%	14%	21%	10%	18%	7%
Threatened with a weapon on school property	9	6	10	6	12	6
Absent because of safety concerns	6	3	6	3	7	4

Source: MMWR, July 30, 2004.

likely to lash out (Aronson, 2000; Mulvey & Cauffman, 2001). Supportive measures within schools, such as the warm teacher–student relationships and the peer befriending already mentioned, could alleviate such situations throughout adolescence.

Because overt violence is rare, it is impossible to know which particular sixth- to twelfth-grade students out of the 24 million in the United States, or the billion in the world, might turn to school violence. Therefore, tertiary prevention is impossible, and secondary prevention may be ineffective or too late. Primary prevention to reduce the climate of violence in the schools is needed, yet most school administrators are oblivious to the harm done by inappropriate measures (Mulvey & Cauffman, 2001). As one psychologist explained:

> Some apparently sensible interventions could produce negative or even disastrous consequences, depending on what is actually going on in the school. . . . A few days after the Columbine tragedy, my 16-year-old grandson came home from high school and said, "Guess what? The principal sent around a notice asking us to report any kids who are dressing strangely, behaving weirdly, appear to be loners, or out of it."
>
> . . . The principal is shining his spotlight on the wrong part of the equation. Here's why: From my classroom research, I have found that the social atmosphere in most schools is competitive, cliquish, and exclusionary. . . . My grandson's high school principal is unwittingly making a bad situation worse by implicitly sanctioning the rejection and exclusion of a sizable group of students whose only sin is unpopularity.
>
> *[Aronson, 2000]*

Fortunately, the same practices that foster motivation can also prevent violence. Students who are engaged in learning, bonding with their teachers and fellow students, and involved in school activities are unlikely to be destructive. They create a protective shield throughout the school, for "students are well aware of the problem children in their own classrooms . . . [but] for such information to flow from students to administrators requires an atmosphere where sharing in good faith is respected and honored" (Mulvey & Cauffman, 2001).

A mismatch between the adolescent mind and the school setting can be dangerous. However, most students do learn, and every reader of this book probably had at least one high school teacher who knew "how to get adolescent fires lit, how to have them develop the complex of dispositions and skills needed to take charge of their lives" (Larson, 2000, p. 170).

Remember that adolescents combine the hypothetical and the experiential, the analytic and the intuitive. Think about teaching Shakespeare's *Hamlet* in high school:

> Steven [the teacher] began his unit on *Hamlet* without even mentioning the name of the play. To help his students grasp the initial outline of the themes and issues of the play, he asked them to imagine that their parents had recently divorced and that their mothers had taken up with a new man. This new man had replaced their father at work, and "there's some talk that he had something to do with the ousting of your dad." Steven then asked students to think about the circumstances that might drive them so mad that they would contemplate murdering another human being. Only then, after students had contemplated these issues and done some writing on them, did Steven introduce the play they would be reading.
>
> *[Bransford et al., 1999, p. 34]*

After discussion, the students understood that the carnage in *Hamlet* is needless, useless, and pointless—the result of partial truths, imperfect analysis, and misinterpreted intuitions. They realized that, whatever their personal circumstances, they did not need to "contemplate murdering another human being." Good teaching not only makes learning exciting but also makes violence less appealing, since analytic thought can overcome emotional impulses.

SUMMING UP

High school education can advance thinking of all kinds. High-stakes testing reflects an effort to equalize achievement and increase accountability, but the tests themselves are controversial. Lack of student motivation is considered the most common high school problem; the ways students prefer to engage with ideas are often disconnected from the learning they need to pass their courses. School violence is relatively rare, but many students and others are afraid of the possibility. Crucial to safe and successful secondary education are classroom and extracurricular activities that encourage student engagement with ideas, with one another, and with teachers.

Postformal Thought

Some developmentalists have described a fifth stage of thinking that appears after Piaget's four stages, a stage that characterizes adult thinking. Called **postformal thought**, this fifth stage is said to concern "problem finding," not "problem solving" (Arlin, 1984, 1989).

postformal thought A possible fifth stage of cognition proposed by developmentalists who believe that adults advance in their ability to combine emotions and logic in complex yet practical ways.

In other words, older adolescents and adults are not content to find solutions to the intellectual problems posed to them by others (mostly teachers) but instead are concerned with social and personal problems. Grappling with those problems attracts more of their brain power than finding answers to questions raised by others.

Overall, after high school, intellectual skills become harnessed to real occupational and interpersonal demands, and conclusions and consequences matter. This makes older adolescents less playful and more practical thinkers, seeking issues of social concern rather than intellectual puzzles to enjoy. Emerging adults want to discover their options and then act, amid the contradictions and inconsistencies of everyday experience. Even such a seemingly straightforward decision as choosing a college major is a cognitive challenge, requiring a combination of emotion and logic (Galotti, 1999).

Emotions and Logic

Thinking about personal matters precludes neither intuition nor analysis. Instead, "postformal logic combines subjectivity and objectivity" (Sinnott, 1998, p. 55), using both emotional and intellectual reasoning. The intellectual readiness to recognize and express complex and contradictory emotions increases throughout adolescence, levels off at about age 30, and decreases at about age 60 (Labouvie-Vief, 2003).

How does this work in practice? Extreme behaviors—such as sensation seeking, binge eating, anorexia, addiction, and suicide—are outgrowths of absolutist thought, or thought at the extremes. If the extreme occurs at the rational end of the spectrum of thinking, a person might label something as totally right or absolutely wrong. If the extreme occurs at the emotional end, a person might perceive him- or herself as uniquely brilliant or "the most vile, worthless and useless person ever to have existed" (quoted in Udovitch, 2002). Neither of these perspectives is a balanced one, combining reason and emotion.

By contrast, an emerging adult might have more balanced thinking, using personal experience and knowledge (Blanchard-Fields, 1999). For example, the despairing adult, contemplating suicide, realizes that a happier day might come;

the self-blaming alcoholic understands that drinking is a choice; the jealous lover remembers that other partners are available. These are all mature responses, beyond the capacity of most adolescents (and many adults).

Cognitive Flexibility

A hallmark of postformal cognition is the awareness that "there are multiple views of the same phenomenon" (Baltes et al., 1998, p. 1093). Each perspective is only one of many, and each problem has many potential solutions (Sinnott, 1998). Because knowledge is dynamic, not static, the best perspective or solution may change, day by day, and conclusions reached years ago may no longer be valid.

Particularly useful is emotional flexibility, the ability to show or hide emotion as appropriate to the situation, including the ability to approach something feared or avoid something desired. This ability correlates with successful adaptation (Bonanno et al., 2004) and is needed to deal with many of the practical problems of adulthood. For example, when adults realize they must overcome their feelings of racism or sexism, they need emotional flexibility to suppress their negative impulses. Many adults cannot or will not do so, but at least it is possible (Dasgupta & Greenwald, 2001).

More difficult, but equally necessary, is the intellectual flexibility to counter the stereotypes other people might have. One highly emotional fear is that someone else assumes that you are stupid (or worse) because of your ethnicity, gender, age, or some other characteristic. The mere possibility of being negatively stereotyped arouses emotions that disrupt cognition. This is called **stereotype threat;** it is an anxiety-producing awareness that one's appearance or behavior might be misused to confirm another person's stereotype about one's race, gender, or other group (Steele, 1997).

stereotype threat The concern that another person might have a negative prejudice about oneself as a member of a particular race, gender, or other group; the resulting anxiety leads to lower achievement.

The stereotype-threat hypothesis is an intriguing one. It could explain some apparent anomalies, such as the fact that few women become engineers or physicists or that many African American men tend to underachieve in academic settings.

Given the multidisciplinary nature of developmental research, many other hypotheses may account for underachievement by members of various groups. Historians focus on the legacy of slavery or male chauvinism; economists point to financial barriers; sociologists describe multifaceted discrimination in academic or employment structures; biologists explore genetic or hormonal differences. Explanations are many; stereotype threat is not the only reason some people do not develop their potential (Cokley, 2003; Sackett et al., 2004). It is, however, a reason worth exploring, as the following explains.

Especially for High School Guidance Counselors Given what you know about adolescent thinking, should you spend more time helping students with college applications, with summer jobs, with family problems, or with high school course selection?

Thinking Like a Scientist

Stereotype Threat

Many scientists have examined the stereotype-threat hypothesis. In one experiment, college men and women were asked to solve 20 difficult math problems (Schmader, 2002). Half the students simply took the test, but the other half were told in advance that the results would reveal gender differences. The average scores of both sexes were similar except for one low-scoring subgroup: women who were told that gender differences would be assessed and who identified strongly with their sex. At least in this study, identifying as women and the threat that their scores would reveal lower female math ability led these women to solve fewer problems than similar women who had not been primed to think of gender differences.

Thinking like a scientist usually includes wondering if the theory applies in other cultures. According to the scientist who developed the theory, it does. Stereotype threat affects "caste-like minorities in industrial and nonindustrial nations throughout the world (e.g., the Maoris of New Zealand, the Baraku of Japan, the Harijans of India, the Oriental Jews of Israel, and the West Indians of Great Britain)" (Steele, 1997, p. 623).

Researchers also wonder if a theory could apply to them. It might, in a small way, apply to me. My mother and my older brother were excellent spellers, but I am not. I blame my brother. When we were children, he implied that his superior spelling proved my stupidity. Could that be related to the fact that, to this day, I devalue spelling, taking pride in my ineptness and proudly erasing my mistakes when my students correct my spelling on the board?

This example is minor compared with the discrimination that others experience or the stereotype threat they anticipate. However, the basic idea—that people devalue whatever skills others expect them not to have—seems valid. It is protective to disconnect one's self-esteem from a stereotyped trait. If African American boys feel unfairly judged by White female teachers, they might conclude that success in school is for women and Whites, not for them (Fordham & Ogbu, 1986).

The final test of any theory is to apply it. A random group of freshmen at Stanford University (all very intelligent, some White and some Black) were enrolled in a training program of three one-hour sessions, supposedly in preparation for mentoring at-risk middle school students (Aronson et al., 2002). Half of them (the experimental group) read research showing that academic achievement is the product of effort, not innate ability, and half (the comparison group) read about multiple intelligences. The students were then asked to write to the middle school students, encouraging them by explaining the research.

Did the students who read that learning was the result of effort feel less threatened by the negative stereotype about inborn ability? Yes. In the school term following the intervention, the African American students in the experimental group had grades that were higher, on average, than those of Black students in the comparison group (B+ versus B) or than the overall average for African Americans. European Americans in the experimental group also scored higher than the comparison group (A– versus B+).

When asked how important they thought academics were (as part of a general survey), the ratings of the European Americans were high but were not affected by the experiment; in contrast, the ratings of the African Americans increased after the experiment (see Table 15.2). Apparently, as the stereotype became less of a personal threat, they could value academic achievement more and study harder.

Ethnic differences in grades and attitudes remained, which is not surprising; a lifetime of stereotype threats does not disappear in just three hours. However, the effect of the intervention suggests that young adults can learn to think differently about themselves. Less stereotype threat can lead to more achievement.

TABLE 15.2 **How Important Are Academics? (Rate from 1 to 7)**

	Average Rating	
	African Americans	**European Americans**
Experimental group	4.77	5.61
Comparison group	3.89	5.67
Students in neither group	3.45	5.71

Source: Aronson et al., 2002.

Teaching and Learning in College

A college education is a wise investment. Whether they live in Asia, Africa, Europe, or the Americas, college-educated adults earn more, live longer, and have better health, emotional and physical, than do those with less education. For example, in the United States, the average income of household heads with a master's degree is more than twice that of those with only a high school diploma (U.S. Bureau of the Census, 2004). Even when compared with other adults of the same income, college graduates everywhere are less likely to smoke, to overeat, to underexercise, and to die young (Gottfredson & Deary, 2004).

Cognition itself changes with higher education. Research over the past 50 years has consistently found that college graduates are not only healthier and wealthier than others but also are deeper, more flexible thinkers.

This is good news for college students and professors alike. But scientists are taught to be skeptical, and in this comparison, alternate explanations abound.

RESPONSE FOR HIGH SCHOOL GUIDANCE COUNSELORS (from page 488): It depends on what your particular students need; schools vary a great deal. However, all students need to talk and think about their choices and options so that they will not act impulsively. Therefore, providing information and a listening ear might be the most important thing you can spend time doing. You will also want to keep all students in challenging and interesting classes until they graduate. Encouraging teachers and administrators to improve educational structures and to increase student motivation is a worthwhile endeavor.

After all, college students are already at an advantage. They tend to have better grades in high school, higher scores on aptitude tests, and wealthier families with fewer divorces; they are also less often delinquent, learning-disabled, or from large families.

The transition to college is difficult for everyone, but again, those who will eventually graduate have an advantage. One recent study of French Canadian students confirmed this observation. Those who had good relationships with their parents in high school (secure, autonomous attachment, not dismissing or enmeshed family bonds) tended to earn better grades in college, even when their high school achievement was taken into account (Larose et al., 2005).

The key question is: Does higher education itself teach students to combine subjective and objective thinking and to seek divergent perspectives? Is this the reason they do better later on? Or does a powerful selection effect account for the later success of college students?

The answer seems to be that college education itself is beneficial. It improves verbal and quantitative abilities, knowledge of specific subject areas, skills in various professions, reasoning ability, and reflectiveness. A comprehensive review concludes:

> Compared to [college] freshmen, seniors have better oral and written communication skills, are better abstract reasoners or critical thinkers, are more skilled at using reason and evidence to address ill-structured problems for which there are no verifiably correct answers, have greater intellectual flexibility in that they are better able to understand more than one side of a complex issue, and can develop more sophisticated abstract frameworks to deal with complexity.
>
> *[Pascarella & Terenzini, 1991, p. 155]*

The research suggests that higher education benefits human development, no matter what the nation or culture. In most nations, however, the majority of young adults never enter college, and of those who do, many leave before they develop the "social know-how" to make college work for them (Deil-Amen & Rosenbaum, 2003, p. 141).

In most nations, only a fraction of high school graduates are admitted to college. In the United States, most begin college but less than half earn a BA degree; the dropout rate is particularly high for community college students—not for intellectual reasons, but for financial and cultural ones (Brint, 2003).

For those who stay, thinking may improve year by year (Clinchy, 1993; King & Kitchener, 1994; Perry, 1981) (see Table 15.3). First-year students tend to believe that clear and perfect truths exist; they get upset if their professors do not explain these truths. They gather facts as if they were nuggets of gold, each one pure and true, separate from other bits of knowledge. One first-year student said he was like a squirrel, "gleaning little acorns of knowledge and burying them for later use" (Bozik, 2002, p. 145).

This initial phase is followed by a wholesale questioning of personal and social values, including doubts about the idea of truth itself. No fact is taken at face value, much less stored intact for future use.

If students stay to graduate, after considering many opposing ideas, they typically commit to some hard-won values, realizing that they need to remain open-minded and that their values might change (Pascarella & Terenzini, 1991; Rest et al., 1999). Facts are neither gold nor dross but are steps toward a greater understanding. This open-mindedness is encouraged by their professors, but they cannot take all the credit. For most emerging adults, college means listening to fellow students, a group that is likely to be far more diverse than their cohort in high school was. That itself makes thinking deeper.

TABLE 15.3 **Scheme of Cognitive and Ethical Development**

Dualism modified	Position 1	Authorities know, and if we work hard, read every word, and learn Right Answers, all will be well.
	Transition	But what about those Others I hear about? And different opinions? And Uncertainties? Some of our own Authorities disagree with each other or don't seem to know, and some give us problems instead of Answers.
	Position 2	True Authorities must be Right, the others are frauds. We remain Right. Others must be different and Wrong. Good Authorities give us problems so we can learn to find the Right Answer by our own independent thought.
	Transition	But even Good Authorities admit they don't know all the answers *yet!*
	Position 3	Then some uncertainties and different opinions are real and legitimate *temporarily,* even for Authorities. They're working on them to get to the Truth.
	Transition	But there are *so many* things they don't know the Answers to! And they won't for a long time.
Relativism discovered	*Position 4a*	Where Authorities don't know the Right Answers, everyone has a right to his own opinion; no one is wrong!
	Transition	Then what right have They to grade us? About what?
	Position 4b	In certain courses Authorities are not asking for the Right Answer. They want us to *think* about things in a certain way, *supporting* opinion with data. That's what they grade us on.
	Position 5	Then *all* thinking must be like this, even for Them. Everything is relative but not equally valid. You have to understand how each context works. Theories are not Truth but metaphors to interpret data with. You have to think about your thinking.
	Transition	But if everything is relative, am I relative, too? How can I know I'm making the Right Choice?
	Position 6	I see I'm going to have to make my own decisions in an uncertain world with no one to tell me I'm Right.
	Transition	I'm lost if I don't. When I decide on my career (or marriage or values), everything will straighten out.
Commitments in relativism developed	Position 7	Well, I've made my first Commitment!
	Transition	Why didn't that settle everything?
	Position 8	I've made several commitments. I've got to balance them—how many, how deep? How certain, how tentative?
	Transition	Things are getting contradictory. I can't make logical sense out of life's dilemmas.
	Position 9	This is how life will be. I must be wholehearted while tentative, fight for my values yet respect others, believe my deepest values right yet be ready to learn. I see that I shall be retracing this whole journey over and over—but, I hope, more wisely.

Source: Perry, 1981.

All the evidence suggests that higher education is "a transforming element in human development" (Benjamin, 2003, p. 11). Most of the research leading to such conclusions arose from earlier cohorts, when most students were full time, of higher socioeconomic status (SES), and not from minority groups. Do the same conclusions fit current college students, who are more often from minority groups, who usually work to pay for their education, and who tend to be part-time students? What is your experience?

SUMMING UP

Toward the end of adolescence, some emerging adults become capable of an advanced form of thinking that combines emotions and logic. This is sometimes called postformal thought, because it follows Piaget's fourth stage of formal operational thinking. Young adult thought is often more flexible, more dynamic, and less absolutist than the thinking of younger individuals. Expectations can have a crucial effect on performance, which is why stereotype threat can be devastating. College education correlates with better health, higher income, and longer life. College probably advances thinking, especially flexible, complex postformal thought. Unfortunately many emerging adults are unable to attend college, for a variety of reasons.

■ SUMMARY

Adolescent Egocentrism

1. Cognition in early adolescence is often characterized by egocentrism, a kind of self-centered thinking. Adolescent egocentrism gives rise to the invincibility fable, the personal fable, and the imaginary audience.

2. Middle school students tend to be bored by school, difficult to teach, and hurtful to each other. Many forms of psychopathology increase at the transition to middle school.

3. Part of the reason for the middle school slump may be that schools are not structured to meet the students' intellectual needs. Teachers tend to be more distant and less lenient. No nation has found a way to engage every student during these years.

Thinking Processes During the Teen Years

4. Formal operational thought is Piaget's term for the last of his four periods of cognitive development. He tested and demonstrated formal operational thought with various problems that might be encountered by students in a high school science or math class, such as figuring out how to adjust weights on a balance scale.

5. Adolescents are no longer earthbound and concrete in their thinking; they prefer to imagine the possible, the probable, and even the impossible, instead of focusing on what is real. They develop hypotheses and explore, using deductive reasoning.

6. Intuitive thinking, also known as experiential or heuristic thinking, becomes more forceful during adolescence. Few teenagers always use logic, although they are capable of logical thinking, because emotional, intuitive thinking is quicker and more satisfying.

Teaching and Learning in High School

7. High schools vary a great deal worldwide. In the United States, the demand for more accountability has led to more high-stakes testing, which has had some unintended consequences, including a higher dropout rate. Some other nations are moving away from high-stakes testing.

8. Many adolescents are apathetic about high school learning and have no way to engage in sports or other extracurricular activities. School violence is relatively rare, but primary prevention is needed to reduce feelings of disengagement. Good teaching combines intuitive and analytic thought by involving the students with the material.

Postformal Thought

9. Many researchers believe that, in late adolescence, the complex and often conflicting demands of daily life produce a new type of thinking called postformal thought, which combines emotions and rational analysis. It is particularly useful in responding to emotionally arousing situations, as when one is being stereotyped.

10. Research indicates that college education not only increases wealth and health but also tends to advance cognition. Students gradually become less inclined to seek absolute truths and more inclined to make their own decisions, using many forms of thinking. They also become more open-minded.

11. From a developmental perspective, the overarching problem with adolescent education is that too few students obtain it. This is particularly true at the college level, since most of the world's emerging adults, and most of the world's developing nations, cannot afford the cognitive opportunities that college offers.

■ KEY TERMS

adolescent egocentrism (p. 466)
invincibility fable (p. 466)
personal fable (p. 466)
imaginary audience (p. 467)
middle school (p. 469)
formal operational thought (p. 472)
hypothetical thought (p. 473)
deductive reasoning (p. 474)
inductive reasoning (p. 474)
intuitive thought (p. 476)
analytic thought (p. 476)
cognitive economy (p. 478)
high-stakes testing (p. 481)
postformal thought (p. 487)
stereotype threat (p. 488)

■ KEY QUESTIONS

1. What are some of the behavioral consequences of adolescent egocentrism?

2. Why are adolescents particularly concerned about the imaginary audience?

3. What are specific differences in the structure of elementary and middle schools?

4. What characteristics of the balance-scale question make it a measure of cognition?

5. How might intuition and analysis lead to opposite conclusions?

6. What are the costs and benefits of earning a diploma from a college-prep high school?

7. What are the advantages and disadvantages of high-stakes tests?

8. What are the most motivating, and least motivating, features of a typical high school?

9. What is the difference between direct discrimination and stereotype threat?

10. What are the cognitive differences between entering and graduating college students?

■ APPLICATIONS

1. Present the four-cards problem to three people of various ages or levels of education. Ask each to describe the reasoning behind his or her solution. Note any signs of analytic or heuristic thinking, relating what your respondents said to what you know about adolescent thought.

2. Talk to a teenager about politics, families, school, or any other topic that might reveal the way that young person thinks. Do you hear any adolescent egocentrism? Intuitive thinking? Systematic thought? Flexibility? Cite examples, comparing the adolescent's processes (not content) with your own thinking.

3. Think of life-changing decisions you have made. In what ways was each decision based on logic and in what ways on emotion? Can you think of a decision you would have made differently if you had known more or analyzed the situation differently?

4. College education is said to foster more flexible thinking and to be "transforming." Is this true of your college experience? Reflect on the impact college has had on your cognition and on that of several of your friends, ideally some of whom you have known since they first entered college.

Chapter Sixteen

Adolescence: Psychosocial Development

A 17-year-old writes:

> I am interested in everything. I like new technology, computers, videos. I have a guitar that I play at home. I usually go to play basketball with my friends. . . . Briefly, I feel good. I am friendly and I have a sense of humor. . . . Love, friendship, honesty and self-assurance are the most important values in a person's life.
>
> *[quoted in van Hoorn et al., 2000, p. 22]*

This adolescent could be male or female and could live almost any place—Tokyo, Topeka, Toronto, or your own hometown. In fact, this boy lives in Pecs, Hungary. He grew up hearing gunfire from nearby Croatia and witnessing a massive social and political revolution in his own country. Yet he adds, without irony, "There were no essential, important events in my life, only that I was born" (quoted in van Hoorn et al., 2000, p. 22).

This young man's feelings, including feeling good, are similar to those of many of his peers in other nations. Adolescents everywhere value "love, friendship, honesty and self-assurance," and they are more influenced by their families and friends than by changes (such as political upheaval) in the wider world around them—the exosystem. Globalization has resulted in a remarkably similar adolescence for many youth, although cultural differences are still significant when they affect family values and economic opportunities (Larson & Wilson, 2004).

This universal experience does not undercut another reality. Not only between nations, but within each community, variations are obvious. For instance, sexual involvement for some adolescents means only private thoughts and for others means an active romance; an individual teen's relationship to authority (including parents) may mean respect or rebellion.

Most adolescents are somewhere between the various extremes. They value love, friendship, honesty, and self-assurance, but their expression of those values changes from day to day, person to person, community to community. Almost all adolescents struggle to find their identities and seek approval from family and friends. This chapter describes their quest and then discusses some problems that teenagers may experience.

Identity

Psychosocial development during adolescence is best understood as a search for **identity**, for a consistent definition of one's self. As Erik Erikson (1963, 1968) described it, life's fifth psychosocial crisis is **identity versus diffusion** (originally called *role confusion*). The search for identity leads to the primary crisis of adolescence—a crisis in which young people

TONY FREEMAN / PHOTOEDIT

I'm a Big Girl Now Young teenagers are likely to use their musical taste, their clothing and hairstyles, and sometimes their facial expression to make it very obvious to parents that they are no longer the obedient, predictable children they once were.

struggle to reconcile "a conscious sense of individual uniqueness" with "an unconscious striving for a continuity of experience . . . and a solidarity with a group's ideals" (Erikson, 1968). The adolescent's inner drive to find his or her unique place within the larger community is what makes this a crisis; finding the appropriate combination of self-assertion and group solidarity requires years of exploration, reflection, and discovery.

The first step is to establish the integrity of personality—that is, to align emotions, thinking, and behavior so that they remain coherent and consistent no matter what the place, time, circumstances, or social relationships. "Two-faced," "wishy-washy," and "hypocritical" are among the worst accusations one adolescent can hurl at another, because integrity is both fervently sought and frustratingly elusive. Indeed, without a sense of continuity and consistency amid biological and social changes, adolescents feel adrift and depressed (Chandler et al., 2003). But identity is not easily found.

Multiple Selves

Particularly in early adolescence, teenagers tend to have several identities. Many adolescents try out **possible selves**—that is, various images of who they really are, who they are in different groups or settings, and who they might become (Markus & Nurius, 1986; Markus et al., 1990). Possible selves are explored more imaginatively than realistically, as young adolescents fantasize about becoming, say, an astronaut or a rap star, without beginning the work that must be done to reach such goals.

Many teenagers know that their behavior changes according to their immediate settings and circumstances: They switch from reserved to rowdy, from cooperative to antagonistic, from loving to manipulative. Recognizing inconsistencies among these multiple selves, they wonder which one is "the real me." As one developmentalist noted, "The tortuous search for the self involves a concern with who or what I am, a task made more difficult given the multiple me's that crowd the landscape" (Harter, 1999, p. 68).

In sorting through their possible selves, young people fear taking on a **false self,** acting in ways contrary to their core being—even if they are not sure what that core being is. False and contradictory selves are most common in early and middle adolescence (Harter et al., 1997). A researcher quotes one 17-year-old, looking back at her possible selves: "I've explored being an intellectual, . . . a class clown, . . . a rebellious delinquent. And I've found advantages and disadvantages to all these, . . . and this was the beginning of my own self-identity" (quoted in Kroger, 2000, p. 59). Gradually, as one possible self becomes the true self, the false selves fade away.

Paths to Identity

Identity achievement is the ultimate goal, reached through "selective repudiation and mutual assimilation of childhood identifications" (Erikson, 1968). That is, adolescents establish their own identities by reconsidering all the goals and values set by their parents and culture, accepting some and rejecting others.

Those who "achieve" identity know who they are. They remain connected to morals and attitudes they have learned, but they are not inescapably bound to any of them. Adolescents seek to maintain a sense of continuity with their past in order to move toward their future (Chandler et al., 2003).

identity A consistent definition of one's self as a unique individual, in terms of roles, attitudes, beliefs, and aspirations.

identity versus diffusion Erikson's fifth stage of psychosocial development, in which adolescents want to know who they are, in sex, religion, politics, and vocation, but find it hard to decide which of many possible roles or identities to adopt.

possible selves The many personalities, sets of behavior, or self-images a person could have. Most adults have chosen one "self" from all the possibilities, but adolescents are often still exploring potential selves.

false self A set of behaviors adopted to combat rejection, to please others, or to try out as a possible self.

identity achievement Knowing who one is as a unique person, accepting some cultural values and rejecting others.

Erikson first labeled this crisis more than 50 years ago, an era that differed from today in politics, developmental research, and adolescent self-concept. Yet, although context, cohort, and various microsystems affect the specifics, the overall search for identity continues (Nurmi, 2004). We now look at four paths to identity as outlined by James Marcia and other more recent researchers: diffusion, foreclosure, negation, and moratorium (Kroger, 2004; Marcia, 1966, 1980; Waterman, 1999).

Diffusion

identity diffusion An adolescent's lack of values, traits, or commitments; the opposite of identity achievement.

The opposite of identity achievement is **identity diffusion,** a person's lack of commitment to any goals or values, an apathy about every role. Diffused young people do not meet the usual demands of adolescence, such as completing school assignments, finding a job, making new friends, and thinking about the future. Instead, they sleep too much, watch mind-numbing television programs, and claim not to care about anything because "nothing matters" or "whatever . . ."

Diffusion is not an identity status so much as a lack of status, an absence of self-definition or commitment. Erikson originally called this status *role confusion,* describing adolescents who are uncertain about which role to take. But some adolescents are more than confused: They are scattered and confused, so Erikson changed the term.

Diffused adolescents may turn from one sexual or platonic relationship to another, with no passion, distress, or commitment. They seem indifferent to school failure, parental criticism, missed deadlines for a job, for college, for anything. Almost every adolescent has moments of diffusion, when things don't matter to them as much as their parents or teachers wish they would. If diffusion becomes an entrenched status, that becomes a serious problem. Diffusion puts the person at risk for clinical depression or chronic delinquency (discussed later).

Foreclosure

foreclosure Erikson's term for premature identity formation, when an adolescent adopts preset roles and values wholesale, without questioning.

Identity **foreclosure** occurs when young people short-circuit their search by not questioning their traditional values or by adopting a preformed identity (Marcia, 1966; Marcia et al., 1993). They might accept roles and customs from their parents or culture, never exploring alternatives in order to forge their own identity. An example might be an adolescent boy who had always anticipated following in his father's footsteps. If his father was a doctor, the son might diligently study chemistry and biology. Then he would take pre-med courses in college and begin medical school right after graduation.

Foreclosure might also be found by joining a strict religious cult or a narrow political cell, if that group has preset rules for members to follow in conducting their daily lives. In the immediate stress of adolescence, foreclosure is a shelter. The danger is that, in adulthood, circumstances might make foreclosed individuals question why they become a doctor, a preacher, or a political fanatic. Then they are adrift, without an anchor of their own choosing.

Some adolescents who seem headed for foreclosure suddenly switch course, as did George Stephanopoulos, who always thought he would become a Greek Orthodox priest, as his father and grandfather were. He writes:

> When I was thirteen, my final eighth-grade assignment was a paper on a potential career. As expected, I wrote on being a priest and brought home my A. . . . I started high school, and it hit me. I was sitting in homeroom one morning shortly before eight, thinking about nothing in particular, when the idea that I wasn't *meant* to be a priest, that I wouldn't bear the family legacy into the next generation, revealed itself with an intensity others must feel when called *to* the priesthood.
>
> *[Stephanopoulos, 1999, pp. 12–13]*

After this insight, he tried to combine his past with a new future. He writes, "Drilled into me were two awkwardly compatible ambitions: public service and professional success. Priests serve; immigrants succeed. I would try to do both" (p. 13). A decade of uncertainty followed. For example, immediately after college, Stephanopoulos impulsively decided to join the Peace Corps as a teacher in Tunisia—but two hours after he agreed, he changed his mind. He finally chose to become a political campaign manager and journalist.

Negative Identity

negative identity Identity taken on reactively, with rebellious defiance, simply because it is the opposite of the one that parents or society expects.

Some adolescents decide that the roles that adults offer are unattainable or unappealing, yet they cannot find alternatives that are truly their own. Their reaction may be a **negative identity,** an identity that is the opposite of the one that is expected. The teacher's child refuses to go to college, the religious leader's child becomes a prostitute or a drug dealer—the crucial factor in negative identity is not the choice itself but the reactionary defiance that underlies it.

One version of negative identity is *oppositional identity* (Ogbu, 1993), which occurs when the adolescent rejects the dominant culture by adopting and exaggerating negative stereotypes. For example, some gay young men proudly call themselves "queer," and some African Americans take pride in being the "baddest."

The culture of a generation may facilitate negative identity, as is demonstrated in the following.

A Case to Study

"Give Him a Break"

A career marine dominated his two sons. The older son, Dennis, was a model adolescent in the early 1960s, becoming a football hero and star student. To find his own identity, he made some revisions in his father's pathway: He went to the Air Force Academy instead of joining the marines, and he did not always agree with his dad.

> Greg [the younger son], in contrast, came of age in the late 1960s, and dressed and behaved according to the customs of the day. Issues like Vietnam dominated the news and the dinner table. . . .
>
> Mostly Greg just absorbed his father's criticism and occasionally shot it back at him. (If anything, his father's words only backfired, pushing Greg further into the counterculture.) But one night . . . Dennis, who was home on leave, joined the rest of the family for dinner. His father, as usual, was laying into Greg about how he dressed (in tie-dye and sandals) and for his "poor" table manners. Finally Dennis had heard enough. "Lay off of him already," he said sternly, certainly uncharacteristic of his usual tone with their father. "Give him a break, why don't you?" . . . .
>
> "Yes, lieutenant!" their father snapped back, now dropping the fork with a clang onto his plate. He turned and marched upstairs.
>
> *[Conley, 2004, p. 111]*

It is easy to admire Greg for resisting his harsh father, who never did give him a break. But full-force resistance can become negative identity, with a lifelong cost. Greg did not establish his own identity, since it was obvious to him that he had to oppose everything his father said or did. As an adult, Greg never managed to hold down a regular job. Even after his father died, Greg kept his distance from his mother and brother. Dennis, in contrast, forged his identity by combining some aspects of his father's values with some of his own, advancing to leadership in the Air Force and then in civilian life, earning an upper-middle-class income.

Negative identity requires a foil, a barricade to beat against. If that obstacle disappears or, as in this case, dies, negative identity collapses. Without a positive identity to replace the negative one, the person is lost.

Moratorium

identity moratorium A pause in identity formation. Alternatives are explored, but final identity is postponed.

Finally, in the process of finding a mature identity, many young people declare an **identity moratorium,** a kind of time-out. In the United States, moratoria are particularly common at about age 18, the age at which young women were once expected to marry and young men were once expected to begin a lifetime career. Such expectations seem beyond reach in today's economic landscape, with expanding globalization, increasing female employment, and an unstable labor market (Larson & Wilson, 2004). Consequently, many adolescents postpone identity decisions, opting instead for a moratorium.

A moratorium is not necessarily harmful. In fact, given the complexity of "finding oneself" in modern society, moratoria are often necessary. Society provides several constructive ways to forestall identity achievement. The most obvious one is college, where students are usually required to take courses in a variety of academic areas. In addition, being a student deflects pressure to settle down, to choose a career, and to find a mate, each of which presupposes that the young person has achieved some identity.

Other institutions that provide an acceptable moratorium are the military, religious mission work, and various internships. Unlike teenagers in diffusion, adolescents in moratorium attempt to fill their roles (student, soldier, or whatever), but they consider it temporary, not their final identity. The U.S. Army, for instance, once advertised "Be all that you can be" but did not say that, once you have become all that you can be, you must reenlist. For most members, the military is a temporary identity status, not the final choice.

Arenas of Identity: Change and Progress

The paths toward identity just reviewed—diffusion, foreclosure, negative identity, moratorium—were described primarily by theorists who were building on Erikson's work. Erikson explicitly described four arenas of identity: religious, sexual, political, and vocational.

Now, half a century later, teenagers still struggle in those four arenas—religious commitment, gender roles, political loyalties, and career options—trying to fit their hopes for the future with beliefs acquired in the past (Gibson-Cline, 2000). The terminology has changed since Erikson's day, but these identities still need to be discovered.

It is important to realize that a person does not achieve identity all at once. For instance, many twenty-first-century adolescents foreclose on religious identity, achieve sexual identity, are diffused politically, and are in moratorium on vocational identity. Further, some aspects of the four arenas of identity are easier to find than others.

In achieving a sexual identity, for example, some teenagers identify as homosexual or heterosexual for both biological and social reasons (Hines, 2004; Moshman, 1999), but many continue to struggle with some aspects of sexual identity. A young man might identify as male but not be interested in certain features of the typical male role; for example, he might not have the expected passion for football and other sports. Meanwhile, his girlfriend might be an avid boxing fan, thus deviating from the traditional female role. Identity is a process more than a status for adolescents (Grotevant, 1998).

Now we will look at each of the four arenas originally described by Erikson. We begin with religious identity because it provides examples that clarify diffusion, foreclosure, negative identity, and socially created moratoria.

Religion

Religious identity is probably as important to adolescents today as it ever was because many are on a "spiritual quest . . . [a] search for meaning and purpose in life" (Levesque, 2002). Finding meaning is not easy, however.

There are six signs that teenagers have successfully found their religious identities. They self-identify as committed Christians, Jews, Muslims, Buddhists, and so on; they specify a subcategory, such as Pentecostal or Orthodox; they

ROB HOWARD / CORBIS

A Religious Life These young adolescents in Ethiopia are studying to be monks. Their monastery is a haven in the midst of civil strife; will the rituals and beliefs also provide them with a way to achieve identity?

belong to a particular fellowship of believers; they pray daily; they worship regularly; and their faith affects their daily life. For example, adolescents with a religious identity often volunteer, with other members of their group to help others (Youniss et al., 1999).

Such commitment, which includes practices as well as beliefs, means that the person is neither diffused nor in moratorium. The religious identity status, in this case, may be either foreclosed or achieved. Foreclosure occurs if the person simply accepts the values and practices of his or her parents, learned in childhood. This is the easiest path, because foreclosure provides certainty amid the confusion of adolescence.

Now consider how to recognize whether a teenager is diffused or in moratorium regarding religious identity. Diffused adolescents are indifferent and alienated—claiming, for instance, not only that all religions are the same but also that none are any good. Those in moratorium are still questioning. They are seekers, perhaps willing to accompany a close friend to a religious ceremony or to accept some ideas temporarily, but they are not certain of anything.

Although some adolescents achieve religious identity by age 18 or younger, others take longer. Many religions encourage youth to struggle with religious questions before making a commitment. For example, those who want to join the clergy undergo years of testing and training before they are allowed to commit their lives. Those seeking the religious sacrament of marriage (rather than a civil ceremony) often must undergo a period of waiting and education. In many religions, such as Mormonism, everyone is expected to receive training and then perform missionary work before settling down to raise a family.

Among the Amish (perhaps the most countercultural American religious group), many adolescents rebel against the simplicity and hard work that characterize the Amish way of life; they typically "venture out into the world" to experience the mainstream American life of movies, automobiles, and fashionable clothing (Stevick, 2001, p. 166). The rebels are not banned by their church; in fact, they usually get together with other rebellious Amish adolescents. They often return with their friends to the fold, choosing the Amish way after their interlude of independence.

Almost every organized religion has special programs for adolescents and young adults, designed for questioning (moratorium) and then commitment. By age 30, seekers are rare, because most people have found their religious identity. (If an adult chooses to be a committed, articulate atheist, that itself is a religious identity.) If 30-year-olds are still without any values of their own, they may be stuck in oppositional or diffused religious identity.

Gender

The term *sexual identity* has, over the past 50 years, been replaced by the term *gender identity*. As you remember from Chapter 10, for social scientists *sex* and *sexual* refer to biological male and female characteristics, and *gender* refers to cultural and social characteristics considered appropriate for males and for females.

Half a century ago, Erikson and other psychoanalytic theorists thought of males and females as opposites (Miller & Simon, 1980). They assumed that, although many adolescents were temporarily confused about their sexual identity, they would soon identify as men or women and adopt sex-appropriate roles (Erikson, 1968; Freud, 1958/2000).

In those days, adolescents anticipated traditional masculine or feminine roles. For example, teenage girls prepared to be wives and mothers, learning how to flirt, to wear lipstick, to walk in high heels. Boys prepared to be good providers and "the man of the house," developing toughness and an "old boy network" via competitive sports, all-male colleges, and military training.

Later research, and a changing cultural environment, revealed the narrowness of those preparations (Lippa, 2002). Sexual identity was renamed **gender identity,** and the term now refers primarily to a person's self-definition as male or female. Usually, but not always, a gender identity leads to a gender role and a sexual orientation (Galambos, 2004).

A **gender role** is the sex-typed occupation and patterns of behavior that a person adopts. The female gender role once meant that women married and became housewives obedient to, and dependent on, their husbands or, as "old maid" daughters, obedient to their parents. Now about half of the world's women are in the labor market, but women's traditional roles are still evident in that mothers are the primary caregivers and chief homemakers, and employed women gravitate to careers such as teacher and nurse more than to such traditionally male careers as engineer and corporate executive.

A related term is **sexual orientation,** a person's sexual attraction to people of the other sex, his or her own sex, or both sexes. This orientation may be relatively strong or weak and may be acted upon, unexpressed, or even unconscious. Sexual orientation may coincide with gender identity: Those who identify as males usually seek female partners, and females usually seek males.

LEE SNIDER / THE IMAGE WORKS

Friendship, Romance, or Passion? Sexual identity is much more complex for today's adolescents than it once was. Behavior, clothing, and hairstyles are often ambiguous. Girls with shorn hair, boys with pierced ears, or same-sex couples embracing are not necessarily homosexual for life—and may not have a homosexual orientation at all.

These three aspects of sexual self-definition—gender identity, gender roles, and sexual orientation—are often, but not always, aligned. They are epigenetic, correlated with biological sex but not entirely determined by either nature or nurture (Hines, 2004). Thus, a woman could have masculine clothes and attitudes, work as a coal miner, and be heterosexual, or a man could consider himself masculine, become a devoted father, and be homosexual.

Scholars differ about the extent to which male–female differences in adult behavior are biological or cultural. One respected team concludes that "the pancultural similarities in sex and gender greatly outweigh cultural differences" (Best & Williams, 2001, p. 22). This argument suggests that biology is far more powerful than culture. In contrast, a scientist who has studied people who, for genetic reasons, have hormones that differ from their apparent sex believes that biology and culture overlap and interact in so many ways that a distinction between "sex" and "gender" cannot be drawn (Hines, 2004). In any case, some of the gender differences that people believe to be biological are, in fact, cultural (Barnett & Rivers, 2004).

Each adolescent makes numerous decisions about gender identity and behavior, selecting from many roles and orientations. For instance, teenagers decide where and when to become sexually active, choosing abstinence or promiscuity or some pattern in between. They discover whom they are attracted to and how strong that attraction is, which may or may not affect the gender roles they choose.

To signify gender identity, teenagers choose jewelry and clothing, college majors and occupations, and ways to talk, move, and laugh. Some girls wear extensive makeup, tight pants, dangling earrings, and see-through blouses to high school classes; other girls wear loose-fitting clothes and avoid adornment of

gender identity Originally, this term meant all the behaviors associated with males or females. Now gender identity is more narrowly defined, as whether people see themselves as masculine or feminine.

gender role A role usually assigned either to men or to women, such as housewife, nurse, man of the house, and soldier.

sexual orientation A person's tendency to be sexually attracted to a person of the other sex (a heterosexual orientation), the same sex (a homosexual orientation), or both sexes (a bisexual orientation).

every kind. Both extremes are possible selves, both are likely to change with maturity, and both are evidence of the search for identity.

A developmental pattern may appear. According to some research, over the years of adolescence teenagers become less flexible in their gender-role concepts of male and female; that is, they become more sex-typed than they were earlier, a pattern called *gender intensification* (Galambos, 2004). Parents, schools, and teenagers themselves may become intensely concerned about masculinity and femininity. For instance, in elementary school math classes, many girls do as well as or better than boys. By college, however, far fewer women than men major in math and science. This imbalance may reflect intense awareness during adolescence of social norms and expectations, which are more gender-typed than biologically based (Barnett & Rivers, 2004).

In emerging adulthood, some people abandon gender norms and others intensify them. For example, if a couple has a traditional wedding, they usually follow their culture in being extremely sex-typed. In the United States and other Western societies, the bride typically wears a long white dress with a veil and carries a bouquet; the groom wears a plain, dark suit. She has bridesmaids, parents who give her away, and a wedding ring to add to her engagement ring; he has a best man and may have one ring, but never two. The particulars vary by culture (Chinese brides wear red), but such sex differences are universal.

Ethnicity

In Erikson's day, political identity referred primarily to whether a person self-identified with a particular political party. Today this type of political identity seems the least important of Erikson's four arenas of identity (religious, gender, political, vocational). In most nations that have been studied, adolescents seem indifferent to political identity and values (Torney-Purta et al., 2001). They are the age group least involved in traditional politics of any kind, including voting.

Since Erikson's time, ethnic identity has become increasingly important, and this change affects social and political values and attitudes. Ethnic politics and even ethnic wars are widespread, and many violent protesters and defenders of ethnic group norms are adolescents (Bernal et al., 2003). Often uprisings are portrayed as political (in Palestine and Ukraine, for instance), and reporters focus on the thousands of young people involved; but such movements seem to be as much a matter of ethnic and national pride as of political partisanship.

In the United States, ethnic identity is particularly acute for the more than one in three teenagers who are not native-born or not of European descent. Many of these young people advertise their ethnicity by wearing particular colors, pendants, or headgear. Issues of ethnic identity may also arise for European Americans, especially those whose families cling to their ties to another nation or who connect ethnicity with religion.

Worldwide, most children are raised in neighborhoods with others of similar background. Their shared childhood experiences allow easy transmission of ethnic behaviors and values—not only in diet, gender roles, and language but even in details such as how to wear shoes or greet a stranger. At puberty, ethnic identity may become crucial, especially if adolescents enroll in a large, multiethnic high school, envision employment in a multicultural society, or become aware of historical or current conflicts within their own nation (Lei, 2003).

Children of immigrants experience the identity crisis with special intensity. Their parents, born and raised in another country and another era, simply "had" an ethnic identity—they never needed to find it, or even give it much thought (Song, 2003). Second-generation immigrants choose their own ethnic identity from among several possibilities. The specifics depend on the context, particularly on how many others of their age and ancestry are nearby and how other

LESTER SLOAN / WOODFIN CAMP & ASSOCIATES

CHARLES GUPTON / THE STOCK MARKET

The Same but Different Traditionally, minority identity in the United States focused on race, with young people of color needing to find their place in a white world. Currently, however, the issue has broadened to be seen as ethnic, not racial. These California high school students look physically similar but are from very different backgrounds: The one in the foreground of the left-hand photo is from Cambodia and the one in the right-hand photo is from Mexico. Each is finding her own bicultural identity. Their backgrounds differ, but the search is universal; many adolescents of European descent also struggle with issues of heritage and self.

people react to them. Context is not just influential, but essential: "Without a context, identity formation and self-development cannot occur" (Trimble et al., 2003, p. 267).

Often the second generation has a broader concept of ethnicity than the original immigrants. For example, youth may identify themselves not as people from a particular place in China (as their parents did) but as Chinese, East Asian, or Asian—or, as some Chinese Americans did when affirmative action was a ballot question in California, as non-White (Song, 2003).

Each identity is a choice, with various manifestations in language and values, in dating patterns and partners, in dress and decorum (Trimble et al., 2003). Ethnic identity has three key characteristics:

- It depends on context and therefore may change.
- It is reciprocal, both a personal choice and a response to others.
- It is multifaceted; people can choose some aspects and reject others.

One who chose was Kevin Johnson, the child of a European American father and a Mexican American mother. He wrote a book called *How Did You Get to Be Mexican?* to explain his adolescent decision to be Mexican—to the consternation of those who thought that his name, appearance, and Anglo childhood negated his Mexican heritage. He criticized his parents for not teaching him Spanish. He married a Mexican American, gave his three children Spanish names, and helped them become bilingual (Johnson, 1999).

Ethnic identity is further complicated if young people fear taking on a false self. Since context matters, many adolescents notice that their speech, attitudes, and even personal tastes depend on whether they are with parents, peers, or strangers. Their friends may accuse them of disloyalty, such as being an "Oreo," a "banana," or an "apple" (white on the inside but black, yellow, or red on the outside) or "gray" (a mixture of white and black).

In fact, ethnic identity is always dynamic and changing. No one matches the prototype precisely, as most adults realize but many adolescents do not. Partly to avoid criticism, youth whose parents are considered to be of different races usually self-identify with whichever group experiences more prejudice (Herman, 2004).

For every adolescent, however, combining past and future is complex. This is powerfully expressed regarding U.S.-born youth of Mexican parents by one such person:

> Questioning their identity, as inevitable as that experience is, is not enough. To have passed through the ambiguities, contradictions, and frustration of cultural schizophrenia is to have passed only the first test in the process . . . we need to embody our own history. *El pueblo que pierde su memoria pierde su destino:* The people who forgets its past, forfeits its future.
>
> *[Gaspar de Alba, 2003, pp. 211–212]*

Vocation

Just as sexual and ethnic identities have become increasingly complex over the past 50 years, so has vocational identity (Csikszentmihalyi & Schneider, 2000). In the past, many American adolescents worked for pay while still in school. Their families needed money, and service jobs (delivering papers, babysitting, yard work) were available. Longitudinal research begun during the Great Depression in the United States found that employed teenagers benefited their families and themselves (Elder, 1974). Many adults of that generation still believe that adolescents should work, to "learn the meaning of a dollar" and to "keep out of trouble."

Research tracing the effect of employment on adolescent development, comparing both sexes and various cultures, surprised many social scientists by concluding that work is not necessarily beneficial. Employment during adolescence is likely to impede identity formation, family relationships, academic achievement, and career success. These impairments are especially likely if work takes more than 20 hours a week and is unconnected to the school curriculum (Greenberger & Steinberg, 1986; Hamilton & Lempert, 1996; Staff et al., 2004).

Adolescent employment varies cross-culturally. In Japan, almost no adolescent is employed or even does significant chores at home, because the family and culture agree that the adolescent's obligation is to study (Stevenson & Lee, 1990). In many African nations, adolescents choose between school and work, with the *less* able teenagers staying in school (Sternberg, 2004).

In Germany, work experience is integral to the curriculum. Most German adolescents choose a particular vocation from the 360 that are offered and are then trained by an employer in conjunction with their schoolwork. The students expect that training will lead to employment. Recently this tradition has begun to break down because employers want flexible, independent employees, not newly trained 18-year-olds, and adolescents are spurning apprenticeships, preferring college to immediate employment (Cook & Furstenburg, 2002).

Even in the United States, diversity is apparent. Many North American teenagers work at boring, dead-end positions—at fast-food restaurants, as household help, or the like—and spend their earnings on entertainment, instead of putting it in the bank. They learn nothing about the joys of challenging work, the responsibilities of paying bills, or their own future vocations. But for some, employment that offers opportunities for learning and promotion, mentoring, good pay, and limited stressors has psychosocial benefits, including development of good work habits (Mortimer, 2003).

No single prescription suits everyone. The developmental effects of adolescent employment are tied to the national economy as well as to the culture. In 2003 fewer 16- to 24-year-olds were employed than in 2001 or 2002, largely because there were fewer jobs overall. This trend affected not only the quantity but also the quality of jobs available to adolescents. The long-term effects of employment vary, although more than 20 hours a week of work during high school is considered harmful no matter what the national picture. If a job does not distract from schoolwork and if it leads to adult employment, it may benefit the teenager and the family (Mortimer, 2003).

For the most part, however, intense work at a job is damaging for adolescent development (Staff et al., 2004). Vocational success in adulthood correlates not with gainful employment during adolescence but with teenage social and academic competence, both of which are achieved more easily *without* steady employment (Roisman et al., 2004).

SUMMING UP

Many adolescents take years to achieve a solid identity, which is the product of exploration and commitment. Erikson described the crisis of identity as occurring in four arenas: religion, sex, politics, and vocation. Many other developmentalists have elaborated on this crisis: Some adolescents seem to care about nothing (identity diffusion), some make premature choices (foreclosure), some simply react against social norms (negative identity), and some take a socially sanctioned hiatus (moratorium). For contemporary youth, each aspect of identity is more complex than it once was. Foreclosure in religious identity seems attractive; sexual identity has become gender identity, gender roles, and sexual orientation; political identity is often intertwined with ethnic and religious identity; and vocational identity is elusive. Life choices and patterns are rarely simple dichotomies (e.g., believer/infidel, male/female, Black/White, worker/student). In current conditions, choices that once were simple are frustratingly elusive.

Social Support

The changing seas of development are never sailed alone. At every turn, a voyager's family, friends, and community provide sustenance, provisions, directions, ballast for stability, and a safe harbor when it is time to rest. Through example or insistence, social forces also provide a reason to move ahead. In adolescence, when the winds of change blow particularly strong, adults and contemporaries are valuable shipmates.

Support from Adults

Adolescence is often characterized as a time of waning adult influence, a period when the values and behaviors of young people become increasingly distant from those of their parents and other adults. There is some validity to this idea, but it need not be true. In fact, when young people feel valued by their communities, trusted by teachers, and connected to adults, they are far less likely to have problems of any kind, from experimenting with drug use to serious delinquency (Benson, 2003).

Parents are crucial for support and guidance (Collins & Laursen, 2004), but in effective communities they are not alone (Leventhal & Brooks-Gunn, 2004). Indeed, "supportive relationships with nonparent adults are considered to be among the key developmental assets predicting positive youth outcomes" (Rhodes & Roffman, 2003, p. 195).

The **generation gap**, as the difference in values and attitudes between the younger and older generations has been called, is not wide. The narrowness of the gap is apparent in values regarding education, politics, and social issues that are shared by adolescents and the adults they know best (Elder & Conger, 2000). For example, religion was once considered a hotspot for adolescent rebellion. Teenagers were expected to reject the God of their elders, to shun church or temple, and so on. However, research finds that contemporary parents have a strong and direct influence on their children's religious beliefs (Martin et al., 2003). Both religion and cultural background are resources in the quest for identity, and adults are often a beacon, or at least a landmark (King & Furrow, 2004; Wagener et al., 2003).

generation gap The difference in values and attitudes between adults of one generation and young people of the next. Although the gap does exist in such preferences as music, clothes, and hair, it is not wide when it comes to core beliefs and values.

generational stake The need of each generation to view family interactions from its own perspective because each has a different investment in the family scenario.

This does not mean that all is harmonious between adults and adolescents. Each age group has its own distinct **generational stake** (Bengtson, 1975). That is, each generation has a natural tendency to view interactions from its own position and perspective. When adults consult with other adults and when adolescents talk with their peers, the two generations tell quite different stories.

Consider a conflict about a curfew. Parents may see this as a management problem, the latest version of trying to get the children to bed on time. But teenagers may consider an early curfew to be evidence of the parents' outmoded values or lack of trust. On a deeper level, what parents believe is loving protection, teenagers may consider controlling domination.

Or consider hairstyles. One Indian American 15-year-old writes:

> I wanted to feel free and independent. . . . I wanted a haircut. But I couldn't make myself do it. A haircut was a big decision. My hair was more than just a bunch of dead cells. It was a symbol of control. For my parents and relatives, long hair is considered an essential part of being a woman. Especially for "good Indian girls."
>
> *[Chikkatur, 1997]*

Torn by these conflicts, one day this young woman decided to and—before she told her family or changed her mind—had her hair cut.

For the next month, as all her relatives criticized her, she alternated between thinking she had made a "huge mistake" and being "glad I cut my hair." She considered her short hair a symbol of her independence, not only from Indian traditions but also from what she perceived as the adult culture that wanted girls to be feminine, under control, and dependent. Her parents, aunts, uncles, and grandparents considered her haircut an assault on their gender and cultural values.

Tweens, Teens, and Their Parents

Overall, parents have a stake in believing that all is well and that their children are loyal to the family, despite a superficial show of rebellion triggered by external influences, such as hormones or peer pressure or Hollywood. By contrast, the younger generation has a stake in perceiving their parents as limited, old-fashioned, and out of touch.

The behavior of many American young people, like the Indian American girl above, may have an evolutionary as well as a cultural role. To improve their

NANCY RICHMOND / THE IMAGE WORKS

Not in My Kitchen Both parents and teenagers are invested in their relationship, but each generation has its own stake in, or perspective on, their interactions. The generational stake may result in bickering, often over minor issues.

? OBSERVATIONAL QUIZ (see answer, page 508): What do you see in the body positions of these two that suggests generational stake?

chances of reproducing, adolescent children may need to break free from parental restraints and find their own mates and peers. Disputes inevitably arise as a young person's drive for independence clashes with the parents' customary control. The depth and specifics of the disagreement depend on many factors, including the child's age and gender.

Parent–adolescent conflict typically is most frequent in the tweens, especially between mothers and daughters (Arnett, 1999; Laursen et. al., 1998). Usually it manifests itself as **bickering** (repeated, petty arguments, more nagging than fighting) about daily routines—cleanliness and clothing or, as one observer wrote, "hair, garbage, dishes and galoshes" (Hill & Holmbeck, 1987). Young adolescents often feel compelled to make a statement—with an exposed belly button, a visible tattoo, or blaring hip-hop beats—to establish that a new stage has arrived. Parents notice, and fear the worst—drug addiction, jail, loss of influence. Bickering follows.

"So I blame you for everything—whose fault is that?"

© THE NEW YORKER COLLECTION 2001 BARBARA SMALLER FROM CARTOONBANK.COM. ALL RIGHTS RESERVED

In some ways, bickering is a consequence of a close relationship. Conflict is more likely to indicate the existence of parent–child attachment than a lack of concern (Smetana et al., 2004). Few parents can resist commenting about dirty socks under the coffee table or a ring through the eyebrow, and few adolescents can calmly listen to "expressions of concern" without feeling they are being unfairly judged (Smetana, 2002).

bickering Petty, peevish arguing, usually repeated and ongoing.

When parents realize that their adolescents are becoming more distant and less affectionate, they typically adjust by granting more autonomy, and, by the later teen years, "friendship and positive affect typically rebound to preadolescent levels" (Collins & Laursen, 2004, p. 337). Normally, adjustment occurs on both sides; the child's physical maturity and emotional independence eventually bring mutual appreciation and respect.

ESPECIALLY FOR MOTHERS Why would young adolescent daughters and their mothers be most likely to bicker?

Culture and Family

In North America, ethnic variation is often found in the *timing* of parent–child conflict. For Asian and Latino teens, stormy relations with parents may surface later in adolescence. Perhaps when cultures encourage dependency in children and emphasize family closeness, the typical teenager's quest for autonomy is delayed (Greenberger & Chen, 1996; Harkness & Super, 2002; Laursen et al., 1998).

Internationally, some cultures value family harmony above all else, and both sides avoid conflict. It is possible that the very idea of adolescent rebellion and young-adult autonomy is a social construction, assumed to be necessary in Western culture but not in other places, notably India (Larson & Wilson, 2004). In contemporary China, most adolescents are willing to defer to the older generation, believing strongly in generational harmony and mutual respect (Fuligni & Zhang, 2004). This raises the question of whether adolescent emotionality, autonomy, and rebellion could be a cultural phenomenon, not the universal result of hormones, puberty, egocentrism, and the search for identity.

If adolescence as described in these chapters is primarily cultural, either Western cultures elicit rebellion or Eastern cultures repress autonomy. The later rebellion of immigrant adolescents, just mentioned, could result from later puberty, closer families, or their slow realization of their new culture's expectations. Multicultural research may soon provide answers.

Too much can be made of cultural, ethnic, or national differences. Parents everywhere care about what their children do and hope that their children will be happy and successful adults. Adolescents everywhere appreciate their parents' concern and expect their guidance in matters of health and safety, education, and employment. Cultural differences emerge only in the particulars (Smetana, 2002). One of these particulars is mate selection: Indian youth expect their parents to choose their mates; Japanese youth expect parental guidance in their romantic choices; U.S. adolescents think that their dates and future spouses should be their own choice (Hasebe et al., 2004; Larson et al., 2003).

Such differences aside, adolescents worldwide consider some choices their own. Virtually none believe that parents should dictate their personal taste in matters such as music and clothes. Adolescents not only resent such intrusion, they react with low self-esteem or greater anger. Both of these reactions may be serious, as explained at the end of this chapter.

In every nation, not only cultural norms but also variations within families affect the timing and severity of parent–child disagreement. Some offspring experience more conflict at age 12, others at 22, others in between. Most research done in Canada, Australia, and the United States finds that some conflict is normal but that too much conflict impairs development. No matter what their socioeconomic status (SES) or ethnicity happens to be, adolescents do not benefit when families are permissive to the point of laxness *or* strict to the point of abuse (Maccoby, 2000; Moore & Brooks-Gunn, 2002).

! Answer to Observational Quiz (from page 506): The mother's folded arms show her determination to keep her son in line. The young man sits on the kitchen counter and wears his cap in the house to stress his independence.

Avoiding extremes can be particularly difficult for single mothers who were teenagers when their children were born. When their children become adolescents, these mothers tend to be either too permissive or too harsh, unable to find the proper balance in dealing with a young person who is as tall, and seems almost as mature, as the young mothers themselves (Borkowski et al., 2002; Loeber et al., 2000).

Another complication arises when older siblings influence their younger brothers and sisters. If older siblings are aggressive, sexually active, or involved in drug use, the younger children are more likely to follow their example than to learn caution from their sibling's mistakes (Bank et al., 2004; Brody, 2004; East & Kiernan, 2001; Whiteman & Buchanan, 2002). Why is that? Are siblings role models? Do parents tire of monitoring and controlling? Do their genes and their circumstances push all siblings in the same direction? Probably all three.

The dangers of permissiveness are magnified in deteriorating communities. The worse a neighborhood is, especially if guns and drugs are easily available and neighbors do not use *collective efficacy* (discussed in Chapter 1) to help teenagers, the stronger the pull of deviant peers and externalizing behavior (Leventhal & Brooks-Gunn, 2004). Therefore, in such communities, parents are under special pressure to provide their teenagers with guidelines, monitoring, and support (Walker-Barnes & Mason, 2001).

In any family and every neighborhood, if conflict results in adolescent runaways or throwaways (kicked out of the house), disaster may follow. Indiscriminate sex, drug abuse, violence, and suicide are common among adolescents who feel completely cut off from their parents (Yoder et al., 1998).

Parent–Teen Closeness

Conflict is only one part of the parent–teen relationship. Other significant aspects include:

- Communication (Do parents and teens talk openly with each other?)
- Support (Do they rely on each other?)
- Connectedness (How emotionally close are they?)
- Control (Do parents encourage or limit adolescent autonomy?)

All these factors are discussed in earlier chapters. No researcher doubts that the first two, communication and support, are helpful, if not essential. Patterns of communication and support set in place during childhood continue into adolescence, buffering some of its turbulence (Collins & Laursen, 2004).

Regarding connectedness and control, simple recommendations may be misleading, because specific circumstances and consequences vary. Closeness and control can be destructive as well as constructive.

One of my students wrote:

> I got pregnant when I was sixteen years old and if it weren't for the support of my parents, I would probably not have my son. And if they hadn't taken care of him, I wouldn't have been able to finish high school or attend college. My parents also helped me overcome the shame that I felt when . . . my aunts, uncles, and especially my grandparents found out that I was pregnant.
>
> *[I., 2004, personal communication]*

My student is grateful to her parents for their constructive help, but others might disagree with her parents' decision to support her and, for that matter, might blame her parents for the fact that she had sex at such a young age.

It is known that a powerful deterrent of delinquency, risky sex, and drug abuse is **parental monitoring**—that is, parental awareness of their child's whereabouts, activities, and companions. Monitoring helps limit alcohol, drugs, and other dangers (Rogers, 1999; Sampson & Laub, 1993). When monitoring is part of a warm, supportive relationship, it leads to better outcomes, including a child with higher grades, less emotional distress, and helpful friends (Fletcher et al., 2004).

However, too much parental interference and control predict adolescent depression and other disorders, and may lead adolescents not only to distrust their parents but also to lie to them. The parental tactic called *psychological control* (the threatened withdrawal of love and support, discussed in Chapter 10) is particularly harmful (Barber, 2002; Pettit et al., 2001).

Apparently, adolescents need some freedom in order to feel competent, trusted, and loved (Barber, 2002). The dilemma: Parents must show concern without interference, caring without suspicion. Connectedness is beneficial, but intrusiveness makes children feel guilty and anxious, and that leads to distress and rebellion (Larson & Gillman, 1999). Parental monitoring itself may be harmful when, instead of indicating a warm connection with the adolescent and honest communication, it derives from a harsh, suspicious approach to parenting (Stattin & Kerr, 2000).

Overall, parent–teen closeness can become oppressive instead of supportive. Remember, however, how this section began: Parents are still quite important in the lives of their adolescents. Too much distance, like too much conflict, is destructive.

Response for Mothers (from page 507): Conflicts typically occur about habits of dress and cleanliness. Mothers are most directly involved with daily enforcement, and daughters are traditionally more docile—so their rebellion produces surprise and resistance in their mothers.

parental monitoring Parents' ongoing awareness of what their children are doing, where, and with whom.

ELLEN SENISI / THE IMAGE WORKS

A Guiding Hand Organized extracurricular activities, with appropriate adult supervision, supplement parental monitoring as a way of helping adolescents stay out of trouble.

Peer Relationships

From hanging out with a large group to whispering with a confidant, relations with peers ease the transition from childhood to adulthood and make life a joy rather than a burden (Erwin, 1998). Peer respect comes to those who look like other peers or who defy adults in ways that other peers admire. All adolescents value the opinions of their contemporaries. This makes them care more about how they look and care less about adult standards and values than their parents might wish—as I know from experience.

IN PERSON

The Berger Women Have Weird Rituals

My oldest daughter, Bethany, wore the same pair of jeans to tenth grade, day after day. She washed them each night by hand, and I put them in the dryer very early each morning. I did not know her reason, but I knew this was urgent for her. My bewildered husband watched us both, asking, "Is this some weird female ritual?" He encouraged her to wear other clothes, to no avail. Years later Bethany told me why: She wanted her classmates to think she didn't care how she looked. If she varied her appearance, they might think she did care, and then they would criticize her.

Rachel phoned to tell me she had pierced her ears again so that she could wear more earrings at once than anyone in my generation. She knew that I had waited until I was married to pierce my ears and that my mother had said I was "barbaric" for doing so. My response to Rachel had elements of my mother. "Does this mean you are going to take drugs?" I asked. She laughed at my naiveté, happy at my disapproval.

At age 15, my daughter Elissa was diagnosed with Hodgkin's disease, a form of cancer. My husband and I weighed divergent opinions from four physicians, each of whom explained why his or her treatment would minimize the risk of premature death. Elissa had different priorities: "I don't care what you choose, as long as I keep my hair." (Her hair fell out temporarily, but now her health is good.)

Sarah, my youngest, refused to wear her jacket during her first year of middle school even on the coldest days. Another weird ritual? Years later she said she wanted her peers to think she was tough.

What strikes me now is how oblivious I was to my children's need for peer respect. That did not occur to me at the time as an explanation for their seemingly bizarre actions. Instead, I reacted as a mother, not a wise developmentalist. As my husband once said, "I knew they would become adolescents, but I did not realize we would become parents of adolescents."

peer pressure Social pressure to conform with one's friends or contemporaries in behavior, dress, and attitude; usually considered a negative force, as when adolescent peers encourage one another to defy adult authority.

Peers are constructive as often as they are destructive, contrary to the stereotype of **peer pressure**—which usually means social pressure to conform to some negative peer activity. The concept of peer pressure ignores three important points:

- Peer standards are not always negative. Indeed, "friends generally encourage socially desirable behaviors" (Berndt & Murphy, 2002, p. 281), such as participating in sports, studying for exams, avoiding smoking, and applying to colleges.
- Peers "serve to bridge the gap between childhood and adulthood" (Bagwell et al., 2002, p. 26), easing the transition between childish modes of behavior and full independence. Thus, peers make maturation smoother and faster.
- Peer pressure is short-lived. It rises dramatically in early adolescence, until about age 14, but then declines. Adolescents gradually become more selective in whom they emulate and what they choose to do.

These three points do not negate another reality: Young people can lead one another into trouble. Collectively, peers sometimes engage in escapades that none of them would dare do alone, providing "deviancy training" for one another (Dishion et al., 2001, p. 82).

Destructive peer pressure is strongest during times of uncertainty. For example, students admire aggressive or drug-experimenting classmates in their first year of high school or when they are experiencing the physical changes of puberty or when they are uncomfortable with heterosexual attraction (Bukowski et al., 2000). Students who are socially rebellious tend to have higher peer respect and self-esteem in some adolescent cultures (Pederson et al., 2005).

Adolescent Friendships: Selection and Facilitation

To understand that peer pressure is sometimes helpful and sometimes not, two concepts are helpful: *selection* and *facilitation*. First, selection: Peers choose one another. Teenagers associate with others whose values and interests they share, particularly in regard to drugs and academics (Hamm, 2000). Then, facilitation: Peers encourage one another to do things that none of them would do alone.

Risk-taking behavior is the clearest example of this aspect of peer pressure. Each college class probably includes several students who took risks in high school that they now consider foolish. One of my students and two of his friends began swimming to a distant island because one of them (the strongest swimmer) suggested it. Not until he was almost halfway there did my student realize that he would have to swim back. He turned around. One of his friends made it to the island; the other was rescued by boat.

The same phenomenon can be seen experimentally. When adolescents drove a car in virtual reality (with wheel, accelerator, and brakes, but only headphones and a video screen) they were less likely to crash when they were alone than when they brought two of their friends to the laboratory to watch them "drive" (Steinberg, 2004).

Selection and facilitation can work in any direction, for better or worse (Lacourse et al., 2003). One teenager finds friends who smoke cigarettes and drink beer, and together they share marijuana and vodka at a party. An opposite example might be the teenager who chooses friends who enjoy math, and together they join the math club and sign up for AP calculus.

Contrary to a common adult misperception, facilitation is indirect and pervasive, a team effort rather than a matter of one rebel leading one innocent astray. A student explained:

> The idea of peer pressure is a lot of bunk. What I heard about peer pressure all the way through school is that someone is going to walk up to me and say, "Here, drink this and you'll be cool." It wasn't like that at all. You go somewhere and everyone else would be doing it and you'd think, "Hey, everyone else is doing it and they seem to be having a good time—now why wouldn't I do this?" In that sense, the preparation of the powers that be, the lessons that they tried to drill into me, they were completely off. They had no idea what we are up against.
>
> *[quoted in Lightfoot, 1997]*

Remember that adolescents choose their peers and are chosen by them; the group accomplishes what the individual members wish. High-functioning adolescents have close friends who themselves are high-achieving and have no major emotional problems. The opposite also holds: Those who are drug users, sexually active, and alienated from school encourage their friends to do the same (Crosnoe & Needham, 2004).

One other aspect of peer relationships should be mentioned, because it shows why parents tend to blame peers for their own child's misbehavior. Friends allow adolescents to experiment with possible selves, aiding identity formation. Thus, middle school students who tell their parents that they must do something, wear something, or be somewhere because "everyone else does it" are trying to lessen their responsibility for whatever they wish to try (Ungar, 2000). Peers, in other words, deflect, and defend against, adult criticism.

The Peer Group for Immigrant Teens

Friends play a special role for the millions of adolescents in North America, Australia, and Western Europe whose parents are immigrants. Such adolescents are numerous in major cities, including one-third of all adolescents in Frankfurt, one-half in Amsterdam, and two-thirds in Los Angeles and New York. Many immigrant children become model youth, earning higher grades and seeming to be better adjusted than children of the same ethnicity whose families are not immigrants (Fuligni, 1997, 1998; Liebkind & Jasinskaja-Lahti, 2000; Salazar et al., 2001).

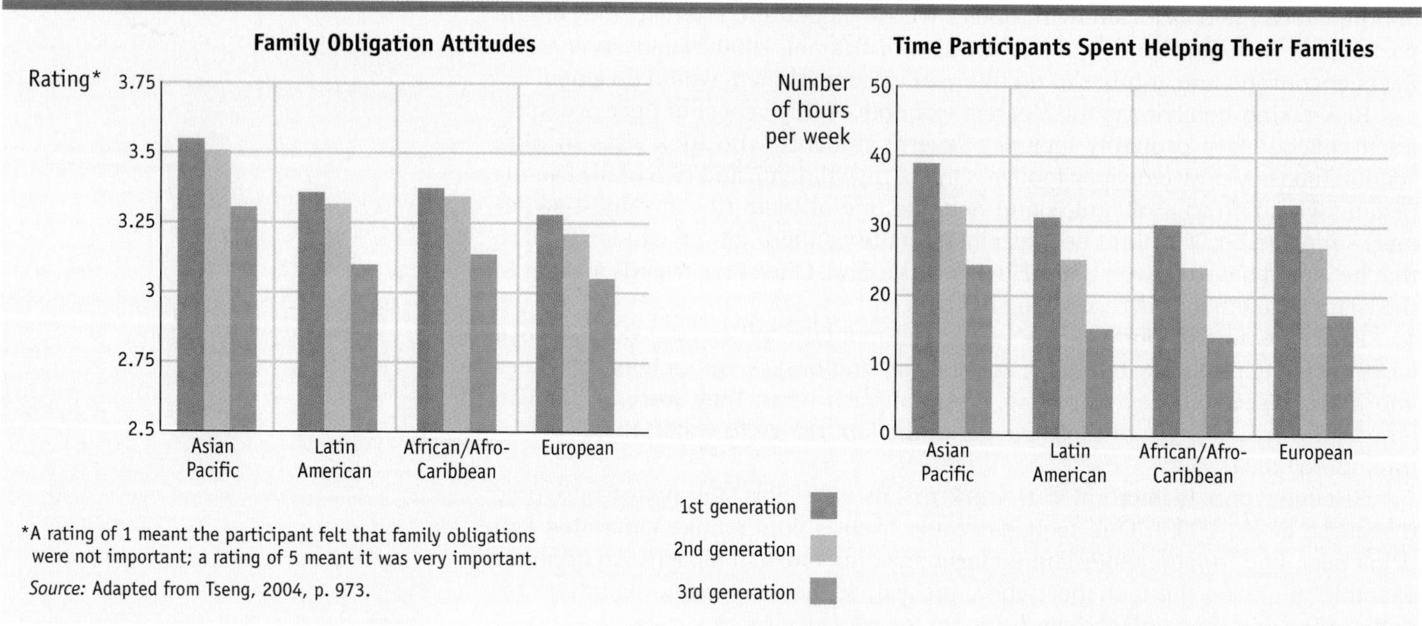

FIGURE 16.1 **A Sense of Duty** Nearly 1,000 U.S. college students from four ethnic groups were asked how important they thought family obligations were and how much time they spent each week helping their families (by, for example, doing household chores, translating for their parents, taking care of siblings, or working in the family business). The responses varied, depending on which ethnic group a participant belonged to and on how long the participant's family had been in the United States. The Asian American participants tended to give the importance of family obligations the highest ratings (left). The first-generation (foreign-born immigrant) students spent the most time—more than 30 hours per week, on average—helping their families (right).

Their parents depend on them, with good reason: They help out at home, and they mediate between the old and new cultures (Tseng, 2004) (see Figure 16.1).

Conflict may arise, however, if the parents' culture differs markedly from that of their children. Immigrant parents may be horrified to see their children growing taller than they are, seeking autonomy via bickering, experimenting with drugs, and rebelling against the authority of their elders. If parents become more restrictive and punitive, the teenagers may become not submissive but defiant.

Friends can help the children of immigrants negotiate conflicting cultures, traditions, and desires, preventing both foreclosure and negative identity, but their parents may not view this support in a favorable light. For instance, Greek Australian adolescents felt that some conflict between themselves and their parents was acceptable, even good, unlike Greek adolescents living in Greece. However, the Greek parents of those Australian youth had attitudes about family harmony that were quite similar to those of Greek adults in Greece (Rosenthal et al., 1989). For the teenagers, talking with their peers helped validate their own experiences.

As another example, consider Layla, whose family lives near Detroit (Sarroub, 2001). Layla's parents were raised in Yemen, but Layla was educated in the United States. At age 15 she was sent to Yemen to marry her father's nephew. She returned to her Michigan public high school, which for her was "both liberating and a sociocultural threat" (Sarroub, 2001, p. 390) and tried to keep her marriage secret (she wore no ring).

Layla respected her parents and adhered to her Islamic religion, but she resisted many aspects of her heritage. For example, she was troubled that her father smoked qaat (a narcotic that is legal in Yemen but illegal in the United States), that he wanted her to wear a long Arab dress (she wore jeans instead), that he did not agree with her plan to get a divorce and go to college. Layla especially resented the fact that Yemeni culture allowed boys more freedom than girls, a tradition evident throughout the developing world (Best & Williams, 2001).

> At times Layla was confused and unhappy at home. She . . . preferred going to school where she could be with her Yemeni friends who understood her problems and with whom she could talk. "They make me feel like really happy. I have friends that have to deal with the same issues." . . . Layla was

> often angry that girls in Yemen were taken out of school. . . . She thought that the boys had been given too much freedom, much more than the girls.
>
> *[Sarroub, 2001, pp. 408–409]*

In general, peers are important for immigrants and nonimmigrants alike. This is particularly apparent in cultures that expect adolescents to seek autonomy. Adolescents need peers to help them grow up. Without peer support, some (especially girls) might submit to parental control, perhaps living at home until an early marriage; others (usually boys) might rebel completely, perhaps joining a gang that provides codes of behavior, standards of dress (e.g., gang colors), and social bonding. As one researcher explains, some Latinos in California join gangs to "satisfy their desire for self-identity" (Arfániarromo, 2001).

Which path an adolescent takes—anything from studious obedience to defiant rebellion—depends on many factors within their family and peer group, including communication, support, connectedness, control, and cultural assimilation (Fuligni, 1998). A wide discrepancy between family background and the current social context pushes many adolescents toward the extreme of either obedience or rebellion (Suarez-Orozco & Suarez-Orozco, 2001).

Other-Sex and Same-Sex Peer Relationships

Many adults worry about boy–girl interactions, assuming that their teenage children will have sexual intercourse if adults are not watching. Adolescent worries are quite different: They worry that they have too few close friends of either sex. In fact, adolescents with high self-esteem usually have several male and female friends who are not romantic partners, and these friendships help them prepare for future romantic relationships (Brown, 2004; Feiring, 1999).

As an Australian researcher named Dexter Dunphy (1968) described adolescent interaction decades ago, heterosexual association during childhood and adolescence usually follows this sequence:

1. Groups of friends, exclusively one sex or the other
2. A loose association of a girls' group and a boys' group, with public interactions
3. Small mixed-sex groups of the advanced members of the larger group
4. A final pairing of couples, with private intimacies

According to subsequent research in many nations, culture affects the timing and manifestation of these stages, but Dunphy's description of the four steps is accurate. The basic sequence seems genetically driven, consistent across decades, across cultures, and even across primate species (Brown, 2004; Connolly et al., 2000; Schlegel & Barry, 1991; Weisfeld, 1999).

In modern developed nations, where signs of puberty begin in the tweens and marriage does not occur until early adulthood or later, each of these stages typically lasts several years. Same-sex groups dominate in elementary school and often continue through middle and high school. Friendship networks that include both sexes are common in later adolescence. Romances appear toward the end of high school.

For instance, 43 percent of eleventh-graders in one large Canadian high school reported having had a romantic relationship; this was almost twice the rate that eleventh-graders had reported two years earlier (Connolly et al., 2000). High schools in other communities find a similar bump, although the particular grade varies. Norms in a particular school also affect peer approval or disapproval of cross-ethnic, cross-age, and same-sex romances, and the incidence of such alliances reflects that cultural view (Brown, 2004).

First romances rarely last more than a few months, with girls more likely to say they have a boyfriend than vice versa. Committed couples with a long-term

JOSÉ LUIS PELAEZ, INC./CORBIS

Young Lovers Young lovers spend as much time together as possible. Their evident closeness might alarm their parents, but any attempt to break up young lovers may backfire, risking early pregnancy and elopement. Parental guidance and good communication are crucial when adolescents become romantically involved.

relationship do not usually form until late high school or beyond. One might hypothesize that socially advanced adolescents would move more quickly through this heterosexual sequence, but the opposite seems more accurate.

Early pairing, especially if it decreases same-sex friendships, signifies emotional trouble (Brown, 2004). One possible reason is that romantic couples spend less time with other friends as well as less time with family, and that cuts off sources of support that are particularly needed in adolescence (Laursen & Williams, 1997). Although romantic partners become a source of emotional support, teenage romances are more about companionship than physical intimacy (Furman et al., 2002), which is one reason teenage couples who break up often remain friends.

For adolescents who are homosexual, complications slow down the formation of friendship and romantic bonds. To begin with, many are reluctant to acknowledge their sexual orientation. In one confidential study of more than 3,000 ninth- to twelfth-grade teenagers, only 0.5 percent identified themselves as gay (males) or lesbian (females) (Garofalo et al., 1999), far fewer than the estimated proportion of adult homosexuals (from 2 to 10 percent, depending on definition).

Retrospectively, homosexual men report that they became aware of their sexual interests at about age 11, but they typically did not tell anyone until age 17 (Maguen et al., 2002). Many young women who will later identify themselves as lesbian spend their teenage years relatively oblivious to, or in denial of, their sexual urges. Unlike gay men, many lesbians first become aware of their homosexuality as part of a close friendship that becomes romantic, usually in late adolescence (Savin-Williams & Diamond, 2004).

Some adolescents, trying to sort out the complexity of gender identity, gender roles, and sexual orientation, are uncertain about their own sexuality. About 10 percent of heterosexual adults report that they had same-sex encounters or desires as adolescents (Laumann et al., 1994). It is not known whether such inclinations are part of normal sexual awakening for all adolescents (only some of whom report it) or whether many homosexual or bisexual individuals decide to pursue an exclusively heterosexual lifestyle in adulthood.

Eleanor Maccoby, an expert on gender differences, finds that "a substantial number of people experiment with same-sex sexuality at some point in their lives, and a small minority settle into a life-long pattern of homosexuality" (Maccoby, 1998, p. 191). Such experimentation is most likely to occur in adolescence, but, because of political conflicts regarding research on adolescent sexuality, it is not known how large "a substantial number" is. Much remains to be discovered (Savin-Williams & Diamond, 2004).

Teenage Sexual Activity

No arena highlights the overlapping influences of parents, peers, and the wider community more clearly than sexuality. Over the millennia, pubertal hormones have always fueled a drive in adolescents to establish families of their own. Although overpopulation may now threaten human survival, genes and hormones do not change in a few generations. Indeed, it can be argued that all adolescents, by nature, are highly sexual beings, whether or not they act on their impulses and whether or not their actions involve conversation and hand-holding or something more (Savin-Williams & Diamond, 2004).

Also over the millennia and in all cultures, parents, peers, and society have been deeply concerned about teenage sexuality, especially what, when, and with whom. Arranged childhood marriages (often to uncles or cousins), no-fault divorces, chastity belts, shotgun weddings, polygamy—each of these has been considered normal in some cultures and bizarre in others. Although adolescents are sexual beings, and although parents, peers, and society are very concerned about adolescent sexual relationships, consistent and reliable guidance is scarce.

Parental Guidance

Parental advice may be pivotal in teenagers' decisions about sex. Many studies have found that if adolescents discuss sex openly with their parents, they take fewer risks, avoid peer pressure to have sex when they do not want to, and believe that their parents provide useful information (Blake et al., 2001; Miller et al., 1997).

Such discussions are rare, largely because of the generational stake. In one study, mothers were asked whether their teens had had sex (Jaccard et al., 1998). Then the teens were asked the same question, in confidence. The difference between the two sets of replies was astounding (see Figure 16.2). For instance, more than a third of the 14-year-olds were sexually active, but less than half of their mothers knew it.

Mothers who were religious and who disapproved of teen sex were less likely than other mothers to know when their children were sexually active, perhaps because they had a higher stake in believing in their children's innocence. Fully 72 percent of all the mothers reported that they had talked with their teens at least once about sex, but only 45 percent of the teens agreed (Jaccard et al., 1998). Thus, at least 27 percent of mother–child pairs disagreed about whether the conversation had taken place—a gap that remained when this study was replicated (Jaccard et al., 2000). Apparently, mothers have a stake in believing they talk to their adolescents about sex, and adolescents have a stake in forgetting such talk, if it occurs.

Parents also underestimate adolescents' capacity to engage in responsible sexual relationships. For example, only 23 percent of the mothers and 33 percent of the fathers in another study thought that most teenagers were capable of using a condom correctly (Eisenberg et al., 2004). In fact, sexually active adolescents are more likely than adults to use condoms correctly. Many experts advise parents to overcome their own ignorance, recognize the needs and the capacities of the younger generation, and then discuss "the social, emotional, familial, and moral consequences" of sexual activity as well as provide practical advice (Jaccard & Dittus, 2000).

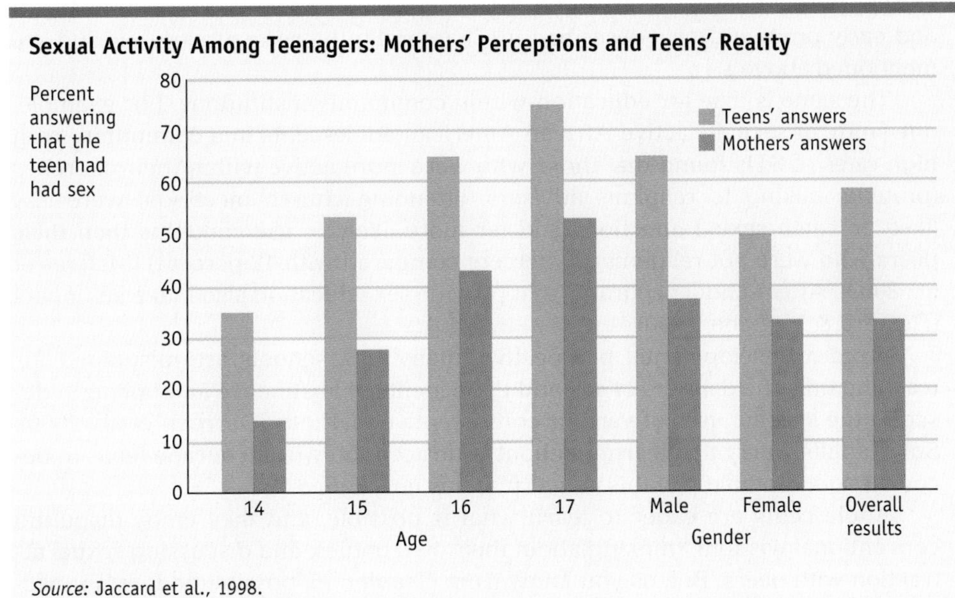

FIGURE 16.2 **Mother Doesn't Always Know** This graph shows the discrepancy between the answers mothers gave to "Is your child sexually active?" and the answers teenagers gave when asked for the truth. Notice which age group and gender had the largest gaps—younger teens and boys!

Especially for Young Adults Suppose your parents never talked to you about sex or puberty. Was that a mistake?

Adolescents look to their parents' behavior as well as to their words. Results from the Add Health survey of 9,000 U.S. teenagers found that, when background factors such as income, ethnicity, and family structure were controlled for, adolescents whose parents smoked cigarettes were one and half times as likely to have sex before age 15 than were adolescents whose parents did not smoke. No effects were found if the parents drank heavily (Wilder & Watt, 2002). This puzzling result needs to be confirmed by other research. The authors speculate that smoking is widely recognized as unhealthy, so adolescents feel free to discount parental admonitions about other health issues, such as early sex.

No one doubts that parents are, ideally, the best sex educators; but most parents want teachers and other adults to provide sex education for their children. Parents typically feel too embarrassed or ill informed to teach their children the specifics they want them to know (Jaccard et al., 2000).

Sex Education in School

Almost all adults (90 percent in the U.S. South; more elsewhere) think that high schools should teach adolescents about sexual matters, including contraception (Landry et al., 2003). Almost all secondary schools worldwide provide sex education; some societies mandate that sex education begin in primary school, and all offer such classes by high school (Landry et al., 2003). In addition to providing facts about disease, reproduction, and puberty, most U.S. high schools teach students how to refuse unwanted sexual activity.

Most European schools also teach how to be sexually responsible, and many provide contraception and confidential counseling. In England these services are available in "youth-friendly" places, not only schools but also fitness clubs and youth centers (Stone & Ingham, 2003). In France, nurses in church-sponsored as well as public schools are legally authorized and culturally encouraged to provide condoms and emergency contraceptive pills (Boonstra, 2000).

Sex education makes developmental sense during adolescence. Teenagers can apply formal operational thinking to understand the sequence of biological sex and to analyze risks. They can use intuitive thinking to respond to emotions and social interaction. Both types of thinking need to be deployed, because passion responds to intuition, not logic. Guided by a masterful teacher, peer discussion of sexual issues can be informative and constructive, helping adolescents analyze possibilities and risks. (The risks of sexually transmitted infections [STIs] and early pregnancy are described in Chapter 14; the risks of early pairing are mentioned above.)

The same is true for education within community institutions. For example, one study of sexually active African American adolescents in a community with high rates of STIs found that those who were more active within their churches (praying, talking to religious advisers, attending church meetings) were less likely to catch sexual infections and far more likely to use condoms than their peers who were not religious (88 percent compared with 12 percent) (McCree et al., 2003). After-school programs that provide sex education also make an impact (Howard & McCabe, 1990).

From a developmental perspective, many U.S. schools are misguided for teaching only the dangers of sex and the benefits of abstinence and failing to describe the specific uses of various contraceptive methods (Darroch et al., 2000). Some adults worry that learning about contraception will encourage teens to become sexually active, but this concern seems unfounded.

Adolescents are eager to learn what is possible, and they enjoy disputing conventional wisdom, thinking about their own bodies, and discussing sexual attraction with peers. But, as you know from Chapter 15, possibility does not necessarily become reality, and discussion does not necessarily lead to action. We noted earlier that peers may slow down rather than speed up a teenager's movement toward private intimacy. The Surgeon General of the United States reviewed more than 100 sex-education programs. He reported that teaching adolescents about contraception

> does not increase adolescent sexual activity, either by hastening the onset of sexual intercourse, increasing the frequency of sexual intercourse, or increasing the number of sexual partners. . . . Some programs increased condom use or contraception use for adolescents who were sexually active.
>
> *[Satcher, 2001]*

Developmentalists agree with most adults in the United States and other nations that sex education belongs in the schools as well as in parent–child conversations. Adolescents learn best about sex from adults they trust. This means that sex education could be included in some seventh-grade curricula (remember that 30 percent of U.S. students are sexually active by age 14), while in other communities the topic can wait until ninth grade (remember that community norms vary).

A longitudinal experiment with ninth-graders in Texas and California (10 schools in the intervention group and 10 in the comparison group) found that a comprehensive sex-education plan worked. The program involved parents, provided referrals for medical care, and delivered a 20-lesson "safer-sex" curriculum over two years; even three years later, condom use increased and sexual intercourse was less frequent (Coyle et al., 2001).

Especially for an Adult Friend of a Teenager If your 14-year-old friend asks you where to get "the pill," what do you say?

However, despite its emphasis on abstinence, the program did not slow down (or speed up) the age of first sexual intercourse, which showed no statistical difference between the experimental and comparison schools. One possible reason, even though the program succeeded in other ways, may be that the program began too late to affect first sexual experiences. By the ninth grade, more than one-fourth of the students in these 20 schools had already had sex.

When sex education in many parts of the world is examined, one crucial factor to emerge is that a multifaceted program should precede sexual activity by a year or more. Otherwise, peers learn from one another, with the first ones to have sex teaching the others or with girls learning from "older men" (often in their 20s) (WHO, 2005).

Peer Influence on Sex

In the United States and some other nations, peers are the main source of information and motivation regarding contraception, abortion, intercourse, and disease. As you know, teenagers are powerfully influenced by their peers through selection and facilitation (Henry, 2004). Variation in age of sexual initiation is substantial, which means that some groups of peers encourage sexual activity and others discourage it.

One recent U.S. survey of ninth- through twelfth-grade students found that a low of 33 percent of Los Angeles girls and a high of 74 percent of Memphis boys were sexually active (MMWR, May 21, 2004). More detailed studies of particular subgroups of Los Angeles girls or Memphis boys might find that the percentages were reversed.

In general, most adolescents are not sexually active until several years after puberty. In early adolescence, they tend to be absorbed in their own growth, monitored by their parents, and uncomfortable with peers of the other sex. Voluntary sexual relationships take years to develop. As already mentioned, early sexual activity signals trouble.

Teens and emerging adults in committed, intimate relationships often discuss decisions about sex, sharing their knowledge and concerns about infections and pregnancy (Kvalem & Traeen, 2000; Manning et al., 2000). Correlational data reveal that, if a romantic partner is someone of the same age and background, sexual intercourse usually occurs only after a long courtship (Ford et al., 2001; Marin, 2000). There is a warning in the flip side of that correlation: Early-maturing adolescents with older partners are likely to become sexually active without protection (Savin-Williams & Diamond, 2004).

Friends can slow down romance and sexual activity as well as facilitate it (Connolly et al., 2000). Teenagers want to be sexually active if they think their peers will respect them more but hesitate to have sex if they think their peers or partners will lose respect for them (Henry et al., 2004).

Response for Young Adults (from page 516): Yes, but maybe you should forgive them. Ideally, parents should talk to their children about sex, presenting honest information and listening to the child's concerns. However, many parents find it very difficult to do this, because they feel embarrassed and ignorant. Try bringing up the subject now; your parents may feel more comfortable discussing it with a young adult than with a child or adolescent.

Some contemporary U.S. teenagers take a "virginity pledge" with their friends, as part of a church program that advocates sexual abstinence until marriage. For them, sexual intercourse is usually postponed until after high school. Crucial to such postponement is that the pledge is voluntary and those who take it feel they are a special group, bonded to one another; in that sense, the pledge is an example of positive peer pressure (Bearman & Bruckner, 2001). There is one problem, however. If pledgers become sexually active, they are less likely to use contraception, so they are at greater risk for pregnancy and STIs.

Adolescents suffer from "pluralistic ignorance" when it comes to sex: None of them are well informed (Cohen & Shotland, 1996). This is not surprising, given what is known about adolescent cognition. Unless encouraged to do so, teenagers do not readily use formal operational thinking for personal decisions. For example, adolescents estimate a high risk of HIV from one act of sexual intimacy, but they think the risk from 10 encounters is not much higher (Linville et al., 1993). As another example, the personal fable lets them deny responsibility: They may blame their partner, their hormones, or even the devil for their sexual urges, as was found by a study of adolescent sex in Latin America (Schifter & Madrigal, 2000).

Particularly troubling in the United States, where most teenage mothers are unwed, is that heuristic thinking makes them underestimate the difficulties of raising a child and overestimate the bonding of sexual intimacy. In one study, the high school girls who were most likely to have a baby thought that their boyfriends would be more committed to them if they became mothers (Ungar, 2000). This is pluralistic ignorance. Unlike 50 years ago, having a baby before age 20 cuts in half a woman's chance of marriage, whether to the baby's father or to someone else (Graefe & Lichter, 2002).

The Media as Teacher

The media are another major source of information—and misinformation—about sex. Sexual talk and actions are common on television (three times per hour, on average [Kunkel et al., 1999]), and even more common in music.

Although the media certainly awaken and exploit sexual urges, and offer models for sexual innuendo and flirting, not much accurate knowledge about sex itself comes from this source. Violence of all kinds, including sexual violence, is far more common on the screen than in real life; but contraception, unwanted births, and induced abortions are very rare on television or in movies (especially in "teen flicks"), even though almost every adolescent has a close friend who has had one or more of these experiences (Roberts et al., 2004).

When teens try to learn about sex on the Internet (as many do), pornography is much easier to find than accurate information. The veracity and intent of Web pages vary markedly. A naive young person has few means of judging the integrity of the source, and, as you remember from Chapter 15, separating fact from fantasy is not easy for adolescents.

Trends in Adolescent Sexuality

The specifics of teen sex have changed markedly over the past few decades. Here are some data:

- *Premarital sex has increased* over the past 30 years. It is rare for a bride and groom to be virgins when they marry.
- *Specific sexual interactions are more varied,* with oral sex more common and coitus less common during adolescence than a decade ago (Savin-Williams & Diamond, 2004).
- *Teen births are decreasing.* This trend is evident on every continent; sometimes the drop is dramatic. Compared with 1960, less than half as many teenagers gave birth in 2004 in places as distant and different as China and the United States.
- *The use of "protection" has increased.* Contraceptive use of all kinds, particularly condoms among adolescent boys, has doubled in most nations since 1990. About 20 percent of U.S. teenage couples now use "dual methods"—usually the pill to prevent pregnancy and condoms to prevent infections (Manlove et al., 2003).

All these facts lead to a conclusion: Although adolescents' bodies have not changed much in the past few centuries, their responses to biological drives are influenced by their social contexts.

Public policy affects seemingly private decisions. For this reason, although every nation has seen a decline in teen births, the actual rates vary a great deal from nation to nation (Teitler, 2002). For example, teenagers in the United States have far more babies than do their peers in any other developed nation (eight times the rate in Japan, twice the rate in Canada and Great Britain)—not because they are having more sex (they are not), but because U.S. teens use less contraception and have fewer abortions.

Educational and economic trends also have an impact. Worldwide, education of women correlates strongly with lower birth rates (LeVine et al., 2001). In the United States, teenagers who have less education and lower cognitive skills tend to have earlier sex and more babies (Shearer et al., 2002). Generally, when the economy plummets, the birth rate declines; this trend was glaringly evident in the United States in the 1930s and in Russia in the 1990s. Sexual activity probably does not decrease, but contraception and abortions increase when jobs are scarce.

Teen births are declining and contraceptive use is increasing worldwide. Nonetheless, sexually transmitted infections (including AIDS), teen births, unsafe abortion, and sexual abuse remain common health hazards for adolescents in many parts of the world (Blum & Nelson-Mmari, 2004). Mortality and sterility rates from all these hazards are far higher in impoverished nations than in wealthier ones (WHO, 2005).

National prosperity does not guarantee adolescent sexual health. In the United States, youth "persistently delay seeking clinical services," and teenage rates of unplanned pregnancies, late abortions, and unwanted births are higher than in any other developed nation (Hock-Long et al., 2003, p. 145). From a developmental perspective, this trend is tragic.

There is hope in this area, however. Apparently, the typical teenager's sexual experiences change from decade to decade and place to place. When it comes to the risks of early sex, psychosocial factors seem more influential than the biological imperative to seek sexual bonding. The fact that biology has changed little over the centuries (except that puberty begins earlier) is not as crucial as the fact that social contexts are created by people. Parents, schools, peers, and the media can make a difference. The hope is that they will.

RESPONSE FOR AN ADULT FRIEND OF A TEENAGER (from page 517): Practical advice is important: Steer your friend to a reputable medical center that provides counseling for adolescents about various methods of avoiding pregnancy (including abstinence). You don't want your friend using ineffective or harmful contraception, or becoming sexually active before he or she is ready. Try to respond to the emotions behind the question, perhaps addressing the ethics and values involved in sexual activity. Remember that adolescents do not always do the things they talk about, nor are they always logical; but they can analyze alternatives and assess consequences if adults lead them in that direction.

SUMMING UP

The social network expands in size and significance during puberty, more often to the benefit of the adolescent than otherwise. Social support comes from many adults: The generation gap is narrower than is widely believed. Parents are particularly crucial. Although adolescents and parents often bicker over small things, parental communication and monitoring are helpful for significant issues, such as future vocation and current sexual practices.

Peers are as likely to aid adolescents in their search for self-esteem and maturity as to encourage self-destructive, antisocial behavior. Immigrant adolescents are often influenced by their friends, as they try to succeed in a culture unlike that which guided their parents. For all teenagers, friends of both sexes are important; romantic commitments usually do not begin until late in adolescence. Accurate information and guidance about sexual relationships are needed, but not always provided, by parents, peers, teachers, and the media.

Sadness and Anger

Adolescence is usually a wonderful time of life, perhaps better for current generations than for earlier ones. As you have seen, the generation gap is narrower than most people think, the teenage pregnancy rate is lower than it was, and friends are usually helpful. Worldwide, more adolescents are in high school, fewer are malnourished, and almost none die of disease (Blum & Nelson-Mmari, 2004). Many developmentalists and cultures consider adolescence a joyful time that should be celebrated, not a problem period when teenagers should be protected.

Nonetheless, for a troubled minority, serious problems emerge. Most adolescent hazards cluster together in the same few people. As an illustration, an adolescent who is, say, unusually rebellious is also at increased risk of dropping out of school, being arrested, and dying accidentally. Similarly, adolescents who use illegal drugs before age 15 are also more vulnerable to depression, unwanted pregnancy, and suicide.

The size of this troubled minority seems to be increasing. Compared with decades ago, there are more unwed mothers, more suicides, more illegal drugs, more teenagers in prison. All these difficulties happen at younger ages than they did 50 years ago, often to youth who have already had problems at school or at home (Farrington, 2004).

Many teenagers are less happy and more angry than they were as children. Some of this is to be expected, an outgrowth of the stresses of puberty, secondary school, social relationships, and greater responsibility. The sad or angry teenager needs guidance and comfort from adults who do not overreact to bouts of crying or cursing. For some individuals, emotions become extreme, pathological, and destructive. If adults merely guide and comfort, the problems may get worse. Differentiating normal from pathological is crucial.

Less Confidence

The general emotional trend in adolescence is more downward than upward, as teenagers become increasingly aware of their bodies, of academic demands, of peer criticism. For example, a cross-sequential study showed that children from ages 6 to 18 feel less competent, on average, each year in most areas of their lives (see Figure 16.3) (Jacobs et al., 2002). Other research, in various places and nations, also finds a drop in self-esteem beginning at about age 12 (e.g., Eccles et al., 1998; Fredricks & Eccles, 2002; Harter, 1999; Marsh, 1989).

The specifics depend on cohort, culture, and domain, but a bumpy decline overall is evident. Day by day, hour by hour, assessments suggest peaks and valleys, not stable moods (Arnett, 1999; Larson & Richards, 1994). This trend is apparent in both sexes; it is a myth that only girls, not boys, lose confidence at adolescence (Barnett & Rivers, 2004).

Some individuals become happier in adolescence, but this is not the usual pattern. At particular risk are those who have been raised to believe they are innately intelligent, skilled, and protected. All this is challenged at adolescence, when almost everyone's grades fall, friendships shift, coaches become more critical, and so on. Unless adolescents develop more realistic goals, they may quit trying, feel hopeless, or lash out (Dweck, 1999)—or, in comorbid fashion, do all three.

As mentioned many times earlier, children and adolescents of low-SES families are particularly vulnerable, partly because of their troubled neighborhoods and partly because their parents are often financially stressed and therefore less effective and responsive. Families high in SES can also experience financial stress and raise adolescents who experience drug abuse, delinquency, and depression (Luthar, 2003).

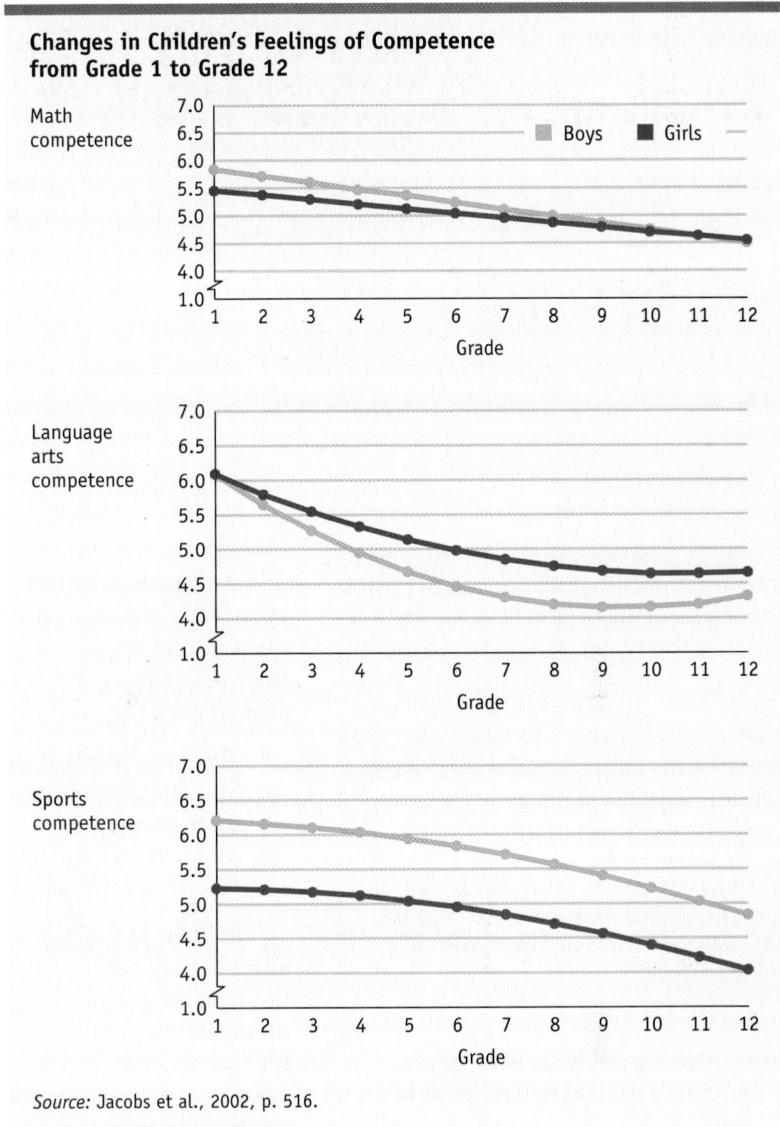

FIGURE 16.3 **All the Children Are Above Average** U.S. children, both boys and girls, feel less and less competent in math, language arts, and sports as they move through grades 1–12. Their scores on tests of feelings of competence could range from 1 to 7, and the fact that the twelfth-grade average was between 4 and 5 indicates that, overall, teenagers still consider themselves above average.

Depression

Some adolescents lack support and guidance from family, friends, or school, and lose faith in their future. A loss of self-esteem may push them not toward realism but toward **clinical depression,** an overwhelming, enduring feeling of sadness and hopelessness that disrupts all normal, regular activities.

Although the signs and causes of clinical depression predate adolescence, including genetic vulnerability and a depressed mother who was the adolescent's primary caregiver in infancy (Cicchetti & Toth, 1998), depression is much more common in adolescence than in childhood. At puberty the rate of clinical depression more than doubles, to about 15 percent, affecting about 1 in 5 teenage girls and 1 in 10 teenage boys (Graber, 2004).

Many researchers wonder why teenagers, especially girls, are so vulnerable (Caspi et al., 2003; Ge et al., 2001; Graber, 2004; Hankin & Abramson, 2001). Individual differences in hormone levels are one explanation, coupled with the psychic stresses of school, friends, sexual drives, and identity crises. Most developmentalists agree that depression is multidimensional: Social and cultural factors (especially peers and parents) can either push people over the edge of despair or protect them. All agree that depressed teenagers need strong support from adults and peers, especially to prevent the most lethal consequence of depression: suicide.

Suicide

Teenagers are just beginning to explore life's possibilities. When trouble comes—failing a class, ending a romance, fighting with a parent—don't they realize that better days lie ahead? Not always. More than one-third (36 percent) of all U.S. adolescent girls say they have felt hopeless in the past year, and one-fifth (21 percent) have seriously thought about suicide (MMWR, May 21, 2004). **Suicidal ideation**—that is, thinking about committing suicide—is so common among high school students that it might be considered normal (Diekstra, 1995).

clinical depression Feelings of hopelessness, lethargy, and worthlessness that last two weeks or more.

suicidal ideation Thinking about suicide, usually with some serious emotional and intellectual or cognitive overtones.

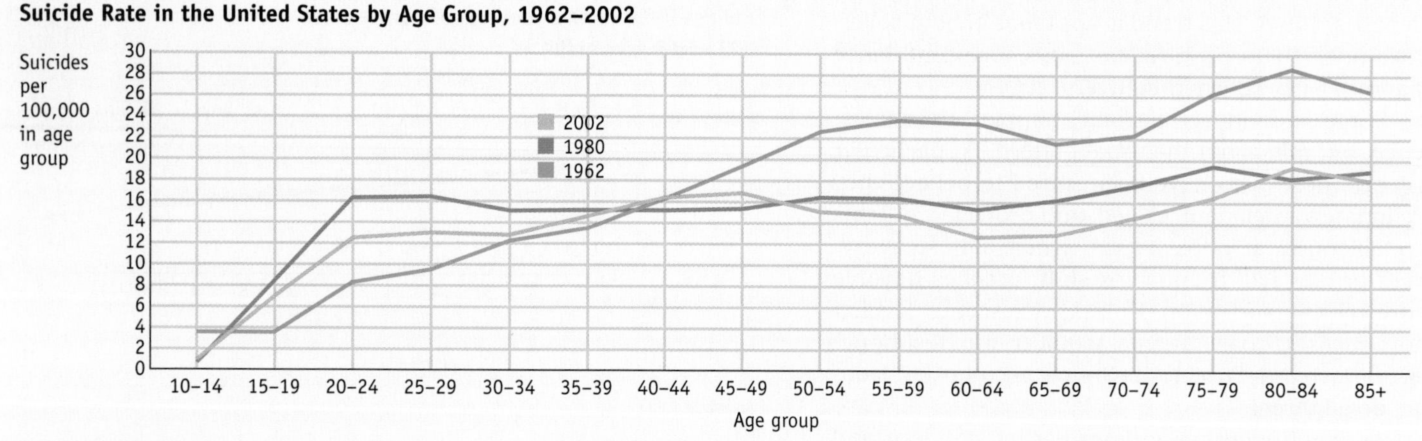

Source: Adapted from Table 3.139, Sourcebook of Criminal Justice Statistics Online, accessed August 2, 2005.

FIGURE 16.4 **So Much to Live For** A historical look at U.S. suicide statistics reveals two trends. First, teenagers are twice as likely to take their own lives as they once were. Second, today young adults are more suicidal and older adults less so. Have increased family and school pressures made adolescence more problematic, while better health care and improved retirement benefits have made the later years of life easier today than they were in 1962?

? OBSERVATIONAL QUIZ (see answer, page 524): In a typical cross-section of 1,000 U.S. 15- to 19-year-olds, how many committed suicide in 2002?

parasuicide Any potentially lethal action against the self that does not result in death.

Just as low self-esteem is common but clinical depression is not, suicidal ideation is common but completed suicides are not. Before delving deeper, we need to correct a misconception. Adolescents under age 20 are *less* likely to kill themselves than adults are. Many people mistakenly think suicide is common in adolescence for four reasons:

- The rate, low as it is, is much higher than it was (see Figure 16.4).
- Statistics often include young adults, who commit suicide far more often than teenagers.
- Most adolescent suicides capture media attention; most adult suicides do not.
- Suicide attempts are more common in adolescence than in adulthood.

Instead of *attempted suicide* or *failed suicide,* experts prefer the term **parasuicide** (any potentially lethal action against the self that does not result in death) because adolescent emotions and confusion make intent unclear, even to the individuals themselves. Some try suicide in the same way that they explore possible selves. After a potentially lethal episode, many feel relieved that they survived. Yet parasuicides should be taken seriously because they are a sign that adolescents may try again and not have the good fortune to be rescued.

Parasuicide is not rare in adolescence. International rates range from 6 to 20 percent, depending partly on culture and age and partly on definition. Here is one specific: Among ninth-graders in U.S. high schools during one year (2003), 15 percent of the girls and 6 percent of the boys tried to kill themselves (see Table 16.1). Whether adolescent suicidal ideation leads to a plan, a parasuicide, or death depends on several factors:

- Availability of lethal means, especially guns
- Lack of parental supervision
- Use of alcohol and other drugs
- Gender
- Cultural attitudes

The first three factors suggest why youth suicide in North America and Europe has doubled since 1960: Adolescents have more guns, experience less adult supervision, and are more prone to use alcohol and drugs than was the case 45 years ago.

Worldwide, parasuicide is higher for females and completed suicide is higher for males. The only exception is in China, where females complete suicide more often than males (because girls tend to use pesticides, which are almost always lethal). One reason for the usual predominance of male suicides is that men

TABLE 16.1 **Suicidal Ideation and Parasuicide Among U.S. High School Students, 2003**

		Seriously Considered Attempting Suicide	Parasuicide (Attempted Suicide)	Parasuicide Requiring Medical Attention	Actual Suicide (ages 14–18)
Overall		16.9%	8.5%	2.9%	Less than 0.01% (about 7 per 100,000)
Girls:	9th grade	22.2	14.7	3.9	
	10th grade	23.8	12.7	3.2	Girls: About 2 per 100,000
	11th grade	20.0	10.0	2.9	
	12th grade	18.0	6.9	2.2	
Boys:	9th grade	11.9	5.8	3.1	
	10th grade	13.2	5.5	2.1	Boys: About 11 per 100,000
	11th grade	12.9	4.6	2.0	
	12th grade	13.2	5.2	1.8	

Source: CDC, National Center for Health Statistics Web site, cdc.gov/nchs/data/hus/hus04trend, Table 59, accessed August 2, 2005.

tend to use the most lethal means—guns rather than pills (Miller & Hemenway, 2001). Guns are more available to those who hunt or join gangs, as males more often do. One California study of 12- to 17-year-olds found that seven times as many boys as girls had their own guns (Sorenson & Vittes, 2004).

Boys are also less likely than girls to ask for help or signal distress (as in parasuicide). This means that adults and peers need to be especially attuned to depressed boys. Remember that disorders often occur together: A depressed boy may appear more angry than sad. Parasuicide decreases when adolescents are taught to recognize when their friends are seriously depressed (Aseltine & DeMartino, 2004)

Adolescent suicide rates vary dramatically among countries and among ethnic groups within countries (see Table 16.2). When continents are compared, Africa and South America have low rates and Europe (especially Eastern Europe) has high rates. As for nations, Japan seems to have one of the lowest rates for teenagers and Hungary one of the highest. Canada and the United States are midway between the extremes. (Such international comparisons can change from year to year, in response not only to shifting culture and changing policy but also to increased accuracy of death certificates.) In Australia, Aboriginal youth are particularly vulnerable, in part because their culture romanticizes suicide (Tatz, 2001). In the United States, Hispanic girls have far higher rates of parasuicides that require medical attention than do African American or European American girls (MMWR, May 21, 2004).

Relatively common in adolescence are **cluster suicides**, which are several suicides committed by members of a group within a brief period of time. When a particular town or school sentimentalizes a teenager's "tragic end," such publicity can trigger suicidal thoughts, parasuicides, and completed suicides in other adolescents (Joiner, 1999). Cluster suicides are found particularly among Native Americans (Beauvais, 2000). In a massive project to reverse this pattern in one tribe, researchers worked to engage the young people in constructive activity and to decrease domestic violence. Parasuicide fell among the tribe's adolescents. The authors note that suicide attempts are a manifestation of depression, anger, and family disintegration, and thus a concerted effort to improve life for families (Indian or not) will also decrease teenage suicide (May et al., 2005).

cluster suicides Several suicides committed by members of a group within a brief period of time.

? **Critical Thinking Question** (see answer, page 524): What might account for the ethnic differences in adolescent suicide rates?

TABLE 16.2 **U.S. Suicide Rates of 15- to 19-Year-Olds by Ethnic Group, 2004**

	Males (rate per 100,000)	Females (rate per 100,000)	Females as Percent of Total
American Indian and Alaskan Native	22.7	9.1	25%
European American	13.4	2.6	16%
Hispanic American	9.1	2.0	20%
African American	6.9	2.3	13%
Asian American	5.7	3.3	29%

Source: National Vital Statistics Report, 53 (17), March 7, 2005, pp. 50–71.

! Answer to Observational Quiz (from page 522): Statistically speaking, none. The rates are given per 100,000 in each age group. This means that fewer than one in 10,000 teens commit suicide in a year.

Some British research has suggested that use of antidepressant drugs by adolescents may increase thoughts of suicide. Research in the United States on fluoxetine (Prozac) refutes this finding. In a study of 439 depressed 12- to 17-year-olds, those who improved most received *both* cognitive-behavioral therapy and medication (March et al., 2004).

The key to reducing adolescent depression and suicide seems to be recognizing the problem when it arises. Clinical depression is not usual or inevitable at any age, yet it often goes unrecognized and untreated (Hollon et al., 2003). Adolescents who lock themselves in their rooms, sobbing or blasting music alone day after day, need help.

More Destruction

LELAND BOBBE / STONE / GETTY IMAGES

If You Were His Father or Mother . . . Would you agree with Anna Freud that teenage rebellion is welcome and beneficial?

Like moments of low self-esteem and thoughts about suicide, bouts of anger are common in adolescence. Many teenagers slam doors, defy parents, and tell friends exactly how badly other friends have behaved. Some do more: They steal, destroy property, or injure others.

Is such behavior normal, particularly for adolescent boys? Most developmentalists who agree with psychoanalytic theory (see Chapter 2) answer "yes." A leading advocate of this view was Anna Freud, who believed that adolescent resistance to parental authority was "welcome . . . beneficial . . . inevitable." Indeed, she was troubled by a lack of defiance. She explained:

> We all know individual children who, as late as the ages of fourteen, fifteen or sixteen, show no such outer evidence of inner unrest. They remain, as they have been during the latency period, "good" children, wrapped up in their family relationships, considerate sons of their mothers, submissive to their fathers, in accord with the atmosphere, idea and ideal of their childhood background. Convenient as this may be, it signifies a delay of their normal development and is, as such, a sign to be taken seriously.
>
> *[A. Freud, 1958/2000, p. 263]*

Contrary to Freud, many psychologists, most teachers, and almost all parents are quite happy if they have well-behaved, considerate teenagers.

Over the past 40 years, longitudinal research has found that many normal teenagers are quite respectful of their parents. Such behavior does not predict a later explosion or psychological breakdown. However, Anna Freud was correct in one respect: Those who are disobedient often settle down once they have jobs and families of their own (Vaillant, 2002; Werner & Smith, 2001). Thus, some anger is common, and explosive anger may not signal a destructive life pattern. To know how serious a rebellion might be, some developmental history is needed.

Especially for Parents of Teenagers Your 13-year-old comes home after a sleepover at a friend's house with a new, weird hairstyle—perhaps cut or colored in a bizarre manner. What do you say and do?

Breaking the Law

Many children are diagnosed as having *conduct disorder,* which involves acting in destructive ways, such as cursing adults, petty stealing, destroying property, and harming animals. Conduct disorder is especially worrisome if it includes active aggression (see pp. 299–300)—when one person intentionally hurts another, either with relational or physical aggression. In adolescence, these children usually become *juvenile delinquents,* who are lawbreakers under age 18.

Misconduct, aggression, and delinquency are more frequent in adolescence than at other ages. Worldwide, arrests are most likely in the second decade of life, rising rapidly at about age 12, peaking at about age 16, and then declining slowly with every passing year (Rutter, 1998). In looking at statistics on adolescent crime, it is useful to separate out the minor, adolescent-only offenses from the more serious ones. Such analysis does not let adolescents off the hook: The arrest rate for violent crimes is twice as high for them as for adults.

! Answer to Critical Thinking Question (from page 523): In every ethnic group, U.S. teenagers born in another nation use guns less often, drink less alcohol, and kill themselves less often than do their U.S.-born peers. This may explain why rates are low among Hispanic and Asian Americans: Many of them are immigrants. It does not explain the low rates among African Americans, however.

These are **incidence** statistics, obtained by determining the age of all arrestees. These data do not indicate **prevalence**—that is, how widespread lawbreaking is. To explain this distinction, suppose that only a few repeat offenders commit almost all the crimes. In this case, the prevalence would be low even though the incidence was high. *If* this were true, and *if* adolescents on the path to a criminal career could be spotted early and then imprisoned, the *incidence* of adolescent crime would plummet, because those few offenders could no longer commit their many crimes. This supposition and strategy have led to attempts to "crack down" and "put away" young criminals.

incidence How often a particular behavior or circumstance occurs.

prevalence How widespread within a population a particular behavior or circumstance is.

Developmentalists over the past decades have found this supposition to be false. Juveniles are mostly experimenters; they have not yet settled on any career, let alone a criminal one (Farrington, 2004). Most break many minor laws (smoking, fighting with a peer) and have no more than one serious brush with the police. Even chronic offenders are usually convicted of a mix of offenses—some minor, some serious. In fact, only 1 of every 100 arrested youths has already been arrested for more than one violent offense. Thus, many adolescent offenders commit one or a few crimes each, rather than a few offenders committing hundreds (Snyder, 1997).

Especially for Police Officers You see some 15-year-olds drinking beer in a local park when they belong in school. What do you do?

Nevertheless, adolescent crime is a serious problem for society and for the delinquents themselves. For one thing, prevalence and incidence are much higher than police records indicate because most lawbreakers are not arrested, or even caught. In one confidential study (Fergusson & Horwood, 2002), the average boy admitted to more than three serious offenses between ages 10 and 20 and the average girl to one—although virtually none of the subjects had been arrested.

JOHN MCCUTCHEN, POOL / AP PHOTO

Do You Know This Boy? His name is Andy Williams. Is he a 15-year-old freshman lost in a large California high school and ignored by his parents? Or is he a crazed killer, who brought his father's revolver to school one day, murdered 2 schoolmates, and wounded 13 more? In fact, he is both, and that was the reason for this court hearing, where the judge decided that Williams should be tried as an adult. Later, Williams pleaded guilty.

? Observational Quiz (see answer, page 527): Who are the adults with Andy?

Gender and ethnic differences are not what they may appear to be. U.S. statistics show that adolescent males are arrested three times more often than females, African Americans three times more often than European Americans, and European Americans three times more often than Asian Americans (U.S. Department of Justice, 2002). Confidential self-reports, however, find much smaller gender and ethnic differences (Rutter et al., 1998). When all illegal acts—including underage drinking, disorderly conduct, breaking a community curfew, playing hooky, sneaking into a movie or onto a bus without paying, and buying cigarettes or beer—are taken into account, virtually every adolescent is a repeat offender.

Make no mistake here. The fact that rebellion is expected or that lawbreaking is common does not mean that juvenile crime is inevitable or insignificant; quite the contrary. Communities need to limit rebellion to relatively harmless actions, not only to halt young criminals before offenses get worse but also to protect young victims. Adolescents are victims two to three times more often than adults, especially of violent crimes (assault, rape, murder) (Hashima & Finkelhor, 1999). (See Appendix A, p. A-17.) Young victims often become perpetrators, and vice versa—yet another reason to halt teenage crime (Bjarnason et al., 1999).

Limiting the Damage

Although it is clear that teenage rebellion should be controlled, it is not clear how this is best accomplished. A useful distinction has been made between the many **adolescence-limited offenders,** whose criminal activity stops by age 21, and the few who are **life-course-persistent offenders,** who become career criminals (Moffitt, 1997).

adolescence-limited offender A person whose criminal activity stops by age 21.

life-course-persistent offender A person whose criminal activity typically begins in early adolescence and continues throughout life; a career criminal.

Adolescence-limited offenders should be kept in check, but the punishment should not compromise their ability to grow up and become model citizens.

Response for Parents of Teenagers (from page 524): Remember: Communicate, do not control. Let your child talk about the meaning of the hairstyle. Remind yourself that a hairstyle in itself is harmless. Don't say "What will people think?" or "Are you on drugs?" or anything that might give your child reason to stop communicating.

Adolescence-limited offenders were not perfect as children, but they were probably not the worst-behaved in their class or the first to use drugs, have sex, or be arrested. By mid-adolescence, their actions may be indistinguishable from those of their life-course-persistent peers, but their past provides hope for their future.

By contrast, life-course-persistent offenders are troubled long before adulthood. They are antisocial in preschool and elementary school, becoming bullies. They may show signs of brain damage—perhaps they were slow to talk, were hyperactive, or had poor emotional control. Their parents either punished them severely or, less often, neglected them completely. They are the first members of their cohort to have sex and to use drugs. By age 14, they are less involved in school activities and more involved with older, lawbreaking youths than other adolescents their age (Connor, 2002; Farrington, 2004; Rutter et al., 1998). Without intervention, they end up in prison, or worse.

Almost all career criminals have this ominous childhood history. However, only about half the children with these characteristics become career criminals. For that reason intervention in early adolescence needs to be carefully targeted, not only to allow the adolescent-limited delinquents to grow out of their rebellion but also to keep life-course-persistent delinquents from getting worse (committing murder instead of theft, for instance). In early adolescence, the progression toward more serious crime can be halted by a cohesive neighborhood, an effective school, a supportive peer group, a stable and responsive family, or a law-abiding best friend (Farrington, 2004).

If neighborhood, school, family, and peers are inadequate, then intensive intervention that teaches life-course-persistent teenage offenders and their families new ways of coping with their biological, cognitive, and psychosocial problems may help. Longitudinal research finds parental retraining to be effective if it begins early in an angry, antisocial child's life, preferably before the first arrest (Reid et al., 2002). Ineffective parenting may not seem harmful in childhood, but the repercussions may become explosively apparent when the children reach puberty (Compton et al., 2003).

Given our developmental understanding of adolescents, punishment must depend on past development as well as on the crime. Residential incarceration in a prison, group home, or juvenile detention center may backfire if young lawbreakers become friends with other deviant youth (Dishion et al., 2002; Mahoney et al., 2001).

If an adolescent is removed from an effective family, supportive school, and prosocial friends and placed in a context where toughness and defiance are required, then antisocial behavior may become habitual. There is a critical developmental distinction here: Younger children learn aggression at home from punitive, unresponsive parents, but adolescents learn such actions from cultural context and peers (McCabe et al., 2001).

One innovative strategy for changing the context is called *therapeutic foster care*, in which violent youth are assigned to foster families trained to teach anger management, school achievement, and responsible self-care. Controlled comparison research finds that therapeutic foster care reduces later arrests by more than half (Chamberlain et al., 2002). This type of foster care is expensive (up to $50,000 per year per youth), but the savings in court, jail, and prison costs are twice that (MMWR, July 2, 2004).

Not surprisingly, in this and all programs for antisocial youth, relationships are crucial. Developing a close attachment with a supportive adult and avoiding associations with deviant peers seem the best ways to keep rebellious youth (adolescence-limited or not) within bounds. Time itself is an agent of change: The adolescents' behavior will either improve (usually) or become more destructive (sometimes) by adulthood.

SUMMING UP

Compared with people of other ages, many adolescents experience sudden and extreme emotions that lead to temporary but powerful sadness and anger. These feelings are usually expressed within supportive families, friendships, neighborhoods, and cultures that contain and channel various outbursts, improving the confidence of depressed youth and limiting the rebellion of delinquents. For some teenagers, however, profound emotions are unchecked or even increased by their social contexts. This can lead to parasuicides (especially for girls), to minor lawbreaking (for both sexes), and, more rarely, to completed suicide and serious lawbreaking (especially for boys). Intervention works best if people recognize the difference between normal and pathological emotion and if intervention not only reduces risks (such as access to guns and drugs) but also helps develop healthy relationships between the adolescent and constructive peers or supportive adults.

! Answer to Observational Quiz (from page 525): They are not Andy's parents, who were not present at this hearing. Andy is flanked by his court-appointed defense attorneys.

Conclusion

Adolescence is usually a wonderful time. Bodies grow taller and stronger and awaken sexually, with all the joys of attraction, intimacy, and love. Minds develop as well, with intellectual excitement and cognitive challenges, as adolescents think more deeply and quickly than ever before. Although there are some bumps in family and peer relationships, respect develops between the generations, and peer friendships, which include people of both sexes and many backgrounds, usually foster happiness and maturity.

Developmentalists agree that adolescence, as an age period, is not a turbulent, rebellious stage, as psychologists once thought it to be. Most adolescents, most of the time, are happy and healthy, worthy of admiration and respect, not suspicion or fear.

Response for Police Officers (from page 525): Avoid both extremes: Don't let them think this situation is either harmless or serious. You might take them to the police station and call their parents in. However, these adolescents are not life-course-persistent offenders; jailing them or grouping them with other lawbreakers might encourage more serious acts of rebellion.

■ SUMMARY

Identity

1. Adolescence is a time for self-discovery, which begins when young people develop multiple selves, trying out various roles and personalities.

2. According to Erikson, adolescents achieve identity in four areas: religion, sex, politics, and vocation. Many adolescents choose foreclosure or moratorium, or experience diffusion before achieving identity. Some react against parental and social pressure by taking on a negative, or oppositional, identity.

3. Religious identity remains important to adolescents, because values are needed for guidance. Most have completed their search for religious identity by age 30, if not before.

4. Adolescents achieve sexual, or gender, identity not only by figuring out their sexual orientation but also by choosing specifics of male or female behavior and roles. Political identity is now usually expressed via ethnic identity, which is increasingly complex in a multiethnic society.

5. Vocational identity is almost impossible to achieve before age 20, since many jobs are unknown to adolescents and since teenage employment rarely leads to a career.

Social Support

6. Adolescents benefit from adult guidance and support. The generation gap is quite narrow, although each generation has its own stake in and perspective on family interactions.

7. Parents continue to influence their growing children, despite bickering over minor issues. Ideally, communication and warmth remain high within the family, while parental control decreases and adolescents develop autonomy. Cultural differences in timing and other patterns emerge, but parental neglect or hostility is always destructive.

8. Friends help adolescents cope with the conflicting demands of school, family, peers, and physical growth. Peer pressure may be either beneficial or harmful, depending on the adolescent's choice of friends.

9. Peers are crucial for immigrant adolescents. Those immigrants who have a strong commitment to family values tend to be successful in school and unlikely to rebel by using drugs or in other ways. Some, however, rebel completely.

10. Heterosexual friendships and romances begin in adolescence and become increasingly important for self-concept and maturation. Whether or not a particular adolescent is romantically attached or sexually active depends on many factors, both personal and cultural.

11. Parents, teachers, and peers all provide some sex education to adolescents, but none necessarily do it well. Worldwide, the teenage birth rate has fallen, partly because individual counseling, more education, and better contraception are available.

Sadness and Anger

12. Almost all adolescents lose some of the confidence they had when they were children. A few individuals become chronically sad and depressed, intensifying problems they had in childhood.

13. Many adolescents think about suicide. Parasuicides are not rare, especially among adolescent girls. Few adolescents actually kill themselves; most who do so are boys. Drugs, alcohol, guns, alienation from parents and peers, and lifelong depression are risk factors for suicide.

14. Almost all adolescents become more independent and angry as part of growing up. According to psychoanalytic theory, emotional turbulence is normal during these years. Often rebelliousness manifests itself in lawbreaking, especially by adolescent boys.

15. Adolescence-limited offenders should be prevented from hurting themselves or others. Life-course-persistent offenders are more difficult to treat, because their problems typically start in early childhood and extend into adulthood. Therapeutic foster care is one treatment that seems effective.

■ KEY TERMS

identity (p. 495)
identity versus diffusion (p. 495)
possible selves (p. 496)
false self (p. 496)
identity achievement (p. 496)
identity diffusion (p. 497)
foreclosure (p. 497)
negative identity (p. 498)
identity moratorium (p. 498)
gender identity (p. 501)
gender role (p. 501)
sexual orientation (p. 501)
generation gap (p. 505)
generational stake (p. 506)
bickering (p. 507)
parental monitoring (p. 509)
peer pressure (p. 510)
clinical depression (p. 521)
suicidal ideation (p. 521)
parasuicide (p. 522)
cluster suicides (p. 523)
incidence (p. 525)
prevalence (p. 525)
adolescence-limited offender (p. 525)
life-course-persistent offender (p. 525)

■ KEY QUESTIONS

1. What is the difference between finding a false self and achieving identity?

2. What factors might make it particularly easy, or particularly difficult, for someone to establish his or her ethnic identity?

3. Give several examples of decisions a person must make in establishing gender identity.

4. What aspects of a high school graduation might help a young person achieve identity?

5. Why and how do parents remain influential during their children's teen years?

6. How and when can peer pressure be helpful and how can it be harmful?

7. What is the usual developmental pattern of relationships between boys and girls?

8. What are the common mistakes that parents make in regard to their adolescent children's sexuality?

9. In what ways can adolescent suicide be considered common and in what ways uncommon?

10. How do personal and cultural factors increase the risk of adolescent suicide?

11. How are adolescence-limited and life-course-persistent offenders similar, and how are they different?

■ APPLICATIONS

1. Is it more difficult to achieve vocational identity today than it used to be? Interview two adults over age 40 and two under age 30. What career goal did each of them have as an adolescent? Did their aspirations change over the years? If so, how and why?

2. Locate a story in your local newspaper about a teenager who committed suicide. Does the article indicate that there were warning signs that were ignored? Does the news report glorify the adolescent's life and death in a way that might encourage cluster suicides?

3. The data suggest that most adolescents have broken the law but that few have been arrested or incarcerated. Is this true for people you know? Ask 10 of your fellow students whether they broke the law when they were under 18. Assure them of confidentiality and ask specific questions (e.g., "Did you ever drink alcohol, buy cigarettes, take something that was not yours?"). What hypothesis about teenage lawbreaking in your cohort can you suggest?

4. As a follow-up to question 3, ask your fellow students about the circumstances. Was lawbreaking done with peers or alone? What response came from police, parents, judges, and peers? Discuss how peers and families affect adolescent behavior.

PART V

Adolescence

BIOSOCIAL

Physical Growth Sometime between the ages of 8 and 14, puberty begins, with increases in various hormones that trigger a host of changes. Within a year of the hormonal increases, the first perceptible physical changes appear—enlargement of the girl's breasts and the boy's testes. About a year later, a growth spurt begins, when boys and girls gain in height, weight, and musculature. Brain growth, like body growth, is uneven, with the limbic system growing faster than the prefrontal cortex.

Sexual Maturation Toward the end of puberty, primary sexual development includes menarche in girls and ejaculation in boys. Secondary sexual characteristics also develop. Males become taller than females and develop deeper voices and characteristic patterns of facial and body hair. Females become wider at the hips; breast development continues for several years. Some teenagers become sexually active too early, risking unwanted pregnancy and sexually transmitted infections. Others use drugs at an age or dose that is harmful to healthy growth, particularly the gateway drugs—tobacco, alcohol, and marijuana. Poor nutrition, in the form of both overeating and undereating, is common.

COGNITIVE

Adolescent Thinking Adolescent thought can deal with the possible as well as the actual, thanks to a newly emerging ability to think hypothetically, to reason deductively, and to explain theoretically. At the same time, adolescent egocentrism, along with feelings of uniqueness and invincibility, can make adolescents extraordinarily self-absorbed, thinking intuitively rather than rationally.

Both logic and intuition advance during adolescence, although few teenagers combine them successfully.

Education Young adolescents tend to be egocentric and to need social encouragement. For this reason, many middle schools are poorly designed for adolescent learning. For many high school students, cognitive growth is slowed down by high-stakes tests, low motivation, and fear of violence at school.

PSYCHOSOCIAL

Identity One goal of adolescence is self-understanding and identity achievement. Achieving identity can be affected by personal factors—including relationships with family and peers. Gender and ethnic identity are especially complex.

Parents and Peers The peer group becomes increasingly important in fostering independence and interaction, particularly with members of the other sex. Parents and young adolescents are often at odds over issues centering on the child's increased assertiveness or lack of self-discipline.

Sadness and Anger Depression and suicidal ideation are common in adolescence, especially among girls, but boys are more likely to actually complete a suicide. Although some emotional problems are common, both parasuicide and law breaking need to be taken seriously. Many adolescents are sad or angry; only a minority are suicidal or likely to become life-course-persistent offenders.

Appendices A–C

Appendix A

Supplemental Charts, Graphs, and Tables

Often, examining specific data is useful, even fascinating, to developmental researchers. The particular numbers reveal trends and nuances not apparent from a more general view. For instance, many people mistakenly believe that the incidence of Down syndrome babies rises sharply for mothers over 35, or that even the tiniest newborns usually survive. Each chart, graph, or table in this appendix probably contains information not generally known.

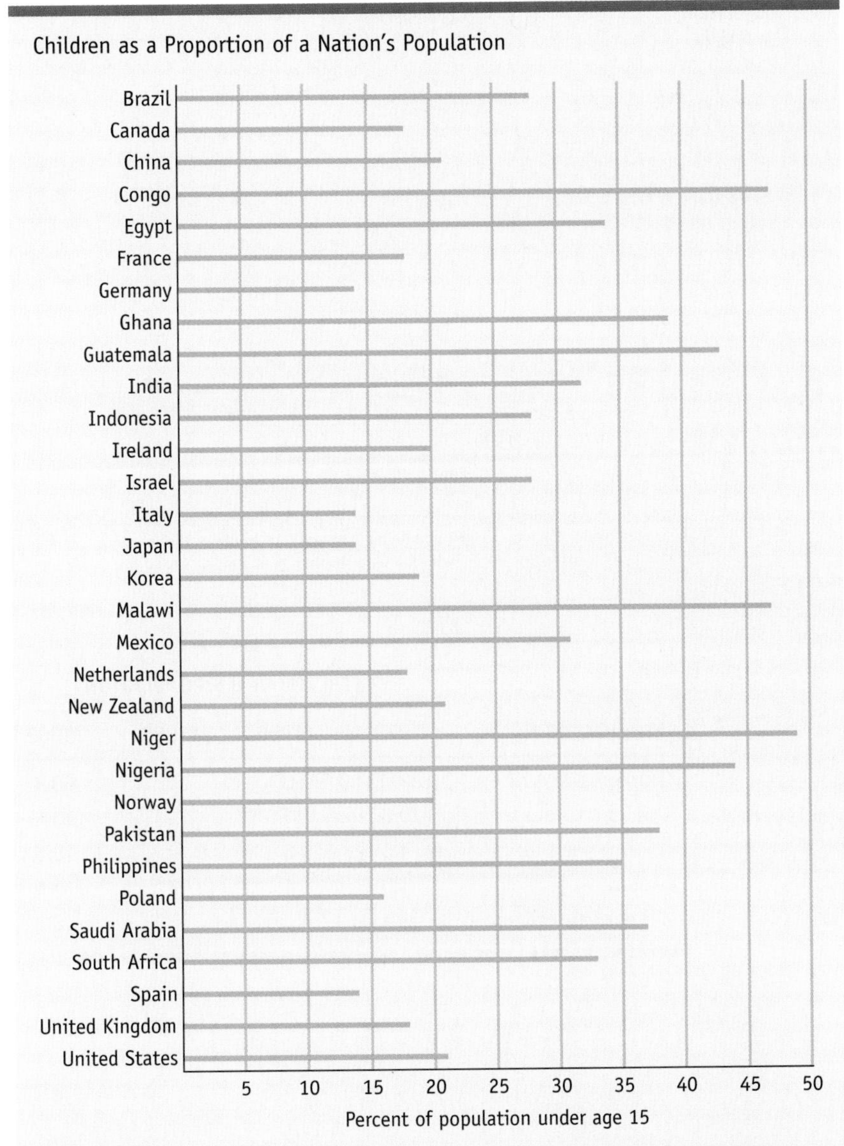

Source: United Nations Secretariat, Statistics Division and Population Division, unstats.un.org, updated April 22, 2005.

More Children, Worse Schools? (Chapter 1)

Nations that have high birth rates also have high death rates, short life spans, and more illiteracy. A systems approach suggests that these variables are connected: For example, the Montessori and Reggio Emilia early-childhood education programs, said to be the best in the world, originated in Italy, and Italy is one of the countries in this graph with the lowest proportion of children under 15.

Ethnic Composition of the U.S. Population (Chapter 2)

Thinking about the ethnic makeup of the U.S. population can be an interesting exercise in social comparison. If you look only at the table, you will conclude that not much has changed over the past 30 years: Whites are still the majority, Native Americans are still a tiny minority, and African Americans are still about 11 percent of the population. However, if you look at the chart, you can see why every group feels that much has changed. Because the proportions of Hispanic Americans and Asian Americans have increased dramatically, European Americans see the current nonwhite population at almost one-third of the total, and African Americans see that Hispanics now outnumber them. There are also interesting regional differences within the United States; for example, Los Angeles County has the largest number of Native Americans (156,000) and the largest number of Asians (1.3 million).

?Observational Quiz (see answer, page A-4): Which ethnic group is growing most rapidly?

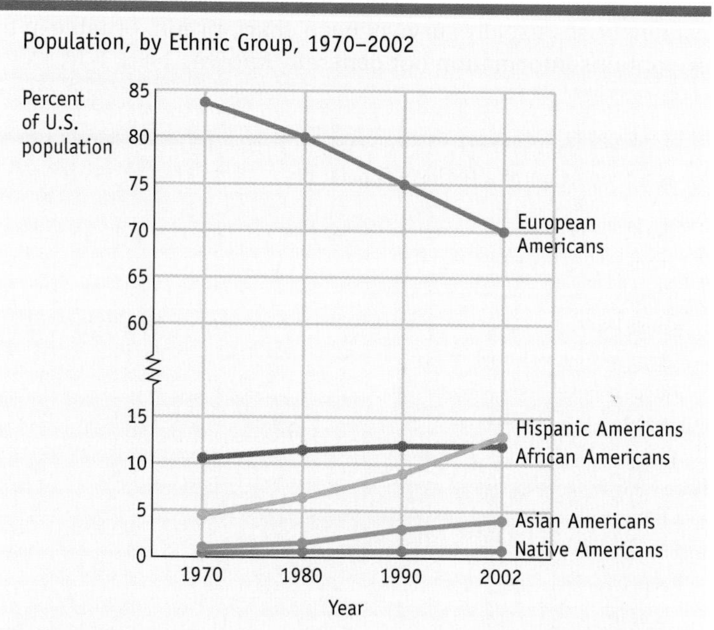

Source: U.S. Bureau of the Census, *Current Population Reports*, March–June 2003.

	PERCENT OF U.S. POPULATION			
ETHNIC ORIGIN	**1970**	**1980**	**1990**	**2002**
European (White)	83.7	80	75	68.4
African (Black)	10.6	11.5	12	13
Latino (Hispanic)	4.5	6.4	9	13.3
Asian	1.0	1.5	3	4.4
Native American	.4	.6	.7	0.9

The Genetics of Blood Types (Chapter 3)

Blood types A and B are dominant traits, and type O is recessive. The percentages given in the first column of this chart represent the odds that a child born to the parents with the various combinations of genotypes will have the genotype given in the second column.

Genotypes of Parents*	Genotype of Offspring	Phenotype	Can Donate Blood to (Phenotype)	Can Receive Blood from (Phenotype)
AA + AA (100%) AA + AB (50%) AA + AO (50%) AB + AB (25%) AB + AO (25%) AO + AO (25%)	AA (inherits one A from each parent)	A	A or AB	A or O
AA + OO (100%) AB + OO (50%) AO + AO (50%) AO + OO (50%) AB + AO (25%) AB + BO (25%)	AO	A	A or AB	A or O
BB + BB (100%) AB + BB (50%) BB + BO (50%) AB + AB (25%) AB + BO (25%) BO + BO (25%)	BB	B	B or AB	B or O
BB + OO (100%) AB + OO (50%) BO + BO (50%) BO + OO (50%) AB + AO (25%) AB + BO (25%)	BO	B	B or AB	B or O
AA + BB (100%) AA + AB (50%) AA + BO (50%) AB + AB (50%) AB + BB (50%) AO + BB (50%) AB + BO (25%) AO + BO (25%)	AB	AB	AB only	A, B, AB, O ("universal recipient")
OO + OO (100%) AO + OO (50%) BO + OO (50%) AO + AO (25%) AO + BO (25%) BO + BO (25%)	OO	O	A, B, AB, O ("universal donor")	O only

*Blood type is not a sex-linked trait, so any of these pairs can be either mother-plus-father or father-plus-mother.
Source: Adapted from Hartl & Jones, 1999.

Odds of Down Syndrome by Maternal Age and Gestational Age (Chapter 4)

The odds of any given fetus, at the end of the first trimester, having three chromosomes at the 21st site (trisomy 21) and thus having Down syndrome is shown in the 10-weeks column. Every year of maternal age increases the incidence of trisomy 21. The number of Down syndrome infants born alive is only half the number who survived the first trimester. Although obviously the least risk is at age 20 (younger is even better), there is no year when the odds suddenly increase (age 35 is an arbitrary cut-off). Even at age 44, less than 4 percent of all newborns have Down syndrome. Other chromosomal abnormalities in fetuses also increase with mother's age, but the rate of spontaneous abortion is much higher, so births of babies with chromosomal defects is not the norm, even for women over age 45.

AGE (YRS)	GESTATION (WEEKS) 10	35	LIVE BIRTHS
20	1/804	1/1,464	1/1,527
21	1/793	1/1,445	1/1,507
22	1/780	1/1,421	1/1,482
23	1/762	1/1,389	1/1,448
24	1/740	1/1,348	1/1,406
25	1/712	1/1,297	1/1,352
26	1/677	1/1,233	1/1,286
27	1/635	1/1,157	1/1,206
28	1/586	1/1,068	1/1,113
29	1/531	1/967	1/1,008
30	1/471	1/858	1/895
31	1/409	1/745	1/776
32	1/347	1/632	1/659
33	1/288	1/525	1/547
34	1/235	1/427	1/446
35	1/187	1/342	1/356
36	1/148	1/269	1/280
37	1/115	1/209	1/218
38	1/88	1/160	1/167
39	1/67	1/122	1/128
40	1/51	1/93	1/97
41	1/38	1/70	1/73
42	1/29	1/52	1/55
43	1/21	1/39	1/41
44	1/16	1/29	1/30

Source: Snijders & Nicolaides, 1996.

Saving Young Lives: Childhood and Adolescent Immunizations (Chapter 5)

Recommended Childhood and Adolescent Immunization Schedule, United States, 2005

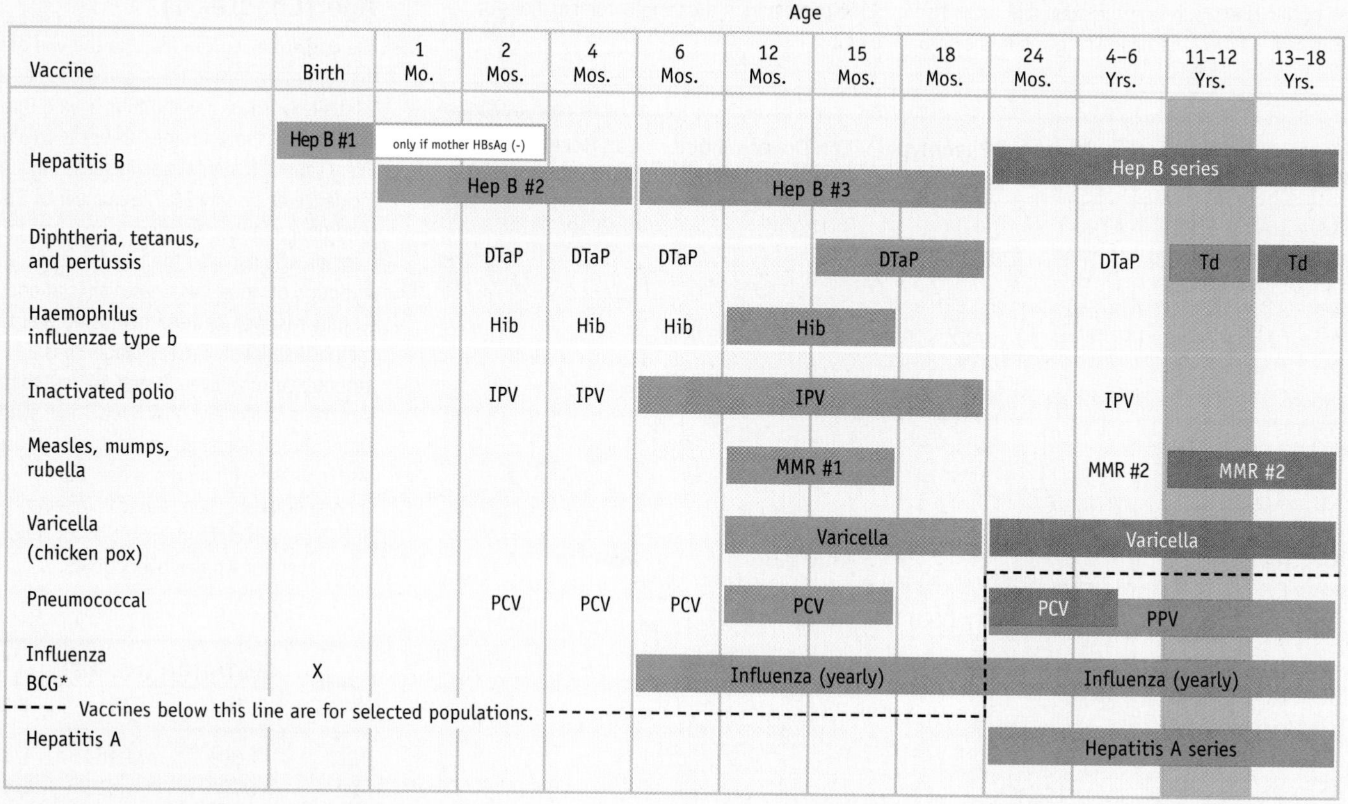

Vaccine	Birth	1 Mo.	2 Mos.	4 Mos.	6 Mos.	12 Mos.	15 Mos.	18 Mos.	24 Mos.	4–6 Yrs.	11–12 Yrs.	13–18 Yrs.
Hepatitis B	Hep B #1	only if mother HBsAg (-)							Hep B series			
		Hep B #2			Hep B #3							
Diphtheria, tetanus, and pertussis			DTaP	DTaP	DTaP		DTaP			DTaP	Td	Td
Haemophilus influenzae type b			Hib	Hib	Hib	Hib						
Inactivated polio			IPV	IPV	IPV					IPV		
Measles, mumps, rubella						MMR #1				MMR #2	MMR #2	
Varicella (chicken pox)						Varicella			Varicella			
Pneumococcal			PCV	PCV	PCV	PCV			PCV	PPV		
Influenza					Influenza (yearly)				Influenza (yearly)			
BCG*	X											
---- Vaccines below this line are for selected populations.												
Hepatitis A									Hepatitis A series			

■ Range of recommended ages for vaccination
■ Catch-up immunization—age groups that warrant special effort to administer those vaccines not given previously
■ Preadolescent assessment

Note: For many diseases, repeated doses are recommended, as shown.
*BCG vaccine is highly recommended in most nations, but is not required in the United States because the prevalence of tuberculosis is low.

Source: CDC Web site (http://cdc.gov/nip/recs/child-schedule), accessed August 12, 2005.

First Sounds and First Words: Similarities Among Many Languages (Chapter 6)

LANGUAGE	BABY'S WORD FOR: Mother	Father
English	mama, mommy	dada, daddy
Spanish	mama	papa
French	maman, mama	papa
Italian	mamma	babbo, papa
Latvian	mama	tēte
Syrian Arabic	mama	baba
Bantu	ba-mama	taata
Swahili	mama	baba
Sanskrit	nana	tata
Hebrew	ema	abba
Korean	oma	apa

! ***Answer to Observational Quiz*** (from page A-2): Asian Americans, whose share of the U.S. population has quadrupled in the past 30 years.

Which Mothers Breast-feed? (Chapter 7)

Differentiating excellent from destructive mothering is not easy, once the child's basic needs for food and protection are met. However, as the Toni and Jacob examples in Chapter 7 make clear, psychosocial development depends on responsive parent–infant relationships. Breast-feeding is one sign of intimacy between mother and infant.

Regions of the world differ dramatically in rates of breast-feeding, with the highest worldwide in Southeast Asia, where half of all 2-year-olds are still breast-fed. In the United States, factors that affect the likelihood of breast-feeding are ethnicity (Latinas are more likely, and African Americans less likely, to breast-feed than European Americans) and maternal age (a positive correlation between age and breast-feeding). The most marked influence of all is the mother's education.

Breast-feeding Rates by Socio-demographic Factors

Socio-demographic factors	Ever Breast-feeding	Breast-feeding at 6 Months	Breast-feeding at 12 Months	Exclusive Breast-feeding* at 3 Months	Exclusive Breast-feeding* at 6 Months
U.S. national	70.9%	36.2%	17.2%	41.1%	14.2%
Sex of baby					
Male	70.7	35.6	16.3	40.3	13.7
Female	71.0	36.8	18.2	41.9	14.8
Birth order					
First born	69.9	37.5	18.5	42.6	14.6
Not first born	72.5	34.1	15.2	38.6	13.6
Race/ethnicity					
Native American	68.6	32.0	14.9	43.7	13.1
Asian/ Pacific Islander	79.3	44.1	22.5	47.8	16.7
African American	54.9	23.9	22.0	29.2	9.8
White	73.8	38.6	18.7	43.2	15.2
Hispanic or Latino	77.8	38.2	20.0	48.6	13.4
Mother's age					
Less than 19	54.5	14.9	6.9	25.1	6.1
20–30	67.6	30.6	14.2	37.5	12.5
More than 30	74.9	42.6	20.7	45.4	16.4
Mother's education					
Less than high school	63.4	28.6	15.2	36.8	10.5
High school	63.5	28.3	13.0	34.3	11.8
Some college	74.4	37.5	17.0	43.0	15.1
College graduate	84.0	51.9	24.8	52.1	19.9
Mother's marital status					
Married	76.8	42.2	20.6	46.2	16.5
Unmarried†	57.8	22.8	9.8	29.9	9.2
Residence					
Central city	69.8	35.4	17.2	40.6	14.0
Urban	74.6	39.6	18.7	44.1	14.9
Suburban and rural	63.8	29.2	13.6	34.6	13.0

*Exclusive breastfeeding is defined as only breast milk and water—no solids or other liquids.
†Unmarried includes never married, widowed, separated, divorced, and deceased.
Source: Adapted from CDC's National Immunization Survey, Table 1; http://www.cdc.gov/breastfeeding/data/NIS_data/socio-demographic.htm, accessed August 17, 2005.

Height Gains from Birth to Age 18 (Chapter 8)

The range of height (on this page) and weight (see page A-7) of children in the United States. The columns labeled "50th" (the fiftieth percentile) show the average; the columns labeled "90th" (the ninetieth percentile) show the size of children taller and heavier than 90 percent of their contemporaries; and the columns labeled "10th" (the tenth percentile) show the size of children who are taller than only 10 percent of their peers. Note that girls are slightly shorter, on average, than boys.

Height by Age Percentiles: 2 to 6 Years

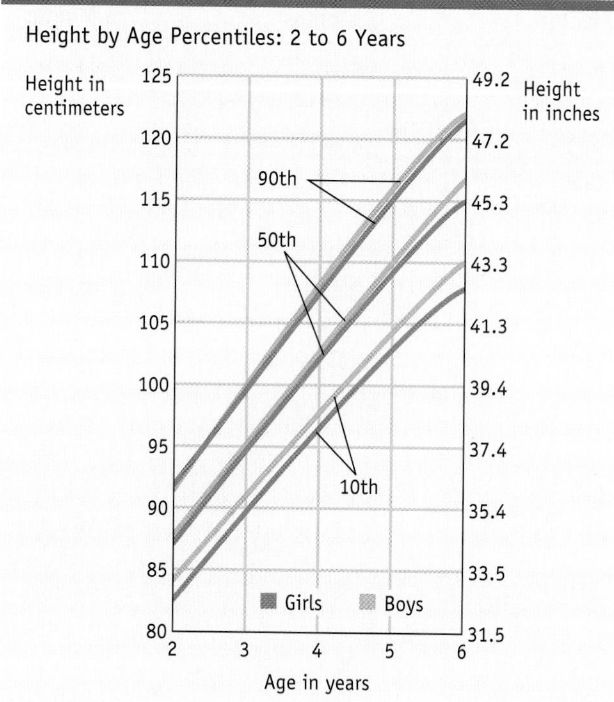

Same Data, Different Form

The columns of numbers in the table at the right provide detailed and precise information about height ranges for every year of childhood. The illustration above shows the same information in graphic form for ages 2–6. The same is done for weight ranges on page A-7. Ages 2–6 are singled out because that is the period during which a child's eating habits are set. Which form of data presentation do you think is easier to understand?

Length in Centimeters (and Inches)

	BOYS: PERCENTILES			GIRLS: PERCENTILES		
AGE	**10th**	**50th**	**90th**	**10th**	**50th**	**90th**
Birth	47.5 (18¾)	50.5 (20)	53.5 (21)	46.5 (18¼)	49.9 (19¾)	52.0 (20½)
1 month	51.3 (20¼)	54.6 (21½)	57.7 (22¾)	50.2 (19¾)	53.5 (21)	56.1 (22)
3 months	57.7 (22¾)	61.1 (24)	64.5 (25½)	56.2 (22¼)	59.5 (23½)	62.7 (24¾)
6 months	64.4 (25¼)	67.8 (26¾)	71.3 (28)	62.6 (24¾)	65.9 (26)	69.4 (27¼)
9 months	69.1 (27¼)	72.3 (28½)	75.9 (30)	67.0 (26½)	70.4 (27¾)	74.0 (29¼)
12 months	72.8 (28¾)	76.1 (30)	79.8 (31½)	70.8 (27¾)	74.3 (29¼)	78.0 (30¾)
18 months	78.7 (31)	82.4 (32½)	86.6 (34)	77.2 (30½)	80.9 (31¾)	85.0 (33½)
24 months	83.5 (32¾)	87.6 (34½)	92.2 (36¼)	82.5 (32½)	86.5 (34)	90.8 (35¾)
3 years	90.3 (35½)	94.9 (37¼)	100.1 (39½)	89.3 (35¼)	94.1 (37)	99.0 (39)
4 years	97.3 (38¼)	102.9 (40½)	108.2 (42½)	96.4 (38)	101.6 (40)	106.6 (42)
5 years	103.7 (40¾)	109.9 (43¼)	115.4 (45½)	102.7 (40½)	108.4 (42¾)	113.8 (44¾)
6 years	109.6 (43¼)	116.1 (45¾)	121.9 (48)	108.4 (42¾)	114.6 (45)	120.8 (47½)
7 years	115.0 (45¼)	121.7 (48)	127.9 (50¼)	113.6 (44¾)	120.6 (47½)	127.6 (50¼)
8 years	120.2 (47¼)	127.0 (50)	133.6 (52½)	118.7 (46¾)	126.4 (49¾)	134.2 (52¾)
9 years	125.2 (49¼)	132.2 (52)	139.4 (55)	123.9 (48¾)	132.2 (52)	140.7 (55½)
10 years	130.1 (51¼)	137.5 (54¼)	145.5 (57¼)	129.5 (51)	138.3 (54½)	147.2 (58)
11 years	135.1 (53¼)	143.33 (56½)	152.1 (60)	135.6 (53½)	144.8 (57)	153.7 (60½)
12 years	140.3 (55¼)	149.7 (59)	159.4 (62¾)	142.3 (56)	151.5 (59¾)	160.0 (63)
13 years	145.8 (57½)	156.5 (61½)	167.0 (65¾)	148.0 (58¼)	157.1 (61¾)	165.3 (65)
14 years	151.8 (59¾)	63.1 (64¼)	173.8 (68½)	151.5 (59¾)	160.4 (63¼)	168.7 (66½)
15 years	158.2 (62¼)	169.0 (66½)	178.9 (70½)	153.2 (60¼)	161.8 (63¾)	170.5 (67¼)
16 years	163.9 (64½)	173.5 (68¼)	182.4 (71¾)	154.1 (60¾)	162.4 (64)	171.1 (67¼)
17 years	167.7 (66)	176.2 (69¼)	184.4 (72½)	155.1 (61)	163.1 (64¼)	171.2 (67½)
18 years	168.7 (66½)	176.8 (69½)	185.3 (73)	156.0 (61½)	163.7 (64½)	171.0 (67¼)

Source: These data are those of the National Center for Health Statistics (NCHS), Health Resources Administration, DHHS. They were based on studies of The Fels Research Institute, Yellow Springs, Ohio. These data were first made available with the help of William M. Moore, M.D., of Ross Laboratories, who supplied the conversion from metric measurements to approximate inches and pounds. This help is gratefully acknowledged.

Weight Gains from Birth to Age 18 (Chapter 8)

These height and weight charts present rough guidelines; a child might differ from these norms and be quite healthy and normal. However, if a particular child shows a discrepancy between height and weight (for instance, at the 90th percentile in height but only the 20th percentile in weight) or is much larger or smaller than most children the same age, a pediatrician should see if disease, malnutrition, or genetic abnormality is part of the reason.

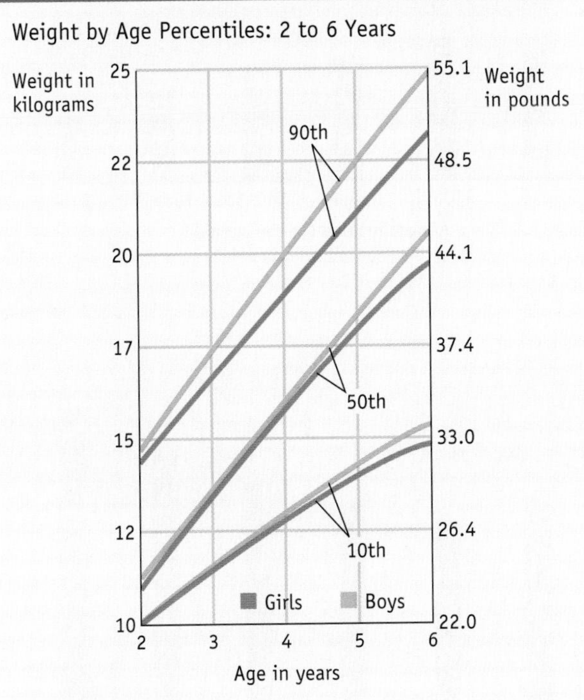

Comparisons

Notice that the height trajectories in the graph on page A-6 are much closer together than the weight trajectories shown in the graph above. By age 18, the height range amounts to only about 6 inches, but there is a difference of about 65 pounds between the 10th and the 90th percentiles.

? ***Critical Thinking Question*** (see answer, page A-8): How can this discrepancy between height and weight ranges be explained?

Weight in Kilograms (and Pounds)

	BOYS: PERCENTILES			GIRLS: PERCENTILES		
AGE	**10th**	**50th**	**90th**	**10th**	**50th**	**90th**
Birth	2.78 (6¼)	3.27 (7¼)	3.82 (8½)	2.58 (5¾)	3.23 (7)	3.64 (8)
1 month	3.43 (7½)	4.29 (9½)	5.14 (11¼)	3.22 (7)	3.98 (8¾)	4.65 (10¼)
3 months	4.78 (10½)	5.98 (13¼)	7.14 (15¾)	4.47 (9¾)	5.40 (12)	6.39 (14)
6 months	6.61 (14½)	7.85 (17¼)	9.10 (20)	6.12 (13½)	7.21 (16)	8.38 (18½)
9 months	7.95 (17½)	9.18 (20¼)	10.49 (23¼)	7.34 (16¼)	8.56 (18¾)	9.83 (21¾)
12 months	8.84 (19½)	10.15 (22½)	11.54 (25½)	8.19 (18)	9.53 (21)	10.87 (24)
18 months	9.92 (21¾)	11.47 (25¼)	13.05 (28¾)	9.30 (20½)	10.82 (23¾)	12.30 (27)
24 months	10.85 (24)	12.59 (27¾)	14.29 (31½)	10.26 (22½)	11.90 (26¼)	13.57 (30)
3 years	12.58 (27¾)	14.62 (32¼)	16.95 (37¼)	12.26 (27)	14.10 (31)	16.54 (36½)
4 years	14.24 (31½)	16.69 (36¾)	19.32 (42½)	13.84 (30½)	15.96 (35¼)	18.93 (41¾)
5 years	15.96 (35¼)	18.67 (41¼)	21.70 (47¾)	15.26 (33¾)	17.66 (39)	21.23 (46¾)
6 years	17.72 (39)	20.69 (45½)	24.31 (53½)	16.72 (36¾)	19.52 (43)	23.89 (52¾)
7 years	19.53 (43)	22.85 (50¼)	27.36 (60¼)	18.39 (40½)	21.84 (48¼)	27.39 (60½)
8 years	21.39 (47¼)	25.30 (55¾)	31.06 (68½)	20.45 (45)	24.84 (54¾)	32.04 (70¾)
9 years	23.33 (51½)	28.13 (62)	35.57 (78½)	22.92 (50½)	28.46 (62¾)	37.60 (83)
10 years	25.52 (56¼)	31.44 (69¼)	40.80 (90)	25.76 (56¾)	32.55 (71¾)	43.70 (96¼)
11 years	28.17 (62)	35.30 (77¾)	46.57 (102¾)	28.97 (63¾)	36.95 (81½)	49.96 (110¼)
12 years	31.46 (69¼)	39.78 (87¾)	52.73 (116¼)	32.53 (71¼)	41.53 (91½)	55.99 (123½)
13 years	35.60 (78½)	44.95 (99)	59.12 (130¼)	36.35 (80¼)	46.10 (101¾)	61.45 (135½)
14 years	40.64 (89½)	50.77 (112)	65.57 (144½)	40.11 (88½)	50.28 (110¾)	66.04 (145½)
15 years	46.06 (101½)	56.71 (125)	71.91 (158½)	43.38 (95¾)	53.68 (118¼)	69.64 (153¼)
16 years	51.16 (112¾)	62.10 (137)	77.97 (172)	45.78 (101)	55.89 (123¼)	71.68 (158)
17 years	55.28 (121¾)	66.31 (146¼)	83.58 (184¼)	47.04 (103¾)	56.69 (125)	72.38 (159½)
18 years	57.89 (127½)	68.88 (151¾)	88.41 (195)	47.47 (104¾)	56.62 (124¾)	72.25 (159¼)

Source: Data are those of the National Center for Health Statistics, Health Resources Administration, DHHS, collected in its Health Examination Surveys.

Day Care and Family Income (Chapter 9)

Note that, in both years, the wealthier families were less likely to have children exclusively in parental care and more likely to have children in center-based care.

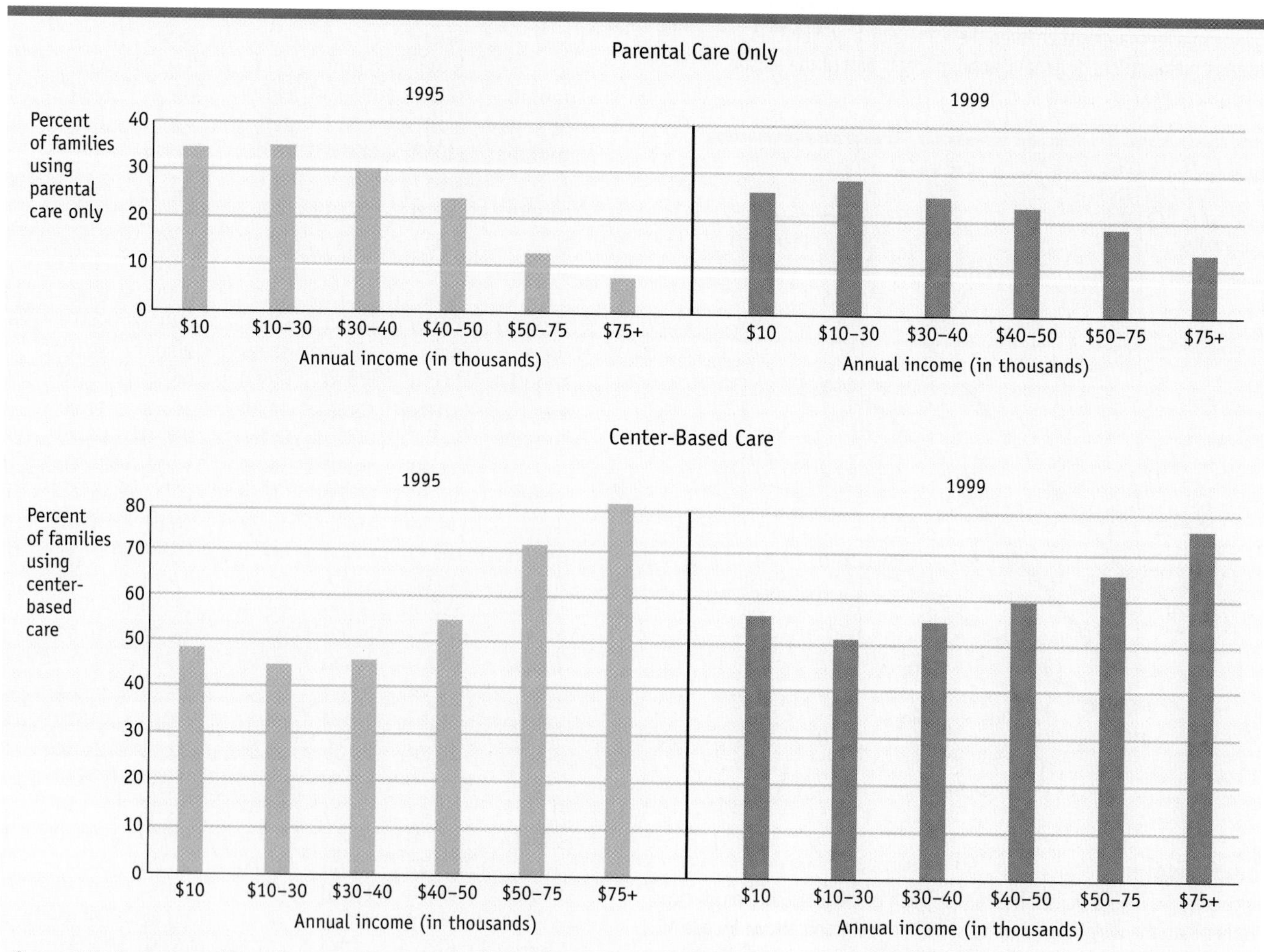

Source: U.S. Department of Education, National Center for Education Statistics Web site, nces.ed.gov, accessed August 15, 2005.

!Answer to Critical Thinking Question (from page A-7): Nutrition is generally adequate in the United States, and that is why height differences are small. But as a result of the strong influence that family and culture have on eating habits, almost half of all North Americans are overweight or obese.

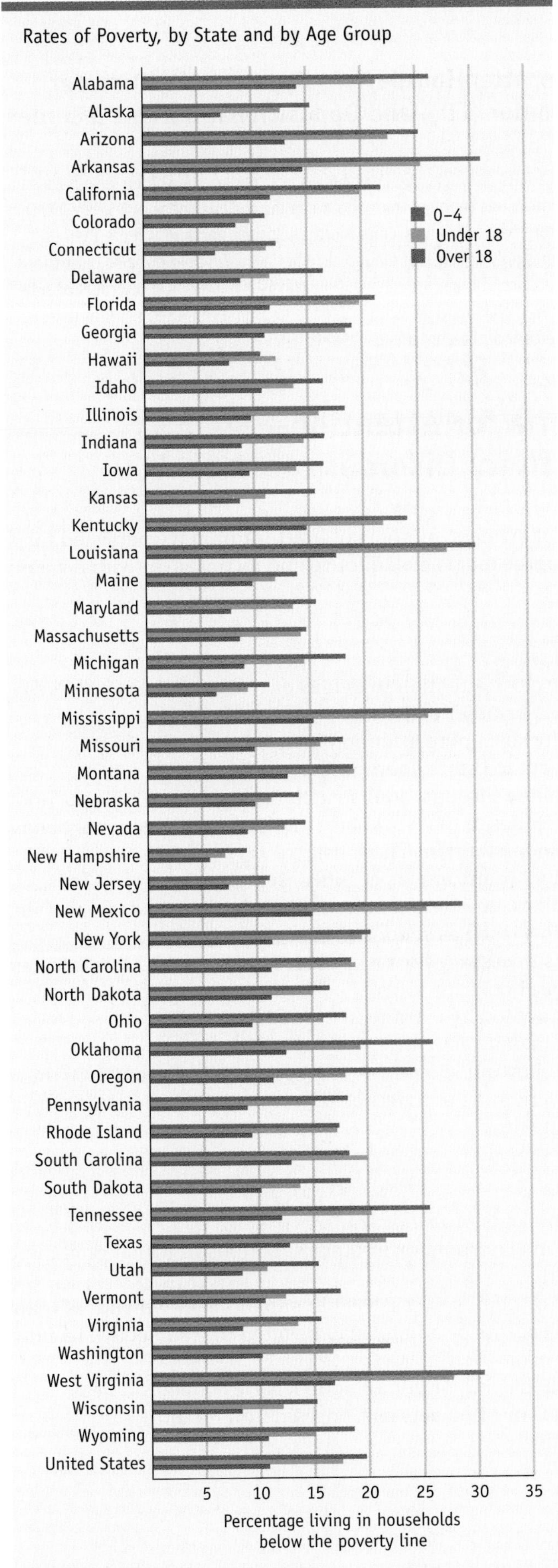

Source: U.S. Bureau of the Census, 2000.

Babies Are the Poorest Americans (Chapter 10)

Is poverty worse for adults than for children? Most developmentalists would say the opposite, and would wonder why every state has more poor children—especially young children—than poor adults.

?*Observational Quiz* (see answer, page A-10): Which state has the highest poverty rate for adults? For children under 18? For children from birth to age 4?

! *Answer to Observational Quiz* (from page A-9): 1. Louisiana, 2. West Virginia, 3. Arkansas. To think about: At which age is poverty the worst and why?

DSM-IV-TR Criteria for Attention-Deficit/Hyperactivity Disorder (ADHD), Conduct Disorder (CD), and Oppositional Defiant Disorder (ODD) (Chapter 11)

The specific symptoms for these various disorders overlap. Many other childhood disorders also have some of the same symptoms. Differentiating one problem from another is the main purpose of DSM-IV-TR. That is no easy task, which is one reason the book is now in its fourth major revision and is more than 900 pages long. Those pages include not only the type of diagnostic criteria shown here but also discussions of prevalence, age and gender statistics, cultural aspects, and prognosis for about 400 disorders or subtypes, 40 of which appear primarily in childhood. Thus, the diagnostic criteria reprinted here for three disorders represent less than 1 percent of the contents of DSM-IV-TR.

Diagnostic Criteria for Attention-Deficit/Hyperactivity Disorder

A. Either (1) or (2):

(1) Six (or more) of the following symptoms of **inattention** have persisted for at least 6 months to a degree that is maladaptive and inconsistent with developmental level:

Inattention

(a) often fails to give close attention to details or makes careless mistakes in schoolwork, work, or other activities
(b) often has difficulty sustaining attention in tasks or play activities
(c) often does not seem to listen when spoken to directly
(d) often does not follow through on instructions and fails to finish schoolwork, chores, or duties in the workplace (not due to oppositional behavior or failure to understand instructions)
(e) often has difficulty organizing tasks and activities
(f) often avoids, dislikes, or is reluctant to engage in tasks that require sustained mental effort (such as schoolwork or homework)
(g) often loses things necessary for tasks or activities (e.g., toys, school assignments, pencils, books, or tools)
(h) is often easily distracted by extraneous stimuli
(i) is often forgetful in daily activities

(2) Six (or more) of the following symptoms of **hyperactivity-impulsivity** have persisted for at least 6 months to a degree that is maladaptive and inconsistent with developmental level:

Hyperactivity

(a) often fidgets with hands or feet or squirms in seat
(b) often leaves seat in classroom or in other situations in which remaining seated is expected
(c) often runs about or climbs excessively in situations in which it is inappropriate (in adolescents or adults, may be limited to subjective feelings of restlessness)
(d) often has difficulty playing or engaging in leisure activities quietly
(e) is often "on the go" or often acts as if "driven by a motor"
(f) often talks excessively

Impulsivity

(g) often blurts out answers before questions have been completed
(h) often has difficulty awaiting turn

(i) often interrupts or intrudes on others (e.g., butts into conversations or games)

B. Some hyperactive-impulsive or inattentive symptoms that caused impairment were present before age 7 years.

C. Some impairment from the symptoms is present in two or more settings (e.g., at school [or work] and at home).

D. There must be clear evidence of clinically significant impairment in social, academic, or occupational functioning.

Diagnostic Criteria for Conduct Disorder

A. A repetitive and persistent pattern of behavior in which the basic rights of others or major age-appropriate societal norms or rules are violated, as manifested by the presence of three (or more) of the following criteria in the past 12 months, with at least one criterion present in the past 6 months:

Aggression to people and animals

(1) often bullies, threatens, or intimidates others
(2) often initiates physical fights
(3) has used a weapon that can cause serious physical harm to others (e.g., a bat, brick, broken bottle, knife, gun)
(4) has been physically cruel to people
(5) has been physically cruel to animals
(6) has stolen while confronting a victim (e.g., mugging, purse snatching, extortion, armed robbery)
(7) has forced someone into sexual activity

Destruction of property

(8) has deliberately engaged in fire setting with the intention of causing serious damage
(9) has deliberately destroyed others' property (other than by fire setting)

Deceitfulness or theft

(10) has broken into someone else's house, building, or car
(11) often lies to obtain goods or favors or to avoid obligations (i.e., "cons" others)
(12) has stolen items of nontrivial value without confronting a victim (e.g., shoplifting, but without breaking and entering; forgery)

Serious violations of rules

(13) often stays out at night despite parental prohibitions, beginning before age 13 years
(14) has run away from home overnight at least twice while living in parental or parental surrogate home (or once without returning for a lengthy period)
(15) is often truant from school, beginning before age 13 years

B. The disturbance in behavior causes clinically significant impairment in social, academic, or occupational functioning.

Diagnostic Criteria for Oppositional Defiant Disorder

A. A pattern of negativistic, hostile, and defiant behavior lasting at least 6 months, during which four (or more) of the following are present:
(1) often loses temper
(2) often argues with adults
(3) often actively defies or refuses to comply with adults' requests or rules
(4) often deliberately annoys people
(5) often blames others for his or her mistakes or misbehavior
(6) is often touchy or easily annoyed by others
(7) is often angry and resentful
(8) is often spiteful or vindictive
Note: Consider a criterion met only if the behavior occurs more frequently than is typically observed in individuals of comparable age and developmental level.

B. The disturbance in behavior causes clinically significant impairment in social, academic, or occupational functioning.

Source: American Psychiatric Association, 2004.

Changes in Ranking of 16 Nations on Science and Math Knowledge Between Fourth and Eighth Grades (Chapter 12)

Only the 16 highest-scoring nations are included in these rankings. Many other countries, such as Chile and Morocco, rank much lower. Still others, including all the nations of Latin America and Africa, do not administer the tests on which these rankings are based. Identical rankings indicate ties between nations on overall scores. International comparisons are always difficult and often unfair, but two general conclusions have been confirmed: Children in East Asian countries tend to be high achievers in math and science, and children in the United States lose ground in science and just hold their own in math between the fourth and eighth grades.

Science Knowledge

Nation	Rank in Fourth Grade	Rank in Eighth Grade	Change in Rank
Singapore	1	1	0
Chinese Taipei	2	2	0
Japan	3	6	–3
Hong Kong	4	4	0
England	5	*	—
United States	6	9	–3
Latvia	7	18	–11
Hungary	8	7	+1
Russian Federation	9	17	–8
Netherlands	10	8	+2
Australia	11	10	+1
New Zealand	12	13	–1
Belgium	13	16	–3
Italy	14	22	–8
Lithuania	15	14	+1
Scotland	16	19	–3

Math Knowledge

Nation	Rank in Fourth Grade	Rank in Eighth Grade	Change in Rank
Singapore	1	1	0
Hong Kong	2	3	–1
Japan	3	5	–2
Chinese Taipei	4	4	0
Belgium	5	6	–1
Netherlands	6	7	–1
Latvia	7	11†	–4
Lithuania	8	13	–5
Russian Federation	9	11†	–2
England	10	*	—
Hungary	11	9	–2
United States	12	12	0
Cyprus	13	26	–13
Moldova	14	25	–11
Italy	15	19	–4
Australia	16	11	+5

*Did not participate.
†Average scale scores were tied.
Source: Third International Mathematics and Science Study (TIMSS), 2003.

Changes in the Average Weekly Amount of Time Spent by 6- to 11-Year-Olds in Various Activities (Chapter 12)

Data can be presented graphically in many ways. The data given here were collected in the same way in 1981 and in 1997, so the changes are real (although the age cutoff in 1997 was 12, not 11). What do you think would be the best way to show this information? What is encouraging and what is problematic in the changes that you see? One possibility is shown below the table: The changes are presented as percentages in a bar graph.

	Average Amount of Time Spent in Activity, per Week		
Activity	**In 1981**	**In 1997**	**Change in Time Spent**
School	25 hrs, 17 min.	33 hrs, 52 min.	+8 hrs, 35 min.
Organized sports	3 hrs, 5 min.	4 hrs, 56 min.	+1 hr, 51 min.
Studying	1 hr, 46 min.	2 hrs, 50 min.	+1 hr, 4 min.
Reading	57 min.	1 hr, 15 min.	+18 min.
Being outdoors	1 hr, 17 min.	39 min.	–38 min.
Playing	12 hrs, 52 min.	10 hrs, 5 min.	–2 hours, 47 min.
Watching TV	15 hrs, 34 min.	13 hrs, 7 min.	–2 hours, 27 min.

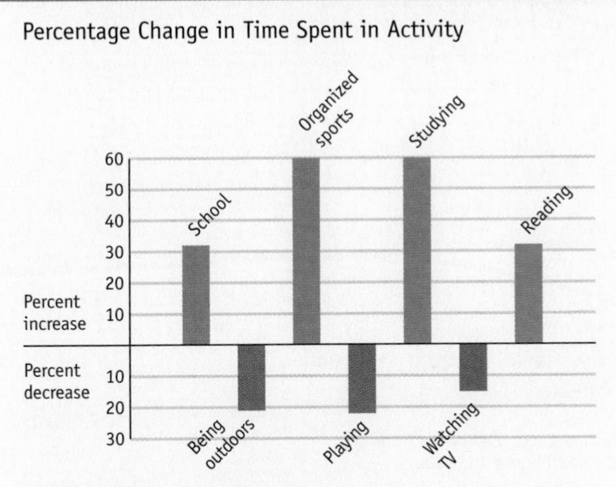

Source: University of Michigan Institute for Social Research, Panel Study of Income Dynamics, Child Development Supplement, as reported in Hofferth, 1999.

Who Is Raising the Children? (Chapter 13)

Most children still live in households with a male/female couple, who may be the children's married or unmarried biological parents, grandparents, stepparents, foster parents, or adoptive parents. However, the proportion of households headed by single parents has risen—by 500 percent for single fathers and by almost 200 percent for single mothers. (In 2004, 52 percent of U.S. households had *no* children under age 18.)

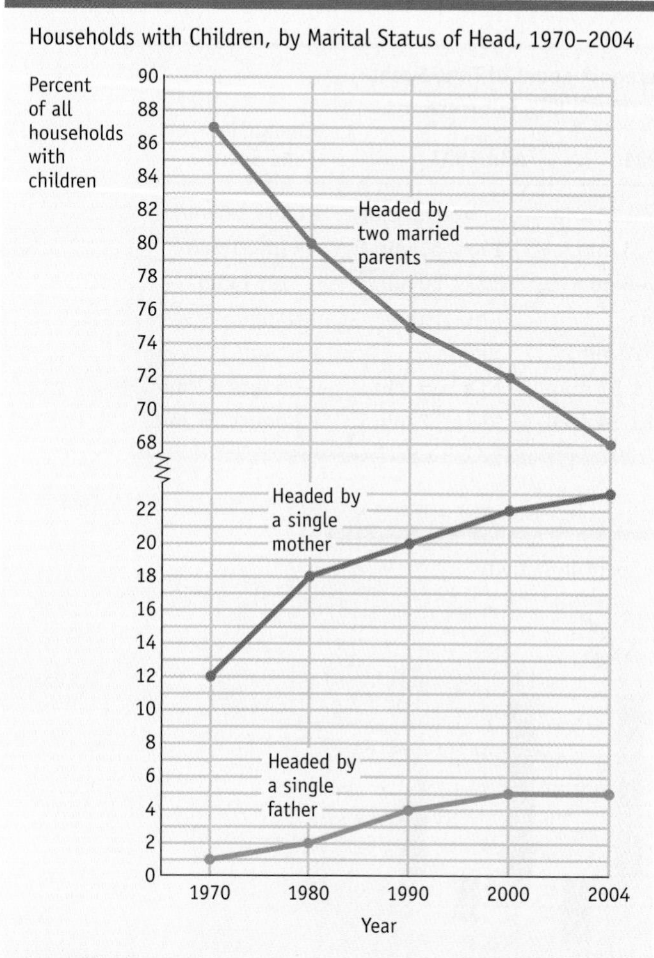

Source: U.S. Bureau of the Census, 1972 and 2002; 2004 data from childstats.ed.gov/americaschildren, accessed August 16, 2005.

Smoking Behavior Among U.S. High School Students, 1991–2003 (Chapter 14)

The data in these two tables reveal many trends. For example, do you see that African American adolescents are much less likely to smoke than Hispanics or European Americans, but that this racial advantage is decreasing? Are you surprised to see that White females smoke more than White males?

Percentage of High School Students Who Reported Smoking Cigarettes

Smoking Behavior	1991	1995	1999	2003
Lifetime (ever smoked)	70.1	71.3	70.4	58.4
Current (smoked at least once in past 30 days)	27.5	34.8	34.8	21.9
Current frequent (smoked 20 or more times in past 30 days)	12.7	16.1	16.8	9.7

Percentage of High School Students Who Reported Current Smoking, by Sex, Race/Ethnicity, and Grade

Characteristic	1991	1995	1999	2003
Sex				
Female	27.3	34.3	34.9	21.9
Male	27.6	35.4	34.7	21.8
Race/ethnicity				
White, non-Hispanic	30.9	38.3	38.6	24.9
Female	*31.7*	*39.8*	*39.1*	*26.6*
Male	*30.2*	*37.0*	*38.2*	*23.3*
Black, non-Hispanic	12.6	19.2	19.7	15.1
Female	*11.3*	*12.2*	*17.7*	*10.8*
Male	*14.1*	*27.8*	*21.8*	*19.3*
Hispanic	25.3	34.0	32.7	18.4
Female	*22.9*	*32.9*	*31.5*	*17.7*
Male	*27.9*	*34.9*	*34.0*	*19.1*
Grade				
9th	23.2	31.2	27.6	17.4
10th	25.2	33.1	34.7	21.8
11th	31.6	35.9	36.0	23.6
12th	30.1	38.2	42.8	26.2

Source: MMWR (2004, June 18)

Sexual Behaviors of U.S. High School Students: Variations Among 20 Selected States, 2003 (Chapter 15)

These percentages, as high as they may seem, are actually lower than they were in the early 1990s. The data in this table reflect responses from students in the 9th to 12th grades. When only high school seniors are surveyed, the percentages are higher. In every state, more than half of all high school seniors have had sexual intercourse, and about 25 percent have had four or more sex partners.

	Ever had sexual intercourse (%)			Had first sexual intercourse before age 13 (%)			Has had four or more sex partners during lifetime (%)			Is currently sexually active* (%)		
State	**Female**	**Male**	**Total**	**Female**	**Male**	**Total**	**Female**	**Male**	**Total**	**Female**	**Male**	**Total**
Alabama	58.2	55.7	**56.9**	4.3	13.6	**9.0**	18.8	23.0	**20.9**	45.6	38.1	**41.9**
Arizona	40.9	45.3	**43.1**	5.2	6.3	**4.3**	10.1	11.9	**10.9**	30.4	31.4	**30.9**
Delaware	56.2	58.5	**57.3**	6.7	15.9	**11.3**	17.8	23.3	**20.6**	44.6	40.7	**42.7**
Florida	46.7	56.1	**51.3**	4.4	12.5	**8.3**	10.8	20.6	**15.6**	35.2	37.2	**36.2**
Idaho	35.7	37.0	**36.4**	3.1	5.6	**4.5**	—	—	—	—	—	—
Maine	42.1	43.5	**42.8**	2.8	6.2	**4.7**	9.8	11.2	**10.6**	32.7	29.7	**31.2**
Massachusetts	41.1	40.8	**41.0**	2.4	7.5	**4.9**	9.0	11.4	**10.1**	31.4	28.2	**29.8**
Michigan	41.9	45.1	**43.5**	4.0	9.7	**6.9**	11.3	15.5	**13.5**	32.8	29.5	**31.1**
Mississippi	57.7	64.2	**61.0**	4.7	18.3	**11.4**	14.9	32.7	**23.6**	46.5	45.9	**46.3**
Missouri	52.8	51.5	**52.2**	4.2	9.6	**7.0**	15.1	18.0	**16.5**	41.6	35.3	**38.4**
Montana	41.7	45.2	**43.6**	2.7	5.9	**8.7**	12.3	15.3	**14.0**	28.9	30.6	**29.9**
Nevada	45.4	47.4	**46.4**	4.2	10.7	**7.5**	16.6	21.4	**19.0**	34.4	30.9	**32.6**
New York	38.5	46.2	**42.4**	3.5	11.0	**7.2**	8.2	17.5	**12.7**	29.9	29.6	**29.7**
North Dakota	43.6	42.0	**42.8**	3.4	5.1	**4.2**	11.7	13.0	**12.4**	35.3	28.0	**31.6**
Ohio	42.7	40.4	**41.7**	4.0	7.8	**6.0**	13.0	12.7	**13.0**	31.9	27.6	**29.8**
South Dakota	43.4	39.6	**41.6**	2.5	5.6	**4.1**	8.8	14.4	**11.7**	30.2	32.0	**28.3**
Tennessee	48.5	51.5	**50.1**	4.0	10.8	**7.4**	12.8	17.6	**15.2**	36.6	34.4	**35.6**
Texas†	45.8	56.7	**51.3**	2.4	11.2	**6.8**	11.6	19.4	**15.6**	36.3	36.3	**36.4**
Wisconsin	37.6	36.0	**36.8**	1.8	3.8	**2.8**	8.0	9.7	**8.9**	29.5	23.6	**26.5**
Wyoming	46.8	44.7	**45.8**	5.6	5.9	**5.8**	16.3	16.0	**16.1**	34.1	29.5	**31.8**

*Active in 3 months prior to survey.
†Excluding Houston.
Source: National Center for Chronic Disease Prevention and Health Promotion, Youth Risk Behavior Surveillance System: http://apps.nccd.cdc.gov/YRBSS, accessed August 17, 2005.

United States Homicide Victim and Offender Rates, by Race and Gender, Ages 14–17 (Chapter 16)

Teenage boys are more often violent offenders than victims. The ratio of victimization to offense has varied for teenage girls over the years. The good news is that rates have decreased dramatically over the past ten years for every category of adolescents—male and female, Black and White. (Similar declines are apparent for Asian and Hispanic Americans.) The bad news is that rates are still higher in the United States than in any other developed nation.

Homicide Victimization Rates per 100,000 Population for 14- to 17-Year-Olds

	Male		Female	
Year	**White**	**Black**	**White**	**Black**
1976	3.7	24.6	2.2	6.4
1981	4.4	23.6	2.4	6.2
1986	4.2	27.4	2.3	6.6
1991	8.7	73.6	2.6	9.6
1996	8.4	53.3	2.1	8.9
2002	3.6	22.6	1.5	6.1

Source: U. S. Bureau of Justice Statistics, 2005.
Tabulations based on FBI Supplementary Homicide Reports and U.S. Census Bureau, Current Population Reports.

Homicide Offending Rates per 100,000 Population for 14- to 17-Year-Olds

	Male		Female	
Year	**White**	**Black**	**White**	**Black**
1976	10.4	72.4	1.3	10.3
1981	10.9	73.1	1.3	8.6
1986	12.3	72.2	1.1	5.6
1991	21.9	199.1	1.3	12.1
1996	17.4	134.8	1.7	7.8
2002	9.2	54.5	.9	3.7

Source: U. S. Bureau of Justice Statistics, 2005.
Tabulations based on FBI Supplementary Homicide Reports and U.S. Census Bureau, Current Population Reports. Rates include both known perpetrators and estimated share of unidentified perpetrators.

All the charts, graphs, and tables in this Appendix offer readers the opportunity to analyze raw data and draw their own conclusions. The same information may be presented in a variety of ways. On this page, you can create your own bar graph or line graph, depicting some noteworthy aspect of the data presented in the three tables. First, consider all the possibilities the tables offer by answering these six questions:

1. Are white male or female teenagers more likely to be victims of homicide?
2. These are annual rates. How many African Americans in 1,000 were likely to commit homicide in 2002?
3. Which age group is *most* likely to commit homicide?
4. Which age group is *least* likely to be victims of homicide?
5. Which age group is *almost equally* likely to be either perpetrators or victims of homicide?
6. Of the four groups of adolescents, which has shown the greatest decline in rates of both victimization and perpetration of homicide over the past decade? Which has shown the least decline?

Answers: 1. Boys—at least twice as often. 2. Less than one. 3. 18–24. 4. 0–13. 5. 25–34. 6. Black males had the greatest decline, and White females had the least (but these two groups have always been highest and lowest, respectively, in every year).
Now—use the grid provided at right to make your own graph.

Overall Rate of Homicide by Age, 2002, United States (Chapter 16)

Late adolescence and early adulthood are the peak times for murders—both as victims and offenders. The question for developmentalists is whether something changes before age 18 to decrease the rates in young adulthood.

Age group	Victims (per 100,000 in age group)	Killers (per 100,000 in age group)
0–13	1.8	0.2
14–17	6.7	15.6
18–24	17.2	29.7
25–34	14.5	16.1
35–49	9.0	7.7
50–64	5.4	3.3

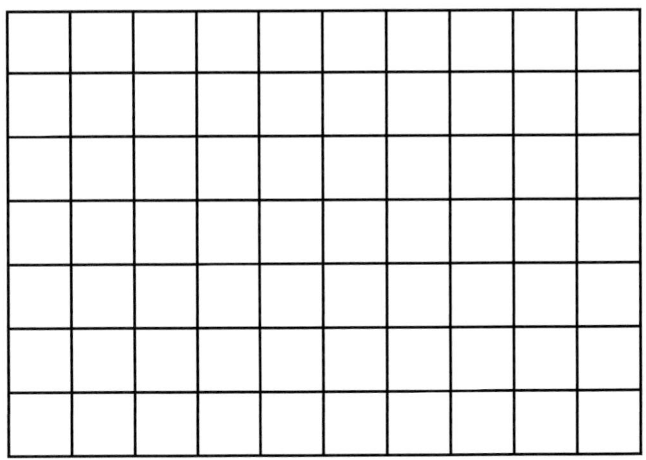

The Human Brain

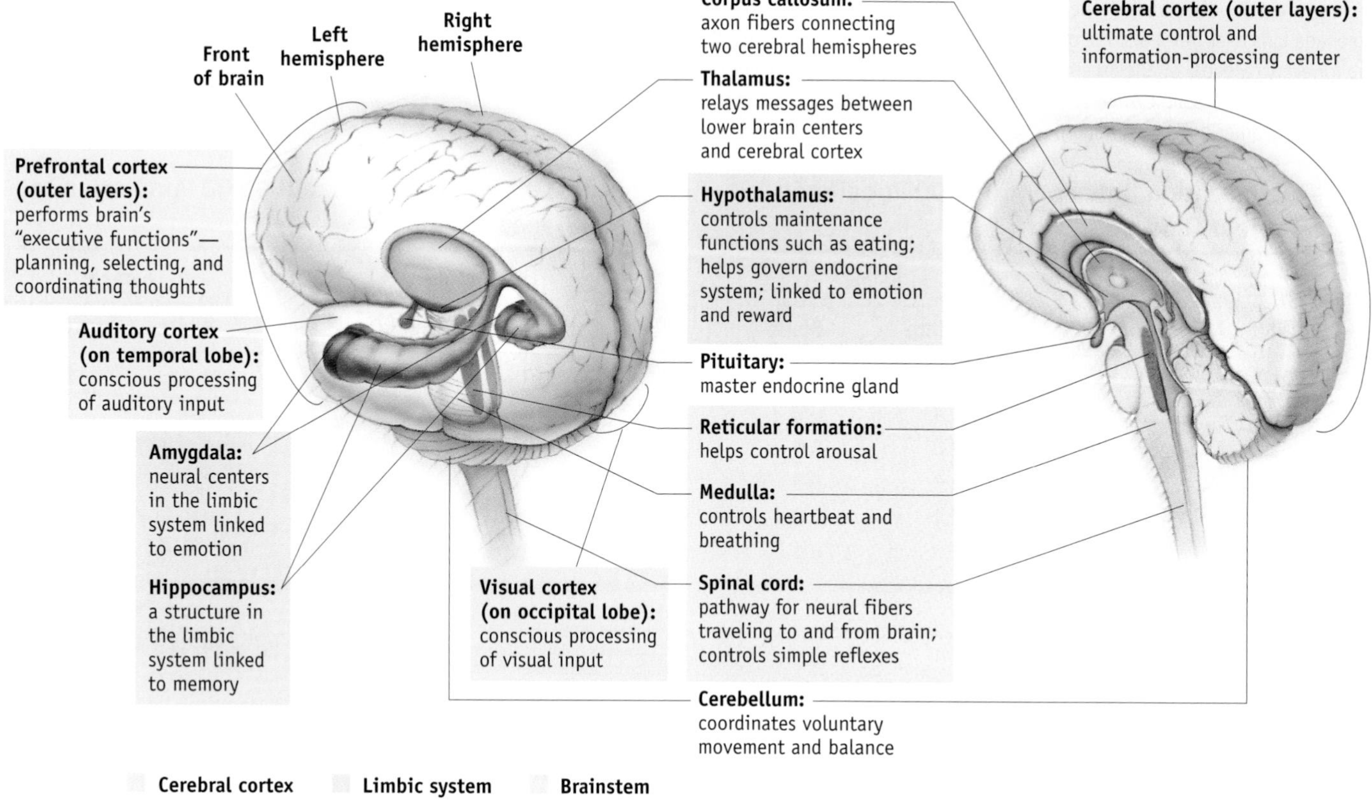

Appendix B
More About Research Methods

The first part of this appendix details some pointers on how to go about gathering more information about human development. The second part expands on Chapter 1's discussion of ways to ensure that research is valid.

Learning More

There are many ways to deepen your understanding of human development, including thinking about your own life and watching the children around you with careful attention to details of expression and behavior. Indeed, such thoughts may become second nature, as you realize how much there is to learn through reflection and observation. But more systematic research, and further book learning, bring insight and understanding that make development even more intriguing.

Library Research

To learn more about a particular topic, focus on readings that are current and scholarly. For instance, if something in a popular magazine or newspaper catches your attention, remember that the writer may have sensationalized, exaggerated, or biased the reporting. You might first check what this textbook says about the topic, and then look at the references cited.

This can begin effective library research. Start with recently published material and then find material from the bibliographies. In addition, there are two collections of abstracts that review current articles from a variety of developmental journals:

- *Psychscan: Developmental Psychology* is published four times a year by the American Psychological Association and includes abstracts of articles from almost 40 scholarly journals, from *Adolescence to Psychological Review*. Volume 24 covers the year 2002.
- *Child Development Abstracts and Bibliography* is published three times a year by the Society for Research in Child Development and is organized topically by author. Included are not only journal articles in biology, cognition, education, personality, and theory but also reviews of major books in the field. Volume 75 covers the year 2001. The online address is www.srcd.org.

"Handbooks," which summarize and evaluate research on various topics, are published every ten years or so. The most recent one in child development is in four volumes: *Handbook of Child Psychology* (1998), William Damon (Ed.), New York: Wiley.

To find the most current research, even before it appears in these abstracts and handbooks, look at the most recent issues of the many research journals. The three that cover all three domains (biosocial, cognitive, and psychosocial) are *Developmental Psychology*, published by the American Psychological Association (750 First St., NE, Washington, DC 20002); *Child Development*, published by Blackwell Publishers for the Society for Research in Child Development (Blackwell Publishers: 350 Main St., Malden, MA 02138; Society for Research in

Child Development: University of Michigan, 505 East Huron St., Suite 301, Ann Arbor, MI 48104-1522); and *Human Development*, published by Karger (P.O. Box CH-4009, Basel, Switzerland). These three journals differ somewhat in the types of articles and studies they publish; together they provide a good overview of development.

These suggestions are only a start. There are hundreds of other professional journals that focus on one aspect or another of human development; many are devoted to a particular age group or topic or to research from a particular nation. All of us who are professors hope you begin with one topic and soon lose track of time and subject, finding your interest drawn from one journal or book to another.

Using the Internet

The Internet is a boon for every student, from the novice just beginning to learn about a particular issue to the experienced researcher who wants today's data about an arcane topic. However, using the Internet carries certain risks. To maximize the benefits and reduce the costs of your Internet research, keep the following two advantages and two disadvantages in mind.

Advantages

It's All There

Virtually everything you might want to know is on the Internet, not only massive government statistics carefully collected and tallied but also very personal accounts of rare maladies. Every journal has a Web site, with tables of contents, usually abstracts of articles, and often full texts. Photos, charts, quizzes, ongoing experiments, newspapers from around the world, videos, and much more are available at the click of a mouse.

Quick and Easy

Just by sitting in front of a computer, any time of the day or night, you can research almost any topic. Every library (especially in colleges) has computers hooked up to the World Wide Web and librarians who can help you get started. Other students, co-workers, family members, and even strangers are experts in one aspect or another of Internet use, and usually they are flattered to be asked for specific suggestions. On your own, alone with your personal computer, you can access the Web and teach yourself everything you need to know, using online tutorials, help buttons, and exploration. This last route takes the most time, but some people learn best by teaching themselves—and do not get discouraged by the inevitable frustration when a particular tactic leads to a dead end.

Disadvantages

There's Too Much

You can spend hours sifting through information that turns out to be useless, trash, or tangential. *Directories* (which list general topics or areas and then move you step by step in the direction you choose) and *search engines* (which give you all the sites that use a particular word or words) sort information to help you find what you want. Each directory or search engine is different, and each provides somewhat different lists; none provides only the most comprehensive and accurate sites. You can take advantage of several search engines at once by using a metasearch engine (such as www://metacrawler.com or www://dogpile.com), but here, too, the selection process may not yield exactly what you want. With experience and help, you will get better at choosing the best sites for you, but resign yourself to sorting through some junk no matter what you do.

From Quality to Quackery

Anybody can put anything on the Web. There is no evaluation of bias, or even of evil; racist hate groups' Web sites and explicit child pornography abound on the Internet. You must evaluate and sift for yourself. Make sure you have several divergent sources for every "fact" you find; consider who put the information on the Internet, and for what reason. As the author of a very useful book on psychology on the Web explains: "There is no such thing as a truly free lunch, and there is no such thing as truly neutral information" (Varnhagen, 2002).

Imagine going to your local newsstand and buying a copy of every magazine and newspaper it carries. Then imagine blindly picking one—and reading it uncritically, as if it were the whole truth. You might be lucky and find a publication that was fairly objective, but more often you would find one that was designed for a particular audience that advocated a particular point of view—pro-gun, pro-environment, pro-sex, pro-Catholic, pro-Conservative, and so on. Or you might find one that assumes that sailing or traveling or crossword puzzles or whatever was the most important activity known to humankind. The Internet has the same problem, only much worse. Every controversial issue in child development has several sites that advocate radically opposite viewpoints; often they do not even suggest that there might be another side to the issue.

The Bottom Line

What these advantages and disadvantages come down to is that everyone will find the Internet useful for every topic, but anyone can waste time and be led astray. If you use the Web for research, also check print resources and more experienced researchers.

If you write a paper using Internet resources, bear in mind that massive plagiarism and prejudiced perspectives are common problems. Cite every source you use (so your reader can check your references) and evaluate objectivity, validity, and credibility even more carefully than you do for print resources. Expect your readers or your professors to be suspicious of Internet-based papers, and allay their fears by making your sources explicit and using published materials as well as electronic ones.

To help you get started, here are ten Internet addresses. They are all useful, but always remember to read with a critical eye.

- www.worthpublishers.com/berger Includes links to Web sites, quizzes, PowerPoint slides, and activities keyed to every chapter of the textbook.
- http://www.psych.umn.edu/psylabs/mtfs/ Describes the findings and ongoing work of the Minnesota Twin Family Study, which seeks to identify the genetic and environmental influences on the development of psychological traits.
- http://embryo.soad.umich.edu The Multidimensional Human Embryo. Presents MRI images of a human embryo at various stages of development, accompanied by brief explanations.
- www.kidshealth.org Web site on children's health, with a large number of articles by experts on various aspects of children's health. Sponsored by the Nemours Foundations.

- www.cdipage.com A useful site, with links and articles on child development and information on common childhood psychological disorders.
- http://www.piaget.org/main.html The Jean Piaget Society. Home page of an international, interdisciplinary organization devoted to "exploring the nature of the developmental construction of human knowledge." Some information about Piaget and his theories is provided, along with references and links to other sites.
- http://ericeece.org/eeceweb.html ERIC Clearinghouse on Elementary and Early Childhood Education: World Wide Web Sites Sponsored or Maintained by ERIC/EECE. Provides links to many education-related sites and provides brief descriptions of each.
- http://education.indiana.edu/cas/adol/adol.html Adolescence Directory online (ADOL) is an electronic guide to information on adolescent issues. It is a service of the Center for Adolescent Studies at Indiana University.
- http://www.psychREF.com Contains an index of references in psychology. Not all of them are relevant to human development, but almost every topic in this text is referenced on this Web site.

Ways to Make Research More Valid

As emphasized throughout this text, the study of development is a science. All social scientists use many methods to make their research more objective and therefore more valid. Several basic techniques are described in Chapter 1, including observation and experiments, correlation and statistical significance, independent and dependent variables, and cross-sectional, longitudinal, and cross-sequential research designs. Six additional terms or techniques pertaining to the validity of research are described here. Understanding them will help you evaluate research read about on the Internet, from library reading, or in textbooks.

Population and Participants

population The entire group of individuals who are of particular concern in a scientific study, such as all the children of the world or all newborns who weigh less than 3 pounds.

participants The people who are studied in a research project.

The entire group of people about whom a scientist wants to learn is called the **population.** Generally, a research population is quite large—not usually the world's entire population of 6 billion, but perhaps all the 4 million babies born in the United States last year, or all the 500,000 Japanese currently over age 65, or even all the 70,000 low-income fifth-graders attending New York City public schools in 2003. The particular individuals who are studied in a specific research project are called the **participants.** Typically, the participants reflect the characteristics of the population. Indeed, every published study reports who the participants were and how they did, or did not, reflect the population.

Sample Size

sample A group of individuals drawn from a specified population. A sample might be the low-birthweight babies born in four particular hospitals that are representative of all hospitals.

To make statements about people in general, scientists study particular participants chosen from the larger population. Each group of research participants, called a **sample,** must be large enough to ensure that if a few extreme cases happen to be included, they do not distort the statistical picture the sample gives of the population. Suppose, for instance, that researchers want to know the average age at which children begin to walk. Since they cannot include every infant in their study, they choose a sample of infants, determine the age of walking for each participant in the sample, and then calculate the sample average. If the sample is typical, the average walking age will be very close to the average for the entire infant population.

The importance of an adequate **sample size** can be seen if we assume, for the moment, that one of the infants in the sample had an undetected disability and did not walk until age 24 months. Assume also that all the other infants walked at 12 months, the current norm. If the sample size was less than 10 infants, then one late walker would add more than a month to the age at which the "average" child is said to walk. However, if the sample contained more than 500 children, the one abnormally late walker would not change the results by even one day.

sample size The number of individuals who are being studied in a single sample in a research project.

Representative Sample

Data collected from one group of participants may not be valid (that is, applicable and accurate) for other people who are different in some significant way, such as gender or ethnic background. Thus, every sample should be a **representative sample**—that is, should consist of people who are typical of the population the researchers wish to learn about. In a study of the average age of walking, for example, the sample population should reflect—in terms of male/female ratio, socioeconomic and ethnic background, and other characteristics—the entire population of infants. Ideally, other factors might be taken into consideration as well. For instance, if there is some evidence that first-born children walk earlier than later-born children, the sample should also be representative of the population's birth order.

representative sample A group of research participants who reflect the relevant characteristics of the larger population whose attributes are under study.

The importance of representative sampling is revealed by its absence in two classic studies of age of walking for infants in the United States (Gesell, 1926; Shirley, 1933). Both studies used a relatively small and unrepresentative sample (all the children were European American and most were middle-class). Partly because the samples were not representative of the general population of infants, both studies arrived at an average walking age of 15 months. This is 3 months later than the current U.S. norm, which was obtained through research on a much larger, more representative sample that included some low-SES children and some children of African and Latino descent—groups known to have high proportions of early-walking children. Another reason the earlier studies found babies walking 3 months later is that infants 80 years ago received much less physical stimulation, so their motor skill development was slowed down. In other words, infants actually did start to walk somewhat later then, perhaps at 13 months, which the researchers would have found if their sample had been representative.

"Blind" Experimenters and Participants

When experimenters have specific expectations about their research findings, those expectations can unintentionally affect the research results. As much as possible, therefore, the people who actually gather the data should be in a state of **"blindness"**—that is, they should be unaware of the purpose of the research.

blindness A situation in which data gatherers and their participants are deliberately kept ignorant of the purpose of the research so that they cannot unintentionally bias the results.

Suppose we are testing the hypothesis that first-born infants walk sooner than later-borns. Ideally, the examiner who measures the participants' walking ability should not know the hypothesis or the infants' age or birth order. The participants in the research should also be kept blind to its purpose, especially when the participants are older children or adults, whose behavior might be influenced by their own expectations.

Operational Definitions

When planning a study, researchers establish *operational definitions* of whatever phenomena they will be examining. That is, they define each variable in terms of specific, observable behavior that can be measured with precision. Even a simple variable, such as whether or not a toddler is walking, requires an operational definition. For example, does "walking" include steps taken while holding onto someone or something, or must the steps be taken without support? Is one unsteady step enough to meet the definition, or must the infant be able to move a certain distance without faltering? For a study on age of first walking to be meaningful, the researchers would need to resolve questions like these in a clear and through definition. In fact, the usual operational definition of walking is "takes at least three steps without holding on."

Understandably, operational definitions become much harder to establish when personality or intellectual variables are being studied. It is nonetheless essential that researchers who are investigating, say, "aggression" or "sharing" or "reading" define the trait in terms that are as precise and measurable as possible. Obviously, the more accurately operational definitions describe the variables to be examined, the more objective and valid the results of the study will be.

Experimental and Comparison Groups

experimental group Research participants who experience the special condition or treatment that is the key aspect of the research.

comparison group Research participants who are comparable to those in the experimental group in every relevant dimension except that they do not experience the special condition or treatment that is the key aspect of the experiment. Also called a *control group.*

To test a hypothesis adequately in an experiment, researchers gather data on two samples that are similar in every important way except one. They compare an **experimental group,** which receives some special experimental treatment, and a **comparison group,** or *control group,* which is matched to the experimental group in every respect but one: It does not receive the experimental treatment.

Suppose a research team hypothesizes that infants who are provided with regular exercise to strengthen their legs begin to walk earlier than babies who do not receive such exercise. In other words, they hypothesize that the independent variable of exercise affects the dependent variable of walking. To find out if this hypothesis is true, the researchers would first select two representative samples of children and examine both groups to make sure they are equivalent in motor skills, such as the ability to roll over and sit up. Then one sample (the experimental group) would receive daily "workouts" devoted to leg-strengthening between, say, their sixth and twelfth months; and the other sample (the control group) would get no special leg exercise. Results for the two groups would then be compared to test the hypothesis.

To put all this together with the techniques discussed in Chapter 1: A researcher might find 1,000 participants *(sample size),* randomly chosen from all babies *(population)* born throughout the United States on a particular day *(representative sample)* and visit them at home once a month from age 8 months to 18 months *(longitudinal research),* seeing *(naturalistic observation)* which ones take three unaided steps *(operational definition)* at what age. Then, in follow-up research with a similar sample, two groups of participants would be matched on every variable except one: The parents of half the babies *(experimental group)* would be shown how to exercise their infants' legs *(independent variable)* and be encouraged, perhaps even paid, to do this every day. These babies' age of walking *(dependent variable)* could be compared with that of the non-exercised babies *(comparison group)* by a researcher who doesn't know *(blind)* which babies are in which group. If differences between the groups emerge, they could be analyzed to see if they exceed random variability (that is, they could be tested for *statistical significance*).

Appendix C
Suggestions for Research Assignments

The best way to study child development is to do some investigation yourself, not only reading the textbook and expressing your ideas in speech and writing but also undertaking some research of your own. Writing a term paper is the usual mode in most college courses: You and your instructor already know the importance of setting a deadline for each stage (topic selection, outline, first draft, final draft), of asking several readers to evaluate your paper (perhaps including other students or a professor), and of having the final version typed with references correctly cited and listed. Some suggestions for effective use of journals and the Internet are given in Appendix B.

The subject of human development is also ideal for more personal study, so suggestions for conducting observations, case studies, surveys, and experiments are offered here.

Learning Through Observation

Much can be learned by becoming more systematic in your observations of the children around you. One way to begin is to collect observations of ten different children, in differing contexts, during the semester. Each profile should be approximately one page and should cover the following four items:

1. *Describe the physical and social context.* You will want to describe where you are, what day and time it is, and how many people you are observing. The weather and age and gender of those who are being observed might also be relevant. For example:

   Neighborhood playground on (street), at about 4:00 P.M. on (day, date), thirty children and ten adults present.

   OR

   Supermarket at (location) on Saturday morning (day, date), about 20 shoppers present.

2. *Describe the specific child who is the focus of your attention.* Estimate age, gender, and so on of the target child and anyone else who interacts with the child. Do not ask the age of the child until after the observation, if at all. Your goal is to conduct a naturalistic observation that is unobtrusive. For example:

   Boy, about 7 years old, playing with four other boys, who seem a year or two older. All are dressed warmly (it is a cold day) in similar clothes.

   OR

   Girl, about 18 months old, in supermarket cart pushed by woman, about 30 years old. The cart is half full of groceries.

3. *Write down everything that the child does or says in three minutes.* (Use a watch with a second hand.) Record gestures, facial expressions, movements, and words. Accurate reporting is the goal, and three minutes becomes a surprisingly long time if you write down everything. For example:

Child runs away about 20 feet, returns, and says, "Try to catch me." Two boys look at him, but they do not move. Boy frowns. He runs away and comes back in 10 seconds, stands about four feet away from the boys, and says, "Anyone want to play tag?" [And so on.]

OR

Child points to a package of Frosted Flakes cereal and makes a noise. (I could not hear if it was a word.) Mother says nothing and pushes the cart past the cereal. Child makes a whining noise, looks at the cereal, and kicks her left foot. Mother puts pacifier in child's mouth. [And so on.]

4. *Interpret what you just observed.* Is the child's behavior typical of children that age? Is the reaction of others helpful or not helpful? What values are being encouraged, and what skills are being mastered? What could have happened differently? This section is your opinion, but it must be based on the particulars you have just observed and on your knowledge of child development, ideally with specific reference to concepts (e.g., the first may be a rejected child; the second child's language development may not be encouraged).

Structuring a Case Study

A case study is more elaborate and detailed than an observation report. Select one child (ask your instructor if family members can be used), and secure written permission from the caregiver and, if the child is old enough, the child him- or herself. Explain that you are not going to report the name of the child, that the material is for your class, that the child or caregiver can stop the project at any time, and that they would be doing you a big favor in helping you learn about child development. Most people are quite happy to help in your education, if you explain this properly.

Gather Your Data

First, collect the information for your paper by using all the research methods you have learned. These methods include:

1. *Naturalistic observation.* Ask the caregiver when the child is likely to be awake and active, and observe the child for an hour during this time. Try to be as unobtrusive as possible; you are not there to play with, or care for, the child. If the child wants to play, explain that you must sit and write for now and that you will play later.

   Write down, minute by minute, everything the child does and that others do with the child. Try to be objective, focusing on behavior rather than interpretation. Thus, instead of writing "Jennifer was delighted when her father came home, and he dotes on her," you should write "5:33: Her father opened the door, Jennifer looked up, smiled, said 'dada,' and ran to him. He bent down, stretched out his arms, picked her up, and said, 'How's my little angel?' 5:34: He put her on his shoulders, and she said, 'Giddy up, horsey.'"

   After your observation, summarize the data in two ways: (a) Note the percentage of time spent in various activities. For instance, "Playing alone, 15 percent; playing with brother, 20 percent; crying, 3 percent." (b) Note the frequency of various behaviors: "Asked adult for something five times; adult granted request four times. Aggressive acts (punch, kick, etc.) directed at brother, 2; aggressive acts initiated by brother, 6." Making notations like these will help you evaluate and quantify your observations. Also, note any circumstances that might have made your observation atypical (e.g., "Jenny's mother said she hasn't been herself since she had the flu a week ago," or "Jenny kept trying to take my pen, so it was hard to write").

Note: Remember that a percentage can be found by dividing the total number of minutes spent on a specific activity by the total number of minutes you spent observing. For example, if, during your 45-minute observation, the child played by herself for periods of 2 minutes, 4 minutes, and 5 minutes, "playing alone" would total 11 minutes. Dividing 11 by 45 yields .244; thus the child spent 24 percent of the time playing alone.

2. *Informal interaction.* Interact with the child for at least half an hour. Your goal is to observe the child's personality and abilities in a relaxed setting. The particular activities you engage in will depend on the child's age and temperament. Most children enjoy playing games, reading books, drawing, and talking. Asking a younger child to show you his or her room and favorite toys is a good way to break the ice; asking an older child to show you the neighborhood can provide insights.
3. *Interview adults responsible for the child's care.* Keep these interviews loose and open-ended. Your goals are to learn (a) the child's history, especially any illnesses, stresses, or problems that might affect development; (b) the child's daily routine, including play patterns; (c) current problems that might affect the child; (d) a description of the child's temperament and personality, including special strengths and weaknesses.

   You are just as interested in adult values and attitudes as in the facts; therefore, you might concentrate on conversing during the interview, perhaps writing down a few words. Then write down all you remember as soon as the interview has been completed.
4. *Testing the child.* Assess the child's perceptual, motor, language, and intellectual abilities by using specific test items you have prepared in advance. The actual items you use will depend on the age of the child. For instance, you might test object permanence in a child between 6 and 24 months old; you would test conservation in a child between 3 and 9 years old. Likewise, testing language abilities might involve babbling with an infant, counting words per sentence with a preschooler, and asking a school-age child to make up a story.

Write Up Your Findings

Second, write the report, using the following steps:

1. Begin by reporting relevant background information, including the child's birth date and sex, age and sex of siblings, economic and ethnic background of the family, and the educational and marital status of the parents.
2. Describe the child's biosocial, cognitive, and psychosocial development, citing supporting data from your research to substantiate any conclusions you have reached. Do *not* simply transcribe your interview, test, or observation data, although you can attach your notes as an appendix, if you wish.
3. Predict the child's development in the next year, the next five years, and the next ten years. List the strengths in the child, the family, and the community that you think will foster optimal development. Also note whatever potential problems you see (either in the child's current behavior or in the family and community support system) that may lead to future difficulties for the child. Include discussion of the reasons, either methodological or theoretical, that your predictions may not be completely accurate.

Finally, show your report to a classmate (your instructor may assign you to a peer mentor) and ask if you have been clear in your description and predictions. Discuss the child with your classmate to see if you should add more details to your report. Your revised case study should be typed and given to your professor, who will evaluate it. If you wish, send me a copy (Professor Kathleen Berger, c/o Worth Publishers, 41 Madison Avenue, New York, NY 10010).

Experiments and Surveys

As you learned in Chapter 1, experiments and surveys are wonderful ways to learn more about development, but each study needs to be very carefully designed and undertaken to avoid bias and to ensure that all the ethical considerations are taken into account. Accordingly, I recommend that an experiment or survey be undertaken by a group of students, not by an individual. Listening carefully to other opinions, using more than one person to collect data, and checking with your professor before beginning the actual study are ways to make sure that your results have some validity.

If you do this, structure your work in such a way that everyone contributes and that contrary opinions are encouraged. (The normal human response is for everyone to agree with everyone else, but, as you learned in Chapter 15, seeking alternate, logical explanations can move an entire group forward to deeper, more analytic thought.) You might designate one person to be the critic, or your group might spend one day designing your study and another day finding problems with the design. (Some problems simply need to be recognized and acknowledged, but some of them can be fixed by changing the design.)

Specific topics for experiments or surveys depend on your group's interests and on your professor's requirements for the course. For ideas, check this book's Subject Index or Study Guide. Since development is multidisciplinary and multicontextual, almost any topic can be related to child development. Just remember to consider theory and practice, change and continuity, social interaction and cultural impact . . . and then try to limit your initial experiment or survey to one small part of this fascinating, ever-changing subject!

Glossary

A

achievement tests Measures of mastery and proficiency in reading, math, science, or any other subject.

adaptation The cognitive processes by which new information is taken in and responded to. Both assimilation and accommodation are kinds of adaptation.

additive gene A gene that, through interaction with other genes, affects a specific trait (such as skin color or height).

adolescence-limited offender A person whose criminal activity stops by age 21.

adolescent egocentrism A characteristic of adolescent thinking that leads young people to focus on themselves to the exclusion of others. A person might believe, for example, that his or her thoughts, feelings, and experiences are unique, more wonderful or more awful than anyone else's.

adrenal glands Two glands, located above the kidneys, that produce hormones (including the "stress hormones" epinephrine [adrenaline] and norepinephrine).

affordance An opportunity for perception and interaction that is offered by people, places, and objects in the environment.

age of viability The age (about 22 weeks after conception) at which a fetus can survive outside the mother's uterus if specialized medical care is available.

aggressive-rejected Rejected by peers because of antagonistic, confrontational behavior.

allele A slight, normal variation of a particular gene. Typically an allele differs in some amino-acid triplets but is the same in most of the genetic code.

amygdala A tiny brain structure that registers emotions, particularly fear and anxiety.

analytic thought Thought that results from analysis, such as a systematic ranking of pros and cons, risks and consequences, possibilities and facts. Analytic thought depends on logic and rationality.

androgyny A balance, within a person, of traditionally male and female psychological characteristics.

anorexia nervosa A serious eating disorder in which a person restricts eating to the point of emaciation and possible starvation. Most victims are high-achieving adolescent females.

anoxia A lack of oxygen that, if prolonged during birth, can cause brain damage or death.

antipathy Feelings of anger, distrust, dislike, or even hatred toward another person.

antisocial behavior Feeling and acting in ways that are deliberately hurtful or destructive to another person.

Apgar scale A quick assessment of a newborn's body functioning. The baby's color, heart rate, reflexes, muscle tone, and respiratory effort are scored (from 0 to 2) twice, at one minute and five minutes after birth, and the total scores are compared with the ideal score (a perfect 10).

apprentice in thinking A person whose cognition is stimulated and directed by older and more skilled members of society.

apprenticeship in thinking In sociocultural theory, the process by which novices develop cognitive competencies. They work with more skilled members of the society, often parents or teachers, who act as tutors or mentors.

aptitude The potential to learn, or master, a particular skill or body of knowledge.

assisted reproductive technology (ART) A general term for the techniques designed to help infertile couples conceive and then sustain a pregnancy.

asthma A chronic disease of the respiratory system in which inflammation narrows the airways from the lungs to the nose and mouth, causing difficulty in breathing. Symptoms include wheezing, rapid breathing, and coughing.

attachment According to Ainsworth (1973), "an affectional tie" that one person forms with another—a tie that binds them together in space and endures over time.

attention-deficit disorder (ADD) A condition in which a person has great difficulty concentrating. Such persons may seem lost in thought, spaced out, daydreaming, or distracted.

attention-deficit/hyperactivity disorder (ADHD) A condition in which a person not only has great difficulty concentrating for more than a few moments but also is inattentive, impulsive, and overactive.

authoritarian parenting Child rearing with high behavioral standards, punishment of misconduct, and low communication.

authoritative parenting Child rearing in which the parents set limits but listen to the child and are flexible.

autism A pervasive developmental disorder marked by an inability to relate to other people normally, extreme self-absorption, and an inability to acquire normal speech.

automatization A process in which repetition of a sequence of thoughts and actions makes the sequence routine so that it no longer requires conscious thought.

autonomy versus shame and doubt Erikson's second crisis of psychosocial development. Toddlers either succeed or fail in gaining a sense of self-rule over their own actions and bodies.

axon A nerve fiber that extends from a neuron and transmits electrical impulses from that neuron to the dendrites of other neurons.

B

babbling The extended repetition of certain syllables, such as *ba-ba-ba,* that begins at about 6 or 7 months of age.

balanced bilingual A person who is equally fluent in two languages, not favoring one or the other.

behavioral teratogens Agents and conditions that can harm the prenatal brain, affecting the future child's intellectual and emotional functioning.

behaviorism A grand theory of human development that studies observable behavior. Behaviorism is also called *learning theory,* because it describes the laws and processes by which behavior is learned.

bickering Petty, peevish arguing, usually repeated and ongoing.

binge drinking Consuming five or more drinks in a row. Some authorities specify four or more drinks in a row as binge drinking for women, since women tend to be smaller than men and to metabolize alcohol more quickly.

binocular vision The ability to focus the two eyes in a coordinated manner in order to see one image.

blended family A family that consists of two adults and the children of the prior relationships of one or both parents and/or the new partnership.

blindness A situation in which data gatherers and their participants are deliberately kept ignorant of the purpose of the research so that they cannot unintentionally bias the results.

body image A person's concept of his or her body's appearance.

bulimia nervosa An eating disorder in which the person, usually an adolescent or young adult female, repeatedly overeats and then purges through induced vomiting or abuse of laxatives.

bullying Repeated, systematic efforts to inflict harm through physical, verbal, or social attack on a weaker person.

bullying aggression Unprovoked, repeated physical or verbal attack, especially on victims who are unlikely to defend themselves.

bully-victim A bully who is, or has been, a victim. Also called *provocative victims* because they deliberately attack a bully.

butterfly effect The idea that a small event or thing can have a large impact if it happens to tip the balance, causing other changes that create a major event.

C

carrier A person whose genotype includes a gene that is not expressed in the phenotype. Carriers pass on those unexpressed genes to half their gametes and thus to half their children, who most likely will be carriers, too. Generally, only when the gene is inherited from both parents does the characteristic appear in the phenotype.

case study A research method in which one individual is studied intensively.

center day care Child care that usually occurs in a place especially designed for the purpose, where several paid providers care for many children. Usually the children are grouped by age, the day-care center is licensed, and providers are trained and certified in child development.

centration A characteristic of preoperational thought in which a person focuses (centers) on one idea, excluding all others.

cerebral palsy A disorder that results from damage to the brain's motor centers. People with cerebral palsy have difficulty with muscle control, which can affect speech and body movements.

cesarean section A surgical birth. Incisions through the mother's abdomen and uterus allow the fetus to be removed quickly, instead of being delivered through the vagina. Also called *c-section* or simply *section.*

child abuse Deliberate action that is harmful to a child's physical, emotional, or sexual well-being.

child-directed speech The high-pitched, simplified, and repetitive way adults speak to infants. Also called *baby talk* or *motherese.*

child maltreatment Intentional harm to, or avoidable endangerment of, anyone under 18 years of age.

child neglect Failure to meet a child's basic physical, educational, or emotional needs.

child sexual abuse Any erotic activity that arouses an adult and excites, shames, or confuses a child, whether or not the victim protests and whether or not genital contact is involved.

child with special needs A child who, because of a physical or mental disability, requires extra help in order to learn.

chromosome A carrier of genes; one of the 46 molecules of DNA (in 23 pairs) that each cell of the human body contains and that, together, contain all the genes. Other species have more or fewer chromosomes.

classical conditioning The learning process that connects a meaningful stimulus (such as the smell of food to a hungry animal) with a neutral stimulus, which had no special meaning before conditioning. Thus, money is neutral to a baby, but adults have been conditioned to want money because they have learned that it is connected to obtaining food and other basic things. (Also called *respondent conditioning.*)

classification The logical principle by which things are organized into groups (or categories or classes) according to some property they have in common.

clinical depression Feelings of hopelessness, lethargy, and worthlessness that last two weeks or more.

clone An organism that has exactly the same genotype as another organism that is already alive.

cluster suicides Several suicides committed by members of a group within a brief period of time.

code of ethics A set of principles that members of a profession or group are expected to follow.

code-switching Changing from one manner of speaking to another, a change that usually involves tone, gestures, pronunciation, sentence length, vocabulary, and sometimes language itself.

cognitive economy The idea that people generally use their minds as efficiently as possible, saving brain power and intellectual work. Although adolescents are capable of intensive, systematic, analytic thought, they often prefer easier and quicker intuitive thought, which is more economical.

cognitive equilibrium In cognitive theory, the condition of mental balance, when people are not confused or bewildered because they can use their existing thought processes to understand current experiences and ideas.

cognitive operation The process of organizing and evaluating thoughts in one's mind to come to a logical conclusion.

cognitive theory A grand theory of human development that focuses on changes in how people think over time. According to this theory, our thoughts shape our attitudes, beliefs, and behaviors.

cohort A group of people born at about the same time. They travel through life together, experiencing the same major historical changes.

comparison group/(control group) The group of participants in a research study who are similar to the experimental group in all relevant ways except that they do not experience the experimental condition (the independent variable).

concrete operational thought Piaget's term for the ability to reason logically about direct experiences and perceptions.

conditioning According to behaviorism, conditioning is the process of learning. The word *conditioning* is used to emphasize the importance of repeated practice, as when an athlete gets in condition by training for many weeks or months. (Sometimes called S–R [*stimulus–response*] *conditioning*.)

conservation The idea that the amount of a substance remains the same (i.e., is conserved) when its appearance changes.

continuity The word that signifies developments over time that appear to persist, unchanging, from one age to the next.

control processes The mechanisms (selective attention, strategic retrieval, metacognition, and emotional regulation) that combine memory, processing speed, and knowledge to regulate the analysis and flow of information within the information-processing system.

conventional moral reasoning Kohlberg's second level of moral reasoning, emphasizing social rules.

corpus callosum A long strip of nerve fibers that connect the left and right hemispheres of the brain.

correlation A number indicating the degree of relationship between two variables, expressed in terms of the likelihood that one variable will (or will not) occur when the other variable does (or does not). A correlation is not an indication that one variable causes the other.

cortex The outer layers of the brain in humans and other mammals. Most thinking, feeling, and sensing involve the cortex.

critical period In prenatal development, the time when a particular organ or other body part of the fetus is most susceptible to damage by teratogens. Also, a time when a certain development *must* happen if it is ever to happen. For example, the period of the embryo is critical for the growth of arms and legs.

cross-sectional research A research design that compares groups of people who differ in age but are similar in other important characteristics.

cross-sequential research A hybrid research method in which researchers first study several groups of people of different ages (a cross-sectional approach) and then follow those groups over the years (a longitudinal approach). (Also called *cohort-sequential* or *time-sequential research*.)

culture of children The particular habits, styles, and values that reflect the set of rules and rituals that characterize children as distinct from adult society.

D

deductive reasoning Reasoning from a general statement, premise, or principle, through logical steps, to figure out (deduce) specifics. Sometimes called "top-down" thinking.

deferred imitation A sequence in which an infant first perceives something that someone else does and then performs the same action a few hours or even days later.

dendrite A nerve fiber that extends from a neuron and receives electrical impulses transmitted from other neurons via their axons.

dependent variable In an experiment, the variable that may change as a result of whatever new condition or situation the experimenter adds. In other words, the dependent variable *depends* on the independent variable.

developmental psychopathology The field that uses insights into typical development to study and treat developmental disorders, and vice versa.

developmental theory A group of ideas, assumptions, and generalizations that interpret and illuminate the thousands of observations about human growth. In this way, developmental theories provide a framework for explaining the patterns and problems of development.

***Diagnostic and Statistical Manual of Mental Disorders* (DSM-IV-R)** The American Psychiatric Association's official guide to the diagnosis (not treatment) of mental disorders ("IV-R" means "fourth edition, revised").

discontinuity The word that signifies developments that appear quite different from those that came before.

disorganized attachment A category of attachment that is marked by inconsistent behavior of the infant in reaction to the caregiver's departure and return.

distal parenting Parenting practices that focus on the intellect more than the body, such as conversing and playing with an object.

dizygotic (DZ) twins Twins who are formed when two separate ova are fertilized by two separate sperm at roughly the same time. Such twins share about half their genes, like any other siblings. (Also called *fraternal twins*.)

DNA (deoxyribonucleic acid) The molecule that contains the chemical instructions for cells to manufacture various proteins.

dominant–recessive pattern The interaction of a pair of alleles in such a way that the phenotype reveals the influence of one allele (the dominant gene) more than that of the other (the recessive gene).

doula A woman who helps with the birth process. Traditionally in Latin America, a doula was like a midwife, the only professional who attended the birth process. Now doulas are likely to work alongside a hospital's medical staff to help the woman through labor and delivery.

Down syndrome A condition in which a person has 47 chromosomes instead of the usual 46, with 3 rather than 2 chromosomes at the 21st position. People with Down syndrome are mentally retarded and often have distinctive characteristics: unusual facial features, heart abnormalities, and language difficulties. (Also called *trisomy*-21.)

drug abuse The ingestion of a drug to the extent that it impairs biological or psychological well-being. Abuse depends on the context; even one-time use can be abusive.

drug addiction A situation in which a person craves more of a drug to feel physically or psychologically at ease.

dynamic perception Perception that is primed to focus on movement and change.

dyslexia Unusual difficulty with reading; thought to be the result of some neurological underdevelopment.

E

eclectic perspective The approach taken by most developmentalists, in which they apply aspects of each of the various theories of development rather than adhering exclusively to one theory.

ecological-systems approach A vision of how development should be studied, with the person considered in all the contexts and interactions that constitute a life.

effortful control The ability to regulate one's emotions and actions through effort, not simply through natural inclination.

egocentrism Piaget's term for children's tendency to think about the world entirely from their own personal perspective.

Electra complex The unconscious desire of girls to replace their mothers and win their father's exclusive love.

embryo The name for the developing organism from about the third through the eighth week after conception.

embryonic period Approximately the third through the eighth week after conception; the period during which the basic forms of all body structures, including internal organs, develop.

emergent literacy The early skills that help children learn to read, such as letter recognition and page sequencing.

emergent theories Theories that bring together information from many disciplines and are becoming comprehensive and systematic in their interpretations of development but are not yet established and detailed enough to be considered grand theories.

emotional intelligence An understanding of how to interpret and express emotions.

emotional regulation Controlling the expression of emotions, so sadness, fear, anger, and so on are not apparent.

empathy The ability to understand the emotions of another person, especially when those emotions differ from one's own.

English-language learner (ELL) A person who is learning English.

epigenetic theory An emergent theory of development that includes both the genetic origins of behavior (within each person and within each species) and the direct, systematic influence that environmental forces have, over time, on genes. The theory focuses on the dynamic interaction, over the decades and centuries, between these two influences.

ESL (English as a second language) An approach to teaching English that puts all children who do not speak English together, giving them an intensive course in basic English so that they can be educated in the same classroom as native English speakers.

estradiol A sex hormone, considered the chief estrogen. Females produce far more estradiol than males do.

ethnic group People whose ancestors were born in the same region, usually sharing a language and religion.

ethnotheory A theory that underlies the values and practices of a culture and that becomes apparent through analysis and comparison of those practices, although it is not usually apparent to the people within the culture.

experience-dependent Refers to brain functions that depend on particular, variable experiences and that therefore may or may not develop in a particular infant.

experience-expectant Refers to brain functions that require basic common experiences (which the infant can be expected to have) in order to develop normally.

experiment A research method in which the researcher tries to determine the cause-and-effect relationship between two variables by manipulating one variable (called the *independent variable*) and then observing and recording the resulting changes in the other variable (called the *dependent variable*).

experimental group The group of participants in a research study who experience the special condition or treatment that is the key aspect of the research.

extended family A family of three or more generations living in one household.

externalizing problems Difficulty with emotional regulation that involves outwardly expressing emotions in uncontrolled ways, such as by lashing out in impulsive anger or attacking other people or things.

extremely low birthweight (ELBW) A body weight at birth of less than 2 pounds (1 kilogram).

F

failure to thrive A situation in which a child stops growing or even loses weight, despite apparently normal health.

false self A set of behaviors adopted to combat rejection, to please others, or to try out as a possible self.

family day care Child care that occurs in a paid caregiver's home and involves six or fewer children of various ages.

family function The way a family works to meet the needs of its members. Children need families to provide basic material necessities, encourage learning, develop self-confidence, nurture friendships, and foster harmony and stability.

family structure The legal and genetic relationships (e.g., nuclear, extended, step) among relatives in the same home.

fast-mapping The speedy and imprecise way in which children learn new words by mentally charting them into categories according to their meaning.

fetal alcohol syndrome (FAS) A cluster of birth defects, including abnormal facial characteristics, slow physical growth, and retarded mental development, caused by the mother's drinking alcohol when pregnant.

fetal period The stage of prenatal development from the ninth week after conception until birth; the period during which the organs of the developing person grow in size and mature in functioning. Brain maturation and weight gain occur throughout this period.

fetus The name for the developing organism from the ninth week after conception until birth.

fine motor skills Physical abilities involving small body movements, especially of the hands and fingers, such as drawing and picking up a coin. (The word *fine* here means "small.")

Flynn Effect The rise in IQ score averages that has occurred over the decades in many nations.

fMRI Functional magnetic resonance imaging, a measuring technique in which the brain's magnetic properties indicate activation anywhere in the brain; fMRI helps locate neurological responses to stimuli.

focus on appearance A characteristic of preoperational thought in which a young child ignores all attributes that are not apparent.

foreclosure Erikson's term for premature identity formation, when an adolescent adopts preset roles and values wholesale, without questioning.

formal operational thought In Piaget's theory, the fourth and final stage of cognitive development, characterized by more systematic logic and the ability to think about abstract ideas.

foster care A legal, publicly supported plan in which a maltreated child is cared for by someone other than the parents.

fragile X syndrome A genetic disorder in which part of the X chromosome seems to be attached to the rest of it by a very thin string of molecules. The actual cause is too many repetitions of a particular part of a gene's code.

G

gamete A reproductive cell; that is, a sperm or ovum that can produce a new individual if it combines with a gamete from the other sex to make a zygote.

gender differences Differences in the roles and behavior of males and females that originate in the culture.

gender identity Originally, this term meant all the behaviors associated with males or females. Now gender identity is more narrowly defined, as whether people see themselves as masculine or feminine.

gender role A role usually assigned to men or women, such as housewife, nurse, man of the house, and soldier.

gene The basic unit for the transmission of heredity, consisting of a string of chemicals coding for the manufacture of certain proteins.

generation gap The difference in values and attitudes between adults of one generation and young people of the next. Although the gap does exist in such preferences as music, clothes, and hair, it is not wide when it comes to core beliefs and values.

generational forgetting The idea that each new generation forgets what the previous generation learned about harmful drugs.

generational stake The need of each generation to view family interactions from its own perspective because each has a different investment in the family scenario.

genetic counseling A program of consultation and testing that enables individuals to learn about their genetic heritage, including conditions that might harm any children they may conceive.

genotype An organism's entire genetic inheritance, or genetic potential.

germinal period The first two weeks of development after conception; characterized by rapid cell division and the beginning of cell differentiation. This is the most hazardous period of development.

gonads The paired sex glands (ovaries in females, testicles in males). The gonads produce hormones and gametes.

goodness of fit A similarity of temperament and values that produces a smooth interaction between the individual and the social context, including family, school, and community.

grammar All the methods—word order, verb forms, and so on—that languages use to communicate meaning, apart from the words themselves.

grand theories Comprehensive theories of psychology, which have traditionally inspired and directed psychologists' thinking about child development. Psychoanalytic theory, behaviorism, and cognitive theory are all grand theories.

gross motor skills Physical abilities involving large body movements, such as walking and jumping. (The word *gross* here means "big.")

growth spurt The relatively sudden and rapid physical growth that occurs during puberty. Each body part increases in size on a schedule: Weight usually precedes height, and the limbs precede the torso.

guided participation In sociocultural theory, the most effective technique used by skilled mentors to help novices learn. They not only provide instruction but also allow direct, shared involvement in the activity.

H

habituation The process of getting used to an object or event through repeated exposure to it.

head-sparing The biological protection of the brain when malnutrition affects body growth. The brain is the last part of the body to be damaged by malnutrition.

hidden curriculum The unofficial, unstated, or implicit rules and priorities that influence the academic curriculum and every other aspect of learning in school.

high-stakes testing An evaluation that is critical in determining success or failure. If one test determines whether a student will graduate or be promoted, that is a high-stakes test.

hippocampus A brain structure that is a central processor of memory, especially the memory of locations.

holophrase A single word that is used to express a complete, meaningful thought.

hormone An organic chemical substance that is produced by one body tissue and conveyed via the bloodstream to another to affect some physiological function. Various hormones influence thoughts, urges, emotions, and behavior.

HPA axis The hypothalamus-pituitary-adrenal axis, a route followed by many kinds of hormones to trigger the changes of puberty and to regulate stress, growth, sleep, appetite, sexual excitement, and various other bodily changes.

human genome The full set of all the 25,000 or so genes that are the instructions to make a human being.

Human Genome Project An international effort to map the complete human genetic code. This effort was virtually completed in 2001, though analysis is ongoing.

human immunodeficiency virus (HIV) The virus that causes AIDS (acquired immune deficiency syndrome), in which the body's immune system is gradually overwhelmed and the individual becomes vulnerable to opportunistic infections. Even with treatment, AIDS eventually leads to death from any of several opportunistic diseases.

hypothalamus A brain area that responds to the amygdala and the hippocampus to produce hormones that activate other parts of the brain and body.

hypothesis A specific prediction that is stated in such a way that it can be tested and either confirmed or refuted.

hypothetical thought Thought that includes propositions and possibilities that may not reflect reality.

I

identification An attempt to defend one's self-concept by taking on the behaviors and attitudes of someone else.

identity The logical principle that certain characteristics of an object remain the same even if other characteristics change. Also, a consistent definition of one's self as a unique individual, in terms of roles, attitudes, beliefs, and aspirations.

identity achievement Knowing who one is as a unique person, accepting some cultural values and rejecting others.

identity diffusion An adolescent's lack of values, traits, or commitments; the opposite of identity achievement.

identity moratorium A pause in identity formation. Alternatives are explored, but final identity is postponed.

identity versus diffusion Erikson's fifth stage of psychosocial development, in which adolescents want to know who they are, in sex, religion, politics, and vocation, but find it hard to decide which of many possible roles or identities to adopt.

imaginary audience The egocentric belief that other people are watching, and taking note of, one's appearance, ideas, and behavior. This belief that "It's all about me" makes people very self-conscious.

immunization A process that stimulates the body's immune system to defend against attack by a particular contagious disease. Immunization may either occur naturally (by having the disease) or be acquired through vaccination (by injection, wearing a patch, or swallowing or inhaling).

implantation Beginning about a week after conception, the burrowing of the zygote into the lining of the uterus, where it can be nourished and protected during growth.

incidence How often a particular behavior or circumstance occurs.

inclusion An approach to educating children with special needs in which they are included in regular classrooms, with "appropriate aids and services" as required by law.

independent variable In an experiment, the variable that is introduced to see what effect it has on the dependent variable. (Also called *experimental variable*.)

individual education plan (IEP) A document specifying educational goals and plans for a child with special needs.

inductive reasoning Reasoning from one or more specific experiences or facts to a general conclusion. Sometimes called "bottom-up" reasoning, induction may be less advanced than deduction.

industry versus inferiority The fourth of Erikson's eight psychosexual development crises, during which children attempt to master many skills, developing a sense of themselves as either industrious or inferior, competent or incompetent.

infertility The inability to produce a baby after at least a year of trying.

information-processing theory A perspective that compares human thinking processes, by analogy, to computer analysis of data, including sensory input, connections, stored memories, and output.

initiative versus guilt Erikson's third psychosocial crisis. Children begin new activities and feel guilty when they fail.

injury control/harm reduction These terms express the belief that accidents are not random and that injuries are less harmful with proper controls in place. In practice, this means anticipating, controlling, and preventing dangerous activities.

insecure-avoidant attachment A pattern of attachment in which one person avoids connection with another, as when an infant seems not to care about a caregiver's presence, departure, or return.

insecure-resistant/ambivalent attachment A pattern of attachment in which anxiety and uncertainty are evident, as when an infant is very upset at separation and both resists and seeks contact on reunion.

instrumental aggression Hurtful behavior that is intended to get or keep something that another person has.

interaction effect The result of a combination of teratogens. Sometimes risk is greatly magnified when the embryo is exposed to more than one teratogen at the same time.

internalizing problems Difficulty with emotional regulation that involves turning one's emotional distress inward, as by feeling excessively guilty, ashamed, or worthless.

intrinsic motivation Goals or drives that come from inside a person, such as the need to feel smart or competent. This contrasts with external motivation, the need for rewards from outside, such as material possessions or someone else's esteem.

intuitive thought Thought that arises from an emotion or a hunch, beyond rational explanation. Past experiences, cultural assumptions, and sudden impulses are the precursors of intuitive thought. Also called *heuristic* or *experiential thought*.

invincibility fable A teenager's conviction, stemming from adolescent egocentrism, that he or she cannot be conquered or even harmed by anything that might vanquish a normal mortal, such as unprotected sex, drug abuse, or high-speed driving.

in vitro fertilization (IVF) Literally, fertilization "in glass"—that is, in a glass laboratory dish, rather than inside a woman's body. Sperm are mixed with ova that have been surgically removed from a woman's ovary. If the combination produces a zygote, it is inserted into the woman's uterus, where it may implant and develop into a baby.

IQ tests Aptitude tests designed to measure intellectual aptitude, or ability to learn in school. Originally intelligence was defined as mental age divided by chronological age, times 100—hence *intelligence quotient* (IQ).

irreversibility The idea that nothing can be undone; the failure to recognize that reversal sometimes restores something back to what existed before a change occurred.

K

kangaroo care Care that occurs when the mother of a low-birthweight infant spends at least an hour a day holding the infant between her breasts, like a kangaroo that carries her immature newborn in a pouch on her abdomen. If the infant is capable, he or she can easily breast-feed.

kinship care A form of foster care in which a relative of the maltreated child becomes the approved caregiver.

knowledge base A body of knowledge in a particular area that makes it easier to master new learning.

kwashiorkor A disease of chronic malnutrition during childhood, in which a deficiency of protein makes the child more vulnerable to other diseases, such as measles, diarrhea, and influenza.

L

language acquisition device (LAD) Chomsky's term for a hypothesized brain structure that enables humans to learn language, including the basic aspects of grammar, vocabulary, and intonation.

latency Freud's term for middle childhood, during which children's emotional drives and psychosocial needs are quiet (latent). Freud thought that sexual conflicts from earlier stages are only temporarily submerged, to burst forth again at puberty.

lateralization Literally, sidedness. Each side of the brain specializes in certain functions, with one side dominant for each activity. The left side of the brain controls the right side of the body, and vice versa.

learning disability A marked delay in a particular area of learning that is not caused by an apparent physical disability, by mental retardation, or by an unusually stressful home environment.

least restrictive environment (LRE) A legal requirement that children with special needs be assigned to the least restrictive context in which they can learn.

life-course-persistent offender A person whose criminal activity typically begins in early adolescence and continues throughout life; a career criminal.

little scientist Piaget's term for the stage-five toddler (age 12 to 18 months), who experiments without anticipating the results.

longitudinal research A research design that follows the same individuals over time, repeatedly assessing their development.

long-term memory The component of the information-processing system in which virtually limitless amounts of information can be stored indefinitely.

low birthweight (LBW) A body weight at birth of less than 5½ pounds (2.5 kilograms). The cause could be slow growth during prenatal development, or birth before 36 weeks of gestation, or both.

M

mainstreaming The practice of teaching children with special needs in the same classrooms as other children.

marasmus A disease of severe protein-calorie malnutrition during early infancy, in which growth stops, body tissues waste away, and the infant eventually dies.

menarche A girl's first menstrual period, signaling that she has begun ovulation. Pregnancy is biologically possible, but ovulation and menstruation are often irregular for years after menarche.

mental retardation Literally, means slow, or late, thinking. In practice, people are considered mentally retarded if they score below 70 on an IQ test and if they are markedly behind their peers in adaptation to daily life.

metacognition "Thinking about thinking," or the ability to evaluate a cognitive task to determine how best to accomplish it, and then to monitor and adjust one's performance on that task.

middle childhood The period between early childhood and early adolescence, roughly age 6 or 7 to 10 or 11.

middle school A term for the years of school between elementary and high school; also called junior high or intermediate school. Some systems have no middle school, only schools for grades 1–8 or 7–12.

minitheories Theories that focus on some specific topic. In development, for example, several theories of how infants learn to talk are minitheories. They are less general and comprehensive than the grand theories, although useful in their own right.

modeling The central process of social learning, by which people observe the actions of others and then copy them.

monozygotic (MZ) twins Literally, "from one zygote." Twins and other multiple births that originate from one zygote that splits apart very early in development. (Also called *identical twins.*)

morality of care In Gilligan's view, the moral stance that nurturance and compassion are more important than absolute judgments of right and wrong.

morality of justice In Gilligan's view, the moral stance that judgments of absolute right and wrong are more important than nurturance and compassion.

mosaic Having a condition (*mosaicism*) that involves having a mixture of cells, some normal and some with an odd number of chromosomes or a series of missing genes.

motor skill Any ability to move a part of the body, from a large leap to a small movement of the eyelid. These are called skills because they are learned, not automatic.

multifactorial Literally, "many factors." In genetics, *multifactorial* means that traits are affected by many influences, both genetic and environmental.

myelination The process by which axons become coated with myelin, a fatty substance that speeds the transmission of nerve impulses from neuron to neuron.

N

naming explosion A sudden increase in an infant's vocabulary, especially in the number of nouns, beginning at about 18 months.

nature A general term for the traits, capacities, and limitations that each individual inherits genetically from his or her parents at the moment of conception.

negative identity Identity taken on reactively, with rebellious defiance, simply because it is the opposite of the one that parents or society expects.

neuron A nerve cell of the central nervous system. Most neurons (billions of them) are in the brain.

No Child Left Behind Act A controversial law, enacted in 2001, that uses multiple assessments and achievement standards to try to improve public education in the United States.

norm An average, or standard, measurement, calculated from the measurements of many individuals within a specific group or population.

nuclear family A family that consists of a father, a mother, and their biological children under age 18.

nurture A general term for all the environmental influences that affect development after an individual is conceived.

O

obese For adults, obesity begins at a BMI of 30. For children, obesity is usually set at the 95th percentile or higher, based on 1980 standards for age and sex.

object permanence The realization that objects (including people) still exist when they cannot be seen, touched, or heard.

Oedipus complex The unconscious desire of young boys to replace their fathers and win their mother's exclusive love.

operant conditioning The learning process by which a particular action is followed by something desired (which makes the person or animal more likely to repeat the action) or by something unwanted (which makes the action less likely to be repeated). A student might study for many hours because, in the past, studying produced intellectual satisfaction, high grades, or parental praise. Such diligence is the result of operant conditioning. (Also called *instrumental conditioning*.)

overregularization Applying grammar rules even when exceptions occur, making the language more "regular" than it actually is.

overweight For adults, "overweight" is based on the weight/height ratio, with a BMI of 25 to 29 classified as overweight. Usually a child who is above the 85th percentile, for his or her age and sex, is overweight.

P

parasuicide Any potentially lethal action against the self that does not result in death.

parental alliance Cooperation between mother and father based on their mutual commitment to their children. In a parental alliance, the parents agree to support each other in their shared parental roles.

parental monitoring Parents' awareness of what their children are doing, where, and with whom.

parent–infant bond The strong, loving connection that forms as parents hold their newborn. Bonding probably begins before birth and continues throughout infancy, so mother–child contact in the first few minutes after birth is helpful but not crucial.

participants The people who are studied in a research project.

peer pressure Social pressure to conform with one's friends or contemporaries in behavior, dress, and attitude; usually considered a negative force, as when adolescent peers encourage one another to defy adult authority.

people preference The innate attraction that human babies have to other humans, evident in visual, auditory, tactile, and other preferences.

percentile A point on a ranking scale of 1 to 99. The 50th percentile is the midpoint; half the people in the group rank higher and half lower. If a child is in the bottom 5 percent, or loses rank from one measurement to the next, that is a cause for concern.

perception The mental processing of sensory information, when the brain interprets a sensation.

permanency planning A plan for the eventual outcome when a child has experienced substantiated maltreatment. A goal is to make a definite plan that avoids repeated changes of caregiver or school, which can be particularly harmful for the child.

permissive parenting Child rearing with high nurturance and communication but rare punishment, guidance, or control.

perseveration The tendency to persevere in, or stick to, one thought or action for a long time.

personal fable A teenager's false belief, stemming from adolescent egocentrism, that he or she is destined to have a unique, heroic, or even legendary life.

pervasive developmental disorders Severe problems, such as autism, that affect many aspects of a young child's psychological growth, causing evident delay of speech, movement, or social skills before age 6.

phallic stage Freud's third stage of development, when the penis becomes the focus of concern and pleasure.

phenotype The observable characteristics of a person, including appearance, personality, intelligence, and all other traits.

phonics approach Teaching reading by first teaching the sounds of each letter and of various letter combinations.

pituitary gland A gland that, in response to a signal from the hypothalamus, produces many hormones, including those that regulate growth and control other glands, among them the adrenal and sex glands.

polygenic Literally, "many genes." Almost all important human traits, including abilities and emotions, are the result of the interaction of many genes.

population The entire group of individuals who are of particular concern in a scientific study, such as all the children of the world or all newborns who weigh less than 3 pounds.

possible selves The many personalities, sets of behavior, or self-images a person could have. Most adults have chosen one "self" from all the possibilities, but adolescents are often still exploring potential selves.

postconventional moral reasoning Kohlberg's third level of moral reasoning, emphasizing moral principles.

postformal thought A possible fifth stage of cognition proposed by developmentalists who believe that adults advance in their ability to combine emotions and logic in complex yet practical ways.

postpartum depression A mother's feelings of sadness, inadequacy, and hopelessness in the days and weeks after giving birth. These feelings are partly physiological (especially hormonal) and partly cultural, particularly if the woman does not receive adequate assistance and encouragement from the baby's father and other helpers.

post-traumatic stress disorder (PTSD) A delayed reaction to a trauma or shock, which may include hyperactivity and hypervigilance, displaced anger, sleeplessness, sudden terror or anxiety, and confusion between fantasy and reality.

preconventional moral reasoning Kohlberg's first level of moral reasoning, emphasizing rewards and punishments.

preformism The belief that the form of development is permanently set before a person is born. Some developments appear in the course of maturation, but it is through time, not experience, that they emerge.

prefrontal cortex The area of cortex at the front of the brain that specializes in anticipation, planning, and impulse control.

preoperational thought Piaget's term for cognitive development between the ages of about 2 and 6, before logical, operational thinking becomes possible.

preterm birth Birth that occurs 3 weeks or more before the full term of pregnancy has elapsed—that is, at 35 or fewer weeks after conception.

prevalence How widespread within a population a particular behavior or circumstance is.

primary circular reactions The first of three types of feedback loops, this one involving the infant's own body. The infant senses motion, sucking, noise, and so on, and tries to understand them.

primary prevention Actions that change overall background conditions to prevent some unwanted event or circumstance, such as injury, disease, or abuse.

primary sex characteristics The parts of the body that are directly involved in reproduction, including the vagina, uterus, ovaries, testicles, and penis.

private speech The internal dialogue that occurs when people talk to themselves (either silently or out loud).

prosocial behavior Feeling and acting in ways that are helpful and kind, without obvious benefit to oneself.

protein-calorie malnutrition A condition in which a person does not consume sufficient food of any kind. This results in several illnesses, weight loss, and sometimes death.

proximal parenting Parenting practices that involve close physical contact with the child's entire body, such as cradling and swinging.

psychoanalytic theory A grand theory of human development that holds that irrational, unconscious drives and motives, often originating in childhood, underlie human behavior.

psychological control A disciplinary technique that involves threatening to withdraw love and support and that relies on a child's feelings of guilt and gratitude to the parents.

puberty The time between the first onrush of hormones and full adult physical development. Puberty usually lasts three to five years. Many more years are required to achieve psychosocial maturity.

Q

qualitative research Research that considers qualities instead of quantities. Descriptions of particular conditions and participants' expressed ideas are often part of qualitative studies.

quantitative research Research that provides data that can be expressed with numbers, such as ranks or scales.

R

race A group of people who are regarded (by themselves or by others) as genetically distinct on the basis of physical appearance.

reaction time The time it takes to respond to a stimulus, either with a reflexive movement (such as an eye blink) or with a thought.

reactive aggression An impulsive retaliation for another person's intentional or accidental actions, verbal or physical.

reciprocity The principle that things may change in opposite ways and thus balance each other out. (Also called *inversion*.)

reflex A responsive movement that seems automatic because it almost always occurs in reaction to a particular stimulus. Newborns have many reflexes, some of which disappear with maturation.

reinforcement A technique for conditioning behavior in which that behavior is followed by something desired, such as food for a hungry animal or a welcoming smile for a lonely person.

relational aggression Actions, such as insults or social rejection, aimed at harming the victim's friendships.

REM sleep Rapid eye movement sleep, a stage of sleep characterized by flickering eyes behind closed lids, dreaming, and rapid brain waves.

reminder session A perceptual experience that helps a person recollect an idea or experience, without testing whether the person remembers it at the moment.

replication The repetition of a scientific study, using the same procedures on another group of participants, to verify or dispute the original study's conclusions.

reported maltreatment Maltreatment about which someone has notified the authorities.

representative sample A group of research participants who reflect the relevant characteristics of the larger population whose attributes are under study.

resilience The ability of some people to endure conditions that are often harmful—such as poverty, mental illness, social disruptions, and low intelligence—and to adapt in ways that make them stronger.

resource room A room in which trained teachers help children with special needs, using specialized curricula and equipment.

reversibility The logical principle that sometimes a thing that has been changed can be returned to its original state by reversing the process by which it was changed.

risk analysis The science of weighing the potential effects of a particular event, substance, or experience to determine the likelihood of harm. In teratology, risk analysis attempts to evaluate everything that affects the chances that a particular agent or condition will cause damage.

rough-and-tumble play Play that mimics aggression through wrestling, chasing, or hitting but in which there is no intent to harm.

S

sample A group of individuals drawn from a specified population. A sample might be the low- birthweight babies born in four particular hospitals that are representative of all hospitals.

sample size The number of individuals who are being studied in a single sample in a research project.

scaffolding Temporary support provided to help a learner master the next task in a given learning process.

science of human development The science that seeks to understand how and why people change or remain the same over time. People of all ages and circumstances are studied.

scientific method A way to answer questions that requires empirical research and data-based conclusions.

scientific observation A method of testing hypotheses by unobtrusively watching and recording participants' behavior in a systematic and objective manner, either in a laboratory or in a natural setting.

secondary circular reactions The second of three types of feedback loops, this one involving people and objects. The infant is responsive to other people and to toys and other objects that can be manipulated.

secondary prevention Actions that avert harm in the immediate situation, such as stopping a car before it hits a pedestrian.

secondary sex characteristics Physical traits that are not directly involved in reproduction but that indicate sexual maturity, such as a man's beard and a woman's breasts.

secure attachment A relationship of trust and confidence. During infancy, secure attachment enables a child to play independently and happily, reassured by the caregiver's proximity.

selective adaptation The process by which humans and other animals gradually adjust to their environment. Specifically, the frequency of a particular genetic trait in a population increases or decreases over generations, depending on whether or not the trait contributes to the survival and reproduction of members of that population.

selective attention The ability to concentrate on one stimulus and exclude others.

self-awareness A person's realization that he or she is a distinct individual, with independent body, mind, and actions.

self-concept A person's understanding of who he or she is. Self-concept includes appearance, personality, and various traits.

self-efficacy In social learning theory, the belief that one is effective. Self-efficacy motivates people to change themselves and their contexts because they believe they are capable of effective action.

self-esteem How a person evaluates his or her own worth, either in specifics (e.g., intelligence, attractiveness) or overall.

self-righting The inborn drive to remedy a developmental deficit.

sensation The response of a sensory system (eyes, ears, skin, tongue, nose) when it detects a stimulus.

sensitive period A time when a certain kind of growth or development is most likely to happen or happens most readily. For example, early childhood is considered to be a sensitive period for language learning.

sensorimotor intelligence Piaget's term for the intelligence of infants during the first period of cognitive development, when babies think by using their senses and motor skills.

sensory memory The component of the information-processing system in which incoming stimulus information is stored for a split second to allow it to be processed. Sometimes called the *sensory register.*

separation anxiety Distress when a familiar caregiver leaves; most obvious between 9 and 14 months.

sex differences Biological differences between males and females, in organs, hormones, and body type.

sexual abuse The use of a nonconsenting person for one's own sexual pleasure.

sexual orientation A person's tendency to be sexually attracted to a person of the other sex (a heterosexual orientation), the same sex (a homosexual orientation), or both sexes (a bisexual orientation).

sexually transmitted infection (STI) A disease spread by sexual contact, including syphilis, gonorrhea, genital herpes, chlamydia, and HIV.

shaken baby syndrome Life-threatening brain damage resulting from internal hemorrhaging and broken neural connections, caused by shaking an infant back and forth, sharply and quickly.

small for gestational age (SGA) A term for a baby whose birthweight is significantly lower than expected, given the time since conception. For example, a 5-pound (2.2-kilogram) newborn is SGA if born on time but not SGA if born two months early. (Also called *small-for-dates.*)

social cognition The ability to understand social interactions, including the causes and consequences of human behavior.

social comparison The tendency to assess one's abilities, achievements, social status, and other attributes by measuring them against those of other people, especially one's peers.

social construction An idea that is built more on shared perceptions of the social order than on objective reality.

social learning Learning by observing others.

social learning theory An extension of behaviorism that emphasizes the power of other people over our behavior. Even without specific reinforcement or punishment, people learn many things via observation and imitation of other people.

social mediation A function of speech by which a person's cognitive skills are refined and extended through both formal instruction and casual conversation.

social referencing Seeking information about an unfamiliar or ambiguous object or event by observing someone else's expressions and reactions. That other person becomes a social reference.

social smile A smile evoked by a human face, normally evident in infants at about 6 weeks after birth.

sociocultural theory An emergent theory that holds that development results from the dynamic interaction between each person and the surrounding social and cultural forces. This theory notes similarities and differences among children growing up in various nations, ethnic groups, and eras.

sociodramatic play Pretend play in which children act out various roles and themes in stories that they create.

socioeconomic status (SES) Part of the socioeconomic context, whereby people are classified as rich, poor, middle class, and so on according to income, education, occupation, and so on.

spermarche A boy's first ejaculation of sperm. Erections can occur as early as infancy, but ejaculation signals sperm production. Spermarche occurs during sleep (in a "wet dream") or via direct stimulation.

spontaneous abortion The naturally occurring termination of a pregnancy before the embryo or fetus is fully developed. (Also called a *miscarriage.*) If the woman chooses to terminate a pregnancy, that is called an *induced abortion.*

static reasoning Thinking that nothing changes: Whatever is now has always been and will ever be.

stereotype threat The concern that another person might have a negative prejudice about oneself as a member of a particular race, gender, or other group; the resulting anxiety leads to lower achievement.

still-face technique An experimental device in which an adult keeps his or her face unmoving and without expression in face-to-face interaction with an infant.

Strange Situation A laboratory procedure to measure attachment by evoking infant reactions to stress.

stranger wariness An infant's expression of concern—a quiet stare, clinging to a familiar person, or sadness—when a stranger appears. This signifies maturation: The baby recognizes the person as strange.

substantiated maltreatment Maltreatment that has been reported, investigated, and verified.

sudden infant death syndrome (SIDS) A situation in which a seemingly healthy infant, at least 2 months of age, suddenly stops breathing and dies unexpectedly while asleep. The cause is unknown, but it is correlated with sleeping on the stomach and having parents who smoke.

suicidal ideation Thinking about suicide, usually with some serious emotional and intellectual or cognitive overtones.

superego In psychoanalytic theory, the judgmental part of the personality that internalizes moral standards of the parents.

survey A research method in which information is collected from a large number of people by personal interview, written questionnaire, or some other means.

synapse The intersection between the axon of one neuron and the dendrites of other neurons.

synchrony A coordinated, rapid, and smooth exchange of responses between caregiver and infant.

T

temperament Inborn differences between one person and another in emotions, activity, and self-control. Temperament is epigenetic, originating in genes but affected by child-rearing practices.

teratogens Agents and conditions, including viruses, drugs, and chemicals, that can impair prenatal development and result in birth defects or even death.

tertiary circular reactions The third of three types of feedback loops, this one involving active exploration and experimentation. The infant explores a range of new activities, varying his or her responses as a way of learning about the world.

tertiary prevention Actions that are taken after an adverse event occurs, aimed at reducing the harm or preventing disability. Immediate and effective medical treatment of illness or injury is tertiary prevention.

testosterone A sex hormone, the best known of the androgens (male hormones); secreted in far greater amounts by males than by females.

theory of mind A person's theory of what other people might be thinking. In order to have a theory of mind, children must realize that other people are not necessarily thinking the same thoughts that they themselves are. Such a realization is seldom possible before age 4.

theory-theory The idea that children attempt to explain everything they see and hear by constructing theories.

threshold effect A situation in which a certain teratogen is relatively harmless in small doses but becomes harmful once exposure reaches a certain level (the threshold).

time-out A disciplinary technique in which a child is separated from other people for a specified time.

TIMSS (Trends in Math and Science Study) An international assessment of math and science skills. Although TIMSS is very useful, scores are not always comparable, since sample selection, test administration, and content validity are hard to keep uniform.

total immersion A strategy for teaching a second language by having all instruction in that language.

transient exuberance The great increase in the number of dendrites that occurs in an infant's brain during the first two years of life.

trust versus mistrust Erikson's first psychosocial stage. Infants learn basic trust if the world is a secure place where their basic needs (for food, comfort, attention, etc.) are met.

23rd pair The chromosome pair that, in humans, determines the zygote's (and hence the person's) sex. The other 22 pairs are autosomes, the same whether the 23rd pair is for a male or female.

V

very low birthweight (VLBW) A body weight at birth of less than 3 pounds (1.3 kilograms).

visual cliff An experimental apparatus that gives an illusion of a sudden drop between one horizontal surface and another.

Wechsler Intelligence Scale for Children (WISC) An IQ test designed for school-age children. The test assesses potential in many areas, including vocabulary, general knowledge, memory, and spatial comprehension.

whole-language approach Teaching reading by early use of all language skills—talking and listening, reading and writing.

withdrawn-rejected Rejected by peers because of timid, withdrawn, and anxious behavior.

working memory The component of the information-processing system in which current conscious mental activity occurs. Sometimes called *short-term memory*.

working model In cognitive theory, a set of assumptions that the individual uses to organize perceptions and experiences.

X-linked Referring to a gene carried on the X chromosome. If a boy inherits an X-linked recessive trait from his mother, he expresses that trait, since the Y from his father has no counteracting gene. Girls are more likely to be carriers of X-linked traits but are less likely to express them.

XX A 23rd pair of two X-shaped chromosomes, an X from the mother and an X from the father. XX zygotes become female embryos, female fetuses, and girls.

XY A 23rd pair of an X-shaped chromosome from the mother and a Y-shaped chromosome from the father. Zygotes that are XY become male embryos, male fetuses, and boys.

Z

zone of proximal development (ZPD) Vygotsky's term for a metaphorical area, or "zone," that includes all the skills, knowledge, and concepts that a learner is close ("proximal") to acquiring but cannot yet master without help.

zygote The single cell formed from the fusing of two gametes, a sperm and an ovum.

References

Abbott, Lesley, & Nutbrown, Cathy (Eds.). (2001). *Experiencing Reggio Emilia: Implications for pre-school provision.* Buckingham, England: Open University Press.

Abikoff, Howard B., & Hechtman, Lily. (1996). Multimodal therapy and stimulants in the treatment of children with ADHD. In Euthymia D. Hibbs & Peter S. Jensen (Eds.), *Psychosocial treatments for child and adolescent disorders: Empirically based strategies for clinical practice.* (pp. 341–369). Washington, DC: American Psychological Association.

Aboud, Frances E., & Amato, Maria. (2001). Developmental and socialization influences on intergroup bias. In Rupert Brown & Samuel L. Gaertner (Eds.), *Blackwell handbook of social psychology: Intergroup processes* (pp. 65–85). Malden, MA: Blackwell.

Aboud, Frances E., & Mendelson, Morton J. (1998). Determinants of friendship selection and quality: Developmental perspectives. In William M. Bukowski, Andrew F. Newcomb, & Willard W. Hartup (Eds.), *The company they keep: Friendship in childhood and adolescence* (pp. 87–112). New York: Cambridge University Press.

Ackerman, Brian P., Brown, Eleanor D., & Izard, Carroll E. (2004). The relations between contextual risk, earned income, and the school adjustment of children from economically disadvantaged families. *Developmental Psychology, 40,* 204–216.

Adam, Emma K. (2004). Beyond quality: Parental and residential stability and children's adjustment. *Current Directions in Psychological Science, 13,* 210–213.

Adams, Marilyn Jager, Treiman, Rebecca, & Pressley, Michael. (1998). Reading, writing, and literacy. In William Damon (Series Ed.) & Irving E. Sigel & K. Ann Renninger (Vol. Eds.), *Handbook of child psychology: Vol. 4. Child psychology in practice* (5th ed., pp. 275–357). New York: Wiley.

Adler, Bill (Ed.). (2001). *Kids' letters to Harry Potter from around the world: An unauthorized collection.* New York: Carroll & Graf.

Adolph, Karen E., Vereijken, Beatrix, & Denny, Mark A. (1998). Learning to crawl. *Child Development, 69,* 1299–1312.

Adolph, Karen E., Vereijken, Beatrix, & Shrout, Patrick E. (2003). What changes in infant walking and why. *Child Development, 74,* 475–497.

Agarwal, Dharam P., & Seitz, Helmut K. (Eds.). (2001). *Alcohol in health and disease.* New York: Dekker.

Aguirre-Molina, Marilyn, Molina, Carlos W., & Zambrana, Ruth Enid (Eds.). (2001). *Health issues in the Latino community.* San Francisco: Jossey Bass.

Ainsworth, Mary D. Salter. (1973). The development of infant-mother attachment. In Bettye M. Caldwell & Henry N. Ricciuti (Eds.), *Review of child development research* (Vol. 3, pp. 1–94). Chicago: University of Chicago Press.

Akhtar, Nameera, Jipson, Jennifer, & Callanan, Maureen A. (2001). Learning words through overhearing. *Child Development, 72,* 416–430.

Akiba, Daisuke, & García Coll, Cynthia. (2004). Effective interventions with children of color and their families: A contextual developmental approach. In Timothy B. Smith (Ed.), *Practicing multiculturalism: Affirming diversity in counseling and psychology* (pp. 123–144). Boston: Pearson/Allyn and Bacon.

Aksan, Nazan, & Kochanska, Grazyna. (2005). Conscience in childhood: Old questions, new answers. *Developmental Psychology, 41,* 506–516.

Alcock, John. (2001). *The triumph of sociobiology.* New York: Oxford University Press.

Alexander, Robin. (2000). *Culture and pedagogy: International comparisons in primary education.* Malden, MA: Blackwell.

Amato, Paul R., & Fowler, Frieda. (2002). Parenting practices, child adjustment, and family diversity. *Journal of Marriage & the Family, 64,* 703–716.

American Psychiatric Association. (2000). *Diagnostic and statistical manual of mental disorders: DSM-IV-TR* (4th ed.). Washington, DC: Author.

Ananth, Cande V., Demissie, Kitaw, Kramer, Michael S., & Vintzileos, Anthony M. (2003). Small-for-gestational-age births among black and white women: Temporal trends in the United States. *American Journal of Public Health, 93,* 577–579.

Anderson, Craig A., Berkowitz, Leonard, Donnerstein, Edward, Huesmann, L. Rowell, Johnson, James D., Linz, Daniel, et al. (2003). The influence of media violence on youth. *Psychological Science in the Public Interest, 4,* 81–110.

Anderson, Craig A., & Bushman, Brad J. (2002). Human aggression. *Annual Review of Psychology, 53,* 27–51.

Anderson, Daniel R., Huston, Aletha C., Schmitt, Kelly L., Linebarger, Deborah L., & Wright, John C. (2001). Early childhood television viewing and adolescent behavior: The recontact study. *Monographs of the Society for Research in Child Development, 66*(1, Serial No. 264).

Anderson, Mark, Johnson, Daniel, & Batal, Holly. (2005). *Sudden infant death syndrome and prenatal maternal smoking: Rising attributed risk in the Back to Sleep era.* Retrieved June 23, 2005, from the World Wide Web: http://www.biomedcentral.com/1741-7015/3/4

Anderson, Robert N., & Smith, Betty L. (2005, March 7). Table 2. Deaths, percentage of total deaths, and death rates for the 10 leading causes of death in selected age groups, by Hispanic origin, race for non-Hispanic population, and sex: United States, 2002. *National Vital Statistics Reports, 53*(17), 50–71.

Andrade, Miriam, & Menna-Barreto, L. (2002). Sleep patterns of high school students living in Sao Paulo, Brazil. In Mary A. Carskadon (Ed.), *Adolescent sleep patterns: Biological, social, and psychological influences* (pp. 118–131). New York: Cambridge University Press.

Andrade, Susan E., Gurwitz, Jerry H., Davis, Robert L., Chan, K. Arnold, Finkelstein, Jonathan A., Fortman, Kris, et al. (2004). Prescription drug use in pregnancy. *American Journal of Obstetrics and Gynecology, 191,* 398–407.

Angelou, Maya. (1970). *I know why the caged bird sings.* New York: Random House.

Angold, Adrian, Erkanli, Alaattin, Egger, Helen L., & Costello, E. Jane. (2000). Stimulant treatment for children: A community perspective. *Journal of the American Academy of Child & Adolescent Psychiatry, 39,* 975–984.

Apgar, Virginia. (1953). A proposal for a new method of evaluation of the newborn infant. *Current Researches in Anesthesia and Analgesia, 32,* 260–267.

Arfániarromo, Albert. (2001). Toward a psychosocial and sociocultural understanding of achievement motivation among Latino gang members in U.S. schools. *Journal of Instructional Psychology, 28,* 123–136.

Arlin, Patricia Kennedy. (1984). Adolescent and adult thought: A structural interpretation. In Michael L. Commons, Francis A. Richards, & Cheryl Armon (Eds.), *Beyond formal operations: Late adolescent and adult cognitive development* (pp. 258–271). New York: Praeger.

Arlin, Patricia Kennedy. (1989). Problem solving and problem finding in young artists and young scientists. In Michael L. Commons, Jan D. Sinnott, Francis A. Richards, & Cheryl Armon (Eds.), *Adult development: Vol. 1. Comparisons and applications of developmental models* (pp. 197–216). New York: Praeger.

Armour-Thomas, Eleanor, & Gopaul-McNicol, Sharon-Ann. (1998). *Assessing intelligence: Applying a bio-cultural model.* Thousand Oaks, CA: Sage.

Arnett, Jeffrey Jensen. (1999). Adolescent storm and stress, reconsidered. *American Psychologist, 54,* 317–326.

Arnett, Jeffrey Jensen. (2002). Adolescents in Western countries in the 21st century: Vast opportunities—for all? In B. Bradford Brown, Reed W. Larson, & T. S. Saraswathi (Eds.), *The world's youth: Adolescence in eight regions of the globe* (pp. 307–343). New York: Cambridge University Press.

Aron, David C., Gordon, Howard S., DiGiuseppe, David L., Harper, Dwain L., & Rosenthal, Gary E. (2000). Variations in risk-adjusted cesarean delivery rates according to race and health insurance. *Medical Care, 38,* 35–44.

Aronson, Elliot. (2000). *Nobody left to hate: Teaching compassion after Columbine.* New York: W. H. Freeman.

Aronson, Joshua, Fried, Carrie B., & Good, Catherine. (2002). Reducing the effects of stereotype threat on African American college students by shaping theories of intelligence. *Journal of Experimental Social Psychology, 38,* 113–125.

Aseltine, Robert H., Jr, & DeMartino, Robert. (2004). An outcome evaluation of the SOS suicide prevention program. *American Journal of Public Health, 94,* 446–451.

Ashman, Sharon B., & Dawson, Geraldine. (2002). Maternal depression, infant psychobiological development, and risk for depression. In Sherryl H. Goodman & Ian H. Gotlib (Eds.), *Children of depressed parents: Mechanisms of risk and implications for treatment* (pp. 37–58). Washington, DC: American Psychological Association.

Aslin, Richard N., & Hunt, Ruskin H. (2001). Development, plasticity, and learning in the auditory system. In Charles A. Nelson & Monica Luciana (Eds.), *Handbook of developmental cognitive neuroscience* (pp. 149–158). Cambridge, MA: MIT Press.

Aslin, Richard N., Jusczyk, Peter W., & Pisoni, David B. (1998). Speech and auditory processing during infancy: Constraints on and precursors to language. In William Damon (Series Ed.) & Deanna Kuhn & Robert S. Siegler (Vol Eds.), *Handbook of child psychology: Vol. 2. Cognition, perception, and language* (5th ed., pp. 147–198). New York: Wiley.

Astington, Janet Wilde, & Gopnik, Alison. (1988). Knowing you've changed your mind: Children's understanding of representational change. In Janet W. Astington, Paul L. Harris, & David R. Olson (Eds.), *Developing theories of mind* (pp. 193–206). New York: Cambridge University Press.

Astington, Janet Wilde, & Jenkins, Jennifer M. (1999). A longitudinal study of the relation between language and theory-of-mind development. *Developmental Psychology, 35,* 1311–1320.

Astuti, Rita, Solomon, Gregg E. A., & Carey, Susan. (2004). Constraints on conceptual development. *Monographs of the Society for Research in Child Development, 69*(3, Serial No. 277), vii-135.

Atkinson, Janette, & Braddick, Oliver. (2003). Neurobiological models of normal and abnormal visual development. In Michelle De Haan & Mark H. Johnson (Eds.), *The cognitive neuroscience of development* (pp. 43–71). New York: Psychology Press.

Aunola, Kaisa, & Nurmi, Jari-Erik. (2004). Maternal affection moderates the impact of psychological control on a child's mathematical performance. *Developmental Psychology, 40,* 965–978.

Bagwell, Catherine L., Schmidt, Michelle E., Newcomb, Andrew F., & Bukowski, William M. (2001). Friendship and peer rejection as predictors of adult adjustment. In William Damon (Series Ed.) & Douglas W. Nangle & Cynthia A. Erdley (Vol. Eds.), *New directions for child and adolescent development: No. 91. The role of friendship in psychological adjustment* (pp. 25–49). San Francisco: Jossey-Bass.

Baildam, Eileen M., Hillier, V. F., Menon, S., Bannister, R. P., Bamford, F. N., Moore, W. M. O., et al. (2000). Attention to infants in the first year. *Child: Care, Health and Development, 26,* 199–216.

Bailey, J. Michael, Kirk, Katherine M., Zhu, Gu, Dunne, Michael P., & Martin, Nicholas G. (2000). Do individual differences in sociosexuality represent genetic or environmentally contingent strategies? Evidence from the Australian Twin Registry. *Journal of Personality & Social Psychology, 78,* 537–545.

Baillargeon, Renée. (1999). Young infants' expectations about hidden objects: A reply to three challenges. *Developmental Science, 2,* 115–132.

Baillargeon, Renée, & DeVos, J. (1991). Object permanence in young infants: Further evidence. *Child Development, 62,* 1227–1246.

Baker, Jeffrey P. (2000). Immunization and the American way: 4 childhood vaccines. *American Journal of Public Health, 90,* 199–207.

Baker, Susan P. (2000). Where have we been and where are we going with injury control? In Dinesh Mohan & Geetam Tiwari (Eds.), *Injury prevention and control* (pp. 19–26). London: Taylor & Francis.

Baldwin, Dare A. (1993). Infants' ability to consult the speaker for clues to word reference. *Journal of Child Language, 20,* 395–418.

Baldwin, Dare A. (2000). Interpersonal understanding fuels knowledge acquisition. *Current Directions in Psychological Science, 9,* 40–45.

Ball, David J. (2004). Policy issues and risk-benefit trade-offs of 'safer surfacing' for children's playgrounds. *Accident Analysis & Prevention, 36,* 661–670.

Ballard, Cortney L., & Wood, Ruth I. (2005). Intracerebroventricular self-administration of commonly abused anabolic-androgenic steroids in male hamsters (Mesocricetus auratus): Nandrolone, drostanolone, oxymetholone, and stanozolol. *Behavioral Neuroscience, 119,* 752–758.

Balmford, Andrew, Clegg, Lizzie, Coulson, Tim, & Taylor, Jennie. (2002). Why conservationists should heed Pokémon [Letter to the editor]. *Science, 295,* 2367.

Baltes, Paul B., Lindenberger, Ulman, & Staudinger, Ursula M. (1998). Life-span theory in developmental psychology. In William Damon (Series Ed.) & Richard M. Lerner (Vol. Ed.), *Handbook of child psychology: Vol. 1. Theoretical models of human development* (5th ed., pp. 1029–1144). New York: Wiley.

Bandura, Albert. (1977). *Social learning theory.* Englewood Cliffs, NJ: Prentice Hall.

Bandura, Albert. (1986). *Social foundations of thought and action: A social cognitive theory.* Englewood Cliffs, NJ: Prentice-Hall.

Bandura, Albert. (1997). The anatomy of stages of change. *American Journal of Health Promotion, 12,* 8–10.

Bandura, Albert, Barbaranelli, Claudio, Vittorio Caprara, Gian, & Pastorelli, Concetta. (2001). Self-efficacy beliefs as shapers of children's aspirations and career trajectories. *Child Development, 72,* 187–206.

Banerjee, Robin, & Lintern, Vicki. (2000). Boys will be boys: The effect of social evaluation concerns on gender-typing. *Social Development, 9,* 397–408.

Banich, Marie T. (1998). Integration of information between the cerebral hemispheres. *Current Directions in Psychological Science, 7,* 32–37.

Banich, Marie T., & Heller, Wendy. (1998). Evolving perspectives on lateralization of function. *Current Directions in Psychological Science, 7,* 1–2.

Bank, Lew, Burraston, Bert, & Snyder, Jim. (2004). Sibling conflict and ineffective parenting as predictors of adolescent boys' antisocial behavior and peer difficulties: Additive and interactional effects. *Journal of Research on Adolescence, 14,* 99–125.

Barber, Brian K. (Ed.). (2002). *Intrusive parenting: How psychological control affects children and adolescents.* Washington, DC: American Psychological Association.

Barber, Brian K., & Olsen, Joseph A. (2004). Assessing the transitions to middle and high school. *Journal of Adolescent Research, 19,* 3–30.

Barber, Bonnie L., Eccles, Jacquelynne S., & Stone, Margaret R. (2001). Whatever happened to the jock, the brain, and the princess? Young adult pathways linked to adolescent activity involvement and social identity. *Journal of Adolescent Research, 16,* 429–455.

Barber, Bonnie L., Jacobson, Kristen C., Miller, Kristelle E., & Petersen, Anne C. (1998). Ups and downs: Daily cycles of adolescent moods. In Anne C. Crouter & Reed Larson (Eds.), *New directions for child and adolescent development: No. 82. Temporal rhythms in adolescence: Clocks, calendars, and the coordination of daily life* (pp. 23–36). San Francisco: Jossey-Bass.

Barinaga, Marcia. (2003). Newborn neurons search for meaning. *Science, 299,* 32–34.

Barnard, Kathryn E., & Martell, Louise K. (1995). Mothering. In Marc H. Bornstein (Ed.), *Handbook of parenting: Vol. 3. Status and social conditions of parenting* (pp. 3–26). Hillsdale, NJ: Erlbaum.

Barnett, Rosalind C., & Rivers, Caryl. (2004). *Same difference: How gender myths are hurting our relationships, our children, and our jobs.* New York: Basic Books.

Barnhill, Gena, Hagiwara, Taku, Myles, Brenda Smith, & Simpson, Richard L. (2000). Asperger syndrome: A study of the cognitive profiles of 37 children and adolescents. *Focus on Autism & Other Developmental Disabilities, 15,* 146–153.

Baron-Cohen, Simon. (1995). *Mindblindness: An essay on autism and theory of mind.* Cambridge, MA: MIT Press.

Baron-Cohen, Simon. (2000). Is Asperger syndrome/high-functioning autism necessarily a disability? *Development & Psychopathology, 12,* 489–500.

Barrett, Martyn. (1999). An introduction to the nature of language and to the central themes and issues in the study of language development. In Martyn Barrett (Ed.), *The development of language* (pp. 1–24). Hove, England: Psychology Press.

Barrett, Martyn, Lyons, Evanthia, & Valle, Arantza del. (2004). The development of national identity and social identity processes: Do social identity theory and self-categorization theory provide useful heuristic frameworks for developmental research? In Mark Bennett & Fabio Sani (Eds.), *The development of the social self* (pp. 159–188). Hove, England: Psychology Press.

Bateman, Belinda, Warner, John O., Hutchinson, Emma, Dean, Tara, Rowlandson, Piers, Gant, Carole, et al. (2004). The effects of a double blind, placebo controlled, artificial food colourings and benzoate preservative challenge on hyperactivity in a general population sample of preschool children. *Archives of Disease in Childhood, 89,* 506–511.

Bates, Elizabeth, Devescovi, Antonella, & Wulfeck, Beverly. (2001). Psycholinguistics: A cross-language perspective. *Annual Review of Psychology, 52,* 369–396.

Bates, John E., Pettit, Gregory S., Dodge, Kenneth A., & Ridge, Beth. (1998). Interaction of temperamental resistance to control and restrictive parenting in the development of externalizing behavior. *Developmental Psychology, 34,* 982–995.

Bates, John E., Viken, Richard J., Alexander, Douglas B., Beyers, Jennifer, & Stockton, Lesley. (2002). Sleep and adjustment in preschool children: Sleep diary reports by mothers relate to behavior reports by teachers. *Child Development, 73,* 62–74.

Bateson, Patrick. (2005). Desirable scientific conduct. *Science, 307*(5710), 645.

Bau, C. H. D., Almeida, S., Costa, F. T., Garcia, C. E. D., Elias, E. P., Ponso, A. C., et al. (2001). DRD4 and DAT1 as modifying genes in alcoholism: Interaction with novelty seeking on level of alcohol consumption. *Molecular Psychiatry, 6,* 7–9.

Bauer, Amy M., Quas, Jodi A., & Boyce, W. Thomas. (2002). Associations between physiological reactivity and children's behavior: Advantages of a multisystem approach. *Journal of Developmental & Behavioral Pediatrics, 23,* 102–113.

Bauer, Patricia J., & Dow, Gina Annunziato. (1994). Episodic memory in 16- and 20-month-old children: Specifics are generalized but not forgotten. *Developmental Psychology, 30,* 403–417.

Bauer, Patricia J., Liebl, Monica, & Stennes, Leif. (1998). PRETTY is to DRESS as BRAVE is to SUITCOAT: Gender-based property-to-property inferences by 4½-year-old children. *Merrill-Palmer Quarterly, 44,* 355–377.

Baumeister, Roy F., Campbell, Jennifer D., Krueger, Joachim I., & Vohs, Kathleen D. (2003). Does high self-esteem cause better performance, interpersonal success, happiness, or healthier lifestyles? *Psychological Science in the Public Interest, 4,* 1–44.

Baumrind, Diana. (1967). Child care practices anteceding three patterns of preschool behavior. *Genetic Psychology Monographs, 75,* 43–88.

Baumrind, Diana. (1971). Current patterns of parental authority. *Developmental Psychology, 4*(1, Pt. 2), 1–103.

Baumrind, Diana. (1991). The influence of parenting style on adolescent competence and substance use. *Journal of Early Adolescence, 11,* 56–95.

BBC News Online. (2005, February 9). *World's smallest baby goes home.* Retrieved May 7, 2005, from the World Wide Web: http://news.bbc.co.uk/1/hi/health/4249147.stm

Beal, Carole R. (1994). *Boys and girls: The development of gender roles.* New York: McGraw-Hill.

Beal, S., & Porter, C. (1991). Sudden infant death syndrome related to climate. *Acta Paediatrica Scandinavica, 80,* 278–287.

Bearison, David J., Minian, Nadia, & Granowetter, Linda. (2002). Medical management of asthma and folk medicine in a Hispanic community. *Journal of Pediatric Psychology, 27,* 385–392.

Bearman, Peter S., & Brückner, Hannah. (2001). Promising the future: Virginity pledges and first intercourse. *American Journal of Sociology, 106,* 859–912.

Bearman, Peter S., Moody, James, & Stovel, Katherine. (2004). Chains of affection: The structure of adolescent romantic and sexual networks. *American Journal of Sociology, 110,* 44–91.

Beauvais, Fred. (2000). Indian adolescence: Opportunity and challenge. In Raymond Montemayor, Gerald R. Adams, & Thomas Gullotta (Eds.), *Advances in adolescent development: Vol. 10. Adolescent diversity in ethnic, economic, and cultural contexts* (pp. 110–140). Thousand Oaks, CA: Sage.

Beck, Martha Nibley. (1999). *Expecting Adam: A true story of birth, rebirth, and everyday magic.* New York: Times Books.

Beckwith, Leila, Cohen, Sarale E., & Hamilton, Claire E. (1999). Maternal sensitivity during infancy and subsequent life events relate to attachment representation at early adulthood. *Developmental Psychology, 35,* 693–700.

Behne, Tanya, Carpenter, Malinda, Call, Josep, & Tomasello, Michael. (2005). Unwilling versus unable: Infants' understanding of intentional action. *Developmental Psychology, 41,* 328–337.

Behrend, Douglas A., Scofield, Jason, & Kleinknecht, Erica E. (2001). Beyond fast mapping: Young children's extensions of novel words and novel facts. *Developmental Psychology, 37,* 698–705.

Behrman, Richard E. (Ed.). (1992). *Nelson textbook of pediatrics* (14th ed.). Philadelphia: Saunders.

Belamarich, Peter, & Ayoob, Keith-Thomas. (2001). Keeping teenage vegetarians healthy and in the know. *Contemporary Pediatrics, 10,* 89–108.

Belizan, Jose M., Althabe, Fernando, Barros, Fernando C., & Alexander, Sophie. (1999). Rates and implications of caesarean sections in Latin America: Ecological study. *British Medical Journal, 319,* 1397–1402.

Belka, David. (2004). Substituting skill learning for traditional games in early childhood. *Teaching Elementary Physical Education, 15,* 25–27.

Belsky, Jay. (2001). Emanuel Miller Lecture: Developmental risks (still) associated with early child care. *Journal of Child Psychology & Psychiatry, 42,* 845–859.

Belsky, Jay, Domitrovich, Celene, & Crnic, Keith. (1997). Temperament and parenting antecedents of individual differences in three-year-old boys' pride and shame reactions. *Child Development, 68,* 456–466.

Belsky, Jay, & Fearon, R. M. Pasco. (2002). Infant-mother attachment security, contextual risk, and early development: A moderational analysis. *Development & Psychopathology, 14,* 293–310.

Belsky, Jay, & Fearon, R. M. Pasco. (2004). Exploring marriage-parenting typologies and their contextual antecedents and developmental sequelae. *Development & Psychopathology, 16,* 501–523.

Belsky, Jay, Steinberg, Laurence, & Draper, Patricia. (1991). Childhood experience, interpersonal development, and reproductive strategy: An evolutionary theory of socialization. *Child Development, 62,* 647–670.

Bem, Sandra Lipsitz. (1993). *The lenses of gender: Transforming the debate on sexual inequality.* New Haven, CT: Yale University Press.

Benes, Francine M. (2001). The development of prefrontal cortex: The maturation of neurotransmitter systems and their interactions. In Charles A. Nelson & Monica Luciana (Eds.), *Handbook of developmental cognitive neuroscience* (pp. 79–92). Cambridge, MA: MIT Press.

Bengtson, Vern L. (1975). Generation and family effects in value socialization. *American Sociological Review, 40,* 358–371.

Benjamin, Georges C. (2004). The solution is injury prevention. *American Journal of Public Health, 94,* 521.

Benjamin, Roger. (2003). *The coming transformation of the American university.* New York: Council for Aid to Education.

Benson, Lee. (2005, June 8). *Little League for 3 years: No tantrums.* Deseret Morning News. Retrieved September 10, 2005, from the World Wide Web: http://deseretnews.com/dn/view/0,1249,600139765,00.html

Benson, Peter L. (2003). Developmental assets and asset-building community: Conceptual and empirical foundations. In Richard M. Lerner & Peter L. Benson (Eds.), *Developmental assets and asset-building communities: Implications for research, policy, and practice* (pp. 19–43). New York: Kluwer/Plenum.

Bentley, Gillian R., & Mascie-Taylor, C. G. Nicholas. (2000). Introduction. In Gillian R. Bentley & C. G. Nicholas Mascie-Taylor (Eds.), *Infertility in the modern world: Present and future prospects* (pp. 1–13). Cambridge, England: Cambridge University Press.

Benton, David. (2004). Role of parents in the determination of the food preferences of children and the development of obesity. *International Journal of Obesity & Related Metabolic Disorders, 28,* 858–869.

Beppu, Satoshi. (2005). Social cognitive development of autistic children: Attachment relationships and understanding the existence of minds of others. In David W. Shwalb, Jun Nakazawa, & Barbara J. Shwalb (Eds.), *Applied developmental psychology: Theory, practice, and research from Japan* (pp. 199–221). Greenwich, CT: Information Age.

Berg, Sandra J., & Wynne-Edwards, Katherine E. (2002). Salivary hormone concentrations in mothers and fathers becoming parents are not correlated. *Hormones & Behavior, 42,* 424–436.

Berger, Joel, Swenson, Jon E., & Persson, Inga-Lill. (2001). Recolonizing carnivores and naïve prey: Conservation lessons from Pleistocene extinctions. *Science, 291,* 1036–1039.

Bering, Jesse M., & Bjorklund, David F. (2004). The natural emergence of reasoning about the afterlife as a developmental regularity. *Developmental Psychology, 40,* 217–233.

Bernal, Guillermo, Trimble, Joseph E., Burlew, Ann Kathleen, & Leong, Frederick T. (Eds.). (2003). *Racial and ethnic minority psychology series: Vol. 4. Handbook of racial & ethnic minority psychology.* Thousand Oaks, CA: Sage.

Berndt, Thomas J. (1999). Friends' influence on children's adjustment to school. In W. Andrew Collins & Brett Laursen (Eds.), *Relationships as developmental contexts* (pp. 85–107). Mahwah, NJ: Erlbaum.

Berndt, Thomas J., & Murphy, Lonna M. (2002). Influences of friends and friendships: Myths, truths, and research recommendations. In Robert V. Kail (Ed.), *Advances in child development and behavior* (Vol. 30, pp. 275–310). San Diego, CA: Academic Press.

Berninger, Virginia Wise, & Richards, Todd L. (2002). *Brain literacy for educators and psychologists.* Amsterdam, The Netherlands: Academic Press.

Berrick, Jill Duerr. (1998). When children cannot remain home: Foster family care and kinship care. *The Future of Children: Protecting Children from Abuse and Neglect, 8*(1), 72–87.

Bertenthal, Bennett I., & Clifton, Rachel K. (1998). Perception and action. In William Damon (Series Ed.) & Deanna Kuhn & Robert S. Siegler (Vol. Eds.), *Handbook of child psychology: Vol. 2. Cognition, perception, and language* (5th ed., pp. 51–102). New York: Wiley.

Best, Deborah L., & Williams, John E. (2001). Gender and culture. In David Matsumoto (Ed.), *The handbook of culture and psychology* (pp. 195–219). London: Oxford University Press.

Betts, Julian R. (1995). Does school quality matter? Evidence from the National Longitudinal Survey of Youth. *Review of Economics & Statistics, 77,* 231–250.

Bialystok, Ellen. (2001). *Bilingualism in development: Language, literacy, and cognition.* New York: Cambridge University Press.

Bigelow, Ann E. (1999). Infants' sensitivity to imperfect contingency in social interaction. In Philippe Rochat (Ed.), *Early social cognition: Understanding others in the first months of life* (pp. 137–154). Mahwah, NJ: Erlbaum.

Bijou, Sidney William, & Baer, Donald Merle. (1978). *Behavior analysis of child development.* Englewood Cliffs, NJ: Prentice-Hall.

Birch, Susan A. J., & Bloom, Paul. (2003). Children are cursed: An asymmetric bias in mental-state attribution. *Psychological Science, 14,* 283–286.

Biro, Frank M., McMahon, Robert P., Striegel-Moore, Ruth, Crawford, Patricia B., Obarzanek, Eva, Morrison, John A., et al. (2001). Impact of timing of pubertal maturation on growth in black and white female adolescents: The National Heart, Lung, and Blood Institute Growth and Health Study. *Journal of Pediatrics, 138,* 636–643.

Bissex, Glenda L. (1980). *Gnys at wrk: A child learns to write and read.* Cambridge, MA: Harvard University Press.

Bjarnason, Thoroddur, Sigurdardottir, Thordis J., & Thorlindsson, Thorolfur. (1999). Human agency, capable guardians, and structural constraints: A lifestyle approach to the study of violent victimization. *Journal of Youth & Adolescence, 28,* 105–119.

Black, Stephen. (2005, February 3). *Visual cliff ethics. Message posted to PSYCHTEACHER discussion list, archived at http://list.kennesaw.edu/archives/psychteacher.html.*

Blackburn, Susan Tucker. (2003). *Maternal, fetal & neonatal physiology: A clinical perspective* (2nd ed.). St. Louis, MO: Saunders.

Blair, Peter S., & Ball, Helen L. (2004). The prevalence and characteristics associated with parent-infant bed-sharing in England. *Archives of Disease in Childhood, 89,* 1106–1110.

Blake, Susan M., Simkin, Linda, Ledsky, Rebecca, Perkins, Cheryl, & Calabrese, Joseph M. (2001). Effects of a parent-child communications intervention on young adolescents' risk for early onset of sexual intercourse. *Family Planning Perspectives, 33,* 52–61.

Blanchard-Fields, Fredda. (1999). Social schemacity and causal attributions. In Thomas M. Hess & Fredda Blanchard-Fields (Eds.), *Social cognition and aging* (pp. 219–236). San Diego, CA: Academic Press.

Blatchford, Peter. (2003). *The class size debate: Is small better?* Maidenhead, Berkshire, England: Open University.

Block, Lauren G., Morwitz, Vicki G., Putsis, William P., Jr., & Sen, Subrata K. (2002). Assessing the impact of antidrug advertising on adolescent drug consumption: Results from a behavioral economic model. *American Journal of Public Health, 92,* 1346–1351.

Bloom, Floyd E., Nelson, Charles A., & Lazerson, Arlyne. (2001). *Brain, mind, and behavior* (3rd ed.). New York: Worth.

Bloom, Lois. (1993). *The transition from infancy to language: Acquiring the power of expression.* New York: Cambridge University Press.

Bloom, Lois. (1998). Language acquisition in its developmental context. In William Damon (Series Ed.) & Deanna Kuhn & Robert S. Siegler (Vol. Eds.), *Handbook of child psychology: Vol. 2. Cognition, perception, and language* (5th ed., pp. 309–370). New York: Wiley.

Bloom, Lois. (2000). Pushing the limits on theories of word learning. *Monographs of the Society for Research in Child Development, 65*(3, Serial No. 262), 124–135.

Bloom, Lois, & Tinker, Erin. (2001). The intentionality model and language acquisition: Engagement, effort, and the essential tension in development. *Monographs of the Society for Research in Child Development, 66*(4, Serial No. 267).

Blum, Deborah. (2002). *Love at Goon Park: Harry Harlow and the science of affection.* Cambridge, MA: Perseus.

Blum, Robert Wm., & Nelson-Mmari, Kristin. (2004). Adolescent health from an international perspective. In Richard M. Lerner & Laurence D. Steinberg (Eds.), *Handbook of adolescent psychology* (2nd ed., pp. 553–586). Hoboken, NJ: Wiley.

Blum-Kulka, Shoshana, & Snow, Catherine E. (Eds.). (2002). *Talking to adults.* Mahwah, NJ: Erlbaum.

Blurton-Jones, Nicholas G. (1976). Rough-and-tumble play among nursery school children. In Jerome S. Bruner, Alison Jolly, & Kathy Sylva (Eds.), *Play: Its role in development and evolution* (pp. 352–363). New York: Basic Books.

Boaler, Jo. (2002). *Experiencing school mathematics: Traditional and reform approaches to teaching and their impact on student learning* (Rev. ed.). Mahwah, NJ: Erlbaum.

Bogin, Barry. (1996). Human growth and development from an evolutionary perspective. In C. Jeya K. Henry & Stanley J. Ulijaszek (Eds.), *Long-term consequences of early environment: Growth, development, and the lifespan developmental perspective* (pp. 7–24). Cambridge, UK: Cambridge University Press.

Bolger, Kerry E., & Patterson, Charlotte J. (2003). Sequelae of child maltreatment: Vulnerability and resilience. In Suniya S. Luthar (Ed.), *Resilience and vulnerability: Adaptation in the context of childhood adversities* (pp. 156–181). New York: Cambridge University Press.

Bolger, Kerry E., Patterson, Charlotte J., & Kupersmidt, Janis B. (1998). Peer relationships and self-esteem among children who have been maltreated. *Child Development, 69,* 1171–1197.

Bonanno, George A., Papa, Anthony, Lalande, Kathleen, Westphal, Maren, & Coifman, Karin. (2004). The importance of being flexible: The ability to both enhance and suppress emotional expression predicts long-term adjustment. *Psychological Science, 15,* 482–487.

Bonner, Barbara L., Crow, Sheila M., & Logue, Mary Beth. (1999). Fatal child neglect. In Howard Dubowitz (Ed.), *Neglected children: Research, practice, and policy* (pp. 156–173). Thousand Oaks, CA: Sage.

Books, Sue. (2004). *Poverty and schooling in the U.S.: Contexts and consequences.* Mahwah, NJ: Erlbaum.

Boom, Jan, Brugman, Daniel, & van der Heijden, Peter G. M. (2001). Hierarchical structure of moral stages assessed by a sorting task. *Child Development, 72,* 535–548.

Boonstra, Heather. (2000). Promoting contraceptive use and choice: France's approach to teen pregnancy and abortion. *The Guttmacher Report on Public Policy, 3*(3), 3–4.

Booth, Alan, & Amato, Paul R. (2001). Parental predivorce relations and offspring postdivorce well-being. *Journal of Marriage & the Family, 63,* 197–212.

Booth, Tony, & Ainscow, Mel (Eds.). (1998). *From them to us: An international study of inclusion in education.* New York: Routledge.

Borgaonkar, Digamber S. (1997). *Chromosomal variation in man: A catalog of chromosomal variants and anomalies* (8th ed.). New York: Wiley-Liss.

Borkowski, John G., Bisconti, Toni, Weed, Keri, Willard, Christine, Keogh, Deborah A., & Whitman, Thomas L. (2002). The adolescent as parent: Influences on children's intellectual, academic, and socioemotional development. In John G. Borkowski, Sharon Landesman Ramey, & Marie Bristol-Power (Eds.), *Parenting and the child's world: Influences on academic, intellectual, and social-emotional development* (pp. 161–184). Mahwah, NJ: Erlbaum.

Borland, Moira. (1998). *Middle childhood: The perspectives of children and parents.* London: Jessica Kingsley.

Bornstein, Marc H. (2002). Parenting infants. In Marc H. Bornstein (Ed.), *Handbook of parenting: Vol. 1. Children and parenting* (2nd ed., pp. 3–43). Mahwah, NJ: Erlbaum.

Bornstein, Marc H., & Cote, Linda R. (2004). Mothers' parenting cognitions in cultures of origin, acculturating cultures, and cultures of destination. *Child Development, 75,* 221–235.

Bornstein, Marc H., Cote, Linda R., Maital, Sharone, Painter, Kathleen, Park, Sung-Yun, Pascual, Liliana, et al. (2004). Cross-linguistic analysis of vocabulary in young children: Spanish, Dutch, French, Hebrew, Italian, Korean, and American English. *Child Development, 75,* 1115–1139.

Bornstein, Marc H., Haynes, O. Maurice, Azuma, Hiroshi, Galperin, Celia, Maital, Sharone, Ogino, Misako, et al. (1998). A cross-national study of self-evaluations and attributions in parenting: Argentina, Belgium, France, Israel, Italy, Japan, and the United States. *Developmental Psychology, 34,* 662–676.

Boulton, Michael, & Smith, Peter K. (1989). Issues in the study of children's rough-and-tumble play. In Marianne N. Bloch & Anthony D. Pellegrini (Eds.), *The ecological context of children's play* (pp. 57–83). Norwood, NJ: Ablex.

Bowerman, Melissa, & Levinson, Stephen C. (2001). Introduction. In Melissa Bowerman & Stephen C. Levinson (Eds.), *Language acquisition and conceptual development* (pp. 1–18). Cambridge, UK: Cambridge University Press.

Bowlby, John. (1969). *Attachment and loss: Vol. 1. Attachment.* New York: Basic Books.

Bowlby, John. (1973). *Attachment and loss: Vol. 2. Separation: Anxiety and anger.* New York: Basic Books.

Bowlby, John. (1988). *A secure base: Clinical applications of attachment theory.* London: Routledge.

Bozik, Mary. (2002). The college student as learner: Insight gained through metaphor analysis. *College Student Journal, 36,* 142–151.

Bradley, Robert H., & Corwyn, Robert F. (2005). Productive activity and the prevention of behavior problems. *Developmental Psychology, 41,* 89–98.

Bradley, Robert H., Corwyn, Robert F., McAdoo, Harriette Pipes, & Garcia Coll, Cynthia. (2001). The home environments of children in the United States Part I: Variations by age, ethnicity, and poverty status. *Child Development, 72,* 1844–1867.

Brandtstädter, Jochen. (1998). Action perspectives on human development. In William Damon (Series Ed.) & Richard M. Lerner (Vol. Ed.), *Handbook of child psychology: Vol. 1. Theoretical models of human development* (5th ed., pp. 807–864). New York: Wiley.

Bransford, John, Brown, Ann L., & Cocking, Rodney R. (Eds.). (1999). *How people learn: Brain, mind, experience, and school.* Washington, DC: National Academy Press.

Braver, Sanford L., Hipke, Kathleen N., Ellman, Ira M., & Sandler, Irwin N. (2004). Strengths-building public policy for children of divorce. In Kenneth I. Maton, Cynthia J. Schellenbach, Bonnie J. Leadbeater, & Andrea L. Solarz (Eds.), *Investing in children, youth, families, and communities: Strengths-based research and policy* (pp. 53–72). Washington, DC: American Psychological Association.

Breggin, Peter R., & Baughman, Fred A., Jr. (2001). Questioning the treatment for ADHD [Letter to the editor]. *Science, 291,* 595.

Brendgen, Mara, Vitaro, Frank, Bukowski, William M., Doyle, Anna Beth, & Markiewicz, Dorothy. (2001).

Developmental profiles of peer social preference over the course of elementary school: Associations with trajectories of externalizing and internalizing behavior. *Developmental Psychology, 37,* 308–320.

Brennan, Robert T., Kim, Jimmy, Wenz-Gross, Melodie, & Siperstein, Gary N. (2001). The relative equitability of high-stakes testing versus teacher-assigned grades: An analysis of the Massachusetts Comprehensive Assessment System (MCAS). *Harvard Educational Review, 71,* 173–216.

Brenner, Ruth A., Trumble, Ann C., Smith, Gordon S., Kessler, Eileen P., & Overpeck, Mary D. (2001). Where children drown, United States, 1995. *Pediatrics, 108,* 85–89.

Bressler, Steven L. (2002). Understanding cognition through large-scale cortical networks. *Current Directions in Psychological Science, 11,* 58–61.

Bretherton, Inge, & Munholland, Kristine A. (1999). Internal working models in attachment relationships: A construct revisited. In Jude Cassidy & Phillip R. Shaver (Eds.), *Handbook of attachment: Theory, research, and clinical applications* (pp. 89–111). New York: Guilford Press.

Briley, Mike, & Sulser, Fridolin (Eds.). (2001). *Molecular genetics of mental disorders: The place of molecular genetics in basic mechanisms and clinical applications in mental disorders.* London: Martin Dunitz.

Brint, Steven. (2003). Few remaining dreams: Community colleges since 1985. *The Annals of the American Academy of Political and Social Science, 586,* 16–37.

Brisk, Maria. (1998). *Bilingual education: From compensatory to quality schooling.* Mahwah, NJ: Erlbaum.

Brody, Gene H. (2004). Siblings' direct and indirect contributions to child development. *Current Directions in Psychological Science, 13,* 124–126.

Bronfenbrenner, Urie. (1977). Toward an experimental ecology of human development. *American Psychologist, 32,* 513–531.

Bronfenbrenner, Urie, & Morris, Pamela A. (1998). The ecology of developmental processes. In William Damon (Series Ed.) & Richard M. Lerner (Vol. Ed.), *Handbook of child psychology: Vol. 1. Theoretical models of human development* (5th ed., pp. 993–1028). New York: Wiley.

Brooks-Gunn, Jeanne. (1991). Maturational timing variations in adolescent girls, antecedents of. In Richard M. Lerner, Anne C. Petersen, & Jeanne Brooks-Gunn (Eds.), *Encyclopedia of adolescence* (pp. 609–618). New York: Garland.

Brooks-Gunn, Jeanne, Han, Wen-Jui, & Waldfogel, Jane. (2002). Maternal employment and child cognitive outcomes in the first three years of life: The NICHD study of early child care. *Child Development, 73,* 1052–1072.

Brown, Bernard. (1999). Optimizing expression of the common human genome for child development. *Current Directions in Psychological Science, 8,* 37–41.

Brown, B. Bradford. (2004). Adolescents' relationships with peers. In Richard M. Lerner & Laurence D. Steinberg (Eds.), *Handbook of adolescent psychology* (2nd ed., pp. 363–394). Hoboken, NJ: Wiley.

Brown, B. Bradford, & Larson, Reed W. (2002). The kaleidoscope of adolescence: Experiences of the world's youth at the beginning of the 21st century. In B. Bradford Brown, Reed W. Larson, & T. S. Saraswathi (Eds.), *The world's youth: Adolescence in eight regions of the globe* (pp. 1–20). New York: Cambridge University Press.

Brown, Christia Spears, & Bigler, Rebecca S. (2005). Children's perceptions of discrimination: A developmental model. *Child Development, 76,* 533–553.

Brown, Kathryn. (2003). The medication merry-go-round. *Science, 299,* 1646–1649.

Brown, Nigel A. (1997). Chemical teratogens: Hazards, tools and clues. In Peter Thorogood (Ed.), *Embryos, genes, and birth defects* (pp. 69–88). New York: Wiley.

Bruck, Maggie, & Ceci, Stephen. (2004). Forensic developmental psychology. *Current Directions in Psychological Science, 13,* 229–232.

Bryan, Elizabeth M. (1999). The death of a twin. In Audrey C. Sandbank (Ed.), *Twin and triplet psychology: A professional guide to working with multiples* (pp. 186–200). New York: Routledge.

Buckner, John C., Bassuk, Ellen L., Weinreb, Linda F., & Brooks, Margaret G. (1999). Homelessness and its relation to the mental health and behavior of low-income school-age children. *Developmental Psychology, 35,* 246–257.

Buehler, Cheryl, & Gerard, Jean M. (2002). Marital conflict, ineffective parenting, and children's and adolescents' maladjustment. *Journal of Marriage & Family, 64,* 78–92.

Buekens, Pierre, Curtis, Siân, & Alayón, Silvia. (2003). Demographic and health surveys: Caesarean section rates in sub-Saharan Africa. *British Medical Journal, 326,* 136.

Bugental, Daphne Blunt, & Happaney, Keith. (2004). Predicting infant maltreatment in low-income families: The interactive effects of maternal attributions and child status at birth. *Developmental Psychology, 40,* 234–243.

Bukowski, William M. (2001). Friendship and the worlds of childhood. In Douglas W. Nangle & Cynthia A. Erdley (Eds.), *New directions for child and adolescent development: No. 91. The role of friendship in psychological adjustment* (pp. 93–105). San Francisco: Jossey-Bass.

Bukowski, William M., Sippola, Lorrie K., & Newcomb, Andrew F. (2000). Variations in patterns of attraction of same- and other-sex peers during early adolescence. *Developmental Psychology, 36,* 147–154.

Bumpass, Larry, & Lu, Hsien-Hen. (2000). Trends in cohabitation and implications for children's family contexts in the United States. *Population Studies, 54,* 29–41.

Burlingham, Dorothy T., & Freud, Anna. (1942). *Young children in war-time: A year's work in a residential war nursery.* London: Allen & Unwin.

Burniat, Walter, Cole, Tim J., Lissau, Inge, & Poskitt, Elizabeth M. E. (Eds.). (2002). *Child and adolescent obesity: Causes and consequences, prevention and management.* New York: Cambridge University Press.

Burton, Sarah, & Mitchell, Peter. (2003). Judging who knows best about yourself: Developmental change in citing the self across middle childhood. *Child Development, 74,* 426–443.

Buschman, Nina A., Foster, G., & Vickers, Pauline. (2001). Adolescent girls and their babies: Achieving optimal birthweight. Gestational weight gain and pregnancy outcome in terms of gestation at delivery and infant birth weight: A comparison between adolescents under 16 and adult women. *Child: Care, Health & Development, 27,* 163–171.

Buss, David M., Haselton, Martie G., Shackelford, Todd K., Bleske, April L., &

Wakefield, Jerome C. (1998). Adaptations, exaptations, and spandrels. *American Psychologist, 53,* 533–548.

Busse, William W., & Lemanske, Robert F. (Eds.). (2005). *Lung biology in health and disease: Vol. 195. Asthma prevention.* Boca Raton, FL: Taylor & Francis.

Butler, Samantha C., Berthier, Neil E., & Clifton, Rachel K. (2002). Two-year-olds' search strategies and visual tracking in a hidden displacement task. *Developmental Psychology, 38,* 581–590.

Byard, Roger W. (2004). *Sudden death in infancy, childhood, and adolescence* (2nd ed.). Cambridge, England: Cambridge University Press.

Bybee, Jane (Ed.). (1998). *Guilt and children.* San Diego, CA: Academic Press.

Cairns, Robert B., & Cairns, Beverley D. (1994). *Lifelines and risks: Pathways of youth in our time.* New York: Cambridge University Press.

Cairns, Robert B., & Cairns, Beverley D. (2001). Aggression and attachment: The folly of separatism. In Arthur C. Bohart & Deborah J. Stipek (Eds.), *Constructive & destructive behavior: Implications for family, school, & society* (pp. 21–47). Washington, DC: American Psychological Association.

Callaghan, Tara, Rochat, Philippe, Lillard, Angeline, Claux, Mary Louise, Odden, Hal, Itakura, Shoji, et al. (2005). Synchrony in the onset of mental-state reasoning: Evidence from five cultures. *Psychological Science, 16,* 378–384.

Callaghan, Tara C., Rochat, Philippe, MacGillivray, Tanya, & MacLellan, Crystal. (2004). Modeling referential actions in 6- to 18-month-old infants: A precursor to symbolic understanding. *Child Development, 75,* 1733–1744.

Calvert, Karin. (2003). Patterns of childrearing in America. In Willem Koops & Michael Zuckerman (Eds.), *Beyond the century of the child: Cultural history and developmental psychology* (pp. 62–81). Philadelphia: University of Pennsylvania Press.

Cameron, Judy, & Pierce, W. David. (2002). *Rewards and intrinsic motivation: Resolving the controversy.* Westport, CT: Bergin & Garvey.

Cameron, Judy L. (2001). Effects of sex hormones on brain development. In Charles A. Nelson & Monica Luciana (Eds.), *Handbook of developmental cognitive neuroscience* (pp. 59–78). Cambridge, MA: MIT Press.

Cameron, Judy L. (2004). Interrelationships between hormones, behavior, and affect during adolescence: Understanding hormonal, physical, and brain changes occurring in association with pubertal activation of the reproductive axis. Introduction to Part III. *Annals of the New York Academy of Sciences, 1021,* 110–123.

Camilli, Gregory, Vargas, Sadako, & Yurecko, Michele. (2003). Teaching children to read: The fragile link between science and federal education policy. *Education Policy Analysis Archives, 11,* 1–52.

Campaign for Fiscal Equity v. State of New York, 719 N.Y.S.2d 475 (2001).

Campbell, Frances A., Pungello, Elizabeth P., Miller-Johnson, Shari, Burchinal, Margaret, & Ramey, Craig T. (2001). The development of cognitive and academic abilities: Growth curves from an early childhood educational experiment. *Developmental Psychology, 37,* 231–242.

Campbell, Thomas F., Dollaghan, Christine A., Rockette, Howard E., Paradise, Jack L., Feldman, Heidi M., Shriberg, Lawrence D., et al. (2003). Risk factors for speech delay of unknown origin in 3-year-old children. *Child Development, 74,* 346–357.

Campos, Joseph J., Frankel, Carl B., & Camras, Linda. (2004). On the nature of emotion regulation. *Child Development, 75,* 377–394.

Campos, Joseph J., Hiatt, Susan, Ramsay, Douglas, Henderson, Charlotte, & Svejda, Marilyn. (1978). The emergence of fear on the visual cliff. In Michael Lewis & Leonard A. Rosenblum (Eds.), *Genesis of behavior: Vol. 1. The development of affect* (pp. 149–182). New York: Plenum Press.

Campos, Paul F. (2004). *The obesity myth: Why America's obsession with weight is hazardous to your health.* New York: Gotham Books.

Canadian Psychological Association. (2000). *Canadian code of ethics for psychologists* (3rd ed.). Ottawa, Ontario, Canada: Author.

Cannon, Tyrone D., Rosso, Isabelle M., Bearden, Carrie E., Sanchez, Laura E., & Hadley, Trevor. (1999). A prospective cohort study of neurodevelopmental processes in the genesis and epigenesis of schizophrenia. *Development & Psychopathology, 11,* 467–485.

Caprara, Gian Vittorio, Barbaranelli, Claudio, & Pastorelli, Concetta. (2001). Prosocial behavior and aggression in childhood and pre-adolescence. In Arthur C. Bohart & Deborah J. Stipek (Eds.), *Constructive & destructive behavior: Implications for family, school, & society* (pp. 187–203). Washington, DC: American Psychological Association.

Caretta, Carla Mucignat, Caretta, Antonio, & Cavaggioni, Andrea. (1995). Pheromonally accelerated puberty is enhanced by previous experience of the same stimulus. *Physiology & Behavior, 57,* 901–903.

Carey, Susan. (1985). *Conceptual change in childhood.* Cambridge, MA: MIT Press.

Carlson, Marcia J., & Corcoran, Mary E. (2001). Family structure and children's behavioral and cognitive outcomes. *Journal of Marriage & the Family, 63,* 779–792.

Carlson, Stephanie M. (2003). Executive function in context: Development, measurement, theory and experience. *Monographs of the Society for Research in Child Development, 68*(3, Serial No. 274), 138–151.

Carpenter, Siri. (1999, August 14). Modern hygiene's dirty tricks: The clean life may throw off a delicate balance in the immune system. *Science News, 156,* 108–110.

Carskadon, Mary A. (2002a). Factors influencing sleep patterns of adolescents. In Mary A. Carskadon (Ed.), *Adolescent sleep patterns: Biological, social, and psychological influences* (pp. 4–26). New York: Cambridge University Press.

Carskadon, Mary A. (2002b). Risks of driving while sleepy in adolescents and young adults. In Mary A. Carskadon (Ed.), *Adolescent sleep patterns: Biological, social, and psychological influences* (pp. 148–158). New York: Cambridge University Press.

Carskadon, Mary A., Acebo, Christine, & Jenni, Oskar G. (2004). Regulation of adolescent sleep: Implications for behavior. *Annals of the New York Academy of Sciences, 1021,* 276–291.

Case, Robbie. (1998). The development of conceptual structures. In William Damon (Series Ed.) & Deanna Kuhn & Robert S. Siegler (Vol. Eds.), *Handbook of child psychology: Vol. 2. Cognition, perception, and language* (5th ed., pp. 745–800). New York: Wiley.

Casey, Betty Jo. (2001). Disruption of inhibitory control in developmental disorders: A mechanistic model of implicated frontostriatal circuitry. In James L. McClelland & Robert S. Siegler (Eds.), *Mechanisms of cognitive development: Behavioral and neural perspectives* (pp. 327–349). Mahwah, NJ: Erlbaum.

Caspi, Avshalom, McClay, Joseph, Moffitt, Terrie, Mill, Jonathan, Martin, Judy, Craig, Ian W., et al. (2002). Role of genotype in the cycle of violence in maltreated children. *Science, 297*, 851–854.

Caspi, Avshalom, Moffitt, Terrie E., Morgan, Julia, Rutter, Michael, Taylor, Alan, Arseneault, Louise, et al. (2004). Maternal expressed emotion predicts children's antisocial behavior problems: Using monozygotic-twin differences to identify environmental effects on behavioral development. *Developmental Psychology, 40*, 149–161.

Caspi, Avshalom, Sugden, Karen, Moffitt, Terrie E., Taylor, Alan, Craig, Ian W., Harrington, HonaLee, et al. (2003). Influence of life stress on depression: Moderation by a polymorphism in the 5-HTT gene. *Science, 301*, 386–389.

Cassidy, Jude, & Shaver, Phillip R. (Eds.). (1999). *Handbook of attachment: Theory, research, and clinical applications.* New York: Guilford Press.

Caughy, Margaret O'Brien, DiPietro, Janet A., & Strobino, Donna M. (1994). Day-care participation as a protective factor in the cognitive development of low-income children. *Child Development, 65*, 457–471.

Cavanaugh, Sean. (2005, January 5). Poor math scores on world stage trouble U.S. *Education Week, 25*, 1, 18.

Cedergren, Marie I. (2004). Maternal morbid obesity and the risk of adverse pregnancy outcome. *Obstetrics & Gynecology, 103*, 219–224.

Center on Education Policy. (2005). *From the capital to the classroom: Year 3 of the No Child Left Behind Act.* Washington, DC: Author.

Cepeda, Nicholas J., Kramer, Arthur F., & Gonzalez de Sather, Jessica C. M. (2001). Changes in executive control across the life span: Examination of task-switching performance. *Developmental Psychology, 37*, 715–730.

Chamberlain, Patricia, Fisher, Philip A., & Moore, Kevin. (2002). Multidimensional treatment foster care: Applications of the OSLC intervention model to high-risk youth and their families. In John B. Reid, Gerald R. Patterson, & James Snyder (Eds.), *Antisocial behavior in children and adolescents: A developmental analysis and model for intervention* (pp. 203–218). Washington, DC: American Psychological Association.

Chandler, Michael J., Lalonde, Christopher E., Sokol, Bryan W., & Hallett, Darcy. (2003). Personal persistence, identity development, and suicide: A study of Native and non-Native North American adolescents. *Monographs of the Society for Research in Child Development, 68*(2, Serial No. 273), vii-130.

Chao, Ruth K. (2001). Extending research on the consequences of parenting style for Chinese Americans and European Americans. *Child Development, 72*, 1832–1843.

Chassin, Laurie, Hussong, Andrea, Barrera, Manuel, Jr., Molina, Brooke S. G., Trim, Ryan, & Ritter, Jennifer. (2004). Adolescent substance use. In Richard M. Lerner & Laurence D. Steinberg (Eds.), *Handbook of adolescent psychology* (2nd ed., pp. 665–696). Hoboken, NJ: Wiley.

Chen, Xinyin, Cen, Guozhen, Li, Dan, & He, Yunfeng. (2005). Social functioning and adjustment in Chinese children: The imprint of historical time. *Child Development, 76*, 182–195.

Chen, Xinyin, Rubin, Kenneth H., & Sun, Yuerong. (1992). Social reputation and peer relationships in Chinese and Canadian children: A cross-cultural study. *Child Development, 63*, 1336–1343.

Chess, Stella, Thomas, Alexander, & Birch, Herbert G. (1965). *Your child is a person: A psychological approach to parenthood without guilt.* Oxford, England: Viking Press.

Chikkatur, Anita. (1997). A shortcut to independence. In Youth Communication, Andrea Estepa, & Philip Kay (Eds.), *Starting with "I": Personal essays by teenagers* (pp. 12–16). New York: Persea Books.

Chisholm, Kim. (1998). A three year follow-up of attachment and indiscriminate friendliness in children adopted from Romanian orphanages. *Child Development, 69*, 1092–1106.

Chomsky, Noam. (1968). *Language and mind.* New York: Harcourt Brace & World.

Chomsky, Noam. (1980). *Rules and representations.* New York: Columbia University Press.

Chow, Gregory E., & Yancey, Michael K. (2001). Labor and delivery: Normal and abnormal. In Frank W. Ling & W. Patrick Duff (Eds.), *Obstetrics and gynecology: Principles for practice* (pp. 423–458). New York: McGraw-Hill.

Christenson, Sandra L., & Thurlow, Martha L. (2004). School dropouts: Prevention considerations, interventions, and challenges. *Current Directions in Psychological Science, 13*, 36–39.

Christoffel, Tom, & Gallagher, Susan Scavo. (1999). *Injury prevention and public health: Practical knowledge, skills, and strategies.* Gaithersburg, MD: Aspen.

Cianciolo, Anna T., & Sternberg, Robert J. (2004). *Intelligence: A brief history.* Malden, MA: Blackwell.

Cicchetti, Dante, & Barnett, Douglas. (1991). Attachment organization in maltreated preschoolers. *Development & Psychopathology, 3*, 397–411.

Cicchetti, Dante, & Sroufe, L. Alan. (2000). The past as prologue to the future: The times, they've been a-changin'. *Development & Psychopathology, 12*, 255–264.

Cicchetti, Dante, & Toth, Sheree L. (1998). Perspectives on research and practice in developmental psychopathology. In William Damon (Series Ed.) & Irving E. Sigel & K. Ann Renninger (Vol. Eds.), *Handbook of child psychology: Vol. 4. Child psychology in practice* (5th ed., pp. 479–483). New York: Wiley.

Cicchetti, Dante, & Walker, Elaine F. (2001). Stress and development: Biological and psychological consequences. *Development and Psychopathology, 13*, 413–418.

Cillessen, Antonius H. N., & Mayeux, Lara. (2004a). From censure to reinforcement: Developmental changes in the association between aggression and social status. *Child Development, 75*, 147–163.

Cillessen, Antonius H. N., & Mayeux, Lara. (2004b). Sociometric status and peer group behavior: Previous findings and current directions. In Janis B. Kupersmidt & Kenneth A. Dodge (Eds.), *Children's peer relations: From development to intervention* (pp. 3–20). Washington, DC: American Psychological Association.

Clark, Eve Vivienne. (1995). Later lexical development and word formation. In Paul Fletcher & Brian MacWhinney (Eds.), *The handbook of child language* (pp. 393–412). Cambridge, MA: Blackwell.

Clarke, Ann M., & Clarke, Alan D. B. (2003). *Human resilience: A fifty year quest.* London: Jessica Kingsley.

Clarke-Stewart, Alison, & Allhusen, Virginia D. (2005). *What we know about childcare.* Cambridge, MA: Harvard University Press.

Clinchy, Blythe McVicker. (1993). Ways of knowing and ways of being: Epistemological and moral development in undergraduate women. In Andrew Garrod (Ed.), *Approaches to moral development: New research and emerging themes.* New York: Teachers College Press.

Cobb, Paul. (2000). Conducting teaching experiments in collaboration with teachers. In Anthony E. Kelly & Richard A. Lesh (Eds.), *Handbook of research design in mathematics and science education* (pp. 307–334). Mahwah, NJ: Erlbaum.

Cobb, Paul, Wood, Terry, & Yackel, Erna. (1993). Discourse, mathematical thinking, and classroom practice. In Ellice A. Forman, Norris Minick, & C. Addison Stone (Eds.), *Contexts for learning: Sociocultural dynamics in children's development* (pp. 91–119). London: Oxford University Press.

Cohen, Deborah, Spear, Suzanne, Scribner, Richard, Kissinger, Patty, Mason, Karen, & Wildgen, John. (2000). "Broken windows" and the risk of gonorrhea. *American Journal of Public Health, 90,* 230–236.

Cohen, Jon. (2004). HIV/AIDS in China: Poised for takeoff? *Science, 304,* 1430–1432.

Cohen, Laurie L., & Shotland, R. Lance. (1996). Timing of first sexual intercourse in a relationship: Expectations, experiences, and perceptions of others. *Journal of Sex Research, 33,* 291–299.

Cohen, Susan A. (2005). U.S. global AIDS policy and sexually active youth: A high-risk strategy. *The Guttmacher Report on Public Policy, 8,* 4–6.

Cokley, Kevin O. (2003). What do we know about the motivation of African American students? Challenging the "anti-intellectual" myth. *Harvard Educational Review, 73,* 524–558.

Colder, Craig R., Mott, Joshua A., & Berman, Arielle S. (2002). The interactive effects of infant activity level and fear on growth trajectories of early childhood behavior problems. *Development & Psychopathology, 14,* 1–23.

Cole, Michael. (1996). *Cultural psychology: A once and future discipline.* Cambridge, MA: Harvard University Press.

Cole, Pamela M., Zahn-Waxler, Carolyn, Fox, Nathan A., Usher, Barbara A., & Welsh, Jean D. (1996). Individual differences in emotion regulation and behavior problems in preschool children. *Journal of Abnormal Psychology, 105,* 518–529.

Coles, Robert. (1990). *The spiritual life of children.* Boston: Houghton Mifflin.

Coles, Robert. (1997). *The moral intelligence of children: How to raise a moral child.* New York: Random House.

Collins, Michael F. (with Kay, Tess). (2003). *Sport and social exclusion.* London: Routledge.

Collins, W. Andrew, & Laursen, Brett. (2004). Parent-adolescent relationships and influences. In Richard M. Lerner & Laurence D. Steinberg (Eds.), *Handbook of adolescent psychology* (2nd ed., pp. 331–361). Hoboken, NJ: Wiley.

Collins, W. Andrew, Maccoby, Eleanor E., Steinberg, Laurence, Hetherington, E. Mavis, & Bornstein, Marc H. (2000). Contemporary research on parenting: The case for nature and nurture. *American Psychologist, 55,* 218–232.

Compas, Bruce E. (2004). Processes of risk and resilience during adolescence: Linking contexts and individuals. In Richard M. Lerner & Laurence D. Steinberg (Eds.), *Handbook of adolescent psychology* (2nd ed., pp. 263–296). Hoboken, NJ: Wiley.

Compian, Laura, Gowen, L. Kris, & Hayward, Chris. (2004). Peripubertal girls' romantic and platonic involvement with boys: Associations with body image and depression symptoms. *Journal of Research on Adolescence, 14,* 23–47.

Compton, Kristi, Snyder, James, Schrepferman, Lynn, Bank, Lew, & Shortt, Joann Wu. (2003). The contribution of parents and siblings to antisocial and depressive behavior in adolescents: A double jeopardy coercion model. *Development & Psychopathology, 15,* 163–182.

Conger, Rand D., Wallace, Lora Ebert, Sun, Yumei, Simons, Ronald L., McLoyd, Vonnie C., & Brody, Gene H. (2002). Economic pressure in African American families: A replication and extension of the family stress model. *Developmental Psychology, 38,* 179–193.

Conley, Dalton. (2004). *The pecking order: Which siblings succeed and why.* New York: Pantheon Books.

Connolly, Jennifer, Furman, Wyndol, & Konarski, Roman. (2000). The role of peers in the emergence of heterosexual romantic relationships in adolescence. *Child Development, 71,* 1395–1408.

Connor, Daniel F. (2002). *Aggression and antisocial behavior in children and adolescents: Research and treatment.* New York: Guilford Press.

Cook, Thomas D., & Furstenberg, Frank F. (2002). Explaining aspects of the transition to adulthood in Italy, Sweden, Germany, and the United States: A cross-disciplinary, case synthesis approach. *Annals of the American Academy of Political & Social Science, 580,* 257–287.

Correa-Chavez, Maricela, Rogoff, Barbara, & Arauz, Rebeca Mejia. (2005). Cultural patterns in attending to two events at once. *Child Development, 76,* 664–678.

Corsaro, William A., & Molinari, Luisa. (2000). Entering and observing in children's worlds: A reflection on a longitudinal ethnography of early education in Italy. In Pia Monrad Christensen & Allison James (Eds.), *Research with children: Perspectives and practices* (pp. 179–200). London: Falmer Press.

Cosby, Ennis. (1997, January 26). Teaching from the heart. *New York Times,* pp. sec. 4, p. 13.

Costello, Anthony, & Manandhar, Dharma (Eds.). (2000). *Improving newborn infant health in developing countries.* London: Imperial College Press.

Covington, Martin V., & Dray, Elizabeth. (2002). The developmental course of achievement motivation: A need-based approach. In Allan Wigfield & Jacquelynne S. Eccles (Eds.), *Development of achievement motivation* (pp. 33–56). San Diego, CA: Academic Press.

Cox, Maureen V. (1993). *Children's drawings of the human figure.* Hillsdale, NJ: Erlbaum.

Cox, Maureen V. (1997). *Drawings of people by the under-5s.* London: Falmer Press.

Coyle, Karin, Basen-Engquist, Karen, Kirby, Douglas, Parcel, Guy, Banspach, Stephen, Collins, Janet, et al. (2001). Safer choices: Reducing teen pregnancy, HIV, and STDs. *Public Health Reports, 116*(Supplement 1), 82–93.

Crain, William C. (2005). *Theories of development: Concepts and applications* (5th ed.). Upper Saddle River, NJ: Prentice Hall.

Crane, J., Wickens, K., Beasley, R., & Fitzharris, P. (2002). Asthma and allergy: A worldwide problem of meanings and management? *Allergy, 57,* 663–672.

Crick, Nicki R., Casas, Juan F., & Ku, Hyon-Chin. (1999). Relational and physical forms of peer victimization in preschool. *Developmental Psychology, 35,* 376–385.

Criss, Michael M., Pettit, Gregory S., Bates, John E., Dodge, Kenneth A., & Lapp, Amie L. (2002). Family adversity, positive peer relationships, and children's externalizing behavior: A longitudinal perspective on risk and resilience. *Child Development, 73,* 1220–1237.

Crombag, Hans S., & Robinson, Terry E. (2004). Drugs, environment, brain, and behavior. *Current Directions in Psychological Science, 13,* 107–111.

Crosnoe, Robert, & Needham, Belinda. (2004). Holism, contextual variability, and the study of friendships in adolescent development. *Child Development, 75,* 264–279.

Crow, James F. (2003). There's something curious about paternal-age effects. *Science, 301,* 606–607.

Csikszentmihalyi, Mihaly, & Schneider, Barbara. (2000). *Becoming adult: How teenagers prepare for the world of work.* New York: Basic Books.

Cullen, Karen Weber, & Zakeri, Issa. (2004). Fruits, vegetables, milk, and sweetened beverages consumption and access to a la carte/snack bar meals at school. *American Journal of Public Health, 94,* 463–467.

Cummings, E. Mark, & Davies, Patrick. (1994). *Children and marital conflict: The impact of family dispute and resolution.* New York: Guilford Press.

Cummings, E. Mark, Goeke-Morey, Marcie C., & Papp, Lauren M. (2003). Children's responses to everyday marital conflict tactics in the home. *Child Development, 74,* 1918–1929.

Curtis, W. John, & Cicchetti, Dante. (2003). Moving research on resilience into the 21st century: Theoretical and methodological considerations in examining the biological contributors to resilience. *Development & Psychopathology, 15,* 773–810.

Curtis, W. John, & Nelson, Charles A. (2003). Toward building a better brain: Neurobehavioral outcomes, mechanisms, and processes of environmental enrichment. In Suniya S. Luthar (Ed.), *Resilience and vulnerability: Adaptation in the context of childhood adversities* (pp. 463–488). New York: Cambridge University Press.

Cycowicz, Yael M., Friedman, David, & Duff, Martin. (2003). Pictures and their colors: What do children remember? *Journal of Cognitive Neuroscience, 15,* 759–768.

Czech, Christian, Tremp, Günter, & Pradier, Laurent. (2000). Presenilins and Alzheimer's disease: Biological functions and pathogenic mechanisms. *Progress in Neurobiology, 60,* 363–384.

Dahl, Ronald E. (2004). Adolescent brain development: A period of vulnerabilities and opportunities. Keynote address. *Annals of the New York Academy of Sciences, 1021,* 1–22.

Dales, Loring, Hammer, Sandra Jo, & Smith, Natalie J. (2001). Time trends in autism and in MMR immunization coverage in California. *Journal of the American Medical Association, 285,* 1183–1185.

Daley, Tamara C., Whaley, Shannon E., Sigman, Marian D., Espinosa, Michael P., & Neumann, Charlotte. (2003). IQ on the rise: The Flynn effect in rural Kenyan children. *Psychological Science, 14,* 215–219.

Damasio, Antonio R. (2003). *Looking for Spinoza: Joy, sorrow, and the feeling brain.* Orlando, FL: Harcourt.

Danel, Isabella, Berg, Cynthia, Johnson, Christopher H., & Atrash, Hani. (2003). Magnitude of maternal morbidity during labor and delivery: United States, 1993–1997. *American Journal of Public Health, 93,* 631–634.

Danielzik, S., Czerwinski-Mast, M., Langnase, K., Dilba, B., & Muller, M. J. (2004). Parental overweight, socioeconomic status and high birth weight are the major determinants of overweight and obesity in 5–7 year-old children: Baseline data of the Kiel Obesity Prevention Study (KOPS). *International Journal of Obesity, 28,* 1494–1502.

Daniluk, Judith C. (1998). *Women's sexuality across the life span: Challenging myths, creating meanings.* New York: Guilford Press.

Danis, Agnes, Bernard, Jean-Marc, & Leproux, Christine. (2000). Shared picture-book reading: A sequential analysis of adult-child verbal interactions. *British Journal of Developmental Psychology, 18,* 369–388.

Darling, Nancy E., & Steinberg, Laurence. (1997). Community influences on adolescent achievement and deviance. In Jeanne Brooks-Gunn, Greg J. Duncan, & J. Lawrence Aber (Eds.), *Neighborhood poverty: Vol. 2. Policy implications in studying neighborhoods* (pp. 120–131). New York: Russell Sage Foundation.

Daro, Deborah. (2002). Public perception of child sexual abuse: Who is to blame? *Child Abuse & Neglect, 26,* 1131–1133.

Darroch, Jacqueline E., Landry, David J., & Singh, Susheela. (2000). Changing emphases in sexuality education in U.S. public secondary schools, 1988–1999. *Family Planning Perspectives, 32,* 204–211, 265.

Dasen, Pierre R. (2003). Theoretical frameworks in cross-cultural developmental psychology: An attempt at integration. In T. S. Saraswati (Ed.), *Cross-cultural perspectives in human development: Theory, research, and applications* (pp. 128–165). New Delhi, India: Sage.

Dasgupta, Nilanjana, & Greenwald, Anthony G. (2001). On the malleability of automatic attitudes: Combating automatic prejudice with images of admired and disliked individuals. *Journal of Personality & Social Psychology, 81,* 800–814.

Datan, Nancy. (1986). Oedipal conflict, platonic love: Centrifugal forces in intergenerational relations. In Nancy Datan, Anita L. Greene, & Hayne W. Reese (Eds.), *Life-span developmental psychology: Intergenerational relations* (pp. 29–50). Hillsdale, NJ: Erlbaum.

Daulaire, Nils, Leidl, Pat, Mackin, Laurel, Murphy, Colleen, & Stark, Laura. (2002). *Promises to keep: The toll of unintended pregnancies on women's lives in the developing world.* Washington, DC: Global Health Council.

David, Barbara, Grace, Diane, & Ryan, Michelle K. (2004). The gender wars: A self-categorization perspective on the development of gender identity. In Mark Bennett & Fabio Sani (Eds.), *The development of the social self* (pp. 135–157). Hove, East Sussex, England: Psychology Press.

Davies, Patrick T., & Cicchetti, Dante. (2004). Toward an integration of family systems and developmental psychopathology approaches. *Development & Psychopathology, 16,* 477–481.

Davis, Elysia Poggi, Parker, Susan Whitmore, Tottenham, Nim, & Gunnar, Megan R. (2003). Emotion, cognition, and the hypothalamic-pituitary-adrenocortical axis: A developmental perspective. In Michelle De Haan & Mark H. Johnson (Eds.), *The cognitive neuroscience of development* (pp. 181–206). New York: Psychology Press.

Dawson, Geraldine, & Ashman, Sharon B. (2000). On the origins of a vulnerability to depression: The influence of the early social environment on the development of psychobiological systems related to risk for affective disorder. In Charles A. Nelson (Ed.), *The Minnesota symposia on child psychology: Vol. 31. The effects of early adversity on neurobehavioral development* (pp. 245–279). Mahwah, NJ: Erlbaum.

De Bellis, Michael D. (2001). Developmental traumatology: The psychobiological development of maltreated children and its implications for research, treatment, and policy. *Development and Psychopathology, 13,* 539–564.

De Bellis, Michael D., Clark, Duncan B., Beers, Sue R., Soloff, Paul H., Boring, Amy M., Hall, Julie, et al. (2000). Hippocampal volume in adolescent-onset alcohol use disorders. *American Journal of Psychiatry, 157,* 737–744.

de Boysson-Bardies, Bénédicte. (1999). *How language comes to children: From birth to two years.* (Malcolm DeBevoise, Trans.). Cambridge, MA: MIT Press.

De Haan, Michelle, & Johnson, Mark H. (2003). Mechanisms and theories of brain development. In Michelle De Haan & Mark H. Johnson (Eds.), *The cognitive neuroscience of development* (pp. 1–18). Hove, England: Psychology Press.

De Lee, Joseph Bolivar. (1938). *The principles and practice of obstetrics* (7th ed.). Philadelphia: Saunders.

de Mey, Langha, Baartman, Herman E. M., & Schulze, Hans-J. (1999). Ethnic variation and the development of moral judgment of youth in Dutch society. *Youth & Society, 31,* 54–75.

de Roiste, Aine, & Bushnell, Ian W. R. (1996). Tactile stimulation: Short- and long-term benefits for pre-term infants. *British Journal of Developmental Psychology, 14*(Pt. 1), 41–53.

de Villiers, Jill G., & de Villiers, Peter A. (2000). Linguistic determinism and the understanding of false beliefs. In Peter Mitchell & Kevin John Riggs (Eds.), *Children's reasoning and the mind* (pp. 191–228). Hove, England: Psychology Press.

Deater-Deckard, Kirby, Dodge, Kenneth A., Bates, John E., & Pettit, Gregory S. (1998). Multiple risk factors in the development of externalizing behavior problems: Group and individual differences. *Development & Psychopathology, 10,* 469–493.

Deci, Edward L., Koestner, Richard, & Ryan, Richard M. (1999). A meta-analytic review of experiments examining the effects of extrinsic rewards on intrinsic motivation. *Psychological Bulletin, 125,* 627–668.

Deil-Amen, Regina, & Rosenbaum, James E. (2003). The social prerequisites of success: Can college structure reduce the need for social know-how? *The Annals of the American Academy of Political and Social Science, 586,* 120–143.

DeKeseredy, Walter S., & Schwartz, Martin D. (1998). *Women abuse on campus: Results from the Canadian National Survey.* Thousand Oaks, CA: Sage.

Delaney, Carol. (2000). Making babies in a Turkish village. In Judy S. DeLoache & Alma Gottlieb (Eds.), *A world of babies: Imagined childcare guides for seven societies* (pp. 117–144). New York: Cambridge University Press.

Demant, Peter. (2003). Cancer susceptibility in the mouse: Genetics, biology and implications for human cancer. *Nature Reviews Genetics, 4,* 721–734.

Demetriou, Andreas, Christou, Constantinos, Spanoudis, George, & Platsidou, Maria. (2002). The development of mental processing: Efficiency, working memory, and thinking. *Monographs of the Society for Research in Child Development, 67*(1, Serial No. 268).

Denham, Susanne A. (1998). *Emotional development in young children.* New York: Guilford Press.

Denham, Susanne A., Blair, Kimberly A., DeMulder, Elizabeth, Levitas, Jennifer, Sawyer, Katherine, Auerbach-Major, Sharon, et al. (2003). Preschool emotional competence: Pathway to social competence. *Child Development, 74,* 238–256.

Dennis, Tracy A., Cole, Pamela M., Zahn-Waxler, Carolyn, & Mizuta, Ichiro. (2002). Self in context: Autonomy and relatedness in Japanese and U.S. mother-preschooler dyads. *Child Development, 73,* 1803–1817.

Derryberry, Douglas, Reed, Marjorie A., & Pilkenton-Taylor, Carolyn. (2003). Temperament and coping: Advantages of an individual differences perspective. *Development & Psychopathology, 15,* 1049–1066.

Dershewitz, Robert A. (2002, December 28). *Another good year for immunizations.* Journal Watch Gastroenterology. Retrieved June 22, 2005, from the World Wide Web: http://gastroenterology.jwatch.org/cgi/content/full/2002/1228/11

Deveraux, Lara L., & Hammerman, Ann Jackoway. (1998). *Infertility and identity: New strategies for treatment.* San Francisco: Jossey-Bass.

Diamond, Adele. (2000). Close interrelation of motor development and cognitive development and of the cerebellum and prefrontal cortex. *Child Development, 71,* 44–56.

Diamond, Adele. (2002). A model system for studying the role of dopamine in prefrontal cortex during early development in humans. In Mark H. Johnson, Yuko Munakata, & Rick O. Gilmore (Eds.), *Brain development and cognition: A reader* (2nd ed., pp. 441–493). Malden, MA: Blackwell.

Diamond, Adele, & Kirkham, Natasha. (2005). Not quite as grown-up as we like to think: Parallels between cognition in childhood and adulthood. *Psychological Science, 16,* 291–297.

Diamond, David M., Dunwiddie, Thomas V., & Rose, G. M. (1988). Characteristics of hippocampal primed burst potentiation in vitro and in the awake rat. *Journal of Neuroscience, 8,* 4079–4088.

Dickson, Nigel, Paul, Charlotte, Herbison, Peter, & Silva, Phil. (1998). First sexual intercourse: Age, coercion, and later regrets reported by a birth cohort. *British Medical Journal, 316,* 29–33.

Diederich, Paul B. (1973). *Research 1960–1970 on methods and materials in reading, II.* Princeton, NJ: Educational Testing Service. (ERIC Document Reproduction Service No. ED072115)

Diekstra, René F. W. (1995). Depression and suicidal behaviors in adolescence: Sociocultural and time trends. In Michael Rutter (Ed.), *Psychosocial disturbances in young people: Challenges for prevention* (pp. 212–243). New York: Cambridge University Press.

Diener, Marissa. (2000). Gift from the gods: A Balinese guide to early child rearing. In Judy S. DeLoache & Alma Gottlieb (Eds.), *A world of babies: Imagined childcare guides* *for seven societies* (pp. 96–116). New York: Cambridge University Press.

Dietz, Tracy L. (1998). An examination of violence and gender role portrayals in video games: Implications for gender socialization and aggressive behavior. *Sex Roles, 38,* 425–442.

DiGirolamo, Ann, Thompson, Nancy, Martorell, Reynaldo, Fein, Sara, & Grummer-Strawn, Laurence. (2005). Intention or experience? Predictors of continued breastfeeding. *Health Education & Behavior, 32,* 208–226.

Dionne, Ginette, Dale, Philip S., Boivin, Michel, & Plomin, Robert. (2003). Genetic evidence for bidirectional effects of early lexical and grammatical development. *Child Development, 74,* 394–412.

DiPietro, Janet A., Hilton, Sterling C., Hawkins, Melissa, Costigan, Kathleen A., & Pressman, Eva K. (2002). Maternal stress and affect influence fetal neurobehavioral development. *Developmental Psychology, 38,* 659–668.

DiPietro, Janet A., Hodgson, Denice M., Costigan, Kathleen A., Hilton, Sterling C., & Johnson, Timothy R. B. (1996). Fetal neurobehavioral development. *Child Development, 67,* 2553-2567.

Dishion, Thomas J., & Bullock, Bernadette Marie. (2002). Parenting and adolescent problem behavior: An ecological analysis of the nurturance hypothesis. In John G. Borkowski, Sharon Landesman Ramey, & Marie Bristol-Power (Eds.), *Parenting and the child's world: Influences on academic, intellectual, and social-emotional development* (pp. 231–249). Mahwah, NJ: Erlbaum.

Dishion, Thomas J., Bullock, Bernadette Marie, & Granic, Isabela. (2002). Pragmatism in modeling peer influence: Dynamics, outcomes and change processes. *Development & Psychopathology, 14,* 969–981.

Dishion, Thomas J., & Owen, Lee D. (2002). A longitudinal analysis of friendships and substance use: Bidirectional influence from adolescence to adulthood. *Developmental Psychology, 38,* 480–491.

Dishion, Thomas J., Poulin, François, & Burraston, Bert. (2001). Peer group dynamics associated with iatrogenic effects in group interventions with high-risk young adolescents. In William Damon (Series Ed.) & Douglas W. Nangle & Cynthia A. Erdley (Vol. Eds.), *New directions for child and adolescent development: No. 91. The role of friendship in psychological adjustment* (pp. 79–92). San Francisco: Jossey-Bass.

Dixon, Roger A., & Lerner, Richard M. (1999). History and systems in developmental psychology. In Marc H. Bornstein & Michael E. Lamb (Eds.), *Developmental psychology: An advanced textbook* (4th ed., pp. 3–45). Mahwah, NJ: Erlbaum.

Donaldson, Margaret C. (1979). *Children's minds* (1st American ed.). New York: Norton.

Douglas, Ann. (2002). *The mother of all pregnancy books.* New York, NY: Hungry Minds.

Doumbo, Ogobara K. (2005). It takes a village: Medical research and ethics in Mali. *Science, 307*(5710), 679–681.

Dounchis, Jennifer Zoler, Hayden, Helen A., & Wilfley, Denise E. (2001). Obesity, body image, and eating disorders in ethnically diverse children and adolescents. In J. Kevin Thompson & Linda Smolak (Eds.), *Body image, eating disorders, and obesity in youth: Assessment, prevention, and treatment* (pp. 67–98). Washington, DC: American Psychological Association.

Dubowitz, Howard. (1999). Neglect of children's health care. In Howard Dubowitz (Ed.), *Neglected children: Research, practice, and policy* (pp. 109–130). Thousand Oaks, CA: Sage.

Dugger, Celia W. (2001, April 22). Abortion in India is tipping scales sharply against girls. *New York Times,* pp. A1, A10.

Duncan, Greg J., & Brooks-Gunn, Jeanne (Eds.). (1997). *Consequences of growing up poor.* New York: Russell Sage Foundation.

Dunn, Judy. (1988). *The beginnings of social understanding.* Cambridge, MA: Harvard University Press.

Dunn, Judy, & Hughes, Claire. (2001). "I got some swords and you're dead!": Violent fantasy, antisocial behavior, friendship, and moral sensibility in young children. *Child Development, 72,* 491–505.

Dunphy, Dexter C. (1963). The social structure of urban adolescent peer groups. *Sociometry, 26,* 230–246.

Durlak, Joseph A. (1998). Common risk and protective factors in successful prevention programs. *American Journal of Orthopsychiatry, 68,* 512–520.

Durrant, Joan E. (1996). Public attitudes toward corporal punishment in Canada. In Detlev Frehsee, Wiebke Horn, & Kai-D. Bussmann (Eds.), *Prevention and intervention in childhood and adolescence: Vol. 19. Family violence against children: A challenge for society* (pp. 19–26). Berlin: de Gruyter.

Duster, Troy. (1999). The social consequences of genetic disclosure. In Ronald A. Carson & Mark A. Rothstein (Eds.), *Behavioral genetics: The clash of culture and biology* (pp. 172—188). Baltimore: Johns Hopkins University Press.

Dutton, Donald G. (2000). Witnessing parental violence as a traumatic experience shaping the abusive personality. In Robert A. Geffner, Peter G. Jaffe, & Marlies Sudermann (Eds.), *Children exposed to domestic violence: Current issues in research, intervention, prevention, and policy development* (pp. 59–67). Binghamton, NY: Haworth Press.

Dweck, Carol S. (1999). *Self-theories: Their role in motivation, personality, and development.* Philadelphia: Psychology Press.

Dybdahl, Ragnhild. (2001). Children and mothers in war: An outcome study of a psychosocial intervention program. *Child Development, 72,* 1214–1230.

East, Patricia L., & Kiernan, Elizabeth A. (2001). Risks among youths who have multiple sisters who were adolescent parents. *Family Planning Perspectives, 33,* 75–80.

Eccles, Jacquelynne S. (2004). Schools, academic motivation, and stage-environment fit. In Richard M. Lerner & Laurence D. Steinberg (Eds.), *Handbook of adolescent psychology* (2nd ed., pp. 125–153). Hoboken, NJ: Wiley.

Eccles, Jacquelynne S., Wigfield, Allan, & Schiefele, Ulrich. (1998). Motivation to succeed. In William Damon (Series Ed.) & Nancy Eisenberg (Vol. Ed.), *Handbook of child psychology: Vol. 3. Social, emotional, and personality development* (5th ed., pp. 1017–1095). New York: Wiley.

Editors. (2004). Preventing early reading failure. *American Educator, 28,* 5.

Edwards, Carolyn, Gandini, Lella, & Forman, George (Eds.). (1998). *The hundred languages of children: The Reggio Emilia approach—advanced reflections* (2nd ed.). Greenwich, CT: Ablex.

Egan, Kieran, & Ling, Michael. (2002). We began as poets: Conceptual tools and the arts in early childhood. In Liora Bresler & Christine Marme Thompson (Eds.), *The arts* *in children's lives: Context, culture, and curriculum* (pp. 93–100). Dordrecht, The Netherlands: Kluwer.

Ehrenberg, Ronald G., Brewer, Dominic J., Gamoran, Adam, & Willms, J. Douglas. (2001). Class size and student achievement. *Psychological Science in the Public Interest, 2,* 1–30.

Eid, Michael, & Diener, Ed. (2001). Norms for experiencing emotions in different cultures: Inter- and intranational differences. *Journal of Personality & Social Psychology, 81,* 869–885.

Eiden, Rina Das, Edwards, Ellen Peterson, & Leonard, Kenneth E. (2002). Mother-infant and father-infant attachment among alcoholic families. *Development & Psychopathology, 14,* 253–278.

Eisbach, Anne O'Donnell. (2004). Children's developing awareness of diversity in people's trains of thought. *Child Development, 75,* 1694–1707.

Eisenberg, Marla E., Bearinger, Linda H., Sieving, Renee E., Swain, Carolyne, & Resnick, Michael D. (2004). Parents' beliefs about condoms and oral contraceptives: Are they medically accurate? *Perspectives on Sexual and Reproductive Health, 36,* 50–57.

Eisenberg, Nancy. (2000). Emotion, regulation, and moral development. *Annual Review of Psychology, 51,* 665–697.

Eisenberg, Nancy, Cumberland, Amanda, Spinrad, Tracy L., Fabes, Richard A., Shepard, Stephanie A., Reiser, Mark, et al. (2001). The relations of regulation and emotionality to children's externalizing and internalizing problem behavior. *Child Development, 72,* 1112–1134.

Eisenberg, Nancy, Spinrad, Tracy L., Fabes, Richard A., Reiser, Mark, Cumberland, Amanda, Shepard, Stephanie A., et al. (2004). The relations of effortful control and impulsivity to children's resiliency and adjustment. *Child Development, 75,* 25–46.

Eisner, Manuel. (2002). Crime, problem drinking, and drug use: Patterns of problem behavior in cross-national perspective. *Annals of the American Academy of Political & Social Science, 580,* 201–225.

El-Sheikh, Mona, & Harger, JoAnn. (2001). Appraisals of marital conflict and children's adjustment, health, and physiological reactivity. *Developmental Psychology, 37,* 875–885.

Elder, Glen H., Jr. (1986). Military times and turning points in men's lives. *Developmental Psychology, 22,* 233–245.

Elder, Glen H., Jr. (1998). The life course as developmental theory. *Child Development, 69,* 1–12.

Elder, Glen H., Jr., & Conger, Rand D. (2000). *Children of the land: Adversity and success in rural America.* Chicago: University of Chicago Press.

Elkind, David. (1967). Egocentrism in adolescence. *Child Development, 38,* 1025–1034.

Elkind, David. (1979). *The child and society: Essays in applied child development.* New York: Oxford University Press.

Ellis, Bruce J., & Garber, Judy. (2000). Psychosocial antecedents of variation in girls' pubertal timing: Maternal depression, stepfather presence, and marital and family stress. *Child Development, 71,* 485–501.

Ellison, Peter Thorpe. (2001). *On fertile ground.* Cambridge, MA: Harvard University Press.

Ellison, Peter Thorpe. (2002). Puberty. In Noël Cameron (Ed.), *Human growth and development* (pp. 65–84). San Diego, CA: Academic Press.

Elmore, Richard, Ablemann, Charles, Even, Johanna, Kenyon, Susan, & Marshall, Joanne. (2004). When accountability knocks, will anyone answer? In Richard F. Elmore (Ed.), *School reform from the inside out: Policy, practice, and performance* (pp. 133–200). Cambridge, MA: Harvard Education Press.

Emler, Nicholas. (1998). Sociomoral understanding. In Anne Campbell & Steven Muncer (Eds.), *The social child* (pp. 293–323). Hove, England: Psychology Press.

Enserink, Martin. (2005). Infectious diseases: A puzzling outbreak of Marburg disease, *Science, 308,* 31–33.

Epstein, Ann S., Schweinhart, Lawrence J., & McAdoo, Leslie. (1996). *Models of early childhood education.* Ypsilanti, MI: High/Scope Press.

Epstein, Seymour. (1994). Integration of the cognitive and the psychodynamic unconscious. *American Psychologist, 49,* 709–724.

Erdley, Cynthia A., & Asher, Steven R. (1998). Linkages between children's beliefs about the legitimacy of aggression and their behavior. *Social Development, 7,* 321–339.

Eriks-Brophy, Alice, & Crago, Martha. (2003). Variation in instructional discourse features: Cultural or linguistic? Evidence from Inuit and Non-Inuit teachers of Nunavik. *Anthropology & Education Quarterly, 34,* 396–419.

Erikson, Erik H. (1963). *Childhood and society* (2nd ed.). New York: Norton.

Erikson, Erik H. (1968). *Identity: Youth and crisis.* New York: Norton.

Erwin, Phil. (1998). *Friendship in childhood and adolescence.* London: Routledge.

Ethics Committee of the American Society for Reproductive Medicine. (2001). Preconception gender selection for nonmedical reasons. *Fertility and Sterility, 75,* 861–864.

Evans, David W., Leckman, James F., Carter, Alice, Reznick, J. Steven, Henshaw, Desiree, King, Robert A., et al. (1997). Ritual, habit, and perfectionism: The prevalence and development of compulsive-like behavior in normal young children. *Child Development, 68,* 58–68.

Evans, Jonathan, Heron, Jon, Francomb, Helen, Oke, Sarah, & Golding, Jean. (2001). Cohort study of depressed mood during pregnancy and after childbirth. *British Medical Journal, 323,* 257–260.

Eveleth, Phyllis B., & Tanner, James M. (1990). *Worldwide variation in human growth* (2nd ed.). Cambridge, England: Cambridge University Press.

Evenson, Kelly R., Huston, Sara L., McMillen, Bradley J., Bors, Philip, & Ward, Dianne S. (2003). Statewide prevalence and correlates of walking and bicycling to school. *Archives of Pediatrics & Adolescent Medicine, 157,* 887–892.

Eyer, Diane E. (1992). *Mother-infant bonding: A scientific fiction.* New Haven, CT: Yale University Press.

Fabes, Richard A., Martin, Carol Lynn, Hanish, Laura D., Anders, Mary C., & Madden-Derdich, Debra A. (2003). Early school competence: The roles of sex-segregated play and effortful control. *Developmental Psychology, 39,* 848–858.

Fackelmann, Kathy A. (1994, November 5). Beyond the genome: The ethics of DNA testing. *Science News, 146,* 298–299.

Fagot, Beverly I. (1995). Parenting boys and girls. In Marc H. Bornstein (Ed.), *Handbook of parenting: Vol. 1. Children and parenting* (pp. 163–183). Hillsdale, NJ: Erlbaum.

Falk, Ruma, & Wilkening, Friedrich. (1998). Children's construction of fair chances: Adjusting probabilities. *Developmental Psychology, 34,* 1340–1357.

Farbrother, Jane E., & Guggenheim, Jeremy A. (2001). Myopia genetics: The family study of myopia. *Optometry Today, 41,* 41–44.

Farrington, David P. (2004). Conduct disorder, aggression, and delinquency. In Richard M. Lerner & Laurence D. Steinberg (Eds.), *Handbook of adolescent psychology* (2nd ed., pp. 627–664). Hoboken, NJ: Wiley.

Feiring, Candice. (1999). Other-sex friendship networks and the development of romantic relationships in adolescence. *Journal of Youth & Adolescence, 28,* 495–512.

Feldman, Ruth, & Eidelman, Arthur I. (2004). Parent-infant synchrony and the social-emotional development of triplets. *Developmental Psychology, 40,* 1133–1147.

Feldman, Ruth, & Eidelman, Arthur I. (2005). Does a triplet birth pose a special risk for infant development? Assessing cognitive development in relation to intrauterine growth and mother-infant interaction across the first 2 years. *Pediatrics, 115,* 443–452.

Feldman, Ruth, Eidelman, Arthur I., & Rotenberg, Noa. (2004). Parenting stress, infant emotion regulation, maternal sensitivity, and the cognitive development of triplets: A model for parent and child influences in a unique ecology. *Child Development, 75,* 1774–1791.

Feldman, Ruth, & Klein, Pnina S. (2003). Toddlers' self-regulated compliance to mothers, caregivers, and fathers: Implications for theories of socialization. *Developmental Psychology, 39,* 680–692.

Feldman, Ruth, Weller, Aron, Sirota, Lea, & Eidelman, Arthur I. (2002). Skin-to-skin contact (kangaroo care) promotes self-regulation in premature infants: Sleep-wake cyclicity, arousal modulation, and sustained exploration. *Developmental Psychology, 38,* 194–207.

Fenson, Larry, Bates, Elizabeth, Dale, Philip, Goodman, Judith, Reznick, J. Steven, & Thal, Donna. (2000). Measuring variability in early child language: Don't shoot the messenger. *Child Development, 71,* 323–328.

Fenson, Larry, Dale, Philip S., Reznick, J. Steven, Bates, Elizabeth, Thal, Donna J., & Pethick, Stephen J. (1994). Variability in early communicative development. *Monographs of the Society for Research in Child Development, 59*(5, Serial No. 242), 1–173.

Ferguson, Mark W. J., & Joanen, Ted. (1982, April 29). Temperature of egg incubation determines sex in *Alligator mississippiensis. Nature, 296,* 850–853.

Fergusson, David M., & Horwood, L. John. (2002). Male and female offending trajectories. *Development & Psychopathology, 14,* 159–177.

Fergusson, David M., & Horwood, L. John. (2003). Resilience to childhood adversity: Results of a 12-year study. In Suniya S. Luthar (Ed.), *Resilience and vulnerability: Adaptation in the context of childhood adversities* (pp. 130–155). New York: Cambridge University Press.

Ferrari, Michel, & Sternberg, Robert J. (1998). The development of mental abilities and styles. In William Damon (Series Ed.) & Deanna Kuhn & Robert S. Siegler (Vol. Eds.), *Handbook of child psychology: Vol. 2. Cognition, perception, and language* (5th ed., pp. 899–946). New York: Wiley.

Field, Tiffany. (2001). Massage therapy facilitates weight gain in preterm infants. *Current Directions in Psychological Science, 10,* 51–54.

Finch, Caleb Ellicott, & Kirkwood, Thomas B. L. (2000). *Chance, development, and aging.* New York: Oxford University Press.

Finn, Jeremy D., Gerber, Susan B., Achilles, Charles M., & Boyd-Zaharias, Jayne. (2001). The enduring effects of small classes. *Teachers College Record, 103,* 145–183.

Fischer, Kurt W., & Bidell, Thomas R. (1998). Dynamic development of psychological structures in action and thought. In William Damon (Series Ed.) & Richard M. Lerner (Vol. Ed.), *Handbook of child psychology: Vol. 1. Theoretical models of human development* (5th ed., pp. 467–561). New York: Wiley.

Fish, Jefferson M. (2002). The myth of race. In Jefferson M. Fish (Ed.), *Race and intelligence: Separating science from myth* (pp. 113–141). Mahwah, NJ: Erlbaum.

Fishbein, Martin, Hall-Jamieson, Kathleen, Zimmer, Eric, von Haeften, Ina, & Nabi, Robin. (2002). Avoiding the boomerang: Testing the relative effectiveness of antidrug public service announcements before a national campaign. *American Journal of Public Health, 92,* 238–245.

Flavell, John H., Green, Frances L., Flavell, Eleanor R., & Grossman, James B. (1997). The development of children's knowledge about inner speech. *Child Development, 68,* 39–47.

Flavell, John H., Miller, Patricia H., & Miller, Scott A. (2002). *Cognitive development* (4th ed.). Upper Saddle River, NJ: Prentice Hall.

Fletcher, Anne C., Steinberg, Laurence, & Williams-Wheeler, Meeshay. (2004). Parental influences on adolescent problem behavior: Revisiting Stattin and Kerr. *Child Development, 75,* 781–796.

Flook, Lisa, Repetti, Rena L., & Ullman, Jodie B. (2005). Classroom social experiences as predictors of academic performance. *Developmental Psychology, 41,* 319–327.

Flores, Glenn, & Zambrana, Ruth Enid. (2001). The early years: The health of children and youth. In Marilyn Aguirre-Molina, Carlos W. Molina, & Ruth E. Zambrana (Eds.), *Health issues in the Latino community* (pp. 77–106). San Francisco: Jossey Bass.

Flynn, James R. (1999). Searching for justice: The discovery of IQ gains over time. *American Psychologist, 54,* 5–20.

Fontanet, Arnaud L., Messele, Tsehaynesh, Dejene, Amare, Enquselassie, Fikre, Abebe, Almaz, Cutts, Felicity T., et al. (1998). Age- and sex-specific HIV-1 prevalence in the urban community setting of Addis Ababa, Ethiopia. *Aids, 12,* 315–322.

Ford, Kathleen, Sohn, Woosung, & Lepkowski, James. (2001). Characteristics of adolescents' sexual partners and their association with use of condoms and other contraceptive methods. *Family Planning Perspectives, 33,* 100–105, 132.

Fordham, Signithia, & Ogbu, John U. (1986). Black students' school success: Coping with the "burden of acting white." *Urban Review, 18,* 176–206.

Fortune-Wood, Jan. (2002). Transitions without school. In Hilary Fabian & Aline-Wendy Dunlop (Eds.), *Transitions in the* *early years: Debating continuity and progression for young children in early education* (pp. 135–145). New York: RoutledgeFalmer.

Fox, Nathan A., Henderson, Heather A., Rubin, Kenneth H., Calkins, Susan D., & Schmidt, Louis A. (2001). Continuity and discontinuity of behavioral inhibition and exuberance: Psychophysiological and behavioral influences across the first four years of life. *Child Development, 72,* 1–21.

Frank, Deborah A., Augustyn, Marilyn, Knight, Wanda Grant, Pell, Tripler, & Zuckerman, Barry. (2001). Growth, development, and behavior in early childhood following prenatal cocaine exposure: A systematic review. *Journal of the American Medical Association, 285,* 1613–1625.

Frankel, Frederick D. (2005). Parent-assisted children's friendship training. In Euthymia D. Hibbs & Peter S. Jensen (Eds.), *Psychosocial treatments for child and adolescent disorders: Empirically based strategies for clinical practice* (2nd ed., pp. 693–715). Washington, DC: American Psychological Association.

Frankenburg, William K., Fandal, A. W., Sciarillo, W., & Burgess, D. (1981). The newly abbreviated and revised Denver Developmental Screening Test. *Journal of Pediatrics, 99,* 995–999.

Fredricks, Jennifer A., Blumenfeld, Phyllis C., & Paris, Alison H. (2004). School engagement: Potential of the concept, state of the evidence. *Review of Educational Research, 74,* 59–109.

Fredricks, Jennifer A., & Eccles, Jacquelynne S. (2002). Children's competence and value beliefs from childhood through adolescence: Growth trajectories in two male-sex-typed domains. *Developmental Psychology, 38,* 519–533.

Fredriksen, Katia, Rhodes, Jean, Reddy, Ranjini, & Way, Niobe. (2004). Sleepless in Chicago: Tracking the effects of adolescent sleep loss during the middle school years. *Child Development, 75,* 84–95.

French, Howard W. (2005, February 17). As girls 'vanish,' Chinese city battles tide of abortions. *New York Times,* pp. A3.

Freud, Anna. (1958). Adolescence. *Psychoanalytic Study of the Child, 13,* 255–278.

Freud, Sigmund. (1935). *A general introduction to psychoanalysis* (Joan Riviere, Trans.). New York: Liveright.

Freud, Sigmund. (1938). *The basic writings of Sigmund Freud* (A. A. Brill, Ed. & Trans.). New York: Modern Library.

Freud, Sigmund. (1964). An outline of psycho-analysis. In James Strachey (Ed. and Trans.), *The standard edition of the complete psychological works of Sigmund Freud* (Vol. 23, pp. 144–207). London: Hogarth Press. (Original work published 1940)

Freud, Sigmund. (1965). *New introductory lectures on psychoanalysis* (James Strachey, Ed. & Trans.). New York: Norton. (Original work published 1933)

Freud, Sigmund. (1966). *The psychopathology of everyday life* (James Strachey, Ed., Alan Tyson, Trans.). New York: Norton. (Original work published 1901)

Frey, Karin S., Hirschstein, Miriam K., Snell, Jennie L., Van Schoiack-Edstrom, Leihua, MacKenzie, Elizabeth P., & Broderick, Carole J. (2005). Reducing playground bullying and supporting beliefs: An experimental trial of the steps to respect program. *Developmental Psychology, 41,* 479–491.

Frick, Paul J., Cornell, Amy H., Bodin, S. Doug, Dane, Heather E., Barry, Christopher T., & Loney, Bryan R. (2003). Callous-unemotional traits and developmental pathways to severe conduct problems. *Developmental Psychology, 39,* 246–260.

Friedlander, Samuel L., Larkin, Emma K., Rosen, Carol L., Palermo, Tonya M., & Redline, Susan. (2003). Decreased quality of life associated with obesity in school-aged children. *Archives of Pediatrics & Adolescent Medicine, 157,* 1206–1211.

Friedman, Michael S., Powell, Kenneth E., Hutwagner, Lori, Graham, LeRoy M., & Teague, W. Gerald. (2001). Impact of changes in transportation and commuting behaviors during the 1996 Summer Olympic Games in Atlanta on air quality and childhood asthma. *Journal of the American Medical Association, 285,* 897–905.

Fuligni, Andrew J. (1997). The academic achievement of adolescents from immigrant families: The roles of family background, attitudes, and behavior. *Child Development, 68,* 351–363.

Fuligni, Andrew J. (1998). Authority, autonomy, and parent-adolescent conflict and cohesion: A study of adolescents from Mexican, Chinese, Filipino, and European backgrounds. *Developmental Psychology, 34,* 782–792.

Fuligni, Andrew J. (2001). A comparative longitudinal approach to acculturation among children from immigrant families. *Harvard Educational Review, 71,* 566–578.

Fuligni, Andrew J., & Zhang, Wenxin. (2004). Attitudes toward family obligation among adolescents in contemporary urban and rural China. *Child Development, 75,* 180–192.

Furman, Wyndol, Simon, Valerie A., Shaffer, Laura, & Bouchey, Heather A. (2002). Adolescents' working models and styles for relationships with parents, friends, and romantic partners. *Child Development, 73,* 241–255.

Galambos, Nancy L. (2004). Gender and gender role development in adolescence. In Richard M. Lerner & Laurence D. Steinberg (Eds.), *Handbook of adolescent psychology* (2nd ed., pp. 233–262). Hoboken, NJ: Wiley.

Galambos, Nancy L., Barker, Erin T., & Almeida, David M. (2003). Parents do matter: Trajectories of change in externalizing and internalizing problems in early adolescence. *Child Development, 74,* 578–594.

Galinsky, Ellen, Howes, Carollee, Kontos, Susan, & Shinn, Marybeth. (1994). *The study of children in family child care and relative care: Highlights of findings.* New York: Families and Work Institute.

Gall, Stanley (Ed.). (1996). *Multiple pregnancy and delivery.* St. Louis, MO: Mosby.

Galotti, Kathleen M. (1999). Making a "major" real-life decision: College students choosing an academic major. *Journal of Educational Psychology, 91,* 379–387.

Galotti, Kathleen M. (2002). *Making decisions that matter: How people face important life choices.* Mahwah, NJ: Erlbaum.

Gantley, M., Davies, D. P., & Murcott, A. (1993). Sudden infant death syndrome: Links with infant care practices. *British Medical Journal, 306,* 16–20.

Garbarino, James, & Collins, Cyleste C. (1999). Child neglect: The family with a hole in the middle. In Howard Dubowitz (Ed.), *Neglected children: Research, practice and policy* (pp. 1–23). Thousand Oaks, CA: Sage.

Garcia, Cristina. (2004). *Monkey hunting.* New York: Ballantine Books.

Gardner, Howard. (1983). *Frames of mind: The theory of multiple intelligences.* New York: Basic Books.

Gardner, Howard. (1999). Are there additional intelligences? The case for naturalist, spiritual, and existential intelligences. In Jeffrey Kane (Ed.), *Education, information, and transformation: Essays on learning and thinking* (pp. 111–131). Upper Saddle River, NJ: Merrill.

Garner, Leon F., Owens, Helen, Kinnear, Robert F., & Frith, Michael J. (1999). Prevalence of myopia in Sherpa and Tibetan children in Nepal. *Optometry and Vision Science, 76,* 282–285.

Garner, Pamela W., & Spears, Floyd M. (2000). Emotion regulation in low-income preschoolers. *Social Development, 9,* 246–264.

Garofalo, Robert, Wolf, R. Cameron, Wissow, Lawrence S., Woods, Elizabeth R., & Goodman, Elizabeth. (1999). Sexual orientation and risk of suicide attempts among a representative sample of youth. *Archives of Pediatrics & Adolescent Medicine, 153,* 487–493.

Garvin, James. (1994). *Learning how to kiss a frog: Advice for those who work with pre- and early adolescents.* Topsfield, MA: New England League of Middle Schools.

Gaspar de Alba, Alicia. (2003). Rights of passage: From cultural schizophrenia to border consciousness in Cheech Marin's Born in East L.A. In Alicia Gaspar de Alba (Ed.), *Velvet barrios: Popular culture & Chicana/o sexualities.* Basingstoke: Palgrave Macmillan.

Gathercole, Susan E., Pickering, Susan J., Ambridge, Benjamin, & Wearing, Hannah. (2004). The structure of working memory from 4 to 15 years of age. *Developmental Psychology, 40,* 177–190.

Gauvain, Mary. (1998). Cognitive development in social and cultural context. *Current Directions in Psychological Science, 7,* 188–192.

Gazelle, Heidi, & Rudolph, Karen D. (2004). Moving toward and away from the world: Social approach and avoidance trajectories in anxious solitary youth. *Child Development, 75,* 829–849.

Gdalevich, Michael, Mimouni, Daniel, & Mimouni, Marc. (2001). Breast-feeding and the risk of bronchial asthma in childhood: A systematic review with meta-analysis of prospective studies. *Journal of Pediatrics, 139,* 261–266.

Ge, Xiaojia, Conger, Rand D., & Elder, Glen H., Jr. (2001). Pubertal transition, stressful life events, and the emergence of gender differences in adolescent depressive symptoms. *Developmental Psychology, 37,* 404–417.

Ge, Xiaojia, Kim, Irene J., Brody, Gene H., Conger, Rand D., Simons, Ronald L., Gibbons, Frederick X., et al. (2003). It's about timing and change: Pubertal transition effects on symptoms of major depression among African American youths. *Developmental Psychology, 39,* 430–439.

Gelles, Richard J. (1999). Policy issues in child neglect. In Howard Dubowitz (Ed.), *Neglected children: Research, practice, and policy* (pp. 278–298). Thousand Oaks, CA: Sage.

Gelman, Susan A. (2003). *The essential child: Origins of essentialism in everyday thought.* New York: Oxford University Press.

Genesee, Fred. (1998). A case study of multilingual education in Canada. In Jasone Cenoz & Fred Genesee (Eds.), *Beyond bilingualism: Multilingualism and multilingual education* (pp. 243–258). Clevedon, England: Multilingual Matters.

Gennetian, Lisa A., & Miller, Cynthia. (2002). Children and welfare reform: A view from an experimental welfare program in Minnesota. *Child Development, 73,* 601–620.

Gentner, Dedre, & Boroditsky, Lera. (2001). Individuation, relativity, and early word learning. In Melissa Bowerman & Stephen C. Levinson (Eds.), *Language acquisition and conceptual development* (pp. 215–256). Cambridge, UK: Cambridge University Press.

Georgieff, Michael K., & Rao, Raghavendra. (2001). The role of nutrition in cognitive development. In Charles A. Nelson & Monica Luciana (Eds.), *Handbook of developmental cognitive neuroscience* (pp. 149–158). Cambridge, MA: MIT Press.

Gergely, György, & Watson, John S. (1999). Early socio-emotional development: Contingency perception and the social-biofeedback model. In Philippe Rochat (Ed.), *Early social cognition: Understanding others in the first months of life* (pp. 101–136). Mahwah, NJ: Erlbaum.

Gerris, Jan, Olivennes, François, & De Sutter, Petra (Eds.). (2004). *Assisted reproductive technologies: Quality and safety.* Boca Raton, FL: Parthenon.

Gershoff, Elizabeth Thompson. (2002). Corporal punishment by parents and associated child behaviors and experiences: A meta-analytic and theoretical review. *Psychological Bulletin, 128,* 539–579.

Gerstadt, Cherie L., Hong, Yoon Joo, & Diamond, Adele. (1994). The relationship between cognition and action: Performance of children 3½–7 years old on a Stroop-like day-night test. *Cognition, 53,* 129–153.

Gibson, Eleanor J. (1969). *Principles of perceptual learning and development.* New York: Appleton-Century-Crofts.

Gibson, Eleanor J. (1988). Levels of description and constraints on perceptual development. In Albert Yonas (Ed.), *Perceptual development in infancy* (pp. 283–296). Hillsdale, NJ: Erlbaum.

Gibson, Eleanor J. (1997). An ecological psychologist's prolegomena for perceptual development: A functional approach. In Cathy Dent-Read & Patricia Zukow-Goldring (Eds.), *Evolving explanations of development: Ecological approaches to organism-environment systems* (pp. 23–54). Washington, DC: American Psychological Association.

Gibson, Eleanor J., & Walk, Richard D. (1960). The "visual cliff." *Scientific American, 202*(4), 64–71.

Gibson, James Jerome. (1979). *The ecological approach to visual perception.* Boston: Houghton Mifflin.

Gibson-Cline, Janice (Ed.). (2000). *Youth and coping in twelve nations: Surveys of 18–20-year-old young people.* New York: Routledge.

Gifford-Smith, Mary E., & Rabiner, David L. (2004). Social information processing and children's social adjustment. In Janis B. Kupersmidt & Kenneth A. Dodge (Eds.), *Children's peer relations: From development to intervention* (pp. 61–79). Washington, DC: American Psychological Association.

Gigerenzer, Gerd, Todd, Peter M., & ABC Research Group. (1999). *Simple heuristics that make us smart.* New York: Oxford University Press.

Gilhooly, Mary. (2002). Ethical issues in researching later life. In Anne Jamieson & Christina R. Victor (Eds.), *Researching ageing and later life: The practice of social gerontology* (pp. 211–225). Philadelphia: Open University Press.

Gilligan, Carol. (1982). *In a different voice: Psychological theory and women's development.* Cambridge, MA: Harvard University Press.

Gilligan, Carol, Murphy, John Michael, & Tappan, Mark B. (1990). Moral development beyond adolescence. In Charles N. Alexander & Ellen J. Langer (Eds.), *Higher stages of human development: Perspectives on adult growth* (pp. 208–225). London: Oxford University Press.

Gilliom, Miles, Shaw, Daniel S., Beck, Joy E., Schonberg, Michael A., & Lukon, JoElla L. (2002). Anger regulation in disadvantaged preschool boys: Strategies, antecedents, and the development of self-control. *Developmental Psychology, 38,* 222–235.

Ginsburg, Herbert P., Klein, Alice, & Starkey, Prentice. (1998). The development of children's mathematical thinking: Connecting research with practice. In William Damon (Series Ed.) & Irving E. Sigel & K. Ann Renninger (Vol. Eds.), *Handbook of child psychology: Vol. 4. Child psychology in practice* (5th ed., pp. 401–476). New York: Wiley.

Girouard, Pascale C., Baillargeon, Raymond H., Tremblay, Richard E., Glorieux, Jacqueline, Lefebvre, Francine, & Robaey, Philippe. (1998). Developmental pathways leading to externalizing behaviors in 5 year olds born before 29 weeks of gestation. *Journal of Developmental & Behavioral Pediatrics, 19,* 244–253.

Gladwell, Malcolm. (2005). *Blink: The power of thinking without thinking.* New York: Little Brown.

Glasgow, Kristan L., Dornbusch, Sanford M., Troyer, Lisa, Steinberg, Laurence, & Ritter, Philip L. (1997). Parenting styles, adolescents' attributions, and educational outcomes in nine heterogeneous high schools. *Child Development, 68,* 507–529.

Glauber, James H., Farber, Harold J., & Homer, Charles J. (2001). Asthma clinical pathways: Toward what end? *Pediatrics, 107,* 590–592.

Glazier, Anne M., Nadeau, Joseph H., & Aitman, Timothy J. (2002). Finding genes that underlie complex traits. *Science, 298,* 2345–2349.

Gleason, Jean Berko, & Ely, Richard. (2002). Gender differences in language development. In Ann McGillicuddy-De Lisi & Richard De Lisi (Eds.), *Advances in applied developmental psychology: Vol. 21. Biology, society, and behavior: The development of sex differences in cognition* (pp. 127–154). Westport, CT: Ablex.

Glover, Evam Kofi, Bannerman, Angela, Pence, Brian Wells, Jones, Heidi, Miller, Robert, Weiss, Eugene, et al. (2003). Sexual health experiences of adolescents in three Ghanaian towns. *International Family Planning Perspectives, 29,* 32–40.

Gogate, Lakshmi J., Bahrick, Lorraine E., & Watson, Jilayne D. (2000). A study of multimodal motherese: The role of temporal synchrony between verbal labels and gestures. *Child Development, 71,* 878–894.

Goldin-Meadow, Susan. (2000). Beyond words: The importance of gesture to researchers and learners. *Child Development, 71,* 231–239.

Goldman, Herbert I. (2001). Parental reports of 'MAMA' sounds in infants: An exploratory study. *Journal of Child Language, 28,* 497–506.

Goleman, Daniel. (1998, August). *Building emotional intelligence.* Paper presented at the 106th Annual Convention of the American Psychological Association, San Francisco, CA.

Golub, Sharon. (1992). *Periods: From menarche to menopause.* Newbury Park, CA: Sage.

Gomes, Uilho A., Silva, Antônio A., Bettiol, Heloisa, & Barbieri, Marco A. (1999). Risk factors for the increasing caesarean section rate in Southeast Brazil: A comparison of two birth cohorts, 1978–1979 and 1994. *International Journal of Epidemiology, 28,* 687–694.

Goodman, Sherryl H., & Gotlib, Ian H. (1999). Risk for psychopathology in the children of depressed mothers: A developmental model for understanding mechanisms of transmission. *Psychological Review, 106,* 458–490.

Goodman, Sherryl H., & Gotlib, Ian H. (2002). Transmission of risk to children of depressed parents: Integration and conclusions. In Sherryl H. Goodman & Ian H. Gotlib (Eds.), *Children of depressed parents: Mechanisms of risk and implications for treatment* (pp. 307–326). Washington, DC: American Psychological Association.

Gopnik, Alison. (2001). Theories, language, and culture: Whorf without wincing. In Melissa Bowerman & Stephen C. Levinson (Eds.), *Language acquisition and conceptual development* (pp. 45–69). Cambridge, UK: Cambridge University Press.

Gordon, Richard Allan. (2000). *Eating disorders: Anatomy of a social epidemic* (2nd ed.). Malden, MA: Blackwell.

Gorenstein, Ethan E., & Comer, Ronald J. (2002). *Case studies in abnormal psychology.* New York: Worth.

Gorski, Peter A. (2002). Racing cain. *Journal of Developmental & Behavioral Pediatrics, 23,* 95.

Goss, David A. (2002). More evidence that near work contributes to myopia development. *Indiana Journal of Optometry, 5,* 11–13.

Gottfredson, Linda S., & Deary, Ian J. (2004). Intelligence predicts health and longevity, but why? *Current Directions in Psychological Science, 13,* 1–4.

Gottlieb, Alma. (2000). Luring your child into this life: A Beng path for infant care. In Judy S. DeLoache & Alma Gottlieb (Eds.), *A world of babies: Imagined childcare guides for seven societies* (pp. 55–90). New York: Cambridge University Press.

Gottlieb, Gilbert. (2002). *Individual development and evolution: The genesis of novel behavior.* Mahwah, NJ: Erlbaum.

Gottlieb, Gilbert. (2003). Probabilistic epigenesis of development. In Jaan Valsiner & Kevin J. Connolly (Eds.), *Handbook of developmental psychology* (pp. 3–17). Thousand Oaks, CA: Sage.

Graber, Julia A. (2004). Internalizing problems during adolescence. In Richard M. Lerner & Laurence D. Steinberg (Eds.), *Handbook of adolescent psychology* (2nd ed., pp. 587–626). Hoboken, NJ: Wiley.

Gradin, Maria, Eriksson, Mats, Holmqvist, Gunilla, Holstein, Åsa, & Schollin, Jens. (2002). Pain reduction at venipuncture in newborns: Oral glucose compared with local anesthetic cream. *Pediatrics, 110,* 1053–1057.

Graefe, Deborah Roempke, & Lichter, Daniel T. (2002). Marriage among unwed mothers: Whites, blacks and Hispanics compared. *Perspectives on Sexual and Reproductive Health, 34,* 286–293.

Graham, John W., & Beller, Andrea H. (2002). Nonresident fathers and their children: Child support and visitation from an economic perspective. In Catherine S. Tamis-LeMonda & Natasha Cabrera (Eds.), *Handbook of father involvement: Multidisciplinary perspectives* (pp. 431–453). Mahwah, NJ: Erlbaum.

Graham, Susan A., Kilbreath, Cari S., & Welder, Andrea N. (2004). Thirteen-month-olds rely on shared labels and shape similarity for inductive inferences. *Child Development, 75,* 409–427.

Granott, Nira, & Parziale, Jim (Eds.). (2002). *Microdevelopment: Transition processes in development and learning.* Cambridge, UK: Cambridge University Press.

Grantham-McGregor, Sally M., & Ani, Cornelius. (2001). Undernutrition and mental development. In John D. Fernstrom, Ricardo Uauy, & Pedro Arroyo (Eds.), *Nutrition and brain* (pp. 1–18). Basel, Switzerland: Karger.

Green, Jonathan, Gilchrist, Anne, Burton, Di, & Cox, Anthony. (2000). Social and psychiatric functioning in adolescents with Asperger syndrome compared with conduct disorder. *Journal of Autism & Developmental Disorders, 30,* 279–293.

Greenberger, Ellen, & Chen, Chuansheng. (1996). Perceived family relationships and depressed mood in early and late adolescence: A comparison of European and Asian Americans. *Developmental Psychology, 32,* 707–716.

Greenberger, Ellen, & Steinberg, Laurence D. (1986). *When teenagers work: The psychological and social costs of adolescent employment.* New York: Basic Books.

Greenfield, Patricia M. (1997). You can't take it with you: Why ability assessments don't cross cultures. *American Psychologist, 52,* 1115–1124.

Greenfield, Patricia M., Keller, Heidi, Fuligni, Andrew, & Maynard, Ashley. (2003). Cultural pathways through universal development. *Annual Review of Psychology, 54,* 461–490.

Greenough, William T. (1993). Brain adaptation to experience: An update. In Mark H. Johnson (Ed.), *Brain development and cognition: A reader* (pp. 319–322). Oxford, UK: Blackwell.

Greenough, William T., Black, James E., & Wallace, Christopher S. (1987). Experience and brain development. *Child Development, 58,* 539–559.

Greenough, William T., & Volkmar, Fred R. (1973). Pattern of dendritic branching in occipital cortex of rats reared in complex environments. *Experimental Neurology, 40,* 491–504.

Greenspan, Stanley I., Wieder, Serena, & Simons, Robin. (1998). *The child with special needs: Encouraging intellectual and emotional growth.* Reading, MA: Addison-Wesley.

Gregg, Norman McAlister. (1941). Congenital cataract following German measles in the mother. *Transactions of the Ophthalmological Society of Australia, 3,* 35–46.

Griebel, Wilfried, & Niesel, Renate. (2002). Co-constructing transition into kindergarten and school by children, parents, and teachers. In Hilary Fabian & Aline-Wendy Dunlop (Eds.), *Transitions in the early years: Debating continuity and progression for young children in early education* (pp. 64–75). New York: RoutledgeFalmer.

Grigorenko, Elena L., & O'Keefe, Paul A. (2004). What do children do when they cannot go to school? In Robert J. Sternberg & Elena L. Grigorenko (Eds.), *Culture and competence: Contexts of life success* (pp. 23–53). Washington, DC: American Psychological Association.

Grolnick, Wendy S., Deci, Edward L., & Ryan, Richard M. (1997). Internalization within the family: The self-determination theory perspective. In Joan E. Grusec & Leon Kuczynski (Eds.), *Parenting and children's internalization of values: A handbook of contemporary theory* (pp. 135–161). New York: Wiley.

Grossmann, Klaus E., & Grossmann, Karin. (1990). The wider concept of attachment in cross-cultural research. *Human Development, 33,* 31–47.

Grosvenor, Theodore. (2003). Why is there an epidemic of myopia? *Clinical and Experimental Optometry, 86,* 273–275.

Grotevant, Harold D. (1998). Adolescent development in family contexts. In William Damon (Series Ed.) & Nancy Eisenberg (Vol. Ed.), *Handbook of child psychology: Vol. 3. Social, emotional, and personality development* (5th ed., pp. 1097–1149). New York: Wiley.

Gu, Dongfeng, Reynolds, Kristi, Wu, Xigui, Chen, Jing, Duan, Xiufang, Reynolds, Robert F., et al. (2005). Prevalence of the metabolic syndrome and overweight among adults in China. *Lancet, 365,* 1398–1405.

Guberman, Steven R. (1996). The development of everyday mathematics in Brazilian children with limited formal education. *Child Development, 67,* 1609–1623.

Guillaume, Michele, & Lissau, Inge. (2002). Epidemiology. In Walter Burniat, Tim J. Cole, Inge Lissau, & Elizabeth M. E. Poskitt (Eds.), *Child and adolescent obesity: Causes and consequences, prevention and management* (pp. 28–49). New York: Cambridge University Press.

Gunnar, Megan R., & Vazquez, Delia M. (2001). Low cortisol and a flattening of expected daytime rhythm: Potential indices of risk in human development. *Development & Psychopathology, 13,* 515–538.

Gurney, James G., Fritz, Melissa S., Ness, Kirsten K., Sievers, Phillip, Newschaffer, Craig J., & Shapiro, Elsa G. (2003). Analysis of prevalence trends of autism spectrum disorder in Minnesota. *Archives of Pediatrics & Adolescent Medicine, 157,* 622–627.

Guzell, Jacqueline R., & Vernon-Feagans, Lynne. (2004). Parental perceived control over caregiving and its relationship to parent-infant interaction. *Child Development, 75,* 134–146.

Hack, Maureen, Flannery, Daniel J., Schluchter, Mark, Cartar, Lydia, Borawski, Elaine, & Klein, Nancy. (2002). Outcomes in young adulthood for very-low-birth-weight infants. *New England Journal of Medicine, 346,* 149–157.

Haden, Catherine A., Ornstein, Peter A., Eckerman, Carol O., & Didow, Sharon M. (2001). Mother-child conversational interactions as events unfold: Linkages to subsequent remembering. *Child Development, 72,* 1016–1031.

Hagerman, Randi Jenssen. (2002). The physical and behavioral phenotype. In Randi Jenssen Hagerman & Paul J. Hagerman (Eds.), *Fragile X syndrome: Diagnosis, treatment, and research* (3rd ed., pp. 3–109). Baltimore: Johns Hopkins University Press.

Hakuta, Kenji, Bialystok, Ellen, & Wiley, Edward. (2003). Critical evidence: A test of the critical-period hypothesis for second-language acquisition. *Psychological Science, 14,* 31–38.

Hala, Suzanne, & Chandler, Michael. (1996). The role of strategic planning in accessing false-belief understanding. *Child Development, 67,* 2948–2966.

Halberstadt, Amy G., & Eaton, Kimberly L. (2003). A meta-analysis of family expressiveness and children's emotion expressiveness and understanding. *Marriage & Family Review, 34,* 35–62.

Haley, David W., & Stansbury, Kathy. (2003). Infant stress and parent responsiveness: Regulation of physiology and behavior during still-face and reunion. *Child Development, 74,* 1534–1546.

Hamer, Dean. (2002). Rethinking behavior genetics. *Science, 298,* 71–72.

Hamilton, Brady E., Martin, Joyce A., & Sutton, Paul P. (2004, November 23). Births: Preliminary data for 2003. *National Vital Statistics Reports, 53*(9), 1–17.

Hamilton, Stephen F., & Lempert, Wolfgang. (1996). The impact of apprenticeship on youth: A prospective analysis. *Journal of Research on Adolescence, 6,* 427–455.

Hamm, Jill V. (2000). Do birds of a feather flock together? The variable bases for African American, Asian American, and European American adolescents' selection of similar friends. *Developmental Psychology, 36,* 209–219.

Hammen, Constance. (2003). Risk and protective factors for children of depressed parents. In Suniya S. Luthar (Ed.), *Resilience and vulnerability: Adaptation in the context of childhood adversities* (pp. 50–75). New York: Cambridge University Press.

Hammond, Christopher J., Andrew, Toby, Mak, Ying Tat, & Spector, Tim D. (2004). A susceptibility locus for myopia in the normal population is linked to the PAX6 gene region on chromosome 11: A genomewide scan of dizygotic twins. *American Journal of Human Genetics, 75,* 294–304.

Hanish, Laura D., & Guerra, Nancy G. (2002). A longitudinal analysis of patterns of adjustment following peer victimization. *Development & Psychopathology, 14,* 69–89.

Hankin, Benjamin L., & Abramson, Lyn Y. (2001). Development of gender differences in depression: An elaborated cognitive vulnerability-transactional stress theory. *Psychological Bulletin, 127,* 773–796.

Hanushek, Eric A. (1999). The evidence on class size. In Susan E. Mayer & Paul E. Peterson (Eds.), *Earning and learning: How schools matter* (pp. 131–168). Washington, DC: Brookings Institution Press/Russell Sage Foundation.

Hardy, John, Singleton, Andrew, & Gwinn-Hardy, Katrina. (2003). Ethnic differences and disease phenotypes. *Science, 300,* 739–740.

Hariri, Ahmad R., Mattay, Venkata S., Tessitore, Alessandro, Kolachana, Bhaskar, Fera, Francesco, Goldman, David, et al. (2002). Serotonin transporter genetic variation and the response of the human amygdala. *Science, 297,* 400–403.

Harkness, Sara, & Super, Charles M. (2002). Culture and parenting. In Marc H. Bornstein (Ed.), *Handbook of parenting: Vol. 2: Biology and ecology of parenting* (2nd ed., pp. 253–280). Mahwah, NJ: Erlbaum.

Harlow, Clara Mears. (1986). The evolution of Harlow research. In Clara Mears Harlow (Ed.), *From learning to love: The selected papers of H. F. Harlow* (pp. xvii-xxxviii). New York: Praeger.

Harlow, Harry F. (1958). The nature of love. *American Psychologist, 13,* 673–685.

Harmon, Amy. (2004, June 20). In new tests for fetal defects, agonizing choices for parents. *New York Times,* pp. A1, A19.

Harris, Judith Rich. (2002). Beyond the nurture assumption: Testing hypotheses about the child's environment. In John G. Borkowski, Sharon Landesman Ramey, & Marie Bristol-Power (Eds.), *Parenting and the child's world: Influences on academic, intellectual, and social-emotional development* (pp. 3–20). Mahwah, NJ: Erlbaum.

Hart, Betty, & Risley, Todd R. (1995). *Meaningful differences in the everyday experience of young American children.* Baltimore: Brookes.

Harter, Susan. (1998). The development of self-representations. In William Damon (Series Ed.) & Nancy Eisenberg (Vol. Ed.), *Handbook of child psychology: Vol. 3. Social, emotional and personality development* (5th ed., pp. 553–618). New York: Wiley.

Harter, Susan. (1999). *The construction of the self: A developmental perspective.* New York: Guilford Press.

Harter, Susan, Waters, Patricia L., & Whitesell, Nancy R. (1997). Lack of voice as a manifestation of false self behavior among adolescents: The school setting as a stage upon which the drama of authenticity is enacted. *Educational Psychologist, 32,* 153–173.

Hartl, Daniel L., & Jones, Elizabeth W. (1999). *Essential genetics* (2nd ed.). Sudbury, MA: Jones and Bartlett.

Hartmann, Donald P., & George, Thomas P. (1999). Design, measurement, and analysis in developmental research. In Marc H. Bornstein & Michael E. Lamb (Eds.), *Developmental psychology: An advanced textbook* (4th ed., pp. 125–198). Mahwah, NJ: Erlbaum.

Hartup, Willard W. (1996). The company they keep: Friendships and their developmental significance. *Child Development, 67,* 1–13.

Hartup, Willard W. (2002). Growing points in developmental science: A summing up. In Willard W. Hartup & Rainer K. Silbereisen (Eds.), *Growing points in developmental science: An introduction* (pp. 329–344). New York: Psychology Press.

Hartup, Willard W., & Stevens, Nan. (1999). Friendships and adaptation across the life span. *Current Directions in Psychological Science, 8,* 76–79.

Harwood, Robin L., Miller, Joan G., & Irizarry, Nydia Lucca. (1995). *Culture and attachment: Perceptions of the child in context.* New York: Guilford Press.

Hasebe, Yuki, Nucci, Larry, & Nucci, Maria S. (2004). Parental control of the personal domain and adolescent symptoms of psychopathology: A cross-national study in the United States and Japan. *Child Development, 75,* 815–828.

Haselager, Gerbert J. T., Cillessen, Antonius H. N., Van Lieshout, Cornelis F. M., Riksen-Walraven, J. Marianne A., & Hartup, Willard W. (2002). Heterogeneity among peer-rejected boys across middle childhood: Developmental pathways of social behavior. *Developmental Psychology, 38,* 446–456.

Hashima, Patricia Y., & Finkelhor, David. (1999). Violent victimization of youth versus adults in the National Crime Victimization Survey. *Journal of Interpersonal Violence, 14,* 799–820.

Haskins, Ron. (2005). Child development and child-care policy: Modest impacts. In David B. Pillemer & Sheldon Harold White (Eds.), *Developmental psychology and social change: Research, history, and policy* (pp. 140–170). New York: Cambridge University Press.

Hassold, Terry J., & Patterson, David (Eds.). (1999). *Down syndrome: A promising future, together.* New York: Wiley-Liss.

Hastie, Peter A. (2004). Problem-solving in teaching sports. In Jan Wright, Lisette Burrows, & Doune MacDonald (Eds.), *Critical inquiry and problem-solving in physical education* (pp. 62–73). London: Routledge.

Haugaard, Jeffrey J. (2000). The challenge of defining child sexual abuse. *American Psychologist, 55,* 1036–1039.

Hawker, David S. J., & Boulton, Michael J. (2000). Twenty years' research on peer victimization and psychosocial maladjustment: A meta-analytic review of cross-sectional studies. *Journal of Child Psychology & Psychiatry, 41,* 441–455.

Hawkins, J. D., Smith, B. H., Hill, K. G., Kosterman, R. , Catalano, R. F., & Abbott, R. D. (2003). Understanding and preventing crime and violence: Findings from the Seattle social development project. In Terence P. Thornberry & Marvin D. Krohn (Eds.), *Taking stock of delinquency: An overview of findings from contemporary longitudinal studies* (pp. 255–312). New York: Kluwer.

Hawley, Patricia H. (1999). The ontogenesis of social dominance: A strategy-based evolutionary perspective. *Developmental Review, 19,* 97–132.

Hay, Dale F., Pawlby, Susan, Sharp, Deborah, Asten, Paul, Mills, Alice, & Kumar, Ramesh 'Channi.' (2001). Intellectual problems shown by 11-year-old children whose mothers had postnatal depression. *Journal of Child Psychology & Psychiatry & Allied Disciplines, 42,* 871–889.

Hayes, Brett K., & Younger, Katherine. (2004). Category-use effects in children. *Child Development, 75,* 1719–1732.

Health Development Agency. (2003). *Teenage pregnancy and parenthood: A review of reviews.* London: National Health Service.

Heath, Andrew C., Slutske, Wendy S., & Madden, Pamela A. F. (1997). Gender differences in the genetic contribution to alcoholism risk and to alcohol consumption patterns. In Richard W. Wilsnack & Sharon C. Wilsnack (Eds.), *Gender and alcohol: Individual and social perspectives* (pp. 114–149). Piscataway, NJ: Rutgers Center of Alcohol Studies.

Hedley, Allison A., Ogden, Cynthia L., Johnson, Clifford L., Carroll, Margaret D., Curtin, Lester R., & Flegal, Katherine M. (2004). Prevalence of overweight and obesity among U.S. children, adolescents, and adults, 1999–2002. *Journal of the American Medical Association, 291,* 2847–2850.

Heimann, Mikael, & Meltzoff, Andrew N. (1996). Deferred imitation in 9- and 14-month-old infants: A longitudinal study of a Swedish sample. *British Journal of Developmental Psychology, 14*(Pt. 1), 55–64.

Helmuth, Laura. (2001). Where the brain tells a face from a place. *Science, 292,* 196–198.

Helwig, Charles C. (1995). Adolescents' and young adults' conceptions of civil liberties: Freedom of speech and religion. *Child Development, 66,* 152–166.

Helwig, Charles C., & Jasiobedzka, Urszula. (2001). The relation between law and morality: Children's reasoning about socially beneficial and unjust laws. *Child Development, 72,* 1382–1393.

Henderson, Heather A., Marshall, Peter J., Fox, Nathan A., & Rubin, Kenneth H. (2004). Psychophysiological and behavioral evidence for varying forms and functions of nonsocial behavior in preschoolers. *Child Development, 75,* 236–250.

Henry, David B. (2004, May). *Peer selection and socialization effects in sexual risk.* Paper presented at the 16th Annual Convention of the American Psychological Society, Chicago.

Herman, Melissa. (2004). Forced to choose: Some determinants of racial identification in multiracial adolescents. *Child Development, 75,* 730–748.

Herman-Giddens, Marcia E., Wang, Lily, & Koch, Gary. (2001). Secondary sexual characteristics in boys: Estimates from the National Health and Nutrition Examination Survey III, 1988–1994. *Archives of Pediatrics & Adolescent Medicine, 155,* 1022–1028.

Hermelin, Beate. (2001). *Bright splinters of the mind: A personal story of research with autistic savants.* Philadelphia: Jessica Kingsley.

Hetherington, E. Mavis, Bridges, Margaret, & Insabella, Glendessa M. (1998). What matters? What does not? Five perspectives on the association between marital transitions and children's adjustment. *American Psychologist, 53,* 167–184.

Hetherington, E. Mavis, & Elmore, Anne Mitchell. (2003). Risk and resilience in children coping with their parents' divorce and remarriage. In Suniya S. Luthar (Ed.), *Resilience and vulnerability: Adaptation in the context of childhood adversities* (pp. 182–212). New York: Cambridge University Press.

Hetherington, E. Mavis, & Kelly, John. (2002). *For better or for worse: Divorce reconsidered.* New York: Norton.

Heuveline, Patrick. (2002). An international comparison of adolescent and young adult mortality. *Annals of the American Academy of Political and Social Science, 580,* 172–200.

Heuveline, Patrick, & Timberlake, Jeffrey M. (2004). The role of cohabitation in family formation: The United States in comparative perspective. *Journal of Marriage & Family, 66,* 1214–1230.

Heyman, Bob, & Henriksen, Mette. (2001). *Risk, age, and pregnancy: A case study of prenatal genetic screening and testing.* New York: Palgrave.

Hill, Andrew J., & Lissau, Inge. (2002). Psychosocial factors. In Walter Burniat, Tim J. Cole, Inge Lissau, & Elizabeth M. E. Poskitt (Eds.), *Child and adolescent obesity: Causes and consequences, prevention and management* (pp. 109–128). New York: Cambridge University Press.

Hill, John P., & Holmbeck, Grayson N. (1987). Familial adaptation to biological change during adolescence. In Richard M. Lerner & Terryl T. Foch (Eds.), *Biological-psychosocial interactions in early adolescence* (pp. 207–223). Hillsdale, NJ: Erlbaum.

Hill, Nancy E., Bush, Kevin R., & Roosa, Mark W. (2003). Parenting and family socialization strategies and children's mental health: Low-income Mexican-American and Euro-American mothers and children. *Child Development, 74,* 189–204.

Hinds, David A., Stuve, Laura L., Nilsen, Geoffrey B., Halperin, Eran, Eskin, Eleazar, Ballinger, Dennis G., et al. (2005). Whole-genome patterns of common DNA variation in three human populations. *Science, 307,* 1072–1079.

Hines, Melissa. (2004). *Brain gender.* Oxford, England: Oxford University Press.

Hobbes, Thomas. (1982). *Leviathan.* London: Penguin. (Original work published 1651)

Hock-Long, Linda, Herceg-Baron, Roberta, Cassidy, Amy M., & Whittaker, Paul G. (2003). Access to adolescent reproductive health services: Financial and structural barriers to care. *Perspectives on Sexual and Reproductive Health, 35,* 144–147.

Hodder, Harbour Fraser. (1997, November-December). The new fertility. *Harvard Magazine, 99,* 54–64, 97–99.

Hodges, Ernest V. E., Boivin, Michel, Vitaro, Frank, & Bukowski, William M. (1999). The power of friendship: Protection against an escalating cycle of peer victimization. *Developmental Psychology, 35,* 94–101.

Hoff, Erika. (2003). The specificity of environmental influence: Socioeconomic status affects early vocabulary development via maternal speech. *Child Development, 74,* 1368–1378.

Hoff, Erika, & Naigles, Letitia. (2002). How children use input to acquire a lexicon. *Child Development, 73,* 418–433.

Hofferth, Sandra. (1999). Changes in American children's time, 1981–1997. University of Michigan's Institute for Social Research, Center Survey (January 1999).

Hofmann, Adele Dellenbaugh. (1997). Adolescent growth and development. In Adele Dellenbaugh Hofmann & Donald Everett Greydanus (Eds.), *Adolescent medicine* (3rd ed., pp. 10–22). Norwalk, CT: Appleton & Lange.

Hogan, Dennis P., Sun, Rongjun, & Cornwell, Gretchen T. (2000). Sexual and fertility behaviors of American females aged 15–19 years: 1985, 1990, and 1995. *American Journal of Public Health, 90,* 1421–4125.

Hoh, Josephine, & Ott, Jurg. (2003). Mathematical multi-locus approaches to localizing complex human trait genes. *Nature Reviews Genetics, 4,* 701–709.

Holden, Constance. (2000). The violence of the lambs. *Science, 289,* 580–581.

Hollich, George J., Hirsh-Pasek, Kathy, Golinkoff, Roberta Michnick, Brand, Rebecca J., Brown, Ellie, Chung, He Len, et al. (2000). Breaking the language barrier: An emergentist coalition model for the origins of word learning. *Monographs of the Society for Research in Child Development, 65*(3, Serial No. 262), v–123.

Hollon, Steven D., Thase, Michael E., & Markowitz, John C. (2002). Treatment and prevention of depression. *Psychological Science in the Public Interest, 3,* 39–77.

Holme, Jennifer Jellison. (2002). Buying homes, buying schools: School choice and the social construction of school quality. *Harvard Educational Review, 72,* 177–205.

Hong, Ying-yi, Morris, Michael W., Chiu, Chi-yue, & Benet-Martinez, Veronica. (2000). Multicultural minds: A dynamic constructivist approach to culture and cognition. *American Psychologist, 55,* 709–720.

Hooley, Jill M. (2004). Do psychiatric patients do better clinically if they live with certain kinds of families? *Current Directions in Psychological Science, 13,* 202–205.

Hosaka, Toru. (2005). School absenteeism, bullying, and loss of peer relationships in Japanese children. In David W. Shwalb, Jun Nakazawa, & Barbara J. Shwalb (Eds.), *Applied developmental psychology: Theory, practice, and research from Japan* (pp. 283–299). Greenwich, CT: Information Age.

Howard, Marion, & McCabe, Judith. (1990). Helping teenagers postpone sexual involvement. *Family Planning Perspectives, 22,* 21–26.

Howe, Christine. (1998). *Conceptual structure in childhood and adolescence: The case of everyday physics.* London: Routledge.

Howe, Mark L. (2004). The role of conceptual recoding in reducing children's retroactive interference. *Developmental Psychology, 40,* 131–139.

Howson, Geoffrey. (2002). Some questions on probability. *Teaching Statistics, 24,* 17–21.

Hrdy, Sarah Blaffer. (2000). *Mother nature: Maternal instincts and how they shape the human species* (1st Ballantine Books ed.). New York: Ballantine Books.

Hsu, Hui-Chin, Fogel, Alan, & Cooper, Rebecca B. (2000). Infant vocal development during the first 6 months: Speech quality and melodic complexity. *Infant & Child Development, 9,* 1–16.

Hubbs-Tait, Laura, Culp, Anne McDonald, Culp, Rex E., & Miller, Carrie E. (2002). Relation of maternal cognitive stimulation, emotional support, and intrusive behavior during Head Start to children's kindergarten cognitive abilities. *Child Development, 73,* 110–131.

Huesmann, L. Rowell, Moise-Titus, Jessica, Podolski, Cheryl-Lynn, & Eron, Leonard D. (2003). Longitudinal relations between children's exposure to TV violence and their aggressive and violent behavior in young adulthood: 1977–1992. *Developmental Psychology, 39,* 201–221.

Hugdahl, Kenneth, & Davidson, Richard J. (Eds.). (2002). *The asymmetrical brain.* Cambridge, MA: MIT Press.

Hulanicka, Barbara. (1999). Acceleration of menarcheal age of girls from dysfunctional families. *Journal of Reproductive & Infant Psychology, 17,* 119–132.

Hulbert, Ann. (2003). *Raising America: Experts, parents, and a century of advice about children.* New York: Knopf.

Humphrey, James Harry. (2003). *Child development through sports.* New York: Haworth Press.

Huston, Aletha C., & Aronson, Stacey Rosenkrantz. (2005). Mothers' time with infant and time in employment as predictors of mother-child relationships and children's early development. *Child Development, 76,* 467–482.

Huttenlocher, Janellen, Levine, Susan, & Vevea, Jack. (1998). Environmental input and cognitive growth: A study using time-period comparisons. *Child Development, 69,* 1012–1029.

Hyde, Kenneth E. (1990). *Religion in childhood and adolescence: A comprehensive review of the research.* Birmingham, AL: Religious Education Press.

Ichikawa, Shin'ichi. (2005). Cognitive counseling to improve students' metacogntion and cognitive skills. In David W. Shwalb, Jun Nakazawa, & Barbara J. Shwalb (Eds.), *Applied developmental psychology: Theory, practice, and research from Japan* (pp. 67–87). Greenwich, CT: Information Age.

Ingold, Tim. (2001). From the transmission of representation to the education of attention. In Harvey Whitehouse (Ed.), *The debated mind: Evolutionary psychology versus ethnography* (pp. 113–153). New York: Berg.

Inhelder, Bärbel, & Piaget, Jean. (1958). *The growth of logical thinking from childhood to adolescence: An essay on the construction of formal operational structures.* New York: Basic Books.

Inhelder, Bärbel, & Piaget, Jean. (1964). *The early growth of logic in the child.* New York: Harper & Row.

Irwin, Scott, Galvez, Roberto, Weiler, Ivan Jeanne, Beckel-Mitchener, Andrea, &

Greenough, William. (2002). Brain structure and the functions of FMR1 protein. In Randi Jenssen Hagerman & Paul J. Hagerman (Eds.), *Fragile X syndrome: Diagnosis, treatment, and research* (3rd ed., pp. 191–205). Baltimore: Johns Hopkins University Press.

Isolauri, Erika, Sutas, Yelda, Salo, Matti K., Isosomppi, Riitta, & Kaila, Minna. (1998). Elimination diet in cow's milk allergy: Risk for impaired growth in young children. *Journal of Pediatrics, 132,* 1004–1009.

Iverson, Jana M., & Fagan, Mary K. (2004). Infant vocal-motor coordination: Precursor to the gesture-speech system? *Child Development, 75,* 1053–1066.

Izard, Carroll E., & Ackerman, Brian P. (2000). Motivational, organizational, and regulatory functions of discrete emotions. In Michael Lewis & Jeannette M. Haviland-Jones (Eds.), *Handbook of emotions* (2nd ed., pp. 253–264). New York: Guilford Press.

Izard, Carroll E., Fine, Sarah, Mostow, Allison, Trentacosta, Christopher, & Campbell, Jan. (2002). Emotion processes in normal and abnormal development and preventive intervention. *Development & Psychopathology, 14,* 761–787.

Jaccard, James, & Dittus, Patricia J. (2000). Adolescent perceptions of maternal approval of birth control and sexual risk behavior. *American Journal of Public Health, 90,* 1426–1430.

Jackson, Debra J., Lang, Janet M., Swartz, William H., Ganiats, Theodore G., Fullerton, Judith, Ecker, Jeffrey, et al. (2003). Outcomes, safety, and resource utilization in a collaborative care birth center program compared with traditional physician-based perinatal care. *American Journal of Public Health, 93,* 999–1006.

Jackson, Yo, & Warren, Jared S. (2000). Appraisal, social support, and life events: Predicting outcome behavior in school-age children. *Child Development, 71,* 1441–1457.

Jacob's father. (1997). Jacob's story: A miracle of the heart. *Zero to Three, 17,* 59–64.

Jacobs, Janis E., Lanza, Stephanie, Osgood, D. Wayne, Eccles, Jacquelynne S., & Wigfield, Allan. (2002). Changes in children's self-competence and values: Gender and domain differences across grades one though twelve. *Child Development, 73,* 509–527.

Jacobvitz, Deborah, Hazen, Nancy, Curran, Melissa, & Hitchens, Kristen. (2004). Observations of early triadic family interactions: Boundary disturbances in the family predict symptoms of depression, anxiety, and attention-deficit/hyperactivity disorder in middle childhood. *Development & Psychopathology, 16,* 577–592.

Jaffee, Sara, Caspi, Avshalom, Moffitt, Terrie E., Belsky, Jay, & Silva, Phil. (2001). Why are children born to teen mothers at risk for adverse outcomes in young adulthood? Results from a 20-year longitudinal study. *Development & Psychopathology, 13,* 377–397.

Jaffee, Sara R., Caspi, Avshalom, Moffitt, Terrie E., Dodge, Kenneth A., Rutter, Michael, Taylor, Alan, et al. (2005). Nature X nurture: Genetic vulnerabilities interact with physical maltreatment to promote conduct problems. *Development & Psychopathology, 17,* 67–84.

Jaffee, Sara R., Caspi, Avshalom, Moffitt, Terrie E., Polo-Tomas, Monica, Price, Thomas S., & Taylor, Alan. (2004). The limits of child effects: Evidence for genetically mediated child effects on corporal punishment but not on physical maltreatment. *Developmental Psychology, 40,* 1047–1058.

Jahns, Lisa, Siega-Riz, Anna Maria, & Popkin, Barry M. (2001). The increasing prevalence of snacking among U.S. children from 1977 to 1996. *Journal of Pediatrics, 138,* 493–498.

Jang, Kerry L., McCrae, Robert R., Angleitner, Alois, Riemann, Rainer, & Livesley, W. John. (1998). Heritability of facet-level traits in a cross-cultural twin sample: Support for a hierarchical model of personality. *Journal of Personality & Social Psychology, 74,* 1556–1565.

Jayakody, Rukmalie, & Kalil, Ariel. (2002). Social fathering in low-income, African American families with preschool children. *Journal of Marriage & Family, 64,* 504–516.

Jenkins, Jennifer M., & Astington, Janet Wilde. (1996). Cognitive factors and family structure associated with theory of mind development in young children. *Developmental Psychology, 32,* 70–78.

Johnson, Dana E. (2000). Medical and developmental sequelae of early childhood institutionalization in Eastern European adoptees. In Charles A. Nelson (Ed.), *The Minnesota symposia on child psychology: Vol. 31. The effects of early adversity on neurobehavioral development* (pp. 113–162). Mahwah, NJ: Erlbaum.

Johnson, Deborah J., Jaeger, Elizabeth, Randolph, Suzanne M., Cauce, Ana Mari, & Ward, Janie. (2003). Studying the effects of early child care experiences on the development of children of color in the United States: Toward a more inclusive research agenda. *Child Development, 74,* 1227–1244.

Johnson, Janice, Im-Bolter, Nancie, & Pascual-Leone, Juan. (2003). Development of mental attention in gifted and mainstream children: The role of mental capacity, inhibition, and speed of processing. *Child Development, 74,* 1594–1614.

Johnson, Jeffrey G., Cohen, Patricia, Smailes, Elizabeth M., Kasen, Stephanie, & Brook, Judith S. (2002). Television viewing and aggressive behavior during adolescence and adulthood. *Science, 295,* 2468–2471.

Johnson, Kevin R. (1999). *How did you get to be Mexican? A white/brown man's search for identity.* Philadelphia: Temple University Press.

Johnson, Mark H. (1998). The neural basis of cognitive development. In William Damon (Series Ed.) & Deanna Kuhn & Robert S. Siegler (Vol. Eds.), *Handbook of child psychology: Vol. 2. Cognition, perception, and language* (pp. 1–49). New York: Wiley.

Johnson, Mark H., & Morton, John. (1991). *Biology and cognitive development: The case of face recognition.* Oxford, UK: Blackwell.

Johnson, Ruth S. (2002). *Using data to close the achievement gap: How to measure equity in our schools.* Thousand Oaks, CA: Corwin Press.

Johnston, Lloyd D., O'Malley, Patrick M., Bachman, Jerald G., & Schulenberg, John E. (2005). *Monitoring the Future national survey results on drug use, 1975–2004: Vol. I. Secondary school students* (NIH Publication No. 05-5727). Bethesda, MD: National Institute on Drug Abuse.

Johnston, Lloyd D., O'Malley, Patrick M., Bachman, Jerald G., & Schulenberg, John E. (2005). *Monitoring the Future national results on adolescent drug use: Overview of key findings, 2004* (NIH Publication No. 05-5726). Bethesda, MD: National Institute on Drug Abuse.

Johnston, Timothy D., & Edwards, Laura. (2002). Genes, interactions, and the development of behavior. *Psychological Review, 109,* 26–34.

Joiner, Thomas E. (1999). The clustering and contagion of suicide. *Current Directions in Psychological Science, 8,* 89–92.

Jones, Edward P. (2003). *The known world.* New York: Amistad.

Jones, Edward P. (2003). *Lost in the city: Stories.* New York: Amistad. (Original work published 1992)

Jones, Howard W., Jr., & Cohen, Jean. (2001). IFFS surveillance 01. *Fertility and Sterility, 76*(5, Supplement 1), 5–36.

Jones, Mary Cover. (1965). Psychological correlates of somatic development. *Child Development, 36,* 899–911.

Joseph, Rhawn. (2000). Fetal brain behavior and cognitive development. *Developmental Review, 20,* 81–98.

Jusczyk, Peter W. (1997). *The discovery of spoken language.* Cambridge, MA: MIT Press.

Kagan, Jerome. (1998). *Galen's prophecy: Temperament in human nature.* Boulder, CO: Westview Press.

Kagan, Jerome. (2002). *Surprise, uncertainty, and mental structures.* Cambridge, MA: Harvard University Press.

Kagan, Jerome, & Herschkowitz, Elinore Chapman. (2005). *Young mind in a growing brain.* Mahwah, NJ: Erlbaum.

Kagan, Jerome, & Snidman, Nancy C. (2004). *The long shadow of temperament.* Cambridge, MA: Belknap Press.

Kagitcibasi, Cigdem. (2003). Human development across cultures: A contextual-functional analysis and implications for interventions. In T. S. Saraswati (Ed.), *Cross-cultural perspectives in human development: Theory, research, and applications* (pp. 166–191). New Delhi, India: Sage.

Kahana-Kalman, Ronit, & Walker-Andrews, Arlene S. (2001). The role of person familiarity in young infants' perception of emotional expressions. *Child Development, 72,* 352–369.

Kahn, Jeffrey P., Mastroianni, Anna C., & Sugarman, Jeremy (Eds.). (1998). *Beyond consent: Seeking justice in research.* New York: Oxford University Press.

Kail, Robert. (2000). Speed of information processing: Developmental change and links to intelligence. *Journal of School Psychology, 38,* 51–61.

Källén, Bengt. (2004). Neonate characteristics after maternal use of antidepressants in late pregnancy. *Archives of Pediatric and Adolescent Medicine, 158,* 312–316.

Kanner, Leo. (1943). Autistic disturbances of affective contact. *Nervous Child, 2,* 217–250.

Kaplan, Bonnie J., Crawford, Susan G., Dewey, Deborah M., & Fisher, Geoff C. (2000). The IQs of children with ADHD are normally distributed. *Journal of Learning Disabilities, 33,* 425–432.

Karpov, Yuriy V., & Haywood, H. Carl. (1998). Two ways to elaborate Vygotsky's concept of mediation. *American Psychologist, 53,* 27–36.

Kaufman, Alan S., & Lichtenberger, Elizabeth O. (2000). *Essentials of WISC-III and WPPSI-R assessment.* New York: Wiley.

Kaufman, Joan, & Charney, Dennis. (2001). Effects of early stress on brain structure and function: Implications for understanding the relationship between child maltreatment and depression. *Development & Psychopathology, 13,* 451–471.

Kazdin, Alan E. (2001). *Behavior modification in applied settings* (6th ed.). Belmont, CA: Wadsworth/Thomson Learning.

Keating, Daniel P. (2004). Cognitive and brain development. In Richard M. Lerner & Laurence D. Steinberg (Eds.), *Handbook of adolescent psychology* (2nd ed., pp. 45–84). Hoboken, NJ: Wiley.

Kegl, Judy, Senghas, Ann, & Coppola, Marie. (1999). Creation through contact: Sign language emergence and sign language change in Nicaragua. In Michel DeGraff (Ed.), *Language creation and language change: Creolization, diachrony, and development* (pp. 179–237). Cambridge, MA: MIT Press.

Keil, Frank C., & Lockhart, Kristi L. (1999). Explanatory understanding in conceptual development. In Ellin Kofsky Scholnick, Katherine Nelson, Susan A. Gelman, & Patricia H. Miller (Eds.), *Conceptual development: Piaget's legacy* (pp. 103–130). Mahwah, NJ: Erlbaum.

Keiley, Margaret Kraatz, Howe, Tasha R., Dodge, Kenneth A., Bates, John E., & Pettit, Gregory S. (2001). The timing of child physical maltreatment: A cross-domain growth analysis of impact on adolescent externalizing and internalizing problems. *Development & Psychopathology, 13,* 891–912.

Kelemen, Deborah, Callanan, Maureen A., Casler, Krista, & Perez-Granados, Deanne R. (2005). Why things happen: Teleological explanation in parent-child conversation. *Developmental Psychology, 41,* 251–264.

Keller, Heidi, Yovsi, Relindis, Borke, Joern, Kartner, Joscha, Jensen, Henning, & Papaligoura, Zaira. (2004). Developmental consequences of early parenting experiences: Self-recognition and self-regulation in three cultural communities. *Child Development, 75,* 1745–1760.

Keller, Monika, Gummerum, Michaela, Wang, Xiao Tien, & Lindsey, Samuel. (2004). Understanding perspectives and emotions in contract violation: Development of deontic and moral reasoning. *Child Development, 75,* 614–635.

Keller, Meret A., & Goldberg, Wendy A. (2004). Co-sleeping: Help or hindrance for young children's independence? *Infant and Child Development, 13,* 369–388.

Kelley, Sue A., Brownell, Celia A., & Campbell, Susan B. (2000). Mastery motivation and self-evaluative affect in toddlers: Longitudinal relations with maternal behavior. *Child Development, 71,* 1061–1071.

Kellman, Philip J., & Banks, Martin S. (1998). Infant visual perception. In William Damon (Series Ed.) & Deanna Kuhn & Robert S. Siegler (Vol. Eds.), *Handbook of child psychology: Vol. 2. Cognition, perception, and language* (5th ed., pp. 103–146). New York: Wiley.

Keltikangas-Jarvinen, Liisa, & Heinonen, Kati. (2003). Childhood roots of adulthood hostility: Family factors as predictors of cognitive and affective hostility. *Child Development, 74,* 1751–1768.

Kendall-Tackett, Kathleen. (2002). The health effects of childhood abuse: Four pathways by which abuse can influence health. *Child Abuse & Neglect, 26,* 715–729.

Keogh, Barbara K. (2004). The importance of longitudinal research for early intervention practices. In Peggy D. McCardle & Vinita Chhabra (Eds.), *The voice of evidence in reading research* (pp. 81–102). Baltimore: Brookes.

Kerig, Patricia K., Fedorowicz, Anne E., Brown, Corina A., & Warren, Michelle. (2000). Assessment and intervention for PTSD in children exposed to violence. In Robert A. Geffner, Peter G. Jaffe, & Marlies Sudermann (Eds.), *Children exposed to domestic violence: Current issues in research, intervention, prevention, and policy develop-*

ment (pp. 161–184). Binghamton, NY: Haworth Press.

Kessler, Seymour. (2000). *Psyche and helix: Psychological aspects of genetic counseling* (Robert G. Resta, Ed.). New York: Wiley-Liss.

Khaleque, Abdul, & Rohner, Ronald P. (2002). Perceived parental acceptance-rejection and psychological adjustment: A meta-analysis of cross-cultural and intracultural studies. *Journal of Marriage & the Family, 64,* 54–64.

Khawaja, Marwan, Jurdi, Rozzet, & Kabakian-Khasholian, Tamar. (2004). Rising trends in cesarean section rates in Egypt. *Birth: Issues in Perinatal Care, 31,* 12–16.

Kiberstis, Paula A. (2005). A surfeit of suspects. *Science, 307,* 369.

Kim, Kenneth, & Smith, Peter K. (1998). Retrospective survey of parental marital relations and child reproductive development. *International Journal of Behavioral Development, 22,* 729–751.

Kim, Karl H. S., Relkin, Norman R., Lee, Kyoung-Min, & Hirsch, Joy. (1997, July 10). Distinct cortical areas associated with native and second languages. *Nature, 388,* 171–174.

Kim-Cohen, Julia, Moffitt, Terrie E., Caspi, Avshalom, & Taylor, Alan. (2004). Genetic and environmental processes in young children's resilience and vulnerability to socioeconomic deprivation. *Child Development, 75,* 651–668.

Kimmel, Michael S. (2004). *The gendered society* (2nd ed.). New York: Oxford University Press.

King, Kendall. (2004). Language policy and local planning in South America: New directions for enrichment bilingual education in the Andes. *International Journal of Bilingual Education & Bilingualism, 7,* 334–347.

King, Pamela Ebstyne, & Furrow, James L. (2004). Religion as a resource for positive youth development: Religion, social capital, and moral outcomes. *Developmental Psychology, 40,* 703–713.

King, Patricia M., & Kitchener, Karen S. (1994). *Developing reflective judgment: Understanding and promoting intellectual growth and critical thinking in adolescents and adults.* San Francisco: Jossey-Bass.

King, Valarie, Harris, Kathleen Mullan, & Heard, Holly E. (2004). Racial and ethnic diversity in nonresident father involvement. *Journal of Marriage & Family, 66,* 1–21.

Kirkwood, Thomas B. L. (2003). Age differences in evolutionary selection benefits. In Ursula M. Staudinger & Ulman Lindenberger (Eds.), *Understanding human development: Dialogues with lifespan psychology* (pp. 45–57). Dordrecht, The Netherlands: Kluwer.

Kitzinger, Sheila. (2001). *Rediscovering birth.* New York: Simon & Schuster.

Klaczynski, Paul A. (2000). Motivated scientific reasoning biases, epistemological beliefs, and theory polarization: A two-process approach to adolescent cognition. *Child Development, 71,* 1347–1366.

Klaczynski, Paul A. (2001). Analytic and heuristic processing influences on adolescent reasoning and decision-making. *Child Development, 72,* 844–861.

Klaus, Marshall H., & Kennell, John H. (1976). *Maternal-infant bonding: The impact of early separation or loss on family development.* St. Louis, MO: Mosby.

Kloo, Daniela, & Perner, Josef. (2003). Training transfer between card sorting and false belief understanding: Helping children apply conflicting descriptions. *Child Development, 74,* 1823–1839.

Klug, William S., & Cummings, Michael R. (2000). *Concepts of genetics* (6th ed.). Upper Saddle River, NJ: Prentice Hall.

Knudsen, Eric I. (1999). Mechanisms of experience-dependent plasticity in the auditory localization pathway of the barn owl. *Journal of Comparative Physiology A: Sensory, Neural, and Behavioral Physiology, 185,* 305–321.

Kochanska, Grazyna, Coy, Katherine C., & Murray, Kathleen T. (2001). The development of self-regulation in the first four years of life. *Child Development, 72,* 1091–1111.

Kochanska, Grazyna, Gross, Jami N., Lin, Mei-Hua, & Nichols, Kate E. (2002). Guilt in young children: Development, determinants, and relations with a broader system of standards. *Child Development, 73,* 461–482.

Kochenderfer-Ladd, Becky, & Skinner, Karey. (2002). Children's coping strategies: Moderators of the effects of peer victimization? *Developmental Psychology, 38,* 267–278.

Kohlberg, Lawrence. (1963). The development of children's orientations toward a moral order: I. Sequence in the development of moral thought. *Vita Humana, 6*(1-2), 11–33.

Kohlberg, Lawrence, Levine, Charles, & Hewer, Alexandra. (1983). *Moral stages: A current formulation and a response to critics.* New York: Karger.

Kolb, Bryan, & Whishaw, Ian Q. (2003). *Fundamentals of human neuropsychology* (5th ed.). New York: Worth.

Koops, Willem. (2003). Imaging childhood. In Willem Koops & Michael Zuckerman (Eds.), *Beyond the century of the child: Cultural history and developmental psychology* (pp. 1–18). Philadelphia: University of Pennsylvania Press.

Kovacs, Donna M., Parker, Jeffrey G., & Hoffman, Lois W. (1996). Behavioral, affective, and social correlates of involvement in cross-sex friendship in elementary school. *Child Development, 67,* 2269–2286.

Kovas, Yulia, Hayiou-Thomas, Marianna E., Oliver, Bonamy, Dale, Philip S., Bishop, Dorothy V. M., & Plomin, Robert. (2005). Genetic influences in different aspects of language development: The etiology of language skills in 4.5-year-old twins. *Child Development, 76,* 632–651.

Kozol, Jonathan. (1991). *Savage inequalities: Children in America's schools.* New York: Crown.

Kraft, Joan Creech, & Willhite, Calvin C. (1997). Retinoids in abnormal and normal embryonic development. In Sam Kacew & George H. Lambert (Eds.), *Environmental toxicology and pharmacology of human development* (pp. 15–40). Washington, DC: Taylor & Francis.

Krashen, Stephen D., Tse, Lucy, & McQuilla, Jeff (Eds.). (1998). *Heritage language development.* Culver City, CA: Language Education Associates.

Krieger, Nancy, Chen, Jarvis T., Waterman, Pamela D., Rehkopf, David H., & Subramanian, S. V. (2005). Painting a truer picture of U.S. socioeconomic and racial/ethnic health inequalities: The Public Health Disparities Geocoding Project. *American Journal of Public Health, 95,* 312–323.

Kroger, Jane. (2000). *Identity development: Adolescence through adulthood.* Thousand Oaks, CA: Sage.

Kroger, Jane. (2004). *Identity in adolescence: The balance between self and other* (3rd ed.). Hove, UK: Routledge.

Kuller, Jeffrey A., Strauss, Robert A., & Cefalo, Robert C. (2001). Preconceptional and prenatal care. In Frank W. Ling & W. Patrick Duff (Eds.), *Obstetrics and gynecology: Principles for practice* (pp. 25–54). New York: McGraw-Hill.

Kunkel, Dale, Cope, Kirstie M., Farinola, Wendy Jo Maynard, Biely, Erica, Rollin, Emma, & Donnerstein, Edward. (1999). *Sex on TV: Content and context: A biennial report to the Kaiser Family Foundation* (#1458). Menlo Park, CA: Kaiser Family Foundation.

Kupersmidt, Janis B., Coie, John D., & Howell, James C. (2004). Resilience in children exposed to negative peer influences. In Kenneth I. Maton, Cynthia J. Schellenbach, Bonnie J. Leadbeater, & Andrea L. Solarz (Eds.), *Investing in children, youth, families, and communities: Strengths-based research and policy* (pp. 251–268). Washington, DC: American Psychological Association.

Kvalem, Ingela Lundin, & Traeen, Bente. (2000). Self-efficacy, scripts of love and intention to use condoms among Norwegian adolescents. *Journal of Youth & Adolescence, 29,* 337–353.

La Leche League International. (1997). *The womanly art of breastfeeding* (6th ed.). New York: Plume.

Labouvie-Vief, Gisela. (2003). Dynamic integration: Affect, cognition, and the self in adulthood. *Current Directions in Psychological Science, 12,* 201–206.

Lacourse, Eric, Nagin, Daniel, Tremblay, Richard E., Vitaro, Frank, & Claes, Michel. (2003). Developmental trajectories of boys' delinquent group membership and facilitation of violent behaviors during adolescence. *Development & Psychopathology, 15,* 183–197.

Ladd, Gary W. (1999). Peer relationships and social competence during early and middle childhood. *Annual Review of Psychology, 50,* 333–359.

Ladd, Gary W., & Pettit, Gregory S. (2002). Parenting and the development of children's peer relationships. In Marc H. Bornstein (Ed.), *Handbook of parenting: Vol. 5. Practical issues in parenting* (2nd ed., pp. 269–309). Mahwah, NJ: Erlbaum.

Lagattuta, Kristin Hansen. (2005). When you shouldn't do what you want to do: Young children's understanding of desires, rules, and emotions. *Child Development, 76,* 713–733.

Lagattuta, Kristin Hansen, & Wellman, Henry M. (2002). Differences in early parent-child conversations about negative versus positive emotions: Implications for the development of psychological understanding. *Developmental Psychology, 38,* 564–580.

Laland, Kevin N., & Brown, Gillian R. (2002). *Sense and nonsense: Evolutionary perspectives on human behaviour.* New York: Oxford University Press.

Lamb, Michael E. (1982). Maternal employment and child development: A review. In Michael E. Lamb (Ed.), *Nontraditional families: Parenting and child development* (pp. 45–69). Hillsdale, NJ: Erlbaum.

Lamb, Michael E. (1998). Nonparental child care: Context, quality, correlates, and consequences. In William Damon (Series Ed.) & Irving E. Sigel & K. Ann Renninger (Vol. Eds.), *Handbook of child psychology: Vol. 4. Child psychology in practice* (5th ed., pp. 73–133). New York: Wiley.

Lamb, Michael E. (2000). The history of research on father involvement: An overview. In H. Elizabeth Peters, Gary W. Peterson, Suzanne K. Steinmetz, & Randal D. Day (Eds.), *Fatherhood: Research, interventions, and policies* (pp. 23–42). New York: Haworth Press.

Lanclos, Donna M. (2003). *At play in Belfast: Children's folklore and identities in Northern Ireland.* New Brunswick, NJ: Rutgers University Press.

Landry, David J., Darroch, Jacqueline E., Singh, Susheela, & Higgins, Jenny. (2003). Factors associated with the content of sex education in U.S. public secondary schools. *Perspectives on Sexual and Reproductive Health, 35,* 261–269.

Langer, Jonas. (2001). The mosaic evolution of cognitive and linguistic ontogeny. In Melissa Bowerman & Stephen C. Levinson (Eds.), *Language acquisition and conceptual development* (pp. 19–44). Cambridge, UK: Cambridge University Press.

Lansford, Jennifer E., Ceballo, Rosario, Abbey, Antonia, & Stewart, Abigail J. (2001). Does family structure matter? A comparison of adoptive, two-parent biological, single-mother, stepfather, and stepmother households. *Journal of Marriage & the Family, 63,* 840–851.

Lansford, Jennifer E., Dodge, Kenneth A., Pettit, Gregory S., Bates, John E., Crozier, Joseph, & Kaplow, Julie. (2002). A 12-year prospective study of the long-term effects of early child physical maltreatment on psychological, behavioral, and academic problems in adolescence. *Archives of Pediatrics & Adolescent Medicine, 156,* 824–830.

Lapsley, Daniel K. (1993). Toward an integrated theory of adolescent ego development: The "new look" at adolescent egocentrism. *American Journal of Orthopsychiatry, 63,* 562–571.

Larcombe, Duncan. (2005). Content matters: Sometimes even more than we think. *American Educator, 29,* 42–43.

Larner, Mary B., Stevenson, Carol S., & Behrman, Richard E. (1998). Protecting children from abuse and neglect: Analysis and recommendations. *The Future of Children: Protecting Children from Abuse and Neglect, 8*(1), 4–22.

Larose, Simon, Bernier, Annie, & Tarabulsy, George M. (2005). Attachment state of mind, learning dispositions, and academic performance during the college transition. *Developmental Psychology, 41,* 281–289.

Larsen, William J. (1998). *Essentials of human embryology.* New York: Churchill Livingstone.

Larson, David E., & Mayo Clinic. (Eds.). (1990). *Mayo Clinic family health book.* New York: Morrow.

Larson, Reed W. (2000). Toward a psychology of positive youth development. *American Psychologist, 55,* 170–183.

Larson, Reed W. (2001). Commentary. *Monographs of the Society for Research in Child Development, 66*(1, Serial No. 264), 148–154.

Larson, Reed W., & Gillman, Sally. (1999). Transmission of emotions in the daily interactions of single-mother families. *Journal of Marriage & the Family, 61,* 21–37.

Larson, Reed W., & Richards, Maryse Heather. (1994). *Divergent realities: The emotional lives of mothers, fathers, and adolescents.* New York: Basic Books.

Larson, Reed W., Verma, Suman, & Dworkin, Jodi. (2003). Adolescence without family disengagement: The daily family lives of Indian middle class teenagers. In T. S. Saraswati (Ed.), *Cross-cultural perspectives in human development: Theory, research, and applications* (pp. 258–286). New Delhi, India: Sage.

Larson, Reed W., & Wilson, Suzanne. (2004). Adolescence across place and time: Globalization and the changing pathways to adulthood. In Richard M. Lerner & Laurence D. Steinberg (Eds.), *Handbook of adolescent psychology* (2nd ed., pp. 299–330). Hoboken, NJ: Wiley.

Laumann, Edward O., Gagnon, John H., Michael, Robert T., & Michaels, Stuart. (1994). *The social organization of sexuality: Sexual practices in the United States.* Chicago: University of Chicago Press.

Laursen, Brett, Coy, Katherine C., & Collins, W. Andrew. (1998). Reconsidering changes in parent-child conflict across adolescence: A meta-analysis. *Child Development, 69,* 817–832.

Laursen, Brett, & Williams, Vickie A. (1997). Perceptions of interdependence and closeness in family and peer relationships among adolescents with and without romantic partners. In Shmuel Shulman & W. Andrew Collins (Eds.), *New directions for child development: No. 78. Romantic relationships in adolescence: Developmental perspectives* (pp. 3–20). San Francisco: Jossey-Bass.

Lavelli, Manuela, & Fogel, Alan. (2005). Developmental changes in the relationship between the infant's attention and emotion during early face-to-face communication: The 2-month transition. *Developmental Psychology, 41,* 265–280.

Law, James. (2000). Factors affecting language development in West African children: A pilot study using a qualitative methodology. *Child: Care, Health & Development, 26,* 289–308.

Layden, Tim. (2004, November 15). Get out and play! *Sports Illustrated, 101,* 80–93.

Lazar, Mitchell A. (2005). How obesity causes diabetes: Not a tall tale. *Science, 307,* 373–375.

Leach, Penelope. (1997). *Your baby & child: From birth to age five* (3rd ed.). New York: Knopf.

Leaper, Campbell. (2002). Parenting girls and boys. In Marc H. Bornstein (Ed.), *Handbook of parenting: Vol. 1. Children and parenting* (2nd ed., pp. 189–225). Mahwah, NJ: Erlbaum.

Leaper, Campbell, & Smith, Tara E. (2004). A meta-analytic review of gender variations in children's language use: Talkativeness, affiliative speech, and assertive speech. *Developmental Psychology, 40,* 993–1027.

Lee, K. (2000). Crying patterns of Korean infants in institutions. *Child: Care, Health and Development, 26,* 217–228.

Lei, Joy L. (2003). (Un)necessary toughness?: Those "loud black girls" and those "quiet Asian boys." *Anthropology & Education Quarterly, 34,* 158–181.

Lenneberg, Eric H. (1967). *Biological foundations of language.* New York: Wiley.

Leonard, Christiana M. (2003). Neural substrate of speech and language development. In Michelle De Haan & Mark H. Johnson (Eds.), *The cognitive neuroscience of development* (pp. 127–156). New York: Psychology Press.

Leonard, Kenneth E., & Blane, Howard T. (Eds.). (1999). *Psychological theories of drinking and alcoholism* (2nd ed.). New York: Guilford.

Leone, Tiziana, Matthews, Zoë, & Dalla Zuanna, Gianpiero. (2003). Impact and determinants of sex preference in Nepal. *International Family Planning Perspectives, 29,* 69–75.

Lepper, Mark R., Greene, David, & Nisbett, Richard E. (1973). Undermining children's intrinsic interest with extrinsic reward: A test of the "overjustification" hypothesis. *Journal of Personality & Social Psychology, 28,* 129–137.

Lerner, Janet W. (2000). *Learning disabilities: Theories, diagnosis, and teaching strategies* (8th ed.). Boston: Houghton Mifflin.

Leroy, Valériane, Karon, John M., Alioum, Ahmadou, Ekpini, Ehounou R., Meda, Nicolas, Greenberg, Alan E., et al. (2002). Twenty-four month efficacy of a maternal short-course zidovudine regimen to prevent mother-to-child transmission of HIV-1 in West Africa. *AIDS, 16,* 631–641.

Leventhal, Tama, & Brooks-Gunn, Jeanne. (2004). Diversity in developmental trajectories across adolescence: Neighborhood influences. In Richard M. Lerner & Laurence D. Steinberg (Eds.), *Handbook of adolescent psychology* (2nd ed., pp. 451–486). Hoboken, NJ: Wiley.

Levesque, Roger J. R. (2002). *Not by faith alone: Religion, law, and adolescence.* New York: New York University Press.

Levine, James A., Lanningham-Foster, Lorraine M., McCrady, Shelly K., Krizan, Alisa C., Olson, Leslie R., Kane, Paul H., et al. (2005). Interindividual variation in posture allocation: Possible role in human obesity. *Science, 307,* 584–586.

LeVine, Robert A., LeVine, Sarah E., & Schnell, Beatrice. (2001). "Improve the women": Mass schooling, female literacy, and worldwide social change. *Harvard Educational Review, 71,* 1–50.

Levinson, David. (1989). *Family violence in cross-cultural perspective.* Newbury Park, CA: Sage.

Lewin, Kurt. (1943). Psychology and the process of group living. *Journal of Social Psychology, 17,* 113–131.

Lewis, Ann, & Lindsay, Geoff. (2000). Emerging issues. In Ann Lewis & Geoff Lindsay (Eds.), *Researching children's perspectives* (pp. 189–197). Philadelphia: Open University Press.

Lewis, Lawrence B., Antone, Carol, & Johnson, Jacqueline S. (1999). Effects of prosodic stress and serial position on syllable omission in first words. *Developmental Psychology, 35,* 45–59.

Lewis, Michael. (1997). *Altering fate: Why the past does not predict the future.* New York: Guilford Press.

Lewis, Michael, & Brooks, Jeanne. (1978). Self-knowledge and emotional development. In Michael Lewis & L. A. Rosenblum (Eds.), *Genesis of behavior: Vol. 1. The development of affect* (pp. 205–226). New York: Plenum Press.

Lewis, Michael, & Ramsay, Douglas. (2004). Development of self-recognition, personal pronoun use, and pretend play during the 2nd year. *Child Development, 75,* 1821–1831.

Lewis, Michael, & Ramsay, Douglas. (2005). Infant emotional and cortisol responses to goal blockage. *Child Development, 76,* 518–530.

Lewit, Eugene M., & Kerrebrock, Nancy. (1998). Child indicators: Dental health. *The Future of Children: Protecting Children from Abuse and Neglect, 8*(1), 133–142.

Liebkind, Karmela, & Jasinskaja-Lahti, Inga. (2000). Acculturation and psychological well-being among immigrant adolescents in Finland: A comparative study of adolescents from different cultural backgrounds. *Journal of Adolescent Research, 15,* 446–469.

Lieu, Tracy A., Ray, G. Thomas, Black, Steven B., Butler, Jay C., Klein, Jerome

O., Breiman, Robert F., et al. (2000). Projected cost-effectiveness of pneumococcal conjugate vaccination of healthy infants and young children. *Journal of the American Medical Association, 283,* 1460–1468.

Lightfoot, Cynthia. (1997). *The culture of adolescent risk-taking.* New York: Guilford Press.

Lillard, Angeline. (1998). Ethnopsychologies: Cultural variations in theories of mind. *Psychological Bulletin, 123,* 3–32.

Lillard, Angeline Stoll. (2005). *Montessori: The science behind the genius.* New York: Oxford University Press.

Lin, B. H., Huang, C. L., & French, S. A. (2004). Factors associated with women's and children's body mass indices by income status. *International Journal of Obesity, 28,* 536–542.

Lindsay, Geoff. (2000). Researching children's perspectives: Ethical issues. In Ann Lewis & Geoff Lindsay (Eds.), *Researching children's perspectives* (pp. 3–20). Philadelphia: Open University Press.

Linville, Patricia W., Fischer, Gregory W., & Fischhoff, Baruch. (1993). AIDS risk perceptions and decision biases. In John B. Pryor & Glenn D. Reeder (Eds.), *The social psychology of HIV infection* (pp. 5–38). Hillsdale, NJ: Erlbaum.

Lippa, Richard A. (2002). *Gender, nature, and nurture.* Mahwah, NJ: Erlbaum.

Lissau, Inge, Overpeck, Mary D., Ruan, W. June, Due, Pernille, Holstein, Bjorn E., & Hediger, Mary L. (2004). Body mass index and overweight in adolescents in 13 European countries, Israel, and the United States. *Archives of Pediatrics & Adolescent Medicine, 158,* 27–33.

Little League Baseball. (2005). *Media guide 2005.* Williamsport, PA: Author.

Little, Peter (Ed.). (2002). *Genetic destinies.* Oxford, England: Oxford University Press.

Lockhart, Kristi L., Chang, Bernard, & Story, Tyler. (2002). Young children's beliefs about the stability of traits: Protective optimism? *Child Development, 73,* 1408–1430.

Loeb, Susanna, Fuller, Bruce, Kagan, Sharon Lynn, & Carrol, Bidemi. (2004). Child care in poor communities: Early learning effects of type, quality, and stability. *Child Development, 75,* 47–65.

Loeber, Rolf, Drinkwater, Matthew, Yin, Yanming, Anderson, Stewart J., Schmidt, Laura C., & Crawford, Anne. (2000). Stability of family interaction from ages 6 to 18. *Journal of Abnormal Child Psychology, 28,* 353–369.

Loeber, Rolf, & Farrington, David P. (2000). Young children who commit crime: Epidemiology, developmental origins, risk factors, early interventions, and policy implications. *Development & Psychopathology, 12,* 737–762.

Loehlin, John C., McCrae, Robert R., Costa, Paul T., & John, Oliver P. (1998). Heritabilities of common and measure-specific components of the Big Five personality factors. *Journal of Research in Personality, 32,* 431–453.

Loland, Sigmund. (2002). *Fair play in sport: A moral norm system.* London: Routledge.

Lombardi, Joan, & Cubbage, Amy Stephens. (2004). Head Start in the 1990s: Striving for quality through a decade of improvement. In Edward Zigler & Sally J. Styfco (Eds.), *The Head Start debates* (pp. 283–295). Baltimore: Brookes.

Lopez, Nestor L., Vazquez, Delia M., & Olson, Sheryl L. (2004). An integrative approach to the neurophysiological substrates of social withdrawal and aggression. *Development & Psychopathology, 16,* 69–93.

Lorenz, Edward. (1972, December). *Predictability: Does the flap of a butterfly's wings in Brazil set off a tornado in Texas?* Paper presented at the American Association for the Advancement of Science, Washington, DC.

Lovaas, O. Ivar. (1987). Behavioral treatment and normal educational and intellectual functioning in young autistic children. *Journal of Consulting & Clinical Psychology, 55,* 3–9.

Lowe, B., Zipfel, S., Buchholz, C., Dupont, Y., Reas, D. L., & Herzog, W. (2001). Long-term outcome of anorexia nervosa in a prospective 21-year follow-up study. *Psychological Medicine, 31,* 881–890.

Luciana, Monica. (2003). Cognitive development in children born preterm: Implications for theories of brain plasticity following early injury. *Development and Psychopathology, 15,* 1017–1047.

Luciana, Monica. (2003). The neural and functional development of human prefrontal cortex. In Michelle De Haan & Mark H. Johnson (Eds.), *The cognitive neuroscience of development* (pp. 157–179). New York: Psychology Press.

Luciana, Monica, Conklin, Heather M., Hooper, Catalina J., & Yarger, Rebecca S. (2005). The development of nonverbal working memory and executive control processes in adolescents. *Child Development, 76,* 697–712.

Lundberg, Shelly, & Rose, Elaina. (2003). Child gender and the transition to marriage. *Demography, 40,* 333–349.

Lundy, Jean E. B. (2002). Age and language skills of deaf children in relation to theory of mind development. *Journal of Deaf Studies & Deaf Education, 7,* 41–56.

Luthar, Suniya S. (2003). The culture of affluence: Psychological costs of material wealth. *Child Development, 74,* 1581–1593.

Luthar, Suniya S., Cicchetti, Dante, & Becker, Bronwyn. (2000). The construct of resilience: A critical evaluation and guidelines for future work. *Child Development, 71,* 543–562.

Luthar, Suniya S., & Zelazo, Laurel Bidwell. (2003). Research on resilience: An integrative review. In Suniya S. Luthar (Ed.), *Resilience and vulnerability: Adaptation in the context of childhood adversities* (pp. 510–549). New York: Cambridge University Press.

Lutz, Donna J., & Sternberg, Robert J. (1999). Cognitive development. In Marc H. Bornstein & Michael E. Lamb (Eds.), *Developmental psychology: An advanced textbook* (4th ed., pp. 275–311). Mahwah, NJ: Erlbaum.

Lye, Steve, & Challis, John R. G. (2001). Parturition. In Richard Harding & Alan D. Bocking (Eds.), *Fetal growth and development* (pp. 241–266). New York: Cambridge University Press.

Lykken, David Thoreson. (1995). *The antisocial personalities.* Hillsdale, NJ: Erlbaum.

Lyons, Peter, & Rittner, Barbara. (1998). The construction of the crack babies phenomenon as a social problem. *American Journal of Orthopsychiatry, 68,* 313–320.

Lyons-Ruth, Karlen, Bronfman, Elisa, & Parsons, Elizabeth. (1999). IV. Maternal frightened, frightening, or atypical behavior and disorganized infant attachment patterns. *Monographs of the Society for Research in Child Development, 64*(3, Serial No. 258), 67–96.

Maccoby, Eleanor E. (1998). *The two sexes: Growing up apart, coming together.* Cambridge, MA: Belknap Press of Harvard University Press.

Maccoby, Eleanor E. (2000). Parenting and its effects on children: On reading and misreading behavior genetics. *Annual Review of Psychology, 51,* 1–27.

Macfie, Jenny, Cicchetti, Dante, & Toth, Sheree L. (2001). The development of dissociation in maltreated preschool-aged children. *Development and Psychopathology, 13,* 233–254.

MacIntyre, U. E., de Villiers, F. P., & Owange-Iraka, J. W. (2001). Increase in childhood asthma admissions in an urbanising population. *South African Medical Journal, 91,* 667–672.

Macpherson, Alison, Roberts, Ian, & Pless, I. Barry. (1998). Children's exposure to traffic and pedestrian injuries. *American Journal of Public Health, 88,* 1840–1843.

Macrae, C. Neil, & Bodenhausen, Galen V. (2000). Social cognition: Thinking categorically about others. *Annual Review of Psychology, 51,* 93–120.

MacWhinney, Brian, & Bornstein, Marc H. (2003). Language and literacy. In Marc H. Bornstein, Lucy Davidson, Corey L. M. Keyes, & Kristin Moore (Eds.), *Well-being: Positive development across the life course* (pp. 331–339). Mahwah, NJ: Erlbaum.

Madsen, Kreesten Meldgaard, Hviid, Anders, Vestergaard, Mogens, Schendel, Diana, Wohlfahrt, Jan, Thorsen, Poul, et al. (2002). A population-based study of measles, mumps, and rubella vaccination and autism. *New England Journal of Medicine, 347,* 1477–1482.

Maehr, Martin L., & Yamaguchi, Ryoko. (2001). Cultural diversity, student motivation and achievement. In Farideh Salili, Chi-Yue Chiu, & Ying-Yi Hong (Eds.), *Student motivation: The culture and context of learning* (pp. 123–148). Dordrecht, The Netherlands: Kluwer.

Magara, Keiichi. (2005). Children's misconceptions: Research on improving understanding of mathematics and science. In David W. Shwalb, Jun Nakazawa, & Barbara J. Shwalb (Eds.), *Applied developmental psychology: Theory, practice, and research from Japan* (pp. 89–108). Greenwich, CT: Information Age.

Magen, Zipora. (1998). *Exploring adolescent happiness: Commitment, purpose, and fulfillment.* Thousand Oaks, CA: Sage.

Maguen, Shira, Floyd, Frank J., Bakeman, Roger, & Armistead, Lisa. (2002). Developmental milestones and disclosure of sexual orientation among gay, lesbian, and bisexual youths. *Journal of Applied Developmental Psychology, 23,* 219–233.

Maguire, Kathleen, & Pastore, Ann L. (2003). *Sourcebook of criminal justice statistics, 2002* (NCJ 203301). Rockville, MD: National Criminal Justice Reference Service.

Mahler, Margaret S., Pine, Fred, & Bergman, Anni. (1975). *The psychological birth of the human infant: Symbiosis and individuation.* New York: Basic Books.

Mahmoud, Adel. (2004). The global vaccination gap. *Science, 305,* 147.

Mahoney, Joseph L., Stattin, Hakan, & Magnusson, David. (2001). Youth recreation centre participation and criminal offending: A 20-year longitudinal study of Swedish boys. *International Journal of Behavioral Development, 25,* 509–520.

Maier, Susan E., Chen, Wei-Jung A., & West, James R. (1996). The effects of timing and duration of alcohol exposure on development of the fetal brain. In Ernest L. Abel (Ed.), *Fetal alcohol syndrome: From mechanism to prevention* (pp. 27–50). Boca Raton, FL: CRC Press.

Malina, Robert M., Bouchard, Claude, & Bar-Or, Oded. (2004). *Growth, maturation, and physical activity* (2nd ed.). Champaign, IL: Human Kinetics.

Mandel, Denise R., Jusczyk, Peter W., & Pisoni, David B. (1995). Infants' recognition of the sound patterns of their own names. *Psychological Science, 6,* 314–317.

Mandler, Jean Matter. (2004). *The foundations of mind: Origins of conceptual thought.* Oxford, England: Oxford University Press.

Mange, Elaine Johansen, & Mange, Arthur P. (1999). *Basic human genetics* (2nd ed.). Sunderland, MA: Sinauer Associates.

Manlove, Jennifer, Ryan, Suzanne, & Franzetta, Kerry. (2003). Patterns of contraceptive use within teenagers' first sexual relationships. *Perspectives on Sexual and Reproductive Health, 35,* 246–255.

Manly, Jody Todd, Kim, Jungmeen E., Rogosch, Fred A., & Cicchetti, Dante. (2001). Dimensions of child maltreatment and children's adjustment: Contributions of developmental timing and subtype. *Development & Psychopathology, 13,* 759–782.

Manning, Wendy D., Longmore, Monica A., & Giordano, Peggy C. (2000). The relationship context of contraceptive use at first intercourse. *Family Planning Perspectives, 32,* 104–110.

Mao, Amy, Burnham, Melissa M., Goodlin-Jones, Beth L., Gaylor, Erika E., & Anders, Thomas F. (2004). A comparison of the sleep-wake patterns of cosleeping and solitary-sleeping infants. *Child Psychiatry and Human Development, 35,* 95–105.

March, John, Silva, Susan, Petrycki, Stephen, Curry, John, Wells, Karen, Fairbank, John, et al. (2004). Fluoxetine, cognitive-behavioral therapy, and their combination for adolescents with depression: Treatment For Adolescents With Depression Study (TADS) randomized controlled trial. *Journal of the American Medical Association, 292,* 807–820.

March, John S., Franklin, Martin E., Leonard, Henrietta L., & Foa, Edna B. (2004). Obsessive-compulsive disorder. In Tracy L. Morris & John S. March (Eds.), *Anxiety disorders in children and adolescents* (2nd ed., pp. 212–240). New York: Guilford Press.

Marcia, James E. (1966). Development and validation of ego-identity status. *Journal of Personality & Social Psychology, 3,* 551–558.

Marcia, James E. (1980). Identity in adolescence. In Joseph Adelson (Ed.), *Handbook of adolescent psychology* (pp. 159–187). New York: Wiley.

Marcia, James E., Waterman, Alan S., Matteson, David R., Archer, Sally L., & Orlofsky, Jacob L. (1993). *Ego identity: A handbook for psychosocial research.* New York: Springer-Verlag.

Marcin, James P., Schembri, Michael S., He, Jingsong, & Romano, Patrick S. (2003). A population-based analysis of socioeconomic status and insurance status and their relationship with pediatric trauma hospitalization and mortality rates. *American Journal of Public Health, 93,* 461–466.

Marcus, Gary F. (2000). *Pabiku* and *Ga Ti Ga*: Two mechanisms infants use to learn about the world. *Current Directions in Psychological Science, 9,* 145–147.

Marcus, Gary F. (2004). *The birth of the mind: How a tiny number of genes creates the complexities of human thought.* New York: Basic Books.

Marin, Barbara Vanoss, Coyle, Karin K., Gomez, Cynthia A., Carvajal, Scott C., & Kirby, Douglas B. (2000). Older boyfriends and girlfriends increase risk of sexual initiation in young adolescents. *Journal of Adolescent Health, 27,* 409–418.

Markus, Hazel, Cross, Susan, & Wurf, Elissa. (1990). The role of the self-system in competence. In Robert J. Sternberg & John Kolligian, Jr. (Eds.), *Competence considered* (pp. 205–225). New Haven, CT: Yale University Press.

Markus, Hazel, & Nurius, Paula. (1986). Possible selves. *American Psychologist, 41,* 954–969.

Marlow, Neil, Wolke, Dieter, Bracewell, Melanie A., & Samara, Muthanna. (2005). Neurologic and developmental disability at six years of age after extremely preterm birth. *New England Journal of Medicine, 352,* 9–19.

Marlow-Ferguson, Rebecca (Ed.). (2002). *World education encyclopedia: A survey of educational systems worldwide* (2nd ed.). Detroit, MI: Gale Group.

Marsh, Herbert W. (1989). Age and sex effects in multiple dimensions of self-concept: Preadolescence to early adulthood. *Journal of Educational Psychology, 81,* 417–430.

Marsh, Herbert W., Hau, Kit-Tai, & Kong, Chit-Kwong. (2000). Late immersion and language of instruction in Hong Kong high schools: Achievement growth in language and nonlanguage subjects. *Harvard Educational Review, 70,* 302–346.

Marsh, Herbert W., Trautwein, Ulrich, Lüdtke, Oliver, Köller, Olaf, & Baumert, Jürgen. (2005). Academic self-concept, interest, grades, and standardized test scores: Reciprocal effects models of causal ordering. *Child Development, 76,* 397–416.

Martin, Andres, & Leslie, Douglas. (2003). Trends in psychotropic medication costs for children and adolescents, 1997–2000. *Archives of Pediatrics & Adolescent Medicine, 157,* 997–1004.

Martin, Carol Lynn. (2000). Cognitive theories of gender development. In Thomas Eckes & Hanns M. Trautner (Eds.), *The developmental social psychology of gender* (pp. 91–121). Mahwah, NJ: Erlbaum.

Martin, Carol Lynn, Eisenbud, Lisa, & Rose, Hilary. (1995). Children's gender-based reasoning about toys. *Child Development, 66,* 1453–1471.

Martin, Carol Lynn, & Fabes, Richard A. (2001). The stability and consequences of young children's same-sex peer interactions. *Developmental Psychology, 37,* 431–446.

Martin, Joyce A., Hamilton, Brady E., Ventura, Stephanie J., Menacker, Fay, & Park, Melissa M. (2002, February 12). Births: Final data for 2000. *National Vital Statistics Reports, 50*(5).

Martin, Joyce A., Hamilton, Brady E., Ventura, Stephanie J., Menacker, Fay, Park, Melissa M., & Sutton, Paul D. (2002, December 18). Births: Final data for 2001. *National Vital Statistics Reports, 51*(2).

Martin, Todd F., White, James M., & Perlman, Daniel. (2003). Religious socialization: A test of the channeling hypothesis of parental influence on adolescent faith maturity. *Journal of Adolescent Research, 18,* 169–187.

Marvin, Robert S. (1997). Ethological and general systems perspectives on child-parent attachment during the toddler and preschool years. In Nancy L. Segal, Glenn E. Weisfeld, & Carol C. Weisfeld (Eds.), *Uniting psychology and biology: Integrative perspectives on human development* (pp. 189–216). Washington, DC: American Psychological Association.

Masten, Ann S. (2001). Ordinary magic: Resilience processes in development. *American Psychologist, 56,* 227–238.

Masten, Ann S. (2004). Regulatory processes, risk, and resilience in adolescent development. *Annals of the New York Academy of Sciences, 1021,* 310–319.

Masten, Ann S., & Coatsworth, J. Douglas. (1998). The development of competence in favorable and unfavorable environments: Lessons from research on successful children. *American Psychologist, 53,* 205–220.

Masterpasqua, Frank, & Perna, Phyllis A. (Eds.). (1997). *The psychological meaning of chaos: Translating theory into practice.* Washington, DC: American Psychological Association.

Maton, Kenneth I., Schellenbach, Cynthia J., Leadbeater, Bonnie J., & Solarz, Andrea L. (Eds.). (2004). *Investing in children, youth, families, and communities: Strengths-based research and policy.* Washington, DC: American Psychological Association.

Matsuda, Fumiko. (2001). Development of concepts of interrelationships among duration, distance, and speed. *International Journal of Behavioral Development, 25,* 466–480.

Matsumoto, David. (2004). Reflections on culture and competence. In Robert J. Sternberg & Elena L. Grigorenko (Eds.), *Culture and competence: Contexts of life success* (pp. 273–282). Washington, DC: American Psychological Association.

Maugh, Thomas H., II. (2002, October 18). 'Sobering' state report calls autism an epidemic. *Los Angeles Times,* pp. A1, 25.

Maughan, Angeline, & Cicchetti, Dante. (2002). Impact of child maltreatment and interadult violence on children's emotion regulation abilities and socioemotional adjustment. *Child Development, 73,* 1525–1542.

Maurer, Daphne, Lewis, Terri L., Brent, Henry P., & Levin, Alex V. (1999). Rapid improvement in the acuity of infants after visual input. *Science, 286,* 108–110.

May, Philip A., Serna, Patricia, Hurt, Lance, & DeBruyn, Lemyra M. (2005). Outcome evaluation of a public health approach to suicide prevention in an American Indian tribal nation. *American Journal of Public Health, 95,* 1238–1244.

Mayberry, Rachel I., & Nicoladis, Elena. (2000). Gesture reflects language development: Evidence from bilingual children. *Current Directions in Psychological Science, 9,* 192–196.

Maynard, Ashley E. (2002). Cultural teaching: The development of teaching skills in Maya sibling interactions. *Child Development, 73,* 969–982.

McBride-Chang, Catherine, & Treiman, Rebecca. (2003). Hong Kong Chinese kindergartners learn to read English analytically. *Psychological Science, 14,* 138–143.

McCabe, Kristen M., Hough, Richard, Wood, Patricia A., & Yeh, May. (2001). Childhood and adolescent onset conduct disorder: A test of the developmental taxonomy. *Journal of Abnormal Child Psychology, 29,* 305–316.

McCardle, Peggy, & Chhabra, Vinita. (2004). The accumulation of evidence: A continuing process. In Peggy D. McCardle & Vinita Chhabra (Eds.), *The voice of evidence in reading research* (pp. 463–478). Baltimore: Brookes.

McCarty, Michael E., & Ashmead, Daniel H. (1999). Visual control of reaching and grasping in infants. *Developmental Psychology, 35,* 620–631.

McCloskey, Laura Ann, & Stuewig, Jeffrey. (2001). The quality of peer relationships among children exposed to family violence. *Development & Psychopathology, 13,* 83–96.

McCourt, Frank. (1996). *Angela's ashes: A memoir.* New York: Scribner.

McCourt, Malachy. (1998). *A monk swimming: A memoir.* New York: Hyperion.

McCrae, Robert R., & Costa, Paul T. (2003). *Personality in adulthood: A five-factor theory perspective* (2nd ed.). New York: Guilford Press.

McCree, Donna Hubbard, Wingood, Gina M., DiClemente, Ralph, Davies, Susan, & Harrington, Katherine F. (2003). Religiosity and risky sexual behavior in African-American adolescent females. *Journal of Adolescent Health, 33,* 2–8.

McEwen, Bruce S. (2000). Effects of adverse experiences for brain structure and function. *Biological Psychiatry, 48,* 721–731.

McGue, Matt. (1995). Mediators and moderators of alcoholism inheritance. In J. Rick Turner, Lon R. Cardon, & John K. Hewitt (Eds.), *Perspectives on individual differences: Behavior genetic approaches in behavioral medicine* (pp. 17–44). New York: Plenum Press.

McGuffin, Peter, Riley, Brien, & Plomin, Robert. (2001). Toward behavioral genomics. *Science, 291,* 1232–1249.

McGuigan, Fiona, & Salmon, Karen. (2004). The time to talk: The influence of the timing of adult-child talk on children's event memory. *Child Development, 75,* 669–686.

McHale, Susan M., Crouter, Ann C., & Whiteman, Shawn D. (2003). The family contexts of gender development in childhood and adolescence. *Social Development, 12,* 125–148.

McKelvie, Pippa, & Low, Jason. (2002). Listening to Mozart does not improve children's spatial ability: Final curtains for the Mozart effect. *British Journal of Developmental Psychology, 20,* 241–258.

McKenna, James J., & Gartner, Lawrence M. (2000). Sleep location and suffocation: How good is the evidence? [Letter to the editor]. *Pediatrics, 105*(4, Pt. 1), 917–919.

McKusick, Victor A. (1994). *Mendelian inheritance in man: A catalog of human genes and genetic disorders* (11th ed.). Baltimore: Johns Hopkins University Press.

McLanahan, Sara, Donahue, Elisabeth, & Haskins, Ron (Eds.). (2005). *The future of children: Marriage and child wellbeing.* Washington, DC: Brookings Institution.

McLoyd, Vonnie C. (1998). Socioeconomic disadvantage and child development. *American Psychologist, 53,* 185–204.

McLoyd, Vonnie C., & Smith, Julia. (2002). Physical discipline and behavior problems in African American, European American, and Hispanic children: Emotional support as a moderator. *Journal of Marriage & the Family, 64,* 40–53.

McQuaid, Elizabeth L., Kopel, Sheryl J., Klein, Robert B., & Fritz, Gregory K. (2003). Medication adherence in pediatric asthma: Reasoning, responsibility, and behavior. *Journal of Pediatric Psychology, 28,* 323–333.

Medved, Michael. (1995, October). Hollywood's 3 big lies. *Reader's Digest, 147,* 155–158.

Meltzoff, Andrew N., & Moore, M. Keith. (1989). Imitation in newborn infants: Exploring the range of gestures imitated and the underlying mechanisms. *Developmental Psychology, 25,* 954–962.

Meltzoff, Andrew N., & Moore, M. Keith. (1999). A new foundation for cognitive development in infancy: The birth of the representational infant. In Ellin Kofsky Scholnick, Katherine Nelson, Susan A. Gelman, & Patricia H. Miller (Eds.), *Conceptual development: Piaget's legacy* (pp. 53–78). Mahwah, NJ: Erlbaum.

Merline, Alicia C., O'Malley, Patrick M., Schulenberg, John E., Bachman, Jerald G., & Johnston, Lloyd D. (2004). Substance use among adults 35 years of age: Prevalence, adulthood predictors, and impact of adolescent substance use. *American Journal of Public Health, 94,* 96–102.

Merrell, Kenneth W., & Gimpel, Gretchen A. (1998). *Social skills of children and adolescents: Conceptualization, assessment, treatment.* Mahwah, NJ: Erlbaum.

Merriman, William E. (1999). Competition, attention, and young children's lexical processing. In Brian MacWhinney (Ed.), *The emergence of language* (pp. 331–358). Mahwah, NJ: Erlbaum.

Merzenich, Michael M. (2001). Cortical plasticity contributing to child development. In James L. McClelland & Robert S. Siegler (Eds.), *Mechanisms of cognitive development: Behavioral and neural perspectives* (pp. 67–95). Mahwah, NJ: Erlbaum.

Midgley, Carol (Ed.). (2002). *Goals, goal structures, and patterns of adaptive learning.* Mahwah, NJ: Erlbaum.

Midobuche, Eva. (2001). More than empty footprints in the sand: Educating immigrant children. *Harvard Educational Review, 71,* 529–535.

Miller, Brent C., Fan, Xitao, Christensen, Mathew, Grotevant, Harold D., & van Dulmen, Manfred. (2000). Comparisons of adopted and nonadopted adolescents in a large, nationally representative sample. *Child Development, 71,* 1458–1473.

Miller, Brent C., Norton, Maria C., Curtis, Thom, Hill, Jeffrey, Schvaneveldt, Paul, & Young, Margaret H. (1997). The timing of sexual intercourse among adolescents: Family, peer, and other antecedents. *Youth and Society, 29,* 54–83.

Miller, Greg. (2002). Gene's effect seen in brain's fear response. *Science, 297,* 319.

Miller, Jon F., Leddy, Mark Gene, & Leavitt, Lewis A. (Eds.). (1999). *Improving the communication of people with Down syndrome.* Baltimore: Brookes.

Miller, Joan G. (2004). The cultural deep structure of psychological theories of social development. In Robert J. Sternberg & Elena L. Grigorenko (Eds.), *Culture and competence: Contexts of life success* (pp. 111–138). Washington, DC: American Psychological Association.

Miller, M., Bowen, Jennifer R., Gibson, Frances L., Hand, Peter J., & Ungerer, Judy A. (2001). Behaviour problems in extremely low birthweight children at 5 and 8 years of age. *Child: Care, Health & Development, 27,* 569–581.

Miller, Matthew, & Hemenway, David. (2001). Firearm prevalence and the risk of suicide: A review. *Harvard Health Policy Review, 2,* 1–3.

Miller, Orlando J., & Therman, Eeva. (2001). *Human chromosomes* (4th ed.). New York: Springer.

Miller, Patricia H. (2002). *Theories of developmental psychology* (4th ed.). New York: Worth.

Miller, Patricia Y., & Simon, William. (1980). The development of sexuality in adolescence. In Joseph Adelson (Ed.), *Handbook of adolescent psychology* (pp. 383–407). New York: Wiley.

Mills, James L., McPartlin, Joseph M., Kirke, Peadar N., Lee, Young J., Conley, Mary R., Weir, Donald G., et al. (1995). Homocysteine metabolism in pregnancies complicated by neural-tube defects. *Lancet, 345,* 149–151.

Min, Pyong Gap. (2000). Korean Americans' language use. In Sandra Lee McKay & Sau-ling Cynthia Wong (Eds.), *New immigrants in the United States: Readings for second language educators* (pp. 306–332). Cambridge, UK: Cambridge University Press.

Mintz, Toben H. (2005). Linguistic and conceptual influences on adjective acquisition in 24- and 36-month-olds. *Developmental Psychology, 41,* 17–29.

Mitchell, Jean, & McCarthy, Helen. (2000). Eating disorders. In Lorna Champion & Mick Power (Eds.), *Adult psychological problems: An introduction* (2nd ed., pp. 103–130). Hove, England: Psychology Press.

Mitchell, Katharyne. (2001). Education for democratic citizenship: Transnationalism, multiculturalism, and the limits of liberalism. *Harvard Educational Review, 71,* 51–78.

Mitchell, Peter, & Kikuno, Haruo. (2000). Belief as construction: Inference and processing bias. In Peter Mitchell & Kevin John Riggs (Eds.), *Children's reasoning and the mind* (pp. 281–299). Hove, England: Psychology Press.

Mix, Kelly S., Huttenlocher, Janellen, & Levine, Susan Cohen. (2002). *Quantitative development in infancy and early childhood.* New York: Oxford University Press.

MMWR. (2002, April 5). Alcohol use among women of childbearing age—United States, 1991–1999. *Morbidity and Mortality Weekly Report, 51*(13), 273–276.

MMWR. (2002, August 16). Prevention of perinatal group B streptococcal disease: Revised guidelines from CDC. *MMWR Recommendations and Reports, 51*(RR11), 1–22.

MMWR. (2002, December 6). State-specific trends in U.S. live births to women born outside the 50 states and the District of Columbia—United States, 1990 and 2000. *Morbidity and Mortality Weekly Report, 51*(48), 1091–1095.

MMWR. (2002, October 25). Nonfatal choking-related episodes among children—United States, 2001. *Morbidity and Mortality Weekly Report, 51,* 945–948.

MMWR. (2002, September 13). Folic acid and prevention of spina bifida and anencephaly: 10 years after the U.S. public health service recommendation. *MMWR Recommendations and Reports, 51*(RR13), 1–3.

MMWR. (2003, June 13). Varicella-related deaths—United States, 2002. *Morbidity and Mortality Weekly Report, 52,* 545–547.

MMWR. (2004, December 24). Alcohol consumption among women who are pregnant or who might become pregnant—United States, 2002. *Morbidity and Mortality Weekly Report, 53,* 1178–1181.

MMWR. (2004, July 2). Therapeutic foster care for the prevention of violence: A report on recommendations of the task force on community preventive services. *MMWR Recommendations and Reports, 53*(RR10), 1–8.

MMWR. (2004, July 30). Violence-related behaviors among high school students—United States, 1991–2003. *Morbidity and Mortality Weekly Report, 53,* 651–655.

MMWR. (2004, June 18). Cigarette use among high school students—United States, 1991–2003. *Morbidity and Mortality Weekly Report, 53,* 499–502.

MMWR. (2004, May 21). Youth risk behavior surveillance—United States, 2003. *MMWR Surveillance Summaries, 53*(SS02), 1–96.

MMWR. (2004, October 15). Newborn screening for cystic fibrosis: Evaluation of benefits and risks and recommendations for state newborn screening programs. *MMWR: Recommendations and Reports, 53*(RR13), 1–36.

MMWR. (2004, October 29). Chlamydia screening among sexually active young female enrollees of health plans—United States, 1999–2001. *Morbidity and Mortality Weekly Report, 53,* 983–985.

MMWR. (2004, September 3). Surveillance for fatal and nonfatal injuries—United States, 2001. *MMWR Surveillance Summaries, 53*(SS07), 1–57.

MMWR. (2004, September 17). Use of vitamins containing folic acid among women of childbearing age—United States, 2004. *Morbidity and Mortality Weekly Report, 53,* 847–850.

MMWR. (2005, January 14). Reducing childhood asthma through community-based service delivery—New York City, 2001–2004. *Morbidity and Mortality Weekly Report, 54,* 11–14.

MMWR. (2005, May 27). Blood lead levels—United States, 1999–2002. *Morbidity and Mortality Weekly Report, 54,* 513–516.

Moats, Louisa C. (2001). Overcoming the language gap: Invest generously in teacher professional development. *American Educator, 25,* 5, 8–9.

Moeller, Thomas G. (2001). *Youth aggression and violence: A psychological approach.* Mahwah, NJ: Erlbaum.

Moffitt, Terrie E. (1997). Adolescence-limited and life-course-persistent offending: A complementary pair of developmental theories. In Terence P. Thornberry (Ed.), *Developmental theories of crime and delinquency* (pp. 11–54). New Brunswick, NJ: Transaction.

Moffitt, Terrie E., Caspi, Avshalom, Belsky, Jay, & Silva, Phil A. (1992). Childhood experience and the onset of menarche: A test of a sociobiological model. *Child Development, 63,* 47–58.

Mohan, Dinesh. (2000). Injury control and safety promotion: Ethics, science, and practice. In Dinesh Mohan & Geetam Tiwari (Eds.), *Injury prevention and control* (pp. 1–12). London: Taylor & Francis.

Molnar, Alex, Smith, Philip, Zahorik, John, Palmer, Amanda, Halbach, Anke, & Ehrle, Karen. (1999). Evaluating the SAGE program: A pilot program in targeted pupil-teacher reduction in Wisconsin. *Educational Evaluation and Policy Analysis, 21,* 165–178.

Monteiro, Carlos A., Conde, Wolney L., & Popkin, Barry M. (2004). The burden of disease from undernutrition and overnutrition in countries undergoing rapid nutrition transition: A view from Brazil. *American Journal of Public Health, 94,* 433–434.

Montessori, Maria. (1966). *The secret of childhood* (M. Joseph Costelloe, Trans.).

Notre Dame, IN: Fides. (Original work published 1936)

Moore, Celia L. (2002). On differences and development. In David J. Lewkowicz & Robert Lickliter (Eds.), *Conceptions of development: Lessons from the laboratory* (pp. 57–76). New York: Psychology Press.

Moore, Ginger A., & Calkins, Susan D. (2004). Infants' vagal regulation in the still-face paradigm is related to dyadic coordination of mother-infant interaction. *Developmental Psychology, 40,* 1068–1080.

Moore, Keith L., & Persaud, Trivedi V. N. (2003). *The developing human: Clinically oriented embryology* (7th ed.). Philadelphia: Saunders.

Moore, Mignon R., & Brooks-Gunn, Jeanne. (2002). Adolescent parenthood. In Marc H. Bornstein (Ed.), *Handbook of parenting: Vol. 3. Being and becoming a parent* (2nd ed., pp. 173–214). Mahwah, NJ: Erlbaum.

Morgan, Ian G. (2003). The biological basis of myopic refractive error. *Clinical and Experimental Optometry, 86,* 276–288.

Morgenstern, Hal, Bingham, Trista, & Reza, Avid. (2000). Effects of pool-fencing ordinances and other factors on childhood drowning in Los Angeles County, 1990–1995. *American Journal of Public Health, 90,* 595–601.

Morris, Jenny. (1998). *Still missing? Vol 1: The experiences of disabled children living away from their families.* London: The Who Cares? Trust.

Morrison, Frederick J., Griffith, Elizabeth M., & Alberts, Denise M. (1997). Nature-nurture in the classroom: Entrance age, school readiness, and learning in children. *Developmental Psychology, 33,* 254–262.

Morrongiello, Barbara A., Fenwick, Kimberley D., & Chance, Graham. (1998). Crossmodal learning in newborn infants: Inferences about properties of auditory-visual events. *Infant Behavior & Development, 21,* 543–553.

Mortensen, Preben Bo, Pedersen, Carsten Bocker, Westergaard, Tine, Wohlfahrt, Jan, Ewald, Henrik, Mors, Ole, et al. (1999). Effects of family history and place and season of birth on the risk of schizophrenia. *New England Journal of Medicine, 340,* 603–608.

Mortimer, Jeylan T. (2003). *Working and growing up in America.* Cambridge, MA: Harvard University Press.

Morton, J. Bruce, & Trehub, Sandra E. (2001). Children's understanding of emotion in speech. *Child Development, 72,* 834–843.

Morton, J. Bruce, Trehub, Sandra E., & Zelazo, Philip David. (2003). Sources of inflexibility in 6-year-olds' understanding of emotion in speech. *Child Development, 74,* 1857–1868.

Moshman, David. (1999). *Adolescent psychological development: Rationality, morality, and identity.* Mahwah, NJ: Erlbaum.

Moshman, David. (2000). Diversity in reasoning and rationality: Metacognitive and developmental considerations. *Behavioral and Brain Sciences, 23,* 689–690.

Moshman, David, & Geil, Molly. (1998). Collaborative reasoning: Evidence for collective rationality. *Thinking & Reasoning, 4,* 231–248.

Moss, Ellen, Cyr, Chantal, & Dubois-Comtois, Karine. (2004). Attachment at early school age and developmental risk: Examining family contexts and behavior problems of controlling-caregiving, controlling-punitive, and behaviorally disorganized children. *Developmental Psychology, 40,* 519–532.

Moster, Dag, Lie, Rolv T., Irgens, Lorentz M., Bjerkedal, Tor, & Markestad, Trond. (2001). The association of Apgar score with subsequent death and cerebral palsy: A population-based study in term infants. *Journal of Pediatrics, 138,* 798–803.

Mpofu, Elias, & van de Vijver, Fons J. R. (2000). Taxonomic structure in early to middle childhood: A longitudinal study with Zimbabwean schoolchildren. *International Journal of Behavioral Development, 24,* 204–212.

Msall, Michael E., Avery, Roger C., Tremont, Michelle R., Lima, Julie C., Rogers, Michelle L., & Hogan, Dennis P. (2003). Functional disability and school activity limitations in 41,300 school-age children: Relationship to medical impairments. *Pediatrics, 111,* 548–553.

Mullis, Ina V. S., Martin, Michael O., Gonzalez, Eugenio J., & Chrostowski, Steven J. (2004). *TIMSS 2003 international mathematics report: Findings from IEA's trends in international mathematics and science study at the eighth and fourth grades.* Chestnut Hill, MA: TIMSS & PIRLS International Study Center, Lynch School of Education, Boston College.

Mullis, Ina V. S., Martin, Michael O., Gonzalez, Eugenio J., & Kennedy, Ann M. (2003). *PIRLS 2001 international report: IEA's study of reading literacy achievement in primary school in 35 countries.* Chestnut Hill, MA: PIRLS International Study Center, Lynch School of Education, Boston College.

Mulvey, Edward P., & Cauffman, Elizabeth. (2001). The inherent limits of predicting school violence. *American Psychologist, 56,* 797–802.

Mumme, Donna L., & Fernald, Anne. (2003). The infant as onlooker: Learning from emotional reactions observed in a television scenario. *Child Development, 74,* 221–237.

Murphy, J. Michael, Wehler, Cheryl A., Pagona, Maria E., Little, Michelle, Kleinman, Ronald E., & Jellinek, Michael S. (2001). Relationship between hunger and psychosocial functioning in low-income American children. In Margaret Hertzig & Ellen Farber (Eds.), *Annual Progress in Child Psychiatry and Child Development 1999* (pp. 215–228). Philadelphia: Brunner-Routledge.

Murphy, Shane M. (1999). *The cheers and the tears: A healthy alternative to the dark side of youth sports today.* San Francisco: Jossey-Bass.

Musick, Kelly. (2002). Planned and unplanned childbearing among unmarried women. *Journal of Marriage & Family, 64,* 915–929.

Mustillo, Sarah, Worthman, Carol, Erkanli, Alaattin, Keeler, Gordon, Angold, Adrian, & Costello, E. Jane. (2003). Obesity and psychiatric disorder: Developmental trajectories. *Pediatrics, 111,* 851–859.

Muter, Valerie, Hulme, Charles, Snowling, Margaret J., & Stevenson, Jim. (2004). Phonemes, rimes, vocabulary, and grammatical skills as foundations of early reading development: Evidence from a longitudinal study. *Developmental Psychology, 40,* 665–681.

Naito, Mika, & Miura, Hisayoshi. (2001). Japanese children's numerical competencies: Age- and schooling-related influences on the development of number concepts and addition skills. *Developmental Psychology, 37,* 217–230.

Nakamura, Suad, Wind, Marilyn, & Danello, Mary Ann. (1999). Review of hazards associated with children placed in adult beds. *Archives of Pediatrics and Adolescent Medicine, 153,* 1019–1023.

Nantais, Kristin M., & Schellenberg, E. Glenn. (1999). The Mozart effect: An artifact of preference. *Psychological Science, 10,* 370–373.

National Academy of Sciences. (1994). *Assessing genetic risks: Implications for health and social policy* (Lori B. Andrews, Jane E. Fullarton, Neil A. Holtzman, & Arno G. Motulsky, Ed.). Washington, DC: National Academy Press.

National Center for Education Statistics. (2005). *The condition of education 2005: Appendix 1—Supplemental table 27-1.* Retrieved September 11, 2005, from the World Wide Web: http://nces.ed.gov/pubs2005/2005094_App1.pdf

National Center for Health Statistics. (2000, September 21). Deaths: Final data for 1999. *National vital statistics reports, 49*(8).

National Center for Health Statistics. (2002, September 16). Deaths: Leading causes for 2000. *National Vital Statistics Reports, 50*(16).

National Center for Health Statistics. (2004, October 12). Deaths: Final data for 2002, table 3. *National Vital Statistics Reports, 53*(5), 21.

National Research Council and Institute of Medicine, Board on Children, Youth, and Families (U.S.), Committee on Integrating the Science of Early Childhood Development. (2000). *From neurons to neighborhoods: The science of early childhood development.* Washington, DC: National Academy Press.

National Task Force on Fetal Alcohol Syndrome and Fetal Alcohol Effect. (2002, September 20). Defining the national agenda for fetal alcohol syndrome and other prenatal alcohol-related effects. *MMWR Recommendations and Reports, 51*(RR-14), 9–12.

Nell, Victor. (2002). Why young men drive dangerously: Implications for injury prevention. *Current Directions in Psychological Science, 11,* 75–79.

Nelson, Adie. (2000). The pink dragon is female: Halloween costumes and gender markers. *Psychology of Women Quarterly, 24,* 137–144.

Nelson, Charles A. (2004). Brain development during puberty and adolescence: Comments on Part II. *Annals of the New York Academy of Sciences, 1021,* 105–109.

Nelson, Charles A., Bloom, Floyd E., Cameron, Judy L., Amaral, David, Dahl, Ronald E., & Pine, Daniel. (2002). An integrative, multidisciplinary approach to the study of brain-behavior relations in the context of typical and atypical development. *Development & Psychopathology, 14,* 499–520.

Nelson, Charles A., & Webb, Sara J. (2003). A cognitive neuroscience perspective on early memory development. In Michelle De Haan & Mark H. Johnson (Eds.), *The cognitive neuroscience of development* (pp. 99–126). New York: Psychology Press.

Nelson, Jennifer A., Chiasson, Mary Ann, & Ford, Viola. (2004). Childhood overweight in a New York City WIC population. *American Journal of Public Health, 94,* 458–462.

Nelson, Katherine. (1996). *Language in cognitive development: The emergence of the mediated mind.* New York: Cambridge University Press.

Nemy, Enid (with Alexander, Ron). (1998, November 2). Metropolitan diary. *New York Times,* pp. B2.

Nesdale, Drew. (2004). Social identity processes and children's ethnic prejudice. In Mark Bennett & Fabio Sani (Eds.), *The development of the social self* (pp. 219–245). Hove, East Sussex, England: Psychology Press.

Nesselroade, John R., & Molenaar, Peter C. M. (2003). Quantitative models for developmental processes. In Jaan Valsiner & Kevin J. Connolly (Eds.), *Handbook of developmental psychology* (pp. 622–639). Thousand Oaks, CA: Sage.

Neuman, Michelle J. (2002). The wider context: An international overview of transition issues. In Hilary Fabian & Aline-Wendy Dunlop (Eds.), *Transitions in the early years: Debating continuity and progression for young children in early education* (pp. 8–22). New York: RoutledgeFalmer.

Newcomb, Andrew F., Bukowski, William M., & Pattee, Linda. (1993). Children's peer relations: A meta-analytic review of popular, rejected, neglected, controversial, and average sociometric status. *Psychological Bulletin, 113,* 99–128.

Newman, Rochelle S. (2005). The cocktail party effect in infants revisited: Listening to one's name in noise. *Developmental Psychology, 41,* 352–362.

Newnham, John P., Doherty, Dorota A., Kendall, Garth E., Zubrick, Stephen R., Landau, Louis L., & Stanley, Fiona J. (2004). Effects of repeated prenatal ultrasound examinations on childhood outcome up to 8 years of age: Follow-up of a randomised controlled trial. *Lancet, 364,* 2038–2044.

Nguyen, Huong Q., Jumaan, Aisha O., & Seward, Jane F. (2005). Decline in mortality due to varicella after implementation of varicella vaccination in the United States. *New England Journal of Medicine, 352,* 450–458.

Nguyen, Simone P., & Murphy, Gregory L. (2003). An apple is more than just a fruit: Cross-classification in children's concepts. *Child Development, 74,* 1783–1806.

NICHD Early Child Care Research Network. (1999). Child care and mother-child interaction in the first 3 years of life. *Developmental Psychology, 35,* 1399–1413.

NICHD Early Child Care Research Network. (2000). The relation of child care to cognitive and language development. *Child Development, 71,* 960–980.

NICHD Early Child Care Research Network. (2001). Child care and children's peer interaction at 24 and 36 months: The NICHD study of early child care. *Child Development, 72,* 1478–1500.

NICHD Early Child Care Research Network. (2003). Does quality of child care affect child outcomes at age 4½? *Developmental Psychology, 39,* 451–469.

NICHD Early Child Care Research Network. (2003). Do children's attention processes mediate the link between family predictors and school readiness? *Developmental Psychology, 39,* 581–593.

NICHD Early Child Care Research Network. (2003). Does amount of time spent in child care predict socioemotional adjustment during the transition to kindergarten? *Child Development, 74,* 976–1005.

NICHD Early Child Care Research Network. (2004). Does class size in first grade relate to children's academic and social performance or observed classroom processes? *Developmental Psychology, 40,* 651–664.

NICHD Early Child Care Research Network. (2004). Are child developmental outcomes related to before- and after-school care arrangements? Results from the NICHD Study of Early Child Care. *Child Development, 75,* 280–295.

NICHD Early Child Care Research Network. (2005). Pathways to reading: The role of oral language in the transition to reading. *Developmental Psychology, 41,* 428–442.

NICHD Early Child Care Research Network (Ed.). (2005). *Child care and child development: Results from the NICHD study of early child care and youth development.* New York: Guilford Press.

Nielsen, David A., Virkkunen, Matti, Lappalainen, Jaakko, Eggert, Monica, Brown, Gerald L., Long, Jeffrey C., et al. (1998). A tryptophan hydroxylase gene marker for suicidality and alcoholism. *Archives of General Psychiatry, 55,* 593–602.

Nieto, Sonia. (2000). *Affirming diversity: The sociopolitical context of multicultural education* (3rd ed.). New York: Longman.

Nishina, Adrienne, & Juvonen, Jaana. (2005). Daily reports of witnessing and experiencing peer harassment in middle school. *Child Development, 76,* 435–450.

Nixon, James. (2000). Injury prevention and children's rights. In Dinesh Mohan & Geetam Tiwari (Eds.), *Injury prevention and control* (pp. 167–180). London: Taylor & Francis.

No Child Left Behind Act of 2001, 20 U.S.C. § 6301 (2002).

Nsamenang, A. Bame. (2002). Adolescence in sub-Saharan Africa: An image constructed from Africa's triple inheritance. In B. Bradford Brown, Reed W. Larson, & T. S. Saraswathi (Eds.), *The world's youth: Adolescence in eight regions of the globe* (pp. 61–104). New York: Cambridge University Press.

Nunan, David, & Lam, Agnes. (1998). Teacher education for multilingual contexts: Models and issues. In Jasone Cenoz & Fred Genesee (Eds.), *Beyond bilingualism: Multilingualism and multilingual education* (pp. 117–140). Clevedon, England: Multilingual Matters.

Nurmi, Jari-Erik. (2004). Socialization and self-development: Channeling, selection, adjustment, and reflection. In Richard M. Lerner & Laurence D. Steinberg (Eds.), *Handbook of adolescent psychology* (2nd ed., pp. 85–124). Hoboken, NJ: Wiley.

O'Connor, Thomas G. (2002). The 'effects' of parenting reconsidered: Findings, challenges, and applications. *Journal of Child Psychology & Psychiatry, 43,* 555–572.

O'Connor, Thomas G., Rutter, Michael, Beckett, Celia, Keaveney, Lisa, Kreppner, Jana M., & English & Romanian Adoptees Study Team. (2000). The effects of global severe privation on cognitive competence: Extension and longitudinal follow-up. *Child Development, 71,* 376–390.

O'Dell, Laura E., Bruijnzeel, Adrie W., Ghozland, Sandy, Markou, Athina, & Koob, George F. (2004). Nicotine withdrawal in adolescent and adult rats. *Annals of the New York Academy of Sciences, 1021,* 167–174.

O'Donoghue, Ted, & Rabin, Matthew. (2001). Risky behavior among youths: Some issues from behavioral economics. In Jonathan Gruber (Ed.), *Risky behavior among youths: An economic analysis* (pp. 29–67). Chicago: University of Chicago Press.

O'Rahilly, Ronan R., & Müller, Fabiola. (2001). *Human embryology & teratology* (3rd ed.). New York: Wiley-Liss.

Oddy, Wendy H. (2004). A review of the effects of breastfeeding on respiratory infections, atopy, and childhood asthma. *Journal of Asthma, 41,* 605–621.

Ogbu, John U. (1993). Differences in cultural frame of reference. *International Journal of Behavioral Development, 16,* 483–506.

Ohring, Richard, Graber, Julia A., & Brooks-Gunn, Jeanne. (2002). Girls' recurrent and concurrent body dissatisfaction: Correlates and consequences over 8 years. *International Journal of Eating Disorders, 31,* 404–415.

Olausson, Petra Otterblad, Haglund, Bengt, Weitoft, Gunilla Ringbäck, & Cnattingius, Sven. (2001). Teenage childbearing and long-term socioeconomic consequences: A case study in Sweden. *Family Planning Perspectives, 33,* 70–74.

Olivo, Warren. (2003). "Quit talking and learn English!": Conflicting language ideologies in an ESL classroom. *Anthropology & Education Quarterly, 34,* 50–71.

Olson, Lynn. (2005, June 22). States raise bar for high school diploma. *Education Week, 24,* 1, 28.

Olson, Sheryl L., Kashiwagi, Keiko, & Crystal, David. (2001). Concepts of adaptive and maladaptive child behavior: A comparison of U.S. and Japanese mothers of preschool-age children. *Journal of Cross-Cultural Psychology, 32,* 43–57.

Olweus, Dan. (1992). Bullying among schoolchildren: Intervention and prevention. In Ray DeV. Peters, Robert Joseph McMahon, & Vernon L. Quinsey (Eds.), *Aggression and violence throughout the life span* (pp. 100–125). Thousand Oaks, CA: Sage.

Olweus, Dan. (1993). Victimization by peers: Antecedents and long-term outcomes. In Kenneth H. Rubin & Jens B. Asendorpf (Eds.), *Social withdrawal, inhibition, and shyness in childhood* (pp. 315–341). Hillsdale, NJ: Erlbaum.

Olweus, Dan. (1999). Norway. In Peter K. Smith, Yohji Morita, Josine Junger-Tas, Dan Olweus, Richard F. Catalano, & Phillip Slee (Eds.), *The nature of school bullying: A cross-national perspective* (pp. 28–48). London: Routledge.

Oosterlaan, Jaap, Logan, Gordon D., & Sergeant, Joseph A. (1998). Response inhibition in AD/HD, CD, comorbid AD/HD + CD, anxious, and control children: A meta-analysis of studies with the stop task. *Journal of Child Psychology & Psychiatry & Allied Disciplines, 39,* 411–425.

Oppenheim, David. (1998). Perspectives on infant mental health from Israel: The case of changes in collective sleeping on the kibbutz. *Infant Mental Health Journal, 19,* 76–86.

Orfield, Gary, & Kornhaber, Mindy L. (2001). *Raising standards or raising barriers? Inequality and high-stakes testing in public education.* New York: Century Foundation Press.

Orford, Jim. (2001). *Excessive appetites: A psychological view of addictions* (2nd ed.). New York: Wiley.

Orsini, Alfonso J. (2005, July 13). Big tests, big sticks: The social contexts of high-stakes testing in China and the United States. *Education Week, 24,* 37–38.

Pang, Jenny W. Y., Heffelfinger, James D., Huang, Greg J., Benedetti, Thomas J., & Weiss, Noel S. (2002). Outcomes of planned home births in Washington State: 1989–1996. *Obstetrics & Gynecology, 100,* 253–259.

Panksepp, Jaak. (1998). Attention deficit hyperactivity disorders, psychostimulants and intolerance of childhood playfulness: A tragedy in the making? *Current Directions in Psychological Science, 7,* 91–98.

Parízková, Jana, & Hills, Andrew P. (2005). *Childhood obesity: Prevention and treatment* (2nd ed.). Boca Raton, FL: CRC Press.

Park, D. J. J., & Congdon, Nathan G. (2004). Evidence for an "epidemic" of myopia. *Annals, Academy of Medicine, Singapore, 33,* 21–26.

Parke, Ross D. (1996). *Fatherhood.* Cambridge, MA: Harvard University Press.

Parke, Ross D., Coltrane, Scott, Duffy, Sharon, Buriel, Raymond, Dennis, Jessica, Powers, Justina, et al. (2004). Economic stress, parenting, and child adjustment in Mexican American and European American families. *Child Development, 75,* 1632–1656.

Parke, Ross D., Ornstein, Peter A., Rieser, John J., & Zahn-Waxler, Carolyn. (1994). The past as prologue: An overview of a century of developmental psychology. In Ross D. Parke, Peter A. Ornstein, John J. Rieser, & Carolyn Zahn-Waxler (Eds.), *A century of developmental psychology* (pp. 1–72). Washington, DC: American Psychological Association.

Parker, Richard. (2002). The global HIV/AIDS pandemic, structural inequalities, and the politics of international health. *American Journal of Public Health, 92,* 343–347.

Parker, Susan W., & Nelson, Charles A. (2005). The impact of early institutional rearing on the ability to discriminate facial expressions of emotion: An event-related potential study. *Child Development, 76,* 54–72.

Parsell, Diana. (2004, November 13). Assault on autism. *Science News, 166,* 311–312.

Parten, Mildred B. (1932). Social participation among pre-school children. *Journal of Abnormal & Social Psychology, 27,* 243–269.

Pascarella, Ernest T., & Terenzini, Patrick T. (1991). *How college affects students: Findings and insights from twenty years of research.* San Francisco: Jossey-Bass.

Pascual-Leone, Alvaro, & Torres, Fernando. (1993). Plasticity of the sensorimotor cortex representation of the reading finger in Braille readers. *Brain, 116,* 39–52.

Patel, Dilip R., & Luckstead, Eugene F. (2000). Sport participation, risk taking, and health risk behaviors. *Adolescent Medicine, 11,* 141–155.

Patrick, Kevin, Norman, Gregory J., Calfas, Karen J., Sallis, James F., Zabinski, Marion F., Rupp, Joan, et al. (2004). Diet, physical activity, and sedentary behaviors as risk factors for overweight in adolescence. *Archives of Pediatrics & Adolescent Medicine, 158,* 385–390.

Patterson, Charlotte J. (2002). Lesbian and gay parenthood. In Marc H. Bornstein (Ed.), *Handbook of parenting: Vol. 3. Being and becoming a parent* (2nd ed., pp. 317–338). Mahwah, NJ: Erlbaum.

Patterson, Gerald R. (1998). Continuities—A search for causal mechanisms: Comment on the special section. *Developmental Psychology, 34,* 1263–1268.

Paulesu, Eraldo, Demonet, J.-F., Fazio, F., McCrory, E., Chanoine, V., Brunswick, N., et al. (2001). Dyslexia: Cultural diversity and biological unity. *Science, 291,* 2165–2167.

Pauli-Pott, Ursula, Mertesacker, Bettina, & Beckmann, Dieter. (2004). Predicting the development of infant emotionality from maternal characteristics. *Development & Psychopathology, 16,* 19–42.

Pedersen, Sara, Seidman, Edward, Yoshikawa, Hirokazu, Rivera, Ann C., Allen, LaRue, & Aber, J. Lawrence. (2005). Contextual competence: Multiple manifestations among urban adolescents. *American Journal of Community Psychology, 35,* 65–82.

Pellegrini, Anthony D., & Galda, Lee. (1998). *The development of school-based literacy: A social ecological perspective.* New York: Routledge.

Pellegrini, Anthony D., & Smith, Peter K. (2001). Physical activity play: The nature and function of a neglected aspect of play. In Margaret Hertzig & Ellen Farber (Eds.), *Annual Progress in Child Psychiatry and Child Development 1999* (pp. 1–36). Philadelphia: Brunner-Routledge.

Peltonen, Leena, & McKusick, Victor A. (2001). Genomics and medicine: Dissecting human disease in the postgenomic era. *Science, 291,* 1224–1229.

Pennington, Bruce F. (2001). Genetic methods. In Charles A. Nelson & Monica Luciana (Eds.), *Handbook of developmental cognitive neuroscience* (pp. 149–158). Cambridge, MA: MIT Press.

Pennington, Bruce Franklin. (2002). *The development of psychopathology: Nature and nurture.* New York: Guilford Press.

Pepler, Debra, Craig, Wendy, Yuile, Amy, & Connolly, Jennifer. (2004). Girls who bully: A developmental and relational perspective. In Martha Putallaz & Karen L. Bierman (Eds.), *Aggression, antisocial behavior, and violence among girls: A developmental perspective* (pp. 90–109). New York: Guilford.

Perfetti, Jennifer, Clark, Roseanne, & Fillmore, Capri-Mara. (2004). Postpartum depression: Identification, screening, and treatment. *Wisconsin Medical Journal, 103*(6), 56–63.

Perner, Josef. (2000). About + belief + counterfactual. In Peter Mitchell & Kevin John Riggs (Eds.), *Children's reasoning and the mind* (pp. 367–401). Hove, England: Psychology Press.

Perner, Josef, Lang, Birgit, & Kloo, Daniela. (2002). Theory of mind and self-control: More than a common problem of inhibition. *Child Development, 73,* 752–767.

Perriello, Vito A., Jr. (2001, September). Aiming for healthy weight in wrestlers and other athletes. *Contemporary Pediatrics, 18*(9), 55–56, 58, 61–62, 65–66, 68, 72–74.

Perry, William G., Jr. (1981). Cognitive and ethical growth: The making of meaning. In Arthur W. Chickering (Ed.), *The modern American college: Responding to the new realities of diverse students and a changing society* (pp. 76–116). San Francisco: Jossey-Bass.

Persaud, Trivedi V. N., Chudley, Albert E., & Skalko, Richard G. (1985). *Basic concepts in teratology.* New York: Liss.

Pérusse, Louis, & Bouchard, Claude. (1999). Role of genetic factors in childhood obesity and in susceptibility to dietary variations. *Annals of Medicine, 31*(Supplement 1), 19–25.

Peterson, James C. (2001). *Genetic turning points: The ethics of human genetic intervention.* Grand Rapids, MI: Eerdmans.

Petitto, Laura Ann, & Marentette, Paula F. (1991). Babbling in the manual mode: Evidence for the ontogeny of language. *Science, 251,* 1493–1496.

Petrou, Stavros, Sach, Tracey, & Davidson, Leslie L. (2001). The long-term costs of preterm birth and low birth weight: Results of a systematic review. *Child: Care, Health & Development, 27,* 97–115.

Pettit, Gregory S. (2004). Violent children in developmental perspective: Risk and protective factors and the mechanisms through which they (may) operate. *Current Directions in Psychological Science, 13,* 194–197.

Pettit, Gregory S., Bates, John E., & Dodge, Kenneth A. (1997). Supportive parenting, ecological context, and children's adjustment: A seven-year longitudinal study. *Child Development, 68,* 908–923.

Pettit, Gregory S., Laird, Robert D., Dodge, Kenneth A., Bates, John E., & Criss, Michael M. (2001). Antecedents and behavior-problem outcomes of parental monitoring and psychological control in early adolescence. *Child Development, 72,* 583–598.

Pew Environmental Health Commission. (2000). *Attack asthma: Why America needs a public health defense system to battle environmental threats.* Baltimore: Johns Hopkins School of Public Health.

Phelps, Elizabeth A., O'Connor, Kevin J., Cunningham, William A., Funayama, E. Sumie, Gatenby, J. Christopher, Gore, John C., et al. (2000). Performance on indirect measures of race evaluation predicts amygdala activation. *Journal of Cognitive Neuroscience, 12,* 729–738.

Philip, John, Silver, Richard K., Wilson, R. Douglas, Thom, Elizabeth A., Zachary, Julia M., Mohide, Patrick, et al. (2004). Late first-trimester invasive prenatal diagnosis: Results of an international randomized trial. *Obstetrics & Gynecology, 103,* 1164–1173.

Phillips, Deborah A., & White, Sheldon H. (2004). New possibilities for research on Head Start. In Edward Zigler & Sally J. Styfco (Eds.), *The Head Start debates* (pp. 263–278). Baltimore: Brookes.

Phipps, Maureen G., & Sowers, MaryFran. (2002). Defining early adolescent childbearing. *American Journal of Public Health, 92,* 125–128.

Piaget, Jean. (1929). *The child's conception of the world* (Joan and Andrew Tomlinson, Trans.). London: K. Paul Trench Trubner.

Piaget, Jean. (1932). *The moral judgment of the child* (Marjorie Gabain, Trans.). London: K. Paul Trench Trubner.

Piaget, Jean. (1952). *The origins of intelligence in children* (M. Cook, Trans.). Oxford, England: International Universities Press. (Original work published 1936)

Piaget, Jean. (1962). *Play, dreams and imitation in childhood* (C. Gattegno & F. M. Hodgson, Trans.). New York: Norton. (Original work published 1945)

Piaget, Jean, & Moreau, Albert. (2001). *The inversion of arithmetic operations* (Robert L. Campbell, Ed. & Trans.). Hove, E. Sussex, England: Psychology Press. (Original work published 1977)

Piaget, Jean, Voelin-Liambey, Daphne, & Berthoud-Papandropoulou, Ioanna. (2001). *Problems of class inclusion and logical implication* (Robert L. Campbell, Ed. & Trans.). Hove, E. Sussex, England: Psychology Press. (Original work published 1977)

Pickett, Kate E., Mookherjee, Jessica, & Wilkinson, Richard G. (2005). Adolescent birth rates, total homicides, and income inequality in rich countries. *American Journal of Public Health, 95,* 1181–1183.

Pinborg, Anja, Loft, Anne, & Nyboe Andersen, Anders. (2004). Neonatal outcome in a Danish national cohort of 8602 children born after in vitro fertilization or intracytoplasmic sperm injection: The role of twin pregnancy. *Acta Obstetricia et Gynecologica Scandinavica, 83,* 1071–1078.

Pinker, Steven. (1994). *The language instinct.* New York: William Morrow.

Piontelli, Alessandra. (2002). *Twins: From fetus to child.* London: Routledge.

Pitt, W. Robert, & Cass, Danny T. (2001). Preventing children drowning in Australia. *Medical Journal of Australia, 175,* 603–604.

Plank, Stephen B., & MacIver, Douglas J. (2003). Educational achievement. In Marc H. Bornstein, Lucy Davidson, Corey L. M. Keyes, & Kristin Moore (Eds.), *Well-being: Positive development across the life course* (pp. 341–354). Mahwah, NJ: Erlbaum.

Plomin, Robert. (2002). Behavioural genetics in the 21st century. In Willard W. Hartup & Rainer K. Silbereisen (Eds.), *Growing points in developmental science: An introduction* (pp. 47–63). Philadelphia: Psychology Press.

Plomin, Robert, DeFries, John C., McClearn, Gerald E., & McGuffin, Peter. (2001). *Behavioral genetics* (4th ed.). New York: Worth.

Plomin, Robert, & McGuffin, Peter. (2003). Psychopathology in the postgenomic era. *Annual Review of Psychology, 54,* 205–228.

Plutchik, Robert. (2003). *Emotions and life: Perspectives from psychology, biology, and evolution.* Washington, DC: American Psychological Association.

Pollack, Harold, & Frohna, John. (2001). A competing risk model of sudden infant death syndrome incidence in two U.S. birth cohorts. *Journal of Pediatrics, 138,* 661–667.

Pollak, Seth D., Cicchetti, Dante, Hornung, Katherine, & Reed, Alex. (2000). Recognizing emotion in faces: Developmental effects of child abuse and neglect. *Developmental Psychology, 36,* 679–688.

Pomerantz, Eva M., & Rudolph, Karen D. (2003). What ensues from emotional distress? Implications for competence estimation. *Child Development, 74,* 329–345.

Pong, Suet-ling, Dronkers, Jaap, & Hampden-Thompson, Gillian. (2003). Family policies and children's school achievement in single- versus two-parent families. *Journal of Marriage and Family, 65,* 681–699.

Ponsonby, Anne-Louise, Dwyer, Terence, Gibbons, Laura E., Cochrane, Jennifer A., & Wang, You-Gan. (1993). Factors potentiating the risk of sudden infant death syndrome associated with the prone position. *New England Journal of Medicine, 329,* 377–382.

Posner, Michael I., & Rothbart, Mary K. (2000). Developing mechanisms of self-regulation. *Development and Psychopathology, 12,* 427–441.

Powlishta, Kimberly. (2004). Gender as a social category: Intergroup processes and gender-role development. In Mark Bennett & Fabio Sani (Eds.), *The development of the social self* (pp. 103–133). Hove, East Sussex, England: Psychology Press.

Prinzie, Peter, Onghena, P., Hellinckx, W., Grietens, H., Ghesquiere, P., & Colpin, H. (2003). The additive and interactive effects of parenting and children's personality on externalizing behaviour. *European Journal of Personality, 17,* 95–117.

Putallaz, Martha, Kupersmidt, Janis B., Cole, John D., McKnight, Kate, & Grimes, Christina L. (2004). A behavioral analysis of girls' aggression and victimization. In Martha Putallaz & Karen L. Bierman (Eds.), *Aggression, antisocial behavior, and violence among girls: A developmental perspective* (pp. 110–134). New York: Guilford.

Quinn, Paul C. (2004). Development of subordinate-level categorization in 3- to 7-month-old infants. *Child Development, 75,* 886–899.

Qvortrup, Jens. (2000). Microanalysis of childhood. In Pia Monrad Christensen & Allison James (Eds.), *Research with children: Perspectives and practices* (pp. 77–97). London: Falmer Press.

Raley, R. Kelly, & Wildsmith, Elizabeth. (2004). Cohabitation and children's family instability. *Journal of Marriage & Family, 66,* 210–219.

Ramey, Craig T., Ramey, Sharon Landesman, Lanzi, Robin Gaines, & Cotton, Janice N. (2002). Early educational interventions for high-risk children: How center-based treatment can augment and improve parenting effectiveness. In John G. Borkowski, Sharon Landesman Ramey, & Marie Bristol-Power (Eds.), *Parenting and the child's world: Influences on academic, intellectual, and social-emotional development* (pp. 125–140). Mahwah, NJ: Erlbaum.

Ramey, Sharon Landesman. (2002). The science and art of parenting. In John G. Borkowski, Sharon Landesman Ramey, & Marie Bristol-Power (Eds.), *Parenting and the child's world: Influences on academic, intellectual, and social-emotional development* (pp. 47–71). Mahwah, NJ: Erlbaum.

Ramey, Sharon Landesman. (2005). Human developmental science serving children and families: Contributions of the NICHD study of early child care. In NICHD Early Child Care Research Network (Ed.), *Child care and child development: Results from the NICHD study of early child care and youth development* (pp. 427–436). New York: Guilford Press.

Rankin, Jane L., Lane, David J., Gibbons, Frederick X., & Gerrard, Meg. (2004). Adolescent self-consciousness: Longitudinal age changes and gender differences in two cohorts. *Journal of Research on Adolescence, 14,* 1–21.

Rao, Raghavendra, & Georgieff, Michael K. (2000). Early nutrition and brain development. In Charles A. Nelson (Ed.), *The Minnesota symposia on child psychology: Vol. 31. The effects of early adversity on neurobehavioral development* (pp. 1–30). Mahwah, NJ: Erlbaum.

Rauscher, Frances H., & Shaw, Gordon L. (1998). Key components of the Mozart effect. *Perceptual & Motor Skills, 86*(3, Pt. 1), 835–841.

Rauscher, Frances H., Shaw, Gordon L., & Ky, Catherine N. (1993, 14 Oct). Music and spatial task performance. *Nature, 365,* 611.

Rayco-Solon, Pura, Fulford, Anthony J., & Prentice, Andrew M. (2005). Differential effects of seasonality on preterm birth and intrauterine growth restriction in rural Africans. *American Journal of Clinical Nutrition, 81,* 134–139.

Rayner, Keith, Foorman, Barbara R., Perfetti, Charles A., Pesetsky, David, & Seidenberg, Mark S. (2001). How psychological science informs the teaching of reading. *Psychological Science in the Public Interest, 2,* 31–74.

Reid, John B., Patterson, Gerald R., & Snyder, James J. (Eds.). (2002). *Antisocial behavior in children and adolescents: A developmental analysis and the Oregon model for intervention.* Washington, DC: American Psychological Association.

Reiss, David, & Neiderhiser, Jenae M. (2000). The interplay of genetic influences and social processes in developmental theory: Specific mechanisms are coming into view. *Development & Psychopathology, 12,* 357–374.

Reiss, David, Neiderhiser, Jenae M., Hetherington, E. Mavis, & Plomin, Robert. (2000). *The relationship code: Deciphering genetic and social influences on adolescent development.* Cambridge, MA: Harvard University Press.

Reiter, Edward O., & Lee, Peter A. (2001). Have the onset and tempo of puberty changed? *Archives of Pediatrics & Adolescent Medicine, 155,* 988–989.

Remage-Healey, Luke, & Bass, Andrew H. (2004). Rapid, hierarchical modulation of vocal patterning by steroid hormones. *Journal of Neuroscience, 24,* 5892–5900.

Renninger, K. Ann, & Amsel, Eric. (1997). Change and development: An introduction. In Eric Amsel & K. Ann Renninger (Eds.), *Change and development: Issues of theory, method, and application.* Mahwah, NJ: Erlbaum.

Repetti, Rena L., Taylor, Shelley E., & Seeman, Teresa E. (2002). Risky families: Family social environments and the mental and physical health of offspring. *Psychological Bulletin, 128,* 330–366.

Research Advisory Committee of the National Council of Teachers of Mathematics. (1989). The mathematics education of underserved and underrepresented groups: A continuing challenge. *Journal for Research in Mathematics Education, 20,* 371–375.

Resnick, Lauren, & Zurawsky, Chris. (2005). Getting back on course: Standards-based reform and accountability. *American Educator, 29,* 8–19, 44.

Rest, James, Narvaez, Darcia, Bebeau, Muriel J., & Thoma, Stephen J. (1999). *Postconventional moral thinking: A neo-Kohlbergian approach.* Mahwah, NJ: Erlbaum.

Retting, Richard A., Ferguson, Susan A., & McCartt, Anne T. (2003). A review of evidence-based traffic engineering measures designed to reduce pedestrian-motor vehicle crashes. *American Journal of Public Health, 93,* 1456–1463.

Reyna, Valerie F. (2004). How people make decisions that involve risk: A dual-processes approach. *Current Directions in Psychological Science, 13,* 60–66.

Reynolds, Arthur J. (2000). *Success in early intervention: The Chicago child-parent centers.* Lincoln, NE: University of Nebraska Press.

Rhodes, Jean E., & Roffman, Jennifer G. (2003). Nonparental adults as asset builders in the lives of youth. In Richard M. Lerner & Peter L. Benson (Eds.), *Developmental assets and asset-building communities: Implications for research, policy, and practice* (pp. 195–209). New York: Kluwer/Plenum.

Rice, Amy L., Sacco, Lisa, Hyder, Adnan, & Black, Robert E. (2000). Malnutrition as an underlying cause of childhood deaths associated with infectious diseases in developing countries. *Bulletin of the World Health Organization, 78,* 1207–1221.

Richardson, Chinué Turner, & Dailard, Cynthia. (2005). Politicizing statutory rape reporting requirements: A mounting campaign? *The Guttmacher Report on Public Policy, 8,* 1–3.

Ridley, Matt. (1999). *Genome: The autobiography of a species in 23 chapters.* New York: HarperCollins.

Ridley, Matt. (2004). *The agile gene: How nature turns on nurture* (1st Perennial ed.). New York: Perennial.

Riordan, Jan (Ed.). (2005). *Breastfeeding and human lactation* (3rd ed.). Sudbury, MA: Jones and Bartlett.

Roberts, Donald F., & Foehr, Ulla G. (2004). *Kids and media in America: Patterns of use at the millennium.* New York: Cambridge University Press.

Roberts, Donald F., Henriksen, Lisa, & Foehr, Ulla G. (2004). Adolescents and media. In Richard M. Lerner & Laurence D. Steinberg (Eds.), *Handbook of adolescent psychology* (2nd ed., pp. 487–521). Hoboken, NJ: Wiley.

Roberts, Robert E., Roberts, Catherine Ramsay, & Chen, Irene Ger. (2002). Impact of insomnia on future functioning of adolescents. *Journal of Psychosomatic Research, 53,* 561–569.

Robin, Daniel J., Berthier, Neil E., & Clifton, Rachel K. (1996). Infants' predictive reaching for moving objects in the dark. *Developmental Psychology, 32,* 824–835.

Robins, Lee N., Helzer, John E., & Davis, Darlene H. (1975). Narcotic use in southeast Asia and afterward. An interview study of 898 Vietnam returnees. *Archives of General Psychiatry, 32,* 955–961.

Robitaille, David F., & Beaton, Albert E. (Eds.). (2002). *Secondary analysis of the TIMSS data.* Boston: Kluwer.

Rochat, Philippe. (2001). *The infant's world.* Cambridge, MA: Harvard University Press.

Rodgers, Kathleen Boyce. (1999). Parenting processes related to sexual risk-taking behaviors of adolescent males and females. *Journal of Marriage & the Family, 61,* 99–109.

Rodier, Patricia M. (2000, February). The early origins of autism. *Scientific American, 282,* 56–63.

Rodkin, Philip C., Farmer, Thomas W., Pearl, Ruth, & Van Acker, Richard. (2000). Heterogeneity of popular boys: Antisocial and prosocial configurations. *Developmental Psychology, 36,* 14–24.

Rogoff, Barbara. (1998). Cognition as a collaborative process. In William Damon (Series Ed.) & Deanna Kuhn & Robert S. Siegler (Vol. Eds.), *Handbook of child psychology: Vol. 2. Cognition, perception, and language* (5th ed., pp. 679–744). New York: Wiley.

Rogoff, Barbara. (2003). *The cultural nature of human development.* New York: Oxford University Press.

Roid, Gale. (2003). *Stanford-Binet intelligence scales, fifth edition.* Itasca, IL: Riverside.

Roisman, Glenn I., Masten, Ann S., Coatsworth, J. Douglas, & Tellegen, Auke. (2004). Salient and emerging developmental tasks in the transition to adulthood. *Child Development, 75,* 123–133.

Rolland-Cachera, Marie Françoise, & Bellisle, France. (2002). Nutrition. In Walter Burniat, Tim J. Cole, Inge Lissau, & Elizabeth M. E. Poskitt (Eds.), *Child and adolescent obesity: Causes and consequences, prevention and management* (pp. 69–92). New York: Cambridge University Press.

Romaine, Suzanne. (1999). Bilingual language development. In Martyn Barrett (Ed.), *The development of language* (pp. 251–275). Hove, England: Psychology Press.

Roschelle, Anne R. (1997). *No more kin: Exploring race, class, and gender in family networks.* Thousand Oaks, CA: Sage.

Rose, Amanda J., & Asher, Steven R. (1999). Children's goals and strategies in response to conflicts within a friendship. *Developmental Psychology, 35,* 69–79.

Rose, Amanda J., & Asher, Steven R. (2004). Children's strategies and goals in response to help-giving and help-seeking tasks within a friendship. *Child Development, 75,* 749–763.

Rose-Jacobs, Ruth, Cabral, Howard, Posner, Michael A., Epstein, Jennifer, & Frank, Deborah A. (2002). Do "we just know?" Masked assessors' ability to accurately identify children with prenatal cocaine exposure. *Journal of Developmental & Behavioral Pediatrics, 23,* 340–346.

Rosenberg, Noah A., Pritchard, Jonathan K., Weber, James L., Cann, Howard M., Kidd, Kenneth K., Zhivotovsky, Lev A., et al. (2002). Genetic structure of human populations. *Science, 298,* 2381–2385.

Rosenthal, Doreen A., Demetriou, Andreas, & Efklides, Anastasia. (1989). A cross-national study of the influence of culture on conflict between parents and adolescents. *International Journal of Behavioral Development, 12,* 207–219.

Rothbart, Mary K., & Bates, John E. (1998). Temperament. In William Damon (Series Ed.) & Nancy Eisenberg (Vol. Ed.), *Handbook of child psychology: Vol. 3. Social, emotional, and personality development* (5th ed., pp. 105–176). New York: Wiley.

Rothbaum, Fred, Pott, Martha, Azuma, Hiroshi, Miyake, Kazuo, & Weisz, John. (2000). The development of close relationships in Japan and the United States: Paths of symbiotic harmony and generative tension. *Child Development, 71,* 1121–1142.

Rovee-Collier, Carolyn. (1987). Learning and memory in infancy. In Joy Doniger Osofsky (Ed.), *Handbook of infant development* (2nd ed., pp. 98–148). New York: Wiley.

Rovee-Collier, Carolyn. (1990). The "memory system" of prelinguistic infants. In Adele Diamond (Ed.), *Annals of the New York Academy of Sciences: Vol. 608. The development and neural bases of higher cognitive functions* (pp. 517–542). New York: New York Academy of Sciences.

Rovee-Collier, Carolyn. (2001). Information pick-up by infants: What is it, and how can we tell? *Journal of Experimental Child Psychology, 78,* 35–49.

Rovee-Collier, Carolyn, & Gerhardstein, Peter. (1997). The development of infant memory. In Nelson Cowan (Ed.), *The development of memory in childhood* (pp. 5–39). Hove, East Sussex, UK: Psychology Press.

Rovee-Collier, Carolyn, & Hayne, Harlene. (1987). Reactivation of infant memory: Implications for cognitive development. In Hayne W. Reese (Ed.), *Advances in child development and behavior* (Vol. 20, pp. 185–238). San Diego, CA: Academic Press.

Rovi, Sue, Chen, Ping-Hsin, & Johnson, Mark S. (2004). The economic burden of hospitalizations associated with child abuse and neglect. *American Journal of Public Health, 94,* 586–590.

Rowland, Andrew S., Umbach, David M., Stallone, Lil, Naftel, A. Jack, Bohlig, E. Michael, & Sandler, Dale P. (2002). Prevalence of medication treatment for attention deficit-hyperactivity disorder among elementary school children in Johnston County, North Carolina. *American Journal of Public Health, 92,* 231–234.

Royal College of Obstetricians and Gynaecologists Clinical Effectiveness Support Unit. (2001). *National sentinel caesarean section audit.* London: RCOG Press.

Rubin, Kenneth H. (2000). *The play observation scale (revised).* College Park, MD: University of Maryland.

Rubin, Kenneth H., Bukowski, William, & Parker, Jeffrey G. (1998). Peer interactions, relationships, and groups. In William Damon (Series Ed.) & Nancy Eisenberg (Vol. Ed.), *Handbook of child psychology: Vol. 3. Social, emotional, and personality development* (5th ed., pp. 619–700). New York: Wiley.

Rubin, Kenneth H., Burgess, Kim B., & Hastings, Paul D. (2002). Stability and social-behavioral consequences of toddlers' inhibited temperament and parenting behaviors. *Child Development, 73,* 483–495.

Ruble, Diane, Alvarez, Jeanette, Bachman, Meredith, Cameron, Jessica, Fuligni, Andrew, Coll, Cynthia Garcia, et al. (2004). The development of a sense of "we": The emergence and implications of children's collective identity. In Mark Bennett & Fabio Sani (Eds.), *The development of the social self* (pp. 29–76). Hove, East Sussex, England: Psychology Press.

Ruble, Diane N., & Martin, Carol Lynn. (1998). Gender development. In William Damon (Series Ed.) & Nancy Eisenberg (Vol. Ed.), *Handbook of child psychology: Vol. 3. Social, emotional, and personality development* (5th ed., pp. 933–1016). New York: Wiley.

Ruffman, Ted, Slade, Lance, & Crowe, Elena. (2002). The relation between children's and mothers' mental state language and theory-of-mind understanding. *Child Development, 73,* 734–751.

Ruffman, Ted, Slade, Lance, Sandino, Juan Carlos, & Fletcher, Amanda. (2005). Are A-not-B errors caused by a belief about object location? *Child Development, 76,* 122–136.

Rumbaut, Rubén G., & Portes, Alejandro (Eds.). (2001). *Ethnicities: Children of immigrants in America.* Berkeley, CA and New York: University of California Press and the Russell Sage Foundation.

Russell, Mark. (2002). South Korea: Institute helps spread use of vaccines in Asia. *Science, 295,* 611–612.

Rust, John, Golombok, Susan, Hines, Melissa, Johnston, Katie, Golding, Jean, & The ALSPAC Study Team. (2000). The role of brothers and sisters in the gender development of preschool children. *Journal of Experimental Child Psychology, 77,* 292–303.

Rutland, Adam, Cameron, Lindsey, Milne, Alan, & McGeorge, Peter. (2005). Social norms and self-presentation: Children's implicit and explicit intergroup attitudes. *Child Development, 76,* 451–466.

Rutstein, Shea O. (2000). Factors associated with trends in infant and child mortality in developing countries during the 1990s. *Bulletin of the World Health Organization, 78,* 1256–1270.

Rutter, Michael. (1998). Some research considerations on intergenerational continuities and discontinuities: Comment on the special section. *Developmental Psychology, 34,* 1269–1273.

Rutter, Michael. (2002). The interplay of nature, nurture, and developmental influences: The challenge ahead for mental health. *Archives of General Psychiatry, 59,* 996–1000.

Rutter, Michael, Giller, Henri, & Hagell, Ann. (1998). *Antisocial behavior by young people.* New York: Cambridge University Press.

Rutter, Michael, & O'Connor, Thomas G. (2004). Are there biological programming effects for psychological development? Findings from a study of Romanian adoptees. *Developmental Psychology, 40,* 81–94.

Rutter, Michael, & Sroufe, L. Alan. (2000). Developmental psychopathology: Concepts and challenges. *Development & Psychopathology, 12,* 265–296.

Rutter, Michael, Thorpe, Karen, Greenwood, Rosemary, Northstone, Kate, & Golding, Jean. (2003). Twins as a natural experiment to study the causes of mild language delay: I: Design; twin-singleton differences in language, and obstetric risks. *Journal of Child Psychology and Psychiatry, 44,* 326–341.

Ryalls, Brigette Oliver. (2000). Dimensional adjectives: Factors affecting children's ability to compare objects using novel words. *Journal of Experimental Child Psychology, 76,* 26–49.

Ryalls, Brigette Oliver, Gul, Robina E., & Ryalls, Kenneth R. (2000). Infant imitation of peer and adult models: Evidence for a peer model advantage. *Merrill-Palmer Quarterly, 46,* 188–202.

Ryan, Michael J. (2005, June 8). *Punching out in Little League.* Boston Herald. Retrieved September 11, 2005, from the World Wide Web: http://news.bostonherald.com/blogs/rapSheet/index.bg?mode=viewid&post_id=190

Sackett, Paul R., Hardison, Chaitra M., & Cullen, Michael J. (2004). On interpreting stereotype threat as accounting for African American-White differences on cognitive tests. *American Psychologist, 59,* 7–13.

Sackett, Paul R., Schmitt, Neal, Ellingson, Jill E., & Kabin, Melissa B. (2001). High-stakes testing in employment, credentialing, and higher education: Prospects in a post-affirmative-action world. *American Psychologist, 56,* 302–318.

Sacks, Oliver W. (1998). *The man who mistook his wife for a hat and other clinical tales.* New York: Simon & Schuster. (Original work published 1970)

Sadeh, Avi, Raviv, Amiram, & Gruber, Reut. (2000). Sleep patterns and sleep disruptions in school-age children. *Developmental Psychology, 36,* 291–301.

Sagi, Abraham, Koren-Karie, Nina, Gini, Motti, Ziv, Yair, & Joels, Tirtsa. (2002). Shedding further light on the effects of various types and quality of early child care on infant-mother attachment relationship: The Haifa study of early child care. *Child Development, 73,* 1166–1186.

Salazar, Lilia P., Schludermann, Shirin M., Schludermann, Eduard H., & Huynh, Cam-Loi. (2000). Filipino adolescents' parental socialization for academic achievement in the United States. *Journal of Adolescent Research, 15,* 564–586.

Salkind, Neil J. (2004). *An introduction to theories of human development.* Thousand Oaks, CA: Sage.

Salmivalli, Christina, Ojanen, Tiina, Haanpaa, Jemina, & Peets, Katlin. (2005). "I'm OK but you're not" and other peer-relational schemas: Explaining individual differences in children's social goals. *Developmental Psychology, 41,* 363–375.

Salzarulo, Piero, & Fagioli, Igino. (1999). Changes of sleep states and physiological activities across the first year of life. In Alex Fedde Kalverboer, Maria Luisa Genta, & J. B. Hopkins (Eds.), *Current issues in developmental psychology: Biopsychological perspectives* (pp. 53–73). Dordrecht, The Netherlands: Kluwer.

Sameroff, Arnold J. (2000). Developmental systems and psychopathology. *Development & Psychopathology, 12,* 297–312.

Sameroff, Arnold J., & MacKenzie, Michael J. (2003). Research strategies for capturing transactional models of development: The limits of the possible. *Development & Psychopathology, 15,* 613–640.

Sampaio, Ricardo C., & Truwit, Charles L. (2001). Myelination in the developing human brain. In Charles A. Nelson & Monica Luciana (Eds.), *Handbook of developmental* *cognitive neuroscience* (pp. 35–44). Cambridge, MA: MIT Press.

Sampson, Robert J., & Laub, John H. (1993). *Crime in the making: Pathways and turning points through life.* Cambridge, MA: Harvard University Press.

Sampson, Robert J., Raudenbush, Stephen W., & Earls, Felton. (1997). Neighborhoods and violent crime: A multilevel study of collective efficacy. *Science, 277,* 918–924.

Sanchez, Maria del Mar, Ladd, Charlotte O., & Plotsky, Paul M. (2001). Early adverse experience as a developmental risk factor for later psychopathology: Evidence from rodent and primate models. *Development & Psychopathology, 13,* 419–449.

Sandler, Irwin, Wolchik, Sharlene, Davis, Caroline, Haine, Rachel, & Ayers, Tim. (2003). Correlational and experimental study of resilience in children of divorce and parentally bereaved children. In Suniya S. Luthar (Ed.), *Resilience and vulnerability: Adaptation in the context of childhood adversities* (pp. 213–240). New York: Cambridge University Press.

Sandstrom, Marlene J., & Zakriski, Audrey L. (2004). Understanding the experience of peer rejection. In Janis B. Kupersmidt & Kenneth A. Dodge (Eds.), *Children's peer relations: From development to intervention* (pp. 101–118). Washington, DC: American Psychological Association.

Sani, Fabio, & Bennett, Mark. (2004). Developmental aspects of social identity. In Mark Bennett & Fabio Sani (Eds.), *The development of the social self* (pp. 77–100). Hove, East Sussex, England: Psychology Press.

Santelli, John S., Lindberg, Laura Duberstein, Abma, Joyce, McNeely, Clea Sucoff, & Resnick, Michael. (2000). Adolescent sexual behavior: Estimates and trends from four nationally representative surveys. *Family Planning Perspectives, 32,* 156–165, 194.

Santora, Marc. (2005, January 30). U.S. is close to eliminating AIDS in infants, officials say. *New York Times,* pp. A1.

Sapp, Felicity, Lee, Kang, & Muir, Darwin. (2000). Three-year-olds' difficulty with the appearance-reality distinction: Is it real or is it apparent? *Developmental Psychology, 36,* 547–560.

Sarroub, Loukia K. (2001). The sojourner experience of Yemeni American high school students: An ethnographic portrait. *Harvard Educational Review, 71,* 390–415.

Satcher, David. (2001). *Women and smoking: A report of the Surgeon General.* Rockville, MD: U.S. Department of Health and Human Services.

Satcher, David. (2001). *The Surgeon General's call to action to promote sexual health and responsible sexual behavior.* Rockville, MD: Office of the Surgeon General.

Savage, Felicity, & Lhotska, Lida. (2000). Recommendations on feeding infants of HIV positive mothers. WHO, UNICEF, UNAIDS guidelines. In Nathan Back, Irun R. Cohen, David Kritchevsky, Abel Lajtha, & Rodolfo Paoletti (Series Eds.) & Berthold Koletzko, Kim Fleischer Michaelsen, & Olle Hernell (Vol. Eds.), *Advances in experimental medicine and biology: Vol. 478. Short and long term effects of breast feeding on child health* (pp. 225–230). Dordrecht, The Netherlands: Kluwer Academic/Plenum.

Savin-Williams, Ritch C., & Diamond, Lisa M. (1997). Sexual orientation as a developmental context for lesbians, gays, and bisexuals: Biological perspectives. In Nancy L. Segal, Glenn E. Weisfeld, & Carol C. Weisfeld (Eds.), *Uniting psychology and biology: Integrative perspectives on human development* (pp. 217–238). Washington, DC: American Psychological Association.

Savin-Williams, Ritch C., & Diamond, Lisa M. (2004). Sex. In Richard M. Lerner & Laurence D. Steinberg (Eds.), *Handbook of adolescent psychology* (2nd ed., pp. 189–231). Hoboken, NJ: Wiley.

Saw, Seang-Mei. (2003). A synopsis of the prevalence rates and environmental risk factors for myopia. *Clinical and Experimental Optometry, 86,* 289–294.

Saxe, Geoffrey B. (1991). *Culture and cognitive development: Studies in mathematical understanding.* Hillsdale, NJ: Erlbaum.

Saxe, Geoffrey B. (1999). Sources of concepts: A cultural-developmental perspective. In Ellin Kofsky Scholnick, Katherine Nelson, Susan A. Gelman, & Patricia H. Miller (Eds.), *Conceptual development: Piaget's legacy* (pp. 253–267). Mahwah, NJ: Erlbaum.

Saylor, Megan M., & Sabbagh, Mark A. (2004). Different kinds of information affect word learning in the preschool years: The case of part-term learning. *Child Development, 75,* 395–408.

Schacter, Daniel L., & Badgaiyan, Rajendra D. (2001). Neuroimaging of priming: New perspectives on implicit and explicit memory. *Current Directions in Psychological Science, 10,* 1–4.

Schaffer, H. Rudolph. (2000). The early experience assumption: Past, present, and future. *International Journal of Behavioral Development, 24,* 5–14.

Schaie, K. Warner. (1996). *Intellectual development in adulthood: The Seattle Longitudinal Study.* New York: Cambridge University Press.

Schardein, James L. (1976). *Drugs as teratogens.* Cleveland, OH: CRC Press.

Scharf, Miri. (2001). A "natural experiment" in childrearing ecologies and adolescents' attachment and separation representations. *Child Development, 72,* 236–251.

Schifter, Jacobo, & Madrigal Pana, Johnny. (2000). *The sexual construction of Latino youth: Implications for the spread of HIV/AIDS.* New York: Haworth Hispanic/Latino Press.

Schlegel, Alice. (2003). Modernization and changes in adolescent social life. In T. S. Saraswati (Ed.), *Cross-cultural perspectives in human development: Theory, research, and applications* (pp. 236–257). New Delhi, India: Sage.

Schlegel, Alice, & Barry, Herbert. (1991). *Adolescence: An anthropological inquiry.* New York: Free Press.

Schmader, Toni. (2002). Gender identification moderates stereotype threat effects on women's math performance. *Journal of Experimental Social Psychology, 38,* 194–201.

Schneider, Wolfgang. (1998). The development of procedural metamemory in childhood and adolescence. In Giuliana Mazzoni & Thomas O. Nelson (Eds.), *Metacognition and cognitive neuropsychology: Monitoring and control processes* (pp. 1–21). Mahwah, NJ: Erlbaum.

Schneider, Wolfgang, & Pressley, Michael. (1997). *Memory development between two and twenty* (2nd ed.). Mahwah, NJ: Erlbaum.

Schore, Allan N. (2001). Effects of a secure attachment relationship on right brain development, affect regulation, and infant mental health. *Infant Mental Health Journal, 22*(1-2), 7–66.

Schult, Carolyn A. (2002). Children's understanding of the distinction between intentions and desires. *Child Development, 73,* 1727–1747.

Schumann, Cynthia Mills, Hamstra, Julia, Goodlin-Jones, Beth L., Lotspeich, Linda J., Kwon, Hower, Buonocore, Michael H., et al. (2004). The amygdala Is enlarged in children but not adolescents with autism; the hippocampus Is enlarged at all ages. *Journal of Neuroscience, 24,* 6392–6401.

Schwab, Jacqueline, Kulin, Howard E., Susman, Elizabeth J., Finkelstein, Jordan W., Chinchilli, Vernon M., Kunselman, Susan J., et al. (2001). The role of sex hormone replacement therapy on self-perceived competence in adolescents with delayed puberty. *Child Development, 72,* 1439–1450.

Schwartz, David, Proctor, Laura J., & Chien, Deborah H. (2001). The aggressive victim of bullying: Emotional and behavioral dysregulation as a pathway to victimization by peers. In Jaana Juvonen & Sandra Graham (Eds.), *Peer harassment in school: The plight of the vulnerable and victimized* (pp. 147–174). New York: Guilford Press.

Schwartz, Jeffrey, & Begley, Sharon. (2002). *The mind and the brain: Neuroplasticity and the power of mental force.* New York: Regan Books.

Schweinhart, Lawrence J., & Weikart, David P. (1997). *Lasting differences: The High/Scope preschool curriculum comparison study through age 23.* Ypsilanti, MI: High/Scope Educational Research Foundation.

Scott, Jacqueline. (2000). Children as respondents: The challenge for quantitative methods. In Pia Monrad Christensen & Allison James (Eds.), *Research with children: Perspectives and practices* (pp. 98–119). London: Falmer Press.

Scovel, Thomas. (1988). *A time to speak: A psycholinguistic inquiry into the critical period for human speech.* New York: Newbury House.

Segal, Nancy L. (1999). *Entwined lives: Twins and what they tell us about human behavior.* New York: Dutton.

Seifer, Ronald, LaGasse, Linda L., Lester, Barry, Bauer, Charles R., Shankaran, Seetha, Bada, Henrietta S., et al. (2004). Attachment status in children prenatally exposed to cocaine and other substances. *Child Development, 75,* 850–868.

Seifer, Ronald, Schiller, Masha, Sameroff, Arnold, Resnick, Staci, & Riordan, Kate. (1996). Attachment, maternal sensitivity, and infant temperament during the first year of life. *Developmental Psychology, 32,* 12–25.

Senechal, Monique, & LeFevre, Jo-Anne. (2002). Parental involvement in the development of children's reading skill: A five-year longitudinal study. *Child Development, 73,* 445–460.

Serpell, Robert, & Haynes, Brenda Pitts. (2004). The cultural practice of intelligence testing: Problems of international export. In Robert J. Sternberg & Elena L. Grigorenko (Eds.), *Culture and competence: Contexts of life success* (pp. 163–185). Washington, DC: American Psychological Association.

Shafir, Eldar, & LeBoeuf, Robyn A. (2002). Rationality. *Annual Review of Psychology, 53,* 491–517.

Shahin, Hashem, Walsh, Tom, Sobe, Tama, Lynch, Eric, King, Mary-Claire, Avraham, Karen, et al. (2002). Genetics of congenital deafness in the Palestinian population: Multiple connexin 26 alleles with shared origins in the Middle East. *Human Genetics, 110,* 284–289.

Shattuck, Roger. (2005). Curriculum first: A case history. *American Educator, 29,* 28–34.

Shatz, Marilyn. (1994). *A toddler's life: Becoming a person.* New York: Oxford University Press.

Shaw, Daniel S., Vondra, Joan I., Hommerding, Katherine Dowdell, Keenan, Kate, & Dunn, Marija G. (1994). Chronic family adversity and early child behavior problems: A longitudinal study of low income families. *Journal of Child Psychology & Psychiatry & Allied Disciplines, 35,* 1109–1122.

Shearer, Darlene L., Mulvihill, Beverly A., Klerman, Lorraine V., Wallander, Jan L., Hovinga, Mary E., & Redden, David T. (2002). Association of early childbearing and low cognitive ability. *Perspectives on Sexual and Reproductive Health, 34,* 236–243.

Sheinberg, Marcia, & Fraenkel, Peter. (2001). *The relational trauma of incest.* New York: Guilford Press.

Sherman, Stephanie. (2002). Epidemiology. In Randi Jenssen Hagerman & Paul J. Hagerman (Eds.), *Fragile X syndrome: Diagnosis, treatment, and research* (3rd ed., pp. 136–168). Baltimore: Johns Hopkins University Press.

Shields, Alexandra E., Fortun, Michael, Hammonds, Evelynn M., King, Patricia A., Lerman, Caryn, Rapp, Rayna, et al. (2005). The use of race variables in genetic studies of complex traits and the goal of reducing health disparities: A transdisciplinary perspective. *American Psychologist, 60,* 77–103.

Shoji, Junichi. (2005). Child abuse in Japan: Developmental, cultural, and clinical perspectives. In David W. Shwalb, Jun Nakazawa, & Barbara J. Shwalb (Eds.), *Applied developmental psychology: Theory, practice, and research from Japan* (pp. 261–279). Greenwich, CT: Information Age.

Shweder, Richard. (2003). *Why do men barbecue? Recipes for cultural psychology.* Cambridge, MA: Harvard University Press.

Shweder, Richard A., Goodnow, Jacqueline, Hatano, Giyoo, LeVine, Robert A., Markus, Hazel, & Miller, Peggy. (1998). The cultural psychology of development: One mind, many mentalities. In William Damon (Series Ed.) & Richard M. Lerner (Vol. Ed.), *Handbook of child psychology: Vol. 1. Theoretical models of human development* (5th ed., pp. 865–937). New York: Wiley.

Siegal, Michael. (2004). Signposts to the essence of language. *Science, 305,* 1720–1721.

Siegel, Judith M., Yancey, Antronette K., Aneshensel, Carol S., & Schuler, Roberleigh. (1999). Body image, perceived pubertal timing, and adolescent mental health. *Journal of Adolescent Health, 25,* 155–165.

Siegler, Robert S. (1998). *Children's thinking* (3rd ed.). Upper Saddle River, NJ: Prentice Hall.

Siegler, Robert S., & Jenkins, Eric. (1989). *How children discover new strategies.* Hillsdale, NJ: Erlbaum.

Silk, Jennifer S., Nath, Sanjay R., Siegel, Lori R., & Kendall, Philip C. (2000). Conceptualizing mental disorders in children: Where have we been and where are we going? *Development & Psychopathology, 12,* 713–735.

Silver, Archie A., & Hagin, Rosa A. (2002). *Disorders of learning in childhood* (2nd ed.). New York: Wiley.

Silverman, Wendy K., & Dick-Niederhauser, Andreas. (2004). Separation anxiety disorder. In Tracy L. Morris & John S. March (Eds.), *Anxiety disorders in children and adolescents* (2nd ed., pp. 164–188). New York: Guilford Press.

Simmons, Roberta G., & Blyth, Dale A. (1987). *Moving into adolescence: The impact of pubertal change and school context.* New York: de Gruyter.

Simon, Herbert A. (2001). Learning to research about learning. In Sharon M. Carver & David Klahr (Eds.), *Cognition and instruction: Twenty-five years of progress* (pp. 205–226). Mahwah, NJ: Erlbaum.

Singer, Dorothy G., & Singer, Jerome L. (2005). *Imagination and play in the electronic age.* Cambridge, MA: Harvard University Press.

Singer, Lynn T. (1999). Advances and redirections in understanding effects of fetal drug exposure. *Journal of Drug Issues, 29,* 253–262.

Singer, Lynn T., Arendt, Robert, Minnes, Sonia, Farkas, Kathleen, Salvator, Ann, Kirchner, H. Lester, et al. (2002). Cognitive and motor outcomes of cocaine-exposed infants. *Journal of the American Medical Association, 287,* 1952–1960.

Singer, Wolf. (2003). The nature-nurture problem revisited. In Ursula M. Staudinger & Ulman Lindenberger (Eds.), *Understanding human development: Dialogues with lifespan psychology* (pp. 437–447). Dordrecht, The Netherlands: Kluwer.

Sinnott, Jan D. (1998). *The development of logic in adulthood: Postformal thought and its applications.* New York: Plenum Press.

Siqueira, Lorena M., Rolnitzky, Linda M., & Rickert, Vaughn I. (2001). Smoking cessation in adolescents: The role of nicotine dependence, stress, and coping methods. *Archives of Pediatrics & Adolescent Medicine, 155,* 489–495.

Sirard, John R., Ainsworth, Barbara E., McIver, Kerri L., & Pate, Russell R. (2005). Prevalence of active commuting at urban and suburban elementary schools in Columbia, SC. *American Journal of Public Health, 95,* 236–237.

Skinner, B. F. (1953). *Science and human behavior.* New York: Macmillan.

Skinner, B. F. (1957). *Verbal behavior.* New York: Appleton-Century-Crofts.

Slobin, Dan I. (2001). Form-function relations: How do children find out what they are? In Melissa Bowerman & Stephen C. Levinson (Eds.), *Language acquisition and conceptual development* (pp. 406–449). Cambridge, UK: Cambridge University Press.

Smedley, Audrey, & Smedley, Brian D. (2005). Race as biology is fiction, racism as a social problem is real: Anthropological and historical perspectives on the social construction of race. *American Psychologist, 60,* 16–26.

Smetana, Judith G. (2002). Culture, autonomy, and personal jurisdiction in adolescent-parent relationships. In Robert V. Kail & Hayne W. Reese (Eds.), *Advances in child development and behavior* (Vol. 29, pp. 51–87). San Diego, CA: Academic Press.

Smetana, Judith G., Metzger, Aaron, & Campione-Barr, Nicole. (2004). African American late adolescents' relationships with parents: Developmental transitions and longitudinal patterns. *Child Development, 75,* 932–947.

Smith, Jacqui, & Baltes, Paul B. (1999). Trends and profiles of psychological functioning in very old age. In Paul B. Baltes & Karl Ulrich Mayer (Eds.), *The Berlin Aging Study: Aging from 70 to 100* (pp. 197–226). New York: Cambridge University Press.

Smith, Jonathan, & Dunworth, Fraser. (2003). Qualitative methodology. In Jaan Valsiner & Kevin J. Connolly (Eds.), *Handbook of developmental psychology* (pp. 603–621). Thousand Oaks, CA: Sage.

Smith, Leslie. (2002). *Reasoning by mathematical induction in children's arithmetic.* Amsterdam, The Netherlands: Pergamon.

Smith, Linda B. (1995). Self-organizing processes in learning to learn words: Development is not induction. In Charles Alexander Nelson (Ed.), *The Minnesota symposia on child psychology: Vol. 28. Basic and applied perspectives on learning, cognition, and development* (pp. 1–32). Hillsdale, NJ: Erlbaum.

Smith, Margaret G., & Fong, Rowena. (2004). *The children of neglect: When no one cares.* New York: Brunner-Routledge.

Smith, Mary Lee, & Glass, Gene V. (1979). *Relationship of class size to classroom processes, teacher satisfaction and pupil affect: A meta-analysis.* San Francisco: Far West Laboratory for Educational Research and Development.

Smith, Peter K., & Ananiadou, Katerina. (2003). The nature of school bullying and the effectiveness of school-based interventions. *Journal of Applied Psychoanalytic Studies, 5,* 189–209.

Smith, Russ. (2005, June 10). *Little League lives.* Wall Street Journal. Retrieved September 11, 2005, from the World Wide Web: http://www.opinionjournal.com/taste/?id=110006802

Snarey, John R. (1993). *How fathers care for the next generation: A four-decade study.* Cambridge, MA: Harvard University Press.

Snijders, R. J. M., & Nicolaides, K. H. (1996). *Ultrasound markers for fetal chromosomal defects.* New York: Parthenon.

Snow, Catherine E. (1984). Parent-child interaction and the development of communicative ability. In Richard L. Schiefelbusch & Joanne Pickar (Eds.), *The acquisition of communicative competence* (pp. 69–107). Baltimore: University Park Press.

Snyder, Howard N. (1998). Appendix: Serious, violent, and chronic juvenile offenders—An assessment of the extent of and trends in officially recognized serious criminal behavior in a delinquent population. In Rolf Loeber & David P. Farrington (Eds.), *Serious & violent juvenile offenders: Risk factors and successful interventions* (pp. 428–444). Thousand Oaks, CA: Sage.

Snyder, James, Schrepferman, Lynn, Oeser, Jessica, Patterson, Gerald, Stoolmiller, Mike, Johnson, Kassy, et al. (2005). Deviancy training and association with deviant peers in young children: Occurrence and contribution to early-onset conduct problems. *Development & Psychopathology, 17,* 397–413.

Snyder, Thomas D., Tan, Alexandra G., & Hoffman, Charlene M. (2004). *Digest of education statistics, 2003* (NCES 2005025). Washington, DC: U.S. Government Printing Office.

Social Security Administration. (2004, May 7). *Popular baby names.* Retrieved March 29, 2005, from the World Wide Web: http://www.ssa.gov/OACT/babynames/

Society for Assisted Reproductive Technology and the American Society for Reproductive Medicine. (2002). Assisted reproductive technology in the United States: 1998 results generated from the American Society for Reproductive Medicine/Society for Assisted Reproductive Technology Registry. *Fertility and Sterility, 77,* 18–31.

Sofie, Cecilia A., & Riccio, Cynthia A. (2002). A comparison of multiple methods for the identification of children with reading disabilities. *Journal of Learning Disabilities, 35,* 234–244.

Song, Miri. (2003). *Choosing ethnic identity*. Cambridge, UK: Polity Press.

Sorenson, Susan B., & Vittes, Katherine A. (2004). Adolescents and firearms: A California statewide survey. *American Journal of Public Health, 94*, 852–858.

Spelke, Elizabeth S. (1993). Object perception. In Alvin I. Goldman (Ed.), *Readings in philosophy and cognitive science* (pp. 447–460). Cambridge, MA: MIT Press.

Spock, Benjamin. (1976). *Baby and child care* (Newly rev., updated, and enl. ed.). New York: Pocket Books.

Sroufe, L. Alan. (1996). *Emotional development: The organization of emotional life in the early years*. Cambridge, UK: Cambridge University Press.

Staff, Jeremy, Mortimer, Jeylan T., & Uggen, Christopher. (2004). Work and leisure in adolescence. In Richard M. Lerner & Laurence D. Steinberg (Eds.), *Handbook of adolescent psychology* (2nd ed., pp. 429–450). Hoboken, NJ: Wiley.

Stanovich, Keith E. (1999). *Who is rational? Studies of individual differences in reasoning*. Mahwah, NJ: Erlbaum.

Stanovich, Keith E. (2000). *Progress in understanding reading: Scientific foundations and new frontiers*. New York: Guilford Press.

Stansfeld, S. A., Berglund, B., Clark, C., Lopez-Barrio, I., Fischer, P., Ohrstrom, E., et al. (2005). Aircraft and road traffic noise and children's cognition and health: A cross-national study. *Lancet, 365*, 1942–1949.

Stattin, Hakan, & Kerr, Margaret. (2000). Parental monitoring: A reinterpretation. *Child Development, 71*, 1072–1085.

Staudinger, Ursula M., & Lindenberger, Ulman. (2003). Why read another book on human development? Understanding human development takes a metatheory and multiple disciplines. In Ursula M. Staudinger & Ulman E. R. Lindenberger (Eds.), *Understanding human development: Dialogues with lifespan psychology* (pp. 1–13). Boston: Kluwer.

Stecher, Brian M., & Bohrnstedt, George W. (2000). *Class size reduction in California: The 1998–99 evaluation findings*. Sacramento, CA: California Department of Education.

Steele, Claude M. (1997). A threat in the air: How stereotypes shape intellectual identity and performance. *American Psychologist, 52*, 613–629.

Steele, Kenneth M., Bass, Karen E., & Crook, Melissa D. (1999). The mystery of the Mozart effect: Failure to replicate. *Psychological Science, 10*, 366–369.

Steinberg, Adria. (1993). *Adolescents and schools: Improving the fit*. Cambridge, MA: Harvard Education Letter.

Steinberg, Laurence. (2004). Risk taking in adolescence: What changes, and why? *Annals of the New York Academy of Sciences, 1021*, 51–58.

Steinberg, Laurence, Lamborn, Susie D., Darling, Nancy, Mounts, Nina S., & Dornbusch, Sanford M. (1994). Over-time changes in adjustment and competence among adolescents from authoritative, authoritarian, indulgent, and neglectful families. *Child Development, 65*, 754–770.

Stephanopoulos, George. (1999). *All too human: A political education*. Boston: Little Brown.

Stern, Daniel N. (1985). *The interpersonal world of the infant: A view from psychoanalysis and developmental psychology*. New York: Basic Books.

Sternberg, Robert J. (1996). *Successful intelligence: How practical and creative intelligence determine success in life*. New York: Simon & Schuster.

Sternberg, Robert J. (2004). Culture and intelligence. *American Psychologist, 59*, 325–338.

Sternberg, Robert J., & Grigorenko, Elena (Eds.). (2004). *Culture and competence: Contexts of life success*. Washington, DC: American Psychological Association.

Sternberg, Robert J., Grigorenko, Elena L., & Bundy, Donald A. (2001). The predictive value of IQ. *Merrill-Palmer Quarterly, 47*, 1–41.

Sternberg, Robert J., Grigorenko, Elena L., & Kidd, Kenneth K. (2005). Intelligence, race, and genetics. *American Psychologist, 60*, 46–59.

Stevenson, Harold W., Chen, Chuansheng, & Lee, Shin-ying. (1993). Mathematics achievement of Chinese, Japanese, and American children: Ten years later. *Science, 259*, 53–58.

Stevenson, Harold W., Lee, Shin-ying, Chen, Chuansheng, Stigler, James W., Hsu, Chen-Chin, & Kitamura, Seiro. (1990). Contexts of achievement: A study of American, Chinese, and Japanese children. *Monographs of the Society for Research in Child Development, 55*(1-2, Serial No. 221), 1–123.

Stevenson, Harold W., & Zusho, Akane. (2002). Adolescence in China and Japan: Adapting to a changing environment. In B. Bradford Brown, Reed W. Larson, & T. S. Saraswathi (Eds.), *The world's youth: Adolescence in eight regions of the globe* (pp. 141–170). New York: Cambridge University Press.

Stevick, Richard A. (2001). The Amish: Case study of a religious community. In Clive Erricker & Jane Erricker (Eds.), *Contemporary spiritualities: Social and religious contexts* (pp. 159–172). London: Continuum.

Stewart, Susan D., Manning, Wendy D., & Smock, Pamela J. (2003). Union formation among men in the U.S.: Does having prior children matter? *Journal of Marriage and Family, 65*, 90–104.

Stewart, Sunita Mahtani, & Bond, Michael Harris. (2002). A critical look at parenting research from the mainstream: Problems uncovered while adapting Western research to non-Western cultures. *British Journal of Developmental Psychology, 20*, 379–392.

Stigler, James W., & Hiebert, James. (1999). *The teaching gap: Best ideas from the world's teachers for improving education in the classroom*. New York: Free Press.

Stiles, Joan. (1998). The effects of early focal brain injury on lateralization of cognitive function. *Current Directions in Psychological Science, 7*, 21–26.

Stipek, Deborah, Feiler, Rachelle, Daniels, Denise, & Milburn, Sharon. (1995). Effects of different instructional approaches on young children's achievement and motivation. *Child Development, 66*, 209–223.

Stone, Nicole, & Ingham, Roger. (2003). When and why do young people in the United Kingdom first use sexual health services? *Perspectives on Sexual and Reproductive Health, 35*, 114–120.

Strachan, David P. (1999). The epidemiology of childhood asthma. *Allergy, 54*(Supplement 49), 7–11.

Strassberg, Zvi, Dodge, Kenneth A., Pettit, Gregory S., & Bates, John E. (1994). Spanking in the home and children's subsequent aggression toward kindergarten peers. *Development & Psychopathology, 6,* 445–461.

Straus, Murray A., & Donnelly, Denise A. (1994). *Beating the devil out of them: Corporal punishment in American families.* New York: Lexington Books.

Strauss, David, & Eyman, Richard K. (1996). Mortality of people with mental retardation in California with and without Down syndrome, 1986–1991. *American Journal on Mental Retardation, 100,* 643–653.

Streissguth, Ann P., & Connor, Paul D. (2001). Fetal alcohol syndrome and other effects of prenatal alcohol: Developmental cognitive neuroscience implications. In Charles A. Nelson & Monica Luciana (Eds.), *Handbook of developmental cognitive neuroscience* (pp. 505–518). Cambridge, MA: MIT Press.

Striano, Tricia. (2004). Direction of regard and the still-face effect in the first year: Does intention matter? *Child Development, 75,* 468–479.

Suarez-Orozco, Carola, & Suarez-Orozco, Marcelo M. (2001). *Children of immigration.* Cambridge, MA: Harvard University Press.

Suomi, Steven J. (2002). Parents, peers, and the process of socialization in primates. In John G. Borkowski, Sharon Landesman Ramey, & Marie Bristol-Power (Eds.), *Parenting and the child's world: Influences on academic, intellectual, and social-emotional development* (pp. 265–279). Mahwah, NJ: Erlbaum.

Susman, Elizabeth J. (1997). Modeling developmental complexity in adolescence: Hormones and behavior in context. *Journal of Research on Adolescence, 7,* 283–306.

Susman, Elizabeth J., & Rogol, Alan. (2004). Puberty and psychological development. In Richard M. Lerner & Laurence D. Steinberg (Eds.), *Handbook of adolescent psychology* (2nd ed., pp. 15–44). Hoboken, NJ: Wiley.

Sutherland, Lisa A. (2003, April). *Health trends in U.S. adolescents over the past 20 years.* Paper presented at the "Translating the Genome" meeting of the Federation of American Societies for Experimental Biology, San Diego, CA.

Sutton-Smith, Brian. (1997). *The ambiguity of play.* Cambridge, MA: Harvard University Press.

Swain, Merrill, & Johnson, Robert Keith. (1997). Immersion education: A category within bilingual education. In Robert Keith Johnson & Merrill Swain (Eds.), *Immersion education: International perspectives* (pp. 1–16). Cambridge, England: Cambridge University Press.

Sweet, Matthew P., Hodgman, Joan E., Pena, Ivette, Barton, Lorayne, Pavlova, Zdena, & Ramanathan, Rangasamy. (2003). Two-year outcome of infants weighing 600 grams or less at birth and born 1994 through 1998. *Obstetrics & Gynecology, 101,* 18–23.

Swenson, Nora C. (2000). Comparing traditional and collaborative settings for language intervention. *Communication Disorders Quarterly, 22,* 12–18.

Szatmari, Peter. (2001). Thinking about autism, Asperger syndrome and PDDNOS. *PRISME, 34,* 24–34.

Szkrybalo, Joel, & Ruble, Diane N. (1999). "God made me a girl": Sex-category constancy judgments and explanations revisited. *Developmental Psychology, 35,* 392–402.

Tamis-LeMonda, Catherine S., Bornstein, Marc H., & Baumwell, Lisa. (2001). Maternal responsiveness and children's achievement of language milestones. *Child Development, 72,* 748–767.

Tanaka, Yuko, & Nakazawa, Jun. (2005). Job-related temporary father absence (Tanshinfunin) and child development. In David W. Shwalb, Jun Nakazawa, & Barbara J. Shwalb (Eds.), *Applied developmental psychology: Theory, practice, and research from Japan* (pp. 241–260). Greenwich, CT: Information Age.

Tangney, June Price. (2001). Constructive and destructive aspects of shame and guilt. In Arthur C. Bohart & Deborah J. Stipek (Eds.), *Constructive & destructive behavior: Implications for family, school, & society* (pp. 127–145). Washington, DC,: American Psychological Association.

Tanner, James Mourilyan. (1990). *Foetus into man: Physical growth from conception to maturity* (Rev. and enl. ed.). Cambridge, MA: Harvard University Press.

Tarter, Ralph E., Vanyukov, Michael, Giancola, Peter, Dawes, Michael, Blackson, Timothy, Mezzich, Ada, et al. (1999). Etiology of early age onset substance use disorder: A maturational perspective. *Development & Psychopathology, 11,* 657–683.

Tatz, Colin Martin. (2001). *Aboriginal suicide is different: A portrait of life and self-destruction.* Canberra, Australia: Aboriginal Studies Press.

Tay, Marc Tze-Hsin, Au Eong, Kah Guan, Ng, C. Y., & Lim, M. K. (1992). Myopia and educational attainment in 421,116 young Singaporean males. *Annals, Academy of Medicine, Singapore, 21,* 785–791.

Taylor, H. Gerry, Klein, Nancy, & Hack, Maureen. (2000). School-age consequences of birth weight less than 750 g: A review and update. *Developmental Neuropsychology, 17,* 289–321.

Taylor, Marjorie, Carlson, Stephanie M., Maring, Bayta L., Gerow, Lynn, & Charley, Carolyn M. (2004). The characteristics and correlates of fantasy in school-age children: Imaginary companions, impersonation, and social understanding. *Developmental Psychology, 40,* 1173–1187.

Teicher, Martin H. (2002, March). Scars that won't heal: The neurobiology of child abuse. *Scientific American, 286,* 68–75.

Teitelbaum, Philip, Teitelbaum, Osnat, Nye, Jennifer, Fryman, Joshua, & Maurer, Ralph G. (1998). Movement analysis in infancy may be useful for early diagnosis of autism. *Proceedings of the National Academy of Sciences, 95,* 13982–13987.

Teitler, Julien O. (2002). Trends in youth sexual initiation and fertility in developed countries: 1960–1995. *Annals of the American Academy of Political & Social Science, 580,* 134–152.

Tenenbaum, Harriet R., & Leaper, Campbell. (2002). Are parents' gender schemas related to their children's gender-related cognitions? A meta-analysis. *Developmental Psychology, 38,* 615–630.

Tester, June M., Rutherford, George W., Wald, Zachary, & Rutherford, Mary W. (2004). A matched case-control study evaluating the effectiveness of speed humps in reducing child pedestrian injuries. *American Journal of Public Health, 94,* 646–650.

Thelen, Esther, & Corbetta, Daniela. (2002). Microdevelopment and dynamic systems: Applications to infant motor development. In Nira Granott & Jim Parziale (Eds.), *Microdevelopment: Transition processes in development and learning* (pp. 59–79). New York: Cambridge University Press.

Thomas, Kathleen M., & Casey, Betty Jo. (2003). Methods for imaging the developing brain. In Michelle De Haan & Mark H. Johnson (Eds.), *The cognitive neuroscience* *of development* (pp. 19–41). New York: Psychology Press.

Thompson, Christine. (2002). Drawing together: Peer influence in preschool-kindergarten art classes. In Liora Bresler & Christine Marme Thompson (Eds.), *The arts in children's lives: Context, culture, and curriculum* (pp. 129–138). Dordrecht, The Netherlands: Kluwer.

Thompson, Ross A. (1998). Early sociopersonality development. In William Damon (Series Ed.) & Nancy Eisenberg (Vol. Ed.), *Handbook of child psychology: Vol. 3. Social, emotional, and personality development* (5th ed., pp. 24–104). New York: Wiley.

Thompson, Ross A., & Nelson, Charles A. (2001). Developmental science and the media: Early brain development. *American Psychologist, 56,* 5–15.

Thompson, Ross A., & Raikes, H. Abigail. (2003). Toward the next quarter-century: Conceptual and methodological challenges for attachment theory. *Development & Psychopathology, 15,* 691–718.

Thompson, Ron A., & Sherman, Roberta Trattner. (1993). *Helping athletes with eating disorders.* Champaign, IL: Human Kinetics.

Thompson, Richard F. (2000). *The brain: A neuroscience primer* (3rd ed.). New York: Worth.

TIMSS. (2004). *Highlights from the Trends in International Mathematics and Science Study: TIMSS 2003* (NCES 2005005). Washington, DC: National Center for Education Statistics.

Tishkoff, Sarah A, & Kidd, Kenneth K. (2004). Implications of biogeography of human populations for 'race' and medicine. *Nature Genetics, 36,* S21-S27.

Tomasello, Michael. (2001). Perceiving intentions and learning words in the second year of life. In Melissa Bowerman & Stephen C. Levinson (Eds.), *Language acquisition and conceptual development* (pp. 132–158). Cambridge, UK: Cambridge University Press.

Torgesen, Joseph K. (2004). Preventing early reading failure—And its devastating downward spiral. *American Educator, 28,* 6–9, 12–13, 17–19, 45–47.

Torney-Purta, Judith, Lehmann, Rainer, Oswald, Hans, & Schulz, Wolfram. (2001). *Citizenship and education in twenty-eight countries: Civic knowledge and engagement at age fourteen.* Amsterdam, The Netherlands: International Association for the Evaluation of Educational Achievement.

Towne, Bradford, Demerath, Ellen W., & Czerwinski, Stefan A. (2002). The genetic epidemiology of growth and development. In Noël Cameron (Ed.), *Human growth and development* (pp. 103–137). San Diego, CA: Academic Press.

Toyama, Miki. (2001). Developmental changes in social comparison in preschool and elementary school children: Perceptions, feelings, and behavior. *Japanese Journal of Educational Psychology, 49,* 500–507.

Trimble, Joseph, Root, Maria P. P., & Helms, Janet E. (2003). Psychological perspectives on ethnic and racial psychology. In Guillermo Bernal, Joseph E. Trimble, Ann Kathleen Burlew, & Frederick T. Leong (Eds.), *Racial and ethnic minority psychology series: Vol. 4. Handbook of racial & ethnic minority psychology* (pp. 239–275). Thousand Oaks, CA: Sage.

Tronick, Edward Z. (1989). Emotions and emotional communication in infants. *American Psychologist, 44,* 112–119.

Tronick, Edward Z., Als, H., Adamson, L., Wise, S., & Brazelton, T. B. (1978). The infant's response to entrapment between contradictory messages in face-to-face interaction. *Journal of the American Academy of Child Psychiatry, 17,* 1–13.

Tronick, Edward Z., & Weinberg, M. Katherine. (1997). Depressed mothers and infants: Failure to form dyadic states of consciousness. In Lynne Murray & Peter J. Cooper (Eds.), *Postpartum depression and child development* (pp. 54–81). New York: Guilford Press.

True, Mary McMahan, Pisani, Lelia, & Oumar, Fadimata. (2001). Infant-mother attachment among the Dogon of Mali. *Child Development, 72,* 1451–1466.

Tsao, Feng-Ming, Liu, Huei-Mei, & Kuhl, Patricia K. (2004). Speech perception in infancy predicts language development in the second year of life: A longitudinal study. *Child Development, 75,* 1067–1084.

Tseng, Vivian. (2004). Family interdependence and academic adjustment in college: Youth from immigrant and U.S.-born families. *Child Development, 75,* 966–983.

Tucker, G. Richard. (1998). A global perspective on multilingualism and multilingual education. In Jasone Cenoz & Fred Genesee (Eds.), *Beyond bilingualism: Multilingualism and multilingual education* (pp. 3–15). Clevedon, England: Multilingual Matters.

Tuerk, Peter W. (2005). Research in the high-stakes era: Achievement, resources, and No Child Left Behind. *Psychological Science, 16,* 419–425.

Turiel, Elliot. (2002). *The culture of morality: Social development, context, and conflict.* New York: Cambridge University Press.

Turley, Ruth N. López. (2003). Are children of young mothers disadvantaged because of their mother's age or family background? *Child Development, 74,* 465–474.

Turner, Lindsey, Mermelstein, Robin, & Flay, Brian. (2004). Individual and contextual influences on adolescent smoking. In Ronald E. Dahl & Linda Patia Spear (Eds.), *Adolescent brain development: Vulnerabilities and opportunities* (Vol. 1021, pp. 175–197). New York: New York Academy of Sciences.

U.S. Bureau of the Census. (1991). *Statistical abstract of the United States: 1991* (111th ed.). Washington, DC: U.S. Government Printing Office.

U.S. Bureau of the Census. (2002). *Statistical abstract of the United States, 2001: The national data book* (121st ed.). Washington, DC: U.S. Department of Commerce.

U.S. Bureau of the Census. (2003). *Statistical abstract of the United States, 2002: The national data book* (122nd ed.). Washington, DC: U.S. Government Printing Office.

U.S. Bureau of the Census. (2004). *Statistical abstract of the United States: 2004–2005: The national data book* (124th ed.). Washington, DC: U.S. Government Printing Office.

U.S. Bureau of the Census. (2005). *Living arrangements of children: 2001* (Current Population Reports, P70-104). Washington, DC: Author.

U.S. Department of Education, Office of Special Education Programs. (2003). *Data tables for OSEP state reported data: Tables AB8, AB10.* Retrieved September 14, 2005, from the World Wide Web: http://www.ideadata.org/arc_toc5.asp#partbLRE

U.S. Department of Health and Human Services. (2004). *Trends in the well-being of America's children and youth, 2003*

(017-022-01571-4). Washington, DC: U.S. Government Printing Office.

U.S. Department Of Health And Human Services, & Administration for Children and Families. (2005, April). *Foster care FY1999-FY2003 entries, exits, and numbers of children in care on the last day of each federal fiscal year.* Retrieved September 7, 2005, from the World Wide Web: http://www.acf.hhs.gov/programs/cb/dis/tables/entryexit2002.htm

U.S. Department of Health and Human Services, Administration on Children, Youth and Families. (2005). *Child Maltreatment 2003*. Washington, DC: U.S. Government Printing Office.

U.S. Department of Health and Human Services. Administration on Children, Youth and Families. (2001). *Child maltreatment 1999: Reports from the states to the National Child Abuse and Neglect Data System*. Washington, DC: U.S. Government Printing Office.

Udovitch, Mim. (2002, September 8). A secret society of the starving. *New York Times Magazine, 151,* 18–22.

Underwood, Marion K. (2004). Gender and peer relations: Are the two gender cultures really all that different? In Janis B. Kupersmidt & Kenneth A. Dodge (Eds.), *Children's peer relations: From development to intervention* (pp. 21–36). Washington, DC: American Psychological Association.

Ungar, Michael T. (2000). The myth of peer pressure. *Adolescence, 35,* 167–180.

UNICEF (United Nations Children's Fund). (2002). *The state of the world's children 2003*. New York: Author.

UNICEF (United Nations Children's Fund). (2003). *The state of the world's children 2004: Infants with low birthweight.* Retrieved September 3, 2005, from the World Wide Web: http://hdr.undp.org/statistics/data/indic/indic_68_1_1.html

Uttal, William R. (2000). *The war between mentalism and behaviorism: On the accessibility of mental processes.* Mahwah, NJ: Erlbaum.

Vaillant, George E. (2002). *Aging well: Surprising guideposts to a happier life from the landmark Harvard Study of Adult Development.* Boston: Little Brown.

Van Hoorn, Judith Lieberman. (2000). *Adolescent development and rapid social change: Perspectives from Eastern Europe.* Albany, NY: State University of New York Press.

Van IJzendoorn, Marinus H. (1992). Intergenerational transmission of parenting: A review of studies in nonclinical populations. *Developmental Review, 12,* 76–99.

Van Leeuwen, Karla, De Fruyt, Filip, & Mervielde, Ivan. (2004). A longitudinal study of the utility of the resilient, overcontrolled, and undercontrolled personality types as predictors of children's and adolescents' problem behaviour. *International Journal of Behavioral Development, 28,* 210–220.

Van Leeuwen, Karla G., Mervielde, Ivan, Braet, Caroline, & Bosmans, Guy. (2004). Child personality and parental behavior as moderators of problem behavior: variable- and person-centered approaches. *Developmental Psychology, 40,* 1028–1046.

Vartanian, Lesa Rae. (2001). Adolescents' reactions to hypothetical peer group conversations: Evidence for an imaginary audience? *Adolescence, 36,* 347–380.

Vasa, Roma A., & Pine, Daniel S. (2004). Neurobiology. In Tracy L. Morris & John S. March (Eds.), *Anxiety disorders in children and adolescents* (2nd ed., pp. 3–26). New York: Guilford Press.

Venn, John J. (Ed.). (2004). *Assessing children with special needs* (3rd ed.). Upper Saddle River, NJ: Pearson.

Verkuyten, Maykel. (2004). Ethnic minority identity and social context. In Mark Bennett & Fabio Sani (Eds.), *The development of the social self* (pp. 189–216). Hove, East Sussex, England: Psychology Press.

Verma, Suman, & Saraswathi, T. S. (2002). Adolescence in India: Street urchins or Silicon Valley millionaires? In B. Bradford Brown, Reed W. Larson, & T. S. Saraswathi (Eds.), *The world's youth: Adolescence in eight regions of the globe* (pp. 105–140). New York: Cambridge University Press.

Verona, Sergiu. (2003). Romanian policy regarding adoptions. In Victor Littel (Ed.), *Adoption update*. New York: Nova Science.

Verté, Sylvie, Geurts, Hilde M., Roeyers, Herbert, Oosterlaan, Jaap, & Sergeant, Joseph A. (2005). Executive functioning in children with autism and Tourette syndrome. *Development & Psychopathology, 17,* 415–445.

Vinden, Penelope G. (1996). Junin Quechua children's understanding of mind. *Child Development, 67,* 1707–1716.

Vizmanos, Barbara, & Martí-Henneberg, Carlos. (2000). Puberty begins with a characteristic subcutaneous body fat mass in each sex. *European Journal of Clinical Nutrition, 54,* 203–208.

Votruba-Drzal, Elizabeth, Coley, Rebekah Levine, & Chase-Lansdale, P. Lindsay. (2004). Child care and low-income children's development: Direct and moderated effects. *Child Development, 75,* 296–312.

Vygotsky, Lev S. (1978). *Mind in society: The development of higher psychological processes* (Michael Cole, Vera John-Steiner, Sylvia Scribner, & Ellen Souberman, Ed.). Cambridge, MA: Harvard University Press. (Original work published 1935)

Vygotsky, Lev S. (1986). *Thought and language* (Alex Kozulin, Ed., Eugenia Hanfmann & Gertrude Vakar, Trans.). Cambridge, MA: MIT Press. (Original work published 1934)

Vygotsky, Lev S. (1987). Thinking and speech (Norris Minick, Trans.). In R. W. Rieber & Aaron S. Carton (Eds.), *The collected works of L. S. Vygotsky* (Vol. 1, pp. 39–285). New York: Plenum Press. (Original work published 1934)

Vygotsky, Lev S. (1994). Principles of social education for deaf and dumb children in Russia (Theresa Prout, Trans.). In Rene van der Veer & Jaan Valsiner (Eds.), *The Vygotsky reader* (pp. 19–26). Cambridge, MA: Blackwell. (Original work published 1925)

Vygotsky, Lev S. (1994). The development of academic concepts in school aged children (Theresa Prout, Trans.). In Rene van der Veer & Jaan Valsiner (Eds.), *The Vygotsky reader* (pp. 355–370). Cambridge, MA: Blackwell. (Original work published 1934)

Wachs, Theodore D. (1999). Celebrating complexity: Conceptualization and assessment of the environment. In Sarah L. Friedman & Theodore D. Wachs (Eds.), *Measuring environment across the life span: Emerging methods and concepts* (pp. 357–392). Washington, DC: American Psychological Association.

Wachs, Theodore D. (2000). *Necessary but not sufficient: The respective roles of single and multiple influences on individual development.* Washington, DC: American Psychological Association.

Wagener, Linda Mans, Furrow, James L., King, Pamela Ebstyne, Leffert, Nancy, & Benson, Peter L. (2003). Religious involvement and developmental resources in youth. *Review of Religious Research, 44,* 271–284.

Wahlsten, Douglas. (2003). Genetics and the development of brain and behavior. In Jaan Valsiner & Kevin J. Connolly (Eds.), *Handbook of developmental psychology* (pp. 18–47). Thousand Oaks, CA: Sage.

Wahlstrom, Kyla L. (2002). Accommodating the sleep patterns of adolescents within current educational structures: An uncharted path. In Mary A. Carskadon (Ed.), *Adolescent sleep patterns: Biological, social, and psychological influences* (pp. 172–197). New York: Cambridge University Press.

Wailoo, Michael, Ball, Helen L., Fleming, Peter, & Ward Platt, Martin. (2004). Infants bed-sharing with mothers. *Archives of Disease in Childhood, 89,* 1082–1083.

Wainright, Jennifer L., Russell, Stephen T., & Patterson, Charlotte J. (2004). Psychosocial adjustment, school outcomes, and romantic relationships of adolescents with same-sex parents. *Child Development, 75,* 1886–1898.

Wainryb, Cecilia, Shaw, Leigh A., Langley, Marcie, Cottam, Kim, & Lewis, Renee. (2004). Children's thinking about diversity of belief in the early school years: Judgments of relativism, tolerance, and disagreeing persons. *Child Development, 75,* 687–703.

Wainryb, Cecilia, & Turiel, Elliot. (1995). Diversity in social development: Between or within cultures? In Melanie Killen & Daniel Hart (Eds.), *Morality in everyday life: Developmental perspectives* (pp. 283–313). New York: Cambridge University Press.

Walcott, Delores D., Pratt, Helen D., & Patel, Dilip R. (2003). Adolescents and eating disorders: Gender, racial, ethnic, sociocultural and socioeconomic issues. *Journal of Adolescent Research, 18,* 223–243.

Waldron, Nancy L., & McLeskey, James. (1998). The effects of an inclusive school program on students with mild and severe learning disabilities. *Exceptional Children, 64,* 395–405.

Walker, Elaine F. (2002). Adolescent neurodevelopment and psychopathology. *Current Directions in Psychological Science, 11,* 24–28.

Walker, Lawrence J. (1988). The development of moral reasoning. *Annals of Child Development, 5,* 33–78.

Walker, Lawrence J., Gustafson, Paul, & Hennig, Karl H. (2001). The consolidation/transition model in moral reasoning development. *Developmental Psychology, 37,* 187–197.

Walker-Barnes, Chanequa J., & Mason, Craig A. (2001). Ethnic differences in the effect of parenting on gang involvement and gang delinquency: A longitudinal, hierarchical linear modeling perspective. *Child Development, 72,* 1814–1831.

Walsh, Froma. (2002). A family resilience framework: Innovative practice applications. *Family Relations, 51,* 130–137.

Wardley, Bridget L., Puntis, John W. L., & Taitz, Leonard S. (1997). *Handbook of child nutrition* (2nd ed.). New York: Oxford University Press.

Warshofsky, Fred. (1999). *Stealing time: The new science of aging.* New York: TV Books.

Waterman, Alan S. (1999). Issues of identity formation revisited: United States and The Netherlands. *Developmental Review, 19,* 462–479.

Watson, John B. (1928). *Psychological care of infant and child.* New York: Norton.

Watson, John B. (1998). *Behaviorism.* New Brunswick, NJ: Transaction. (Original work published 1924)

Wayne, Andrew J., & Youngs, Peter. (2003). Teacher characteristics and student achievement gains: A review. *Review of Educational Research, 73,* 89–122.

Webb, Wilse B. (1994). Sleep as a biological rhythm: A historical view. *Sleep: Journal of Sleep Research & Sleep Medicine, 17,* 188–194.

Wechsler, David. (2003). *Wechsler intelligence scale for children—Fourth edition (WISC-IV).* San Antonio, TX: The Psychological Corporation.

Weikart, David P. (Ed.). (1999). *What should young children learn? Teacher and parent views in 15 countries.* Ypsilanti, MI: High/Scope Press.

Weinstock, Marta. (1997). Does prenatal stress impair coping and regulation of hypothalamic-pituitary-adrenal axis? *Neuroscience & Biobehavioral Reviews, 21,* 1–10.

Weisfeld, Glenn E. (1999). *Evolutionary principles of human adolescence.* New York: Basic Books.

Weissbluth, Marc. (1999). *Healthy sleep habits, happy child* (Rev. ed.). New York: Ballantine.

Weizman, Zehava Oz, & Snow, Catherine E. (2001). Lexical output as related to children's vocabulary acquisition: Effects of sophisticated exposure and support for meaning. *Developmental Psychology, 37,* 265–279.

Wellman, Henry M., Cross, David, & Watson, Julanne. (2001). Meta-analysis of theory-of-mind development: The truth about false belief. *Child Development, 72,* 655–684.

Welner, Kevin Grant. (2001). *Legal rights, local wrongs: When community control collides with educational equity.* Albany, NY: State University of New York Press.

Welti, Carlos. (2002). Adolescents in Latin America: Facing the future with skepticism. In B. Bradford Brown, Reed W. Larson, & T. S. Saraswathi (Eds.), *The world's youth: Adolescence in eight regions of the globe* (pp. 276–306). New York: Cambridge University Press.

Wendland-Carro, Jacqueline, Piccinini, Cesar A., & Millar, W. Stuart. (1999). The role of an early intervention on enhancing the quality of mother-infant interaction. *Child Development, 70,* 713–721.

Werner, Emmy E., & Smith, Ruth S. (1992). *Overcoming the odds: High risk children from birth to adulthood.* Ithaca, NY: Cornell University Press.

Werner, Emmy E., & Smith, Ruth S. (2001). *Journeys from childhood to midlife: Risk, resilience, and recovery.* Ithaca, NY: Cornell University Press.

Wertsch, James V. (1998). *Mind as action.* New York: Oxford University Press.

Wertsch, James V., & Tulviste, Peeter. (1992). L. S. Vygotsky and contemporary developmental psychology. *Developmental Psychology, 28,* 548–557.

West, Sheila, & Sommer, Alfred. (2001). Prevention of blindness and priorities for the future. *Bulletin of the World Health Organization, 79,* 244–248.

West, Steven L., & O'Neal, Keri K. (2004). Project D.A.R.E. outcome effectiveness revisited. *American Journal of Public Health, 94,* 1027–1029.

Wheeler, Mary E., & Fiske, Susan T. (2005). Controlling racial prejudice: Social-cognitive goals affect amygdala and stereotype activation. *Psychological Science, 16,* 56–63.

Wheeler, Patricia G., Bresnahan, Karen, Shephard, Barbara A., Lau, Joseph, & Balk, Ethan M. (2004). Short stature and functional impairment: A systematic review. *Archives of Pediatrics & Adolescent Medicine, 158,* 236–243.

White, Aaron M., Ghia, Amol J., Levin, Edward D., & Swartzwelder, H. Scott. (2000). Binge pattern ethanol exposure in adolescent and adult rats: Differential impact on subsequent responsiveness to ethanol. *Alcoholism: Clinical & Experimental Research, 24,* 1251–1256.

White, Aaron M., & Swartzwelder, H. Scott. (2004). Hippocampal function during adolescence: A unique target of ethanol effects. *Annals of the New York Academy of Sciences, 1021,* 206–220.

Whitehurst, Grover J., & Massetti, Greta M. (2004). How well does Head Start prepare children to learn to read? In Edward Zigler & Sally J. Styfco (Eds.), *The Head Start debates* (pp. 251–262). Baltimore: Brookes.

Whiteman, Shawn D., & Buchanan, Christy M. (2002). Mothers' and children's expectations for adolescence: The impact of perceptions of an older sibling's experience. *Journal of Family Psychology, 16,* 157–171.

Whitfield, Keith E., & McClearn, Gerald. (2005). Genes, environment, and race: Quantitative genetic approaches. *American Psychologist, 60,* 104–114.

Wiener, Judith, & Schneider, Barry H. (2002). A multisource exploration of the friendship patterns of children with and without learning disabilities. *Journal of Abnormal Child Psychology, 30,* 127–141.

Wigfield, Allan, Eccles, Jacquelynne S., Yoon, Kwang Suk, Harold, Rena D., Arbreton, Amy J. A., Freedman-Doan, Carol, et al. (1997). Change in children's competence beliefs and subjective task values across the elementary school years: A 3-year study. *Journal of Educational Psychology, 89,* 451–469.

Wilder, Esther I., & Watt, Toni Terling. (2002). Risky parental behavior and adolescent sexual activity at first coitus. *Milbank Quarterly, 80,* 481–524.

Willatts, Peter. (1999). Development of means-end behavior in young infants: Pulling a support to retrieve a distant object. *Developmental Psychology, 35,* 651–667.

Williams, Benjamin R., Ponesse, Jonathan S., Schachar, Russell J., Logan, Gordon D., & Tannock, Rosemary. (1999). Development of inhibitory control across the life span. *Developmental Psychology, 35,* 205–213.

Winsler, Adam, Carlton, Martha P., & Barry, Maryann J. (2000). Age-related changes in preschool children's systematic use of private speech in a natural setting. *Journal of Child Language, 27,* 665–687.

Winsler, Adam, Díaz, Rafael M., Espinosa, Linda, & Rodríguez, James L. (1999). When learning a second language does not mean losing the first: Bilingual language development in low-income, Spanish-speaking children attending bilingual preschool. *Child Development, 70,* 349–362.

Wishart, Jennifer G. (1999). Learning and development in children with Down's syndrome. In Alan Slater & Darwin Muir (Eds.), *The Blackwell reader in developmental psychology* (pp. 493–508). Malden, MA: Blackwell.

Witt, Whitney P., Riley, Anne W., & Coiro, Mary Jo. (2003). Childhood functional status, family stressors, and psychosocial adjustment among school-aged children with disabilities in the United States. *Archives of Pediatrics & Adolescent Medicine, 157,* 687–695.

Wolfe, David A., Wekerle, Christine, Reitzel-Jaffe, Deborah, & Lefebvre, Lorrie. (1998). Factors associated with abusive relationships among maltreated and nonmaltreated youth. *Development and Psychopathology, 10,* 61–85.

Wollons, Roberta Lyn (Ed.). (2000). *Kindergartens and cultures: The global diffusion of an idea.* New Haven, CT: Yale University Press.

Wong, Sheila, Chan, Kingsley, Wong, Virginia, & Wong, Wilfred. (2002). Use of chopsticks in Chinese children. *Child: Care, Health & Development, 28,* 157–161.

Wong, Sau-ling Cynthia, & Lopez, Miguel G. (2000). English language learners of Chinese background: A portrait of diversity. In Sandra Lee McKay & Sau-ling Cynthia Wong (Eds.), *New immigrants in the United States: Readings for second language educators* (pp. 263–305). Cambridge, UK: Cambridge University Press.

Woodward, Amanda L., & Markman, Ellen M. (1998). Early word learning. In William Damon (Series Ed.) & Deanna Kuhn & Robert S. Siegler (Vol. Eds.), *Handbook of child psychology: Vol. 2. Cognition, perception and language* (5th ed., pp. 371–420). New York: Wiley.

Woolley, Jacqueline D., & Boerger, Elizabeth A. (2002). Development of beliefs about the origins and controllability of dreams. *Developmental Psychology, 38,* 24–41.

World Health Organization. (2000). *New data on the prevention of mother-to-child transmission of HIV and their policy implications—Conclusions and recommendations.* Retrieved September 3, 2005, from the World Wide Web: http://www.who.int/child-adolescent-health/New_Publications/CHILD_HEALTH/MTCT_Consultation.htm

World Health Organization. (2003). *World atlas of birth defects* (2nd ed.). Geneva, Switzerland: Author.

World Health Organization. (2005). *Sexually transmitted infections among adolescents: Issues in adolescent health and development.* Geneva, Switzerland: Author.

Wright, Jan, Burrows, Lisette, & MacDonald, Doune. (2004). *Critical inquiry and problem-solving in physical education.* London: Routledge.

Wyman, Peter A., Cowen, Emory L., Work, William C., Hoyt-Meyers, Lynn, Magnus, Keith B., & Fagen, Douglas B. (1999). Caregiving and developmental factors differentiating young at-risk urban children showing resilient versus stress-affected outcomes: A replication and extension. *Child Development, 70,* 645–659.

Xu, Fujie, Schillinger, Julia A., Markowitz, Lauri E., Sternberg, Maya R., Aubin, Mark R., & St. Louis, Michael E. (2000). Repeat *Chlamydia trachomatis* infection in women: Analysis through a surveillance case registry in Washington state, 1993–1998. *American Journal of Epidemiology, 152,* 1164–1170.

Yates, Tuppett M., Egeland, Byron, & Sroufe, L. Alan. (2003). Rethinking resilience: A developmental process perspective. In Suniya S. Luthar (Ed.), *Resilience and vulnerability: Adaptation in the context of*

childhood adversities (pp. 243–266). New York: Cambridge University Press.

Yeung, W. Jean, Linver, Miriam R., & Brooks-Gunn, Jeanne. (2002). How money matters for young children's development: Parental investment and family processes. *Child Development, 73,* 1861–1879.

Yoder, Kevin A., Hoyt, Dan R., & Whitbeck, Les B. (1998). Suicidal behavior among homeless and runaway adolescents. *Journal of Youth & Adolescence, 27,* 753–771.

Yoos, H. Lorrie, Kitzman, Harriet, & Cole, Robert. (1999). Family routines and the feeding process. In Daniel B. Kessler & Peter Dawson (Eds.), *Failure to thrive and pediatric undernutrition: A transdiciplinary approach* (pp. 375–384). Baltimore: Brookes.

Young-Hyman, Deborah, Schlundt, David G., Herman-Wenderoth, Leanna, & Bozylinski, Khristine. (2003). Obesity, appearance, and psychosocial adaptation in young African American children. *Journal of Pediatric Psychology, 28,* 463–472.

Youniss, James, McLellan, Jeffrey A., & Yates, Miranda. (1999). Religion, community service, and identity in American youth. *Journal of Adolescence, 22,* 243–253.

Zahn-Waxler, Carolyn. (2000). The development of empathy, guilt, and internalization of distress: Implications for gender differentiation in internalizing and externalizing problems. In Richard J. Davidson (Ed.), *Anxiety, depression, and emotion* (pp. 222–265). New York: Oxford University Press.

Zeedyk, M. Suzanne, Wallace, Linda, & Spry, Linsay. (2002). Stop, look, listen, and think? What young children really do when crossing the road. *Accident Analysis & Prevention, 34,* 43–50.

Zehler, Annette M., Fleischman, Howard L., Hopstock, Paul J., Stephenson, Todd G., Pendzick, Michelle L., & Sapru, Saloni. (2003). *Descriptive study of services to LEP students and LEP students with disabilities: Vol. 1. Research report.* Arlington, VA: Development Associates.

Zehr, Mary Ann. (2004, January 14). Report updates portrait of LEP students. *Education Week, 23,* 3.

Zeifman, Debra, Delaney, Sarah, & Blass, Elliott M. (1996). Sweet taste, looking, and calm in 2- and 4-week-old infants: The eyes have it. *Developmental Psychology, 32,* 1090–1099.

Zelazo, Philip David, Frye, Douglas, & Rapus, Tanja. (1996). An age-related dissociation between knowing rules and using them. *Cognitive Development, 11,* 37–63.

Zigler, Edward, & Styfco, Sally J. (2001). Can early childhood intervention prevent delinquency? A real possibility. In Arthur C. Bohart & Deborah J. Stipek (Eds.), *Constructive & destructive behavior: Implications for family, school, & society* (pp. 231–248). Washington, DC: American Psychological Association.

Zigler, Edward, & Styfco, Sally J. (Eds.). (2004). *The Head Start debates.* Baltimore: Brookes.

Zigler, Edward F., Kagan, Sharon Lynn, & Hall, Nancy Wilson (Eds.). (1996). *Children, families, and government: Preparing for the twenty-first century.* New York: Cambridge University Press.

Zito, Julie Magno, Safer, Daniel J., dosReis, Susan, Gardner, James F., Magder, Laurence, Soeken, Karen, et al. (2003). Psychotropic practice patterns for youth: A 10-year perspective. *Archives of Pediatrics & Adolescent Medicine, 157,* 17–25.

Name Index

Subject Index